Psychology

Fourth Canadian Edition

A Journey

DENNIS COON

JOHN O. MITTERER
Brock University

PATRICK BROWN
Western University

RAJESH MALIK
Dawson College

SUSANNE MCKENZIE
Dawson College

NELSON / EDUCATION

NELSON / EDUCATION

Psychology: A Journey, Fourth Canadian Edition

by Dennis Coon, John O. Mitterer, Patrick Brown, Rajesh Malik, and Susanne McKenzie

Vice President, Editorial Higher Education:
Anne Williams

Executive Editor:
Lenore Taylor-Atkins

Marketing Manager:
Ann Byford

Developmental Editors:
Leah Blain and Sandy Matos

Photo Researcher:
Lynn McLeod

Permissions Coordinator:
Lynn McLeod

Content Production Manager:
Claire Horsnell

Production Service:
MPS Limited

Copy Editor:
Julia Cochrane

Proofreader:
Jennifer McIntyre

Indexer:
Sonya Dintaman

Senior Manufacturing Coordinator:
Joanne McNeil

Design Director:
Ken Phipps

Managing Designer:
Franca Amore

Interior Design:
Dianna Little

Cover Design:
Trinh Truong

Cover Image:
Masterfile

Compositor:
MPS Limited

Printer:
RR Donnelley

Library and Archives Canada Cataloguing in Publication

Psychology: a journey/Dennis Coon . . . [et al.]. —4th Canadian ed.

Includes bibliographical references and index.ISBN 978-0-17-650372-7

1. Psychology—Textbooks. I. Coon, Dennis

BF121.P8323 2013   150
C2012-905098-9

PKG ISBN-13: 978-0-17-666253-0
PKG ISBN-10: 0-17-666253-7

Photo credits for Boxed Features in the text: Human Diversity (tropical fish): Carlos Davila/Getty Images; Brain Waves (breaking surf): © Ocean/Corbis; Study Break (check mark): iStockphoto; Test Your Knowledge (sailing boats): courtesy Sandy Matos; Using Psychology (mountains and pasture): John Wang /Getty Images; The Clinical File (Lighthouse, Peggy's Cove, NS): Thinkstock.

Photo Credits for Table of Contents: p. iii (group of students): © Digital Vision/Alamy; p. iv (Canadian fan): CP Photo/Tom Hanson; p. v (EEG recording): AJPhoto/Photo Researchers, Inc.; p. vi (mother and child): digitalskillet/Shutterstock; p. vii (soccer players): Charles Platiau/Reuters/Corbis; (group of students): Wavebreakmedia Ltd/Shutterstock; p. viii (orca and trainer): © Gary Crabbe/Alamy; p. ix (the Obama family): Ralf-Finn Hestoft/Corbis; (robot and Rubik's cube): Bela Szandelszky/AP Images; p. x (roller coaster): Chad Slattery/Getty Images; p. xi (Pierre Elliott Trudeau): Hulton Archive/Getty Images; p. xii (punk girl): PhotoDisc/Getty Images; (yoga class): PhotoDisc/Getty Images; p. xiii (Freud's couch): © Peter Aprahamian/CORBIS; p. xiv (couple): Jeff Greenberg/PhotoEdit.

Brief Contents

Contents

Preface xv
About the Authors xxvii

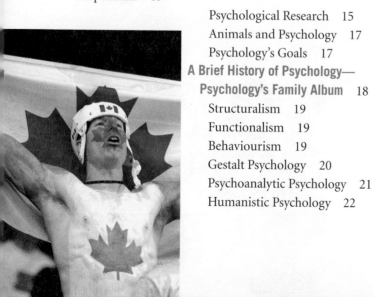

CHAPTER 2   Brain and Behaviour   53

CHAPTER 3   Human Development   92

Chapter 4   Sensation and Perception   133

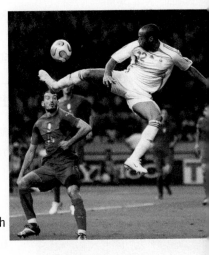

CHAPTER 5   States of Consciousness   183

CHAPTER 6   Conditioning and Learning   230

CHAPTER 7   Memory   269

CHAPTER 8   Intelligence, Cognition, Language, and Creativity   307

CHAPTER 9   Motivation and Emotion   350

CHAPTER 10   Personality   395

CHAPTER 13   Therapies   513

CHAPTER 14   Social Behaviour   554

APPENDIX

Preface

TO THE STUDENT—THE JOURNEY BEGINS

Psychology is an exciting field. It is at once familiar, exotic, surprising, and challenging. Most of all, psychology is changing. Indeed, this book is just a snapshot of a colourful passing scene. Yet, change is what makes psychology fascinating: What could be more intriguing than our evolving understanding of human behaviour?

Psychology is about each of us. Psychology asks, "How can we step outside ourselves to look objectively at how we live, think, feel, and act?" Psychologists believe the answer is through careful thought, observation, and inquiry, so those principles inform all that follows in this text.

Each chapter of this book takes you into a different realm of psychology, such as personality, abnormal behaviour, memory, consciousness, and human development. Each realm is complex and fascinating, with many pathways, landmarks, and detours to discover. The title of this book, *Psychology: A Journey*, reflects the fact that learning is an adventure. Like any journey of discovery, your tour of psychology will help you to better understand yourself, others, and the world around you. It's definitely a trip worth taking.

We hope you will find human behaviour as fascinating as we do. In the pages that follow, we have done all that we can to make your first journey through psychology enjoyable and worthwhile. The delight we have found in our own students' curiosity, insights, imagination, and interests will be apparent to you as you explore psychology. Please view this book as a long letter from us to you. It is, in a very real sense, written about you, for you, and to you.

TO THE INSTRUCTOR—A CONCISE SURVEY OF PSYCHOLOGY

Psychology: A Journey was written to provide a concise but complete first course in psychology. It is organized into 14 chapters so that the entire field can be covered in a single term, at the rate of one chapter per week. With that in mind, we were prompted to select only the best material from the vast quantity available. Nevertheless, the book manages to cover not only essential topics at the core of psychology but also many others at the cutting edge of current knowledge.

The publication of the fourth Canadian edition of *Psychology: A Journey* is a direct result of feedback from instructors and students. New information, anecdotes, perspectives, and narratives appear throughout this edition. Readers will find out about past and current research in Canada, about statistics that are relevant to Canadians, and about examples that illustrate the diversity of the Canadian cultural experience. The result is a concise text that is readable, relevant, and motivating.

Marcel Proust wrote, "The real voyage of discovery consists not in seeing new landscapes but in having new eyes." It is in this spirit that we invite you to make full use of this book to help you promote an interest in human behaviour, including an appreciation of the practical applications of psychology, the richness of human diversity, and the field of positive psychology.

Readability and Narrative Emphasis

Selecting a textbook is half the battle in teaching a successful course. A good text does much of the work of imparting information to students. This frees class time for discussion, extra topics, and media presentations. It also leaves students asking for more. When a book overwhelms students or damps their enthusiasm, teaching and learning suffer.

Growing numbers of students who enter introductory courses are poor or reluctant readers. No matter how interesting the text, its value is lost if students fail to read it. That's why we've worked hard to make this a clear, readable, and engaging text. We want students to read this book with genuine interest and enthusiasm, not merely as an obligation.

To encourage students to read, we made a special effort to weave narrative threads through every chapter. Everyone loves a good story, and the story of psychology is among the most compelling to be told. In every chapter of *Psychology: A Journey,* we have used intriguing anecdotes and running examples to propel reading and sustain interest. As students explore concepts, they are asked to think about ideas and relate them to their own experiences. For example, the discussion of dreams in Chapter 5 looks at a survey of typical dreams of Canadian university students.

Practical Applications

An important question to ask about introductory psychology is "What will students remember next year? Or in ten years?" Consequently, *Psychology: A Journey* is designed to give students a clear grasp of major concepts without burying them in details. At the same time, it offers an overview that reflects psychology's rich heritage of ideas. We think students will find this book informative and intellectually stimulating. Moreover, we have emphasized the many ways that psychology relates to practical problems in daily life.

A major feature of this book is the *Psychology in Action* section found in each chapter. This high-interest discussion bridges the gap between theory and practical application. We believe it is fair for students to ask, "Does this mean anything to me? Can I use it? Why should I learn it if I can't use it?" The Psychology in Action features spell out how students can use psychology to solve problems and manage their own behaviour. This allows students to see the benefits of adopting new ideas, and it breathes life into psychology's concepts.

An Integrated Study Guide

The chapters of this text are divided into short segments by a special feature called *Study Break.* Each Study Break asks students to relate concepts to their own experiences, to quiz themselves, and to think critically about the principles they are learning. In addition, each chapter concludes with a feature called *Test Your Knowledge.* The multiple-choice questions in Test Your Knowledge provide a way for students to judge how well they are doing in their studies by taking a sample test at the end of the chapter. The questions are comparable in difficulty to in-class exams.

Taken together, the Study Break and Test Your Knowledge features are essentially an integrated study guide. If students would like more feedback and practice, more learning resources are available on the *Psychology: A Journey* CourseMate, described below.

Electronic Resources

To encourage further exploration, a section called *Interactive Learning* is included at the end of each chapter of this book. The websites listed there offer a wealth of information on topics related to psychology, and easy access is ensured through hyperlinks to these sites that are available via the *Psychology: A Journey* CourseMate.

Human Diversity

Today's students reflect the multicultural, multifaceted nature of contemporary society. In *Psychology: A Journey*, students will find numerous discussions of human diversity, including differences in race, ethnicity, culture, gender, abilities, sexual orientation, and age. Too often, such differences needlessly divide people into opposing groups. Our aim throughout this text is to discourage stereotyping, prejudice, discrimination, and intolerance. We've tried to make this book gender-neutral and sensitive to diversity issues. All pronouns and examples involving females and males are equally divided by gender. In artwork, photographs, and examples we have tried to portray the rich diversity of humanity. Many topics and examples encourage students to appreciate social, physical, and cultural differences and to accept them as a natural part of being human.

Positive Psychology

In January 2000, Martin Seligman and Mihaly Csikszentmihalyi co-edited a special issue of *American Psychologist* devoted to optimal functioning, happiness, and "positive psychology." Over the past 100 years, psychologists have paid ample attention to the negative side of human behaviour. This is easy to understand because we urgently need to find remedies for human problems. However, Seligman and Csikszentmihalyi have urged us to also study positive psychology. What do we know, for instance, about love, happiness, creativity, well-being, self-confidence, and achievement? Throughout this book, we have attempted to answer such questions for students. Our hope is that students who read this book will gain an appreciation for the potential we all have for optimal functioning. Also, of course, we hope that they will leave introductory psychology with emotional and intellectual tools they can use to enhance their lives.

How Chapter Features Support the SQ4R Method

This text is designed around the SQ4R study-reading method. In addition to helping students learn psychology, its format promotes valuable study skills. Notice how the steps of the SQ4R method—*survey, question, read, recite, reflect,* and *review*—are incorporated into the chapter structure.

Survey

Our goal in the initial pages of each chapter is to help students form a cognitive map of upcoming topics before they start reading. Each chapter begins with a short preview that arouses interest, provides an entry point into the main topic of the chapter, and focuses attention so that students will read with a purpose. Next, a list of *Survey Questions* provides a focused overview of the chapter. The same Survey Questions appear again in the main body of the text to help students structure their learning. Later, the Survey Questions are used to organize the Chapter Summary. In this way, students are given a consistent framework for studying and learning.

Question

Throughout each chapter, italicized *Guide Questions* serve as organizers that prompt students to look for important ideas as they read. Guide Questions also establish a dialogue in which the questions and reactions of students are anticipated. This dialogue clarifies difficult points—in a lively give-and-take between questions and responses.

Read

We've made every effort to make this a clear, readable text. In terms of formal readability measures, this is a highly readable text. To further aid comprehension, we've used a full array of traditional learning aids. These include boldface terms, bullet summaries, a robust illustration program, summary tables, a name index, a subject index, and a detailed glossary.

A running glossary aids understanding by providing precise definitions in the page margins. In this way, students get clear definitions when and where they need them. The running glossary also makes it easier for students to find, study, and review important terms.

Several times per chapter, boxed highlights discuss recent research (*Clinical File*), multicultural perspectives (*Human Diversity*), how to apply psychology (*Using Psychology*), the latest in neuroscience research (*Brainwaves*), and how to distinguish empirically evaluated research from common-sense beliefs (*Critical Thinking*). These highlights are stimulating but non-intrusive supplements to the main text. They enrich the presentation and encourage students to think about what they're learning.

Recite

Every few pages, a *Study Break* provides opportunities for students to test their understanding and recall of psychological principles they just learned. The Study Breaks are small, built-in study guides that include a *Learning Check* (a short, non-comprehensive quiz). Learning Checks help students actively process information and assess their progress. However, Learning Check questions are not as difficult as in-class tests, so students who miss any questions are encouraged to backtrack and clarify their understanding before they read more. In this way, completing Learning Checks serves as a form of recitation to enhance learning.

Reflect

Cognitive psychologists tell us that elaborative rehearsal is one of the best ways to form lasting memories. Through elaborative rehearsal we make new information more meaningful by relating it to familiar knowledge. To help students use elaborative rehearsal, each Study Break includes a series of *Reflect* questions. These questions encourage students to associate new concepts with meaningful personal experiences and prior knowledge.

A course in psychology naturally contributes to critical thinking. To further promote critical thinking abilities, we have included *Critical Thinking* boxes throughout the book, and each Study Break includes one or more *Critical Thinking* questions. These questions challenge students to think critically and analytically about psychology. Each is followed by a brief answer, which students can compare with their own thoughts. Many of the answers are based on research and are informative in their own right.

Review

As noted above, all important terms appear in a running glossary, which aids review. As also noted, a Psychology in Action section completes each chapter. This feature shows students how psychological concepts relate to practical problems, including problems in their own lives. The information in the Psychology in Action features helps reinforce learning by illustrating psychology's practicality. It also encourages students to review and extend the ideas they have learned.

To help students consolidate their learning, the *Chapter in Review* section restates all of the major ideas presented earlier in the chapter. This section begins with a list of *Major Points* that summarize the "take-home" concepts every student should be able to remember 10 years after reading this text. Next, a point-by-point *Summary* provides a detailed synopsis of the chapter. As mentioned before, the Summary is organized around the same Survey Questions found at the beginning of the chapter. This brings the SQ4R process full circle and reinforces the learning objectives for the chapter. Every chapter concludes with Test Your Knowledge, the brief multiple-choice test described earlier. Students who miss any questions are urged to review further, using various supplements available with this text.

Critical Thinking

The active, questioning nature of the SQ4R method is itself an inducement to think critically. Many of the Guide Questions that introduce topics in the text act as models of critical thinking. More important, Chapter 1 contains a brief discussion of critical thinking skills and a rational appraisal of pseudo-psychologies. In reality, the presentation of research methods in Chapter 1 is a short course on how to think clearly about behaviour. It is supplemented by suggestions about how to critically evaluate claims in the popular media. Chapter 8, "Intelligence, Cognition, Learning, and Creativity," discusses many topics that focus on thinking skills. Throughout the text, many boxed highlights promote critical thinking and healthy skepticism. As mentioned earlier, every Study Break includes Critical Thinking questions. Taken together, these features help students gain thinking skills of lasting value.

What's New in the Fourth Canadian Edition?

Thanks to psychology's vitality and suggestions from professors, this edition has improved in many ways. Canadian research, examples, and statistics have been integrated into every chapter of the text, and key topics have been introduced and updated throughout. The following is a list of just some of the new information and examples you will read about in the fourth Canadian edition.

- In **Chapter 1**, we have included more information on neuroscience and neuropsychologists; refocused the discussion of participant bias and researcher bias, with additional current references; and redefined the word "psyche" to include the soul, as developed by Aristotle, Plato, and others.
- In **Chapter 2**, we have also included a new Using Psychology box called "You Can Change Your Mind, But Can You Change Your Brain?" This chapter has been expanded to reflect the growing importance of neuroscience to psychology. A new section on saltatory conduction has also been added. The section on exploring brain function has been reworked. The section on fMRI has been enhanced with the inclusion of a discussion of lie detection and a new figure. The section on lobes of the cerebral cortex has been reorganized, as has the section on handedness.
- **Chapter 3** includes more material on adolescence, adulthood, later life, and successful aging. Ethnic differences in parenting are also discussed. In addition, the material on Piaget's stages has been condensed into a table.
- **Chapter 4** includes discussion of two blind people who use echolocation to "see" their environment, enabling them to walk around obstacles. It also explores how blindness impacts young people's social life and how social concerns prevent elderly blind people from seeking help they may need, and describes how researchers in Montréal are studying tone deafness.
- In **Chapter 5**, we have reorganized the section on sleep and dreams to include a new approach to explaining dreams: the neurocognitive theory. The section on hypnosis has been reorganized and the discussion of stage hypnosis has been moved to the end of the subsection. We have also revised the section on meditation to include a discussion on changes in the brain produced by practising meditation, and expanded the discussion of how drugs work in the brain. This new discussion includes a Canadian study, the first of its kind, that investigates the effects of cannabis on chronic pain.
- **Chapter 6** includes a new Critical Thinking Box that explores animals' awareness of the passage of time.
- **Chapter 7** includes new material on a young Canadian woman who suffered brain damage shortly after birth that seriously impaired her episodic memory but who nonetheless taught herself memory techniques that enabled her to graduate from high school. We also discuss a memory patient in Toronto who learned how to *use* new tools but could not remember the learning experience, and research at the University of Waterloo showing that you can improve memory for material to be learned just by reading it out loud.

- In **Chapter 8**, New Canadian research of note is discussed in a new Human Diversity box that looks at how becoming bilingual offers advantages beyond simply being able to converse in another language—it also improves executive control of cognitive processes. Also new is a discussion of evidence that infants as young as eight months old have some ability to make statistical inferences.

- **Chapter 9** begins with a look at a perennial issue for students, procrastination. This new material features both some cross-cultural comparisons and a useful tip on how students can avoid procrastination. The chapter includes a new Human Diversity box describing recent research on the Canadian college student experience of and attitudes towards casual sex. Notable new Canadian research discussed in this chapter describes studies of hunger among Aboriginal people and weight problems in the general population, including some remarkable new data on how Canadians compare to Americans on obesity. New research from the University of Toronto suggests one way to fight overeating—don't look at what other people are eating—while researchers at the Hospital for Sick Children in Toronto have developed a media-literacy program aimed at improving body satisfaction among students. Also, research from Newfoundland and Labrador used teenaged boys as examples of the power of intrinsic motivation in a study of skateboarders persisting in the fact of failure until they learned a new trick.

- In **Chapter 10**, the section on the HEXACO model of personality and the material on the role of gender and the treatment of androgyny have been updated and reorganized. The section on the hereditary aspects of personality, refers to the work of Kerry Jang, who leads the largest research program involving twins in Canada.

- In **Chapter 11** we have included current information on Russell Williams, as well as two new boxes on mental health: "Crazy for a Day" and "Sick of Being Sick." Incidence statistics of some disorders have been updated. The sections on mood disorders and schizophrenia have been updated and reorganized. When this chapter was being prepared, the DSM-5 was still under revision; its publication was expected around May of 2013. Therefore, the decision was to base our discussion of the psychological disorders on the existing classification system: DSM-IV-TR. Since this is a college-level introductory psychology textbook, we have not stressed the diagnostic criteria in any significant detail. Rather, the emphasis has been to get across to students basic ideas regarding the symptoms of the most common psychological disorders as well as their causes. Nevertheless, DSM-5 will introduce numerous changes to how disorders are classified and diagnosed, and we would like students reading this book to know something about the new manual. To accomplish this objective, relevant and up-to-date information about DSM-5 will be made available on Nelson's website at the following URL: www.nelson.com/psychologyjourney4ce.

- **Chapter 12** has two new boxes. Using Psychology examines the reasons people find it difficult to alter unhealthy behaviours. A new Critical Thinking box discusses the shift toward a biopsychosocial model of health promotion.

- In **Chapter 13**, the material on distance therapies and the role of digital media has been updated. The material on medical therapies has been updated and a new section on *Interpersonal Therapy* has been added. The section "Locating a Therapist" has been changed based on comments received from reviewers. We have also included two new boxes: a Critical Thinking box called "How Do We Know Therapy Actually Works?" and a Clinical File box called "Overcoming the Gambler's Fallacy."

- **Chapter 14** begins with a look at the *Roots of Empathy* program, which teaches children to think about other people's feelings using regular classroom visits by a baby and the baby's parent. The children are encouraged to imagine what life is like for the baby and for the parent. New material also includes a study of the relationship of the "Dark Triad" of personality to different styles of humour and an analysis of self-disclosure on Facebook that suggests the practice can make things worse for people with low self-esteem.

A Complete Course—Teaching and Learning Supplements

A rich array of supplements accompanies *Psychology: A Journey*, including several that make use of the latest technologies. These supplements are designed to make teaching and learning more effective. Many are available free to professors or students. Others can be packaged with this text at a discount.

Student Support Materials

Introductory students must learn a multitude of abstract concepts, which can make a first course in psychology difficult. The materials listed here will greatly improve students' chances for success.

Multimedia CD-ROMs

Interactive CD-ROMs make it possible for students to directly experience some of the phenomena they are studying. The following CDs from Nelson Education Ltd. provide a wealth of engaging modules and exercises.

Psyk.Trek® 3.0: A Multimedia Introduction to Psychology

(ISBN 0-495-09035-2) Available as a CD-ROM for Windows and Macintosh or in an online version, this student tutorial is organized into 65 individual learning modules that parallel the core content of any introductory psychology course. Version 3.0 includes new modules on Forgetting (in the Memory unit), Attachment (in the Human Development unit), and Conformity and Obedience (in the Social Psychology unit). Students using *Psyk.Trek® 3.0* will find studying fun as they create illusions, run simulated experiments, view videos, and quiz themselves on the content of the introductory psychology course. *Psyk.Trek® 3.0* also includes an interactive study guide and a multimedia glossary with an audio pronunciation guide.

Sniffy™ The Virtual Rat Lite, Version 2.0

(ISBN 0-534-63357-9) There's no better way to master the basic principles of learning than working with a real laboratory rat. However, this is usually impractical in introductory psychology courses. *Sniffy™ the Virtual Rat* offers a fun, interactive alternative to working with lab animals. This innovative and entertaining software teaches students about operant and classical conditioning by allowing them to condition a virtual rat. Users begin by training Sniffy to press a bar to obtain food. Then they progress to studying the effects of reinforcement schedules and simple classical conditioning. In addition, special Mind Windows enable students to visualize how Sniffy's experiences in the Skinner box produce learning. The *Sniffy™* CD-ROM includes a Lab Manual that shows students how to set up various operant and classical conditioning experiments.

Internet Resources

The Internet provides new ways to exchange information and enhance education. In psychology, Nelson Education Ltd. is at the forefront in making use of this exciting technology.

CourseMate CourseMate

Bundled with each copy of the fourth Canadian edition of *Psychology: A Journey*, Nelson Education's Psychology CourseMate brings course concepts to life with interactive learning and exam preparation tools that integrate with the textbook. Students activate their knowledge through quizzes, games, and flashcards, among many other tools.

Psychology: A Journey CourseMate includes

- an interactive eBook, with highlighting, note taking, and search capabilities
- interactive learning tools including
  - quizzes
  - flashcards
  - videos
  - and more!

Essential Teaching Resources

As every professor knows, teaching an introductory psychology course is a tremendous amount of work. The supplements listed here should make life easier for you, as well as making it possible for you to concentrate on the more creative and rewarding facets of teaching.

Nelson Education Teaching Advantage

The **Nelson Education Teaching Advantage** (**NETA**) program delivers research-based instructor resources that promote student engagement and higher-order thinking to enable the success of Canadian students and educators.

Instructors today face many challenges. Resources are limited, time is scarce, and a new kind of student has emerged: one who is juggling school with work, has gaps in his or her basic knowledge, and is immersed in technology in a way that has led to a completely new style of learning. In response, Nelson Education has gathered a group of dedicated instructors to advise us on the creation of richer and more flexible ancillaries that respond to the needs of today's teaching environments.

The members of our editorial advisory board, who have experience across a variety of disciplines and are recognized for their commitment to teaching, are as follows:

Norman Althouse, Haskayne School of Business, University of Calgary

Brenda Chant-Smith, Department of Psychology, Trent University

Scott Follows, Manning School of Business Administration, Acadia University

Jon Houseman, Department of Biology, University of Ottawa

Glen Loppnow, Department of Chemistry, University of Alberta

Tanya Noel, Department of Biology, York University

Gary Poole, Director, Centre for Teaching and Academic Growth and School of Population and Public Health, University of British Columbia

Dan Pratt, Department of Educational Studies, University of British Columbia

Mercedes Rowinsky-Geurts, Department of Languages and Literatures, Wilfrid Laurier University

David DiBattista, Department of Psychology, Brock University

Roger Fisher, PhD

In consultation with the editorial advisory board, Nelson Education Ltd. has completely rethought the structure, approaches, and formats of our key textbook ancillaries. We've also increased our investment in editorial support for our ancillary authors. The result is NETA and its key components: *NETA Engagement, NETA Assessment, NETA Presentation,* and *NETA Digital*. Each component includes one or more ancillaries prepared according to our best practices and a document explaining the theory behind the practices.

NETA Engagement presents materials that help instructors deliver engaging content and activities to their classes. Instead of Instructor's Manuals that regurgitate chapter outlines and key terms from the text, NETA Enriched Instructor's Manuals (EIMs) provide genuine assistance to teachers. The EIMs answer questions like "What should students learn?," "Why should students care?," and "What are some common student misconceptions and stumbling blocks?" EIMs not only identify the topics that cause students the most difficulty but also describe techniques and resources to help students master these concepts. Dr. Roger Fisher's *Instructor's Guide to Classroom Engagement (IGCE)* accompanies every EIM. (Information about the NETA EIM prepared for *Psychology: A Journey* is included in the description of the Instructor's Resource CD (IRCD) below.)

NETA Assessment relates to testing materials: not just Nelson's Test Banks and Computerized Test Banks, but also in-text self-tests, web quizzes, and homework programs such as CourseMate. Under *NETA Assessment,* Nelson's authors create multiple-choice questions that reflect research-based best practices for constructing effective questions and testing not just recall but also higher-order thinking. Our guidelines were developed by David DiBattista, a 3M National Teaching Fellow, whose recent research as a professor of psychology at Brock University has focused on multiple-choice testing. All Test Bank authors receive training at workshops conducted by Professor DiBattista, as do the copyeditors assigned to each Test Bank. A copy of *Multiple Choice Tests: Getting Beyond Remembering,* Professor DiBattista's guide to writing effective tests, is included with every Nelson Test Bank/Computerized Test Bank package. (Information about the NETA Test Bank prepared for *Psychology: A Journey* is included in the description of the IRCD below.)

NETA Presentation has been developed to help instructors make the best use of PowerPoint in their classrooms. With a clean and uncluttered design developed by Maureen Stone of StoneSoup Consulting, NETA Presentation features slides with improved readability, more multi-media and graphic materials, activities to use in class, and tips for instructors on the Notes page. A copy of *NETA Guidelines for Classroom Presentations,* by Maureen Stone, is included with each set of PowerPoint slides. (Information about the NETA PowerPoint prepared for *Psychology: A Journey* is included in the description of the IRCD below.)

NETA Digital is a framework based on Arthur Chickering and Zelda Gamson's seminal work, "Seven Principles for Good Practice in Undergraduate Education" (1987), and the follow-up work by Chickering and Stephen C. Ehrmann, "Implementing the Seven Principles: Technology as Lever" (1996). This aspect of the NETA program guides the writing and development of our digital products to ensure that they appropriately reflect the core goals of contact, collaboration, multimodal learning, time on task, prompt feedback, active learning, and high expectations. The resulting focus on pedagogical utility, rather than technological wizardry, ensures that all of our technology supports better outcomes for students.

Instructor's Resource CD (IRCD)

Key instructor ancillaries are provided on the *Instructor's Resource CD* (ISBN 978-0-17-666270-7), giving instructors the ultimate tool for customizing lectures and presentations. The IRCD includes the following:

- **NETA Engagement:** The Enriched Instructor's Manual was written by Jason Daniels. It is organized according to the textbook chapters and addresses eight key educational concerns, such as typical stumbling blocks students face and how to address them.

- **NETA Assessment:** The Test Bank was written by Jonah Santa-Barbara. It includes over 1600 multiple-choice questions written according to NETA guidelines for effective construction and development of higher-order questions. Also included are 15 fill-in-the-blank and 15 essay/short-answer questions. Test Bank files are provided in Word format for easy editing and in PDF format for convenient printing, whatever your system.

  The Computerized Test Bank by ExamView® includes all the questions from the Test Bank. The easy-to-use ExamView software is compatible with Microsoft Windows and Mac OS. Create tests by selecting questions from the question bank, modifying these questions as desired, and adding new questions you write yourself. You can administer quizzes online and export tests to WebCT, Blackboard, and other formats.

- **NETA Presentation:** Microsoft® PowerPoint® lecture slides for every chapter have been created by Corey Isaacs. There is an average of 25 slides per chapter, many featuring key figures, tables, and photographs from *Psychology: A Journey.* NETA principles of clear design and engaging content have been incorporated throughout.
- **Image Library:** This resource consists of digital copies of figures and short tables used in the book. Instructors may use these jpegs to create their own PowerPoint® presentations.
- **DayOne:** Day One—Prof InClass is a PowerPoint® presentation that you can customize to orient your students to the class and their text at the beginning of the course.

Cengage Film and Video Library for Introductory Psychology

Adopters can select from a variety of continually updated film and video options. Please contact your local Nelson sales representative for the most current listing of top-quality selections from well-known video producers.

Psychology Digital Video Library Version 3.0

This CD-ROM (ISBN 0-495-09063-8) contains a diverse selection of more than 100 classic and contemporary clips, including "The Action Potential of a Neuron," "Understanding Addiction," and many more! The digital library offers a convenient way to access an appropriate clip for every lecture. An accompanying Digital Video Handbook offers a detailed description, approximate running time, and references to related media clips. It also offers objective quizzing and critical-thinking questions for each clip, as well as instructions on how to embed clips into your PowerPoint® presentations. This CD-ROM is available exclusively to instructors who adopt Nelson psychology texts.

Summary

We sincerely hope that teachers and students will consider this book and its supporting materials a refreshing change from the ordinary. Creating it has been quite an adventure. In the pages that follow, we think students will find an attractive blend of the theoretical and the practical, plus many of the most exciting ideas in psychology. Most of all, we hope that students using this book discover that reading a college textbook can be entertaining and enjoyable.

Acknowledgments

Psychology is a cooperative effort requiring the talents and energies of a large community of scholars, teachers, researchers, and students. Like most endeavours in psychology, this book reflects the efforts of many people.

To all the professional reviewers who gave their time and expertise we extend our sincere thanks. We wish to thank the following reviewers (and others who preferred to remain anonymous)—their sage advice helped make the Fourth Canadian Edition of this concise, interactive text a reality:

Kristen Buscaglia, Niagara College

Shauna Moore, Durham College

Ruth Rodgers, University of Ontario Institute of Technology

Suzanne Tebbutt, Conestoga College

Karen White, Vanier College

Frank Winstan, Vanier College

We would like to dedicate this new edition to our students—present, past, and future: this is really for you.

Producing the fourth Canadian edition of *Psychology: A Journey* and its supplements was a formidable task, requiring the work of many talented people. We are especially indebted to Dennis Coon, John Mitterer, and the talented individuals at Cengage who collaborated to produce the original text on which this edition is based.

Patrick Brown

I would like to thank Lenore Taylor-Atkins and all at Nelson for their work on this project. It was a pleasure to work with them and with copyeditor Julia Cochrane, content production manager Claire Horsnell, and especially developmental editor Leah Blain, for her patience. I would also like to thank Louise and Stephanie for their unstinting support throughout this process.

Rajesh Malik

First and foremost, my sincere thanks go to the executive editor, Lenore Taylor-Atkins, for her keen sense of planning and foresight. I would also like to thank Sandy Matos, developmental editor, for providing excellent support during the painstaking process of preparing the manuscript. She was always available for consultation, for advice, and, occasionally, for consolation! Leah Blain began the same fine work that Sandy continued, for which she deserves a special mention. Julia Cochrane conducted the copy editing of the manuscript admirably. My thanks also go to Claire Horsnell and Preeti Longia Sinha for making the book production and proofreading processes almost painless. I would also like to acknowledge the enormous support and valuable comments of my co-authors, Patrick and Sue, on earlier drafts of my chapters. Finally, a big thank-you to my family for allowing me to ignore them for long periods, which enabled me to complete the manuscript on time.

Sue McKenzie

Thanks to Lenore Taylor-Atkins, Sandy Matos and Leah Blain for all their work in the production of this fourth edition. Julia Cochrane didn't miss a trick as copy editor. I appreciate her painstaking work and share her enjoyment of Indian food. Claire Horsnell, content production manager, thanks for your great sense of style. I also enjoyed working with Preeti Longia Sinha, the project manager. Last, but never least, to my husband, Bob, my children and grandchildren, and, most of all, all my students for all those years. It was always about you.

About the Authors

After earning a doctorate in psychology from the University of Arizona, Dennis Coon taught for 22 years at Santa Barbara City College, California. Throughout his career, Dr. Coon has especially enjoyed the challenge of teaching introductory psychology. He and his wife, Sevren, now live in Tucson, Arizona, where he continues to teach, write, edit, and consult. Dr. Coon is the author of *Introduction to Psychology*, as well as *Essentials of Psychology*. Together, these texts have been used by over two million students. Dr. Coon frequently serves as a reviewer and consultant to publishers, and he edited the best-selling trade book *Choices*. In his leisure hours, Dr. Coon enjoys hiking, photography, painting, woodworking, and music. He also designs, builds, and plays classical and steel string acoustic guitars. He has published articles on guitar design and occasionally offers lectures on this topic, in addition to his more frequent presentations on psychology. His return to Arizona has made it possible for him to fulfill a lifelong dream of using operant conditioning to teach scorpions to tap dance.

John O. Mitterer was awarded his Ph.D. in cognitive psychology from McMaster University. Currently, Dr. Mitterer teaches at Brock University, where he has taught over 20 000 introductory psychology students. He is the recipient of the 2003 Brock University Distinguished Teaching Award, a 2003 Ontario Confederation of University Faculty Associations (OCUFA) Teaching Award, a 2004 National 3M Teaching Fellowship, and the 2005 Canadian Psychological Association Award for Distinguished Contributions to Education and Training in Psychology.

Dr. Mitterer's primary research focus is on basic cognitive processes in learning and teaching. He consulted for a variety of companies, such as Bell Northern Research, Unisys Corporation, IBM Canada, and computer-game developer Silicon Knights. His professional focus, however, is on applying cognitive principles to the improvement of undergraduate education. In support of his introductory psychology course, he has been involved in the production of textbooks and ancillary materials, such as CD-ROMs and websites, for both students and instructors. Dr. Mitterer has published and lectured on undergraduate instruction throughout Canada and the United States.

In his spare time, Dr. Mitterer strives to become a better golfer and to attain his life goal of seeing all the bird species in the world. To this end he recently travelled to Papua New Guinea, Brazil, Australia, and South Africa.

Patrick Brown studied linguistics at the University of Ottawa and psychology at the University of Waterloo, receiving M.A. and Ph.D. degrees. During a postdoctoral fellowship in the Department of Neurology, College of Medicine, at the University of Florida, he studied the influence of brain damage on perception of, and memory for, emotion. He taught for three years at Laurentian University in Sudbury before going to the Department of Psychology at Western University in London, Ontario, where he has taught cognition, research methods, and statistics since 1990.

Born and raised in India, Rajesh Malik came to Canada at the age of 20. He obtained his doctorate degree in psychology from Concordia University and currently teaches in the Department of Psychology at Dawson College. Within his chosen field, he is particularly interested in the topics of consciousness, hypnosis, and psychological disorders. He is passionate about classical music, reads literature and philosophy with deep interest, and remains a committed vegetarian.

Sue McKenzie received a B.A. from Northwestern University and M.A. and Ph.D. degrees from McGill. In 2008, she retired after teaching psychology at Dawson College in Montréal since the college opened in 1969. She and her husband, Bob, have three grown children and two grandchildren. When not skiing, visiting her grandsons or singing in a women's barbershop chorus, she likes to weave. On a loom.

The Psychology of Studying

Even excellent students can improve their study skills. Students who get good grades tend to work *smarter,* not just longer or harder (Santrock & Halonen, 2007). To help you get a good start, let's look at several ways to improve studying.

THE SQ4R METHOD—HOW TO TAME A TEXTBOOK

How much do you typically remember after you've read a textbook chapter? If the answer is "Nada," "Huh?" or simply "Not enough," it may be time to try the SQ4R method. SQ4R stands for *survey, question, read, recite, reflect,* and *review.* These six steps can help you learn as you read, remember more, and review effectively:

S = *Survey.* Skim through a chapter before you begin reading it. Start by looking at topic headings, figure captions, and summaries. Try to get an overall picture of what lies ahead. Because this book is organized into short sections, you can survey just one section at a time if you prefer.

Q = *Question*. As you read, turn each topic heading into one or more questions. For example, when you read the heading "Stages of Sleep" you might ask: "Is there more than one stage of sleep?" "What are the stages of sleep?" "How do they differ?" Asking questions helps you read with a purpose.

R1 = *Read*. The first R in SQ4R stands for read. As you read, look for answers to the questions you asked. Read in short "bites," from one topic heading to the next, and then stop. For difficult material you may want to read only a paragraph or two at a time.

R2 = *Recite*. After reading a small amount, you should pause and recite or rehearse. That is, try to mentally answer your questions. Better yet, summarize what you just read in brief notes. Making notes will show you what you know and don't know, so you can fill gaps in your knowledge (Peverly et al., 2003).

If you can't summarize the main ideas, skim over the section again. Until you can remember what you just read, there's little point to reading more.

After you've studied a short "bite" of text, turn the next topic heading into questions. Then read to the following heading. Remember to look for answers as you read and to recite or take notes before moving on. Ask yourself repeatedly, "What is the main idea here?" Repeat the question-read-recite cycle until you've finished an entire chapter (or just from one Study Break to the next, if you want to read shorter units).

R3 = *Reflect*. As you read, try to relate new facts, terms, and concepts to information you already know well or to your own experiences. You've probably noticed that it is especially easy to remember ideas that are personally meaningful, so try to relate the ideas or concepts you encounter to your own life. This may be the most important step in the SQ4R method. The more genuine interest you can bring to your reading, the more you will learn (Hartlep & Forsyth, 2000).

R4 = *Review*. When you're done reading, skim back over the chapter, or read your notes. Then check your memory by reciting and quizzing yourself again. Try to make frequent, active review a standard part of your study habits. (See Figure I.1.)

Does this really work? Yes. Using a reading strategy improves learning and course grades (Taraban, Rynearson, & Kerr, 2000). Simply reading straight through a chapter can give you "intellectual indigestion." That's why it's better to stop often to think, question, recite, reflect, review, and "digest" information as you read.

How to Use *Psychology: A Journey*

You can apply the SQ4R method to any text. However, this book is specifically designed to help you actively learn psychology.

Survey

Each chapter opens with a preview called *Journey into Psychology*, followed by a list of *Survey Questions*. You can use these features to identify important ideas as you begin reading. The previews should help you get interested in the topics you will be reading about, and Survey Questions are a good guide to the kinds of information you should look for as you read. After you've studied these features, take a few minutes to do your own survey of the chapter. Doing so will help you build a "mental map" of upcoming topics.

▶▶**FIGURE I.1** The SQ4R method promotes active learning and information processing. You should begin with a survey of the chapter or a shorter section, depending on how much you plan to read. Then you should proceed through cycles of questioning, reading, reflecting, and relating, and conclude with a review of the section or the entire chapter.

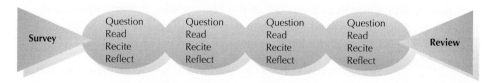

Question

How can I use the SQ4R method to make reading more interesting and effective? One of the key steps is to ask yourself lots of questions while you read. The Survey Questions are repeated throughout each chapter to help you recognize key topics. In addition, questions like the one that began this paragraph appear throughout each chapter. They will help you focus on seeking information as you read. However, be sure to ask your own questions, too. Try to actively interact with your textbooks as you read.

Read

As an aid to reading, important terms are printed in **boldface type** and defined where they first appear. (Some are followed by pronunciations—capital letters show which syllables are accented.) You'll also find a *running glossary* on the page you are reading so you'll never have to guess about the meaning of technical terms. If you need to look up a term from a lecture or another chapter, check the main *Glossary*. This "mini-dictionary" is located near the end of the book. Perhaps you should take a moment to find it now.

Reflect

Every few pages, a learning guide called a *Study Break* provides chances to think, rehearse, reflect, and test your memory. (Don't forget to also take notes or recite on your own.) If you want to study chapters in smaller "bites," Study Breaks make good stopping points.

This book also encourages you to reflect more deeply about what you are reading. Near the end of each chapter, you'll find a section called *Psychology in Action*. These discussions are filled with practical ideas you can put to use in your own life. *Using Psychology* boxes also invite you to relate psychology to your own life. *Critical Thinking* boxes will help you reflect on intriguing questions and apply critical thinking skills to psychology. In addition, *Human Diversity* boxes encourage you to reflect on the rich variability of human experience, *Brain Waves* boxes invite you to reflect on how the brain relates to psychology, and *The Clinical File* encourages you to reflect on ways that psychology can be applied to treat clinical problems.

Review

Each chapter concludes with a summary, called *Chapter in Review*, to help you identify key ideas to remember. Each Chapter in Review begins with a list of *Major Points* that make up the most important concepts or "big ideas" of the chapter. A point-by-point *Summary* reviews the chapter in some detail. These summaries are organized around the same Survey Questions you read at the beginning of the chapter. You can also return to the glossary items throughout each chapter for further review. The *Interactive Learning* section provides a list of websites related to the chapter material that you may find useful.

On the last page of every chapter you will find a brief quiz called *Test Your Knowledge*. You can use this quiz to get a preliminary idea about how well you remember ideas and concepts from your reading. But don't stop studying just because you do well on one of these quizzes. Additional review and practice will add greatly to your understanding—not to mention your test scores.

Table I.1 summarizes how this text helps you apply the **SQ4R method.** Even with all this help, there is still much more you can do on your own.

SQ4R method An active study-reading technique based on these steps: survey, question, read, recite, reflect, and review.

Active listener A person who knows how to maintain attention, avoid distractions, and actively gather information from lectures.

■ Table I.1 Using the SQ4R Method

Survey
Preview
Survey Questions
Figure Captions
Chapter in Review

Question
Topic Headings
Survey Questions
In-text Dialogue Questions

Read
Topic Headings
Boldface Terms
Running Glossary (in margins)
Figures and Tables

Recite
Learning Check Questions (in Study Breaks)
Practice Quizzes (online)
Notes (make them while reading)

Reflect
Reflect Questions (in Study Breaks)
Critical Thinking Questions (in Study Breaks)
Boxed Features (throughout the text)

Review
Chapter in Review
Boldface Terms
Running Glossary (in margins)
Tables
Test Your Knowledge
Practice Quizzes (online)
Study Guide

EFFECTIVE NOTE-TAKING—GOOD STUDENTS, TAKE NOTE!

Reading strategies may be good for studying, but what about taking notes in class? Sometimes it's hard to know what's important. Like effective reading, good notes come from actively seeking information. People who are **active listeners** avoid distractions and skilfully gather ideas.

Here's a listening/note-taking plan that works for many students. The letters LISAN, pronounced like the word *listen,* will help you remember the steps.

L = *Lead. Don't follow.* Try to anticipate what your teacher will say by asking yourself questions. Questions can come from study guides, reading assignments, or your own curiosity.

I = *Ideas.* Every lecture is based on a core of ideas. Usually, an idea is followed by examples or explanations. Ask yourself often, "What is the main idea now? What ideas support it?"

S = *Signal words.* Listen for words that tell you what direction the instructor is taking. For instance, here are some signal words:

There are three reasons why …	Here come ideas.
Most important is …	Main idea
On the contrary …	Opposite idea
As an example …	Support for main idea
Therefore …	Conclusion

A = *Actively listen.* Sit where you can get involved and ask questions. Bring questions you want answered from the last lecture or from your text. Raise your hand at the beginning of class or approach your professor before the lecture. Do anything that helps you stay active, alert, and engaged.

N = *Note-taking.* Students who take accurate lecture notes tend to do well on tests (Williams & Eggert, 2002). However, don't try to be a tape recorder. Listen to everything, but be selective and write down only key points. If you are too busy writing, you may not grasp what your professor is saying. When you're taking notes, it might help to think of yourself as a reporter who is trying to get a good story (Ryan, 2001).

Actually, most students take reasonably good notes—and then don't use them! Many students wait until just before exams to review. By then, their notes have lost much of their meaning. If you don't want your notes to seem like "chicken scratches," it pays to review them every day (Rowe, 2007).

Using and Reviewing Your Notes

When you review, you will learn more if you take the extra steps listed here (Knaus & Ellis, 2002; Rowe, 2007; Santrock & Halonen, 2007).

- As soon as you can, improve your notes by filling in gaps, completing thoughts, and looking for connections among ideas.
- Remember to link new ideas to what you already know.
- Summarize your notes. Boil them down and *organize* them.
- After each class session, write down at least seven major ideas, definitions, or details that are likely to become test questions. Then make up questions from your notes and be sure you can answer them.

Summary

The letters LISAN are a guide to active listening, but listening and good note-taking are not enough. You must also review, organize, reflect, and extend, thinking about new ideas. Use active listening to get involved in your classes and you will undoubtedly learn more (Rowe, 2007).

STUDY STRATEGIES—MAKING A HABIT OF SUCCESS

Grades depend nearly as much on effort as they do on "intelligence." However, don't forget that good students work more *efficiently,* not just harder. Many study practices are notoriously poor, such as recopying lecture notes, studying class notes but not the textbook (or the textbook but not class notes), outlining chapters, answering study questions with the book open, and "group study" (which often becomes a party). The best students emphasize *quality:* They study their books and notes in depth and attend classes regularly. It's a mistake to blame poor grades on events "beyond your control." Students who are motivated to succeed usually get better grades (Perry et al., 2001). Let's consider a few more things you can do to improve your study habits.

Study in a Specific Place

Ideally, you should study in a quiet, well-lighted area free of distractions. If possible, you should also have at least one place where you *only study.* Do nothing else at that spot: Keep magazines, iPods, friends, cell phones, pets, posters, video games, puzzles, food, lovers, sports cars, elephants, pianos, televisions, kazoos, and other distractions out of the area. In this way, the habit of studying will become strongly linked with one specific place. Then, rather than trying to force yourself to study, all you have to do is go to your study area. Once there, you'll find it is relatively easy to get started.

Use Spaced Study Sessions

It is reasonable to review intensely before an exam. However, you're taking a big risk if you are only "cramming" (learning new information at the last minute). **Spaced practice** is much more efficient (Anderson, 2005). Spaced practice consists of a large number of relatively short study sessions. Long, uninterrupted study sessions are called **massed practice**. (If you "massed up" your studying, you probably messed it up too.)

Cramming places a big burden on memory. Usually, you shouldn't try to learn anything new about a subject during the last day before a test. It is far better to learn small amounts every day and review frequently (Anderson, 2005).

Try Mnemonics

Learning has to start somewhere, and memorizing is often the first step. Let's consider just one technique here.

A **mnemonic** is a memory aid. Most mnemonics link new information to ideas or images that are easy to remember. For example, what if you want to remember that the Spanish word for duck is *pato* (pronounced POT-oh)? To use a mnemonic, you could picture a duck in a pot or a duck wearing a pot for a hat. Likewise, to remember that the cerebellum controls coordination, you might picture someone named "Sarah Bellum" who is very coordinated. For best results, make your mnemonic images exaggerated or bizarre, vivid, and interactive (Macklin & McDaniel, 2005). There are many ways to create mnemonics. If you would like to learn more about memory strategies, see Chapter 7.

Mnemonics make new information more familiar and memorable. Forming an image of a duck wearing a pot for a hat might help you remember that *pato* is the Spanish word for duck.

Test Yourself

A great way to improve grades is to take practice tests before the real one in class. In other words, studying should include **self-testing**, in which you pose questions to yourself. You can use flash cards, Learning Check questions, Test Your Knowledge questions, online quizzes, a study guide, or other means. As you study, ask many questions and be sure you can answer them. Studying without self-testing is like practising for a soccer game without running drills.

For more convenient self-testing, your professor may make a *Study Guide* or a separate booklet of *Practice Quizzes* available. You can use either to review for tests. Practice quizzes are also available on the Book Companion website, as described later. However, don't use practice quizzes as a substitute for studying your textbook and lecture notes. Trying to learn from quizzes alone will probably *lower* your grades. It is best to use quizzes to find out what topics you need to study more (Brothen & Wambach, 2001).

Overlearning Continuing to study and learn after you first think you've mastered a topic.

Self-regulated learning Active, self-guided learning.

Overlearn

Many students *underprepare* for exams, and most *overestimate* how well they will do. A solution to both problems is **overlearning**, in which you continue studying beyond your initial mastery of a topic. In other words, plan to do extra study and review *after* you think you are prepared for a test. One way to overlearn is approach all tests as if they will be essays. That way, you will learn more completely, so you really know your stuff.

SELF-REGULATED LEARNING—ACADEMIC ALL-STARS

Think of a topic you are highly interested in, such as music, sports, fashion, cars, cooking, politics, or movies. Whatever the topic, you have probably learned a lot about it—painlessly. How could you make your school work more like voluntary learning? An approach called self-regulated learning might be a good start. **Self-regulated learning** is active, self-guided study (Hofer & Yu, 2003). Here's how you can change passive studying into self-regulated learning:

1. *Set specific, objective learning goals.* Try to begin each learning session with specific goals in mind. What knowledge or skills are you trying to master? What do you hope to accomplish? (Knaus & Ellis, 2002).
2. *Plan a learning strategy.* How will you accomplish your goals? Make daily, weekly, and monthly plans for learning. Then put them into action.
3. *Be your own teacher.* Effective learners silently give themselves guidance and ask themselves questions. For example, as you are learning, you might ask yourself, "What are the important ideas here? What do I remember? What don't I understand? What do I need to review? What should I do next?"
4. *Monitor your progress.* Self-regulated learning depends on self-monitoring. Exceptional learners keep records of their progress toward learning goals (pages read, hours of studying, assignments completed, and so forth). They quiz themselves, use study guides, and find other ways to check their understanding while learning.
5. *Reward yourself.* When you meet your daily, weekly, or monthly goals, reward your efforts in some way, such as going to a movie or downloading a new album. Be aware that self-praise also rewards learning. Being able to say, "Hey, I did it!" or "Good work!" and know that you deserve it can be very rewarding. In the long run, success, self-improvement, and personal satisfaction are the real payoffs for learning.
6. *Evaluate your progress and goals.* It is a good idea to frequently evaluate your performance records and goals. Are there specific areas of your work that need improvement? If you are not making good progress toward long-range goals, do you need to revise your short-term targets?
7. *Take corrective action.* If you fall short of your goals, you may need to adjust how you budget your time. You may also need to change your learning environment to deal with distractions such as watching TV, daydreaming, talking to friends, or testing the structural integrity of the walls with your stereo system.

If you discover that you lack necessary knowledge or skills, ask for help, take advantage of tutoring programs, or look for information beyond your courses and textbooks. Knowing how to regulate and control learning can be a key to lifelong enrichment and personal empowerment.

PROCRASTINATION—AVOIDING THE LAST-MINUTE BLUES

All of these study techniques are fine. But what can I do about procrastination? A tendency to procrastinate is almost universal. (When campus workshops on procrastination are offered, many students never get around to signing up!) Even when procrastination doesn't lead to failure, it can cause much suffering. Procrastinators work only under pressure, skip classes, give false reasons for late work, and feel ashamed of their last-minute efforts. They also tend to feel frustrated, bored, and guilty more often (Blunt & Pychyl, 2005).

Why do so many students procrastinate? Many students equate grades with their *personal worth*. That is, they act as if grades tell whether they are good, smart people who will succeed in life. By procrastinating they can blame poor work on a late start, rather than a lack of ability (Beck, Koons, & Milgrim, 2000). After all, it wasn't their best effort, was it? Perfectionism is a related problem. If you expect the impossible, it's hard to start an assignment. Students with high standards often end up with all-or-nothing work habits (Onwuegbuzie, 2000).

Time Management

Most procrastinators must eventually face the self-worth issue. Nevertheless, most can improve by learning study skills and better time management. We have already discussed general study skills, so let's consider time management in a little more detail.

A **weekly time schedule** is a written plan that allocates time for study, work, and leisure activities. To prepare your schedule, make a chart showing all of the hours in each day of the week. Then fill in times that are already committed: sleep, meals, classes, work, team practices, lessons, appointments, and so forth. Next, fill in times when you will study for various classes. Finally, label the remaining hours as open or free times.

Each day, you can use your schedule as a checklist. That way you'll know at a glance which tasks are done and which still need attention (Knaus & Ellis, 2002).

You may also find it valuable to make a **term schedule** that lists the dates of all quizzes, tests, reports, papers, and other major assignments for each class.

The beauty of sticking to a schedule is that you know you are making an honest effort. It will also help you avoid feeling bored while you are working or guilty when you play.

Be sure to treat your study times as serious commitments, but respect your free times, too. And remember, students who study hard and practise time management *do* get better grades (Rau & Durand, 2000).

Goal Setting

As mentioned earlier, students who are active learners set **specific goals** for studying. Such goals should be clear-cut and measurable (Knaus & Ellis, 2002). If you find it hard to stay motivated, try setting goals for the term, the week, the day, and even for single study sessions. Also, be aware that more effort early in a course can greatly reduce the "pain" and stress you will experience later. If your professors don't give frequent assignments, set your own day-by-day goals. That way, you can turn big assignments into a series of smaller tasks that you can actually complete (Ariely & Wertenbroch, 2002). An example would be reading, studying, and reviewing eight pages a day to complete a 40-page chapter in five days. For this book, reading from one Study Break to the next each day might be a good pace. Remember, many small steps can add up to an impressive journey. (See Figure I.2 for a summary of study skills.)

Make Learning an Adventure

A final point to remember is that you are more likely to procrastinate if you think a task will be unpleasant (Pychyl et al., 2000). Learning can be hard work. Nevertheless, many students find ways to make schoolwork interesting and enjoyable. Try to approach your schoolwork as if it were a game, a sport, an adventure, or simply a way to become a better person. The best educational experiences are challenging, yet fun (Ferrari & Scher, 2000).

Virtually every topic is interesting to someone, somewhere. You may not be particularly interested in the sex life of South American tree frogs. However, a biologist might be fascinated. (Another tree frog might be, too.) If you wait for teachers to "make" their courses interesting, you are missing the point. Interest is a matter of *your attitude*.

Weekly time schedule A written plan that allocates time for study, work, and leisure activities during a one-week period.
Term schedule A written plan that lists the dates of all major assignments for each of your classes for an entire term.
Specific goal A goal with a clearly defined and measurable outcome.

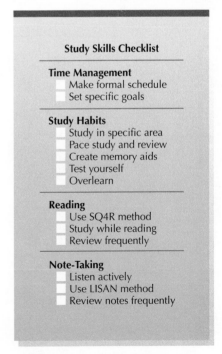

Study Skills Checklist

Time Management
- [ ] Make formal schedule
- [ ] Set specific goals

Study Habits
- [ ] Study in specific area
- [ ] Pace study and review
- [ ] Create memory aids
- [ ] Test yourself
- [ ] Overlearn

Reading
- [ ] Use SQ4R method
- [ ] Study while reading
- [ ] Review frequently

Note-Taking
- [ ] Listen actively
- [ ] Use LISAN method
- [ ] Review notes frequently

▶▶**FIGURE I.2** Study skills checklist.

TAKING TESTS—ARE YOU "TEST WISE"?

If I read and study effectively, is there anything else I can do to improve my grades? You must also be able to show what you know on tests. Here are some suggestions for improving your test-taking skills.

General Test-Taking Skills

You'll do better on all types of tests if you observe the following guidelines (Wood & Willoughby, 1995):

1. Read all directions and questions carefully. They may give you good advice or clues.
2. Quickly survey the test before you begin.
3. Answer easy questions before spending time on more difficult ones.
4. Be sure to answer all required questions.
5. Use your time wisely.
6. Ask for clarification when necessary.

Objective Tests

Several additional strategies can help you do better on objective tests. Objective tests (multiple-choice and true–false items) require you to recognize a correct answer among wrong ones or a true statement versus a false one. Here are some strategies for taking objective tests.

1. First, relate the question to what you know about the topic. Then read the alternatives. Does one match the answer you expected to find? If none match, reexamine the choices and look for a *partial* match.
2. Read *all* the choices for each question before you make a decision. Here's why: If you immediately think that *a* is correct and stop reading, you might miss seeing a better answer like "both *a* and *d*."
3. Read rapidly and skip items you are unsure about. You may find "free information" in later questions that will help you answer difficult items.
4. Eliminate certain alternatives. With a four-choice multiple-choice test, you have one chance in four of guessing right. If you can eliminate two alternatives, your guessing odds improve to 50–50.
5. Unless there is a penalty for guessing, be sure to answer any skipped items. Even if you are not sure of the answer, you may be right. If you leave a question blank, it is automatically wrong. When you must guess, don't choose the longest answer or the letter you've used the least. Both strategies lower scores more than random guessing does.
6. There is a bit of folk wisdom that says "Don't change your answers on a multiple-choice test. Your first choice is usually right." This is *false*. If you change answers, you are more likely to gain points than to lose them. This is especially true if you are uncertain of your first choice or it was a hunch, and if your second choice is more reflective (Higham & Gerrard, 2005).
7. Remember, you are searching for the one *best* answer to each question. Some answers may be partly true, yet flawed in some way. If you are uncertain, try rating each multiple-choice alternative on a 1-to-10 scale. The answer with the highest rating is the one you are looking for.
8. Few circumstances are *always* or *never* present. Answers that include superlatives such as *most, least, best, worst, largest,* or *smallest* are often false.

Essay Tests

Essay questions are weak spots for students who lack organization, don't support their ideas, or don't directly answer the question (Rowe, 2007). When you take an essay exam, try the following:

1. Read the question carefully. Be sure to note key words, such as *compare, contrast, discuss, evaluate, analyze,* and *describe.* These words all demand a certain focus to your answer.
2. Think about your answer for a few minutes and list the main points you want to make. Just write them as they come to mind. Then rearrange the ideas in a logical order and begin writing. Elaborate plans or outlines are not necessary.
3. Don't beat around the bush or pad your answer. Be direct. Make a point and support it. Get your list of ideas into words.
4. Look over your essay for errors in spelling and grammar. Save this for last. Your *ideas* are of first importance. You can work on spelling and grammar separately if they affect your grades.

Short-Answer Tests

Tests that ask you to fill in a blank, define a term, or list specific items can be difficult. Usually, the questions themselves contain little information. If you don't know the answer, you won't get much help from the questions.

The best way to prepare for short-answer tests is to overlearn the details of the course. As you study, pay special attention to lists of related terms.

Again, it is best to start with the questions you're sure you know. Follow that by completing items you think you probably know. Questions you have no idea about can be left blank.

Again, for your convenience, Figure I.2 provides a checklist summary of the main study skills we have covered.

USING DIGITAL MEDIA—NETTING NEW KNOWLEDGE

The Internet and digital media are providing exciting new ways to explore topics ranging from amnesia to zoophobia.

Back in the stone age, researching a project or paper usually meant a trip to the library, where you could spend hours sifting through card catalogues or rummaging through the stacks, breathing in the musty aroma of old books, only to find that someone else had checked out the critical information you so desperately needed (just ask your instructors, or your parents). Today, with a computer and Internet access, you can do most of your research from the comfort of your own room. You can find out more than you would ever want to know about just about any topic—all you have to do is google it. And it's all true, too—or is it?

Just how accurate is the information you find on the Internet? The answer to this question is, the information available on the Internet is only as reliable as its source. Reputable sources of psychological information include the American and Canadian Psychological Associations (see page 11), university psychology department web pages, and online resources such as Health Canada. If information on a web page is not attributed to a reliable source, such as a scholarly research journal, be very careful about using it, as you have no way to determine its accuracy. Apply the same critical thinking skills that you use to evaluate information from newspapers, magazines, and television: Keep an open mind, ask questions, be aware of biases (your own included), and beware of overly complicated explanations.

The Book Companion Website

How would I find information about psychology on the Internet? Your first stop on the Internet should be the companion website for this book at **www.psychologyjourney4ce.nelson.com**. Here's what you'll find there:

Online Quizzes. You can use these chapter-by-chapter multiple-choice quizzes to practise for tests and check your understanding.

Interactive Activities. The demonstrations and mini-experiments in this feature allow you to directly experience various psychological principles.

Internet Resources. This area is a "launching pad" that will take you to other psychology-related sites on the Internet. If a site sounds interesting, a click of the mouse will link you to it.

Online Flash Cards. The online flash cards allow you to practise terms and concepts interactively.

Psych in the News. This section features a news item or current event that is explored from a psychological perspective. After you've thought about a topic, you can share your opinions with others in an online discussion.

Discussion Forum. In the Discussion Forum, you'll have a chance to share your ideas with those of psychology students from all over the country.

Research and Teaching Showcase. Here you'll find regularly updated summaries of presentations, articles, and other teaching and research materials.

Archives. Using the Archives, you can quickly search for current and past articles from Psych in the News and the Research and Teaching Showcase.

The Book Companion website gives you online access to a variety of valuable learning aids and interesting materials.

Be sure to visit the Book Companion website for important information about how to improve your grades and enhance your appreciation of psychology.

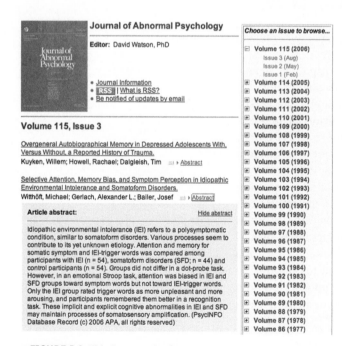

▶**FIGURE I.3** This is a sample abstract from the PsycINFO database. If you search for the term *idiopathic environmental intolerance*, you will find this article and many more in PsycINFO. (This record is reprinted with permission of the American Psychological Association, publisher of the PsycINFO Database, all rights reserved. May not be reproduced without prior permission.)

CourseMate

The more you study, the better the results. Make the most of your study time by accessing everything you need to succeed in one place. Read your textbook, take notes, review flashcards, watch videos, and take practice quizzes—online with CourseMate.

Psych Sites

You'll find a list of interesting websites you may want to explore at the end of each chapter in this book. The sites we've listed are generally of high quality. However, be aware that information on the Internet is not always accurate. It is wise to approach all websites with a healthy dose of skepticism.

PsycINFO

Psychological knowledge can also be found in specialized online databases. One of the best is PsycINFO, offered by the American Psychological Association (APA). **PsycINFO** provides summaries of the scientific and scholarly literature in psychology. Each record in PsycINFO consists of an abstract (short summary), plus notes about the author, title, source, and other details (see Figure I.3). All entries are indexed using key terms. Thus, you can search for various topics by entering words such as *drug abuse, postpartum depression,* or *creativity.*

You can gain access to PsycINFO in several ways. Many colleges and universities subscribe to PsycINFO or to a related CD-ROM version called PsycLIT. If this is the case, you can usually search PsycINFO from a terminal in the library or computer centre—for free. PsycINFO can also be accessed through the Internet, either directly or through APA's PsycDIRECT service. For more information on how to gain access to PsycINFO, check this website: *www.apa.org/pubs/databases/psycinfo/index.aspx.*

The American Psychological Association (APA) Website

The APA maintains an online library of free general-interest articles on aging, anger, children and families, depression, divorce, emotional health, kids and the media, sexuality, stress, women and men, and other topics. They are well worth consulting when you have questions about psychological issues. You'll find them at *www.apa.org.* For links to recent articles in newspapers and magazines, be sure to check the APA's PsycPORT page at *www.apa.org/news/psycport/index.aspx.*

The Canadian Psychological Association (CPA)

The objectives of the Canadian Psychological Association are as follows:

- to improve the health and welfare of all Canadians
- to promote excellence and innovation in psychological research, education, and practice
- to promote the advancement, development, dissemination, and application of psychological knowledge
- to provide high-quality services to members

The CPA publishes three journals (*The Canadian Journal of Experimental Psychology, The Canadian Journal of Behavioural Science,* and *Canadian Psychology*); fact sheets designed to give the general public trustworthy information about various psychological concerns and problems; and a quarterly newsletter (*Psynosis*) that is available online.

On the CPA website you will find information for students in psychology, links to psychology departments at Canadian universities, and other useful information. You can find all this and more at *www.cpa.ca.*

Please take some of the "digital journeys" described here. You might be surprised by the fascinating information that awaits you. Investigating psychology on your own is one of the best ways to enrich an already valuable course.

A Final Word

There is a distinction in Zen between "live words" and "dead words." Live words come from personal experience; dead words are "about" a subject. This book can only be a collection of dead words unless you accept the challenge of making an intellectual journey. You will find many helpful, useful, and exciting ideas in the pages that follow. To make them yours, you must set out to *actively* learn as much as you can. The ideas presented here should get you off to a good start. Good luck!

For more information, consult any of the following books.

Hettich, P. I. (2005). *Connect College to Career: Student Guide to Work and Life Transition.* Belmont, CA: Wadsworth.

Knaus, W. J., & Ellis, A. (2002). *The Procrastination Workbook: Your Personalized Program for Breaking Free from the Patterns That Hold You Back.* Oakland, CA: New Harbinger Press.

Rosnow, R. L. (2006). *Writing Papers in Psychology: A Student Guide to Research Papers, Essays, Proposals, Posters, and Handouts* (7th ed.). Belmont, CA: Wadsworth.

Rowe, B. (2007). *College Awareness Guide: What Students Need to Know to Succeed in College.* Upper Saddle River, NJ: Prentice Hall.

Santrock, J. W., & Halonen, J. S. (2007). *Connections to College Success.* Belmont, CA: Wadsworth.

STUDY BREAK **Study Skills**

Reflect

Which study skills do you think would help you the most? Which techniques do you already use? Which do you think you should try? To what extent do you already engage in self-regulated learning? What additional steps could you take to become a more active, goal-oriented learner?

Learning Check

1. The four R's in SQ4R stand for "read, recite, reflect, and review." T or F?
2. When using the LISAN method, students try to write down as much of a lecture as possible so that their notes are complete. T or F?
3. Spaced study sessions are usually superior to massed practice. T or F?
4. According to recent research, you should almost always stick with your first answer on multiple-choice tests. T or F?
5. To use the technique known as overlearning, you should continue to study after you feel you have begun to master a topic. T or F?
6. Setting learning goals and monitoring your progress are important parts of _____ learning.
7. Procrastination is related to seeking perfection and equating self-worth with grades. T or F?

Critical Thinking

8. How are the SQ4R method and the LISAN method related?

Answers

1. T 2. F 3. T 4. F 5. T 6. self-regulated 7. T 8. Both encourage people to actively seek information as a way of learning more effectively.

chapter 1

Jupiterimages/Thinkstock

Introducing Psychology and Research Methods

JOURNEY INTO PSYCHOLOGY: THE MYSTERIES OF HUMAN BEHAVIOUR

Look around you. Newspapers, radio, magazines, television, and the Internet are loaded with psychological information. Psychology is an ever-changing panorama of people and ideas. Really, you can't call yourself educated without knowing something about it. And, while we might envy those who have walked on the Moon or explored the ocean's depths, the ultimate frontier still lies closer to home. What could be more fascinating than a journey of self-discovery?

As you read this book, think of it as a travel guide. Ultimately, each person's path through life is unique. Nevertheless, psychology can show you much about human behaviour, so you

Psychology The scientific study of behaviour and mental processes.

will better understand yourself and others. And studying psychology will certainly help you make sense of the vast amount of psychological information that assaults us every day. Your guide awaits you. We hope you enjoy the journey.

Survey Questions

- What is psychology? What are its goals?
- What are the historical roots of modern psychology?
- What are the major trends and specialties in psychology today?
- What is the scientific method? Why is the scientific method important to psychologists?
- How do psychologists collect information?
- What is an experiment? Why do psychologists use experiments to answer questions about behaviour and mental processes?
- What other research methods do psychologists use?
- Why is it important for psychologists to consider ethical issues when doing research?
- What is critical thinking? Why is it important?
- How do psychological explanations differ from other (unscientific) explanations of behaviour?
- Can you trust the psychological information you find on the Internet and in popular media?

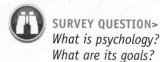

SURVEY QUESTION>
What is psychology?
What are its goals?

PSYCHOLOGY—SPOTLIGHT ON BEHAVIOUR

Psychology touches many areas of our lives. Psychology is about happiness, memory, stress, therapy, love, persuasion, hypnosis, perception, death, conformity, creativity, learning, personality, aging, intelligence, sexuality, emotion, and much more.

Psychology is both a science and a profession. Some psychologists are scientists, who do research to create new knowledge. Others are teachers, who pass this knowledge on to students. Still others apply psychology to solve problems in mental health, education, business, sports, law, and medicine. Later we will return to the profession of psychology. For now, let's focus on how knowledge is created. Whether they work in a lab, a classroom, or a clinic, all psychologists rely on information gained from scientific research.

Defining Psychology

The word *psychology* comes from the roots *psyche*, which means "mind," or "soul," and *logos*, meaning "knowledge or study." However, when was the last time you saw or touched a "mind"? Because the mind can't be studied directly, **psychology** is now defined as the scientific study of behaviour and mental processes.

What behaviours are we talking about here? Anything you do—eating, sleeping, talking, or sneezing—is a behaviour. So are snowboarding, gambling, watching television, learning French, basket weaving, and reading this book. Naturally, we are interested in

© Jeff Greenberg/Photo Edit

Psychologists are highly trained professionals. In addition to the psychological knowledge they possess, psychologists learn specialized skills in counselling and therapy, measurement and testing, research and experimentation, statistics, diagnosis, treatment, and many other areas.

overt behaviours (observable actions and responses). But psychologists also study covert behaviours. These are private, internal activities, such as thinking, remembering, and other mental events (Jackson, 2008).

Empiricism

When it comes to human behaviour, it seems we are all expert people watchers. "Common-sense" theories abound. However, you may be surprised to learn how often self-appointed authorities and long-held common-sense beliefs about human behaviour are wrong. For example, have you ever heard that blind people have amazingly accurate organs of touch? Or that the more motivated you are, the better you will do at solving a complex problem? It turns out that these common-sense beliefs, and many others, are wrong (Landau & Bavaria, 2003).

Because common sense is flawed, psychologists have a special respect for **empirical evidence** (information gained from direct observation), especially when it is collected in a scientific fashion. Unlike our personal experience, scientific observation is systematic, or carefully planned. When possible, we study behaviour directly, by collecting **data** (observed facts) so that we can draw valid conclusions. Would you say it's true, for instance, that you can't teach an old dog new tricks? Why argue about it? A psychologist could simply get 10 "new" dogs, 10 "used" dogs, and 10 "old" dogs and then try to teach them all a new trick to find out!

Here's an example of gathering empirical evidence: Have you ever wondered whether people become more hostile when it's boiling hot outside? John Simister and Cary Cooper (2005) decided to find out. They obtained data on temperatures and criminal activity in Los Angeles over a four-year period. When they graphed air temperature and the frequency of aggravated assaults, a clear relationship emerged. Assaults and temperatures rise and fall more or less in parallel (so there may be something to the phrase "hot under the collar").

Isn't the outcome of this study fairly predictable? Not if you started out believing otherwise. Sometimes the results of studies match our personal observations and common-sense beliefs and sometimes they come as a surprise. In this instance, you may have guessed the outcome. Your suspicions were confirmed by scientific observation. However, hostile actions that require more extreme physical exertion, such as fistfights, might become less likely at very high temperatures. Without systematically gathering data, we wouldn't know for sure whether overheated people become sluggish or more aggressive when it gets hot.

Psychological Research

Researchers in many fields, such as history, law, art, and business, are interested in human behaviour. How is psychology different? Psychology's great strength is that it uses **scientific observation** to systematically answer questions about behaviour (Stanovich, 2007).

This is also what separates scientific psychology from the "pop" psychology found in books, popular magazines, and TV programs.

Sometimes ethical or practical concerns make it impossible to study a topic. More often, questions go unanswered for lack of a suitable **research method** (a systematic procedure for answering scientific questions). For example, at one time we believed people who said they never dreamed. Then the EEG (electroencephalograph) was developed to measure brain waves. Certain EEG patterns, and the presence of eye movements, can reveal when a person is dreaming. People who "never dream," it turns out, dream frequently. If they are awakened during a dream, they vividly remember it. Thus, the EEG (see Figure 1.1) helped make the study of dreaming more scientific.

Overt behaviour An action or response that is directly observable.

Covert behaviour A response that is internal or hidden from view (such as a thought or an emotional reaction).

Empirical evidence Facts or information based on direct observation or experience.

Data Observed facts or evidence (*data:* plural; *datum:* singular).

Scientific observation An empirical investigation that is structured to answer questions about the world.

Research method A systematic approach to answering scientific questions.

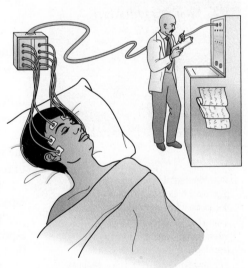

▸▸**FIGURE 1.1** The scientific study of dreaming was made possible by use of the EEG, a device that records the tiny electrical potentials generated by the brain as a person sleeps. The EEG converts these electrical signals to a written record of brain activity. Certain shifts in brain activity, coupled with the presence of rapid eye movements, are strongly related to dreaming. (See Chapter 5 for more information.)

Photodisc/Getty Images

Greg Epperson/Shutterstock

CP Photo/Tom Hanson

The variety and complexity of human behaviour make psychological investigation challenging. How would you explain the behaviours shown here?

Developmental psychologist A psychologist interested in human growth and development from conception until death.

Learning theorist A psychologist interested in variables affecting learning and in theories of learning.

Personality theorist A psychologist who studies personality traits, dynamics, and theories.

Sensation and perception psychologist A psychologist who studies the sense organs and the process of perception.

Comparative psychologist A psychologist primarily interested in studying and comparing the behaviour of different species, especially animals.

What kinds of topics do research psychologists study? Here's a sample of what various research psychologists might say about their work.

"I am a **developmental psychologist.** I study the course of human growth and development, from conception until death. I'm especially interested in how young children develop the ability to think, speak, perceive, and act.

"I'm also interested in how people get to be the way they are. Like other **learning theorists,** I study how and why learning occurs in humans and animals. Right now I'm investigating how patterns of reward affect learning in pigeons."

"I'm a **personality theorist.** I study personality traits, motivation, and individual differences. I am especially interested in the personality profiles of highly creative university students."

"As a **sensation and perception psychologist,** I investigate how we come to know the world through our senses. I am using a perceptual theory to study how we are able to recognize faces."

"**Comparative psychologists** study and compare the behaviour of different species, especially animals. Personally, I'm fascinated by the echolocation abilities of porpoises."

"**Neuropsychologists** are interested in how behaviour is related to biological processes, especially activities in the nervous system. I've been doing some exciting research on how the brain controls hunger."

"**Social psychologists** explore human social behaviour, such as attitudes, persuasion, riots, conformity, leadership, racism, and friendship. My own interest is interpersonal attraction. I place two strangers in a room and analyze how strongly they are attracted to each other."

"**Cultural psychologists** study the ways in which culture affects human behaviour. The language you speak, the foods you eat, how your parents disciplined you, what laws you obey, whom you regard as 'family,' whether you eat with a spoon or your fingers—these and countless other details of behaviour are strongly influenced by culture."

"*Gender psychologists* study differences between females and males. I want to understand how gender differences are influenced by biology, child rearing, education, and stereotypes."

"*Evolutionary psychologists* are interested in how our behaviour is guided by patterns that evolved during the long history of humankind. I am studying some interesting trends in male and female mating choices that don't seem to be merely learned or based on culture."

"*Forensic psychologists* apply psychological principles to legal issues. I am interested in improving the reliability of eyewitness testimony during trials."

This small sample should give you an idea of the diversity of psychological research. It also hints at some of the kinds of information we will cover later in this book.

Some of the most interesting research with animals has focused on attempts to teach primates to communicate with sign language. Such research has led to better methods for teaching language to aphasic children (children with serious language impairment). (See Chapter 8 for more information.)

Animals and Psychology

Research involving animals was mentioned in some of the preceding examples. Why is that? It may surprise you to learn that psychologists are interested in the behaviour of any living creature—from flatworms to humans. Indeed, some comparative psychologists have spent their entire careers studying rats, cats, dogs, turtles, or chimpanzees.

Psychological studies involving animals include many different types of research (Ord et al., 2005). **Animal models** are used to discover principles that apply to human behaviour. Studying animals has helped us better understand obesity, memory, stress, psychosis, therapy, aging, and many other topics. Psychology also benefits animals. The care of endangered species in zoos, for example, relies on behavioural studies.

Psychology's Goals

What do psychologists hope to achieve? As scientists, our ultimate goal is to benefit humanity (O'Neill, 2005). Specifically, the goals of psychology are to describe, understand, predict, and control behavior. What do psychology's goals mean in practice? Let's see.

Description

Answering psychological questions often begins with a careful description of behaviour. **Description**, or naming and classifying, is typically based on making a detailed record of behavioural observations.

But a description doesn't explain anything, does it? Right. Useful knowledge begins with accurate description, but descriptions fail to answer the important "why" questions. Why do more women attempt suicide, and why do more men complete it? Why are people more aggressive when they are uncomfortable? Why are bystanders often unwilling to help in an emergency?

Understanding

Psychology's second goal is met when we can explain an event. That is, **understanding** usually means we can state the causes of a behaviour. Take our last "why" question as an example: Research on "bystander apathy" has shown that people often fail to help when other possible helpers are nearby. Why? Because a "diffusion of responsibility" occurs. Basically, no one feels personally obligated to pitch in. Generally, the more potential helpers there are, the less likely it is that anyone will help (Darley, 2000; Darley & Latané, 1968). Now we can explain a perplexing problem.

Prediction

Psychology's third goal, **prediction**, is the ability to forecast behaviour accurately. Notice that our explanation of bystander apathy makes a prediction about the chances of getting help. Anyone who has ever been stuck in a snowbank will recognize the accuracy of this prediction: Having many potential helpers nearby is no guarantee that anyone will pick up a shovel and help dig you out.

Neuropychologist A psychologist who studies the relationship between behaviour and biological processes, especially activity in the nervous system.

Social psychologist A psychologist particularly interested in human social behaviour.

Cultural psychologist A psychologist who studies the ways in which culture affects human behaviour.

Animal model In research, using animal behaviour to discover principles that may apply to human behaviour.

Description In scientific research, the process of naming and classifying.

Understanding In psychology, when the causes of a behaviour can be stated.

Prediction An ability to accurately forecast behaviour.

STUDY BREAK **The Science of Psychology**

Reflect

At first, many students think that psychology is primarily about abnormal behaviour and psychotherapy. Did you? How would you describe the field now?

Learning Check

To check your memory, see if you can answer these questions. If you miss any, skim over the preceding material before continuing, to make sure you understand what you just read.

1. Psychology is the _____ study of _____ and _____ processes.

2. Information gained through direct observation and measurement is called _____ evidence.

3. In psychological research, animal _____ may be used to discover principles that apply to human behaviour.

4. Which of the following questions relates most directly to the goal of understanding behaviour?
   a. Do the scores of men and women differ on tests of thinking abilities?
   b. Why does a blow to the head cause memory loss?

c. Will productivity in a business office increase if room temperature is raised or lowered?

d. What percentage of university students suffer from test anxiety?

Match the following research areas with the topics they cover.

5. _____	Developmental psychology	A. Attitudes, groups, leadership
6. _____	Learning	B. Conditioning, memory
7. _____	Personality	C. The psychology of law
8. _____	Sensation and perception	D. Brain and nervous system
9. _____	Neuropsychology	E. Child psychology
10. _____	Social psychology	F. Individual differences, motivation
11. _____	Comparative psychology	G. Animal behaviour
		H. Processing sensory information

Critical Thinking

12. All sciences are interested in controlling the phenomena they study. T or F?

Answers

1. scientific, behaviour, mental 2. empirical 3. models 4. b 5. E 6. B 7. F 8. H 9. D 10. A 11. G 12. False. Astronomy and archaeology are examples of sciences that do not share psychology's fourth goal.

Control Altering conditions that influence behaviour in predictable ways.

Control

Description, explanation, and prediction seem reasonable, but is control a valid goal for psychology? Control may seem like a threat to your personal freedom. However, to a psychologist, **control** simply means altering the conditions that influence behaviour in some predictable way. If someone makes changes in a classroom that help children learn better, that person has exerted control. If a clinical psychologist helps a person overcome a terrible fear of heights, control is involved. Control is also involved in designing airplanes to keep pilots from making fatal errors. However, psychological control must be used wisely, humanely, and ethically.

In summary, psychology's goals are a natural outgrowth of our desire to understand behaviour. Basically, they boil down to asking the following questions:

- What is the nature of this behaviour? (description)
- Why does it occur? (understanding and explanation)
- Can we forecast when it will occur? (prediction)
- What conditions affect it? (control)

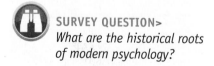 **SURVEY QUESTION>**
What are the historical roots of modern psychology?

A BRIEF HISTORY OF PSYCHOLOGY—PSYCHOLOGY'S FAMILY ALBUM

Psychology began centuries ago as a branch of philosophy, the study of knowledge, reality, and human nature. In many Canadian universities, psychology remained connected with philosophy departments until after World War II (Adair, Paivio, & Ritchie, 1996).

Psychology's history as a separate science began in 1879 in Leipzig, Germany. There, the "father of psychology," Wilhelm Wundt (VILL-helm Voont), set up the first psychological laboratory to study conscious experience. How, he wondered, do we form sensations, images, and feelings? To find out, Wundt observed and measured stimuli of various kinds (lights, sounds, weights). A **stimulus** is any physical energy that affects a person and evokes a response (*stimulus:* singular; *stimuli* [STIM-you-lie]: plural). Wundt then used **introspection,** or "looking inward," and careful measurement to probe his reactions to various stimuli. (If you stop reading right now and carefully examine your thoughts, feelings, and sensations, you will have done some introspecting.) Over the years, Wundt studied vision, hearing, taste, touch, memory, time perception, and many other subjects. By insisting on careful observation and measurement, he answered some interesting questions and got psychology off to a good start.

Structuralism

Wundt's ideas were carried to North America by Edward B. Titchener. Titchener called Wundt's ideas **structuralism** because they dealt with the structure of mental life. Essentially, the structuralists hoped to analyze experience into basic "elements" or "building blocks," using introspection as their primary tool.

For instance, an observer might hold an apple and decide that she had experienced the elements "hue" (colour), "roundness," and "weight." Another example of the kind of question that might have interested a structuralist is: What basic tastes mix together to create complex flavours as different as liver, lime, bacon, and chocolate chip peanut butter surprise?

It soon became clear that introspection was a poor way to answer many questions. Why? Because the structuralists frequently disagreed. And when they did, there was no way to settle differences. If two people came up with different lists of basic taste sensations, for example, who could say which was right? Despite such limitations, "looking inward" is still used in studies of hypnosis, meditation, problem solving, moods, and many other topics (Mayer & Hanson, 1995).

Functionalism

William James, an American scholar, broadened psychology to include animal behaviour, religious experience, abnormal behaviour, and other interesting topics. James's brilliant first book, *Principles of Psychology* (1890), helped establish the field as a serious discipline (Simon, 1998).

The term **functionalism** comes from an interest in how the mind functions to adapt us to our environment. James regarded consciousness as an ever-changing stream or flow of images and sensations—not a set of lifeless building blocks, as the structuralists claimed.

The functionalists admired Charles Darwin, who proposed that creatures evolve in ways that favour their survival. According to Darwin's principle of **natural selection,** physical characteristics that help animals adapt to their environments are retained in evolution. Similarly, the functionalists wanted to find out how the mind, perception, habits, and emotions help us adapt and survive.

Behaviourism

Functionalism was soon challenged by **behaviourism,** the study of overt, observable behaviour. Behaviourist John B. Watson objected strongly to the study of the "mind" or "conscious experience." "Introspection," he said, "is unscientific." Watson realized that he could study

Wilhelm Wundt, 1832–1920. Wundt is credited with making psychology an independent science, separate from philosophy. Wundt's original training was in medicine, but he became deeply interested in psychology. In his laboratory, Wundt investigated how sensations, images, and feelings combine to make up personal experience.

William James, 1842–1910. William James was the son of philosopher Henry James, Sr., and the brother of novelist Henry James. During his long academic career, James taught anatomy, physiology, psychology, and philosophy at Harvard University. James believed strongly that ideas should be judged in terms of their practical consequences for human conduct.

Stimulus Any physical energy that has some effect on an organism and that evokes a response.

Introspection To look within; to examine one's own thoughts, feelings, or sensations.

Structuralism The school of thought concerned with analyzing sensations and personal experience into basic elements.

Functionalism The school of psychology concerned with how behaviour and mental abilities help people adapt to their environments.

Natural selection Darwin's theory that evolution favours those plants and animals best suited to their living conditions.

Behaviourism The school of psychology that emphasizes the study of overt, observable behaviour.

John B. Watson, 1878–1958. Watson's intense interest in observable behaviour began with his doctoral studies in biology and neurology. Watson became a psychology professor at Johns Hopkins University in 1908 and advanced his theory of behaviourism. He remained at Johns Hopkins until 1920, when he left for a career in the advertising industry!

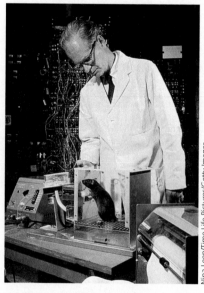

B. F. Skinner, 1904–1990. Skinner studied simple behaviours under carefully controlled conditions. The "Skinner box" you see here has been widely used to study learning in simplified animal experiments. In addition to advancing psychology, Skinner hoped that his radical brand of behaviourism would improve human life.

animals even though he couldn't ask them questions or know what they were thinking. He simply observed the relationship between stimuli (events in the environment) and an animal's **responses** (any muscular action, glandular activity, or other identifiable behaviour). Why not, he asked, apply the same objectivity to studying humans (Watson, 1994)?

Watson soon adopted Russian physiologist Ivan Pavlov's (ee-VAHN PAV-lahv) concept of conditioning to explain most behaviour. (A **conditioned response** is a learned reaction to a particular stimulus.) Watson enthusiastically proclaimed, "Give me a dozen healthy infants, well-formed, and my own special world to bring them up in and I'll guarantee to take any one at random and train him to become any type of specialist I might select— doctor, lawyer, artist, merchant-chief, and yes, beggarman and thief" (Watson, 1913).

Would most psychologists agree with Watson's claim? Today, most would consider it an overstatement. Just the same, behaviourism helped make psychology a natural science, rather than a branch of philosophy (Richelle, 1995).

One of the best-known modern behaviourists, B. F. Skinner (1904–1990), believed that our behaviour is controlled by rewards, or positive reinforcers. To study learning, Skinner created his famous conditioning chamber, or "Skinner box." With it, he could present stimuli to animals and record their responses (see Chapter 6, page 241, "Operant Conditioning"). Many of Skinner's ideas about learning grew out of work with rats and pigeons. Nevertheless, he believed that the same laws of behaviour apply to all organisms, including humans. As a "radical behaviourist," Skinner also believed that mental events are not needed to explain behaviour (Schultz & Schultz, 2008).

Skinner was convinced that a "designed culture" based on positive reinforcement could encourage desirable behaviour. (Contrary to common belief, Skinner disliked the use of punishment.) It is essential, he said, to change our behaviour before overpopulation, pollution, or nuclear war shatters humanity. Too often, misguided rewards lead us into destructive actions.

Gestalt Psychology

Imagine that you just played "Happy Birthday" on a tuba. Next, you play it on a violin. None of the tuba's sounds are duplicated by the violin, but the melody is still completely recognizable— as long as the relationship between notes remains the same.

Now, what would happen if you played the notes of "Happy Birthday" in the correct order, but at a rate of one per hour? What would we have? Nothing! The separate notes would no longer be a melody. Perceptually, the melody is somehow more than the individual notes that define it.

It was observations like these that launched the Gestalt school of thought. **Gestalt psychologists** studied thinking, learning, and perception in whole units, not by analyzing experiences into parts. Their slogan was "The whole is greater than the sum of its parts" (see Figure 1.2).

Response Any muscular action, glandular activity, or other identifiable aspect of behaviour.

Conditioned response A reflex response that has become associated with a new stimulus.

Gestalt psychology The school of psychology emphasizing the study of thinking, learning, and perception in whole units, not by analysis into parts.

▶▶**FIGURE 1.2** The design you see here is entirely made up of broken elements. However, as the Gestalt psychologists discovered, our perceptions have a powerful tendency to form meaningful patterns. Because of this tendency, you will probably see a triangle in this design, even though it is only an illusion. Your whole perceptual experience exceeds the sum of its parts.

Women in Psychology

Women were actively discouraged from seeking advanced degrees in the late 1800s (Bohan, 1990). Even so, by 1906 in the United States, about one psychologist in every ten was a woman. Who were these "foremothers" of psychology? Three who became well known are Mary Calkins, Christine Ladd-Franklin, and Margaret Washburn.

Mary Calkins did valuable research on memory. She was also the first woman president of the American Psychological Association, in 1905. Christine Ladd-Franklin studied colour vision. In 1906, she was ranked as one of the 50 most important psychologists in the

United States. In 1908, Margaret Washburn published an influential textbook on animal behaviour titled *The Animal Mind*.

The first woman to be awarded a Ph.D. in psychology was Margaret Washburn, in 1894. Over the next 15 years, many more women followed her pioneering lead. Today, two out of three graduate students in psychology are women. And, in recent years, nearly a majority of university graduates with a major in psychology have been women. Clearly, psychology has become fully open to both men and women (Hyde, 2004; Martin, 1995).

Mary Calkins, 1863–1930.

Christine Ladd-Franklin, 1847–1930.

Margaret Washburn, 1871–1939.

Max Wertheimer (VERT-hi-mer), a German psychologist, was the first person to advance the Gestalt viewpoint. It is a mistake, he said, to analyze psychological events into pieces, or "elements," as the structuralists did. Like a melody, many experiences cannot be broken into smaller units. For this reason, studies of perception and personality have been especially influenced by the Gestalt viewpoint.

Were all the early psychologists men? So far, no women have been mentioned. For the most part, men dominated science and education at the beginning of the 20th century. Nevertheless, women have contributed to psychology from the beginning (Minton, 2000). Take a moment to read Human Diversity: "Women in Psychology," above for more information.

Psychoanalytic Psychology

As psychology grew more scientific, an Austrian doctor named Sigmund Freud was developing his own theories. Freud believed that mental life is like an iceberg: Only a small part is exposed to view. He called the area of the mind that lies outside of personal awareness the **unconscious**. According to Freud, our behaviour is deeply influenced by unconscious thoughts, impulses, and desires—especially those concerning sex and aggression. Freud's ideas opened new horizons in art, literature, and history, as well as psychology (Robins, Gosling, & Craik, 1998).

Freud theorized that many unconscious thoughts are threatening; hence, they are **repressed** (held out of awareness). But sometimes, he said, they are revealed by dreams, emotions, or slips of the tongue. ("Freudian slips" are often humorous, as when a student who is tardy for class says, "I'm sorry I couldn't get here any later.")

Unconscious The region of the mind that is beyond awareness—especially impulses and desires not directly known to a person.

Repression The unconscious process by which memories, thoughts, or impulses are held out of awareness.

Max Wertheimer, 1880–1941. Wertheimer first proposed the Gestalt viewpoint to help explain perceptual illusions. He later promoted Gestalt psychology as a way to understand not only perception, problem solving, thinking, and social behaviour but also art, logic, philosophy, and politics.

Psychoanalysis A Freudian approach to psychotherapy emphasizing the exploration of unconscious conflicts.

Psychodynamic theory Any theory of behaviour that emphasizes internal conflicts, motives, and unconscious forces.

Humanism An approach to psychology that focuses on human experience, problems, potentials, and ideals.

Determinism The idea that all behaviour has prior causes that would completely explain one's choices and actions if all such causes were known.

Free will The idea that human beings are capable of freely making choices or decisions.

Self-image The total subjective perception of oneself.

Self-evaluation Positive and negative feelings held toward oneself.

Frame of reference A mental perspective used for judging and evaluating events.

Self-actualization The process of fully developing one's personal potential.

Sigmund Freud, 1856–1939. For over 50 years, Freud probed the unconscious mind. In doing so, he altered modern views of human nature. His early experimentation with a "talking cure" for hysteria is regarded as the beginning of psychoanalysis. Through psychoanalysis, Freud added psychological treatment methods to psychiatry.

Archives of the History of American Psychology, The University of Akron

Freud believed that all thoughts, emotions, and actions are determined. In other words, nothing is an accident: If we probe deeply enough we will find the causes of every thought or action. Freud was also among the first to appreciate that childhood affects adult personality ("The child is father to the man"). Most of all, perhaps, Freud is known for creating **psychoanalysis,** the first "talking therapy." Freud's method of psychotherapy explores unconscious conflicts and emotional problems (see Chapter 13, page 516). Today, his ideas have been altered so much that few strictly psychoanalytic psychologists are left. However, Freud's legacy is still evident in various **psychodynamic theories,** which emphasize internal motives, conflicts, and unconscious forces (Westen, 1998).

Humanistic Psychology

Humanism is a view that focuses on understanding subjective human experience. As a group, humanistic psychologists are interested in human problems, potentials, and ideals.

How is the humanistic approach different from others? Carl Rogers, Abraham Maslow, and other humanists rejected the Freudian idea that personality is ruled by unconscious forces. They were also uncomfortable with the behaviourist emphasis on environmental control. Both views have a strong undercurrent of **determinism** (the idea that behaviour is determined by forces beyond our control). In contrast, the humanists stress **free will,** the ability to make voluntary choices. Of course, past experiences affect us. Nevertheless, humanists believe that people can freely choose to live more creative, meaningful, and satisfying lives.

Humanists helped stimulate interest in psychological needs for love, self-esteem, belonging, self-expression, creativity, and spirituality. Such needs, they believe, are as important as our biological urges for food and water. For example, newborn infants deprived of human love may die just as surely as they would if deprived of food.

How scientific is the humanistic approach? At first, humanists tended to be less interested in treating psychology as an objective, behavioural science. Instead, they stressed subjective factors, such as one's self-image, self-evaluation, and frame of reference. (**Self-image** is your perception of your own body, personality, and capabilities. **Self-evaluation** refers to the positive and negative feelings you have about yourself. A **frame of reference** is a mental or emotional perspective used for evaluating events.) Today, although humanists still seek to understand how people perceive themselves and experience the world, they collect data and seek evidence to support their ideas through research, as most other psychologists do (Schneider, Bugental, & Pierson, 2001).

Maslow's concept of self-actualization is a special feature of humanism. **Self-actualization** refers to fully developing one's potential and becoming the best person possible. According to humanists, everyone has this potential. Humanists seek ways to help it emerge. Table 1.1 shows a summary of psychology's early development.

Archives of the History of American Psychology, The University of Akron

Abraham Maslow, 1908–1970. As a founder of humanistic psychology, Maslow was interested in studying people of exceptional mental health. Such self-actualized people, he believed, make full use of their talents and abilities. Maslow offered his positive view of human potential as an alternative to the schools of behaviourism and psychoanalysis.

■ Table 1.1	The Early Development of Psychology

Date	Notable Events
1875	• First psychology course offered by William James at Harvard University
1878	• First American Ph.D. in psychology awarded
1879	• Wilhelm Wundt establishes first psychology laboratory in Germany
1883	• First American psychology laboratory founded at Johns Hopkins University
1885	• First Canadian psychology textbook published by the Rev. William Lyall
1886	• First American psychology textbook published by John Dewey
1890	• William James publishes *Principles of Psychology*
1891	• James Mark Baldwin establishes the first psychology laboratory at the University of Toronto
1892	• American Psychological Association founded
1894	• Margaret Washburn the first woman to be awarded a Ph.D. in psychology
1895	• Sigmund Freud publishes first studies
1898	• Edward Titchener advances psychology based on introspection
1900	• Freud publishes *The Interpretation of Dreams*
1905	• Mary Calkins elected first woman president of the American Psychological Association
1906	• Ivan Pavlov reports his research on conditioning
1912	• Max Wertheimer and others advance Gestalt viewpoint
1913	• John Watson presents behaviouristic view
1939	• Canadian Psychological Association founded
1968	• Mary Wright elected first woman president of the Canadian Psychological Association

Cognitive psychology The area of psychology concerned with human thinking and information processing.

PSYCHOLOGY TODAY—THREE VIEWS OF BEHAVIOUR

At one time, loyalty to each school of thought was fierce, and clashes were common. Today, viewpoints such as functionalism and Gestalt psychology have blended into newer, broader perspectives. Also, some early systems, such as structuralism, have disappeared entirely. Certainly, loyalties and specialties still exist. But today, many psychologists are *eclectic* (ee-KLEK-tik) because they realize that a single perspective is unlikely to fully explain all the complexities of human behaviour. The three broad views that shape modern psychology are the *biological, psychological,* and *sociocultural* perspectives (see Table 1.2).

The Biological Perspective

The biological perspective seeks to explain our behaviour in terms of mechanisms such as brain processes, evolution, and genetics. By using new techniques for studying the brain, neuropsychologists are producing exciting new insights about how the brain relates to thinking, feelings, perception, abnormal behaviour, and other topics. Neuropsychologists and others who study the brain and nervous system, such as biologists and biochemists, form the broader field of neuroscience. *Evolutionary psychologists* attempt to explain our current behaviour by looking back at human history to learn how evolutionary principles and genetics affect us.

The Psychological Perspective

The psychological perspective views behaviour as the result of psychological processes within each person. This view continues to emphasize objective observation, just as the early behaviourists did. However, the psychological perspective now includes **cognitive psychology,** which seeks to explain how mental processes affect our thoughts, actions, and feelings. Cognitive psychology has gained prominence in recent years as researchers have devised ways to objectively study covert behaviours, such as thinking, memory, language, perception, problem solving, consciousness, and creativity. With a renewed interest in thinking, it can be said that psychology has finally "regained consciousness" (Robins, Gosling, & Craik, 1999).

<SURVEY QUESTION
What are the major trends and specialties in psychology today?

McGill University Archives

Donald O. Hebb, 1904–1985. Born in Nova Scotia, Hebb received a B.A. from Dalhousie University and worked as a school principal while studying for an M.A. at McGill University. After receiving a Ph.D. from Harvard, he worked at the Montreal Neurological Institute and Queen's University before returning to McGill as a professor of psychology. His book *The Organization of Behavior* (1949) paved the way for the current emphasis on understanding the brain. His ideas continue to have a major influence on both cognitive psychology and cognitive neuropsychology.

■ Table 1.2 **Contemporary Ways to Look at Behaviour**

Biological Perspective

Neuropsychological View

Key Idea: *Human and animal behaviour is the result of internal physical, chemical, and biological processes.*
Seeks to explain behaviour through activity of the brain and nervous system, physiology, genetics, the endocrine system, and biochemistry; neutral, reductionistic, mechanistic view of human nature.

Evolutionary View

Key Idea: *Human and animal behaviour is the result of the process of evolution.*
Seeks to explain behaviour through evolutionary principles based on natural selection; neutral, reductionistic, mechanistic view of human nature.

Psychological Perspective

S ➤ R

Behaviouristic View

Key Idea: *Behaviour is shaped and controlled by one's environment.*
Emphasizes the study of observable behaviour and the effects of learning; stresses the influence of external rewards and punishments; neutral, scientific, somewhat mechanistic view of human nature.

Cognitive View

Key Idea: *Much human behaviour can be understood in terms of the mental processing of information.*
Concerned with thinking, knowing, perception, understanding, memory, decision making, and judgment; explains behaviour in terms of information processing; neutral, somewhat computer-like view of human nature.

Psychodynamic View

Key Idea: *Behaviour is directed by forces within one's personality that are often hidden or unconscious.*
Emphasizes internal impulses, desires, and conflicts—especially those that are unconscious; views behaviour as the result of clashing forces within the personality; somewhat negative, pessimistic view of human nature.

Humanistic View

Key Idea: *Behaviour is guided by one's self-image, by subjective perceptions of the world, and by needs for personal growth.*
Focuses on subjective, conscious experience, human problems, potentials, and ideals; emphasizes self-image and self-actualization to explain behaviour; positive, philosophical view of human nature.

Sociocultural Perspective

Sociocultural View

Key Idea: *Behaviour is influenced by one's social and cultural context.*
Emphasizes that behaviour is related to the social and cultural environment within which a person is born, grows up, and lives from day to day; neutral, interactionist view of human nature.

Freudian psychoanalysis continues to evolve into the broader *psychodynamic view.* Although many of Freud's ideas have been challenged, psychodynamic psychologists continue to trace human behaviour to unconscious processes. They also seek to develop therapies to help people lead happier, fuller lives. Humanistic psychologists do, too, but they stress subjective, conscious experience and the positive side of human nature.

Psychologists have always paid attention to the negative side of human behaviour. This is easy to understand because of the pressing need to solve human problems. However, psychologists have recently begun to ask: What do we know about love, happiness, creativity, well-being, self-confidence, and achievement? Together, such topics make up **positive psychology,** the study of human strengths, virtues, and optimal behaviour (Compton, 2005; Seligman & Csikszentmihalyi, 2000). Many topics from positive psychology can be found in this book. Ideally, they will help make your own life more positive and fulfilling (Simonton & Baumeister, 2005).

The Sociocultural Perspective

As you can see, it is helpful to view human behaviour from more than one perspective. This is also true in another sense. We are a multicultural society, made up of people from many different nations. How has this affected psychology? Let us introduce you to Jerry, whose parents came to Canada from Japan. Jerry is married to Anne, whose family arrived in Quebec during the Irish potato famine. They live in Vancouver with their children. Last year, this is how they spent New Year's Day.

> We woke up in the morning and went to mass at St. Brigid's, which has a gospel choir. . . . Then we went to the Japanese Community Centre for the Oshogatsu New Year's program and saw Buddhist archers shoot arrows to ward off evil spirits for the year. Next, we ate traditional rice cakes as part of the New Year's service and listened to a young storyteller who was visiting from Japan. On the way home, we stopped in Chinatown for tea and after that we ate poutine. (Adapted from Njeri, 1991)

Jerry and his family reflect the Canadian social reality: Cultural diversity is the norm. According to the 2006 census, 16.2 percent of Canadians identify themselves as members of a visible minority (Statistics Canada, 2008).

The Impact of Culture

In the past, psychology was based mostly on the cultures of North America and Europe. Now, we must ask: Do the principles of Western psychology apply to people in all cultures? Are some psychological concepts invalid in other cultures? Are any universal? As psychologists have probed such questions, one thing has become clear: Most of what we think, feel, and do is influenced in one way or another by the social and cultural worlds in which we live (Lehman, Chiu, & Schaller, 2004).

Cultural Relativity

Imagine that you are a psychologist. Your client, Linda, who is an Aboriginal Canadian, tells you that spirits live in the trees near her home. Is she abnormal? If you fail to take her cultural beliefs into account, you may misjudge Linda's mental health status. **Cultural relativity** (the idea that behaviour must be judged relative to the values of the culture in which it occurs) can greatly affect the diagnosis of mental disorders (Alarcon, 1995; Draguns, Gielen, & Fish, 2004). Cases like Linda's teach us to be wary of using inappropriate standards when judging others or comparing groups.

A Broader View of Diversity

In addition to cultural differences, age, ethnicity, gender, religion, disability, and sexual orientation all affect the **norms** that guide behaviour. (Norms are rules that define acceptable and expected behaviour for members of various groups.) All too often, the unstated standard for judging what is "average," "normal," or "correct" is the behaviour of Caucasian, middle-class males (Reid, 2002). To fully understand human behaviour, psychologists need to know how people differ, as well as the ways in which we are all alike. For the same reason, an appreciation of human diversity can enrich your life, as well as your understanding of psychology (Denmark, Rabinowitz, & Sechzer, 2005).

In a moment, we will further explore what psychologists do. First, here are some questions to enhance your learning.

Positive psychology The study of human strengths, virtues, and optimal behaviour.

Cultural relativity The idea that behaviour must be judged relative to the values of the culture in which it occurs.

Norms Rules that define acceptable and expected behaviour for members of a group.

✓ STUDY BREAK   History and Major Perspectives

Reflect

Which school of thought most closely matches your own view of behaviour? Do you think any of the early schools offer a complete explanation of why we behave as we do? What about the three contemporary perspectives? Can you explain why so many psychologists are eclectic?

Learning Check

Match:

_____ 1. Philosophy

_____ 2. Wundt

_____ 3. Structuralism

_____ 4. Functionalism

_____ 5. Behaviourism

_____ 6. Gestalt

A. Against analysis; studied whole experiences

B. "Mental chemistry" and introspection

C. Emphasizes self-actualization and personal growth

D. Interested in unconscious causes of behaviour

E. Interested in how the mind aids survival

F. First woman Ph.D. in psychology

_____ 7. Psychodynamic

_____ 8. Humanistic

_____ 9. Cognitive

_____ 10. Washburn

_____ 11. Neuropsychology

G. Studied stimuli and responses, conditioning

H. Part of psychology's "long past"

I. Concerned with thinking, language, problem solving

J. Used introspection and careful measurement

K. Relates behaviour to the brain, physiology, and genetics

12. Cultural relativity refers to the fact that some universal behaviour patterns are not related to culture. T or F?

13. Universal norms exist for judging the behaviour of people in various cultural and social groups. T or F?

Critical Thinking

14. Modern sciences, such as psychology, are built on observations that can be verified by two or more independent observers. Did structuralism meet this standard? Why or why not?

Answers

1. H 2. J 3. B 4. E 5. G 6. A 7. D 8. C 9. I 10. F 11. K 12. F 13. F 14. No, it did not. The downfall of structuralism was that each observer examined the contents of his or her own mind—which is something that no other person can observe.

PSYCHOLOGISTS—GUARANTEED NOT TO SHRINK

What are the differences among various kinds of mental health professionals? Certainly, they're not all "shrinks." Each has a specific blend of training and skills.

A **psychologist** is highly trained in the methods, factual knowledge, and theories of psychology. Psychologists usually have a master's degree or a doctorate. These degrees typically require from three to eight years of postgraduate training. Psychologists may teach, do research, give psychological tests, or serve as consultants to business, industry, government, or the military.

Public impressions of psychologists are often inaccurate. Perhaps this occurs because so many stereotyped images appear in movies and on television. For example, in the film *Prime*, a therapist listens to a patient describe the intimate details of her relationship with a man without telling the patient that the man is her son. No ethical therapist would ever engage in such behaviour. Other films have featured psychologists who are more disturbed than their patients (*Anger Management*) or are bumbling buffoons (*Analyze This*). Television shows with a major psychological focus include *Criminal Minds, In Treatment, Lie to Me* (based loosely on the work of Paul Eckman, who did groundbreaking work on the relationship between facial expressions and their underlying emotions), and *The Mentalist.* Such portrayals may be dramatic and entertaining, but they can seriously distort the public's perception of responsible and hard-working psychologists. Real psychologists follow an ethical code that stresses respect for people's privacy, dignity, confidentiality, and welfare (Canadian Code of Ethics for Psychologists, 2000). Psychology has also hit reality TV. Shows such as *Hoarders* and *Intervention* focus on obsessive-compulsive disorders and addictions. Even without media distortions, misconceptions about psychologists and what they do are

Psychologist A person highly trained in the methods, factual knowledge, and theories of psychology.

common. In reality, not all psychologists are therapists in private practice. They are also employed in schools, businesses, governments, and social agencies.

One public perception of psychologists is accurate: Most do help people in one way or another. Psychologists interested in emotional problems specialize in clinical or counselling psychology. **Clinical psychologists** treat psychological problems or do research on psychotherapy and mental disorders. **Counselling psychologists** treat milder emotional and behavioural disturbances. Counselling psychology used to be limited to problems such as poor adjustment at work or school. Now, many counselling psychologists are doing psychotherapy. As a result, differences between counselling and clinical psychology are beginning to fade.

Other Mental Health Professionals

A **psychiatrist** is a medical doctor who specializes in treating mental disorders. Most psychiatrists are "talking doctors" who primarily do psychotherapy.

To be a **psychoanalyst,** you must have a moustache and goatee, spectacles, a German accent, and a well-padded couch—or so the TV and movie stereotype goes. Actually, to become a psychoanalyst, you must have an M.D. or Ph.D. degree plus further specialized training in the theory and practice of Freudian psychoanalysis. In other words, either a physician or a psychologist may become a psychoanalyst by completing more training in a specific type of psychotherapy.

Counsellors may also do mental health work. A **counsellor** is an adviser who helps solve problems with marriage, career, school, work, or the like. Counsellors may be trained in practical helping skills and may do family or sex therapy, for example, but generally do not treat serious mental health problems and are not permitted to practise as psychologists. The term *psychologist* is reserved for people licensed in their province or territory to practise psychology. British Columbia, Saskatchewan, Manitoba, Ontario, and Québec restrict the designation as a psychologist to those with doctoral degrees (known as "doctoral psychologists" in Saskatchewan). The designation of "psychological associate" is used in British Columbia, Manitoba, and Ontario for practitioners with master's degrees. The remaining provinces and the territories require at least a master's degree in psychology or a related field. Most provinces also require a period of supervised practical training, with the length of training depending on whether the person has a master's or a doctoral degree.

Psychiatric social workers and psychiatric nurses play an important role in many mental health programs. **Psychiatric social workers** apply social science principles to help patients in clinics and hospitals. Many social workers hold an M.S.W. (Master of Social Work). **Psychiatric nurses** may also provide counselling and other mental health services, in addition to nursing care. Both social workers and nurses may assist psychologists and psychiatrists as part of a team. Their typical duties include evaluating patients and families; conducting group psychotherapy; or visiting a patient's home, school, or job to alleviate problems.

Specialties in Psychology

Do all psychologists do therapy and treat abnormal behaviour? No. Although many are clinical and counselling psychologists, the rest are found in other specialties. Currently, the Canadian Psychological Association has 30 sections, each reflecting special skills or areas of interest. These areas are listed in Table 1.3. Many psychologists are employed full-time at colleges or universities, where they teach and do research, consulting, or therapy. Some do **basic research**, in which they seek knowledge for the sake of knowledge. For example, a psychologist might study memory purely out of a desire to understand how it works. Others do **applied research** to solve immediate practical problems, such as finding ways to improve the memory of eyewitnesses to crimes. Some do research of both types (see Table 1.4).

In the film *Prime*, Meryl Streep plays a therapist who listens to her patient, played by Uma Thurman, describe intimate details of her relationship with a man. However, the therapist neglects to tell her patient that the man is her son. No ethical therapist would ever engage in such behaviour. Such premises are typical of the way psychologists and psychotherapy are misrepresented in the media.

Clinical psychologist A psychologist who specializes in the treatment of psychological and behavioural disturbances or who does research on such disturbances.

Counselling psychologist A psychologist who specializes in the treatment of milder emotional and behavioural disturbances.

Psychiatrist A medical doctor with additional training in the diagnosis and treatment of mental and emotional disorders.

Psychoanalyst A mental health professional (usually a medical doctor) trained to practise psychoanalysis.

Counsellor A mental health professional who specializes in helping people with problems not involving serious mental disorder (e.g., marriage counsellors, career counsellors, and school counsellors).

Psychiatric social worker A mental health professional trained to apply social science principles to help patients in clinics and hospitals.

Psychiatric nurse A nurse with specialized training in mental health.

Basic research Scientific study undertaken without concern for immediate practical application.

Applied research Scientific study undertaken to solve immediate practical problems.

■ Table 1.3 **Sections of the Canadian Psychological Association**

Aboriginal Psychology	International and Cross-Cultural Psychology
Addiction Psychology	Psychoanalytic and Psychodynamic Psychology
Adult Development and Aging	Industrial/Organizational Psychology
Brain and Cognitive Science	Psychologists in Education
Clinical Psychology	Psychology in the Military
Clinical Neuropsychology	Psychopharmacology
Community Psychology	Religion
Counselling Psychology	Rural and Northern Psychology
Criminal Justice Psychology	Sexual Orientation and Gender Identity
Developmental Psychology	Social and Personality
Environmental Psychology	Sport and Exercise
Extremism and Terrorism	Students
Family Psychology	Teaching
Health Psychology	Traumatic Stress
History and Philosophy Section	Section for Women and Psychology (SWAP)

■ Table 1.4 **Kinds of Psychologists and What They Do**

Specialty		Typical Activities
Neuropsychologist	A*, B	Does research on the brain, nervous system, and other physical origins of behaviour
Clinical	A	Does psychotherapy; investigates clinical problems; develops methods of treatment
Cognitive	B	Studies human thinking and information-processing abilities
Community	A	Promotes community-wide mental health through research, prevention, education, and consultation
Comparative	B	Studies and compares the behaviour of different species, especially animals
Consumer	A	Researches packaging, advertising, marketing methods, and characteristics of consumers
Counselling	A	Does psychotherapy and personal counselling; researches emotional disturbances and counselling methods
Cultural	B	Studies the ways in which culture, subculture, and ethnic group membership affect behaviour
Developmental	A, B	Conducts research on infant, child, adolescent, and adult development; does clinical work with disturbed children; acts as consultant to parents and schools
Educational	A	Investigates classroom dynamics, teaching styles, and learning; develops educational tests; evaluates educational programs
Engineering	A	Does applied research on the design of machinery, computers, airlines, automobiles, and so on, for business, industry, and the military
Environmental	A, B	Studies the effects of urban noise, crowding, attitudes toward the environment, and human use of space; acts as a consultant on environmental issues
Forensic	A	Studies problems of crime and crime prevention, rehabilitation programs, prisons, courtroom dynamics; selects candidates for police work
Gender	B	Does research on differences between males and females, the acquisition of gender identity, and the role of gender throughout life
Health	A, B	Studies the relationship between behaviour and health; uses psychological principles to promote health and prevent illness
Industrial/ Organizational	A	Selects job applicants; does skills analysis; evaluates on-the-job training; improves work environments and human relations in organizations and work settings
Learning	B	Studies how and why learning occurs; develops theories of learning
Medical	A	Applies psychology to manage medical problems, such as the emotional impact of illness, self-screening for cancer, compliance in taking medicine
Personality	B	Studies personality traits and dynamics; develops theories of personality and tests for assessing personality traits
School	A	Does psychological testing, referrals, and emotional and vocational counselling of students; detects and treats learning disabilities; improves classroom learning
Sensation and perception	B	Studies the sense organs and the process of perception; investigates the mechanisms of sensation; develops theories about how perception occurs
Social	B	Investigates human social behaviour, including attitudes, conformity, persuasion, prejudice, friendship, aggression, helping, and so forth

*Research in this area is typically applied (A), basic (B), or both (A, B).

STUDY BREAK **Psychologists and Their Specialties**

Reflect

You're going to meet four psychologists at a social gathering. How many would you expect to be therapists in private practice? Odds are that only two will be clinical (or counselling) psychologists and only one of these will work in private practice. On the other hand, at least one out of the four (and probably two) will work at a college or university.

Learning Check

See if you can answer these questions before continuing.

1. Which of the following can prescribe drugs?
   a. a psychologist   b. a psychiatrist
   c. a psychotherapist   d. a counsellor

2. A psychologist who specializes in treating human emotional difficulties is called a _____ psychologist.

3. Roughly 40 percent of psychologists specialize in counselling psychology. T or F?

4. Who among the following would most likely be involved in the detection of learning disabilities?
   a. a consumer psychologist   b. a forensic psychologist
   c. an experimental psychologist   d. a school psychologist

Critical Thinking

5. If most psychologists work in applied settings, why is basic research still of great importance?

Answers

1. b 2. clinical or counselling 3. F 4. d 5. Because practitioners benefit from basic psychological research in the same way that physicians benefit from basic research in biology. Discoveries in basic science form the knowledge base that leads to useful applications.

In a moment we'll take a closer look at how research is done. Before that, here's a chance to do a little research on how much you've learned.

SCIENTIFIC RESEARCH—HOW TO THINK LIKE A PSYCHOLOGIST

Systematic recording of facts and events is at the heart of all sciences. To be scientific, **observations** must be systematic, so that they reveal something about behaviour (Stanovich, 2007). To use an earlier example, little would be gained if you drove around a city during the summer and made haphazard observations of aggressive behaviour.

<SURVEY QUESTION
What is the scientific method? Why is the scientific method important to psychologists?

The Scientific Method

The **scientific method** is a form of critical thinking based on careful collection of evidence, accurate description and measurement, precise definition, controlled observation, and repeatable results (Jackson, 2008). In its ideal form the scientific method has six elements:

1. Making observations
2. Defining a problem
3. Proposing a hypothesis
4. Gathering evidence/testing the hypothesis
5. Publishing results
6. Theory building

Hypothesis Testing

What exactly is a hypothesis? A **hypothesis** is a tentative explanation of an event or relationship between events. In common terms, a hypothesis is a testable hunch or educated guess about behaviour. For example, you might hypothesize that frustration encourages aggression. How could you test this hypothesis? First you would have to decide how you are going to frustrate people. (This part might be fun.) Then you would need to find a way to measure whether they become more aggressive. (Not so much fun if you plan to be nearby.) Your observations would then provide evidence to confirm or disconfirm the hypothesis.

Observation Gathering data directly by recording facts or events.

Scientific method Testing the truth of a proposition by careful measurement and controlled observation.

Hypothesis The predicted outcome of an experiment or an educated guess about the relationship between variables.

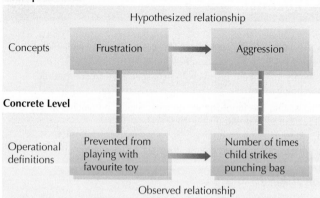

Conceptual Level

Hypothesized relationship

Concepts — Frustration → Aggression

Concrete Level

Operational definitions — Prevented from playing with favourite toy → Number of times child strikes punching bag

Observed relationship

▸▸**FIGURE 1.3** Operational definitions are used to link concepts with concrete observations. Do you think the examples given are reasonable operational definitions of frustration and aggression? Operational definitions vary in how well they represent concepts. For this reason, many different experiments may be necessary to draw clear conclusions about hypothesized relationships in psychology.

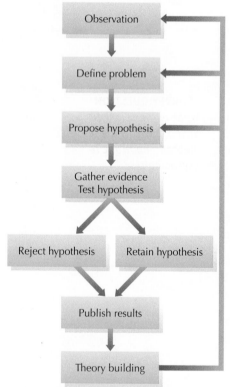

Observation → Define problem → Propose hypothesis → Gather evidence Test hypothesis → Reject hypothesis / Retain hypothesis → Publish results → Theory building

▸▸**FIGURE 1.4** Psychologists use the logic of science to answer questions about behaviour. Specific hypotheses can be tested in a variety of ways, including naturalistic observation, correlational studies, controlled experiments, clinical studies, and the survey method. Psychologists revise their theories to reflect the evidence they gather. New or revised theories then lead to new observations, problems, and hypotheses.

Operational Definitions

Because we cannot see or touch frustration, it must be defined operationally. An **operational definition** states the exact procedures used to represent or measure a concept. Operational definitions allow abstract ideas to be tested in real-world terms. For example, you might define frustration as "interrupting an adult before he or she can finish a puzzle and win a $100 prize." And aggression might be defined as "the number of times a frustrated individual insults the person who prevented work on the puzzle" (see also Figure 1.3). Covert behaviours are operationally defined in terms of overt behaviour in order to permit scientific study.

Clever Hans

Several steps of the scientific method can be illustrated with the story of Clever Hans, a famous "wonder horse" (Rosenthal, 1965). Clever Hans seemed to solve difficult math problems, which he answered by tapping his hoof. If you asked Hans, "What is 12 times 2, minus 18," Hans would tap his hoof six times. This was so astonishing that a scientist (Oskar Pfungst) decided to find out if Hans really could do arithmetic. Assume that you are Pfungst and that you are just itching to discover how Hans really does his trick.

Can a Horse Add?

Your investigation of Hans's math skills would probably begin with careful observation of both the horse and his owner. Assume that these observations fail to reveal any obvious cheating. Then the problem becomes more clearly defined: What signals Hans to start and stop tapping his hoof? Your first hypothesis might be that the owner is giving Hans a signal. Your proposed test would be to make the owner leave the room. Then someone else could ask Hans questions. Your test would either confirm or deny the owner's role. This evidence would support or eliminate the cheating hypothesis. By changing the conditions under which you observe Hans, you have controlled the situation to gain more information from your observations.

Incidentally, Hans could still answer when his owner was out of the room. But a brilliant series of controlled observations by psychologist Oskar Pfungst revealed Hans's secret. If Hans couldn't see the questioner, he couldn't answer. It seems that questioners always lowered their heads (to look at Hans's hoof) after asking a question. This was Hans's cue to start tapping. When Hans had tapped the correct number, a questioner would always look up to see if Hans was going to stop. This was Hans's cue to stop tapping!

Theories

What about theory formulation? Since Clever Hans's ability to do math was an isolated problem, no theorizing was involved. However, in actual research, a **theory** acts as a map of knowledge. Good theories summarize observations, explain them, and guide further research (see Figure 1.4). Without theories of forgetting, personality, stress, mental illness, and the like, psychologists would drown in a sea of disconnected facts (Stanovich, 2007).

Publication

Scientific information must always be publicly available. The results of psychological studies are usually published in professional journals (see Table 1.5). That way, anyone willing to make appropriate observations can see whether a claim is true (Leary, 2004).

■ Table 1.5   **Outline of a Research Report**

- **Abstract** Research reports begin with a very brief summary of the study and its findings. The abstract allows you to get an overview without reading the entire article.
- **Introduction** The introduction describes the question to be investigated. It also provides background information by reviewing prior studies on the same or related topics, highlighting important theoretical or methodological issues.
- **Method** This section tells how and why observations were made. It also describes the specific procedures used to gather data so that other researchers can duplicate the study to see if they get the same results.
- **Results** The outcome of the investigation is presented. Data may be graphed, summarized in tables, or statistically analyzed.
- **Discussion** The results of the study are discussed in relation to the original question. Implications of the study are explored and further studies may be proposed.

Operational definition Defining a scientific concept by stating the specific actions or procedures used to measure it. For example, "hunger" might be defined as "the number of hours of food deprivation."

Theory A system of ideas designed to interrelate concepts and facts in a way that summarizes existing data and predicts future observations.

Naturalistic observation Observing behaviour as it unfolds in natural settings.

Correlational method Making measurements to discover relationships between events.

Experimental method Investigating behaviour through controlled experimentation.

Clinical method Studying psychological problems and therapies in clinical settings.

Survey method Using questionnaires and surveys to poll large groups of people.

Summary

Now let's summarize more realistically. All the basic elements of the scientific method are found in the example that follows.

- **Observation:** Susanne, a psychologist, observes that some people who design computer video games seem to experience less work-related stress than others do.
- **Defining a Problem:** Susanne's problem is to identify the ways in which high-stress and low-stress game designers are different.
- **Observation:** Susanne carefully questions game designers about how much stress they experience. These additional observations suggest that low-stress designers feel they have more control over their work.
- **Proposing a Hypothesis:** Susanne hypothesizes that having control over difficult tasks reduces stress.
- **Gathering Evidence/Testing the Hypothesis:** Susanne designs an experiment in which two groups of people must solve a series of very difficult problems. One group is required to solve the problems at a pace dictated by Susanne. The other group is allowed to set its own pace. While working, the second group reports lower stress levels than the first. This suggests that Susanne's hypothesis is correct.
- **Publishing Results:** In a scholarly article, Susanne carefully describes the question she investigated, the methods she used, and the results of her experiment. The article is published in the *Canadian Journal of Experimental Psychology.*
- **Theory Building:** Drawing on the results of similar experiments, Susanne and other psychologists create a theory to explain why having control over a task helps reduce stress.

RESEARCH METHODS

Psychologists gather evidence and test hypotheses in many ways: They observe behaviour as it unfolds in natural settings (**naturalistic observation**), they make measurements to discover relationships between events (**correlational method**), they use the powerful technique of controlled experimentation (**experimental method**), they study psychological problems and therapies in clinical settings (**clinical method**), and they use questionnaires to poll large groups of people (**survey method**). Let's see how each of these is used to advance psychological knowledge.

<SURVEY QUESTION
How do psychologists collect information?

NATURALISTIC OBSERVATION—PSYCHOLOGY STEPS OUT!

Instead of waiting for a chance encounter, psychologists may actively observe behaviour in a **natural setting** (the typical environment in which a person or animal lives). The work of Jane Goodall provides a good example. She and her staff have been observing chimpanzees in Tanzania since 1960. A quotation from her book *In the Shadow of Man* captures the excitement of a scientific discovery:

> Quickly focusing my binoculars, I saw that it was a single chimpanzee, and just then he turned in my direction. . . . He was squatting beside the red earth mound of a termite nest, and as I watched I saw him carefully push a long grass stem into a hole in the mound. After a moment he withdrew it and picked something from the end with his mouth. I was too far away to make out what he was eating, but it was obvious that he was actually using a grass stem as a tool [see Figure 1.5]. (Van Lawick-Goodall, 1971)

Notice that naturalistic observation only provides descriptions of behaviour. In order to *explain* observations, we may need information from other research methods. Just the same, Goodall's discovery helped us realize that humans are not the only tool-making animals (Nakamichi, 2004).

Chimpanzees in zoos use objects as tools. Doesn't that demonstrate the same thing? Not necessarily. Naturalistic observation allows us to study behaviour that hasn't been tampered with or altered by outside influences. Only by observing chimps in their natural environment can we tell if they use tools without human interference.

▸▸**FIGURE 1.5** A special moment in Jane Goodall's naturalistic study of chimpanzees. A chimp uses a grass stem to extract a meal from a termite nest. Goodall's work also documented the importance of long-term emotional bonds between chimpanzee mothers and their offspring, as well as fascinating differences in the behaviour and "personalities" of individual chimps (Goodall, 1990).

© Hugo Van Lawick/NGS Image Collection

Limitations

Doesn't the presence of human observers in an animal colony affect the animals' behaviour? Yes. A major problem is the **observer effect**, which refers to changes in a subject's behaviour caused by an awareness of being observed. Naturalists must be very careful to keep their distance and avoid "making friends" with the animals they are observing. Likewise, if you were interested in differences between aggressive and non-aggressive school children, you couldn't simply stroll onto a playground and start taking notes. As a stranger, your presence would probably change the children's behaviour. Whenever possible, this problem is minimized by concealing the observer. Another solution is to use hidden recorders. For example, a naturalistic study of traffic accidents was done with video cameras installed in 100 cars (Dingus et al., 2006). It turns out that most accidents are caused by failing to look at the traffic in front of the car (eyes forward!). Hidden stationary video cameras have also provided valuable observations of many animal species. As recording devices have become miniaturized, it has even become possible to attach "critter cams" directly to many species, allowing observations in a wide range of natural environments. For example, zoologist Christian Rutz and his colleagues outfitted shy New Caledonian crows with "crow cams" to better understand their use of tools to forage for food (Rutz et al., 2007). Apparently, humans and other primates are not the only tool-using species.

Observer bias is a related problem in which observers see what they expect to see or record only selected details (Jackson, 2008). Teachers in one classic study were told to watch elementary school children (all normal) who had been labelled as learning disabled, mentally retarded, emotionally disturbed, or normal. The results were troubling: Teachers gave the children very different ratings, depending on the labels used (Foster & Ysseldyke, 1976). In some situations, observer bias can have serious consequences (Spano, 2005). An example is studies of the effectiveness of psychotherapy, where therapists tend to get better results with the type of therapy they favour (Lambert, 1999).

Natural setting The environment in which an organism typically lives.

Observer effect Changes in behaviour brought about by an awareness of being observed.

Observer bias The tendency of an observer to distort observations or perceptions to match his or her expectations.

The Anthropomorphic Error

A special trap that must be avoided while observing animals is the **anthropomorphic** (AN-thro-po-MORE-fik) **error**. This is the error of attributing human thoughts, feelings, or motives to animals—especially as a way of explaining their behaviour (Wynne, 2004).

The temptation to assume that an animal is "angry," "jealous," "bored," or "guilty" can be strong, but it can lead to false conclusions. If you have pets at home, you probably already know how difficult it is to avoid anthropomorphizing. For example, if your dog growls at your girlfriend every time she visits, you might assume the dog doesn't like her. But maybe she wears a perfume that bothers the dog's nose.

Recording Observations

Psychologists doing naturalistic studies make a special effort to minimize bias by keeping a formal log of data and observations called an **observational record**. As suggested in the study of traffic accidents, video recording often provides the best record of all.

Despite its problems, naturalistic observation can supply a wealth of information and raise many interesting questions. In most scientific research it is an excellent starting point.

CORRELATIONAL STUDIES—IN SEARCH OF THE PERFECT RELATIONSHIP

Let's say a psychologist notes an association between the IQs of parents and those of their children, or between beauty and social popularity, or between anxiety and test performance, or even between crime and the weather. In each instance, two observations or events are **correlated** (linked together in an orderly way). The study of crime and temperature mentioned earlier in this chapter is an example of a correlational study.

A **correlational study** finds the degree of relationship, or correlation, between two existing traits, behaviours, or events. First, two factors of interest are measured. Then a statistical technique is used to find their degree of correlation. For example, we could find the correlation between the number of hours slept at night and afternoon sleepiness. If the correlation is large, knowing how long a person sleeps at night would allow us to predict his or her degree of sleepiness in the afternoon. Likewise, afternoon sleepiness could be used to predict the duration of nighttime sleep.

Correlation Coefficients

How is the degree of correlation expressed? The strength and direction of a relationship can be expressed as a **coefficient of correlation**. This is simply a number falling somewhere between +1.00 and −1.00. If the number is zero or close to zero, the association between two measures is weak or non-existent. For example, the correlation between shoe size and intelligence is zero. (Sorry, size 12 readers.) If the correlation is +1.00, a perfect positive relationship exists; if it is −1.00, a perfect negative relationship has been discovered.

Correlations in psychology are rarely perfect. But the closer the coefficient is to +1.00 or −1.00, the stronger the relationship. For example, identical twins tend to have almost identical IQs. In contrast, the IQs of parents and their children are only generally similar. The correlation between the IQs of parents and children is 0.35; between identical twins it's 0.86.

What do the terms "positive" and "negative" correlation mean? A **positive correlation** shows that increases in one measure are matched by increases in the other (or decreases correspond to decreases). For example, there is a positive correlation between high school grades and university grades; students who do better in high school tend to do better in university (and the reverse). In a **negative correlation,** increases in the first measure are

Anthropomorphic error The error of attributing human thoughts, feelings, or motives to animals, especially as a way of explaining their behaviour.

Observational record A detailed summary of observed events or a video recording of observed behaviour.

Correlation The existence of a consistent, systematic relationship between two events, measures, or variables.

Correlational study A non-experimental study designed to measure the degree of relationship (if any) between two or more events, measures, or variables.

Coefficient of correlation A statistical index ranging from +1.00 to −1.00 that indicates the direction and degree of correlation.

Positive correlation A statistical relationship in which increases in one measure are matched by increases in the other (or decreases correspond to decreases).

Negative correlation A statistical relationship in which increases in one measure are matched by decreases in the other.

Causation The act of causing some effect.

Experiment A formal trial undertaken to confirm a fact or principle.

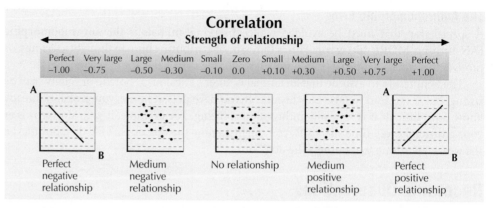

Correlation
Strength of relationship

Perfect	Very large	Large	Medium	Small	Zero	Small	Medium	Large	Very large	Perfect
−1.00	−0.75	−0.50	−0.30	−0.10	0.0	+0.10	+0.30	+0.50	+0.75	+1.00

Perfect negative relationship

Medium negative relationship

No relationship

Medium positive relationship

Perfect positive relationship

▶▶**FIGURE 1.6** The correlation coefficient tells how strongly two measures are related. These graphs show a range of relationships between two measures, A and B. If a correlation is negative, increases in one measure are associated with decreases in the other. (As B gets larger, A gets smaller.) In a positive correlation, increases in one measure are associated with increases in the other. (As B gets larger, A gets larger.) The centre-left graph ("medium negative relationship") might result from comparing anxiety level (B) with test scores (A): Higher anxiety is associated with lower scores. The centre graph ("no relationship") would result from plotting a person's shoe size (B) and the length of her hair (A). The centre-right graph ("medium positive relationship") could be a plot of grades in high school (B) and grades in university (A) for a group of students: Higher grades in high school are associated with higher grades in university.

associated with decreases in the second (see Figure 1.6). We might observe, for instance, that students who spend hours playing games online get lower grades than those who spend less time playing these games.

Wouldn't that prove that playing too many computer games causes lower grades? It might seem so, but we cannot be sure without performing an experiment.

Correlation and Causation

Correlational studies help us discover relationships and make predictions. However, correlation does not demonstrate **causation** (a cause-and-effect relationship) (Halpern, 2003). It could be, for instance, that students who are uninterested in their classes have more time for computer games because they don't spend much time studying. If so, then both their lack of study and lower grades would result from disinterest, not excessive game playing. Just because one thing appears to be related to another does not mean that a cause-and-effect connection exists.

Here is another example of mistaking correlation for causation: What if a psychologist discovers that the blood of schizophrenic patients contains a certain chemical not found in other people? Does this show that the chemical causes schizophrenia? It may seem so, but schizophrenia could cause the chemical to form. Or both schizophrenia and the chemical might be caused by some unknown third factor. Just because one thing appears to cause another does not mean that it does. The best way to be confident that a cause-and-effect relationship exists is to perform a controlled experiment. You'll learn how in the next section.

SURVEY QUESTION>
What is an experiment? Why do psychologists use experiments to answer questions about behaviour and mental processes?

THE PSYCHOLOGY EXPERIMENT—WHERE CAUSE MEETS EFFECT

To get beyond description and fully understand behaviour, psychologists must be able to explain why we act the way we do. To truly discover the causes of behaviour, we must conduct **experiments**. An experiment is a formal trial undertaken to confirm or disconfirm a hypothesis about the causes of behaviour. Psychologists carefully control conditions in

STUDY BREAK **Scientific Research, Naturalistic Observation, and Correlation**

Reflect

You probably hypothesize daily about why people act the way they do. Do you seek to verify your hypotheses? Usually we observe others to determine whether our "educated guesses" about them are correct. But casual observation can be misleading. To really test a hypothesis, systematic observation and formal research methods are necessary.

Learning Check

1. Most of psychology can rightfully be called common sense because psychologists prefer naturalistic observation to controlled observation. T or F?
2. A hypothesis is any careful observation made in a controlled experiment. T or F?
3. Two major problems in naturalistic observation are the effects of the observer and observer bias. T or F?
4. The _____ error involves attributing human feelings and motives to animals.

5. Correlation typically does not demonstrate causation. T or F?
6. Which correlation coefficient represents the strongest relationship?

a. −0.86　　　　　　　　b. +0.66

c. +0.10　　　　　　　　d. +0.09

Critical Thinking

7. Can you think of some additional "common-sense" statements that contradict each other?
8. Attributing mischievous motives to a car that is not working properly is a thinking error similar to anthropomorphizing. T or F?
9. Adults who often ate Frosted Flakes cereal as children now have half the cancer rate seen in adults who never ate Frosted Flakes. What do you think explains this strange correlation?

Answers

1. F 2. F 3. T 4. anthropomorphic 5. T 6. a 7. There are many examples. Here are a few more to add to the ones you thought of: "You can't make a silk purse out of a sow's ear," versus "Clothes make the man (or woman)." "He (or she) who hesitates is lost," versus "Haste makes waste." "Birds of a feather flock together," versus "Opposites attract." 8. True. It appears to be difficult for humans to resist thinking of other species and even machines in human terms. 9. The correlation is related to an age bias in the group of people studied. Older adults have higher cancer rates than younger adults, and Frosted Flakes weren't available during the childhoods of older people. Thus, Frosted Flakes appear to be related to cancer, when age is the real connection (Tierny, 1987).

experiments to identify cause-and-effect relationships. To perform an experiment you would do the following:

1. Directly vary a condition you think might affect behaviour.
2. Create two or more groups of subjects. These groups should be alike in all ways except for the condition you are varying.
3. Record whether varying the condition has any effect on behaviour.

Suppose you want to find out whether talking on a cell phone while driving affects driving ability. First, you would form two groups of people. Then you could give the members of one group a test of driving ability while they are talking on a cell phone. The second group would take the same test while not using a cell phone. By comparing average driving ability scores for the two groups, you could tell if cell phone use affects driving ability.

As you can see, the simplest psychological experiment is based on two groups of **experimental subjects** (animals or people whose behaviour is investigated). One group is called the *experimental group*; the other becomes the *control group.* The control group and the experimental group are treated exactly alike except for the condition you intentionally vary. This condition is called the *independent variable.*

Variables and Groups

A **variable** is any condition that can change and that might affect the outcome of the experiment. Identifying causes and effects in an experiment involves three types of variables:

1. **Independent variables** are conditions altered or varied by the experimenter, who sets their size, amount, or value. Independent variables are suspected causes for differences in behaviour.

Experimental subjects Humans or animals whose behaviour is investigated in an experiment.

Variable Any condition that changes or can be made to change; a measure, event, or state that may vary.

Independent variable In an experiment, the condition being investigated as a possible cause of some change in behaviour. The values that this variable takes are chosen by the experimenter.

Dependent variable In an experiment, the condition (usually a behaviour) that is affected by the independent variable.

Extraneous variables Conditions or factors excluded from influencing the outcome of an experiment.

Experimental group In a controlled experiment, the group of subjects exposed to the independent variable or experimental condition.

Control group In a controlled experiment, the group of subjects exposed to all experimental conditions or variables *except* the independent variable.

Random assignment The use of chance (e.g., flipping a coin) to assign subjects to experimental and control groups.

2. **Dependent variables** measure the results of the experiment. That is, they reveal the effects that independent variables have on behaviour. Such effects are often revealed by measures of performance, such as test scores.

3. **Extraneous variables** are conditions that a researcher wishes to prevent from affecting the outcome of the experiment.

We can apply these terms to our cell phone use/driving ability experiment in this way: Cell phone use is the independent variable—we want to know whether talking on a cell phone affects driving ability. Driving ability (defined by scores on the driving test) is the dependent variable—we want to know whether the ability to drive depends on whether a person is using a cell phone. All other conditions that could affect driving ability are extraneous. Examples are the number of hours slept the night before the test, familiarity with the car (or simulated car) being used for the test, and driving experience.

So the **experimental group** consists of subjects exposed to the independent variable (talking on a cell phone while driving in the preceding example). Members of the **control group** are exposed to all the same conditions except the independent variable.

Let's examine another simple experiment. Suppose you notice that you seem to study better while listening to music on your iPod. This suggests the hypothesis that music improves learning. We could test this idea by forming an experimental group that studies with music. A control group would study without music. Then we could compare their scores on a test.

Is a control group really needed? Can't people just study with music on to see if they do better? Without a control group it would be impossible to tell if music had any effect on learning. The control group provides a point of reference for comparison with scores of the experimental group. If the average test score of the experimental group is higher than the average of the control group, we can conclude that music improves learning. If there is no difference, it's obvious that the independent variable had no effect on learning.

In this experiment, the amount learned (indicated by scores on the test) is the dependent variable. We are asking: Does the independent variable affect the dependent variable? (Does music affect or influence learning?)

CONTROL GROUP   OUT OF CONTROL GROUP

Courtesy of Pearl S. Mueller

Experimental Control

How do we know that the people in one group aren't more intelligent than those in the other group? It's true that personal differences might affect the experiment. However, they can be controlled by randomly assigning people to groups. **Random assignment** means that a subject has an equal chance of being in either the experimental group or the control group. Randomization evenly balances personal differences in the two groups. In our musical experiment, this could be done by simply flipping a coin for each subject: Heads, and the subject is in the experimental group; tails, it's the control group. This would result in few differences in the number of people in each group who are geniuses or dunces, hungry, hungover, tall, music lovers, or whatever.

Other *extraneous,* or outside, variables—such as the amount of study time, the sex of subjects, the temperature in the room, the time of day, the amount of light, and so forth—must also be prevented from affecting the outcome of an experiment. But how? Usually this is done by making all conditions (except the independent variable) exactly alike for both groups. When all conditions are the same for both groups—except the presence or absence of music—then a difference in the amount learned must be caused by the music (see Figure 1.7).

Possible subjects

Random assignment controls for subject differences

Experimental group — **Control group**

Study and testing conditions — Identical conditions to control extraneous variables — Study and testing conditions

Music included — Independent variable **(Cause)** — **No music**

Behaviour (test scores) — Dependent variable **(Effect)** — **Behaviour** (test scores)

Is there a difference?

▶▶**FIGURE 1.7** Elements of a simple psychological experiment to assess the effects of music during study on test scores.

Cause and Effect

Now let's summarize more formally. In an experiment, two or more groups of subjects are treated differently with respect to the independent variable. In all other ways they are treated the same. That is, extraneous variables are equalized for all groups in the experiment. The effect of the independent variable (or variables) on some behaviour (the dependent variable) is then measured. In a carefully controlled experiment, the independent variable is the only possible *cause* for any effect noted in the dependent variable. This allows clear cause-and-effect connections to be identified (see Figure 1.8).

Placebo Effects—Sugar Pills and Saltwater

Let's do an experiment to see whether caffeine (a stimulant) affects learning: Before studying, we explain to the members of our experimental group what our hypothesis is and that they will take a caffeine pill. Control group members are told nothing and get nothing. Later, we assess how much each subject learned. Does this experiment seem valid? Actually, it has several serious flaws.

Why? The experimental group took the drug and the control group didn't, so differences in the amount they learned must have been caused by the drug, right? No, because the drug wasn't the only difference between the groups. For a start, because of what they were told, participants in the experimental group most likely expected to learn more. Any observed differences between groups, then, may reflect differences in expectation, not the actual effect of the drug. In a well-designed experiment, you must be careful about what you tell participants. Small bits of information might create **research participant bias,** or changes in participants' behaviour caused by the influence of their expectations. Also, people in the experimental group swallowed a pill, and control subjects did not. This is another form of research participant bias. Without using a placebo (plah-SEE-bo), it is impossible to tell if the drug affects learning. It could be that those who swallowed a pill expected to do better. This alone might have affected their performance, even if the pill didn't.

What is a placebo? Why would it make a difference? A **placebo** is a fake pill or injection. Inert substances such as sugar pills and saline (saltwater) injections are common placebos. Thus, if a placebo has any effect, it must be based on suggestion, rather than chemistry (Thompson, 2005).

The **placebo effect** (changes in behaviour caused by belief that one has taken a drug) can be powerful. For instance, a saline injection is 70 percent as effective as morphine in reducing pain. That's why doctors sometimes prescribe placebos—especially for complaints that seem to have no physical basis. Placebos have been shown to affect pain, anxiety, depression, alertness, tension, sexual arousal, cravings for alcohol, and many other processes (Wampold et al., 2005).

How could an inert substance have any effect? Placebos alter our expectations about our own emotional and physical reactions. Because we associate taking medicine with feeling better, we expect placebos to make us feel better too (Stewart-Williams, 2004). After a person takes a placebo, there is a reduction in brain activity linked with pain, so the effect is not imaginary (Wager et al., 2004).

Controlling Research Participant Bias

To control for research participant bias, we could use a **single-blind experiment**. In this case, subjects do not know if they are receiving a real drug or a placebo. All subjects get the same instructions and everyone gets a pill or injection. People in the experimental group get a real drug and people in the control group get a placebo. Because subjects are unaware (or "blind") as to whether they received the drug, their expectations are the same. Any difference in their behaviour must be caused by the drug.

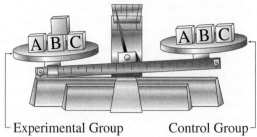

Dependent Variable

Experimental Group   Control Group

☐ Extraneous Variables
☐ Independent Variable

▸▸**FIGURE 1.8** Experimental control is achieved by balancing extraneous variables for the experimental group and the control group. For example, the average age (A), education (B), and intelligence (C) of group members could be made the same for both groups. Then we could apply the independent variable to the experimental group. If their behaviour (the dependent variable) changes (in comparison with the control group), the change must be caused by the independent variable.

Research participant bias Changes in the participants' behaviour caused by the influence of their expectations.

Placebo An inactive substance given in the place of a drug in psychological research.

Placebo effect Changes in behaviour due to expectations that a drug (or other treatment) will have some effect.

Single-blind experiment An arrangement in which subjects remain unaware of whether they are in the experimental group or the control group, although the researcher knows.

> **Researcher bias** Changes in subjects' behaviour caused by the unintended influence of a researcher's actions.
>
> **Self-fulfilling prophecy** A prediction that prompts people to act in ways that make the prediction come true.
>
> **Double-blind experiment** An arrangement in which both participants and researchers are unaware of whether subjects are in the experimental group or the control group.

Researcher Bias

How could a researcher influence subjects? As we saw above, when we explained our hypothesis to the subjects, we likely biased the results of the experiment. Even if the researcher uses a single-blind procedure to avoid deliberately biasing the participants, **researcher bias** (changes in behaviour caused by the unintended influence of the researcher) is a common problem in psychological research. In essence, experimenters run the risk of finding what they expect to find. This occurs because humans are very sensitive to hints about what is expected of them (Rosenthal, 1994).

Researcher bias even applies outside the laboratory. Psychologist Robert Rosenthal (1973) reports an example of how expectations can influence people: At the U.S. Air Force Academy Preparatory School, 100 airmen were randomly assigned to 5 different math classes. Their teachers did not know about this random placement. Instead, each teacher was told that his or her students had unusually high or low ability. Students in the classes labelled "high ability" improved much more in math scores than those in "low-ability" classes. Yet, initially, all of the classes had students of equal ability.

Apparently, the teachers subtly communicated their expectations to students. Most likely, they did this through tone of voice, body language, and giving encouragement or criticism. Their "hints," in turn, created a **self-fulfilling prophecy** that affected the students. A self-fulfilling prophecy is a prediction that prompts people to act in ways that make the prediction come true. In short, people sometimes become what we prophesy for them. It is wise to remember that others tend to live up or down to our expectations for them (Jussim & Harber, 2005).

Because of both research participant bias and researcher bias, it is common to keep both participants and researchers "blind." In a **double-blind experiment,** neither subjects nor

---

 STUDY BREAK   THE PSYCHOLOGY EXPERIMENT

Reflect

In a sense, we all conduct little experiments to detect cause-and-effect connections. If you are interested in cooking, for example, you might try cooking rice in vegetable stock one time but not another. The question then becomes: Does the use of vegetable stock (the independent variable) improve the flavour (the dependent variable)? By comparing rice cooked with water (the control group) to rice cooked with stock (the experimental group), you could find out if stock is worth using. Can you think of at least one informal experiment you've run in the last month? What were the variables? What was the outcome?

Learning Check

1. To understand cause and effect, a simple psychological experiment is based on creating two groups: the _____ group and the _____ group.

2. Here are three types of variables to consider in an experiment: _____ variables (which are manipulated by the experimenter); _____ variables (which measure the outcome of the experiment); and _____ variables (factors to be excluded in a particular experiment).

3. A researcher performs an experiment to learn if room temperature affects the amount of aggression displayed by

college students under crowded conditions in a simulated prison environment. In this experiment, the independent variable is which of the following?
   a. room temperature
   b. the amount of aggression
   c. crowding
   d. the simulated prison environment

4. A procedure used to control both the placebo effect and researcher bias in drug experiments is
   a. the correlation method
   b. extraneous prophecy
   c. double-blind technique
   d. random assignment of subjects

Critical Thinking

5. There is a loophole in the statement "I've been taking vitamin C tablets, and I haven't had a cold all year. Vitamin C is great!" What is the loophole?

6. How would you determine if sugary breakfasts affect children's activity levels and their ability to learn in school?

7. People who believe strongly in astrology have personality characteristics that actually match, to a degree, those predicted by their astrological signs. Can you explain why this occurs?

Answers

1. experimental, control 2. independent, dependent, extraneous 3. a 4. c 5. The statement implies that vitamin C prevented colds. However, not getting a cold could just be a coincidence. A controlled experiment with a group given vitamin C and a control group not taking vitamin C would be needed to learn if vitamin C actually has any effect on susceptibility to colds. 6. An actual experiment on this question used a double-blind design in which children were given a breakfast drink containing 50 grams of sucrose (sugar), a placebo (aspartame), or only a very small amount of sucrose. Observed changes in activity levels and in scores on a learning task did not support the view that sugar causes major changes in children's behaviour (Rosen et al., 1988). 7. Belief in astrology can create a self-fulfilling prophecy in which people alter their behaviours and self-concepts to match their astrological signs (van Rooij, 1994).

researchers know who has received a drug and who has taken a placebo. This keeps researchers from unconsciously influencing subjects. Typically, someone else prepares the pills or injections so researchers don't know until after testing who got what. Not only does this control for research participant bias but it also keeps researchers from unconsciously influencing participants. Double-blind testing has shown that about 50 percent of the effectiveness of antidepressant drugs such as Prozac is due to the placebo effect (Kirsch & Sapirstein, 1998). Much of the current popularity of herbal and holistic remedies is also based on the placebo effect (Seidman, 2001).

THE CLINICAL METHOD—DATA BY THE CASE

Many experiments are impractical, unethical, or impossible to do. In instances such as these, information may be gained from a **case study** (an in-depth focus on all aspects of a single subject). Clinical psychologists rely heavily on case studies.

Case studies may sometimes be thought of as **natural clinical tests** (accidents or other natural events that provide psychological data). Gunshot wounds, brain tumours, accidental poisonings, and similar disasters provide much information about the human brain. One remarkable case from the history of psychology is reported by Dr. J. M. Harlow (1868). Phineas Gage, a young foreman on a work crew, had a six-kilogram steel rod blown through the front of his brain by a dynamite explosion (see Figure 1.9). Amazingly, he survived the accident. Within two months Gage could walk, talk, and move normally. But the injury changed his personality, at least at first. (According to some reports, his personality returned to normal after a few months.) Instead of the honest and dependable worker he had been before, Gage became a surly, foul-mouthed liar. Dr. Harlow carefully recorded all details of what was perhaps the first in-depth case study of an accidental frontal lobotomy (the destruction of front brain matter). Gage's story also illustrates how information may become distorted over time, and how these distortions pass into the historical record as fact. Over a number of years, Dr. Harlow's original reports were transformed by successive newspaper accounts of Gage's life, some of which may have had little basis in fact (Macmillan, 2000; Macmillan & Lena, 2010).

Not all people would have the same reaction to a similar injury. This is why psychologists prefer controlled experiments and often use lab animals for studies of the brain. Case studies lack formal control groups. This, of course, limits the conclusions that can be drawn from clinical observations. Nonetheless, when a purely psychological problem is under study, the clinical method may be the *only* source of information.

When a carpenter named Michael Melnick suffered a similar injury, he recovered completely, with no sign of lasting ill effects. Melnick's very different reaction to a similar injury shows why psychologists prefer controlled experiments and often use lab animals for studies of the brain. Case studies lack formal control groups. This, of course, limits the conclusions that can be drawn from clinical observations. Despite their limitations, case studies often provide insights into human behaviour that couldn't be obtained by any other method. They are especially valuable for studying rare events, such as unusual mental disorders, childhood "geniuses," or "rampage" school shootings (Harding, Fox, & Mehta, 2002). Also, case studies of psychotherapy have provided many useful ideas about how to treat emotional problems (Wedding & Corsini, 2005).

SURVEY METHOD—HERE, HAVE A SAMPLE

Sometimes psychologists would like to ask everyone in the world a few well-chosen questions: "Do you drink alcoholic beverages? How often per week?" "What form of discipline did your parents use when you were a child?" "What is the most creative thing you've done?"

<SURVEY QUESTION
What other research methods do psychologists use?

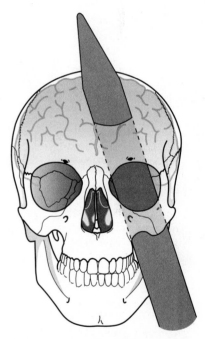

▸▸ **FIGURE 1.9** Some of the earliest information on the effects of damage to frontal areas of the brain came from a case study of the accidental injury of Phineas Gage.

Case study An in-depth focus on all aspects of a single person.

Natural clinical test A natural event that provides data on a psychological phenomenon.

Survey method The use of public polling techniques to answer psychological questions.

Representative sample A small, randomly selected part of a larger population that accurately reflects characteristics of the whole population.

Population An entire group of animals, people, or objects belonging to a particular category (for example, all college or university students or all married women).

Biased sample A subpart of a larger population that does not accurately reflect characteristics of the whole population.

Courtesy bias The tendency to give "polite" answers—especially the tendency to alter answers so as not to hurt an interviewer's feelings.

The answers to such questions can reveal much about people's behaviour. But because it is impossible to question everyone, doing a survey is often more practical.

In the **survey method,** public polling techniques are used to answer psychological questions. Typically, people in a representative sample are asked a series of carefully worded questions. A **representative sample** is a small group that accurately reflects a larger population. A good sample must include the same proportion of men, women, young, old, occupations, ethnicity, political affiliations, and so on as found in the population as a whole.

A **population** is an entire group of animals, people, or objects belonging to a particular category (for example, all college or university students or all married women). Ultimately, we are interested in entire populations. But by selecting a smaller sample, we can draw conclusions about the larger group without polling each and every person. Representative samples are often obtained by *randomly* selecting who will be included. (Notice that this is similar to randomly assigning subjects to groups in an experiment.)

How accurate is the survey method? Surveys conducted by firms such as Ipsos-Reid and Leger Marketing are usually quite accurate. However, if a survey is based on a biased sample, it may paint a false picture. A **biased sample** does not accurately reflect the population from which it was drawn. Surveys done by magazines, websites, and online information services can be quite biased. Surveys on the use of illicit drugs done by *Flare* and *Maclean's* would probably produce very different results—neither of which would represent the general population. That's why psychologists using the survey method go to great lengths to ensure that their samples are representative. Fortunately, people can often be polled by telephone, which makes it easier to obtain large samples. Also, recent studies have shown that even if one person out of three refuses to answer survey questions, the results are still likely to be valid (Hutchinson, 2004).

Internet Surveys

Recently, psychologists have started doing surveys and experiments on the Internet. Web-based research has the advantage of low cost, and it can reach very large groups of people. However, psychologists are well aware that samples obtained through websites are not necessarily representative. Nevertheless, Internet studies have provided interesting information about topics such as anger, decision making, religion, racial prejudice, what disgusts people, sexual attitudes, and much more. Biased samples can limit web-based research, but psychologists are finding ways to gather valid information with it (Birnbaum, 2004; Whitaker, 2007).

Social Desirability

Even well-designed surveys may be limited by another problem. If a psychologist were to ask you detailed questions about your sexual history and current sexual behaviour, how accurate would your replies be? Would you exaggerate? Would you be embarrassed? Replies to survey questions are not always accurate or truthful. Many people show a distinct **courtesy bias** (a tendency to give "polite" or socially desirable answers). For example, answers to questions concerning sex, alcohol or drug use, income, and church attendance tend to be less than truthful. Likewise, the week after an election, more people will say they voted than actually did (Hutchinson, 2004).

Summary

Despite their limitations, surveys frequently produce valuable information. The survey method can be a powerful research tool. Like other methods, it has limitations, but new techniques and strategies are providing valuable information about our behaviour (Tourangeau, 2004; Kahneman et al., 2004).

ETHICS AND PSYCHOLOGICAL RESEARCH

<SURVEY QUESTION
Why is it important for psychologists to consider ethical issues when doing research?

One question you may be asking yourself after reading this discussion of research methods is, "But is it ethical?" Is it ethical to use animals as research subjects? Is it ethical to use deception as part of a research project? Imagine if you were a subject in the study of students at the U.S. Air Force Academy Prep School mentioned earlier. How would you feel when you learned that you were in the group that had "unusually low" mathematical ability? And what about the teachers? Imagine how they must have felt when they learned that they had been deceived!

The issue of research ethics is an important one for psychologists. So important, in fact, that the three major federal agencies that distribute grant money have developed a code of conduct that governs all research in Canada. The Social Sciences and Humanities Research Council of Canada (SSHRC), the Canadian Institutes of Health Research (CIHR), and the Natural Sciences and Engineering Research Council of Canada (NSERC), or the Tri-Council, as they are known, require that all colleges and universities have committees to review all research proposals to ensure that the research is carried out according to strict ethical guidelines.

Research with Human Subjects

Any research carried out on human beings must respect the dignity and welfare of the participants. Participation is strictly voluntary, and people must be informed about the purpose of the study, including any potential risks, so that they can give *informed consent*. Researchers must also minimize any potential harm to the participants. And researchers undertake to keep any personal or sensitive information about the participants strictly confidential.

So how does deception fit into these guidelines? It seems that the use of deception, or deliberately misinforming people, would be unethical. And it is. Generally, the Tri-Council does not support the use of deception, except in limited circumstances. The researcher must show that the potential benefit or value of the research justifies the use of deception, that alternative procedures have been considered, and that participants will be completely informed of the true aim and design of the study.

Research with Animal Subjects

Animals are used as subjects in many different areas of psychological research, including research on the brain, brain functioning, and the relationship of the brain to behaviour; research on sexual behaviour; and research on learning. Depending on the study, they may be unharmed or may undergo various types of brain or other operations. Some studies require the animal's death so that areas of the brain or other organs may be examined to determine the effects of a procedure (see, e.g., the discussion on stress in Chapter 12). Animals are used as research subjects for many reasons. Some questions, although important, cannot ethically be answered by experimental research on human beings (e.g., studying the effects of smoking during pregnancy). In some cases, such as learning, comparable behaviours in humans are either too complex or complicated by other factors (we don't usually worry that a rat had a fight with his girlfriend on the night before a big experiment). It is also useful to study animals in order to extend our knowledge to other species, such as studying sex differences. And in many cases, people study animals just because they are interested in animal behaviour (Jane Goodall, for instance).

Just as the Tri-Council has specified ethical standards for research with humans, the Canadian Council on Animal Care (CCAC) has established guidelines for the use of animals in research. These guidelines require that researchers ensure that discomfort is minimal, that as few animals as possible are used, and that the benefits of the research are maximized.

In addition, the guidelines specify that all care be taken of the animals when they are not actively participating in the research (e.g., that social animals, such as chimpanzees and rats, are not isolated in individual cages) and that all animals be provided with an enriched environment. Also, the CCAC requires that humane methods be used if the research requires that the animals be put to death.

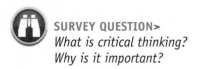

SURVEY QUESTION>
What is critical thinking? Why is it important?

SUMMARY—SCIENCE AND CRITICAL THINKING

Is so much emphasis on research really necessary in psychology? In a word, yes. As we have seen, science is a powerful way of asking questions about the world and getting trustworthy answers. Your awareness of this fact should help make you a more critical observer of human behaviour. Table 1.6 summarizes many of the important ideas we have covered.

Most of us would be skeptical when buying a used car. But all too often, we may be tempted to "buy" outrageous claims about topics such as the occult, the Bermuda Triangle, UFOs, Tarot cards, healing crystals, and so forth. Likewise, most of us easily accept our ignorance of subatomic physics. But because we deal with human behaviour every day, we tend to think that we already know what is true in psychology.

■ **Table 1.6 Comparison of Psychological Research Methods**

	Advantages	Disadvantages
Naturalistic observation	Behaviour is observed in a natural setting, much information is obtained, and hypotheses and questions for additional research are formed.	Little or no control is possible; observed behaviour may be altered by the presence of the observer; observations may be biased; and causes cannot be conclusively identified.
Correlational method	Relationships can be shown to exist; predictions can be made; the method can be used in a lab, a clinic, or a natural setting.	Little or no control is possible, relationships may be coincidental, and cause-and-effect relationships cannot be confirmed.
Experimental method	Clear cause-and-effect relationships can be identified, powerful controlled observations can be staged, and there is no need to wait for a natural event.	Results may be somewhat artificial, and some natural behaviour is not easily studied in the laboratory (field experiments may avoid these objections).
Clinical method	This method takes advantage of "natural clinical trials" and allows investigation of rare or unusual problems or events.	Little or no control is possible, a control group is not provided for comparison, subjective interpretation is often necessary, and a single case may be misleading or unrepresentative.
Survey method	This method allows information about large numbers of people to be gathered and can address questions not answered by other approaches.	Obtaining a representative sample is critical and can be difficult to do, answers may be inaccurate, and people may not do what they say.

For these and many more reasons, learning to think critically is one of the lasting benefits of a university education. **Critical thinking** refers to an ability to evaluate, compare, analyze, critique, and synthesize information. Critical thinkers are willing to ask the hard questions, including those that challenge conventional wisdom. For example, many people believe that punishment (a spanking) is a good way to reinforce learning in children. Actually, nothing could be further from the truth (Gershoff, 2002). That's why a critical thinker would immediately ask, "Does punishment work? If so, when? Under what conditions does it not work? What are its drawbacks? Are there better ways to guide learning?"

> **Critical thinking** An ability to evaluate, compare, analyze, critique, and synthesize information.

Thinking about Behaviour

The core of critical thinking is a willingness to actively *evaluate* ideas. Critical thinkers analyze the evidence supporting their beliefs and probe for weaknesses in their reasoning. They question assumptions and look for alternative conclusions. True knowledge, they recognize, comes from constantly revising and enlarging our understanding of the world.

Critical thinking is built upon four basic principles (Browne & Keeley, 2007):

1. *Few "truths" transcend the need for empirical testing.* It is true that religious beliefs and personal values may be held without supporting evidence. But most other ideas can be evaluated by applying the rules of logic and evidence.
2. *Evidence varies in quality.* Judging the quality of evidence is crucial. Imagine that you are a juror in a courtroom, judging claims made by two battling lawyers. To decide correctly, you can't just weigh the amount of evidence. You must also critically evaluate the quality of the evidence. Then you can give greater weight to the most credible facts.
3. *Authority or claimed expertise does not automatically make an idea true.* Just because a teacher, celebrity, or authority is convinced or sincere doesn't mean you should automatically believe him or her. It is unscientific and self-demeaning to just take the word of an "expert" without asking, "What evidence convinced her or him? How good is it? Is there a better explanation?"
4. *Critical thinking requires an open mind.* Be prepared to consider daring departures and go wherever the evidence leads. However, it is possible to be so "open-minded" that you simply become gullible. Critical thinkers try to strike a balance between open-mindedness and healthy skepticism. Being open-minded means that you consider all possibilities before drawing a conclusion. It is the ability to change your views under the impact of new and more convincing evidence (Bartz, 2002).

To put these principles into action, here are some questions to ask over and over again as you evaluate new information (Browne & Keeley, 2007):

1. What claims are being made?
2. What test of these claims (if any) has been made?
3. Who did the test? How good is the evidence?
4. What were the nature and quality of the tests? Are they credible? Can they be repeated?
5. How reliable and trustworthy were the investigators? Do they have conflicts of interest? Do their findings appear to be objective? Has any other independent researcher duplicated the findings?
6. Finally, how much credibility can the claim be given? High, medium, low, provisional?

A course in psychology naturally enriches thinking skills. To add to the process, all upcoming chapters include Critical Thinking questions like the ones you have seen here. Tackling these questions will sharpen your thinking abilities and make learning more lively. For an immediate thinking challenge, let's take a critical look at several non-scientific systems that claim to explain behaviour.

SURVEY QUESTION>
How do psychological explanations differ from other (unscientific) explanations of behaviour?

PSEUDO-PSYCHOLOGIES—PLANETS AND PERSONALITY

What are false psychologies? Why do they sometimes seem to work? A **pseudo-psychology** (SUE-doe-psychology) is any unfounded system that resembles psychology. Many pseudo-psychologies give the appearance of science but are actually false. (*Pseudo* means "false.") Pseudo-psychologies change little over time because their followers seek evidence that supports and avoid evidence that contradicts their beliefs. Scientists, in contrast, actively look for contradictions as a way to advance knowledge. They are skeptical critics of their own theories (Schick & Vaughn, 2010).

How about an example of a pseudo-psychology? At first glance, a pseudo-psychology called *graphology* might seem reasonable. Graphologists claim that personality traits are revealed through our handwriting (**graphology**). Based on such claims, some companies use graphologists to select job candidates. This is troubling because graphologists score close to zero on tests of accuracy in rating personality (Furnham, Chamorro-Premuzic, & Callahan, 2003). In fact, graphologists do no better than untrained college students in rating personality and job performance (Neter & Ben-Shakhar, 1989). Ironically enough, two researchers from the University of Western Ontario found that a graphological society concluded that handwriting analysis should not be used to select people for jobs (Simner & Goffin, 2003). (By the way, graphology's failure at revealing personality should be separated from its proven value for detecting faked documents.)

This might seem harmless, except that this false system has been used to determine who is hired, given bank credit, or selected for juries. In these and similar situations, pseudo-psychologies do, in fact, harm people.

Astrology is probably the most popular pseudo-psychology. **Astrology** holds that the positions of the stars and planets at the time of one's birth determine personality traits and affect behaviour. Like other pseudo-psychologies, astrology has repeatedly been shown to have no scientific validity (Hartmann, Reuter, & Nyborg, 2006; Kelly, 1999).

If pseudo-psychologies have no scientific basis, how do they survive and why are they popular? There are several reasons.

Uncritical Acceptance

If you have ever had your astrological chart done or your handwriting analyzed as a way of finding out more about your personality, you may have been impressed with its apparent accuracy. However, such perceptions are typically based on **uncritical acceptance** (the tendency to believe positive or flattering descriptions of yourself). Naturally, when your personality is described in desirable terms, it is hard to deny that the description has the "ring of truth."

Positive Instances

Even when a personality description contains a mixture of good and bad traits, it may seem accurate. To find out why, read the following personality description.

Your Personality Profile

You have a strong need for other people to like you and for them to admire you. You have a tendency to be critical of yourself. You have a great deal of unused energy which you have not turned to your advantage. While you have some personality weaknesses, you are generally able to compensate for them. Your sexual adjustment has presented some problems for you. Disciplined and controlled on the outside, you tend to be worrisome and insecure inside. At times you have serious doubts as to whether you have made the right decision or done the right thing. You prefer a certain amount of change and variety and become dissatisfied when hemmed in by restrictions and limitations. You pride yourself on being an independent thinker and do not accept other opinions without satisfactory proof. You have found it unwise to be too frank in revealing

Pseudo-psychology Any false and unscientific system of beliefs and practices that is offered as an explanation of behaviour.

Graphology A false system based on the belief that handwriting can reveal personality traits.

Astrology A false system based on the belief that human behaviour is influenced by the positions of stars and planets.

Uncritical acceptance The tendency to believe generally positive or flattering descriptions of oneself.

> **Fallacy of positive instances** The tendency to remember or notice information that fits one's expectations, while forgetting discrepancies.
>
> **Barnum effect** The tendency to consider a personal description accurate if it is stated in very general terms.

yourself to others. At times you are extroverted, affable, sociable, while at other times you are introverted, wary, and reserved. Some of your aspirations tend to be pretty unrealistic.*

Does this describe your personality? When this summary was read individually to college students, only 5 out of 79 felt that the description was inaccurate.

Reread the description and you will see that it contains both sides of several personality dimensions. Its apparent accuracy is an illusion based on the **fallacy of positive instances,** in which we remember or notice things that confirm our expectations and forget the rest. All pseudo-psychologies thrive on this effect. For example, you can always find "Leo characteristics" in a Leo. If you look, however, you could also find "Gemini characteristics," "Scorpio characteristics," or whatever. (See Using Psychology: "The Barnum Effect.")

Astrology's popularity shows that many people have difficulty separating valid psychology from systems that seem valid but are not. The goal of this discussion, then, has been to make you a more critical observer of human behaviour and to clarify what is, and what is not, psychology. Pseudo-psychologies may seem like no more than a nuisance, but they can

USING PSYCHOLOGY

The Barnum Effect

Pseudo-psychologies also take advantage of the **Barnum effect,** which is a tendency to consider personal descriptions accurate if they are stated in general terms (Kida, 2006). P. T. Barnum, the famed circus showman, had a formula for success: "Always have a little something for everybody." Like the all-purpose personality profile, palm readings, fortunes, horoscopes, and other products of pseudo-psychology are stated in such general terms that they can hardly miss.

Cathy Fichten and Betty Sunerton, two psychology teachers at Dawson College in Montréal, devised a classroom exercise to teach research methodology to students in their introductory psychology classes. Students were asked to validate horoscopes that appeared in a Montréal newspaper using a 10-point rating scale of personal usefulness ("How personally useful would this forecast have been for you if you had read it yesterday?"). Some students were told that the forecasts were for their own zodiac signs, while others rated the same forecasts without knowing the signs. Although students who thought they were rating their own horoscopes rated them as more personally useful than those who did not, the results were not replicated when the procedure was repeated using the same day's horoscopes from a Toronto newspaper. In other words, daily forecasts were not valid (Fichten & Sunerton, 1983). When

students who said they read their own horoscopes at least three times a week were asked to match daily horoscopes with their appropriate astrological signs, they did no better than chance. Fichten and Sunerton repeated the exercise several times in their classes and eventually published the results.

A few months after their research was reported in a peer-reviewed psychology journal, one of Fichten's students came to her waving a copy of a widely circulated tabloid. Under a screaming bold headline ("Horoscopes really true, says psychologist") was an article that summarized the research methodology accurately but conveniently omitted the word "not" when describing the results. In addition, the phrase "Dr. Fichten said" was used repeatedly throughout the article (*The Star*, October 11, 1983, p. 32). However, Fichten was never interviewed by anyone from the tabloid. The tabloid article was later quoted as a source of "scientific" information on the validity of horoscope predictions by a horoscope magazine.

It didn't stop there. For months after, Fichten received phone calls and letters from people looking for "expert" information about their horoscopes, including one woman who wanted advice on who to marry and an 80-year-old woman looking for guidance from the stars about her will (Fichten, personal communication).

*Reprinted with permission of author and publisher from: R. E. Ulrich, T. J. Stachnik, and N. R. Stainton, "Student acceptance of generalized personality interpretations," *Psychological Reports*, 13, 1963, p. 831–834.

STUDY BREAK   Clinical and Survey Methods/Critical Thinking

Reflect

It is unusual to get through a day without encountering people who believe in pseudo-psychologies or who make unscientific or unfounded statements. How stringently do you evaluate your own beliefs and the claims made by others? Critical thinking requires effort and discipline, but high-quality information is the reward.

Learning Check

1. Case studies can often be thought of as natural tests and are frequently used by clinical psychologists. T or F?

2. For the survey method to be valid, a representative sample of people must be polled. T or F?

3. Belief in astrology is based on the fallacy of positive instances, which is a failure to
   a. collect relevant correlations
   b. make use of introspection
   c. distinguish between observation and inference
   d. engage in critical thinking

4. The fallacy of positive instances refers to graphology's accepted value for the detection of forgeries. T or F?

5. Personality descriptions provided by pseudo-psychologies are stated in general terms that provide "a little something for everybody." This fact is the basis of the
   a. palmist's fallacy
   b. uncritical acceptance pattern
   c. fallacy of positive instances
   d. Barnum effect

Critical Thinking

6. A psychologist conducting a survey at a shopping mall (The Gallery of Wretched Excess) flips a coin before stopping passersby. If the coin shows heads, he interviews the person; if it shows tails, he skips that person. Has the psychologist obtained a random sample?

Answers

1. T 2. T 3. b 4. F 5. d 6. The psychologist's coin flips might produce a reasonably good sample of people at the mall. The real problem is that people who go to the mall may be mostly from one part of town, from upper-income groups, or from some other non-representative group. The psychologist's sample is likely to be seriously flawed.

---

do harm. For instance, people seeking treatment for psychological disorders may become the victims of self-appointed "experts" who offer ineffective, pseudo-scientific "therapies" (Kalal, 1999; Lilienfeld et al., 2005). Valid psychological principles are based on observation and evidence, not fads, opinions, or wishful thinking.

A Look Ahead

To help you get the most out of psychology, each chapter of this text includes a Psychology in Action section like the one that follows. There you will find ideas you can actually use, now or in the future. To complete our discussion, let's take a critical look at information reported in the popular press. You should find this an interesting way to conclude our first tour of psychology and its methods.

Psychology in Action

SURVEY QUESTION>
Can you trust the psychological information you find on the Internet and in popular media?

PSYCHOLOGY IN THE NEWS—SEPARATING FACT FROM FICTION

Psychology is a popular topic in magazines and newspapers. Unfortunately, much of what you will read is based on wishful thinking rather than science. Here are some suggestions for separating high-quality information from misleading fiction.

Suggestion 1

Be Skeptical

Reports in the popular press tend to be made uncritically and with a definite bias toward reporting "astonishing" findings. Remember, if it sounds unbelievable, it usually is.

Example 1: Some years ago, news articles described an amazing new "sixth sense" called "dermo-optical perception." A few gifted people, the articles claimed, could use their fingertips to identify colours and read print while blindfolded.

In reality, such "abilities" are based on what stage magicians call a "nose peek." It is impossible to prepare a blindfold (without damaging the eyes) that does not leave a tiny space on each side of the nose. Were the people who claimed to have "X-ray eyes" taking nose peeks? Apparently they were, because "dermo-optical abilities" disappeared as soon as the opportunity to peek was controlled.

Example 2: The Internet is a great source of misinformation. One recent classic was a story about a health department in Oregon seeking a Klingon interpreter for mental health patients who only speak in the fictional language used in the *Star Trek* movies. This tale started when a newspaper reported that Klingon was on a list of languages that some psychiatric patients claimed they could speak. The article specifically noted that "in reality, no patient has yet tried to communicate in Klingon." Nevertheless, as the story spread around the Web, the idea that a hospital was looking for someone fluent in Klingon had become a "fact" (O'Neill, 2003). When in doubt, check out www.snopes.com for the latest in urban legends, Internet hoaxes, and scams.

Suggestion 2

Consider the Source of Information

It should come as no surprise that information used to sell a product often reflects a desire for profit rather than the objective truth. Here is a typical advertising claim: "Independent laboratory tests prove that no pain reliever is stronger or more effective than Brand X." A statement like this usually means that there was no difference between the products tested. No other pain reliever was stronger or more effective. But none were weaker either.

Keep the source in mind when reading the claims of makers of home biofeedback machines, sleep-learning devices, subliminal tapes, and the like. Remember that psychological services may be merchandised as well. Be wary of expensive courses that promise instant mental health and happiness, a better memory, ESP or psychic ability, control of the unconscious mind, weight loss, and so on. They are usually promoted with a few testimonials and many unsupported claims (Lilienfeld et al., 2005).

Psychic claims should be viewed with special caution. Stage mentalists make a living by deceiving the public. Understandably, they are highly interested in promoting belief in their non-existent powers. The same is true of the so-called psychic advisers promoted in TV commercials. These charlatans make use of the Barnum effect (described earlier) to create an illusion that they know private information about people who call them.

Suggestion 3

Ask Yourself if There Was a Control Group

The key importance of a control group in any experiment is frequently overlooked by the unsophisticated—an error to which you are no longer susceptible! The popular press is full of reports of "experiments" performed without control groups: "Talking to Plants Speeds Growth"; "Special Diet Controls Hyperactivity in Children"; "Food Shows Less Spoilage in Pyramid Chamber"; "Graduates of Fire-Walking Seminar Risk Their Soles."

Fire-walking is based on simple physics, not on any form of supernatural psychological control. The temperature of the coals may be as high as 650°C (1200°F). However, coals are like the air in a hot oven: They are very inefficient at transferring heat during brief contact.

Consider the last example for a moment. In recent years, expensive commercial courses have been promoted to teach people to walk barefoot on hot coals. (Why anyone would want to do this is itself an interesting question.) Firewalkers supposedly protect their feet with a technique called "neurolinguistic programming." Many people have paid good money to learn the technique, and most do manage a quick walk on the coals. But is the technique necessary? And is anything remarkable happening? We need a comparison group!

Fortunately, physicist Bernard Leikind has provided one. Leikind showed with volunteers that anyone (with reasonably callused feet) can walk over a bed of coals without being burned. The reason is that the coals, which are light, fluffy carbon, transmit little heat when touched. The principle involved is similar to briefly putting your hand in a hot oven. If you touch a pan, you will be burned because metal transfers heat efficiently. But if your hand stays in the heated air you'll be fine because air transmits little heat (Mitchell, 1987). Mystery solved.

Suggestion 4

Look for Errors in Distinguishing between Correlation and Causation

As you now know, it is dangerous to presume that one thing caused another just because they are correlated. In spite of this, you will see many claims based on questionable correlations. Here's an example of mistaking correlation for causation: The late Jeanne Dixon, an astrologer, once answered a group of prominent scientists—who had declared that there is no scientific foundation for astrology—by saying, "They would do well to check the records at their local police stations, where they will learn that the rate of violent crime rises and falls with lunar cycles." Dixon, of course, believed that the moon affects human behaviour.

If it is true that violent crime is more frequent at certain times of the month, doesn't that prove her point? Far from it. Increased crime could be due to darker nights, the fact that many people expect others to act crazier, or any number of similar factors. More important, direct studies of the alleged "lunar effect" have shown that it doesn't occur (Dowling, 2005). Moonstruck criminals, along with "moon madness," are a fiction (Iosif & Ballon, 2005). If we told you that sales of snow-removal equipment were correlated with deaths from heart attacks, would you think twice before going to your local Canadian Tire store to replace the shovel that broke last year?

Suggestion 5

Be Sure to Distinguish between Observation and Inference

If you see a person crying, is it correct to assume that she or he is sad? Although it seems reasonable to make this assumption, it is actually quite risky. We can observe objectively that the person is crying, but to infer sadness may be in error. It could be that the individual has just peeled 10 onions. Or maybe he or she just won a million-dollar lottery or is trying contact lenses for the first time.

Psychologists, politicians, physicians, scientists, and other experts often go far beyond the available facts in their claims. This does not mean that their inferences, opinions, and interpretations have no value; the opinion of an expert on the causes of mental illness, criminal behaviour, learning problems, or whatever can be revealing. But be careful to distinguish between fact and opinion.

Suggestion 6

Beware of Oversimplifications, Especially Those Motivated by Monetary Gain

Courses or programs that offer a "new personality in three sessions," "six steps to love and fulfillment in marriage," or newly discovered "secrets of unlocking the powers of the mind" should be immediately suspect.

Suggestion 7

Remember, "For Example" Is Not Proof

After reading this chapter, you should be sensitive to the danger of selecting single examples. If you read, "Law student passes bar exam using sleep-learning device," don't rush out to buy one. Systematic research has shown that these devices are of little or no value (Druckman & Bjork, 1994; Wood et al., 1992). A corollary to this suggestion is to ask: Are the reported observations important or widely applicable?

Examples, anecdotes, single cases, and testimonials are all potentially deceptive. Unfortunately, individual cases tell nothing about what is true in general (Stanovich, 2007). For instance, studies of large groups of people show that smoking increases the likelihood of lung cancer. It doesn't matter if you know a lifelong heavy smoker who is 94 years old. The general finding is the one to remember.

Summary

We are all bombarded daily with such a mass of new information that it is difficult to absorb it. The available knowledge, even in a limited area such as psychology, biology, medicine, or contemporary rock music, is so vast that no single person can completely know and comprehend it. With this situation in mind, it becomes increasingly important that you become a critical, selective, and informed consumer of information.

 STUDY BREAK **Psychology in the Media**

Reflect

Do you tend to assume that a statement must be true if it is in print, on television, on the Internet, or made by an authority? How actively do you evaluate and question claims found in the media? Could you be a more critical consumer of information? Should you be a more critical consumer of information?

Learning Check

1. Newspaper accounts of dermo-optical perception have generally reported only the results of carefully designed psychological experiments. T or F?

2. Stage mentalists and psychics often use deception in their acts. T or F?

3. Blaming the lunar cycle for variations in the rate of violent crime is an example of mistaking correlation for causation. T or F?

4. If a law student uses a sleep-learning device to pass the bar exam, it proves that the device works. T or F?

Critical Thinking

5. Many parents believe that children become "hyperactive" when they eat too much sugar, and some early studies seemed to confirm this connection. However, we now know that eating sugar rarely has any such effect on children. Why do you think that sugar appears to cause hyperactivity?

Answers

1. F 2. T 3. T 4. F 5. This is another case of mistaking correlation for causation. Children who are hyperactive may eat more sugar (and other foods) to fuel their frenetic activity levels.

CHAPTER IN REVIEW

Major Points

- Psychology is the science of behaviour and mental processes. Psychology provides objective answers to questions about human behaviour.

- Psychologists gather scientific data in order to describe, understand, predict, and control behaviour.

- The scientific method consists of highly refined procedures for observing the natural world, testing hypotheses, and drawing valid conclusions.

- Psychologists use several specialized research methods. Each has strengths and weaknesses, so all are needed to fully investigate human behaviour.

- Experimentation is the most powerful way to identify cause-and-effect relationships.

- Critical thinking is central to the scientific method, to psychology, and to effective behaviour in general.

- The popular media are rife with inaccurate information. It is essential to critically evaluate information, no matter what its source may be.

Summary

What is psychology? What are its goals?

- Psychology is the scientific study of behaviour.

- Some major areas of research in psychology are comparative, learning, sensation, perception, personality, biopsychology, motivation and emotion, social, cognitive, developmental, gender, and cultural psychology.

- Psychologists may be directly interested in animal behaviour, or they may study animals as models of human behaviour.

- As a science, psychology's goals are to describe, understand, predict, and control behaviour.

What are the historical roots of modern psychology?

- Historically, psychology is an outgrowth of philosophy.

- The first psychological laboratory was established in Germany by Wilhelm Wundt, who tried to study conscious experience.

- The first school of thought in psychology was structuralism, a kind of "mental chemistry" based on introspection and analysis.

- Structuralism was followed by functionalism, behaviourism, and Gestalt psychology.

- Psychodynamic approaches, such as Freud's psychoanalytic theory, emphasize the unconscious origins of behaviour.

- Humanistic psychology accentuates subjective experience, human potentials, and personal growth.

What are the major trends and specialties in psychology today?

- Three main streams of thought in modern psychology are the biological perspective, including neuropsychology and evolutionary psychology; the psychological perspective, including behaviourism, cognitive psychology, the psychodynamic approach, and humanism; and the sociocultural perspective.

- Although psychologists, psychiatrists, psychoanalysts, and counsellors all work in the field of mental health, their training and methods differ considerably.

- Clinical and counselling psychologists, who do psychotherapy, represent only two of dozens of specialties in psychology.

- Psychological research may be basic or applied.

What is the scientific method? Why is the scientific method important to psychologists?

- Important elements of a scientific investigation include observing, defining a problem, proposing a hypothesis, gathering evidence/testing the hypothesis, publishing results, and forming a theory.

- Before they can be investigated, psychological concepts must be given operational definitions.

How do psychologists collect information?

- Naturalistic observation is a starting place in many investigations.

- Three problems with naturalistic observation are the effects of the observer on the observed, observer bias, and an inability to explain observed behaviour.

- In the correlational method, relationships between two traits, responses, or events are measured.

- A correlation coefficient is computed to gauge the strength of the relationship. Correlations allow prediction, but they do not demonstrate cause-and-effect connections.

- Cause-and-effect relationships are best identified by controlled experiments.

What is an experiment? Why do psychologists use experiments to answer questions about behaviour and mental processes?

- In an experiment, two or more groups of subjects are formed. These groups differ only with regard to the independent variable (condition of interest as a cause in the experiment).

- Effects on the dependent variable are then measured. All other conditions (extraneous variables) are held constant.

- In experiments that involve drugs, a placebo must be given to control for the effects of expectations (participant bias). If a double-blind procedure is used, neither subjects nor experimenters know who received a drug.

- A related problem is researcher bias (a tendency for researchers to unwittingly influence the outcome of an experiment). Expectations can create a self-fulfilling prophecy, in which a person changes in the direction of the expectation.

What other research methods do psychologists use?

- The clinical method employs case studies, which are in-depth records of a single subject. Case studies provide important information on topics that cannot be studied in any other way.

- In the survey method, people in a representative sample are asked a series of carefully worded questions.

Why is it important for psychologists to consider ethical issues when doing research?

- The Social Sciences and Humanities Research Council (SSHRC), the Canadian Institutes of Health Research (CIHR), and the Natural Sciences and Engineering Research Council of Canada (NSERC) (also known as the Tri-Council) require all colleges and universities to have ethics review boards to ensure that all research is carried out in accordance with current standards and ethical guidelines.

- Research with human subjects must respect the dignity and integrity of the subjects. Subjects are entitled to all information necessary for informed consent. Potential harm should be minimized.

- Deception may be used only when the researchers can show that the benefits of using deception far outweigh any potential harm to the subjects.

- Ethical standards of research with animal subjects require that the animals be well cared for and adequately housed in clean cages. Pain or other discomfort must be minimal.

What is critical thinking? Why is it important?

- Critical thinking is the ability to evaluate, compare, analyze, critique, and synthesize information.

- To judge the validity of a claim, it is important to gather evidence for and against the claim and to evaluate the quality of the evidence.

How do psychological explanations differ from other (unscientific) explanations of behaviour?

- Numerous pseudo-psychologies exist. These false systems are frequently confused with valid psychology. Belief in pseudo-psychologies is based in part on uncritical acceptance, the fallacy of positive instances, and the Barnum effect.

Can you trust the psychological information you find on the Internet and in popular media?

- Information in the mass media varies greatly in quality and accuracy.

- It is wise to approach such information with skepticism and caution. This is especially true with regard to the source of information, uncontrolled observation, correlation and causation, inferences, oversimplification, single examples, and unrepeatable results.

Interactive Learning

Please visit *http://www.psychologyjourney4ce.nelson.com* for a list of weblinks to relevant psychology sites.

 CourseMate

Access the interactive eBook and chapter-specific interactive learning tools, including flashcards, quizzes, videos, and more, in your Psychology CourseMate at NelsonBrain.com.

psyk.trek 1. History and Methods.

TEST YOUR KNOWLEDGE

The questions that follow are only a sample of what you need to know. If you miss any of the items, review the entire chapter and the Study Breaks. Another way to prepare for tests is to use the Study Guide and the Practice Exams that are available with this text.

1. According to the textbook, which of the following is the best definition of *psychology*?
   a. Psychology is the study of the mind and mental processes.
   b. Psychology is the knowledge of philosophy and mental processes.
   c. Psychology is the study of personality and mental processes.
   d. Psychology is the science of behaviour and mental processes.

2. Which of the following is most interested in the growth of young children?
   a. a learning theorist
   b. a personality theorist
   c. a comparative psychologist
   d. a developmental psychologist

3. Research explains why people remember better when they relate new information to familiar ideas. Which of psychology's goals is met by this research?
   a. description
   b. understanding
   c. prediction
   d. control

4. Which two schools of thought have largely disappeared from contemporary psychology?
   a. functionalism, behaviourism
   b. structuralism, cognitive
   c. functionalism, structuralism
   d. structuralism, humanism

5. What does behaviourism study?
   a. unconscious behaviour
   b. conscious behaviour
   c. observable behaviour
   d. introspective behaviour

6. Which of the following is *least* likely to treat serious behavioural and emotional disturbances?
   a. a psychologist
   b. a counsellor
   c. a psychiatrist
   d. a psychoanalyst

7. A psychotherapist is working with a person of a different ethnicity. Two things she should be aware of that affect behaviour are cultural relativity and which of the following?
   a. anthropomorphic errors
   b. operational definitions
   c. sampling errors
   d. social norms

8. You have identified an interesting problem or question to study. Before you begin your research, what will you need to establish?
   a. the variables' correlation coefficients
   b. the variables' operational definitions
   c. the variables' double-blind controls
   d. the variables' new theories

9. A psychologist wants to see whether having control over difficult tasks reduces stress. What will this psychologist be testing?
   a. an experimental hypothesis
   b. an operational definition
   c. an empirical definition theory
   d. an anthropomorphic error

10. What technique do psychologists use to answer questions about behaviour?
    a. experimentation
    b. naturalistic observation
    c. the survey method
    d. the clinical method

11. Which research methods have problems of observer bias and the observer effect?
    a. experiment observations
    b. naturalistic studies
    c. surveys
    d. clinical studies

12. The outcome of a psychology experiment is revealed by measuring changes in behaviour. What type of variables are these measures?
    a. independent variables
    b. correlational variables
    c. dependent variables
    d. extraneous variables

13. What are double-blind experiments designed to control?
    a. the placebo effect and researcher bias
    b. the anthropomorphic fallacy and courtesy bias
    c. random assignment and researcher bias
    d. courtesy bias and the placebo effect

14. In psychological research, which of the following is most likely to lead to the use of representative samples?
    a. naturalistic studies
    b. the survey method
    c. the experimental method
    d. the clinical method

15. Which method is most likely used when investigating amnesia?
    a. the survey method
    b. field experiments
    c. a double-blind experiment
    d. a case study

16. A magazine article claims special diets can control hyperactivity in children. What would make these claims meaningful?
    a. The author is an expert on hyperactivity.
    b. The diets have been tested empirically.
    c. The diets are based on animal research.
    d. The author is an expert on children's diets.

17. A researcher is looking for a way to improve children's math learning. What kind of research is the researcher most likely to engage in?
    a. basic research
    b. applied research
    c. pure research
    d. group research

18. Which of the following is one of the three major ethical issues that researchers must be sensitive about?
    a. deception
    b. financial cost
    c. invasion of personal beliefs
    d. inconsequential harm

19. What is an advantage of naturalistic observation?
    a. Causes of behaviour can be identified.
    b. Behaviour is *not* influenced by outside sources.
    c. Correlation can be carefully determined.
    d. Hypotheses can be carefully tested.

20. Danny takes a herbal supplement for ankle pain. His pain seems to decrease, and he tells everyone how effective the supplement is. What is another explanation for his pain reduction?
    a. the placebo effect
    b. the replication effect
    c. the experimenter effect
    d. the observer effect

ANSWERS   1.d 2.d 3.b 4.c 5.c 6.b 7.d 8.b 9.a 10.a 11.b 12.c 13.a 14.d 15.d 16.b 17.b 18.a 19.b 20.a

chapter 2

Brain and Behaviour

JOURNEY INTO PSYCHOLOGY: FINDING MUSIC IN TOFU

It's hard to watch and hear a gifted musician without thinking about the brain. Listening to a recording of the famous Canadian pianist Glenn Gould performing Bach's *Goldberg Variations* makes you wonder, what was so special about his brain that led him to play music so exquisitely? If Gould had been an athlete, you would definitely say he was "in the zone." His performance of Bach is unforgettable. Of course, in everything from rock to rap, musicians regularly make music that no machine could duplicate. A virtual Bryan Adams? A mechanical Eric Clapton? A synthetic Shania Twain? Certainly not. That's why music is a good example of the central role the brain plays in all that is human.

Your brain is about the size of a grapefruit. It weighs around 1.5 kilograms and looks a lot like tofu. The next time you are in a market that sells beef brains, stop and have a look. What you will see is similar to your own brain, only smaller. How could such a squishy little blob of tissue allow us to make music of exquisite beauty? To seek a cure for cancer? To fall in love? Or to read a book like this one?

Each nerve cell in your brain is linked to as many as 15 000 others. This network makes it possible to process immense amounts of information. In fact, there may be more possible pathways between the neurons in your brain than there are atoms in the entire universe! Undeniably, the human brain is the most amazing of all computers.

Scientists use the power of the brain to study the brain. Yet even now we must wonder if the brain will ever completely understand itself. Nevertheless, it is clear that answers to many age-old questions about the mind, consciousness, and knowledge lie buried within the brain, waiting to be discovered. Let's visit this fascinating realm.

 Survey Questions

- How do nerve cells operate and communicate?
- How is the nervous system organized, and what are the functions of its major parts?
- How do we know how the brain works? What are the methods by which scientists study the brain?
- How is the brain organized, and what do its higher structures do?
- Why are the brain's association areas important? What happens when they are injured?
- What kinds of behaviours are controlled by the subcortex?
- How does the glandular system affect behaviour?
- How do right- and left-handed individuals differ?

NEURONS—BUILDING A "BIOCOMPUTER"

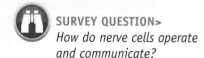 **SURVEY QUESTION>**
How do nerve cells operate and communicate?

While they may seem far removed from your daily life, 100 billion tiny **neurons** (NOOR-ons: individual nerve cells) make up your brain. Neurons carry information from the senses to the brain, where they process it. They also activate muscles and glands. Yet, a single neuron is not very smart—it takes at least several just to make you blink.

When a musician such as Bruce Springsteen plays a guitar riff, literally billions of neurons may be involved. Your brainpower arises because individual neurons link to one another in tight clumps and long "chains." Each neuron receives messages from many others and sends its own message on. Everything you think, feel, or do can be traced back to electrical impulses flashing through spidery networks of neurons. When neurons form vast networks, they produce intelligence and consciousness. Let's see how neurons operate and how the nervous system is "wired."

Parts of a Neuron

What does a neuron look like? What are its main parts? No two neurons are exactly alike, but most have four basic parts (see Figure 2.1). The **dendrites** (DEN-drytes), which look like tree roots, receive messages from other neurons. The **soma** (SOH-mah: cell body) houses the nucleus, which, in turn, contains our DNA or genetic material. It can also receive messages from other neurons and send messages away from it. The resulting message, or the nerve impulse, travels down a thin fibre called the **axon** (AK-sahn).

Neuron An individual nerve cell.
Dendrites Neuron fibres that receive incoming messages.
Soma (cell body) The part of a neuron that contains the nucleus, which, in turn, carries the genetic material.
Axon A thin fibre that carries information away from the cell body of a neuron.

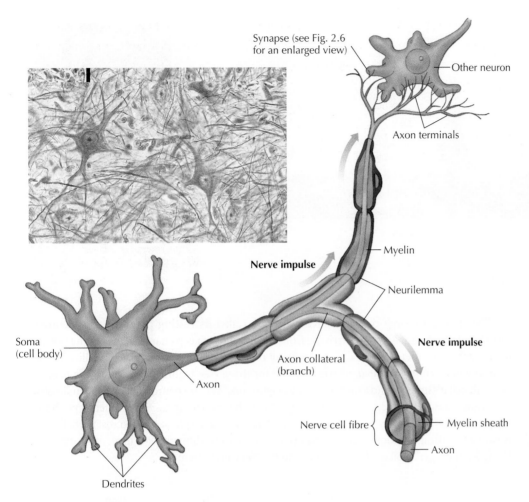

Synapse (see Fig. 2.6 for an enlarged view)

Other neuron

Axon terminals

Myelin

Neurilemma

Nerve impulse

Nerve impulse

Soma (cell body)

Axon

Axon collateral (branch)

Nerve cell fibre

Myelin sheath

Axon

Dendrites

▶▶**FIGURE 2.1** An example of a neuron, or nerve cell, showing several of its important features. The right foreground shows a nerve cell fibre in cross section, and the upper left inset gives a more realistic picture of the shape of neurons. The nerve impulse usually travels from the dendrites and soma to the branching ends of the axon. The neuron shown here is a motor neuron. Motor neurons originate in the brain or spinal cord and extend their axons to the muscles or glands of the body.

 Log on to CourseMate to access this interactive figure

Some axons are only 0.1 millimetres long. (That's about the width of a pencil line.) Others stretch up to a metre through the nervous system (from the base of your spine to your big toe, for instance). Like miniature cables, axons carry messages through the brain and nervous system. Altogether, your brain has about 4.6 million kilometres of axons in it (Rosenzweig, Breedlove, & Watson, 2004).

Axons "branch out" into smaller fibres ending in bulb-shaped **axon terminals.** By forming connections with the dendrites and somas of other neurons, axon terminals allow information to pass from neuron to neuron.

Now let's summarize with a metaphor. Imagine that you are standing in a long line of people holding hands. A person on the far right end of the line wants to silently send a message to the person on the left end. She does this by pressing the hand of the person to her left, who presses the hand of the person to his left, and so on. The message arrives at your right hand (your dendrites). You decide whether to pass it on (you are the soma). The message goes out through your left arm (the axon). With your left hand (the axon terminals), you squeeze the hand of the person to your left, and the message moves on.

The Nerve Impulse

Electrically charged molecules called *ions* (EYE-ons) are found inside each neuron (Figure 2.2). Other ions lie outside the cell. Some ions have a positive electrical charge, and some are negative. When a neuron is inactive, more of these "plus" charges exist outside the neuron and more "minus" charges exist inside. As a result, the inside of each neuron in your brain has an electrical charge of about −70 millivolts. (A millivolt is one-thousandth of a volt.) This charge allows each neuron in your brain to act like a tiny biological battery.

Axon terminals Bulb-shaped structures at the ends of axons that form connections with the dendrites and somas of other neurons.

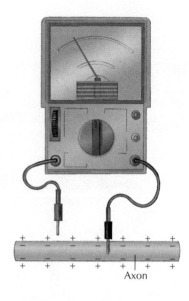

Axon

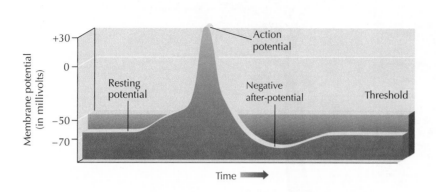

▸▸**FIGURE 2.2** Activity in an axon can be measured by placing electrical probes inside and outside the axon. (The scale is exaggerated here. Such measurements require ultra-small electrodes, as described later in this chapter.) At rest, the inside of an axon is about –60 to –70 millivolts, compared with the outside. Electrochemical changes in a nerve cell generate an action potential. When positively charged sodium ions (Na^+) rush into the cell, its interior briefly becomes positive. This is the action potential. After the action potential, an outward flow of positive potassium ions (K^+) restores the negative potential inside the axon. (See Figure 2.3 for further explanation.)

The electrical charge of an inactive neuron is called its **resting potential.** But neurons seldom get much rest: Messages arriving from other neurons keep changing the resting potential to higher or lower amounts. If the electrical potential changes to about –50 millivolts, the neuron will reach its *threshold*, or trigger point for firing (see Figure 2.2). It's as if the neuron says, "Ah-ha! It's time to send a message to my neighbours." When a neuron reaches –50 millivolts, an **action potential,** or nerve impulse, sweeps down the axon at up to 320 kilometres per hour (see Figure 2.3). That may seem fast, but it still takes at least a split second to react. That's one reason why hitting a major league fastball is one of the most difficult feats in all of sports. (See Using Psychology: "Dollars, Drag Racing, and the Nervous System.")

Resting potential The electrical charge of a neuron at rest.

Action potential The nerve impulse.

1. In its resting state, the axon has a negatively charged interior.

2. During an action potential, positively charged atoms (ions) rush into the axon. This briefly changes the electrical charge inside the axon from negative to positive. Simultaneously, the charge outside the axon becomes negative.

3. The action potential advances as positive and negative charges reverse in a moving zone of electrical activity that sweeps down the axon.

▸▸**FIGURE 2.3** The inside of an axon normally has a negative electrical potential. The fluid surrounding an axon is normally positive. As an action potential passes along the axon, these charges reverse, so that the interior of the axon briefly becomes positive.

4. After an action potential passes, positive ions rapidly flow out of the axon to quickly restore its negative charge. An outward flow of additional positive ions returns the axon to its resting state.

USING PSYCHOLOGY

Dollars, Drag Racing, and the Nervous System

In the sport of drag racing, victory depends on a driver's reaction time. When a light signals the start of a race, the driver must react as quickly as possible, usually in less than a half second. To test your own reaction time, have a friend hold a five-dollar bill from the top, as shown in Figure 2.4. Spread your thumb and fingers about 5 centimetres apart and place them around the bill, about halfway down its length. Watch the bill intently. Without warning, your friend should release the bill. When you see it begin to move, try to catch it by pressing your thumb and fingers together. Most likely, the bill will slip through your fingers. It takes a split second for you to see the bill's movement, process that information in your brain, and send signals to your hand, causing it to move. Because neural processing takes time, our experiences and reactions lag slightly behind events in the world. In fact, your sense of control over your actions is partly an illusion. For instance, if you decide to wiggle your finger, your brain will begin a series of events that leads to finger movement. This activity will start before you begin to feel that you are intentionally moving your finger (Obhi & Haggard, 2004)!

▶▶**FIGURE 2.4**

Bank of Canada

What happens during an action potential? The axon membrane has tiny tunnels called **ion channels.** Normally, these channels are blocked by molecules that act like "gates" or "doors." During an action potential, the gates pop open. This allows sodium ions (Na$^+$) to rush into the axon (Carlson, 2010). The channels open up first near the soma. Then, gate after gate opens down the axon as the action potential zips along (see Figure 2.5).

Each action potential is an all-or-nothing event (a nerve impulse occurs completely or not at all). You might find it helpful to picture the axon as a row of dominoes set on end. Tipping over the dominoes is an all-or-nothing act. Once the first domino drops, a wave of

Ion channels Tiny holes in the axon membrane.

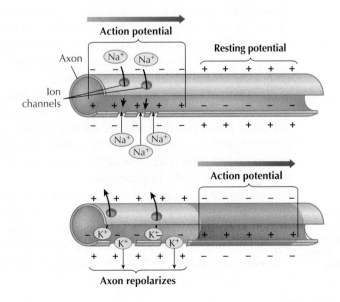

▶▶**FIGURE 2.5** The interior of an axon. The right end of the top axon is at rest. Thus, it has a negative charge inside. An action potential begins when ion channels open and sodium ions (Na$^+$) rush into the axon. In this drawing, the action potential would travel from left to right along the axon. In the lower axon, the action potential has moved to the right. After it passes, potassium ions (K$^+$) flow out of the axon. This quickly renews the negative charge inside the axon, so it can fire again. Sodium ions that enter the axon during an action potential are pumped out more slowly. Removing them restores the original resting potential.

Negative after-potential A drop in electrical charge below the resting potential.

Saltatory conduction The process by which nerve impulses conducted down the axons of neurons coated with myelin jump from gap to gap in the myelin layer.

Synapse (synaptic cleft) The microscopic space between two neurons, over which messages pass. It is also referred to as synaptic cleft.

Neurotransmitter Any chemical released by a neuron that alters activity in other neurons.

falling blocks will zip rapidly to the end of the line. Similarly, when a nerve impulse is triggered near the soma, a wave of activity (the action potential) travels down the length of the axon. This is what happened in long chains of neurons as Glenn Gould's brain told his hands what to do next, note after note.

After each nerve impulse, the cell briefly drops below its resting level, and it becomes less willing to fire. This **negative after-potential** occurs because potassium ions (K^+) flow out of the neuron while the membrane gates are open (see Figure 2.5). After a nerve impulse, ions flow both into and out of the axon, recharging it for more action. In our model, it takes an instant for the row of dominoes to be set up again. Soon, the axon is ready for another wave of activity.

Saltatory Conduction

The axons of some neurons (such as the one pictured in Figure 2.1) are coated with a fatty layer called *myelin* (MY-eh-lin). Small gaps in the myelin help nerve impulses move faster. Instead of passing down the entire length of the axon, the action potential leaps from gap to gap in a process called **saltatory conduction.** (The Latin word *saltare* means "to hop" or "leap.") Without the added speed of saltatory action potentials, it would probably be impossible to brake in time to avoid many automobile accidents (or hit that professional tennis serve). When the myelin layer is damaged, a person may suffer from numbness, weakness, or paralysis. That is, in fact, what happens in multiple sclerosis, a disease that occurs when the immune system attacks and destroys the myelin in a person's body.

Synapses and Neurotransmitters

How does information move from one neuron to another? The nerve impulse is primarily electrical. That's why electrically stimulating the brain affects behaviour. To prove the point, researcher José Delgado once entered a bullring with a cape and a radio transmitter. The bull charged. Delgado retreated. At the last instant the speeding bull stopped short. Why? Because Delgado's radio activated electrodes (metal wires) placed deep within the bull's brain. These, in turn, stimulated "control centres" that brought the bull to a halt (Delgado, 1969).

The nerve impulse is not what relays a message from one neuron to another. This is because there is a microscopic gap called a **synapse** (SIN-aps) (or synaptic cleft) (see Figure 2.6) that exists between two neurons, and electrical impulses cannot flow through physical gaps. You can think about this problem in the following way: You receive electricity from your local power corporation, which generates power many kilometres away from your home. Your home is connected to the power plant through a complex network of wires. A cut in the system of wires anywhere along the intricate maze will disrupt your electrical supply. If we think of neurons as pieces of wire, then an electrical impulse will come to a halt when it reaches the end of the neuronal path.

So if a neuron cannot communicate with its neighbours via an electrical impulse, how does it manage to send its message across the gap? When an action potential reaches the tips of the axon terminals, chemical substances called **neurotransmitters** (NOOR-oh-TRANS-mitters) are released. After crossing the synaptic gap, these chemicals affect the activity of the next neuron.

Let's return to our metaphor of people standing in a line. To be the example, you and the others shouldn't be holding hands. Instead, each person should have a toy squirt gun in his or her left hand. To pass along a message, you squirt the right hand of the person to your left. When that person notices this "message," he or she squirts the right hand of the person to the left, and so on.

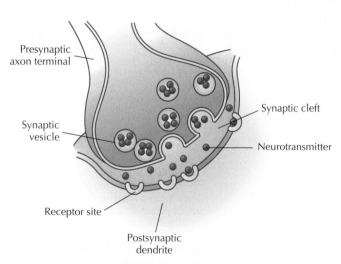

Presynaptic axon terminal

Synaptic vesicle

Synaptic cleft

Neurotransmitter

Receptor site

Postsynaptic dendrite

▶▶ **FIGURE 2.6** A highly magnified view of the synapse shown in Figure 2.1. Neurotransmitters are stored in tiny sacs called synaptic vesicles. When a nerve impulse arrives at an axon terminal, the vesicles move to the surface and release neurotransmitters. These transmitter molecules cross the synaptic cleft to affect the next neuron. The size of the gap is exaggerated here; it is actually only about 0.00004 centimetres. Transmitter molecules vary in their effects: Some excite the next neuron and some inhibit its activity.

When chemical molecules cross over a synapse, they attach to special receiving areas on the next neuron (see Figure 2.6). These tiny **receptor sites** on the cell membrane are sensitive to neurotransmitters. The sites are found in large numbers on nerve somas and dendrites. Muscles and glands have receptor sites, too.

Do neurotransmitters always trigger an action potential in the next neuron? No. Some transmitters excite the next neuron (move it closer to firing). Others inhibit it (make firing less likely).

After accomplishing their work on receptor sites, some of the neurotransmitter molecules are broken down in the synaptic cleft by certain chemical substances in a process known as **degradation.** Yet more transmitter molecules are picked up for reuse by the vesicles in a process called **reuptake.** Both of these processes ensure that neurotransmitter substances don't remain active for too long.

More than 100 neurotransmitter chemicals are found in the brain. Some examples are acetylcholine, epinephrine, norepinephrine, serotonin, dopamine, histamine, and various amino acids. Many drugs imitate, duplicate, or inhibit (block) these neurotransmitters, or interfere with the degradation or reuptake processes. For example, **acetylcholine** (ah-SEET-ul-KOH-leen) normally activates muscles. Without acetylcholine, our musical genius Glenn Gould couldn't even move, much less play Bach. That's exactly why the drug *curare* (cue-RAH-ree) causes paralysis. By attaching to receptor sites on muscles, curare competes with acetylcholine. This prevents acetylcholine from activating muscle cells. As a result, a person or animal given curare cannot move—a fact known to South American Indigenous people of the Amazon River Basin, who use curare as an arrow poison for hunting.

Another very important neurotransmitter is called **dopamine** (DOE-pa-MEEN). Dopamine is always involved when we experience the rewarding qualities of food and sex as well as the powerful effects of certain drugs, such as cocaine and amphetamines (Crombag & Robinson, 2004). When dopamine-producing neurons in a certain area of the brain degenerate, we develop Parkinson's disease. On the other hand, schizophrenia is related, at least in part, to overactivity of dopamine in some areas of the brain and to a lack in other regions (Conklin & Iacono, 2002). Anti-psychotic drugs work by blocking the dopamine receptor sites, which makes dopamine less active as a neurotransmitter.

The neurotransmitter *norepinephrine* (NOR-eh-pi-NEF-rin) controls heart rate, respiration, and blood pressure. Its overactivity also contributes to the development of overwhelming feelings of anxiety. On the other hand, the presence of *gamma aminobutyric acid* (gama a-ME-no-byu-TER-ik as-id) (GABA) helps to combat anxiety and gives us a sense of tranquillity (Durand & Barlow, 2010).

Finally, **serotonin** (SE-ro-TOE-nin) also plays a crucial role in many behaviours and psychological processes. Its deficiency is believed to be a factor in depression. A well-known antidepressant, Prozac, used to combat depression belongs to a category of drugs known as selective serotonin reuptake inhibitors (SSRIs). These drugs work by inhibiting the reuptake process involving serotonin, which causes more of the neurotransmitter molecules to be available in the brain (Jacobs, 2004). (Further discussion of neurotransmitters is found in Chapters 5 and 11.)

Why are there so many neurotransmitters? Good question. Some neurotransmitters are used by specific "pathways" that interlink regions of the brain. It is as if different pathways speak different languages. Perhaps this helps prevent confusing "cross-talk," or intermixing of messages.

Neural Regulators

More subtle brain activities are affected by chemicals called **neuropeptides** (NOOR-oh-PEP-tides). These chemicals are regarded by many as neurotransmitters, but the way they work is quite different. After they attach themselves to the postsynaptic receptors, they set in motion a chain of events that involves several other chemical substances as well as genes. By working their magic gradually, they affect those behaviours that require some time to build up. Neuropeptides affect memory, pain, emotion, pleasure, mood, hunger, sexual behaviour,

Receptor sites Areas on the surface of neurons and other cells that are sensitive to neurotransmitters or hormones.

Degradation A chemical process by which neurotransmitter molecules are broken down into other chemicals and thus rendered inactive.

Reuptake A process in which neurotransmitter molecules are picked up by synaptic vesicles for reuse.

Acetylcholine A neurotransmitter released by neurons to activate muscles.

Dopamine A neurotransmitter implicated in Parkinson's disease and schizophrenia.

Serotonin A neurotransmitter implicated in depression.

Neuropeptides Brain chemicals, such as enkephalins and endorphins, that regulate the activity of neurons.

Enkephalins Opiate-like brain chemicals that regulate reactions to pain and stress.

Endorphins Chemicals that are similar in structure and painkilling effect to opiate drugs, such as morphine.

Neurogenesis The production of new neurons from precursor cells.

and other basic processes. For example, when you touch something hot, you jerk your hand away. The messages for this action are carried by neurotransmitters. At the same time, painful stimulation causes the brain to release **enkephalins** (en-KEF-ah-lins). These opiate-like neural regulators relieve pain and stress. Related chemicals called **endorphins** (en-DORF-ins) are released by the pituitary gland. Together, these chemicals reduce the pain so that it is not too disabling (Drolet et al., 2001).

Such discoveries help to explain the painkilling effect of placebos (fake pills or injections), which raise endorphin levels (Stewart-Williams, 2004). A release of endorphins also seems to underlie "runner's high," masochism, acupuncture, the euphoria sometimes associated with childbirth and painful initiation rites, and even sport parachuting (Janssen & Arntz, 2001). In each case, pain and stress cause the release of endorphins. These in turn induce feelings of pleasure or euphoria similar to being "high" on morphine (Ulett, 1992). People who say they are "addicted" to running or other sports may be closer to the truth than they realize.

Ultimately, brain regulators may help to explain depression, schizophrenia, drug addiction, and other puzzling problems. For example, women who suffer from severe premenstrual pain and distress have unusually low endorphin levels (Straneva et al., 2002).

Neural Networks

Let's put together what we now know about the nerve impulse and synapses to see how *neural networks* process information in our brains. Figure 2.7 shows a small part of a neural network. Five neurons synapse with a single neuron that, in turn, connects with three more neurons. At the point in time depicted in the diagram, the single neuron A is receiving three excitatory messages and two inhibitory ones. At any instant, an actual neuron may receive hundreds or thousands of messages. Does it fire an impulse? It depends: If several "exciting" messages arrive close in time, the neuron will fire—but only if it doesn't get too many "inhibiting" messages that push it *away* from its trigger point. In this way, messages are *combined* before a neuron "decides" to fire its all-or-nothing action potential.

Let's try another metaphor. You are out shopping for new blue jeans with five friends. Three of them think you should buy the jeans (your best friend is especially positive), and two think you shouldn't. Because, on balance, their input is positive, you go ahead and buy the jeans. Maybe you even tell some other friends they should buy these jeans as well. Similarly, any single neuron in a neural network "listens" to the neurons that synapse with it and combines that input into an output. After the neuron recovers from the resulting action potential, it again combines the inputs, which may well have changed in the meantime, into another output, and another, and another.

In this way, each neuron in your brain functions as a tiny computer. Compared to the average laptop computer, a neuron is terribly simple and slow. But multiply these events by 100 billion neurons and 100 trillion synapses, all operating at the same time, and you have an amazing computer—one that could easily fit inside a shoebox.

New Knowledge about the Brain

Until about a decade ago, it was widely believed that we are born with all the neurons we will ever have. This led to the depressing idea that we all go slowly downhill. Although it is true that the brain loses lots of nerve cells every day, it grows new neurons to replace at least some of them. This process is called **neurogenesis** (NOOR-oh-JEN-uh-sis: the production of new nerve cells) (Gould, Reeves, & Gross, 1999). Each day, thousands of new cells originate deep within the brain, move to the surface, and link up with other neurons to become part of the brain's circuitry. This was stunning news to brain scientists, who must now figure out what the new cells do. Most likely they are involved in learning, memory, and our ability to adapt to changing circumstances. In fact, Liisa Galea, of the University of

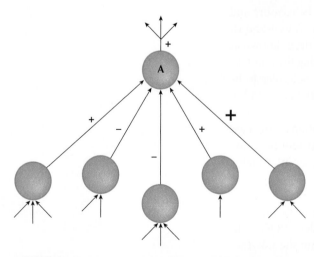

▶▶**FIGURE 2.7** A small neural network. Neuron A receives inputs from three excitatory connections (+) and two inhibitory connections (–) and combines the inputs into a "decision" to launch an action potential, which may help trigger further synaptic transmissions in other neurons.

British Columbia, has observed the formation of new neurons in an important region of the brain called the hippocampus. This area is responsible for spatial learning and memory. Experimenting with meadow voles (a type of rodent), Galea's research indicated that the brains of these small animals increased the production of neurons under certain conditions. For example, when they roam quite freely in their natural habitat, the voles need to learn detailed information about their surroundings. This led these creatures' brains to manufacture more neurons. The new neurons probably help the voles with the acquisition of important information about their environment (Ormerod & Galea, 2001).

There are at least two other ways of boosting the production of new neurons in the hippocampus of adult rats—both of them contribute to improved spatial ability, including giving them the opportunity to engage in physical exercise and keeping them in a stimulating environment (Olson et al., 2006).

The discovery of neurogenesis in adult brains has raised new hopes that some types of brain damage can be repaired. Doctors have tested a new method to treat strokes. Their attempts involve injecting immature cells called **stem cells** into damaged areas of the brain. If the technique is successful, the new cells should link up with existing neurons and repair some of the stroke damage (Borlongan, Sanberg, & Freeman, 1999).

In a promising experiment, some scientists have recently reported success in reversing paralysis in rats whose spinal cords had been injured. Researchers first created motor neurons from stem cells with the aid of crucial chemical ingredients. These neurons were then transplanted into the spinal cords of rats who were paralyzed in one leg. To ensure the survival of the newly formed neurons, rats were also given a host of chemical substances. These neurons then made a direct path toward the muscle in the paralyzed leg. Out of the 4000 neurons that resulted from this procedure, only a few dozen remained fully functional, but enough did their job so that most of the treated animals were able to move the affected leg and could walk with it. This is the first time scientists have succeeded in constructing new, functioning neuronal circuits. It would be interesting to see whether this procedure can be used successfully with other animals, including humans, and whether it would work effectively in other parts of the nervous system (Griffith, 2007). Research of this kind may help those who suffer from degenerative conditions such as Lou Gehrig's disease (Vastag, 2001).

Besides discovering that the brain is capable of growing new neurons, we are also becoming aware of the brain's great potential to develop new synaptic connections and thus change during its owner's entire lifetime. This is known as **neuroplasticity.** Canadian scientists have found that aged rats can grow new synaptic connections when they spend some time in complex environments. More surprisingly, when infant rats were given brief tactile stimulation daily for three weeks, they managed to develop better motor and cognitive skills in adulthood, and there were notable corresponding changes in their brains' structure. Furthermore, positive events during a mother's pregnancy can lead her offspring to develop more synaptic connections in adulthood. Similar changes may occur among humans. Even the drugs we take, the type of food we eat, the injuries we incur, and the diseases we develop are all known to change the structure of the brain and, consequently, our behaviour. One reason that someone addicted to drugs may find it difficult to give up this dependence may very well be because of the ways in which the brain organization has been altered by the drugs themselves (Kolb, Robbin, & Terry, 2003).

A method to help stroke survivors relies on just this idea: An approach called constraint-induced movement therapy is used to speed recovery. In this case, a person's good, unaffected arm is restrained, forcing them to use the impaired arm for hours at a time. By employing this strategy the stroke survivor would change the structure of their brain and thus regain more strength and ability in the affected arm (Taub, 2004).

In sum, the brain is not a static organ as was once believed. It appears to grow when demands are placed on it—as when we decide to acquire a new language in adulthood or learn a musical instrument—but it also changes for the worse if we engage in self-defeating acts. Our behaviour changes the brain, and these changes in turn alter our behaviour (See Using Psychology, "You Can Change Your Mind, but Can You Change Your Brain?")

Stem cells Immature cells that differentiate into various types of mature cells in the body, including neurons.

Neuroplasticity The capacity of the brain to reorganize its neural pathways by developing new synaptic links.

You Can Change Your Mind, But Can You Change Your Brain?

You can always change your mind. But does that have anything to do with your brain? Philosophers have debated the relationship of the mind to the brain (and the rest of the body) for centuries. Biopsychologists believe that every mental event involves a brain event.

In one study, people suffering from spider phobias (an intense fear of spiders) could actually touch spiders after undergoing therapy. Images of their brains revealed reduced activity in brain areas related to the phobia (Paquette et al., 2003). Not only did they change their minds about spiders, they literally changed their brains.

Another study focused on patients with language difficulties caused by damage to the left sides of their brains. To aid their recovery, the patients were trained in language comprehension, which did, in fact, improve their ability to understand language. In addition, brain images revealed that the right sides of their brains had become more active, to compensate for their left-brain damage (Musso et al., 1999). Again, a learning experience changed their brains.

Every time you learn something, you are reshaping your living brain. There is even a fancy phrase to describe what you are doing: *self-directed neuroplasticity*. Just think: As you study this psychology textbook, you are changing your mind—and your brain— about psychology.

THE NERVOUS SYSTEM—WIRED FOR ACTION

SURVEY QUESTION>
How is the nervous system organized, and what are the functions of its major parts?

Jamal and Vicki are playing catch with a Frisbee. This may look fairly simple. However, to merely toss the Frisbee or catch it, a huge amount of information must be sensed, interpreted, and directed to countless muscle fibres. As they entertain themselves, Jamal's and Vicki's neural circuits are ablaze with activity. Let's explore the "wiring diagram" that makes their Frisbee game possible.

Neurons and Nerves

Are nerves the same as neurons? No. **Nerves** are collections of axons. You can easily see nerves without magnification, whereas you would need a microscope to see a typical neuron.

Nerves in the peripheral nervous system can regrow if they are damaged. The axons of most neurons in nerves outside the brain and spinal cord are covered by a thin layer of cells called the **neurilemma** (NOOR-rih-LEM-ah). (Return to Figure 2.1.) The neurilemma forms a "tunnel" that damaged nerve fibres (axons) can follow as they repair themselves. Nerve fibres in this region can sometimes regenerate following an injury to a nerve.

Subparts of the Nervous System

As you can see in Figures 2.8 and 2.9, the **central nervous system (CNS)** consists of the brain and spinal cord. The brain is the central "computer" of the nervous system. Jamal must use this "computer" to anticipate when and where the Frisbee will arrive. Jamal's brain communicates with the rest of his body through a large "cable" called the spinal cord. From there, messages flow through the **peripheral nervous system (PNS).** This intricate network of nerves carries information to and from the CNS.

The Peripheral Nervous System

The peripheral system can be divided into two major parts. The **somatic system** carries messages to and from the sense organs and skeletal muscles. In general, it controls voluntary behaviour, such as when Vicki tosses the Frisbee or B. B. King plays the blues. In contrast, the **autonomic system** serves the internal organs and glands of the body. The word *autonomic* means "self-governing." Activities governed by the autonomic nervous system (ANS) are mostly "vegetative" or automatic, such as heart rate, digestion, and perspiration. Thus, messages carried by the somatic system can make your hand move, but they cannot cause your eyes to dilate. Likewise, messages carried by the ANS can stimulate digestion, but they

Nerve A bundle of axons or nerve fibres.

Neurilemma A layer of cells that encases many axons.

Central nervous system (CNS) The brain and spinal cord.

Peripheral nervous system (PNS) All parts of the nervous system outside the brain and spinal cord.

Somatic system Nerves linking the spinal cord with the body and sense organs.

Autonomic system Nerves carrying information to and from the internal organs and glands.

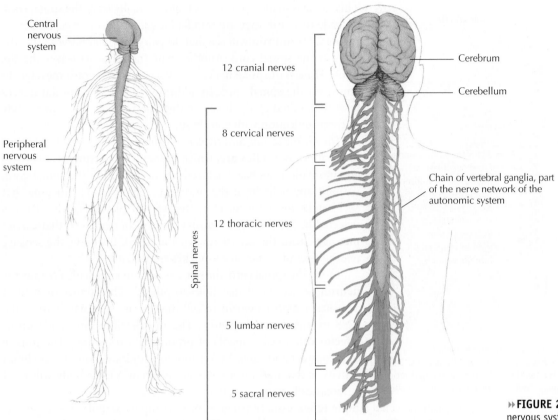

Central nervous system

Peripheral nervous system

12 cranial nerves

8 cervical nerves

12 thoracic nerves

5 lumbar nerves

5 sacral nerves

Spinal nerves

Cerebrum

Cerebellum

Chain of vertebral ganglia, part of the nerve network of the autonomic system

(a)

(b)

▸▸**FIGURE 2.8** (a) Central and peripheral nervous systems. (b) Spinal nerves, cranial nerves, and the autonomic nervous system.

cannot help you write a letter. If Jamal feels a flash of anger when he misses a catch, a brief burst of activity will spread through his autonomic system.

The autonomic nervous system can be divided into the sympathetic and parasympathetic branches. Both are related to responses involved in emotions, such as sweating, heart rate, and other involuntary behaviour (see Figure 2.10). The ANS and the somatic system work together to coordinate the body's internal reactions with events in the world outside. For example, if a snarling dog lunges at you, the somatic system will control your leg muscles so you can run. At the same time, the autonomic system will raise your blood pressure, quicken your heart, and so forth.

How do the branches of the autonomic system differ? The **sympathetic system** is an "emergency" system. It prepares the body for "fight or flight" during times of danger or high emotion. In essence, it arouses the body for action. Imagine someone who has a winning lottery ticket for $5 million and ends up misplacing it. No doubt that person's sympathetic nervous system would become quite active when they first notice that the lottery ticket is not where it should be.

The **parasympathetic system** quiets the body and returns it to a lower level of arousal. It is most active soon after an emotional event. The parasympathetic branch also helps to keep vital functions such as heart rate, breathing, and digestion at moderate levels.

Of course, both branches of the ANS are always active. At any given moment, their combined activity determines if your body is relaxed or aroused.

The Spinal Cord

As mentioned earlier, the spinal cord acts like a cable connecting the brain to other parts of the body. If you were to cut through this "cable," you would see columns of white matter in areas that have lots of myelin.

Sympathetic system The branch of the autonomic system that arouses the body.
Parasympathetic system The branch of the autonomic system that quiets the body.

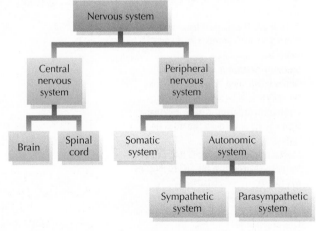

Nervous system

Central nervous system

Peripheral nervous system

Brain

Spinal cord

Somatic system

Autonomic system

Sympathetic system

Parasympathetic system

▸▸**FIGURE 2.9** Subparts of the nervous system.

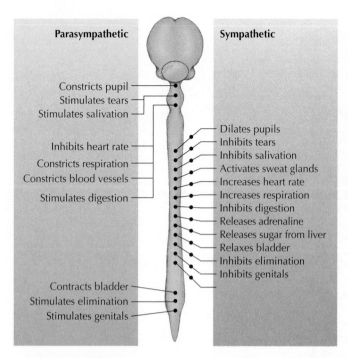

Parasympathetic

- Constricts pupil
- Stimulates tears
- Stimulates salivation
- Inhibits heart rate
- Constricts respiration
- Constricts blood vessels
- Stimulates digestion
- Contracts bladder
- Stimulates elimination
- Stimulates genitals

Sympathetic

- Dilates pupils
- Inhibits tears
- Inhibits salivation
- Activates sweat glands
- Increases heart rate
- Increases respiration
- Inhibits digestion
- Releases adrenaline
- Releases sugar from liver
- Relaxes bladder
- Inhibits elimination
- Inhibits genitals

▸▸**FIGURE 2.10** Sympathetic and parasympathetic branches of the autonomic nervous system. Both branches control involuntary actions. The sympathetic system generally activates the body. The parasympathetic system generally quiets it. The sympathetic branch relays through clusters of cell bodies outside the spinal cord.

This tissue is made up of axons that eventually leave the spinal cord. Outside the cord, they are bundled together into nerves. Return to Figure 2.8b and you will see that 30 pairs of spinal nerves leave the sides of the spinal cord. Another pair (not shown) leaves the tip. These 31 pairs of **spinal nerves** carry sensory and motor messages to and from the spinal cord. In addition, 12 pairs of **cranial nerves** leave the brain directly. Together, these nerves keep your entire body in communication with your brain.

How is the spinal cord related to behaviour? The simplest behaviour pattern is a **reflex arc,** which occurs when a stimulus provokes an automatic response. Such reflexes occur within the spinal cord, without any help from the brain (see Figure 2.11). Imagine that Vicki steps on a thorn. (Yes, they're still playing catch.) Pain is detected in her foot by a **sensory neuron** (a nerve cell that carries messages from the senses toward the CNS). Instantly, the sensory neuron fires off a message to Vicki's spinal cord.

Inside the spinal cord, the sensory neuron joins with a **connector neuron** (a nerve cell that links to others). The connector neuron activates a **motor neuron** (a cell that carries commands from the CNS to muscles and glands). The muscle fibres are made up of **effector cells** (cells capable of producing a response). The muscle cells contract and cause Vicki's foot to withdraw. Note that no brain activity is required for a reflex arc to occur. Vicki's body will react automatically to protect itself.

In reality, even a simple reflex usually triggers more complex activity. For example, the muscles of Vicki's other leg must contract to support her as she shifts her weight. Even this can be done by the spinal cord, but it involves many more cells and several spinal nerves. Also, the spinal cord normally informs the brain of the actions it has taken. As her foot pulls away from the thorn, Vicki will feel the pain and think, "Ouch, what was that?"

Perhaps you have realized how adaptive it is to have a spinal cord capable of responding on its own. Such automatic responses leave the brains of our Frisbee

Spinal nerves Major nerves that carry sensory and motor messages in and out of the spinal cord.

Cranial nerves Major nerves that leave the brain without passing through the spinal cord.

Reflex arc The simplest behaviour, in which a stimulus provokes an automatic response.

Sensory neuron A nerve cell that carries information from the senses toward the CNS.

Connector neuron A nerve cell that serves as a link between two other nerve cells.

Motor neuron A nerve cell that carries motor commands from the CNS to muscles and glands

Effector cells Cells in muscles and glands that are capable of producing some type of response.

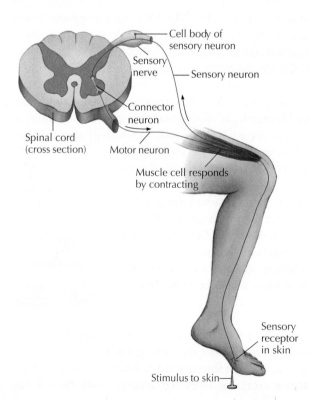

- Cell body of sensory neuron
- Sensory nerve
- Sensory neuron
- Connector neuron
- Spinal cord (cross section)
- Motor neuron
- Muscle cell responds by contracting
- Sensory receptor in skin
- Stimulus to skin

▸▸**FIGURE 2.11** A simple sensory-motor (reflex) arc. A simple reflex is set in motion by a stimulus to the skin (or other part of the body). The nerve impulse travels to the spinal cord and then back out to a muscle, which contracts. Reflexes provide an "automatic" protective device for the body.

aces free to deal with more important information—such as the location of trees, lampposts, and attractive onlookers—as they take turns making grandstand catches.

A serious injury to the brain or spinal cord is usually permanent. However, scientists are starting to make progress in repairing damaged neurons in the CNS. Imagine what that could mean to a person who needs a wheelchair. Although it is unwise to raise false hopes, solutions to such problems are beginning to emerge (Baisden, 1995). Medical researchers have begun the first human trials in which nerve grafts will be used to repair damaged spinal cords (Féron et al., 2005). Just the same, it is wise to take good care of your own CNS. That means using seatbelts when you drive, a helmet if you ride a motorcycle or a bicycle, and protective gear for sports, as well as avoiding activities that pose a risk to the spinal cord.

In a few moments, we will probe more deeply into the brain. Before we do, it might be wise to explore some of the research tools biopsychologists use. Uncovering the brain's mysteries has not been easy. Let's consider some of the basics.

CP Photo/Boris Spremo

Each year spinal cord injuries rob many thousands of people, like the late actor Christopher Reeve and Canadian Rick Hansen, of the ability to move. Yet there is growing hope that nerve-grafting techniques may some day make it possible for some of them to walk again.

RESEARCH METHODS—CHARTING THE BRAIN'S INNER REALMS

Biopsychology is the study of how biological processes, especially those occurring in the nervous system, relate to behaviour. In their research, many biopsychologists try to learn which parts of the brain control particular mental or behavioural functions, such as being able to recognize faces or move your hands. That is, they try to learn where functions are localized (located) in the brain. Many techniques have been developed to help identify brain structures and the functions they control.

<SURVEY QUESTION
How do we know how the brain works? What are the methods by which scientists study the brain?

Studying the Brain

Many of the functions of the brain have been identified by **clinical studies.** Such studies examine changes in personality, behaviour, or sensory capacity caused by brain diseases or injuries. If damage to a particular part of the brain consistently leads to a particular loss of function, then we say the function is localized in that structure. Presumably, that part of the brain controls the same function in all of us.

Consider, for example, the story of Kate Adamson (Adamson, 2004). At the age of 33, she had a stroke that caused catastrophic damage to her brainstem. This event left her with *locked-in syndrome:* Just before the stroke she was fine, and the next moment she was totally paralyzed, trapped in her own body and barely able to breathe. As you can see, this clinical case suggests that our brainstems play a role in controlling vital life functions, such as movement and breathing.

But what happened to Kate? Oh, yes. Unable to move a muscle, but still fully awake and aware, Kate thought she was going to die. Her doctors, who thought she was *brain dead* (Laureys & Boly, 2007), did not administer painkillers as they inserted breathing and feeding tubes down her throat. However, in time Kate discovered that she could communicate by blinking her eyes. After a recovery that has been miraculous by any measure, she even went on to appear before the U.S. Congress.

A related experimental technique is based on **ablation** (ab-LAY-shun: surgical removal) of parts of the brain (see Figure 2.12). When ablation causes changes in behaviour or sensory capacity, we gain insight into the purpose of the missing "part." An alternative approach is to use electrical stimulation to "turn on" brain structures. For example, the surface of the

Clinical study An intensive investigation of a single person, especially one suffering from some injury or disease.

Ablation Surgical removal of tissue.

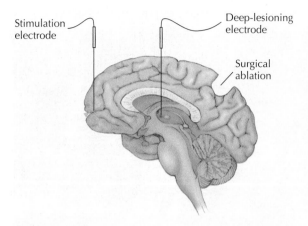

Stimulation electrode

Deep-lesioning electrode

Surgical ablation

▶▶**FIGURE 2.12** The functions of brain structures are explored by selectively activating or removing them. Brain research is often based on electrical stimulation, but chemical stimulation is also used at times.

Electrode Any device (such as a wire, needle, or metal plate) used to electrically stimulate nerve tissue or to record its activity.

Deep lesioning Removal of tissue within the brain by use of an electrode.

Electrical stimulation of the brain (ESB) Direct electrical stimulation and activation of brain tissue.

Micro-electrode An electrode small enough to record the activity of a single neuron.

Electroencephalograph (EEG) A device that records electrical activity in the brain.

brain can be activated by touching it with a small electrified wire called an **electrode.** When this is done during brain surgery, the patient can tell what effect the stimulation had. (The brain has no pain receptors, so surgery can be done while a patient is awake. Only local painkillers are used for the scalp and skull.) In fact, such experiments were carried out in Montréal by a famous neurosurgeon, Wilder Penfield. While performing surgery on people with epilepsy, Penfield stimulated certain brain areas. Patients heard sounds, parts of their bodies moved automatically, or they were reminded of certain events from their past, depending on what area of the brain was stimulated (Penfield & Perot, 1963).

Even structures below the surface of the brain can be activated or removed. In **deep lesioning** (LEE-zhuning), a thin wire electrode, insulated except at the tip, is lowered into a target area inside the brain (see Figure 2.12). An electric current is then used to destroy a small amount of brain tissue. Again, changes in behaviour give clues about the function of the affected area. Using a weaker current, it is also possible to activate target areas rather than remove them. This is called **electrical stimulation of the brain (ESB).** ESB can call forth behaviour with astonishing power. It can instantly bring about aggression, alertness, escape, eating, drinking, sleeping, movement, euphoria, memories, speech, tears, and more. By using ESB, researchers are creating a three-dimensional brain map. This "atlas" shows the sensory, motor, and emotional responses that can be elicited from various parts of the brain. It promises to be a valuable guide for medical treatment, as well as for exploring the brain (Carter, 1998; Yoshida, 1993).

Could ESB be used to control a person against his or her will? It might seem that ESB could be used to control a person like a robot. But the details of emotions and behaviours elicited by ESB are modified by personality and circumstances. Sci-fi movies to the contrary, it would be impossible for a ruthless dictator to enslave people by "radio-controlling" their brains.

To find out what individual neurons are doing, we need to do a micro-electrode recording. A **micro-electrode** is an extremely thin glass tube filled with a salty fluid. The tip of a micro-electrode is small enough to detect the electrical activity of a single neuron. Watching the action potentials of just one neuron provides a fascinating glimpse into the true origins of behaviour. (The action potential shown in Figure 2.2 was recorded with a micro-electrode.)

What about the bigger picture? Is it possible to record what the brain is doing as a whole? Yes, it is, with electroencephalography (ee-LEK-tro-in-SEF-ah-LOG-ruh-fee). This technique measures the waves of electrical activity produced by the brain. Small disk-shaped metal plates are placed on a person's scalp. Electrical impulses from the brain are detected by these electrodes and sent to an **electroencephalograph (EEG).** The EEG amplifies these very weak signals (brain waves) and records them on a moving sheet of paper or a computer screen (see Figure 2.13). Various brainwave patterns can identify the presence of tumours, epilepsy, and other diseases. The EEG also reveals changes in brain activity during sleep, daydreaming, and other mental states.

New Images of the Living Brain

Many of the brain's riddles have been solved with the methods just described, plus others based on drugs and brain chemistry. Yet each technique lets us see only a part of the whole picture. What if we could "peek" inside an intact brain while a person is

AJPhoto/Photo Researchers, Inc.

▶▶**FIGURE 2.13** An EEG recording.

thinking, perceiving, and reacting? Rather than seeing individual musical notes, or small musical phrases, what if we could see the brain's entire ongoing symphony? Computer-enhanced images are now making this age-old dream possible. Let's look through some of these newly opened "windows" into the human biocomputer.

CT Scan

Computerized scanning equipment has virtually revolutionized the study of brain diseases and injuries. At best, conventional X-rays produce only shadowy images of the brain. **Computed tomographic (CT) scanning** is a specialized type of X-ray that does a much better job of making the brain visible. In a CT scan, X-ray information is collected by a computer and formed into an image of the brain. A CT scan can reveal the effects of strokes, injuries, tumours, and other brain disorders. These, in turn, can be related to a person's behaviour.

MRI Scan

Magnetic resonance imaging (MRI) uses a very strong magnetic field, rather than X-rays, to produce an image of the body's interior. During an MRI scan, the body is placed inside a magnetic field. Processing by a computer then creates a three-dimensional model of the brain or body. Any two-dimensional plane, or slice, of the body can be selected and displayed as an image on a computer screen. This allows us to peer into the living brain almost as if it were transparent (see Figure 2.14).

A **functional MRI (fMRI) scan** goes one step further by making brain activity visible. For example, the motor areas on the surface of the brain would be highlighted in an fMRI image as Glenn Gould moved his fingers on the piano. Such images are allowing scientists to pinpoint areas in the brain responsible for thoughts, feelings, and actions.

Psychiatrist Daniel Langleben and his colleagues (2005) have used fMRI images to tell whether a person is lying. As Figure 2.15 shows, the front of the brain tends to be more active when a person is lying, rather than telling the truth. This may occur because it takes extra effort to lie, and the resulting extra brain activity is detected with fMRI. Clearly, it is just a matter of time until even brighter beacons are flashed into the shadowy inner world of thought.

PET Scan

Positron emission tomography (PET) provides detailed images of activity both *near* and *below* the surface of the brain. A **PET scan** detects positrons (subatomic particles) emitted by weakly radioactive glucose (sugar) as it is consumed by the brain. Since the brain runs on glucose, a PET scan shows which areas are using more energy. Higher energy use corresponds to higher activity. Thus, by placing positron detectors around the head and

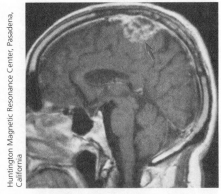

Huntington Magnetic Resonance Center, Pasadena, California

▸▸**FIGURE 2.14** An MRI scan reveals a brain tumour (see arrow). Notice how it is possible to display a precise "slice" from the middle of the three-dimensional MRI data.

Computed tomographic (CT) scanning A computer-enhanced X-ray image of the brain or body.

Magnetic resonance imaging (MRI) scan A three-dimensional image of the body, based on its response to a magnetic field.

Functional MRI (fMRI) scan A scan that records brain activity.

PET scan Positron emission tomography scan; a computer-generated image of brain activity based on glucose consumption in the brain.

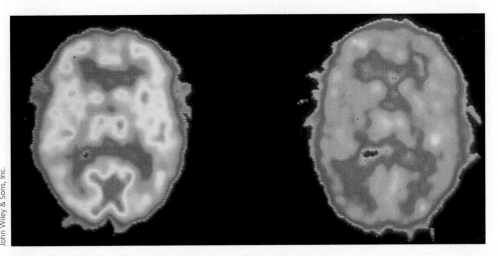

Adapted from Langleben et al, HUMAN BRAIN MAPPING Copyright © 2005 Daniel Langleben. Reprinted by permission of John Wiley & Sons, Inc.

▸▸**FIGURE 2.15** Participants were asked to tell the truth or to lie while fMRI images of their brains were taken. When compared with telling the truth (shown in blue), areas toward the front of the brain were active during lying (shown in red).

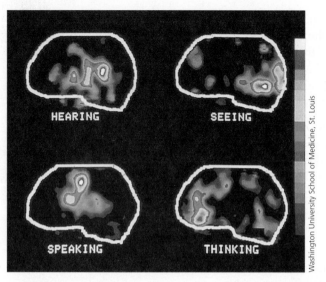

FIGURE 2.16 These PET images show scans of the left side of the brain made while a person heard a word, saw a word, repeated a word aloud, and said a word related to the one that was seen (Petersen et al., 1988).

Washington University School of Medicine, St. Louis

sending data to a computer, it is possible to create a moving, colour picture of changes in brain activity. As you can see in Figure 2.16, PET scans reveal that very specific brain areas are active when you are reading a word, hearing a word, saying a word, or thinking about the meaning of a word (see Figure 2.17).

Is it true that most people use only 10 percent of their brain capacity? This is one of the lasting myths about the brain. Brain scans show that all parts of the brain are active during waking hours. Obviously, some people make better use of their innate brain power than others do. Another way to conceptualize this issue is by noting that we use 100 percent of both our hands, but we use them to accomplish different tasks. Glenn Gould used his to create exceptional music, Wilder Penfield used his to perform intricate brain surgery, and Paul Bernardo used his to commit unspeakable crimes. Similarly, all of our brain is put to use but in very different ways for different purposes. In summary, there are no great hidden or untapped reserves of mental capacity in a normally functioning brain.

✔ STUDY BREAK Neurons, the Nervous System, and Brain Research

Reflect

To cope with all the technical terms in this chapter, it might help to think of neurons as strange little creatures. How do they act? What excites them? How do they communicate? To remember the functions of major branches of the nervous system, think about what you couldn't do if each part were missing.

You suspect that a certain part of the brain is related to memory. How could you use clinical studies, ablation, deep lesioning, and ESB to study the structure? You are interested in finding out how single neurons in the optic nerve respond when the eye is exposed to light. What technique will you use? You want to know which areas of the brain's surface are most active when a person sees a face. What methods will you use?

Learning Check

1. The _____ and _____ are receiving areas where information from other neurons is accepted.

2. Nerve impulses are carried down the _____ to the _____.

3. The _____ potential becomes an _____ potential when a neuron passes the threshold for firing.

4. Neuropeptides are transmitter substances that help to regulate the activity of neurons. T or F?

5. The somatic and autonomic systems are part of the _____ nervous system.

6. Sodium and potassium ions flow through ion channels in the synapse to trigger a nerve impulse in the receiving neuron. T or F?

7. The simplest behaviour sequence is a _____.

8. The parasympathetic nervous system is most active during times of high emotion. T or F?

9. Which of the following research techniques has the most in common with clinical studies of the effects of brain injuries?
   a. EEG recording   b. deep lesioning
   c. micro-electrode recording   d. PET scan

10. CT scans cannot determine which part of your brain plays a role in speech because CT scans
   a. use X-rays   b. reveal brain structure, not brain activity
   c. reveal brain activity, not brain structure   d. use magnetic fields

Critical Thinking

11. What effect would you expect a drug to have if it blocked the passage of neurotransmitters across the synapse?

12. Deep lesioning is used to ablate an area in the hypothalamus of a rat. After the operation, the rat seems to lose interest in food and eating. Why would it be a mistake to conclude that the ablated area is a "hunger centre"?

Answers

1. dendrites, soma   2. axon, axon terminals   3. resting, action   4. T   5. peripheral   6. F   7. reflex arc   8. F   9. b   10. b   11. Such a drug could have wide-ranging effects. If the drug blocked excitatory synapses, it would depress brain activity. If it blocked inhibitory messages, it would act as a powerful stimulant.   12. Because other factors might explain the apparent loss of appetite. For example, the taste or smell of food might be affected, or the rat might simply have difficulty swallowing. It is also possible that hunger originates elsewhere in the brain and the ablated area merely relays messages that cause the rat to eat.

THE CEREBRAL CORTEX—MY, WHAT A BIG BRAIN YOU HAVE!

In many ways, we are pretty unimpressive creatures. Animals surpass humans in almost every category of strength, speed, and sensory sensitivity. The one area in which we excel is intelligence.

Do humans have the largest brains? Surprisingly, no. Elephant brains weigh about 6 kilograms, and whale brains 9 kilograms. At about 1.5 kilograms, the human brain seems puny—until we compare brain weight to body weight. We then find that an elephant's brain is 1/1000 of its weight; the ratio for sperm whales is 1 to 10 000. The ratio for humans is 1 to 60. If someone tells you that you have a "whale of a brain," be sure to find out if he or she means size or ratio!

So having a larger brain doesn't necessarily make a human smarter? That's right. While a small positive correlation exists between intelligence and brain size, overall size alone does not determine human intelligence (Johnson et al., 2008; Witelson, Beresh, & Kigar, 2006). In fact, many parts of your brain are surprisingly similar to corresponding brain areas in other animals, such as lizards. It is your larger **cerebral** (seh-REE-brel or ser-EH-brel) **cortex** that sets you apart.

The cerebral cortex, which looks a little like a giant, wrinkled walnut, consists of the two large hemispheres that cover the upper part of the brain. The two hemispheres are divided into smaller areas known as lobes. Parts of various lobes are responsible for the ability to see, hear, move, think, and speak. Thus, a map of the cerebral cortex is in some ways like a map of human behaviour.

The cerebral cortex covers most of the brain with a mantle of *grey matter* (spongy tissue made up mostly of cell bodies). The cortex in many primitive animals is small and smooth. In humans it is twisted and folded, and it is the largest brain structure. The fact that humans are more intelligent than other animals is related to this **corticalization** (KORE-tih-kal-ih-ZAY-shun), or increase in the size and wrinkling of the cortex.

Although the cortex is only 3 millimetres thick, it contains 70 percent of the neurons in the central nervous system. It is largely responsible for our ability to use language, make tools, acquire complex skills, and live in complex social groups (Gibson, 2002). Without the cortex, we humans wouldn't be much smarter than toads.

According to folklore, a person with a large head and a high forehead is likely to be intelligent. But brain efficiency has as much to do with intelligence as brain size does (Gazzaniga, 1995).

Psychologist Richard J. Haier and his colleagues found that the brains of people who perform well on mental tests consume less energy than those of poor performers (Haier et al., 1988). Haier measured brain activity with a PET scan. Recall that a PET scan records the amount of glucose (sugar) used by neurons. The harder the neurons work, the more sugar they use. By using harmless, radioactively labelled glucose, it is possible to record an image of how hard the brain is working (see Figure 2.18).

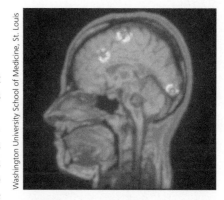

Washington University School of Medicine, St. Louis

▸▸**FIGURE 2.17** The bright spots you see here were created by a PET scan. They are similar to the spots in Figure 2.16. However, here they have been placed over an MRI scan so that the brain's anatomy is visible. The three bright spots are areas in the left brain related to language. The spot on the right is active during reading. The top-middle area is connected with speech. The area to the left, in the frontal lobe, is linked with thinking about a word's meaning (Montgomery, 1989).

◂**SURVEY QUESTION**
How is the brain organized, and what do its higher structures do?

Cerebral cortex The outer layer of the brain.

Corticalization An increase in the relative size of the cerebral cortex.

Cerebral hemispheres The right and left halves of the cerebrum.

Corpus callosum The bundle of fibres connecting the cerebral hemispheres.

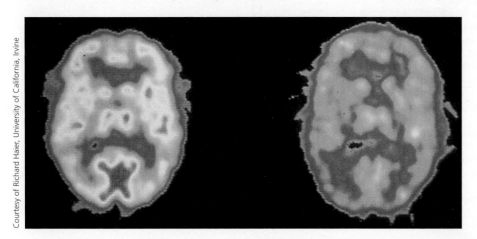

Courtesy of Richard Haier, University of California, Irvine

▸▸**FIGURE 2.18** In the images you see here, red, orange, and yellow indicate high consumption of glucose; green, blue, and pink show areas of low glucose use. The PET scan of the brain on the left shows that a man who solved 11 out of 36 reasoning problems burned more glucose than the man on the right, who solved 33.

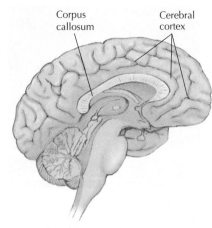

Corpus callosum · Cerebral cortex

▶▶**FIGURE 2.19** The corpus callosum is the major "cable system" through which the right and left cerebral hemispheres communicate. Hutchinson and her colleagues found that the corpus callosum is larger in musicians than it is in non-musicians (Hutchinson et al., 2003). When a person plays a violin or piano, the two hemispheres must communicate rapidly as they coordinate the movements of both hands. Presumably, the size of the corpus callosum can be altered by early experience, such as musical training.

What did PET scans reveal when subjects took a difficult reasoning test? Surprisingly, the brains of those who scored lowest on the test used the most glucose. Although we might assume that smart brains are hard-working brains, the reverse appears to be true. Brighter subjects actually used less energy than poor performers did. Haier believes this shows that intelligence is related to brain efficiency: Less efficient brains work harder and still accomplish less. We've all had days like that!

Cerebral Hemispheres

The cortex is composed of two sides, or **cerebral hemispheres** (half-globes). The two hemispheres are connected by a thick band of fibres called the **corpus callosum** (KORE-pus kah-LOH-sum) (see Figure 2.19). The left side of the brain mainly controls the right side of the body. Likewise, the right brain mainly controls left body areas. When our friend Marge had a stroke, her right hemisphere suffered damage. (A stroke occurs when an artery carrying blood to the brain becomes blocked, causing some brain tissue to die.) In Marge's case, the stroke caused some paralysis and loss of sensation on the left side of her body (for more details about the condition, see Clinical File: "A Stroke of Bad Luck" for more details).

A Stroke of Bad Luck

One morning Bryan Kolb lost his left hand. Up early to feed his cat, he could not see his hand, or anything else on his upper left side. Kolb, a Canadian biopsychologist, instantly realized that he had suffered a right hemisphere stroke. He drove to the hospital, where he argued with the doctors about his own diagnosis. (He was right, of course!) He eventually resumed his career and even wrote a fascinating account of his case (Kolb, 1990).

Strokes and other brain injuries can hit like a thunderbolt. Almost instantly, victims realize that something is wrong. You would, too, if you suddenly found that you couldn't move, or feel parts of your body, or see, or speak. However, some brain injuries are not so obvious. Many involve less dramatic, but equally disabling, changes in personality, thinking, judgment, or emotions (Banich, 2004; Borod et al., 2002). Although major brain injuries are easy enough to spot, psychologists also look for more subtle signs that the brain is not working properly. Neurological soft signs, as they are called, include clumsiness, an awkward gait, poor hand-eye coordination, and other problems with perception or fine muscle control (Stuss & Levine, 2002). These telltale signs are "soft" in the sense that they aren't direct tests of the brain, like an EEG or a CT scan. Bryan Kolb initially diagnosed himself entirely with soft signs. Likewise, soft signs help psychologists to diagnose problems ranging from childhood learning disorders to full-blown psychosis (Ward, 2006).

Even more subtle changes in behaviour may follow brain injuries. For example, damage to the right hemisphere can cause a curious problem called *spatial neglect*. Affected patients pay no attention to the left side of visual space (see Figure 2.20). Often, the patient will not eat food on the left side of a plate. Some even refuse to acknowledge a paralyzed left arm as their own (Springer & Deutsch, 1998). If you point to the "alien" arm, the patient is likely to say, "Oh, that's not my arm. It must belong to someone else."

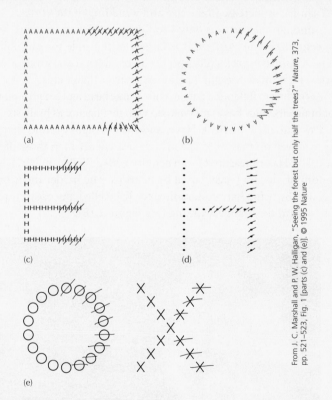

(a)   (b)   (c)   (d)   (e)

From J. C. Marshall and P. W. Halligan, "Seeing the forest but only half the trees?" *Nature,* 373, pp. 521–523, Fig. 1 (parts (c) and (e)). © 1995 Nature

▶▶**FIGURE 2.20** Spatial neglect. A patient with right-hemisphere damage was asked to copy a selection of model drawings. Notice how he neglected the left side in his drawings. Similar neglect occurs in other patients with right-hemisphere damage.

Hemispheric Specialization

In 1981, Roger Sperry (1914–1994) won a Nobel Prize for his remarkable discovery that the right and left brain hemispheres perform differently on tests of language, perception, music, and other abilities.

How is it possible to test only one side of the brain? One way is to work with people who've had a **"split-brain" operation.** In this rare type of surgery, the corpus callosum is cut to control severe epilepsy (Gazzaniga, 2005). The result is essentially a person with two brains in one body. After the surgery, it is a simple matter to send information to one hemisphere or the other (see Figure 2.21).

"Split Brains"

After the right and left brain are separated, each hemisphere will have its own separate perceptions, concepts, and impulses to act.

How does a split-brain person function after the operation? Having two "brains" in one body can create some interesting dilemmas. When one split-brain patient dressed himself, he sometimes pulled his pants down with one hand and up with the other. Once, he grabbed his wife with his left hand and shook her violently. Gallantly, his right hand came to her aid and grabbed the aggressive left hand (Gazzaniga, 1970). However, such conflicts are actually rare. That's because both halves of the brain normally have about the same experience at the same time. Also, if a conflict arises, one hemisphere usually overrides the other.

Split-brain effects are easiest to see in specialized testing. For example, we could flash a dollar sign to the right brain and a question mark to the left brain of a patient named Tom. (Figure 2.21 shows how this is possible.) Next, Tom is asked to draw what he saw, using his left hand, out of sight. Tom's left hand draws a dollar sign. If Tom is then asked to point with his right hand to a picture of what his hidden left hand drew, he will point to a question mark (Sperry, 1968). In short, for the split-brain person, one hemisphere may not know what is happening in the other. This has to be the ultimate case of the "right hand not knowing what the left hand is doing"! Figure 2.22 provides another example of split-brain testing.

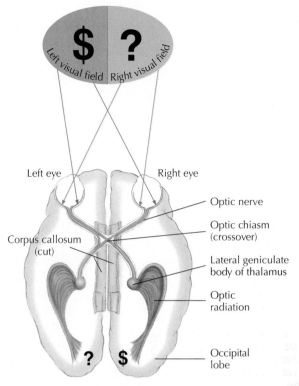

▶▶**FIGURE 2.21** Basic nerve pathways of vision. Notice that the left portion of each eye connects only to the left half of the brain; likewise, the right portion of each eye connects to the right brain. When the corpus callosum is cut, a "split brain" results. Then visual information can be directed to one hemisphere or the other by flashing it in the right or left visual field as the person stares straight ahead.

Left Brain		Right Brain	
■ Language	■ Time sense	■ Nonverbal	■ Recognition and
■ Speech	■ Rhythm	■ Perceptual skills	expression of emotion
■ Writing	■ Ordering of complex	■ Visualization	■ Spatial skills
■ Calculation	movements	■ Recognition of	■ Simple language
		patterns, faces,	comprehension
		melodies	

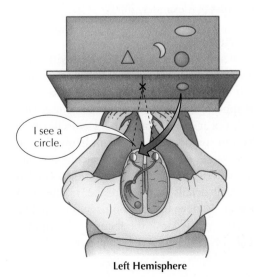

Left Hemisphere

I see a circle.

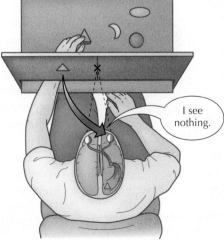

Right Hemisphere

I see nothing.

▶▶**FIGURE 2.22** If a circle is flashed to the left brain and a split-brain patient is asked to say what she or he saw, the circle is easily named. The person can also pick out the circle by touching shapes with the right hand, out of sight under a tabletop (shown semi-transparent in the drawing). However, the left hand will be unable to identify the shape. If a triangle is flashed to the right brain, the person cannot say what was seen (speech is controlled by the left hemisphere). The person will also be unable to identify the correct shape by touch with the right hand. Now, however, the left hand will have no difficulty picking out the hidden triangle. Separate testing of each hemisphere reveals distinct specializations, as listed above the drawing.

So far we have described patients whose corpus callosum has been cut for a reason. Let's now turn to a unique group of people who have what could be called a natural split brain. In some babies, the corpus callosum fails to develop, either partially or completely. Among many different causes of this condition is a rare combination of genes. Known as Andermann's syndrome or Charlevoix disease, it is prevalent in the Saguenay Lac St. Jean and Charlevoix regions of Quebec, mainly because people there have tended to marry within a close-knit circle of families for centuries (Andermann et al., 1972).

We usually do not know that someone lacks a corpus callosum until a problem is suspected and the person is sent for a test with one of the brain-imaging methods described earlier. Maryse Lassonde at the University of Montréal has studied this group of people extensively. She has found that, in contrast to surgically created split-brain individuals, those who lack a corpus callosum (known as *acallosals*) do not show as many sensory deficits (Lassonde, 1994). For example, people born without a corpus callosum do much better at identifying objects presented to either hemisphere than individuals whose brains are surgically split. You may wonder why acallosal persons perform better than surgical split-brain individuals, even though their hemispheres do not appear to be linked. It may be that other brain structures have partly taken over the functions that are normally performed by the corpus callosum. One hemisphere may be able to share information with its counterpart through other pathways in the brain. Callosal surgery is typically performed in adulthood, and by the time we reach this stage, our brains may not be as flexible as the brains of children, which may compensate for a missing corpus callosum by giving some of its functions over to other brain structures (Bayard et al., 2004).

Right Brain/Left Brain

We stated earlier that the hemispheres differ in abilities; in what ways are they different? The brain divides its work in interesting ways. Roughly 95 percent of us use our left brain for language (speaking, writing, and understanding). In addition, the left hemisphere is superior at math; judging time and rhythm; and coordinating the order of complex movements, such as those needed for speech.

In contrast, the right hemisphere can produce only the simplest language and numbers. Working with the right brain is like talking to a child who can say only a dozen words or so. To answer questions, the right hemisphere must use nonverbal responses, such as pointing at objects (see Figure 2.23).

Although it is poor at producing language, the right brain has it own talents. The right brain is especially good at perceptual skills, such as recognizing patterns, faces, and melodies; putting together a puzzle; or drawing a picture. It also helps you express emotions and detect the emotions that other people are feeling (Stuss & Alexander, 2000).

One Brain, Two Styles

In general, the left hemisphere is mainly involved with analysis (breaking information into parts). It also processes information *sequentially* (in order, one item after the next). The right hemisphere appears to process information *simultaneously* and *holistically* (all at once) (Springer & Deutsch, 1998).

To summarize, you could say that the right hemisphere is better at assembling pieces of the world into a coherent picture; it sees overall patterns and general connections. The left brain focuses on small details (see Figure 2.23). The right brain sees the wide-angle view; the left zooms in on specifics. The focus of the left brain is local; the focus of the right is global (Heinze et al., 1998; Hellige, 1993; Huebner, 1998).

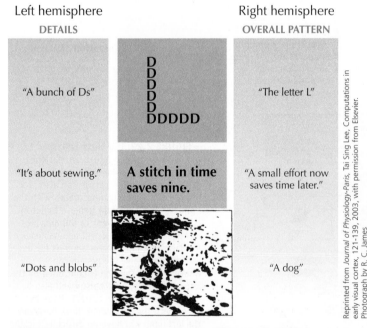

Left hemisphere
DETAILS

Right hemisphere
OVERALL PATTERN

"A bunch of Ds"

DDDDD (arranged as large L)

"The letter L"

"It's about sewing."

A stitch in time saves nine.

"A small effort now saves time later."

"Dots and blobs"

"A dog"

Reprinted from *Journal of Physiology-Paris*, Tai Sing Lee, Computations in early visual cortex, 121-139, 2003, with permission from Elsevier. Photograph by R. C. James

▸▸**FIGURE 2.23** The left and right brain have different information-processing styles. The right brain gets the big picture; the left focuses on small details.

Do people normally do puzzles or draw pictures with just the right hemisphere? Do they do other things with only the left? Numerous books have been written about how to use the right brain to manage, teach, draw, ride horses, learn, cook, and even make love (Carter, 1998). But such books drastically oversimplify right- and left-brain differences. People normally use both sides of the brain at all times. It's true that some tasks may make more use of one hemisphere or the other. But in most real-world activities, the hemispheres share the work. Each does the parts it does best and shares information with the other side. Popular books and courses that claim to teach "right-brain thinking" ignore the fact that everyone already uses the right brain for thinking (Clark, Boutros, & Mendez, 2005). To do anything well requires the talents and processing abilities of both hemispheres. A smart brain is one that grasps both the details and the overall picture at the same time (Ornstein, 1997). Notice, for instance, that during a concert Glenn Gould would have used his left brain to judge time and rhythm and coordinate the order of his hand movements. At the same time, he would have used his right brain to recognize and organize melodies.

Lobes of the Cerebral Cortex

In addition to the two big hemispheres, the cerebral cortex can be divided into several smaller **lobes** (areas bordered by major grooves or fissures or defined by their functions) (see Figure 2.24).

The Occipital Lobes

At the back of the brain, we find the **occipital** (awk-SIP-ih-tal) **lobes,** the primary visual area of the cortex. Patients with tumours (cell growths that interfere with brain activity) in the occipital lobes experience blind spots in their vision.

Do the visual areas of the cortex correspond directly to what is seen? Images are mapped onto the cortex, but the map is greatly stretched and distorted (Carlson, 2010). It is important to avoid thinking of the visual area as being like a little TV screen in the brain. Visual information creates complex patterns of activity in nerve cells; it does not make a TV-like image.

The Parietal Lobes

Bodily sensations register in the **parietal lobes** (puh-RYE-ih-tal), located just above the occipital lobes. Touch, temperature, pressure, and other somatic sensations flow into the **primary somatosensory** (SO-mat-oh-SEN-so-ree) **area** on the parietal lobes. Again, we find that the map of bodily sensations is distorted. The drawing in Figure 2.25 shows that the cortex reflects the *sensitivity* of body areas, not their size. For example, the lips are large in the drawing because of their great sensitivity, while the back and trunk, which are less sensitive, are much smaller. Notice that the hands are also large in the map of body sensitivity—which is obviously an aid to musicians, typists, watchmakers, massage therapists, lovers, and brain surgeons.

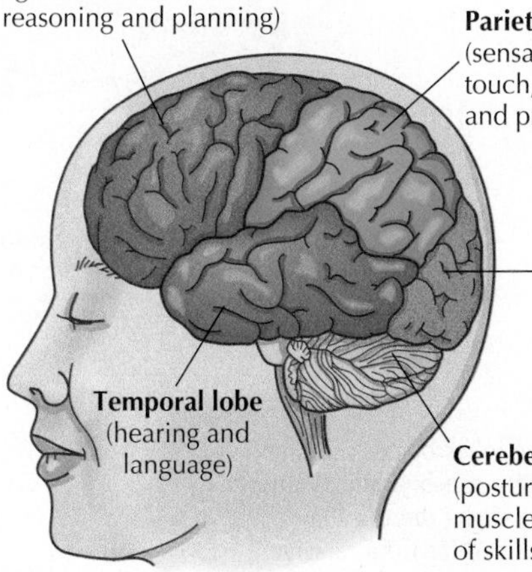

The Temporal Lobes

The **temporal lobes** are located on each side of the brain, above the ears. Auditory information projects directly to the **primary auditory cortex** of the temporal lobes, making it the first site where hearing registers. If we did a PET scan of your brain while we played your favourite song, the primary auditory cortex would be the first to light up. Likewise, if we could stimulate the auditory area of your temporal lobe, you would "hear" a series of sound sensations.

Lobes of the cerebral cortex Areas on the cortex bordered by major fissures or defined by their functions.

Occipital lobes The portion of the cerebral cortex where vision registers in the brain.

Parietal lobes The area of the brain where bodily sensations register.

Primary somatosensory area The receiving area for bodily sensations.

Temporal lobes Areas that include the sites where hearing registers in the brain.

Primary auditory cortex Part of the temporal lobe where auditory information is first registered in the brain.

Frontal lobe
(sense of smell, motor control, and higher mental abilities such as reasoning and planning)

Parietal lobe
(sensation, such as touch, temperature, and pressure)

Occipital lobe
(vision)

Temporal lobe
(hearing and language)

Cerebellum
(posture, coordination, muscle tone, and memory of skills and habits)

▸▸**FIGURE 2.24** Many of the lobes of the cerebral cortex are defined by larger fissures on its surface. Others are regarded as separate areas because their functions are quite different.

 Log on to CourseMate to access this interactive figure

Frontal lobes The brain area associated with movement, the sense of smell, and higher mental functions.
Primary motor cortex The brain area associated with control of movement.
Prefrontal cortex The very front of the frontal lobes; involved in sense of self, reasoning, and planning.

For most people, the left temporal lobe also contains a language "centre." (For 5 percent of all people, the area is on the right temporal lobe.) Damage to the temporal lobe can severely limit the ability to use language. (More on this later.)

The Frontal Lobes

The **frontal lobes** are associated with higher mental abilities. This area is also responsible for the control of movement. Specifically, an arch of tissue over the top of the brain, called the **primary motor cortex,** directs the body's muscles. If this area is stimulated with an electrical current, various parts of the body will twitch or move. Like the somatosensory area, the motor cortex corresponds to the importance of bodily areas, not to their size. The hands, for example, get more area than the feet (see Figure 2.25). If you've ever wondered why your hands are more dextrous than your feet, it's partly because more motor cortex is devoted to the hands. Incidentally, due to neuroplasticity, learning and experience can alter these "motor maps." For instance, violin, viola, and cello players have larger "hand maps" in the cortex (Hashimoto et al., 2004).

The very front of the frontal lobes is known as the **prefrontal cortex.** This part of the brain is related to more complex behaviours. If the frontal lobes are damaged, a person's personality and emotional life may change dramatically. Remember Phineas Gage, the railroad foreman described in Chapter 1? It's likely that Gage's personality changed after he suffered brain damage because the prefrontal cortex generates our sense of self, including

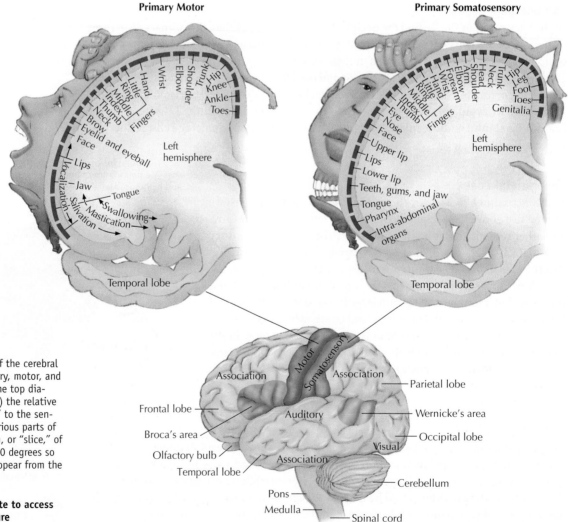

FIGURE 2.25 The lobes of the cerebral cortex and the primary sensory, motor, and association areas on each. The top diagrams show (in cross section) the relative amounts of cortex "assigned" to the sensory and motor control of various parts of the body. (Each cross section, or "slice," of the cortex has been turned 90 degrees so that you see it as it would appear from the back of the brain.)

 Log on to CourseMate to access this interactive figure

an awareness of our current emotional state (Moran et al., 2006; Kawasaki et al., 2005). Reasoning or planning may also be affected (Goel & Dolan, 2004). Patients with frontal lobe damage often get "stuck" on mental tasks and repeat the same wrong answers over and over (Goel & Grafman, 1995). PET scans suggest that much of what we call intelligence is related to increased activity in the frontal areas of the cortex (Duncan et al., 2000). Note that drug abuse is one way in which this important area of the brain may be damaged (Liu et al., 1998).

Association Areas

Only a small part of the cerebral cortex directly controls the body and receives information from the senses. All the surrounding areas, which are called the **association cortex,** combine and process information from the senses. If you see a rose, the association areas will help you recognize it and name it. The association cortex also contributes to higher mental abilities. For example, a person with damage to association areas on the left hemisphere may suffer an **aphasia** (ah-FAZE-yah: impaired ability to use language).

One type of aphasia is related to **Broca's** (BRO-cahs) **area,** a "speech centre" on the left frontal lobe (Ward, 2006). Damage to Broca's area causes great difficulty in speaking or writing. Typically, a patient's grammar and pronunciation are poor and speech is slow and laboured. For example, the person may say "bife" for bike, "seep" for sleep, or "zokaid" for zodiac. Generally, the person knows what she or he wants to say but can't seem to utter the words (Geschwind, 1979).

A second language site, called **Wernicke's** (VER-nick-ees) **area** (see Figure 2.25), lies on the left temporal lobe. If it is damaged, the person has problems with the meaning of words, not their pronunciation. Someone with Broca's aphasia might say "tssair" when shown a picture of a chair. In contrast, a Wernicke's patient might say "stool" (Ward, 2006).

One of the most fascinating results of brain injury is **agnosia** (ag-KNOW-zyah: an inability to identify seen objects). This condition is sometimes referred to as "mindblindness." For example, if we show Marie, an agnosia patient, a candle, she will describe it as "a long narrow object that tapers at the top." Marie can even draw the candle accurately, but she cannot name it. However, if she is allowed to *feel* the candle, she will name it immediately (Farah, 2004). In short, Marie can still see colour, size, and shape. She just can't perceive the meanings of objects.

Are agnosias limited to objects? No. A fascinating type of agnosia is **facial agnosia** or **prosopagnosia** (PROS-o-pag-NO-sia), the inability to perceive familiar faces. Patients with facial agnosia won't be able to recognize their family members when they visit them in the hospital or when they are shown their pictures. However, as soon as family members speak, they will recognize them immediately by their voices. In a more extreme form of facial agnosia, people are unable to distinguish faces as different from other objects, and in rare cases, some may not even recognize their own faces.

Areas devoted to recognizing faces lie on the underside of the occipital lobes. Why would part of the brain be set aside solely for identifying faces? From an evolutionary standpoint it is not really so surprising. After all, we are social animals, for whom facial recognition is very important. This specialization is just one example of what an incredible organ of consciousness we possess.

In summary, the bulk of our daily experience and all of our understanding of the world can be traced to the sensory, motor, and association areas of the cortex. The human brain is among the most advanced and sophisticated of the brain-bearing species on Earth. This, of course, is no guarantee that this marvellous "biocomputer" will be put to good use. Still, we must stand in awe of the potential it represents.

See Human Diversity: "His and Her Brains?" for some interesting differences between men's and women's brains.

<SURVEY QUESTION
Why are the brain's association areas important? What happens when they are injured?

Association cortex All areas of the cerebral cortex that are not primarily sensory or motor in function.

Aphasia A speech disturbance resulting from brain damage.

Broca's area The language area of the brain related to grammar and pronunciation.

Wernicke's area The area of the brain related to language comprehension.

Agnosia The inability to identify seen objects.

Facial agnosia (prosopagnosia) The inability to perceive familiar faces.

His and Her Brains?

Are men's and women's brains specialized in different ways? In a word, yes (Cahill, 2006). Many physical differences between male and female brains have been found, although their effects still need to be better understood. In one series of studies, researchers observed brain activity while people did language tasks. Both men and women showed increased activity in Broca's area, on the left side of the brain, exactly as expected.

Surprisingly, however, the left and the right brain were activated in more than half the women tested (Shaywitz et al., 1995). Using both sides of the brain for language may be a big advantage. When Broca's area is damaged, some women can use the right side of their brains to compensate for the loss, which allows them to resume speaking (Hochstenbach et al., 1998). A man with similar damage might be permanently impaired. Thus, when a man says, "I have half a mind to tell you what I think," he may be stating a curious truth. Despite this difference, the two sexes performed equally well on a task that involved sounding out words (Shaywitz et al., 1995). The researchers concluded that nature has given the brain different routes to the same ability (see Figure 2.26.)

In a study of men and women with similar IQ scores, brain images revealed major differences in brain areas involved in intelligence (Haier et al., 2004). In general, the men had more grey matter (neuron cell bodies), while the women had more white matter (axons coated in myelin). Further, the women had more grey and white matter concentrated in their frontal lobes than the men did. The men's grey matter was split between their frontal and parietal lobes, while their white matter was mostly in the temporal lobes. Whatever else these differences mean, they show that the human brain can be specialized in different ways to arrive at the same capabilities (Piefke et al., 2005).

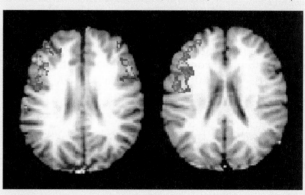

Shaywitz, et al., 1995 NMR Research/ Yale Medical School

▶▶**FIGURE 2.26** Language tasks activate the left side of the brain in men and both sides in many women.

✓ STUDY BREAK Cerebral Cortex and Lobes of the Brain

Reflect

Learning the functions of the brain lobes is like learning areas on a map. Try drawing a map of the cortex. Can you label all the different "countries" (lobes)? Can you name their functions? Where is the primary motor cortex? The somatosensory area? Broca's area? Keep redrawing the map until it becomes more detailed and you can do it easily.

Learning Check

See if you can match the following

_____ 1. Corpus callosum

_____ 2. Occipital lobes

_____ 3. Parietal lobes

_____ 4. Temporal lobes

_____ 5. Frontal lobes

_____ 6. Association cortex

_____ 7. Aphasias

_____ 8. Corticalization

_____ 9. Left hemisphere

_____ 10. Right hemisphere

_____ 11. "Split brain"

A. Primary visual area

B. Language, speech, writing

C. Primary motor cortex and abstract thinking

D. Spatial skills, visualization, pattern recognition

E. Speech disturbances

F. Causes sleep

G. Increased ratio of cortex in brain

H. Bodily sensations

I. Treatment for severe epilepsy

J. Hearing

K. Fibres connecting the cerebral hemispheres

L. Cortex that is not sensory or motor in function

Critical Thinking

12. If you wanted to increase the surface area of the cerebrum so that more cerebral cortex would fit within the skull, how would you do it?

13. If your brain were removed, replaced by another, and moved to a new body, which would you consider to be yourself: your old body with the new brain or your new body with the old brain?

Answers

1. K 2. A 3. H 4. J 5. C 6. L 7. E 8. G 9. B 10. D 11. I 12. One solution would be to gather the surface of the cortex into folds, just as you might if you were trying to fit a large piece of cloth into a small box. This is, in fact, probably why the cortex is more convoluted (folded or wrinkled) in primates. 13. While there is no "correct" answer to this question, your personality, knowledge, personal memories, and self-concept all derive from brain activity—which makes a strong case for your old brain in a new body being more nearly the "real you."

THE SUBCORTEX—AT THE CORE OF THE (BRAIN) MATTER

A person can lose large portions of the cerebral cortex and still survive. Not so with the brain areas below the cortex. Any serious damage could be fatal.

Why are the lower brain areas so important? The **subcortex** lies immediately below the cerebral hemispheres. This area can be divided into the brainstem (or hindbrain), the midbrain, and the forebrain. (The forebrain also includes the cerebral cortex, which we have already discussed because of its size and importance.) For our purposes, the midbrain can be viewed as a link between the forebrain and the brainstem. Therefore, let's focus on the rest of the subcortex (see Figure 2.27).

The Hindbrain

As the spinal cord joins the brain, it widens into the brainstem. The **brainstem** consists mainly of the *medulla* (meh-DUL-ah) and the pons. The **medulla** contains centres important for the reflex control of vital life functions, including heart rate, breathing, and swallowing. At the same time, it controls reflexes involved in breathing, sneezing, coughing, and vomiting. Various drugs, diseases, or injuries can disrupt the medulla and end or endanger life. That's why a karate chop to the back of the neck can be extremely dangerous.

The **pons,** which looks like a small bump on the brainstem, acts as a bridge between the medulla and other brain areas. In addition to connecting with many other locations, including the cerebellum (ser-ah-BEL-uhm), the pons influences sleep and arousal.

The cerebellum, another hindbrain structure, which looks like a miniature cerebral cortex, lies at the base of the brain. The **cerebellum** primarily regulates posture, muscle tone, and muscular coordination. It also stores memories related to skills and habits (Christian & Thompson, 2005). Again we see that experience shapes the brain: Musicians, who practise special motor skills throughout their lives, have larger than average cerebellums (Hutchinson et al., 2003).

Subcortex All brain structures below the cerebral cortex.
Brainstem The lower brain, including the medulla, pons, and reticular formation.
Medulla The structure that connects the brain with the spinal cord and controls vital life functions.
Pons The area on the brainstem that acts as a bridge between the medulla and other structures.
Cerebellum The brain structure that controls posture and coordination.

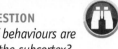

<SURVEY QUESTION
What kinds of behaviours are controlled by the subcortex?

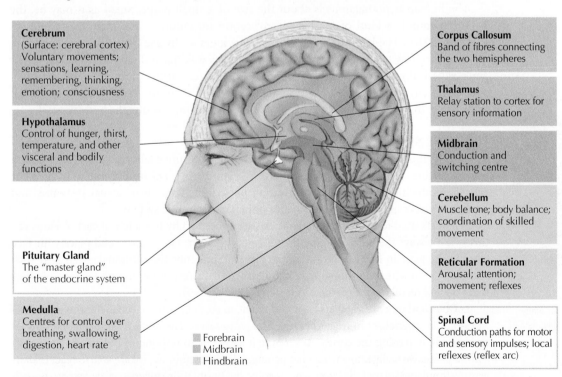

Cerebrum
(Surface: cerebral cortex)
Voluntary movements; sensations, learning, remembering, thinking, emotion; consciousness

Hypothalamus
Control of hunger, thirst, temperature, and other visceral and bodily functions

Pituitary Gland
The "master gland" of the endocrine system

Medulla
Centres for control over breathing, swallowing, digestion, heart rate

Corpus Callosum
Band of fibres connecting the two hemispheres

Thalamus
Relay station to cortex for sensory information

Midbrain
Conduction and switching centre

Cerebellum
Muscle tone; body balance; coordination of skilled movement

Reticular Formation
Arousal; attention; movement; reflexes

Spinal Cord
Conduction paths for motor and sensory impulses; local reflexes (reflex arc)

☐ Forebrain
☐ Midbrain
☐ Hindbrain

▶▶**FIGURE 2.27** This simplified drawing shows the main structures of the human brain and describes some of their most important features. (You can use the colour code in the foreground to identify which areas are part of the forebrain, midbrain, and hindbrain.)

 Log on to CourseMate to access this interactive figure

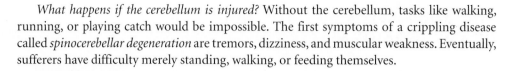

Reticular formation (RF) A network of neurons in the brainstem associated with attention and alertness.

Reticular activating system (RAS) The part of the reticular formation that activates the cerebral cortex.

Thalamus The brain structure that relays sensory information to the cerebral cortex.

Hypothalamus The small area of the brain that regulates emotional behaviours and motives.

Limbic system The system in the forebrain that is closely linked with emotional response.

Amygdala The part of the limbic system associated with fear responses.

What happens if the cerebellum is injured? Without the cerebellum, tasks like walking, running, or playing catch would be impossible. The first symptoms of a crippling disease called *spinocerebellar degeneration* are tremors, dizziness, and muscular weakness. Eventually, sufferers have difficulty merely standing, walking, or feeding themselves.

Reticular Formation

A network of fibres and cell bodies called the **reticular** (reh-TICK-you-ler) **formation** (**RF**) lies inside the medulla and brainstem. As messages flow into the brain, the RF gives priority to some, while turning others aside. By doing so, the RF influences attention. It also modifies outgoing commands to the body. In this way, the RF affects muscle tone; posture; and movements of the eyes, face, head, body, and limbs.

Keeping us vigilant, alert, and awake is another important task of the RF. Incoming messages from the sense organs branch into a part of the RF called the **reticular activating system (RAS).** The RAS bombards the cortex with stimulation, keeping it active and alert. For instance, let's say a sleepy driver rounds a bend and sees a deer standing in the road. The driver snaps to attention and applies the brakes. He can thank his RAS for arousing the rest of his brain and averting an accident. If you're getting sleepy while reading this chapter, try pinching your ear—a little pain will cause the RAS to momentarily arouse your cortex.

The Forebrain

Like hidden gemstones, two of the most important parts of your body lie buried deep within your brain. The *thalamus* (THAL-uh-mus) and an area just below it called the *hypothalamus* (HI-po-THAL-uh-mus) are key parts of the forebrain (see Figure 2.27).

How could these be any more important than other areas already described? The **thalamus** acts as a final "switching station" for sensory messages on their way to the cortex. Vision, hearing, taste, and touch all pass through this small, football-shaped structure. Thus, injury to even small areas of the thalamus can cause deafness; blindness; or loss of any other sense, except smell.

The human hypothalamus is about the size of a small grape. Small as it may be, the **hypothalamus** is a kind of master control centre for emotion and many basic motives (Carlson, 2010). The hypothalamus affects behaviours as diverse as sex, rage, temperature control, hormone release, eating and drinking, sleep, waking, and emotion. The hypothalamus is basically a "crossroads" that connects many areas of the brain. It is also the "final path" for many kinds of behaviour leaving the brain. That is, the hypothalamus is the last place where many behaviours are organized or "decided on," causing the body to react.

The Limbic System

As a group, the hypothalamus, parts of the thalamus, the amygdala, the hippocampus, and other structures make up the limbic system (see Figure 2.28). The **limbic system** has a major role in producing emotion and motivating behaviour. Rage, fear, sexual response, and intense arousal can be localized to various points in the limbic system.

Scientists used to think that all emotions are processed by the cerebral cortex. However, this is not always the case. Imagine this test of willpower: Go to a zoo and place your face close to the glass in front of a rattlesnake display. Suddenly, the rattlesnake strikes at your face. Do you flinch? Even though you know you are safe, researcher Joseph LeDoux predicts that you will recoil from the snake's attack (LeDoux, 1999).

LeDoux and other researchers have found that an area of the brain called the **amygdala** (ah-MIG-duh-la) specializes in triggering fear. The amygdala receives sensory information directly and quickly, bypassing the cortex. As a result, it allows us to respond to potentially dangerous stimuli before we really know what's happening. Like other animals, we are able to react to dangerous stimuli before we fully know what is going on. In situations where true danger exists, such as in military combat, the amygdala's rapid response may aid survival. However, disorders of the brain's fear system can be very disruptive. An example is the war veteran who involuntarily dives

Rod Planch/Photo Researchers, Inc.

The limbic system is responsible for many of our emotional responses. The amygdala, in particular, produces rapid fear, which can help protect us from danger. If you unexpectedly saw a rattlesnake, it is likely that you would instantly jump back in fear, without having to first think about whether you were in danger.

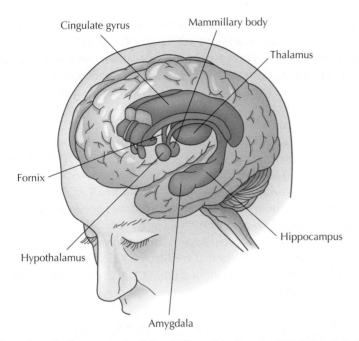

Cingulate gyrus Mammillary body Thalamus Fornix Hypothalamus Amygdala Hippocampus

▶▶**FIGURE 2.28** Parts of the limbic system are shown in this highly simplified drawing. Although only one side is shown, the hippocampus and the amygdala extend out into the temporal lobes at each side of the brain. The limbic system is a sort of "primitive core" of the brain, strongly associated with emotion.

Log on to CourseMate to access this interactive figure

into the bushes when she hears a car backfire (Fellous & LeDoux, 2005; LaBar & LeDoux, 2002). The role of the amygdala in emotion may also explain why people who suffer from phobias and disabling anxiety often feel afraid without knowing why (LeDoux, 1999).

People who suffer damage to the amygdala become insensitive to emotion. An armed robber could hold a gun to the person's head and the person wouldn't feel fear. Such people are also unable to "read" or understand other people's emotions. Many lose their ability to relate normally to friends, family, and co-workers (Goleman, 1995).

Some parts of the limbic system have taken on additional, higher-level functions. A part called the **hippocampus** (HIP-oh-CAMP-us) is important for forming lasting memories (Kumaran & Maguire, 2005). The hippocampus lies inside the temporal lobes, which is why stimulating the temporal lobes can produce memory-like or dreamlike experiences. The hippocampus also helps us navigate through space. Your right hippocampus will become more active, for instance, if you mentally plan a drive across town (Maguire, Frackowiak, & Frith, 1997).

In the 1950s, Canadian psychologists at McGill University discovered that animals will learn to press a lever to deliver a rewarding dose of electrical stimulation to the limbic system. The animals act like the stimulation is satisfying or pleasurable. Indeed, several areas of the limbic system act as reward, or "pleasure," pathways. Many are found in the hypothalamus, where they overlap with areas that control thirst, sex, and hunger. Commonly abused drugs, such as cocaine, amphetamines, heroin, nicotine, marijuana, and alcohol, activate many of the same pleasure pathways. According to Roy Wise, this appears to explain, in part, why these drugs are so powerfully rewarding (Wise & Rompre, 1989). You might also be interested to know that music you would describe as "thrilling" activates pleasure systems in your brain. This may explain some of the appeal of music that can send shivers down your spine (Blood & Zatorre, 2001). (It may also explain why people will pay so much for concert tickets!)

Punishment, or "aversive," areas have also been found in the limbic system. When these locations are activated, animals show discomfort and will work hard to turn off the stimulation. Since much of our behaviour is based on seeking pleasure and avoiding pain, these discoveries continue to fascinate psychologists.

The Magnificent Brain

We have seen that the human brain is an impressive assembly of billions of sensitive cells and nerve fibres. It controls vital bodily functions, keeps track of the external world, issues commands to the muscles and glands, responds to current needs, creates the magic of consciousness, and regulates its own behaviour—all at the same time.

Hippocampus The part of the limbic system associated with storing memories.

Endocrine system Glands whose secretions pass directly into the bloodstream or lymph system.

Hormone A glandular secretion that affects bodily functions or behaviour.

A final note of caution is now in order. For the sake of simplicity, we have assigned functions to each "part" of the brain as if it were a computer. This is only a half-truth. In reality, the brain is a vast information-processing system. Incoming information scatters all over the brain and converges again as it goes out through the spinal cord to muscles and glands. The overall system is much, much more complicated than our discussion of separate "parts" implies.

In addition, the brain constantly revises its circuits in response to changing life experiences (Kolb, Gibb, & Gorny, 2003).

We began our exploration of the brain with a virtuoso performance. Imagine the other extreme of being completely unable to move or speak. Even though you would remain alert and intelligent, you would be unable to communicate your simplest thoughts and feelings to others. Each year, this is the fate of thousands of people, like Kate Adamson, who are paralyzed by stroke, disease, or injury. In a very real sense, these people are *locked in*, prisoners in their own bodies (Smith & Delargy, 2005).

What if they could "will" a computer to speak for them? Right on! Researchers have developed brain–computer interfaces that translate a patient's EEG recordings into commands that can be used to control a computer (Hinterberger et al., 2003) and even access the Internet (Karim et al., 2006).

SURVEY QUESTION>
How does the glandular system affect behaviour?

THE ENDOCRINE SYSTEM—HORMONES AND BEHAVIOUR

Our behaviour is not solely a product of the nervous system. The endocrine (EN-duh-krin) glands serve as a second great communication system in the body. The **endocrine system** is made up of glands that pour chemicals directly into the bloodstream or lymph system (see Figure 2.29). These chemicals, called **hormones,** are carried throughout the body, where they affect both internal activities and visible behaviour. Like other such chemicals, hormones activate cells in the body. To respond, the cells must have receptor sites for the hormone.

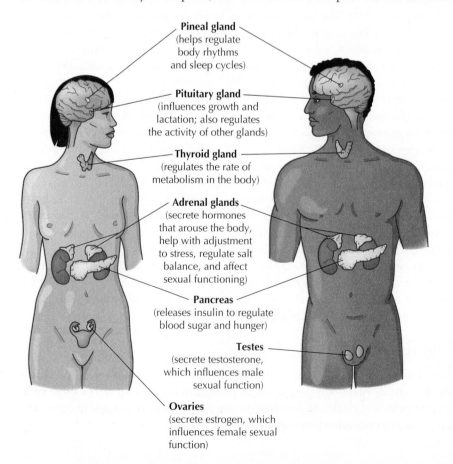

Pineal gland
(helps regulate body rhythms and sleep cycles)

Pituitary gland
(influences growth and lactation; also regulates the activity of other glands)

Thyroid gland
(regulates the rate of metabolism in the body)

Adrenal glands
(secrete hormones that arouse the body, help with adjustment to stress, regulate salt balance, and affect sexual functioning)

Pancreas
(releases insulin to regulate blood sugar and hunger)

Testes
(secrete testosterone, which influences male sexual function)

Ovaries
(secrete estrogen, which influences female sexual function)

▸▸**FIGURE 2.29** Location of the endocrine glands in the male and female.

 Log on to CourseMate to access this interactive figure

How do hormones affect behaviour? Although we are seldom aware of them, hormones affect us in many ways. Here is a brief sample: Pregnancy and motherhood cause the release of hormones that lead to the dramatic changes involved in maternal behaviour (Kingsley & Lambert, 2006). Hormone output from the adrenal glands rises during stressful situations; androgens ("male" hormones) are related to the sex drive in both males and females; hormones secreted during times of high emotion intensify memory formation; at least some of the emotional turmoil of adolescence is due to elevated hormone levels; different hormones prevail when you are angry, rather than fearful. Something as routine as watching a movie can alter hormone levels. After watching violent scenes from the movie *The Godfather*, for instance, men had higher levels of the male hormone testosterone. For both men and women, watching a romantic film boosted a hormone that's linked to relaxation and reproduction (Schultheiss, Wirth, & Stanton, 2004). Since these are just samples, let's consider some additional effects hormones have on the body and behaviour.

The pituitary is a pea-sized globe hanging from the base of the brain (return to Figure 2.29). One of the pituitary's more important roles is to regulate growth. During childhood, the pituitary secretes a hormone that speeds body development. If too little **growth hormone** is released, a person may remain far smaller than average. If this condition is not treated, a child may be 15–30 centimetres shorter than age-mates. As adults, some will be **hypopituitary** (HI-po-pih-TU-ih-ter-ee) **dwarfs.** Such individuals are perfectly proportioned, but tiny. Regular injections of growth hormone can raise a hypopituitary child's height by quite a few centimetres, usually to the short side of average.

Too much growth hormone produces **gigantism** (excessive bodily growth). Secretion of too much growth hormone late in the growth period causes **acromegaly** (AK-row-MEG-uh-lee), a condition in which the arms, hands, feet, and facial bones become enlarged. Acromegaly produces prominent facial features, which some people have used as a basis for careers as character actors, wrestlers, and the like.

The pituitary also governs the functioning of other glands (especially the thyroid, adrenal glands, ovaries, and testes). These glands in turn regulate such bodily processes as metabolism, responses to stress, and reproduction. In women, the pituitary controls milk output following pregnancy.

The **pituitary gland** is often called the "master gland" because it influences other endocrine glands. But the master has a master: The pituitary is directed by the hypothalamus, which lies directly above it. In this way, the hypothalamus can affect glands throughout the body. This, then, is the major link between the brain and hormones (Carlson, 2010).

The **pineal** (pin-EE-ul) **gland** releases a hormone called **melatonin** (mel-ah-TONE-in) in response to daily variations in light. Melatonin levels in the bloodstream rise at dusk and peak around midnight. They fall again as morning approaches. This light-driven cycle helps control body rhythms and sleep cycles. As far as the brain is concerned, it's bedtime when melatonin levels rise (Kalat, 2009).

Flight crews often suffer severe disruptions in their sleep cycles. For example, a crew that leaves Vancouver at 4 p.m., bound for London in England, will arrive in about nine hours. Crew members' bodies, which are on Vancouver time, will act as if it is 1 a.m. Yet in London, it will be 9 a.m.

Studies show that melatonin can be used to minimize jet lag. To reset the body's clock in a new time zone, a small amount of melatonin can be taken about an hour before bedtime. This dose is continued for as many days as necessary to ease jet lag. The same treatment can be used for rotating work shifts (Arendt, 1994; Boivin & James, 2002; Brown, 1994).

The **thyroid gland,** located in the neck, regulates metabolism. As you may remember from a biology course, metabolism is the rate at which energy is produced and expended in the body. By altering metabolism, the thyroid can have a sizable effect on personality. A person suffering from **hyperthyroidism** (an overactive thyroid) tends to be thin, tense, excitable, and nervous. An underactive thyroid (**hypothyroidism**) in an adult can cause inactivity, sleepiness, slowness, depression, and obesity (Joffe, 2006). In infancy,

Growth hormone A hormone secreted by the pituitary gland that promotes bodily growth.

Hypopituitary dwarfism Shortness and smallness caused by too little growth hormone.

Gigantism Excessive bodily growth caused by too much growth hormone.

Acromegaly Enlargement of the arms, hands, feet, and face caused by excess growth hormone late in the human growth period.

Pituitary gland The "master gland," whose hormones influence other endocrine glands.

Pineal gland The gland in the brain that helps regulate body rhythms and sleep.

Melatonin The hormone released by the pineal gland in response to daily cycles of light and dark.

Thyroid gland The endocrine gland that helps regulate the rate of metabolism.

Hyperthyroidism Faster metabolism and excitability caused by an overactive thyroid gland.

Hypothyroidism Slower metabolism and sluggishness caused by an underactive thyroid gland.

Actors Vern Troyer (left) and Matthew McGrory (right) represent extremes of size. Underactivity of the pituitary gland may produce a dwarf; overactivity a giant. Verne Troyer, best known for playing Mini-Me in the Austin Powers movies, has enjoyed an impressive career as an actor. Until his premature death in 2005, actor Matthew McGrory was best known for his role of Karl the Giant in the 2003 movie *Big Fish*.

hypothyroidism limits development of the nervous system, leading to severe mental retardation.

When you are frightened or angry, some important reactions prepare your body for action: Your heart rate and blood pressure rise, stored sugar is released into the bloodstream for quick energy, your muscles tense and receive more blood, and your blood is prepared to clot more quickly in case of injury. As we discussed earlier, these changes are controlled by the autonomic nervous system. Specifically, the sympathetic branch of the ANS causes the hormones *epinephrine* and *norepinephrine* to be released by the adrenal glands. (Epinephrine is also known as adrenaline, which may be more familiar to you.) **Epinephrine** (ep-eh-NEF-rin), which is associated with fear, tends to arouse the body. **Norepinephrine** also tends to arouse the body, but it is linked with anger.

The **adrenal glands** are located just under the back of the ribcage, atop the kidneys. The **adrenal medulla,** or inner core of the adrenal glands, is the source of epinephrine and norepinephrine. The **adrenal cortex,** or outer "bark" of the adrenal glands, produces a set of hormones called *corticoids* (KOR-tih-coyds). One of their jobs is to regulate salt balance in the body. A deficiency of certain corticoids in humans can evoke a powerful craving for the taste of salt. The corticoids also help the body adjust to stress, and they are a secondary source of sex hormones.

An oversecretion of the adrenal sex hormones can cause *virilism* (exaggerated male characteristics). For instance, a woman may grow a beard or a man's voice may become so low it is difficult to understand. Oversecretion early in life can cause premature puberty (full sexual development during childhood). One of the most remarkable cases on record is that of a five-year-old Peruvian girl who gave birth to a son (Strange, 1965).

While we are on the topic of sex hormones, there is a related issue worth mentioning. One of the principal androgens, or "male" hormones, is testosterone, which is supplied in small amounts by the adrenal glands. (The testes are the main source of testosterone in males.) Perhaps you have heard about the use of anabolic steroids by athletes who want to "bulk up" or promote muscle growth. Most of these drugs are synthetic versions of testosterone.

Although there is some disagreement about whether steroids actually improve athletic performance, it is widely accepted that they may cause serious side effects. Problems including voice deepening or baldness in women and shrinkage of the testicles, sexual impotence, or breast enlargement in men (Millman & Ross, 2003). Dangerous increases in hostility and aggression ("roid rage") have been linked with steroid use (Hartgens & Kuipers, 2004). Also common when steroids are used by younger adolescents is an increased risk of heart attack and stroke, liver damage, or stunted growth (Bahrke, Yesalis, & Brower, 1998). Understandably, all major sports organizations ban the use of anabolic steroids.

Do hormones produce differences in men's and women's behaviour? According to a well-respected Canadian psychologist, Doreen Kimura, the answer is yes. In general, research shows that men and women excel at different tasks. For example, on average, men perform better on mathematical reasoning; spatial tasks (e.g., being able to rotate three-dimensional objects in one's head, learning new routes based on geometric information); and gross motor skills (e.g., guiding an object to a target and intercepting an object). Women, on the other hand, are better at verbal skills (e.g., solving word puzzles); arithmetic calculations;

Epinephrine An adrenal hormone that tends to arouse the body; epinephrine is associated with fear; also known as *adrenaline*.

Norepinephrine An adrenal hormone that tends to arouse the body; norepinephrine is associated with anger; also known as *noradrenaline*.

Adrenal glands Endocrine glands that arouse the body, regulate salt balance, adjust the body to stress, and affect sexual functioning.

Adrenal medulla The inner core of the adrenal glands; a source of epinephrine and norepinephrine.

Adrenal cortex The outer layer of the adrenal glands; produces hormones that affect salt intake, reactions to stress, and sexual development.

fine motor tasks (e.g., inserting pegs into holes on a board); and remembering landmarks along a route. Kimura argues that these sex differences are related to the different hormones male and female fetuses are exposed to (Kimura & Clarke, 2002). During prenatal development, the male fetus receives higher levels of androgens and the female fetus gets more estrogen. As a result, the brains of the two sexes develop somewhat differently.

Kimura also reports that women's hormone levels during the menstrual cycle affect their performance on a variety of tasks. When estrogen levels are high, as around the middle of the cycle, women tend not to do as well on spatial tasks, but their verbal and fine motor abilities are at their peak. Spatial ability improves when estrogen levels are lower, as during the menstrual phase. In males, testosterone is higher in the morning and declines during the day and is higher in the fall than in the spring, and their performance on tasks of spatial ability is better when testosterone levels are lower.

The strongest evidence for Kimura's position comes from research on rats. Female rats tend to learn a route by relying on various landmarks located along a particular route, whereas male rats appear to use geometric cues. This parallels the differences between men and women. If male rats are castrated after birth, their androgen levels decrease, and their ability to learn a maze is subsequently diminished. On the other hand, if female rats are administered the male androgens after birth, their spatial performance improves as a result. Hormonal manipulations during adulthood have no detrimental or beneficial effects (Kimura, 1996, 1999). Although animal data are intriguing, it is a huge leap from rodents to humans. We must take into account the strong influence of social and cultural factors on men's and women's behaviour.

© Bettmann/CORBIS

Canadian sprinter Ben Johnson is one of many athletes who have been disqualified, banned from competing, or stripped of medals for steroid use.

What then can we conclude about the relationship of hormone levels and the behavioural differences between men and women? Could men's and women's performance on various tasks not be explained by the different ways in which they are socialized? After all, women have not received the same opportunities men have enjoyed for so long. Women have traditionally not received much encouragement to pursue scientific careers. It is little wonder, then, that their performance on tasks of mathematical reasoning and spatial ability does not equal that of men. This is exactly what Kimura's critics argue. In defence of her position, Kimura does point out that although differences between the sexes on various abilities have shrunk, important discrepancies still remain. Noteworthy among them are women's superiority in verbal skills and men's advantage in high-level mathematics (Kimura, 2002, 2004). In closing, it should be remembered that some of the evidence Kimura puts forward is correlational. No one has convincingly demonstrated in humans a direct causal link between sex hormones and mental ability. Nevertheless, Kimura's ideas have provoked debate about an age-old issue from an interesting angle. Exactly how hormones and socialization shape our behaviour is a complicated issue, and both are probably important. At this time, however, it would be imprudent to emphasize one over the other.

But if Kimura is right, men should not take their physics and engineering exams early in the morning or during the autumn months, and women should avoid them during the middle of their menstrual cycle. Any chance of convincing your professors?

In our brief discussion of the endocrine system, we have considered only a few of the more important glands. Nevertheless, this should give you an appreciation of how completely behaviour and personality are tied to the ebb and flow of hormones in the body.

A Look Ahead

In the upcoming Psychology in Action section, we will return to the brain to see how hand preference relates to brain organization. You'll also find out if being right- or left-handed affects your chances of living to a ripe old age. As we close this chapter, we hope you will agree with us that we live in exciting times as far as research about the brain is concerned. To cite yet another example of research, doctors Roy Bakay and Philip Kennedy have inserted special electrodes into the motor cortex of paralyzed patients. When the patient thinks certain thoughts, bursts of activity in the brain are detected by the implanted wires. Instantly, these signals are transmitted to a computer, where they control the movements of a cursor on the screen. Patients are now learning to select icons on the screen that tell the computer to say phrases such as "Please turn the light on" or "See you later; nice talking to you" (Kennedy & Bakay, 1998).

The human brain is just beginning to understand itself. What an adventure the next decade of brain research will be.

 STUDY BREAK **Subcortex and Endocrine System**

Reflect

If Mr. Medulla met Ms. Cerebellum at a party, what would they say their roles are in the brain? Would a marching band in a "reticular formation" look like a network? Would it get your attention? If you were standing in the final path for behaviour leaving the brain, would you be in the thalamus? Or in the hy-path-alamus (please forgive the misspelling)? When you are emotional do you wave your limbs around (and does your limbic system become more active)?

Name as many of the endocrine glands as you can. Which did you leave out? Can you summarize the functions of each of the glands?

Learning Check

1. Three major divisions of the brain are the brainstem or _____, the _____, and the _____.
2. Reflex centres for heartbeat and respiration are found in the
   a. cerebellum   b. thalamus
   c. medulla   d. reticular formation
3. A portion of the reticular formation, known as the RAS, serves as an _____ system in the brain.
   a. activating   b. adrenal
   c. adjustment   d. aversive

4. The _____ is a final relay, or "switching station," for sensory information on its way to the cortex.
5. "Reward" and "punishment" areas are found throughout the _____ system, which is also related to emotion.
6. Undersecretion from the thyroid can cause
   a. dwarfism   b. gigantism
   c. obesity   d. mental retardation
7. The body's ability to resist stress is related to the action of the adrenal _____.

Critical Thinking

8. Subcortical structures in humans are quite similar to corresponding lower brain areas in other animals. Why would knowing this allow you to predict, in general terms, what functions are controlled by the subcortex?
9. Where in all the brain's "hardware" do you think the mind is found? What is the relationship between mind and brain?

Answers

1. hindbrain, midbrain, forebrain 2. c 3. a 4. thalamus 5. limbic 6. c, d (in infancy) 7. cortex 8. Because the subcortex must be related to basic functions common to all complex animals: motives, emotions, sleep, attention, and vegetative functions, such as heartbeat, breathing, and temperature regulation. The subcortex also routes incoming information from the senses and outgoing commands to the muscles. 9. This question, known as the mind–body problem, has challenged thinkers for centuries. One view is that mental states are "emergent properties" of brain activity. That is, brain activity forms complex patterns that are, in a sense, more than the sum of their parts. Or, to use a rough analogy, if the brain were a musical instrument, then mental life would be like music played on that instrument.

Psychology in Action

HANDEDNESS—ARE YOU SINISTER OR DEXTEROUS?

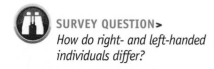 **SURVEY QUESTION>**
How do right- and left-handed individuals differ?

In the English language, "what's right is right," but what's left may be wrong. We have left-handed compliments, people with two left feet, those who are out in left field, and the left-handed. On the other hand (so to speak), we have the right way, the right angle, the right-hand man (or woman), righteousness, and the right-handed.

The Sinister Hand

Left-handedness has a long and undeserved bad reputation. Southpaws have been accused of being clumsy, stubborn (for refusing to use their right hands), and maladjusted. But as any lefty will tell you, and psychology has confirmed, none of this is true. The supposed clumsiness of lefties is merely a result of living in a right-handed world: If it can be gripped, turned, folded, held, or pulled, it's probably designed for the right hand. Even toilet handles are on the right side.

What causes **handedness** (a preference for the right or left hand)? Why are there more right-handed than left-handed people? How do left-handed and right-handed people differ? Does being left-handed create any problems—or benefits? The answers to these questions lead us back to the brain, where handedness begins. Let's see what research has revealed about handedness, the brain, and you.

Assessing Handedness

Write your name on a sheet of paper, first using your right hand and then using your left. You were probably much more comfortable writing with your dominant hand. This is interesting because there's no real difference in the strength or dexterity of the hands themselves. The agility of your dominant hand is an outward expression of superior motor control on one side of the brain. If you are right-handed, there is literally more area on the left side of your brain devoted to controlling your right hand. If you are left-handed, the reverse applies (Annett, 2002).

The preceding exercise implies that you are either entirely right- or entirely left-handed. But handedness is a matter of degree, asserts Stanley Coren (1992), a psychologist and emeritus professor of cognitive science at the University of British Columbia. To better assess your handedness, complete the following questions adapted from the Waterloo Handedness Questionnaire (Brown et al., 2006) by circling an answer for each of the questions. The more "Rights" you circle, the more right-handed you are.

Are You Right- or Left-Handed?

1. Which hand would you use to spin a top? — Right   Left   Either
2. With which hand would you hold a paintbrush to paint a wall? — Right   Left   Either
3. Which hand would you use to pick up a book? — Right   Left   Either
4. With which hand would you use a spoon to eat soup? — Right   Left   Either
5. Which hand would you use to flip pancakes? — Right   Left   Either
6. Which hand would you use to pick up a piece of paper? — Right   Left   Either
7. Which hand would you use to draw a picture? — Right   Left   Either
8. Which hand would you use to insert and turn a key in a lock? — Right   Left   Either
9. Which hand would you use to insert a plug into an electrical outlet? — Right   Left   Either
10. Which hand would you use to throw a ball? — Right   Left   Either
11. In which hand would you hold a needle while sewing? — Right   Left   Either
12. Which hand would you use to turn on a light switch? — Right   Left   Either
13. With which hand would you use the eraser at the end of a pencil? — Right   Left   Either
14. Which hand would you use to saw a piece of wood with a hand saw? — Right   Left   Either
15. Which hand would you use to open a drawer? — Right   Left   Either
16. Which hand would you turn a doorknob with? — Right   Left   Either

> **Handedness** A preference for the right or left hand in most activities.

Courtesy of Wendy Yano

Left-handers have an advantage in sports such as fencing and boxing. Most likely, their movements are less familiar to opponents, who usually face right-handers (Coren, 1992).

Sidedness A combination of preference for hand, foot, eye, and ear.

Dominant hemisphere A term usually applied to the side of a person's brain that produces language.

17. Which hand would you use to hammer a nail?	Right	Left	Either
18. With which hand would you use a pair of tweezers?	Right	Left	Either
19. Which hand do you use for writing?	Right	Left	Either
20. With which hand would you turn the dial of a combination lock?	Right	Left	Either

About 90 percent of all humans are right-handed; 10 percent are left-handed. A majority of people (about 75 percent) are strongly right- or left-handed. The rest show some inconsistency in hand preference. Which are you?

Is there such a thing as being left-footed? Excellent question. Do you have "two left feet"? **Sidedness** is often measured by assessing hand, foot, eye, *and* ear preference (Greenwood et al., 2006). We also generally prefer breathing through one nostril over the other and even have a preference for which direction we lean our head when kissing (Barrett, Greenwood, & McCullagh, 2006). (Do you kiss "right"?) Nevertheless, handedness remains the single most important behavioural indicator of sidedness.

If a person is strongly left-handed, does that mean the right hemisphere is dominant? Not necessarily. It's true that the right hemisphere controls the left hand, but a left-handed person's language-producing, **dominant hemisphere** may be on the opposite side of the brain.

Brain Dominance

About 97 percent of right-handers process speech in the left hemisphere and are left-brain dominant (see Figure 2.30). A good 68 percent of left-handers produce speech from the left hemisphere, just as right-handers do. About 19 percent of all lefties and 3 percent of righties use their right brain for language. Some left-handers (approximately 13 percent) use both sides of the brain for language processing. All told, 94 percent of the population uses the left brain for language (Coren, 1992).

Is there any way for a person to tell which of his or her hemispheres is dominant? One interesting clue is based on the way you write. Right-handed individuals who write with a straight hand, and lefties who write with a hooked hand are usually left-brain dominant for language. Left-handed people who write with their hand below the line and righties who use a hooked position are usually right-brain dominant (Levy & Reid, 1976). Another hint is provided by the hand gestures. If you gesture mostly with your right hand as you talk, you probably process language in your left hemisphere. Gesturing with your left hand is associated with right-brain language processing (Hellige, 1993). Are your friends right-brained or left-brained? (See Figure 2.31.)

Before you leap to any conclusions, be aware that writing position is not foolproof. The only sure way to check brain dominance is to do a medical test that involves briefly anaesthetizing one cerebral hemisphere at a time (Kirveskari, Salmelin, & Hari, 2006).

Causes of Handedness

Is handedness inherited from parents? Yes, at least partly. Clear hand preferences are apparent even before birth, evident from fetal ultrasound images. According to psychologist Peter Hepper, prenatal handedness preferences persist for at least 10 years after birth (Hepper,

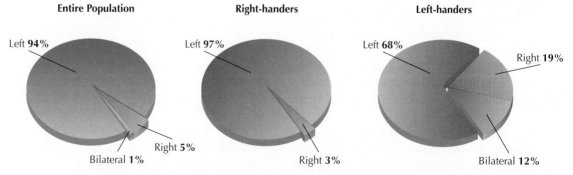

▸▸**FIGURE 2.30** Language is controlled by the left side of the brain in the majority of right- and left-handers.

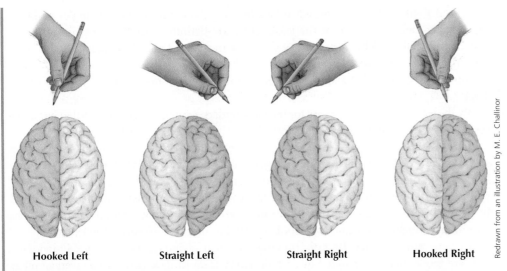

Redrawn from an illustration by M. E. Challinor

| Hooked Left | Straight Left | Straight Right | Hooked Right |

▸▸FIGURE 2.31 Research suggests that the hand position used in writing may indicate which brain hemisphere is used for language.

Wells, & Lynch, 2005). This suggests that handedness cannot be dictated. Parents should never try to force a left-handed child to use the right hand. To do so may create speech or reading problems.

Studies of identical twins show that hand preferences are not directly inherited like eye colour or skin colour (Ooki, 2005; Reiss et al., 1999). Yet, two left-handed parents are more likely to have a left-handed child than two right-handed parents are (McKeever, 2000). The best evidence to date shows that handedness is influenced by a single gene on the X (female) chromosome (Jones & Martin, 2001).

However, environmental factors such as learning, birth traumas, and social pressure to use the right hand can also affect which hand you end up favouring (Bailey & McKeever, 2004; McKeever et al., 2000). In the past, many left-handed children were forced to use their right hand for writing, eating, and other skills. This is especially true in collectivist cultures like India and Japan, where left-handedness is viewed as especially negative. Not surprisingly, the proportion of left-handers in these societies is only about half that found in individualist cultures such as Canada and the United States (Ida & Mandal, 2003).

Are there any drawbacks to being left-handed? A minority of lefties owe their hand preference to birth traumas (such as prematurity, low birth weight, and breech birth). These individuals have a higher incidence of allergies, learning disorders, and other problems (Betancur et al., 1990). Similarly, people with inconsistent handedness (as opposed to consistent left-handers) may be at risk for more immune-related diseases (Bryden, Bruyn, & Fletcher, 2005).

Is it true that right-handed people live longer than left-handed people? It is true that there is a shortage of very old lefties. One possible explanation lies in the widespread finding that left-handers are more accident-prone (Dutta & Mandal, 2005). However, the supposed clumsiness of lefties may well be a result of living in a right-handed world. One study showed that left-handed locomotive engineers have higher accident rates and suggested that the cause was the design of locomotive controls (Bhushan & Khan, 2006). As we noted before, if it can be gripped, turned, or pulled, it's probably designed for the right hand. However, the shortage of very old lefties may just reflect the fact that, in the past, more left-handed children were forced to become right-handed. That makes it look like many lefties don't survive to old age. In reality, they do, but many of them are masquerading as righties (Martin & Freitas, 2002)!

Advantage Left

Actually, there are some clear advantages to being left-handed. Throughout history a notable number of artists have been lefties, from Leonardo da Vinci and Michelangelo to Pablo Picasso and M. C. Escher. Conceivably, because the right hemisphere is superior at imagery

■ Table 2.1   Sports and Handedness

Sport	Handedness Advantage
Baseball	No overall left or right advantage
Boxing	Left
Fencing	Left
Basketball	Mixed and ambidextrous
Ice hockey	Mixed and ambidextrous
Field hockey	Mixed and ambidextrous
Tennis	Strong left or strong right
Squash	Strong left or strong right
Badminton	Strong left or strong right

(Adapted with the permission of The Free Press, a Division of Simon & Schuster, Inc., from *THE LEFT-HANDER SYNDROME* by Stanley Coren. Copyright © 1992, 1993 by Stanley Coren. All rights reserved.)

and visual abilities, there is some advantage to using the left hand for drawing or painting (Springer & Deutsch, 1998). At the least, lefties are definitely better at visualizing three-dimensional objects. This may be why there are more left-handed architects, artists, and chess players than would be expected (Coren, 1992).

Similarly, being right-handed does not guarantee sports superiority, as you can see in Table 2.1.

By the way, chalk up a few more for the left-handers, who have also done well in handball (Dane & Erzurumluoglu, 2003) and professional tennis (Holtzen, 2000).

Lateralization refers to specialization in the abilities of the brain hemispheres. One striking feature of lefties is that they are generally less lateralized than the right-handed. In fact, even the physical size and shape of their cerebral hemispheres are more alike. If you are a lefty, you can take pride in the fact that your brain is less lopsided than most! In general, left-handers are more symmetrical on almost everything, including eye dominance, fingerprints, and even foot size (Polemikos & Papaeliou, 2000).

In some situations, less lateralization may be a real advantage. For instance, individuals who are moderately left-handed or ambidextrous seem to have better than average pitch memory, which is a basic musical skill. Correspondingly, more musicians are ambidextrous than would normally be expected (Springer & Deutsch, 1998).

Math abilities may also benefit from fuller use of the right hemisphere. Students who are extremely gifted in math are much more likely to be left-handed or ambidextrous (Benbow, 1986). Even where ordinary arithmetic skills are concerned, lefties seem to excel (Annett, 2002; Annett & Manning, 1990).

The clearest advantage of being left-handed shows up when there is a brain injury. Because of their milder lateralization, left-handed individuals typically experience less language loss after damage to either brain hemisphere, and they recover more easily (Geschwind, 1979). Maybe having "two left feet" isn't so bad after all.

Lateralization Differences between the two sides of the body; especially, differences in the abilities of the brain hemispheres.

✓ STUDY BREAK   Handedness and Brain Lateralization

Reflect

Think for a moment about what you "knew" about handedness and left-handed people before you read this section. Which of your beliefs were correct? How has your knowledge about handedness changed?

Learning Check

1. About 97 percent of left-handed people process language on the left side of the brain, the same as right-handed people do. T or F?
2. Left-handed individuals who write with their hand below the line are likely to be right-brain dominant. T or F?
3. In general, left-handed individuals show less lateralization in the brain and throughout the body. T or F?

Critical Thinking

4. Reports that left-handed people tend to die younger were flawed in an important way: The average age of people in the left-handed group was younger than that of subjects in the right-handed group. Why would this make a difference in the conclusions drawn?

Answers

1. F 2. T 3. T 4. Because we can't tell if handedness or average age accounts for the difference in death rates. For example, if we start with a group of 20- to 30-year-old people, the average age of death has to be between 20 and 30. If we start with a group of 30- to 40-year-old people, in which some die, the average age of death has to be between 30 and 40. Thus, the left-handed group might have an earlier average age at death simply because the group members were younger to start with.

CHAPTER IN REVIEW

Major Points

- Biopsychologists study how processes in the body, brain, and nervous system relate to behaviour.

- Ultimately, all behaviour can be traced to the activity of neurons. Sensations, thoughts, feelings, motives, actions, memories, and all other human capacities are associated with brain activities and structures.

- To map the brain, researchers activate or disable specific areas and observe changes in behaviour.

- Bioelectrical recordings and computer-generated images of brain activity provide further insights into the structure and function of the brain.

- Endocrine glands serve as a chemical communication system within the body. Behaviour is greatly influenced by the ebb and flow of hormones in the bloodstream.

- Brain dominance and brain activity determine if you are right-handed, left-handed, or ambidextrous.

Summary

How do nerve cells operate and communicate?

- The nervous system is made up of linked neurons that pass information from one to another through synapses.

- The neuronal axons, axon terminals, dendrites, and soma facilitate the sending and receiving of messages in the nervous system.

- The firing of an action potential (nerve impulse) is electrical. Communication between neurons is chemical.

- Neurotransmitters cross the synapse, attach to receptor sites, and excite or inhibit the receiving cell.

- Chemicals called neuropeptides also regulate activity in the brain.

- By combining information, neurons act as simple computers, which become very powerful when they operate together as neural networks.

- The brain's circuitry is not static. The brain can "rewire" itself and even grow new nerve cells in response to changing environmental conditions.

How is the nervous system organized, and what are the functions of its major parts?

- The nervous system can be divided into the central nervous system and the peripheral nervous system, which includes the somatic (bodily) and autonomic (involuntary) nervous systems.

- The brain carries out most of the "computing" in the nervous system.

- The spinal cord connects the brain to the peripheral nervous system and can process simple reflex arcs.

- The peripheral nervous system carries sensory information to the brain and motor commands to the body.

- "Vegetative" and automatic bodily processes are controlled by the autonomic nervous system, which has a sympathetic branch and a parasympathetic branch.

- Neurons and nerves in the peripheral nervous system can often regenerate. At present, damage in the central nervous system is usually permanent, although scientists are working on ways to repair damaged neural tissue.

How do we know how the brain works? What are the methods by which scientists study the brain?

- Brain research relies on clinical studies, electrical stimulation, ablation, deep lesioning, electrical recording, micro-electrode recording, and EEG recording.

- Computer-enhanced images are providing three-dimensional pictures of the living human brain and its activity. Examples of such techniques are CT scans, MRI scans, and PET scans.

How is the brain organized, and what do its higher structures do?

- The human brain is marked by advanced corticalization, or enlargement of the cerebral cortex.

- The left cerebral hemisphere contains speech or language "centres" in most people. It also specializes in writing, calculating, judging time and rhythm, and ordering complex movements.

- The right hemisphere is largely non-verbal. It excels at spatial and perceptual skills; visualization; and recognition of patterns, faces, and melodies.

- "Split brains" have been created in animals and humans by cutting the corpus callosum. The split-brain individual shows a remarkable degree of independence between the right and left hemispheres.

- Some individuals are born with a partial or complete absence of the corpus callosum. In such cases, one hemisphere is able to share some sensory information with its counterpart.

- The most basic functions of the lobes of the cerebral cortex are as follows: occipital lobes—vision; parietal lobes—bodily sensation; frontal lobes—motor control, speech, and abstract thought; temporal lobes—hearing and language. Damage to any of these areas will impair the named functions.

Why are the brain's association areas important? What happens when they are injured?

- Association areas on the cortex are neither sensory nor motor in function. They are related to more complex skills such as language, memory, recognition, and problem solving.

- Damage to either Broca's area or Wernicke's area causes speech and language problems known as aphasias.

What kinds of behaviours are controlled by the subcortex?

- The brain can be subdivided into the forebrain, midbrain, and hindbrain. The subcortex includes several crucial brain structures found at all three levels, below the cortex.

- The medulla contains centres essential for reflex control of heart rate, breathing, and other "vegetative" functions.

- The cerebellum maintains coordination, posture, and muscle tone.

- The reticular formation (RF) directs sensory and motor messages, and part of it, known as the reticular activating system (RAS), acts as an activating system for the cerebral cortex.

- The thalamus carries sensory information to the cortex. The hypothalamus exerts powerful control over eating, drinking, sleep cycles, body temperature, and other basic motives and behaviours.

- The limbic system is related to emotions. It also contains distinct reward and punishment areas and an area known as the hippocampus that is important for forming memories.

How does the glandular system affect behaviour?

- The endocrine system provides chemical communication in the body by releasing hormones into the bloodstream. Endocrine glands influence mood, behaviour, and personality.

- Many of the endocrine glands are influenced by the pituitary (the "master gland"), which is in turn influenced by the hypothalamus.

- Sex hormones may affect the behaviour of men and women differently, but studies on this issue are not conclusive at present.

How do right- and left-handed individuals differ?

- Hand dominance ranges from strongly left-handed to strongly right-handed, with mixed handedness and ambidexterity in between. Ninety percent of the population is right-handed, and 10 percent is left-handed.

- The vast majority of people are right-handed and therefore left-brain dominant for motor skills. Ninety-seven percent of right-handed persons and 68 percent of left-handed persons also produce speech from the left hemisphere.

- In general, left-handed persons are less strongly lateralized in brain function than are right-handed persons.

Interactive Learning

Please visit *http://www.psychologyjourney4ce.nelson.com* for a list of weblinks to relevant psychology sites.

CourseMate

Access the interactive eBook and chapter-specific interactive learning tools, including flashcards, quizzes, videos, and more, in your Psychology CourseMate at NelsonBrain.com.

psyk.trek 2. Biological Bases of Behaviour, Psyck.Trek Simulations: 2. Hemispheric Specialization.

TEST YOUR KNOWLEDGE

The questions that follow are only a sample of what you need to know. If you miss any of the items, review the entire chapter and the Study Breaks. Another way to prepare for tests is to use the Study Guide and the Practice Exams that are available with this text.

1. What two items are linked at the point where information is passed from one neuron to another?
   a. neurilemma and myelin
   b. neurilemma and dendrites
   c. axon terminals and dendrites
   d. axon terminals and myelin

2. What regulates the activity of neurons and thus affects memory, pain, moods, hunger, and other processes?
   a. neuropeptides   b. neurilemmas
   c. resting potentials   d. dendrites

3. Josh is experiencing depression. He is likely to have low levels of which neurotransmitter?
   a. dopamine   b. acetylcholine
   c. serotonin   d. endorphins

4. What process refers to the brain growing new neurons to replace those that have been lost?
   a. neurogenesis   b. neurilemmal regeneration
   c. autonomic regeneration d. neuropeptosis

5. Nerves are made of which of the following?
   a. action potentials   b. neurotransmitters
   c. synapses   d. axons

6. What is the somatic nervous system part of?
   a. the peripheral nervous system (PNS)
   b. the autonomic nervous system (ANS)
   c. the sympathetic nervous system
   d. the parasympathetic system

7. What quiets the body and returns it to a lower level of arousal after an emotional event?
   a. the parasympathetic system
   b. the peripheral nervous system
   c. the spinal nervous system
   d. the sympathetic nervous system

8. What records the electrical activity of a single neuron?
   a. an electroencephalography (EEG)
   b. electrical stimulation of the brain (ESB)
   c. a micro-electrode
   d. surface ablation

9. Which research technique provides an image of ongoing brain activity?
   a. electrical stimulation of the brain (ESB)
   b. deep lesioning
   c. positron emission tomography (PET)
   d. surface ablation

10. Among animals and humans, with what is greater corticalization associated?
    a. increased muscular coordination
    b. increased intelligence
    c. increased fight-or-flight responses
    d. increased conduction speed in the axon

11. The left hemisphere of the brain processes information sequentially, making it superior at which of the following skills?
    a. recognizing patterns   b. holistic thinking
    c. expressing and detecting emotions   d. analysis

12. In a "split-brain" operation, the two cerebral hemispheres are separated due to the cutting of which of the following?
    a. the corpus callosum   b. the chiasm
    c. the lobes   d. the reticulums

13. Impaired hearing can result from damage to which lobes of the brain?
    a. the frontal lobes   b. the temporal lobes
    c. the occipital lobes   d. the parietal lobes

14. What is caused by damage to Broca's area?
    a. a loss of coordination
    b. disturbed sleep patterns
    c. aphasia
    d. an inability to remember recent events

15. What term refers to structures in the brain that play a major role in producing emotion and motivating behaviour?
    a. the thalamic branch of the reticular activating system (RAS)
    b. the cerebellar activating system
    c. the medial brainstem
    d. the limbic system

16. Which part of the brain is *most* involved in forming long-lasting memories?
    a. the amygdala   b. the hippocampus
    c. the thalamus   d. the hypothalamus

17. Which endocrine gland *most* influences the activities of other glands?
    a. the pituitary gland   b. the adrenal gland
    c. the pineal gland   d. the thyroid gland

18. Which glands can have problems that cause dwarfism and gigantism?
    a. the pituitary gland
    b. the adrenal glands
    c. the pineal gland
    d. the thyroid gland

19. Where is speech processed for the majority of both right-handed and left-handed people?
    a. the right brain hemisphere
    b. the corpus callosum
    c. the left brain hemisphere
    d. the hippocampus

20. What is one consistent finding about left-handed people?
    a. Their brains are less lateralized.
    b. They are more likely to die at an early age.
    c. They are unable to use the right brain to produce language.
    d. They are less likely to be ambidextrous.

ANSWERS   1.c 2.a 3.c 4.a 5.d 6.a 7.a 8.c 9.c 10.b 11.d 12.a 13.b 14.c 15.d 16.b 17.a 18.a 19.c 20.a

iStockphoto/Thinkstock

chapter 3

Human Development

JOURNEY INTO PSYCHOLOGY: A STAR IS BORN—HERE'S AMY!

Olivia has just given birth to her first child, Amy. Frankly, at the moment, Amy looks something like a prune—pudgy arms, stubby legs, and lots of wrinkles. She also has the face of an angel—at least in her parents' eyes. As Olivia and her husband, Tom, look at Amy, they wonder how her life will unfold. What kind of a person will she be?

What if we could skip ahead through Amy's childhood and observe her at various ages? What could we learn? Seeing the world through her eyes would be both instructive and fascinating. Children are newcomers to the societies in which they live. Because of this, their attempts to figure out how the world works can make us more acutely aware of things that we take for granted. For example, younger children are very literal in their use of language. That's why one three-year-old who thought her bath was too hot asked her father to "make it warmer, Daddy." At first, her father was confused. The bath was already pretty hot. But then he realized that what she really meant was "bring the water closer to the temperature we call *warm*." It makes perfectly good sense if you look at it that way.

Today we can merely guess about Amy's future. However, developmental psychologists have studied many thousands of children, adolescents, and adults. Their findings tell a fascinating story about human growth and development. Let's let Olivia, Tom, and Amy represent parents and children everywhere, as we see what psychology can tell us about the challenges of growing up. Tracing Amy's development might even help answer two very important questions: How did I become the person I am today, and who will I become tomorrow?

 Survey Questions

- How do heredity and environment affect development?
- What can newborn babies do?
- What is maturation? What influence does maturation have on a child's early development?
- Why is the emotional bond between parent and child so important?
- What are parenting styles? How important are different parenting styles to a child's development?
- How do children acquire language?
- How do children learn to think?
- What are the challenges of adolescence and adulthood? Why is the transition from adolescence to adulthood especially challenging?
- How do we develop morals and values?
- What are the typical tasks and dilemmas that confront people through their lifespan?
- What are the challenges in later adulthood and old age?
- What is the most effective way to discipline a child?

HEREDITY AND ENVIRONMENT—THE NURTURE OF NATURE

When we think of development, we naturally think of children "growing up" into adults. But even as adults we never really stop growing. **Developmental psychology,** the study of progressive changes in behaviour and abilities, involves every stage of life from conception to death (or "the womb to the tomb"). Heredity and environment also affect us throughout life. Some events in a person's life, such as achieving sexual maturity, are mostly governed by heredity. Others, such as learning to swim or use a computer, are primarily a matter of environment. But which is more important, heredity or environment? Let's consider some arguments on both sides of the nature–nurture debate.

But which is more important, heredity or environment? Actually, neither. Canadian biopsychologist D. O. Hebb (1904–1985) once offered a useful analogy: To define the area of a rectangle, what is more important, height or width? Of course, both dimensions are absolutely essential. If either is reduced to zero, there is no rectangle. Similarly, if Amy grows up to become an attractive, popular, intelligent girl and graduates first in her class, her success will be due to both heredity and environment.

<SURVEY QUESTION
How do heredity and environment affect development?

Developmental psychology The study of progressive changes in behaviour and abilities from conception to death.

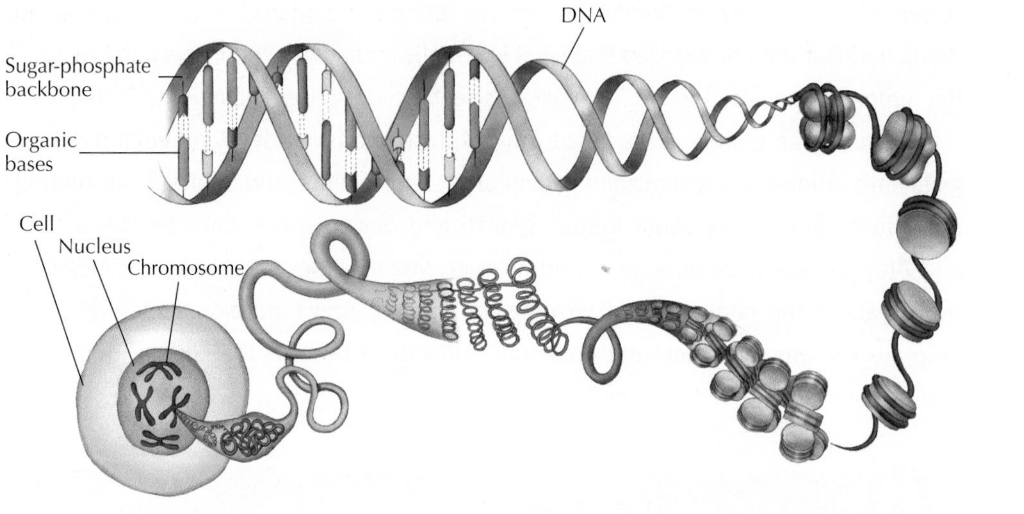

▸▸**FIGURE 3.1** *(Top left)* Linked molecules (organic bases) make up the "rungs" on DNA's twisted "molecular ladder." The order of these molecules serves as a code for genetic information. The code provides a genetic blueprint that is unique for each individual (except identical twins). The drawing shows only a small section of a DNA strand. An entire strand of DNA is composed of billions of smaller molecules. *(Bottom left)* The nucleus of each cell in the body contains chromosomes made up of tightly wound coils of DNA. (Don't be misled by the drawing: Chromosomes are microscopic in size, and the chemical molecules that make up DNA are even smaller.)

DNA

Sugar-phosphate backbone

Organic bases

Cell
Nucleus
Chromosome

Heredity ("nature") The transmission of physical and psychological characteristics from parents to offspring through genes.

Conception The union of an ovum and a sperm cell.

DNA Deoxyribonucleic acid, a molecular structure that contains coded genetic information.

Chromosomes Threadlike "coloured bodies" in the nucleus of each cell that are made up of DNA.

Genes Specific areas on a strand of DNA that carry hereditary information.

Polygenic characteristics Personal traits or physical properties that are influenced by many genes working in combination.

Dominant gene A gene whose influence will be expressed each time the gene is present.

Recessive gene A gene whose influence will be expressed only when it is paired with a second recessive gene.

Human growth sequence The pattern of physical development from conception to death.

Temperament The hereditary aspects of personality, including sensitivity, activity levels, prevailing mood, irritability, and adaptability.

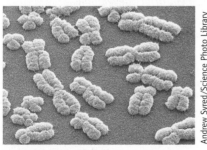

▸▸**FIGURE 3.2** This image, made with a scanning electron microscope, shows several pairs of human chromosomes. (Colours are artificial.)

Andrew Syred/Science Photo Library

While heredity gives each of us a variety of potentials and limitations, these are, in turn, affected by environmental influences, such as learning, nutrition, disease, and culture. Thus, the person you are today reflects a constant *interaction,* or interplay, between the forces of nature and nurture (Gopnik, Meltzoff, & Kuhl, 2000). Let's look in more detail at this dance between heredity and environment.

Heredity

Heredity ("nature") refers to the genetic transmission of physical and psychological characteristics from parents to their children. An incredible number of personal features are set at **conception,** when a sperm cell and an ovum (egg) unite.

How does heredity operate? The nucleus of every human cell contains **DNA,** deoxyribonucleic (dee-OX-see-RYE-bo-new-KLEE-ik) acid. DNA is a long, ladderlike chain of pairs of chemical molecules (see Figure 3.1). The order of these molecules, or organic bases, acts as a code for genetic information. The DNA in each cell contains a record of all the instructions needed to make a human—with room left over. A major scientific milestone was reached in 2003 with the completion of the Human Genome Project, a project designed to completely determine the sequence of all 3 billion chemical base pairs in human DNA (U.S. Department of Energy Office of Science, 2005).

Human DNA is organized into 46 **chromosomes.** (The word *chromosome* means "coloured body.") These threadlike structures hold the coded instructions of heredity (see Figure 3.2). Notable exceptions are sperm cells and ova, which contain only 23 chromosomes. Thus, Amy received 23 chromosomes from Tom and 23 from Olivia. This is her genetic heritage.

Among the 23 chromosomes that Amy received from each of her parents was a sex chromosome. Ova contain only X chromosomes, while sperm cells contain either X or Y chromosomes. Because she is a girl, Amy has two X chromosomes. Her cousin Phillipe has an X chromosome from his mother and a Y chromosome from his father.

Genes are small areas of the DNA code. Each of the 25 000 genes in your cells affects a particular process or personal characteristic. Sometimes, a single gene is responsible for an inherited feature, such as Amy's hair colour. Most characteristics, however, are **polygenic** (pol-ih-JEN-ik), or controlled by many genes working in combination.

Genes may be dominant or recessive. When a gene is **dominant,** the feature it controls will appear every time the gene is present. When a gene is **recessive,** it must be paired with a second recessive gene before its effect will be expressed. Examples of traits controlled by a single dominant gene include the ability to roll your tongue inwards (try it!), a dimple in your chin, and hair on the back of the middle finger joints.

Dominant genes also include pigmented irises, dark hair, curly hair, extra fingers or toes, and type A and B blood. Recessive genes include non-pigmented irises, light hair colour, straight hair, and type O blood. Some genes are linked to the sex chromosomes (usually the X). If such a gene is dominant, any child receiving it will have the condition or disorder. Some forms of deafness, for example, are due to X-linked dominant genes. Others are known as X-linked recessive. Examples of X-linked recessive traits or conditions include red-green colour-blindness, hemophilia (a blood-clotting disorder), and Duchenne muscular dystrophy (the most common form of muscular dystrophy). Since the genes for these conditions are located on the X chromosome, the disorders are much more common in males than in females. For a girl to have hemophilia, for example, her father must have the disease, and her mother must also possess the trait on one of her X chromosomes. Since these genes are rare in the general population, this is unlikely to occur.

If genes for pigmented irises are dominant, why do two dark-eyed parents sometimes have a blue-eyed child? If both parents have genes for pigmented irises (dark eyes), their children can only be dark-eyed. But what if each parent has genes for both pigmented irises and non-pigmented irises? In that case the parents would both have dark eyes. Yet, there is one chance in four that any child will get only genes for non-pigmented irises. In this case the blue layer at the back of the iris shows through. Along the same lines, genetics can sometimes be used to predict the chances that a child will be born with various inherited problems.

Genetic Programming

Heredity exerts a powerful influence on the **human growth sequence,** or overall pattern of physical development (see Table 3.1). To a degree, genetic instructions affect body size and shape, height, intelligence, athletic potential, personality traits, sexual orientation, and a host of other details (Cummings, 2006).

Temperament

How soon do hereditary differences appear? Some appear right away. For instance, newborn babies differ noticeably in **temperament.** This is the physical core of personality. It includes sensitivity, irritability, distractibility, and typical mood (Kagan, 2004; Wachs, 2006). About 40 percent of all newborns are **easy children,** who are relaxed and agreeable. Ten percent are **difficult children,** who are moody, intense, and easily angered. **Slow-to-warm-up children** (about 15 percent) are restrained, unexpressive, or shy. The remaining children do not fit neatly into a single category (Chess & Thomas, 1986). (Perhaps we should call them "generic" children?)

Imagine that we start with some infants who are very shy and some who are very bold. By the time they are four or five years old, most of these children will be only moderately shy or bold. This suggests that inherited temperaments are modified by learning (Kagan, 1999). In other words, nurture immediately enters the picture.

Environment

Environment ("nurture") refers to the sum of all external conditions that affect a person. The environments in which a child grows up can have a powerful impact on development. Humans today are genetically very similar to cave dwellers who lived 30 000 years ago (Cochran & Harpending, 2009; Hawks et al., 2007). Nevertheless, a bright baby born today could learn to become almost anything—a ballet dancer, an engineer, a rapper, or a biochemist who likes to paint in watercolours. But an Upper Paleolithic baby could have become only a hunter or a food gatherer. Score one for the environmentalists!

Early experiences can have very lasting effects. For example, children who are abused may suffer lifelong emotional problems (Goodwin, Fergusson, & Horwood, 2005). At the same time, extra

Jupiter Images

Did you know that most people clasp their hands together with their left thumb on top? This trait is carried on a single dominant gene.

Easy child A child who is temperamentally relaxed and agreeable.

Difficult child A child who is temperamentally moody, intense, and easily angered.

Slow-to-warm-up child A child who is temperamentally restrained and unexpressive.

Environment ("nurture") The sum of all external conditions affecting development, especially the effects of learning.

© Myrleen Ferguson/ Photo Edit

Twins who have identical genes (identical twins) demonstrate the powerful influence of heredity. Even when they are reared apart, identical twins are strikingly alike in motor skills, physical development, and appearance. At the same time, twins are less alike as adults than they were as children, which shows environmental influences are at work (McCartney, Bernieri, & Harris, 1990).

■ Table 3.1 Human Growth Sequence

Prenatal period
- From conception to birth
Germinal period
Zygote: First 2 weeks after conception
Embryonic period
Embryo: 2-8 weeks after conception
Fetal period
Fetus: From 8 weeks after conception to birth

Neonatal period
- *Neonate:* From birth to a few weeks after birth

Infancy
Infant: From a few weeks after birth until child is walking securely; some children walk securely at less than a year, while others may not be able to until age 17–18 months

Early childhood
Toddler: From about 15–18 months until about 2–2.5 years

Preschool child: From age 2–3 to about age 6

Middle childhood
School-age child: From about age 6 to age 12

Pubescence
Adolescent: Period of about 2 years before puberty

Puberty
Point of development at which biological changes of pubescence reach a climax marked by sexual maturity

Adolescence
From the beginning of pubescence until full social maturity is reached (difficult to fix duration of this period)

Adulthood
Adult: From adolescence to death; sometimes subdivided into other periods as shown at left
- Young adulthood (19–25)
- Adulthood (26–40)
- Maturity (41 +)

Senescence
Adult (senile), "old age": No defined limit that would apply to all people; extremely variable; characterized by marked physiological and psychological deterioration

care can sometimes reverse the effects of a poor start in life (Bornstein & Tamis-LeMonda, 2001). In short, environmental forces guide human development, for better or worse, throughout life.

Sensitive Periods

Why do some experiences have more lasting effects than others? Part of the answer lies in **sensitive periods.** These are times when children are more sensitive to environmental influences. Events that occur during a sensitive period can permanently alter the course of development (Cynader, 1994). For instance, if a woman has German measles during early pregnancy, her child may be born with heart defects, cataracts, or hearing loss. Later in the pregnancy, the child would escape without damage.

Often, certain events must occur during a sensitive period for a person to develop normally. As we will see later, for instance, forming a loving bond with a caregiver early in life seems to be crucial for optimal development.

Sensitive period During development, a period of increased sensitivity to environmental influences. Also, a time during which certain events must take place for normal development to occur.

Prenatal Influences

The impact of nurture actually starts before birth. Although the **intrauterine environment** (interior of the womb) is highly protected, environmental conditions can affect the developing child. For example, when Olivia was pregnant, Amy's fetal heart rate and movements increased when loud sounds or vibrations penetrated the womb (Kisilevsky et al., 2004).

If Olivia's health or nutrition had been poor, or if she had contracted German measles, syphilis, or HIV, or used drugs, or was exposed to X-rays or atomic radiation, Amy might have been harmed. In such cases, babies can suffer from **congenital problems** or "birth defects." These problems affect the developing fetus and become apparent at birth. In contrast, **genetic disorders** are inherited from parents. Examples are sickle-cell anemia, hemophilia, cystic fibrosis, muscular dystrophy, albinism, and some forms of mental retardation.

How is it possible for the embryo or the fetus to be harmed? No direct intermixing of blood takes place between a mother and her unborn child. Yet, some substances—especially drugs—do reach the fetus. Anything capable of causing birth defects is called a **teratogen** (te-RAT-uh-jen). If the mother is addicted to morphine, heroin, or methadone, the baby may be born with an addiction. Repeated heavy drinking during pregnancy causes *fetal alcohol spectrum disorder (FASD)* (Connor et al., 2006). Affected infants are usually smaller than normal (and so are their brains), with distinct facial features and psychological characteristics that reflect brain dysfunction (Guerrini, Thompson, & Gurling, 2007). As they get older, most children with FASD catch up in height and weight, and their facial deformities diminish. However, the intellectual, academic, and behavioural deficits persist in varying degrees into adulthood (Guerrini et al., 2007). Behaviours such as poor judgment, distractibility, and lack of awareness of social cues are common (Schonfeld, Mattson, & Riley, 2005). In addition to illicit drugs and alcohol, some prescription drugs are not safe to take during pregnancy. For example, the antibiotic tetracycline can discolour the permanent teeth. In short, when a pregnant woman takes drugs, her unborn child does too.

Tobacco is also harmful. Tobacco smoking greatly reduces the oxygen supply to the fetus. Heavy smokers risk miscarrying or having premature, underweight babies who are more likely to die soon after birth (Cnattingius, 2004). Children of smoking mothers score lower on tests of language and mental ability (Huijbregts et al., 2006). In other words, an unborn child's future can go "up in smoke." That goes for marijuana as well (Viveros et al., 2005).

Deprivation and Enrichment

After a child is born, the effects of environment can be clearly seen when conditions of deprivation or enrichment exist. **Deprivation** refers to a lack of normal stimulation, nutrition, comfort, or love. **Enrichment** exists when an environment is deliberately made more complex and intellectually stimulating.

What happens when children suffer severe deprivation? Tragically, a few mistreated children have spent their first years in closets, attics, and other restricted environments. When first discovered, these children are usually mute, retarded, and emotionally damaged. Fortunately, such extreme deprivation is unusual. Nevertheless, milder levels of perceptual, intellectual, or emotional deprivation occur in many families, especially those that must cope with poverty. Poverty can affect the development of children in at least two ways (Sobolewski & Amato, 2005). First, poor parents may not be able to give their children needed resources, such as nutritious meals and access to health care or home computers and learning materials (Bradley & Corwyn, 2002). As a result, impoverished children tend to have more health problems, and they may lag in cognitive development and achievement at school. Second, the stresses of poverty can also be hard on parents, leading to marriage problems, less positive parenting, and poorer parent–child relationships. The resulting emotional turmoil can damage a child's socioemotional development. In the extreme, it may increase the risk of mental illness and delinquent behaviour (Bradley & Corwyn, 2002).

Can an enriched environment enhance development? To answer this question, psychologists have created enriched environments that are unusually novel, complex, and stimulating. Enriched environments may be the "soil" from which brighter children grow. To illustrate, let's begin with an experiment in which rats were raised in a sort of "rat wonderland." The walls of

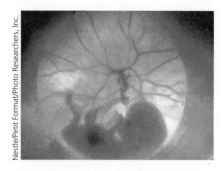

Nestle/Petit Format/Photo Researchers, Inc.

Due to the rapid growth of basic structures, the developing fetus is sensitive to a variety of diseases, drugs, and sources of radiation. This is especially true during the first trimester (three months) of gestation (pregnancy).

Intrauterine environment The physical and chemical environment within the uterus during prenatal development.

Congenital problems Problems or defects that originate during prenatal development in the womb.

Genetic disorders Problems caused by defects in the genes or by inherited characteristics.

Teratogen Radiation, a drug, or any other substance capable of altering fetal development in ways that cause birth defects.

Deprivation In development, the loss or withholding of normal stimulation, nutrition, comfort, love, and so forth; a condition of lacking.

Enrichment Deliberately making an environment more novel, complex, and perceptually or intellectually stimulating.

their cages were decorated with coloured patterns, and each cage was filled with platforms, ladders, and cubbyholes. When the rats reached adulthood, they were superior at learning mazes. In addition, they had larger, heavier brains, with a thicker cortex (Benloucif, Bennett, & Rosenzweig, 1995). Of course, it's a long leap from rats to people, but an actual increase in brain size is impressive. If stimulation can enhance the "intelligence" of a lowly rat, it seems reasonable to assume that human infants also benefit from enrichment. *Is there any evidence that this is actually the case?* Yes, many studies have shown that enriched environments improve abilities or enhance development. Tom and Olivia will be wise to nourish Amy's mind as well as her body (Beeber et al., 2007).

What can parents do to enrich a child's environment? Parents can encourage exploration through stimulating play and by paying attention to what holds a baby's interest. One of the simplest and most effective things a parent can do is to read to a child. Results from a long-term Canadian study (the National Longitudinal Study of Children and Youth) suggest that children whose parents read to them several times a day when they are two and three years old do better in kindergarten and Grade 1 than children who are not read to (Lipps & Yiptong-Avila, 1999).

There is also value in actively enriching sensory experiences. Babies should be surrounded by colours; music; people; and things to see, taste, smell, and touch. It makes perfect sense to take babies outside, to hang mobiles over their cribs, to place mirrors nearby, to play music for them, or to rearrange their rooms now and then. The presence of stimulating play materials in the home, together with responsive parents, is strongly related to how quickly children progress (Beeber et al., 2007)

Reciprocal Influences

Because of differences in temperament, some babies are more likely than others to smile, cry, vocalize, reach out, or pay attention. This means that babies rapidly become active participants in their own development. Growing infants alter their parents' behaviour at the same time as they are changed by it. For example, Amy is an easy baby who smiles frequently and is easily fed. This encourages Olivia to touch, feed, and sing to Amy. Olivia's affection rewards Amy, causing her to smile more. Soon, a dynamic relationship blossoms between mother and child. If Amy were a difficult baby who cried a lot and didn't like to be held, do you think a different dynamic relationship would blossom between mother and child? Difficult children make parents unhappy and elicit more negative parenting (Schoppe-Sullivan et al., 2007).

 STUDY BREAK   Heredity and Environment

Reflect

Do you think that heredity or environment best explains who you are today? Can you think of clear examples of the ways in which heredity and environmental forces have affected your development?

What kind of temperament did you have as an infant? How did it affect your relationship with your parents or caregivers?

What advice would you give a friend who has just become pregnant? Be sure to consider the prenatal environment and sensitive periods.

Learning Check

1. Areas of the DNA molecule called genes are made up of dominant and recessive chromosomes. T or F?
2. Most inherited characteristics can be described as polygenic. T or F?
3. Which of the following represents a correct sequence?

a. zygote, fetus, embryo, neonate, infant
b. zygote, embryo, neonate, fetus, infant
c. embryo, zygote, fetus, neonate, infant
d. zygote, embryo, fetus, neonate, infant

4. "Slow-to-warm-up" children can be described as restrained, unexpressive, or shy. T or F?
5. A _____ is a time of increased sensitivity to environmental influences.
6. As a child develops, there is a continuous _____ between the forces of heredity and environment.

Critical Thinking

7. Environmental influences can interact with hereditary programming in an exceedingly direct way. Can you guess what it is?

Answers

1. F 2. T 3. d 4. T 5. sensitive period 6. interaction 7. Environmental conditions sometimes turn specific genes on or off, thus directly affecting the expression of genetic tendencies (Gottlieb, 1998).

A person's **developmental level** is his or her current state of physical, emotional, and intellectual development. To summarize, three factors combine to determine your developmental level at any stage of life. These are heredity, environment, and your own behaviour, each tightly interwoven with the others.

THE NEWBORN BABY—THE BASIC MODEL COMES WITH OPTIONS

At birth the human **neonate** (NEE-oh-NATE: newborn infant) will die if not cared for by adults. Newborn babies cannot lift their heads, turn over, or feed themselves. Does this mean they are inert and unfeeling? Definitely not! Neonates like Amy can see, hear, smell, taste, and respond to pain and touch. Although their senses are less acute, babies are very responsive. Amy will follow a moving object with her eyes and will turn in the direction of sounds.

Newborn babies also have a number of adaptive reflexes (Siegler, DeLoache, & Eisenberg, 2006). To elicit the **grasping reflex,** press an object in the neonate's palm and he will grasp it with surprising strength. Many infants, in fact, can hang from a raised bar, like little trapeze artists. The grasping reflex aids survival by helping infants avoid falling. You can observe the **rooting reflex** (reflexive head turning and nursing) by touching Amy's cheek. Immediately, she will turn toward your finger and open her mouth, as if searching for something.

How is such turning adaptive? The rooting reflex helps infants find a breast. Then, when a nipple is placed in the infant's mouth, the **sucking reflex** (rhythmic nursing) helps him obtain needed food. Like other reflexes, this is a genetically programmed action (Koepke & Bigelow, 1997). At the same time, food rewards nursing by reducing the feeling of hunger. As a result, babies quickly learn to nurse more actively. Again, we see how nature–nurture interactions alter a baby's behaviour. Interestingly enough, some adults retain the rooting reflex, even though it is no longer adaptive.

The **Moro reflex** is also interesting. If Amy's position is changed abruptly or if she is startled by a loud noise, she will make a hugging motion. This reaction has been compared to the movements baby monkeys use to cling to their mothers.

The World of the Neonate

Thirty years ago, many people thought of newborn babies as mere bundles of reflexes, like the ones just described. But infants are capable of much more. Did you know, for example, that babies are born mimics (Meltzoff, 2005)? As early as 20 days old, babies will imitate adults opening their mouths, pursing their lips, or sticking out their tongues at them. And by nine months of age, infants can imitate actions a day after seeing them (Heimann & Meltzoff, 1996).

How intelligent are neonates? Babies are smarter than many people think. From the earliest days of life, babies seem to be trying to learn how the world works. They immediately begin to look at, touch, taste, and otherwise explore their surroundings. From an evolutionary perspective, a baby's mind is designed to soak up information at an amazing pace (Meltzoff & Prinz, 2002).

In the first months of life, babies are increasingly able to think, to learn from what they see, to make predictions, and to search for explanations. For example, Jerome Bruner (1983) observed that three- to eight-week-old babies seem to understand that a person's voice and body should be connected. If a baby hears his mother's voice coming from where she is standing, the baby will remain calm. If her voice comes from a loudspeaker about a metre away, the baby will become agitated and begin to cry.

Another look into the private world of infants can be drawn from testing their vision. However, such testing is a challenge because infants cannot talk.

A device called a **looking chamber** tells us what infants can see and what holds their attention. Imagine that Amy is placed on her back inside the chamber, facing a lighted area above. Next, two objects are placed in the chamber. By observing the movements of Amy's

<SURVEY QUESTION
What can newborn babies do?

Developmental level An individual's current state of physical, emotional, and intellectual development.

Neonate A term used for newborn infants during the first weeks following birth.

Grasping reflex A neonatal reflex consisting of grasping objects placed in the palms.

Rooting reflex A neonatal reflex elicited by a light touch to the cheek, causing the infant to turn toward the object and attempt to nurse.

Sucking reflex A neonatal reflex elicited by touching the mouth, whereupon the infant makes rhythmic sucking movements.

Moro reflex A neonatal reflex evoked by a sudden loss of support or the sounding of a loud noise; in response, the arms are extended and then brought toward each other.

Looking chamber An experimental apparatus used to test infant perception by presenting visual stimuli and observing infant responses.

Newborn babies display a special interest in the human face. A preference for seeing their mother's face develops rapidly and encourages social interactions between mother and baby.

Maturation The physical growth and development of the body and nervous system.
Cephalocaudal From head to toe.
Proximodistal From the centre of the body to the extremities.
Readiness A condition that exists when maturation has advanced enough to allow the rapid acquisition of a particular skill.

eyes and the images they reflect, we can tell what she is looking at. Such tests show that adult vision is about 30 times as sharp, but babies can see large patterns, shapes, and edges.

Robert Fantz found that three-day-old babies prefer complex patterns, such as checkerboards and bull's-eyes, to simpler coloured rectangles. Other researchers have learned that infants are excited by circles, curves, and bright lights (Brown, 1990). Immediately after birth, Amy will be aware of changes in the position of objects (Slater et al., 1991). When she is six months old, she will be able to recognize categories of objects that differ in shape or colour. By nine months of age she will be able to tell the difference between dogs and birds or other groups of animals (Mandler & McDonough, 1998), and by one year, Amy will see as well as her parents (Sigelman & Rider, 2009).

Neonates can most clearly see objects about 18–23 cm away from them (Kellman & Arterberry 2006). It is as if they are best prepared to see the people who love and care for them (Gopnik et al., 2000). Perhaps that's why babies have a special fascination with human faces. Just hours after they are born, babies begin to prefer seeing their mother's face, rather than a stranger's (Walton, Bower, & Bower, 1992). And just a few days after birth, babies will pay more attention to a person who is gazing directly at them, rather than one who is looking away (Farroni et al., 2004).

In a looking chamber, most infants will spend more time looking at a human face pattern than a face with the features mixed up or a coloured oval. When real human faces are used, infants prefer familiar faces to unfamiliar faces. However, this reverses at about age two. At that time, unusual objects begin to interest the child. For instance, Jerome Kagan (1971) showed face masks to two-year-olds. Kagan found that the toddlers were fascinated by a face with eyes on the chin and a nose in the middle of the forehead. He believes the babies' interest came from a need to understand why the scrambled face differed from what they had come to expect. Such behaviour is further evidence that babies actively try to make sense of their surroundings (Gopnik et al., 2000).

Maturation

SURVEY QUESTION>
What is maturation? What influence does maturation have on a child's early development?

The emergence of many basic abilities is closely tied to **maturation** (physical growth and development of the body, brain, and nervous system). Maturation will be especially evident as Amy learns motor skills, such as crawling and walking. Of course, the rate of maturation varies from child to child. Nevertheless, the order of maturation is almost universal. For instance, Amy will be able to sit without support before she has matured enough to crawl. Indeed, infants around the world typically sit before they crawl, crawl before they stand, and stand before they walk (see Figure 3.3).

1. Fetal posture (newborn)
2. Holds chin up (1 month)
3. Holds chest up (2 months)
4. Sits when supported (4 months)
5. Sits alone (7 months)
6. Stands holding furniture (9 months)
7. Crawls (10 months)
8. Walks if led (11 months)
9. Stands alone (11 months)
10. Walks alone (12 months)

▶▶**FIGURE 3.3** Motor development. Most infants follow an orderly pattern of motor development. Although the order in which children progress is similar, there are large individual differences in the ages at which each ability appears. The ages listed are averages for North American children. It is not unusual for many of the skills to appear one or two months earlier than average or several months later. Parents should not be alarmed if a child's behaviour differs somewhat from the average.

What about my cousin Emo, who never crawled? Like cousin Emo, a few children substitute rolling, creeping, or shuffling for crawling. A very few move directly from sitting to standing and walking. Even so, an orderly sequence of motor development remains evident. In general, increased muscular control spreads in a pattern that is **cephalocaudal** (SEF-eh-lo-KOD-ul: from head to toe) and **proximodistal** (PROK-seh-moe-DIS-tul: from the centre of the body to the extremities). That is, a baby gains control of head and neck muscles before he can control his legs and feet. Even if cousin Emo flunked Elementary Crawling, his motor development followed the standard top-down, centre-outward pattern (Piek, 2006).

Motor Development

While maturation has a big impact, motor skills don't simply "emerge." Amy must learn to control her actions. Babies who are trying to crawl or walk actively try out new movements and select those that work. Amy's first efforts may be flawed—a wobbly crawl ending in a belly flop or some shaky first steps. However, with practice, babies "tune" their movements to be smoother and more effective. Such learning is evident from the very first months of life (Piek, 2006; Thelen, 2000). (See Figure 3.4.)

Readiness

At what ages will Amy be ready to feed herself, walk alone, or say goodbye to diapers? Such milestones tend to be governed by a child's **readiness** for rapid learning. That is, minimum levels of maturation must occur before some skills can be learned. It is impossible, for instance, to teach children to walk or use a toilet before they have matured enough to control their bodies. Parents are asking for failure when they try to force a child to learn skills too early.

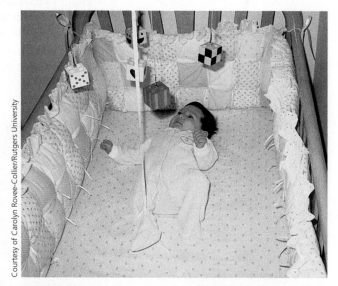

Courtesy of Carolyn Rovee-Collier/Rutgers University

▶▶**FIGURE 3.4** Psychologist Carolyn Rovee-Collier has shown that babies as young as three months old can learn to control their movements. In her experiments, babies lie on their backs under a colourful crib mobile. A ribbon is tied around the baby's ankle and connected to the mobile. Whenever babies spontaneously kick their legs, the mobile jiggles and rattles. Within a few minutes, infants learn to kick faster. Their reward for kicking is a chance to see the mobile move (Hayne & Rovee-Collier, 1995).

Basic emotions The first distinct emotions to emerge in infancy.

Social smile Smiling elicited by social stimuli, such as seeing a parent's face.

Much needless grief can be avoided by respecting a child's personal rate of growth. Consider the eager parents who toilet trained an 18-month-old child in 10 trying weeks of false alarms and "accidents." If they had waited until the child was 24 months old, they might have succeeded in just three weeks with far less effort. Parents may control when toilet training starts, but maturation tends to dictate when it will be completed (Schum et al., 2002). Most Canadian parents toilet train their children between 2 and 3 (Rathus & Longmuir, 2012)

Emotional Development

Early emotional development also follows a pattern closely tied to maturation (Panksepp & Pasqualini, 2005). Even the **basic emotions** of anger, fear, and joy—which appear to be unlearned—take time to develop. General excitement is the only emotion newborn infants clearly express. Researchers do not agree on whether newborns are born with specific emotions (Soussignan & Schall, 2005). However, as Tom and Olivia can tell you, a baby's emotional life blossoms rapidly. One researcher (Bridges, 1932) observed that all the basic human emotions appear before age two. Katharine Bridges found that emotions appear in a consistent order and that the first basic split is between pleasant and unpleasant.

Experts do not yet agree on how quickly emotions unfold (Oster, 2005). For example, psychologist Carroll Izard thinks that infants can express several basic emotions as early as 10 weeks of age. When Izard looks carefully at the faces of babies, he sees abundant signs of emotion (see Figure 3.5). The most common infant expression, he found, is not excitement, but *interest*—followed by *joy, anger,* and *sadness* (Izard et al., 1995).

If Izard is right, then emotions are "hard-wired" by heredity and related to evolution. Perhaps that's why smiling is one of a baby's most common reactions. Smiling probably helps babies survive by inviting parents to care for them (Izard et al., 1995).

At first, a baby's smiling is haphazard. By two to three months, however, infants smile more frequently when another person is nearby (Rathus & Langmuir, 2012). This **social smile** is especially rewarding to parents. On the other hand, when new parents see and hear a crying baby, they feel annoyed, irritated, disturbed, or unhappy. Babies the world over, it seems, rapidly become capable of letting others know what they like and dislike.

Human infants are transformed from helpless babies to independent persons with dazzling speed. Early growth is extremely rapid. By her third year, Amy will have her own unique personality, and she will be able to stand, walk, talk, and explore. At no other time after birth does development proceed more rapidly. During the same period, Amy's relationships with other people will expand as well. Before we explore that topic, here's a chance to rehearse what you've learned.

| Interest | Joy | Anger | Sadness |

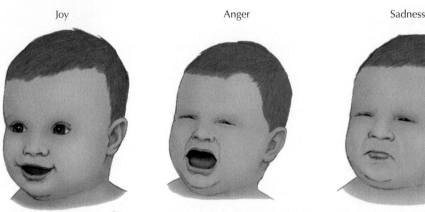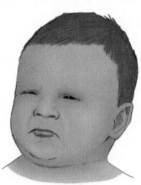

▸▸**FIGURE 3.5** Infants display many of the same emotional expressions as adults do. Carroll Izard believes such expressions show that distinct emotions appear within the first months of life. Other theorists argue that specific emotions come into focus more gradually, as an infant's nervous system matures. Either way, parents can expect to see a full range of basic emotions by the end of a baby's first year. Over the first two years, children become increasingly active in initiating emotional exchanges with parents (Grolnick, Cosgrove, & Bridges, 1996).

STUDY BREAK   The Neonate and Maturation

Reflect

What infant reflexes have you observed? How would maturation affect the chances of teaching an infant to eat with a spoon? Can you give an example of how heredity and environment interact during motor development?

    To know what a baby is feeling, would it be more helpful to be able to detect delight and distress (Bridges) or joy, anger, and sadness (Izard)?

Learning Check

1. If an infant is startled, he or she will make movements similar to an embrace. This is known as the
   a. grasping reflex   b. rooting reflex
   c. Moro reflex   d. adaptive reflex
2. During infancy, a capacity for imitating others first becomes evident at about nine months of age. T or F?

3. After age two, infants tested in a looking chamber show a marked preference for familiar faces and simpler designs. T or F?
4. The orderly sequence observed in the unfolding of many basic responses can be attributed to _____.
5. General excitement or interest is the clearest emotional response present in newborn infants, but meaningful expressions of delight and distress appear soon after. T or F?
6. Neonates display a social smile as early as 10 days after birth. T or F?

Critical Thinking

7. If you were going to test newborn infants to see if they prefer their own mother's face to that of a stranger, what precautions would you take?

Answers: 1. c 2. F 3. F 4. maturation 5. T 6. F 7. In one study of the preferences of newborns, the hair colour and complexion of strangers was matched to that of the mothers. Also, only the mother's or stranger's face was visible during testing. And, finally, a scent was used to mask olfactory (smell) cues so that an infant's preference could not be based on the mother's familiar odour (Bushnell, Sai, & Mullin, 1989).

SOCIAL DEVELOPMENT—BABY, I'M STUCK ON YOU

Like all humans, babies are social creatures. Their early **social development** lays a foundation for relationships with parents, siblings, friends, and relatives (Shaffer & Kipp, 2010). A first basic step into the social world involves becoming aware of oneself as a separate person. When you look in a mirror, you recognize the image staring back as your own—except, perhaps, early on Monday mornings. Would Amy recognize herself at age one? At age two? Like many such events, initial **self-awareness** depends on maturation of the nervous system. Most infants are 18 months old before they recognize themselves (Nielsen & Dissanayake, 2004).

Attachment

The real core of social development is found in the **emotional attachment,** or close emotional bond, that human babies form with their **primary caregivers.** There is a sensitive period (roughly the first year of life) during which this must occur for optimal development. Returning to Amy's story, we find that attachment keeps her close to Olivia, who provides safety, stimulation, and a secure "home base" from which Amy can go exploring.

    Mothers usually begin to cultivate a parent–child bond within hours of giving birth. For example, they touch their own infants more and hold them closer than they do other babies (Kaitz et al., 1995). For their part, as babies mature, they become more and more capable of bonding with their mothers. For the first few months, babies respond more or less equally to everyone. By two or three months, most babies prefer their mothers to strangers. By around seven months, babies generally become truly attached to their mothers, crawling after them if they can. Shortly thereafter, they begin to form attachments to other people as well, such as father, grandparents, or siblings (Sigelman & Rider, 2009).

    A direct sign that an emotional bond has formed appears around 8 to 12 months of age. At that time Amy will display **separation anxiety** (crying and signs of fear) when she is left alone or left with a stranger. (Mild separation anxiety is normal. When it is more intense, it may reveal a problem. See Clinical File: "Beyond Homesickness" for details.) You may have heard that bonding

<SURVEY QUESTION
Why is the emotional bond between parent and child so important?

Social development The development of self-awareness, attachment to parents or caregivers, and relationships with other children and adults.

Self-awareness Consciousness of oneself as a person.

Emotional attachment An especially close emotional bond that infants form with their parents, caregivers, or others.

Primary caregiver The person primarily responsible for the care of an infant; usually the infant's mother or father.

Separation anxiety Distress displayed by infants when they are separated from their parents or principal caregivers.

Chris Lowe/Index Stock Imagery

A sense of self, or self-awareness, develops gradually up until about age 18 months. Psychologists have devised some ingenious methods to assess infant self-awareness. A dot of red lipstick is placed on the child's nose and she is placed in front of a mirror. Not until the age of 18 months do most infants begin to touch their own noses when looking in the mirror (Keller et al., 2005). Before children develop self-awareness, they do not recognize their own image in a mirror. Typically, they think they are looking at another child. Some children try to hug the child in the mirror or go behind it looking for the child they see there (Lewis, 1995).

Secure attachment A type of attachment characterized by mild distress at leave-taking and being readily soothed at reunion with the parent or caregiver.

Avoidant attachment A form of insecure attachment characterized by indifference to both leave-taking and reunion with the parent or caregiver.

Ambivalent/resistant attachment A type of insecure attachment characterized by severe distress on leave-taking coupled with ambivalent behaviour at reunion.

is especially powerful during the first few hours after birth (Klaus & Kennell, 1982). However, careful studies have generally failed to support a "superglue" version of the bonding concept. While long-term infant attachments are a reality, "instant bonding" appears to be a myth (Eyer, 1994). Ultimately, it is more important that secure attachment occur than *when* it occurs.

Attachment Quality

Canadian psychologist Mary Ainsworth believed the quality of attachment is revealed by how babies act when their mothers return after a brief separation. She noted two patterns of attachment—secure and insecure attachment. Infants who are **securely attached** have a stable and positive emotional bond. They are upset by the mother's absence and seek to be near her when she returns. There are two major types of insecure attachment—avoidant attachment and ambivalent/resistant attachment. **Avoidant attachment** infants tend to show the least distress when the mother is absent. They appear to be indifferent to leave-takings and tend to ignore the mother when she returns. **Ambivalent/resistant** babies are the most emotional. They show severe signs of distress when their mothers leave and are ambivalent when they return, alternately clinging to their mothers and pushing them away (Rathus & Longmuir, 2012).

Attachment can have lasting effects. Infants who are securely attached at the age of one year show more resiliency, curiosity, problem-solving ability, and social competence in preschool (Collins & Gunnar, 1990). In contrast, attachment failures can be quite damaging. Consider, for example, the plight of children raised in severely overcrowded Romanian orphanages and later adopted by Canadian families. These children got almost no attention from adults for at least the first eight months of their lives. Psychologist Kim Chisholm and her colleagues followed many of these children for several years. Many were poorly attached to their new parents. Some, for instance, readily wandered off with strangers (Chisholm et al., 1995). She also found that parents reported more behaviour problems in their adopted children (Chisholm, 1998). In short, for some children, the lack of affection early in life may leave long-lasting emotional scars (O'Conner et al., 2003).

Attachment is related to the quality of infant care (Belsky, 2006). Parents of secure infants are more affectionate, cooperative, and predictable than parents of insecure infants and respond more sensitively to their infants' smiles and cries (Harel & Scher, 2003). Poor attachment is seen when a parent's actions are inappropriate, inadequate, intrusive, over-stimulating, or rejecting. An example is the mother who tries to play with a drowsy infant or who ignores a baby who is looking at her and vocalizing. And the link between sensitive caregiving and secure attachment appears to apply across cultures (Posada et al., 2002).

THE CLINICAL FILE

Beyond Homesickness

Anyone who's ever worked at a sleep-away camp knows the look: Sad-eyed, anxious, and forlorn, a homesick child is easy to spot. But such distress can be more serious than the "summer-camp blues." At some point in their lives, about 12 percent of all children suffer from *separation anxiety disorder (SAD)*. Separation anxiety peaks at three ages—five to six, seven to nine, and 12 to 14 years (Rathus & Longmuir, 2012). These children are miserable when they are separated from their parents, whom they cling to or constantly follow. Some fear that they will get lost and never see their parents again. They are reluctant to leave home, sleep over at a friend's house, or go on errands. Seventy-five percent refuse to go to school, which can be a serious handicap.

What causes separation anxiety disorder? Some children are more vulnerable to the disorder, indicating a genetic component (Cronk et al., 2005). As you might expect, environmental stressors also play a role. The problem may begin after a child faces such stresses as illness, the death of a relative or pet, moving to a new neighbourhood, or changing schools. Whatever the triggering event, separation anxiety should not be ignored. It can seriously impair emotional development. If separation anxiety is intense or lasts for more than a month, parents should seek professional help for their child (Masi, Mucci, & Millepiedi, 2001).

What about attachment to fathers? Fathers of securely attached infants tend to be outgoing, agreeable, and happy in their marriage. The more affectionate the interaction between father and infant, the stronger the attachment (Thompson, Easterbrooks, & Padilla-Walker, 2003). In general, children who grow up in a warm family atmosphere are likely to have fewer problems later in childhood and adolescence (Belsky, 1996; Gomez & McLaren, 2007; Pougnet et al., 2011).

As you can see, a baby's **affectional needs** (needs for love and affection) are every bit as important as more obvious needs for food, water, and physical care. Parents are sometimes afraid of "spoiling" babies with too much attention or affection. However, for the first year or two this is nearly impossible (Konner, 1991). As a matter of fact, a later capacity to experience warm and loving relationships may depend on it.

Daycare

Does commercial child care interfere with the quality of attachment? A study by the late Margaret McKim of the University of Saskatchewan looked at the effects of daycare on attachment in 189 infants and toddlers. High-quality daycare did not adversely affect attachment to parents. In fact, attachment seems to be more dependent on the child's temperament and the mother's sensitivity than on the kind of care the child receives (McKim et al., 1999). Children receiving high-quality daycare also have better cognitive skills and language abilities (Burchinal et al., 2000). A long-term Canadian study (the National Longitudinal Survey of Children and Youth) found that 40 percent of kindergarten children who attended early childhood programs or daycare centres were judged by their teachers to be near the top of their class, compared with 24 percent of children who stayed at home with a parent (Lipps & Yiptong-Avila, 1999).

Thus, high-quality daycare can actually improve children's social and mental skills (Scarr, 1998; Geoffroy et al., 2010). However, all the positive effects just noted are reversed for low-quality daycare. One study of 155 four- and five-year-old children attending daycare centres in Montreal found that while children in high-quality centres showed positive effects, those in low-quality centres showed increased anger and defiance (Hausfather et al., 1997). If they have a choice, parents should carefully evaluate and monitor the quality of daycare their children are receiving (Barnet & Barnet, 1998). Poor-quality daycare can actually create behaviour problems that didn't exist beforehand (Pierrehumbert et al., 2002).

What should parents look for when they evaluate the quality of child care? Low-quality daycare is risky because it may weaken attachment. Parents seeking quality should look for at least (1) a small number of children per caregiver, (2) small overall group size (12 to 15), (3) trained caregivers, (4) minimal staff turnover, and (5) a stable daycare experience (Howes, 1997). (Also, avoid any daycare centre with the word *zoo, menagerie,* or *stockade* in its name.)

Play and Social Skills

A chance to **play** with other children is one of the side benefits of daycare. For instance, in one corner, a two-year-old stacks coloured blocks, pounds on them with a toy truck, and then chews on the truck. On the other side of the room some five-year-olds have built a "store" out of cardboard boxes. For the next half hour, one child is the "owner" and the others are "customers." With just three years' difference in age, we see a dramatic change in how children play.

Naturally, play is fun for children. However, it's also serious business. Children use play to explore the world and to practise skills—especially social skills. By the time children are 4 or 5, they will have progressed from **solitary play** (playing alone) to **cooperative play** (in which two or more children must coordinate their actions). Children engaged in cooperative play take parts or play roles, follow rules, and lead or follow others. Playing this way helps them learn to handle cooperation and competition, conflicts, power, role taking, and communication.

Mary D. Salter Ainsworth, 1913–1999. One of the most influential developmental psychologists of the 20th century, Mary Ainsworth earned a Ph.D. from the University of Toronto in 1939. A major in the Canadian Army during World War II, she spent two years as the superintendent of Women's Rehabilitation for the Department of Veterans Affairs. After the war, she returned to the University of Toronto as an assistant professor. In 1950, she went to England to work with John Bowlby, and then in 1954 to Uganda, where she studied infant–mother attachment. She received the G. Stanley Hall Award for her contributions to developmental psychology in 1984.

Affectional needs Emotional needs for love and affection.

Play Any activity done for sheer enjoyment.

Solitary play Playing alone.

Cooperative play Play in which two or more children must coordinate their actions; if children don't cooperate, the game ends.

STUDY BREAK Social Development

Reflect

Think of a child you know who seems to be securely attached and one who seems to be insecurely attached. How do the children differ? Do their parents treat them differently?

Do you think you were securely or insecurely attached as a child? Are there any parallels in your relationships today?

Learning Check

1. Clear signs of self-awareness or self-recognition are evident in most infants by the time they reach eight months of age. T or F?
2. The development of separation anxiety in an infant corresponds to the formation of an attachment to parents. T or F?

3. In Mary Ainsworth's system for rating the quality of attachment, secure attachment is revealed by a lack of distress when an infant is left alone with a stranger. T or F?
4. Children usually play in small groups before they have developed enough confidence to play alone (solitary play). T or F?

Critical Thinking

5. Can emotional bonding begin before birth?
6. Attachment quality is usually attributed to the behaviour of parents or caregivers. How might infants contribute to the quality of attachment?

Answers

1. F 2. T 3. F 4. F 5. It certainly can for parents. When a pregnant woman begins to feel fetal movements, she becomes acutely aware that a baby is coming to life inside her. Likewise, prospective parents who hear a fetal heartbeat at the doctor's office or see an ultrasound image of the fetus begin to become emotionally attached to the unborn child (Konner, 1991). 6. An infant's behaviour patterns, temperament, and emotional style may greatly influence parents' behaviour. As a result, infants can affect attachment as much as parents do (Oatley & Jenkins, 1992).

Cooperative play is a big step toward participating in social life. It's easy for adults to dismiss play as silly or trivial. However, play is one of the most important activities of childhood (Kaplan, 1998).

PARENTING STYLES

SURVEY QUESTION>
What are parenting styles? How important are different parenting styles to a child's development?

Parents have different approaches to rearing their children. Researchers of parental patterns of child-rearing have found it useful to classify them according to two broad dimensions: warmth–coldness and restrictiveness–permissiveness (Baumrind, 2005). Warm parents are less likely to use physical discipline than cold parents (Bender et al., 2007). Cold parents may not enjoy their children and may have few feelings of affection for them. They are likely to complain about their children's behaviour, saying that they are "bad." Children of warm and accepting parents are more likely to develop internal standards of behaviour (Bender et al., 2007). Parental warmth is also related to a child's social and emotional well-being (Lau et al., 2006).

Psychologist Diana Baumrind (1991; 2005) has studied the effects of three major styles of parenting. See if you recognize the styles she describes.

Authoritarian parents enforce rigid rules and demand strict obedience to authority. Typically, they view children as having few rights but adultlike responsibilities. The child is expected to stay out of trouble and to accept, without question, what parents regard as right or wrong. ("Do it because I say so.") The children of authoritarian parents are usually obedient and self-controlled. But they also tend to be emotionally stiff, withdrawn, apprehensive, and lacking in curiosity. One 22-year-long study found that children whose parents are critical, harsh, or authoritarian often become self-absorbed adults. They also have higher rates of violence and drug abuse (Dubow, Huesmann, & Eron, 1987; Weiss et al., 1992).

Overly permissive parents give little guidance, allow too much freedom, or don't hold children accountable for their actions. Typically, the child has rights similar to an adult's but few responsibilities. Rules are not enforced, and the child usually gets his or her way. ("Do whatever you want.") Permissive parents tend to produce dependent, immature children who misbehave frequently. Such children are aimless and likely to "run amok."

Authoritarian parents Parents who enforce rigid rules and demand strict obedience to authority.

Overly permissive parents Parents who give little guidance, allow too much freedom, or do not require the child to take responsibility.

Baumrind describes **authoritative parents** as those who supply firm and consistent guidance, combined with love and affection. Such parents balance their own rights with those of their children. They control their children's behaviour in a caring, responsive, non-authoritarian way. ("Do it for this reason.") This style produces children who are *resilient* (good at bouncing back after bad experiences) and develop the strengths they need to thrive even in difficult circumstances (Kim-Cohen et al., 2004; Masten, 2001). The children of authoritative parents are competent, self-controlled, independent, assertive, and inquiring. They know how to manage their emotions and use positive coping skills (Eisenberg, Geller, & Schmidt, 2003; Lynch et al., 2004).

Effects of Child Discipline

When parents fail to provide **discipline** (guidance regarding acceptable behaviour), children become antisocial, aggressive, and insecure. Effective discipline is fair but loving, authoritative yet sensitive. It socializes a child without destroying the bond of love and trust between parent and child.

Types of Discipline

Parents typically discipline children in one of three ways. **Power assertion** refers to physical punishment or a show of force, such as taking away toys or privileges (see Chapter 6, page 244, for more on punishment). As an alternative, some parents use **withdrawal of love** (withholding affection) by refusing to speak to a child, by threatening to leave, by rejecting the child, or by otherwise acting as if the child is temporarily unlovable. **Management techniques** combine praise, recognition, approval, rules, reasoning, and the like to encourage desirable behaviour. Each of these approaches can control a child's behaviour, but their side effects differ considerably.

What are the side effects? Power-oriented techniques—particularly harsh or severe physical punishment—are associated with fear, hatred of parents, and a lack of spontaneity and warmth. Severely punished children also tend to be defiant, rebellious, and aggressive (Patterson, 1982). Despite its drawbacks, power assertion is the most popular mode of discipline (Papps et al., 1995).

Withdrawal of love produces children who tend to be self-disciplined. You could say that such children have developed a good conscience. Often, they are described as "model" children or as unusually "good." But as a side effect, they are also frequently anxious, insecure, and dependent on adults for approval.

Management techniques also have limitations. Most important is the need to carefully adjust to a child's level of understanding. Younger children don't always see the connection between rules, explanations, and their own behaviour. Nevertheless, management techniques receive a big plus in another area. Psychologist Stanley Coopersmith (1968) found a direct connection between discipline and a child's self-esteem.

Self-Esteem

If you regard yourself as a worthwhile person, you have **self-esteem.** High self-esteem is essential for emotional health. Individuals with low self-esteem don't think much of themselves as people. In elementary school, children with high self-esteem tend to be more popular, cooperative, and successful in class. Children with low self-esteem are more withdrawn and tend to perform below average (Amato & Fowler, 2002).

How does discipline affect self-esteem? Coopersmith found that low self-esteem is related to physical punishment and the withholding of love. And why not? What message do children receive if a parent beats them or tells them they are not worthy of love?

Thus, it is best to minimize physical punishment and avoid unnecessary withdrawal of love. High self-esteem, on the other hand, is promoted by management techniques. Children who feel that their parents support them emotionally tend to have high self-esteem (Amato & Fowler, 2002; Nielsen & Metha, 1994).

Authoritative parents Parents who supply firm and consistent guidance combined with love and affection.

Discipline A framework of guidelines for acceptable behaviour.

Power assertion The use of physical punishment or coercion to enforce child discipline.

Withdrawal of love Withholding affection to enforce child discipline.

Management techniques Combining praise, recognition, approval, rules, and reasoning to enforce child discipline.

Self-esteem Regarding oneself as a worthwhile person; a positive evaluation of oneself.

Courtesy George Brown College

Fathering typically makes a contribution to early development that differs in emphasis from mothering.

Maternal and Paternal Influences

Don't mothers and fathers parent differently? Yes. Although **maternal influences** (all the effects a mother has on her child) generally have a greater impact, fathers do make a unique contribution to parenting. Although fathers are spending more and more time with their children, mothers still do most of the nurturing and caretaking, especially of young children (Craig, 2006).

Studies of **paternal influences** (the sum of all effects a father has on his child) find that fathers are more likely to play with their children and tell them stories. In contrast, mothers are typically responsible for the physical and emotional care of their children (Craig, 2006).

It might seem that the father's role as a playmate makes him less important. Not so. From birth onward, fathers pay more visual attention to children than mothers do. Fathers are much more tactile (lifting, tickling, and handling the baby); more physically arousing (engaging in rough-and-tumble play); and more likely to engage in unusual play (imitating the baby, for example) (Crawley & Sherrod, 1984; Paquette et al., 2003). In comparison, mothers speak to infants more; play more conventional games (such as peek-a-boo); and, as noted, spend much more time in caregiving. Amy's playtime with Tom is actually very valuable. Young children who spend a lot of time playing with their fathers tend to be more competent in many ways (Tamis-LeMonda et al., 2004).

Overall, fathers can be as affectionate, sensitive, and responsive as mothers are. Nevertheless, infants tend to get very different views of males and females. Females, who offer comfort, nurturance, and verbal stimulation, tend to be close at hand. Males may come and go, and when they are present, action, exploration, and risk-taking prevail. It's no wonder, then, that the caregiving styles of mothers and fathers have a major impact on children's sex role development (Lindsay, Mize, & Pettit, 1997; Videon, 2005).

Culture

Do ethnic differences in parenting affect children in distinctive ways? Diana Baumrind's work provides a good overall summary of the effects of parenting. However, her conclusions are probably most valid for families whose roots lie in Europe. Child-rearing in other ethnic groups often reflects different customs and beliefs. For example, Asian and South Asian cultures value interdependence, conformity to social norms, filial piety (respect for one's parents and ancestors), and deference to parental authority (Shariff, 2009; Yoo & Miller, 2011). Emotional restraint is important, and parents, especially fathers, are discouraged from expressing emotions toward their children. Rather, parents demonstrate their care and concern by teaching their children to behave in morally and socially acceptable ways. Children are expected to respect, honour, and obey their parents absolutely (Yoo & Miller, 2011). Middle Eastern cultures expect children to be polite, obedient to authority, disciplined, and conforming. Fathers tend to be strong authority figures who demand absolute obedience so that the family will not be shamed by a child's unacceptable behaviour. Family honour is paramount. Children are raised to respect their parents, older relatives, and other adults (Erickson & Al-Timimi, 2001). Cultural differences are especially apparent with respect to the meaning attached to a child's behaviour. Is a particular behaviour "good" or "bad"? Should it be encouraged or discouraged? The answer will depend greatly on parents' cultural values (Rubin, 1998; Leyendecker et al., 2005).

To sum up, child-rearing is done in a remarkable variety of ways around the world. In fact, many of the things we do in North America, such as forcing young children to sleep alone, would be considered odd or wrong in other cultures. In the final analysis, parenting can only be judged if we know what culture or ethnic community a child is being prepared to enter (Leyendecker et al., 2005).

Maternal influences The total of all psychological effects mothers have on their children.

Paternal influences The aggregate of all psychological effects fathers have on their children.

LANGUAGE DEVELOPMENT—FAST-TALKING BABIES

There's something almost miraculous about a baby's first words. As infants, how did we manage to leap into the world of language? As will soon be apparent, social development provides a foundation for language learning. But before we probe that connection, let's begin with a quick survey of language development.

<SURVEY QUESTION
How do children acquire language?

Language Acquisition

Language development is closely tied to maturation. As every parent knows, babies can cry from birth on. By one month of age, they use crying to gain attention. Typically, parents can tell if an infant is hungry, angry, or in pain from the tone of the crying (Kaplan, 1998). Around six to eight weeks of age, babies begin **cooing** (the repetition of vowel sounds like "oo" and "ah"). Crying and cooing are innate but can be modified by experience (Volterra et al., 2004). Cooing increases as parents respond by smiling and imitating their infants.

By seven months of age, Amy's nervous system will mature enough to allow her to grasp objects, smile, laugh, sit up, and **babble.** In the babbling stage, the consonants *b, d, m,* and *g* are combined with the vowel sounds to produce meaningless language sounds: *dadadadada* or *babababa*. As the infant babbles, parents will often repeat the syllables produced. This repetition apparently helps infants discriminate these sounds from others and encourages them to imitate their parents (Elkind, 2007; Tamis-LeMonda et al., 2004). At first, babbling is the same around the world. But soon, the language spoken by parents begins to have an influence. That is, Chinese babies start to babble in a way that sounds like Chinese, Mexican babies babble in Spanish-like sounds, and so forth (Gopnik, Meltzoff, & Kuhl, 2000). Babbling is not limited to hearing babies making sounds. Deaf (and hearing) infants of deaf parents who learn sign language as their first language make hand gestures that are the manual equivalent of babbling (Petitto & Marentette, 1991).

At about one year of age, children can stand alone for a short time and respond to real words such as *no* and *hi*. Soon afterward, the first connection between words and objects forms, and children may address their parents as "Mama" or "Dada." At any given time,

Cooing Spontaneous repetition of vowel sounds by infants.

Babbling The repetition by infants of meaningless language sounds (including both vowel and consonant sounds).

children understand more words than they can use. For example, one study found that one-year-olds could speak an average of 13 words but understood the meaning of 84 (Tamis-LeMonda et al., 2004). By age 18 months to two years, Amy will have learned to stand and walk alone; her vocabulary may include from 24 to 200 words. At first, there is a **single-word stage,** during which children use one word at a time, such as "go," "juice," or "up." Soon after, words are arranged in simple two-word sentences called **telegraphic speech:** "Want-Teddy," "Mama-gone."

Language and the Terrible Twos

At about the same time that children begin to put two or three words together, they become much more independent. Two-year-olds understand some of the commands parents make, but they are not always willing to carry them out. Amy may assert her independence by saying "No drink," "Me do it," and the like. It can be worse, of course. A two-year-old may look at you intently, make eye contact, listen as you shout "No, no," and still pour her juice on the cat.

During their second year, children become increasingly capable of mischief and temper tantrums (Kaplan, 1998). Thus, calling this time "the terrible twos" is not entirely inappropriate. One-year-olds can do plenty of things parents don't want them to do. However, it's usually two-year-olds who do things *because* you don't want them to (Gopnik, Meltzoff, & Kuhl, 2000).

After age two, the child's comprehension and use of words take a dramatic leap forward (Fernald, Perfors, & Marchman, 2006). From this point on, vocabulary and language skills grow at a phenomenal rate. By Grade 1, Amy will be able to understand around 8000 words and use about 4000. She will have truly entered the world of language.

The Roots of Language

What accounts for this explosion of language development? One possibility is that language recognition is innate. Linguist Noam Chomsky (1975, 1986) has long claimed that humans have a **biological predisposition,** or hereditary readiness, to develop language. According to Chomsky, language patterns are inborn, much like a child's ability to coordinate walking. If such inborn language recognition does exist, it may explain why children around the world use a limited number of patterns in their first sentences. Typical patterns include these (Mussen et al., 1979):

Identification:	"See kitty."
Non-existence:	"Allgone milk."
Possession:	"My doll."
Agent-action:	"Mama give."
Negation:	"Not ball."
Question:	"Where doggie?"

Does Chomsky's theory explain why language develops so rapidly? Perhaps. But many psychologists feel that Chomsky underestimates the importance of learning (Tomasello, 2003). **Psycholinguists** (specialists in the psychology of language) have shown that language is not magically "switched on" by adult speech. Imitation of adults and rewards for correctly using words (as when a child asks for a cookie) are an important part of language learning. Also, babies actively participate in language learning by asking questions, such as "What dis?" (Domingo & Goldstein-Alpern, 1999).

"All right now, give Mommy the super-glue."

Single-word stage In language development, the period during which a child begins to use single words.

Telegraphic speech In language development, the formation of simple, two-word sentences that "telegraph" (communicate) a simple idea.

Biological predisposition The presumed hereditary readiness of humans to learn certain skills, such as how to use language, or a readiness to behave in particular ways.

Psycholinguist A specialist in the psychology of language and language development.

When a child makes a language error, parents typically repeat the child's sentence, with needed corrections (Bohannon & Stanowicz, 1988), or ask a clarifying question to draw the child's attention to the error (Saxton, Houston-Price, & Dawson, 2005). More important still is the fact that parents and children begin to communicate long before the child can speak. Months of shared effort precede a child's first word. From this point of view, an infant's "language dance" reflects a readiness to interact socially with parents, not innate language recognition. The next section explains why.

Early Communication

How do parents communicate with infants before they can talk? Parents go to a great deal of trouble to get babies to smile and vocalize (see Figure 3.6). In doing so, they quickly learn to change their actions to keep the infant's attention, arousal, and activity at optimal levels. A familiar example is the "I'm-Going-to-Get-You Game." In it, the adult says, "I'm gonna getcha. … I'm gonna getcha. … Gotcha!" Through such games, adults and babies come to share similar rhythms and expectations (Carroll, 2008). Soon a system of shared **signals** is created, including touching, vocalizing, gazing, and smiling. These help lay a foundation for later language use. Specifically, signals establish a pattern of "conversational" **turn-taking** (alternate sending and receiving of messages):

Olivia	Amy
	(smiles)
"Oh, what a nice little smile!"	
"Yes, isn't that nice?"	
"There."	
"There's a nice little smile."	(burps)
"Well, pardon you!"	
"Yes, that's better, isn't it?"	
"Yes."	(vocalizes)
"Yes."	(smiles)
"What's so funny?"	

From the outside, such exchanges may look meaningless. In reality, they represent real communication. Amy's vocalizations and attention enable her to interact emotionally with Olivia and Tom. Infants as young as four months engage in vocal turn-taking with adults (Jaffe et al., 2001). The more children interact with parents, the faster they learn to talk and develop thinking abilities (Dickinson & Tabors, 2001). Unmistakably, social relationships contribute to early language learning.

Signal In early language development, any behaviour, such as touching, vocalizing, gazing, or smiling, that allows non-verbal interaction and turn-taking between parent and child.

Turn-taking In early language development, the tendency of parent and child to alternate in the sending and receiving of signals or messages.

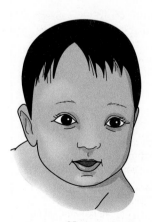
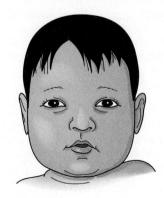
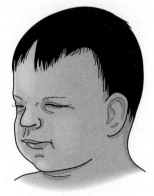

85	50	20
Medium high positive	Neutral attention	Avert

▶▶**FIGURE 3.6** Infant engagement scale. These samples from a 90-point scale show various levels of infant engagement, or attention. Babies participate in prelanguage "conversations" with parents by giving and withholding attention and by smiling, gazing, or vocalizing. (From Beebe et al., 1982.)

As with motherese, parents use a distinctive style when singing to an infant, according to University of Toronto professor emerita Sandra Trehub. Even people who speak another language can tell if a tape-recorded song was sung to an infant or an adult, or if the person was just pretending to sing to an infant. Likewise, lullabies remain recognizable when electronic filtering removes words (Trehub, Unyk, & Trainor, 1993a, 1993b; Trehub et al., 1997).

digitalskillet/Shutterstock

Parentese

When they talk to infants, parents use an exaggerated pattern of speaking called **motherese** or **parentese.** Typically, they raise their tone of voice; use short, simple sentences; and repeat themselves more (Kidd & Bavin, 2007; Snedeker, Geren, & Shafto, 2007). They also slow their rate of speaking and use exaggerated voice inflections: "Did Amy eat it A-L-L UP?"

What is the purpose of such changes? Parents are apparently trying to help their children learn language. When a baby is still babbling, parents tend to use long, adult-style sentences. But as soon as the baby says its first word, they switch to parentese. By the time babies are four months old, they prefer parentese over normal speech (Cooper et al., 1997).

In addition to being simpler, parentese has a distinct "musical" quality (Trainor & Desjardins, 2002). No matter what language mothers speak, the melodies, pauses, and inflections they use to comfort, praise, or give warning are universal. Psychologist Anne Fernald has found that mothers around the world talk to their babies with similar changes in pitch. For instance, we praise babies with a rising, then falling pitch ("BRA-vo!" "GOOD girl!"). Warnings are delivered in a short, sharp rhythm ("Non, non!" "Not!"). To give comfort, parents use low, smooth, drawn-out tones ("Oooh poor baaa-by." "Oooh pauvre petit."). A high-pitched, rising melody is used to call attention to objects ("See the pretty BIRDIE?") (Fernald, 1989).

Parentese helps parents get babies' attention, communicate with them, and teach them language (Thiessen, Hill, & Saffran, 2005). Later, as a child's speaking improves, parents tend to adjust their speech to the child's language ability. Especially from 18 months to four years of age, parents seek to clarify what a child says and prompt the child to say more.

In summary, some elements of language are innate. Nevertheless, our inherited tendency to learn language does not determine if we will speak English or Vietnamese, French, or Russian. Environmental forces also influence whether a person develops simple or sophisticated language skills. The first seven years of life are an extremely important period in language learning (Eliot, 1999). Indeed, it appears that if a child doesn't learn a language during

Motherese (or parentese) A pattern of speech used when talking to infants, marked by a higher-pitched voice; short, simple sentences; repetition; slower speech; and exaggerated voice inflections.

Transformation The mental ability to change the shape or form of a substance (such as clay or water) and to perceive that its volume remains the same.

Assimilation In Piaget's theory, the application of existing mental patterns to new situations (i.e., the new situation is assimilated to existing mental schemes).

Accommodation In Piaget's theory, the modification of existing mental patterns to fit new demands (i.e., mental schemes are changed to accommodate new information or experiences).

✓ STUDY BREAK   Language Development

Reflect

In order, see if you can name and imitate the language abilities you had as you progressed from birth to age two years. Now see if you can label and imitate some basic elements of parentese.

In your own words, state at least one argument for and one argument against Chomsky's view of language acquisition.

You are going to spend a day with a person who speaks a different language than you do. Do you think you would be able to communicate with the other person? How does this relate to language acquisition?

Learning Check

1. The development of speech and language usually occurs in which order?
   a. crying, cooing, babbling, telegraphic speech
   b. cooing, crying, babbling, telegraphic speech
   c. babbling, crying, cooing, telegraphic speech
   d. crying, babbling, cooing, identification
2. Simple, two-word sentences are characteristic of _____ speech.
3. Noam _____ has advanced the idea that language acquisition is built on innate patterns.
4. Prelanguage turn-taking and social interactions would be of special interest to a psycholinguist. T or F?
5. The style of speaking known as _____ is higher in pitch and has a musical quality.

Critical Thinking

6. The children of professional parents hear more words per hour than the children of welfare parents, and they also tend to score higher on tests of mental abilities. How else could their higher scores be explained?

Answers

1. a 2. telegraphic 3. Chomsky 4. T 5. motherese or parentese 6. Children in professional homes receive many educational benefits that are less common in welfare homes. Yet, even when such differences are taken into account, brighter children tend to come from richer language environments (Hart & Risley, 1999).

this period, he may never learn one at all (LaPointe, 2005; Uylings, 2006). Clearly, a full flowering of speech requires careful cultivation.

COGNITIVE DEVELOPMENT—HOW DO CHILDREN LEARN TO THINK?

<SURVEY QUESTION
How do children learn to think?

Now that we have Amy talking, let's move on to a broader view of intellectual development.

How different is a child's understanding of the world from that of an adult? Generally speaking, their thinking is less abstract. Children use fewer generalizations, categories, and principles. They also tend to base their understanding on particular examples and objects they can see or touch.

Before children reach the age of six or seven, their thinking is very concrete. Younger children cannot make **transformations** in which they must mentally change the shape or form of a substance (such as clay or water). Let's visit Amy at age five: If you show her a short, wide glass full of milk and a tall, narrow glass (also full), she will tell you that the taller glass contains more milk. Amy will tell you this even if she watches you pour milk from the short glass into an empty, tall glass. She is not bothered by the fact that the milk appears to be transformed from a smaller to a larger amount. Instead, she responds only to the fact that taller seems to mean more (see Figure 3.7). After about age seven, children are no longer fooled by this situation. Perhaps that's why seven has been called the "age of reason." From age seven on, we see a definite trend toward more logical, adultlike thought (Flavell, 1992).

Is there any pattern to the growth of intellect in childhood? According to the Swiss psychologist and philosopher Jean Piaget (1951, 1952), there is.

Piaget's Theory of Cognitive Development

Jean Piaget (Jahn pea-ah-JAY) (1896–1980) believed that all children pass through a series of distinct stages in intellectual development. Many of his ideas came from observing his own children as they solved various thought problems. Piaget's ideas have had a profound effect on our view of children (Feldman, 2004).

Mental Adaptations

Piaget hypothesized that cognitive processes develop in an ordered sequence of stages. Some children move more quickly through these stages than others, but the sequence remains the same (Siegler & Alibali, 2005). He believed that children absorb new events into their existing concepts of the world through the processes of assimilation and accommodation. **Assimilation** refers to using existing mental patterns in new situations. Let's say that a plastic hammer is Benjamin's favourite toy. He holds the hammer properly and loves to pound on blocks with it. For his birthday Benjamin gets an oversized toy wrench. If he uses the wrench for pounding, it has been assimilated to an existing knowledge structure.

In **accommodation,** existing ideas are modified to fit new requirements. For instance, a younger child might think that a dime is worth less than a (larger) nickel, because it is smaller. However, as children begin to spend money, they must alter their ideas about what "more" and "less" mean. Thus, new situations are assimilated to existing ideas, and new ideas are created to accommodate new experiences.

Piaget's ideas have deeply affected our view of children. Table 3.2 is a brief summary of what he found.

▶▶ **FIGURE 3.7** Children under age seven intuitively assume that a volume of liquid increases when it is poured from a short, wide container into a taller, thinner one. This boy thinks the tall container holds more than the short one. Actually, each holds the same amount of liquid. Children make such judgments based on the height of the liquid, not its volume.

Jean Piaget—philosopher, psychologist, and keen observer of children.

Sensorimotor stage The stage of intellectual development during which sensory input and motor responses become coordinated.

Object permanence The concept, gained in infancy, that objects continue to exist even when they are hidden from view.

Preoperational stage The period of intellectual development during which children begin to use language and think symbolically, yet remain intuitive and egocentric in their thought.

Intuitive thought Thinking that makes little or no use of reasoning and logic.

Egocentric thought Thought that is self-centred and fails to consider the viewpoints of others.

Concrete operational stage The period of intellectual development during which children become able to use the concepts of time, space, volume, and number, but in ways that remain simplified and concrete, rather than abstract.

Reversibility of thought Recognition that relationships involving equality or identity can be reversed (for example, if A = B, then B = A).

Conservation In Piaget's theory, mastery of the concept that the weight, mass, and volume of matter remain unchanged (are conserved) even when the shape or appearance of objects changes.

Abstract principles Concepts and ideas removed from specific examples and concrete situations.

Formal operations stage The period of intellectual development characterized by thinking that includes abstract, theoretical, and hypothetical ideas.

Theory of mind A child's current state of knowledge about the mind, including his or her understanding of desires, beliefs, thoughts, intentions, feelings, and so forth.

■ Table 3.2 **Piaget's Stages**

The Sensorimotor Stage (0 to 2 Years)

In the **sensorimotor stage,** infants progress from responding to events with simple reflexes (such as grasping and sucking) to goal-oriented behaviour. Infants are mainly concerned with learning to coordinate motor movements with information from their senses. Some time during the first year, they begin to actively pursue disappearing objects. By age two, they can anticipate the movement of an object behind a screen. The appearance of **object permanence** is an important aspect of sensorimotor development. Object permanence is the awareness that an object or person continues to exist even when out of the infant's sight.

In general, developments in this stage indicate that the child's ideas about the world are becoming more stable.

The Preoperational Stage (2 to 7 Years)

The **preoperational stage** is characterized by the use of symbolic thought—using symbols to represent objects and the relationships among them. Probably the most important symbolic activity of young children is language. Although preoperational children can form mental images or ideas, they cannot easily transform these images in their minds.

Although children think symbolically and use language, before the age of six or seven their thinking is still very concrete and **intuitive** (they make little use of reasoning and logic). Children have a tendency to confuse words with the objects they represent. To children, the name of an object is as much a part of the object as its size, shape, and colour.

During this time, the child is also quite **egocentric** (unable to take the viewpoint of other people). The child's ego seems to stand at the centre of his or her world. Such egocentrism explains why young children can seem exasperatingly selfish or uncooperative at times. (See Clinical File: "A Child's Theory of Mind.")

The Concrete Operational Stage (7 to 11 Years)

In the **concrete operational stage,** children show the beginnings of adult logic but generally focus on tangible or concrete objects rather than abstract ideas (thus the name "concrete" operations). They begin to use such concepts as time, space, and number. The hallmark of this stage is the ability to carry out such mental operations as reversing thoughts.

Reversibility of thought allows children in the concrete operational stage to recognize that if 4 × 2 equals 8, then 2 × 4 does, too.

The development of mental operations allows mastery of **conservation** (the concept that mass, weight, and volume remain unchanged when the shape of an object changes). Children have learned conservation when they understand that turning a round ball of clay into a long, thin snake does not change the amount of clay. The original amount is conserved despite the change in shape (see Figure 3.7).

The Formal Operations Stage (11 Years and Up)

Younger children are limited to dealing with concrete objects and specific situations, but adolescents and adults can consider abstract ideas and see the world as it could be. They can consider **abstract principles,** think hypothetically, and use inductive and deductive reasoning.

According to Piaget, full adult intellectual ability is attained during the **formal operations stage.** Not everyone reaches this level of thinking. Many adults can think formally about some topics, but their thinking becomes concrete when the topic is unfamiliar. This implies that formal thinking may be more a result of culture and learning than of maturation. In any case, after late adolescence, improvements in intellect are based on gaining knowledge, experience, and wisdom, rather than on any leaps in basic thinking capacity.

Piaget Today

Piaget's theory is a valuable "road map" for understanding how children think. However, many psychologists are convinced that Piaget gave too little credit to the effects of learning. For example, children of pottery-making parents can correctly answer questions about the conservation of clay at an earlier age than Piaget would have predicted. According to learning theorists, children continuously gain specific knowledge; they do not undergo stagelike leaps in general mental ability (Siegler, 2004). On the other hand, the growth in connections between brain cells occurs in waves that parallel some of Piaget's stages

A Child's Theory of Mind—Other People, Other Minds

Why are young children so egocentric? In many instances, it's because they have a limited understanding of mental states, such as desires, beliefs, thoughts, intentions, and feelings. In other words, it could be said that they have a very simplified **theory of mind** (Flavell, 1999).

The following example is based on theory-of-mind research. Imagine that you show five-year-old Nicky a candy box. "What do you think is inside?" you ask. "Candy," Nicky replies. Then you let Nicky look inside, where he finds a surprise: The box contains crayons, not candy. "Nicky," you ask, "what will your friend Max think is inside the box if I show it to him?" "Candy!" Nicky replies, amused at the thought that Max is going to get fooled, too.

Now imagine that we try the procedure again, this time with Shelia, who is only three years old. Like Nicky, Shelia thinks she will find candy in the box. She opens the box and sees the crayons.

Now we ask Shelia what she thinks Max will expect to find in the box. "Crayons," she replies. Because Shelia knows that there are crayons in the box, she assumes that everyone else does, too. It's as if only one reality exists for Shelia. She doesn't seem to understand that the minds of other people contain different information, beliefs, thoughts, and so forth (Gopnik, Meltzoff, & Kuhl, 1999). However, this conclusion may be more a limitation in the design of the experiments used to study how young children perceive the world around them. McGill psychologist Kristine Onishi found that 15-month-old infants use perceptions and beliefs to explain the behaviour of others (Onishi & Baillargeon, 2005).

By the age of four, children have gained a rich understanding of mental life. As their "theory of mind" becomes more accurate, they are able to participate more fully in the complex psychological world in which we all live.

(see Figure 3.8). Thus, the truth may lie somewhere between Piaget's stage theory and modern learning theory.

On a broad scale, many of Piaget's observations have held up well. However, his explanations for the growth of thinking abilities in childhood continue to be debated (Feldman, 2004). Where early infancy is concerned, even Piaget's observations may need revision. It looks like Piaget greatly underestimated the thinking abilities of infants.

Infant Cognition

What evidence is there that Piaget underestimated infant abilities? Piaget believed that infants under the age of one year cannot think. Babies, he said, have no memory of people and objects that are out of sight. Yet we now know that infants begin forming representations of the world very early in life. For example, babies as young as three months of age appear to know that objects are solid and do not disappear when out of view (Baillargeon, 2004).

Why did Piaget fail to detect the thinking skills of infants? Most likely, he mistook babies' limited *physical skills* for mental incompetence. Piaget's tests required babies to search for objects or reach out and touch them. Newer, more sensitive methods are uncovering abilities Piaget missed. One such method takes advantage of the fact that babies, like adults, act surprised when they see something "impossible" or unexpected occur. To make use of this effect, psychologist Renée Baillargeon (2004) puts on little "magic shows" for infants. In her "theatre," babies watch as possible and impossible events occur with toys or other objects. Some three-month-old infants act surprised and gaze longer at impossible events. An example is seeing two solid objects appear to pass through each other. By the time they are eight months old, babies can remember where objects are (or should be) for at least one minute.

Piaget believed that abilities like those described above emerge only after a long period of sensorimotor development. However, evidence continues to mount that babies are born with the capacity to form concepts about the world, or acquire this ability early in life (Aguiar & Baillargeon, 1998, 1999). It looks as if further study is likely to refine and amend the ideas that grew from Piaget's research.

Another criticism of Piaget is that he underestimated the impact of culture on mental development. The next section tells how Amy will go about mastering the intellectual tools valued by her culture.

3 to 6 years

7 to 15 years

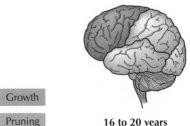

Growth

Pruning

16 to 20 years

▶▶**FIGURE 3.8** Between the ages of three and six a tremendous wave of growth occurs in connections among neurons in the frontal areas of the brain. This corresponds to the time when children make rapid progress in their ability to think symbolically. Between ages 7 and 15, peak synaptic growth shifts to the temporal and parietal lobes. During this period children become increasingly adept at using language, a specialty of the temporal lobes. In the late teens, the brain actively destroys unneeded connections, especially in the frontal lobes. This pruning of synapses sharpens the brain's capacity for abstract thinking. (Courtesy of Dr. Paul Thompson, Laboratory of Neuro Imaging, UCLA School of Medicine.)

Zone of proximal development The range of tasks a child cannot yet master alone, but that she or he can accomplish with the guidance of a more capable partner.

Scaffolding The process of adjusting instruction so that it is responsive to a beginner's behaviour and supports the beginner's efforts to understand a problem or gain a mental skill.

Vygotsky's Sociocultural Theory

While Piaget stressed the role of maturation in cognitive development, Russian scholar Lev Vygotsky (1896–1934) focused on the impact of sociocultural factors. Vygotsky's key insight is that children's thinking develops through dialogues with more capable persons (Vygotsky, 1962, 1978).

How does that relate to intellectual growth? So far, no one has ever published *A Child's Guide to Life on Earth.* Instead, children must learn about life from various "tutors," such as parents, teachers, and older siblings. Even if *A Child's Guide to Life on Earth* did exist, we would need a separate version for every culture. It is not enough for children to learn how to think. They must also learn specific intellectual skills valued by their culture.

Like Piaget, Vygotsky believed that children actively seek to discover new principles. However, Vygotsky emphasized that many of a child's most important "discoveries" are guided by skilful tutors. Developmental psychologists David Shaffer and Katherine Kipp (2010) offer the following example:

> Tonya, a 4-year-old, has just received her first jigsaw puzzle as a birthday present. She attempts to work the puzzle but gets nowhere until her father comes along, sits down beside her, and gives her some tips. He suggests that it would be a good idea to put together the corners first, points to the pink area at the edge of one corner piece and says, "Let's look for another pink piece." When Tonya seems frustrated, he places two interlocking pieces near each other so that she will notice them, and when Tonya succeeds, he offers words of encouragement. As Tonya gradually gets the hang of it, he steps back and lets her work more and more independently. (p. 283)

Interactions like this are most helpful when they take place within a child's **zone of proximal development.**

What did Vygotsky mean by that? The word *proximal* means close or nearby. Vygotsky realized that, at any given time, some tasks are just beyond a child's reach. The child is close to having the mental skills needed to do the task, but the task is a little too complex to be mastered alone. However, children working within this zone can make rapid progress if they receive sensitive guidance from a skilled partner (LeBlanc & Bearison, 2004).

Vygotsky also emphasized a process he called **scaffolding.** A scaffold is a framework or temporary support. Vygotsky believed that adults help children learn how to think by scaffolding, or supporting, their attempts to solve problems or discover principles (Daniels, 2005). To be most effective, scaffolding must be responsive to a child's needs. For example, as Tonya's father helped her with the puzzle, he tailored his hints and guidance to match her evolving abilities. The two of them worked together, step by step, so that Tonya could better understand how to assemble a puzzle. In a sense, Tonya's father set up a series of temporary bridges that helped her move into new mental territory. As predicted by Vygotsky's theory, the cognitive skills of three- to six-year-olds are closely related to the amount of scaffolding provided by their mothers (Dieterich et al., 2006).

During their collaborations with others, children learn important cultural beliefs and values. For example, imagine that a boy wants to know how many Pokémon cards he has. His mother helps him stack and count the cards, moving each card to a new stack as they count it. She then shows him how to write the number on a slip of paper so he can remember it. This teaches the child not only about counting but also that writing is valued in our culture. In other parts of the world, a child learning to count might be shown how to make notches on a stick or tie knots in a cord.

Summary

Vygotsky saw that grown-ups play a crucial role in what children know. As they try to decipher the world, children rely on adults to help them understand how things work. Vygotsky further noticed that adults unconsciously adjust their behaviour to give children the information they need to solve problems that interest the child. In this way, children use adults to learn about their culture and society (Gopnik, Meltzoff, & Kuhl, 2000; LeBlanc & Bearison, 2004).

ADOLESCENCE AND YOUNG ADULTHOOD—THE BEST OF TIMES, THE WORST OF TIMES

Adolescence and young adulthood are a time of change, youthful exploration, and exuberance. They can also be a time of worry and problems, especially in today's world. It might even be fair to describe this period as "the best of times, the worst of times." During adolescence, a person's identity and moral values come into sharper focus even as the transition to adulthood is occurring at ever-later ages.

Adolescence is the culturally defined period between childhood and adulthood. Socially, the adolescent is no longer a child, yet not quite an adult. Almost all cultures recognize this transitional status. However, the length of adolescence varies greatly from culture to culture. For example, most 14-year-old girls in North America live at home and go to school. In contrast, many 14-year-old females in rural villages of many poorer countries are married and have children. In our culture, 14-year-olds are adolescents. In others, they may be adults.

Is marriage the primary criterion for adult status in North America? No, it's not even one of the top three criteria. Today, the most widely accepted standards are (1) taking responsibility for oneself, (2) making independent decisions, and (3) becoming financially independent. In practice, this typically means breaking away from parents by taking a job and setting up a separate residence (Arnett, 2001).

Puberty

Many people confuse adolescence with puberty. However, puberty is a *biological* event, not a social status. During **puberty,** hormonal changes promote rapid physical growth and sexual maturity. Biologically, most people reach reproductive maturity in their early teens. Social and intellectual maturity, however, may lie years ahead. Young adolescents often make decisions that affect their entire lives, even though they are immature mentally and socially. The high rates of teenage pregnancy and drug abuse are prime examples. Despite such risks, most people do manage to weather adolescence without developing any serious psychological problems (Steinberg, 2001).

How much difference does the timing of puberty make? For boys, maturing early is generally beneficial. Typically, it enhances their self-image and gives them an advantage socially and athletically. Early-maturing boys tend to be more relaxed, dominant, self-assured, and popular. However, early puberty does carry some risks because early-maturing boys are also more likely to get into trouble with drugs, alcohol, and antisocial behaviour (Steinberg, 2001).

For girls, the advantages of early maturation are less clear-cut. In elementary school, fast-maturing girls are *less* popular and have poorer self-images, perhaps because they are larger and heavier than their classmates (Deardorff et al., 2007). By Grade 8, however, early development includes sexual features. This leads to a more positive body image, *greater* peer prestige, and adult approval (Brooks-Gunn & Warren, 1988). Early-maturing girls tend to date sooner and are more independent and more active in school. However, like their male counterparts, they are also more often in trouble at school and more likely to engage in early sex (Flannery, Rowe, & Gulley, 1993).

As you can see, there are costs *and* benefits associated with early puberty. One added cost of early maturation is that it may force premature identity formation. When Amy is a teenager and she begins to look like an adult, she may be treated like an adult. Ideally, this change can encourage greater maturity and independence. However, if the search for identity ends too soon, it may leave Amy with a distorted, poorly formed sense of self (Figure 3.9).

<SURVEY QUESTION
What are the challenges of adolescence and adulthood? Why is the transition from adolescence to adulthood especially challenging?

Adolescence The culturally defined period between childhood and adulthood.
Puberty The biologically defined period during which a person matures sexually and becomes capable of reproduction.

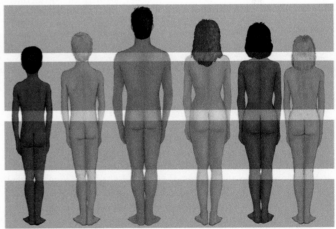

▶▶**FIGURE 3.9** Dramatic differences in physical size and maturity are found in adolescents of the same age. The girls pictured are all 13, the boys 16. Maturation that occurs earlier or later than average can affect the "search for identity." (Adapted from "Growing Up" by J.M. Tanner. Copyright © September 1973 by Scientific American, Inc. All rights reserved.)

Hypothetical possibilities
Suppositions, guesses, or projections.

The Search for Identity

Identity formation is a key task of adolescence (Schwartz, 2008). Of course, problems of identity occur at other times, too. But in a very real sense, puberty signals that it's time to begin forming a new, more mature self-image. Many problems stem from unclear standards about the role adolescents should play within society. Are they adults or children? Should they be autonomous or dependent? Should they work or play? Such ambiguities make it difficult for young people to form clear images of themselves and of how they should act (Alsaker, 1995).

Answering the question "Who am I?" is also spurred by cognitive development. After adolescents have attained the stage of formal operations, they are better able to ask questions about their place in the world and about morals, values, politics, and social relationships. Then too, being able to think about **hypothetical possibilities** allows the adolescent to contemplate the future and ask more realistically, "Who will I be?" (Côté, 2006b). (See Human Diversity: "Ethnic Diversity and Identity.")

The Transition to Adulthood

Adulthood is usually defined by what people do rather than how old they are. Marriage has long been considered a key factor in adulthood (Carroll, Still, & Newby-Clark, 2007). Other criteria have included holding a full-time job and living independently. Today, the transition to adulthood is more often characterized by adjustment issues, including settling on one's values and beliefs, accepting responsibility for oneself, becoming financially independent, and establishing an equal relationship with one's parents (Gottleib et al., 2007). The challenge of adult identity formation is further complicated by the fact that more and more young people are deferring young adulthood, preferring to prolong identity explorations into their twenties before they commit to long-term choices in love and work (Arnett, 2000, 2004; Arnett & Tanner, 2006). According to sociologist James Côté, Western industrialized societies, like Canada, are becoming increasingly tolerant of this period of extended adolescence (Côté, 2006a). (See Critical Thinking "The Twixters.")

Amy may live with Olivia and Tom until her mid-twenties, delaying her transition to adulthood. Alternatively, she may make the transition to young adulthood during the

HUMAN DIVERSITY

Ethnic Diversity and Identity

Ethnic heritage can have a powerful influence on personal identity (Phinney & Ong, 2007). For adolescents of different ethnicities, the question is often not just "Who am I?" Rather, there are many other questions: "Who am I at home? Who am I at school? Who am I with friends from my neighbourhood?" Adolescents who belong to ethnic minority groups such as Black or Islamic Canadians confront two sets of cultural values: the values of the dominant culture (primarily European and Christian heritage) and those of their own ethnic group (Phinney & Alipuria, 2006).

As ethnic minorities continue to grow in status and prominence, adolescents are less and less likely to feel rejected or excluded because of their ethnic heritage as they try to find their place in society. This is fortunate because adolescents of different ethnicities have often faced degrading stereotypes concerning their intelligence, sexuality, social status, manners, and

so forth. The result can be lowered self-esteem and confusion about roles, values, and personal identity (de las Fuentes & Vasquez, 1999).

In forming an identity, adolescents of different ethnicities face the question of how they should think of themselves. Is Lori Canadian or Chinese or both? The answer typically depends on how strongly adolescents identify with their family and ethnic community. Teens who take pride in their ethnic heritage have higher self-esteem, a better self-image, and a stronger sense of personal identity (Costigan et al., 2010). They are also less likely to engage in drug use (Marsiglia et al., 2004) or violent behaviour (French, Kim, & Pillado, 2006).

Group pride, positive models, and a more tolerant society could do much to keep a broad range of options open to *all* adolescents.

The Twixters

Kirsten is a "twixter": twentysomething, still living at home, not yet married, with no children, and no settled career. In England, twixters are called "kippers" (kids in parents' pockets eroding retirement savings). In Australia they are "boomerang kids" (they always come back home). And in Germany they are "Nesthocker" (nest squatters). Are twixters adolescents who are taking longer to find their identity? Or are they young adults avoiding their need to enter the adult world? Are they self-indulgent individuals trapped in a "maturity gap" (Galambos, Barker, & Tilton-Weaver, 2003)? Or are they part of a developmental stage that could be called "emerging adulthood" (Arnett, 2000; Arnett & Tanner, 2006)?

According to Arnett, emerging adulthood represents a new stage in human development, fitting between adolescence and young adulthood in Erikson's (1968) model (Arnett, 2000, 2004). Other developmental psychologists suggest that, rather than representing a true developmental stage, the transition from adolescent to adult has been prolonged, usually for economic and/or social reasons. For example, in Canada, changes in the timing of transition from adolescent to young adult have been noted since the early 1970s (Côté & Bynner, 2008). Perhaps 30 isn't the new 20 after all.

traditional 18-to-21 period. Regardless, she will eventually face the primary adult issues of marriage, children, and career. How she manages, especially in her core relationships, will determine whether she feels a sense of intimacy or feels isolated from others.

In many ways, adolescence and young adulthood are more emotionally turbulent than midlife or old age. One important aspect of the emotional turbulence of adolescence and young adulthood is the struggle with right and wrong—in other words, the need to develop moral values.

MORAL DEVELOPMENT—GROWING A CONSCIENCE

When one of the authors of this book (SM) was a fourth-year university student, she was asked to take an exam for a friend who desperately needed to pass a course. Did she do it? (NO!) Would you? This is a *moral* question, or question of conscience.

Moral development starts in childhood and continues into adulthood (Turiel, 2006). Through this process, we acquire values, beliefs, and thinking patterns that guide responsible behaviour. Moral values are especially likely to come into sharper focus during adolescence, as capacities for self-control and abstract thinking increase (Hart & Carlo, 2005). Let's take a brief look at this interesting aspect of personal development.

<SURVEY QUESTION
How do we develop morals and values?

Levels of Moral Development

How are moral values acquired? In his influential account, psychologist Lawrence Kohlberg (1981) held that we learn moral values through thinking and reasoning. To study moral development, Kohlberg posed dilemmas to children of different ages. The following is one of the moral dilemmas he used (Kohlberg, 1969; adapted):

A woman was near death from cancer, and there was only one drug that might save her. It was discovered by a druggist who was charging 10 times what it cost to make the drug. The sick woman's husband could only pay $1000, but the druggist wanted $2000. He asked the druggist to sell it cheaper or to let him pay later. The druggist said no. So the desperate husband broke into the store to steal the drug for his wife. Should he have done that? Was it wrong or right? Why?

Moral development The development of values, beliefs, and thinking abilities that act as a guide regarding what is acceptable behaviour.

Each child was asked what action the husband should have taken. Kohlberg classified the reasons given for each choice and identified three levels of moral development. Each is based not so much on the choices made, but on the reasoning used to arrive at a choice.

At the lowest, **preconventional,** level, moral thinking is guided by the consequences of actions (punishment, reward, or an exchange of favours). For example, a person at this level might reason that "The man shouldn't steal the drug because he could get caught and sent to jail" (avoiding punishment) or "It won't do him any good to steal the drug because his wife will probably die before he gets out of jail" (self-interest).

At the second, or **conventional,** level, reasoning is based on a desire to please others or to follow accepted authority, rules, and values. For example, a person at this intermediate level might say "He shouldn't steal the drug because others will think he is a thief. His wife would not want to be saved by thievery" (avoiding disapproval) or "Although his wife needs the drug, he should not break the law to get it. Everyone has to obey the law. His wife's condition does not justify stealing" (traditional morality of authority).

At the highest, or **postconventional,** level, moral behaviour is directed by self-chosen ethical principles that tend to be general, comprehensive, or universal. People at this level place a high value on justice, dignity, and equality. For example, a highly principled person might say "He should steal the drug and then inform the authorities that he has done so. He will have to face a penalty, but he will have saved a human life" (self-chosen ethical principles).

Does everyone eventually reach the highest level? People advance at different rates, and many fail to reach the postconventional level of moral reasoning. In fact, many do not even reach the conventional level.

The preconventional level is most characteristic of young children and delinquents (Forney, Forney, & Crutsinger, 2005). Conventional, group-oriented morals are typical of older children and most adults (Commons, Galaz-Fontes, & Morse, 2006). Kohlberg estimated that only about 20 percent of the adult population achieves postconventional morality, representing self-direction and higher principles.

Evaluation of Kohlberg's Theory

There is evidence to support Kohlberg's view that children's moral judgements develop in an upward sequence (Boom, Wouters, and Keller, 2007). Postconventional thought first occurs (when it does) during adolescence, along with formal operational thinking (Patenaude, Niyonsenga, & Fafard, 2003). Kohlberg believed that these stages of moral development represent an unfolding of an innate sequence and are therefore universal. Others believe that he underestimated the influence of social, cultural, and educational institutions on the development of moral reasoning (Dawson, 2002).

Kohlberg found that men and women reached different levels of moral development. Men, he found, were more likely to reach a level of moral reasoning that emphasized justice, law, and order, while women were more likely to focus on care and concern for others (keep in mind that Kohlberg thought these stages were innate).

This view was strongly criticized by Carol Gilligan (1982). Rather than reflect an inherent superiority of male moral reasoning over female moral reasoning, Gilligan and others have argued that these differences reflect differences in the ways males and female are socialized through their lives (Gilligan, 1982; Jorgensen, 2006). Socialization can also *decrease* levels of moral reasoning—a study of medical students at the Université de Sherbrooke in Quebec found that their levels of moral reasoning actually declined over the first three years of their medical education (Patenaude et al., 2003).

Developing a "moral compass" is an important part of growing up. Many of the choices we make every day involve fundamental questions of right and wrong. Being able to think clearly about such questions is essential to becoming a responsible adult.

Preconventional moral reasoning Moral thinking based on the consequences of one's choices or actions (punishment, reward, or an exchange of favours).

Conventional moral reasoning Moral thinking based on a desire to please others or to follow accepted rules and values.

Postconventional moral reasoning Moral thinking based on carefully examined and self-chosen moral principles.

Developmental milestone A significant turning point or marker in personal development.

Life stages Widely recognized periods of life corresponding to broad phases of development.

Developmental task Any personal change that must take place for optimal development.

Psychosocial dilemma A conflict between personal impulses and the social world.

STUDY BREAK Cognitive Development and Moral Development

Reflect

You are going to make cookies with children of various ages. See if you can name each of Piaget's stages and give an example of what a child in that stage might be expected to do.

You have been asked to help a child learn to use a pocket calculator to do simple addition. How would you go about identifying the child's zone of proximal development for this task? How would you scaffold the child's learning?

At what stage of moral development do you think most criminals function?

Learning Check

Match each item with one of the following stages.

  a. Sensorimotor   b. Preoperational
  c. Concrete operational   d. Formal operations

1. _____ egocentric thought
2. _____ abstract or hypothetical thought
3. _____ purposeful movement
4. _____ intuitive thought
5. _____ conservation
6. _____ reversibility of thought
7. _____ object permanence
8. _____ non-verbal development
9. Assimilation refers to applying existing thought patterns or knowledge to new situations. T or F?
10. Newer methods for testing infant thinking abilities frequently make note of whether an infant is _____ by seemingly _____ events.
11. Vygotsky called the process of providing a temporary framework of supports for learning new mental abilities _____.
12. According to Kohlberg, the conventional level of moral development is marked by a reliance on outside authority. T or F?
13. Self-interest and avoiding punishment are elements of postconventional morality. T or F?

Critical Thinking

14. Using Piaget's theory as a guide, decide at what age you would expect a child to recognize that a Styrofoam cup has weight.

Answers

1. B 2. D 3. A 4. B 5. C 6. C 7. A 8. A 9. T 10. surprised, impossible 11. scaffolding 12. T 13. F 14. Seventy-five percent of four- to six-year-olds say that a Styrofoam cup has no weight after lifting it! Most children judge weight intuitively (by the way an object feels) until they begin to move into the concrete operational stage (Smith, Carey, & Wiser, 1985).

THE STORY OF A LIFETIME—ROCKY ROAD OR GARDEN PATH?

<SURVEY QUESTION
What are the typical tasks and dilemmas that confront people through their lifespan?

At the beginning of this chapter, we noted that developmental psychologists are interested in every phase of life, from the womb to the tomb. Thus far, we have concentrated on Amy's first few years because development during childhood can have such a large impact on a person's life. It is not possible here to completely satisfy Olivia and Tom's curiosity about what Amy's life will be like. Nevertheless, we can at least sketch the general outlines of her life to come. Every life is marked by a number of **developmental milestones.** These are notable events, markers, or turning points in personal development (Kail & Cavanaugh, 2010). Some examples are graduating from school, voting for the first time, getting married, watching a child leave home (or move back!), the death of a parent, becoming a grandparent, retirement, and one's own death.

Perhaps the best way to get a preview of Amy's life is to consider some of the major psychological challenges she is likely to encounter. Each of us can take pride in being "one of a kind." There is really no such thing as a "typical person" or a "typical life." Nevertheless, broad similarities can be found in the **life stages** of infancy, childhood, adolescence, young adulthood, middle adulthood, and old age. Each stage confronts a person with new **developmental tasks** that must be mastered for optimal development. Examples are learning to read in childhood, adjusting to sexual maturity in adolescence, and establishing a vocation as an adult.

Erikson's Psychosocial Dilemmas

In an influential book titled *Childhood and Society* (1963), personality theorist Erik Erikson (1903–1994) suggests that we face a specific psychosocial dilemma, or "crisis," at each stage of life. A **psychosocial dilemma** is a conflict between personal impulses and the social world.

Personality theorist Erik Erikson (1903–1994) is best known for his life stage theory of human development. His last book, *Vital Involvement in Old Age,* published in 1986, described his ideas about successful aging.

Sarah Putnum Photography

■ Table 3.3 Erikson's Psychosocial Dilemmas

Age	Characteristic Dilemma
Birth to 1 year	Trust versus mistrust
1 to 3 years	Autonomy versus shame and doubt
3 to 5 years	Initiative versus guilt
6 to 12 years	Industry versus inferiority
Adolescence	Identity versus role confusion
Young adulthood	Intimacy versus isolation
Middle adulthood	Generativity versus stagnation
Late adulthood	Integrity versus despair

Trust versus mistrust A conflict about learning to trust others and the world.

Autonomy versus shame and doubt A conflict between growing self-control and feelings of shame or doubt.

Initiative versus guilt A conflict between learning to take initiative and overcoming feelings of guilt about doing so.

Industry versus inferiority A conflict in middle childhood centred on lack of support for industrious behaviour, which can result in feelings of inferiority.

Identity versus role confusion A conflict concerning the need to establish a personal identity.

Resolving each dilemma creates a new balance between a person and society. A string of "successes" produces healthy development and a satisfying life. Unfavourable outcomes throw us off balance, making it harder to deal with later crises. Life becomes a "rocky road," and personal growth is stunted. Table 3.3 lists Erikson's dilemmas.

What are the major developmental tasks and life crises? A brief description of each psycho-social dilemma follows.

Stage One, First Year of Life: Trust versus Mistrust

During the first year of life, children are completely dependent on others. Erikson believes that a basic attitude of trust or mistrust is formed at this time. **Trust** is established when babies are given adequate warmth, touching, love, and physical care. **Mistrust** is caused by inadequate or unpredictable care and by parents who are cold, indifferent, or rejecting. Basic mistrust may later cause insecurity, suspiciousness, or an inability to relate to others. Notice that trust comes from the same conditions that help babies become securely attached to their parents.

Stage Two, One to Three Years: Autonomy versus Shame and Doubt

In stage two, children express their growing self-control by climbing, touching, exploring, and trying to do things for themselves. Tom and Olivia can foster Amy's sense of **autonomy** by encouraging her to try new skills. However, her first efforts may be crude, involving spilling, falling, wetting, and other "accidents." If Tom and Olivia ridicule or overprotect Amy, they may cause her to **doubt** her abilities and feel **shameful** about her actions.

Stage Three, Three to Five Years: Initiative versus Guilt

In stage three, children move beyond simple self-control and begin to take initiative. Through play, children learn to make plans and carry out tasks. Parents reinforce **initiative** by giving children freedom to play, ask questions, use imagination, and choose activities. Feelings of **guilt** about initiating activities are formed if parents criticize severely, prevent play, or discourage a child's questions.

Stage Four, 6 to 12 Years: Industry versus Inferiority

Many events of middle childhood are symbolized by that fateful day when you first entered school. With dizzying speed your world expanded beyond your family, and you faced a whole series of new challenges.

Erikson describes the elementary school years as the child's "entrance into life." In school, children begin to learn skills valued by society, and success or failure can affect a child's feelings of adequacy. Children learn a sense of **industry** if they win praise for productive activities, such as building, painting, cooking, reading, and studying. If a child's efforts are regarded as messy, childish, or inadequate, feelings of **inferiority** result. For the first time, teachers, classmates, and adults outside the home become as important as parents in shaping attitudes toward oneself.

Stage Five, Adolescence: Identity versus Role Confusion

Adolescence is often a turbulent time. Caught between childhood and adulthood, the adolescent faces some unique problems. Erikson considers a need to answer the question "Who am I?" the primary task during this stage of life. As Amy matures mentally and physically, she will have new feelings, a new body, and new attitudes (see Figure 3.9). Like other adolescents, she will need to build a consistent **identity** out of her talents, her values, her life history, her relationships, and the demands of her culture (Côté & Levine, 2002). Her conflicting experiences as a student, friend, athlete, worker, daughter, lover, and so forth must be integrated into a unified sense of self (more on this later). People who fail to develop a sense of identity suffer from **role confusion,** an uncertainty about who they are and where they are going.

Stage Six, Young Adulthood: Intimacy versus Isolation

What does Erikson believe is the major conflict in early adulthood? In stage six, the individual feels a need for intimacy in his or her life. After establishing a stable identity, a person is prepared to share meaningful love or deep friendship with others. By **intimacy,** Erikson means an ability to care about others and to share experiences with them. In line with Erikson's view, 75 percent of college-age men and women rank a good marriage and family life as important adult goals (Bachman & Johnson, 1979). And yet, marriage or sexual involvement is no guarantee of intimacy: Many adult relationships remain superficial and unfulfilling. Failure to establish intimacy with others leads to a deep sense of **isolation** (feeling alone and uncared for in life). This often sets the stage for later difficulties.

The challenges of young adulthood are quite daunting. More and more young people today are deferring young adulthood, preferring to prolong identity explorations into their twenties before they commit to long-term choices in love and work (Arnett, 2000, 2004; Arnett & Tanner, 2006).

Stage Seven, Middle Adulthood: Generativity versus Stagnation

According to Erikson, an interest in guiding the next generation is the main source of balance in mature adulthood. Erikson called this quality **generativity.** It is expressed by caring about oneself, one's children, and future generations. Generativity may be achieved by guiding one's own children or by helping other children (as a teacher, clergyperson, or coach, for example). Productive or creative work can also express generativity. In any case, a person's concerns and energies must broaden to include the welfare of others and of society as a whole. Failure to do this is marked by a **stagnant** concern with one's own needs and comforts. Life loses meaning, and the person feels bitter, dreary, and trapped (Friedman, 2004).

Stage Eight, Late Adulthood: Integrity versus Despair

What does Erikson see as the conflicts of old age? Old age is a time of reflection. According to Erikson, when Amy grows old she must be able to look back over her life with acceptance and satisfaction. People who have lived richly and responsibly develop a sense of **integrity** (self-respect). This allows them to face aging and death with dignity. If previous life events are viewed with regret, the elderly person experiences **despair** (heartache and remorse). In this case, life seems like a series of missed opportunities. The person feels like a failure and knows it's too late to reverse what has been done. Aging and the threat of death then become sources of fear and depression.

Middle and Late Adulthood: Will You Still Need Me When I'm 64?

Middle adulthood is generally considered to encompass the years from 40 to 65, with 60 to 65 as a transition to old age. As people live longer, and in better health, for many, "you're only as old as you feel." Erikson's dilemmas are not the only challenges of adulthood. Others are all too familiar: marital strife, divorce, career difficulties, unemployment, health problems, financial pressures, legal conflicts, and personal tragedies—to name but a few. How do people maintain a state of well-being as they run the gauntlet of modern life? Research suggests that six major factors contribute to adults' well-being: self-acceptance, positive relations with others, personal freedom, control over one's environment, purposive living, and continuing to grow and develop as a person (Ryff, 1995; Ryff, Singer, & Palmersheim, 2004). For many adults, age-related declines are offset by positive relationships. Sharing life's joys and sorrows with others, coupled with a better understanding of how the world works, may help carry people through midlife and into their later years (Ryff & Singer, 2000).

A Midlife Crisis

So what about that midlife crisis that everyone makes fun of? More people go through a "midcourse correction" at midlife (Lachman, 2004) than a full-blown crisis. The stereotypical male midlife crisis—buy a sports car, ditch the wife and kids, and marry a "trophy" wife—is probably more Hollywood fiction than reality (Rathus & Longmuir, 2012).

According to Erikson, an interest in future generations characterizes optimal adult development.

<SURVEY QUESTION
What are the challenges in later adulthood and old age?

Intimacy versus isolation The challenge of establishing intimacy with others, versus feeling a sense of isolation.

Generativity versus stagnation A conflict in which stagnant self-interest is countered by interest in guiding the next generation.

Integrity versus despair A conflict in old age between feelings of integrity and the despair of viewing previous life events with regret.

Ageism Discrimination or prejudice based on a person's age.

After the late 50s, personal development is complicated by physical aging. However, it is wrong to believe that most elderly people are sickly, infirm, or senile. (Nowadays, 60 is the new 40, an idea that at least two of your authors wholeheartedly agree with!) Only about 5 percent of those older than 65 are in nursing homes. Mentally, many elderly persons are at least as capable as the average young adult. On intellectual tests, top scorers over the age of 65 match the average for men younger than 35. What sets these silver-haired stars apart? Typically they are people who have continued to work and remain intellectually active (Salthouse, 2004). Gerontologist Warner Schaie (1994, 2005) found that you are most likely to stay mentally sharp in old age if

1. You remain healthy.
2. You live in a favourable environment (you are educated and have a stimulating occupation, above-average income, and an intact family).
3. You are involved in intellectually stimulating activities (reading, travel, cultural events, continuing education, clubs, professional associations).
4. You have a flexible personality.
5. You are married to a smart spouse.
6. You maintain your perceptual processing speed.
7. You were satisfied with your accomplishments in midlife.

Aging and Ageism

You have almost certainly encountered ageism in one way or another. **Ageism,** which refers to discrimination or prejudice based on age, can oppress the young as well as the old. For instance, a person applying for a job may just as well be told "You're too young" as "You're too old." In some societies ageism is expressed as respect for the elderly. In Japan, for instance, aging is seen as positive, and greater age brings more status and respect. In most Western nations, however, ageism tends to have a negative impact on older individuals (Ng, 2002).

Ageism is often expressed through patronizing language. Older people are frequently spoken to in an overly polite, slow, loud, and simple way, implying that they are infirm, even when they are not (Nelson, 2005). Popular stereotypes of the "dirty old man," "meddling old woman," "senile old fool," and the like also help perpetuate myths about aging. But such stereotypes are clearly wrong: A tremendous diversity exists among the elderly—ranging from the infirm to aerobic-dancing grandmothers.

In many occupations, older workers perform well in jobs that require *both* speed and skill. Of course, people do experience a gradual loss of *fluid abilities* (those requiring speed or rapid learning) as they age, but often this can be offset by many *crystallized abilities* (learned knowledge and skills), such as vocabulary and stored-up facts, which may actually improve—at least into the 60s (Schaie, 2005). Overall, very little loss of job performance occurs as workers grow older. In the professions, wisdom and expertise can usually more than compensate for any loss of mental quickness (Ericsson, 2000). Basing retirement solely on a person's age makes little sense.

Successful Aging

What are the keys to successful aging? They are not unlike the elements of well-being at midlife. Four psychological characteristics shared by the healthiest, happiest older people are the following (de Leon, 2005):

- Optimism, hope, and an interest in the future
- Gratitude and forgiveness: an ability to focus on what is good in life
- Empathy: an ability to share the feelings of others and see the world through their eyes
- Connection with others: an ability to give and receive social support

STUDY BREAK   Psychosocial Dilemmas

Reflect

See if you can think of a person you know who is facing one of Erikson's psychosocial dilemmas. Now see if you can think of specific people who seem to be coping with each of the other dilemmas.

Learning Check

As a way to improve your memory, you might find it helpful to summarize Erikson's eight life stages. Complete this do-it-yourself summary and compare your answers with those given below.

Stage	Crisis	Favourable Outcome
First year of life	1. ____ vs.	Faith in the environment and in others
	2. ____	
Ages 1 to 3	3. Autonomy vs. ____	Feelings of self-control and adequacy
Ages 3 to 5	4. ____ vs. guilt	Ability to begin one's own activities
Ages 6 to 12	5. Industry vs. ____	Confidence in productive skills, learning how to work

Adolescence	6. ____ vs. role confusion	An integrated image of oneself as a unique person
Young adulthood	7. Intimacy vs. ____	An ability to form bonds of love and friendship with others
Middle adulthood	8. Generativity vs. ____	Concern for family, society, and future generations
Late adulthood	9. ____ vs.	A sense of dignity and fulfillment, willingness to face death
	10. ____	

Critical Thinking

11. Trying to make generalizations about development throughout life is complicated by at least one major factor. What do you think it is?

Answers

1. trust 2. mistrust 3. shame or doubt 4. initiative 5. inferiority 6. identity 7. isolation 8. stagnation 9. integrity 10. despair 11. Different cohorts (groups of people born in the same year) live in different historical times. People born in various decades may have very different life experiences. This makes it difficult to identify universal patterns (Stewart & Ostrove, 1998).

Actually, these are excellent guidelines for well-being at any stage of adulthood.

In summary, enlightened views of aging call for an end to the forced obsolescence of the elderly. As a group, older people represent a valuable source of skill, knowledge, and energy we can't afford to cast aside. As we face the challenges of this planet's uncertain future, we need all the help we can get!

To squeeze a lifetime into a few pages, we had to ignore countless details. Although much is lost, the net effect is a clearer picture of an entire life cycle. Is Erikson's description an exact map of Amy's future—or your own? Probably not. Still, the dilemmas we have discussed reflect major psychological events in the lives of many. Knowing about them may allow you to anticipate typical trouble spots in life. You may also be better prepared to understand the problems and feelings of friends and relatives at various stages in the life cycle.

Psychology in Action

EFFECTIVE PARENTING—RAISING HEALTHY CHILDREN

When parents fail to give children a good start in life, everybody suffers—the child, the parents, and society as a whole. Children need to grow up with a capacity for love, joy, fulfillment, responsibility, and self-control. Most people discipline their children in the same way they were disciplined. Unfortunately, this means many parents make the same mistakes their parents did (Covell, Grusec, & King, 1995).

Two key ingredients of effective parenting are communication and discipline. In each area, parents must strike a balance between freedom and guidance.

<SURVEY QUESTION
What is the most effective way to discipline a child?

Consistency With respect to child discipline, the maintenance of stable rules of conduct.

Consistency

Individual parents may limit behaviour in ways that are more "strict" or less "strict." But this choice is less important than **consistency** (maintaining stable rules of conduct). Consistent discipline gives a child a sense of security and stability. Inconsistency makes the child's world seem insecure and unpredictable.

What does consistent discipline mean in practice? To illustrate the errors parents often make, let's consider some examples of inconsistency (Fontenelle, 1989). The following are mistakes to avoid.

- Saying one thing and doing something else: You tell the child, "Bart, if you don't eat your Brussels sprouts you can't have any dessert." Then you feel guilty and offer him some dessert anyway.
- Making statements you don't mean: "If you don't quiet down, I'm going to stop the car and make you walk home."
- Changing *no* to *yes*, especially to quiet a nagging child: A good example is the parent who first refuses to buy the child a toy and later gives in and buys it.
- Contradicting the rules your spouse has set for the child: Parents need to agree on guidelines for child discipline and not undermine each other's efforts.
- Responding differently to the same misbehaviour: One day a child is given a time-out for fighting with his sister. The next day the fighting is overlooked.

Inconsistency makes children feel angry and confused because they cannot control the consequences of their own behaviour. Inconsistency also gives children the message "Don't believe what I say because I usually don't mean it."

Using Discipline Constructively

At one time or another, most parents use power assertion, withdrawal of love, or management techniques to control their children. Each mode of discipline has its place. However, physical punishment and withdrawal of love should always be used with caution. Here are some guidelines.

1. Parents should separate disapproval of the act from disapproval of the child. Instead of saying, "I'm going to punish you because you are bad," say, "I'm upset about what you did."
2. State specifically what misbehaviour you are punishing. Explain why you have set limits on this kind of conduct.
3. Punishment should never be harsh or injurious. Don't physically punish a child while you are angry. Also remember that the message "I don't love you right now" can be more painful and damaging than any spanking.
4. Punishment is most effective when it is administered immediately. This statement is especially true for younger children.
5. Spanking and other forms of physical punishment are not particularly effective for children under age two. The child will only be confused and frightened. Spankings also become less effective after age five because they tend to humiliate the child and breed resentment.
6. Many psychologists believe that children should never be spanked. If you do use physical punishment, reserve it for situations that pose an immediate danger to younger children, for example, when a child runs into the street.
7. Remember, too, that it is usually more effective to reward children when they are being good than it is to punish them for misbehaviour.

The Parent–Child Relationship

The heart of child management is the relationship between parents and their children. Parenting experts Don Dinkmeyer and Gary McKay (1997) believe that there are four basic ingredients of positive parent–child interactions.

- *Mutual respect.* Effective parents try to avoid nagging, hitting, debating with, and talking down to their children. They also avoid doing things for their children that children can do for themselves. (Constantly stripping children of opportunities to learn and take responsibility prevents them from becoming independent and developing self-esteem.)
- *Shared enjoyment.* Effective parents spend some time each day with their children, doing something that both the parent and the child enjoy.
- *Love.* This goes almost without saying, but many parents assume their children know that they are loved. It is important to show them you care—in words and by actions such as hugging.
- *Encouragement.* Children who get frequent encouragement come to believe in themselves. Effective parents don't just praise their children for success, winning, or good behaviour. They also recognize a child's progress and attempts to improve. Show you have faith in your children by letting them try things on their own and by encouraging their efforts.

After age five, management techniques are the most effective form of discipline, especially techniques that emphasize communication and the relationship between parent and child.

Communicating Effectively with Children

Creative communication is another important ingredient of successful child management (Bath, 1996). Child expert Haim Ginott (1965) believed that distinguishing between feelings and behaviour is the key to clear communication. Since children (and parents, too) do not choose how they feel, it is important to allow free expression of feelings.

Accepting Feelings   The child who learns to regard some feelings as "bad," or unacceptable, is being asked to deny a very real part of his or her experience. Ginott encouraged parents to teach their children that all feelings are appropriate; it is only actions that are subject to disapproval. Many parents are unaware of just how often they block communication and the expression of feelings in their children. Consider this typical conversation excerpted from Ginott's book (1965):

Son: I am stupid, and I know it. Look at my grades in school.
Father: You just have to work harder.
Son: I already work harder and it doesn't help. I have no brains.
Father: You are smart, I know.
Son: I am stupid, I know.
Father: (loudly) You are not stupid!
Son: Yes, I am!
Father: You are not stupid. Stupid!

By debating with the child, the father misses the point that his son feels stupid. It would be far more helpful for the father to encourage the boy to talk about his feelings.

How could he do that? He might say, "You really feel that you are not as smart as others, don't you? Do you feel this way often? Are you feeling bad at school?" In this way, the child is given a chance to express his emotions and to feel understood. The father might conclude by saying, "Look, son, in my eyes you are a fine person. But I understand how you feel. Everyone feels stupid at times."

Encouragement   Again, it is valuable to remember that supportive parents encourage their children. Encouragement sounds like this (Dinkmeyer, McKay, & Dinkmeyer, 1997):

"It looks like you enjoyed that."
"I have confidence in you; you'll make it."
"It was thoughtful of you to ___."
"Thanks. That helped a lot."
"You really worked hard on that."
"You're improving. Look at the progress you've made."

I-Messages   Communication with a child can also be the basis of effective discipline. Child psychologist Thomas Gordon (2000) believes that parents should send I-messages to their children, rather than you-messages.

What's the difference? **You-messages** take the form of threats, name-calling, accusing, bossing, lecturing, or criticizing. Generally, you-messages tell children what's "wrong" with them. An **I-message** tells children what effect their behaviour had on you. To illustrate the difference, consider this example. After a hard day's work, Susan wants to sit down and rest awhile. She begins to relax with a newspaper when her five-year-old daughter starts banging loudly on a toy drum. Most parents would respond with a you-message, such as "You go play outside this instant" (bossing) or "Don't ever make such a racket when someone is reading" (lecturing).

Gordon suggests sending an I-message such as "I am very tired, and I would like to read. I feel upset and can't read with so much noise." This forces the child to accept responsibility for the effects of her actions.

To summarize, an I-message states the behaviour to which you object. It then clearly tells the child the consequence of his or her behaviour and how that makes you feel. Here's a "fill-in-the-blanks" I-message: "When you [state the child's behaviour], I feel [state your feelings] because [state the consequences of the child's behaviour]." For example, "When you go to Jenny's without telling me, I worry that something might have happened to you because I don't know where you are" (Dinkmeyer et al., 1997).

Using Natural and Logical Consequences

Sometimes events automatically discourage misbehaviour. For example, a child who refuses to eat dinner will get uncomfortably hungry. A child who throws a temper tantrum may gain nothing but a sore throat and a headache if the tantrum is ignored (Fontenelle, 1989). In such instances, the child's actions have **natural consequences** (intrinsic effects). In situations that don't produce natural consequences, parents can set up **logical consequences** (rational and

You-message Threatening, accusing, bossing, lecturing, or criticizing another person (as in, "You always..." or "You never...").

I-message A message that states the effect someone else's behaviour had on you (as in, "I think..." or "I feel...").

Natural consequences The effects that naturally tend to follow a particular behaviour.

Logical consequences Reasonable consequences that are defined by parents.

reasonable effects). For example, a parent might say, "We'll go to the zoo when you've picked up all these toys," or "You can play with your dolls as soon as you've taken your bath," or "You two can stop arguing or leave the table until you're ready to join us."

The concept of logical, parent-defined consequences can be combined with I-messages to handle many day-to-day instances of misbehaviour. The key idea is to use an I-message to set up consequences and then give the child a choice to make: "Michelle, we're trying to watch TV. You may settle down and watch with us or go play elsewhere. You decide which you'd rather do" (Dinkmeyer et al., 1997).

How could Susan have dealt with her five-year-old—the one who was banging on a drum? A response that combines an I-message with logical consequences would be "I would like for you to stop banging on that drum; otherwise, please take it outside." If the child continues to bang on the drum inside the house, then she has caused the toy to be put away. If she takes it outside, she has made a decision to play with the drum in a way that respects her mother's wishes. In this way, both parent and child have been allowed to maintain a sense of self-respect and a needless clash has been averted.

After you have stated consequences and let the child decide, be sure to respect the child's choice. If the child repeats the misbehaviour, you can let the consequences remain in effect longer. But later, give the child another chance to cooperate.

With all child management techniques, remember to be firm, kind, consistent, respectful, and encouraging. And most of all, try every day to live the message you wish to communicate.

✔ STUDY BREAK Parenting and Child Discipline

Reflect

What do you think are the best ways to balance freedom and restraint in child discipline? Parents can probably never be completely consistent. Think of a time when your parents were inconsistent in disciplining you. How did it affect you?

To what extent do the four basic ingredients of positive parent–child interactions apply to any healthy relationship?

Think of a you-message you have recently given a child, family member, roommate, or spouse. Can you change it into an I-message?

Learning Check

1. Effective discipline gives children freedom within a structure of consistent and well-defined limits. T or F?
2. One good way to maintain consistency in child management is to overstate the consequences for misbehaviour. T or F?

3. Spankings and other physical punishments are most effective for children under the age of two. T or F?
4. Giving recognition for progress and attempts to improve is an example of parental _____.
5. I-messages are a gentle way of accusing a child of misbehaviour. T or F?
6. In situations where natural consequences are unavailable or do not discourage misbehaviour, parents should define logical consequences for a child. T or F?

Critical Thinking

7. Several Scandinavian countries have made it illegal for parents to spank their own children. Does this infringe on the rights of parents?

Answers

1. T 2. F 3. F 4. encouragement 5. F 6. T 7. Such laws are based on the view that it should be illegal to physically assault any person, regardless of their age. While parents may believe they have a "right" to spank their children, it can be argued that children need special protection because they are small, powerless, and dependent.

CHAPTER IN REVIEW

Major Points

- You are a product of both your genetic heritage and the environment in which you have lived.

- Infant development is strongly influenced by heredity. However, environmental factors such as nutrition, parenting, and learning are also important.

- Forming an emotional bond with a caregiver is a crucial event during infancy.

- Learning to use language is a cornerstone of early intellectual development.

- Piaget's stage theory provides a valuable map of how thinking abilities unfold.

- Vygotsky's theory reminds us that a child's mind is shaped by culture and human relationships.

- Acquiring moral standards depends, in part, on the development of thinking and reasoning abilities.

- Erik Erikson identified a series of challenges that occur across the lifespan. These range from the need to gain trust in infancy to the need to live with integrity in old age.

- Effective child discipline is consistent, humane, encouraging, and based on respectful communication.

Summary

How do heredity and environment affect development?

- The nature–nurture controversy concerns the relative contributions to development of heredity (nature) and environment (nurture).

- Hereditary instructions are carried by the chromosomes and genes in each cell of the body. Most characteristics are polygenic and reflect the combined effects of dominant and recessive genes.

- Heredity is also involved in differences in temperament. Most infants fall into one of three temperament categories: easy children, difficult children, and slow-to-warm-up children.

- During sensitive periods in development, infants experience an increased sensitivity to specific environmental influences.

- Prenatal development is subject to environmental influences in the form of diseases; drugs; and the mother's diet, health, and emotions. Various teratogens can cause prenatal damage to the fetus, resulting in congenital problems.

- Early perceptual, intellectual, and emotional deprivation seriously retards development.

- Deliberate enrichment of the environment has a beneficial effect on development in infancy.

- Heredity and environment are inseparable and interacting forces. Therefore, a child's developmental level reflects heredity, environment, and the effects of the child's own behaviour.

What can newborn babies do?

- The human neonate has a number of adaptive reflexes, including the grasping, rooting, sucking, and Moro reflexes. Neonates show immediate evidence of learning and of appreciating the consequences of their actions.

- Tests in a looking chamber reveal a number of visual preferences in the newborn. The neonate is drawn to bright lights and circular or curved designs.

- Infants prefer human face patterns, especially familiar faces. In later infancy, interest in the unfamiliar emerges.

What is maturation? What influence does maturation have on a child's early development?

- Maturation of the body and nervous system underlies the orderly sequence of motor, cognitive, emotional, and language development.

- The rate of maturation, however, varies from person to person. Also, learning contributes greatly to the development of basic motor skills.

- Emotions develop in a consistent order from the generalized excitement observed in newborn babies. Three of the basic emotions—fear, anger, and joy—may be unlearned.

- Many early skills are subject to the principle of readiness.

Why is the emotional bond between parent and child so important?

- Emotional attachment of human infants is a critical early event.

- Infant attachment is reflected by separation anxiety. The quality of attachment can be classified as secure, avoidant, or ambivalent/resistant.

- High-quality daycare does not appear to harm children. Low-quality daycare can be risky.

- Meeting a baby's affectional needs is as important as meeting needs for physical care.

What are parenting styles? How important are different parenting styles to a child's development?

- Studies suggest that caregiving styles have a substantial impact on emotional and intellectual development.

- Three major parental styles are authoritarian, permissive, and authoritative. When judged by its effects on children, authoritative parenting appears to benefit children the most.

- Effective parental discipline tends to emphasize child management techniques (especially communication), rather than power assertion or withdrawal of love.

- Whereas mothers typically emphasize caregiving, fathers tend to function as playmates for infants.

How do children acquire language?

- Language development proceeds from control of crying, to cooing, to babbling, to the use of single words, to telegraphic speech.

- The underlying patterns of telegraphic speech suggest a biological predisposition to acquire language. This innate predisposition is augmented by learning.

- Prelanguage communication between parent and child involves shared rhythms, non-verbal signals, and turn-taking.

- Motherese or parentese is a simplified, musical style of speaking used by parents to help their children learn language.

How do children learn to think?

- The intellect of a child is less abstract than that of an adult. Jean Piaget theorized that intellectual growth occurs through a combination of assimilation and accommodation.

- Piaget also held that children go through a fixed series of cognitive stages. The stages and their approximate age ranges are sensorimotor (0–2), preoperational (2–7), concrete operational (7–11), and formal operations (11 to adult).

- Learning principles provide an alternative explanation that assumes cognitive development is continuous; it does not occur in stages.

- Recent studies of infants under the age of one year suggest that they are capable of thought well beyond that observed by Piaget.

- Lev Vygotsky's sociocultural theory emphasizes that a child's mental abilities are advanced by interactions with more competent partners. Mental growth takes place in a child's zone of proximal development, where a more skilful person may scaffold the child's progress.

What are the challenges of adolescence and adulthood? Why is the transition from adolescence to adulthood especially challenging?

- Adolescents must form their identity and values at a time when they are also dealing with puberty.

- Identity formation is even more challenging for adolescents of different ethnicities.

- In Western industrialized societies, the transition to adulthood is further complicated as it is increasingly delayed well into the twenties.

How do we develop morals and values?

- Lawrence Kohlberg identified preconventional, conventional, and postconventional levels of moral reasoning.

- Most people function at the conventional level of morality, but some never get beyond the selfish, preconventional level. Only a minority of people attain the highest, or postconventional, level of moral reasoning.

What are the typical tasks and dilemmas that confront people through their lifespan?

- According to Erikson, each life stage provokes a specific psychosocial dilemma.

- In addition to the dilemmas identified by Erikson, we recognize that each life stage requires successful mastery of certain developmental tasks.

What are the challenges in later adulthood and old age?

- Physical aging begins fairly early in adulthood. Every adult must find ways to cope successfully with aging.

- Midlife course corrections are common. Only a minority of people have a midlife crisis.

- Successful lives are based on happiness, purpose, meaning, and integrity.

- Ageism refers to prejudice, discrimination, and stereotyping on the basis of age. It affects people of all ages but is especially damaging to older people. Most ageism is based on stereotypes, myths, and misinformation.

What is the most effective way to discipline a child?

- Responsibility, mutual respect, consistency, love, encouragement, and clear communication are features of effective parenting.

- Much misbehaviour can be managed by the use of I-messages and the application of natural and logical consequences.

Interactive Learning

Please visit *http://www.psychologyjourney4ce.nelson.com* for a list of weblinks to relevant psychology sites.

CourseMate

Access an interactive e-book and chapter-specific interactive learning tools, including flashcards, quizzes, videos, and more, in your psychology CourseMate. Visit NELSONbrain.com to use CourseMate.

psyk.trek 9. Human Development

TEST YOUR KNOWLEDGE

The questions that follow are only a sample of what you need to know. If you miss any of the items, review the entire chapter and the Study Breaks. Another way to prepare for tests is to use the Study Guide and the Practice Exams that are available with this text.

1. In the nature–nurture debate, the word *nature* refers to which of the following?
   a. senescence
   b. sensitive periods
   c. prenatal teratogens
   d. heredity

2. How is the influence of heredity on early child development most clearly shown?
   a. by differences in temperament
   b. by the existence of sensitive periods
   c. by congenital problems
   d. by the effects of teratogens

3. Cephalocaudal and proximodistal patterns show the effects of which of the following on motor development?
   a. enriched environments
   b. maturation
   c. scaffolding
   d. sensitive periods

4. What type of attachment is shown by a baby who turns away from his mother when she returns after a brief separation?
   a. avoidant
   b. ambivalent/resistant
   c. solitary-ambivalent
   d. maternal-disaffectional

5. What term does psychologist Diana Baumrind use to describe parents who enforce rigid rules and demand strict obedience?
   a. authoritative
   b. permissive-repressive
   c. proactive-reactive
   d. authoritarian

6. Turn-taking with non-verbal signals is a first step toward which of the following?
   a. secure attachment
   b. verbal expansion
   c. using language
   d. gaining an ability to make transformations

7. According to Jean Piaget, during which stage does a child master conservation?
   a. the formal operations stage
   b. the preoperational stage
   c. the concrete operational stage
   d. the sensorimotor stage

8. According to Lev Vygotsky, what process do adults use to help children learn how to think?
   a. reversible thinking
   b. scaffolding
   c. accommodation
   d. egocentric reasoning

9. According to Erik Erikson, what is the dilemma faced by most three- to five-year-olds?
   a. autonomy versus shame and doubt
   b. initiative versus guilt
   c. trust versus mistrust
   d. industry versus inferiority

10. What type of child discipline takes the form of threats, name-calling, accusing, bossing, lecturing, or criticizing?
    a. I-messages
    b. you-messages
    c. logical consequences
    d. natural consequences

11. In infancy, an early step toward social development can be seen within which of the following?
    a. the emergence of self-awareness
    b. the emergence of the Moro reflex
    c. the emergence of sensitive periods
    d. the emergence of motor development

12. Which parenting style has a healthy balance between the rights of parents and the rights of children?
    a. authoritative
    b. permissive
    c. authoritarian
    d. consistent

13. Which of the following is a clear sign that infant attachment is beginning to develop?
    a. social smiles
    b. separation anxiety
    c. social scaffolding
    d. affectional needs

14. What form of discipline tends to make children insecure, anxious, and hungry for approval?
    a. withdrawal of love
    b. management techniques
    c. power assertion
    d. authoritative techniques

15. Jean Piaget believed that a child's understanding of the world grows through the mental processes of assimilation and which of the following?
    a. intuition
    b. egocentrism
    c. accommodation
    d. reversibility

16. A child sees a butterfly for the first time and calls it a "bird." This behaviour is an example of which developmental process?
    a. assimilation
    b. accommodation
    c. conservation
    d. egocentrism

17. A child sees a butterfly for the first time and calls it a "bird." Her mother tells her that it is a butterfly. Now, she calls butterflies by their right name. What is this scenario an example of?
    a. assimilation
    b. accommodation
    c. conservation
    d. egocentrism

18. According to Erikson, when a child enters adolescence, what will his major developmental task demands centre on?
    a. developing trust in others
    b. achieving intimacy with another
    c. acquiring personal autonomy
    d. developing a sense of self

19. Suppose you were to observe motor development in infants across cultures. Where would you find the most similarities in this type of development?
    a. in the ages at which abilities appear
    b. in boys rather than in girls
    c. in the order in which abilities appear
    d. in girls rather than in boys

20. By what age do all human emotions appear?
    a. 6 months
    b. 12 months
    c. 18 months
    d. 24 months

David Madison/Corbis

chapter 4

Sensation and Perception

JOURNEY INTO PSYCHOLOGY: CAN HUMANS ACT LIKE BATS?

It is now well established that blindness is often accompanied by increased sensitivity in other senses, such as hearing. Mel Goodale and his colleagues at Western University in London, Ontario, studied two blind people who are able to navigate well enough to mountain bike, hike, and play basketball (Thaler, Arnott, & Goodale, 2011). How can blind people do this? They emit little click sounds that reflect off objects in their environment and then detect the echoes to learn about those objects. This is called echolocation.

The two echolocators in the study are known as EB (for "early blind") and LB (for "late blind"). EB lost his sight at 13 months, and LB at 14 years. EB and LB both had a tiny microphone placed in each ear. Then they emitted clicks in their usual way, both indoors and outdoors. The idea was that when they emitted the clicks the reflected sound waves returning to their ears would be picked up by the microphones and recorded. Then, with the echolocators in an fMRI scanner, the recordings were played back over headphones. This playback simulated the blind person's experience when they emitted clicks and detected echoes in the real world. The remarkable finding was that the playback of reflected clicks produced activation in visual processing areas of the brain.

EB and LB were able to distinguish between echoes reflected from cars, trees, and poles, and to distinguish those from sound stimuli that did not contain reflected echoes. The effects were stronger in EB than in LB, probably because of EB's greater skill in using the click echoes to navigate, a function of longer experience, since he had been blind for 42 years at the time of testing, to LB's 13 years. Nonetheless, both EB and LB had developed the skill on their own and used it daily in their ordinary activities. This study provides fascinating evidence that when one sense is lost at an early age, parts of the brain normally dedicated to that sense may instead be used to support another sense.

We begin this chapter with the first step, a look at how the senses operate. Then we'll explore the second step, perception, when our brain assembles sensations into a meaningful "picture" of events. Our perceptions create faces, melodies, works of art, and illusions out of the raw material of sensation. Let's see how this takes place.

Survey Questions

- In general, how do sensory systems function?
- How does the visual system function?
- What are the mechanisms of hearing?
- How do the chemical senses operate?
- What are the somesthetic senses?
- Why are we more aware of some sensations than others?
- In general, how do we construct our perceptions?
- How is it possible to see depth and judge distance?
- How is perception altered by expectations, motives, emotions, and learning?
- Is extrasensory perception possible?
- How can I learn to perceive events more accurately?

SENSORY SYSTEMS—THE FIRST STEP

SURVEY QUESTION>
In general, how do sensory systems function?

Transducers Devices that convert one kind of energy into another.

Sensation A sensory impression; also, the process of detecting physical energies with the sensory organs.

Perception The mental process of organizing sensations into meaningful patterns.

The primary function of the senses is to act as biological **transducers,** devices that convert one kind of energy into another (Fain, 2003). Each sense translates a specific type of external energy into patterns of activity (action potentials) in neurons. Then the brain processes these messages. Information arriving from the sense organs creates **sensations.** When the brain organizes sensations into meaningful patterns, we speak of **perception.** It is fascinating to realize that "seeing" and "hearing" take place in your brain, not in your eyes or ears.

Before we move on to perception, let's further explore sensation. Consider, for example, vision, which gives us amazingly wide access to the world. In one instant you can view a star light years away, and in the next, you can peer into the microscopic universe of a dewdrop. Yet, vision also narrows what we can possibly observe. Like the other senses, vision acts as a *data reduction system.* It selects and analyzes information in order to code and send to the brain only the most important data (Goldstein, 2010).

Selection

How does data reduction take place? Considerable selection occurs because sensory receptors do not transduce all of the energies they encounter. For example, a guitar transduces string vibrations into sound waves. Pluck a string and the guitar will produce a sound. However, stimuli that don't cause the string to move will have no effect. If you shine a light on the string, or pour cold water on it, the guitar will remain silent. (The owner of the guitar, however, might get quite loud at this point!) In a similar way, the eye transduces electromagnetic radiation, the ear transduces sound waves, and so on. Many other types of stimuli cannot be sensed directly because we lack sensory receptors to transduce their energy. For example, humans cannot sense the bioelectric fields of other living creatures, but sharks have special organs that can (Fields, 2007). (Do they *hear* the fields or *feel* them or what?)

Further, sense receptors transduce only part of their target energy range (Fain, 2003). For example, your eyes transduce only a tiny fraction of the entire range of electromagnetic energies—the part we call the *visible spectrum.* The eyes of honeybees can transduce, and therefore see, parts of the electromagnetic spectrum invisible to humans. The ears of bats can transduce echoing sound waves that humans can't hear. This ability, called *echolocation,* allows bats to fly in pitch darkness. As described earlier, humans can learn to echolocate well enough for a blind person to mountain bike. As you can see, our rich sensory experiences are only a small part of what *could* be sensed and what some animals *can* sense.

Analysis

What we experience is also influenced by **sensory analysis.** As they process information, the senses divide the world into important **perceptual features** (basic stimulus patterns). The visual system, for example, has a set of *feature detectors* that are attuned to very specific stimuli, such as lines, shapes, edges, spots, colours, and other patterns (Hubel & Wiesel, 2005). Look at Figure 4.1 and notice how eye-catching the single vertical line is among a group of slanted lines. This effect, which is called *pop-out,* occurs because your visual system is highly sensitive to these perceptual features (Adler & Orprecio, 2006).

Similarly, frog eyes are highly sensitive to small, dark, moving spots. In other words, they are basically "tuned" to detect bugs flying nearby (Lettvin, 1961). But the insect (spot) must be moving, or the frog's "bug detectors" won't work. A frog could starve to death surrounded by dead flies.

Our sensitivity to perceptual features is an innate characteristic of the nervous system. Like other inborn capacities, this sensitivity is also influenced by experiences early in life. For instance, Colin Blakemore and Graham Cooper of Cambridge University raised kittens in a room with only vertical stripes on the walls. Another set of kittens saw only horizontal stripes. When returned to normal environments, the "horizontal" cats could easily jump onto a chair, but when walking on the floor, they bumped into chair legs. "Vertical" cats, on the other hand, easily avoided chair legs, but they missed when trying to jump to horizontal surfaces. The cats raised with vertical stripes were "blind" to horizontal lines, and the "horizontal" cats acted as if vertical lines were invisible (Blakemore & Cooper, 1970). Other experiments show that there is an actual decrease in brain cells tuned to the missing features (Grobstein & Chow, 1975). However, as the two echolocators described at the beginning of the chapter show, instead of brain cells being lost it is possible for them to be recruited for another sensory modality.

Sensory Coding

As they select and analyze information, sensory systems *code* it. **Sensory coding** refers to converting important features of the world into neural messages understood by the brain (Hubel & Wiesel, 2005). To see coding at work, try closing your eyes for a moment. Then take your fingertips and press firmly on your eyelids. Apply enough pressure to "squash" your eyes slightly. Do this for about 30 seconds and observe what happens. (Readers with eye problems or contact lenses should not try this.)

> **Sensory analysis** Separation of sensory information into important elements.
> **Perceptual features** Basic elements of a stimulus, such as lines, shapes, edges, or colours.
> **Sensory coding** Codes used by the sense organs to transmit information to the brain

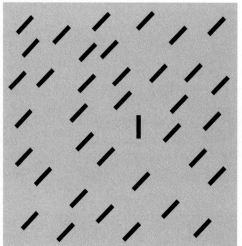

▸▸**FIGURE 4.1** Visual pop-out. Pop-out is so basic that babies as young as three months old respond to it. (Adapted from Adler & Orprecio, 2006.)

▶▶**FIGURE 4.2** An artificial visual system.

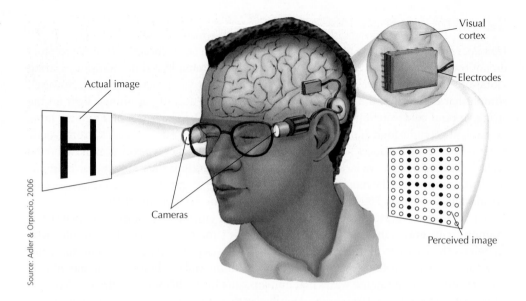

Did you "see" stars, checkerboards, and flashes of colour? These are called *phosphenes* (FOSS-feens: visual sensations caused by mechanical excitation of the retina). They occur because the eye's receptor cells, which normally respond to light, are also somewhat sensitive to pressure. Notice, though, that the eye is prepared to code stimulation—including pressure—only into visual features. As a result, you experience light sensations, not pressure. Also important in producing this effect is *sensory localization* in the brain.

Sensory localization means that the type of sensation you experience depends on which brain area is activated. Some brain areas receive visual information, others receive auditory information, and still others receive taste or touch (see Chapter 2). Knowing which brain areas are active tells us, in general, what kinds of sensations you are feeling.

Sensory localization may some day make it possible to artificially restore sight, hearing, or other senses. In fact, researchers have already used a miniature television camera to send electrical signals to the brain (Figure 4.2) (Dobelle, 2000; Warren & Normann, 2005). In July 2006, a woman named Cheri Robinson became the 16th person in the world with an implant of this type. She can now "see" 100 dots of light. Like a sports scoreboard, these lights can be used to form crude letters (Dobelle, 2000). Eventually, a larger number of dots could make reading and "seeing" large objects, such as furniture and doorways, possible.

Before we move on to discuss perception, let's look in more detail at our various senses, beginning with vision, the most magnificent sensory system of all.

VISION—CATCHING SOME RAYS

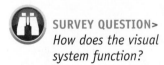

SURVEY QUESTION>
How does the visual system function?

What are the basic dimensions of light and vision? The *visible spectrum* (the spread of electromagnetic energies to which the eyes respond) is made up of a narrow range of wavelengths of electromagnetic radiation. Visible light starts at "short" wavelengths of 400 *nanometres* (NAN-oh-MEE-ter: one billionth of a metre), which we sense as purple or violet. Longer light waves produce blue, green, yellow, orange, and red, which has a wavelength of 700 nanometres (Figure 4.3).

The term *hue* refers to the basic colour categories of red, orange, yellow, green, blue, indigo, and violet. As just noted, various hues (or colour sensations) correspond to the wavelength of the light that reaches our eyes (Mather, 2008). White light, in contrast, is a mixture of many wavelengths. Hues (colours) from a narrow band of wavelengths are very *saturated,* or "pure." (An intense "fire-engine" red is more saturated than a muddy "brick" red.) A third dimension of vision, *brightness,* corresponds roughly to the amplitude, or height, of light waves. Waves of

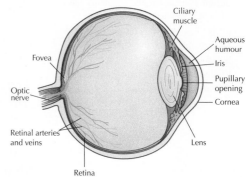

»**FIGURE 4.3** The visible spectrum.

greater amplitude are "taller," carry more energy, and cause the colours we see to appear brighter or more intense. For example, the same "brick" red would look bright under intense, high-energy illumination and drab under dim light.

Structure of the Eye

Although the visual system is much more complex than any digital camera, both cameras and eyes have a *lens* to focus images on a light-sensitive layer at the back of a closed space. In a camera, it is a layer of light-sensitive pixels in the digital image sensor. In the eye, it is a layer of *photoreceptors* (light-sensitive cells) in the **retina,** an area about the size and thickness of a postage stamp (Figure 4.4).

How does the eye focus? Most focusing is done at the front of the eye, by the *cornea,* a clear membrane that bends light inward. The lens makes additional, smaller adjustments. Your eye's focal point changes when muscles attached to the lens alter its shape. This process is called **accommodation.** In cameras, focusing is done more simply—by changing the distance between the lens and the image sensor.

Visual Problems

Focusing is also affected by the shape of the eye. If your eye is too short, nearby objects will be blurred, but distant objects will be sharp. This is called **hyperopia** (HI-per-OPE-ee-ah: farsightedness). If your eyeball is too long, images fall short of the retina and you won't be able to focus distant objects. This results in **myopia** (my-OPE-ee-ah: nearsightedness). When the cornea or the lens is misshapen, part of vision will be focused and part will be fuzzy. In this case, the eye has more than one focal point, a problem called **astigmatism** (ah-STIG-mah-tiz-em). All three visual defects can be corrected by placing glasses (or contact lenses) in front of the eye to change the path of light (Figure 4.5).

As people age, the lens becomes less flexible and less able to accommodate. The result is **presbyopia** (prez-bee-OPE-ee-ah: old vision, or farsightedness due to aging). Perhaps you have seen a grandparent or older friend reading a newspaper at arm's length because of

Retina The light-sensitive layer of cells at the back of the eye.

Accommodation Changes in the shape of the lens of the eye.

Hyperopia Difficulty focusing nearby objects (farsightedness).

Myopia Difficulty focusing distant objects (nearsightedness).

Astigmatism Defects in the cornea, lens, or eye that cause some areas of vision to be out of focus.

Presbyopia Farsightedness caused by aging.

»**FIGURE 4.4** The human eye—a simplified view.

Log on to CourseMate to access this interactive figure

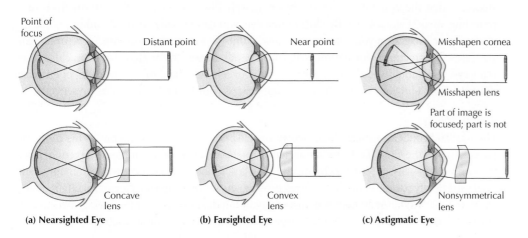

(a) **Nearsighted Eye**   (b) **Farsighted Eye**   (c) **Astigmatic Eye**

»**FIGURE 4.5** Visual defects and corrective lenses: (a) A myopic (longer than usual) eye. The concave lens spreads light rays just enough to increase the eye's focal length. (b) A hyperopic (shorter than usual) eye. The convex lens increases refraction (bending), returning the point of focus to the retina. (c) An astigmatic (lens or cornea not symmetrical) eye. In astigmatism, parts of vision are sharp and parts are unfocused. Lenses to correct astigmatism are non-symmetrical.

Blindness and Social Interaction

As the Canadian population ages, vision problems are likely to increase in significance. One study by researchers from the University of Sherbrooke and the University of Montréal showed that a large group of elderly women with visual impairment had significantly lower participation in daily activities than a control group (Desrosiers et al., 2009). Participation rates were most strongly related to depression and to the women's perception of the quality of their own distance vision. Solving these problems is not simply a matter of providing services. Elderly people have particular issues that must be addressed. For example, researchers from the University of Waterloo and Western University interviewed 34 elderly people suffering low vision to find out why they were not using available services (Spafford et al., 2010). The number one reason was lack of knowledge about those services, a problem even in the Internet era because elderly people are less likely to use computers or have access to the Internet. As people more comfortable with computers age, that issue is likely to be replaced by what is currently the second most important reason for not using available services: motivation to appear independent. For elderly people, maintaining independence can

be an important goal, one that might make them reluctant to admit they need low-vision services.

Of course, it is not just older people who have vision problems. Young people with low vision or blindness face different problems than elderly people, particularly in the area of social relations. One of the most important tasks of young adulthood is finding a life partner. That usually involves being out in society. Social challenges faced by young Canadians with vision impairments were assessed in a recent study by CNIB researchers (Gold, Shaw, & Wolffe, 2010). Using a sample of 300 people from across Canada, Gold and her colleagues showed that blind and low-vision young people engage more in leisure activities that involve no or only moderate social engagement. This was a particular problem for the men in the sample—women with low vision were more likely to have a partner and more likely to have dated than men with low vision. Nonetheless, the Internet appears to help these younger low-vision and blind Canadians interact socially—75 percent of them reported socializing via the Internet, an impressive figure given that the data were collected before the explosion of new social media avenues such as Facebook and Twitter.

Cones Visual receptors for colours and daylight visual acuity.

Rods Visual receptors for dim light that produce only black and white sensations.

Visual acuity The sharpness of visual perception.

presbyopia. While holding a newspaper farther away may not seem like a major difficulty, decreasing vision with aging can have more important consequences, such as compromising social interaction. You can learn more about this aspect of aging in the Clinical File: "Blindness and Social Interaction." If you now wear glasses for nearsightedness, you may need bifocals as you age. Bifocal lenses correct near vision *and* distance vision.

Rods and Cones

The eye has two types of "image sensors," consisting of receptor cells called *rods* and *cones* (Mather, 2008). The 5 million **cones** in each eye work best in bright light. They also produce colour sensations and fine details. In contrast, the **rods,** numbering about 120 million, can't detect colours (Figure 4.6). Pure rod vision is black and white. However, the rods are much more sensitive to light than the cones are. The rods therefore allow us to see in very dim light.

Surprisingly, the retina has a "hole" in it: Each eye has a *blind spot* because there are no receptors where the optic nerve passes out of the eye and blood vessels enter (Figure 4.7a). The blind spot shows that vision depends greatly on the brain. If you close one eye, part of what you see will fall on the blind spot of your open eye. Why isn't there a gap in your vision? The answer is that the visual cortex of the brain actively fills in the gap with patterns from surrounding areas (Figure 4.7b). By closing one eye, you can visually "behead" other people by placing their images on your blind spot. (Just a hint for some classroom fun.) The brain can also "erase" distracting information. Roll your eyes all the way to the right and then close your right eye. You should clearly see your nose in your left eye's field of vision. Now, open your right eye again and your nose will nearly disappear as your brain disregards its presence.

Visual Acuity

The rods and cones also affect **visual acuity,** or sharpness. The cones lie mainly at the centre of the eye. In fact, the *fovea* (FOE-vee-ah: a small, cup-shaped area in the middle of the retina) contains only cones—about 50 000 of them. Like high-resolution digital sensors made of many small pixels, the tightly packed cones in the fovea produce the sharpest images. Normal acuity is designated as 20/20 vision: At 20 metres in distance, you can distinguish what the average person can see at 20 metres (Figure 4.8). If your vision is 20/40, you can see at 20 metres only what the

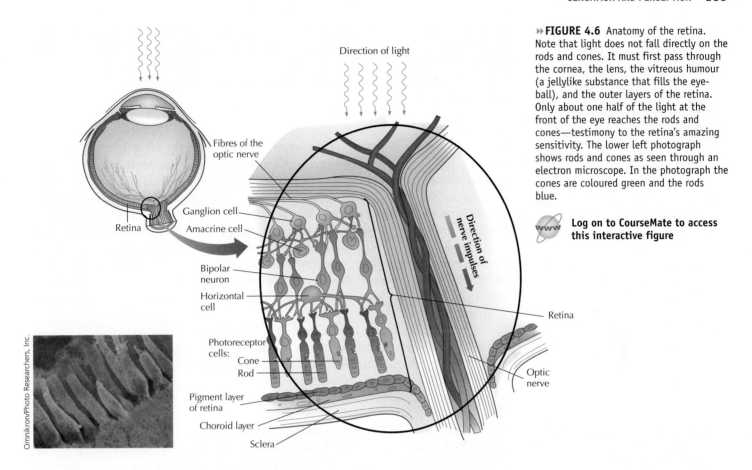

Direction of light

FIGURE 4.6 Anatomy of the retina. Note that light does not fall directly on the rods and cones. It must first pass through the cornea, the lens, the vitreous humour (a jellylike substance that fills the eyeball), and the outer layers of the retina. Only about one half of the light at the front of the eye reaches the rods and cones—testimony to the retina's amazing sensitivity. The lower left photograph shows rods and cones as seen through an electron microscope. In the photograph the cones are coloured green and the rods blue.

Log on to CourseMate to access this interactive figure

FIGURE 4.7 Experiencing the blind spot. (a) With your right eye closed, stare at the upper right cross. Hold the book about 30 centimetres from your eye and slowly move it back and forth. You should be able to locate a position that causes the black spot to disappear. When it does, it has fallen on the blind spot. With a little practice, you can learn to make people or objects you dislike disappear too!
(b) Repeat the procedure described, but stare at the lower cross. When the white space falls on the blind spot, the black lines will appear to be continuous. This may help you understand why you do not usually experience a blind spot in your visual field.

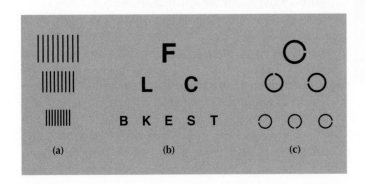

FIGURE 4.8 Tests of visual acuity. Here are some common tests of visual acuity. In (a), sharpness is indicated by the smallest grating still seen as individual lines. The Snellen chart (b) requires that you read rows of letters of diminishing size until you can no longer distinguish them. The Landolt rings (c) require no familiarity with letters. All that is required is a report of which side has a break in it.

Peripheral vision Vision at the edges of the visual field.

Trichromatic theory A theory of colour vision based on three cone types: red, green, and blue.

Opponent-process theory The theory of colour vision based on three coding systems (red or green, yellow or blue, black or white).

average person can see at 40 metres. If your vision is 20/200, everything is a blur and you need glasses! Vision that is 20/12 would mean that you can see at 20 metres what the average person must be 8 metres nearer to see, indicating better than average acuity. American astronaut Gordon Cooper, who claimed to see railroad lines in northern India from 100 miles (160 kilometres) above, had 20/12 vision.

Peripheral Vision

What is the purpose of the rest of the retina? Areas outside the fovea also receive light, creating a large region of **peripheral** (side) **vision.** The rods are most numerous about 20 degrees from the centre of the retina, so much of our peripheral vision is rod vision. Although rod vision is not very high resolution, the rods are quite sensitive to *movement* in peripheral vision. To experience this characteristic of the rods, look straight ahead and hold your hand beside your head, at about 90 degrees. Wiggle your finger and slowly move your hand forward until you can detect motion. You will become aware of the movement before you can actually "see" your finger. Seeing "out of the corner of the eye" is important for sports, driving, and walking down dark alleys. People who suffer from *tunnel vision* (a loss of peripheral vision) feel as if they are wearing blinders (Godnig, 2003).

The rods are also highly responsive to dim light. Because most rods are 20 degrees to each side of the fovea, the best night vision comes from looking *next to* an object you wish to see. Test this yourself some night by looking at, and next to, a very dim star.

Colour Vision

How do the cones produce colour sensations? The **trichromatic** (TRY-kro-MAT-ik) **theory** of colour vision holds that there are three types of cones, each most sensitive to either red, green, or blue. Other colours result from combinations of these three.

A basic problem with the trichromatic theory is that four colours of light—red, green, blue, and yellow—seem to be primary (you can't get them by mixing other colours). Also, why is it impossible to have a reddish green or a yellowish blue? These problems led to the development of a second view, known as the **opponent-process theory,** which states that vision analyzes colours into "either-or" messages (Goldstein, 2010). That is, the visual system can produce messages for either red or green, yellow or blue, black or white. Coding one colour in a pair (red, for instance) seems to block the opposite message (green) from coming through. As a result, a reddish green is impossible, but a yellowish red (orange) can occur.

According to opponent-process theory, fatigue caused by making one response produces an afterimage of the opposite colour as the system recovers. *Afterimages* are visual sensations that persist after a stimulus is removed—like seeing a spot after a flashbulb goes off. To see an afterimage of the type predicted by opponent-process theory, look at Figure 4.9 and follow the instructions there.

Which colour theory is correct? Both! The three-colour theory applies to the retina, where three different types of *visual pigments* (light-sensitive chemicals) have been found in cones. As predicted, each pigment is most sensitive to light in roughly the red, green, or blue region. The three types of cones fire nerve impulses at different rates to produce various colour sensations (Figure 4.10).

In contrast, the opponent-process theory better explains what happens in optic pathways and the brain *after* information leaves the eye. For example, some nerve

▶▶**FIGURE 4.9** Negative afterimages. Stare at the dot near the middle of the flag for at least 30 seconds. Then look immediately at a plain sheet of white paper or a white wall. You will see the Canadian flag in its normal colours. Reduced sensitivity to green and black in the visual system, caused by prolonged staring, results in the appearance of complementary colours. Project the afterimage of the flag on other coloured surfaces to get additional effects.

cells in the brain are excited by the colour red and inhibited by the colour green. So both theories are "correct." One explains what happens in the eye itself. The other explains how colours are analyzed after messages leave the eye (Gegenfurtner & Kiper, 2003).

Colour-Blindness and Colour Weakness

Do you know anyone who regularly draws hoots of laughter by wearing clothes of wildly clashing colours? Or someone who sheepishly tries to avoid saying what colour an object is? If so, you probably know someone who is colour-blind.

What is it like to be colour-blind? What causes colour-blindness? A person who is **colour-blind** cannot perceive colours. It is as if the world were a black-and-white movie. The colour-blind person either lacks cones or has cones that do not function normally (Deeb, 2004). Such total colour-blindness is rare. In **colour weakness,** or partial colour-blindness, a person can't see certain colours. Approximately 8 percent of Caucasian males (but fewer Asian, African, and First Nations males and less than 1 percent of women) are red-green colour-blind (Delpero et al., 2005). These people see reds and greens as the same colour, usually a yellowish brown (see Figure 4.11). Another type of colour weakness, involving yellow and blue, is extremely rare (Hsia & Graham, 1997). (See Using Psychology: "Are You Colour-Blind?")

How can colour-blind individuals drive? Don't they have trouble with traffic lights? Red-green colour-blind individuals have normal vision for yellow and blue, so the main problem is telling red lights from green. In practice, that's not difficult. The green light is brighter than the red, and the relative positions of the colours are consistent—in some jurisdictions, green is on top and red is on the bottom, while in other places green is on the right and red is on the left. Also, "red" traffic signals have yellow light mixed in with the red and a "green" light that is really blue-green.

Dark Adapting to Dim Light

What happens when the eyes adjust to a dark room? **Dark adaptation** is the dramatic increase in retinal sensitivity to light that occurs after a person enters the dark (Goldstein, 2010). Consider walking into a theatre. If you enter from a brightly lit lobby, you

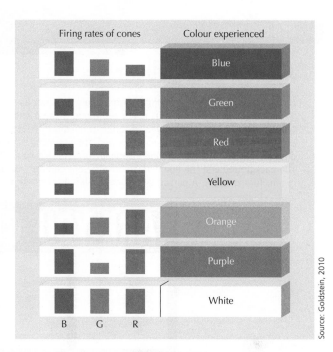

▸▸**FIGURE 4.10** Firing rates of blue, green, and red cones in response to different colours. The taller the coloured bar, the higher the firing rates for that type of cone. As you can see, colours are coded by differences in the activity of all three types of cones in the normal eye. (Adapted from Goldstein, 2010.)

Source: Goldstein, 2010

> **Colour-blindness** A total inability to perceive colours.
>
> **Colour weakness** An inability to distinguish some colours.
>
> **Dark adaptation** Increased retinal sensitivity to light.

(a)

(b)

(c)

Michael Newman/PhotoEdit

▸▸**FIGURE 4.11** Colour-blindness and colour weakness. (a) Photograph illustrates normal colour vision. (b) Photograph is printed in blue and yellow and gives an impression of what a red-green colour-blind person sees. (c) Photograph simulates total colour-blindness. If you are totally colour-blind, all three photos will look nearly identical.

Are You Colour-Blind?

How can I tell if I am colour-blind? Surprisingly, it is not as obvious as you might think; some of us reach adulthood without knowing. The *Ishihara test* is commonly used to measure colour-blindness and colour weakness. In the test, numbers and other designs made of dots are placed on a background also made of dots (Figure 4.12). The background and the numbers are of different colours (red and green, for example). A person who is colour-blind sees only a jumble of dots. If you have normal colour vision, you can detect the numbers or designs (Mollon, Pokorny, & Knoblauch, 2003). The chart below Figure 4.12 lists what is seen by people with normal colour vision and colour-blindness. Because this chart is just a replica, it is not a definitive test of colour-blindness. Nevertheless, if you can't see all of the embedded designs, you may be colour-blind or colour weak.

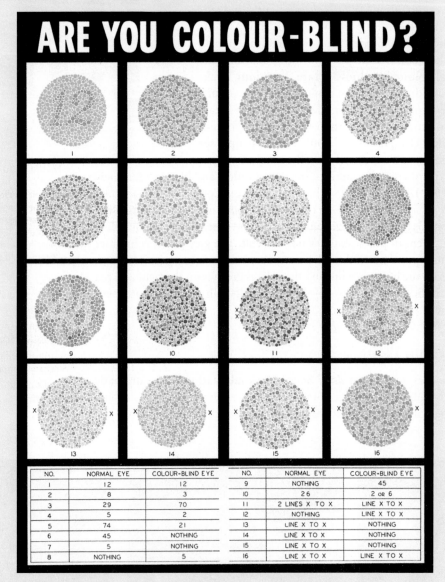

NO.	NORMAL EYE	COLOUR-BLIND EYE	NO.	NORMAL EYE	COLOUR-BLIND EYE
1	12	12	9	NOTHING	45
2	8	3	10	26	2 OR 6
3	29	70	11	2 LINES X TO X	LINE X TO X
4	5	2	12	NOTHING	LINE X TO X
5	74	21	13	LINE X TO X	NOTHING
6	45	NOTHING	14	LINE X TO X	NOTHING
7	5	NOTHING	15	LINE X TO X	NOTHING
8	NOTHING	5	16	LINE X TO X	LINE X TO X

▶▶**FIGURE 4.12** A replica of the Ishihara test for colour-blindness.

practically need to be led to your seat. After a short time, however, you can see the entire room in detail (including the couple kissing over in the corner). It takes about 30 to 35 minutes of complete darkness to reach maximum visual sensitivity (Figure 4.13). At that point, your eye will be 100 000 times as sensitive to light.

What causes dark adaptation? Like the cones, the rods contain a light-sensitive visual pigment. When struck by light, visual pigments *bleach*, or break down chemically. The afterimages you have seen after looking at a flashbulb are a result of this bleaching. In fact, a few seconds of exposure to bright white light can completely wipe out dark adaptation. That's why you should be sure to avoid looking at oncoming headlights when you are driving at night—especially the new bluish-white xenon lights. To restore light sensitivity, the visual pigments in the rods must recombine, which takes time.

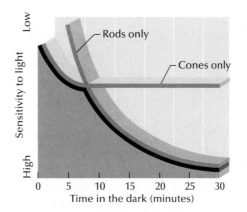

▶▶**FIGURE 4.13** Typical course of dark adaptation. The black line shows how the threshold for vision lowers as a person spends time in the dark. (A lower threshold means that less light is needed for vision.) The green line shows that the cones adapt first, but they soon cease adding to light sensitivity. Rods, shown by the red line, adapt more slowly. However, they continue to add to improved night vision long after the cones are fully adapted.

✔ STUDY BREAK Sensory Systems and Vision

Reflect

How does sensation affect what you are experiencing right now? What if data reduction didn't occur? What if you could transduce other energies? What if your senses were tuned to detect different perceptual features? How would the sensory world you live in change? What would it be like to be a bat?

Pretend you are a beam of light. What will happen to you at each step as you pass into the eye and land on the retina? What will happen if the eye is not perfectly shaped? How will the retina know you've arrived? How will it tell what colour of light you are? What will it tell the brain about you?

Learning Check

1. Sensory receptors are biological _____, or devices for converting one type of energy to another.
2. Lettvin found that a frog's eyes are especially sensitive to phosphenes. T or F?
3. Important features of the environment are transmitted to the brain through a process known as _____.
   a. phosphenation   b. coding
   c. detection   d. programming

4. Match:
   _____ Myopia   **A.** Farsightedness
   _____ Hyperopia   **B.** Elongated eye
   _____ Presbyopia   **C.** Farsightedness due to aging
   _____ Astigmatism   **D.** Lack of cones in the fovea
                             E. Misshapen cornea or lens
5. In dim light, vision depends mainly on the _____. In brighter light, colour and fine detail are produced by the _____.
6. The fovea has the greatest visual acuity due to the large concentration of rods found there. T or F?
7. The eyes become more sensitive to light at night because of a process known as _____.

Critical Thinking

8. William James once said, "If a master surgeon were to cross the auditory and optic nerves, we would hear lightning and see thunder." Can you explain what James meant?
9. Sensory transduction in the eye takes place first in the cornea, then in the lens, then in the retina. True or false? Explain your answer.

ANSWERS

1. transducers 2. F 3. b 4. b, C, A, E 5. rods, cones 6. F 7. dark adaptation 8. The explanation is based on sensory localization: Even if a lightning flash caused rerouted messages from the eyes to activate auditory areas of the brain, we would nevertheless experience a sound sensation. Likewise, if the ears transduced a thunderclap, and sent impulses to the visual area, a sensation of light would occur. 9. False. The cornea and lens bend and focus light rays, but they do not change light to another form of energy. No change in the type of energy takes place until the retina converts light to nerve impulses.

HEARING—GOOD VIBRATIONS

<**SURVEY QUESTION**
What are the mechanisms of hearing?

Rock, classical, jazz, rap, country, hip-hop—whatever your musical taste, you have probably been moved by the riches of sound. Hearing also collects information from all around the body, such as detecting the approach of an unseen car (Yost, 2007). Vision, in all its glory, is limited to stimuli in front of the eyes.

What is the stimulus for hearing? If you throw a stone into a quiet pond, a circle of waves will spread in all directions. In much the same way, sound travels as a series of invisible waves of *compression* (peaks) and *rarefaction* (RARE-eh-fak-shun: valleys) in the air. Any vibrating object—a tuning fork, the string of a musical instrument, or the vocal

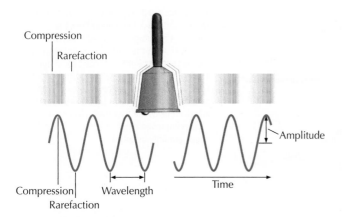

Compression

Rarefaction

Amplitude

Compression

Rarefaction   Wavelength

Time

▸▸**FIGURE 4.14** Waves of compression in the air, or vibrations, are the stimulus for hearing. The frequency of sound waves determines their pitch. The amplitude determines loudness.

cords—will produce sound waves (rhythmic movement of air molecules). Other materials, such as fluids and solids, can also carry sound. But sound does not travel in a vacuum or the airless realm of outer space.

The *frequency* of sound waves (the number of waves per second) corresponds to the perceived *pitch* (higher or lower tone) of a sound. The *amplitude,* or physical "height," of a sound wave tells how much energy it contains. Psychologically, amplitude corresponds to sensed *loudness* (sound intensity) (Figure 4.14).

Although we'll talk about various forms of deafness below, note that pitch perception can be impaired in people with otherwise normal hearing. Isabelle Peretz and her colleagues at the University of Montréal study *congenital amusia,* or "tone deafness," in hearing subjects. Julie Ayotte, Isabelle Peretz, and Krista Hyde (2002) found a set of people who had never suffered brain damage, have no general learning disability, had taken music lessons during childhood, but have a history of musical failure. They have a music-specific disorder of pitch perception (see also Hyde & Peretz, 2003, 2004, 2005). These people are not able to tell which of two examples of a melody has a wrong note, nor to distinguish a dissonant melody from a harmonious one or to detect pitch differences smaller than one semitone. While in general people are better at making pitch discriminations in musical stimuli than in speech stimuli, in congenital amusia the reverse pattern is found: They're better at pitch discrimination in speech than in music (Tillmann et al., 2011). Isabel Peretz and her colleagues developed an online test for congenital amusia (Peretz et al., 2008). This test can be taken in 15 minutes. Work with this test so far has confirmed that the disorder involves only insensitivity to musical pitch, not a deficit in musical timing or in spatial processing (Tillmann et al., 2010).

How We Hear Sounds

How are sounds converted to nerve impulses? Hearing involves an elaborate chain of events that begins with the *pinna* (PIN-ah: the visible, external part of the ear). In addition to being a good place to hang earrings or balance pencils, the pinna acts like a funnel to concentrate sounds. After they are guided into the ear canal, sound waves collide with the *tympanic membrane* (eardrum), setting it in motion. This, in turn, causes three small bones (the *auditory ossicles*) (OSS-ih-kuls) to vibrate (Figure 4.15). The ossicles are the malleus (MAL-ee-us), incus, and stapes (STAY-peas). Their common names are the hammer, anvil, and stirrup. The ossicles link the eardrum with the *cochlea* (KOCK-lee-ah: a snail-shaped organ that makes up the inner ear). The stapes is attached to a membrane on the cochlea called the *oval window.* As the oval window moves back and forth, it makes waves in a fluid inside the cochlea.

Inside the cochlea, tiny **hair cells** detect waves in the fluid. The hair cells are part of the **organ of Corti** (KOR-tee), which makes up the centre part of the cochlea (Figure 4.16). A set of *stereocilia* (STER-ee-oh-SIL-ih-ah), or "bristles," atop each hair cell brush against the tectorial membrane when waves ripple through the fluid surrounding the organ of Corti. As the stereocilia are bent, nerve impulses are triggered, which then flow to the brain.

How are higher and lower sounds detected? The **frequency theory** of hearing states that as pitch rises, nerve impulses of a corresponding frequency are fed into the auditory nerve. That is, an 800-hertz tone produces 800 nerve impulses per second. (*Hertz* refers to the number of vibrations per second.) This explains how sounds up to about 4000 hertz reach the brain. But what about higher tones? **Place theory** states that higher and lower tones excite specific areas of the cochlea. High tones register most strongly at the base of the cochlea (near the oval window). Lower tones, on the other hand, mostly move hair cells

Hair cells Receptor cells within the cochlea that transduce vibrations into nerve impulses.

Organ of Corti The centre part of the cochlea, containing hair cells, canals, and membranes.

Frequency theory Tones up to 4000 hertz are converted to nerve impulses that match the frequency of each tone.

Place theory Higher and lower tones excite specific areas of the cochlea.

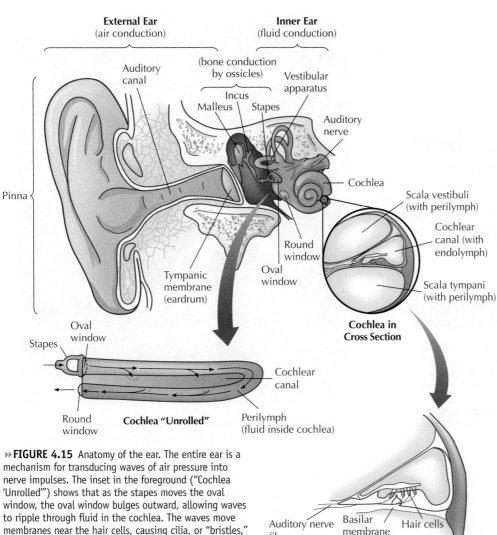

Log on to CourseMate to access this interactive figure

»FIGURE 4.15 Anatomy of the ear. The entire ear is a mechanism for transducing waves of air pressure into nerve impulses. The inset in the foreground ("Cochlea 'Unrolled'") shows that as the stapes moves the oval window, the oval window bulges outward, allowing waves to ripple through fluid in the cochlea. The waves move membranes near the hair cells, causing cilia, or "bristles," on the tips of the cells to bend. The hair cells then generate nerve impulses that are carried to the brain. (See an enlarged cross section of the cochlea in Figure 4.16.)

near the narrow outer tip of the cochlea (Figure 4.17). Pitch is signalled by the area of the cochlea most strongly activated. Place theory also explains why hunters sometimes lose hearing in a narrow pitch range. "Hunter's notch," as it is called, occurs when hair cells are damaged in the area affected by the pitch of gunfire.

Hearing Loss

What causes other types of hearing loss? The two most common types of hearing loss afflict some 278 million people worldwide (Tennesen, 2007). **Conductive hearing loss** occurs when the transfer of vibrations from the outer ear to the inner ear is weak. For example, the eardrums or ossicles may be damaged or immobilized by disease or injury. In many cases, conductive hearing loss can be overcome with a hearing aid, which makes sounds louder and clearer.

One cause of conductive hearing loss is a chronic inflammation of the middle ear due to infection. Called otitis media, it is particularly common in North American Aboriginal children. Although reliable data are difficult to come by because of variation in the make-up of samples and of diagnostic criteria, in a careful analysis of a great many reports Alan Bowd of Lakehead University in Thunder Bay, Ontario, suggested that otitis media is endemic among Aboriginal

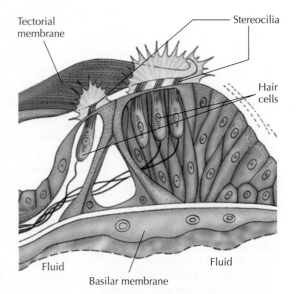

»FIGURE 4.16 A closer view of the hair cells shows how movement of fluid in the cochlea causes the bristling "hairs" or cilia to bend, generating a nerve impulse.

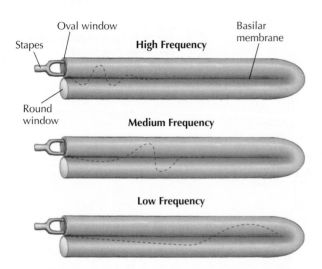

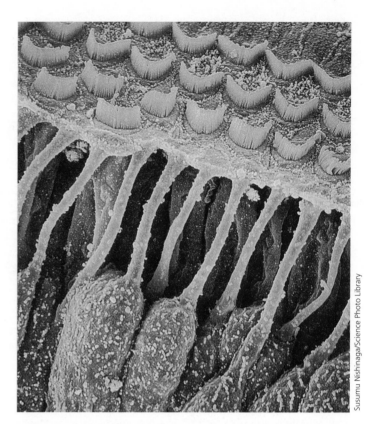

▶▶**FIGURE 4.17** Here we see a simplified side view of the cochlea "unrolled." Remember that the basilar membrane is the elastic "roof" of the lower chamber of the cochlea. The organ of Corti, with its sensitive hair cells, rests atop the basilar membrane. The coloured line shows where waves in the cochlear fluid cause the greatest deflection of the basilar membrane. (The amount of movement is exaggerated in the drawing.) Hair cells respond most in the area of greatest movement, which helps identify sound frequency.

▶▶**FIGURE 4.18** A highly magnified electron microscope photo of the cilia (orange bristles) on the top of human hair cells. (Colours are artificial.)

children in Canada's north, with rates as much as 40 times those in the urban south (Bowd, 2005). High rates of otitis media and hearing loss were also found in a recent study of First Nations elementary school children in Nova Scotia by researchers from Dalhousie University in Halifax (Langan et al., 2007).

Sensorineural hearing loss results from damage to the inner ear hair cells or auditory nerve. Many jobs, hobbies, and pastimes can cause **noise-induced hearing loss,** a form of sensorineural hearing loss that occurs when very loud sounds damage hair cells (as in hunter's notch). The hair cells, which are about as thin as a cobweb, are very fragile (Figure 4.18). If you work in a noisy environment or enjoy loud music, motorcycling, snowmobiling, hunting, or similar pursuits, you may be risking noise-induced hearing loss. Dead hair cells are never replaced: When you abuse them, you lose them. By the time you are 65, more than 40 percent of them will be gone, mainly those that transduce high pitches (Chisolm, Willott, & Lister, 2003).

How loud must a sound be to be hazardous? Daily exposure to 85 decibels or more may cause permanent hearing loss (Mather, 2008). *Decibels* are a measure of sound intensity. Every 20 decibels increases the sound pressure by a factor of 10. In other words, a rock concert at 120 decibels is 1000 times as strong as a voice at 60 decibels. Even short periods at 120 decibels can cause temporary hearing loss. Brief exposure to 150 decibels (a jet airplane nearby) may cause permanent hearing loss. You might find it interesting to check the decibel ratings of some of your activities in Figure 4.19. Be aware that amplified musical concerts, earbuds, and boom box car stereos can also damage your hearing.

Artificial Hearing

Hearing aids are of no help in cases of sensorineural hearing loss because auditory messages are blocked from reaching the brain. In many cases, however, the auditory nerve is actually intact. This finding has spurred the development of cochlear implants that bypass hair cells

Sensorineural hearing loss Loss of hearing caused by damage to the inner ear hair cells or auditory nerve.

Noise-induced hearing loss Damage caused by exposing the hair cells to excessively loud sounds.

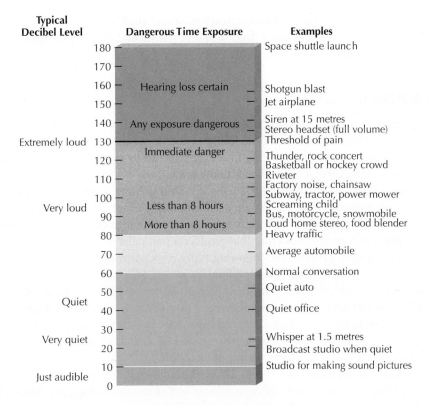

Typical Decibel Level	Dangerous Time Exposure	Examples
180		Space shuttle launch
170	Hearing loss certain	
160		Shotgun blast
150		Jet airplane
140	Any exposure dangerous	Siren at 15 metres
		Stereo headset (full volume)
Extremely loud 130		Threshold of pain
120	Immediate danger	Thunder, rock concert
		Basketball or hockey crowd
110		Riveter
		Factory noise, chainsaw
100		Subway, tractor, power mower
	Less than 8 hours	Screaming child
Very loud 90		Bus, motorcycle, snowmobile
	More than 8 hours	Loud home stereo, food blender
80		Heavy traffic
70		Average automobile
60		Normal conversation
50		Quiet auto
Quiet 40		Quiet office
30		
Very quiet 20		Whisper at 1.5 metres
		Broadcast studio when quiet
10		Studio for making sound pictures
Just audible 0		

▸▸**FIGURE 4.19** The loudness of sound is measured in decibels. Zero decibels is the faintest sound most people can hear. Sounds of 110 decibels are uncomfortably loud. Prolonged exposure to sounds above 85 decibels may damage the inner ear. Rock music, which may be 120 decibels, has caused hearing loss in musicians and may affect audiences as well. Sounds of 130 decibels pose an immediate danger to hearing.

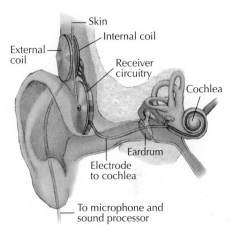

▸▸**FIGURE 4.20** A cochlear implant, or "artificial ear."

and stimulate the auditory nerves directly (Figure 4.20). Wires from a microphone carry electrical signals to an external coil. A matching coil under the skin picks up the signals and carries them to one or more areas of the cochlea. The latest implants make use of place theory to separate higher and lower tones. This has allowed some formerly deaf persons to hear human voices, music, and other higher-frequency sounds. About 60 percent of all multichannel implant patients can understand some spoken words and appreciate music (Leal et al., 2003; Tye-Murray, Spencer, & Woodworth, 1995). Some deaf children with implants learn to speak. Those who receive a cochlear implant before age two learn spoken language at a near normal rate (Dorman & Wilson, 2004).

At present, artificial hearing remains crude. All but the most successful cochlear implant patients describe the sound as "like a radio that isn't quite tuned in." In fact, 30 percent of all adults who have tried implants have given up on them. But cochlear implants are improving. And even now it is hard to argue with enthusiasts like Kristen Cloud. Shortly after Kristen received an implant, she was able to hear a siren and avoid being struck by a speeding car. She says, simply, "The implant saved my life."

SMELL AND TASTE—THE NOSE KNOWS WHEN THE TONGUE CAN'T TELL

Unless you are a wine taster, a perfume blender, a chef, or a gourmet, you may think of **olfaction** (smell) and **gustation** (taste) as minor senses. Certainly you could survive without these *chemical senses* (receptors that respond to chemical molecules). But don't be deceived; life without these senses can be difficult (Drummond, Douglas, & Olver, 2007).

Olfaction The sense of smell.
Gustation The sense of taste.

<SURVEY QUESTION
How do the chemical senses operate?

One person, for instance, almost died because he couldn't smell the smoke when his apartment building caught fire. Besides, olfaction and gustation add pleasure to our lives. Let's see how they operate.

The Sense of Smell

Smell receptors respond to airborne molecules. As air enters the nose, it flows over roughly 5 million nerve fibres embedded in the lining of the upper nasal passages (Figure 4.21). Receptor proteins on the surface of the fibres are sensitive to various airborne molecules. When a fibre is stimulated, it sends signals to the brain.

How are different odours produced? This is still an unfolding mystery. One hint comes from a type of *dysosmia* (dis-OZE-me-ah: defective smell), a sort of "smell blindness" for a single odour. Loss of sensitivity to specific types of odours suggests there are receptors for specific odours. Indeed, the molecules that produce a particular odour are quite similar in shape. Specific shapes produce the following types of odours: floral, camphoric, musky, minty, and etherish (like ether or cleaning fluid).

Does this mean that there are five different types of olfactory receptors? Actually, in humans, about 1000 types of smell receptors are believed to exist (Bensafi et al., 2004). It appears that different-shaped "holes," or "pockets," exist on the surface of olfactory receptors. Like a piece fits in a puzzle, chemicals produce odours when part of a molecule matches a hole of the same shape. This is the **lock and key theory of olfaction.**

Further, molecules trigger activity in different *combinations* of odour receptors. Thus, humans can detect at least 10 000 different odours. Just as you can make many thousands of words from the 26 letters of the alphabet, many combinations of receptors are possible, resulting in many different odours. Scents are also identified, in part, by the *location* of the receptors in the nose that are activated by a particular odour. And, finally, the *number of activated receptors* tells the brain how strong an odour is (Bensafi et al., 2004). The brain uses these distinctive patterns of messages it gets from the olfactory receptors to recognize particular scents (Laurent et al., 2001).

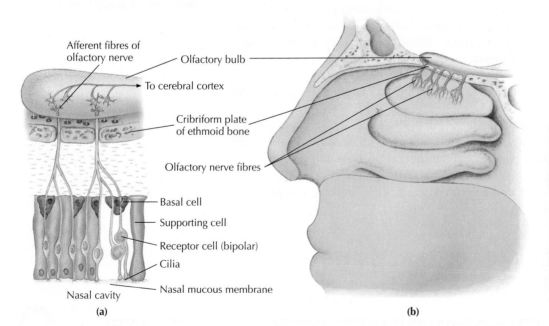

Afferent fibres of olfactory nerve
Olfactory bulb
To cerebral cortex
Cribriform plate of ethmoid bone
Olfactory nerve fibres
Basal cell
Supporting cell
Receptor cell (bipolar)
Cilia
Nasal cavity
Nasal mucous membrane
(a)
(b)

With permission Richard M. Costanzo, PhD., Virginia Commonwealth University

(c)

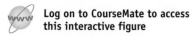

Log on to CourseMate to access this interactive figure

▸▸**FIGURE 4.21** Receptors for the sense of smell (olfaction). (a) Olfactory nerve fibres respond to gaseous molecules. Receptor cells are shown in cross section to the left. (b) Olfactory receptors are located in the upper nasal cavity. (c) This is an image of the sensing end of an olfactory receptor cell, showing cilia that detect odour molecules.

What causes dysosmia? Five people out of 100 experience some degree of dysosmia (Bramerson et al., 2004). Risks include infections, allergies, and blows to the head (which may tear the olfactory nerves). Exposure to such chemicals as ammonia, paints, solvents, and hairdressing potions can also cause dysosmia. If you value your sense of smell, be careful what you breathe (Drummond et al., 2007; Herz, 2001).

Taste and Flavours

There are at least four basic taste sensations: *sweet, salt, sour,* and *bitter.* We are most sensitive to bitter, less sensitive to sour, even less sensitive to salt, and least sensitive to sweet. This order may have helped prevent poisonings when most humans foraged for food, because bitter and sour foods are more likely to be inedible.

Most experts now believe that a fifth taste quality exists (Chandrashekar et al., 2006). The Japanese word *umami* (oo-MAH-me) describes a pleasant savoury or "brothy" taste associated with certain amino acids in chicken soup, some meat extracts, kelp, tuna, human milk, cheese, and soybeans. The receptors for *umami* are sensitive to glutamate, a substance found in monosodium glutamate (MSG) (Sugimoto & Ninomiya, 2005).

If there are only four or five tastes, how can there be so many different flavours? Flavours seem more varied because we tend to include sensations of texture, temperature, smell, and even pain ("hot" chilli peppers) along with taste. Smell is particularly important in determining flavour (Shepherd, 2006). If you plug your nose and eat small bits of apple, potato, and onion, they will "taste" almost exactly alike. That's why food loses its "taste" when you have a cold. It is probably fair to say that subjective flavour is half smell.

Taste buds (taste-receptor cells) are located mainly on the top side of the tongue, especially around the edges. However, a few are found elsewhere inside the mouth

Taste bud The receptor organ for taste.

✓ STUDY BREAK — Hearing, Smell, and Taste

Reflect

Close your eyes and listen to the sounds around you. As you do, try to mentally trace the events necessary to convert vibrations in the air into the sounds you are hearing. Review the discussion of hearing if you leave out any steps.

What is your favourite food odour? What is your favourite taste? Can you explain how you are able to sense the aroma and taste of foods?

Learning Check

1. The frequency of a sound wave corresponds to how loud it is. T or F?
2. Which of the following is not a part of the cochlea?
   a. ossicles   b. pinna
   c. tympanic membrane   d. all of the above
3. According to the place theory of hearing, higher tones register most strongly near the base of the cochlea. T or F?
4. Sensorineural hearing loss occurs when the auditory ossicles are damaged. T or F?

5. Daily exposure to sounds with a loudness of _____ decibels may cause permanent hearing loss.
6. Cochlear implants have been used primarily to overcome
   a. conductive hearing loss   b. hunter's notch
   c. sensorineural hearing loss d. tinnitus
7. Olfaction appears to be at least partially explained by the _____ _____ _____ theory of molecule shapes and receptor sites.
8. *Umami* is a type of "smell blindness" for a particular odour. T or F?

Critical Thinking

9. Why do you think your voice sounds so different when you hear a tape recording of your speech?
10. Smell and hearing differ from vision in a way that may aid survival. What is it?

Answers

1. F 2. d 3. T 4. F 5. 85 6. c 7. lock and key 8. F 9. The answer lies in another question: How else might vibrations from the voice reach the cochlea? Other people hear your voice only as it is carried through the air. You hear not only that sound but also vibrations conducted by the bones of your skull. 10. Both smell and hearing can detect stimuli (including signals of approaching danger) around corners, behind objects, and behind the head.

➠**FIGURE 4.22** Receptors for taste.
(a) The tongue is covered with small protrusions called *papillae*. (b) Most taste buds are found around the top edges of the tongue (shaded area). However, some are located elsewhere, including under the tongue. Stimulation of the central part of the tongue causes no taste sensations. All four primary taste sensations occur anywhere that taste buds exist. (c) An enlarged drawing shows that taste buds are located near the base of papillae. (d) Detail of a taste bud. These receptors also occur in other parts of the digestive system, such as the lining of the mouth.

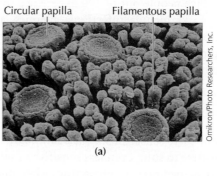

Circular papilla   Filamentous papilla

(a)

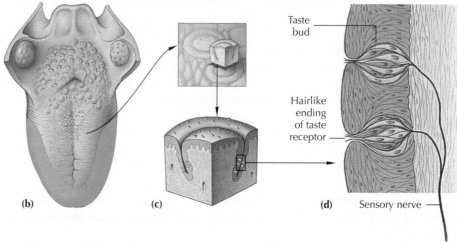

Taste bud

Hairlike ending of taste receptor

(b)   **(c)**   **(d)**   Sensory nerve

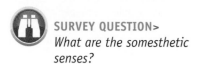

Somesthetic senses Sensations produced by the skin, muscles, joints, viscera, and organs of balance.
Skin senses The senses of touch, pressure, pain, heat, and cold.
Kinesthetic senses The senses of body movement and positioning.
Vestibular senses The senses of balance, position in space, and acceleration.

SURVEY QUESTION>
What are the somesthetic senses?

(Figure 4.22). As food is chewed, it dissolves and enters the taste buds, where it sets off nerve impulses to the brain (Northcutt, 2004). Much like smell, sweet and bitter tastes appear to be based on a lock and key match between molecules and intricately shaped receptors. Saltiness and sourness, however, are triggered by a direct flow of charged atoms into the tips of taste cells (Lindemann, 2001).

THE SOMESTHETIC SENSES—FLYING BY THE SEAT OF YOUR PANTS

A gymnast "flying" through a routine on the uneven bars may rely as much on the **somesthetic senses** as on vision (*soma* means "body," *esthetic* means "feel"). Even the most routine activities, such as walking, running, and passing a sobriety test, would be impossible without the **skin senses** (touch); the **kinesthetic senses** (receptors in muscles and joints that detect body position and movement); and the **vestibular senses** (receptors in the inner ear for balance, gravity, and acceleration). Because of their importance, let's begin with the skin senses.

The Skin Senses

It's difficult to imagine what life would be like without the sense of touch, but the plight of Ian Waterman gives a hint. After an illness, Waterman permanently lost all feeling below his neck. Now, in order to know what position his body is in, he has to be able to see it. If he moves with his eyes closed, he has no idea where he is moving. If the lights go out in a room, he's in big trouble (Gallagher, 2004).

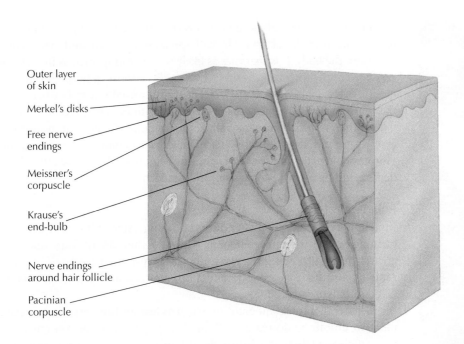

Outer layer
of skin

Merkel's disks

Free nerve
endings

Meissner's
corpuscle

Krause's
end-bulb

Nerve endings
around hair follicle

Pacinian
corpuscle

▶▶**FIGURE 4.23** The skin senses include touch, pressure, pain, cold, and warmth. This drawing shows different forms the skin receptors can take. The only clearly specialized receptor is the Pacinian corpuscle, which is highly sensitive to pressure. Free nerve endings are receptors for pain and any of the other sensations. For reasons that are not clear, cold is sensed near the surface of the skin, and warmth is sensed deeper (Carlson, 2007).

 Log on to CourseMate to access this interactive figure

Skin receptors produce at least five different sensations: *light touch, pressure, pain, cold, and warmth.* Receptors with particular shapes appear to specialize somewhat in various sensations (Figure 4.23). However, free nerve endings alone can produce all five sensations (Carlson, 2007). Altogether, the skin has about 200 000 nerve endings for temperature, 500 000 for touch and pressure, and 3 million for pain.

Does the number of receptors in an area of skin relate to its sensitivity? Yes. Your skin could be "mapped" by applying heat, cold, touch, pressure, or pain to points all over your body. Such testing would show that the number of skin receptors varies, and that sensitivity generally matches the number of receptors in a given area. Generally speaking, important areas such as the lips, tongue, face, hands, and genitals have a higher density of receptors. Of course, the sensation you ultimately feel will depend on brain activity.

Pain

The number of pain receptors also varies, right? Yes, like the other skin senses, pain receptors vary in their distribution. About 230 pain points per square centimetre are found behind the knee, 180 per centimetre on the buttocks, 60 on the pad of the thumb, and 40 on the tip of the nose.

Pain carried by *large nerve fibres* is sharp, bright, and fast and seems to come from specific body areas (McMahon & Koltzenburg, 2005). This is the body's **warning system.** Give yourself a small jab with a pin and you will feel this type of pain. As you do this, notice that warning pain quickly disappears. Much as we may dislike warning pain, it is usually a signal that the body has been, or is about to be, damaged. Without warning pain, we would be unable to detect or prevent injury. Children who are born with a rare inherited insensitivity to pain repeatedly burn themselves, break bones, bite off parts of their tongues, and become ill without knowing it (Cox et al., 2006). As you might imagine, empathy for pain is more complex in people with congenital insensitivity to pain (CIP) (Danziger, Prkachin, & Willer, 2006). People who have a normal experience of pain do not need to be especially empathic to have some understanding of another person's pain. In contrast, among people suffering from CIP, those who score high on a test of emotional empathy are able to understand someone else's pain.

A second type of somatic pain is carried by *small nerve fibres.* This type of pain is slower, nagging, aching, widespread, and very unpleasant (McMahon & Koltzenburg, 2005). It gets worse if the pain stimulus is repeated. This is the body's **reminding system.** It reminds the brain that the body has been injured. For instance, lower back pain often has this quality. Sadly, the reminding system can cause agony long after an injury has healed or, in terminal illnesses, when the reminder is useless.

Warning system Pain based on large nerve fibres; warns that bodily damage may be occurring.

Reminding system Pain based on small nerve fibres; reminds the brain that the body has been injured.

Weightlessness presents astronauts with a real challenge in sensory adaptation.

JSC/NASA

A particularly troubling condition is known as fibromyalgia syndrome, a chronic disorder characterized by widespread muscle pain and many tender points on the body. It is six times as likely to occur in women as in men and can interfere with normal daily activities. Because it is both chronic and painful, it's expensive to treat: A recent study carried out in Quebec found that fibromyalgia patients cost the Quebec health plan 47 percent more per patient than non-fibromyalgia patients and required 70 percent more physician visits and interventions (Lachaine, Beauchemin, & Landry, 2010). Fibromyalgia patients also were significantly more likely to have other disorders, including anxiety, depression, and headache.

Pain Control

In some cultures, people endure tattooing, stretching, cutting, and burning with little apparent pain. How do they do it? Very likely the answer lies in a reliance on psychological factors that anyone can use to reduce pain, such as anxiety reduction, control, and attention (Mailis-Gagnon & Israelson, 2005).

In general, unpleasant emotions such as fear and anxiety increase pain; pleasant emotions decrease it (Rainville, 2004). Anytime you anticipate pain (such as a trip to the doctor, dentist, or tattoo parlour), you can lower anxiety by making sure you are *fully informed*. Be sure everything that will happen is explained. In general, the more control you *feel* over a painful stimulus, the less pain is experienced (Vallerand, Saunders, & Anthony, 2007). To apply this principle, you might arrange a signal so your doctor, dentist, or body piercer will know when to start and stop a painful procedure. Finally, distraction also reduces pain. Instead of listening to the whir of a dentist's drill, for example, you might imagine that you are lying in the sun at a beach, listening to the roar of the surf. Or take an iPod along and crank up your favourite tunes (Bushnell, Villemure, & Duncan, 2004). At home, music can also be a good distractor from chronic pain (Mitchell et al., 2007).

The Vestibular System

Although space flight might look like fun, there is about a 70 percent chance that you will throw up during your first experience in orbit. ("Weightless Wonder" is NASA's official nickname for the high-flying airplane that provides short periods of weightlessness to train astronauts. Unofficially it is called the "Vomit Comet.")

But why? Weightlessness and space flight affect the vestibular system, often causing severe motion sickness. Within the vestibular system, fluid-filled sacs called *otolith* (OH-toe-lith) *organs* are sensitive to movement, acceleration, and gravity (Figure 4.24). The otolith organs contain tiny crystals in a soft, gelatin-like mass. The tug of gravity or rapid head movements can cause the mass to shift. This, in turn, stimulates hairlike receptor cells, allowing us to sense gravity, acceleration, and movement through space (Lackner & DiZio, 2005).

Three fluid-filled tubes called the *semicircular canals* are the sensory organs for balance. If you could climb inside these tubes, you would find that head movements cause the fluid to swirl about. As the fluid moves, it bends a small "flap," or "float," called the

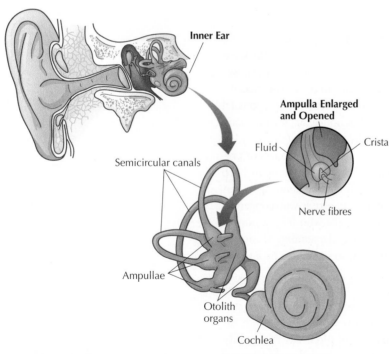

▶▶**FIGURE 4.24** The vestibular system. (See text for explanation.)

crista, that detects movement in the semicircular canals. The bending of each crista again stimulates hair cells and signals head rotation.

What causes motion sickness? According to **sensory conflict theory,** dizziness and nausea occur when sensations from the vestibular system don't match sensations from the eyes and body (Flanagan, May, & Dobie, 2004). On solid ground, information from the vestibular system, vision, and kinesthesis usually matches. However, in a heaving, pitching boat, car, or airplane, a serious mismatch can occur—causing disorientation and heaving of another kind.

Why would sensory conflict cause nausea? You can probably blame (or thank) evolution. Many poisons disturb the vestibular system, vision, and the body. Therefore, we may have evolved so that we react to sensory conflict by vomiting to expel poison. To minimize such conflicts, try to keep your head still, fix your vision on a distant immobile object, and lie down if you can (Harm, 2002).

ADAPTATION, ATTENTION, AND GATING—TUNING IN AND TUNING OUT

You are bombarded by sights, sounds, odours, tastes, and touch sensations. Which are you aware of? Each of the senses we have described is continuously active. Even so, many sensory events never reach awareness because of *sensory adaptation, selective attention,* and *sensory gating.* Let's see how information is filtered by these processes.

Sensory Adaptation

Think about walking into a house where fried squid, sauerkraut, and head cheese were prepared for dinner. You would probably pass out at the door, yet people who had been in the house for some time wouldn't be aware of the food odours. Why? Because sensory receptors respond less to unchanging stimuli, a process called **sensory adaptation.** When exposed to a constant odour, receptors send fewer and fewer nerve impulses to the brain, until the odour is no longer noticed. Adaptation to pressure from a wristwatch, waistband, ring, or glasses is based on the same principle: Sensory receptors generally respond best to *changes* in stimulation.

Selective Attention

As you sit reading this page, receptors for touch and pressure in the seat of your pants are sending nerve impulses to your brain. Although these sensations have been present all along, you were probably not aware of them until just now. This "seat-of-the-pants phenomenon" is an example of **selective attention** (voluntarily focusing on a specific sensory input). Selective attention appears to be based on the ability of brain structures to select and divert incoming sensory messages (Mather, 2008). We are able to "tune in on" a single sensory message while excluding others.

Another familiar example of this is the "cocktail party effect." When you are in a group of people, surrounded by voices, you can select and attend to the voice of the person you are facing. Or if that person gets dull, you can eavesdrop on conversations all over the room. (Be sure to smile and nod your head occasionally!) Actually, no matter how interesting your companion may be, your attention will probably shift away if you hear your own name spoken somewhere in the room (Conway, Cowan, & Bunting, 2001). We do find what others say about us to be very interesting, don't we?

At times, we can even suffer from *inattentional blindness* (blindness caused by not attending to a stimulus) (Most et al., 2005). Not seeing something that is plainly before your eyes is most likely to occur when your attention is narrowly focused

Sensory conflict theory Explains motion sickness as the result of a mismatch between information from vision, the vestibular system, and kinesthesis.

Sensory adaptation A decrease in sensory response to an unchanging stimulus.

Selective attention Giving priority to a particular incoming sensory message.

<SURVEY QUESTION
Why are we more aware of some sensations than others?

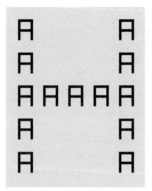

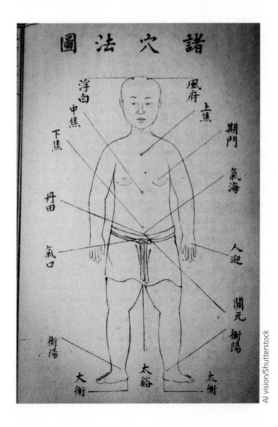 **FIGURE 4.25** The attentional "bottle-neck," or "spotlight," can be widened or narrowed. If you focus on local details in this drawing, you will see the letter *A* repeated 13 times. If you broaden your field of attention to encompass the overall pattern, you will see the letter *H*. (After Lamb & Yund, 1996.)

(Mack, 2002). Inattentional blindness is vividly illustrated by a study in which participants were shown a film of two basketball teams, one wearing black shirts and the other wearing white. Observers were asked to watch the film closely and count how many times a basketball passed between members of one of the teams, while ignoring the other team. As observers watched and counted, a person wearing a gorilla suit walked into the middle of the basketball game, faced the camera, thumped its chest, and walked out of view. Half the observers failed to notice this rather striking event (Simons & Chabris, 1999).

You might find it helpful to think of selective attention as a *bottleneck,* or narrowing in the information channel linking the senses to perception. When one message enters the bottleneck, it seems to prevent others from passing through (see Figure 4.25). Imagine, for instance, that you are driving a car and approaching an intersection. You need to be sure the traffic light is still green. Just as you are about to check it, your passenger points to a friend at the side of the road. If you then fail to notice the light just changed to red, an accident may be just seconds away.

Sensory Gating

What makes selective attention possible? Selective attention appears to be based on the ability of brain structures to select and divert incoming sensory messages (Mather, 2008). But what about messages that haven't reached the brain? Is it possible that some are blocked while others are allowed to pass? Evidence suggests there are *sensory gates* that control the flow of incoming nerve impulses in just this way. In particular, **sensory gating** refers to facilitating or blocking sensory messages in the spinal cord (Melzack & Katz, 2004; Melzack & Wall, 1996).

A fascinating example of sensory gating is provided by McGill University psychologist Ronald Melzack together with British neuroscientist Patrick Wall (1996), who studied "pain gates" in the spinal cord. Melzack and Wall noticed, as you may have, that one type of pain will sometimes cancel another. Their **gate control theory** suggests that pain messages from different nerve fibres pass through the same neural "gate" in the spinal cord. If the gate is

(*Right*) An acupuncturist's chart. (*Left*) Thin stainless steel needles are inserted into areas defined by the chart. Modern research has begun to explain the pain-killing effects of acupuncture (see text). Acupuncture's claimed ability to cure diseases is more debatable.

The Matrix: Do Phantoms Live Here?

In the popular *Matrix* films, at the turn of this century, Neo, as played by Keanu Reeves, discovers that machines have imprisoned humans in a phantom world called the Matrix, in order to steal human energy for their own use. Actually, the idea of a "matrix" is not totally far-fetched. Your own brain may create a *neuromatrix* that allows you to perceive your own body.

A person who suffers an amputation doesn't need to believe in the Matrix to encounter phantoms. Most amputees have *phantom limb* sensations, including pain, for months or years after losing a limb (Fraser, 2002; Halbert, Crotty, & Cameron, 2002). Because the phantom limb feels so "real," a patient with a recently amputated leg may inadvertently try to walk on it, risking further injury. Sometimes, phantom limbs feel like they are stuck in awkward positions. For instance, one man can't sleep on his back because his missing arm feels like it is twisted behind him.

What causes phantom limbs? Gate control theory cannot explain phantom limb pain (Hunter, Katz, & Davis, 2003). Since pain can't be coming from the missing limb (after all, it's missing!), it cannot

pass through pain gates to the brain. Instead, according to Ronald Melzack (1999; Melzack & Katz, 2006), over time the brain creates a body image called the *neuromatrix*. This internal model of the body generates our sense of bodily self. Although amputation may remove a limb, as far as the neuromatrix in the brain is concerned, the limb still exists. Functional magnetic resonance imaging (fMRI) confirms that sensory and motor areas of the brain are more active when a person feels a phantom limb (Rosen et al., 2001). Even though pain signals no longer come from the amputated limb, the neuromatrix evidently interprets other sensory experiences as pain from the missing limb (Giummarra et al., 2007).

Sometimes the brain gradually reorganizes to adjust for the sensory loss (Wu & Kaas, 2002). For example, a person who loses an arm may at first have a phantom arm and hand. After many years, the phantom may shrink, until only a hand is felt at the shoulder. Perhaps more vividly than others, people with phantom limbs are reminded that the sensory world we experience is constructed, moment by moment, not by some futuristic machines, but by our own brain activity.

"closed" by one pain message, other messages may not be able to pass through (Melzack & Katz, 2004; Melzack & Wall, 1996).

How is the gate closed? Messages carried by large, fast nerve fibres seem to close the spinal pain gate directly. Doing so can prevent slower, "reminding system" pain from reaching the brain. As a pain control technique, this is called *counterirritation*. Pain clinics use it by applying a mild electrical current to the skin. This sends *mild* pain messages to the spinal cord and brain, which may effectively close the neurological gates to reduce more agonizing pain (Köke et al., 2004). For more extreme pain, the electrical current can be applied directly to the spinal cord (Linderoth & Foreman, 2006).

You can use counterirritation to control your own pain. For instance, if you are having a tooth filled, try pinching yourself or digging a fingernail into a knuckle while the dentist is working. Focus your attention on the pain you are creating, and increase it any time the dentist's work becomes more painful. This strategy may seem strange, but it works.

Messages from small, slow fibres seem to take a different route. After going through the pain gate, they pass on to a "central biasing system" in the brain. Under some circumstances, the brain then sends a message back down the spinal cord, closing the pain gates (Figure 4.26). Melzack and Wall believe that gate control theory explains the painkilling effects of acupuncture (but see Brainwaves: "The Matrix: Do Phantoms Live Here?").

Conclusion and a Look Ahead

The senses supply raw data to the brain, but the information remains mostly meaningless until it is interpreted. It's as if the senses provide only the jumbled pieces of a complex puzzle. Melzack's (1999) concept of a neuromatrix is one theory of how the brain tries to make sense of sensory input. In the remainder of this chapter, we will further explore some perceptual processes that help us put the puzzle together. But first, here's a chance to rehearse what you've learned.

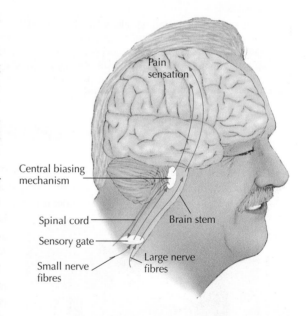

▶▶**FIGURE 4.26** Diagram of a sensory gate for pain. A series of pain impulses going through the gate may prevent other pain messages from passing through. Or pain messages may relay through a "central biasing mechanism" that exerts control over the gate, closing it to other impulses.

Sensory gating Alteration of sensory messages in the spinal cord.

Gate control theory Pain messages pass through neural "gates" in the spinal cord.

STUDY BREAK   Somesthetic Senses, Adaptation, Attention, and Gating

Reflect

Stand on one foot with your eyes closed. Now touch the tip of your nose with your index finger. Which of the somesthetic senses did you use to perform this feat?

Imagine you are on a boat ride with a friend who starts to feel queasy. Can you explain to your friend what causes motion sickness and what she or he can do to prevent it?

As you sit reading this book, which sensory inputs have undergone adaptation? What new inputs can you become aware of by shifting your focus of attention?

Think about a strategy you have used for reducing pain at the doctor or dentist or in some other painful situation. Did you alter anxiety, control, or attention? Can you think of any ways in which you have used counterirritation to lessen pain?

Learning Check

1. Which of the following is a somesthetic sense?
   a. gustation   b. olfaction
   c. rarefaction   d. kinesthesis
2. Warning pain is carried by _____ nerve fibres.
3. Head movements are detected primarily in the semicircular canals; gravity by the otolith organs. T or F?

4. Sensory conflicts appear to explain nausea caused by poisoning, but not the nausea associated with motion sickness. T or F?
5. *Sensory adaptation* refers to a decrease in sensory response that accompanies a constant or unchanging stimulus. T or F?
6. The brain-centred ability to influence what sensations we will receive is called
   a. sensory gating   b. central adaptation
   c. selective attention   d. sensory biasing
7. The painkilling effects of acupuncture appear to result from _____.
8. Like heightened anxiety, increased control tends to increase subjective pain. T or F?
9. Phantom limb pain cannot be explained by gate control theory. T or F?

Critical Thinking

10. Drivers are less likely to become carsick than passengers are. Why might this be?
11. What special precautions would you have to take to test the ability of acupuncture to reduce pain?

Answers

1. d 2. large 3. T 4. F 5. T 6. c 7. sensory gating 8. F 9. T 10. Drivers experience less sensory conflict because they control the car's motion. This allows them to anticipate the car's movements and to coordinate their head and eye movements with those of the car. 11. At the very least, you would have to control for the placebo effect by giving fake acupuncture to control group members. However, a true double-blind study would be difficult to do. Acupuncturists would always know if they were giving a placebo treatment or the real thing, which means they might unconsciously influence subjects.

PERCEPTION—THAT SECOND STEP

SURVEY QUESTION>
In general, how do we construct our perceptions?

Gala Contemplating the Mediterranean Sea Which at Eighteen Metres Becomes the Portrait of Abraham Lincoln,(Homage to Rothko) 1976 (oil on photographic paper), Dali, Salvador (1904-89)/Museo Dali, Figueres, Spain/Index/The Bridgeman Art Library

Imagine what it would be like to have your vision restored after a lifetime of blindness. Actually, a first look at the world can be disappointing because the newfound ability to *sense* the world does not guarantee that it can be *perceived*. Newly sighted persons must *learn* to identify objects; to read clocks, numbers, and letters; and to judge sizes and distances (Gregory, 2003). For instance, Mr. SB was a cataract patient who had been blind since birth. After an operation restored his sight at age 52, Mr. SB struggled to use his vision.

Mr. SB soon learned to tell time from a large clock and to read block letters he had known only from touch. At a zoo, he recognized an elephant from descriptions he had heard. However, handwriting meant nothing to him for more than a year after he regained sight, and many objects were meaningless until he touched them. Thus, Mr. SB slowly learned to organize his *sensations* into meaningful *perceptions*. Cases like those of Mr. SB show that your experiences are **perceptual constructions,** or mental models of external events, that *are actively created by your brain*.

Visual perception involves finding meaningful patterns in complex stimuli. If you look closely at this painting, "Gala Contemplating the Mediterranean Sea Which at Eighteen Metres Becomes the Portrait of Abraham Lincoln (Homage to Rothko)" (1976), by the artist Salvador Dali, you will see that it is entirely made up of small squares. An infant or newly sighted person would see only a jumble of meaningless colours. But because the squares form a familiar pattern, you should easily see Abraham Lincoln's face.

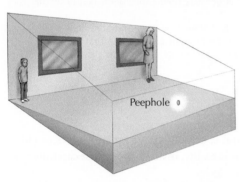

▶▶**FIGURE 4.27** It is difficult to look at this simple drawing without perceiving depth. Yet the drawing is nothing more than a collection of flat shapes. Turn this page counterclockwise 90 degrees and you will see three Cs, one within another. When the drawing is turned sideways, it seems nearly flat. However, if you turn the page upright again, a sense of depth will reappear. Clearly, you have used your knowledge and expectations to *construct* an illusion of depth. The drawing itself would be only a flat design if you didn't invest it with meaning.

▶▶**FIGURE 4.28** The Ames room. From the front, the room looks normal; actually, the right-hand corner is very short, and the left-hand corner is very tall. In addition, the left side of the room slants away from viewers. The diagram shows the shape of the room and reveals why people appear to get bigger as they cross the room toward the nearer, shorter right corner.

Of course, perceptions can be misconstrued as they are filtered through our needs, expectations, attitudes, values, and beliefs (Figure 4.27). We don't just believe what we see. We also see what we believe.

Illusions

Perceptual misconstruction is responsible for many *illusions*. In an **illusion,** length, position, motion, curvature, or direction is consistently misjudged. For example, because we have seen thousands of rooms shaped roughly like a box, we habitually construct perceptions based on this assumption. This need not be true, however. An *Ames room* (named for the man who designed it) is a lopsided space that appears square when viewed from a certain location (Figure 4.28). This illusion is achieved by carefully distorting the proportions of the walls, floor, ceiling, and windows. Because the left corner of the Ames room is farther from a viewer than the right, a person standing in that corner looks very small; one standing in the nearer, shorter right corner looks very large. A person who walks from the left to the right corner will seem to "magically" grow larger.

To detect an illusion, you may have to engage in some **reality testing**—for example, you could measure a drawing or apply a straight-edge to it. Reality testing involves obtaining additional information to check your perceptions. Figure 4.29 shows a powerful illusion

▶▶**FIGURE 4.29** The limits of pure perception. Even simple designs are easily misperceived. Fraser's spiral is actually a series of concentric circles. The illusion is so powerful that people who try to trace one of the circles sometimes follow the illusory spiral and jump from one circle to the next. (After Seckel, 2000.)

THE CLINICAL FILE

Staying in Touch with Reality

Just imagine that, often, and without warning, you hear a voice shouting, "Buckets of blood!" or see blood spattering across the walls of your bedroom. Chances are people would think you are mentally disturbed. Hallucinations are a major symptom of psychosis, dementia, epilepsy, migraine headaches, alcohol withdrawal, and drug intoxication (Spence & David, 2004). They are also one of the clearest signs that a person has "lost touch with reality."

Yet consider the case of mathematician John Nash (the subject of *A Beautiful Mind,* the winner of the 2002 Oscar for best film). Even though Nash suffered from schizophrenia, he eventually learned to use his *reality testing* to sort out which of his experiences were perceptions and which were hallucinations. Unlike John Nash, most people who experience full-blown hallucinations have a limited ability to engage in reality testing (Hohwy & Rosenberg, 2005).

Curiously, "sane hallucinations" also occur. *Charles Bonnet syndrome* is a rare condition that afflicts mainly older people who are partially blind, but not mentally disturbed. Animals, buildings, plants, people, and other objects may seem to appear and disappear in front of their eyes. One older man suffering from partial blindness and leukemia complained of seeing animals in his house, including cattle and bears (Jacob et al., 2004). However, people experiencing "sane hallucinations" can more easily tell that their hallucinations aren't real because their capacity for reality testing is not impaired.

Such unusual experiences show how powerfully the brain seeks meaningful patterns in sensory input and the role that reality testing plays in our normal perceptual experience.

Hallucination An imaginary sensation, such as seeing, hearing, or smelling something that does not exist in the external world.

Bottom-up processing Organizing perceptions by beginning with low-level features.

Top-down processing Applying higher-level knowledge to rapidly organize sensory information into a meaningful perception.

called Fraser's spiral. What appears to be a spiral is actually made up of a series of closed circles. Most people cannot spontaneously see this reality. Instead, they must carefully trace one of the circles to confirm what is "real" in the design.

Note that illusions are distorted perceptions of stimuli that actually exist. In a **hallucination,** people perceive objects or events that have no external reality (Lepore, 2002). For example, they hear voices that are not there (see Clinical File: "Staying in Touch with Reality"). If you think you are experiencing an illusion or a hallucination, try reality testing. If you think you see a metre-tall butterfly, you can confirm you are hallucinating by trying to touch its wings.

Let's explore the process of perceptual construction and some factors that shape or even distort it.

Bottom-Up and Top-Down Processing

Moment by moment, our perceptions are typically constructed in both *bottom-up* and *top-down* fashion. Think about the process of building a house: Raw materials, such as lumber, doors, tiles, carpets, screws, and nails, must be painstakingly fit together. At the same time, a building plan guides how the raw materials are assembled.

Our brain builds perceptions in similar ways. In **bottom-up processing,** we start constructing at the "bottom," with raw materials. That is, we begin with small sensory units (features) and build upward to a complete perception. The reverse also occurs. In **top-down processing,** preexisting knowledge is used to rapidly organize features into a meaningful whole (Goldstein, 2010). If you put together a jigsaw puzzle you've never seen before, you are relying mainly on bottom-up processing: You must assemble small pieces until a recognizable pattern begins to emerge. Top-down processing is like putting together a puzzle you have solved many times: After only a few pieces are in place, your past experience gives you the plan to rapidly fill in the final picture.

Both types of processing are illustrated by Figure 4.30. Also, look ahead to Figure 4.33. The first time you see this photo, you will probably process it bottom-up, picking out features until it becomes recognizable. The next time you see it, because of top-down processing, you should recognize it instantly.

An excellent example of perceptual construction is found in the Gestalt organizing principles.

▶▶ **FIGURE 4.30** Check out this abstract design. If you process it "bottom-up," you will likely see only three small dark geometric shapes near the edges. Would you like to try some top-down processing? Knowing the title of the design will allow you to apply your knowledge and see it in an entirely different way. The title? It's *Special K.* Can you see it now?

Gestalt Organizing Principles

How are sensations organized into perceptions? The Gestalt psychologists (see Chapter 1) proposed that the simplest organization involves grouping some sensations into an object, or figure, that stands out on a plainer background. **Figure–ground organization** is probably inborn, because it is the first perceptual ability to appear after cataract patients like Mr. SB regain sight. In normal figure–ground perception, only one figure is seen. In *reversible figures*, however, figure and ground can be switched. In Figure 4.31 it is equally possible to see either a wineglass on a dark background or two facial profiles on a light background. As you shift from one pattern to the other, you should get a clear sense of what figure–ground organization means.

Are there other Gestalt organizing principles? The Gestalt psychologists identified several other principles that bring some order to your perceptions (Figure 4.32).

1. **Nearness.** All other things being equal, stimuli that are near each other tend to be grouped together (Quinn, Bhatt, & Hayden, 2008). Thus, if three people stand near each other and a fourth person stands 3 metres away, the adjacent three will be seen as a group and the distant person as an outsider (see Figure 4.32a).

▸▸**FIGURE 4.31** A reversible figure–ground design. Do you see two faces in profile, or a wineglass?

▸▸**FIGURE 4.32** How we organize perceptions.

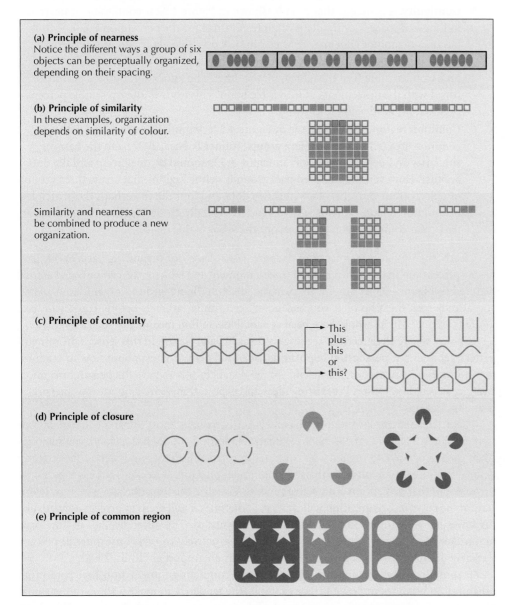

(a) **Principle of nearness**
Notice the different ways a group of six objects can be perceptually organized, depending on their spacing.

(b) **Principle of similarity**
In these examples, organization depends on similarity of colour.

Similarity and nearness can be combined to produce a new organization.

(c) **Principle of continuity**
This plus this or this?

(d) **Principle of closure**

(e) **Principle of common region**

Figure–ground organization Part of a stimulus appears to stand out as an object (figure) against a less prominent background (ground).

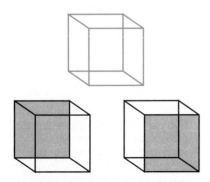

»FIGURE 4.33 A challenging example of perceptual organization. Once the camouflaged insect (known as a giant walkingstick) becomes visible, it is almost impossible to view the picture again without seeing the insect.

Perceptual hypothesis An initial guess regarding how to organize (perceive) a stimulus pattern.

2. **Similarity.** "Birds of a feather flock together"; stimuli that are similar in size, shape, colour, or form tend to be grouped together (see Figure 4.32b). Picture two bands marching side by side. If their uniforms are different colours, the bands will be seen as two separate groups, not as one large group.

3. **Continuation, or continuity.** Perceptions tend toward simplicity and continuity. In Figure 4.32c it is easier to visualize a wavy line on a squared-off line than it is to see a complex row of shapes.

4. **Closure.** Closure refers to the tendency to *complete* a figure so that it has a consistent overall form. Each of the drawings in Figure 4.32d has one or more gaps, yet each is perceived as a recognizable figure. The "shapes" that appear in the two right drawings in Figure 4.32d are *illusory figures* (implied shapes that are not actually bounded by an edge or an outline). Even young children see these shapes, despite knowing that they are "not really there." Illusory figures reveal that our tendency to form shapes—even with minimal cues—is powerful.

5. **Contiguity.** A principle that can't be shown in Figure 4.32 is contiguity, or nearness in time *and* space. Contiguity is often responsible for the perception that one thing has *caused* another (Buehner & May, 2003). A psychologist friend of ours demonstrates this principle in class by knocking on his head with one hand while knocking on a wooden table (out of sight) with the other. The knocking sound is perfectly timed with the movements of his visible hand. This leads to the irresistible perception that his head is made of wood.

6. **Common region.** As you can see in Figure 4.32e, stimuli that are found within a common area tend to be seen as a group (Palmer & Beck, 2007). On the basis of similarity and nearness, the stars in Figure 4.32e should be one group and the dots another. However, the coloured backgrounds define regions that create three groups of objects (four stars, two stars plus two dots, and four dots). Perhaps the principle of common region explains why we tend to mentally group together people from a particular country, state, province, or other geographic region.

Clearly, the Gestalt principles offer us some basic "plans" for organizing parts of our day-to-day perceptions in top-down fashion. Take a moment and look for the camouflaged animal pictured in Figure 4.33. (Camouflage patterns break up figure–ground organization.) Have you already seen this photo? If you had never seen similar animals before, could you have located this one? Mr. SB would have been at a total loss to find meaning in such a picture.

In a way, we are all detectives, seeking patterns in what we see. In this sense, a meaningful pattern represents a **perceptual hypothesis,** or initial plan or guess about how to organize sensations. Have you ever seen a "friend" in the distance, only to have the person turn into a stranger as you drew closer? Preexisting ideas and expectations *actively* guide our interpretation of sensations (Most et al., 2005).

The active, constructive nature of perception is perhaps most apparent for *ambiguous stimuli* (patterns allowing more than one interpretation). If you look at a cloud, you may discover dozens of ways to organize its contours into fanciful shapes and scenes. Even clearly defined stimuli may permit more than one interpretation. Look at Necker's cube in Figure 4.34 if you doubt that perception is an active process. Visualize the top cube as a wire box. If you stare at the cube, its organization will change. Sometimes it will seem to project upward, like the lower left cube; other times it will project downward. The difference lies in how your brain interprets the same information. In short, we actively *construct* meaningful perceptions; we do not passively record the events and stimuli around us (Rolls, 2008).

In some instances, a stimulus may offer such conflicting information that perceptual organization becomes impossible. For example, the tendency to make a three-dimensional object out of a drawing is frustrated by the "three-pronged widget" (Figure 4.35, left), an

»FIGURE 4.34 Necker's cube.

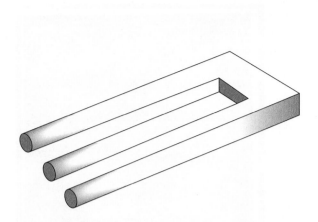

"Disappearing Column" © Shigeo Fukuda, 1985

▶▶**FIGURE 4.35** (Left) An impossible figure—the "three-pronged widget." (Right) It might seem that including more information in a drawing would make perceptual conflicts impossible. However, Japanese artist Shigeo Fukuda has shown otherwise.

impossible figure. Such patterns cannot be organized into stable, consistent, or meaningful perceptions. If you cover either end of the drawing in Figure 4.35 (left), it makes sense perceptually. However, a problem arises when you try to organize the entire drawing. Then, the conflicting information it contains prevents you from forming a stable perception.

Learning to organize his visual sensations was only one of the hurdles Mr. SB faced in learning to see. In the next section, we will consider some others.

> **Size constancy** The perceived size of an object remains constant, despite changes in its retinal image.
>
> **Shape constancy** The perceived shape of an object is unaffected by changes in its retinal image.

Perceptual Constancies

When Mr. SB first regained his vision, he could judge distance only in familiar situations (Gregory, 1990). One day he was found crawling out of a hospital window to get a closer look at traffic on the street. It's easy to understand his curiosity, but he had to be restrained. His room was on the fourth floor!

Why would Mr. SB try to crawl out of a fourth-storey window? Couldn't he at least tell distance from the size of the cars? No, you must be visually familiar with objects to use their size to judge distance. Try holding your left hand a few centimetres in front of your nose and your right hand at arm's length. Your right hand should appear to be about half the size of your left hand. Still, you know your right hand did not suddenly shrink, because you have seen it many times at various distances. We call this **size constancy:** The perceived size of an object remains the same, even though the size of its image on the retina changes.

To perceive your hand accurately, you had to draw on past experience to provide a top-down plan for constructing your perception. Some of these plans are so basic they seem to be *native* (inborn). An example is the ability to see a line on a piece of paper. Likewise, even newborn babies show some evidence of size constancy (Granrud, 2006; Slater, Mattock, & Brown, 1990). However, many of our perceptions are *empirical,* or based on prior experience. For instance, cars, houses, and people look like toys when seen from a great distance or from an unfamiliar perspective, such as from the top of a skyscraper. This suggests that although some size constancy is innate, it is also affected by learning (Granrud, 2004).

In **shape constancy,** the shape of an object remains stable, even though the shape of its retinal image changes. You can demonstrate shape constancy by looking at this page from directly overhead and then from an angle. Obviously, the page is rectangular, but most of the images that reach your eyes are distorted. Yet, though the book's image changes, your perception of its shape remains constant. (For additional examples, see Figure 4.36.) On the highway, alcohol intoxication impairs size and shape constancy, adding to the accident rate among drunk drivers (Farrimond, 1990).

Let's say that you are outside in bright sunlight. Beside you, a friend is wearing a grey skirt and a white blouse. Suddenly a cloud shades the Sun. It might seem that the blouse would grow dimmer, but it still appears to be bright white. This happens because the blouse

Mark Richards/PhotoEdit

Almost everyone's family album has at least one photo like this. Extreme viewing angles can make maintaining size constancy difficult, even for familiar objects.

▶▶**FIGURE 4.36** Shape constancy. (a) When a door is open, its image actually forms a trapezoid. Shape constancy is indicated by the fact that it is still perceived as a rectangle. (b) With great effort you may be able to see this design as a collection of flat shapes. However, if you maintain shape constancy, the distorted pentagrams strongly suggest the surface of a sphere.

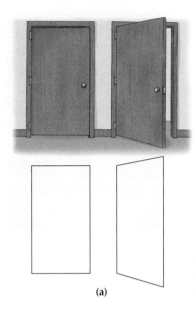

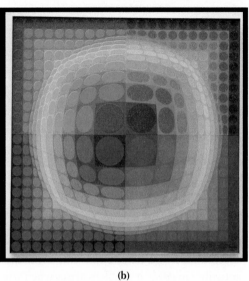

Paz-Ket (oil on canvas) by Victor Vasarely (1908–97); Museo de Bellas Artes, Bilbao, Spain/The Bridgeman Art Library. Nationality/copyright status: French/in copyright until 2068

(a)

(b)

> **Brightness constancy** The apparent (or relative) brightness of objects remains the same as long as they are illuminated by the same amount of light.

continues to reflect a larger *proportion* of light than nearby objects. **Brightness constancy** refers to the fact that the brightness of objects appears to stay the same as lighting conditions change. However, this holds true only if the blouse and other objects are all illuminated by the same amount of light. You could make an area on your friend's grey skirt look whiter than the shaded blouse by shining a bright spotlight on the skirt.

To summarize, the energy patterns reaching our senses are constantly changing, even when they come from the same object. Without size, shape, and brightness constancy we would live in a confusing world in which objects would seem to shrink and grow, change shape as if made of rubber, and light up or fade like neon lamps.

One of the most amazing perceptual feats is our capacity to create three-dimensional space from flat retinal images. We'll explore that topic in a moment, but first here's a chance to rehearse what you've learned.

 STUDY BREAK **Perceptual Construction, Gestalt Organizing Principles, and Perceptual Constancies**

Reflect

As you look around the area in which you are now, how are the Gestalt organizing principles helping to organize your perceptions? Try to find a specific example for each principle.

If you needed to explain the perceptual constancies to a friend, what would you say? Why are the constancies important for maintaining a stable perceptual world?

Learning Check

1. The Ames room is used to test infants for depth perception. T or F?
2. In top-down processing of information, individual features are analyzed and assembled into a meaningful whole. T or F?
3. The first and most basic perceptual organization to emerge when sight is restored to a blind person is
   a. continuity
   b. nearness constancy
   c. recognition of numbers and letters
   d. figure–ground
4. At times, meaningful perceptual organization represents a _____, or "guess," held until the evidence contradicts it.
5. The design known as Necker's cube is a good example of an impossible figure. T or F?
6. Which among the following are subject to basic perceptual constancy?
   a. figure–ground organization
   b. size
   c. ambiguity
   d. brightness
   e. continuity
   f. closure
   g. shape
   h. nearness

Critical Thinking

7. People who have taken psychedelic drugs, such as LSD or mescaline, often report that the objects and people they see appear to be changing in size, shape, and brightness. This suggests that such drugs disrupt what perceptual process?

Answers

1. F 2. F 3. d 4. hypothesis 5. F 6. b, d, g 7. perceptual constancies (size, shape, and brightness)

DEPTH PERCEPTION—WHAT IF THE WORLD WERE FLAT?

Close one of your eyes, hold your head very still, and stare at a single point across the room. If you don't move your head or eyes, your surroundings will appear to be almost flat, like a painting or photograph. But even under these conditions you will still have some sense of depth. Now, open both eyes and move your head and eyes as usual. Suddenly, the "3-D" perceptual world returns. How are we able to perceive depth and space?

Depth perception is the ability to see three-dimensional space and to accurately judge distances. Without depth perception, another form of perceptual construction, you would not be able to drive a car or ride a bicycle, play catch, shoot baskets, thread a needle, or simply navigate around a room (Howard & Rogers, 2001a). The world would look like a flat surface.

Mr. SB had trouble with depth perception after his sight was restored. Is depth perception learned? Studies done with a visual cliff suggest that depth perception is partly learned and partly innate (Witherington et al., 2005). Basically, a visual cliff is a glass-topped table (Figure 4.37). On one side a checkered surface lies directly beneath the glass. On the other side, the checkered surface is 1.2 metres below. This makes the glass look like a tabletop on one side and a cliff, or drop-off, on the other.

To test for depth perception, 6- to 14-month-old infants were placed in the middle of the visual cliff. This gave them a choice of crawling to the shallow side or to the deep side. (The glass prevented them from doing any "skydiving" if they chose the deep side.) Most infants chose the shallow side. In fact, most refused the deep side even when their mothers tried to call them toward it (Gibson & Walk, 1960).

If the infants were at least six months old when they were tested, isn't it possible that they had learned to perceive depth? Yes. More recent research has shown that depth perception begins to develop as early as two weeks of age (Yonas, Elieff, & Arterberry, 2002). It is very likely that at least a basic level of depth perception is innate. Yet, the development of depth perception is not complete until about six months, suggesting that it depends on both brain maturation and individual experience.

But don't some older babies crawl off tables or beds? As soon as infants become active crawlers, they refuse to cross the deep side of the visual cliff. However, older infants who have just learned to walk must again learn to avoid the "deep" side of the visual cliff (Witherington et al., 2005). Besides, even babies who perceive depth may not be able to catch themselves if they slip. A lack of coordination—not an inability to see depth—probably explains most "crash landings" after about four months of age.

We learn to construct our perception of three-dimensional space by using a variety of *depth cues.* **Depth cues** are features of the environment and messages from the body that supply information about distance and space. Some cues require two eyes (*binocular cues*), whereas others will work with just one eye (*monocular cues*).

<SURVEY QUESTION
How is it possible to see depth and judge distance?

> **Depth perception** The ability to see three-dimensional space and to accurately judge distances.
> **Depth cues** Perceptual features that impart information about distance and three-dimensional space.

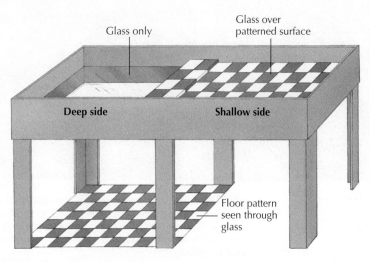

▸▸**FIGURE 4.37** Human infants and newborn animals refuse to go over the edge of the visual cliff.

Stereoscopic vision Perception of space and depth caused chiefly by the fact that the eyes receive different images.

Binocular Depth Cues

The most basic source of depth perception is *retinal disparity* (a discrepancy in the images that reach the right and left eyes). Retinal disparity, which is a binocular cue, is based on the fact that the eyes are about 6.5 centimetres apart. Because of this, each eye receives a slightly different view of the world. When the two images are fused into one overall image, **stereoscopic vision** (three-dimensional sight) occurs (Howard & Rogers, 2001b). The result is a powerful sensation of depth (Figure 4.38 and Figure 4.39).

Convergence is a second binocular depth cue. When you look at a distant object, the lines of vision from your eyes are parallel. You are normally not aware of it, but whenever you estimate a distance under 15 metres (as when you play catch or shoot garbage can hoops with the first draft

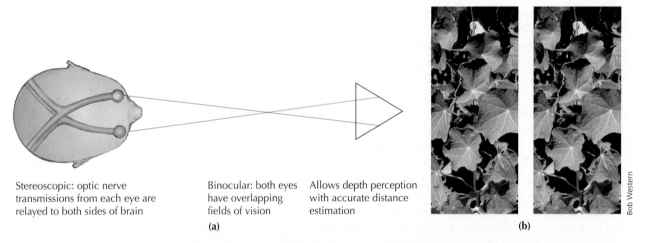

Stereoscopic: optic nerve transmissions from each eye are relayed to both sides of brain

Binocular: both eyes have overlapping fields of vision

Allows depth perception with accurate distance estimation

(a)

(b)

Bob Western

▸▸**FIGURE 4.38** (a) Stereoscopic vision. (b) The photographs show what the right and left eyes would see when viewing a plant. Hold the page about 15 to 20 centimetres from your eyes. Allow your eyes to cross and focus on the overlapping image between the two photos. Then try to fuse the leaves into one image. If you are successful, the third dimension will appear like magic.

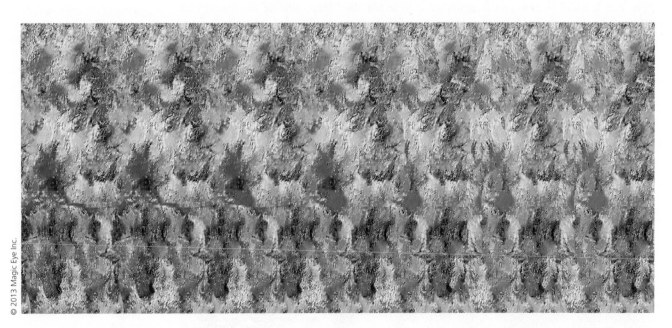

© 2013 Magic Eye Inc.

▸▸**FIGURE 4.39** This computer-generated art creates a 3-D illusion by superimposing two patterns. There are mismatches between some areas of the two patterns. This simulates retinal disparity and creates a sensation of depth. To get the 3-D effect, hold the stereogram about 20 centimetres from the end of your nose. Relax your eyes and look *through* the art, as if you were focusing on something in the distance. If you're patient, you may see a 3-D fawn.

of your essay), you are using convergence. How? Nerves that control muscles attached to the eyeball feed information on eye position to the brain to help it judge distance (Figure 4.40).

You can feel convergence by exaggerating it: Focus on your fingertip and bring it toward your eyes until they almost cross. You can actually feel the muscles that control eye movement working harder and harder as your fingertip gets closer.

Can a person with one eye perceive depth? Yes, but not as well as a person with two eyes. Overall, stereoscopic vision is 10 times as good for judging depth as perception based on just one eye (Rosenberg, 1994). If you closed one eye, you would still be able to drive, although it would be more difficult than usual. It would be possible because your single eye could still make use of monocular depth cues.

Monocular Depth Cues

As their name implies, monocular depth cues can be perceived with just one eye. One such cue is *accommodation,* the bending of the lens to focus on nearby objects. Sensations from muscles attached to each lens flow back to the brain. Changes in these sensations help us judge distances within about 1.2 metres of the eyes. This information is available even if you are just using one eye, so accommodation is a monocular cue. Beyond 1.2 metres, accommodation has limited value. Obviously, it is more important to a watchmaker or a person trying to thread a needle than it is to a hockey player or someone driving an automobile.

Other monocular depth cues are referred to as pictorial depth cues, because a good movie, painting, or photograph can create a convincing sense of depth where none exists.

How is the illusion of depth created on a two-dimensional surface? **Pictorial depth cues** are features found in paintings, drawings, and photographs that impart information about space, depth, and distance. To understand how these cues work, imagine that you are looking outdoors through a window. If you trace everything you see onto the glass, you will have an excellent drawing, with convincing depth. If you then analyze what is on the glass, you will find the following features:

1. **Linear perspective.** This cue is based on the apparent convergence of parallel lines in the environment. If you stand between two railroad tracks, they appear to meet near the horizon, even though they actually remain parallel. Because you know they are parallel, their convergence implies great distance (Figure 4.41a).

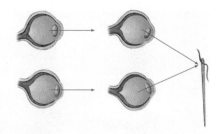

FIGURE 4.40 The eyes must converge, or turn in toward the nose, to focus close objects. The eyes shown are viewed from above the head.

Pictorial depth cues Features found in paintings, drawings, and photographs that impart information about space, depth, and distance.

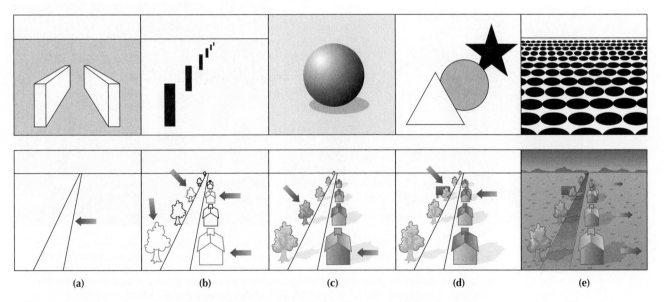

FIGURE 4.41 (a) Linear perspective. (b) Relative size. (c) Light and shadow. (d) Overlap. (e) Texture gradients. Drawings in the top row show fairly "pure" examples of each of the pictorial depth cues. In the bottom row, the pictorial depth cues are used to assemble a more realistic scene.

▸▸**FIGURE 4.42** On a dry lake bed, relative size is just about the only depth cue available for judging the camera's distance from this vintage aircraft. What do you estimate the distance to be? For the answer, look ahead to Figure 4.46.

2. **Relative size.** If an artist wishes to depict two objects of the same size at different distances, the artist makes the more distant object smaller (Figure 4.41b). Special effects in films create sensational illusions of depth by rapidly changing the image size of planets, airplanes, monsters, and so on. (Also see Figure 4.42.)

3. **Height in the picture plane.** Objects that are placed higher (closer to the horizon line) in a drawing tend to be perceived as more distant. In the upper frame of Figure 4.41b, the black columns look like they are receding into the distance partly because they become smaller, but also because they move higher in the drawing.

4. **Light and shadow.** Most objects are lighted in ways that create clear patterns of light and shadow. Copying such patterns of light and shadow can give a two-dimensional design a three-dimensional appearance (Figure 4.41c). (Also see Figure 4.43 for more information on light and shadow.)

5. **Overlap.** Overlap (or *interposition*) occurs when one object partially blocks another object. Hold your hands up and ask a friend across the room which is nearer. Relative size will give the answer if one hand is much nearer to your friend than the other. But if one hand is only slightly closer than the other, your friend may not be able to tell—until you slide one hand in front of the other. Overlap then removes any doubt (Figure 4.41d).

6. **Texture gradients.** Changes in texture also contribute to depth perception. If you stand in the middle of a cobblestone street, the street will look coarse near your feet. However, its texture will get smaller and finer if you look into the distance (Figure 4.41e).

7. **Aerial perspective.** Smog, fog, dust, and haze add to the apparent distance of an object. Because of aerial perspective, distant objects tend to be hazy, washed out in colour, and lacking in detail. Aerial haze is often most noticeable when it is missing. If you have ever seen a distant mountain range on a crystal-clear day, it might have looked like it was only a few kilometres away.

▸▸**FIGURE 4.43** (*Left*) When judging depth, we usually assume that light comes mainly from one direction, usually from above. Squint a little to blur the image you see here. You should perceive a collection of globes v outward. If you turn this page upside down, the globes should become cavities. (*Right*) The famed Dutch artist M. C. Escher violated our assumptions about light to create the dramatic illusions of depth found in his 1955 lithograph "Convex and Concave." In this print, light appears to come from all sides of the scene.

8. **Relative motion.** Relative motion, also known as *motion parallax* (PAIR-ah-lax), can be seen by looking out a window and moving your head from side to side. Notice that nearby objects appear to move a sizable distance as your head moves. Trees, houses, and telephone poles that are farther away appear to move slightly in relation to the background. Distant objects such as hills, mountains, and clouds don't seem to move at all.

When combined, pictorial cues can create a powerful illusion of depth. (See Table 4.1 for a summary of all the depth cues we have discussed.)

Is motion parallax really a pictorial cue? Strictly speaking it is not, except in the two-dimensional world of movies, television, and animated cartoons. However, when parallax is present, we almost always perceive depth. Much of the apparent depth of a good movie comes from relative motion captured by the camera. Figure 4.44 illustrates the defining feature of motion parallax. Imagine that you are on a bus and watching the passing scenery (with your gaze at a right angle to the road). Under these conditions, nearby objects will appear to rush *backward*. Those farther away, such as distant mountains, will seem to move very little or not at all. Objects that are more remote, such as the Sun and the Moon, will appear to move in the *same* direction you are travelling. (That's why the Moon appears to "follow" you when you take a stroll at night.)

The Moon Illusion

How do the depth perception cues relate to daily experience? We constantly use both pictorial cues and bodily cues to sense depth and judge distances. Consider an intriguing effect called the *Moon illusion* (perceiving the Moon as larger when it is low in the sky). When the Moon is on the horizon, it tends to look like a loonie. When it is directly overhead, it looks more like a dime. In fact, the Moon is not magnified by the atmosphere. But the Moon *looks* nearly twice as large when it's low in the sky (Ross & Plug, 2002). This occurs, in part, because the Moon's *apparent distance* is greater when it is near the horizon than when it is overhead (Kaufman & Kaufman, 2000).

But if it seems farther away, shouldn't it look smaller? No. When the Moon is overhead, few depth cues surround it. In contrast, when you see the Moon on the horizon, it is behind houses, trees, telephone poles, and mountains. These objects add numerous depth cues, which cause the horizon to seem more distant than the sky overhead. Picture two balloons, one 3 metres away and the second 6 metres away. Suppose the more distant balloon is inflated until its image on your retina matches the image of the nearer balloon. How do we know the more distant balloon is larger? Because its image is the same size as a balloon that is closer. Similarly, the moon makes the same-size image on the horizon as it does overhead. However, the horizon seems more distant because more depth cues are

■ Table 4.1 **Summary of Visual Depth Cues**

Binocular Cues
- Retinal disparity
- Convergence

Monocular Cues
- Accommodation
- Pictorial depth cues
  - Linear perspective
  - Relative size
  - Height in the picture plane
  - Light and shadow
  - Overlap
  - Texture gradients
  - Aerial perspective
  - Relative motion (motion parallax)

Direction of travel

▶▶**FIGURE 4.44** The apparent motion of objects viewed during travel depends on their distance from the observer. Apparent motion can also be influenced by an observer's point of fixation. At middle distances, objects closer than the point of fixation appear to move backward; those beyond the point of fixation appear to move forward. Objects at great distances, such as the Sun and the Moon, always appear to move forward.

▸▸**FIGURE 4.45** The Ponzo illusion may help you understand the Moon illusion. Picture the two white bars as resting on the railroad tracks. In the drawing, the upper bar is the same length as the lower bar. However, because the upper bar appears to be farther away than the lower bar, we perceive it as longer. The same logic applies to the Moon illusion.

▸▸**FIGURE 4.46** Before you can use familiar size to judge distance, objects must actually be the size you assume they are. Either these men are giants, or the model airplane was closer than you may have thought when you looked at Figure 4.42.

Apparent-distance hypothesis An explanation of the Moon illusion stating that the horizon seems more distant than the night sky.

Müller-Lyer illusion Two equal-length lines tipped with inward- or outward-pointing V's appear to be of different lengths.

present. As a result, the horizon Moon must be perceived as larger (Kaufman & Kaufman, 2000). (See Figure 4.45.)

This explanation is known as the **apparent-distance hypothesis** (the horizon seems more distant than the night sky). You can test it by removing depth cues while looking at a horizon Moon. Try looking at the Moon through a rolled-up paper tube, or make your hands into a "telescope" and look at the next large Moon you see. It will immediately appear to shrink when viewed without depth cues (Ross & Plug, 2002).

Can all illusions be explained? Not in all cases, or to everyone's satisfaction. In general, size and shape constancy, habitual eye movements, continuity, and perceptual habits combine in various ways to produce the illusions in Figure 4.47. Rather than attempt to explain all of them, let's focus on one deceptively simple example.

Consider the drawing in Figure 4.47a. This is the familiar **Müller-Lyer** (MEOO-ler-LIE-er) **illusion** in which the horizontal line with arrowheads appears shorter than the line with V's. A quick measurement will show that they are the same length. How can we explain this illusion? Evidence suggests it is based on a lifetime of experience with the edges and corners of rooms and buildings. Richard Gregory (2000) believes you see the horizontal line with the V's as if it were the corner of a room viewed from inside (Figure 4.48). The line with arrowheads, on the other hand, suggests the corner of a room or building seen from outside. In other words, cues that suggest a three-dimensional space alter our perception of a two-dimensional design (Enns & Coren, 1995).

Earlier, to explain the Moon illusion, we said that if two objects make images of the same size, the more distant object must be larger. This is known formally as *size–distance invariance* (the size of an object's image is precisely related to its distance from the eyes). Gregory believes the same concept explains the Müller-Lyer illusion. If the V-tipped line looks farther away than the arrowhead-tipped line, you must compensate by seeing the V-tipped line as longer. This explanation presumes that you have had years of experience with straight lines, sharp edges, and corners—a pretty safe assumption in our culture.

Is there any way to show that past experience causes the illusion? If we could test someone who saw only curves and wavy lines as a child, we would know if experience with a "square" culture is important. Fortunately, the Zulus, a group of people in South Africa, live in a "round" culture. In their daily lives, traditional Zulus rarely encounter a straight line: Their

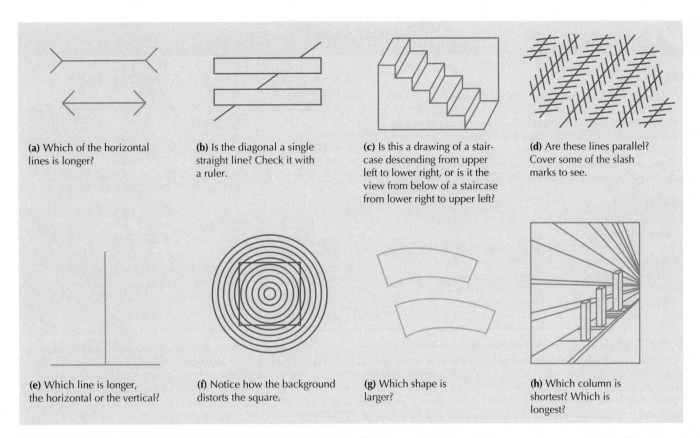

(a) Which of the horizontal lines is longer?

(b) Is the diagonal a single straight line? Check it with a ruler.

(c) Is this a drawing of a staircase descending from upper left to lower right, or is it the view from below of a staircase from lower right to upper left?

(d) Are these lines parallel? Cover some of the slash marks to see.

(e) Which line is longer, the horizontal or the vertical?

(f) Notice how the background distorts the square.

(g) Which shape is larger?

(h) Which column is shortest? Which is longest?

▸▸**FIGURE 4.47** Some interesting perceptual illusions. Such illusions reveal that perceptual misconstructions are a normal part of visual perception.

houses are shaped like rounded mounds and arranged in a circle, tools and toys are curved, and there are few straight roads or square buildings.

What happens if a Zulu looks at the Müller-Lyer design? The typical Zulu villager does not experience the illusion. At most, he or she sees the V-shaped line as *slightly* longer than the other (Gregory, 1990). This seems to confirm the importance of perceptual habits in determining our view of the world.

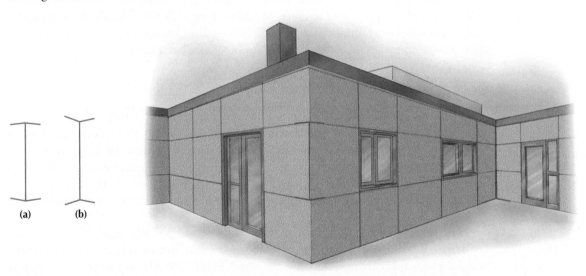

(a)   **(b)**

▸▸**FIGURE 4.48** Why does line (b) in the Müller-Lyer illusion look longer than line (a)? Probably because it looks more like a distant corner than a nearer one. Because the vertical lines form images of the same length, the more "distant" line must be perceived as larger. As you can see in the drawing on the right, additional depth cues accentuate the Müller-Lyer illusion. (After Enns & Coren, 1995.)

STUDY BREAK Depth Perception

Reflect

Part of the rush of excitement produced by action movies and video games is based on the sense of depth they create. Return to the list of pictorial depth cues. What cues have you seen used to portray depth? Try to think of specific examples in a movie or game you have seen recently.

If you spent a year hiking the Amazon River Basin, what effect might it have on your perception of the Müller-Lyer illusion?

Learning Check

1. The visual cliff is used to test for infant sensitivity to linear perspective. T or F?
2. Write an *M* or a *B* after each of the following to indicate if it is a monocular or binocular depth cue.

accommodation _____ convergence _____
retinal disparity _____ linear perspective _____
motion parallax _____ overlap relative size _____

3. Which of the depth cues listed in Question 2 are based on muscular feedback? _____
_____
4. Interpretation of pictorial depth cues requires no prior experience. T or F?
5. The Moon's image is greatly magnified by the atmosphere near the horizon. T or F?
6. Size–distance relationships appear to underlie which two illusions? _____ and _____

Critical Thinking

7. What hearing ability would you say is most closely related to stereoscopic vision?
8. What size object do you think you would have to hold at arm's length to cover up a full Moon?

Answers

1. F 2. accommodation (M), convergence (M), retinal disparity (B), linear perspective (M), motion parallax (M), overlap (M), relative size (M) 3. accommodation/convergence 4. F 5. F 6. Moon illusion, Müller-Lyer illusion 7. If you close your eyes, you can usually tell the direction and perhaps the location of a sound source, such as a hand-clap. Locating sounds in space depends heavily on having two ears, just as stereoscopic vision depends on having two eyes. 8. The most popular answers range from a quarter to a softball. Actually, a pea held in the outstretched hand will cover a full Moon (Kunkel, 1993). If you listed an object larger than a pea, be aware that perceptions, no matter how accurate they seem, may distort reality.

PERCEPTUAL LEARNING—PERCEPTION FROM THE TOP DOWN

SURVEY QUESTION>
How is perception altered by expectations, motives, emotions, and learning?

We use Gestalt organizing principles, perceptual constancies, and depth cues to construct our visual perceptions. All of these processes, and others, make up the common, partly inborn, core of our perceptual abilities. In addition, we each have specific life experiences that can, in top-down fashion, affect our perceptions. For instance, what you perceive can be altered by *perceptual expectancies,* motives, emotions, and *perceptual habits.*

Perceptual Expectancies

What is a perceptual expectancy? If you are a runner in the starting blocks at a track meet, you are *set* to respond in a certain way. If a car backfires, runners at a track meet may jump the gun. Likewise, past experience, motives, context, or suggestions may create a **perceptual expectancy** (or **set**) that prepares you to perceive in a certain way. As a matter of fact, we all frequently jump the gun when perceiving. In essence, an expectancy is a perceptual hypothesis we are *very likely* to apply to a stimulus—even if applying it is inappropriate.

Perceptual sets often lead us to see what we *expect* to see. For example, let's say you are driving across the vast expanse of Northern Ontario. You are very low on gas. Finally, you see a sign approaching. On it are the words FUEL AHEAD. You relax, knowing you will not be stranded. But as you draw nearer, the words on the sign become FOOD AHEAD. Most people have had similar experiences in which expectations altered their perceptions. To observe perceptual expectancies firsthand, perform the demonstration described in Figure 4.49.

Perceptual expectancy (or set) A readiness to perceive in a particular manner, induced by strong expectations.

View I

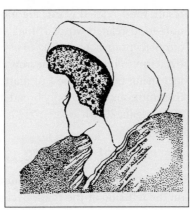

View II

View III

▸▸**FIGURE 4.49** "Young woman/old woman" illustrations. As an interesting demonstration of perceptual expectancy, show some of your friends view I and some view II (cover all other views). Next show your friends view III and ask them what they see. Those who saw view I should see the old woman in view III; those who saw view II should see the young woman in view III. Can you see both? (After Leeper, 1935.)

Perceptual expectancies are frequently created by *suggestion.* In one study (wine snobs take note), participants given a taste of what they were told was a $90 wine reported that it tasted better than what they were told was a $10 wine. Functional MRI images confirmed that brain areas related to pleasure were indeed more active when participants tasted what they thought was the more expensive wine (Plassmann et al., 2008). The twist is that exactly the same wine was served in both cases. Suggesting that the wine was expensive created a perceptual expectancy that it would taste better. And so it did (advertisers also take note).

Motives, Emotions, and Perception

The Human Diversity box "Do They See What We See?" describes one form of cultural influence on perception. Our motives and emotions also play a role in shaping our perceptions. For example, if you are hungry, your motives will concern food. As a

HUMAN DIVERSITY

Do They See What We See?

According to psychologist Richard Nisbett and his colleagues, people from different cultures perceive the world differently. European North Americans are individualistic people for whom a sense of personal control over their lives is important. In contrast, East Asians are collectivist people who tend to focus on their personal relationships and social responsibilities. As a consequence, European North Americans tend to explain actions in terms of internal factors while East Asians tend to explain actions in terms of the social context (Norenzayan & Nisbett, 2000).

Do such cultural differences affect our everyday perception of objects and events? They may sometimes do so. In one study, American and Japanese participants were shown drawings of everyday scenes, such as a farm. Later, they saw a slightly changed version of the scene. Some of the changes were made to the focal point, or figure, of the scene. Other changes altered the surrounding context, or ground, of the scene. Americans, it turns out, were better at detecting changes in the figure of a scene. Japanese participants were better at finding alterations in the background (Nisbett & Miyamoto, 2005).

To explain this difference, Chua, Boland, and Nisbett (2005) presented American and Chinese participants with pictures of a figure (such as a tiger) placed on a ground (such as a jungle) and monitored their eye-movement patterns. The Americans focused their eye movements on the figure; Chinese participants made more eye movements around the ground. In other words, Westerners are more likely to focus on a particular object in a scene, whereas Easterners are more likely to divide attention across a set of objects. This difference in perceptual style even influences the artistic and aesthetic preferences expressed in Eastern and Western art (Masuda et al., 2008).

Charles Platiau/Reuters/Corbis

In many sports, expert players are much better than beginners at paying attention to key information. Compared with novices, experts scan actions and events more quickly, and they focus on only the most meaningful information. This helps experts to make decisions and react more quickly (Bard, Fleury, & Goulet, 1994).

Perceptual learning Changes in perception that can be attributed to prior experience; a result of changes in how the brain processes sensory information.

result, food-related words are more likely to gain your attention than non–food-related words (Mogg et al., 1998). Emotions can also shape our perceptions. According to psychologist Barbara Fredrickson, negative emotions generally narrow our perceptual focus, or "spotlight," increasing the likelihood of inattentional blindness. In contrast, positive emotions can actually broaden the scope of attention (Fredrickson & Branigan, 2005).

Perceptual Learning

England is one of the few countries in the world where people drive on the left side of the road. Because of this reversal, it is not unusual for visitors to step off curbs in front of cars—after carefully looking for traffic in the *wrong* direction. As this example suggests, learning has a powerful impact on top-down processing in perception.

How does learning affect perception? The term **perceptual learning** refers to changes in the brain that alter how we construct sensory information into percepts (Fahle & Poggio, 2002). For example, to use a computer, you must learn to pay attention to specific stimuli, such as icons and cursors. We also learn to tell the difference between stimuli that seemed identical at first. An example is the novice chef who discovers how to tell the difference between dried basil, oregano, and tarragon. In other situations, we learn to focus on just one part of a group of stimuli. This saves us from having to process all the stimuli in the group. For instance, a linebacker in football may be able to tell if the next play will be a run or a pass by watching one or two key players, rather than the entire opposing team (Seitz & Watanabe, 2005).

In general, learning creates *perceptual habits* (ingrained patterns of organization and attention) that affect our daily experience. Stop for a moment and look at Figure 4.50. The left face looks somewhat unusual, to be sure. But the distortion seems mild—until you turn the page upside down. Viewed normally, the face looks quite grotesque. Why is there a difference? Apparently, most people have little experience with upside-down faces. Perceptual learning, therefore, has less impact on our perceptions of an upside-down face. With a face in the normal position, you know what to expect and where to look. Also, you tend to see the entire face as a recognizable pattern. When a face is inverted, we are forced to perceive its individual features separately (Caharel et al., 2006).

▶▶**FIGURE 4.50** The effects of prior experience on perception. The doctored face looks far worse when viewed right-side up because it can be related to past experience.

Based on National Archives of Canada/Pittaway & Jarvis/C-000686

STUDY BREAK Perceptual Expectancies, Motives, Emotions, and Perceptual Learning

Reflect

You have almost certainly misperceived a situation at some time because of a perceptual expectancy or the influence of your motives and emotions. How were your perceptions influenced?

How has perceptual learning affected your ability to safely drive a car? For example, what do you pay attention to at intersections? Where do you habitually look as you are driving?

Learning Check

1. When a person is prepared to perceive events in a particular way, it is said that a perceptual expectancy or ____ exists.

2. People around the world perceive in the same way regardless of culture. T or F?
3. Perceptual habits may become so ingrained that they lead us to misperceive a stimulus. T or F?
4. Perceptual learning seems to program the brain for sensitivity to important ____ of the environment.

Critical Thinking

5. Cigarette advertisements in the United States are required to carry a warning label about the health risks of smoking. How have tobacco companies made these labels less visible?

Answers

1. set 2. F 3. T 4. features 5. Advertisers place health warnings in the corners of ads, where they attract the least possible attention. Also, the labels are often placed on "busy" backgrounds so that they are partially camouflaged. Finally, the main images in ads are designed to strongly attract attention. This further distracts readers from seeing the warnings. Over time, perceptual learning renders these warnings practically invisible.

In the next section, we will go beyond normal perception to ask, Is extrasensory perception possible? Before we do that, here's a chance to answer the question, Is remembering the preceding discussion possible?

EXTRASENSORY PERCEPTION—DO YOU BELIEVE IN MAGIC?

Once, during the middle of the night, a woman away for a weekend visit suddenly had a strong impulse to return home. When she arrived, she found the house on fire with her husband asleep inside (Rhine, 1953). How could she have known? Could she have used **extrasensory perception (ESP)**—the purported ability to perceive events in ways that cannot be explained by known sensory capacities?

About half of the general public believes in the existence of ESP (Wiseman & Watt, 2006). ESP and other paranormal events are treated as accepted facts in many movies and television programs. Stage entertainers routinely "astound" their audiences. There is even a discipline, *parapsychology,* that studies ESP and other **psi phenomena** (events that seem to defy accepted scientific laws). (Psi is pronounced like "sigh.") Parapsychologists seek answers to the questions raised by three basic forms that ESP could take:

1. **Telepathy.** The purported ability to communicate directly with another person's mind. When the other person is dead, the communications are called *mediumship.*
2. **Clairvoyance.** The purported ability to perceive events or gain information in ways that appear unaffected by distance or normal physical barriers.
3. **Precognition.** The purported ability to perceive or accurately predict future events. Precognition may take the form of prophetic dreams that foretell the future. While we are at it, we might as well toss in another purported psi ability:
4. **Psychokinesis.** The purported ability to exert influence over inanimate objects (such as bending spoons) by willpower ("mind over matter"). (Psychokinesis cannot be classed as a type of ESP, but it is frequently studied by parapsychologists.)

<SURVEY QUESTION
Is extrasensory perception possible?

Extrasensory perception (ESP)
The purported ability to perceive events in ways that cannot be explained by known capacities of the sensory organs.

Psi phenomena Events that seem to lie outside the realm of accepted scientific laws.

▸▸**FIGURE 4.51** ESP cards used by J. B. Rhine, an early experimenter in parapsychology.

An Appraisal of ESP

Do psychologists also believe in ESP? Regardless of all of this enthusiasm, psychologists as a group are highly skeptical about psi abilities. Let's have a look at the evidence for and against extrasensory perception. The formal investigation of psi events owes much to the late J. B. Rhine, who tried to study ESP objectively. Many of Rhine's experiments made use of *Zener cards* (a deck of 25 cards, each bearing one of five symbols) (Figure 4.51). In a typical clairvoyance test, people try to guess the symbols on the cards as they are turned up from a shuffled deck. In a typical telepathy test, a *receiver* tries to guess the correct symbol by reading the mind of a *sender* looking at a card. Pure guessing in these tests will produce an average score of 5 "hits" out of 25 cards. Rhine and others since have reported results much greater than might be expected by chance alone.

Doesn't evidence like that settle the issue? No it doesn't, for a number of reasons, including fraud, poorly designed experiments, and chance.

Fraud

Fraud continues to plague parapsychology. The need for skepticism is especially great any time there's money to be made from purported psychic abilities. Stage demonstrations of ESP are based on deception and tricks, as are other "for-profit" parapsychology enterprises. For example, the owners of the "Miss Cleo" TV-psychic operation were convicted of felony fraud in 2002. "Miss Cleo," supposedly a Jamaican-accented psychic, was really just an actress from Los Angeles. People who paid $4.99 a minute for a "reading" from "Miss Cleo" actually reached one of several hundred operators. These people were hired to do "cold readings" through ads that read, "No experience necessary." Despite being entirely faked, the "Miss Cleo" scam brought in more than $1 billion before it was shut down.

Anyone can learn to do "cold readings" well enough to produce satisfied customers (Wood et al., 2003). *Cold reading* is a set of techniques that are used to lead people to believe in the truth of what a psychic or medium is saying about them. These include a reliance on many of the same techniques used by astrologers, such as uncritical acceptance, positive instances, and the Barnum effect. (Remember Chapter 1?)

The "psychic" begins a "reading" by making general statements about a person. The psychic then plays "hot and cold" by attending to the person's facial expressions, body language, or tone of voice. When the psychic is "hot" (on the right track), he or she continues to make similar statements about the person. If the person's reactions signal that the psychic is "cold," the psychic drops that topic or line of thought and tries another (Hyman, 2007).

Poorly Designed Experiments

Unfortunately, some of Rhine's most dramatic early experiments used badly printed Zener cards that allowed the symbols to show faintly on the back. It is also very easy to cheat, by marking cards with a fingernail or by noting marks on the cards caused by normal use. Even if this were not the case, there is evidence that early experimenters sometimes unconsciously gave people cues about cards with their eyes, facial gestures, or lip movements. In short, none of the early studies in parapsychology were done in a way that eliminated the possibility of deliberate fraud or the accidental "leakage" of helpful information (Alcock, Burns, & Freeman, 2003).

"I see a girl, I see a marriage, I see her not understanding you, I see a beer belly. Do you want me to go on?"

Chance

Is that why most psychologists remain skeptical about psi abilities? Probably the most important reason has to do with chance. Remember the woman who had a premonition that something bad was about to happen to her husband? She returned home early to find her house on fire with him sleeping inside. An apparent clairvoyant or telepathic experience like this is certainly striking, but it does not confirm the existence of ESP. Such *coincidences* occur quite often. On any given night, many, many people might act on a "premonition." If, by coincidence, one person's hunch turns out to be correct, it may be *reinterpreted* as precognition or clairvoyance (Marks, 2000; Wiseman & Watt, 2006). Then you read about it in the news the next day. No one reports the vast majority of false premonitions, which will simply be forgotten.

Inconsistency in psi research is a related problem. For every published study with positive results, there are many others that fail and are never reported (Alcock, 2003). Even experimental "successes" are weak. Many of the most spectacular findings in parapsychology simply cannot be *replicated* (reproduced or repeated) (Hyman, 1996a). Furthermore, improved research methods usually result in fewer positive results (Hyman, 1996b; O'Keeffe & Wiseman, 2005).

Even when a person does seems to show evidence of psi ability, it is rare—in fact, almost unheard of—for him or her to maintain that ability over any sustained period of time (Alcock, Burns, & Freeman, 2003). This is likely because a person who only temporarily scores above chance has just received credit for a **run of luck** (a statistically unusual outcome that could occur by chance alone).

To understand the run-of-luck criticism, imagine that you flip a coin 100 times and record the results. You then flip another coin 100 times, again recording the results. The two lists are compared. For any ten pairs of flips, we would expect heads or tails to match five times. Let's say that you go through the list and find a set of ten pairs where nine out of ten matched. This is far above chance expectation. But does it mean that the first coin "knew" what was going to come up on the second coin? The idea is obviously silly. Now, what if a person guesses 100 times what will come up on a coin? Again, we might find a set of 10 guesses that matches the results of flipping the coin. Does this mean that the person, for a time, had precognition—then lost it?

Implications

After close to 130 years of investigation, it is still impossible to say conclusively whether psi events occur. As we have seen, a close look at psi experiments often reveals serious problems of evidence, procedure, and scientific rigour (Alcock, Burns, & Freeman, 2003; Hyman, 2007; Stokes, 2001). The more closely psi experiments are examined, the more likely it is that claimed successes will evaporate (Alcock, 2003; Stokes, 2001). As one critic put it, positive ESP results usually mean "Error Some Place" (Marks, 2000).

What would it take to scientifically demonstrate the existence of ESP? Quite simply, a set of instructions that would allow any competent, unbiased observer to produce a psi event under standardized conditions that rule out any possibility of fraud or chance (Schick & Vaughn, 2001).

Of course, in many ESP tests, the outcome is beyond debate. A good example is provided by ESP experiments done through newspapers, radio, and television. In these mass-media studies, people attempted to identify ESP targets from a distance. The results of more than 1.5 million ESP trials done through the mass media are easy to summarize: There was no significant ESP effect (Milton & Wiseman, 1999). Zero. Zip. Nada. Clearly, provincial lottery organizations have nothing to fear!

A Look Ahead

In this chapter we have moved from basic sensations to the complexities of perceiving people and events. We have also probed some of the controversies concerning ESP. In the Psychology in Action section, we will return to "everyday" perception, for a look at perceptual awareness.

> **Run of luck** A statistically unusual outcome (as in getting five heads in a row when flipping a coin) that could still occur by chance alone.

STUDY BREAK   Extrasensory Perception

Reflect

Let's say that a friend of yours is an avid fan of TV shows that feature paranormal themes. See if you can summarize for her or him what is known about ESP. Be sure to include evidence for and against the existence of ESP and some of the thinking errors associated with non-skeptical belief in the paranormal.

Learning Check

1. Four purported psi events investigated by parapsychologists are clairvoyance, telepathy, precognition, and _____.
2. The _____ cards were used by J. B. Rhine in early tests of ESP.
3. Natural, or "real-life," occurrences are regarded as the best evidence for the existence of ESP. T or F?

4. Skeptics attribute positive results in psi experiments to statistical runs of luck. T or F?
5. Replication rates are very high for ESP experiments. T or F?

Critical Thinking

6. What would you estimate is the chance that two people will have the same birthday (day and month, but not year) in a group of 30 people?
7. A "psychic" on television offers to fix broken watches for viewers. Moments later, dozens of viewers call the station to say that their watches miraculously started running again. What have they overlooked?

Answers

1. psychokinesis 2. Zener 3. F 4. T 5. F 6. Most people assume that this would be a relatively rare event. Actually there is a 71 percent chance that two people will share a birthday in a group of 30. Most people probably underestimate the natural rate of occurrence of many seemingly mysterious coincidences (Alcock, Burns, & Freeman, 2003). 7. When psychologists handled watches awaiting repair at a store, 57 percent began running again, with no help from a "psychic." Believing the psychic's claim also overlooks the impact of big numbers: If the show reached a large audience, at least a few "broken" watches would start working merely by chance.

Psychology in Action

BECOMING A BETTER EYEWITNESS TO LIFE

SURVEY QUESTION>
How can I learn to perceive events more accurately?

Even in broad daylight, eyewitness testimony is untrustworthy. In 2001 an airliner crashed near Kennedy International Airport in New York. Hundreds of people saw the plane go down. Half of them said the plane was on fire. Flight recorders showed there was no fire. One witness in five saw the plane make a right turn. An equal number saw it make a left turn! As one investigator noted, the best witness may be a "kid under 12 years old who doesn't have his parents around." Adults, it seems, are easily swayed by their expectations.

In the courtroom, eyewitness testimony can be a key to proving guilt or innocence. The claim "I saw it with my own eyes" still carries a lot of weight with a jury. Too many jurors (unless they have taken a psychology course) tend to assume that eyewitness testimony is nearly infallible (Durham & Dane, 1999). Even U.S. judges are vulnerable to overoptimism about eyewitness testimony (Wise & Safer, 2004). But, to put it bluntly, eyewitness testimony is frequently wrong (Wells & Olson, 2003).

What about witnesses who are certain that their perceptions were accurate? Should juries believe them? Actually, having confidence in your testimony has almost no bearing on its accuracy (Brewer & Wells, 2006)! Psychologists are gradually convincing lawyers, judges, and police that eyewitness errors are common (Yarmey, 2003). Even so, thousands of people have been wrongly convicted (Scheck, Neufeld, & Dwyer, 2000).

Unfortunately, perception rarely provides an "instant replay" of events. Impressions formed when a person is surprised, threatened, or under stress are especially prone to distortion (Yuille & Daylen, 1998). One study of eyewitness cases found that the *wrong person* was chosen from police line-ups 25 percent of the time (Levi, 1998).

Wouldn't the victim of a crime remember more than a mere witness? Not necessarily. A revealing study found that eyewitness accuracy is virtually the same for witnessing a crime (seeing a pocket calculator stolen) as it is for being a victim (seeing one's own watch stolen) (Hosch & Cooper, 1982). Placing more weight on the testimony of victims may be a serious mistake. In many crimes, victims fall prey to *weapon focus*. Understandably, they fix their entire attention on the knife, gun, or other weapon used by an attacker. In doing so, they fail to notice details of appearance, dress, or other clues to identity (Pickel, French, & Betts, 2003). Additional factors that consistently lower eyewitness accuracy are summarized in Table 4.2 (Kassin et al., 2001; Wells & Olson, 2003).

■ Table 4.2   **Factors Affecting the Accuracy of Eyewitness Perceptions**

Sources of Error	Summary of Findings
1. Wording of questions	An eyewitness's testimony about an event can be affected by how the questions put to that witness are worded.
2. Postevent information	Eyewitness testimony about an event often reflects not only what was actually seen, but also information obtained later on.
3. Attitudes, expectations	An eyewitness's perception and memory for an event may be affected by his or her attitudes and expectations.
4. Alcohol intoxication	Alcohol intoxication impairs later ability to recall events.
5. Cross-racial perceptions	Eyewitnesses are better at identifying members of their own race than they are at identifying people of other races.
6. Weapon focus	The presence of a weapon impairs an eyewitness's ability to accurately identify the culprit's face.
7. Accuracy-confidence	An eyewitness's confidence is not a good predictor of his or her accuracy.
8. Exposure time	The less time an eyewitness has to observe an event, the less well she or he will perceive and remember it.
9. Unconscious transference	Eyewitnesses sometimes identify as a culprit someone they have seen in another situation or context.
10. Colour perception	Judgments of colour made under monochromatic light (such as an orange street light) are highly unreliable.
11. Stress	Very high levels of stress impair the accuracy of eyewitness perceptions.

Source: Adapted from Kassin et al., 2001.

Implications

Now that DNA testing is available, more than 200 people who were convicted of murder, rape, and other crimes in the United States have been exonerated. Most of these innocent people were convicted mainly on the basis of eyewitness testimony. Each also spent *years* in prison before being cleared (Foxhall, 2000). Canada is not immune to such miscarriages of justice. DNA testing has led to convictions being overturned in a number of high-profile cases, including those of Guy-Paul Morin, David Milgaard, Kyle Unger, and Simon Marshall. How often are everyday perceptions as inaccurate or distorted as those of an emotional eyewitness? The answer we have been moving toward is "very frequently." Bearing this in mind may help you be more tolerant of the views of others and more cautious about your own objectivity. It may also encourage more frequent *reality testing* on your part.

If you have ever concluded that someone was angry, upset, or unfriendly without checking the accuracy of your perceptions, you have fallen into a subtle trap. Personal objectivity is an elusive quality, requiring frequent reality testing to maintain. At the very least, it pays to ask a person what he or she is feeling when you are in doubt. Clearly, most of us could learn to be better "eyewitnesses" to daily events.

Positive Psychology: Perceptual Awareness

Do some people perceive things more accurately than others? Humanistic psychologist Abraham Maslow (1969) believed that some people perceive themselves and others with unusual accuracy. Maslow characterized these people as especially alive, open, aware, and mentally healthy. He found that their perceptual styles were marked by immersion in the present; a lack of self-consciousness; freedom from selecting, criticizing, or evaluating; and a general "surrender" to experience. The kind of perception Maslow described is like that of a mother with her newborn infant, a child at Christmas, or two people in love.

In daily life, we quickly habituate (respond less) to predictable and unchanging stimuli. **Habituation** is a type of learning—basically, we learn to cease paying attention to familiar stimuli. For instance, when you download a new song, the music initially holds your attention all the way through. But when the song becomes "old," it may play without your really attending to it. When a stimulus is repeated *without change,* our response to it habituates, or decreases. Interestingly, creative people habituate *more slowly* than average. We might expect that they would rapidly become bored with a repeated stimulus. Instead, it seems that creative people actively attend to stimuli, even those that are repeated (Colin, Moore, & West, 1996).

Habituation A decrease in perceptual response to a repeated stimulus.

Dishabituation The reversal of habituation.

The Value of Paying Attention

Whereas the average person has not reached perceptual restriction of the "if you've seen one tree, you've seen them all" variety, the fact remains that most of us tend to look at a tree and classify it into the perceptual category of "trees in general" without really appreciating the miracle standing before us. How, then, can we bring about **dishabituation** (a reversal of habituation) on a day-to-day basis? Does perceptual clarity require years of effort? Fortunately, a more immediate avenue is available. The deceptively simple key to dishabituation is this: Pay attention. The following story summarizes the importance of attention:

> One day a man of the people said to Zen Master Ikkyu: "Master, will you please write for me some maxims of the highest wisdom?"
>
> Ikkyu immediately took his brush and wrote the word "Attention."
>
> "Is that all?" asked the man. "Will you not add something more?"
>
> Ikkyu then wrote twice running: "Attention. Attention."
>
> "Well," remarked the man rather irritably, "I really don't see much depth or subtlety in what you have just written."
>
> Then Ikkyu wrote the same word three times running: "Attention. Attention. Attention."
>
> Half angered, the man demanded, "What does that word 'Attention' mean anyway?"
>
> And Ikkyu answered gently: "Attention means attention." (Kapleau, 1966)

To this we can add only one thought, provided by the words of poet William Blake: "If the doors of perception were cleansed, man would see everything as it is, infinite."

How to Become a Better "Eyewitness" to Life

Here's a summary of ideas from this chapter to help you maintain and enhance perceptual awareness and accuracy:

1. *Remember that perceptions are constructions of reality.* Learn to regularly question your own perceptions. Are they accurate? Could another interpretation fit the facts? What assumptions are you making? Could they be false? How might your assumptions be distorting your perceptions?

2. *Break perceptual habits and interrupt habituation.* Each day, try to get away from habitual, top-down processing and do some activities in new ways. For example, take different routes when you travel to work or school. Do routines, such as brushing your teeth or combing your hair, with your non-preferred hand. Try to look at friends and family members as if you have just met them for the first time.

3. *Seek out-of-the-ordinary experiences.* The possibilities here range from trying foods you don't normally eat to reading opinions very different from your own. Experiences ranging from a quiet walk in the woods to a trip to an amusement park may be perceptually refreshing.

4. *Beware of perceptual sets.* Anytime you pigeonhole people, objects, or events, there is a danger that your perceptions will be distorted by expectations or preexisting categories. Be especially wary of labels and stereotypes. Try to see people as individuals, and events as unique, one-time occurrences.

5. *Be aware of the ways in which motives and emotions influence perceptions.* It is difficult to avoid being swayed by your own interests, needs, desires, and emotions. But be aware of this trap and actively try to see the world through the eyes of others. Taking the other person's perspective is especially valuable in disputes or arguments. Ask yourself, "How does this look to her or him?"

6. *Make a habit of engaging in reality testing.* Actively look for additional evidence to check the accuracy of your perceptions. Ask questions, seek clarifications, and find alternative channels of information. Remember that perception is not automatically accurate. You could be wrong—we all are frequently.

7. *Pay attention.* Make a conscious effort to pay attention to other people and your surroundings. Don't drift through life in a haze. Listen to others with full concentration. Watch their facial expressions. Make eye contact. Try to get in the habit of approaching perception as if you are going to have to testify later about what you saw and heard.

 STUDY BREAK **Perceptual Awareness and Accuracy**

Reflect

Because perceptions are constructions or models of external events, we should all engage in more frequent reality testing. Can you think of a recent event when a little reality testing would have saved you from misjudging a situation?

In order to improve your own perceptual awareness and accuracy, which strategies would you emphasize first?

Learning Check

1. Most perceptions can be described as active constructions of external reality. T or F?

2. Inaccuracies in eyewitness perceptions obviously occur in "real life," but they cannot be reproduced in psychology experiments. T or F?

3. Accuracy scores for facts provided by witnesses to staged crimes may be as low as 25 percent correct. T or F?

4. Victims of crimes are more accurate eyewitnesses than are impartial observers. T or F?

5. *Reality testing* is another term for dishabituation. T or F?

Critical Thinking

6. Why do you think very high levels of stress would impair the accuracy of eyewitness testimony?

Answers

1. T 2. F 3. T 4. F 5. F 6. High levels of stress can have an effect on eyewitness testimony in several ways. First, stress-related arousal could make certain items more important than others, as a result of which those items might get more than their share of attention. Second, arousal may influence top-down processing. It may affect the kind of knowledge brought to bear to speed up perception. Third, it may cause unrealistic evaluations of focal objects, which can then become part of the stored information about an event or person that is the basis for later testimony.

CHAPTER IN REVIEW

Major Points

- Sensory systems select, analyze, and transduce information from the surrounding world.
- All of the senses rely on a complex series of mechanical, chemical, and neural events to generate messages understood by the brain.
- Sensory adaptation, selective attention, and sensory gating significantly modify our experiences.
- Perception is an active process of assembling sensations into meaningful patterns.
- We unconsciously use Gestalt organizing principles and perceptual constancies to construct perceptions.
- Our wondrous ability to perceive three-dimensional space is based on binocular and monocular depth cues.
- Perception is greatly affected by expectations, motives, emotions, and learning.
- Perceptual accuracy can be improved by conscious effort and an awareness of factors that contribute to erroneous perceptions.

Summary

In general, how do sensory systems function?

- Because of transduction, selectivity, limited sensitivity, feature detection, and coding patterns, the senses act as data reduction systems.
- Sensation can be partially understood in terms of sensory localization in the brain.

How does the visual system function?

- The eye is a visual system, not a photographic one. The entire visual system is structured to analyze visual information.
- Four common visual defects are myopia, hyperopia, astigmatism, and presbyopia.
- The rods and cones are photoreceptors in the retina of the eye.
- The rods specialize in peripheral vision, night vision, seeing black and white, and motion detection. The cones specialize in colour vision, acuity, and daylight vision.
- Colour vision is explained by the trichromatic theory in the retina and by the opponent-process theory in the visual system beyond the eyes.
- Total colour-blindness is rare, but 8 percent of males and 1 percent of females are red-green colour-blind or colour-weak.

- Dark adaptation is caused mainly by an increase in the amount of visual pigments in the rods.

What are the mechanisms of hearing?

- Sound waves are the stimulus for hearing. They are transduced by the eardrum; the auditory ossicles; the oval window; the cochlea; and, ultimately, the hair cells.
- The frequency theory and place theory of hearing together explain how pitch is sensed.
- Two basic types of hearing loss are conductive hearing loss and sensorineural hearing loss. Noise-induced hearing loss is a common form of sensorineural hearing loss caused by exposure to loud noise.

How do the chemical senses operate?

- Olfaction (smell) and gustation (taste) are chemical senses responsive to airborne or liquefied molecules.
- The lock and key theory of olfaction partially explains smell. In addition, the location of the olfactory receptors in the nose helps identify various scents.
- Sweet and bitter tastes are based on a lock and key coding of molecule shapes. Salty and sour tastes are triggered by a direct flow of ions into taste receptors.

What are the somesthetic senses?

- The somesthetic senses include the skin senses, vestibular senses, and kinesthetic senses (receptors that detect muscle and joint positioning).
- The skin senses are touch, pressure, pain, cold, and warmth. Sensitivity to each is related to the number of receptors found in an area of skin.
- Distinctions can be made between warning pain and reminding pain.
- Pain is greatly affected by anxiety, attention, and control over a stimulus. Pain can be reduced by controlling these factors.
- According to sensory conflict theory, motion sickness is caused by a mismatch of visual, kinesthetic, and vestibular sensations. Motion sickness can be avoided by minimizing sensory conflict.

Why are we more aware of some sensations than others?

- Incoming sensations are affected by sensory adaptation (a reduction in the number of nerve impulses sent), by selective attention (selection and diversion of messages in the brain), and by sensory gating (blocking or alteration of messages flowing toward the brain).

- Selective gating of pain messages takes place in the spinal cord, as explained by gate control theory. Gate control theory cannot explain phantom limb pain.

In general, how do we construct our perceptions?

- Perception is an active process of constructing sensations into a meaningful mental representation of the world.

- Perceptions are based on simultaneous bottom-up and top-down processing. Complete percepts are assembled out of small sensory features in "bottom-up" fashion, guided by preexisting knowledge applied "top-down" to help organize features into a meaningful whole.

- Separating figure and ground is the most basic perceptual organization.

- The following Gestalt principles also help organize sensations: nearness, similarity, continuity, closure, contiguity, and common region.

- A perceptual organization may be thought of as a hypothesis held until evidence contradicts it.

- In vision, the image projected on the retina is constantly changing, but the external world appears stable and undistorted because of size, shape, and brightness constancy.

How is it possible to see depth and judge distance?

- A basic, innate capacity for depth perception is present soon after birth.

- Depth perception depends on binocular cues of retinal disparity and convergence.

- Depth perception also depends on the monocular cue of accommodation. Monocular "pictorial" depth cues also underlie depth perception. They are linear perspective, relative size, height in the picture plane, light and shadow, overlap, texture gradients, aerial haze, and motion parallax.

- The Moon illusion can be explained by the apparent-distance hypothesis, which emphasizes that many depth cues are present when the Moon is near the horizon, and few are present when it is overhead.

How is perception altered by expectations, motives, emotions, and learning?

- Suggestion, motives, emotions, attention, and prior experience combine in various ways to create perceptual sets, or expectancies.

- Personal motives and values often alter perceptions by changing the evaluation of what is seen or by altering attention to specific details.

- Perceptual learning influences the top-down organization and interpretation of sensations.

- One of the most familiar of all illusions, the Müller-Lyer illusion, seems to be related to perceptual learning, linear perspective, and size–distance invariance relationships.

Is extrasensory perception possible?

- Parapsychology is the study of purported psi phenomena, including telepathy (including mediumship), clairvoyance, precognition, and psychokinesis.

- Research in parapsychology remains controversial because of a variety of problems and shortcomings. The bulk of the evidence to date is against the existence of ESP.

How can I learn to perceive events more accurately?

- Eyewitness testimony is surprisingly unreliable. Eyewitness accuracy is further damaged by weapon focus and a number of similar factors.

- When a stimulus is repeated without change, our response to it undergoes habituation.

- Perceptual accuracy is enhanced by reality testing, dishabituation, and conscious efforts to pay attention.

- It is also valuable to break perceptual habits, to broaden frames of reference, to beware of perceptual sets, and to be aware of the ways in which motives and emotions influence perceptions.

Interactive Learning

Please visit http://www.psychologyjourney4ce.nelson.com for a list of weblinks to relevant psychology sites.

CourseMate

Access the interactive eBook and chapter-specific interactive learning tools, including flashcards, quizzes, videos, and more, in your Psychology CourseMate at NelsonBrain.com.

psyk.trek 3. Sensation and Perception, Psyk.Trek Simulations: 3. The Poggendorff Illusion.

The questions that follow are only a sample of what you need to know. If you miss any of the items, review the entire chapter and the Study Breaks. Another way to prepare for tests is to use the Study Guide and the Practice Exams that are available with this text.

1. What process refers to the senses dividing the world into basic perceptual features and sensory patterns?
   a. sensory localization
   b. sensory analysis
   c. accommodation
   d. phosphenation

2. Which of the following is characterized by black and white vision and a high degree of sensitivity to movement?
   a. rod vision
   b. cone vision
   c. the blind spot
   d. the fovea

3. What best explains coloured afterimages?
   a. trichromatic theory
   b. the effects of astigmatism
   c. sensory localization
   d. opponent-process theory

4. Sounds are ultimately transduced by movements of which of the following parts of the ear?
   a. the pinna
   b. the malleus
   c. the cochlea
   d. hair cells

5. The lock and key model is helpful in partially explaining which of the following processes?
   a. motion sickness
   b. olfaction and gustation
   c. dark adaptation
   d. colour-blindness

6. A mild surface pain can greatly reduce more agonizing pain. What explanation is this reaction consistent with?
   a. gate control theory
   b. sensory theory adaptation
   c. sensory conflict theory
   d. perceptual constancy theory

7. Which of the following is *least* likely to contribute to the formation of a perceptual figure?
   a. continuity
   b. closure
   c. similarity
   d. separation

8. What is the clearest example of a binocular depth cue?
   a. linear perspective
   b. retinal disparity
   c. aerial perspective
   d. motion parallax

9. To what is top-down perceptual processing closely related?
   a. perceptual expectancies
   b. the Müller-Lyer illusion
   c. size–distance invariances
   d. precognition

10. A good antidote to perceptual habituation can be found in conscious efforts to do which of the following?
   a. reverse sensory gating
   b. pay attention
   c. achieve visual constancy
   d. counteract shape accommodation

11. The type of sensation you experience depends on which area of the brain is activated. What is this phenomenon known as?
   a. the common region
   b. place theory
   c. sensory localization
   d. somesthetic sensation

12. Dark adaptation is due mainly to increases in which of the following?
   a. photoreceptors
   b. rods
   c. convergence
   d. top-down processing

13. What is suggested by the sensory disorder called anosmia?
   a. receptors for specific odours
   b. retinal blind spots
   c. five basic taste sensations
   d. reversible figures

14. On what does our sense of balance depend?
   a. figure–ground organization
   b. accommodation
   c. the cornea
   d. semicircular canals

15. What term refers to changes in the brain that alter how we process sensory information?
   a. perceptual learning
   b. visual acuity
   c. counterirritation
   d. linear perspective

16. What bypasses the hair cells and stimulates the auditory nerves directly?
   a. ambiguous stimuli
   b. otolith organs
   c. auditory ossicles
   d. cochlear implants

17. What term refers to a reduction in receptor response to unchanging stimuli?
   a. nerve deafness
   b. stereopsis
   c. adaptation
   d. invariance

18. What is the perceptual effect of the frequency of a sound-producing vibration?
   a. pitch
   b. loudness
   c. contiguity
   d. gustation

19. What is helped by variation in sensitivity to the four basic taste sensations?
   a. recognizing kin
   b. enhancing flavours
   c. avoiding poison
   d. activating receptors

20. What produces visual acuity?
   a. cones in the periphery
   b. cones in the fovea
   c. rods in the periphery
   d. rods in the fovea

chapter 5

Jupiterimages/Thinkstock

States of Consciousness

JOURNEY INTO PSYCHOLOGY: A VISIT TO SEVERAL STATES (OF CONSCIOUSNESS)

In New Zealand, a Maori tohunga (priest) performs a night-long ritual to talk to the spirits who created the world during the mythical period the Aborigines call Dreamtime.

In Toronto, three businessmen head for a popular tavern after a particularly stressful day.

In the southwestern part of the United States, a Navajo elder gives his congregation peyote tea, a sacrament in the Native American Church, as a drumbeat resounds in the darkness.

In New Delhi, India, a man sits cross-legged in a deep trance in order to experience a state of oneness with the universe.

In Northern Ireland, a nun living in a convent spends an entire week in silent prayer and contemplation.

In Los Angeles, an aspiring actor consults a hypnotist for help in reducing her stage fright.

In Vancouver, an artist spends two hours in a flotation chamber, trying to clear her head before she returns to work on a large painting.

At a park in Amsterdam, a group of street musicians smoke a joint and sing for spare change.

In Montreal, one of your authors pours himself another cup of tea in an attempt to stay alert.

What do all these people have in common? Each person seeks to alter consciousness—in different ways, to different degrees, and for different reasons. As these examples suggest, consciousness can take many forms. In the discussion that follows, we will begin with the familiar realms of sleep and dreaming and then move to more exotic states of consciousness.

Survey Questions

- What is an altered state of consciousness?
- What are the effects of sleep loss or changes in sleep patterns?
- What are the different stages of sleep?
- What are the causes of sleep disorders and unusual sleep events?
- Do dreams have meaning?
- How is hypnosis done, and what are its limitations?
- What is meditation? Does it have any benefits?
- What are the effects of the more commonly used psychoactive drugs?
- How are dreams used to promote personal understanding?

STATES OF CONSCIOUSNESS—THE MANY FACES OF AWARENESS

SURVEY QUESTION>
What is an altered state of consciousness?

Consciousness Mental awareness of sensations, perceptions, memories, and feelings.

Waking consciousness A state of normal, alert awareness.

Altered state of consciousness (ASC) A condition of awareness distinctly different in quality or pattern from waking consciousness.

To be conscious means to be aware. **Consciousness** consists of all the sensations, perceptions, memories, and feelings you are aware of at any instant (Hobson, 2001; Robinson, 2008). (See Critical Thinking: "What Is It Like to Be a Bat?"). We spend most of our lives in **waking consciousness,** a state of clear, organized alertness. In waking consciousness we perceive time, places, and events as real, meaningful, and familiar. But states of consciousness related to fatigue, delirium, hypnosis, and drugs may differ markedly from "normal" awareness. Everyone experiences at least some altered states, such as sleep, dreaming, and daydreaming (Blackmore, 2004). In everyday life, changes in consciousness may also accompany long-distance running, listening to music, and making love, for example.

Altered States of Consciousness

How are altered states distinguished from normal awareness? During an **altered state of consciousness (ASC),** changes occur in the quality and pattern of mental activity. Typically,

What Is It Like to Be a Bat?

Imagine hurtling through the air on leather wings while shrieking noisily. Suddenly, the echo of your own voice draws your attention to a moth that is frantically trying to evade you. You careen after it, twisting through the pitch-black jungle. Dodging trees and other bats, you catch the moth and savour your first meal of the still young night.

In his famous essay, *What Is It Like to Be a Bat?*, Thomas Nagel (1974) points out that we can learn a lot about bats from an objective, *third-person* point of view. Scientifically, we know that bats use echolocation (they emit sounds and interpret the echoes to locate objects) to hunt insects at night. But what does that *feel* like from a subjective, *first-person* point of view? Have you ever been curious about what it is like to be a bat, or

a dog, or a cat? What runs through Rover's mind when he sniffs other dogs? Does Rover have dreams? Are they as strange as ours? Do cats ever worry about the future? Do they like music? Do animals feel joy?

According to Nagel, we cannot directly know the first-person experience of animals (or even other people, for that matter). The difficulty of knowing other minds is why the early behaviourists distrusted introspection. (Remember Chapter 1?) A key challenge for psychology is to use objective studies of the brain and behaviour to help us understand the mind and consciousness, which are basically private phenomena (Blackmore, 2004; Koch, 2004). This chapter summarizes some of what we have learned about states of consciousness.

---

there are distinct shifts in perceptions, emotions, memory, time sense, thinking, feelings of self-control, and suggestibility (Siegel, 2005).

Are there other causes of ASCs? In addition to those already mentioned, we could add these: sensory overload (for example, a rave, Mardi Gras crowd, or mosh pit); monotonous stimulation (such as "highway hypnotism" on long drives); unusual physical conditions (high fever, hyperventilation, dehydration, sleep loss, near-death experiences); and restricted sensory input. In some instances, altered states of awareness have important cultural significance. (See Human Diversity: "Consciousness and Culture" for more information.) In this chapter, we will focus on sleep, dreaming, hypnosis, meditation, and the effects of drugs. Let's begin with questions about sleep, the most familiar ASC.

Biological rhythm Any repeating cycle of biological activity, such as sleep and waking cycles or changes in body temperature.

Circadian rhythms Cyclical changes in bodily functions and arousal levels that recur on a schedule of about 24 hours. These cycles are governed by internal biological clocks. One such clock regulates sleep and wakefulness.

Microsleep A brief shift in brainwave patterns to those of sleep.

Sleep deprivation Being prevented from getting desired or needed amounts of sleep.

Consciousness and Culture

Throughout history, people have found ways to alter consciousness (Siegel, 2005). A dramatic example is the sweat lodge ceremony of many First Nations peoples. During the ritual, several men sit in total darkness inside a small chamber heated by coals. Cedar smoke, bursts of steam, and the scent of sage fill the air. The men chant rhythmically. The heat builds. At last they can stand it no more. The door is thrown open. Cooling night breezes rush in. And then? The cycle begins again—often to be repeated four or five times more.

The ritual "sweats" of the ceremony are meant to cleanse the mind and body. When they are especially intense, they bring altered awareness and personal revelation.

People seek some altered states for pleasure, as is often true of drug intoxication. Yet, as the

© Arne Hodalic/CORBIS

sweat lodge ceremony illustrates, many cultures regard altered consciousness as a pathway to personal enlightenment. Indeed, all cultures and most religions recognize and accept some alterations of consciousness. However, the meaning given to these states varies greatly—from signs of "madness" and "possession" by spirits to life-enhancing breakthroughs. Thus, cultural conditioning greatly affects what altered states we recognize, seek, consider normal, and attain (de Rios & Grob, 2005).

In many cultures, rituals of healing, prayer, purification, or personal transformation are accompanied by altered states of consciousness. Many First Nations groups in Canada practise sweat ceremonies.

SURVEY QUESTION>
What are the effects of sleep loss or changes in sleep patterns?

Sleep Quiz

1. People can learn to sleep for just a few hours a night and still function well. T or F?
2. Everyone dreams every night. T or F?
3. The brain rests during sleep. T or F?
4. Resting during the day can replace lost sleep. T or F?
5. As people get older, they sleep more. T or F?
6. Alcohol may help a person get to sleep, but it disturbs sleep later during the night. T or F?
7. If a person goes without sleep long enough, death will occur. T or F?
8. Dreams mostly occur during deep sleep. T or F?
9. A person prevented from dreaming would soon go crazy. T or F?
10. Sleepwalking occurs when a person acts out a dream. T or F?

Answers

1. F, 2. T, 3. F, 4. F, 5. F, 6. T, 7. T, 8. F, 9. F, 10. F

SLEEP—A NICE PLACE TO VISIT

Many of us will spend some 25 years of life asleep. Contrary to popular belief, you are not totally unresponsive during sleep. For instance, you are more likely to awaken if you hear your own name spoken, instead of another. Likewise, a sleeping mother may ignore a jet thundering overhead but wake at the slightest whimper of her child. It's even possible to do simple tasks while asleep. In one experiment, people learned to avoid an electric shock by touching a switch each time a tone sounded. Eventually, they could do it without waking. (This is much like the basic survival skill of turning off your alarm clock without waking.) Of course, sleep does impose limitations. Don't expect to learn math, a foreign language, or other complex skills while asleep—especially if the snooze takes place during class (Froufe & Schwartz, 2001). But do expect that a good sleep will help you remember what you learned the day before (Fenn, Nusbaum, & Margoliash, 2003; Saxvig et al., 2008).

Because sleep is familiar, many people think they know all about it. Before reading more, test your knowledge with the Sleep Quiz. Were you surprised by any of the answers? Let's see what we know about our "daily retreat from the world."

The Need for Sleep

How strong is the need for sleep? Sleep is an innate **biological rhythm** or **circadian** (sur-KAY-dee-un) **rhythm** that can never be entirely ignored (Lavie, 2001; Mistlberger, 2005). Of course, sleep will give way temporarily, especially at times of great danger. However, there are limits to how long humans can go without sleep. A rare disease that prevents sleep always ends the same way: The patient falls into a stupor, followed by coma, followed by death (Oliwenstein, 1993). (See Figure 5.1.)

Imagine placing an animal on a moving treadmill suspended over a pool of water. This is not a very good way to sleep! Even so, sleep will always win. Under these conditions, animals soon drift into repeated microsleeps (Goleman, 1982). A **microsleep** is a brief shift in brain activity to the pattern normally recorded during sleep. When you drive, remember that microsleeps can lead to macro-accidents. Even if your eyes are open, you can fall asleep for a few seconds. Roughly 2 out of every 100 highway crashes are caused by sleepiness (Lyznicki et al., 1998). By the way, if you are struggling to stay awake while driving, you should stop, quit fighting it, and take a short nap. Although coffee helps a little (Kamimori et al., 2005), briefly giving in to sleep helps much more (Horne & Reyner, 1996).

▶▶**FIGURE 5.1** Not all animals sleep, but like humans, those that do have powerful sleep needs. For example, dolphins must voluntarily breathe air, which means they face the choice of staying awake or drowning. The dolphins solve this problem by sleeping on just one side of their brains at a time! The other half of the brain, which remains awake, controls breathing (Jouvet, 1999).

Sleep Deprivation

How long could a person go without sleep? With few exceptions, four days or more without sleep becomes hell for everyone. For example, a disc jockey named Peter Tripp once stayed awake for about 200 hours in order to raise money for charity. After 100 hours, he began to hallucinate: He saw cobwebs in his shoes and watched in terror as a tweed coat became a suit of "furry worms." By the end of his ordeal, Tripp was unable to distinguish between his waking nightmares, hallucinations, and reality (Luce, 1965). Despite Tripp's breakdown, longer sleepless periods are possible. The world record is held by Randy Gardner—who at age 17 went 268 hours (11 days) without sleep. Surprisingly, Randy needed only 14 hours of sleep to recover. It is not necessary to completely replace lost sleep. As Randy found, most symptoms of **sleep deprivation** (sleep loss) are reversed by a single night's sleep.

What are the costs of sleep loss? Age and personality make a big difference. Although Tripp's behaviour became quite bizarre, Randy was less impaired. However, make no mistake: Sleep is a necessity. At various times, Randy's speech was slurred, and he couldn't concentrate, remember clearly, or name common objects (Coren, 1996). Sleep loss also causes trembling hands, drooping eyelids, inattention, irritability, staring, increased pain sensitivity, and general discomfort (Naitoh, Kelly, & Englund, 1989).

Most people who have not slept for two or three days can still do interesting or complex mental tasks (Binks, Waters, & Hurry, 1999). But they have trouble paying attention, staying alert, and following simple or boring routines. For a driver, pilot, or machine operator, this can spell disaster (Fairclough & Graham, 1999). If a task is monotonous (such as factory work or air traffic control), no amount of sleep loss is safe (Gillberg & Akerstedt, 1998). In fact, if you lose just one hour of sleep a night, it can affect your mood, your memory, your ability to pay attention, and even your health (Everson, 1998; Maas, 1999). (See The Clinical File: "Teenage Sleep Zombies.")

How can you tell how much sleep you really need? Pick a day when you feel well rested. Then sleep that night until you wake without an alarm clock. If you feel rested when you wake up, that's your natural sleep need. If you're sleeping fewer hours than you need, you're building up a sleep debt every day (Maas, 1999).

Severe sleep loss can cause a temporary **sleep-deprivation psychosis** (loss of contact with reality) like Peter Tripp suffered. Confusion, disorientation, delusions, and hallucinations are typical of this reaction. Hallucinations and delusions rarely appear before 60 hours of wakefulness (Naitoh, Kelly, & Englund, 1989).

Sleep Patterns

Sleep was described as an innate biological rhythm. What does that mean? **Sleep patterns** (daily rhythms of sleep and waking) are very stable. Usually they will continue for many days, even when clocks and light-dark cycles are removed, such as in a cave or a submarine (Palinkas, Suedfeld, & Steel, 1995). However, under such conditions humans eventually shift to a sleep-waking cycle that averages 25 hours, not 24. This suggests that external time markers, especially light and dark, help tie our sleep rhythms to a normal 24-hour day (see Figure 5.2). Otherwise, many of us would drift into our own unusual sleep cycles.

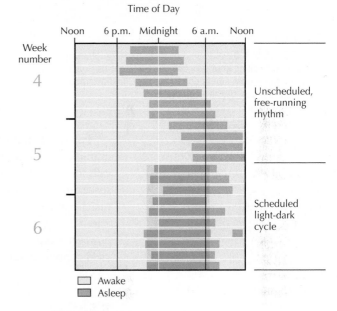

▶▶**FIGURE 5.2** Sleep rhythms. Bars show periods of sleep during the fourth, fifth, and sixth weeks of an experiment with a human subject. During unscheduled periods, the subject was allowed to select times of sleep and lighting. The result was a sleep rhythm of about 25 hours. Notice how this free-running rhythm began to advance around the clock. When periods of darkness were scheduled (coloured area), the rhythm quickly resynchronized with 24-hour days. (Adapted from Czeisler et al., 1981.)

THE CLINICAL FILE

Teenage Sleep Zombies

Did you ever have to fight to stay awake in a high school class? Hypersomnia (HI-per-SOM-nee-ah: excessive daytime sleepiness) is a common problem during adolescence (Carskadon, Acebo, & Jenni, 2004). The reason? Rapid physical changes during puberty increase the need for sleep. However, the quality and quantity of sleep time tend to decrease during the teen years (Fukuda & Ishihara, 2001). At a time when they need more sleep, many adolescents get less.

If teenagers are sleep deprived, why don't they just sleep more? As children enter puberty, they begin to stay up later at night. However, they must get up early to attend school, regardless of when they went to bed. As a result, many teens are seriously sleep-deprived during the week. Then, on the weekend, they sleep longer and get up late in the morning (Laberge et al., 2001). After sleeping extra amounts for two days, many teens have difficulty falling asleep Sunday night. On Monday, they have to get up early for school, and the sleep loss cycle begins again.

What can be done about teenage sleep deprivation? Psychologists have persuaded some school districts to start classes later so that high school students can sleep longer. Preliminary studies suggest that this schedule improves learning and reduces behaviour problems. It looks like some of the "storm and stress" of adolescence may be ordinary grouchiness caused by sleep loss (Mitru, Millrood, & Mateika, 2002).

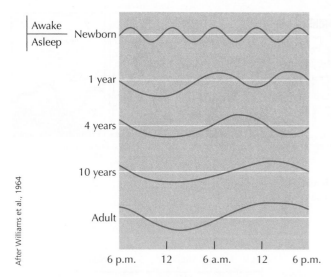

After Williams et al., 1964

▶▶**FIGURE 5.3** Development of sleep patterns. Short cycles of sleep and waking gradually become the night-day cycle of an adult. While most adults don't take naps, mid-afternoon sleepiness is a natural part of the sleep cycle.

What is the normal range of sleep? A few individuals can get by on only an hour or two of sleep a night—and feel perfectly fine. However, this is rare. Eight percent of the population are considered **short sleepers,** getting five hours of sleep or less. Fifteen percent of Canadians average less than 6.5 hours of sleep per night (Statistics Canada, 2001). On the other end of the scale we find **long sleepers,** who doze nine hours or more and tend to be daytime worriers (Grandner & Kripke, 2004; McCann & Stewin, 1988). The majority of us sleep on a familiar seven- to eight-hour-per-night schedule. For a few people, however, it is quite normal to sleep as much as 11 hours a night. Urging everyone to sleep eight hours would be like advising everyone to wear medium-size shoes.

Total sleep time declines throughout life. Those over the age of 50 average only six hours of sleep a night. In contrast, infants spend about 16 to 18 hours a day sleeping, usually in two- to four-hour cycles.

As they mature, most children go through a "nap" stage and eventually settle into a steady cycle of sleeping once a day (see Figure 5.3). Some people, of course, maintain the afternoon "siesta" as an adult pattern. Perhaps we all should: Mid-afternoon sleepiness is a natural part of the sleep cycle. Brief, well-timed naps can help maintain alertness in people like truck drivers and hospital interns, who often must fight drowsiness to stay alert (Garbarino et al., 2004).

It is very tempting to try to reduce sleep time. However, people on *shortened* cycles—for example, three hours of sleep to six hours awake—often can't get to sleep when the cycle calls for it. That's why astronauts continue to sleep on their normal Earth schedule while in space. Adapting to longer-than-normal days is more promising. Such days can be tailored to match natural sleep patterns, which have a ratio of 2 to 1 between time awake and time asleep. For instance, one study showed that 28-hour "days" work for some people. Overall, however, sleep is a "gentle tyrant." Sleep patterns may be bent and stretched, but they rarely yield entirely to human whims (Åkerstedt, 2007).

STAGES OF SLEEP—THE NIGHTLY ROLLER-COASTER RIDE

SURVEY QUESTION>
What are the different stages of sleep?

What causes sleep? Early sleep experts thought that something in the bloodstream must cause sleep. But conjoined twins, whose bodies are joined at birth, show that this is false. It's not unusual for one twin to be asleep while the second is awake. During waking hours, a **sleep hormone** (sleep-promoting chemical) collects in the brain and spinal cord, not in the blood. If this substance is extracted from one animal and injected into another, the second animal will sleep deeply for many hours (Cravatt et al., 1995). Notice, however, that this explanation is incomplete. For example, why would a well-rested person have to fight to stay awake during a boring midday meeting?

Whether you are awake or asleep right now depends on the balance between separate sleep and wakefulness systems. Brain circuits and chemicals in one of the systems promote sleep. A network of neurons in the other system responds to chemicals that inhibit sleep. The two systems see-saw back and forth, switching the brain between sleep and wakefulness (Lavie, 2001). Note that the brain does not "shut down" during sleep. Rather, the pattern of activity changes. The total amount of activity remains fairly constant (Steriade & McCarley, 1990).

Stages of Sleep

What happens when you fall asleep? The changes that come with sleep can be measured with an **electroencephalograph** (eh-LEK-tro-en-SEF-uh-lo-graf), or **EEG.** The brain generates tiny electrical signals (brainwaves) that can be amplified and recorded. When you are awake

Sleep-deprivation psychosis A major disruption of mental and emotional functioning brought about by sleep loss.

Sleep patterns The order and timing of daily sleep and waking periods.

Short sleeper A person averaging five hours of sleep or less per night.

Long sleeper A person who averages nine hours of sleep or more per night.

Sleep hormone A sleep-promoting substance found in the brain and spinal cord.

Electroencephalograph (EEG) A device that records electrical activity in the brain.

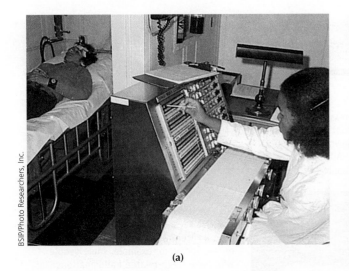

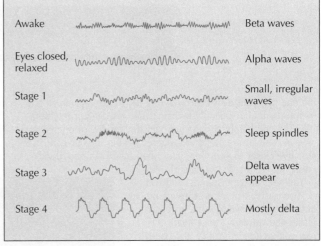

(a)

(b)

▸▸**FIGURE 5.4** (a) Photograph of an EEG recording session. The man in the background is asleep.
(b) Changes in brainwave patterns associated with various stages of sleep. Actually, most types of waves
are present at all times, but they occur more or less frequently in various sleep stages.

and alert, the EEG reveals a pattern of small, fast waves called **beta** (see Figure 5.4).
Immediately before sleep, the pattern shifts to larger and slower waves called **alpha**. (Alpha
waves also occur when you are relaxed and allow your thoughts to drift.) As the eyes close,
breathing becomes slow and regular, the pulse rate slows, and body temperature drops. After
this, four separate slow-wave **sleep stages** occur.

Stage 1

As you begin to lose conscious awareness and enter **light sleep** (stage 1 sleep), your heart
rate slows even more. Breathing becomes more irregular. The muscles of your body relax.
This may trigger a reflex muscle contraction throughout the body called a **hypnic jerk**
(HIP-nik: sleep). (This is quite normal, so have no fear about admitting to your friends that
you fell asleep with a hypnic jerk.) In stage 1 sleep, the EEG is made up mainly of small,
irregular waves with some alpha waves. Persons awakened at this time may or may not say
they were asleep.

Stage 2

As sleep deepens, body temperature drops further. Also, the EEG begins to include **sleep
spindles,** which are short bursts of distinctive brainwave activity (Fogel et al., 2007).
Within four minutes after spindles appear, most people will say, if awakened, that they
were asleep.

Stage 3

In stage 3, a new brainwave called delta begins to appear. **Delta waves** are very large and slow.
They signal a move to deeper sleep and a further loss of consciousness (Shafton, 1995).

Stage 4

Most people reach **deep sleep** (the deepest level of normal sleep) in about an hour.
Stage 4 brainwaves are almost pure delta, and the sleeper is in a state of oblivion. If you
make a loud noise during stage 4, the sleeper will wake up in a state of confusion and may
not remember the noise. (See Clinical File: "Abducted by Space Aliens?" for other waking
hallucinations.) After spending some time in stage 4, the sleeper returns (through stages 3
and 2) to stage 1. Further shifts between deeper and lighter sleep occur throughout the
night (see Figure 5.5).

Beta waves Small, fast brainwaves
associated with being awake and alert.

Alpha waves Large, slow brainwaves
associated with relaxation and falling
asleep.

Sleep stages Levels of sleep
identified by brainwave patterns and
behavioural changes.

Light sleep Stage 1 sleep, marked by
small, irregular brainwaves and some
alpha waves.

Hypnic jerk A reflex muscle twitch
throughout the body that often occurs
as one is falling asleep.

Sleep spindles Distinctive bursts of
brainwave activity that indicate a
person is asleep.

Delta waves Large, slow brainwaves
that occur in deeper sleep (stages 3
and 4).

Deep sleep Stage 4 sleep; the
deepest form of normal sleep.

Abducted by Space Aliens?

Imagine opening your eyes shortly before dawn, attempting to roll over in your bed, and suddenly realizing that you are entirely paralyzed. While lying helplessly on your back and unable to cry out for help, you become aware of sinister figures lurking in your bedroom. As they move closer to your bed, your heart begins to pound violently and you feel as if you are suffocating. You hear buzzing sounds, and feel electrical sensations shooting throughout your body. Within moments, the visions vanish and you can move once again. Terrified, you wonder what has just happened (McNally & Clancy, 2005, p. 114).

Sleep paralysis, which normally prevents us from moving during REM sleep, can also occur just as you begin to wake up. During such episodes, people sometimes have hypnopompic (HIP-noh-POM-pik: "upon awakening") hallucinations. According to Canadian psychologist Al Cheyne, these hallucinations may include bizarre experiences, such as sensing that an alien being is in your bedroom; feeling something

Swiss artist Henry Fuseli drew on hypnopompic imagery as an inspiration for his famous painting *The Nightmare*.

Detroit Institute of the Arts/SuperStock

pressing on your chest, suffocating you; or feeling like you are floating out of your body (Cheyne, 2005; Cheyne, Rueffer, & Newby-Clark, 1999).

Although most of us shrug off these weird experiences, some people try to make sense of them. Earlier in history, people interpreted these hallucinated intruders as angels, demons, or witches and believed that their out-of-body experiences were real. However, as our culture changes, so do our interpretations of sleep experiences. Today, for example, some people who have sleep-related hallucinations believe they have been abducted by aliens or sexually abused (McNally & Clancy, 2005).

Folklore and legends often develop as attempts to explain human experiences, including some of the stranger aspects of sleep. By studying hypnopompic hallucinations, psychologists hope to offer natural explanations for many experiences that might otherwise seem supernatural or paranormal (Cheyne et al., 1999).

Rapid eye movements (REMs) Swift eye movements during sleep.

REM sleep Sleep marked by rapid eye movements and a return to stage 1 EEG patterns.

The Dual Process Hypothesis of Sleep

There is much more to a night's sleep than a simple descent into stage 4. Fluctuations in other sleep hormones cause recurring cycles of deeper and lighter sleep throughout the night (Steiger, 2007). During these repeated periods of lighter sleep, a curious thing happens: The sleeper's eyes occasionally move under the eyelids. (If you ever get a chance to watch a sleeping child, roommate, or spouse, you may see these eye movements.) **Rapid eye movements,** or **REMs,** are associated with dreaming (Figure 5.5). In addition, **REM sleep** is marked by a return of fast, irregular EEG patterns similar to

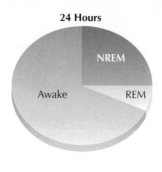

(a)

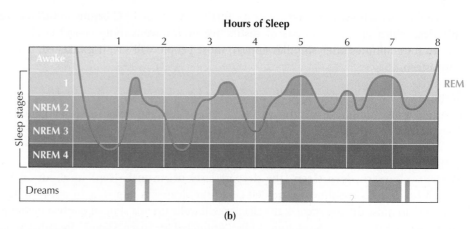

(b)

▶▶**FIGURE 5.5** (a) Average proportion of time adults spend daily in REM sleep and NREM sleep. REM periods add up to about 20 percent of total sleep time. (b) Typical changes in stages of sleep during the night. Notice that dreams mostly coincide with REM periods.

stage 1 sleep. In fact, the brain is so active during REM sleep that it looks as if the person is awake (Rock, 2004).

Earlier, we noted some of the biological benefits of sleep. According to the *dual process hypothesis of sleep,* REM and NREM sleep have two added purposes: They help "refresh" the brain and store memories (Ficca & Salzarulo, 2004).

REM and NREM Sleep

The two most basic states of sleep are REM sleep with its associated dreaming and **non-REM (NREM) sleep,** which occurs during stages 1, 2, 3, and 4 (Jouvet, 1999). NREM sleep is dream-free about 90 percent of the time. Your first period of stage 1 sleep is usually free of REMs and dreams. Later returns to stage 1 are usually accompanied by rapid eye movements. Dreams during REM sleep tend to be longer, clearer, more detailed, more bizarre, and more "dreamlike" than thoughts and images that occur in NREM sleep (Hobson, Pace-Schott, & Stickgold, 2000). Also, brain areas associated with imagery and emotion become more active during REM sleep. This may explain why REM dreams tend to be more vivid than those that occur during NREM sleep (Braun, Balkin, & Herscovitch, 1998).

What is the function of NREM sleep? Dreamless slow-wave NREM sleep increases after physical exertion and may help us recover from bodily fatigue. It also appears to "calm" the brain during the earlier part of a night's sleep (Tononi & Cirelli, 2003).

According to the dual process hypothesis, we are bombarded by information throughout the day, which causes our neural networks to become more and more active. As a result, our brains require more and more energy to continue functioning. Slow-wave sleep early in the night brings overall brain activation levels back down, allowing a "fresh" approach to the next day.

Consider for a moment the amazing jumble of events that make up a day. Some experiences are worth remembering (like what you are reading right now, of course), and others are not so important (like what you were thinking when you put on your socks). As slow-wave sleep reduces overall activation in the brain, less important experiences may fade away and be forgotten. If you wake up feeling clearer about what you studied the previous night, it might be because your brain doesn't "sweat the small stuff"!

The Function of REM Sleep

What, then, is the purpose of REM sleep? According to the dual process hypothesis, while NREM sleep "calms" the brain, REM sleep appears to "sharpen" our memories of the previous day's more important experiences (Saxvig et al., 2008). Daytime stress tends to increase REM sleep, which may rise dramatically when there is a death in the family, trouble at work, a marital conflict, or other emotionally charged events. The value of increased REM sleep is that it helps us sort and retain memories, especially memories about strategies for solving problems (Walker & Stickgold, 2006). This is why, after studying for a long period, you may remember more if you go to sleep, rather than pulling an all-nighter. (REMember to get some REM!)

REM sleep patterns can be affected in some diseases involving the brain. One example is Alzheimer's disease. At the Sacré-Coeur Hospital in Montreal, Jacques Montplaisir and his colleagues have demonstrated that patients with early signs of Alzheimer's disease spend less time in REM sleep, their REM EEG activity slows down in comparison to those who don't have Alzheimer's, and they also may lack muscle paralysis during REM (Gagnon et al., 2006; Montplaisir et al., 1995). Furthermore, patients also experience more stage 1 sleep but decreased slow-wave sleep (Petit et al., 2004). Identifying abnormal patterns of brainwave activity that occur as Alzheimer's gets progressively worse may eventually help doctors predict which patients are likely to develop more severe forms of Alzheimer's. At the same time, this type of research may also tell us a great deal about how the brain operates during REM sleep in general.

Non-REM (NREM) sleep Non–rapid eye movement sleep characteristic of stages 2, 3, and 4.

REM Sleep and Dreaming

Early in life, REM sleep may stimulate the developing brain. Newborn babies have lots of new experiences to process, so they spend a hearty eight or nine hours a day in REM sleep. That's about 50 percent of their total sleep time.

Roughly 85 percent of the time, people awakened during REMs report vivid dreams. Some eye movements correspond to dream activities. Dream that you are watching a tennis match, and you will probably move your eyes from side to side. However, people who were born blind still have REMs, so eye movements are not just a result of "watching" dream images (Shafton, 1995). REM sleep is easy to observe in pets such as dogs and cats. Watch for eye and face movements and irregular breathing. (You can forget about your pet iguana, though. Reptiles show no signs of REM sleep.)

Dreams during REM sleep tend to be longer, clearer, more detailed, more bizarre, and more "dreamlike" than thoughts and images that occur in NREM sleep (Hobson et al., 2000). Brain areas associated with imagery and emotion become more active during REM sleep. As we have already seen, this may explain why REM dreams tend to be more vivid than NREM dreams (Braun et al., 1998; Rock, 2004).

Speaking very loosely, it's as if the dreaming brain were reviewing messages left on voice mail, to decide which are worth keeping. During the day, when information is streaming in, the brain may be too busy to efficiently select useful memories. When the conscious brain is "offline," we are better able to build new memories.

What happens to the body when a person dreams? REM sleep is a time of high emotion. The heart beats irregularly. Blood pressure and breathing waver. Both males and females appear to be sexually aroused: Men usually have an erection, and genital blood flow increases in women. This occurs for all REM sleep, so it is not strictly related to erotic dreams (Jouvet, 1999).

During REM sleep, your body becomes quite still, as if you were paralyzed. Imagine for a moment the results of acting out some of your recent dreams. Very likely, REM-sleep paralysis prevents some hilarious—and dangerous—nighttime escapades. When it fails, some people thrash violently, leap out of bed, and may attack their bed partners. A lack of muscle paralysis during REM sleep is called **REM behaviour disorder** (Ochoa & Pulido, 2005). One patient suffering from the disorder tied himself to his bed every night. That way, he couldn't jump up and crash into furniture or walls (Shafton, 1995). Sometimes sleep paralysis can go a little too far. See The Clinical File: "Abducted by Space Aliens?" to find out why.

Does everyone dream? Most people dream four or five times a night, but not all people remember their dreams. "Non-dreamers" are often surprised by their dreams when first awakened during REM sleep. Dreams are usually spaced about 90 minutes apart. The first dream lasts only about 10 minutes; the last averages 30 minutes and may run as long as 50. Dreams, therefore, occur in real time, not as a "flash" (Shafton, 1995).

How important is REM sleep? Is it essential for normal functioning? To answer these questions, sleep expert William Dement awakened volunteers each time they entered REM sleep. Soon, their need for "dream time" grew more urgent. By the fifth night, many had to be awakened 20 or 30 times to prevent REM sleep. When the volunteers were finally allowed to sleep undisturbed, they dreamed extra amounts. This effect, called a **REM rebound,** explains why alcoholics have horrible nightmares after they quit drinking. Alcohol suppresses REM sleep and sets up a powerful rebound when it is withdrawn. It's worth remembering that while alcohol and other depressant drugs may help a person get to sleep, they greatly reduce sleep quality (Stein & Friedmann, 2005).

Dement's volunteers complained of memory lapses, poor concentration, and daytime anxiety. For a while, it was thought that people deprived of REM sleep might go crazy. But this is now known as the "REM myth." Later experiments showed that missing any sleep stage can cause a rebound for that stage. In general, daytime disturbances are related to the total amount of sleep lost, not to the type of sleep lost (Devoto et al., 1999).

In a moment we will survey some sleep problems—if you are still awake. First, here are a few questions to check your memory of our discussion so far.

REM behaviour disorder A failure of normal muscle paralysis, leading to violent actions during REM sleep.

REM rebound The occurrence of extra rapid eye movement sleep following REM sleep deprivation.

STUDY BREAK Altered States and Sleep

Reflect

Make a quick list of some altered states of consciousness you have experienced. What do they have in common? How are they different? What conditions caused them?

Imagine that you are a counsellor at a sleep clinic. You must explain the basics of sleep and dreaming to a new client who knows little about these topics. Can you do it?

Learning Check

1. Changes in the quality and pattern of mental activity define
   - a. an EEG
   - b. REM
   - c. SIDS
   - d. an ASC
2. Delusions and hallucinations typically continue for several days after a sleep-deprived individual returns to normal sleep. T or F?
3. Alyssa experiences a microsleep while driving. Most likely, this indicates that she
   - a. was producing mostly beta waves
   - b. had high levels of sleep hormones in her bloodstream
   - c. switched from delta waves to alpha waves
   - d. was sleep deprived

4. Older adults, and particularly the elderly, sleep more than children do because the elderly are more easily fatigued. T or F?
5. Alpha waves are to presleep drowsiness as _____ are to stage 4 sleep.
6. Rapid eye movements indicate that a person is in deep sleep. T or F?
7. Which of the following would normally be most incompatible with moving your arms and legs while asleep?
   - a. REM sleep
   - b. sleep spindles
   - c. delta waves
   - d. NREM sleep

Critical Thinking

8. Why might it be better for the unscheduled human sleep-waking cycle to average more than 24 hours, instead of less?
9. In addition to helping store memories, what biological advantages might sleeping provide?

Answers

1. d 2. F 3. d 4. F 5. delta waves 6. F 7. a 8. Sleep experts theorize that the 25-hour average leaves a little "slack" in the cycle. External time markers can then retard the body cycle slightly to synchronize it with light–dark cycles. If the body cycle were shorter than 24 hours, we all might have to "stretch" every day to adjust. 9. Lowering body activity and metabolism during sleep may help conserve energy and lengthen life. Also, natural selection may have favoured sleep because animals that remained active at night probably had a higher chance of being killed.

SLEEP DISTURBANCES—SHOWING NIGHTLY: SLEEP WARS!

Sleep quality has taken a beating in North America. Artificial lighting, frenetic schedules, exciting pastimes, smoking, drinking, overstimulation, and many other factors have contributed to a near epidemic of sleep problems. Sleep disturbances are a serious risk to health and happiness (Shneerson, 2005). Sleep clinics treat thousands of people each year who suffer from sleep disorders or complaints. These disturbances range from daytime sleep attacks to sleepwalking and terrifying nightmares. (See Table 5.1.) Let's explore some of the more interesting problems these people face.

<SURVEY QUESTION
What are the causes of sleep disorders and unusual sleep events?

Insomnia

Staring at the ceiling at 2 a.m. is pretty low on most people's list of favourite pastimes. **Insomnia** includes difficulty in going to sleep, frequent nighttime awakenings, waking too early, or a combination of these problems (Bond & Wooten, 1996). Insomnia lowers people's ability to work, and it damages their health and relationships (Walsh & Uestuen, 1999).

One Canadian survey found 3.3 million people to have had insomnia in 2002 (Tjepkema, 2005). In another recent study, 13.4 percent of adults were noted to have suffered from chronic insomnia (Morin et al., 2011). Women, older individuals, and people with poor physical and mental health were more likely than others to experience insufficient nightly sleep. Surprisingly, French-speaking persons reported fewer problems than the English-speaking population, but they consumed medications and natural products more often to combat their nocturnal difficulties.

Insomnia Difficulty in getting to sleep or staying asleep.

■ Table 5.1   Sleep Disorders—Things That Go Wrong in the Night

Hypersomnia Excessive daytime sleepiness. This can result from depression, insomnia, narcolepsy, sleep apnea, sleep drunkenness, periodic limb movements, drug abuse, and other problems.

Insomnia Difficulty in getting to sleep or staying asleep; also, not feeling rested after sleeping.

Narcolepsy Sudden, irresistible, daytime sleep attacks that may last anywhere from a few minutes to half an hour. Victims may fall asleep while standing, talking, or even driving.

Nightmare disorder Vivid, recurrent nightmares that significantly disturb sleep.

Periodic limb movement syndrome Muscle twitches (primarily affecting the legs) that occur every 20 to 40 seconds and severely disturb sleep.

REM behaviour disorder A failure of normal muscle paralysis, leading to violent actions during REM sleep.

Restless legs syndrome An irresistible urge to move the legs in order to relieve sensations of creeping, tingling, prickling, aching, or tension.

Sleep apnea During sleep, the cessation of breathing for 20 seconds or more until the person wakes a little, gulps in air, and settles back to sleep; this cycle may be repeated hundreds of times per night.

Sleep drunkenness A slow transition to clear consciousness after awakening; sometimes associated with irritable or aggressive behaviour.

Sleep terror disorder The repeated occurrence of night terrors that significantly disturb sleep.

Sleep–wake schedule disorder A mismatch between the sleep–wake schedule demanded by a person's bodily rhythm and that demanded by the environment.

Sleepwalking disorder Repeated incidents of leaving bed and walking about while asleep

(Carney, Geyer, & Berry, 2005; Shneerson, 2005.)

Causes and Treatment of Insomnia

Worry, stress, and excitement can cause **temporary insomnia** (a brief episode of insomnia) and a self-defeating cycle. First, excess mental activity ("I can't stop turning things over in my mind") and heightened arousal block sleep. Then, frustration and anger over not being able to sleep cause more worry and arousal. This further delays sleep, which causes more frustration, and so on (Espie, 2002). A good way to beat this cycle is to avoid fighting it. It is usually best to get up and do something useful or satisfying when you have difficulty sleeping. (Reading a textbook might be a good choice of useful activities.) Return to bed only when you begin to feel that you are struggling to stay awake. If sleeping problems last for more than three weeks, then a diagnosis of **chronic insomnia** can be made.

Drug-dependency insomnia (sleep loss caused by withdrawal from sleeping pills) can also occur. North Americans spend a billion dollars a year on sleeping pills. There is real irony in this expense. Non-prescription sleeping pills such as Sominex, Nytol, and Sleep-Eze have little sleep-inducing effect. Barbiturates are even worse. These prescription drugs decrease both stage 4 sleep and REM sleep, drastically lowering sleep quality. In addition, many users become "sleeping-pill junkies," who need an ever-greater number of pills to get to sleep. Victims must be painstakingly weaned from their sleep medicines. Otherwise, terrible nightmares and "rebound insomnia" may drive them back to drug use. It's worth remembering that although alcohol and other depressant drugs may help a person get to sleep, they also greatly reduce sleep quality (Nau & Lichstein, 2005).

Behavioural Remedies for Insomnia

If sleeping pills are a poor way to treat insomnia, what can be done? Sleep specialists prefer to treat insomnia with lifestyle changes and behavioural techniques (Montgomery & Dennis,

Temporary insomnia A brief episode of insomnia.

Chronic insomnia Insomnia that persists for more than three weeks.

Drug-dependency insomnia Insomnia that follows withdrawal from sleeping pills.

2004). Treatment for chronic insomnia usually begins with a careful analysis of a patient's sleep habits, lifestyle, stress levels, and medical problems. All the approaches you see here are helpful for treating insomnia (Nau & Lichstein, 2005). According to University of Laval researchers, sleep restriction and stimulus control are the most effective among the methods listed here (Lacks & Morin, 1992).

1. Sleep Restriction   Even if you miss an entire night's sleep, do not sleep late in the morning, nap more than an hour, sleep during the evening, or go to bed early the following night. Try to restrict sleep to your normal bedtime hours. That way, you will avoid fragmenting your sleep rhythms (Lacks & Morin, 1992; Shneerson, 2005).

2. Stimulus Control   Insisting on a regular schedule helps establish a firm body rhythm, greatly improving sleep. This is best achieved by exercising **stimulus control,** which refers to linking a response with specific stimuli. It is important to get up and go to sleep at the same time each day, including weekends (Bootzin & Epstein, 2000). (Many people upset their sleep rhythms by staying up late on weekends.) In addition, insomniacs are told to avoid doing anything but sleeping when they are in bed. They are not to study, eat, watch TV, read, pay the bills, worry, or even think in bed. (Lovemaking is okay, however.) In this way, only sleeping and relaxation become associated with going to bed at specific times (Bootzin & Epstein, 2000).

3. Paradoxical Intention   Another helpful approach is to remove the pressures of *trying* to go to sleep. Instead, the goal becomes trying to keep the eyes open (in the dark) and stay awake as long as possible (Nau & Lichstein, 2005). This allows sleep to come unexpectedly and lowers performance anxiety (Espie, 2002).

4. Relaxation   Learn a physical or mental strategy for relaxing, such as deep-muscle relaxation (see Chapter 13), meditation, or blotting out worries with calming images. It is also helpful to schedule time in the early evening to write down worries or concerns and plan what to do about them the next day, in order to set them aside before going to bed.

5. Exercise   Strenuous exercise during the day promotes sleep. It is best if done about six hours before bedtime (Maas, 1999). Exercise in the evening is helpful only if it is very light.

6. Food Intake   What you eat can affect how easily you get to sleep. Eating starchy foods increases the amount of *tryptophan* (TRIP-tuh-fan: an amino acid) reaching the brain. More tryptophan, in turn, increases the amount of serotonin in the brain, which is associated with relaxation, a positive mood, and sleepiness. Thus, to promote sleep, try eating a starchy snack, such as cookies, bread, pasta, oatmeal, pretzels, or dry cereal. If you really want to drop the bomb on insomnia, try eating a baked potato (which may be the world's largest sleeping pill!) (Sahelian, 1998).

7. Stimulants   Avoid stimulants such as coffee and cigarettes. Also remember that alcohol, while not a stimulant, impairs sleep quality.

Sleepwalking and Sleeptalking

Sleepwalking is eerie and fascinating. Somnambulists (som-NAM-bue-lists: those who sleepwalk) avoid obstacles, descend stairways, and on rare occasions may step out of windows or in front of automobiles. The sleepwalker's eyes are usually open, but a blank face and shuffling feet reveal that the person is still asleep. A parent who finds a child sleepwalking should gently guide the child back to bed. Awakening a sleepwalker does no harm, but it is not necessary.

Stimulus control Linking a particular response with specific stimuli.

Sleeptalking Speaking that occurs during NREM sleep.

Nightmare A highly unpleasant and undesirable dream that takes place during REM sleep.

Night terror A state of panic that occurs during NREM sleep.

Sleepwalkers have been observed jumping into lakes, urinating in garbage pails or closets (phew!), shuffling furniture around, and even brandishing weapons (Schenck & Mahowald, 2005).

As strange as it may sound, some people attempt to engage in sexual activity with another person while they are asleep. This condition is officially known as sexsomnia, in which a sleeping individual appears to be fully aroused but consciously unaware of the act being undertaken (Shapiro, Trajanovic, & Fedoroff, 2003).

Can a sleepwalker become violent? Usually not, but consider the rare and tragic case involving a young Canadian man who drove about 23 kilometres to the home of his in-laws. Upon his arrival, he brandished a kitchen knife, stabbed his mother-in-law to death, viciously beat up his father-in-law, and was injured himself in the scuffle. The sleepwalker was subjected to an intense medical and psychological examination, and evidence was sought to determine whether he had carried out these acts consciously. His defence lawyers argued that the savage attacks were not premeditated and that they occurred during an episode of nocturnal somnambulism, in a state of unawareness. The evidence included the following points: (1) the young man had good relations with his parents-in-law; (2) he and his family had a history of sleep-related problems, including sleepwalking; (3) he had no history of aggression against anyone; and (4) his sleep EEG patterns were somewhat unusual and similar to those of people who engage in sleepwalking. The jury was convinced, and the man was acquitted of all criminal charges. The case reached as far as the Supreme Court, but the verdict of not guilty was upheld throughout the appeal process (Broughton et al., 1994).

Violent acts during sleepwalking, however, are extremely rare. Most somnambulists engage in very innocuous activities, such as sitting up in bed, ambling about the room, turning on the lights in the house, or going to the refrigerator for a snack.

Does sleepwalking occur during dreaming? No. Remember that people are normally immobilized during REM sleep. EEG studies have shown that somnambulism occurs during NREM stages 3 and 4 (Stein & Ferber, 2001). **Sleeptalking** also occurs mostly in NREM stages of sleep. The link with deep sleep explains why sleeptalking makes little sense and why sleepwalkers are confused and remember little when awakened (American Psychiatric Association, 2000).

Nightmares and Night Terrors

A **nightmare** is a highly unpleasant and undesirable dream that takes place during REM sleep. Women, children, and adolescents report more nightmares than men. Frequently occurring nightmares (one a week or more) are associated with high levels of psychological distress (Levin & Fireman, 2002). People who suffer from one or more psychological disorders (e.g., depression, post-traumatic stress disorder, schizophrenia) also experience elevated numbers of nightmares (Levin & Nielsen, 2007).

Stage 4 sleep is the realm of night terrors. These frightening episodes are quite different from nightmares. During **night terrors,** a person suffers from total panic and may experience hallucinations involving frightening images. An attack may last 15 or 20 minutes. When it is over, the person awakens drenched in sweat, but only vaguely remembers the terror. Since night terrors occur during NREM sleep (when the body is not immobilized), victims may sit up, scream, get out of bed, or run around the room. Sufferers remember little afterward. (Other family members, however, may have a story to tell.) Night terrors are most common in childhood, but they continue to plague about 2 out of every 100 adults (Kataria, 2004; Ohayon, Guilleminault, & Priest, 1999).

How to Eliminate a Nightmare

Is there any way to stop a recurring nightmare? A bad nightmare can be worse than any horror movie. You can leave a theatre, but we often remain trapped in terrifying dreams. Nevertheless, most nightmares can be banished by following three simple steps. First, write down your nightmare, describing it in detail. Next, change the dream any way you wish, being sure to spell out the details of the new dream. The third step is **imagery rehearsal,** in which you mentally rehearse the changed dream before you fall asleep again (Krakow & Zadra, 2006). Imagery rehearsal may work because it makes upsetting dreams familiar while a person is awake and feeling safe. Or perhaps it mentally "reprograms" future dream content. In any case, the technique has helped many people (Krakow & Krakow, 2002). Lucid dreaming is another technique that can reduce the severity of nightmares (see the Psychology in Action section at the end of the chapter).

Sleep Apnea

Some sage once said, "Laugh and the whole world laughs with you; snore and you sleep alone." Nightly "wood sawing" is often harmless, but it can signal a serious problem. A person who snores loudly, with short silences and loud gasps or snorts, may suffer from apnea (AP-nee-ah: interrupted breathing). In **sleep apnea,** breathing stops for periods of 20 seconds to 2 minutes. As the need for oxygen becomes intense, the person wakes a little and gulps in air. She or he then settles back to sleep. But soon, breathing stops again. This cycle is repeated hundreds of times a night. As you might guess, apnea victims are extremely sleepy during the day (Collop, 2005).

What causes sleep apnea? Some cases occur because the brain stops sending signals to the diaphragm to maintain breathing. Another cause is blockage of the upper air passages. The most effective treatments are the use of a CPAP (continuous positive airway pressure) mask to aid breathing during sleep, weight loss, and surgery for breathing obstructions (Collop, 2005).

DREAMING—A SEPARATE REALITY?

Dream Theories

How meaningful are dreams? Some theorists believe that dreams have deeply hidden meanings. Others regard dreams as nearly meaningless. Yet others hold that dreams reflect our waking thoughts, fantasies, and emotions (A.T. Beck, 2004). Let's examine all three views.

Psychoanalytic Dream Theory

Sigmund Freud's landmark book, *The Interpretation of Dreams* (1900), first advanced the idea that many dreams are based on **wish fulfillment** (an expression of unconscious desires). Freud's proposal was that dreams express unconscious desires and conflicts as disguised **dream symbols** (images that have deeper symbolic meaning). Understanding a dream requires analyzing the dream's obvious, visible meaning (*manifest content*) to uncover its hidden, symbolic meaning (*latent content*). For instance, a woman who dreams of stealing her best friend's wedding ring and placing it on her own hand may be unwilling to consciously admit that she is sexually attracted to her best friend's husband. Similarly, a journey might symbolize death, and horseback riding or dancing, sexual intercourse.

Freud's **psychoanalytic theory** of dreaming emphasizes internal conflicts and unconscious forces. While many of his ideas may seem persuasive, there is evidence against them. For example, volunteers in a study of starvation showed no particular increase in dreams about food and eating, directly or indirectly. People who have been victimized by traumatic experiences such as rape or wartime brutalities relive their experiences in dreams. In general, dreams show few signs of expressing hidden wishes (Fischer & Greenberg, 1996).

Do all dreams have hidden meanings? Probably not. Even Freud realized that some dreams are trivial "day residues" or carryovers from ordinary waking events. On the other hand, dreams do tend to reflect a person's current concerns.

Imagery rehearsal Mentally rehearsing and changing a nightmare in order to prevent it from reoccurring.

Sleep apnea Repeated interruption of breathing during sleep.

Wish fulfillment The Freudian belief that many dreams express unconscious desires.

Dream symbols Images in dreams that serve as visible signs of hidden ideas, desires, impulses, emotions, relationships, and so forth.

Psychoanalytic dream theory A theory that emphasizes internal conflicts, motives, and unconscious forces.

<SURVEY QUESTION
Do dreams have meaning?

According to Freudian theory, dream imagery often has symbolic meaning. How would you interpret Henri Rousseau, *The Dream* (left) and Belgian artist René Magritte's *The Castle of the Pyrenees* (right)? The fact that dreams don't have a single unambiguous meaning is one of the shortcomings of Freudian dream theory.

The Activation-Synthesis Hypothesis

Psychiatrists Allan Hobson and Robert McCarley have a radically different view of dreaming called the **activation-synthesis hypothesis.** They have shown that during REM sleep several lower brain centres are "turned on" (*activated*) in more or less random fashion. At the same time, sensory input to the brain is mostly blocked, and most of the major motor systems are inactivated, so no movement occurs. Struggling to interpret the random activation of information, certain brain areas search through stored memories and manufacture (*synthesize*) a dream (Hobson, 2000, 2005). However, frontal areas of the cortex, which control higher mental abilities, are mostly shut down during REM sleep. Consequently, the emotional areas of the brain become more assertive. This explains why dreams are more primitive and more bizarre than daytime thoughts (Hobson, 2000).

How does that help explain dream content? Let's use the classic chase dream as an example. In such dreams we feel we are running, but, in reality, we are not going anywhere. This occurs because the brain is told the body is running, but it gets no feedback from the motionless legs. To make sense of everything, according to the activation-synthesis hypothesis, the brain creates a chase drama. A similar process probably explains dreams of floating or flying.

So dreams have no meaning? The activation-synthesis hypothesis doesn't rule out the idea that dreams have some meaning. Because dreams are created from memories and past experiences, parts of dreams can sometimes reflect each person's mental life, emotions, and concerns (Hobson, 2000).

Neurocognitive Dream Theory

Can't dreams just be about normal, day-to-day stuff? Yes, they can. William Domhoff offers a third view of dreaming. According to his **neurocognitive dream theory,** dreams actually have much in common with waking thoughts and emotions. Most dreams reflect ordinary waking concerns. Domhoff believes this is true because many brain areas that are active when we are awake remain active during dreaming (Domhoff, 2001, 2003). From this perspective, our dreams are a conscious expression of REM sleep processes that are sorting and storing daily experiences. Thus, we shouldn't be surprised if a student who is angry at a teacher dreams of embarrassing the teacher in class, a lonely person dreams of romance, or a hungry child dreams of food. It is not necessary to seek deep symbolic meanings to understand these dreams.

Activation-synthesis hypothesis
A theory to explain how dream content is affected by random neuronal activity and the brain's own attempt to make sense of it.

Neurocognitive dream theory
A proposal that dreams reflect everyday waking thoughts and emotions.

Which dream theory is the most widely accepted? Each theory has strengths and weaknesses. However, studies of dream content do support neurocognitive theory's focus on the continuity between dreams and waking thought. Rather than being exotic or bizarre, most dreams reflect everyday events (Hall, 1966; Pesant & Zadra, 2006). For example, athletes tend to dream about the previous day's athletic activities (Erlacher & Schredl, 2004). In general, the favourite dream setting is a familiar room in a house. Action usually takes place between the dreamer and two or three other emotionally important people—friends, enemies, loved ones, or employers. Dream actions are also mostly familiar: running, jumping, riding, sitting, talking, and watching. About half of all dreams have sexual elements. Dreams of flying, floating, and falling occur less frequently. However, note that such dreams also lend support to the activation-synthesis hypothesis, because they are not everyday events. (Unless you are a trapeze artist.)

Among Canadian university students, the two most common dream themes were sex and being chased and followed without physical injury. Although men and women dreamed mostly about similar ideas, there were a few notable differences. Nightmares were reported more often by women, sexual experiences were reported more frequently by men, and being chased was more common for women. Men's dreams had a more positive flavour to them and contained references to magical and mythical ideas, whereas women's dreams had a somewhat negative flavour and were characterized by thoughts of failure and lack of control (Nielsen et al., 2003). The reason for such gender patterns is not clear, but differences in the way men and women are socialized is one possibility for these findings.

Are most dreams happy or sad? If you ask people in the morning what they dreamed about, they mention more unpleasant emotions than pleasant emotions (Merritt et al., 1994). However, it may be that dreams of fear, anger, or sadness are easier to remember. When people are awakened during REM sleep, they report equal numbers of positive and negative emotions (Fosse, Stickgold, & Hobson, 2001).

STUDY BREAK Sleep Disturbances and Dreaming

Reflect

Almost everyone suffers from insomnia at least occasionally. Are any of the techniques for combatting insomnia similar to strategies you have discovered on your own?

How many sleep disturbances can you name (including those listed in Table 5.1)? Have you experienced any of them? Which do you think would be most disruptive?

Do you think the activation-synthesis hypothesis provides an adequate explanation of your own dreams? Have you had dreams that seem to reflect Freudian wish fulfillment? Do you think your dreams have symbolic meaning or reflect everyday concerns?

Learning Check

1. Which of the following is not a behavioural remedy for insomnia?
   a. daily hypersomnia   b. stimulus control
   c. deep-muscle relaxation   d. paradoxical intention
2. Eating a snack that is nearly all starch can promote sleep because it increases _____ in the brain.
   a. beta waves   b. tryptophan
   c. EEG activity   d. hypnic cycling

3. Night terrors, sleepwalking, and sleeptalking all occur during stage 1, NREM sleep. T or F?
4. Sleep _____ is cessation of breathing during sleep.
5. People who suffer from sudden daytime sleep attacks have which sleep disorder?
   a. narcolepsy   b. REM behaviour disorder
   c. somnambulism   d. sleep spindling
6. According to the activation-synthesis hypothesis of dreaming, dreams are constructed from _____ to explain messages received from nerve cells controlling eye movement, balance, and bodily activity.
7. Sharpening memories and facilitating their storage is one function of
   a. activation-synthesis cycles b. REM sleep
   c. deep sleep   d. NREM sleep

Critical Thinking

8. Even without being told that somnambulism is an NREM event, you could have predicted that sleepwalking doesn't occur during dreaming. Why?

Answers

1. a 2. b 3. F 4. apnea 5. a 6. memories 7. b 8. Because people are immobilized during REM sleep and REM sleep is strongly associated with dreaming. This makes it unlikely that sleepwalkers are acting out dreams.

Even if many dreams can be viewed as just a different form of thought, many psychologists continue to believe that some dreams have deeper meaning (White & Taytroe, 2003; Wilkinson, 2006). There seems to be little doubt that dreams can make a difference in our lives: Veteran sleep researcher William Dement once dreamed that he had lung cancer. In the dream a doctor told Dement he would die soon. At the time, Dement was smoking two packs of cigarettes a day. He says, "I will never forget the surprise, joy, and exquisite relief of waking up. I felt reborn." Dement quit smoking the following day. (For more information about dreaming, see the Psychology in Action section later in this chapter.)

HYPNOSIS—LOOK INTO MY EYES

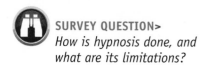

SURVEY QUESTION>
How is hypnosis done, and what are its limitations?

"Your body is becoming heavy. You can barely keep your eyes open. You are so tired you can't move. Relax. Let go. Relax. Close your eyes and relax." These are the last words a textbook should ever say to you, and the first a hypnotist might say.

Interest in hypnosis began in the 1700s with Franz Mesmer, whose name gave us the term **mesmerize** (to hypnotize). Mesmer, an Austrian physician, believed he could cure various diseases with magnets. Mesmer's strange "treatments" are related to hypnosis because they were actually based on the power of suggestion, not "animal magnetism" (Waterfield, 2002). For a time, Mesmer enjoyed quite a following. In the end, however, his theories of animal magnetism were rejected and he was recognized as a fraud.

The term **hypnosis** was later coined by an English surgeon named James Braid. The Greek word *hypnos* means "sleep," and Braid used it to describe the hypnotic state. Today we know that hypnosis is not sleep. Confusion about this point remains because some hypnotists give the suggestion, "Sleep, sleep." However, EEG records made during hypnosis differ from those seen when a person is asleep (Barabasz, 2000).

Inducing Hypnosis

How is hypnosis done? Could I be hypnotized against my will? Hypnotists use many different methods. Still, all techniques encourage a person (1) to focus attention on what is being said, (2) to relax and feel tired, (3) to "let go" and accept suggestions easily, and (4) to use vivid imagination (Druckman & Bjork, 1994). Basically, you must cooperate to become hypnotized. Many theorists believe that all hypnosis is really **self-hypnosis** (autosuggestion). From this perspective, a hypnotist merely helps another person to follow a series of suggestions. These suggestions, in turn, alter sensations, perceptions, thoughts, feelings, and behaviours (Druckman & Bjork, 1994; Kirsch & Lynn, 1995).

What does it feel like to be hypnotized? You might be surprised at some of your actions during hypnosis. Bear in mind that personal experiences vary widely. You might have mild feelings of floating, sinking, anaesthesia, or separation from your body. A key element in hypnosis is the **basic suggestion effect** (a tendency of hypnotized persons to carry out suggested actions as if they were involuntary). Hypnotized persons feel like their actions and experiences are automatic—they seem to happen without effort (Kihlstrom, 1985). Here is how one person described his hypnotic session:

> I felt lethargic, my eyes going out of focus and wanting to close. My hands felt real light....I felt I was sinking deeper into the chair....I felt like I wanted to relax more and more....My responses were more automatic. I didn't have to wish to do things so much or want to do them....I just did them....I felt floating...very close to sleep. (Hilgard, 1968)

Contrary to the way hypnosis is portrayed in movies, hypnotized people generally remain in control of their behaviour and aware of what is going on. For instance, most

Mesmerize To hypnotize.

Hypnosis An altered state of consciousness characterized by narrowed attention and increased suggestibility.

Self-hypnosis A state of hypnosis attained without the aid of a hypnotist; autosuggestion.

Basic suggestion effect The tendency of hypnotized persons to carry out suggested actions as if they were involuntary.

people will not act out hypnotic suggestions that they consider immoral or repulsive (such as disrobing in public or harming someone) (Kirsch & Lynn, 1995).

Hypnotic susceptibility One's capacity for becoming hypnotized.

Hypnotic Susceptibility

Can everyone be hypnotized? About eight people out of ten can be hypnotized, but only one or two out of ten will be good hypnotic subjects. People who are imaginative and prone to fantasy tend to respond well to hypnosis (Kallio & Revonsuo, 2003). But people who lack these traits may also be hypnotized to some degree. If you are willing to be hypnotized, chances are good that you could be. Hypnosis depends more on the efforts and abilities of the hypnotized person than the skills of the hypnotist (Kirsch & Lynn, 1995). But make no mistake, people who are hypnotized are not merely faking their responses (Perugini et al., 1998).

Hypnotic susceptibility refers to how easily a person can become hypnotized. It can be measured by giving a series of suggestions and counting the number to which a person responds. A typical hypnotic test is the *Stanford Hypnotic Susceptibility Scale,* shown in Table 5.2. (See also Figure 5.6.) If you were to score high on the scale today, you probably would do the same years from now. Hypnotizability is very stable over time (Piccione, Hilgard, & Zimbardo, 1989).

Effects of Hypnosis

What can (and cannot) be achieved with hypnosis? Many abilities have been tested during hypnosis, leading to the following conclusions (Burgess & Kirsch, 1999; Chaves, 2000):

1. *Superhuman acts of strength.* Hypnosis has no more effect on physical strength than instructions that encourage a person to make his or her best effort.
2. *Memory.* There are some claims that hypnosis can enhance memory (Wagstaff et al., 2004). However, it frequently increases the number of false memories as well. For this reason, many jurisdictions now bar persons from testifying in court if they were hypnotized to improve their memory of a crime they witnessed.
3. *Amnesia.* A person told not to remember something heard during hypnosis may claim not to remember. In some instances, this may be nothing more than a deliberate attempt to avoid thinking about specific ideas. However, brief memory loss of this type actually does seem to occur, as has been pointed out by psychologists at the University of Waterloo (Bowers & Woody, 1996).

■ Table 5.2 Stanford Hypnotic Susceptibility Scale

Suggested Behaviour	Criterion of Passing
1. Postural sway	Falls without forcing
2. Eye closure	Closes eyes without forcing
3. Hand lowering (left)	Lowers at least 15 centimetres by end of 10 seconds
4. Immobilization	Arm (right arm) rises less than 2.5 centimetres in 10 seconds
5. Finger lock	Incomplete separation of fingers at end of 10 seconds
6. Arm rigidity (left arm)	Less than 5 centimetres of arm bending in 10 seconds
7. Hands moving together	Hands at least as close as 15 centimetres after 10 seconds
8. Verbal inhibition (name)	Name unspoken in 10 seconds
9. Hallucination (fly)	Any movement, grimacing, acknowledgment of effect
10. Eye catalepsy	Eyes remain closed at end of 10 seconds
11. Posthypnotic (changes chairs)	Any partial movement response
12. Amnesia test	Three or fewer items recalled

(Adapted from Weitzenhoffer & Hilgard, 1959.)

Dennis Coon

▸▸**FIGURE 5.6** In one test of hypnotiz-ability, subjects attempt to pull their hands apart after hearing suggestions that their fingers are "locked" together.

4. *Pain relief.* Hypnosis can relieve both acute (immediate) and chronic pain (Keefe, Abernethy, & Campbell, 2005; Patterson, 2004). Therefore, it can be especially useful in situations where chemical painkillers cannot be used or are ineffective. One such situation is control of phantom limb pain. (Phantom limb pain is a recurring pain that amputees sometimes feel coming from the missing limb.)

5. *Age regression.* Given the proper suggestions, some hypnotized people appear to "regress" to childhood. However, most theorists now believe that "age-regressed" subjects are only acting out a suggested role.

6. *Sensory changes.* Hypnotic suggestions concerning sensations are among the most effective. Given the proper instructions, a person can be made to smell a small bottle of ammonia and respond as if it were a wonderful perfume. It is also possible to alter colour vision, hearing sensitivity, time sense, perception of illusions, and many other sensory responses.

Hypnosis is a valuable tool. It can help people relax, feel less pain, and make good prog-ress in psychotherapy (Chapman, 2006). Generally, hypnosis is more successful at changing subjective experience than it is at modifying behaviours such as smoking or overeating.

If hypnosis isn't sleep, then what is it? That's a good question. Hypnosis is often defined as an altered state of consciousness, characterized by narrowed attention and an increased openness to suggestion (Kallio & Revonsuo, 2003; Kosslyn et al., 2000). Notice that this defi-nition assumes that hypnosis is a distinct state of consciousness.

The best-known state theory of hypnosis was proposed by Ernest Hilgard (1904–2001), who argued that hypnosis causes a dissociative state, or "split" in awareness. To illustrate, he asked hypnotized subjects to plunge one hand into a painful bath of ice water. Subjects told to feel no pain said they felt none. The same subjects were then asked if there was any part of their mind that did feel pain. With their free hand, many wrote, "It hurts," or "Stop it, you're hurting me," while they continued to act pain-free (Hilgard, 1977, 1994). Thus, one part of the hypno-tized person says there is no pain and acts as if there is none. Another part, which Hilgard calls the hidden observer, is aware of the pain but remains in the background. The **hidden observer** is a detached part of the hypnotized person's awareness that silently observes events.

In contrast, non-state theorists argue that hypnosis is not a distinct state at all. Instead it is merely a blend of conformity, relaxation, imagination, obedience, and role-playing (Kirsch, 2005). Again, many theorists believe that all hypnosis is really self-hypnosis (autosuggestion).

One way to establish whether hypnosis qualifies as an altered state of consciousness is to find out if something special is happening in the brains of hypnotized persons. This is exactly what Pierre Rainville of the University of Montreal has been attempting to accom-plish. With the help of PET scans, he has shown how different brain centres act when people are hypnotized. For example, during a hypnotic state, as volunteers were told to relax, their occipital lobes showed increased blood flow and the thalamus showed a decrease. However, when they were asked to concentrate really hard on the current situation and to ignore irrel-evant stimuli in their environment, the brain centres involved in paying attention—the thalamus, the frontal lobes, and the brainstem—appeared to be hard at work (Rainville et al., 2002). Furthermore, when volunteers were subjected to a painful stimulus but were given a hypnotic suggestion, "it really won't hurt!" they did not rate the pain as unpleasant. More important, however, researchers observed changes in brain activity levels in a centre called the ACC. This region plays a role in how we emotionally evaluate pain. The brain regions associated with the intensity of pain, the somatosensory cortex, showed no changes in blood flow, clearly indicating that pain was being registered in the somatosensory area but did not seem to bother the volunteers, as shown by blood flow changes in the ACC (Rainville et al., 1997). Finally, MRI tests have revealed the size of the corpus callosum to be larger among highly hypnotizable subjects than low hypnotizable persons. It is not clear what role the size of the corpus callosum plays in hypnotizability, but a relationship of some sort does appear to exist between the two (Horton et al., 2004). This kind of research is still prelimi-nary, but it does suggest that different brain areas may be responding as people are hypno-tized and are given suggestions to perform various tasks (Rainville & Price, 2003).

Hidden observer A detached part of the hypnotized person's awareness that silently observes events.

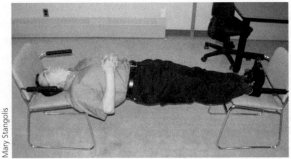

▶▶**FIGURE 5.7** Arrange three chairs as shown. Have someone recline as shown. Ask him or her to lift slightly while you remove the middle chair. Accept the applause gracefully! (Concerning hypnosis and similar phenomena, the moral, of course, is "Suspend judgment until you have something solid to stand on.")

Stage Hypnosis

How do stage entertainers use hypnosis to get people to do strange things? They don't. Little or no hypnosis is needed to do a good hypnosis act. **Stage hypnosis** is often merely a simulation of hypnotic effects. Stage hypnotists make use of several features of the stage setting to perform their act (Barber, 2000).

1. *Waking suggestibility.* We are all more or less open to suggestion, but on stage people are unusually cooperative because they don't want to "spoil the act." As a result, they will readily follow almost any instruction given by the entertainer.
2. *Selection of responsive subjects.* Participants in stage hypnotism (all volunteers) are first "hypnotized" as a group. Thus, anyone who doesn't yield to instructions is eliminated.
3. *The hypnosis label disinhibits.* Once a person has been labelled "hypnotized," he or she can sing, dance, act silly, or whatever, without fear of embarrassment. On stage, being "hypnotized" takes away personal responsibility for one's actions.
4. *The hypnotist as a "director."* After volunteers loosen up and respond to a few suggestions, they find that they are suddenly the stars of the show. Audience response to the antics on stage brings out the "ham" in many people. All the "hypnotist" needs to do is direct the action.
5. *The stage hypnotist uses tricks.* Stage hypnosis is about 50 percent taking advantage of the situation and 50 percent deception. One of the more impressive stage tricks is to rigidly suspend a person between two chairs. This is astounding only because the audience does not question it. Anyone can do it, as is shown in the photographs and instructions in Figure 5.7. Try it!

In short, stage "hypnotists" entertain; they rarely hypnotize.

MEDITATION AND SENSORY DEPRIVATION—CHILLING, THE HEALTHY WAY

Meditation refers to mental exercises that are used to alter consciousness. In general, these exercises focus attention and interrupt the typical flow of thoughts, worries, and analysis. People who use meditation to reduce stress often report less daily physical arousal and anxiety (Andresen, 2000). PET and fMRI scans reveal changes in the activity of the frontal lobes of the brain during meditation, which suggests that it may represent a distinct state of consciousness (Cahn & Polich, 2006). Practising meditation can produce profound structural changes in the brain. Long-term meditators show greater thickness in regions of the brain involved in learning and memory, regulation of emotions, and empathy. These include the highly evolved areas of the cerebral cortex as well as the more primitive brainstem (Hölzel et al., 2011; Vestergaard-Poulsen et al., 2009).

> **Stage hypnosis** The use of hypnosis to entertain; often, merely a simulation of hypnosis for that purpose.
> **Meditation** A mental exercise for producing relaxation or heightened awareness.

<SURVEY QUESTION
What is meditation? Does it have any benefits?

Concentrative meditation Mental exercise based on attending to a single object or thought.

Mindfulness meditation Mental exercise based on widening attention to become aware of everything experienced at any given moment.

Mantra A flowing word or sound repeated silently during concentrative meditation.

Relaxation response The pattern of internal bodily changes that occurs at times of relaxation.

Meditation takes two major forms. In **concentrative meditation,** attention is given to a single focal point, such as an object, a thought, or one's own breathing. In contrast, **mindfulness meditation** is "open," or expansive. In this case, attention is widened to embrace a total, non-judgmental awareness of the world (Lazar, 2005). An example is losing all self-consciousness while walking in the wilderness with a quiet and receptive mind. Mindfulness meditation is more difficult to practise than concentrative meditation (Smith, 1986). For this reason, we will discuss concentrative meditation as a practical self-control method.

Performing Concentrative Meditation

How is concentrative meditation done? The basic idea is to sit still and quietly focus on some external object or on a repetitive internal stimulus, such as your own breathing or humming (Blackmore, 2004). As an alternative, you can silently repeat a **mantra** (a word used as the focus of attention). Typical mantras are smooth, flowing sounds that are easily repeated. A widely used mantra is the word "om." A mantra could also be a phrase from a familiar prayer. If other thoughts arise as you repeat a mantra, just return attention to it as often as necessary to maintain meditation.

The Relaxation Response

The benefits of meditation include lowered heart rate, blood pressure, muscle tension, and other signs of stress. Medical researcher Herbert Benson believes that the core of meditation is the **relaxation response**—an innate physiological pattern that opposes the body's fight-or-flight mechanism. Benson feels, quite simply, that most of us have forgotten how to relax deeply. People in his experiments have learned to produce the relaxation response by following these instructions:

> Sit quietly in a comfortable position. Close your eyes. Deeply relax all your muscles, beginning at your feet and progressing up to your face. Keep them deeply relaxed.
>
> Breathe through your nose. Become aware of your breathing. As you breathe out, say the word "one" silently to yourself.
>
> Do not worry about whether you are successful in achieving a deep level of relaxation. Maintain a passive attitude and permit relaxation to occur at its own pace. Expect distracting thoughts. When these distracting thoughts occur, ignore them and continue repeating "one." (Adapted from Benson, 1977; Lazar et al., 2000).

Effects of Meditation

What effects does meditation have other than producing relaxation? Many extravagant claims have been made about meditation. For example, members of the Transcendental Meditation (TM) movement have stated that 20 minutes of meditation is as restful as a full night's sleep. This, however, is simply an exaggeration.

Long-term meditators have claimed that the practice improves memory, alertness, creativity, and intuition. Again, such claims must be regarded as unproven. Most are based on personal testimonials or poorly controlled studies. A major problem with most studies of TM is that they use devoted meditators. It is quite likely that the beliefs and lifestyles of these people influence the results of the studies as much as meditation does (Druckman & Bjork, 1994).

While many of the claimed benefits of meditation appear to be overstated, meditation does reliably elicit the relaxation response (Janowiak & Hackman, 1994). Meditation may be beneficial for people who find it difficult to "turn off" upsetting thoughts when they need to relax. For example, college students who tried meditation as part of a study felt happier, less anxious, and less depressed after just two weeks of twice-a-day meditation (Smith, Compton, & West, 1995). More promising and encouraging results were obtained in a study conducted in Alberta, which showed meditation to be effective in the reduction of emotional problems among cancer patients. Compared with a control group, those who meditated over seven weeks experienced a substantial decrease in stress, depression, anger, and irritability, as well as a variety of physical symptoms, and were consequently found to be in a better mood (Speca et al., 2000). We will also note that compared with non-meditators, long-term meditators show marked brainwave changes as evidenced by EEG recordings (Lutz et al., 2004).

According to Roger Walsh and Shauna Shapiro (2006), meditation has benefits beyond relaxation. Practised regularly, meditation may foster mental well-being and positive mental skills such as clarity, concentration, and calm. In this sense, meditation may have much in common with psychotherapy. Indeed, research has shown that mindfulness meditation relieves a variety of psychological disorders, from insomnia to excessive anxiety. It can also reduce aggression and the illegal use of psychoactive drugs (Walsh & Shapiro, 2006). Regular meditation may even help people develop self-awareness and maturity (Travis, Arenander, & DuBois, 2004).

Sensory Deprivation

The relaxation response can also be produced by brief sensory deprivation. **Sensory deprivation (SD)** refers to any major reduction in the amount or variety of sensory stimulation.

What happens when stimulation is greatly reduced? A hint comes from reports by prisoners in solitary confinement, Arctic explorers, high-altitude pilots, long-distance truck drivers, and radar operators. When faced with limited or monotonous stimulation, people sometimes have bizarre sensations, dangerous lapses in attention, and distorted perceptions. Initial experiments involving sensory deprivation were conducted at McGill University in the 1950s. Subjects were offered a high monetary reward to spend as many days as they could in small cubicles with a severe reduction in sensory input. Under these confining conditions, volunteers could not last very long, and the experiment was over within two or three days. It was quite common for subjects to be confused and restless and to experience hallucinations; their performance on intellectual tasks was severely hampered (Bexton, Heron, & Scott, 1954).

> **Sensory deprivation (SD)** Any major reduction in the amount or variety of sensory stimulation.
>
> **REST** Restricted environmental stimulation therapy.
>
> **Psychoactive drug** A substance capable of altering attention, memory, judgment, time sense, self-control, mood, or perception.
>
> **Stimulant** A substance that increases activity in the body and nervous system.
>
> **Depressant** A substance that decreases activity in the body and nervous system.
>
> **Physical dependence** Physical addiction, as indicated by the presence of drug tolerance and withdrawal symptoms.
>
> **Withdrawal symptoms** Physical illness and discomfort following the withdrawal of a drug.
>
> **Drug tolerance** A reduction in the body's response to a drug.

 STUDY BREAK **Hypnosis, Meditation, and Sensory Deprivation**

Reflect

How have your beliefs about hypnosis changed after reading the preceding section? Can you think of specific examples in which hypnosis was misrepresented? For example, in high school assemblies, stage acts, movies, or TV dramas?

Various activities can produce the relaxation response. When do you experience states of deep relaxation, coupled with a sense of serene awareness? What similarities do these occurrences have to meditation?

Have you experienced any form of sensory restriction or sensory deprivation? How did you react? Would you be willing to try REST in order to break a bad habit?

Learning Check

1. The term *hypnotism* was coined by a British surgeon named
   a. Franz Mesmer   b. James Stanford
   c. T. A. Kreskin   d. James Braid
2. Only two out of ten people can be hypnotized. T or F?
3. Which of the following can most definitely be achieved with hypnosis?
   a. unusual strength   b. pain relief
   c. improved memory   d. sleeplike brainwaves

4. The focus of attention in concentrative meditation is "open," or expansive. T or F?
5. Mantras are words said silently to oneself to end a session of meditation. T or F?
6. Research conducted by Herbert Benson indicates that careful selection of a mantra is necessary to obtain the physical benefits of meditation. T or F?
7. The most immediate benefit of meditation appears to be its capacity for producing the relaxation response. T or F?
8. Prolonged periods of extreme sensory deprivation lower anxiety and induce deep relaxation. T or F?

Critical Thinking

9. What kind of control group would you need in order to identify the true effects of hypnosis?
10. Regular meditators report lower levels of stress and a greater sense of well-being. What other explanations must we eliminate before this effect can be regarded as genuine?

Answers

1. d 2. F 3. b 4. F 5. F 6. F 7. T 8. F 9. Most experiments on hypnosis include a control group in which people are asked to simulate being hypnotized. Without such controls, the tendency of subjects to cooperate with experimenters makes it difficult to identify true hypnotic effects. 10. Studies on the effects of meditation must control for the placebo effect and the fact that those who meditate may not be a representative sample of the general population. Studies controlling for such factors still show that meditation is beneficial (Pagano & Warrenburg, 1983).

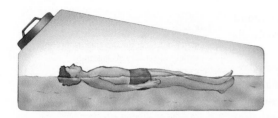

▶▶FIGURE 5.8 A sensory isolation chamber. Small flotation tanks like the one pictured have been used by psychologists to study the effects of mild sensory deprivation. Subjects float in darkness and silence. The shallow, body-temperature water contains several hundred kilograms of Epsom salts, so that subjects float near the surface. Mild sensory deprivation produces deep relaxation.

Not surprisingly, the effects of this experiment were quite devastating for the people involved. Psychologists have also explored the possible benefits of mild sensory restriction. Much of this work has involved small isolation tanks like the one pictured in Figure 5.8.

Brief periods of sensory restriction can be very relaxing. An hour or two spent in a flotation tank, for instance, causes a large drop in blood pressure, muscle tension, and other signs of stress (van Dierendonck & Te Nijenhuis, 2005). Of course, it could be argued that a warm bath has the same effect. Nevertheless, brief sensory deprivation appears to be one of the surest ways to induce deep relaxation (Suedfeld & Borrie, 1999).

Mild sensory deprivation can also help people quit smoking, lose weight, and reduce their use of alcohol and drugs (Borrie, 1990–91; Cooper, Adams, & Scott, 1988; Suedfeld, 1990). Psychologist Peter Suedfeld calls such benefits restricted environmental stimulation therapy, or **REST**. REST also shows promise as a way to stimulate creative thinking (Norlander, Bergman, & Archer, 1998).

Other researchers have reported that REST sessions can enhance performance in skilled sports, such as gymnastics, tennis, basketball, darts, and marksmanship (Druckman & Bjork, 1994; Norlander, Bergman, & Archer, 1999). There is also evidence that REST can relieve chronic pain and reduce stress (Bood et al., 2006). Clearly, there is much yet to be learned from studying "nothingness" (Suedfeld & Borrie, 1999).

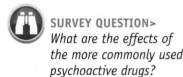

SURVEY QUESTION>
What are the effects of the more commonly used psychoactive drugs?

DRUG-ALTERED CONSCIOUSNESS— THE HIGH AND LOW OF IT

Facts about Drugs

Alcohol, heroin, amphetamines, barbiturates, marijuana, cocaine, LSD, caffeine, nicotine…. The list of mind-altering drugs—legal and illegal—is extensive. The surest way to alter human consciousness is to administer a **psychoactive drug** (a substance capable of altering attention, judgment, memory, time sense, self-control, emotion, or perception) (Julien, 2005).

Most psychoactive drugs can be placed on a scale ranging from stimulation to depression. A **stimulant** increases activity in the body and nervous system. A **depressant** does the reverse. Figure 5.9 shows various drugs and their approximate effects. A more complete summary of frequently abused psychoactive drugs is given in Table 5.3.

Dependence

Drug dependence falls into two broad categories. When a person compulsively uses a drug to maintain bodily comfort, a **physical dependence** (addiction) exists. Physical dependence occurs most often with drugs that cause **withdrawal symptoms** (physical illness that follows removal of a drug) (Julien, 2005). Withdrawal from drugs such as alcohol, barbiturates, and opiates can be extremely unpleasant. Quitting opiates, for example, causes violent flulike symptoms of nausea, vomiting, diarrhea, chills, sweating, and cramps (Feldman & Meyer, 1996). Addiction is often accompanied by a **drug tolerance** (reduced response to a drug). This leads users to take larger and larger doses to get the desired effect.

It's fascinating to note that withdrawal from alcohol, nicotine, caffeine, food, gambling, and even a love relationship can all produce similar symptoms. This may occur because a variety of rewards activate the same pleasure pathways in the brain. In this sense, a person may be "addicted" to food, sex, or love, as well as to drugs (Gilbert, Gilbert, & Schultz, 1998).

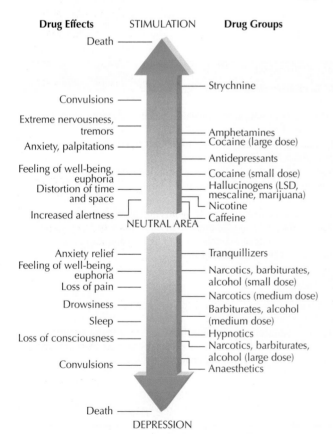

▶▶FIGURE 5.9 Spectrum and continuum of drug action. Many drugs can be rated on a stimulation–depression scale according to their effects on the central nervous system. Although LSD, mescaline, and marijuana are listed here, the stimulation–depression scale is less relevant to these drugs. The principal characteristic of such hallucinogens is their mind-altering quality.

■ Table 5.3 **Comparison of Psychoactive Drugs**

Name	Classification	Medical Use	Usual Dose	Duration of Effect	Effects Sought
Alcohol	Depressant	Solvent, antiseptic	Varies	1–4 hours	Sense alteration, anxiety reduction, sociability
Amphetamines	Stimulant	Relief of mild depression; control of appetite and narcolepsy	2.5–5 milligrams	4 hours	Alertness, activeness
Barbiturates	Depressant	Sedation; relief of high blood pressure, hyperthyroidism	50–100 milligrams	4 hours	Anxiety reduction, euphoria
Benzodiazepines	Depressant	Tranquilizer	2–100 milligrams	1–8 hours	Anxiety relief
Caffeine	Stimulant	Counteract depressant drugs; treatment of migraine headaches	Varies	Varies	Wakefulness, alertness
Cocaine	Stimulant, local anaesthetic	Local anaesthesia	Varies	Varies, brief periods	Excitation, talkativeness
Codeine	Depressant	Ease pain and coughing	30 milligrams	4 hours	Euphoria, prevent withdrawal discomfort
Heroin	Depressant	Pain relief	Varies	4 hours	Euphoria, prevent withdrawal discomfort
LSD	Hallucinogen	Experimental study of mental function, alcoholism	100–500 milligrams	10 hours	Insightful experiences, exhilaration, distortion of senses
Marijuana (THC)	Depressant; in high doses, hallucinogen	Treatment of glaucoma and side effects of chemotherapy	1–2 cigarettes	4 hours	Relaxation; increased euphoria, perceptions, sociability
MDMA	Stimulant/ hallucinogen	None	1–6 milligrams or more	4–6 hours	Excitation, euphoria
Mescaline	Hallucinogen	None	350 micrograms	12 hours	Insightful experiences, exhilaration, distortion of senses
Methadone	Depressant	Pain relief	10 milligrams	4–6 hours	Prevent withdrawal discomfort
Morphine	Depressant	Pain relief	15 milligrams	6 hours	Euphoria, prevent withdrawal discomfort
PCP	Hallucinogen	None	2–10 milligrams	4–6 hours, plus 12-hour recovery	Euphoria
Psilocybin	Hallucinogen	None	25 milligrams	6–8 hours	Insightful experiences, exhilaration, distortion of senses
Tobacco (nicotine)	Stimulant	Emetic (nicotine)	Varies	Varies	Alertness, calmness, sociability

Note: Persons who inject drugs under non-sterile conditions run a high risk of contracting AIDS, hepatitis, abscesses, or circulatory disorders.

■ Table 5.3 *continued.*

Long-Term Symptoms	Physical Dependence Potential	Psychological Dependence Potential	Organic Damage Potential
Cirrhosis, toxic psychosis, neurologic damage, addiction	Yes	Yes	Yes
Loss of appetite and narcolepsy hallucinations, toxic psychosis	Yes	Yes	Yes
Addiction with severe withdrawal symptoms, possible convulsions, toxic psychosis	Yes	Yes	Yes
Irritability, confusion, depression, sleep disorders	Probably	Yes	No
Insomnia, heart arrhythmias, high blood pressure	No?	Yes	Yes
Depression, convulsions	Yes	Yes	Yes
Addiction, constipation, loss of appetite	Yes	Yes	No
Addiction, constipation, loss of appetite	Yes	Yes	No
May intensify existing psychosis, panic reactions	No	No?	No?
Possible lung cancer, other health risks	No	Yes	Yes
Personality change, hyperthermia, liver damage	No	No?	No?
May intensify existing psychosis, panic reactions	Yes	No	No
Addiction, constipation, loss of appetite	Yes	Yes	No
Addiction, constipation, loss of appetite	Yes	Yes	No*
Unpredictable behaviour, suspicion, hostility, psychosis	Debated	Yes	Yes
May intensify existing psychosis, panic reactions	No	No?	No?
Emphysema, lung cancer, mouth and throat cancer, cardiovascular damage, loss of appetite	Yes	Yes	Yes

How Drugs Affect the Brain

How do drugs alter consciousness? Psychoactive drugs influence the activity of neurons. Typically, drugs imitate or alter neurotransmitters, the chemicals that carry messages between neurons. Some drugs cause more neurotransmitters to be released, increasing the activity of neurons. Ecstasy, amphetamine, and some antidepressants are examples of drugs that have this effect. Other drugs, such as cocaine, slow the removal of neurotransmitters after they are released. This prolongs the action of transmitter chemicals and typically has a stimulating effect. Yet other drugs, such as nicotine and opiates, directly stimulate neurons by mimicking neurotransmitters. Another possibility is illustrated by alcohol and tranquillizers. These drugs affect certain types of neurons that cause relaxation and relieve anxiety. Some drugs fill receptor sites on neurons and block incoming messages. Other possibilities also exist, which is why drugs can have such a wide variety of effects on the brain (Julien, 2005).

Nearly all addictive drugs stimulate the brain's reward circuitry, producing feelings of pleasure (Kalat, 2013). In particular, addictive drugs stimulate a brain region called the *nucleus accumbens* to release the neurotransmitter dopamine, which results in intensified feelings of pleasure (Figure 5.10). As one expert put it, addictive drugs fool brain-reward pathways: As a result, the reward pathway signals, "That felt good. Let's do it again. Let's remember exactly how we did it." This creates a compulsion to repeat the drug experience. It's the hook that eventually snares the addict (Restak, 2001). Adolescents are especially susceptible to addiction because brain systems that restrain risk-taking are not as mature as those that reward pleasure-seeking (Chambers, Taylor, & Potenza, 2003).

When a person develops a **psychological dependence,** he or she feels that a drug is necessary to maintain feelings of comfort or well-being. Usually, the person intensely craves the drug and its rewarding qualities (Feldman & Meyer, 1996). Psychological dependence can be just as powerful as physical addiction. That's why some psychologists define addiction as any compulsive habit pattern. By this definition, a person who has lost control over drug use, for whatever reason, is addicted (Marlatt et al., 1988). In fact, most people who answer yes to both of the following questions have an alcohol or drug problem and should seek professional help (Brown et al., 1997):

- In the last year, did you ever drink or use drugs more than you meant to?
- Have you felt you wanted or needed to cut down on your drinking or drug use in the last year?

Polydrug Abuse

There is one more pattern of drug abuse that bears mentioning: the abuse of more than one drug at the same time. Polydrug abuse accounts for the vast majority of deaths due to drug overdose. When mixed, the effects of different drugs are multiplied by **drug interactions** (one drug enhances the effect of another), which are responsible for thousands of fatal drug overdoses every year (Goldberg, 2006). This is true whether the mixed drugs are legally or illegally obtained.

Drugs of Abuse

Note in Table 5.3 that the drugs most likely to lead to physical dependence are alcohol, amphetamines, barbiturates, cocaine, codeine, heroin, methadone, morphine, and tobacco (nicotine). Using any of the drugs listed in Table 5.3 can result in psychological dependence. Note, too, that people who take drugs intravenously are at high risk for developing hepatitis and HIV/AIDS. The discussion that follows focuses on the drugs most often abused by students.

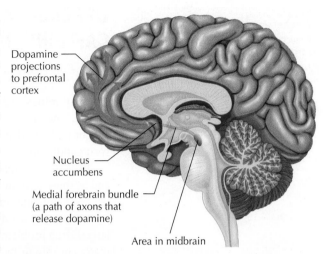

Dopamine projections to prefrontal cortex

Nucleus accumbens

Medial forebrain bundle (a path of axons that release dopamine)

Area in midbrain

▸▸**FIGURE 5.10** Addictive drugs increase dopamine activity in the medial forebrain bundle and the nucleus accumbens, stimulating the frontal cortex and giving rise to intensified feelings of pleasure.

Psychological dependence Drug dependence that is based primarily on emotional or psychological needs.

Drug interaction A combined effect of two drugs that exceeds the addition of one drug's effects to the other.

Amphetamines A class of synthetic drugs having stimulant effects on the nervous system.

Amphetamine psychosis A severe disruption of psychological functioning caused by abuse of amphetamines.

UPPERS—AMPHETAMINES, COCAINE, CAFFEINE, NICOTINE

Amphetamines

Amphetamines are synthetic stimulants. Common street names for amphetamine are "speed," "bennies," "dexies," "go," and "uppers." These drugs were once widely prescribed for weight loss and depression. Today, the main legitimate medical use of amphetamines is to treat childhood hyperactivity and overdoses of depressant drugs.

Illicit use of amphetamines is widespread, however, especially by people seeking to stay awake and by those who think drugs can improve mental or physical performance (Iversen, 2006).

Methamphetamine is a more potent variation of amphetamine. It can be snorted, injected, or eaten. Of the various types of amphetamine, methamphetamine has created the largest drug problem. "Bergs," "glass," "meth," or "crystal," as it is known on the street, can be made cheaply in backyard labs and sold for massive profits. In addition to ruining lives through addiction, it has fuelled a violent criminal subculture.

Amphetamines rapidly produce a drug tolerance. Most abusers begin with one or two pills a day and end up taking dozens to get the same effect. Eventually, some users switch to injecting Methedrine ("speed") directly into the bloodstream. True speed freaks typically go on binges lasting several days, after which they "crash" from lack of sleep and food.

Abuse

How dangerous are amphetamines? Amphetamines pose many dangers. To stay high, the abuser must take more and more of the drug as the body's tolerance grows. Higher doses can cause nausea, vomiting, dangerously high blood pressure, fatal heart arrhythmias, and crippling strokes. Also, it is important to realize that amphetamines speed up the use of bodily resources; they do not magically supply energy. Hence, the after-effects of an amphetamine binge can include crippling fatigue, depression, terrifying nightmares, confusion, uncontrolled irritability, and aggression. Repeatedly overextending the body with stimulants may lead to self-starvation, sores and ulcers, chronic chest infections, liver disease, and brain hemorrhage. Amphetamines can also cause a loss of contact with reality known as **amphetamine psychosis.** Affected users suffer from paranoid delusions that someone is out to get them. Acting on these delusions, they may become violent, resulting in self-injury or injury to others (Iversen, 2006).

A potent new smokable form of crystal methamphetamine has recently added to the risks of stimulant abuse. This drug, known as "ice" on the street, is highly addictive. Like "crack," the smokable form of cocaine, it produces an intense high. But also like crack, crystal methamphetamine leads very rapidly to compulsive abuse and severe drug dependence.

MDMA ("Ecstasy")

The drug MDMA (methylenedioxymethamphetamine, or "Ecstasy") is also chemically similar to amphetamine. In addition to producing a rush of energy, users say it makes them feel closer to others and heightens sensory experiences. Ecstasy causes neurons to release extra amounts of serotonin. The physical effects of MDMA include dilated pupils, elevated blood pressure, jaw clenching, loss of appetite, and elevated body temperature (Braun, 2001). Some users believe that Ecstasy increases sexual pleasure. However, it impairs erection in 40 percent of men, and it can retard orgasm in both men and women (Zemishlany, Aizenberg, & Weizman, 2001).

Abuse

The use of Ecstasy has doubled in North America in the last five years. At least 1 in 20 university and college students have tried Ecstasy. What are the consequences of such widespread use? Serious problems are beginning to surface. Every year, emergency room doctors see more MDMA cases, including a steady increase in MDMA-related deaths. Some of these incidents are caused by elevated body temperature (hyperthermia) or heart arrhythmias, which can lead to collapse.

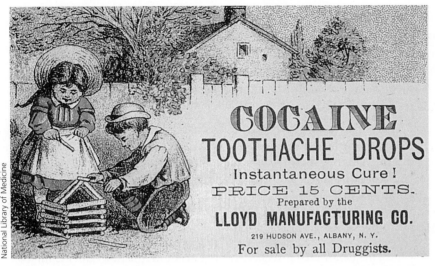

Cocaine was the main ingredient in many non-prescription elixirs before the turn of the 20th century. Today cocaine is recognized as a powerful and dangerous drug. Its high potential for abuse has damaged the lives of countless users.

Ecstasy users at "rave" parties try to prevent over-heating by drinking water to cool themselves. This may help to a small degree, but the risk of fatal heat exhaustion is real. MDMA can also cause severe liver damage, which can be fatal (Braun, 2001). In addition, Ecstasy users are more likely to abuse alcohol and other drugs, to neglect studying, to party excessively, and to engage in risky sex (Strote, Lee, & Wechsler, 2002).

What about the long-term effects of Ecstasy use? Feelings of anxiety or depression can persist for months after a person stops taking Ecstasy. In addition, heavy users typically do not perform well in tests of learning and memory and show some signs of underlying brain damage (Quednow et al., 2006). Fortunately, however, the long-term psychological consequences are not as severe as once feared (Advisory Council on the Misuse of Drugs, 2009).

Cocaine

Cocaine is a powerful central nervous system stimulant extracted from the leaves of the coca plant. Cocaine produces feelings of alertness, euphoria, well-being, power, boundless energy, and pleasure (Julien, 2005).

Cocaine has a long history of use and misuse. At the turn of the 20th century, dozens of non-prescription potions and cure-alls contained cocaine. It was during this time that Coca-Cola was indeed the "real thing." From 1886 until 1906, when the United States Pure Food and Drug Act was passed, Coca-Cola contained cocaine (which has since been replaced with caffeine). Recent statistics show that 7 percent of Canadians had used cocaine at least once in their lives, and 0.7 percent had used the drug during the previous year (Health Canada, 2012).

How does cocaine differ from amphetamines? The two are very similar in their effects on the central nervous system. The main difference is that amphetamine lasts several hours; cocaine is snorted and quickly metabolized, so its effects last only about 15 to 30 minutes.

Abuse

Cocaine's capacity for abuse and social damage rivals that of heroin. When rats and monkeys are given free access to cocaine, they find it irresistible. Many, in fact, end up dying of convulsions from self-administered overdoses of the drug. Even casual or first-time users run a risk because cocaine can cause convulsions, heart attack, or stroke (Lacayo, 1995). Cocaine increases the levels of the neurotransmitters dopamine and norepinephrine (see Chapter 2). Norepinephrine arouses the brain, and dopamine produces a "rush" of pleasure. This combination is so power-fully rewarding that cocaine users run a high risk of becoming compulsive abusers (Ridenour et al., 2005). The highly publicized death of American basketball star Len Bias is a case in point.

A person who stops using cocaine does not experience heroin-like withdrawal symptoms. But cocaine can be highly addictive. The brain adapts to cocaine abuse in ways that upset its chemical balance, causing depression when cocaine is withdrawn. First, there is a jarring "crash" of mood and energy. Within a few days, the person enters a long period of fatigue, anxiety, paranoia, boredom, and **anhedonia** (an-he-DOH-nee-ah: an inability to feel plea-sure). Before long, the urge to use cocaine grows overwhelming. So, while cocaine does not fit the classic pattern of physical addiction, there is little doubt about its potential for compulsive abuse. Even a person who gets through withdrawal may crave cocaine months or years later (Withers et al., 1995). Many authorities estimate that if cocaine were cheaper, nine out of ten users would progress to compulsive abuse. In fact, rock cocaine (or "crack"), which is cheaper, produces very high abuse rates. Here are some signs of cocaine abuse (Pursch, 1983):

Cocaine A crystalline drug derived from coca leaves; used as a central nervous system stimulant and local anaesthetic.

Anhedonia An inability to feel pleasure.

Caffeine A natural drug with stimulant properties; found in coffee and tea and added to artificial beverages and medicines.

Caffeinism Excessive consumption of caffeine, leading to dependence and a variety of physical and psychological complaints.

Nicotine A potent stimulant drug found primarily in tobacco; nicotine is a known carcinogen.

- *Compulsive use.* If cocaine is available—say, at a party—you will undoubtedly use it. You can't say no to it.
- *Loss of control.* Once you have had some cocaine, you will keep using it until you are exhausted or the cocaine is gone.
- *Disregarding consequences.* You don't care if the rent gets paid, your job is endangered, your lover disapproves, or your health is affected—you'll use cocaine anyway.

Clearly, cocaine's capacity for abuse and social damage rivals that of heroin. Anyone who thinks she or he has a cocaine problem should seek advice at a drug clinic or a Cocaine Anonymous meeting. Quitting cocaine is extremely difficult (Sinha et al., 2006). Nevertheless, three out of four cocaine abusers who remain in treatment do succeed in breaking their dependence (Simpson et al., 1999).

Caffeine

Caffeine is the most frequently used psychoactive drug in North America. **Caffeine** stimulates the brain by blocking chemicals that normally inhibit or slow nerve activity (Julien, 2005). Its effects become apparent with doses as small as 50 milligrams, the amount found in about one half-cup of brewed coffee. Caffeine can lead to sweating, talkativeness, tinnitus (ringing in the ears), and hand tremors in some people (Nehlig, 2004). Psychologically, caffeine suppresses fatigue or drowsiness and increases feelings of alertness (Smith, Clark, & Gallagher, 1999). Some people have a hard time starting a day (or writing another paragraph) without it.

How much caffeine did you consume today? Although it is common to think of coffee as the major source of caffeine, there are many others. Caffeine is found in tea, many soft drinks (especially colas), chocolate, and cocoa (see Table 5.4). Over 2000 non-prescription drugs also contain caffeine, including stay-awake pills, cold remedies, and many name-brand aspirin products. Many popular energy drinks also contain caffeine.

Abuse

Are there any serious drawbacks to using caffeine? Serious abuse may result in an unhealthy dependence on caffeine known as **caffeinism.** Insomnia, irritability, loss of appetite, chills, racing heart, and elevated body temperature are all signs of caffeinism. Many people with these symptoms drink 15 to 20 cups of coffee a day.

Caffeine can pose a variety of health risks. It encourages the growth of breast cysts in women, and it may contribute to bladder cancer and heart problems. Pregnant women should consider giving up caffeine entirely because of a suspected link between caffeine and birth defects. Pregnant women who consume six or more cups of coffee a day double their risk of having a miscarriage (Cnattingius et al., 2000).

On the other hand, recent studies have linked the consumption of coffee to many positive health benefits, including a lower risk of suffering from depression and a reduced risk of dying earlier than non-drinkers due to cardiovascular diseases, respiratory diseases, diabetes, and infections (Freedman et al., 2012). Coffee contains hundreds of compounds—antioxidants being the most important health-promoting substances—that may explain these positive findings.

Finally, although it is customary to think of caffeine as a non-drug, people who consume coffee or tea regularly and try to kick the habit may experience signs of withdrawal, such as anxiety, fatigue, headaches, and flulike symptoms (Juliano & Griffiths, 2004). About half of all caffeine users show some signs of dependence (Hughes et al., 1998). It is wise to remember that caffeine is a drug and to use it in moderation.

Nicotine

Nicotine is a natural stimulant found mainly in tobacco. Next to caffeine, it is the most widely used psychoactive drug (Julien, 2005).

How does nicotine compare with other stimulants? Nicotine is a potent drug. It is so toxic that it is sometimes used to kill insects! In large doses, it causes stomach pain,

■ Table 5.4   **Average Caffeine Content of Various Foods and Beverages**

Instant coffee (150 mL): 64 mg

Percolated coffee (150 mL): 108 mg

Drip coffee (150 mL): 145 mg

Decaffeinated coffee (150 mL): 3 mg

Black tea (150 mL): 42 mg

Canned iced tea (500 mL): 30 mg

Cocoa drink (175 mL): 8 mg

Chocolate drink (235 mL): 14 mg

Sweet chocolate (30 g): 20 mg

Colas (355 mL): 50 mg

One in six deaths in Canada are caused by smoking.

vomiting and diarrhea, cold sweats, dizziness, confusion, and muscle tremors. In very large doses, nicotine may cause convulsions, respiratory failure, and death. For a non-smoker, 50 to 75 milligrams of nicotine taken in a single dose could be lethal. (Chain-smoking about 17 to 25 cigarettes will produce this dosage.) Most first-time smokers get sick on one or two cigarettes. In contrast, a heavy smoker may inhale 40 cigarettes a day without feeling ill. This indicates that regular smokers build up a tolerance for nicotine (Perkins, 1995; Stolerman & Jarvis, 1995).

Abuse

Is it true that nicotine can be addicting? A vast array of evidence confirms that nicotine is addictive. For many smokers, withdrawal from nicotine causes headaches, sweating, cramps, insomnia, digestive upset, irritability, and a sharp craving for cigarettes (Killen & Fortmann, 1997). These symptoms may last from two to six weeks and may be worse than heroin withdrawal. Indeed, relapse patterns are nearly identical for alcoholics, heroin addicts, and smokers who try to quit (Stolerman & Jarvis, 1995). A staggering eight out of ten people who quit smoking relapse within a year (Jarvik, 1995).

Impact on Health

How serious are the health risks of smoking? A burning cigarette releases a large variety of potent **carcinogens** (car-SIN-oh-jins: cancer-causing substances). Lung cancer and other cancers caused by smoking are now considered the single most preventable cause of death in Canada and the United States. Among men, 97 percent of lung cancer deaths are caused by smoking. For women, 74 percent of all lung cancers are due to smoking. Here are some sobering facts about smoking:

Smoking Facts

- Every cigarette reduces a smoker's life expectancy by seven minutes.
- More people die every year from tobacco use than from motor vehicle injuries, murders, suicides, alcohol use, illegal drug use, and HIV/AIDS *combined* (NCCDPHP, 2004).
- In Canada, one in six deaths are caused by smoking. In 2002, there were 37 209 deaths due to tobacco use, which is estimated to have led to a total of 515 607 years of potential life lost (Rehm et al., 2006).

Carcinogen A substance capable of causing cancer.

A study of students in Grades 5 to 12 found that those who smoke are less likely than non-smokers to believe the health warning labels on cigarette packs (Cecil, Evans, & Stanley, 1996). Smokers in general are less likely to believe that smoking poses a serious risk to health.

Mary Stangolis

- Tobacco cost the Canadian economy a staggering $17 billion in 2002 (Rehm et al., 2006).
- Forty percent of all smokers who develop throat cancer try smoking again.
- Each year, only one out of five smokers who try to quit smoking succeed.
- Some tobacco companies manipulate nicotine levels in their cigarettes to keep smokers addicted.
- Daily exposure to second-hand smoke at home or work causes a 24 to 39 percent increase in cancer risk to non-smokers.

If you think smoking is harmless, or that there's no connection between smoking and cancer, you're kidding yourself. The scientific link between tobacco smoking and cancer is undeniable. Skeptics please note: Wayne McLaren, who portrayed the rugged "Marlboro Man" in U.S. cigarette ads, died of lung cancer at age 51.

Smokers don't just risk their own health, they also endanger those who live and work nearby. Second-hand smoke causes 20 percent of all lung cancers. Non-smoking women who are married to smokers suffer a 30 percent increase in their risk of developing lung cancer. It is particularly irresponsible of smokers to expose young children to second-hand smoke (Abramson, 1993). Canadian government officials are starting to agree: At the end of 2007, Wolfville, Nova Scotia, became the first Canadian municipality to ban smoking in a vehicle when a child is in it; following its lead, some provinces have recently passed similar legislation, and others are seriously considering it.

Quitting Smoking

Is it better for a person to quit smoking abruptly or taper down gradually? For many years, smokers were advised to quit cold turkey. The current view is that quitting all at once isn't as effective as tapering off. Going cold turkey makes quitting an all-or-nothing proposition. Smokers who smoke even one cigarette after "quitting forever" tend to feel they've failed. Many figure they might just as well resume smoking. Those who quit by tapering off accept that success may take many attempts, spread over several months. However, switching to "light" cigarettes is not a good way to quit gradually. Heavy smokers tend to adjust their smoking to

© Mim Friday/Alamy

Although smoking cigarettes still claims many lives every year, the message about the harmful effects of inhaling tobacco seems to be getting through. As a result, the number of people smoking cigarettes has been declining steadily in Western countries.

Strategies to Stop Smoking

If you smoke but would like to quit, here are some basic steps you can take: (1) Delay having a first cigarette in the morning. Then try to delay a little longer each day. (2) Gradually reduce the total number of cigarettes you smoke each day. (3) Quit completely, but for just one week. Then quit again, a week at a time, for as many times as necessary to make it stick (Pierce, 1991).

You will probably be most successful at strategy number 2 if you schedule a gradual reduction in smoking. To begin, count the number of cigarettes you smoke per day. For the first week your goal will be to smoke only two-thirds of that "baseline" number each day. In addition, you should divide the 16 waking hours in each day by the number of cigarettes you will smoke that day. For example, if you plan to smoke 16 cigarettes per day, then you only get to smoke one per hour. When a scheduled "smoking time" arrives, smoke only for five minutes, whether you finish the cigarette or not. Don't smoke any "missed" cigarettes later.

During the second week, you should smoke only one-third as many cigarettes as you did during your baseline. Again, divide each 16-hour day by the number of cigarettes, so you can plan how much time to allow between smoking periods.

During week three, reduce your cigarette allowance to 20 percent of the original baseline number.

In the fourth week, stop smoking entirely.

Gradually stretching the time periods between cigarettes is a key part of this program. Scheduled smoking apparently helps people learn to cope with the urge to smoke. As a result, people using this method are more likely to succeed. Also, they more often remain permanent non-smokers than people using other approaches (Cinciripini, Wetter, & McClure, 1997).

keep bodily levels of nicotine constant. Thus, when they smoke lighter cigarettes, they smoke more. This can do extra damage, because light cigarettes have as much tar as regular cigarettes (Kozlowski et al., 1998).

Using Psychology: "Strategies to Stop Smoking" summarizes several ways to quit smoking. Whatever approach is taken, quitting smoking is not easy. It does help, though, if you get a spouse or partner to support your efforts (Cohen & Lichtenstein, 1990). Also, as we have noted, anyone trying to quit should be prepared to make several attempts before succeeding. But the good news is millions of people have quit.

DOWNERS—SEDATIVES, TRANQUILLIZERS, AND ALCOHOL

The most widely used downers, or depressant drugs, are alcohol, barbiturates, and benzodiazepine (ben-zoe-die-AZ-eh-peen) tranquillizers. These drugs are much alike in their effects. In fact, barbiturates and tranquillizers are sometimes referred to as "solid alcohol." Let's examine the properties of each.

Barbiturates

Barbiturates are sedative drugs that depress brain activity. Common barbiturates include amobarbital, pentobarbital, secobarbital, and tuinal. On the street they are known as "downers," "blue heavens," "yellow jackets," "lows," "goof balls," "reds," "pink ladies," "rainbows," or "tooies." Medically, they are used to calm patients or to induce sleep. In mild doses, barbiturates have an effect similar to alcohol intoxication. Higher doses can cause severe mental confusion or even hallucinations. Barbiturates are often taken in excess amounts because a first dose may be followed by others, as the user becomes uninhibited or forgetful. Overdoses first cause unconsciousness. Then they severely depress brain centres that control heartbeat and breathing. The result is death (McKim, 2007).

Barbiturate One of a large group of sedative drugs that depress activity in the nervous system.

Tranquillizer A drug that lowers anxiety and reduces tension.

GHB

Would you swallow a mixture of degreasing solvent and drain cleaner to get high? Apparently, a lot of people would. A mini-epidemic of GHB (gamma-hydroxybutyrate) use took place in the early twenty-first century, especially at nightclubs and raves. GHB ("goop," "scoop," "max," "Georgia Home Boy") is a central nervous system depressant that relaxes and sedates the body. Users describe its effects as being similar to alcohol. Mild GHB intoxication tends to produce euphoria, a desire to socialize, and a mild loss of inhibitions. GHB's intoxicating effects typically last three to four hours, depending on the dosage.

Abuse

At lower dosages, GHB can relieve anxiety and produce relaxation. However, as the dose increases, its sedative effects may result in nausea, a loss of muscle control, and either sleep or a loss of consciousness. Higher dosages can cause coma, breathing failure, and death. GHB inhibits the gag reflex, so some users choke to death on their own vomit. Potentially fatal doses of GHB are only three times the amount typically taken by users. This narrow margin of safety has led to numerous overdoses, especially when GHB was combined with alcohol.

Clinical evidence increasingly suggests that GHB is addictive and a serious danger to users. Two out of three frequent users have lost consciousness after taking GHB. Heavy users who stop taking GHB have withdrawal symptoms that include anxiety, agitation, tremor, delirium, and hallucinations (Miotto et al., 2001).

As if the preceding weren't enough reason to be leery of GHB, here's one more to consider: GHB is often manufactured in homes with recipes and ingredients purchased on the Internet. As mentioned earlier, it can be produced by combining degreasing solvent with drain cleaner (Falkowski, 2000). If you want to degrease your brain, GHB will do the trick.

Tranquillizers

A **tranquillizer** is a drug that lowers anxiety and reduces tension. Doctors prescribe benzodiazepine tranquillizers to alleviate nervousness and stress. Valium is the best-known drug in this family; others are Xanax, Halcion, and Librium. Even at normal doses these drugs can cause drowsiness, shakiness, and confusion. When used at too high a dose or for too long a time, benzodiazepines have strong addictive potential (McKim, 2007).

A drug sold under the trade name Rohypnol (ro-HIP-nol) has added to the problem of tranquillizer abuse. This drug, which is related to Valium, is cheap and potent. It lowers inhibitions and produces relaxation or intoxication. Large doses induce short-term amnesia and sleep. "Roofies," as they are known on the street, are odourless and tasteless. They have been used to spike drinks, which are given to the unwary. Drugged victims are then sexually assaulted or raped while they are unconscious (Navarro, 1995).

Abuse

Repeated use of barbiturates can cause physical dependence. Some abusers suffer severe emotional depression that may end in suicide. Similarly, when tranquillizers are used at too high a dose or for too long a time, addiction may occur. Many people have learned the hard way that their legally prescribed tranquillizers are as dangerous as many illicit drugs (McKim, 2007).

Combining barbiturates or tranquillizers with alcohol is extremely risky. When mixed, the effects of both drugs are multiplied by a drug interaction. Drug interactions are responsible for many hundreds of fatal drug overdoses every year. All too often, depressants are gulped down with alcohol or added to a spiked punch bowl. This is the lethal brew that left a young woman named Karen Ann Quinlan in a coma that lasted ten years, ending with her death. It is no exaggeration to restate that mixing depressants with alcohol can be deadly.

Alcohol

Alcohol is the common name for ethyl alcohol, the intoxicating element in fermented and distilled liquors. Contrary to popular belief, alcohol is not a stimulant. The noisy animation at drinking parties is due to alcohol's effect as a depressant. As Figure 5.11 shows, small amounts of alcohol reduce inhibitions and produce feelings of relaxation and euphoria. Larger amounts cause ever-greater impairment of the brain until the drinker loses consciousness. Alcohol is also not an aphrodisiac. Rather than enhancing sexual arousal, it usually impairs performance, especially in males. As William Shakespeare observed long ago, drink "provokes the desire, but it takes away the performance."

Abuse

Alcohol, the world's favourite depressant, breeds our biggest drug problem. Over 200 million people in Canada and the United States use alcohol. An estimated 25 million have serious drinking problems. An alarming trend is the high level of alcohol abuse among adolescents and young adults. By the time Canadian students are in Grade 12, a great number of them use alcohol either alone or in combination with other drugs (Leatherdale & Burkhalter, 2012). Fifty percent of male college students and 40 percent of college women have engaged in binge drinking. For fraternity and sorority members, the figure jumps to 84 percent. **Binge drinking** is defined as downing five or more drinks in a short time. Apparently, many students think it's entertaining to get completely wasted and throw up on their friends. Binge drinking is a serious sign of alcohol abuse (Wechsler et al., 1999).

Our society bears a heavy cost attributable to alcohol. Alcohol abuse claimed the lives of 4258 Canadians in 2002, and it was responsible for a total of 1 587 054 days of hospital care for patients. Alcohol also played a role in 761 638 criminal offences, which corresponds to 30.4 percent of all such cases in this country (Rehm et al., 2006).

Positive reinforcement—drinking for pleasure—motivates most people who consume alcohol. What sets alcohol abusers apart is that they also drink to cope with negative emotions, such as anxiety and depression. That's why alcohol abuse increases with the level of stress in people's lives. People who drink to cope with bad feelings run a great risk of becoming alcoholics (Kenneth, Carpenter, & Hasin, 1998).

Recognizing Problem Drinking

What are the signs of alcohol abuse? Because alcohol abuse is such a common problem, it is important to recognize the danger signals. If you can answer yes to even one of the following questions, you may have a problem with drinking (adapted from the College Alcohol Problems Scale, revised; Maddock et al., 2001):

As a result of drinking alcoholic beverages I...
1. engaged in unplanned sexual activity.
2. did not use protection when engaging in sex.
3. drove under the influence of alcohol.
4. engaged in illegal activities associated with drug use.
5. felt sad, blue, or depressed.
6. was nervous or irritable.
7. felt bad about myself.
8. had problems with appetite or sleeping.

Alcohol The common name for ethyl alcohol, the intoxicating element in fermented and distilled liquors.
Binge drinking Consuming five or more drinks in a short time.

▸▸**FIGURE 5.11** The behavioural effects of alcohol are related to blood alcohol content and the resulting suppression of higher mental function. The legal federal blood alcohol limit for drivers in Canada is 0.08 (80 milligrams of alcohol in 100 millilitres of blood), and many provinces impose a stricter limit of 0.05.

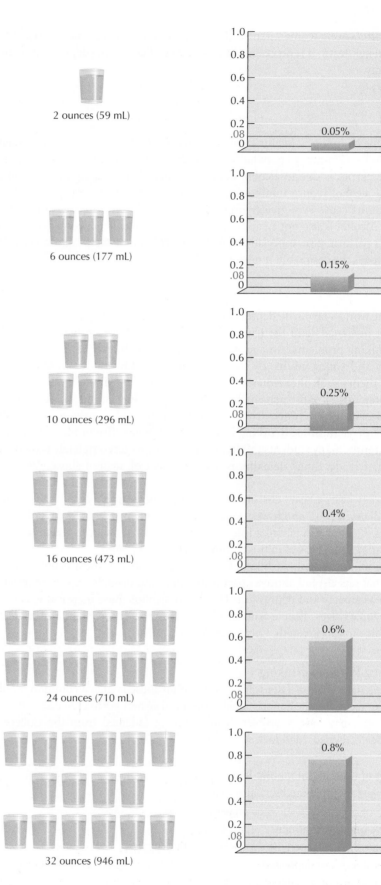

Moderated Drinking

Many social-recreational drinkers could do a far better job of managing their use of alcohol. Almost everyone has been to a party spoiled by someone who drank too much too fast. Those who avoid overdrinking have a better time, and so do their friends. But how do you avoid drinking too much? After all, as one wit once observed, "The conscience dissolves in alcohol." It takes skill to regulate drinking in social situations, where the temptation to drink can be strong. If you choose to drink, here are some guidelines that may be helpful (adapted from Miller & Munoz, 2005; Vogler & Bartz, 1992):

Paced Drinking

1. Think about your drinking beforehand and plan how you will manage it.
2. Drink slowly, eat while drinking or drink on a full stomach, and make every other drink (or more) a non-alcoholic beverage.
3. Limit drinking primarily to the first hour of a social event or party.
4. Practise how you will politely but firmly refuse drinks.
5. Learn how to relax, meet people, and socialize without relying on alcohol.

Binge drinking and alcohol abuse have become serious problems among college and university students. Many alcohol abusers regard themselves as "moderate" drinkers, which suggests that they are in denial about how much they actually drink (Grant & Dawson, 1997).

And remember, research has shown that you are likely to overestimate how much your fellow students are drinking (Maddock & Glanz, 2005). So don't let yourself be lured into overdrinking just because you have the (probably false) impression that other students are drinking more than you. Limiting your own drinking may help others as well. When people are tempted to drink too much, their main reason for stopping is that "other people were quitting and deciding they'd had enough" (Johnson, 2002).

Treatment

Treatment for alcohol dependence begins with sobering up the person and cutting off the supply. This phase is referred to as **detoxification** (literally, "to remove poison"). It frequently produces all the symptoms of drug withdrawal and can be extremely unpleasant. The next step is to try to restore the person's health. Heavy abuse of alcohol usually causes severe damage to body organs and the nervous system. After alcoholics have "dried out," and some degree of health has been restored, they may be treated with tranquillizers, antidepressants, or psychotherapy. Unfortunately, the success of these procedures has been limited.

One mutual-help approach that has been fairly successful is Alcoholics Anonymous (AA). AA acts on the premise that it takes a former alcoholic to understand and help a current alcoholic. The organization emphasizes a sense of spirituality and community. Participants at AA meetings admit that they have a problem, share feelings, and resolve to stay "dry" one day at a time. Other group members provide support for those struggling to end dependency. (Cocaine Anonymous and Narcotics Anonymous use the same approach.)

Eighty-one percent of those who remain in AA over one year get through the following year without a drink. However, AA's success rate may simply reflect the fact that members join voluntarily, meaning they have admitted they have a serious problem (Morgenstern et al., 1997). Sadly, it seems that alcohol abusers will often not face their problems until they have "hit rock bottom." If they are willing, though, AA presents a practical approach to the problem (Vaillant, 2005).

Other groups offer a rational, non-spiritual approach to alcohol abuse that better fits the needs of some people. Examples include Rational Recovery and Secular Organizations for Sobriety (SOS). Other alternatives to AA include medical treatment, group therapy, and

Detoxification In the treatment of alcoholism, the withdrawal of the patient from alcohol.

Marijuana The leaves and flowers of the hemp plant, *Cannabis sativa*.

Hashish Resinous material scraped from the leaves of the hemp plant; hashish has a high concentration of THC.

THC Tetrahydrocannabinol, the main active chemical in marijuana.

Hallucinogen A substance that alters or distorts sensory impressions.

individual psychotherapy (Buddie, 2004). There is a strong tendency for abusive drinkers to deny they have a problem. The sooner they seek help, the better.

MARIJUANA AND HALLUCINOGENS—WHAT'S IN THE POT?

Marijuana and hashish (cannabis) are derived from the hemp plant *Cannabis sativa*. **Marijuana** consists of the leaves and flowers of the hemp plant. **Hashish** is a resinous material scraped from cannabis leaves. The main active chemical in marijuana is **tetrahydrocannabinol** (tet-rah-hydro-cah-NAB-ih-nol), or **THC.** THC is a mild **hallucinogen** (hal-LU-sin-oh-jin: a substance that alters sensory impressions).

Cannabis is the most widely used illegal drug in Canada. A survey completed in 2010 found that 10.7 percent of Canadians over the age of 14 years had used it in the previous year, and 41.5 percent had used it at least once in their lives (Health Canada, 2012). These statistics show a decline of about 3 percentage points since 2004 in both past-year and lifetime users (Adlaf, Begin, & Sawka, 2005).

Marijuana

Marijuana's psychological effects include a sense of euphoria or well-being, relaxation, altered time sense, and perceptual distortions. At high dosages, however, paranoia, hallucinations, and delusions can occur (Ksir, Hart, & Ray, 2006). All considered, marijuana intoxication is relatively subtle by comparison to drugs such as LSD and alcohol (Kelly et al., 1990). Despite this, driving a car while high on marijuana can be extremely hazardous. As a matter of fact, driving under the influence of any intoxicating drug is dangerous.

No overdose deaths have been reported from marijuana. However, marijuana cannot be considered harmless. Particularly worrisome is the fact that THC accumulates in the body's fatty tissues, especially in the brain and reproductive organs. Scientists have located a specific receptor site on the surface of neurons where THC binds to produce its effects (see Figure 5.12). These receptor sites are found in large numbers in the cerebral cortex, which is the seat of human consciousness (Julien, 2005). In addition, THC receptors are found in areas involved in the control of skilled movement. Naturally occurring chemicals similar to THC may help the brain cope with pain and stress. However, when THC is used as a drug, high dosages can cause paranoia, hallucinations, and dizziness.

Does marijuana produce physical dependence? Yes, according to recent studies (Lichtman & Martin, 2006). Frequent users of marijuana find it very difficult to quit, so dependence is a risk (Budney & Hughes, 2006). But marijuana's potential for abuse lies primarily in the realm of psychological dependence, not physical.

Dangers of Marijuana Use

There have been very alarming reports in the press about the dangers of marijuana. Are they accurate? As one pharmacologist put it, "Those reading only *Good Housekeeping* would have to believe that marijuana is considerably more dangerous than the black plague." Unfortunately, an evaluation of marijuana's risks has been clouded by emotional debate. Let's see if we can make a realistic appraisal.

In the past it was widely reported that marijuana causes brain damage, genetic damage, and a loss of motivation. Each of these charges can be criticized for being based on poorly done or inconclusive research. However, that doesn't mean that marijuana gets a clean bill of health. For about a day after a person smokes marijuana, his or her attention, coordination, and short-term memory are affected (Pope, Gruber, & Yurgelun-Tod, 1995). When surveyed at age 29, non-users are healthier, earn more, and are more satisfied with their

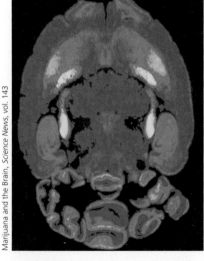

Marijuana and the Brain, *Science News*, vol. 143

▶▶**FIGURE 5.12** This thin slice of a rat's brain has been washed with a radioactive THC-like drug. Yellowish areas show where the brain is rich in THC receptors.

lives than people who smoke marijuana regularly (Ellickson, Martino, & Collins, 2004). Note the correlational nature of this latter finding: Increased levels of life satisfaction, health, and wealth are negatively related to marijuana use. Don't assume causation here (see Chapter 1).

Does marijuana affect overall intelligence? To answer this question, Peter Fried and his colleagues at Carleton University followed 77 people for about a decade. They noted the amount of marijuana use and administered an IQ test on different occasions over the study period. Heavy users (smoking at least five joints weekly) had significant declines in IQ scores compared to when they were non-users. Interestingly, however, heavy users who had quit the drug did not show intellectual deficits. Finally, current light smokers also showed no declines in IQ scores (Fried et al., 2002). Before you jump to the conclusion that only current heavy marijuana users are negatively affected, you must keep in mind two important points: First, this study assessed global or overall IQ levels, and global IQ scores may not be sensitive enough to pick up deficits in individual cognitive abilities, such as attention, memory, and so on. Second, this was one small study, and scientific consensus comes about through many studies that find similar results, so we need more research on this issue. What we can say for now is that the final truth about the impact of marijuana on intelligence is still to be unearthed.

Health Risks

Marijuana's long-term effects include the following health risks.

1. Marijuana smoke contains 50 percent more cancer-causing hydrocarbons and 16 times as much tar as tobacco smoke does. Thus, smoking several "joints" a week may be the equivalent of smoking a dozen cigarettes a day. In regular users, marijuana increases the risk of a variety of cancers, including prostate and cervical cancer (Hashibe et al., 2005).

2. Marijuana temporarily lowers sperm production in males, and users produce more abnormal sperm. This could be a problem for a man who is marginally fertile and wants to have a family (Schuel et al., 1999).

3. In experiments with female monkeys, THC causes abnormal menstrual cycles and disrupts ovulation. Other animal studies show that THC causes a higher rate of miscarriages and that it can reach the developing fetus. As is true for so many other drugs, it appears that marijuana should be avoided during pregnancy.

4. THC can suppress the body's immune system, possibly increasing the risk of disease (Turkington, 1986).

5. In some animals, marijuana causes genetic damage within cells of the body. It is not known to what extent this happens in humans, but it does suggest that marijuana may be detrimental to health (Zimmerman & Zimmerman, 1990).

6. Activity levels in the cerebellum are lower than normal in marijuana abusers. This may explain why chronic marijuana users tend to show some loss of coordination (Volkow et al., 1996).

7. There is some evidence that THC damages parts of the brain important for memory (Chan et al., 1998).

8. Children whose mothers smoked marijuana during pregnancy show lowered ability to succeed in challenging, goal-oriented activities (Fried & Smith, 2001; Noland et al., 2005).

Does marijuana have any medical benefits? It is claimed that smoking marijuana can relieve the excruciating pain experienced by glaucoma sufferers, can help increase the appetite of those suffering from HIV/AIDS (and thus combat weight-loss problems linked with the illness), and can reduce the nausea associated with chemotherapy in the treatment of cancer. There are many anecdotal reports about the alleged medical benefits of marijuana, but only a few controlled scientific studies on this issue have been performed to date. One

McGill University study compared the effects of smoked marijuana on chronic pain. People who smoked THC once daily for five days experienced more pain reduction and had improved quality of sleep than those who puffed on a placebo. This and other investigations are pointing to the definite medical benefits of using cannabis (Russell, 2007).

The Canadian government has passed legislation that allows people with certain conditions, including multiple sclerosis, spinal cord injury, cancer, HIV/AIDS, severe arthritis, and epilepsy, to smoke marijuana as a therapeutic agent. They must, however, obtain permission from the authorities before using the drug. Under the new law, people suffering from serious illnesses can apply to either grow their own marijuana or have someone else cultivate the plant for them (Health Canada, n.d.).

There have been plenty of emotional arguments on marijuana's potential health benefits. Some believe that the drug is a panacea for all sorts of medical problems, while others insist that marijuana is devoid of any healing properties, is a great menace to society, and therefore should remain banned. It is only through further well-designed scientific investigations that we can ever hope to learn the facts about this drug. All we can do at the moment is wait and let researchers reveal to us what's really in the pot.

Hallucinogens

The drug LSD (lysergic acid diethylamide) is perhaps the best-known hallucinogen. Even when taken in tiny amounts, LSD can produce hallucinations and psychosis-like disturbances in thinking and perception. Two other common hallucinogens are mescaline (peyote) and psilocybin ("magic mushrooms"). Incidentally, the drug PCP (phencyclidine) can have hallucinogenic effects. However, PCP, which is an anaesthetic, also has stimulant and depressant effects. This potent combination can cause extreme agitation; disorientation; violence; and, too often, tragedy.

Summary

Why is drug abuse such a common problem? People seek drug experiences for many reasons, ranging from curiosity and a desire to belong to a group, to a search for meaning or an escape from feelings of inadequacy. The best predictors of adolescent drug use and abuse are drug use by peers, parental drug use, delinquency, parental maladjustment, poor self-esteem, social non-conformity, and stressful life changes. A study conducted by Richard Tremblay and his colleagues at the University of Montreal found that adolescents who abuse drugs tend to be maladjusted, violent, alienated, impulsive, and emotionally distressed (Masse & Tremblay, 1997; Van Lier et al., 2009). Antisocial behaviour, school failure, and risky sexual behaviour are also commonly associated with drug abuse (Ary et al., 1999). Such patterns make it clear that taking drugs is a symptom, rather than a cause, of personal and social maladjustment (Ksir et al., 2006).

Many abusers turn to drugs in a self-defeating attempt to cope with life. All the frequently abused drugs produce immediate feelings of pleasure. The negative consequences follow much later. This combination of immediate pleasure and delayed punishment allows abusers to feel good on demand. In time, of course, most of the pleasure goes out of drug abuse, and the abuser's problems get worse. But if an abuser merely feels better (however briefly) after taking a drug, drug taking can become compulsive (Barrett, 1985). In contrast, people who stop using drugs often say that they quit because the drawbacks had come to exceed the benefits (Toneatto et al., 1999).

Although a large sum of money has been spent on drug enforcement in recent years, there has been an increase in the overall level of drug use in North America. Most drug use begins in early adolescence (Chen & Kandel, 1995). Given this fact, some experts believe that prevention through education and early intervention is the answer to drug problems (Julien, 2005). What do you think?

Cengage owned

Artists have tried at times to capture the effects of hallucinogens. Here, the artist depicts visual experiences he had while under the influence of LSD.

STUDY BREAK **Psychoactive Drugs**

Reflect

What legal drugs did you use in the last year? Did any have psychoactive properties? How do psychoactive drugs differ from other substances in their potential for abuse?

Learning Check

1. Which of the drugs listed below are known to cause a physical dependence?
   a. heroin
   b. morphine
   c. codeine
   d. methadone
   e. barbiturates
   f. alcohol
   g. LSD
   h. amphetamines
   i. nicotine
   j. cocaine
2. Amphetamine psychosis is similar to extreme _____, in which the individual feels threatened and suffers from delusions.
3. Cocaine is very similar to which of the following in its effects on the central nervous system?
   a. alcohol
   b. codeine
   c. cannabis
   d. amphetamine

4. The combination of _____ or _____ and alcohol can be fatal.
5. One drink starts a chain reaction leading to a second and a third in the crucial phase of problem drinking. T or F?
6. This country's biggest drug problem centres on abuse of
   a. marijuana
   b. alcohol
   c. LSD
   d. cocaine
7. Most experts now acknowledge that marijuana is physically addicting. T or F?

Critical Thinking

8. Many governments around the world continue to fund anti-smoking campaigns and smoking-related health research at the same time as subsidizing tobacco growers. Can you explain this contradiction?
9. Why do you think there is such a contrast between the laws regulating marijuana and those regulating alcohol and tobacco?

Answers

1. All but g 2. paranoia 3. d 4. barbiturates, tranquillizers 5. T 6. b 7. F 8. Neither can we. 9. Drug laws in Western societies reflect cultural values and historical patterns of use. Inconsistencies in the law often cannot be justified on the basis of pharmacology, health risks, or abuse potential.

Psychology in Action

EXPLORING AND USING DREAMS

Dream theorist Calvin Hall (1974) thought of dreams as plays and the dreamer as a playwright. Hall admitted that dream images and ideas tend to be more primitive than waking thoughts. Nevertheless, much can be learned by simply considering the setting, cast of characters, plot, and emotions portrayed in a dream.

Another dream theorist, Rosalind Cartwright, suggests that dreams are primarily "feeling statements." According to her, the overall emotional tone (underlying mood) of a dream is a major clue to its meaning. Is the dream comical, threatening, joyous, or depressing? Were you lonely, jealous, frightened, in love, or angry? Cartwright believes that exploring everyday dream life can be a source of personal enrichment and personal growth (Cartwright & Lamberg, 1992).

In many ways, dreams can be thought of as a message from yourself to yourself. Thus, the way to understand dreams is to remember them, write them down, look for the messages they contain, and become deeply acquainted with your own symbol system. Here's how.

How to Catch a Dream

1. Before retiring, plan to remember your dreams. Keep a pen and paper or a voice recorder beside your bed.
2. If possible, arrange to awaken gradually without an alarm. Natural awakening almost always follows soon after a REM period.
3. If you rarely remember your dreams, you may want to set an alarm clock to go off an hour before you usually awaken. Although less desirable than awakening naturally, this may let you catch a dream.

<SURVEY QUESTION
How are dreams used to promote personal understanding?

■ Table 5.5	Effects of Selected Drugs on Dreaming
Drug	**Effect**
Alcohol	Decrease
Amphetamines	Decrease
Barbiturates	Decrease
Caffeine	None
Cocaine	Decrease
LSD	Slight increase
Marijuana	Slight increase or no effect
Opiates	Decrease
Valium	Decrease

iStockphoto

4. Upon awakening, lie still and review the dream images with your eyes closed. Try to recall as many details as possible.

5. If you can, make your first dream record (whether by writing or by recording) with your eyes closed. Opening your eyes will disrupt dream recall.

6. Review the dream again and record as many additional details as you can remember. Dream memories disappear quickly. Be sure to describe feelings as well as the plot, characters, and actions of the dream.

7. Put your dreams into a permanent dream diary. Keep dreams in chronological order and review them periodically. This procedure will reveal recurrent themes, conflicts, and emotions. It almost always produces valuable insights.

8. Remember, a number of drugs suppress dreaming (see Table 5.5).

Dream Work

Because each dream has several possible meanings or levels of meaning, there is no fixed way to work with it. Telling the dream to others and discussing its meaning can be a good start. Describing it may help you relive some of the feelings in the dream. Also, family members or friends may be able to offer interpretations you are unaware of. Watch for verbal or visual puns and other playful elements in dreams. For example, if you dream that you are in a wrestling match and your arm is pinned behind your back, it may mean that you feel someone is "twisting your arm" in real life.

The meaning of most dreams will yield to a little detective work. Rosalind Cartwright suggests asking a series of questions about dreams you would like to understand (Cartwright & Lamberg, 1992):

Probing Dreams

1. Who was in the dream? Were there humans, animals, or mythical characters? Do you recognize any of the characters?

2. What social interactions were taking place? Were those interactions friendly? Aggressive? Sexual?

3. What activities were taking place? Were they physical activities or not?

4. Was there striving? Was the striving successful or not?

5. Was the dream about good fortune or misfortune?

6. What emotions were present in the dream? Was there anger, apprehension, confusion, happiness, or sadness?

7. What were the physical surroundings like? What was the setting? Were there any physical objects present? (Adapted from the Hall-Van de Castle system of dream content analysis; Domhoff, 2003.)

How would you try to find the meaning of a dream? A traditional approach is to look for symbolic messages as well as literal meanings. If you find yourself wearing a mask in a dream, for instance, it could relate to important roles that you play at school, work, or home. It could also mean that you want to hide or that you are looking forward to a costume party. However, to interpret a dream accurately you need to learn your own "vocabulary" of dream images and meanings. Keeping a dream diary is the first step toward gaining valuable insights.

Using Your Dreams

It is possible to learn to use our dreams for our own purposes. For example, as discussed below, nightmare sufferers can use special dream techniques to modify their own nightmares (Germain et al., 2004; Krakow & Zadra, 2006). Similarly, it is possible to use your dreams to enhance creativity (Stickgold & Walker, 2004).

History gives us many examples of dreams that have served as a pathway to creativity and discovery. A striking example is provided by Dr. Otto Loewi, a pharmacologist and recipient of a Nobel prize. Loewi had spent years studying the chemical transmission of nerve impulses. A tremendous breakthrough in his research came when he dreamed of an experiment three nights in a row. The first two nights he woke up and scribbled the experiment on a pad. But the next morning, he couldn't tell what the notes meant. On the third night, he got up after having the dream. This time, instead of making notes, he went straight to his laboratory and performed the crucial experiment. Loewi later said that if the experiment had occurred to him while awake he would have rejected it.

Loewi's experience gives some insight into using dreams to produce creative solutions. Inhibitions are reduced during dreaming, which may be especially useful in solving problems that require a fresh point of view.

Being able to take advantage of dreams for problem solving is improved if you "set" yourself before retiring. Before you go to bed, try to think intently about a problem you wish to solve. Steep yourself in the problem by stating it clearly and reviewing all relevant information. Then use the suggestions listed in the previous section to catch your dreams. While this method is not guaranteed to produce a novel solution or a new insight, it is certain to be an adventure. About half of a group of college students using the method for one week recalled a dream that helped them solve a personal problem (Barrett, 1993).

Lucid Dreaming

If you would like to press further into the territory of dreams, you may want to learn lucid dreaming, a relatively rare but fascinating experience. Have you ever been aware in your dream that you were dreaming? If you answered yes to the above question, you are what psychologists call a lucid dreamer. Many people have had at least one **lucid dream** in their lives, but only about 20 percent have them regularly (Blackmore, 1991).

Stephen La Berge and his colleagues at the Stanford University Sleep Research Center have used a unique approach to show that lucid dreams are real and that they occur during REM sleep. In the sleep lab, lucid dreamers agree to make prearranged signals when they become aware they are dreaming. One such signal is to look up abruptly in a dream, causing a distinct upward eye movement. Another signal is to clench the right and left fists (in the dream) in a prearranged pattern. In other words, lucid dreamers can partially overcome REM sleep paralysis. Such signals show very clearly that lucid dreaming and voluntary action in dreams is possible (La Berge, 1981, 1985; Moss, 1989).

How would a person go about learning to have lucid dreams? Dream researcher Stephen La Berge found he could greatly increase lucid dreaming by following this simple routine: When you awaken spontaneously from a dream, take a few minutes to try to memorize it. Next, engage in 10 to 15 minutes of reading or any other activity requiring full wakefulness. Then, while lying in bed and returning to sleep, say to yourself, "Next time I'm dreaming, I want to remember I'm dreaming." Finally, visualize yourself lying in bed asleep while in the dream you just recalled. At the same time, picture yourself realizing that you are dreaming. Follow this routine each time you awaken (substitute a dream memory from another occasion if you don't awaken from a dream). Researchers have also found that stimulation from the vestibular system tends to increase lucidity. Thus, sleeping in a hammock, on a boat, or on a waterbed might increase the number of lucid dreams you have (Leslie & Ogilvie, 1996).

Why would anyone want to have more lucid dreams? Researchers are interested in lucid dreams because they provide a tool for understanding dreaming (Paulsson & Parker, 2006). Using subjects who can signal while they are dreaming makes it possible to explore dreams with firsthand data from the dreamer's world itself.

Lucid dream A dream in which the dreamer feels awake and capable of normal thought and action.

One interesting application of lucid dreaming is in the treatment of nightmares. Researchers at the Sacré-Coeur Hospital in Montreal have taught people who have serious nightmares how to create lucid dreams, that is, to become aware that they are having a dream or, perhaps, a nightmare. After realizing that they were having a recurrent nightmare, clients were encouraged to change the direction of their terrifying dream to something that was not so unpleasant. Once people had succeeded in recognizing that they were dreaming and were able to alter the course of the unwanted dreams, the frequency and severity of their nightmares decreased substantially (Zadra & Pihl, 1997).

Consider yet another example of how lucid dreams can lead to emotional growth. A recently divorced woman kept dreaming that she was being swallowed by a giant wave. Rosalind Cartwright asked the woman to try swimming the next time the wave engulfed her. She did, with great determination, and the nightmare lost its terror. More important, her revised dream made her feel that she could cope with life again. For reasons such as this, people who have lucid dreams tend to feel a sense of emotional well-being (Wolpin et al., 1992).

The phenomenon of lucid dreaming raises intriguing questions about the nature of consciousness. To what extent do the rules that operate under waking consciousness—the ability to use logic, to have a coherent sense of oneself and one's surroundings—also operate during the nightly drama? If we can control the content of our dreams, should we still call dreams "dreams"? Is dreaming not just an extension of our waking consciousness, or vice versa? We do not have enough information to be able to answer these questions precisely, but we can certainly dream!

 STUDY BREAK   **Exploring and Using Dreams**

Reflect

Some people are very interested in remembering and interpreting their dreams. Others pay little attention to dreaming. What importance do you place on dreams? Do you think dreams and dream interpretation can increase self-awareness?

Learning Check

1. Calvin Hall's approach to dream interpretation emphasizes the setting, cast, plot, and emotions portrayed in a dream. T or F?
2. Rosalind Cartwright stresses that dreaming is a relatively mechanical process having little personal meaning. T or F?
3. Both alcohol and LSD cause a slight increase in dreaming. T or F?
4. Recent research shows that lucid dreaming occurs primarily during NREM sleep or micro-awakenings. T or F?

Critical Thinking

5. The possibility of having a lucid dream raises an interesting question: If you were dreaming right now, how could you prove it?

Answers

1. T 2. F 3. F 4. F 5. In waking consciousness, our actions have consequences that produce immediate sensory feedback. Dreams lack such external feedback. Thus, trying to walk through a wall or doing similar tests would reveal if you were dreaming.

CHAPTER IN REVIEW

Major Points

- Consciousness and altered states of awareness are core features of mental life.

- Sleep is necessary for survival; dreaming appears to contribute to memory consolidation and perhaps to general mental and emotional health.

- Sleep loss and sleep disorders are serious health problems that should be corrected when they persist.

- Dreams are at least as meaningful as waking thoughts. Whether they have deeper, symbolic meaning is still debated.

- Hypnosis is useful but not "magical." Hypnosis can change private experiences more readily than behaviours or habits.

- Meditation can be used to alter consciousness, as well as to reliably produce deep relaxation.

- Psychoactive drugs, which alter consciousness, are highly prone to abuse.

- Collecting and interpreting your dreams can promote self-awareness.

Summary

What is an altered state of consciousness?

- States of awareness that differ from normal, alert, waking consciousness are called altered states of consciousness (ASCs). Altered states are especially associated with sleep and dreaming, hypnosis, sensory deprivation, and psychoactive drugs.

- Cultural conditioning greatly affects what altered states a person recognizes, seeks, considers normal, and attains.

What are the effects of sleep loss or changes in sleep patterns?

- Sleep is an innate biological rhythm essential for survival. Higher animals and people deprived of sleep experience involuntary microsleeps.

- Moderate sleep loss mainly affects vigilance and performance on routine or boring tasks. Extended sleep loss can produce a temporary sleep-deprivation psychosis.

- Sleep patterns show some flexibility, but seven to eight hours remains average. The amount of daily sleep decreases steadily from birth to old age. Once-a-day sleep patterns, with a 2-to-1 ratio of waking and sleep, are most efficient for most people.

What are the different stages of sleep?

- Sleep occurs in four stages. Stage 1 is light sleep, and stage 4 is deep sleep. The sleeper alternates between stages 1 and 4 (passing through stages 2 and 3) several times each night.

- There are two basic sleep states, rapid eye movement (REM) sleep and non-REM (NREM) sleep. REM sleep is much more strongly associated with dreaming than non-REM sleep is.

- Dreaming and REMs occur mainly during light sleep, similar to stage 1. Dreaming is accompanied by emotional arousal but relaxation of the skeletal muscles.

- People deprived of dream sleep show a REM rebound when allowed to sleep without interruption. However, total sleep loss seems to be more important than loss of a single stage.

- In addition to several other possible functions, REM sleep appears to aid in the processing of memories.

What are the causes of sleep disorders and unusual sleep events?

- Sleepwalking and sleeptalking occur during NREM sleep. Night terrors occur in NREM sleep, whereas nightmares occur in REM sleep.

- Sleep apnea (interrupted breathing) is one source of insomnia and daytime hypersomnia (sleepiness).

- Insomnia may be temporary or chronic. When it is treated through the use of drugs, sleep quality is often lowered and drug-dependency insomnia may develop.

- Behavioural approaches to managing insomnia, such as sleep restriction and stimulus control, are quite effective.

Do dreams have meaning?

- Most dream content is about familiar settings, people, and actions. Dreams involve negative emotions more often than positive emotions.

- The Freudian, or psychoanalytic, view is that dreams express unconscious wishes, frequently hidden by dream symbols.

- Many theorists have questioned Freud's view of dreams. For example, the activation-synthesis hypothesis portrays dreaming as a physiological process.

How is hypnosis done, and what are its limitations?

- Hypnosis is an altered state characterized by narrowed attention and increased suggestibility.

- Hypnosis appears capable of producing relaxation, controlling pain, and altering perceptions. Stage hypnotism uses deception to simulate hypnosis.

What is meditation? Does it have any benefits?

- Concentrative meditation can be used to focus attention, alter consciousness, and reduce stress. Major benefits of meditation are its ability to interrupt anxious thoughts and to elicit the relaxation response.

- Brief exposure to sensory deprivation can also elicit the relaxation response. Under proper conditions, sensory deprivation may help break long-standing habits.

What are the effects of the more commonly used psychoactive drugs?

- A psychoactive drug is a substance that affects the brain in ways that alter consciousness. Most psychoactive drugs can be placed on a scale ranging from stimulation to depression.

- Drugs may cause a physical dependence (addiction) or a psychological dependence, or both. All psychoactive drugs can lead to psychological dependence.

- Stimulant drugs are readily abused because of the period of depression that often follows stimulation. The greatest risks are associated with amphetamines, cocaine, and nicotine, but even caffeine can be a problem. Nicotine includes the added risk of lung cancer, heart disease, and other health problems.

- Barbiturates and tranquillizers are depressant drugs whose action is similar to that of alcohol. Mixing barbiturates or tranquillizers and alcohol may result in a fatal drug interaction.

- Alcohol is the most heavily abused drug in common use today. The development of a drinking problem is usually marked by an initial phase of increasing consumption; a crucial phase, in which a single drink can set off a chain reaction; and a chronic phase, in which a person lives to drink and drinks to live.

- Marijuana is subject to an abuse pattern similar to alcohol. Studies have linked chronic marijuana use with lung cancer, various mental impairments, and other health problems.

- Drug abuse is related to a variety of factors, especially personal and social maladjustment, attempts to cope, the immediate reinforcing qualities of psychoactive drugs, peer group influences, and expectations about the value and effects of drugs.

- Proposed remedies for drug abuse have ranged from severe punishment to legalization. The search for a solution continues.

How are dreams used to promote personal understanding?

- Dreams may be used to promote self-understanding. Hall emphasized the setting, cast, plot, and emotions of a dream. Cartwright's view of dreams as feeling statements is also helpful.

- Dreams may be used for creative problem solving, especially when dream awareness is achieved through lucid dreaming.

Interactive Learning

Please visit http://www.psychologyjourney4ce.nelson.com for a list of weblinks to relevant psychology sites.

CourseMate

Access the interactive eBook and chapter-specific interactive learning tools, including flashcards, quizzes, videos, and more, in your Psychology CourseMate at NelsonBrain.com.

psyk.trek 4. Consciousness

TEST YOUR KNOWLEDGE

The questions that follow are only a sample of what you need to know. If you miss any of the items, review the entire chapter and the Study Breaks. Another way to prepare for tests is to use the Study Guide and the Practice Exams that are available with this text.

1. What is defined by changes in the quality and pattern of mental activity?
   a. an electroencephalograph (EEG)
   b. an alpha wave
   c. a beta wave
   d. an altered state of consciousness (ASC)

2. Alyssa experiences a microsleep while driving. What does her behaviour most likely indicate?
   a. Alyssa was producing mostly beta waves.
   b. Alyssa had high levels of sleep hormones in her bloodstream.
   c. Alyssa switched from delta waves to alpha waves.
   d. Alyssa was sleep deprived.

3. What is produced by a person who is in deep sleep?
   a. beta waves   b. alpha waves
   c. delta waves   d. rapid eye movements (REMs)

4. Which of the following is normally *not* compatible with moving your arms and legs while asleep?
   a. rapid eye movement (REM) sleep
   b. sleep spindles
   c. delta waves
   d. non-rapid eye movement (NREM) sleep

5. What sleep disorder leads to sudden daytime sleep attacks?
   a. narcolepsy   b. REM behaviour disorder
   c. somnambulism   d. sleep spindling

6. What sleep disorder is treated by sleep restriction and stimulus control?
   a. sleep apnea   b. sleeptalking
   c. night terrors   d. insomnia

7. Which of the following includes the function of sorting and integrating memories?
   a. stage 1 sleep   b. REM sleep
   c. deep sleep   d. NREM sleep

8. Which explanation of dream content includes the concepts of wish fulfillment and dream symbols?
   a. the activation-synthesis hypothesis
   b. neurocognitive dream theory
   c. imagery rehearsal theory
   d. psychoanalytic theory

9. Tests of hypnotic susceptibility measure a person's tendency to respond to which of the following?
   a. suggestion   b. imagery rehearsal
   c. stimulus control   d. activation-synthesis
      techniques

10. According to research, hypnosis cannot produce which of the following?
    a. unusual strength   b. changes in memory
    c. pain relief   d. sensory changes

11. During hypnosis, which brain lobes show increased activity in PET scans when people are asked to relax?
    a. the occipital lobes   b. the temporal lobes
    c. the frontal lobes   d. the parietal lobes

12. Which terms do *not* belong together?
    a. concentrative meditation—relaxation response
    b. sensory deprivation—relaxation response
    c. receptive meditation—mantra
    d. sensory deprivation—altered state of consciousness

13. What is affected when addictive drugs stimulate the brain's reward circuitry?
    a. neurotransmitters   b. alpha waves
    c. tryptophan levels   d. delta spindles

14. What is drug tolerance most closely associated with?
    a. psychological dependence b. marijuana
    c. withdrawal symptoms   d. anhedonia

15. In terms of its effects on the nervous system, cocaine is most similar to which of the following?
    a. marijuana   b. benzodiazepine
    c. serotonin   d. amphetamines

16. Use of which drug has the major risks of hyperthermia and severe liver damage?
    a. marijuana
    b. benzodiazepine
    c. methylenedioxymethamphetamine (MDMA)
    d. gamma-hydroxybutyrate (GHB)

17. Which of the following combinations can lead to a dangerous drug interaction?
    a. marijuana and amphetamines
    b. barbiturates and alcohol
    c. alcohol and cocaine
    d. marijuana and tetrahydrocannabinol (THC)

18. Treatment for alcohol dependence begins with sobering up the person and cutting off the supply. What is this treatment process called?
    a. "hitting bottom"   b. the crucial phase
    c. detoxification   d. clinical anhedonia

19. Drug abuse is partly explained by the fact that psychoactive drugs produce immediate pleasure and which of the following?
    a. somnambulism   b. self-esteem
    c. delayed punishment   d. brain carcinogens

20. Which of the following causes a decrease in the frequency of dreams?
    a. LSD   b. alcohol
    c. caffeine   d. chocolate

chapter 6

Conditioning and Learning

JOURNEY INTO PSYCHOLOGY: WHAT DID YOU LEARN TODAY?

Imagine that one night you and a friend go out for dinner to a great new restaurant that everyone's talking about. Feeling adventurous, or maybe amorous, you order raw oysters for the first time. They take a little getting used to, but you quickly learn to appreciate them, and happily scarf down three orders. Later that night, you awaken from a sound sleep only to find that you are horribly nauseated. You make it to the bathroom just in time. For a while, you alternate between running to the bathroom and staggering back to bed. Finally, you give up and, taking your blanket, curl up in a miserable heap on the bathroom floor. Although for a while you think you are going to die, in a day or two you're back to normal—at least until the next time someone offers you a raw oyster. To your surprise, you suddenly feel sick. You can't even look at oysters.

Your reaction to oysters is a result of classical conditioning, one of the topics of this chapter.

Now, let's say that you are at school and you feel like you are "starving to death." You locate a vending machine and deposit your last loonie to buy a chocolate bar. Then you press the button, and ... nothing happens. Being civilized and in complete control, you press the other buttons and try the coin return. Still nothing. Impulsively, you give the machine a little kick (just to let it know who's the boss). Then, as you turn away, out pops a chocolate bar plus 25 cents in change. Once this happens, chances are good that you will repeat the "kicking response" in the future. If it pays off several times more, kicking vending machines may become a regular feature of your behaviour. In this case, learning is based on operant conditioning (also called instrumental learning).

Classical and operant conditioning reach into every corner of our lives. Are you ready to learn more about learning? If so, read on!

 Survey Questions

- What is learning?
- What is classical conditioning? How does it occur?
- How are emotions affected by conditioning?
- What is operant conditioning? How does it occur?
- What are the different kinds of operant reinforcement?
- Can patterns of reward influence our behaviour?
- How does punishment affect behaviour?
- What is cognitive learning?
- Does learning occur by imitation?
- Can we use the principles of conditioning to help solve practical problems?

WHAT IS LEARNING—DOES PRACTICE MAKE PERFECT?

Most behaviour is learned. Imagine if you suddenly lost all you had ever learned. What could you do? You would be unable to read, write, or speak. You couldn't feed yourself, find your way home, drive a car, play the bassoon, or "party." Needless to say, you would be totally incapacitated.

Learning is obviously important. What's a formal definition of learning? **Learning** is a relatively permanent change in behaviour due to experience (Powell, Symbaluk & Honey, 2009). Notice that this definition excludes both temporary changes and more permanent changes caused by motivation, fatigue, maturation, disease, injury, or drugs. Each of these can alter behaviour, but none qualify as learning.

Types of Learning

As the opening vignette illustrates, there are different types of learning. **Associative learning** occurs whenever an organism forms a simple association among various stimuli and/or responses. Humans share the capacity for associative learning with many other species,

<SURVEY QUESTION
What is learning?

Learning Any relatively permanent change in behaviour that can be attributed to experience.

Associative learning The formation of simple associations between various stimuli and responses.

Cognitive learning Higher-level learning involving thinking, knowing, understanding, and anticipation.

Reinforcement Any event that increases the probability that a particular response will occur.

Response Any identifiable behaviour.

Antecedents Events that precede a response.

Consequences Effects that follow a response.

including dogs, rats, and beetles. In a moment, we will explore two types of associative learning—classical conditioning and operant conditioning.

Humans also engage in **cognitive learning,** which refers to understanding, knowing, anticipating, or otherwise making use of information-rich higher mental processes. The more complex forms of cognitive learning, such as learning from written language (like this book), are unique to humans. However, some animal species do engage in simpler forms of cognitive learning.

Associative Learning

Isn't learning the result of practice? It depends on what you mean by practice. Merely repeating a response will not necessarily produce learning. You could close your eyes and swing a tennis racquet hundreds of times without learning anything about tennis. Reinforcement is the key to most learning. **Reinforcement** refers to any event that increases the probability that a response will occur again. A **response** is any identifiable behaviour. Responses may be observable actions, such as blinking, eating a piece of candy, or turning a doorknob. They can also be internal, such as having a faster heartbeat.

To teach a dog a trick, you could reinforce correct responses by giving the dog some food each time it sits up. Similarly, you could teach a child to be neat by praising her for picking up her toys. Learning can also occur in other, less obvious ways. For instance, if a boy gets bitten by a dog, he may learn to fear dogs. In this case, the boy's fear is strengthened by the pain he feels immediately after seeing the dog. Later, you'll discover how such varied experiences lead to learning.

Antecedents and Consequences

Unlocking the secrets of learning begins with noting what happens before and after a response. Events that precede a response are called **antecedents.** For example, Ashleigh, who is three, has learned that when she hears a truck pull into the driveway, it means that Daddy is home. Ashleigh runs to the front door, where she gets a hug from her father. Effects that follow a response are **consequences.** The hug is what reinforces Ashleigh's tendency to run to the door. As this suggests, paying careful attention to the "before and after" of learning is a key to understanding it.

There are two basic kinds of learning: classical and operant conditioning (see Figure 6.1). Classical conditioning is based on what happens *before* a response, while operant conditioning is based on what comes *after* a response occurs. Let's look at each one in more detail.

▸▸**FIGURE 6.1** In classical conditioning, a stimulus that does not produce a response is paired with a stimulus that does elicit a response. After many such pairings, the stimulus that previously had no effect begins to produce the same response on its own. In the example shown, a horn precedes a puff of air to the eye. Eventually, the horn alone will produce an eye-blink. In operant conditioning, a response that is followed by a reinforcing consequence becomes more likely to occur on future occasions. In the example shown, a dog learns to sit up when it hears a whistle.

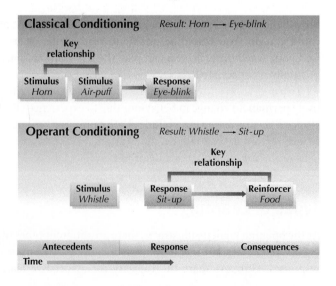

CLASSICAL CONDITIONING—DOES THE NAME PAVLOV RING A BELL?

How was classical conditioning discovered? At the beginning of the 20th century, something happened in the lab of Russian physiologist Ivan Pavlov that brought him the Nobel Prize. The event now seems so trivial that a lesser person might have ignored it: Pavlov's subjects drooled at him.

Actually, Pavlov was studying digestion. To observe salivation, he placed meat powder or some tidbit on a dog's tongue. After doing this many times, Pavlov noticed that his dogs were salivating before the food reached their mouths. Later, the dogs began to salivate even when they saw Pavlov enter the room (Hergenhahn, 2009). Pavlov believed that salivation is an automatic, inherited **reflex.** The dogs were *supposed* to salivate when he put food in their mouths, but they were *not supposed* to salivate when they merely saw him. This was a change in behaviour due to experience. For the animals to salivate at the mere sight of food, some type of learning had to have occurred. Pavlov called it conditioning (see Figure 6.2). Because of its importance in psychology's history, it is now called **classical conditioning** (also known as Pavlovian conditioning or respondent conditioning).

<SURVEY QUESTION
What is classical conditioning? How does it occur?

▶▶**FIGURE 6.2** An apparatus for classical conditioning. A tube carries saliva from the dog's mouth to a lever that activates a recording device (far left). During conditioning, various stimuli can be paired with a dish of food placed in front of the dog. The device pictured here is more elaborate than the one Pavlov used in his early experiments.

Pavlov's Experiment

How did Pavlov study conditioning? After Pavlov observed that his dogs seemed to salivate in anticipation of receiving the meat powder, he began to study the phenomenon more closely (see Figure 6.2). To begin, he rang a bell. At first, the bell was a neutral stimulus (it did not evoke salivation). Immediately after Pavlov rang the bell, he would place meat powder on the dog's tongue, which caused reflex salivation. This sequence was repeated many times: bell, meat powder, salivation; bell, meat powder, salivation. Eventually (as conditioning took place), the dogs began to salivate when they heard the bell (see Figure 6.3). By association, the bell began to elicit the same response as food. To show this, Pavlov sometimes rang the bell alone. The dog would salivate, even when no food was present.

The bell in Pavlov's experiment starts out as a **neutral stimulus (NS).** In time, the bell becomes a **conditioned stimulus (CS)** (a stimulus that, because of learning, will

Reflex An innate, automatic response to a stimulus (for example, an eye-blink).

Classical conditioning A form of learning in which reflex responses are associated with new stimuli.

Neutral stimulus (NS) A stimulus that does not evoke a response.

Conditioned stimulus (CS) A stimulus that evokes a response because it has been repeatedly paired with an unconditioned stimulus.

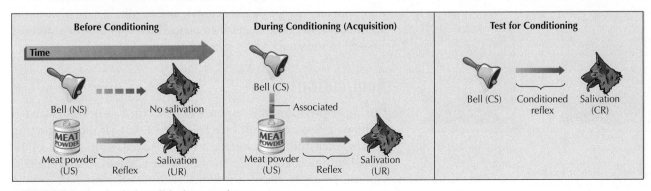

▶▶**FIGURE 6.3** The classical conditioning procedure.

■ Table 6.1   Elements of Classical Conditioning

Element	Symbol	Description	Example
Neutral stimulus	NS	A stimulus that does not elicit a response	Bell
Unconditioned stimulus	US	A stimulus innately capable of eliciting a response	Meat powder
Conditioned stimulus	CS	A stimulus that elicits a response because it has been repeatedly paired with an unconditioned stimulus	Bell
Unconditioned response	UR	An innate reflex response elicited by an unconditioned stimulus	Reflex salivation
Conditioned response	CR	A learned response elicited by a conditioned stimulus	Salivation

Unconditioned stimulus (US) A stimulus innately capable of eliciting a response.

Unconditioned response (UR) An innate reflex response elicited by an unconditioned stimulus.

Conditioned response (CR) A learned response elicited by a conditioned stimulus.

Acquisition The period in conditioning during which a response is reinforced.

elicit a response). The meat powder is an **unconditioned stimulus (US)** (a stimulus innately capable of eliciting a response). Notice that the dog did not have to learn to respond to the US. Such stimuli naturally elicit reflexes or emotional reactions.

Since a reflex is innate, or "built in," it is called an **unconditioned** (non-learned) **response (UR).** Reflex salivation was the UR in Pavlov's experiment. Besides salivation, other examples of reflex responses include contraction of the pupil in response to a bright light and extension of the lower leg when the area just below the knee is tapped. Babies have several reflexes, which are described in Chapter 3 (page 99); the reflex arc is explained in Chapter 2 (page 64).

When Pavlov's bell also produced salivation, the dog was making a new response. Thus, salivation had become a **conditioned** (learned) **response (CR)** (see Figure 6.3). Table 6.1 summarizes the important elements of classical conditioning.

It's hard to keep all these terms straight. Are they really necessary? Yes, because they help us recognize similarities in various instances of learning. Let's return to the example in Figure 6.1. A puff of air to the surface of your eye will reliably elicit a blink (it's a reflex). If a horn is sounded before every puff of air, eventually you will blink when you hear the horn.

We can summarize the terms in this example as follows:

Before Conditioning	*Example*
US ⟶ UR	Puff of air ⟶ eye-blink
NS ⟶ no effect	Horn ⟶ no effect

After conditioning	*Example*
CS ⟶ CR	Horn ⟶ eye-blink

PRINCIPLES OF CLASSICAL CONDITIONING— TEACH YOUR LITTLE BROTHER TO SALIVATE

To observe conditioning, you could ring a bell, squirt lemon juice into a child's mouth (we'll call him Randy), and condition salivation to the bell. Randy's reactions might then be used to explore other aspects of classical conditioning. Let's see how this occurs.

Acquisition

During **acquisition,** the response to be learned must be associated with any relevant stimuli (see Figure 6.4). Classical conditioning occurs when the CS is followed by, or paired with, an unconditioned stimulus. For Randy, the bell is the CS; salivating is the UR; and the sour lemon juice is an unconditioned stimulus (US). To elicit salivating to the bell, we must link the bell with the lemon juice. Conditioning will be most rapid if the

FIGURE 6.4 Acquisition and extinction of a conditioned response. (After Pavlov, 1927.)

US (lemon juice) follows immediately after the CS (the bell). With most reflexes, the optimal delay between CS and US is from one-half second to about five seconds (Chance, 2009).

Higher-Order Conditioning

Once a response is learned, it can bring about **higher-order conditioning** (Lefrançois, 2006). In this case, a well-learned CS is used to bring about further learning. That is, the CS has become strong enough to be used like an unconditioned stimulus. Let's illustrate again with our salivating child.

As a result of earlier learning, the bell now makes Randy salivate. (No more lemon juice is needed.) To go a step further, you could clap your hands and then ring the bell. (Again, without the lemon juice.) Through higher-order conditioning, Randy would soon learn to salivate when you clapped your hands.

Higher-order conditioning extends learning one or more steps beyond the original conditioned stimulus. Many advertisers use this effect by pairing images that evoke good feelings (such as people smiling and having fun) with pictures of their products. Obviously, they hope that you will learn, by association, to feel good when you see their products (Priluck & Till, 2004). Can you think of any examples of this?

Expectancies

Pavlov believed that classical conditioning did not involve any higher mental processes. Today, many psychologists believe that classical conditioning is related to information that might aid our survival. According to this **informational view,** we look for associations among events. Doing so creates new mental **expectancies,** or expectations about how events are interconnected.

How does classical conditioning alter expectancies? Notice that the conditioned stimulus reliably precedes the unconditioned stimulus. Because it does, the CS predicts the US (Rescorla, 1987). During conditioning, the brain learns to expect that the US will follow the CS. As a result, the brain prepares the body to respond to the US. Here's an example: When you are about to get a shot with a hypodermic needle, your muscles tighten and there is a catch in your breathing. Why? Because your body is preparing for pain. You have learned to expect that getting poked with a needle will hurt. This expectancy, which was acquired during classical conditioning, changes your behaviour.

Extinction and Spontaneous Recovery

After conditioning has occurred, what would happen if the US no longer followed the CS? If the US never again follows the CS, conditioning will fade away. Let's return to our boy Randy and the bell. If you ring the bell many times and do not follow it with lemon juice, his expectancy that "bell precedes lemon juice" will weaken. As it does, Randy will lose his tendency to salivate when he hears the bell. Thus, we see that a classically conditioned response can be weakened by removing the unconditioned stimulus (see Figure 6.4). This process is called **extinction.**

If conditioning takes a while to build up, shouldn't it take time to reverse? Yes. In fact, it may take several extinction sessions to completely reverse conditioning. Let's say that we ring the bell until Randy quits responding. It might seem that extinction is complete. However, he will probably respond to the bell again on the following day, at least at first (Rescorla, 2004). The reappearance of a response following its apparent extinction is called **spontaneous recovery.** It explains why people who have had a terrifying automobile accident may need many slow, calm rides before their fear of driving extinguishes.

Higher-order conditioning Classical conditioning in which a conditioned stimulus is used to bring about further learning; that is, a CS is used as if it were a US.

Informational view A perspective that explains learning in terms of information imparted by events in the environment.

Expectancy An anticipation concerning future events or relationships.

Extinction The weakening of a conditioned response through removal of the unconditioned stimulus.

Spontaneous recovery The reappearance of a learned response after its apparent extinction.

Generalization

Stimulus generalization The tendency to respond to stimuli similar but not identical to a conditioned stimulus.

Stimulus discrimination The learned ability to respond differently to similar stimuli.

After conditioning, other stimuli that are similar to the CS may also elicit a response. This is called **stimulus generalization.** For example, we might find that Randy salivates to the sound of a ringing telephone or doorbell, even though they were never used as conditioning stimuli.

It is easy to see the value of stimulus generalization. Consider the child who burns her finger while playing with matches. Most likely, lighted matches will become conditioned fear stimuli for her. But will she fear only matches? Because of stimulus generalization, she should also have a healthy fear of flames from lighters, fireplaces, stoves, and so forth. It's fortunate that generalization extends learning to related situations. Otherwise, we would be far less adaptable.

As you may have guessed, stimulus generalization has limits. As stimuli become less like the original CS, responding decreases. If you condition a person to blink each time you play a particular note on a piano, blinking will decline as you play higher or lower notes. If the notes are much higher or lower, the person will not respond at all (see Figure 6.5). Stimulus generalization explains why some stores carry imitations of nationally known products. For many customers, positive attitudes conditioned to real products tend to generalize to cheaper knockoffs (Till & Priluck, 2000).

Discrimination

Let's consider one more idea with our salivating child (who by now must be ready to hide in the closet). Suppose Randy is again conditioned with a bell as the CS. As an experiment, we occasionally sound a buzzer instead of the bell, but never follow it with the US (lemon juice). At first, the buzzer produces salivation (because of generalization). But after hearing the buzzer several times more, the child will stop responding to it. Randy has now learned to discriminate, or respond differently, to the bell and the buzzer. In essence, his generalized response to the buzzer has extinguished.

Stimulus discrimination is the ability to respond differently to various stimuli. As an example, you might remember the feelings of anxiety or fear you had as a child when your mother's or father's voice changed to its you're-about-to-get-yelled-at tone. (Or the dreaded give-me-that-remote-right-now tone.) Most children quickly learn to discriminate voice tones associated with punishment from those associated with praise or affection.

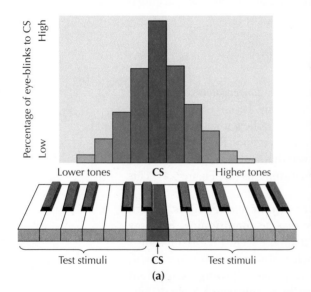

(a)

(b)

▸▸**FIGURE 6.5** (a) Stimulus generalization. Stimuli similar to the CS also elicit a response. (b) This cat has learned to salivate when it sees a cat food box. Because of stimulus generalization, it also salivates when it is shown a similar-looking box.

CLASSICAL CONDITIONING IN HUMANS— AN EMOTIONAL TOPIC

How much human learning is based on classical conditioning? At its simplest, classical conditioning depends on reflex responses. As mentioned earlier, a reflex is a dependable, inborn stimulus-and-response connection. For example, your hand reflexively draws back from pain. Bright light causes the pupil of the eye to contract. A puff of air directed at your eye will make you blink. (See Clinical File: "Blink if Your Brain Is Healthy.") Various foods elicit salivation. Any of these reflexes, and others as well, can be associated with a new stimulus. At the very least, you have probably noticed how your mouth waters when you see or smell a bakery. Even pictures of food may make you salivate (a photo of a sliced lemon is great for this).

Conditioned Emotional Responses

Of larger importance, perhaps, are the more subtle ways that conditioning affects us. In addition to simple reflexes, more complex emotional, or "gut," responses may be linked to new stimuli. For instance, if your face reddened when you were punished as a child, you may blush now when you are embarrassed or ashamed. Or think about the effects of associating pain with a dentist's office during your first visit. On later visits, did your heart pound and your palms sweat before the dentist even began to drill?

Many involuntary, autonomic nervous system responses ("fight-or-flight" reflexes) are linked with new stimuli and situations by classical conditioning. For example, conditioned responses aggravate many cases of hypertension (high blood pressure). Traffic jams, arguments with a partner, and similar situations can become conditioned stimuli that trigger a dangerous rise in blood pressure (Reiff, Katkin, & Friedman, 1999).

Of course, emotional conditioning also applies to animals. One of the most common mistakes people make with pets (especially dogs) is hitting them if they do not come when called. Calling the animal then becomes a conditioned stimulus for fear and withdrawal. No wonder the pet disobeys when called on future occasions. Parents who belittle, scream at, or physically abuse their children make the same mistake.

Learned Fears

Fears are adaptive responses that allow us to respond quickly to a threatening situation. When a fear gets out of hand, it is known as a phobia. A **phobia** is a fear that persists even when no realistic danger exists. Some phobias are also based on emotional conditioning. Fears of animals, water, heights, thunder, fire, bugs, elevators, and the like are common.

<SURVEY QUESTION
How are emotions affected by conditioning?

Phobia An intense and unrealistic fear of some specific object or situation.

THE CLINICAL FILE

Blink If Your Brain Is Healthy

Dementia is a terrifying mental disorder. Imagine how it must feel to lose your ability to read, think, carry on a conversation, recognize friends and family members, and do ordinary tasks. Dementia is caused by a number of different diseases and conditions of the brain, including many associated with aging. Eventually, people with dementia suffer major declines in memory, judgment, language, and thinking. Yet, in its early stages, dementia may be nearly invisible.

It is important to detect dementia as soon as possible so that treatment can begin early. Early treatment may slow the progress of the disorder. However, most screening tests for dementia are based on higher mental abilities, such as memory or reasoning. By the time a person has problems in these areas, dementia is usually fairly advanced.

There is evidence, however, that classical conditioning might be used to identify people in the early stages of dementia (as much as six years before any signs of cognitive impairment). Research has found that people who later go on to develop dementia are slower to develop a classically conditioned eye-blink than those who do not develop the disorder (Woodruff-Pak, 2001).

▸▸**FIGURE 6.6** Hypothetical example of a CER becoming a phobia. Child approaches dog (a) and is frightened by it (b). Fear generalizes to other household pets (c) and later to virtually all furry animals (d).

(a)

(b)

(c)

(d)

Conditioned emotional response (CER) An emotional response that has been linked to a previously non-emotional stimulus by classical conditioning.

Desensitization Reducing fear or anxiety by repeatedly exposing a person to emotional stimuli while the person is deeply relaxed.

Psychologists believe that many phobias begin as **conditioned emotional responses (CERs).** (A CER is a learned emotional reaction to a previously neutral stimulus.) People who have phobias can sometimes trace their fears to a time when they were frightened, injured, or upset by a particular stimulus, although not everyone with a specific phobia can identify the original experience (Coelho & Purkis, 2009). Many phobias, for example, spider phobia, start in childhood (King, Muris, & Ollendick, 2005). Just one bad experience with a spider may condition fears that last for years (de Jong & Muris, 2002).

Stimulus generalization and higher-order conditioning can broaden CERs to other stimuli (Gewirtz & Davis, 1998). As a result, what began as a limited fear may become a disabling phobia (see Figure 6.6).

During a CER, the area of your brain known as the amygdala becomes more active, producing feelings of fear. The amygdala is part of the limbic system, which is responsible for other emotions as well (see Chapter 2). Cognitive learning has little effect on these lower brain areas (Olsson, Nearing, & Phelps, 2007). Perhaps that's why merely reading about how to control fears cannot readily ease fears and phobias. However, conditioned fears do respond to a therapy called **desensitization.** This is done by gradually exposing the phobic person to feared stimuli while he or she remains calm and relaxed. For example, people who have a fear of heights (acrophobia) may slowly be taken to ever-higher elevations until their fears extinguish (Wiederhold & Wiederhold, 2005). (See Chapter 13 for more information about therapies based on learning principles.)

Undoubtedly, we acquire many of our likes, dislikes, and fears as CERs. As noted before, advertisers try to achieve the same effect by pairing products with pleasant images and music. So do many students on a first date.

Vicarious, or Second-Hand, Conditioning

Conditioning also occurs indirectly, which adds to its impact on us. Let's say, for example, that you watch another person get an electric shock. Each time, a signal light comes on before the shock is delivered. Even if you don't receive a shock yourself, you will soon develop a CER to the light (Bandura & Rosenthal, 1966). Children who learn to fear thunder by watching their parents react to it have undergone similar conditioning. Similarly, people who counsel traumatized victims of sexual abuse can develop vicarious trauma (Way et al., 2004; Rothschild & Rand, 2006).

Vicarious classical conditioning occurs if we learn to respond emotionally to a stimulus by observing another person's emotional reactions (Olsson et al., 2007). Such "second-hand" learning affects feelings in many situations. How, for instance, does a child learn to fear snakes and respond emotionally to mere pictures of them? Being told that "snakes are dangerous" may not explain the child's emotional response. More likely, the child has observed others reacting fearfully to the word snake or to snake images on television (King et al., 2005). As children grow up, the emotions of parents, friends, and relatives may add to fears of snakes, caves, spiders, heights, and other terrors. Even horror movies filled with screaming actors may have a similar effect.

The emotional attitudes we develop toward foods, political parties, ethnic groups, escalators—whatever—are probably conditioned not only by direct experiences but also vicariously. No one is born prejudiced—attitudes are learned. Parents may do well to look in a mirror if they wonder how or where a child "picked up" a particular fear or emotional attitude.

Conditioned Taste Aversions

Remember the student described at the beginning of this chapter who became ill after eating oysters and afterwards felt sick at the sight of them? This is an example of a **conditioned taste aversion,** a negative response to a specific food. This is also due to classical conditioning. Conditioned taste aversions develop when a novel or unfamiliar food is associated with an unpleasant reaction (in this case, nausea and vomiting). It doesn't matter whether the food actually caused the illness or not. The unfamiliar food, like the oysters in this example, is the conditioned stimulus. The unconditioned stimulus is whatever caused the illness in the first place—a virus, too much alcohol, a bad oyster, whatever. The vomiting is the unconditioned response, and the nausea you feel when you now see or smell oysters is the conditioned response. The association is made specifically to the food—its taste and smell—and not to other aspects of the situation, such as the pattern on the china or the person you were with (fortunately). And it is usually unfamiliar foods, or those you eat infrequently, rather than familiar ones, that cause the development of taste aversions (but see also Clinical File: "Coping with Chemo").

Classical Conditioning and Tolerance to Drugs

Emeritus Professor of Psychology Shepard Siegel and his colleagues at McMaster University have done extensive research on the role of classical conditioning in the development of tolerance to drugs. When a person uses drugs, certain physiological responses compensate for the effects of

> **Vicarious classical conditioning**
> Classical conditioning brought about by observing another person react to a particular stimulus.
>
> **Conditioned taste aversion** A learned aversive response to a specific food.

THE CLINICAL FILE

Coping with Chemo

Our hearts go out to children with cancer. Even the treatment, chemotherapy, makes them miserable because it causes nausea and vomiting. In a cruel twist, after a few treatments, nausea can occur even when no chemotherapy is scheduled. Typically, it is triggered by certain sights or tastes, like the sight of the treatment centre or the taste of a food the child ate before an earlier chemotherapy session.

In classical conditioning terms, chemotherapy is a US that leads to nausea, which is a UR. The sight of the treatment centre or the taste of food eaten before treatment is initially a neutral stimulus that becomes associated with nausea and vomiting, making it a CS. These sights or tastes can now elicit anticipatory nausea (a CR) even at times when the child doesn't receive chemotherapy (Chance, 2006).

In nature, many species are *biologically prepared* to associate specific locations and tastes with nausea. If animals eat

contaminated food, get sick, and vomit, later the same locations or tastes may trigger anticipatory nausea and vomiting. These reactions discourage animals from eating potentially dangerous food. Unfortunately, conditioned nausea only complicates treatment for young cancer patients (and older ones, too). If Gina eats pizza, her favourite meal, before she has a chemotherapy session, the taste of pizza may come to make her feel sick.

Is there any way to prevent conditioned nausea? No, but classical conditioning can provide some relief (Taylor, 2002). Meals eaten before chemotherapy can be strongly flavoured with an unusual taste, such as peppermint. The unique flavour overshadows other tastes, which don't become linked with nausea (Bovbjerg et al., 1992). In this way, Gina can continue to enjoy her favourite meal.

STUDY BREAK   Classical Conditioning

Reflect

US, CS, UR, CR—How will you remember these terms? First, you should note that we are talking about either a stimulus (S) or a response (R). What else do we need to know? Each S or R can be either conditioned (C) or unconditioned (U).

Can a stimulus evoke a response before any learning has occurred? If it can, then it's a US. Do you have to learn to respond to the stimulus? If you do, then it's a CS.

Does a response occur without being learned? If it does, then it's a UR. If it has to be learned, then it's a CR.

Learning Check

1. In learning, antecedents are the effects that follow a response. T or F?
2. Classical conditioning was studied extensively by the Russian physiologist _____.
3. Classical conditioning is strengthened when the _____ follows the _____.

a. CS, US	b. US, CS
c. UR, CR	d. CS, CR

4. The informational view says that classical conditioning is based on changes in mental _____ about the CS and US.
5. Training that inhibits (or weakens) a conditioned response is called _____.
6. Psychologists theorize that many phobias begin when a CER generalizes to other, similar situations. T or F?
7. Conditioning brought about by observing pain, joy, or fear in others is called _____ conditioning.

Critical Thinking

8. Lately you have been getting a shock of static electricity every time you touch a door handle. Now you find yourself flinching every time you open any door. Can you analyze this situation in terms of classical conditioning?

Answers

1. F 2. Ivan Pavlov 3. b 4. expectancies 5. extinction 6. T 7. vicarious 8. Door handles have become conditioned stimuli that elicit the reflex withdrawal and muscle tensing that normally follows getting a shock. This conditioned response has also generalized to other handles. The CS would be the sight of the door handle, the US is the shock. The UR is flinching in response to the pain of the shock, and the CR is flinching when your hand approaches any door handle.

Operant conditioning Learning based on the consequences of responding.

Law of effect Responses that lead to desirable effects are repeated; those that produce undesirable results are not.

the drug. For example, if the drug causes the heart to beat more slowly, physiological changes in the body speed up the heart rate to compensate. Because these physiological responses occur at the same time as the drug use, they become classically conditioned to injection of the drug. That is, the drug is an unconditioned stimulus for these responses. Since these changes compensate to some extent for the effects of the drug, the person will need more of the drug to experience the same effects. Environmental cues, such as the location and the paraphernalia used to prepare the drugs for injection, also become associated with these compensatory responses by classical conditioning. When people use drugs in unfamiliar settings, the compensatory responses normally elicited by these environmental cues do not occur, and the drug user may suffer a fatal overdose even though the amount of drug taken is within their tolerance level. Classical conditioning can also explain why people may experience drug cravings after they are released from detoxification programs and return to their old haunts. Previously conditioned environmental cues can elicit compensatory physiological responses, which are interpreted as withdrawal symptoms and trigger the cravings (Ramos et al., 2002; Siegel, 1999, 2002; Siegel et al., 2000).

OPERANT CONDITIONING—CAN PIGEONS PLAY PING-PONG?

SURVEY QUESTION>
What is operant conditioning? How does it occur?

As stated earlier, in **operant conditioning** (or instrumental learning) we associate responses with their consequences. The basic principle is simple: Acts that are reinforced tend to be repeated (Mazur, 2006). Pioneer learning theorist Edward L. Thorndike called this the **law of effect,** that is, the probability of a response recurring is altered by the effect it has (Schultz & Schultz, 2008). Learning is strengthened each time a response is followed by a satisfying state of affairs. You are likely to keep telling a joke if people laugh at it. If the first three people who hear the joke groan, you may never tell it again.

Classical conditioning is passive. It simply "happens to" the learner when a US follows a CS. In operant conditioning, the learner actively "operates on" the environment.

■ Table 6.2 Comparison of Classical and Operant Conditioning

	Classical Conditioning	Operant Conditioning
Nature of response	Involuntary, reflex	Spontaneous, voluntary
Cause of learning	Pairing of the CS and US is responsible for learning	Response is strengthened by consequences
Role of learner	Passive (response is elicited by US)	Active (response is emitted)
Nature of learning	Neutral stimulus becomes a CS through association with a US	Probability of response is altered by consequences that follow it
Learned expectancy	US will follow CS	Response will have a specific effect

Thus, operant conditioning involves primarily the learning of voluntary responses. For example, waving your hand in class to get a teacher's attention is a learned operant response. It is reinforced by gaining the teacher's attention. (See Table 6.2 for a further comparison of classical and operant conditioning.)

Positive Reinforcement

The idea that reward affects learning is certainly nothing new to parents (and other trainers of small animals). However, parents, as well as teachers, politicians, supervisors, and even you, may use reward in ways that are inexact or misguided. A case in point is the term *reward*. To be correct, it is better to say *reinforcer*. Why? Because rewards do not always increase response. If you try to give licorice candy to a child as a "reward" for good behaviour, it will work only if the child likes licorice. What is reinforcing for one person may not be for another. As a practical rule of thumb, psychologists define an **operant reinforcer** as any event that follows a response and increases the probability that the response will recur.

Acquiring an Operant Response

Most laboratory studies of instrumental learning take place in a **conditioning chamber,** an apparatus designed for the study of operant conditioning in animals. This device is also sometimes called a Skinner box, after B. F. Skinner, who invented it (see Figure 6.7). A look into a typical Skinner box will clarify the process of operant conditioning.

The Adventures of Mickey Rat

A hungry rat is placed in a small, cagelike chamber. The walls are bare except for a metal lever and a tray into which food pellets can be dispensed (see Figure 6.7).

Frankly, there's not much to do in a Skinner box. This increases the chances that our rat will make the response we want to reinforce, which is pressing the bar. Also, hunger keeps the animal motivated to seek food and actively emit, or freely give off, a variety of responses. Now let's see what happens.

Further Adventures of Mickey Rat

For a while our rat walks around, grooms, sniffs at the corners, or stands on his hind legs—all typical rat behaviours. Then it happens. He places his paw on the lever. Click! The lever depresses, and a food pellet drops into the tray. The rat walks to the tray, eats the pellet, and then grooms himself. Up and exploring the cage again, he leans on the lever. Click! After a trip to the food tray, he returns to the bar and sniffs it, then puts his foot on it. Click! Soon the rat settles into a smooth pattern of frequent bar pressing.

Notice that the rat did not acquire a new skill in this situation. He was already able to depress the bar. Reinforcers alter only how frequently he presses the bar. In operant conditioning, reinforcement is used to alter the frequency of responses, or to mould them into new patterns.

Operant reinforcer Any event that reliably increases the probability or frequency of responses it follows.

Conditioning chamber An apparatus designed to study operant conditioning in animals; a Skinner box.

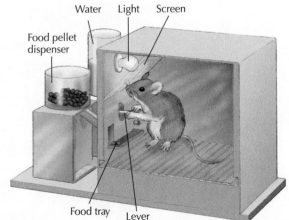

Water Light Screen

Food pellet dispenser

Food tray Lever

▶▶**FIGURE 6.7** The Skinner box. This simple device, invented by B. F. Skinner, allows careful study of operant conditioning. When the rat presses the bar, a pellet of food or a drop of water is automatically released. (A photograph of a Skinner box appears in Chapter 1 on page 20.)

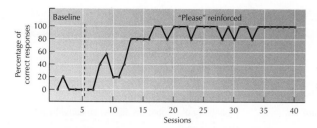

▸▸FIGURE 6.8 Reinforcement and human behaviour. The percentage of times that an emotionally disturbed child said "Please" when he wanted an object was increased dramatically by reinforcing him for making a polite request. Reinforcement produced similar improvements in saying "Thank you" and "You're welcome," and the boy applied these terms in new situations as well. (Adapted from Matson et al., 1990.)

Information and Contingency

Like classical conditioning, operant learning is based on information and expectancies. In operant conditioning, we learn to expect that a certain response will have a certain effect at certain times (Pierce & Cheney, 2004). That is, we learn that a particular stimulus is associated with a particular response that is associated with reinforcement (Hergenhahn & Olson, 2005). From this point of view, a reinforcer tells a person or an animal that a response was "right" and worth repeating.

Figure 6.8 shows how operant reinforcement can change behaviour. The results are from an effort to teach an emotionally disturbed nine-year-old child to say "Please," "Thank you," and "You're welcome." As you can see, during the initial, baseline period, the child rarely used the word *please.* Typically, he just grabbed objects and became angry if he couldn't have them. However, when he was reinforced for saying "Please," he soon learned to use the word nearly every time he wanted something. When the child said "Please," he was reinforced in three ways: He received the object he asked for (a crayon, for example); he was given a small food treat, such as a piece of candy, popcorn, or a grape; and he was praised for his good behaviour (Matson et al., 1990).

Contingent Reinforcement

Operant reinforcement works best when it is **response contingent.** That is, it must be given only after a desired response has occurred. If the disturbed child had received reinforcers haphazardly, his behaviour wouldn't have changed at all. In situations ranging from studying to working hard on the job, contingent reinforcement also affects the performance of responses. Figure 6.9 shows the performance of 38 Major League Baseball pitchers who signed multi-year contracts for large salaries. When salary was no longer contingent on good performance, there was a rapid decline in innings pitched and in the number of wins. During the same six-year period, the performance of pitchers on one-year contracts remained fairly steady. In similar ways, operant principles greatly affect behaviour in homes, schools, and businesses. It is always worthwhile to arrange reinforcers so that they encourage productive and responsible behaviour.

The Timing of Reinforcement

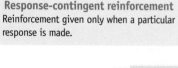

Response-contingent reinforcement Reinforcement given only when a particular response is made.

Operant reinforcement is most effective when it rapidly follows a correct response (Mazur, 2006). For rats in a Skinner box, very little learning occurs when the delay between bar pressing and receiving food reaches 50 seconds. If the food reward is delayed more than a minute and a half, no learning occurs (see Figure 6.10). In general, you will be most successful if you present

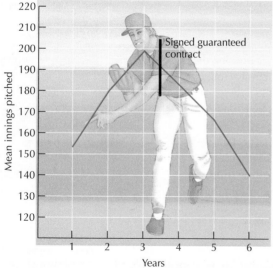

▸▸FIGURE 6.9 Average number of innings pitched by Major League Baseball pitchers before and after signing long-term guaranteed contracts. (Data from O'Brien et al., 1981.)

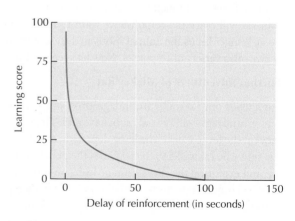

▸▸FIGURE 6.10 The effect of delay of reinforcement. Notice how rapidly the learning score drops when the reward is delayed. Animals learning to press a bar in a Skinner box showed no signs of learning if the delay between the bar press and the food reward was more than 100 seconds (Perin, 1943).

a reinforcer immediately after a response you wish to change. Thus, a child who is helpful or courteous should be praised immediately for her good behaviour.

Let's say I work hard all term in a class to get an A, but I only get the grade at the end of the term. Wouldn't the delay in reinforcement keep me from learning anything? No, for several reasons. First, as a human you can anticipate future reward. Second, you get reinforced by quiz and test grades all through the semester. Third, a single reinforcer can often maintain a long **response chain** (a linked series of actions that lead to reinforcement). For instance, the long series of events necessary to prepare a meal is rewarded by the final eating. A violin maker may carry out thousands of steps for the final reward of hearing a first musical note. Tying a shoe is a short but familiar response chain.

Superstitious Behaviour

Reinforcers affect not only the response they follow but also other responses that occur shortly before. This helps explain many human superstitions. If a golfer taps her club on the ground three times and then hits an unusually fine shot, what happens? The successful shot reinforces not only the correct swing but also the three taps. If this happens a few times more, the golfer may superstitiously tap her club three times before every shot. During operant training, animals often develop similar unnecessary responses. Some examples of actual superstitious behaviours of professional baseball players include drawing four lines in the dirt before getting in the batter's box, eating chicken before each game, and always playing in the same athletic supporter—for four years (phew!) (Burger & Lynn, 2005).

Superstitious behaviours are repeated because they appear to produce reinforcement, even though they are actually unnecessary (Burger & Lynn, 2005). If you walk under a ladder and then break a leg, you may avoid ladders in the future. Each time you avoid a ladder and nothing bad happens, your superstitious action is reinforced. Belief in magic can also be explained along such lines. Rituals to bring rain, ward off illness, or produce abundant crops very likely earn the faith of participants because they occasionally appear to succeed. Besides, better safe than sorry! Do you engage in any behaviours that could be classified as superstitious?

Shaping

How is it possible to reinforce responses that rarely occur? Even in a barren Skinner box, it could take a long time for a rat to accidentally press the bar and get a food pellet. We might wait forever for more complicated responses to occur. For example, you would have to wait a long time for a duck to accidentally walk out of its cage, turn on a light, play a toy piano, turn off the light, and walk back to its cage. If this is what you wanted to reward, you would never get the chance. And if your duck was waiting to get fed, it might starve first.

Then how are the animals on TV and at amusement parks taught to perform complicated tricks? The answer lies in **shaping,** which is the gradual moulding of responses to a desired pattern. Let's look again at our friend, Mickey Rat.

Mickey Rat Shapes Up

Assume that our rat has not yet learned to press the bar. He also shows no signs of interest in the bar. Instead of waiting for the first accidental bar press, we can shape his behaviour. At first, we settle for just getting him to face the bar. Any time he turns toward the bar, he is reinforced with a bit of food. Soon Mickey spends much of his time facing the bar. Next, we reinforce him every time he takes a step toward the bar. If he turns toward the bar and walks away, nothing happens. But when he faces the bar and takes a step forward, click! His responses are being shaped.

By changing the rules about what makes a successful response, we can gradually train the rat to approach the bar and press it. In other words, **successive approximations** (ever-closer matches) to a desired response are reinforced during shaping. B. F. Skinner once taught two

Response chain A linked series of separate actions that lead to reinforcement.
Superstitious behaviour A behaviour repeated because it seems to produce reinforcement, even though it is actually unnecessary.
Shaping Gradually moulding responses to a final desired pattern.
Successive approximations A series of steps or ever-closer matches to a desired response pattern.

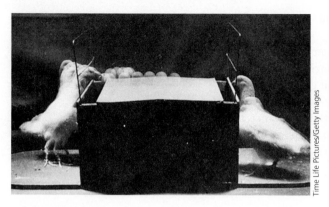

Time Life Pictures/Getty Images

▸▸**FIGURE 6.11** Operant conditioning principles were used to train these pigeons to play Ping-Pong.

pigeons to play Ping-Pong in this way (see Figure 6.11). Shaping applies to humans, too. Let's say you want to study more, clean the house more often, or exercise more. In each case, it would be best to set a series of gradual, daily goals. Then you can reward yourself for small steps in the right direction (Watson & Tharp, 2007).

Operant Extinction

What happens if no more food arrives? Would the rat stop pressing the bar? Yes, but not immediately. Learned responses that are not reinforced gradually fade away. This process is called **operant extinction.** Just as acquiring an operant response takes time, so does extinction. For example, if a TV program repeatedly bores you, watching the program will probably extinguish over time.

Even after extinction seems complete, the previously reinforced response may return. If a rat is removed from a Skinner box after extinction and given a short rest, the rat will press the bar again when returned to the box. Similarly, a few weeks after they give up on buying lottery tickets, many people are tempted to try again.

Does extinction take as long the second time? If reinforcement is still withheld, a rat's bar pressing will extinguish again, usually more quickly. The brief return of an operant response after extinction is another example of spontaneous recovery (mentioned earlier regarding classical conditioning). Spontaneous recovery is very adaptive. After a rest period, the rat responds again in a situation that produced food in the past: "Just checking to see if the rules have changed!"

Marked changes in behaviour occur when reinforcement and extinction are combined. For example, parents often unknowingly reinforce children for **negative attention seeking** (using misbehaviour to gain attention). Children are generally ignored when they are playing quietly. They get attention when they become louder and louder, yell "Hey, Mom!" at the top of their lungs, throw tantrums, kick a toy across the room, or break something. Granted, the attention they get is often a scolding, but any attention is a powerful reinforcer. Parents report dramatic improvements when they ignore their children's disruptive behaviour and praise or attend to a child who is quiet or playing constructively.

Negative Reinforcement

Until now, we have focused on **positive reinforcement,** which occurs when a pleasant or desirable event follows a response. Are there other ways that operant learning could be reinforced? The time has come to consider **negative reinforcement,** which occurs when making a response removes an unpleasant event. Don't be fooled by the word *negative.* Remember our definition of reinforcement on page 232. Negative reinforcement also increases responding. However, it does so by taking away an unpleasant stimulus or ending discomfort.

Let's say that you have a headache and take a pain reliever. Your pill taking will be negatively reinforced if the headache stops. That is, the next time you have a headache, you will most likely reach for the medicine bottle. Likewise, a rat could be taught to press a bar to get food (positive reinforcement), or the rat could be given a continuous mild shock (through the floor of its cage) that is turned off by a bar press (negative reinforcement). Either way, bar pressing would increase. Why? Because it leads to a desired state of affairs (food or an end to pain). Often, positive and negative reinforcement combine. If you are uncomfortably hungry, eating a meal is reinforced by the good-tasting food (positive reinforcement) and by an end to nagging hunger (negative reinforcement).

Punishment

Many people mistake negative reinforcement for punishment. They are not the same. **Punishment** is any event following a response that *decreases* its likelihood of occurring again. As noted, negative reinforcement, like positive reinforcement, *increases* responding.

Operant extinction The weakening or disappearance of a non-reinforced operant response.

Negative attention seeking Using misbehaviour to gain attention.

Positive reinforcement When a response is followed by a reward or other positive event.

Negative reinforcement When a response is followed by an end to discomfort or by the removal of an unpleasant event.

Punishment Any event that follows a response and decreases the likelihood of it occurring again.

■ Table 6.3 **Behavioural Effects of Various Consequences**

	Consequence of Making a Response	Example	Effect on Response Probability
Positive reinforcement	Positive event begins	Food given	Increase
Negative reinforcement	Negative event ends	Pain stops	Increase
Positive punishment	Negative event begins	Pain begins	Decrease
Negative punishment (response cost)	Positive event ends	Food removed	Decrease
Non-reinforcement	Nothing	—	Decrease

Response cost Removal of a positive reinforcer after a response is made.
Primary reinforcers Non-learned reinforcers; usually those that satisfy physiological needs.
Intra-cranial stimulation Direct electrical stimulation and activation of brain tissue.

The difference can be seen in this example. Let's say you live in an apartment and your neighbour's stereo is blasting so loudly that your ears hurt. If you pound on the wall and the volume suddenly drops (negative reinforcement), future wall pounding will be more likely. But if you pound on the wall and the volume increases (punishment), or if the neighbour comes over and pounds on you (more punishment), wall pounding becomes less likely.

As another example, consider a drug user undergoing withdrawal. Taking the drug will temporarily end painful withdrawal symptoms. Drug taking is therefore negatively reinforced. If the drug made the pain worse (punishment), the person would quickly stop taking it. Punishment that weakens a response through the application of an unpleasant event or stimulus is also known as positive punishment.

Isn't it also punishing to have privileges, money, or other positive things taken away for making a particular response? Yes. Punishment also occurs when a reinforcer or positive state of affairs is removed, such as losing privileges. This second type of punishment is called negative punishment or **response cost.** Parents who "ground" their teenage children for misbehaviour are applying response cost. Parking tickets and other fines are also based on response cost. For your convenience, Table 6.3 summarizes four basic consequences of making a response.

If the terms are still unclear, remember first that both types of reinforcement *increase* responding and both types of punishment *decrease* responding. Positive reinforcement occurs when you add something. For example, food is given (added) after a response. In negative reinforcement, something is subtracted. For example, a response causes an electric shock to end (pain is subtracted or taken away). Punishment can also be positive or negative. Responding will decrease if it is followed by a negative event (for example, pain is added) (positive punishment) or if a positive event is subtracted (for example, food is removed) (negative punishment).

OPERANT REINFORCERS—WHAT'S YOUR PLEASURE?

For humans, an effective operant reinforcer may be anything from a candy to a pat on the back. In categorizing such reinforcers, useful distinctions can be made between primary reinforcers, secondary reinforcers, and feedback. Operant reinforcers of all types have a large impact on our lives. Let's examine them in more detail.

<SURVEY QUESTION
What are the different kinds of operant reinforcement?

Primary Reinforcers

Primary reinforcers are natural, non-learned, and rooted in biology: They produce comfort, end discomfort, or fill an immediate physical need. Food, water, and sex are obvious examples. Every time you open the refrigerator, walk to a drinking fountain, turn up the heat, or order a double latte, your actions reflect primary reinforcement.

In addition to obvious examples, there are other less natural primary reinforcers. One of the most powerful is **intra-cranial stimulation (ICS).** ICS involves direct activation of "pleasure centres" in the brain (Olds & Fobes, 1981) (see Brainwaves: "Tickling Your Own Fancy").

Tickling Your Own Fancy

Suppose you could have an electrode permanently implanted in your brain and connected to an iPod-style controller. Twirl the controller and electrical impulses stimulate one of your brain's "pleasure centres." The very few humans who have ever had a chance to try direct brain stimulation report feeling intense pleasure that is better than food, water, sex, drugs, or any other primary reinforcer (Heath, 1963). (See Figure 6.12.)

Most of what we know about intracranial self-stimulation (ICSS) comes from studying rats with similar implants (Olds & Fobes, 1981). A rat "wired for pleasure" can be trained to press the bar in a Skinner box to deliver electrical stimulation to its own limbic system (refer back to Figure 2.27, page 78). Some rats will press the bar thousands of times per hour to obtain brain stimulation. After 15 to 20 hours of constant pressing, animals sometimes collapse from exhaustion. When they revive, they begin pressing again. If the reward circuit is not turned off, an animal will ignore food, water, and sex in favour of bar pressing.

Many natural primary reinforcers activate the same pleasure pathways in the brain that make ICSS so powerful (McBride, Murphy, & Ikemoto, 1999). So do psychoactive drugs, such as alcohol, marijuana and cocaine (Eisler, Justice, Jr., & Neill, 2004; Rodd et al., 2005; Rahman et al., 2008). One shudders to think what might happen if brain implants were easy and practical to do. (They are not.) Every company from Playboy to Microsoft would have a device

on the market, and we would have to keep a closer watch on politicians than usual!

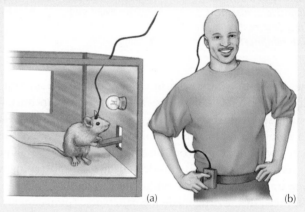

▶▶**FIGURE 6.12** In the apparatus shown in (a), the rat can press a bar to deliver mild electric stimulation to a "pleasure centre" in the brain. Humans have also been "wired" for brain stimulation, as shown in (b). However, in humans, this has been done only as an experimental way to restrain uncontrollable outbursts of violence. Implants have not been done merely to produce pleasure.

Secondary reinforcer A learned reinforcer; often one that gains reinforcing properties by association with a primary reinforcer.

Token reinforcer A tangible secondary reinforcer such as money, gold stars, poker chips, and the like.

Much of the early research on the brain's mechanisms of reward was carried out at McGill University by James Olds and Peter Milner.

Secondary Reinforcers

Although some human learning is still strongly tied to food, water, and other primary reinforcers, most of us also respond to a much broader range of rewards and reinforcers. Money, praise, attention, approval, success, affection, grades, and the like all serve as learned or **secondary reinforcers.**

How does a secondary reinforcer work? Some secondary reinforcers are simply associated with a primary reinforcer. For example, if you would like to train a dog to follow you ("heel") when you take a walk, you could reward the dog with small food treats for staying close by your side. If you praise the dog each time you give it a treat, praise will become a secondary reinforcer. In time, you will be able to skip giving treats and simply praise your pup for doing the right thing. The same principle applies to children. One reason that parents' praise becomes a secondary reinforcer is because it is frequently associated with food, candy, hugs, and other primary reinforcers.

Tokens

Secondary reinforcers that can be exchanged for primary reinforcers gain their value more directly (Mazur, 2006). Money itself obviously has little or no value of its own. You can't eat it, drink it, or sleep with it. However, it can be exchanged for food, water, lodging, and other necessities.

A **token reinforcer** is a tangible secondary reinforcer, such as money, gold stars, poker chips, and the like. In a series of classic experiments, chimpanzees were taught to work for tokens.

The chimps were first trained to put poker chips into a "Chimp-O-Mat" vending machine. Each chip dispensed a few grapes or raisins. Once the animals had learned to exchange tokens for food, they would learn new tasks to earn the chips (Cowles, 1937; Wolfe, 1936).

A major advantage of tokens is that they don't lose reinforcing value as quickly as primary reinforcers do. For instance, if you use candy to reinforce a child for correctly naming things, the child might lose interest once she or he is satiated (fully satisfied) or no longer hungry. It would be better to use tokens as immediate rewards for learning. Later, the child could exchange the tokens for food, toys, or a trip to the movies.

Tokens have been used in similar ways with troubled children and adults in special programs, and even in ordinary elementary school classrooms (Spiegler & Guevremont, 2003; Alberto & Trautman, 2009)). (See Figure 6.13.) In each case, the goal is to provide an immediate reward for learning. Typically, tokens may be exchanged for food, desired goods, special privileges, or trips to movies, amusement parks, and so forth. Many parents find that tokens greatly reduce discipline problems with younger children. For example, during the week children can earn points or gold stars for good behaviour. If they earn enough tokens, on Sunday they are allowed to choose one item out of a "grab bag" of small treats.

Social Reinforcers

As we have noted, the desire for attention and approval, which are called **social reinforcers,** often influences human behaviour. This fact can be used in a classic, if somewhat mischievous, demonstration. If you try this, and your teacher catches on, you didn't learn it here!

Shaping a Teacher

For this activity, at least one-half of the students in a classroom must participate. First, select a target behaviour. This should be something like "lecturing from the right side of the room." (Keep it simple, in case your teacher is a slow learner.) Begin training in this way: Each time the instructor turns toward the right or takes a step in that direction, participating students should look really interested. Also, smile, ask questions, lean forward, and make eye contact. If the teacher turns to the left or takes a step in that direction, participating students should lean back, yawn, check their split ends, close their eyes, or generally look bored. Soon, without being aware of why, the instructor should be spending most of his or her time each class period lecturing from the right side of the classroom.

This trick has been a favourite of psychology students for decades. In one case, a professor delivered all his lectures from the right side of the room while toying with the cords from the Venetian blinds. (The students added the cords the second week!) The point to remember from this example is that attention and approval can change the behaviour of children, family members, friends, roommates, and co-workers. Be aware of what you are reinforcing.

Feedback

His eyes, driven and blazing, dart from side to side. His right hand twitches, dances, rises, and strikes, hitting its target again and again. At the same time, his left hand furiously spins in circular motions. Does this describe some strange neurological disorder? Actually, it depicts 10-year-old Mark as he plays his favourite motion-control video game, a virtual snowboarding adventure!

> **Social reinforcers** Reinforcers, such as attention and approval, provided by other people.

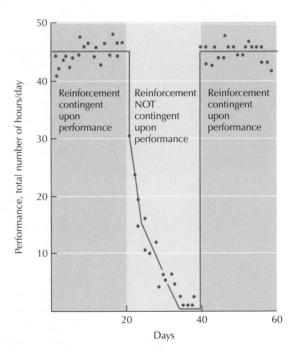

▶▶**FIGURE 6.13** Reinforcement in a token economy. This graph shows the effects of using tokens to reward socially desirable behaviour in a psychiatric hospital ward. Desirable behaviour was defined as cleaning, bed making, attending therapy sessions, and so forth. Tokens earned could be exchanged for basic amenities such as meals, snacks, coffee, game-room privileges, or weekend passes. The graph shows more than 24 hours per day because it represents the total number of hours of desirable behaviour performed by all patients in the ward. (Adapted from Ayllon & Azrin, 1965.)

Feedback Information returned to a person about the effects a response has had; also known as knowledge of results.

Knowledge of results (KR) Informational feedback.

Programmed instruction Any learning format that presents information in small amounts, gives immediate practice, and provides continuous feedback to learners.

Computer-assisted instruction (CAI) Learning aided by computer-presented information, exercises, and feedback.

How did Mark learn the complex movements needed to excel at virtual snowboarding? After all, he was not rewarded with food or money. The answer lies in the fact that Mark's favourite game provides feedback, a key element that underlies learning. **Feedback** (information about the effect the response had) is particularly important in human cognitive learning (Lefrançois, 2006). Humans readily learn responses that have a desired effect or that bring a goal closer.

Every time a player does something, a video game responds instantly with sounds, animated actions, and a higher or lower score. The machine's responsiveness and the information flow it provides can be very motivating if you want to win. The same principle applies to many other learning situations: If you are trying to learn to use a computer, to play a musical instrument, to cook, or to solve math problems, feedback when you achieved a desired result can be reinforcing in its own right. Whenever you are trying to learn a complex skill, it pays to get as much feedback as possible (Jaehnig & Miller, 2007).The adaptive value of information helps explain why much human learning occurs without obvious reinforcement by food, water, and the like. Humans readily learn responses that merely have a desired effect or that bring a goal closer. Let's explore this idea further.

Knowledge of Results

Imagine that you are asked to throw darts at a target. Each dart must pass over a screen that prevents you from telling if you hit the target. Even if you threw 1000 darts, we would expect little improvement in your performance, because no feedback is provided. Feedback is particularly important in human learning. Mark's video game did not explicitly reward him for correct responses. Yet, because it provided feedback, rapid learning took place.

How can feedback be applied? Increased feedback (also called **knowledge of results,** or **KR**) almost always improves learning and performance (Horn et al., 2005). If you want to learn to play a musical instrument, to sing, to speak a second language, or to deliver a speech, audio-recorded feedback can be very helpful. In sports, video is used to improve everything from tennis serves to pick-off moves in baseball. (Recorded replays of this kind are most helpful when a skilled coach directs attention to key details.)

Learning Aids

Since increased feedback almost always improves learning and performance, it makes sense to design learning aids to supply effective feedback (Horn et al., 2005).

How do these techniques make use of feedback? Feedback is most effective when it is frequent, immediate, and detailed. **Programmed instruction** teaches students in a format that presents information in small amounts, gives immediate practice, and provides continuous feedback to learners. Frequent feedback keeps learners from practising errors. It also lets students work at their own pace. To get a sense of this format, finish reading the next few paragraphs and then complete the Study Break when you encounter it (just like you do with all of the Study Breaks, right?). Work through the questions one at a time, checking each answer as you go. (You can find the correct answers upside down at the end of the Study Break.) In this way, your correct (or incorrect) responses will be followed by immediate feedback.

Programmed instruction is usually done on a computer or through the Web, but it can also be presented in book form (Emurian, 2005; McDonald, Yanchar, & Osguthorpe, 2005). You may know it as **computer-assisted instruction (CAI)** or drill-and-practise.

In addition to giving immediate feedback, the computer can analyze why an answer is wrong and what might be done to correct it (Timmerman & Kruepke, 2006).

Although the final level of skill or knowledge is not necessarily higher than that gained by conventional methods, CAI can save teachers and learners much time and effort.

STUDY BREAK   **Operant Conditioning**

Reflect

How have your thoughts about the effects of "rewards" changed now that you've read about operant conditioning? Can you explain the difference between positive reinforcement, negative reinforcement, and punishment? Can you give an example of each concept from your own experience?

A friend of yours punishes his dog all the time. What advice would you give him about how to use reinforcement, extinction, and shaping instead of punishment?

Learning Check

1. Responses in operant conditioning are _____, whereas those in classical conditioning are passive, _____ responses.
2. Changing the rules in small steps, so that an animal (or person) is gradually trained to respond as desired, is called _____.
3. Positive reinforcers increase the rate of responding and negative reinforcers decrease it. T or F?

4. Primary reinforcers are those learned through classical conditioning. T or F?
5. Superstitious responses are those that are
   a. shaped by secondary reinforcement
   b. extinguished
   c. prepotent
   d. unnecessary to obtain reinforcement
6. Knowledge of results, or KR, is also known as _____.

Critical Thinking

7. How might operant conditioning principles be used to encourage people to pick up litter? (What rewards could be offered, and how might the cost of rewards be kept low?)

Answers

1. voluntary, involuntary or emitted, elicited   2. shaping   3. F   4. F   5. d   6. feedback   7. A strategy that has been used with some success is to hold drawings for various prizes, such as movie or concert passes. Each time a person turns in a specific amount of litter, he or she receives one chance (a token) to enter in the drawing. Giving refunds for cans and bottles is another way to reinforce recycling of litter.

In addition, people often do better with feedback from a computer because they can freely make mistakes and learn from them (Luyben, Hipworth & Pappas, 2003). Some CAI programs, known as *serious games,* use **instructional games** in which stories, competition with a partner, sound effects, and gamelike graphics increase interest and motivation (Michael & Chen, 2006) (see Figure 6.14). In **educational simulations,** students explore an imaginary situation or "microworld" that simulates real-world problems. By seeing the effects of their choices, students discover basic principles of physics, biology, psychology, or other subjects (Grabe, 2006).

Let's pause now for some learning exercises so you can get some feedback about your mastery of the preceding ideas.

Instructional games Educational computer programs designed to resemble video games in order to motivate learning.

Educational simulations Computer programs that simulate real-world settings or situations to promote learning.

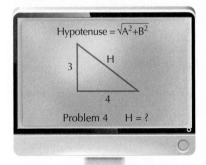  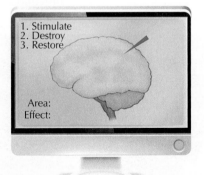

▶▶**FIGURE 6.14** Computer-assisted instruction. The screen on the left shows a typical drill-and-practise math problem, in which students must find the hypotenuse of a triangle. The centre screen presents the same problem as an instructional game to increase interest and motivation. In the game, a child is asked to set the proper distance on a ray gun in the hovering space ship to "vaporize" an attacker. The screen on the right depicts an educational simulation. Here, students place a "probe" at various spots in a human brain. They then "stimulate," "destroy," or "restore" areas. As each area is altered, it is named on the screen, and the effects on behaviour are described. This allows students to explore basic brain functions on their own.

PARTIAL REINFORCEMENT—CASINOS: HUMAN SKINNER BOXES?

SERENDIPITY (n): to discover one thing while looking for another.

B. F. Skinner, so the story goes, was studying operant conditioning when he ran short of food pellets. In order to continue, he arranged for a pellet to reward every other response. Thus began the formal study of **schedules of reinforcement** (plans for determining which responses will be reinforced). Until now, we have treated operant reinforcement as if it were continuous. **Continuous reinforcement** means that a reinforcer follows every correct response. This is fine in the lab, but it has little to do with the real world. Most of our responses are rewarded inconsistently. In daily life, learning is usually based on **partial reinforcement,** where reinforcers do not follow every response.

Partial reinforcement can be given in several patterns. Each has a distinct effect on behaviour. In addition to these (which will be explored in a moment), there is a general effect of partial reinforcement: Responses acquired by partial reinforcement are highly resistant to extinction. This is called the **partial reinforcement effect.**

How can getting reinforced only part of the time make a habit stronger? If you have ever visited a casino, you have probably seen row after row of people playing slot machines. To gain insight into partial reinforcement, imagine that you are visiting the Montréal Casino. You put a token in a slot machine and press the button. A pile of tokens spills into the tray. Using one of your newly won coins, you press the button again. Another payoff! Let's say this continues for 15 minutes. Every press is followed by a payoff. Suddenly each press is followed by nothing. Obviously, you would respond several times more before giving up. However, when continuous reinforcement is followed by extinction, the message soon becomes clear: no more payoffs.

Contrast this with partial reinforcement. Again, imagine that this is your first encounter with a slot machine. You put a token in the machine five times without a payoff. You are just about to quit, but decide to play once more. Bingo! The machine returns $20. After this, payoffs continue on a partial schedule; some are large, and some are small. All are unpredictable. Sometimes you hit two in a row, and sometimes 20 or 30 plays go unrewarded.

Now let's say the payoff mechanism is turned off again. How many times do you think you would respond this time before your button-pressing behaviour extinguished? Since you have developed the expectation that any play may be "the big one," it will be hard to resist just one more play … and one more … and one more. Also, since partial reinforcement includes long periods of non-reward, it will be harder to discriminate between periods of reinforcement and extinction. It is no exaggeration to say that the partial reinforcement effect has left many people penniless. Even psychologists visiting casinos may get "cleaned out"—and they should know better!

Schedules of Partial Reinforcement

Partial reinforcement can be given in many different patterns (Domjan, 2006). Reinforcement can be given after a certain number of responses have been emitted (ratio schedules), or after a certain amount of time has passed (interval schedules). Let's consider the four most basic patterns, which have some interesting effects on the way we behave.

Fixed Ratio

What would happen if a reinforcer followed only every other response? Or what if we followed every third, fourth, fifth, or some other number of responses with reinforcement? Each of these patterns is a **fixed-ratio (FR) schedule** (a set number of correct responses must be made to obtain a reinforcer). Notice that in an FR schedule the *ratio* of reinforcers to

Schedule of reinforcement A rule or plan for determining which responses will be reinforced.

Continuous reinforcement A schedule in which every correct response is followed by a reinforcer.

Partial reinforcement A schedule in which only a portion of responses are reinforced.

Partial reinforcement effect Responses acquired with partial reinforcement are more resistant to extinction.

Fixed-ratio (FR) schedule A set number of correct responses must be made to get a reinforcer. For example, a reinforcer is given for every four correct responses.

The one-armed bandit (slot machine) is a dispenser of partial reinforcement.

© Jonathan Drake/epa/Corbis

responses is fixed: FR-2 means that every other response is rewarded; FR-3 means that every third response is reinforced; in an FR-10 schedule, exactly 10 responses must be made to obtain a reinforcer.

Fixed-ratio schedules produce very high response rates (see Figure 6.15). A hungry rat on an FR-10 schedule will quickly run off 10 responses, pause to eat, and then run off 10 more. A similar situation occurs when workers are paid on a piecework basis. When a fixed number of items must be produced for a set amount of pay, work output is high.

Variable Ratio

In a **variable-ratio (VR) schedule,** a varied number of correct responses must be made to get a reinforcer. Instead of reinforcing, for example, every fourth response (FR-4), a person or animal on a VR-4 schedule gets rewarded on average every fourth response. Sometimes two responses must be made to obtain a reinforcer; sometimes it's five, sometimes four, and so on. The actual number varies, but it averages out to four (in this example). Variable-ratio schedules also produce high response rates.

VR schedules seem less predictable than FR schedules. Does that have any effect on extinction? Yes. Since reinforcement is less predictable, VR schedules tend to produce greater resistance to extinction than fixed-ratio schedules. Playing a slot machine is an example of behaviour maintained by a variable-ratio schedule. Another would be a child asking for a "treat" at the supermarket. The number of times the child must ask before getting reinforced varies (depending on his or her parent's patience), so the child becomes quite persistent. Golf, tennis, and many other sports are also reinforced on a variable ratio basis: An average of perhaps one good shot in five to ten may be all that's needed to create a golf fanatic.

Fixed Interval

In another pattern, reinforcement is given only when a correct response is made after a fixed amount of time has passed. This time interval is measured from the last reinforced response. Responses made during the time interval are not reinforced. In a **fixed-interval (FI) schedule,** the first correct response made after the time period has passed is reinforced. Thus, a rat on an FI-30-second schedule has to wait 30 seconds after the last reinforced response before a bar press will pay off again. The rat can press the bar as often as it wants during the interval, but it will not be rewarded until 30 seconds have elapsed.

Fixed interval schedules produce moderate response rates. These are marked by spurts of activity mixed with periods of inactivity. Animals working on an FI schedule seem to develop a keen sense of the passage of time (Eckerman, 1999). For example, let's return to Mickey Rat:

Mickey Rat Takes a Break

Mickey Rat, trained on an FI-60-second schedule, has just been reinforced for a bar press. What does he do? He saunters around the cage, grooms himself, hums, whistles, reads magazines, and polishes his nails. After 50 seconds, he walks to the bar and gives it a press—just testing. After 55 seconds, he gives it two or three presses, but there's still no payoff. Fifty-eight seconds, and he settles down to rapid pressing, 59 seconds, 60 seconds, and he hits the reinforced press. After one or two more presses (unrewarded), he wanders off again for the next interval. (See also Critical Thinking: "Are Animals Stuck in Time?")

Is getting paid every two weeks an FI schedule? Pure examples of fixed-interval schedules are rare, but getting paid biweekly at work does come close. Notice, however, that most people do not work faster just before payday, as an FI schedule predicts. A closer parallel would be having a test every five weeks in your psychology class. Right after a test, your work would probably drop to zero for a week or more. Then, as the next test draws near, a work frenzy occurs as you try to catch up on your reading (Chance, 2009). (If you don't believe this, keep track of the number of hours you study per week and see what happens just before a test.)

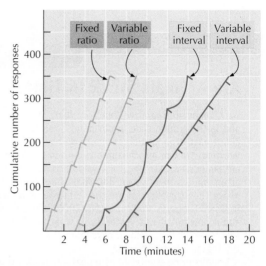

▸▸**FIGURE 6.15** Typical response patterns for reinforcement schedules. Results such as these are obtained when a cumulative recorder is connected to a Skinner box. The device consists of a moving strip of paper and a mechanical pen that jumps upward each time a response is made. Rapid responding causes the pen to draw a steep line; a horizontal line indicates no response. Small tick marks on the lines show when a reinforcer was given.

Variable-ratio (VR) schedule The number of correct responses that must be made to get a reinforcer varies. For example, a reinforcer is given after three to seven correct responses; the actual number changes randomly.

Fixed-interval (FI) schedule A reinforcer is given only when a correct response is made after a set amount of time has passed since the last reinforced response. Responses made during the time interval are not reinforced.

CRITICAL THINKING

Are Animals Stuck in Time?

We humans are *cognitive time travellers,* regularly zooming back and forth through time in our minds. You can, for example, think about past events, such as what you had for breakfast this morning. We can also imagine events in the future. Brides-to-be are famous for planning their weddings down to the last detail, often months in advance. But what about animals? Are they cognitive time travellers or are they less cognitive and hence "stuck in time" (Roberts, 2002; Zentall, 2005)? Does your dog ever think about how hot it was yesterday or what he plans to do tomorrow? To answer such questions, psychologists have used operant conditioning as a research tool.

Conditioning studies have repeatedly shown that animals are sensitive to the passage of time (Zentall, 2005). For example, pigeons and rats reinforced on fixed-interval schedules stop responding immediately after they receive a reinforcer and do not start again until just before the next scheduled reinforcement (Roberts, 2002). In one study, pigeons were put in a Skinner box with a pecking key on each wall. They quickly learned to peck only at Key 1 if it was 9:30 in the morning and at Key 3 if it was 4:00 in the afternoon (Saksida & Wilkie, 1994).

Another study focused on scrub jays. These birds are hoarders; they store excess food at different locations and then go back later to eat it. Scrub jays were allowed to hoard some nuts in one location and some worms in another. If they were released four hours later, they went directly to the worms. However, if they were released five days later, they went straight for the nuts. Worms are a scrub jay's favourite food, which explains their choice after four hours. But worms decay after a day or so, while nuts stay edible. It seems that the jays knew exactly where they stored each type of food and how much time had passed (Clayton, Yu, & Dickinson, 2001).

While these studies are suggestive, they are part of an ongoing debate about animal cognition, including whether or not animals are stuck in time (Roberts & Roberts, 2002). Nevertheless, be careful if you forget to feed your dog at his usual mealtime. If he has been conditioned to think it's time to eat, he may settle for your favorite flip-flops instead of dog food!

Variable-interval (VI) schedule A reinforcer is given for the first correct response made after a varied amount of time has passed since the last reinforced response. Responses made during the time interval are not reinforced.

Stimulus control Stimuli that are present when an operant response is acquired tend to control when and where the response is made.

Variable Interval

Variable-interval (VI) schedules are a variation on fixed intervals. Here, reinforcement is given for the first correct response made after a varied amount of time has passed. On a VI-30-second schedule, reinforcement is available after an interval that averages 30 seconds.

VI schedules produce slow, steady rates of response and tremendous resistance to extinction. When you dial a phone number and get a busy signal, reward (getting through) is on a VI schedule. You may have to wait 30 seconds or 30 minutes. If you are like most people, you will doggedly dial over and over again until you get a connection (or, at least, let the phone company dial it for you). Success in fishing is also on a VI schedule—which may explain the bulldog tenacity of many anglers (Chance, 2009). To maximize studying, some professors take advantage of this by scheduling frequent, unannounced class quizzes or tests. If some of your professors do this, what effect does it have on your behaviour?

STIMULUS CONTROL—RED LIGHT, GREEN LIGHT

When you are driving, your behaviour at intersections is controlled by stop signs and traffic lights. In a similar fashion, many of the stimuli we encounter each day act like stop or go signals that guide our behaviour. To state the idea more formally, stimuli that consistently precede a rewarded response tend to influence when and where the response will occur. This effect is called **stimulus control.** See how it works with our friend Mickey Rat:

Lights Out for Mickey Rat

While learning the bar-pressing response, Mickey has been in a Skinner box illuminated by a bright light. During several training sessions, the light is alternately turned on and off. When the light is on, a bar press will produce food. When the light is off, bar pressing goes unrewarded. We soon observe that the rat presses vigorously when the light is on but ignores the bar when the light is off.

In this example, the light signals what consequences will follow if a response is made. Evidence for stimulus control could be shown by turning the food delivery on when the light is off. A well-trained animal might never discover that the rules had changed (Powell et al., 2009). A similar example of stimulus control would be a child learning to ask for candy when her or his mother is in a good mood, but not asking at other times. Likewise, we pick up phones that are ringing or vibrating, but rarely answer ones that are silent and still.

Generalization

Two important aspects of stimulus control are *generalization* and *discrimination*. Let's return to the example of the vending machine to illustrate these concepts. First, generalization.

Is generalization the same in operant conditioning as it is in classical conditioning? Basically, yes. **Operant stimulus generalization** is the tendency to respond to stimuli similar to those that preceded operant reinforcement. That is, a reinforced response tends to be made again when similar antecedents are present. Assume, for instance, that you have been reliably rewarded for kicking one particular vending machine. Your kicking response tends to occur in the presence of that machine. It has come under stimulus control. Now let's say that there are three other machines on campus identical to the one that pays off when you kick it. Because they are similar, your kicking response will very likely transfer to them. If each of these machines also pays off when kicked, your kicking response may generalize to other machines only mildly similar to the original. Similarly, generalization explains why young children may temporarily call all men Daddy—much to the embarrassment of their parents.

Discrimination

Meanwhile, back at the vending machine…. As stated earlier, to discriminate means to respond differently to similar stimuli. Because one vending machine reinforced your kicking response, you began kicking other identical machines (generalization). Because these also paid off, you began kicking similar machines (more generalization). If kicking these new machines has no effect, the kicking response that generalized to them will extinguish because of non-reinforcement. Thus, your response to machines of a particular size and colour is consistently rewarded, whereas the same response to different machines is extinguished. Through **operant stimulus discrimination** you have learned to differentiate between antecedent stimuli that signal reward and non-reward. As a result, your response pattern will shift to match these **discriminative stimuli** (stimuli that precede rewarded and non-rewarded responses).

Stimulus discrimination is also aptly illustrated by the "sniffer" dogs that locate drugs and explosives at airports and border crossings. Operant discrimination is used to teach these dogs to recognize contraband. During training, they are reinforced only for approaching containers baited with drugs or explosives.

Stimulus discrimination clearly has an impact on human behaviour. Learning to recognize different automobile brands, birds, animals, wines, types of music, and even the answers on psychology tests all depends, in part, on operant discrimination learning.

A discriminative stimulus that many drivers are familiar with is a police car on a highway. This stimulus is a clear signal that a specific set of reinforcement contingencies applies. As you have probably observed, the approach of what might be a police car brings about rapid reductions in driving speed, lane changes, tailgating, and other kinds of bad driving. In Montreal, one suburb hired a man to wear an orange vest, stand at the side of a high-traffic residential street, and wave his arm at passing cars as if he were holding a radar gun. Drivers' responses were immediate (McKenzie, 2011).

I use different ring tones for different people on my cell phone. Is this an example of using discriminative stimuli? Absolutely! Suppose you use one ring tone for people you want to speak to, another for people you don't, and a third for calls from strangers. In no time at all, you will show different telephone answering behaviour in response to the different ring tones.

Operant stimulus generalization The tendency to respond to stimuli similar to those that preceded operant reinforcement.

Operant stimulus discrimination The tendency to make an operant response when stimuli previously associated with reward are present and to withhold the response when stimuli associated with non-reward are present.

Discriminative stimuli Stimuli that precede rewarded and non-rewarded responses in operant conditioning.

© Gary Crabbe/Alamy

Stimulus control. Operant shaping was used to teach this whale to "bow" to an audience. Fish were used as reinforcers. Notice the trainer's hand signal, which serves as a discriminative stimulus to control the performance.

STUDY BREAK Partial Reinforcement and Stimulus Control

Reflect

Think of something you do that is reinforced only part of the time. Do you pursue this activity persistently? How have you been affected by partial reinforcement?

See if you can think of at least one everyday example of the four basic schedules of reinforcement.

Some doors that are meant to be pushed outward have metal plates on them. Those that are meant to be pulled inward have handles. Do these discriminative stimuli affect your behaviour? (If they don't, how's your nose doing?)

Learning Check

1. Two aspects of stimulus control are _____ and _____.
2. Responding tends to occur in the presence of discriminative stimuli associated with reinforcement and tends not to occur in the presence of discriminative stimuli associated with non-reinforcement. T or F?
3. Stimulus generalization refers to making an operant response in the presence of stimuli similar to those that preceded reinforcement. T or F?

4. When a reward follows every response, it is called
   a. continuous reinforcement   b. fixed reinforcement
   c. ratio reinforcement   d. controlled reinforcement
5. Partial reinforcement tends to produce slower responding and reduced resistance to extinction. T or F?
6. The schedule of reinforcement associated with playing slot machines and other types of gambling is
   a. fixed ratio   b. variable ratio
   c. fixed interval   d. variable interval

Critical Thinking

7. A business owner who pays employees an hourly wage wants to increase productivity. How could the owner make more effective use of reinforcement?
8. How could you use conditioning principles to teach a dog or a cat to come when called?
9. Is the beep on voice mail or answering machines a discriminative stimulus?

Answers

1. generalization, discrimination 2. T 3. T 4. a 5. F 6. b 7. Continuing to use fixed-interval rewards (hourly wage or salary) would guarantee a basic level of income for employees. To reward extra effort, the owner could add some fixed-ratio reinforcement (such as incentives, bonuses, commissions, or profit sharing) to employees' pay. 8. An excellent way to train a pet to come when you call is to give a distinctive call or whistle each time you feed the animal. This makes the signal a secondary reinforcer and a discriminative stimulus for reward (food). It also helps to directly reinforce an animal with praise, petting, or food for coming when called. 9. Yes, it is. The beep is a signal that speaking will pay off (your message will be recorded). Most of us are well conditioned to "wait for the beep" before talking.

PUNISHMENT—PUTTING THE BRAKES ON BEHAVIOUR

SURVEY QUESTION>
How does punishment affect behaviour?

Spankings, reprimands, fines, jail sentences, firings, failing grades, and the like are commonly used to control behaviour. Clearly, the story of learning is unfinished without a return to the topic of punishment. Recall that **punishment** lowers the probability that a response will occur again. To be most effective, punishment must be given contingently (only after an undesired response occurs).

Punishers, like reinforcers, are best defined by observing their effects on behaviour. A **punisher** is any consequence that reduces the frequency of a target behaviour. It is not always possible to know ahead of time what will act as a punisher for a particular person. For example, when Jason's mother reprimanded him for throwing toys, he stopped doing it. In this instance, the reprimand was a punisher. However, Chris is starved for attention of any kind from his parents. For Chris, a reprimand, or even a spanking, might actually reinforce toy throwing. Remember, too, that a punisher can be either the onset of an unpleasant event or the removal of a positive state of affairs (response cost).

Variables Affecting Punishment

How effective is punishment? Many people assume that punishment stops unacceptable behaviour. Is this always true? Actually, the effectiveness of punishers depends greatly on their timing, consistency, and intensity. Punishment works best when it occurs as the response is being made, or immediately afterward (timing), and when it is given each time a response occurs (consistency). Thus, if simply refusing to feed your dog table scraps is not enough to stop it

Punishment The process of suppressing a response.
Punisher Any event that decreases the probability or frequency of responses it follows.

from jumping at you when you sit at a table, you could effectively (and humanely) punish it by spraying water on its nose each time it jumps up. About 10 to 15 such treatments are usually enough. This would not be the case if you applied punishment haphazardly or long after the jumping happened. If you discover that your dog dug up a tree and ate it while you were gone, punishing the dog hours later will do little good. Likewise, the commonly heard childhood threat "Just wait 'til your father comes home; then you'll be sorry" only makes the father a feared brute; it doesn't effectively punish an undesirable response.

Severe punishment (following a response with an intensely aversive or unpleasant stimulus) can be extremely effective in stopping behaviour. If three-year-old Beavis sticks his finger in a light socket and gets a shock, that may be the last time he ever tries it. More often, however, punishment only temporarily suppresses a response. If the response is still reinforced, punishment may be particularly ineffective. Responses suppressed by **mild punishment** usually reappear later.

This fact was demonstrated by slapping rats on the paw as they were bar pressing in a Skinner box. Two groups of well-trained rats were placed on extinction. One group was punished with a slap for each bar press, while the other group was not. It might seem that the slap would cause bar pressing to extinguish more quickly. Yet, this was not the case, as you can see in Figure 6.16. Punishment temporarily slowed responding, but it did not cause more rapid extinction. Slapping the paws of rats or hands of children has little permanent effect on a reinforced response.

Similarly, if seven-year-old Alissa sneaks a snack from the refrigerator before dinner and is punished for it, she may pass up snacks for a short time. But since snack sneaking was also rewarded by the sneaked snack, she will probably try sneaky snacking again later. It is worth stating again, however, that intense punishment may permanently suppress responding, even for actions as basic as eating. Animals severely punished while eating may never eat again (Bertsch, 1976).

Side Effects of Punishment

What are the drawbacks of using punishment? The basic problem with punishment is that it is **aversive** (painful or uncomfortable). As a result, people and situations associated with punishment tend, through classical conditioning, to become feared, resented, or disliked. The aversive nature of punishment makes it especially poor to use when teaching children to eat politely or in toilet training.

Escape and Avoidance

A second major problem is that aversive stimuli encourage escape and avoidance learning. In **escape learning** we learn to make a response in order to end an aversive stimulus. For example, if you work with a loud and obnoxious person, you may at first escape from conversations with him to obtain relief. (Notice that escape learning is based on negative reinforcement.) Later you may dodge him altogether. This is an example of **avoidance learning** (making a response in order to postpone or prevent discomfort). Each time you sidestep him, your avoidance is again reinforced by a sense of relief. (Notice that this is positive reinforcement.) In many situations involving frequent punishment, similar desires to escape and avoid are activated. For example, children who run away from punishing parents (escape) may soon learn to lie about their behaviour (avoidance) or to spend as much time away from home as possible (also an avoidance response).

Aggression

A third problem with punishment is that it can greatly increase aggression. Animals react to pain by attacking whoever or whatever else is around. A common example is the faithful dog that nips its owner during a painful procedure at the veterinarian's office. Likewise, humans who are in pain have a tendency to lash out at others.

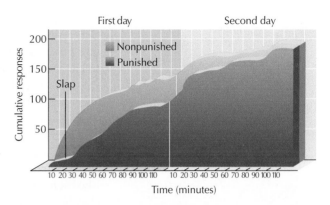

▸▸**FIGURE 6.16** The effect of punishment on extinction. Immediately after punishment, the rate of bar pressing is suppressed, but by the end of the second day, the effects of punishment have disappeared. (After B. F. Skinner, *The Behavior of Organisms*. © 1938. D. Appleton-Century Co., Inc. Reprinted by permission of Skinner Foundation.)

Severe punishment Intense punishment; punishment capable of suppressing a response for long periods.

Mild punishment Punishment that has a relatively weak effect—especially punishment that only temporarily slows responding.

Aversive stimulus A stimulus that is painful or uncomfortable.

Escape learning Learning to make a response in order to end an aversive stimulus.

Avoidance learning Learning to make a response in order to postpone or prevent discomfort.

We also know that one of the most common responses to frustration is aggression. Generally speaking, punishment is painful, frustrating, or both. Punishment, therefore, sets up a powerful environment for learning aggression. When a child is spanked, the child may feel angry, frustrated, and hostile. What if the child then goes outside and hits a brother, a sister, or a neighbour? The danger is that aggressive acts may feel good because they release anger and frustration. If so, aggression has been rewarded and will tend to occur again in other frustrating situations.

One Canadian study found that children who are physically punished are more likely to engage in aggressive, impulsive, antisocial behaviour, at both age two and age eight (Thomas, 2004). Similarly, a classic study of angry adolescent boys found that they were severely punished at home. This suppressed their misbehaviour at home but made them more aggressive elsewhere. Parents were often surprised to learn that their "good boys" were in trouble for fighting at school (Bandura & Walters, 1959). Fortunately, at least for younger children, if parents change to less punitive parenting, their children's levels of aggression will decline (Thomas, 2004).

In the classroom, physical punishment, yelling, and humiliation are generally ineffective. Positive reinforcement, in the form of praise, approval, and reward, is much more likely to quell classroom disruptions, defiance, and inattention (Alberto & Troutman, 2009).

Using Punishment Wisely

In light of its drawbacks, should punishment be used to control behaviour? Parents, teachers, animal trainers, and the like have three basic tools to control simple learning: (1) Reinforcement strengthens responses; (2) non-reinforcement causes responses to extinguish; (3) punishment suppresses responses. (Consult Figure 6.17 if you need to refresh your memory about the different types of reinforcement and punishment.) These tools work best in combination.

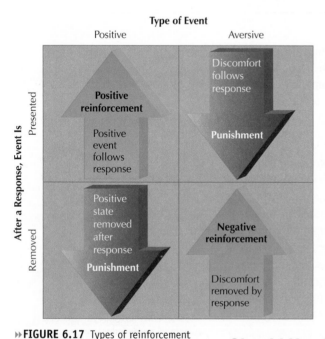

►►FIGURE 6.17 Types of reinforcement and punishment. The impact of an event depends on whether it is presented or removed after a response is made. Each square defines one possibility: Arrows pointing upward indicate that responding is increased; downward-pointing arrows indicate that responding is decreased. (Adapted from Kazdin, 1975.)

If punishment is used at all, it should always be mild. But remember that mild punishment will be ineffective if reinforcers are still available in the situation. That's why it is best to also reward an alternative, desired response. For example, a child who has a habit of taking toys from her sister should not just be reprimanded for it. She should also be praised for cooperative play and sharing her toys with others. Punishment tells a person or an animal that a response was "wrong." However, it does not say what the "right" response is, so it does not teach new behaviours. If reinforcement is missing from the formula, punishment becomes less effective.

In a situation that poses immediate danger, such as when a child reaches for something hot or a dog runs into the street, mild punishment may prevent disaster. Punishment in such cases works best when it produces actions incompatible with the response you want to suppress. Let's say a child reaches toward a stove burner. Would a swat on the bottom serve as an effective punisher? Maybe. It would be better, however, to slap the child's outstretched hand so it will be withdrawn from the source of danger. See Using Psychology: "If You Must Punish, Here's How" for some additional tips on using punishment.

Should You Punish or Not?

To summarize, the most common error in using punishment is to rely on it alone for training or discipline. The overall emotional adjustment of a child or pet disciplined mainly by reward is usually superior to one disciplined mainly by punishment. Frequent punishment makes a person or an animal unhappy, confused, anxious, aggressive, and fearful.

If You Must Punish, Here's How

There are times when punishment may be necessary to manage the behaviour of an animal, a child, or even another adult. If you feel that you must punish, here are some tips to keep in mind.

1. *Avoid punishment whenever you can.* Make liberal use of positive reinforcement, especially praise, to encourage good behaviour. Also, try extinction first: See what happens if you ignore a problem behaviour or shift attention to a desirable activity and then reinforce it with praise.

2. *Punish immediately if at all possible.* Of course, immediate punishment is not always possible. With older children and adults, you can bridge the delay by clearly stating what act you are punishing. If you cannot punish a younger child or an animal immediately, wait for the next instance of misbehaviour.

3. *Use the minimum punishment necessary to suppress misbehaviour.* Often, a verbal rebuke or a scolding is enough. Never use harsh physical punishment. Taking away privileges or other positive reinforcers (response cost) is usually best for older children and adults. Frequent punishment may lose its

effectiveness, and harsh or excessive punishment has serious negative side effects.

4. *Be consistent.* Be very clear about what you regard as misbehaviour. Punish every time the misbehaviour occurs. Don't punish for something one day and ignore it the next. If you are usually willing to give a child three chances, don't change the rule and explode without warning after a first offence. Both parents should try to punish their children for the same things and in the same way.

5. *Expect anger from a punished person.* Briefly acknowledge this anger, but be careful not to reinforce it. Be willing to admit your mistake if you wrongfully punish someone or if you punished too severely.

6. *Punish with respect.* Allow the punished person to retain self-respect. For instance, do not punish a person in front of others, if at all possible. A strong, trusting relationship tends to minimize behaviour problems. Ideally, others should want to behave well to get your praise, not because they fear punishment.

Parents and teachers should be aware that using punishment can be habit forming. When children are being noisy, messy, disrespectful, or otherwise misbehaving, the temptation to punish them can be strong. The danger is that punishment often works. When it does, a sudden end to the adult's irritation acts as a negative reinforcer (for the adult). This encourages the adult to use punishment more often in the future (Alberto & Troutman, 2009). Immediate silence may be "golden," but its cost can be very high with regard to a child's emotional health. "Sparing the rod" will not spoil a child.

✓ STUDY BREAK   Punishment

Reflect

Think of how you were punished as a child. Was the punishment immediate? Was it consistent? What effect did these factors have on your behaviour? Was the punishment effective? Which of the side effects of punishment have you witnessed or experienced?

Learning Check

1. Negative reinforcement increases responding; punishment suppresses responding. T or F?
2. Three factors that greatly influence the effects of punishment are timing, consistency, and _____.
3. Mild punishment tends to only temporarily _____ a response that is also reinforced.
   a. enhance
   b. aggravate
   c. replace
   d. suppress

4. Three undesired side effects of punishment are (1) conditioning of fear and resentment, (2) encouragement of aggression, and (3) the learning of escape or _____ responses.
5. Using punishment can be habit forming because putting a stop to someone else's irritating behaviour can _____ the person who applies the punishment.

Critical Thinking

6. Using the concept of partial reinforcement, can you explain why inconsistent punishment is especially ineffective?
7. Escape and avoidance learning have been applied to encourage automobile seat belt use. Can you explain how?

Answers

1. T 2. intensity 3. d 4. avoidance 5. negatively reinforce 6. An inconsistently punished response will continue to be reinforced on a partial schedule, which makes it even more resistant to extinction. 7. Many automobiles have an unpleasant buzzer or persistent chime that sounds if the engine is running and the driver's seat belt is not fastened. Most drivers quickly learn to fasten the belt to stop the annoying sound. This is an example of escape conditioning. Avoidance conditioning is evident when a driver learns to buckle up before starting the car.

COGNITIVE LEARNING—BEYOND CONDITIONING

Is all learning just a connection between stimuli and responses? Some learning can be thought of this way. But, as we have seen, even basic conditioning has "mental" elements. As a human, you can anticipate future rewards or punishments and react accordingly. Here's why: There is no doubt that human learning includes a large cognitive, or mental, dimension. As humans, we are greatly affected by information, expectations, perceptions, mental images, and the like.

Loosely speaking, cognitive learning refers to our understanding, knowing, anticipating, or otherwise making use of information-rich higher mental processes. Cognitive learning extends beyond basic conditioning to involve memory, thinking, problem solving, and language. Since these topics are covered in later chapters, our discussion here is limited to a first look at learning beyond conditioning.

Cognitive Maps

How do you navigate around the city you live in? Have you constructed an overall mental picture of how the place where you live is laid out? This internal "map" acts as a guide even when you must detour or take a new route (Foo et al., 2005). A **cognitive map** is an internal representation of an area, such as a maze, city, campus, or building. Even the lowly rat—not exactly a mental giant—learns where food is found in a maze, not just which turns to make to reach the food (Tolman, Ritchie, & Kalish, 1946), although some research suggests that rats' cognitive maps are specific to the original maze and do not transfer to a new situation (Olthof et al., 1999). If you have ever learned your way through some of the levels found in a video game, you will have a good idea of what a cognitive map is. In a sense, cognitive maps also apply to other kinds of knowledge. For instance, it could be said that you have been developing a "map" of the field of psychology while reading this book. This may be why students sometimes find it helpful to draw pictures or diagrams of how they envision concepts fitting together.

Latent Learning

Cognitive learning is also shown by latent (hidden) learning. **Latent learning** occurs without obvious reinforcement and remains hidden until reinforcement is provided (Davidson, 2000). Here's an example from a classic animal study: Two groups of rats were allowed to explore a maze. The animals in one group found food at the far end of the maze. Soon they learned to rapidly make their way through the maze. Rats in the second group were unrewarded and showed no signs of learning. But later, when the "uneducated" rats were given food in the maze, they ran the maze as quickly as the rewarded group (Tolman & Honzik, 1930). Although there was no outward sign of it, the unrewarded animals had learned their way around the maze. Their learning, therefore, remained latent at first (see Figure 6.18).

It's easy to get lost when visiting a new city if you don't have a cognitive map of the area. Printed maps help, but they may still leave you puzzled until you begin to form a mental representation of major landmarks and directions.

Cognitive map Internal images or other mental representations of an area (maze, city, campus, and so forth) that underlie an ability to choose alternative paths to the same goal.

Latent learning Learning that occurs without obvious reinforcement and that remains unexpressed until reinforcement is provided.

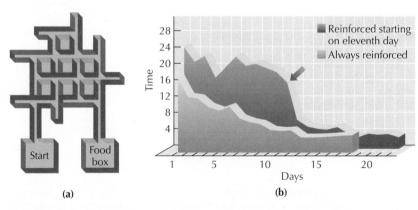

(a)　　　　(b)

▶▶**FIGURE 6.18** Latent learning. (a) The maze used by Tolman and Honzik to demonstrate latent learning by rats. (b) Results of the experiment. Notice the rapid improvement in performance that occurred when food was made available to the previously unreinforced animals. This indicates that learning had occurred but that it remained hidden or unexpressed. (Adapted from Tolman & Honzik, 1930.)

How did they learn if there was no reinforcement? Just satisfying curiosity can be enough to reward learning (Harlow & Harlow, 1962). In humans, latent learning is related to higher-level abilities, such as anticipating future reward. For example, if you give an attractive classmate a ride home, you may make mental notes about how to get to his or her house, even if a date is only a remote future possibility.

Discovery Learning

Much of what is meant by cognitive learning is summarized by the word *understanding*. Each of us has, at times, learned ideas by **rote** (repetition and memorization). Although rote learning is efficient, many psychologists believe that learning is more lasting and flexible when people discover facts and principles on their own. In **discovery learning,** skills are gained by insight and understanding instead of by rote. Discovery learning is an important element of computerized educational simulations and instructional games, as mentioned earlier (Swaak, de Jong, & van Joolingen, 2004).

As long as learning occurs, what difference does it make if it is by discovery or by rote? Figure 6.19 illustrates the difference. Two groups of students were taught to calculate the area of a parallelogram. Some were encouraged to see that a "piece" of a parallelogram could be "moved" to create a rectangle. Later, they were better able to solve unusual problems. Students who simply memorized a rule were confused by the same problems (Wertheimer, 1959). As this implies, discovery leads to a better understanding of new or unusual problems. Whenever possible, people should try new strategies and discover new solutions during learning.

Best of all, perhaps, is guided discovery, in which students who are solving problems are given enough freedom to actively think about them and enough guidance that they gain useful knowledge (Mayer, 2004).

> **Rote learning** Learning that takes place mechanically, through repetition and memorization, or by learning rules.
> **Discovery learning** Learning based on insight and understanding.

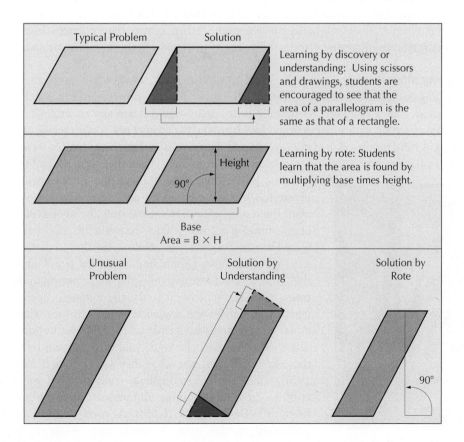

▸▸**FIGURE 6.19** Learning by understanding and by rote. For some types of learning, understanding may be superior, although both types of learning are useful. (After Wertheimer, 1959.)

MODELLING—DO AS I DO, NOT AS I SAY

SURVEY QUESTION>
Does learning occur by imitation?

> **Observational learning** Learning achieved by watching and imitating the actions of another or noting the consequences of those actions.
>
> **Model** A person who serves as an example in observational learning.

Many skills are learned by what Albert Bandura (1971) calls observational learning, or modelling. **Observational learning** is achieved by watching and imitating the actions of another person or by noting the consequences of the person's actions (Lefrançois, 2006). In other words, modelling is any process in which information is imparted by example, before direct practice is allowed (Rosenthal & Steffek, 1991). Humans share the capacity for observational learning with many other mammals, including gorillas (Meunier, Monfardini, & Boussaoud, 2007).

The value of learning by observation is obvious: Imagine trying to tell someone how to tie a shoe, do a Zumba step, or play a guitar. Bandura believes that anything that can be learned from direct experience can be learned by observation. Often, this allows a person to skip the tedious trial-and-error stage of learning.

Observational Learning

It seems obvious that we learn by observation, but how does it occur? By observing a **model** (someone who serves as an example), a person may (1) learn new responses, (2) learn to carry out or avoid previously learned responses (depending on what happens to the model for doing the same thing), or (3) learn a general rule that can be applied to various situations (Lefrançois, 2006).

For observational learning to occur, several things must take place. First, the learner must pay attention to the model and remember what was done. (A beginning auto mechanic might be interested enough to watch an entire tune-up, but unable to remember all the steps.) Next, the learner must be able to reproduce the modelled behaviour. (Sometimes this is a matter of practice, but it may be that the learner will never be able to perform the behaviour. We all admire the feats of world-class gymnasts, but there aren't many of us who could reproduce those moves, no matter how much we practise.) If a model is successful at a task or rewarded for a response, the learner is more likely to imitate the behaviour. In general, models who are attractive, trustworthy, capable, admired, powerful, or high in status also tend to be imitated (Bandura & Walters, 1963; Brewer & Wann, 1998). Finally, once a new response is tried, normal reinforcement determines if it will be repeated thereafter. (Notice the similarity to latent learning, described earlier.)

Imitating Models

Modelling has a powerful effect on behaviour. In a classic experiment, children watched an adult attack a large blow-up "Bo-Bo the Clown" doll. Some children saw an adult sit on the doll, punch it, hit it with a hammer, and kick it around the room. Others saw a movie of these actions. A third group saw a cartoon version of the aggression. Later, the children were frustrated by having some attractive toys taken away from them. Then they were allowed to play with the Bo-Bo doll. Most imitated the adult's attack (see Figure 6.20). Some even added new aggressive acts of their own! Interestingly, the cartoon was only slightly less effective in encouraging aggression than the live adult model and the filmed model (Bandura, Ross, & Ross, 1963).

Then do children blindly imitate adults? No. Remember that observational learning only prepares a person to duplicate a response. Whether it is actually imitated depends on whether the model was rewarded or punished for what was done. When parents tell a child to do one thing, but model a completely different behaviour, children tend to imitate what the parents do, and not what they say (Bryan & Walbek, 1970). Thus, through modelling, children learn not only attitudes, gestures, emotions, and personality traits but also fears, anxieties, and bad habits. A good example is the adolescent smoker, who is much more likely to begin smoking if his or her parents, siblings, and friends smoke (Wilkinson & Abraham, 2004). And children who witness

Observational learning often imparts much information that would be difficult to obtain by reading instructions or memorizing rules.

Chris Stein/Getty Images

Courtesy of Albert Bandura.

▶▶**FIGURE 6.20** A nursery school child imitates the aggressive behaviour of an adult model he has just seen in a movie.

domestic violence are more likely to commit it themselves (Hutton, 2003; Murrell, Christoff, & Henning, 2007).

Now, consider a typical situation: Little Owen has just been interrupted at play by his younger brother, Liam. Angry and frustrated, he decks Liam, who starts to cry. This behaviour interrupts his father's TV watching. Father promptly spanks Owen, saying, "This will teach you to hit your little brother." And it will. Because of modelling effects, it is unrealistic to expect a child to "do as I say, not as I do." The message the father has given the child is clear: "You have frustrated me; therefore, I will hit you." The next time Owen is frustrated, it won't be surprising if he imitates his father and hits his brother.

Modelling and the Media

Speaking of television, do the media promote observational learning? Canadian children spend approximately 15 hours a week watching television (Statistics Canada, 2007). Adding in video games, movies, the Internet, music, books, and magazines, children and teens spend up to 44 hours a week engaged with various media (Active Healthy Kids Canada, 2011).

Children watching Saturday morning cartoons see a chilling 26 or more violent acts each hour (Pogatchnik, 1990). Even G-rated cartoons average 10 minutes of violence per hour (Yokota & Thompson, 2000). In short, typical TV viewers are exposed to a massive dose of media violence, which tends to promote observational learning of aggression (Bushman & Anderson, 2001).

Televised Aggression

The last finding comes as no surprise. Studies show conclusively that if large groups of children watch a great deal of televised violence, they will be more prone to behave aggressively (Anderson et al., 2003; Bushman & Anderson, 2001). In other words, not all children will become more aggressive, but many will. A group of primary school students with known television-viewing habits were later contacted in early adulthood (Huesmann et al., 2003). Those who watched more violence on television as elementary school students were more aggressive as adults 15 years later. *Does the same conclusion apply to other media?* Oh, yes. Children tend to imitate what they observe in all media. From professional wrestling (Bernthal, 2003) to rap music (Wingood et al., 2003) to video games (Carnagey & Anderson, 2004), children have plenty of opportunity to observe and imitate both the good and the bad. (See Critical Thinking: "You Mean Video Games Might Be Bad for Me?" for some recent evidence.)

Is it fair to say, then, that televised violence causes aggression in viewers (especially children)? Fortunately, that would be an exaggeration (Kirsh, 2005). Media violence can make aggression more likely, but it does not invariably "cause" it to occur for any given child. Many other factors affect the chances that hostile thoughts will be turned into actions. Youngsters who believe that aggression is an acceptable way to solve problems, who believe that TV violence is realistic, and who identify with TV characters are most likely to copy televised aggression (Huesmann et al., 2003).

In view of such findings, it is understandable that Canada, among other countries, has restricted the amount of permissible violence on television.

© Photos 12/Alamy

TV heroes can act as powerful models for observational learning of aggression.

CRITICAL THINKING

You Mean Video Games Might Be Bad for Me?

Today's kids can experience more gore in a day than most people used to experience in a lifetime, even during military combat. For example, in *Manhunt,* you kill people violently with plastic bags and piano wires and stab them in the eyes with broken bottles; *Manhunt 2* includes more of the same, as well as graphic torture scenes where you're doing the torturing.

What effects do such experiences have on people who play violent video games? Reviews have concluded that violent video games increase aggressive behaviour in children and young adults (Bushman & Anderson, 2001; Anderson, 2004). As with TV, young children are especially susceptible to fantasy violence in video games (Anderson et al., 2003; Bensley & Van Eenwyk, 2001).

One study illustrates the impact of video game violence. First, college students played a violent (*Mortal Kombat*) or non-violent (*PGA Tournament Golf*) video game. Next, they competed with

another student (actually an actor) in a task that allowed aggression and retaliation to take place. Students who played *Mortal Kombat* were much more likely to aggress by punishing their competitor with a blast of loud noise than those playing a non-violent game (Bartholow & Anderson, 2002). (Don't mess with someone who just played *Mortal Kombat!*)

How does video game violence increase aggressive behaviour? One possibility is that repeated exposure to violence desensitizes players, making them less likely to react negatively to violence and, hence, more prone to engage in it (Bartholow, Sestir, & Davis, 2005; Funk, 2005). Another possibility is that by practising violence against other people, players may learn to be aggressive in real life (Unsworth & Ward, 2001). There is also evidence that playing violent video games directly alters brain functioning in the regions associated with cognitive function and emotional control (Wang et al., 2011).

A Look Ahead

Conditioning principles are often derived from animal experiments. However, it should be apparent that the same principles apply to human behaviour. Perhaps the best way to appreciate this fact is to observe how reinforcement affects your own behaviour. With this in mind, the upcoming Psychology in Action section proposes a personal experiment in operant conditioning. We'll also consider steps you can take to better manage your learning at school. Don't miss these coming attractions!

✔ STUDY BREAK   Cognitive Learning and Imitation

Reflect

Try to think of at least one personal example of each of these concepts: cognitive map, latent learning, discovery learning.

Describe a skill you have learned primarily through observational learning. How did modelling help you learn?

What entertainment or sports personalities did you identify with when you were a child? How did this affect your behaviour?

Learning Check

1. An internal representation of relationships is referred to as a

_____ _____.

2. Learning that suddenly appears when a reward or incentive for performance is given is called
   a. discovery learning   b. latent learning
   c. rote learning   d. reminiscence
3. Psychologists use the term _____ to describe observational learning.

4. If a model is successful, rewarded, attractive, or high in status, his or her behaviour is
   a. difficult to reproduce   b. less likely to be attended to
   c. more likely to be imitated   d. subject to positive transfer
5. Children who observed a live adult behave aggressively became more aggressive; those who observed movie and cartoon aggression did not. T or F?
6. Children are most likely to imitate TV characters with whom they identify, but this applies primarily to characters who are non-violent. T or F?
7. Psychological research indicates that televised violence causes aggressive behaviour in children. T or F?

Critical Thinking

8. Draw a map of your school's campus as you picture it now. Draw a map of the campus as you pictured it after your first visit. Why do the maps differ?
9. Children who watch many aggressive programs on television tend to be more aggressive than average. Why doesn't this observation prove that televised aggression causes aggressive behaviour?

Answers

1. cognitive map 2. b 3. modelling 4. c 5. F 6. F 7. F 8. Your cognitive map of the campus has undoubtedly become more accurate and intricate over time as you have added details to it. Your drawings should reflect this change. 9. Because the observation is based on a correlation. Children who are already aggressive may choose to watch more aggressive programs, rather than being made aggressive by them. It took experimental studies to verify that televised aggression promotes aggression by viewers.

Psychology in Action

BEHAVIOURAL SELF-MANAGEMENT

This discussion could be the start of one of the most personal applications of psychology in this book. Here is an invitation for you to carry out a self-management project of your own. Would you like to increase the number of hours you spend studying each week? Would you like to exercise more, attend more classes, lose weight, concentrate longer, stop smoking, or read more books? All these activities and many others can be improved by following the steps described here.

<SURVEY QUESTION
Can we use the principles of conditioning to help solve practical problems?

Self-Managed Behaviour—A Rewarding Project

The principles of operant conditioning can be adapted to manage your own behaviour. Here's how:

1. *Choose a target behaviour.* Identify the behaviour you want to change.
2. *Record a baseline.* Record how much time you currently spend performing the target behaviour, or count the number of desired or undesired responses you make each day.
3. *Establish goals.* Remember the principle of shaping, and set realistic goals for gradual improvement on each successive week. Also, set daily goals that add up to the weekly goal.
4. *Choose reinforcers.* If you meet your daily goal, what reward will you allow yourself? Daily rewards might be watching television, eating a chocolate bar, socializing with friends, playing a musical instrument, or whatever you enjoy. Also establish a weekly reward. If you reach your weekly goal, what reward will you allow yourself? A movie? A dinner out? A weekend hike? (However, if your goal is to lose weight, you should not reward yourself with food!)
5. *Record your progress.* Keep accurate records of the amount of time spent each day on the desired activity or the number of times you make the desired response.
6. *Reward successes.* If you meet your daily goal, collect your reward. If you fall short, be honest with yourself and skip the reward. Do the same for your weekly goal.
7. *Make adjustments.* Adjust your plan as you learn more about your behaviour. Overall progress will reinforce your attempts at self-management.

If you have trouble finding rewards, or if you don't want to use the entire system, remember that anything done often can serve as reinforcement. This is known as the **Premack principle.** It is named after David Premack, a psychologist who popularized its use. For example, if you watch television every night and want to study more, make it a rule not to turn on the set until you have studied for an hour (or whatever length of time you choose). Then lengthen the requirement each week. Here is a sample of one student's plan:

1. Target behaviour: number of hours spent studying for school.
2. Recorded baseline: an average of 25 minutes per day for a weekly total of about three hours.
3. Goal for the first week: an increase in study time to 40 minutes per day; weekly goal of about four and a half hours total study time. Goal for second week: 50 minutes per day and almost six hours per week. Goal for third week: one hour per day and seven hours per week. Ultimate goal: to reach and maintain 14 hours per week study time.
4. Daily reward for reaching goal: one hour of guitar playing in the evening; no playing if the goal is not met. Weekly reward for reaching goal: going to a movie or downloading an album.

Self-Recording

Even if you find it difficult to give and withhold rewards, you are likely to succeed. Simply knowing that you are reaching a desired goal can be reward enough. The key to any self-management program, therefore, is **self-recording** (keeping records of response frequencies). The concept was demonstrated by students in a psychology course. Some of the

Premack principle Any high-frequency response can be used to reinforce a low-frequency response.
Self-recording Self-management based on keeping records of response frequencies.

jacomstephens/iStockPhoto

students recorded their study time and graphed their daily and weekly study behaviour. Even though no extra rewards were offered, these students earned better grades than others who were not required to keep records (Johnson & White, 1971).

As discussed earlier, feedback is also valuable for changing personal behaviour. Feedback can help you decrease bad habits as well as increase desirable responses. Keep track of the number of times daily that you arrive late to class, smoke a cigarette, watch an hour of TV, drink a cup of coffee, bite your fingernails, swear, or whatever you are interested in changing. A simple tally on a piece of paper will do, or you can get a small mechanical counter like those used to keep golf scores or count calories. Record-keeping helps break patterns, and the feedback can be motivating as you begin to make progress.

Good Ways to Break Bad Habits

How can I use learning principles to break a bad habit? By using the methods we have discussed, you can reinforce yourself for decreasing unwanted behaviours, such as swearing, nail biting, criticizing others, smoking, drinking coffee, excess TV watching, or any other behaviour you choose to target. However, breaking bad habits may require some additional techniques. Here are four strategies to help you change bad habits.

Alternative Responses

A good strategy for change is to try to get the same reinforcement with a new response.

Example: Marta often tells jokes at the expense of others. Her friends sometimes feel hurt by her sharp-edged humour. Marta senses this and wants to change. What can she do? Usually, Marta's joke telling is reinforced by attention and approval. She could just as easily get the same reinforcement by giving other people praise or compliments. Making a change in her behaviour should be easy because she will continue to receive the reinforcement she seeks.

Extinction

Try to discover what is reinforcing an unwanted response and remove, avoid, or delay the reinforcement.

Example: Tiffany has developed a habit of taking longer and longer "breaks" to watch TV when she should be studying. Obviously, TV watching is reinforcing her break taking. To improve her study habits, Tiffany could delay reinforcement by studying at the library or some other location a good distance from her TV. This won't work if she takes her laptop with her and watches TV in the library on her laptop.

Response Chains

Break up response chains that precede an undesired behaviour. The key idea is to scramble the chain of events that leads to an undesired response (Watson & Tharp, 2007).

Example: Almost every night Steve comes home from work, turns on the TV, and eats a whole bag of cookies or chips. He then takes a shower and changes clothes. By dinnertime he has lost his appetite. Steve realizes he is substituting junk food for dinner. Steve could solve the problem by breaking the response chain that precedes dinner. For instance, he could shower immediately when he gets home or he could avoid turning on the television until after dinner. He could also not buy cookies or chips. If they aren't there, he can't eat them.

Cues and Antecedents

Try to avoid, narrow down, or remove stimuli that elicit the bad habit.

Example: Saul wants to cut down on smoking. He has taken many smoking cues out of his surroundings by removing ashtrays, matches, and extra cigarettes from his house and car. Saul should try narrowing antecedent stimuli even more. He could begin by smoking only outside, and never in his car. He could then limit his smoking to home. Then to only one room at home. Then to one chair at home. If he succeeds in getting this far, he may want to limit his smoking to only one unpleasant place, such as a bathroom, basement, or garage (Riley et al., 2002).

Contracting

If you try the techniques described here and have difficulty sticking with them, you may want to try a fifth technique, **behavioural contracting.** In a behavioural contract, you state a specific problem behaviour you want to control or a goal you want to achieve. Also state the rewards you will receive, privileges you will forfeit, or punishments you must accept. The contract should be typed, printed out, and signed by you and a person you trust.

A behavioural contract can be quite motivating, especially when mild punishment is part of the agreement. Here's an example reported by Nurnberger and Zimmerman (1970): A student working on his Ph.D. had completed all requirements but his dissertation, yet for two years he had not written a single page. A contract was drawn up for him in which he agreed to meet weekly deadlines on the number of pages he would complete. To make sure he would meet the deadlines, he wrote post-dated cheques. These were to be cashed if he failed to reach his goal for the week. The cheques were made out to organizations he despised. From the time he signed the contract until he finished his degree, the student's work output was greatly improved.

If you discover that you lack necessary knowledge or skills, ask for help, take advantage of tutoring programs, or look for sources of information beyond your courses and textbooks. Knowing how to regulate and control learning can be a key to lifelong enrichment and personal empowerment.

> **Behavioural contract** A formal agreement stating behaviours to be changed and consequences that apply.

Getting Help

Attempting to manage or alter your own behaviour may be more difficult than it sounds. If you feel you need more information, consult the book listed below. You will also find helpful advice in the Psychology in Action section of Chapter 13, page 544. If you do try a self-modification project or self-regulated learning, but find it impossible to reach your goals, be aware that professional advice is available.

Where to Obtain More Information

- Watson, D. L., and Tharp, R. G. *Self-directed Behavior: Self Modification for Personal Adjustment.* 9th ed. Pacific Grove, CA: Wadsworth-Brooks/Cole, 2007.

 STUDY BREAK **Behavioural Self-Management**

Reflect

Even if you don't expect to carry out a self-management project right now, outline a plan for changing your own behaviour. Be sure to describe the behaviour you want to change, set goals, and identify reinforcers.

To what extent do you already engage in self-regulated learning? What additional steps could you take to become a more active, goal-oriented learner?

Learning Check

1. After a target behaviour has been selected for reinforcement, it's a good idea to record a baseline so you can set realistic goals for change. T or F?
2. Self-recording, even without the use of extra rewards, can bring about desired changes in target behaviours. T or F?

3. The Premack principle states that behavioural contracting can be used to reinforce changes in behaviour. T or F?
4. A self-management plan should make use of the principle of shaping by setting a graduated series of goals. T or F?
5. A key aspect of self-_____ learning is feedback, which means you should find ways to _____ your progress.
6. Self-instruction refers to the process of comparing short-term performance to long-term goals. T or F?

Critical Thinking

7. How does setting daily goals in a behavioural self-management program help maximize the effects of reinforcement?

Answers

1. T 2. T 3. F 4. T 5. regulated, monitor 6. F 7. Daily performance goals and rewards reduce the delay of reinforcement, which maximizes its impact.

CHAPTER IN REVIEW

Major Points

- Conditioning is a fundamental type of learning that affects many aspects of daily life.

- In classical conditioning, a neutral stimulus is repeatedly paired with a stimulus that reliably provokes a response. By association, the neutral stimulus also begins to elicit a response.

- In operant conditioning, responses that are followed by reinforcement occur more frequently.

- To understand why people behave as they do, it is important to identify how their responses are being reinforced.

- Cognitive learning involves acquiring higher-level information, rather than just linking stimuli and responses.

- We also learn by observing and imitating the actions of others.

- Behavioural principles can be used to manage one's own behaviour.

Summary

What is learning?

- Learning is a relatively permanent change in behaviour due to experience. Learning resulting from conditioning depends on reinforcement. Reinforcement increases the probability that a particular response will occur.

- Classical conditioning and operant conditioning are two basic types of learning.

- In classical conditioning, a previously neutral stimulus begins to elicit a response through association with another stimulus.

- In operant conditioning, the frequency and pattern of voluntary responses are altered by their consequences.

What is classical conditioning? How does it occur?

- In classical conditioning, a neutral stimulus (NS) is associated with an unconditioned stimulus (US).

- The US causes a reflex called the unconditioned response (UR). If the NS is consistently paired with the US, it becomes a conditioned stimulus (CS) capable of producing a conditioned (learned) response (CR).

- When the CS is followed by the US, conditioning is reinforced (strengthened).

- From an informational view, conditioning creates expectancies, which alter response patterns. That is, the CS creates an expectancy that the US will follow.

- Higher-order conditioning occurs when a well-learned conditioned stimulus is used as if it were an unconditioned stimulus, bringing about further learning.

- When the CS is repeatedly presented alone, conditioning is extinguished (weakened or inhibited). After extinction seems to be complete, a rest period may lead to the temporary reappearance of a conditioned response. This is called spontaneous recovery.

- Through stimulus generalization, stimuli similar to the conditioned stimulus will also produce a response. Generalization gives way to stimulus discrimination when an organism learns to respond to one stimulus but not to similar stimuli.

How are emotions affected by conditioning?

- Conditioning applies to visceral or emotional responses as well as simple reflexes. As a result, conditioned emotional responses (CERs) also occur.

- Irrational fears called phobias may be CERs. Conditioning of emotional responses can occur vicariously (second-hand) as well as directly.

What is operant conditioning? How does it occur?

- Operant conditioning occurs when a voluntary action is followed by a reinforcer. Reinforcement in operant conditioning increases the frequency or probability of a response. This result is based on the law of effect.

- Complex operant responses can be taught by reinforcing successive approximations to a final desired response. This is called shaping. It is particularly useful in training animals.

- If an operant response is not reinforced, it may extinguish (disappear). But after extinction seems complete, it may temporarily reappear (spontaneous recovery).

What are the different kinds of operant reinforcement?

- In positive reinforcement, a reward or a pleasant event follows a response. In negative reinforcement, a response that ends discomfort becomes more likely.

- Primary reinforcers are "natural," physiologically based rewards.

- Secondary reinforcers are learned. They typically gain their reinforcing value by direct association with primary reinforcers or because they can be exchanged for primary reinforcers. Tokens and money gain their reinforcing value in this way.

- Feedback, or knowledge of results, aids learning and improves performance. It is most effective when it is immediate, detailed, and frequent.

- Programmed instruction breaks learning into a series of small steps and provides immediate feedback. Computer-assisted instruction (CAI) does the same and also provides added information when needed.

Can patterns of reward influence our behaviour?

- Delayed reinforcement is less effective, but long chains of responses may be built up so that a single reinforcer maintains many responses.

- Superstitious behaviours often become part of response chains because they appear to produce reinforcement.

- Reward or reinforcement may be given continuously (after every response) or on a schedule of partial reinforcement. Partial reinforcement produces greater resistance to extinction.

- The four most basic schedules of reinforcement are fixed ratio, variable ratio, fixed interval, and variable interval. Each produces a distinct pattern of responding.

- Stimuli that precede a reinforced response tend to control the response on future occasions (stimulus control). Two aspects of stimulus control are generalization and discrimination.

- In generalization, an operant response tends to occur when stimuli similar to those preceding reinforcement are present.

- In discrimination, responses are given in the presence of discriminative stimuli associated with reinforcement.

How does punishment affect behaviour?

- Punishment decreases responding. Punishment occurs when a response is followed by the onset of an aversive event or by the removal of a positive event (response cost).

- Punishment is most effective when it is immediate, consistent, and intense.

- The undesirable side effects of punishment include the conditioning of fear to punishing agents and situations associated with punishment, the learning of escape and avoidance responses, and the encouragement of aggression.

What is cognitive learning?

- Cognitive learning involves higher mental processes, such as understanding, knowing, or anticipating. Even in relatively simple learning situations, animals and people seem to form cognitive maps (internal representations of relationships).

- In latent learning, learning remains hidden or unseen until a reward or incentive for performance is offered.

- Discovery learning emphasizes insight and understanding, in contrast to rote learning.

Does learning occur by imitation?

- Much human learning is achieved through observation, or modelling. Observational learning is influenced by the personal characteristics of the model and the success or failure of the model's behaviour.

- Television characters can act as powerful models for observational learning. Televised violence increases the likelihood of aggression by viewers.

Can we use the principles of conditioning to help solve practical problems?

- When managing your own behaviour, self-reinforcement, self-recording, feedback, and behavioural contracting are all helpful.

- Four strategies that can help change bad habits are reinforcing alternative responses, promoting extinction, breaking response chains, and avoiding antecedent cues.

- In school, self-regulated learners typically do all of the following: They set learning goals, plan learning strategies, use self-instruction, monitor their progress, evaluate themselves, reinforce successes, and take corrective action when required.

Interactive Learning

Please visit http://www.psychologyjourney4ce.nelson.com for a list of weblinks to relevant psychology sites.

CourseMate

Access an interactive e-book and chapter-specific interactive learning tools, including flashcards, quizzes, videos, and more, in your psychology CourseMate. Visit Nelsonbrain.com to use CourseMate.

psyk.trek 5. Learning, Psyk.Trek Simulations: 4. Shaping in Operant Conditioning.

The questions that follow are only a sample of what you need to know. If you miss any of the items, review the entire chapter and the Study Breaks. Another way to prepare for tests is to use the Study Guide and the Practice Exams that are available with this text.

1. To what does the concept of reinforcement apply?
   a. antecedents of behaviour   b. neutral stimuli and rewards
   c. consequences of behaviour   d. spontaneous recovery

2. According to the informational view, what does classical conditioning create?
   a. new expectancies   b. new unconditioned responses
   c. new unconditioned stimuli   d. new generalizations

3. What can *some* phobias be thought of as?
   a. Neutral stimulus–conditioned response (NS–CR) connections
   b. desensitization gradients
   c. extinction responses
   d. conditioned emotional responses (CERs)

4. Within learning, the law of effect defines the role of which of the following?
   a. antecedent stimuli   b. stimulus generalization
   c. operant reinforcers   d. stimulus approximations

5. How does negative reinforcement affect responding?
   a. It increases responding.   b. It decreases responding.
   c. It reverses responding.   d. It extinguishes responding.

6. Response cost is a form of which of the following?
   a. discrimination conditioning   b. generalization
   c. higher-order conditioning   d. punishment

7. Which of the following is a correct match?
   a. token reinforcer—primary reinforcement
   b. token reinforcer—secondary reinforcement
   c. social reinforcer—primary reinforcement
   d. social reinforcer—secondary reinforcement

8. What schedules have moderate response rates that are marked by spurts of activity and periods of inactivity?
   a. fixed-rate (FR) schedules   b. variable-rate (VR) schedules
   c. fixed-interval (FI) schedules   d. variable-interval (VI) schedules

9. Children who watch a great deal of televised violence are more prone to be aggressive. What best explains this effect?
   a. negative reinforcement
   b. shaping and successive approximations
   c. observational learning
   d. vicarious classical conditioning

10. In a behavioural management strategy, what does self-recording apply to personal habits?
    a. vicarious conditioning   b. feedback
    c. behavioural contracting   d. the Premack principle

11. You smell cookies baking and your mouth waters. While the smell of the cookies is a conditioned stimulus, your salivation is which of the following?
    a. a conditioned stimulus (CS)   b. a conditioned response (CR)
    c. a consequence   d. a reflex

12. Three-year-old Josh was chased by a dog, and now he is afraid of all dogs. What explains Josh's fear?
    a. extinction   b. stimulus generalization
    c. spontaneous recovery   d. higher-order conditioning

13. When does operant reinforcement work best?
    a. when it is delayed   b. when it is antecedent
    c. when it is response contingent   d. when it is aversive

14. "Sniffer" dogs locate drugs and explosives. What kind of training teaches them to identify these substances?
    a. classical extinction   b. classical desensitization
    c. vicarious feedback   d. operant discrimination

15. Bad habits can be altered by finding ways to remove, avoid, or delay the reinforcement that follows unwanted behaviours. What best describes this strategy?
    a. seeking alternative ways of reacting
    b. using operant extinction
    c. breaking up response chains
    d. narrowing cues and antecedents

16. Every day when you come home from school, you drop your coat and books in the middle of the living room. Your mother yells at you until you pick up your stuff. What is at work to support your mother's yelling?
    a. positive reinforcement   b. negative reinforcement
    c. punishment   d. modelling

17. Every day when you come home from school, you drop your coat and books in the middle of the living room. Your father yells at you until you pick up your stuff. What is at work to support your behaviour of picking up your stuff?
    a. positive reinforcement   b. negative reinforcement
    c. punishment   d. modelling

18. What can weaken conditioned responses?
    a. spontaneous recovery
    b. stimulus generalization
    c. extinction
    d. following the conditioned stimulus (CS) with an unconditioned stimulus (US)

19. What shares the same principles as computer-assisted instruction (CAI)?
    a. negative reinforcement
    b. higher-order conditioning
    c. programmed instruction
    d. stimulus generalization

20. Your niece has a temper tantrum in the store while you are shopping. If you buy her a toy, what is the effect?
    a. She is discouraged from tantrums in the future.
    b. She is encouraged to have more destructive behaviours.
    c. She is encouraged to have more tantrums in the future.
    d. She is discouraged from more destructive behaviours.

ANSWERS   1.c 2.a 3.d 4.c 5.a 6.d 7.b 8.c 9.c 10.b 11.b 12.b 13.c 14.d 15.c 16.a 17.b 18.c 19.c 20.c

Memory

JOURNEY INTO PSYCHOLOGY: OVERCOMING MEMORY LOSS

In this chapter, we'll consider some remarkable feats of memory—both by people with intact brains and by people who have suffered some form of brain damage. Among the most compelling of the latter group is HC, a young woman studied by Shayna Rosenbaum of York University in Toronto and her colleagues at the Rotman Research Institute. HC was born prematurely, at 32 weeks, and suffered a loss of oxygen to her brain soon afterwards. This partially destroyed her hippocampus, a structure important for storing memories of experiences. As a result, HC is poor at remembering episodes of her own life—she has impaired episodic memory—but she has normal knowledge of the world (semantic memory). Most remarkably, HC graduated from high school and took one year of training at a technical college before switching into a culinary degree program.

Memory The mental system for receiving, encoding, storing, organizing, altering, and retrieving information.

HC has difficulty learning new information, which should be a major problem to overcome. Nonetheless, she overcame it—she figured out that repetition was important for her to securely store information in long-term memory. And she learned to use a handheld computer to keep track of things like appointments and new people that she meets.

Recently, Rosenbaum and her colleagues at Rotman made a startling discovery while testing HC's ability to remember faces and words (Rose et al., 2012). The face recognition test was particularly challenging: A face was presented for a second and a half. Then two faces were presented: the studied face and a morphed face made 50 percent from the studied face and 50 percent from a different face. On each trial, the task was to say which of the two the studied face was. The remarkable finding was that HC was much better at this task if the studied face was familiar than if it was unfamiliar. Shown Paris Hilton's face, she could do the task very well. Shown a stranger's face, she was much worse.

HC is better at working-memory tasks if the stimuli are already securely stored in long-term memory (LTM). In that case, when a stimulus appears, she can somehow "tag" the trace in LTM and later, when tested, retrieve the tagged items for recall. But this strategy will obviously not work for things that are not already in LTM.

In a very real sense, who we are is determined by what we remember *and* what we forget (Behrend, Beike, & Lampinen, 2004). As you read this chapter on **memory** and forgetting, you'll almost certainly discover ways to improve your memory.

 Survey Questions

- How does memory work?
- What are the features of short-term memory?
- What are the features of long-term memory?
- How is memory measured?
- Why do we forget?
- How does the brain form and store memories?
- What are "photographic" memories?
- How can I improve my memory?
- Are there any tricks to help me with my memory?

STAGES OF MEMORY—DO YOU HAVE A MIND LIKE A SIEVE?

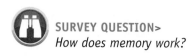 **SURVEY QUESTION>** *How does memory work?*

Why are we always forgetting stuff? To understand forgetting, we first need to understand remembering. Do you remember what you had for breakfast this morning? Or any of what happened last month? Of course you do. But how is it possible for us to so easily travel back in time? Let's begin with a look at some basic memory concepts.

Many people think of memory as "a dusty storehouse of facts." In reality, human **memory** is an active system that receives, stores, organizes, alters, and recovers information (Baddeley, Eysenck, & Anderson, 2009). To be stored for a long time, information must pass through

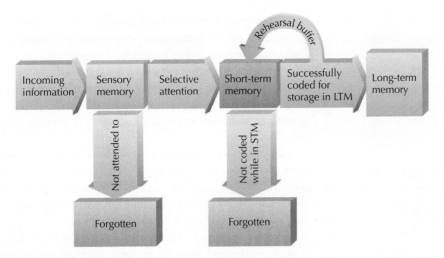

Encoding Converting information into a form in which it will be retained in memory.

Storage Holding information in memory for later use.

Retrieval Recovering information from storage in memory.

Sensory memory The first stage of memory, which holds an exact record of incoming information for a few seconds or less.

Iconic memory A mental image or visual representation.

Echoic memory A brief continuation of sensory activity in the auditory system after a sound is heard.

►►**FIGURE 7.1** The Atkinson-Schiffrin model. Remembering is thought to involve at least three steps. Incoming information is first held for a second or two by sensory memory. Information selected by attention is then transferred to temporary storage in short-term memory (STM). If new information is not rapidly encoded, or rehearsed, it is forgotten. If it is transferred to long-term memory (LTM), it becomes relatively permanent, although retrieving it may be a problem. The preceding is a useful, but highly simplified, *model* of memory; it may not be literally true of what happens in the brain (Atkinson & Schiffrin, 1968; Goldstein, 2008).

sensory memory, short-term memory, and long-term memory. These stages are summarized by the *Atkinson-Schiffrin model* of memory shown in Figure 7.1 (Atkinson & Schiffrin, 1968; Goldstein, 2008).

In some general ways, each of these three memory systems acts like a computer (Figure 7.2). Incoming information is first **encoded,** or changed into a usable form. This step is like typing data into a computer. Next, information is **stored,** or held, in the memory system. Finally, information must be **retrieved,** or taken out of storage, to be useful. If you're going to remember all of the 9856 new terms on your next psychology exam, you must successfully move them through sensory memory, short-term memory, and long-term memory. Let's trace the interesting series of memory events that must occur before you can pass that exam.

Sensory Memory

Let's say you sit down to memorize a few terms from this textbook. How will you remember them? Information is first encoded in **sensory memory,** which can hold an exact copy of what you see or hear, for a few seconds or less. We are normally unaware of the functioning of our sensory memories. For instance, look at a flower and then quickly close your eyes. If you are lucky, a fleeting visual image of the flower will persist. **Iconic** (eye-KON-ick) **memories** (sensory images) typically last for about one-half second (Keysers et al., 2005). Similarly, when you hear information, sensory memory stores it as an echoic memory for up to two seconds (Haenschel et al., 2005). An **echoic memory** is a brief flurry of activity in the auditory system. In general, sensory memory holds information just long enough to move it to the second memory system, short-term memory (Neath & Surprenant, 2003).

Short-Term Memory

Not everything we see or hear stays in memory. Imagine that a radio is playing in the background as you read this chapter. Will you remember what the announcer says, too? Probably not, because *selective attention* (focusing on a selected portion of sensory input) controls

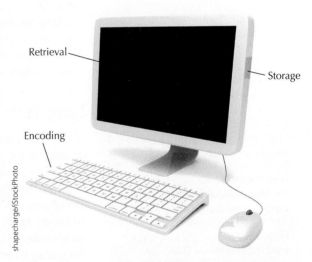

shapecharge/iStockPhoto

►►**FIGURE 7.2** In some ways, a computer acts like a mechanical memory system. Both systems process information, and both allow encoding, storage, and retrieval of data.

EDY | DRAMA | VIDEOS YOU'VE FORGOTTEN YOU'VE SEEN ALREADY | ACTION

© Mick Stevens/The New Yorker Collection/www.cartoonbank.com

what information is retrieved from sensory memory and moved on to short-term memory. **Short-term memory (STM)** stores small amounts of information. We are consciously aware of short-term memories for a dozen seconds or so (Jonides et al., 2008). By paying attention to your textbook, you will place some psychological terms in short-term memory (while you ignore the voice on the radio saying, "Try Drizzle Diapers today").

How are short-term memories encoded? Short-term memories can be encoded as images. But more often they are encoded *phonetically* (by sound), especially in recalling words and letters (Page et al., 2007). If you are introduced to Tim at a party and you forget his name, you are more likely to call him by a name that sounds like Tim (Jim, Kim, or Slim, for instance) than by a name that sounds different, such as Bob or Mike. On a psychology exam you may be lucky if you don't write "axon potential" instead of "action potential," or "depression" instead of "repression"!

Short-term memory briefly stores small amounts of information. When you dial a phone number or briefly remember a shopping list, you are using STM. Notice that unless you *rehearse* information (silently say it over and over to yourself), it is quickly "dumped" from STM and forever lost. Short-term memory prevents our minds from storing useless names, dates, telephone numbers, and other trivia.

As you may have noticed when dialling a telephone, STM is very sensitive to *interruption*, or *interference*. You've probably had something like this happen: Someone leaves a phone number on your voice mail. You repeat the number to yourself as you start to dial. Someone asks you a question. You answer, turn to the phone, and find that you have forgotten the number. Notice again that STM can handle only small amounts of information. It is very difficult to do more than one task at a time in STM (Miyake, 2001; Oberauer & Göthe, 2006).

Working Memory

Short-term memory is often used for more than just storing information. When STM is combined with other mental processes, it acts more like a sort of "mental scratchpad," or **working memory**, where we do much of our thinking. That is, working memory briefly holds the information we need when we are thinking and solving problems (Holmes & Adams, 2006). Whenever you read a book, do mental arithmetic, put together a puzzle, plan a meal, or follow directions, you are using working memory (Baddeley, 2003).

Long-Term Memory

If STM is so limited, how do we remember for longer periods? Information that is important or meaningful is transferred to **long-term memory (LTM)**, which acts as a lasting storehouse for knowledge. LTM contains everything you know about the world—from aardvark to zebra, math to *Mad Men*, facts to fantasy. Yet, there appears to be no danger of running out of room. LTM can store nearly limitless amounts of information. In fact, the more you know, the easier it becomes to add new information to memory. This is the reverse of what we would expect if LTM could be "filled up" (Goldstein, 2008). It is also one of many reasons for getting an education.

Are long-term memories also encoded as sounds? They can be. But, typically, long-term memories are encoded on the basis of *meaning*, not sound. If you make an error in LTM, it will probably be related to meaning. For example, if you are trying to recall the phrase *test*

Short-term memory (STM) The memory system used to hold small amounts of information for relatively brief time periods.

Working memory Another name for short-term memory, especially when it is used for thinking and problem solving.

Long-term memory (LTM) The memory system used for relatively permanent storage of meaningful information.

anxiety for your psychology exam, you are more likely to mistakenly say *test nervousness* or *test worry* than *text anxiety* or *tent anxiety*.

If you can link information in STM to knowledge already stored in LTM, it gains meaning. This makes it easier to remember. If you can relate the definition of *test anxiety* to a memory of a time when you or a friend were nervous about taking a test, you are more likely to remember the definition. As another example, try to memorize this story:

> With hocked gems financing him, our hero bravely defied all scornful laughter. "Your eyes deceive," he had said. "An egg, not a table, correctly typifies this unexplored planet." Now three sturdy sisters sought proof. Forging along, days became weeks as many doubters spread fearful rumours about the edge. At last from nowhere welcome winged creatures appeared, signifying momentous success. (Adapted from Dooling & Lachman, 1971.)

This odd story emphasizes the impact that meaning has on memory. People given the title of the story were able to remember it far better than those not given a title. See if the title helps you as much as it did them: "Columbus Discovers America."

The Relationship between STM and LTM

Although sensory memory is involved every time we store information, we are most likely to notice STM and LTM. To summarize the traditional view of their connection, picture short-term memory as a small desk at the front of a huge warehouse full of filing cabinets (LTM). As information enters the warehouse, it is first placed on the desk. Because the desk is small, it must be quickly cleared off to make room for new information. Unimportant items are simply tossed away. Meaningful or personally important information is placed in the files (LTM). When we want to use knowledge from LTM to answer a question, the information is returned to STM. Or, in our analogy, a folder is taken out of the files (LTM) and moved to the desk (STM), where it can be used.

Now that you have a general picture of memory, it is time to explore STM and LTM in more detail. But first, here's a chance to rehearse what you've learned.

✔ STUDY BREAK Memory Systems

Reflect

Think of a time today when you used short-term memory (such as briefly remembering a phone number, a URL, or someone's name). For how long did you retain the information? How did you encode it? How much do you remember now?

How is long-term memory helping you read this sentence? If the words weren't already stored in LTM, could you read at all? How else have you used LTM today?

Learning Check

Match: **A.** Sensory memory   **B.** STM   **C.** LTM

1. _____ Information tends to be encoded phonetically
2. _____ Holds information for a few seconds or less
3. _____ Stores an iconic memory or echoic memory
4. _____ Permanent, unlimited capacity
5. _____ Temporarily holds small amounts of information
6. _____ Selective attention determines its contents

7. STM is improved by interruption, or interference, because attention is more focused at such times. T or F?

Critical Thinking

8. Why is sensory memory important to filmmakers?

Answers

1. B 2. A 3. A 4. C 5. B 6. B 7. F 8. Without sensory memory, a movie would look like a series of still pictures. The split-second persistence of visual images helps blend one motion-picture frame into the next.

SHORT-TERM MEMORY—DO YOU KNOW THE MAGIC NUMBER?

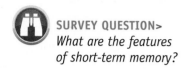

SURVEY QUESTION>
What are the features of short-term memory?

To make good use of your memory, it is valuable to know more about the quirks and characteristics of both STM and LTM. Let's start with a closer look at STM.

How much information can be held in short-term memory? For an answer, read the following numbers once. Then close the book and write as many as you can in the correct order.

8　5　1　7　4　9　3

This is called a digit-span test. It is a measure of attention and short-term memory. If you were able to correctly repeat seven digits, you have an average short-term memory. Now try to memorize the following list, again reading it only once.

7　1　8　3　5　4　2　9　1　6　3　4

This series was probably beyond your short-term memory capacity. Psychologist George Miller found that short-term memory is limited to the "magic number" seven (plus or minus two) **information bits** (Miller, 1956). A bit is a single meaningful "piece" of information, such as a digit. It is as if short-term memory has seven "slots" or "bins" into which separate items can be placed. Actually, a few people can remember up to nine bits, and for some types of information five bits is the limit. Thus, an *average* of seven information bits can be stored in short-term memory (Neath & Surprenant, 2003). When all of the "slots" in STM are filled, there is no room for new information. This is why phone numbers typically have no more than seven digits—even before psychologists had developed the concept of STM, people knew from experience that phone numbers longer than seven digits were difficult to work with.

Chunking

Before we continue, try your short-term memory again, this time on letters. Read the following letters once, and then look away and try to write them in the proper order.

T　V　I　B　M　U　S　N　Y　M　C　A

Notice that there are 12 letters, or "bits" of information. If you studied the letters one at a time, this should be beyond the seven-item limit of STM. However, you may have noticed that some of the letters can be grouped, or *chunked*, together. For example, you may have noticed that NY is the abbreviation for New York. If so, the two bits N and Y became one chunk. **Information chunks** are made up of bits of information grouped into larger units.

Does chunking make a difference? Yes. Chunking recodes (reorganizes) information into units that are already in LTM. In a classic experiment that used lists like this one, people remembered best when the letters were read as familiar meaningful chunks: TV, IBM, USN, YMCA (Bower & Springston, 1970). If you recoded the letters this way, you organized them into four *chunks* of information and probably remembered the entire list. If you didn't, go back and try it again; you'll notice a big difference.

Chunking suggests that STM holds about five to seven of whatever units we are using. A single chunk could be made up of numbers, letters, words, phrases, or familiar sentences. Picture STM as a small desk again. Through chunking, we combine several items into one "stack" of information. This allows us to place seven stacks on the desk, where before there was only room for seven separate items. While you are studying, try to find ways to link two, three, or more separate facts or ideas into larger chunks, and your short-term memory will improve. In fact, some psychologists believe that STM may actually hold only four items, unless some chunking has occurred (Cowan, 2005; Jonides et al., 2008). The clear message is that creating information chunks is the key to making good use of your short-term memory (Gobet, 2005).

Information bits Meaningful units of information, such as numbers, letters, words, or phrases.
Information chunks Information bits grouped into larger units.

Rehearsing Information

How long are short-term memories stored? They disappear very rapidly. However, you can prolong a memory by silently repeating it, a process called **maintenance rehearsal.** In a sense, rehearsing information allows you to "hear" it many times, not just once (Nairne, 2002). You have probably used maintenance rehearsal to keep a phone number active in your mind while looking at your cell phone and dialling it.

Elaborative encoding, which makes information more meaningful, is a far better way to form lasting memories. Elaborative encoding links new information to memories that are already in LTM. When you are studying, you will remember more if you elaborate on the meaning of the information. As you read, try to reflect frequently. Ask yourself "why" questions, such as, "Why would that be true?" (Toyota & Kikuchi, 2005; Willoughby et al., 1997). Also, try to relate new ideas to your own experiences and knowledge (Hartlep & Forsyth, 2000). In doing so, you'll be taking advantage of what Tim Rogers at the University of Calgary called the **self-reference effect.** We remember best when we encode new information on the basis of meaning rather than superficial features. And this effect is strongest if the meaning is personally relevant. If you see a dog in the park, you'll remember it better if you think of it chasing a cat than if you focus on the colour of its fur. But you'll do better still if you remember it chasing *your* cat. That's the self-reference effect (Rogers, Kuiper, & Kirker, 1977).

What if rehearsal is prevented, so a memory cannot be recycled or moved to LTM? Without maintenance rehearsal, STM storage is quite brief. In one experiment, subjects heard meaningless syllables like "xar," followed by a number like 67. As soon as subjects heard the number, they began counting backward by threes (to prevent them from repeating the syllable). After a delay of between 12 and 18 seconds, their memory for the syllables fell to zero (Peterson & Peterson, 1959). That's why if you are introduced to someone and that person's name slips out of STM, it is gone forever. To avoid embarrassment, pay careful attention to the name, repeat it to yourself several times, and try to use it in the next sentence or two—before you lose it (Neath & Surprenant, 2003).

> **Maintenance rehearsal** Silently repeating or mentally reviewing information to hold it in short-term memory.
>
> **Elaborative encoding** Encoding that links new information with existing memories and knowledge.
>
> **Self-reference effect** Memory works better when you encode for meaning and emphasize personal relevance of the material.

LONG-TERM MEMORY—A BLAST FROM THE PAST

An electrode touched the patient's brain. Immediately she said, "Yes, sir, I think I heard a mother calling her little boy somewhere. It seemed to be something happening years ago. It was somebody in the neighborhood where I live." A short time later the electrode was applied to the same spot. Again the patient said, "Yes, I hear the same familiar sounds, it seems to be a woman calling, the same lady" (Penfield, 1958). A woman made these statements while she was undergoing brain surgery. There are no pain receptors in the brain, so the patient was awake as her brain was electrically stimulated (Figure 7.3). When activated, some brain areas seemed to produce vivid memories of long-forgotten events.

<SURVEY QUESTION
What are the features of long-term memory?

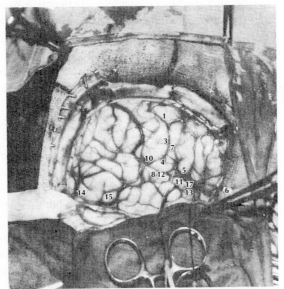

▶▶FIGURE 7.3 Exposed cerebral cortex of a patient undergoing brain surgery. Numbers represent points that reportedly produced "memories" when electrically stimulated. A critical evaluation of such reports suggests that they are more like dreams than memories. This fact raises questions about claims that long-term memories are permanent. (From Wilder Penfield, *The Excitable Cortex in Conscious Man*, 1958. Courtesy of the author and Charles C. Thomas Publisher, Springfield, Illinois.)

Permanence

Are all our experiences permanently recorded in memory? Results like those described led neurosurgeon Wilder Penfield to claim that the

Constructive processing
Reorganizing or updating memories on the basis of logic, reasoning, or the addition of new information.

brain records the past like a "strip of movie film, complete with sound track" (Penfield, 1957). But as you already know, this is an exaggeration, since many events never get past sensory or short-term memory. Also, brain stimulation produces memory-like experiences in only about 3 percent of cases. Most reports resemble dreams more than memories, and many are clearly imaginary. Memory experts now believe that long-term memories are only *relatively* permanent (Goldstein, 2008).

Try It Yourself: How's Your Memory?

To better appreciate the next topic, pause for a moment and read the words you see here. Read through the list once. Then continue reading the next section of this chapter.

| bed | dream | blanket | doze | pillow | nap | snore | mattress | alarm |
| clock | rest | slumber | nod | sheet | bunk | cot | cradle | groggy |

Constructing Memories

There's good reason for doubting that all our experiences are permanently recorded. As new long-term memories are stored, older memories are often updated, changed, lost, or *revised* (Baddeley et al., 2009). To illustrate this point, Elizabeth Loftus and John Palmer (1974) showed people a filmed automobile accident. Afterwards, some participants were asked to estimate how fast the cars were going when they "smashed" into each other. For others, the words "bumped," "contacted," or "hit" replaced "smashed." One week later, each person was asked, "Did you see any broken glass?" Those asked earlier about the cars that "smashed" into each other were more likely to say yes. (No broken glass was shown in the film.) The new information ("smashed") was included in memories and altered them.

Try It Yourself: Old or New?

Now, without looking back to the list of words you read a few minutes ago, see if you can tell which of the following are "old" words (items from the list you read) and which are "new" words (items that weren't on the list). Mark each of the following words as old or new:

sofa   sleep   lamp   kitchen

Updating memories is called **constructive processing.** Gaps in memory, which are common, may be filled in by logic, guessing, or new information (Schacter, Norman, & Koutstaal, 1998). Indeed, it is possible to have "memories" for things that never happened (such as remembering broken glass at an accident when there was none) (Loftus, 2003a, 2003b). In one study, people who had visited a Disney resort were shown several fake ads for Disney that featured Bugs Bunny. Later, about 16 percent of the people who saw these fake ads claimed that they had met Bugs at Disneyland. This is impossible, of course, because Bugs Bunny is a Warner Brothers character that would never be found at Disneyland (Braun, Ellis, & Loftus, 2002).

A different kind of constructive process was observed in a study at Western University in London, Ontario. Mitchell Callan based his studies on the Just World Hypothesis (Lerner, 1977, 1980), which is the belief that the world we live in is one susceptible to a universal force of justice—a world in which people get what they deserve. In one study, Callan gave participants one or another of two stories about a man named Roger who had won a large amount of money on a lottery. One group read that Roger was a caring, generous person and a good employee. The other group read that Roger was an uncaring, selfish person and a lazy, unpleasant employee. Later, when asked to recall exactly how much money Roger had won, people who read about "good" Roger gave a larger number than people who read about "bad" Roger. In other words, the belief in a just world influenced the reconstruction of the news story people read (Callan et al., 2009).

Try It Yourself: And Now, the Results

Return now and look at the labels you wrote on the "old or new" word list. Contrary to what you may think you "remembered," all of the listed words are "new." None were on the original list!

Eyewitness memories are notoriously inaccurate. By the time witnesses are asked to testify in court, information they learned after an incident may blend into their original memories.

If you thought you "remembered" that "sleep" was on the original list, you had a false memory. The word *sleep* is associated with most of the words on the original list, which creates a strong impression that you saw it before (Roediger & McDermott, 1995).

As the preceding examples show, thoughts, inferences, and mental associations may be mistaken for true memories (Loftus, 2003a, 2003b). People in Elizabeth Loftus's experiments who had these *pseudomemories* (false memories) were often quite upset to learn they had given false "testimony" (Loftus & Ketcham, 1994).

False long-term memories are a common problem in police work. For example, a witness may select a photo of a suspect from police files or see a photo in the news. Later, the witness identifies the suspect in a lineup or in court. Did the witness really remember the suspect from the scene of the crime? Or was it from the more recently seen photograph?

Does new information "overwrite" existing memories? No, the real problem is that we often can't remember the *source* of a memory (Simons et al., 2004). This can lead witnesses to "remember" a face that they actually saw somewhere other than the crime scene (Ruva, McEvoy, & Bryant, 2007). Many tragic cases of mistaken identity occur this way. One famous example involved memory expert Donald Thomson. After appearing live on Australian television, he was accused of rape. It turns out that the victim was watching him on TV when the actual rapist broke into her apartment (Schacter, 1996, 2001). She correctly remembered his face but attributed it to the wrong source.

Is there any way to avoid such problems? Forensic psychologists have tried a variety of techniques to help improve the memory of witnesses. Critical Thinking "Telling Wrong from Right in Forensic Memory" examines research on this important question.

To summarize, forming and using long-term memories is an active, creative, highly personal process. Our memories are coloured by emotions, judgments, and quirks of personality. If you and a friend were joined at the hip and you went through life side-by-side, you would still have different memories. What we remember depends on what we pay attention to, what we regard as meaningful or important, and what we feel strongly about (Schacter, 2000).

Organizing Memories

Long-term memory stores huge amounts of information during a lifetime. How are we able to quickly find specific memories? The answer is that each person's "memory index" is highly organized.

Do you mean that information is arranged alphabetically, as in a dictionary? Not a chance! If we ask you to name a black and white animal that lives on ice, is related to a chicken, and cannot fly, you don't have to go from aardvark to zebra to find the answer. You will probably think of only black-and-white birds living in the Antarctic. *Voilà*, the answer is a penguin.

Information in LTM may be arranged according to rules, images, categories, symbols, similarity, formal meaning, or personal meaning (Baddeley et al., 2009). In recent years, psychologists have begun to develop a picture of the *structure,* or organization, of memories. *Memory structure* refers to the pattern of associations among items of information. For example, assume that you are given two statements, to which you must answer yes or no: (1) *A canary is an animal.* (2) *A canary is a bird.* Which do you answer more quickly? Most people can say that *A canary is a bird* faster than they can recognize that *A canary is an animal* (Collins & Quillian, 1969).

Telling Wrong from Right in Forensic Memory

Imagine that you are a forensic psychologist, investigating a crime. Unfortunately, your witness can't remember much of what happened. As a "memory detective," what can you do to help?

Could hypnosis improve the witness's memory? It might seem so. In one California case, 26 children were abducted from a school bus and held captive for ransom. Under hypnosis, the bus driver recalled the licence plate number of the kidnappers' van. This memory helped break the case. Such successes seem to imply that hypnosis can improve memory. But does it?

Research has shown that hypnosis increases false memories more than it does true ones. In one classic experiment by Jane Dywan and the late Ken Bowers at the University of Waterloo, 80 percent of the new memories produced by hypnotized subjects were *incorrect* (Dywan & Bowers, 1983). This is in part because a hypnotized person is more likely than normal to use imagination to fill in gaps in memory. Also, if a questioner asks misleading or suggestive questions, hypnotized persons tend to weave the information into their memories (Scoboria et al., 2002). To make matters worse, even when a memory is completely false, the hypnotized person's confidence in it can be unshakable (Burgess & Kirsch, 1999).

Thus, hypnosis sometimes uncovers more information, as it did with the bus driver (Schreiber & Schreiber, 1999). However, in the absence of corroborating evidence, there is no sure way to tell which of these memories are false and which are true (Newman & Thompson, 2001).

Is there a better way to improve eyewitness memory? To help police detectives, R. Edward Geiselman and Ron Fisher created the **cognitive interview**, a technique for jogging the memory of eyewitnesses (Fisher & Geiselman, 1987). The key to this approach is recreating the crime scene. Witnesses revisit the scene in their imaginations or in person. That way, aspects of the crime scene, such as sounds, smells, and objects, provide helpful retrieval cues (stimuli associated with a memory). Back in the context of the crime, the witness is encouraged to recall events in different orders and from different viewpoints. Every new memory, no matter how trivial it may seem, can serve as a cue to trigger the retrieval of yet more memories. (Later in this chapter, we will see why such cues are so effective for jogging memories.)

When used properly, the cognitive interview produces 35 percent more correct information than standard questioning (Davis, McMahon, & Greenwood, 2005; Geiselman et al., 1986). This improvement comes without adding to the number of false memories elicited, as occurs with hypnosis. The result is a procedure that is more effective in actual police work and in different cultures (Ginet & Py, 2001; Kebbell & Wagstaff, 1998; Stein & Memon, 2006).

Some police detectives, following the advice of psychologists, recreate crime scenes to help witnesses remember what they saw. Typically, people return to the scene at the time of day the crime occurred. They are also asked to wear the same clothing they wore and go through the same motions as they did before the crime. With so many memory cues available, witnesses sometimes remember key items of information they hadn't recalled before.

Cognitive interview The use of various cues and strategies to improve the memory of eyewitnesses.

Network model A model of memory that views it as an organized system of linked information.

Why should this be so? Psychologists believe that a **network model** of memory explains why. According to this view, LTM is organized as a network of linked ideas (Figure 7.4). When ideas are more strongly associated, it takes a shorter chain of associations to connect them. The "closer" two items are in the network, the less time it takes to answer. In terms of information links, *canary* is probably "close" to *bird* in your "memory files." *Animal* and *canary* are farther apart. Remember, though, this has nothing to do with alphabetical order. We are talking about a system of linked meanings.

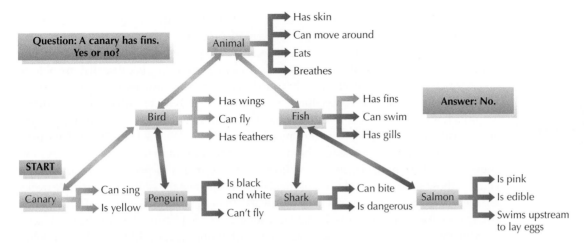

▸▸**FIGURE 7.4** A hypothetical network of facts about animals shows what is meant by the structure of memory. Small networks of ideas such as this are probably organized into larger and larger units and higher levels of meaning. (Adapted from *Journal of Verbal Learning and Verbal Behavior*, 8, Allan M. Collins & M. Ross Quillian, "Retrieval time from semantic memory," 240–247, Copyright © 1969 with permission from Elsevier.)

Redintegration

Networks of associated memories may also help explain a common experience: Imagine finding a picture taken on your sixth birthday or tenth Christmas. As you look at the photo, one memory leads to another, which leads to another, and another. Soon you have unleashed a flood of seemingly forgotten details. This process is called *redintegration* (ruh-DIN-tuh-GRAY-shun).

Redintegration seems to spread through the "branches" of memory networks. The key idea in redintegration is that one memory serves as a cue to trigger another. As a result, an entire past experience may be reconstructed from one small recollection. Many people find that redintegration can be touched off by distinctive odours from the past—from a farm visited in childhood, Grandma's kitchen, the seashore, the perfume or aftershave of a former lover, and so on (Willander & Larsson, 2006).

Skill Memory and Fact Memory

How many types of long-term memory are there? It is becoming clear that more than one type of long-term memory exists. For example, a curious thing happens to many people who develop amnesia. Amnesic patients may be unable to learn a telephone number, an address, or a person's name. Yet the same patients can learn to solve complex puzzles in a normal amount of time (Cavaco et al., 2004) (Figure 7.5). These and other observations have led many psychologists, notably Paul Kolers at the University of Toronto, to conclude that long-term memories fall into at least two categories (Kolers, 1975). One is called *procedural memory* (or skill memory). The other is *declarative memory* (also sometimes called fact memory).

Skills **Procedural memory** includes basic conditioned responses and learned actions, such as those involved in typing, driving, or swinging a golf club. Memories such as these can be fully expressed only as actions (or "know-how"). It is likely that skill memories register in "lower" brain areas, especially the cerebellum. They represent the more basic "automatic" elements of conditioning, learning, and memory (Hermann et al., 2004).

Facts **Declarative memory** stores specific factual information, such as names, faces, words, dates, and ideas. Declarative memories are expressed as words or symbols. For example, knowing that *Peter* Jackson directed the *Lord of the Rings* trilogy, while *Randy* Jackson judges on *American Idol* is a declarative memory. This is the type of memory that a person with

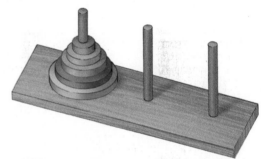

▸▸**FIGURE 7.5** The tower puzzle. In this puzzle, all the coloured disks must be moved to another post, without ever placing a larger disk on a smaller one. Only one disk may be moved at a time, and a disk must always be moved from one post to another (it cannot be held aside). An amnesic patient learned to solve the puzzle in 31 moves, the minimum possible. Even so, each time he began, he protested that he did not remember ever solving the puzzle before and that he did not know how to begin. Evidence like this suggests that memories for skills are distinct from memories for facts.

Redintegration The process by which memories are reconstructed or expanded by starting with one memory and then following chains of association to other, related memories.

Procedural memory Long-term memories of conditioned responses and learned skills.

Declarative memory That part of long-term memory containing specific factual information.

Semantic memory A subpart of declarative memory that records impersonal knowledge about the world.

Episodic memory A subpart of declarative memory that records personal experiences that are linked with specific times and places.

Tip-of-the-tongue (TOT) state The feeling that a memory is available but not quite retrievable.

amnesia lacks and that most of us take for granted. Declarative memory can be further divided into *semantic memory* and *episodic memory* (Tulving, 2002).

One important question about the relation between procedural and declarative memories arises in connection with our use of tools. Tools are interesting because they are objects about which we can have declarative knowledge, but they are also associated with particular behaviours—we have procedural knowledge about how to behave toward them. Shumita Roy of York University and Norman Park of the Baycrest Centre in Toronto taught an amnesia patient, DA, to use a set of novel complex tools (Roy & Park, 2010). They then tested DA's declarative knowledge about the tools and his skill in using the tools. Over the course of three training sessions, DA showed improvements in performance in tool use equal to those shown by six control participants. He retained the skill at testing three weeks after learning. However, DA was markedly worse than the controls on tests of his declarative knowledge about the tools: Presented with a greyscale picture of a tool, he was essentially unable to answer questions about its use, what objects it could be used on, or what colour it was.

Semantic Memory

Much of our basic factual knowledge about the world is almost totally immune to forgetting. The names of objects, the days of the week or months of the year, simple math skills, the seasons, words and language, and other general facts are all quite lasting. Such impersonal facts make up a part of LTM called **semantic memory,** which serves as a mental dictionary or encyclopedia of basic knowledge.

Episodic Memory

Semantic memory has no connection to times or places. It would be rare, for instance, to remember when and where you first learned the names of the seasons. In contrast, **episodic memory** is an "autobiographical" record of personal experiences. It stores life events (or "episodes") day after day, year after year. Can you remember your seventh birthday? Your first date? What you did yesterday? All are episodic memories. Note that episodic memories are about the "what," "where," and "when" of our lives. More than simply storing information, they allow us to mentally travel back in time and *re-experience* events (Tulving, 2002).

Episodic memory can be compromised both by accidental damage to the brain and by congenital disorders. One famous memory patient, KC, has been studied by researchers in Toronto, including Endel Tulving of the Rotman Research Institute and Shayna Rosenbaum of York University. While KC can remember lots of facts about family and friends, such as names and addresses, he can't recall any of the events of his life; high school graduation, a brother's wedding, and even the death of another brother in a boating accident were all lost to him (Tulving et al., 1988; Rosenbaum, Murphy, & Rich, 2012). Congenital disorders can also influence episodic memory: researchers at The Hospital for Sick Children in Toronto found impaired episodic memory in a group of young adults with spina bifida meningomyelocele (SBM), a congenital disorder of the nervous system. These young adults had no loss of semantic or working memory (Dennis et al., 2007).

Are episodic memories as lasting as semantic memories? In general, episodic memories are more easily forgotten than semantic memories. In fact, it is the forgetting of episodic information that results in the formation of semantic memories. At first, you remembered when and where you were when you learned the names of the seasons (Mommy! Daddy! Guess what I learned in kindergarten today!). Over time, you forgot the episodic details but will likely remember the season names for the rest of your life.

Do animals have episodic memory similar to that of humans? There is reason to think that they do not. William Roberts of the Western University in Ontario carried out a very clever experiment to answer this question (Roberts et al., 2008). He put rats into a radial maze (with eight arms extending like the spokes of a wheel). On test trials, one arm either

STUDY BREAK STM and LTM

Reflect

Telephone numbers in Canada and the United States are divided into an area code (three digits) and a seven-digit number that is divided into three digits plus four more. Can you relate this practice to STM? How about to chunking and recoding?

Think about how you've used your memory in the past hour. See if you can identify an example of each of the following: a procedural memory, a declarative memory, a semantic memory, and an episodic memory.

Learning Check

1. Information is best transferred from STM to LTM when a person engages in
   a. maintenance chunking   b. maintenance recoding
   c. elaborative networking   d. elaborative encoding
2. Constructive processing is often responsible for creating pseudomemories. T or F?
3. Electrical stimulation of the brain has shown conclusively that all memories are stored permanently, but not all memories can be retrieved. T or F?

4. Memories elicited under hypnosis are more vivid, complete, and reliable than normal. T or F?
5. The existence of redintegration is best explained by _____ models of memory.
   a. network   b. integrative
   c. implicit   d. chunking
6. Which of the following is a synonym for skill memory?
   a. semantic memory   b. declarative memory
   c. episodic memory   d. procedural memory

Critical Thinking

7. Parents sometimes warn children not to read comic books, fearing that they will learn less in school if they "fill their heads up with junk." Why is this warning unnecessary?

Answers

1. d 2. T 3. F 4. F 5. a 6. d 7. Because the more information you have in long-term memory, the greater the possibilities for linking new information to it. Generally, the more you know, the more you can learn—even if some of what you know is "junk."

---

contained a piece of cheese or was empty. The actual state of that arm depended upon what was there in an earlier "study" phase. In one condition, rats could predict at test what was in that arm on the basis of a memory of *when* they found the cheese (in the study phase). In another condition, the prediction at test depended upon *how long ago* they found the cheese. To see the difference, consider the intervals midnight to 4 a.m. and 10 a.m. to 2 p.m. If we ask when these intervals start, the answers are different for the two intervals. If we ask how long the intervals last, the answers are the same. The data clearly showed that rats could use only the "how long ago" cue, not the "when" cue. Roberts and his colleagues concluded that animals cannot "time travel" using episodic memory the way humans do—that is, they cannot move at will to particular points in time using episodic memory. They only have access to information about how long ago something happened.

How Many Types of Memory?

In answer to the question posed at the beginning of this section, it is very likely that three kinds of long-term memories exist: procedural memory and two types of declarative memory, semantic and episodic (Figure 7.6).

MEASURING MEMORY—THE ANSWER IS ON THE TIP OF MY TONGUE

You either remember something or you don't, right? Wrong. Partial memories are common. For instance, have you ever tried to remember something only to find yourself stuck in a **tip-of-the-tongue (TOT) state?** This is the feeling that a memory is available but not quite retrievable (Schwartz, 2002). It is as if an answer or a memory is just out of reach—on the "tip of your tongue."

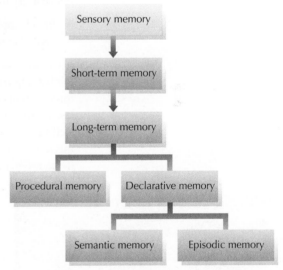

▶▶**FIGURE 7.6** In the model shown here, long-term memory is divided into procedural memory (learned actions and skills) and declarative memory (stored facts). Declarative memories can be either semantic (impersonal knowledge) or episodic (personal experiences associated with specific times and places).

<**SURVEY QUESTION**
How is memory measured?

Recall To supply or reproduce memorized information with a minimum of external cues.

Serial position effect The tendency to make the most errors in remembering the middle items of an ordered list.

Recognition memory An ability to correctly identify previously learned information

Because memory is not an all-or-nothing event, there are several ways of measuring it. Three commonly used methods of measuring memory are *recall*, *recognition*, and *relearning*. Let's see how they differ.

Recalling Information

What is the name of the first song on your favourite album? Who won the Stanley Cup last year? Who wrote *Hamlet*? If you can answer these questions, you are using **recall,** a direct retrieval of facts or information. Tests of recall often require *verbatim* (word-for-word) memory. If, after studying a poem, you recite it without looking at it, you are recalling the poem. If you complete a fill-in-the-blank question, you are using recall. When you answer an essay question by providing facts and ideas, you are also using recall, even though you didn't learn your essay verbatim.

Recall is obviously important to college students, so if someone came up with a way to improve recall by 15 to 20 percent, that would be worth knowing about. In fact, according to psychologist Colin MacLeod and his colleagues at the University of Waterloo, someone has come up with such a technique. In fact, they did so over 40 years ago but hardly anyone noticed! MacLeod et al. (2010) call it the production effect. It was first reported by Hopkins & Edwards (1972). The technique is so simple as to be almost impossible to believe, but it works: The trick is, when you want to improve your memory for some material, read it out loud. An important condition is that the technique only works if you do not read everything out loud. So if there is a particular part of a lecture or chapter that you really want to improve your recall on—definitions, for example—read those parts out loud, but silently read the rest of the chapter.

The order in which information is memorized has an interesting effect on recall. To experience it, try to memorize the following list, reading it only once:

> bread, apples, soda, ham, cookies, rice, lettuce, beets, mustard, cheese, oranges, ice cream, crackers, flour, eggs

If you are like most people, it will be hardest for you to recall items from the middle of the list. Figure 7.7 shows the results of a similar test. Notice that most errors occur with middle items of an ordered list. This is the **serial position effect.** You can remember the last items on a list because they are still in STM. The first items are also remembered well because they entered an "empty" short-term memory. This allows you to rehearse the items so they move into long-term memory (Addis & Kahana, 2004). The middle items are neither held in short-term memory nor moved to long-term memory, so they are often lost.

Recognizing Information

Try to write down everything you can remember learning from a class you took last year. If you actually did this, you might conclude that you had learned very little. However, a more sensitive test based on recognition could be used. In **recognition memory,** previously learned material is correctly identified. For instance, you could take a multiple-choice test on facts and ideas from the course. Because you would have to recognize only correct answers, you would probably find that you had learned a lot.

Recognition memory can be amazingly accurate for pictures and photographs (Whitehouse, Maybery, & Durkin, 2006). In one classic study, people viewed 2560 photographs at a rate of one every 10 seconds. Each person was then shown 280 pairs of photographs. Each pair included an "old" picture (from the first set of photos) and a similar "new" image. Subjects could tell 85 to 95 percent of the time which photograph they had seen before (Haber, 1970). This finding may explain why we rarely need to see our friends' vacation photos more than once.

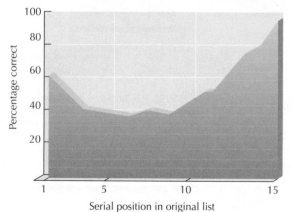

▶▶**FIGURE 7.7** The serial position effect. The graph shows the percentage of subjects correctly recalling each item in a 15-item list. Recall is best for the first and last items. (Data from Craik, 1970.)

Recognition is usually superior to recall. That's why people so often say, "I may forget a name, but I never forget a face." (You can't recall the name but you can recognize the face.) That's also why police departments use photographs or a lineup to identify criminal suspects. Witnesses who disagree when they try to recall a suspect's height, weight, age, or eye colour often agree completely when they merely need to recognize the person.

Is recognition always superior? It depends greatly on the kind of *distractors* used (Flowe & Ebbese, 2007). These are false items included with an item to be recognized. If distractors are very similar to the correct item, memory may be poor. A reverse problem occurs when only one choice looks like it could be correct. This can produce a *false positive*, or false sense of recognition, like the false memory you had earlier when you thought you remembered seeing the word *sleep*.

Many hundreds of people have been put in jail on the basis of mistaken eyewitness memories (Wells, Memon, & Penrod, 2006). There have been instances in which witnesses described a criminal as black, tall, or young. Then a lineup was held in which a suspect was the only Black person among Caucasians, the only tall suspect, or the only young person. In such cases a false identification is very likely. To avoid tragic mistakes, it's better to have *all* the distractors look like the person witnesses described. Also, to reduce false positives, witnesses should be warned that the culprit *may not be present*. It's also better to show witnesses one photo at a time (a sequential lineup). For each photo, the witness must decide whether the person is the culprit before another photo is shown (Wells, 2001; Wells & Olsen, 2003).

Police lineups make use of the sensitivity of recognition memory. However, unless great care is taken, false identifications are still possible (Wells, 2001).

Relearning Learning again something that was previously learned; used to measure memory of prior learning.

Explicit memory A memory that a person is aware of having; a memory that is consciously retrieved.

Relearning Information

In another classic experiment, a psychologist read a short passage in Greek to his son every day when the boy was between 15 months and three years of age. At age eight, the boy was asked if he remembered the Greek passage. He showed no evidence of recall. He was then shown selections from the passage he heard and selections from other Greek passages. Could he recognize the one he heard as an infant? "It's all Greek to me!" he said, indicating a lack of recognition (and drawing a frown from everyone in the room).

Had the psychologist stopped, he might have concluded that no memory of the Greek remained. However, the child was then asked to memorize the original quotation and others of equal difficulty. This time his earlier learning became evident. The boy memorized the passage he had heard in childhood 25 percent faster than the others (Burtt, 1941). As this experiment suggests, **relearning** is typically the most sensitive measure of memory.

When a person is tested by relearning, how do we know a memory still exists? As with the boy described, relearning is measured by a *savings score* (the amount of time saved when relearning information). Let's say it takes you 1 hour to memorize all the names in a telephone book. (It's a small town.) Two years later you relearn them in 45 minutes. Because you "saved" 15 minutes, your savings score would be 25 percent (15 divided by 60 times 100). Savings of this type are a good reason for studying a wide range of subjects. It may seem that learning algebra, history, or a foreign language is wasted if you don't use the knowledge immediately. But when you do need such information, you will be able to relearn it quickly.

Explicit and Implicit Memories

Who were the last three prime ministers of Canada? What did you have for breakfast today? What is the title of Arcade Fire's latest album? Explicit memory is used in answering each of these questions. **Explicit memories** are past experiences that are consciously

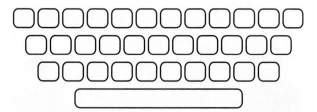

Can you label the letter keys on this blank keyboard? If you can, you probably used implicit memory to do it.

Implicit memory A memory that a person does not know exists; a memory that is retrieved unconsciously.

brought to mind. Recall, recognition, and the tests you take in school rely on explicit memories.

In contrast, **implicit memories** lie outside of awareness (Roediger & Amir, 2005). That is, we are not aware that a memory exists. For example, if you know how to type, it is apparent that you know where the letters are on the keyboard. But how many typists could correctly label blank keys in a drawing of a keyboard? Many people find that they cannot directly remember such information, even though they "know" it. Nevertheless, implicit memories—such as unconsciously knowing where the letters are on a keyboard—greatly influence our behaviour (Neath & Surprenant, 2003). An amusing demonstration of implicit memory was carried out at McMaster University in Hamilton, Ontario. In a third-year memory course, during a lecture, the professor discussed the difference between unavailable and inaccessible memories. Each year from 1996 to 2007, the professor used the name of an American state as an example, always choosing one known to be relatively unfamiliar to Canadian students. Four to eight weeks later, he asked the class to write down the names of all the states. Each year, the state mentioned in the earlier lecture was named more frequently than it would have been had it not been mentioned in passing weeks earlier. But with only one or two exceptions, none of the students remembered that earlier mention (Thomson, Milliken, & Smilek, 2010).

Priming

How is it possible to show that a memory exists if it lies outside of awareness? Psychologists first noticed implicit memory while studying memory loss caused by brain injuries. Let's say, for example, that a patient is shown a list of common words, such as *chair*, *tree*, *lamp*, *table*, and so on. Later, the patient fails to recall any words from the list.

Now, instead of asking the patient to explicitly recall the list, we could "prime" his memory by giving him the first two letters of each word. "Just say whatever word comes to mind that begins with these letters," we tell him. Of course, many words could be

---

✔ STUDY BREAK   Measuring Memory

Reflect

Have you experienced a TOT state recently? Were you able to retrieve the word you were searching for? If not, what could you remember about it?

Do you prefer tests based primarily on recall or recognition? Have you observed a savings effect while relearning information you studied in the past (such as in high school)?

Can you think of things you do that are based on implicit memories? For instance, how do you know which way to turn various handles in your house, apartment, or dorm? Do you have to explicitly think, "Turn it to the right" before you act?

What kinds of information are you good at remembering? Why do you think your memory is better for those topics?

Learning Check

1. Four techniques for measuring or demonstrating memory are
   _____   _____
   _____   _____

2. Essay tests require _____ of facts or ideas.
3. As a measure of memory, a savings score is associated with
   a. recognition   b. priming
   c. relearning   d. reconstruction
4. The two most sensitive tests of memory are
   a. recall and redintegration   b. recall and relearning
   c. recognition and relearning   d. recognition and digit-span
5. Priming is used to reveal which type of memories?
   a. explicit   b. sensory
   c. skill   d. implicit

Critical Thinking

6. When asked to explain why they may have failed to recall some information, people often claim it must be because the information is no longer in their memory. Why does the existence of implicit memories challenge this explanation?

Answers

1. recall, recognition, relearning, priming 2. recall 3. c 4. c 5. d 6. It is possible to have an implicit memory that cannot be consciously recalled. Memories like these (available in memory even though they are not consciously accessible) show that failing to recall something does not guarantee it is no longer in memory (Allik, 2000).

made from each pair of letters. For example, the first item (from "chair") would be the letters CH. The patient could say "child," "chalk," "chain," "check," or many other words. Instead, he says "chair," a word from the original list. The patient is not aware that he is remembering the list, but as he gives a word for each letter pair, almost all are from the list. Apparently, the letters **primed** (activated) hidden memories, which then influenced his answers.

Similar effects have been found for people with normal memories. As the preceding example suggests, implicit memories are often revealed by giving a person limited cues, such as the first letter of words or partial drawings of objects. The person is just saying whatever comes to mind. But the same information would not be brought to mind by a deliberate attempt to recall it (Rueckl & Galantucci, 2005).

> **Priming** Facilitating the retrieval of an implicit memory by using cues to activate hidden memories.
>
> **Curve of forgetting** A graph that shows the amount of memorized information remembered after varying lengths of time.

FORGETTING IN LTM—WHY WE, UH, LET'S SEE; WHY WE, UH . . . FORGET!

We don't expect sensory memories and short-term memories to remain with us for long. But when you deliberately encode and store information in long-term memory, you want it to stay there (after all, it's supposed to be *long*-term). For example, when you study for an exam, you count on your long-term memory to retain the information at least until you take your exam.

Why do we forget long-term memories? The more you know about how we "lose" memories, the better you will be able to hang on to them. Most forgetting tends to occur immediately after memorization. Herman Ebbinghaus (1885) famously tested his own memory at various intervals after learning. To be sure he would not be swayed by prior learning, he memorized *nonsense syllables*. These are meaningless three-letter words such as "cef," "wol," and "gex." The importance of using meaningless words is shown by the fact that "Vel," "Fab," and "Duz" are no longer used on memory tests in the United States, where they are now familiar as brand names. People who recognize these words as detergent names find them very easy to remember. This is another reminder that relating new information to what you already know can improve memory.

By waiting various lengths of time before testing himself, Ebbinghaus plotted a **curve of forgetting.** This graph shows the amount of information remembered after varying lengths of time (Figure 7.8). Notice that forgetting is rapid at first, followed by a slow decline (Hintzman, 2005). The same applies to meaningful information, but the forgetting curve is stretched over a longer time. As you might expect, recent events are recalled more accurately than those from the remote past (O'Connor et al., 2000). Thus, you are more likely to remember that *The Artist* won the "Best Picture" Academy Award for 2011 than you are to remember that *The Departed* won it for 2006.

As a student, you should note that a short delay between studying and taking a test minimizes forgetting. However, this is no reason for cramming. Most students make the error of *only* cramming. If you cram, you don't have to remember for very long, but you may not learn enough in the first place. If you use short, daily study sessions and review intensely before a test, you will get the benefit of good preparation and a minimum time lapse.

The Ebbinghaus curve shows less than 30 percent remembered after only two days have passed. Is forgetting really that rapid? No, not always. Meaningful information is not lost nearly as quickly as nonsense syllables. After three years, students who took a university psychology course had forgotten about 30 percent of the facts they learned. After that, little more forgetting occurred (Conway, Cohen, & Stanhope, 1992). Actually, as learning grows stronger, some knowledge may become nearly permanent (Berntsen & Thomsen, 2005).

<SURVEY QUESTION
Why do we forget?

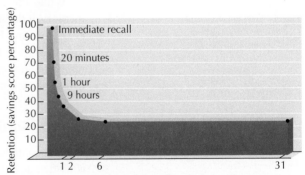

▶▶FIGURE 7.8 The curve of forgetting. This graph shows the amount remembered (measured by relearning) after varying lengths of time. Notice how rapidly forgetting occurs. The material learned was nonsense syllables. Forgetting curves for meaningful information also show early losses followed by a long gradual decline, but, overall, forgetting occurs much more slowly. (After Ebbinghaus, 1885.)

Card Magic!

▸▸**FIGURE 7.9** Pick a card from the six cards in Figure 7.9, above. Look at it closely and be sure you can remember which card is yours. Now, snap your fingers and look at the cards in Figure 7.10, below. Poof! Only five cards remain, and the card you chose has disappeared. Obviously, you could have selected any one of the six cards in Figure 7.9. How did we know which one to remove?

▸▸**FIGURE 7.10** This trick is based entirely on an illusion of memory. Recall that you were asked to concentrate on one card among the six cards in Figure 7.9. That prevented you from paying attention to the other cards, so they weren't stored in your memory (Mangels, Picton, & Craik, 2001; Naveh-Benjamin, Guez, & Sorek, 2007). The five cards you see above are all new (none are shown in Figure 7.9). Because you couldn't find it in the "remaining five," your card seemed to disappear. What looked like "card magic" is actually memory magic. Now return to "When Encoding Fails" and continue reading to learn more about forgetting.

While the Ebbinghaus curve gives a general picture of forgetting from long-term memory, it doesn't explain it. For explanations, we must search further. (Before we do, look at Discovering Psychology: "Card Magic!" where you will find an interesting demonstration.) Earlier in this chapter we pointed out that three processes are involved in successfully remembering: encoding, storage, and retrieval. Conversely, forgetting can be due to the failure of any one of these three processes.

When Encoding Fails

Can you accurately draw and label a Canadian penny? Which animal appears on a nickel? What is written at the top of a penny? In an interesting experiment, Ray Nickerson and Marilyn Adams (1979) asked a large group of students to draw a U.S. penny. Few could. In fact, few could even recognize a drawing of a real penny among fakes. (Can you?) (See Figure 7.11.)

The most obvious reason for forgetting is also the most commonly overlooked. Few of us ever encode the details of a penny. Similarly, we may not encode the details of what we are reading in a book or studying for an exam. In such cases, we "forget" because of **encoding failure.** That is, a memory was never formed in the first place (the card trick you just saw is another example). If you are bothered by frequent forgetting or absent-mindedness, it is wise to ask yourself, "Have I been encoding the information in the first place?" (Schacter, 2001). By the way, if you like to study while watching television or texting, beware. Dividing

Encoding failure Failure to store sufficient information to form a useful memory.

▶▶**FIGURE 7.11** Correct and incorrect images of U.S. pennies were some of the distractor items used in a study of recognition memory and encoding failure. Penny (a) is correct but was seldom recognized. Pennies (g) and (j) were popular wrong answers. (Adapted from Nickerson & Adams, 1979.)

your attention between studying and other activities can also lead to encoding failure (Naveh-Benjamin, Guez, & Sorek, 2007). It's worth noting that talking in a lecture while the professor is speaking creates a divided attention situation not just for the student doing the talking but also for other students in earshot. Researchers at the University of Toronto recently demonstrated that encoding is harmed in such a situation, precisely because resources that should be used for encoding the lecture material into memory are diverted to perceptual processing. That is, separating the lecturer's voice out from the hubbub of conversation takes more cognitive resources (Heinrich, Schneider, & Craik, 2008).

Actively thinking about the information you are learning (elaborative encoding) is a good way to prevent encoding failure (Hall et al., 2007). You'll find more memory strategies later in this chapter in Improving Memory—Keys to the Memory Bank and also in the Psychology in Action section, Mnemonics—Memory Magic, at the end of the chapter.

When Memory Storage Fails

One view of forgetting holds that **memory traces** (changes in nerve cells or brain activity) decay (fade or weaken) over time. **Memory decay** appears to be a factor in the loss of sensory memories. Such fading also applies to short-term memory. Information stored in STM seems to initiate a brief flurry of activity in the brain that quickly dies out. Short-term memory therefore operates like a leaky bucket: New information constantly pours in, but it rapidly fades away and is replaced by still newer information. Let's say that you are trying to remember a short list of letters, numbers, or words after seeing or hearing them once. If it takes you more than four to six seconds to repeat the list, you will forget some of the items (Dosher & Ma, 1998).

Disuse

Does decay also occur in long-term memory? There is evidence that memories not retrieved and "used" or rehearsed become weaker over time (Schacter, 2001). That is, some long-term memory traces may fade from **disuse** (infrequent retrieval) and eventually become too weak to retrieve. However, disuse alone cannot fully explain forgetting.

Disuse doesn't seem to account for our ability to recover seemingly forgotten memories through redintegration, relearning, and priming. It also fails to explain why some unused memories fade, whereas others are carried for life. A third contradiction will be recognized by anyone who has spent time with the elderly. People growing senile may become so forgetful that they can't remember what happened a week ago. Yet, at the same time that your Uncle Oscar's recent memories are fading, he may have vivid memories of trivial and long-forgotten events from the past. "Why, I remember it as clearly as if it were yesterday," he will say, forgetting that the story he is about to tell is one he told earlier the same day (twice). In short, disuse offers no more than a partial explanation of long-term forgetting.

Memory traces Physical changes in nerve cells or brain activity that take place when memories are stored.

Memory decay The fading or weakening of memories assumed to occur when memory traces become weaker.

Disuse The theory that memory traces weaken when memories are not periodically used or retrieved.

External cues like those found in a photograph, in a scrapbook, or during a walk through an old neighbourhood often aid recall of seemingly lost memories. For many veterans, finding a familiar name engraved in the Vietnam Veterans Memorial unleashes a flood of memories.

When Retrieval Fails

If encoding failure and storage failure don't fully explain forgetting from long-term memory, what does? If you have encoded and stored information, that leaves retrieval failure as a likely cause of forgetting. Even if memories are **available** (stored in your memory), you still have to be able to **access** them (locate or retrieve them) in order to remember. For example, you've probably had the experience of knowing you know the answer to an exam question (you knew it was available) but being unable to retrieve it during the exam (it was inaccessible) (Landau & Leynes, 2006). You know what happens next, right? As you leave the exam, the answer "pops" into your head!

Cue-Dependent Forgetting

One reason retrieval may fail is because **memory cues** (stimuli associated with a memory) are missing when the time comes to retrieve information. For instance, if you were asked, "What were you doing on Monday afternoon of the third week in May, two years ago?" your reply might be, "Come on, how should I know?" However, if you were reminded, "That was the day the courthouse burned," or "That was the day Stacy had her automobile accident," you might remember immediately.

The presence of appropriate cues almost always enhances memory (Nairne, 2002). For example, memory will tend to be better if you study in the same room where you will be tested. Because this is often impossible, when you study, try to visualize the room where you will be tested. Doing so can enhance memory later (Jerabek & Standing, 1992). Similarly, people remember better if the same odour (such as lemon or lavender) is present when they study and are tested (Parker, Ngu, & Cassaday, 2001). If you wear a particular perfume or cologne while you prepare for a test, it might be wise to wear it when you take the test.

State-Dependent Learning

The bodily state that exists during learning can be a strong retrieval cue for later memory, an effect known as **state-dependent learning** (Neath & Surprenant, 2003). Being very thirsty, for instance, might prompt you to remember events that took place on another occasion when you were thirsty. Because of such effects, information learned under the influence of a drug is best remembered when the drugged state occurs again (Slot & Colpaert, 1999). However, this is a laboratory finding. In school, it's far better to study with a clear mind in the first place.

A similar effect applies to emotional states (Wessel & Wright, 2004). For instance, Gordon Bower (1981) found that people who learned a list of words while in a happy mood recalled them better when they were again happy. People who learned while they felt sad remembered best when they were sad (Figure 7.12). Similarly, if you are in a happy mood you are more likely to remember recent happy events. If you are in a bad mood you will tend to have unpleasant memories. Such links between emotional cues and memory could explain why couples who quarrel often end up remembering—and rehashing—old arguments.

Interference

Further insight into forgetting comes from a classic experiment in which college students learned lists of nonsense syllables. After studying, students in one group slept for eight hours and were then tested for memory of the lists. A second group stayed awake for eight hours and went about business as usual. When members of the second group were tested, they remembered less than the group that slept

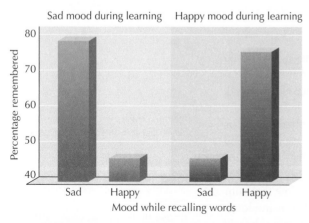

▶▶ FIGURE 7.12 The effect of mood on memory. Subjects best remembered a list of words when their mood during testing was the same as their mood was when they learned the list. (Adapted from Bower, 1981.)

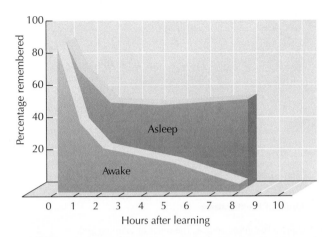

▸▸FIGURE 7.13 The amount of forgetting after a period of sleep or of being awake. Notice that sleep causes less memory loss than activity that occurs while one is awake. (After Jenkins & Dallenbach, 1924.)

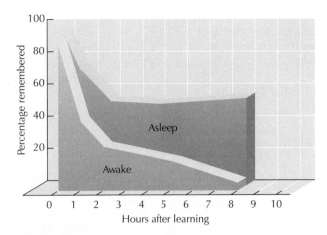

▸▸FIGURE 7.14 Effects of interference on memory. A graph of the approximate relationship between percentage recalled and number of different word lists memorized. (Adapted from Underwood, 1957.)

(Figure 7.13). This difference is based on the fact that new learning can interfere with the ability to retrieve previous learning. (Sleep can improve memory in another way: REM sleep and dreaming appear to help us form certain types of memories. See Chapter 5.) **Interference** refers to the tendency for new memories to impair retrieval of older memories (and the reverse). It seems to apply to both short-term and long-term memory (Lustig, May, & Hasher, 2001; Nairne, 2002).

It is not completely clear if new memories alter existing memory traces or if they make it harder to retrieve earlier memories. In any case, there is no doubt that interference is a major cause of forgetting (Neath & Surprenant, 2003). College students who memorized 20 lists of words (one list each day) were able to recall only 15 percent of the last list. Students who learned only one list remembered 80 percent (Underwood, 1957) (Figure 7.14).

The sleeping students remembered more because retroactive interference was held to a minimum. **Retroactive interference** refers to the tendency for new learning to inhibit retrieval of old learning. Avoiding new learning prevents retroactive interference. This doesn't exactly mean you should hide in a closet after you study for an exam. However, you should avoid studying other subjects until the exam. Sleeping after study can help you retain memories, and reading, writing, or even watching TV may cause interference.

Experimental group:	Learn A	Learn B	Test A
Control group:	Learn A	Rest	Test A

Retroactive interference is easily demonstrated in the laboratory by this arrangement:

Imagine yourself as a member of the experimental group. In task A, you learn a list of telephone numbers. In task B, you learn a list of Social Insurance numbers. How do you score on a test of task A (the telephone numbers)? If you do not remember as much as the control group that learns *only* the task A list, then retroactive interference has occurred. The second thing learned interfered with memory of the first thing learned; the interference went "backward," or was "retroactive" (Figure 7.15).

Proactive interference is the second type of interference. **Proactive interference** occurs when prior learning inhibits recall of later learning. A test for proactive interference would take this form:

Experimental group:	Learn A	Learn B	Test B
Control group:	Rest	Learn B	Test B

Interference The tendency for new memories to impair retrieval of older memories, and the reverse.

Retroactive interference The tendency for new memories to interfere with the retrieval of old memories.

Proactive interference The tendency for old memories to interfere with the retrieval of newer memories.

Suppression A conscious effort to put something out of mind or to keep it from awareness.

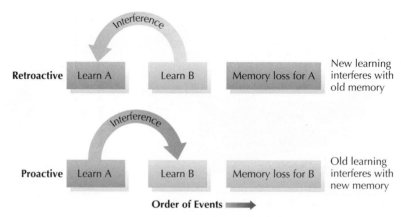

▶▶**FIGURE 7.15** Retroactive and proactive interference. The order of learning and testing shows whether interference is retroactive (backward) or proactive (forward).

Let's assume that the experimental group remembers less than the control group on a test of the task B list. In that case, learning list A interfered with memory for list B.

Then proactive interference goes "forward"? Yes. For instance, if you cram for a psychology exam and then later the same night cram for a history exam, your memory for the second subject studied (history) will be less accurate than if you had studied only history. (Because of retroactive interference, your memory for psychology would probably also suffer.) The greater the similarity in the two subjects studied, the more interference takes place. The moral, of course, is don't procrastinate in preparing for exams. The more you can avoid competing information, the more likely you are to recall what you want to remember (Anderson & Bell, 2001; Wixted, 2004).

Repression and Suppression of Memories

Take a moment to scan over the events of the past few years of your life. What kinds of things most easily come to mind? Many people remember happy, positive events better than disappointments and irritations (Moore & Zoellner, 2007). That poorer recall for negatively toned material is called repression, or motivated forgetting. Through repression, memories that are painful, threatening, or embarrassing are held out of consciousness (Anderson et al., 2004). An example is provided by soldiers who have repressed some of the horrors they saw during combat (Karon & Widener, 1997).

The forgetting of past failures, upsetting childhood events, the names of people you dislike, or appointments you don't want to keep may reveal repression. People prone to repression tend to be extremely sensitive to emotional events. As a result, they use repression to protect themselves from threatening thoughts (McNally, Clancy, & Barrett, 2004). See Clinical File: "The Recovered Memory/False Memory Debate" for further cautions.

If I try to forget a test I failed, am I repressing it? No. Repression can be distinguished from **suppression,** an active, conscious attempt to put something out of mind. By not thinking about the test, you have merely suppressed a memory. If you choose to, you can remember the test. Clinicians consider true repression an *unconscious* event and one of the major psychological defences we use against emotional threats. When a memory is repressed, we may be unaware that forgetting has even occurred.

Although some psychologists have questioned whether repression exists (Court & Court, 2001), evidence suggests that we can choose to actively suppress upsetting memories (Anderson, 2001). If you have experienced a painful emotional event, you will probably

How could anyone lose something as large as a car? If you park your car in a different place every day, you may have experienced forgetting caused by interference. Today's memory about your car's location is easily confused with memories from yesterday, and the day before, and the day before that.

Andy Reynolds/Getty Images

The Recovered Memory/False Memory Debate

Many sexually abused children develop problems that persist into adulthood. In some instances, they repress all memory of the abuse. According to some psychologists, uncovering these hidden memories can be an important step toward regaining emotional health (Colangelo, 2007).

Although the preceding may be true, the search for repressed memories of sexual abuse has itself been a problem. Families have been torn apart by accusations of sexual abuse that later turned out to be completely false (Porter, Spencer, & Birt, 2003). For example, Gary Ramona lost his marriage and his $400 000-a-year job when his daughter Holly alleged that he molested her throughout her childhood. To prove to Holly that her memories were true, the therapists gave her the drug Amytal and told her that it was a "truth drug." (Amytal is a hypnotic drug that induces a twilight state of consciousness. People do not automatically tell the truth while under its influence.) Ramona sued Holly's therapists, claiming that they had been irresponsible. After reviewing the evidence, a jury awarded Gary Ramona $500 000 in damages. In a way, Gary Ramona was lucky. Most people who are falsely accused have no way to prove their innocence (Loftus & Ketcham, 1994).

Why would anyone have false memories about such disturbing events? Several popular books and some misguided therapists have

Gary Ramona's life was shattered by "recovered" memories that turned out to be false.

AP Images/Al Francis

actively encouraged people to find repressed memories of abuse. Hypnosis, guided visualization, suggestion, age regression, and similar techniques can elicit fantasies that are mistaken for real memories. As we saw earlier, it is easy to create false memories, especially by using hypnosis (Loftus, 2003b; Loftus & Bernstein, 2005).

In an effort to illustrate how easy it is to create false memories and to publicize *false memory syndrome,* memory expert Elizabeth Loftus once deliberately implanted a false memory in actor Alan Alda. As the host of the television series *Scientific American Frontiers,* he was scheduled to interview Loftus. Before the interview, Alda was asked to fill out a questionnaire about his tastes in food. When Alda arrived, Loftus told him that his answers revealed that he must once have gotten sick after eating hard-boiled eggs (which was false). Later that day, at a picnic, Alda would not eat hard-boiled eggs (Loftus, 2003a).

Certainly, some memories of abuse that return to awareness are genuine and must be dealt with. However, there is little doubt that some "recovered" memories are pure fantasy. No matter how real a recovered memory may seem, it could be false, unless it can be verified by others, or by court or medical records (Olio, 2004). The saddest thing about such claims is that they deaden public sensitivity to actual abuse.

---

avoid all thoughts associated with it. This tends to keep cues out of mind that could trigger a painful memory. In time, your active suppression of the memory may become true repression (Anderson & Green, 2001).

> **Consolidation** The process by which relatively permanent memories are formed in the brain.

MEMORY AND THE BRAIN—SOME "SHOCKING" FINDINGS

One possibility overlooked in our discussion of forgetting is that memories may be lost as they are being formed (Papanicolaou, 2006). For example, a head injury may cause a "gap" in memories preceding the accident. *Retrograde amnesia,* as this is called, involves forgetting events that occurred before an injury or trauma. In contrast, *anterograde amnesia* involves forgetting events that follow an injury or trauma (Behrend et al., 2004). (We will discuss an example of this type of amnesia in a moment.)

<SURVEY QUESTION
How does the brain form and store memories?

Consolidation

We can explain retrograde amnesia by assuming that it takes time to form a lasting memory, a process called **consolidation** (Vogel, Woodman, & Luck, 2006). You can think of consolidation as being somewhat like writing your name in wet concrete. Once the concrete is set, the information (your name) is fairly lasting. But while it is setting, it can be wiped out (amnesia) or scribbled over (interference).

Hippocampus A brain structure associated with emotion and the transfer of information from short-term memory to long-term memory.

Consider a classic experiment on consolidation, in which a rat is placed on a small platform. The rat steps down to the floor and receives a painful electric shock. After one shock, the rat can be returned to the platform repeatedly, but it will not step down. Obviously, the rat remembers the shock. Would it remember if consolidation were disturbed?

Curiously, one way to prevent consolidation is to give a different kind of shock called *electroconvulsive shock* (ECS). ECS is a mild electric shock to the brain. It will destroy any memory that is being formed at the time of the shock. If each painful shock is followed by ECS, the rat will step down over and over. Each time, ECS will erase the memory of the painful shock. (ECS is employed as a psychiatric treatment for severe depression in humans.)

What would happen if ECS were given several hours after the learning? Recent memories are more easily disrupted than older memories. If enough time is allowed to pass between learning and ECS, the memory will be unaffected because consolidation is already complete. That's why people with mild head injuries lose only memories from just before the accident, while older memories remain intact (Baddeley et al., 2009).

Where does consolidation take place in the brain? Actually, many parts of the brain are responsible for memory, but the **hippocampus** is particularly important (Sutherland et al., 2006). The hippocampus acts as a sort of "switching station" between short-term and long-term memory (Squire, 2004). The hippocampus does this, in part, by growing new neurons (nerve cells) and by making new connections within the brain (Eichenbaum & Fortin, 2005).

If the hippocampus is damaged, patients usually develop anterograde amnesia and show a striking inability to consolidate new memories (Zola & Squire, 2001). A man described by Montreal neuropsychologist Brenda Milner (1965) provides a dramatic example. Two years after an operation damaged his hippocampus, the 29-year-old HM continued to give his age as 27 and reported that the operation had just taken place. His memory of events before the operation remained clear, but he found forming new long-term memories almost impossible. When his parents moved to a new house a few blocks away on the same street, he could not remember the new address. Month after month, he read the same magazines over and over without finding them familiar. If you had met this man, he would have seemed fairly normal because he still had short-term memory. But if you had left the room and returned 15 minutes later, he would have acted as if he had never seen you before. Lacking the ability to form new lasting memories, he lived eternally in the present until his death in 2008 at the age of 82 (Bohbot & Corkin, 2007; Corkin, 2002).

Memory and Emotion

Do you remember when you first learned about the terrorist attacks on New York City and Washington in 2001? Can you recall lots of detail, including how you reacted? If so, you have a flashbulb memory for 9/11. A flashbulb memory is an especially vivid image that seems to be frozen in memory at times of emotionally significant personal or public events. Depending on your age, you may also have a flashbulb memory for the *Challenger* or *Columbia* space shuttle disasters, or the death of Princess Diana (Curci & Luminet, 2006; Sharot et al., 2007).

Are flashbulb memories handled differently by the brain? Powerful experiences activate the limbic system, the part of the brain that processes emotions. Heightened activity in the limbic system, in turn, appears to intensify memory consolidation (LaBar, 2007; Kensinger, 2007). As a result, flashbulb memories tend to form at times of intense emotion.

Although flashbulb memories are often related to public tragedies, memories of both positive and negative events can have flashbulb clarity

Ralf-Finn Hestoft/Corbis

Do you have a flashbulb memory for the November 4, 2008, election victory of U.S. President Obama? You do if someone alerted you about the news and you remember that person's call. You do if you saw the news on TV and you have clear memories of how you reacted.

(Paradis et al., 2004; Rubin, 1985). Would you consider any of the following to be a flashbulb memory? Your first kiss, a special date, or your prom night? How about a time you had to speak in front of a large audience? A car accident you were in or witnessed?

The term **flashbulb memories** was first used to describe recollections that seemed to be unusually vivid and permanent (Brown & Kulik, 1977). It has become clear, however, that flashbulb memories are not always accurate (Greenberg, 2004; Kensinger, 2007). More than anything else, what sets flashbulb memories apart is that we tend to place great *confidence* in them—even when they are wrong (Niedzwienska, 2004). Perhaps that's because we review emotionally charged events over and over and tell others about them. Also, public events such as wars, earthquakes, and elections reappear many times in the news, which highlights them in memory. Over time, flashbulb memories tend to crystallize into consistent, if not entirely accurate, landmarks in our lives (Schmolck, Buffalo, & Squire, 2000).

Some memories go beyond flashbulb clarity and become so intense that they may haunt a person for years. Extremely traumatic experiences, such as military combat, can produce so much limbic system activation that the resulting memories and "flashbacks" leave a person emotionally handicapped (Nemeroff et al., 2006).

Long-Term Memory and the Brain

Somewhere within the 1.5-kilogram mass of the human brain lies all we know: postal codes, faces of loved ones, history, favourite melodies, the taste of an apple, and much, much more. Where is this information? According to neuroscientist Richard Thompson (2005), many parts of the brain become active when we form long-term memories, but some areas are more important for each type of memory.

For example, patterns of blood flow in the cerebral cortex (the wrinkled outer layer of the brain) can be used to map brain activity. Figure 7.16 shows the results of measuring blood flow while people were thinking about a semantic memory or an episodic memory. The resulting pattern indicates that we use the front of the cortex for episodic memory. Back areas are more associated with semantic memory (Tulving, 2002).

Let's summarize (and simplify greatly). Earlier we noted that the hippocampus handles memory consolidation (Zola & Squire, 2001). Once declarative long-term memories are formed, they appear to be stored in the cortex of the brain (episodic in the front, semantic in the back) (Squire, 2004). Long-term procedural (skill) memories are stored in the cerebellum, a part of the brain that is also responsible for muscular coordination (Hermann et al., 2004).

> **Flashbulb memories** Memories created at times of high emotion that seem especially vivid.

An *aplysia*. The relatively simple nervous system of this sea animal allows scientists to study memory as it occurs in single nerve cells.

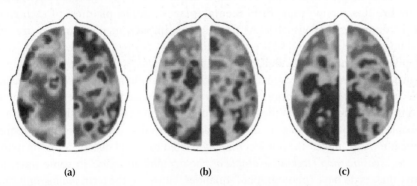

(a)　　　　　(b)　　　　　(c)

▸▸**FIGURE 7.16** Patterns of blood flow in the cerebral cortex (wrinkled outer layer of the brain) change as areas become more or less active. Thus, blood flow can be used to draw "maps" of brain activity. This drawing, which views the brain from the top, shows the results of measuring cerebral blood flow while people were thinking about a semantic memory (a) or an episodic memory (b). In the map, green indicates areas that are more active during semantic thinking. Reds show areas of greater activity during episodic thinking. The brain in view (c) shows the difference in activity between views (a) and (b). The resulting pattern suggests that the front of the cortex is related to episodic memory. Areas toward the back and sides of the brain, especially the temporal lobes, are more associated with semantic memory (Gabrieli, 1998; Tulving, 1989, 2002).

© Tulving, E. (1989). Remembering and knowing the past. *American Scientist,* 77(4), 361-367.

STUDY BREAK **Forgetting**

Reflect

Do you know someone whose name you have a hard time remembering? Do you like or dislike that person? Do you think your difficulty is an instance of repression? Suppression? Interference? Encoding failure?

Have you had a flashbulb memory? How vivid is the memory today? How accurate do you think it is?

Learning Check

1. According to the Ebbinghaus curve of forgetting, we forget slowly at first and then a rapid decline occurs. T or F?
2. Which explanation seems to account for the loss of short-term memories?
   a. decay   b. disuse
   c. repression   d. interference
3. When memories are available but not accessible, forgetting may be cue dependent. T or F?
4. When learning one thing makes it more difficult to recall another, forgetting may be caused by _____.
5. You are asked to memorize long lists of telephone numbers. You learn a new list each day for 10 days. When tested on list 3,

you remember less than a person who learned only the first three lists. Your larger memory loss is probably caused by
   a. disuse   b. retroactive interference
   c. regression   d. proactive interference
6. If you consciously succeed at putting a painful memory out of mind, you have used
   a. redintegration   b. suppression
   c. negative rehearsal   d. repression
7. Retrograde amnesia results when consolidation is speeded up. T or F?

Critical Thinking

8. Based on state-dependent learning, why do you think that music often strongly evokes memories?
9. You must study French, Spanish, psychology, and biology in one evening (poor thing!). What do you think would be the best order in which to study these subjects so as to minimize interference?

Answers

1. F 2. a and d 3. T 4. interference 5. b 6. b 7. F 8. Music tends to affect the mood that a person is in, and moods tend to affect memory (Miranda & Kihlstrom, 2005). 9. Any order that separates French from biology and psychology from Spanish would be better (for instance: French, psychology, Spanish, biology).

EXCEPTIONAL MEMORY—WIZARDS OF RECALL

SURVEY QUESTION>
What are "photographic" memories?

In this section, we will explore exceptional memories. Is superior memory a biological gift, such as having a "photographic" memory? Or do excellent memorizers merely make better-than-average use of normal memory capacities?

Can you remember how many doors there are in your house or apartment? To answer a question like this, many people form **mental images** (mental pictures) of each room and count the doorways they visualize. As this example implies, many memories are stored as mental images (Roeckelein, 2004).

Stephen Kosslyn, Thomas Ball, and Brian Reiser (1978) found an interesting way to show that memories do exist as images. Participants first memorized a sort of treasure map similar to the one shown in Figure 7.17a. They were then asked to picture a black dot moving from one object, such as one of the trees, to another, such as the hut at the top of the island. Did people really form an image to do this task? It seems they did. As shown in Figure 7.17b, the time it took to "move" the dot was directly related to actual distances on the map.

Is the "treasure map" task an example of photographic memory? In some ways, internal memory images do have "photographic" qualities. However, the term *photographic memory* is more often used to describe a memory ability called eidetic imagery.

Eidetic Imagery

Mental images Internal images or visual depictions used in memory and thinking.

Eidetic imagery The ability to retain a "projected" mental image long enough to use it as a source of information.

Eidetic (eye-DET-ik) **imagery** occurs when a person has visual images clear enough to be "scanned" or retained for at least 30 seconds. Internal memory images can be "viewed" mentally with the eyes closed. In contrast, eidetic images are "projected" out in front of a person. That is, they are best "seen" on a plain surface, such as a blank piece of paper. In this respect,

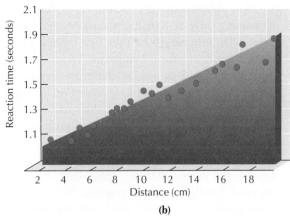

(a) **(b)**

▶▶**FIGURE 7.17** (a) "Treasure map" similar to the one used by Kosslyn, Ball, and Reiser (1978) to study images in memory. (b) This graph shows how long it took subjects to move a visualized spot various distances on their mental images of the map. (See text for explanation.)

eidetic images are somewhat like the after-images you might have after looking at a flashbulb or a brightly lit neon sign (Haber & Haber, 2000).

In one series of tests, children were shown a picture from *Alice's Adventures in Wonderland* (Figure 7.18). To test your eidetic imagery, look at the picture and read the instructions there.

Now, let's see how much you remember. Can you say (without looking again) which of Alice's apron strings is longer? Are the cat's front paws crossed? How many stripes are on the cat's tail? After the picture was removed from view, one 10-year-old boy was asked what he saw. He replied, "I see the tree, gray tree with three limbs. I see the cat with stripes around its tail." Asked to count the stripes, the boy replied, "There are about 16" (a correct count!). The boy then went on to describe the remainder of the picture in striking detail (Haber, 1969).

Don't be disappointed if you didn't do too well when you tried your eidetic skills. Eidetic memory is more common in childhood and becomes rare by adulthood (Haber & Haber, 2000).

A Case of Photographic Memory

Let's return now to the concept of mental images. In rare instances, such images may be so vivid that it is reasonable to say that a person has "photographic memory." But forgetting is also important. If you didn't have selective memory, you would recall all the ingredients on your cereal box, every street number you've ever seen, and countless other scraps of information. Regardless, few people in history have possessed such amazing memory abilities. Instead, most people with good memories have learned effective strategies for remembering. Let's investigate further.

Strategies for Remembering

At first, a student volunteer named Steve could remember seven digits. Could he improve with practice? For 20 months Steve practiced memorizing ever-longer lists of digits. Ultimately, he was able to memorize approximately 80 digits, like this sample:

9284204805084226895399019025291280799970660657471731060108058526972 60
26357332135

▶▶**FIGURE 7.18** A test picture like that used to identify children with eidetic imagery. To test your eidetic imagery, look at the picture for 30 seconds. Then look at a blank surface and try to "project" the picture onto it. If you have good eidetic imagery, you will be able to see the picture in detail. Return now to the text and try to answer the questions there. (Redrawn from an illustration in Lewis Carroll's *Alice's Adventures in Wonderland*.)

8 7 3 7 9 2 6 8
2 0 1 1 7 4 9 5
0 1 7 5 8 7 8 3
1 9 4 7 6 0 6 9
3 6 1 6 8 1 5 4
4 5 2 4 0 2 9 7

▸▸**FIGURE 7.19** This number matrix is similar to the ones contestants in the World Memory Championship had to memorize. To be scored as correct, digits had to be recalled in their proper positions (Wilding & Valentine, 1994a).

How did Steve do it? Basically, he worked by chunking digits into meaningful groups containing three or four digits each. Steve's avid interest in long-distance running helped greatly. For instance, to him the first three digits above represented 9 minutes and 28 seconds, a good time for a 2-mile run. When running times wouldn't work, Steve used other associations, such as ages or dates, to chunk digits (Ericsson & Chase, 1982). It seems apparent that Steve's success was based on learned strategies. By using similar memory systems, other people have trained themselves to equal Steve's feat (Bellezza, Six, & Phillips, 1992). In fact, the ability to organize information into chunks underlies expertise in many fields (Gobet, 2005).

Psychologist Anders Ericsson believes that exceptional memory is merely a learned extension of normal memory. As evidence, he notes that Steve's short-term memory did not improve during months of practice. For example, Steve could still memorize only seven consonants. Steve's phenomenal memory for numbers grew as he figured out new ways to chunk digits upon encoding and store them in LTM. Steve began with a normal memory for digits. He extended his memory by diligent practice. Clearly, exceptional memory can be learned (Ericsson et al., 2004).

Memory Champions

Each year the World Memory Championship is held in England. Contestants must rapidly memorize daunting amounts of information, such as long lists of unrelated words and numbers (see Figure 7.19). Psychologists John Wilding and Elizabeth Valentine saw this event as an opportunity to study exceptional memory and persuaded the contestants to take some additional memory tests. These ranged from ordinary (recall a story), to challenging (recall the telephone numbers of six different people), to diabolical (recall 48 numerals arranged in rows and columns) (Maguire et al., 2003; Wilding & Valentine, 1994a).

Exceptional memorizers were found to

- Use memory strategies and techniques
- Have specialized interests and knowledge that make certain types of information easier to encode and recall
- Have naturally superior memory abilities, often including vivid mental images
- Not have superior intellectual abilities or different brains

The first two points confirm what we learned from Steve's acquired memory ability. Many of the contestants, for example, actively used memory strategies, including special memory "tricks" called *mnemonics* (nee-MON-iks). Specialized interests and knowledge also helped for some tasks. For example, one contestant, a mathematician, was exceedingly good at memorizing numbers (Wilding & Valentine, 1994a).

Several of the memory contestants were able to excel on tasks that prevented the use of learned strategies and techniques. This observation implies that superior memory ability can be a "gift" as well as a learned skill. Wilding and Valentine conclude that exceptional memory may be based on either natural ability or learned strategies. Usually it requires both.

IMPROVING MEMORY—KEYS TO THE MEMORY BANK

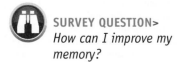

SURVEY QUESTION>
How can I improve my memory?

Let's see how you can improve your memory. To begin, there is very little you can do to improve your brain's ability to store long-term memories. The jury is still out on the use of herbs (such as *Ginkgo biloba*) and vitamins (such as vitamin E) to improve human memory (McDaniel, Maier, & Einstein, 2002). However, until there's a memory pill, you can immediately use learned strategies to improve memory encoding and memory retrieval. Most super memorizers use these strategies to augment whatever natural talents they have. Some of their strategies are described in the remainder of this section. Later, mnemonics are explored in this chapter's Psychology in Action section. Please do remember to read it.

Encoding Strategies

One way to improve your memory is to be sure to fully encode information. That way you can avoid forgetting due to encoding failure. Here are some steps you can take to become a better encoder.

Elaborative Encoding

The more you *rehearse* (mentally review) information as you read, the better you will remember it. But remember that maintenance rehearsal alone is not very effective. Elaborative encoding, in which you rehearse by looking for connections to existing knowledge, is far better. Repeatedly thinking about facts helps link them together in memory. To learn college-level information, you must make active use of more reflective rehearsal strategies (Santrock & Halonen, 2007).

Selection

The Dutch scholar Erasmus said that a good memory should be like a fish net: It should keep all the big fish and let the little ones escape. If you boil down the paragraphs in most textbooks to one or two important terms or ideas, your memory chores will be more manageable. Practise very selective marking in your texts and use marginal notes to further summarize ideas. Most students mark their texts too much instead of too little. If everything is underlined, you haven't been selective. And, very likely, you didn't pay much attention in the first place (Peterson, 1992).

Organization

Assume that you must memorize the following list of words: north, man, red, spring, woman, east, autumn, yellow, summer, boy, blue, west, winter, girl, green, south. This rather difficult list could be reorganized into *chunks* as follows: north-east-south-west, spring-summer-autumn-winter, red-yellow-green-blue, man-woman-boy-girl. Organizing class notes and summarizing chapters can be quite helpful (Hettich, 2005). You may even want to summarize your summaries, so that the overall network of ideas becomes clearer and simpler. Summaries improve memory by encouraging better encoding of information (Hadwin, Kirby, & Woodhouse, 1999).

Whole versus Part Learning

If you have to memorize a speech, is it better to try to learn it from beginning to end? Or in smaller parts like paragraphs? Generally it is better to practise whole packages of information rather than smaller parts (*whole learning*). This is especially true for fairly short, organized information. An exception is that learning parts may be better for extremely long, complicated information. In *part learning*, subparts of a larger body of information are studied (such as sections of a textbook chapter). To decide which approach to use, remember to study the *largest meaningful amount of information* you can at one time.

For very long or complex material, try the *progressive-part method*, by breaking a learning task into a series of short sections. At first, you study part A until it is mastered. Next, you study parts A and B; then A, B, and C; and so forth. This is a good way to learn the lines of a play, a long piece of music, or a poem (Ash & Holding, 1990). After the material is learned, you should also practise by starting at points other than A (at C, D, or B, for example). This helps prevent getting "lost" or going blank in the middle of a performance.

Serial Position

Whenever you must learn something in order, be aware of the serial position effect. As you will recall, this is the tendency to make the most errors in remembering the middle of a list. If you are introduced to a long line of people, the names you are likely to forget will be those in the middle, so you should make an extra effort to attend to them. You should also give extra practice to the middle of a list, poem, or speech. Try to break long lists of information into short sublists, and make the middle sublists the shortest of all.

▸▸FIGURE 7.20 Actors can remember large amounts of complex information for many months, even when learning new roles in between. During testing, they remember their lines best when they are allowed to move and gesture as they would when performing. Apparently their movements supply cues that aid recall (Noice & Noice, 1999).

Cues

The best *memory cues* (stimuli that aid retrieval) are those that were present during encoding (Anderson, 2005). For example, students in one study had the daunting task of trying to recall a list of 600 words. As they read the list (which they did not know they would be tested on), the students gave three other words closely related in meaning to each listed word. In a test given later, the words each student supplied were used as cues to jog memory. The students recalled an astounding 90 percent of the original word list (Mantyla, 1986).

Now read the following sentence:

The fish bit the swimmer.

If you were tested a week from now, you would be more likely to recall the sentence if you were given a memory cue. And, surprisingly, the word *shark* would work better as a reminder than *fish* would. The reason for this is that most people think of a shark when they read the sentence. As a result, *shark* becomes a potent memory cue (Schacter, 2000).

The preceding example shows, once again, that it often helps to *elaborate* information as you learn. When you study, try to use new names, ideas, or terms in several sentences. Also, form images that include the new information and relate it to knowledge you already have. Your goal should be to knit meaningful cues into your memory code to help you retrieve information when you need it (Figure 7.20).

Overlearning

Numerous studies have shown that memory is greatly improved when you *overlearn* or continue to study beyond bare mastery. After you have learned material well enough to remember it once without error, you should continue studying. Overlearning is your best insurance against going blank on a test because of being nervous.

Spaced Practice

To keep boredom and fatigue to a minimum, try alternating short study sessions with brief rest periods. This pattern, called **spaced practice,** is generally superior to **massed practice,** in which little or no rest is given between learning sessions (see the Introduction of this book for more on this). By improving attention and consolidation, three 20-minute study sessions can produce more learning than one hour of continuous study (Neath & Surprenant, 2003).

Perhaps the best way to make use of spaced practice is to *schedule* your time. To make an effective schedule, designate times during the week before, after, and between classes when you will study particular subjects. Then treat these times just as if they were classes you have to attend.

Retrieval Strategies

Once you have successfully encoded information, you still have to retrieve it. Here are some strategies to help you avoid retrieval failure.

Retrieval Practice

Learning proceeds best when feedback allows you to check your progress. Feedback can help you identify ideas that need extra practice. In addition, knowing that you have remembered or answered correctly is rewarding. A prime way to provide feedback for yourself while studying is *recitation*. If you are going to remember something, eventually you will have to retrieve it. Recitation refers to summarizing aloud while you are learning. Recitation forces you to practise retrieving information. When you are reading a text, you should stop frequently and try to remember what you have just read by restating it in your own words. In

Spaced practice A practice schedule that alternates study periods with brief rests.

Massed practice A practice schedule in which studying continues for long periods, without interruption.

one classic experiment, the best memory score was earned by a group of students who spent 80 percent of their time reciting and only 20 percent reading (Gates, 1958). Maybe students who talk to themselves aren't crazy after all.

If you have spaced your practice and overlearned, retrieval practice in the form of review will be like icing on your study cake. Reviewing shortly before an exam cuts down the time during which you must remember details that may be important for the test. When reviewing, hold the amount of new information you try to memorize to a minimum. It may be realistic to take what you have actually learned and add a little more to it at the last minute by cramming. But remember that more than a little new learning may interfere with what you already know.

Using a Strategy to Aid Recall

Successful retrieval is usually the result of a planned *search* of memory (Herrmann et al., 2006). For example, one study found that students were most likely to recall names that eluded them if they made use of partial information (Reed & Bruce, 1982). The students were trying to answer questions such as, "He is best remembered as the scarecrow in the Judy Garland movie *The Wizard of Oz*." (The answer is Ray Bolger.) Partial information that helped students remember included impressions about the length of the name, letter sounds within the name, similar names, and related information (such as the names of other characters in the movie). A similar helpful strategy is to go through the alphabet, trying each letter as the first sound of a name or word you are seeking.

The *cognitive interview* described earlier in this chapter (see Critical Thinking "Telling Wrong from Right in Forensic Memory") offers some further hints for recapturing context and jogging memories:

1. Say or write down *everything* you can remember that relates to the information you are seeking. Don't worry about how trivial any of it seems; each bit of information you remember can serve as a cue to bring back others.

2. Try to recall events or information in different orders. Let your memories flow out backward or out of order, or start with whatever impressed you the most.

3. Recall from different viewpoints. Review events by mentally standing in a different place. Or try to view information as another person would remember it. When taking a test, for instance, ask yourself what other students or your professor would remember about the topic.

4. Mentally put yourself back in the situation where you learned the information. Try to mentally recreate the learning environment or relive the event. As you do, include sounds, smells, details of weather, nearby objects, other people present, what you said or thought, and how you felt as you learned the information (Fisher & Geiselman, 1987; Milne & Bull, 2002).

Extend How Long You Remember

When you are learning new information, practise retrieval repeatedly. As you do, gradually lengthen the amount of time that passes before you test yourself again. For example, if you are studying German words on flash cards, look at the first card and then move it a few cards back in the stack. Do the same with the next few cards. When you get to the first "old" card, test yourself on it and check the answer. Then, move it farther back in the stack. Do the same with other "old" cards as they come up. When "old" cards come up for the third time, put them clear to the back of the stack (Cull, Shaughnessy, & Zechmeister, 1996).

Sleep and Memory

Remember that sleeping after study reduces interference. However, unless you are a "night person," late evening may not be a very efficient time for you to study. Also, you obviously can't sleep after every study session or study everything just before you sleep. That's why your study schedule should include ample breaks between subjects, as described earlier. (See "Spaced Practice.") The breaks and free time in your schedule are as important as your study periods.

STUDY BREAK   Improving Memory

Reflect

What kinds of information are you good at remembering? Why do you think your memory is better for these topics?

Return to the topic headings in the preceding pages that list techniques for improving memory. Place a check mark next to those that you have used recently. Review any you didn't mark and think of a specific example of how you could use each technique at school, at home, or at work.

Learning Check

1. Children with eidetic imagery typically have no better than average long-term memory. T or F?
2. For most people, having an especially good memory is based on
   a. maintenance rehearsal   b. constructive processing
   c. phonetic imagery   d. learned strategies
3. As new information is encoded, it is helpful to elaborate on its meaning and connect it to other information. T or F?

4. Organizing information while studying has little effect on memory because long-term memory is already highly organized. T or F?
5. To improve memory, it is reasonable to spend as much or more time reciting as reading. T or F?
6. The cognitive interview helps people remember more by providing
   a. memory cues   b. a serial position effect
   c. phonetic priming   d. massed practice

Critical Thinking

7. What advantages are there to taking notes as you read a textbook, as opposed to underlining words in the text?

Answers

1. T 2. d 3. T 4. F 5. T 6. a 7. Note-taking is a form of elaborative encoding and recitation; it facilitates the organization and selection of important ideas, and your notes can be used for review.

Hunger and Memory

People who are hungry almost always score lower on memory tests. So Mother was right, it's a good idea to make sure you've had a good breakfast or lunch before you take tests at school (Smith, Clark, & Gallagher, 1999). And a cup of coffee won't hurt your test performance, either (Smith, 2005).

A Look Ahead

Psychologists still have much to learn about the nature of memory and how to improve it. For now, one thing stands out clearly: People who have good memories excel at organizing information and making it meaningful. Sometimes, however, you are faced with the need to memorize information without much inherent meaning. For example, a shopping list is just a list of more or less unrelated items. There isn't much of a meaningful relationship between carrots, rolls of toilet paper, TV dinners, and cookies except that you need more of them. With this in mind, the Psychology in Action discussion for this chapter tells how you can use mnemonics to better memorize when meaning-based memory strategies, like those described in this section, are not helpful.

Psychology in Action

MNEMONICS—MEMORY MAGIC

SURVEY QUESTION>
Are there any tricks to help me with my memory?

Just imagine the poor biology or psychology student who is required to learn the names of the 12 cranial nerves (in order, of course). Although the spinal nerves connect the brain to the body through the spinal cord, the cranial nerves do so directly. Just in case you wanted to know, their names are olfactory, optic, oculomotor, trochlear, trigeminal, abducens, facial, vestibulocochlear, glossopharyngeal, vagus, spinal accessory, and hypoglossal.

As you might imagine, most of us find it difficult to successfully encode this list. In the absence of any obvious meaningful relationship among these terms, it is difficult to apply the memory strategies we discussed earlier in the chapter and tempting to resort to *rote* learning (learning by simple repetition). Fortunately, there *is* an alternative: mnemonics (Baddeley et al., 2009; Neath & Surprenant, 2003). A **mnemonic** is any kind of memory system or aid (see the Introduction of this book for more on this). The superiority of mnemonic learning as opposed to rote learning has been demonstrated many times (Carney & Levin, 2003; Manalo, 2002).

Some mnemonic systems are so common that almost everyone knows them. If you are trying to remember how many days there are in a month, you may find the answer by reciting, "Thirty days hath September…." Physics teachers often help students remember the colours of the spectrum by giving them the mnemonic "Roy G. Biv": **R**ed, **O**range, **Y**ellow, **G**reen, **B**lue, **I**ndigo, **V**iolet. The budding sailor who has trouble telling port from starboard may remember that "port" and "left" both have four letters or may remind herself, "I *left* port." And what beginning musician hasn't remembered the notes represented by the lines and spaces of the musical staff by learning "F-A-C-E" and "**E**very **G**ood **B**oy **D**oes **F**ine"?

Generations of students have learned the names of the spinal nerves by memorizing the sentence "**O**n **O**ld **O**lympus's **T**owering **T**op **A F**amous **V**ocal **G**erman **V**iewed **S**ome **H**ops." This mnemonic, which uses the first letter of each of the cranial nerves to generate a nonsense sentence, indeed produces better recall of the cranial nerves. Such *acrostics* are even more effective if you make up your own (Bloom & Lamkin, 2006). By practising mnemonics you should be able to greatly improve your memory with little effort.

Here, then, are some basic principles of mnemonics:

1. **Make things meaningful.** In general, transferring information from short-term memory to long-term memory is aided by making it meaningful. If you encounter technical terms that have little or no immediate meaning for you, *give* them meaning, even if you have to stretch the term to do so. (This point is clarified by the examples following this list.)

2. **Make information familiar.** Another way to get information into long-term memory is to connect it to information already stored there. If some facts or ideas in a chapter seem to stay in your memory easily, associate other, more difficult facts with them.

3. **Use mental pictures.** Visual pictures, or images, are generally easier to remember than words. Turning information into mental pictures is therefore very helpful. Make these images as vivid as possible (Neath & Surprenant, 2003).

4. **Form bizarre, unusual, or exaggerated mental associations.** Forming images that make sense is better in most situations. However, when associating two ideas, terms, or especially mental images, you may find that the more outrageous and exaggerated the association, the more likely you are to remember. Bizarre images make stored information more *distinctive* and therefore easier to retrieve (Worthen & Marshall, 1996). Imagine, for example, that you have just been introduced to Mr. Rehkop. To remember his name, you could picture him wearing a police uniform. Then replace his nose with a ray gun. This bizarre image will provide two hints when you want to remember Mr. Rehkop's name: *ray* and *cop*. This technique works for other kinds of information, too. College students who used exaggerated mental associations to remember the names of unfamiliar animals outperformed students who just used rote memory (Carney & Levin, 2001). Bizarre images mainly help improve immediate memory, and they work best for fairly simple information (Fritz et al., 2007; Robinson-Riegler & McDaniel, 1994). Nevertheless, they can be a first step toward learning.

A sampling of typical applications of mnemonics should make these four points clearer to you:

Example 1: Let's say you have some new vocabulary words to memorize in French. You can learn them with little effort by using the **keyword method,** in which a familiar word or image is used to link two other words or items (Fritz et al., 2007; Pressley, 1987). To remember that the word *livre* (pronounced LEE-vre) means book, you can link it to a

Mnemonic Any kind of memory system or aid.

Keyword method As an aid to memory, using a familiar word or image to link two items.

Commercial Eye/Getty Images

Mnemonics can be an aid in preparing for tests. However, because mnemonics help most in the initial stages of storing information, it is important to follow through with other elaborative learning strategies.

"key" word in English: *Livre* sounds a bit like "lever." Therefore, to remember that *livre* means book, you might visualize a huge lever being used to lift a giant box of books. You should try to make this image as vivid and exaggerated as possible, with the box of books accidentally falling off the lever and pages flying everywhere. Similarly, for the word *carte* (which means "map"), you might imagine a shopping *cart* filled with maps.

If you link similar keywords and images for the rest of the list, you may not remember them all, but you will get most without much more practice. As a matter of fact, if you have formed the *livre* and *carte* images just now, it is going to be almost impossible for you to ever see these words again without remembering what they mean.

Exaggerated mental images can link two words or ideas in ways that aid memory. Here, the keyword method is used to link the English word *map* with the French word *carte*.

What about a year from now? How long do keyword memories last? Mnemonic memories work best in the short run. Later, they may be more fragile than conventional memories. That's why it's usually best to use mnemonics during the initial stages of learning (Carney & Levin, 2003). To create more lasting memories, you'll need to use the techniques discussed earlier in this chapter.

Example 2: Suppose you have to learn the names of all the bones and muscles in the human body for biology. To remember that the jawbone is the *mandible*, you can associate it to a *man nibbling*, or maybe you can picture a *man dribbling* a basketball with his jaw (make this image as ridiculous as possible). If the muscle name *latissimus dorsi* gives you trouble, familiarize it by turning it into "*the ladder misses the door, sigh.*" Then picture a ladder glued to your back where the muscle is found. Picture the ladder leading up to a small door at your shoulder. Picture the ladder missing the door. Picture the ladder sighing like an animated character in a cartoon.

This seems like more to remember, not less, and it seems like it would cause you to misspell things. Mnemonics are an aid, not a complete substitute for normal memory. Mnemonics are not likely to be helpful unless you make extensive use of *images* (Willoughby et al., 1997). Your mental pictures will come back to you easily. As for misspellings, mnemonics can be thought of as a built-in hint in your memory. Often, when taking a test, you will find that the slightest hint is all you need to remember correctly. A mnemonic image is like having someone leaning over your shoulder who says, "Psst, the name of that muscle sounds like 'ladder misses the door, sigh.'" If misspelling continues to be a problem, try to create memory aids for spelling, too.

Here are two more examples to help you appreciate the flexibility of a mnemonic approach to studying.

Example 3: Your art history teacher expects you to be able to name the artist when you are shown slides as part of exams. You have seen many of the slides only once before in class. How will you remember them? As the slides are shown in class, make each artist's name into an object or image. Then picture the object *in* the paintings done by the artist. For example, you can picture Van Gogh as a *van* (automobile) *going* through the middle of each Van Gogh painting. Picture the van running over things and knocking things over. Or, if you remember that Van Gogh cut off his ear, picture a giant bloody ear in each of his paintings.

Example 4: If you have trouble remembering history, try to avoid thinking of it as something from the dim past. Picture each historical personality as a person you know right now (a friend, teacher, parent, and so on). Then picture these people doing whatever the historical figures did. Also, try visualizing battles or other events as if they were happening in your town, or make parks and schools into countries. Use your imagination.

How can mnemonics be used to remember things in order? Here are three helpful techniques:

1. **Form a story or a chain.** To remember lists of ideas, objects, or words in order, try forming an exaggerated association (mental image) connecting the first item to the second, then the second to the third, and so on. To remember the following short list in order—elephant, doorknob, string, watch, rifle, oranges—picture a full-size *elephant* balanced on a *doorknob* playing with a *string* tied to him. Picture a *watch* tied to the string, and a *rifle* shooting *oranges* at the watch. This technique can be used quite successfully for lists of 20 or more items. In one test, people who used a linking mnemonic did much better at remembering lists of 15 and 22 errands (Higbee et al., 1990). Try it next time you go shopping and leave your list at home. Another helpful strategy is to make up a short story that links all the items on a list you want to remember (McNamara & Scott, 2001).

2. **Take a mental walk.** Ancient Greek orators had an interesting way to remember ideas in order when giving a speech. Their method was to take a mental walk along a familiar path. As they did, they associated topics with the images of statues found along the walk. You can do the same thing by "placing" objects or ideas along the way as you mentally take a familiar walk (Neath & Surprenant, 2003).

3. **Use a system.** As we have already seen, many times, the first letters or syllables of words or ideas can be formed into another word that will serve as a reminder of order. "Roy G. Biv" is an example. As an alternative, learn the following: 1 is a bun, 2 is a shoe, 3 is a tree, 4 is a door, 5 is a hive, 6 is sticks, 7 is heaven, 8 is a gate, 9 is a line, 10 is a hen. To remember a list in order, form an image associating bun with the first item on your list. For example, if the first item is *frog*, picture a "frog-burger" on a bun to remember it. Then, associate shoe with the second item, and so on.

If you have never used mnemonics, you may still be skeptical, but give this approach a fair trial. Most people find they can greatly extend their memory through the use of mnemonics. But remember, like most things worthwhile, remembering takes effort.

✓ STUDY BREAK   Mnemonics

Reflect

The best mnemonics are your own. As an exercise, see if you can create a better acrostic for the 12 cranial nerves. One student generated **O**ld **O**tto **O**ctavius **T**ried **T**rigonometry **A**fter **F**acing **V**ery **G**rim **V**irgins' **S**ad **H**usbands (Bloom & Lamkin, 2006).

Go through the glossary items in this chapter and make up mnemonics for any terms you have difficulty remembering. Here is an example to help you get started. An iconic memory is a visual image: Picture an *eye* in a *can* to remember that iconic memories store visual information.

Learning Check

1. Memory systems and aids are referred to as _____.
2. Which of the following is least likely to improve memory?
   a. using exaggerated mental images
   b. forming a chain of associations
   c. turning visual information into verbal information
   d. associating new information with information that is already known or familiar
3. Bizarre images make stored information more distinctive and therefore easier to retrieve. T or F?
4. In general, mnemonics improve memory for related words or ideas only. T or F?

Critical Thinking

5. How are elaborative encoding and mnemonics alike?

Answers

1. mnemonics 2. c 3. T 4. F 5. Both attempt to relate new information to information stored in LTM that is familiar or already easy to retrieve.

CHAPTER IN REVIEW

Major Points

- Remembering is an active process. Our memories are frequently lost, altered, revised, or distorted.
- The best way to remember depends, to an extent, on which memory system you are using.
- Remembering is not an all-or-nothing process. Even when you think you can't recall anything, some information may continue to exist in memory.
- Understanding how and why forgetting occurs will allow you to make better use of your memory.
- Some people have naturally superior memories, but everyone can learn to improve his or her memory.
- Memory systems (mnemonics) greatly improve immediate memory. However, conventional learning tends to create the most lasting memories.

Summary

How does memory work?

- Memory is an active, computer-like system that encodes, stores, and retrieves information.
- The three stages of memory (sensory memory, short-term memory, and long-term memory) hold information for increasingly longer periods.
- Sensory memories are encoded as iconic memories or echoic memories. Short-term memories tend to be encoded by sound, and long-term memories by meaning.

What are the features of short-term memory?

- Selective attention determines what information moves from sensory memory, which is exact but very brief, on to STM.
- STM has a capacity of about five to seven bits of information, but this can be extended by chunking, or recoding. Short-term memories are brief and very sensitive to interruption, or interference; however, they can be prolonged by maintenance rehearsal.

What are the features of long-term memory?

- LTM serves as a general storehouse for meaningful information. Elaborative encoding helps us form lasting, long-term memories.
- Long-term memories are relatively permanent. LTM seems to have an almost unlimited storage capacity.

- Constructive processing tends to alter memories. Remembering is an active process. Our memories are frequently lost, altered, revised, or distorted.
- LTM is highly organized. The structure of memory networks is the subject of current research.
- In redintegration, memories are reconstructed as one bit of information leads to others, which then serve as cues for further recall.
- LTM contains procedural (skill) and declarative (fact) memories. Declarative memories can be semantic or episodic.

How is memory measured?

- The tip-of-the-tongue state shows that memory is not an all-or-nothing event. Memories may therefore be revealed by recall, recognition, relearning, or priming.
- In recall, memories are retrieved without explicit cues, as in an essay exam. Recall of listed information often reveals a serial position effect.
- A common test of recognition is the multiple-choice question.
- In relearning, material that seems to be forgotten is learned again, and memory is revealed by a savings score.
- Recall, recognition, and relearning measure mainly explicit memories. Other techniques, such as priming, are necessary to reveal implicit memories.

Why do we forget?

- Forgetting can occur because of failures of encoding, of storage, or of retrieval.
- Herman Ebbinghaus found that forgetting is most rapid immediately after learning, as shown by the curve of forgetting.
- Failure to encode information is a common cause of "forgetting."
- Forgetting in sensory memory and STM is due to a failure of storage through a weakening (decay) of memory traces. Decay of memory traces may also explain some LTM losses.
- Failures of retrieval occur when information that resides in memory is nevertheless not retrieved.
- A lack of memory cues can produce retrieval failure. State-dependent learning is related to the effects of memory cues.

- Much forgetting in STM and LTM is caused by interference. In retroactive interference, new learning interferes with the ability to retrieve earlier learning. Proactive interference occurs when old learning interferes with the retrieval of new learning.

- Memories can be consciously suppressed and they may be unconsciously repressed.

- Extreme caution is warranted when "recovered" memories are the only basis for believing that a person was sexually abused during childhood.

How does the brain form and store memories?

- Lasting memories are recorded by changes in the activity, structure, and chemistry of brain cells.

- It takes time to consolidate memories. In the brain, memory consolidation takes place in the hippocampus. Until they are consolidated, long-term memories are easily destroyed.

- Intensely emotional experiences can result in flashbulb memories.

- After memories have been consolidated, they appear to be stored in the cortex of the brain.

- Memories are recorded in the brain through nerve cells and how they interconnect.

What are "photographic" memories?

- Eidetic imagery (photographic memory) occurs when a person is able to project an image onto a blank surface.

- Eidetic imagery is rarely found in adults. However, many adults have internal memory images, which can be very vivid.

How can I improve my memory?

- Although it's true that some people have naturally superior memories, everyone can learn to improve his or her memory.

- Exceptional memory may be based on natural ability or learned strategies. Usually it involves both.

- Excellent memory abilities are based on using strategies and techniques that make learning efficient and that compensate for natural weaknesses in human memory.

- Memory can be improved through better encoding strategies, such as elaborating, selecting, and organizing information, as well as whole learning, the progressive part method, encoding memory cues, overlearning, and spaced practice.

- Memory can also be improved through better retrieval strategies, such as using feedback, recitation, rehearsal, and active search strategies.

- When you are studying or memorizing, you should also keep in mind the effects of serial position, sleep, and hunger.

Are there any tricks to help me with my memory?

- Mnemonic systems use mental images and unusual associations to link new information with familiar memories already stored in LTM.

- Effective mnemonics tend to rely on mental images and bizarre or exaggerated mental associations.

Interactive Learning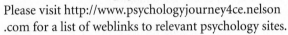

Please visit http://www.psychologyjourney4ce.nelson.com for a list of weblinks to relevant psychology sites.

CourseMate

Access an interactive e-book and chapter-specific interactive learning tools, including flashcards, quizzes, videos, and more, in your psychology CourseMate. Visit Nelsonbrain.com to use CourseMate.

psyk.trek 6. Memory, Psyk.Trek Simulations: 5. Memory processes I, 6. Memory Processes II

TEST YOUR KNOWLEDGE

The questions that follow are only a sample of what you need to know. If you miss any of the items, review the entire chapter and the Study Breaks. Another way to prepare for tests is to use the Study Guide and the Practice Exams that are available with this text.

1. Selective attention controls information that moves from sensory memory to which of the following?
   a. phonetic memory
   b. iconic memory
   c. short-term memory (STM)
   d. long-term memory (LTM)

2. What is the primary way in which information is stored in long-term memory (LTM)?
   a. by meaning
   b. by sounds and phonetics
   c. by icons and echoes
   d. by how it will be retrieved

3. What does the digit-span test primarily measure?
   a. long-term memory (LTM)
   b. elaborative rehearsal
   c. recoding
   d. short-term memory (STM)

4. Which of the following is a type of skill memory?
   a. semantic memory
   b. declarative memory
   c. episodic memory
   d. procedural memory

5. What type of memory test is most likely to reveal a serial position effect?
   a. recall
   b. recognition
   c. relearning
   d. implicit

6. For most people, what is an especially good memory based on?
   a. maintenance rehearsal
   b. constructive processing
   c. phonetic imagery
   d. learned strategies

7. A saxophone player learns three new pieces of music, one after the other, in a single afternoon. The next day he is least able to remember the third piece. What term refers to this effect?
   a. state-dependent learning
   b. the time decay of memory traces
   c. proactive interference
   d. disuse of memory cues

8. What memories are considered to be the reverse of flashbulb memories?
   a. repressed memories
   b. proactive memories
   c. retroactive memories
   d. episodic memories

9. What is most likely to disrupt memory consolidation?
   a. rehearsal
   b. electroconvulsive shock (ECS)
   c. overlearning
   d. sleep

10. What is the keyword method?
    a. a cognitive interviewing technique
    b. a massed practice strategy
    c. a mnemonic technique
    d. the first step in the progressive part method

11. Items encoded into short-term memory are most likely to be confused if they are similar in which of the following?
    a. meaning
    b. shape
    c. name
    d. location

12. What term refers to a fleeting mental image that lasts for about half a second after you close your eyes?
    a. a photographic memory
    b. an icon
    c. an episodic memory
    d. a short-term memory

13. What type of memory do we use for thinking and problem solving?
    a. working memory
    b. semantic memory
    c. procedural memory
    d. strategy memory

14. What term refers to filling in gaps in memory by using logic or reasoning?
    a. pseudo-memory
    b. self-reference effect
    c. constructive processing
    d. consolidation

15. Episodic memories, which make it possible for us to travel back in time, are more easily forgotten than are which of the following?
    a. procedural memories
    b. declarative memories
    c. short-term memories
    d. semantic memories

16. What do you use when you predict whether you will be able to remember something?
    a. the tip-of-the-tongue process
    b. the savings score
    c. implicit memory
    d. the feeling of knowing

17. Which of the following is illustrated by someone unconsciously knowing the location of letters on a keyboard?
    a. implicit memory
    b. explicit memory
    c. eidetic imagery
    d. priming

18. What best explains why recent events are recalled more accurately than events from the remote past?
    a. the forgetting curve
    b. encoding failure
    c. mnemonic strategies
    d. disuse

19. Sam couldn't recall meeting Sarah until she reminded him that they met at the graduation party in their last year of high school. What is this scenario an example of?
    a. state-dependent learning
    b. suppression
    c. cue-dependent forgetting
    d. order effects

20. Suffering a severe head injury, Frank is unable to remember anything from his past. He has what type of neurological issue?
    a. anterograde amnesia
    b. retrograde amnesia
    c. repression
    d. retrograde aplysia

ANSWERS   1.c 2.a 3.d 4.d 5.a 6.d 7.c 8.a 9.b 10.c 11.c 12.b 13.a 14.c 15.d 16.d 17.a 18.a 19.c 20.b

chapter 8

Intelligence, Cognition, Language, and Creativity

JOURNEY INTO PSYCHOLOGY:
SURPRISING BABIES

If you were asked to list your least favourite academic subject, statistics might be near the top of the list. If it is, you may be surprised to learn that statistical thinking is natural for human beings and that even infants as young as eight months old can do it.

Psychologists Fei Xu and Vashti Garcia at the University of British Columbia in Vancouver devised a clever way to test infants' ability to think statistically. They knew that infants will look longer at something that surprises them than at

Yellow Dog Productions/Getty Images

something they expected. In one study, with eight-month-old infants watching her, the experimenter closed her eyes and took a sample of five balls out of a large box. It's important to note that the experimenter closed her eyes to show the infants that she was not choosing balls by colour. Infants know that when your eyes are closed you can't see anything. After pulling either four red and one white or one red and four white balls, she showed the infants the contents of the large box, which consisted of mostly red balls with a few white ones mixed in. If infants have any ability to make inferences from a sample to a population, they should be surprised—and therefore should look longer—when shown the mostly red population after seeing a sample of four white balls and one red one. That is exactly what happened.

Xu and Stephanie Denison (2009) asked whether infants would modify their inference from sample to population if the experimenter looked into the box and deliberately chose all white balls. Now, when shown the population of mostly red balls, the infants did not look longer—they seemed to understand that they should not make an inference to the population because the sample was not randomly chosen.

Finally, Denison and Xu (2010) showed that infants could also change their expectation on the basis of physical information. In this case, one large box contained balls of one colour with Velcro strips on them and another large box contained balls of a different colour without Velcro. The infants were allowed to play with the boxes and learned that (for example) the red balls were immobile—that is, could not be removed from their box–while the green balls were removable. The physical fact—Velcro made red balls immobile—would make a red sample surprising. The statistical fact—the population was mostly red—would make a sample of green balls surprising. The question was, which constraint would dominate? In the experiments, the physical fact won. Eleven-month-old infants were not surprised to see green balls taken out of a mostly red box when they knew that the red balls were fixed to the box by Velcro.

All of these results show that infants as young as eight months old make sensible inferences from samples to populations, and vice versa. Infants also integrate different sources of knowledge, adjusting their inferences based on additional information about either the experimenter's demonstrated preference for one colour or about physical constraints on ball selection. We hope this evidence that inferential reasoning occurs naturally even in infants will make your experience of statistics classes less intimidating in the future. For now, though, the finding makes an important point about human cognition to introduce this chapter: There is a lot to learn during childhood, so it's a good thing that we get started when we're so young.

A final thought: At the end of their testing session, each infant in all Xu's experiments was given a diploma. Not even one year old and they've already graduated from their first statistics course!

Survey Questions

- How is human intelligence defined and measured?
- How much does intelligence vary from person to person?
- What are some controversies in the study of intelligence?
- What is the nature of thought?
- In what ways are images related to thinking?
- What are concepts?
- What is the role of language in thinking?
- What do we know about problem solving?
- What is creative thinking?
- How accurate is intuition?
- What can be done to improve thinking and promote creativity?

HUMAN INTELLIGENCE—THE IQ AND YOU

What do we mean when we say that Stephen Hawking is "intelligent"? Can intelligence be measured? Can intelligence tests predict life success? What are the consequences of having extremely high or low intelligence? These questions and others concerning intelligence have fascinated psychologists for over 100 years (Flynn, 2007). Let's see what has been learned and what issues are still debated.

Like many important concepts in psychology, intelligence cannot be observed directly. Nevertheless, we feel certain it exists. Let's compare two children:

> When she was 14 months old, Anne wrote her own name. She taught herself to read at age two. At age five, she astounded her kindergarten teacher by bringing a notebook computer to class—on which she was reading an encyclopedia. At 10 she breezed through an entire high school algebra course in 12 hours.
>
> Billy, who is 10 years old, can write his name and can count, but he has trouble with simple addition and subtraction problems and finds multiplication impossible. He has been held back in school twice and is still incapable of doing the work his eight-year-old classmates find easy.

Anne is considered a genius; Billy, a slow learner. There seems little doubt that they differ in intelligence.

Wait! Anne's ability is obvious, but how do we know that Billy isn't just lazy? That's the same question that Alfred Binet faced in 1904 (Jarvin & Sternberg, 2003). The French minister of education in Paris wanted to find a way to distinguish slower students from the more capable (or the capable but lazy). In a flash of brilliance, Binet and an associate created a test made up of "intellectual" questions and problems. Next, they learned which questions an average child could answer at each age. By giving children the test, they could tell if a child was performing up to his or her potential (Kaufman, 2000).

Binet's approach gave rise to modern intelligence tests. At the same time, it launched an ongoing debate. Part of the debate is related to the basic difficulty of defining intelligence (Sternberg, Grigorenko, & Kidd, 2005).

Defining Intelligence

Isn't there an accepted definition of intelligence? Broadly speaking, yes. **Intelligence** is the global capacity to act purposefully, to think rationally, and to deal effectively with the environment. The core of intelligence is usually thought to consist of a small set of *general mental*

<SURVEY QUESTION
How is human intelligence defined and measured?

Intelligence An overall capacity to think rationally, act purposefully, and deal effectively with the environment.

Modern intelligence tests are widely used to measure intellectual abilities. When properly administered, such tests provide an operational definition of intelligence.

abilities (called the *g*-factor) in the areas of reasoning, problem solving, knowledge, memory, and successful adaptation to one's surroundings (Gottfredson, 2007). Although opponents of intelligence testing sometimes suggest that psychologists cannot agree on how to define intelligence, in fact there is wide agreement on this question (Hunt & Carlson, 2007; Gottfredson, 1997; Lubinski, 2004; Neisser et al., 1996). There is, however, a long-standing debate on how we can measure intelligence. Many psychologists accept an operational definition of intelligence. By selecting test items, a psychologist is saying in a very direct way, "This is what I mean by intelligence."

Measuring Intelligence

American psychologists quickly saw the value of Alfred Binet's test. In 1916, Lewis Terman and others at Stanford University revised it for use in North America. After more revisions, the *Stanford-Binet Intelligence Scales, Fifth Edition* (SB5) continues to be widely used. The SB5 is made up primarily of age-ranked questions. Naturally, these questions get a little harder at each age level. The SB5 is appropriate for people from age 2 to 85+ years (Roid, 2003).

The SB5 measures five cognitive factors (types of mental abilities) that make up general intelligence. These are *fluid reasoning, knowledge, quantitative reasoning, visual-spatial processing,* and *working memory.* Each factor is measured with verbal questions (those involving words and numbers) and non-verbal questions (items that use pictures and objects). Let's see what each factor looks like.

Fluid Reasoning

Fluid reasoning is tested with questions like the following:

How are an apple, a plum, and a banana different from a beet?

An apprentice is to a master as a novice is to an _____.

"I knew my bag was going to be in the last place I looked, so I looked there first."—What is silly or impossible about that?

Other items ask people to fill in the missing shape in a group of shapes and to tell a story that explains what's going on in a series of pictures.

Knowledge

The knowledge factor assesses what a person knows about a wide range of topics.

Why is yeast added to bread dough?

What does "cryptic" mean?

What is silly or impossible about this picture? (For example, a bicycle has square wheels.)

Quantitative Reasoning

Test items for quantitative reasoning measure a person's ability to solve problems involving numbers. Here are some samples:

If I have six marbles and you give me another one, how many marbles will I have?

Given the numbers 3, 6, 9, 12, what number would come next?

If a shirt is being sold for 50 percent of the normal price, and the price tag is $60, what is the cost of the shirt?

Visual-Spatial Processing

People who have visual-spatial skills are good at putting picture puzzles together and copying geometric shapes (such as triangles, rectangles, and circles). Visual-spatial processing questions ask test takers to reproduce patterns of blocks and choose pictures that show how a piece of paper would look if it were folded or cut. Verbal questions can also require visual-spatial abilities:

Suppose that you are going east, then turn right, then turn right again, and then turn left. In which direction are you facing now?

Working Memory

The working memory part of the SB5 measures the ability to use short-term memory. Some typical memory tasks include the following:

Correctly remember the order of coloured beads on a stick.

After hearing several sentences, name the last word from each sentence.

Repeat a series of digits (forward or backward) after hearing them once.

If you were to take the SB5, it would yield a score for your general intelligence, verbal intelligence, non-verbal intelligence, and each of the five cognitive factors (Bain & Allin, 2005).

The Wechsler Tests

Is the Stanford-Binet the only intelligence test? A widely used alternative is the *Wechsler Adult Intelligence Scale—Third Edition* (WAIS-III). A version for children is called the *Wechsler Intelligence Scale for Children—Fourth Edition* (WISC-IV) (Baron, 2005).

Although the Wechsler tests are similar to the Stanford-Binet, there are some differences as well. For one thing, the WAIS-III was specifically designed to test adult intelligence. The original Stanford-Binet was better suited for children and adolescents. The latest Stanford-Binet (the SB5) can now be used for all ages, but the WAIS was the first "adult" intelligence test. Like the Stanford-Binet, the Wechsler tests yield a single overall intelligence score. In addition, the WAIS and WISC give separate scores for **performance** (non-verbal) **intelligence** and **verbal** (language- or symbol-oriented) **intelligence.** (Note that this feature was also recently added to the SB5.) The abilities measured by the Wechsler tests and some sample test items are listed in Table 8.1.

> **Performance intelligence**
> Intelligence measured by solving puzzles, assembling objects, completing pictures, and other tasks requiring the test taker to do something.
> **Verbal intelligence** Intelligence measured by answering questions involving vocabulary, general information, arithmetic, and other tasks requiring the test taker to say something.

■ **Table 8.1   Sample Items Similar to Those Used on the WAIS-III**

Verbal Subtests	Sample Items
Information	How many wings does a bird have? Who wrote Paradise Lost?
Digit span	Repeat from memory a series of digits, such as 3 1 0 6 7 4 2 5, after hearing it once.
General	What is the advantage of keeping money in the bank?
Comprehension	Why is copper often used in electrical wires?
Arithmetic	Three men divided 18 golf balls equally among themselves. How many golf balls did each man receive? If 2 apples cost 15¢, what is the cost of a dozen apples?
Similarities	In what way are a lion and a tiger alike? In what way are a saw and a hammer alike?
Vocabulary	The test consists simply of asking, "What is a _____?" or "What does _____ mean?" The words cover a wide range of difficulty or familiarity.

Performance Subtests	Description of Item
Picture arrangement	Arrange a series of cartoon panels to make a meaningful story.
Picture completion	What is missing from these pictures?
Block design	Copy designs with blocks (as shown at right).
Object assembly	Put together a jigsaw puzzle.
Digit symbol	Fill in the symbols:

1	2	3	4
X	III	I	0

3	4	1	3	4	2	1	2

Mental age The average mental ability people display at a given age.

Chronological age A person's age in years.

Intelligence quotient (IQ) An index of intelligence defined as a person's mental age divided by his or her chronological age and multiplied by 100.

Deviation IQ An IQ obtained statistically from a person's relative standing in his or her age group, that is, how far above or below average the person's score was relative to other scores.

Artificial intelligence (AI) Any artificial system (often a computer program) that is capable of humanlike problem solving or intelligent responding.

Intelligence Quotients

What is an IQ score? Imagine that a child named Yuan can answer questions an average seven-year-old can answer. How smart is she? Actually, we can't say yet, because we don't know how old Yuan is. If she is 10, she's not very smart. If she's 5, she is very bright. Thus, to estimate a child's intelligence we need to compare her **mental age** (average intellectual performance) and her **chronological age** (age in years). This yields an **intelligence quotient,** or **IQ.** When the Stanford-Binet was first used, IQ was defined as mental age (MA) divided by chronological age (CA) and multiplied by 100. (Multiplying by 100 and rounding changes the IQ into a whole number, rather than a decimal.)

$$\frac{\text{MA}}{\text{CA}} \times 100 = \text{IQ}$$

Deviation IQs

Although IQ scores were originally calculated as shown above, that method is no longer used. Instead, modern tests use **deviation IQs.** Tables supplied with the test are used to convert a person's relative standing in the group to an IQ score. That is, they tell how far above or below average the person's score falls. For example, if you score at the 50th percentile, half the people your age who take the test score higher than you and half score lower. In this case, your IQ score is 100. If you score at the 84th percentile, your IQ score is 115. If you score at the 97th percentile, your IQ score is 130. (For more information, see the Behavioural Statistics appendix near the end of this book.)

Group Tests

The SB5 and the Wechsler tests are individual intelligence tests that must be given to a single person by a trained specialist. In contrast, group intelligence tests can be given to a large group of people with minimal supervision. Group tests usually require people to read; to follow instructions; and to solve problems of logic, reasoning, mathematics, or spatial skills. If you're wondering if you have ever taken an intelligence test, the answer may be yes if you have taken the SAT. The well-known *SAT Reasoning Test* measures aptitudes for language, math, and reasoning. The SAT is designed to predict students' chances for success in college. Because it measures a number of different mental aptitudes, it can also be used to estimate general intelligence (Frey & Detterman, 2004).

Artificial Intelligence

While most efforts have focused on measuring intelligence in humans, a small group of psychologists and computer scientists have taken an entirely different approach. Their basic idea is to build machines that display **artificial intelligence (AI).** This usually refers to creating computer programs capable of doing things that require intelligence when done by people (Russell & Norvig, 2003). The resulting programs may then help us understand how people do those same things.

Consider, for example, Aaron Sloman's robot, the "Cubinator," which solves Rubik's Cube puzzles. Sloman hopes the Cubinator's expertise will help him better understand how humans do mathematics (Sloman, 2008).

How smart are computers and robots? Don't worry, they are not very smart yet. Let's say you are exchanging text messages with someone you don't know. You are allowed to make any comments and ask any questions you like, for as long as you like. In reality, the "person" you are communicating with is a computer. Do you think a computer could fool you into believing it was human? You may be surprised to learn that, to date, no machine has come close to passing this test (Moor, 2003). If it did, would that qualify it as "intelligent"? Not necessarily. One problem is that humans have a kind of bias to see patterns in the behaviour of even totally random systems.

Bela Szandelszky/AP Images

The "Cubinator" solving a Rubik's Cube at the 2007 Rubik's Cube World Championships. The winner, in 10 seconds, was a person. The Cubinator took 26 seconds. To what extent is the way the Cubinator comes up with solutions helpful for understanding how humans do it?

Those patterns make it look like the system is intelligently controlled. Some people, for example, believe they see patterns in the random numbers drawn by provincial lotteries. This bias may cause us to see humanlike "intelligence" even in the behaviour of simple machines.

The challenge computers face is that we humans can mentally "shift gears" from one topic to another with incredible flexibility. In contrast, machine "intelligence" is currently "blind" outside its underlying set of rules. As a tiny example, u cann understnd wrds thet ar mizpeld. Computers are very literal and easily stymied by such errors.

Regardless, AI has been successful at very specific tasks (such as playing chess or solving Rubik's Cubes). Much of current AI is based on the fact that many tasks—from harmonizing music to diagnosing disease—can be reduced to a set of rules applied to a collection of information. AI is valuable in situations where speed, vast memory, and persistence are required. In fact, AI programs are better at some tasks than humans are. An example is world chess champion Garry Kasparov's loss, in 1997, to a computer called Deep Blue.

Artificial Intelligence and Cognition

Although AI is a long way from duplicating general human intelligence, AI systems like the Cubinator offer a way to probe some of our specific cognitive skills, or intelligences. For instance, computer simulations and expert systems provide good examples of how AI is being used as a research tool.

Computer simulations are programs that attempt to duplicate specific human behaviours, especially thinking, decision making, and problem solving. Here, the computer acts as a "laboratory" for testing models of cognition. If a computer program behaves as humans do (including making the same errors), then the program may be a good model of how we think. As one example, Derek Besner, of the University of Waterloo, tested a computer simulation of basic processes in reading (Besner, Wartak, & Robidoux, 2008). He wanted to see whether the model would be influenced by variations in the quality of the visual stimulus (how clear the words to be read were) in the same way that people are affected. In fact, the computer model was more sensitive to these variations than people are, suggesting that the cognitive model on which the simulation was based needs more development.

Expert systems are computer programs that respond as a human expert would (Giarratano & Riley, 2005). They have demystified some human abilities by converting complex skills into clearly stated rules a computer can follow. Expert systems can predict the weather, analyze geological formations, diagnose disease, play chess, read, tell when to buy or sell stocks, and perform many other tasks.

Now let's a look at how much measured intelligence varies from person to person.

VARIATIONS IN INTELLIGENCE— CURVED LIKE A BELL

IQ scores are classified as shown in Figure 8.1. The distribution (or scattering) of IQ scores approximates a **normal** (bell-shaped) **curve.** That is, most scores fall close to the average and very few are found at the extremes.

The Mentally Gifted

How high is the IQ of a genius? Only 2 people out of 100 score above 130 on IQ tests. These bright individuals are usually described as "gifted." Less than one half of 1 percent of the population scores above 140. These people are certainly gifted or perhaps even "geniuses." However, some psychologists reserve the term

> **Normal curve** A bell-shaped curve characterized by a large number of scores in a middle area, tapering to very few extremely high and low scores.

<SURVEY QUESTION
How much does intelligence vary from person to person?

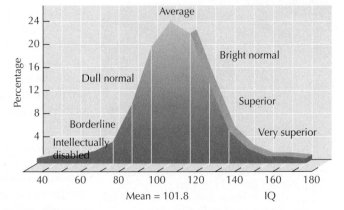

FIGURE 8.1 Distribution of Stanford-Binet Intelligence Test scores for 3184 children. (After Terman & Merrill, 1937/1960.)

Giftedness The possession of either a high IQ or special talents or aptitudes.

Intellectual disability (formerly mental retardation) The presence of a developmental disability, a formal IQ score below 70, or a significant impairment of adaptive behaviour.

It is wise to remember that there are many ways in which a child may be gifted. Many schools now offer Gifted and Talented Education programs for students with a variety of special abilities—not just for those who score well on IQ tests.

genius for people with even higher IQs or those who are exceptionally creative (Hallahan & Kauffman, 2006).

Gifted Children

Do high IQ scores in childhood predict later ability? To directly answer this question, Lewis Terman selected 1500 children with IQs of 140 or more. Terman followed this gifted group (the "Termites" as he called them) into adulthood and found that most were quite successful. A majority finished college, earned advanced degrees, or held professional positions, and many had written books or scientific articles (Terman & Oden, 1959).

In general, the correlation between IQ scores and school grades is 0.50, a sizable association. The link would be even stronger, but motivation, special talents, off-campus learning, and many other factors also affect grades. The same is true of real-world success beyond school. IQ is not at all good at predicting success in art, music, writing, or dramatics. Creativity is much more strongly related to doing well in these areas (Preckel, Holling, & Wiese, 2006; Runco, 2004). IQ is also not especially good at predicting success in science and leadership, but that may be because only people with relatively high IQs become scientists or leaders. In the absence of much variation in IQ in those fields, we can't tell whether success and IQ are correlated. Regardless, when people score in the gifted range, their chances for high achievement do seem to rise (Shurkin, 1992).

Were all the Termites superior as adults? No. Although most were mentally healthy and successful, some had committed crimes, were unemployable, or were emotionally troubled. Remember that a high IQ reveals *potential*. It does not guarantee success. Nor does a lower IQ guarantee failure. Nobel prize–winning physicist Richard Feynman, whom many regarded as a genius, had an IQ of 122 (Michalko, 1998).

How did Terman's more successful Termites differ from the less successful? Most of them had educated parents who taught them to value learning. They also had *intellectual determination,* which is a desire to know, to excel, and to persevere (Winner, 2003). Thus, successful gifted persons tend to be persistent and motivated to learn. What you do is always more important than what you should be able to do.

Identifying Gifted Children

How might a parent spot an unusually bright child? Early signs of giftedness are not always purely "intellectual." **Giftedness** can be the possession of either a high IQ or special talents or aptitudes, such as creativity.

The following signs may reveal that a child is gifted: a tendency to seek out older children and adults; an early fascination with explanations and problem solving; talking in complete sentences as early as two or three years of age; an unusually good memory; precocious talent in art, music, or number skills; an early interest in books, along with early reading (often by age three); or showing of kindness, understanding, and cooperation toward others (Alvino & Editors, 1996; Distin, 2006).

In the next section, we will discuss intellectual disability. Before you begin, take a few moments to read the Clinical File: "Meet the Rain Man," where you will find information about a remarkable mixture of brilliance and intellectual disability.

Intellectual Disability

A person with mental abilities far below average is termed **intellectually disabled.** Intellectual disability begins at an IQ of approximately 70 or below. However, a person's ability to perform *adaptive behaviours* (basic skills such as dressing,

The Rain Man

Kim Peek was the model for Dustin Hoffman's character in the 1988 Academy Award–winning movie *Rain Man.* Kim began memorizing books at 18 months of age. Eventually, he was able to recite from memory more than 9000 books. He knew all the ZIP codes and area codes in the United States and could give accurate travel directions between any two major U.S. cities. He could also discuss hundreds of pieces of classical music in detail and even learned to play some of that music. Amazingly, though, for someone with such skills, Kim had difficulty with abstract thinking and tests of general intelligence. He was poorly coordinated and could not button his own clothes (Treffert & Christensen, 2005).

Kim Peek had *savant syndrome,* in which a person of limited intelligence shows exceptional mental ability in one or more narrow areas, such as mental arithmetic, calendar calculations, art, or music (Young, 2005).

Do savants have special mental powers not shared by most people? According to

Richard Green

Once, four months after reading a Tom Clancy novel, *The Hunt for Red October,* Kim was asked about a character, a Russian radio operator. He immediately named the character, gave the page number on which a description appeared, and accurately recited several paragraphs about the character (Treffert & Christensen, 2005).

one theory, many savants have suffered some form of damage to their left hemispheres, freeing them from the "distractions" of language, concepts, and higher-level thought. This allows them to focus with crystal clarity on music, drawing, prime numbers, licence plates, TV commercials, or other specific information (Young, 2005). Another theory holds that the performances of many savants result from intense practice (Miller, 1999). Perhaps each of us harbours embers of mental brilliance that intense practice could fan into full flame (Snyder et al., 2006).

Although savant syndrome hasn't been fully explained, it does show that extraordinary abilities can exist apart from general intelligence.

---

eating, communicating, shopping, and working) also figures into evaluating this disability (American Psychiatric Association, 2000; Hallahan & Kauffman, 2006). (See Table 8.2.)

Intellectually disabled persons have no handicap where feelings are concerned. They are easily hurt by rejection, teasing, or ridicule. Likewise, they respond warmly to love and acceptance. They have a right to self-respect and a place in the community (Montreal Declaration on Intellectual Disabilities, 2004). This is especially important during childhood, when support from others adds greatly to the person's chances of becoming a well-adjusted member of society.

■ Table 8.2   Levels of Intellectual Disability

IQ Range	Degree of Intellectual Disability	Educational Classification	Required Level of Support
50–55 to 70	Mild	Educable	Intermittent
35–40 to 50–55	Moderate	Trainable	Limited
20–25 to 35–40	Severe	Dependent	Extensive
Below 20–25	Profound	Life support	Pervasive

(American Psychiatric Association, 2000; Hodapp, 1994.)

These youngsters are participants in the Special Olympics—an athletic event for the intellectually disabled. It is often said of the Special Olympics that "everyone is a winner—participants, coaches, and spectators."

It's worth noting some recent Canadian studies that increase our understanding of the emotional lives of people with intellectual disabilities. A major contributor to this research is Yona Lunsky at the Centre for Addiction and Mental Health at the University of Toronto (e.g., Lunsky & Palucka, 2004). Lunsky (2003) reported that, just as in the general population, depression is more common among women with intellectual disability than among men of similar mental status. The risk factors associated with depression are similar for people with intellectual disability as for the general population—unemployment, poor social support, abusive situations, and relationship discord. Lunsky (2004) measured a number of variables in a sample of 99 adults with borderline IQ to moderate intellectual disability in southern Ontario. One-third of the sample reported that they sometimes think life is not worth living, one-quarter of them said they were thinking of killing themselves, and one in ten reported having made an attempt to do so. Those who reported suicidal ideation reported suffering more loneliness, stress, depression, and anxiety, and less social support than those who did not. Lunsky and Gracey (2009) reported on the experiences of women with intellectual disability during visits to hospital emergency departments. The women spoke about their feelings of not being respected, what it was like to be physically restrained, and the apparent discomfort of emergency room staff in treating people with intellectual disability. Notwithstanding their intellectual disability, in other words, these were people with rich and complex emotional lives, responding very much as do people in the general population. Of course, the emotional lives of people with intellectual disability are not uniformly negative. In a study of nine Toronto women with intellectual disability aged 47 to 65 years, Lunsky found that these women were relatively happy and optimistic about their futures. They were challenged, but with support felt that they could meet their challenges (Canrinus & Lunsky, 2003).

Causes of Intellectual Disability

What causes intellectual disability? About half of all cases of intellectual disability are organic, or related to physical disorders (Das, 2000). These include *genetic abnormalities,* such as missing genes, extra genes, or defective genes; *fetal damage* (prenatal damage from teratogens such as disease, infection, or drugs); and *birth injuries* (such as lack of oxygen during delivery). *Metabolic disorders,* which affect energy production and use in the body, also cause intellectual disability. Malnutrition and exposure to lead, PCBs, and other toxins early in childhood can also cause organic intellectual disability (Beirne-Smith, Patton, & Shannon, 2006).

In 30 to 40 percent of cases, no known biological problem can be identified, which does not mean that there isn't a biological problem—only that if there is we cannot yet identify it. In many such instances, the degree of intellectual disability is mild, in the 50 to 70 IQ range. Often, other family members are also mildly intellectually disabled. *Familial intellectual disability,* as this is called, occurs mostly in very poor households where nutrition, intellectual stimulation, medical care, and emotional support may be inadequate. On this basis, it is tempting to argue that familial intellectual disability may be based largely on an impoverished environment. In fact, however, a number of large-scale programs have put that idea to the test, of which the most well-known is the U.S. government's *Head Start* program, which has run continuously since 1964. Head Start offers short-term interventions, from a few months to two years, aimed at improving health, learning, and social skills in preschoolers. Head Start has been studied intensively for many years, and the general conclusion is that it has little lasting effect on IQ. Improvements in academic achievement seen in children in the program typically disappear within the first two years of school and are smallest for the most disadvantaged children (Currie & Thomas, 1995; see also National Forum on Early Childhood Policy and Programs, 2010).

QUESTIONING INTELLIGENCE—HOW INTELLIGENT IS THE IDEA OF INTELLIGENCE?

The idea that intelligence can be defined in terms of a small set of general mental abilities and measured with IQ tests like the SB5 or the Wechsler scales has been controversial for several reasons. To begin, not every culture values the intellectual skills assessed by these tests. (For a glimpse at how some other cultures define "intelligence," see Human Diversity "Intelligence—How Would a Fool Do It?") In view of such differences, psychologists have tried to create "culture-fair" intelligence tests. Some have questioned the value of defining intelligence in terms of any general intelligence factor. Others have wondered whether intelligence is mainly inherited from our parents or shaped through life experiences. However, among psychologists who do research on intelligence and its measurement, there is wide agreement that tests like the SB5 and the Wechsler do a good job of assessing intellectual capacity.

<SURVEY QUESTION
What are some controversies in the study of intelligence?

Culture and Intelligence

Imagine giving the SB5 to a young Pulawat islander, living in the South Pacific. If navigating from island to island is what he values and is good at, then what would it mean if he got a low IQ score? As noted earlier, cultural values, knowledge, language patterns, and

HUMAN DIVERSITY

Intelligence—How Would a Fool Do It?

You have been asked to sort some objects into categories. Wouldn't it be smart to put the clothes, containers, implements, and foods in separate piles? Not necessarily. When members of the Kpelle culture in Liberia were asked to sort objects, they grouped them together by function. For example, a potato (food) would be placed together with a knife (implement). When the Kpelle were asked why they grouped the objects this way, they often said that that was how a wise man would do it. The researchers finally asked the Kpelle, "How would a fool do it?" Only then did the Kpelle sort the objects into the nice, neat categories we Westerners prefer.

This anecdote, related by cultural psychologist Patricia Greenfield (1997), raises serious questions about general definitions of intelligence. For example, among the Cree of northern Canada, "smart" people are the ones who have visual skills needed to find food on the frozen tundra (Darou, 1992). For the Puluwat people in the South Pacific, being smart means having the ocean-going navigation skills necessary to get from island to island (Sternberg, 2004). And so it goes, as each culture teaches its children the kinds of "intelligence" valued in that culture—how the wise man (or woman) would do it, not the fool (Correa-Chávez, Rogoff, & Arauz, 2005).

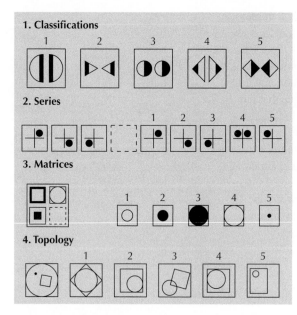

1. Classifications

2. Series

3. Matrices

4. Topology

▸▸**FIGURE 8.2** Sample items from a culture-fair test. **1.** Which pattern is different from the remaining four? (Number 3.) **2.** Which of the five figures on the right would properly continue the three on the left? (Number 5.) **3.** Which of the figures on the right should go in the square on the left to make it look right? (Number 2.) **4.** At left, the dot is outside the square and inside the circle. In which of the figures on the right could you put a dot outside the square and inside the circle? (Number 3.) ("Cultural Fair Test Sample Items," from R. B. Cattell, Culture Free Intelligence Test, Scale 1, Handbook. Courtesy Hogrefe Ltd.)

Culture-fair test A test (such as an intelligence test) designed to minimize the importance of skills and knowledge that may be more common in some cultures than in others.

traditions can greatly affect performance on tests designed for Western cultures (Neisser et al., 1996; Sternberg & Grigorenko, 2005). To avoid this problem, some psychologists have tried to develop culture-fair tests that do not disadvantage certain groups. A **culture-fair test** is designed to minimize the importance of skills and knowledge that may be more common in some cultures than in others. (For a sample of culture-fair test items, see Figure 8.2.)

Culture-fair tests attempt to measure intelligence as much as possible without being influenced by a person's verbal skills, cultural background, and educational level. Their value lies not just in testing people from other cultures. They are also useful for testing children in North America who come from poor communities, rural areas, or ethnic minority families (Stephens et al., 1999). However, no intelligence test can be entirely free of cultural influences. For instance, our culture is very "visual," because children are constantly exposed to television, movies, video games, and the like. Thus, compared with children in developing countries, a child who grows up in Canada may be better prepared to take *both* non-verbal tests and traditional IQ tests.

Multiple Intelligences

Defining intelligence as a *g*-factor (general ability factor) has been controversial. Some psychologists have suggested that we need a broader definition of intelligence. One such psychologist is Howard Gardner of Harvard University. Gardner (2003, 2004) theorizes that there are actually eight distinctly different kinds of intelligence. These are different mental "languages" that people use for thinking. Each is listed below, with examples of pursuits that make use of them:

1. *Language* (linguistic abilities)—writer, lawyer, comedian
2. *Logic and math* (numeric abilities)—scientist, accountant, programmer
3. *Visual and spatial* (pictorial abilities)—engineer, inventor, artist
4. *Music* (musical abilities)—composer, musician, music critic
5. *Bodily-kinesthetic* (physical abilities)—dancer, athlete, surgeon
6. *Intrapersonal* (self-knowledge)—poet, actor, minister
7. *Interpersonal* (social abilities)—psychologist, teacher, politician
8. *Naturalist* (an ability to understand the natural environment)—biologist, shaman, organic farmer

Although Gardner's ideas have been received with enthusiasm by parents and teachers (who are understandably keen to find something that each child can do well and thus be counted as intelligent), the scientific case to be made for multiple intelligences theory is very weak.

Beth Visser of Brock University in St. Catharines, Ontario, and her colleagues selected some existing tests that measure the multiple intelligences Gardner has described (Visser, Ashton, & Vernon, 2006). They chose two separate tests for each of Gardner's hypothesized intelligences and gave them to a large sample of adults. Visser and her colleagues found that performance on many of these tests, including the two tests of spatial abilities, was strongly correlated with the general intelligence factor, *g*. Some tests, such as those of bodily-kinesthetic abilities, did not correlate with *g*, partly because the tests of those abilities were just not very good tests (they had low reliability, so it was pretty much impossible for them to correlate with other tests). In addition, the tests that did not correlate with *g* were tests of abilities that do not require much cognitive processing. Because bodily-kinesthetic ability has so little cognitive content and does not correlate with *g*, it should not be considered a form of intelligence.

A second major problem with multiple intelligences theory, discussed by Arthur Jensen (2008), is that Gardner has never produced usable tests of the types of intelligence he espouses, which has discouraged research to test his theory. This is a particularly serious problem because Gardner often responds to critics such as Visser and her colleagues by arguing that their tests do not capture the abilities his theory is about. Since he does not then offer better ways of measuring the multiple intelligences, such criticism has the effect of making his theory untestable and therefore of very limited scientific value.

The verdict of the intelligence testing community is that Gardner's ideas are interesting, but his **multiple intelligences** probably reduce to things like motivation, initiative, socialization, and acquired knowledge (Buckhalt, 2002).

Let's end this section with a look at the controversial question of how much intelligence is inherited from our parents.

IQ and Heredity

Is intelligence inherited? Most researchers in the area agree that there is a large genetic component to intelligence (Haworth et al., 2010; Neisser et al., 1996; Plomin et al., 2001). As Figure 8.3 shows, the similarity in IQ scores among relatives grows in proportion to how close they are on the family tree. A useful test of the inheritability of intelligence is provided by studies of families having one adopted child and one biological child. As Figure 8.3 shows, parents contribute genes and environment to their biological child. With an adopted child they contribute only environment. If intelligence is highly genetic, the IQs of biological children should be more like their parents' IQs than are the IQs of adopted children, which is very clearly the case. Adopted children are more similar to their biological mothers than to their adoptive mothers, even if they have never met their biological mothers. In a 16-year study of adopted children, parent–child correlations for intelligence were higher for children and biological parents than for children and adoptive parents (Plomin et al., 1997). In this study, there was essentially no relation at all between the IQs of adoptive parents and of the children they adopted, after early childhood. Similarly, McGue and his colleagues (1993) found an average correlation of zero for adoptive siblings tested as adults.

Does this indicate that intelligence is hereditary? Not entirely. Brothers, sisters, and parents share similar environments as well as similar heredity. To separate nature and nurture, **twin studies** may be done. Such studies compare the IQs of twins who were raised together or separated at birth. This allows us to estimate how much heredity and environment affect intelligence.

Twin Studies

Further evidence comes from studies of **identical twins** (twins who developed from the same egg) and **fraternal twins** (twins who developed from two simultaneously fertilized eggs). Identical twins are genetically identical, while fraternal twins share 50 percent of their genes, as do non-twin siblings. We'll consider three questions: (1) Are the IQs of identical twins more similar than the IQs of fraternal twins? (2) Are the IQs of fraternal twins more similar than the IQs of pairs of non-twin siblings? (3) Are the IQs of non-twin siblings more similar than the IQs of unrelated children raised in the same home?

At the top of Figure 8.3 you can see that identical twins who grow up in the same family have highly correlated IQs. This is what we would expect with identical heredity and very similar environments. In studies of more than 10 000 pairs of twins, the average correlation of IQ scores for the identical twins was 0.86, while for

Multiple intelligences Howard Gardner's controversial theory that there are several specialized types of intellectual ability.

Twin study A comparison of the characteristics of twins who were raised together or separated at birth; used to identify the relative impact of heredity and environment.

Identical twins Twins who develop from a single egg and therefore have identical genes.

Fraternal twins Twins conceived from two separate eggs. Fraternal twins are no more alike genetically than other siblings.

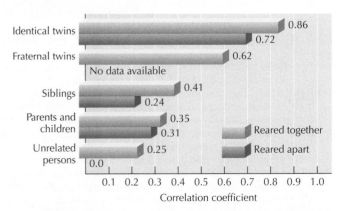

▶▶**FIGURE 8.3** Approximate correlations between IQ scores for persons with varying degrees of genetic and environmental similarity. Notice that the correlations grow smaller as the degree of genetic similarity declines. Also note that a shared environment increases the correlation in all cases. (Estimates from Bouchard, 1983; Henderson, 1982.)

the fraternal twins it was 0.60 (Plomin et al., 2001). Note that the test-retest correlation for intelligence test scores is about 0.90—meaning that two identical twins are almost as similar as any one person is to himself or herself. Now, let's consider what happens when identical twins are reared apart. As you can see, the correlation drops, but only from 0.86 to 0.75. Obviously, these correlations suggest an important role for genetics, but environment is also having an effect.

In fact, studies involving tests of twins at one point in time don't give the whole picture. In a recent study of 11 000 pairs of twins from four countries, Haworth et al. (2010) found that the genetic contribution to intelligence increases through childhood, from explaining 41 percent of the individual difference variability at age 9 to explaining 66 percent at age 17. This means that as children grow up, environment makes less of a difference to their intellectual ability—that ability is more determined by their genes. How can this be? According to Robert Plomin, this is the "nature of nurture" effect: As children grow up they become increasingly able to select and shape their own environment. How they do this is determined by their genes.

IQ and Environment

How much can environment alter intelligence? We've already talked about the U.S. Head Start program. Other programs that offer more resources to individual children have also been tried. The two most well-known of these intensive programs aimed at improving IQ in at-risk children are the Milwaukee Project and the Abecedarian Project. Both programs provided treatment five days a week for up to five years. Neither program had much positive effect on IQ, and what effect was found tended to be limited to skills practised during the program—that is, the effects did not generalize to new tasks. Nonetheless, a different sort of claim about an effect of experience on IQ is discussed in Critical Thinking: "You Mean Video Games Might Be Good for Me?" (As always, caution is in order: Note that the idea discussed in that box is not a demonstration that video game playing increases intelligence but a suggestion that the observed increase in IQ scores over time might be partially produced by video games.)

IQ and Race

Most psychologists have concluded that there is no scientific answer to the question of why racial groups differ in average IQ in North America. A commission of eminent

CRITICAL THINKING

You Mean Video Games Might Be Good for Me?

Test results from Westernized nations have shown an average gain of 15 IQ points during the past 30 years (Dickens & Flynn, 2001; Flynn, 2007). This change was not the result of any deliberate program, so what produced it? Writer Steven Johnson (2005) believes that popular culture is responsible. He points out that video games, the Internet, and even television are becoming more complex. As a result, they demand ever-greater cognitive effort from us.

For example, early video games, such as *Pong* and *Pac Man,* offered simple, repetitive visual experiences. In contrast, today's popular games, such as *The World of Warcraft* and *Second Life,* offer rich, complicated experiences that can take many hours of intense problem solving to complete. Furthermore, players must usually figure out the rules by themselves.

According to Johnson (2005), other forms of popular culture have also become more complex, including the Internet, computer software, and even popular television. For example, while television dramas of the past typically wrapped up a story in a single weekly episode, modern dramas weave plot lines and characters through an entire season of programs. In the end, popular culture may well be inviting us to read, reflect, and problem solve more than ever before (Jaeggi et al., 2008). However, it is also possible that over the past 30 years young people have had more freedom and resources to shape their environments in ways that please them. If so, and if as Robert Plomin suggests, our genes control how we shape our environment, then we may yet find that the "Flynn effect" is explainable at least in part in terms of genetics. (Before you uncritically embrace video games, read Critical Thinking: "You Mean Video Games Might Be Bad for Me?" in Chapter 6.)

STUDY BREAK Intelligence

Reflect

If you were going to write an intelligence test, what kinds of questions would you include? How much would they resemble the questions found on the SB5, the WAIS-III, or culture-fair tests? Can you think of any type of question that wouldn't favour the mental skills emphasized by some culture, somewhere in the world?

How has your understanding of the following concepts changed: IQ, giftedness, intellectual disability?

A friend says to you, "I think intelligence is entirely due to environment." What could you tell your friend to make sure she or he is better informed?

Learning Check

1. Which modern intelligence test originated with attempts to measure the mental abilities of children in Paris?
   a. SB5   b. WAIS
   c. SAT   d. WISC
2. If we define intelligence by writing a test, we are using a(n) _____ definition.
3. By definition, a person has average intelligence when
   a. MA = CA   b. CA = 100
   c. MA = 100   d. MA × CA = 100

4. The WAIS-III is a group intelligence test. T or F?
5. The distribution of IQs approximates a _____ (bell-shaped) curve.
6. Many cases of intellectual disability without known organic causes appear to be _____.
7. The claim that heredity accounts for racial differences in average IQ ignores environmental differences and the cultural bias inherent in standard IQ tests. T or F?
8. From a practical point of view, intelligence can most readily be increased by
   a. genetics   b. teaching adaptive behaviours
   c. stimulating environments   d. applying deviation IQs

Critical Thinking

9. Is it ever accurate to describe a machine as "intelligent"?
10. Some people treat IQ as if it were a fixed number, permanently stamped on the forehead of each child. Why is this view in error?

Answers 1. a 2. operational 3. a 4. F 5. normal 6. familial 7. T 8. c 9. Rule-driven expert systems may appear "intelligent" within a narrow range of problem solving. However, they are "stone stupid" at everything else. This is usually not what we have in mind when discussing human intelligence. 10. Because one's IQ depends on the intelligence test used to measure it: Change the test and you will change the score. Also, heredity establishes a range of possibilities; it does not automatically preordain a person's intellectual capacities.

---

psychologists tasked by the American Psychological Association to address the question of racial differences in average IQ put it this way: "Thus the issue ultimately comes down to a personal judgment: How different are the relevant life experiences of Whites and Blacks in the United States today? At present, this question has no scientific answer" (Neisser et al., 1996, p. 95).

> **Cognition** The process of thinking or mentally processing information (images, concepts, words, rules, and symbols).

Summary

To sum up, few psychologists seriously believe that heredity is not a factor in intelligence, and all acknowledge that environment affects it. Estimates of the impact of each factor continue to vary, though most researchers agree that about 50 percent of variability in IQ scores within any group is due to genetic influences, with the other 50 percent then being due to environment. The importance of environment decreases as children grow, becoming relatively small in adulthood.

WHAT IS THINKING?—BRAINS OVER BRAWN

We have seen that intelligence consists of various mental abilities. Let's explore some of them in more detail. How do concepts, language, and mental images make abstract, intelligent thinking possible?

Cognition refers to mentally processing information. Our thoughts take many forms, including daydreaming, problem solving, and reasoning (to name but a few). Although thinking is not limited to humans, imagine trying to teach an animal to match the feats of

<SURVEY QUESTION
What is the nature of thought?

Image Most often, a mental representation that has picturelike qualities; an icon.

Concept An idea representing a category of related objects or events.

Language Words or symbols, and rules for combining them, that are used for thinking and communication.

Shakuntala Devi, who once set a world record for mental calculation by multiplying two randomly chosen 13-digit numbers (7 686 369 774 870 times 2 465 099 745 779) in her head, giving the answer in 28 seconds. (That's 18 947 668 104 042 434 089 403 730 if you haven't already figured it out.)

Some Basic Units of Thought

At its most basic, thinking is an *internal representation* (mental expression) of a problem or situation. Picture a chess player who mentally tries out several moves before actually touching a chess piece. By *planning* her moves, she can avoid many mistakes. Imagine planning what to study for an exam, what to say at a job interview, or how to get to your hotel for your school break holiday. Better yet, in each of these cases imagine what might happen if you couldn't, or didn't, plan at all.

The power of being able to mentally represent problems is dramatically illustrated by chess grandmaster Miguel Najdorf, who once simultaneously played 45 chess games while blindfolded. How did Najdorf do it? Like most people, he used the basic units of thought: images, concepts, and language (or symbols). **Images** are picturelike mental representations. **Concepts** are ideas that represent categories of objects or events. **Language** consists of words or symbols and rules for combining them. Thinking often involves all three units. For example, blindfolded chess players rely on visual images; concepts ("Game 2 begins with a strategy called an English opening"); and the notational system, or "language," of chess.

In a moment we will delve further into imagery, concepts, and language. Be aware, however, that thinking involves attention, pattern recognition, memory, decision making, intuition, knowledge, and more. The rest of this chapter is just a sample of what cognitive psychology is about.

MENTAL IMAGERY—DOES A FROG HAVE LIPS?

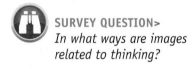

SURVEY QUESTION>
In what ways are images related to thinking?

Almost everyone has visual and auditory images. More than half of us have imagery for movement, touch, taste, smell, and pain. Thus, mental images are sometimes more than just "pictures." For example, your image of a bakery may also include its delicious aroma. Some people even have a rare form of imagery called *synesthesia* (sin-es-THEE-zyah). For these individuals, images cross normal sensory barriers (Kadosh & Henik, 2007). For one such person, spiced chicken tastes "pointy"; for another, pain is the colour orange; and, for a third, human voices unleash a flood of colours and tastes (Dixon, Smilek, & Merikle, 2004; Robertson & Sagiv, 2005). Despite such variations, most of us use images to think, remember, and solve problems. For instance, we may use mental images to

- Make a decision or solve a problem (choosing what clothes to wear; figuring out how to arrange furniture in a room)
- Change feelings (thinking of pleasant images to get out of a bad mood; imagining yourself as thin to stay on a diet)
- Improve a skill or prepare for some action (using images to improve a tennis stroke; mentally rehearsing how you will ask for a raise)
- Aid memory (picturing Mr. Cook wearing a chef's hat, so you can remember his name)

The Nature of Mental Images

Mental images are not flat, like photographs. Researcher Stephen Kosslyn showed this by asking people, "Does a frog have lips and a stubby tail?" Unless you often kiss frogs, you will probably tackle this question by using mental images. Most people picture a frog, "look" at its mouth, and then mentally "rotate" the frog in mental space to check its tail (Kosslyn, 1983). Mental rotation is partly based on imagined movements (Figure 8.4). That is, we mentally "pick up" an object and turn it around (Wraga et al., 2005).

"Reverse Vision"

What happens in the brain when a person has visual images? Seeing something in your "mind's eye" is similar to seeing real objects. Information from the eyes normally activates the brain's primary visual area, creating an image (Figure 8.5). Other brain areas then help us recognize the image by relating it to stored knowledge. When you form a mental image, the system works in reverse. Brain areas where memories are stored send signals back to the visual cortex, where once again an image is created (Ganis, Thompson, & Kosslyn, 2004; Kosslyn, 2005). For example, if you visualize a friend's face right now, the area of your brain that specializes in perceiving faces will become more active (O'Craven & Kanwisher, 2000).

As is often the case, a simple picture becomes more complex as we learn more. In this case, a recent study by Jason Lerch of the Montreal Neurological Institute and some Italian researchers described two patients who had suffered left temporal lobe damage that left them with deficits in mental imagery ability (Moro et al., 2008). The patients were asked to do things such as say whether a given animal's tail or legs were long or short in relation to their body, or to draw an object from memory. Their performance on these tasks was severely impaired, but neither patient had damage to the primary visual cortex or showed any visual deficit. That is, their vision worked just as well as ever, but they had essentially lost the ability to generate visual mental images. The exact opposite pattern has been found in patients who have severe damage to the primary visual cortex, rendering them cortically blind, who nonetheless are still able to create and use visual images. Such patients have been reported in both England (patient SBR; Bridge et al., 2011) and Italy (patient PB; Zago et al., 2010). These patients suggest that we do not yet have the full story on the connection between vision and mental imagery.

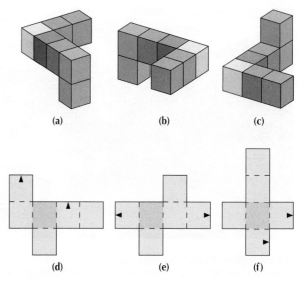

▸▸FIGURE 8.4 Imagery in thinking. *(Top)* Subjects were shown a drawing similar to (a) and drawings of how (a) would look in other positions, such as (b) and (c). Subjects could recognize (a) after it had been "rotated" from its original position. However, the more (a) was rotated in space, the longer it took to recognize it. This result suggests that people actually formed a three-dimensional image of (a) and rotated the image to see if it matched (Shepard, 1975). *(Bottom)* Try your ability to manipulate mental images: Picture each of these shapes as a piece of paper that can be folded to make a cube. After they have been folded, on which cubes do the arrow tips meet? (Kosslyn, 1985).

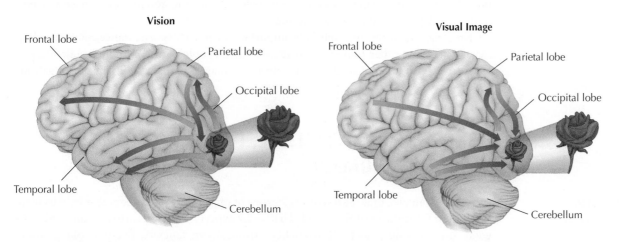

▸▸FIGURE 8.5 When you see a flower, its image is represented by activity in the primary visual area of the cortex, at the back of the brain. Information about the flower is also relayed to other brain areas. If you form a mental image of a flower, information follows a reverse path. The result, once again, is activation of the primary visual area.

The Guggenheim Museum in Bilbao, Spain, was designed by Toronto-born architect Frank Gehry. Could a person lacking mental imagery design such a masterpiece? Three people out of 100 find it impossible to produce mental images, and 3 out of 100 have very strong imagery. Most artists, architects, designers, sculptors, and filmmakers have excellent visual imagery.

Using Mental Images

How are images used to solve problems? We use *stored images* (information from memory) to apply past experiences to problem solving. Let's say you are asked, "In how many ways can you use an empty egg carton?" You might begin by picturing uses you have already seen, such as sorting buttons. To give more original answers, you will probably need to use *created* images, which are assembled or invented, rather than simply remembered. Thus, an artist may picture a completed sculpture before beginning work. People with good imaging abilities tend to score higher on tests of creativity (Morrison & Wallace, 2001). In fact, Albert Einstein, Thomas Edison, Lewis Carroll, and many other of history's most original intellects relied heavily on imagery (West, 1991).

Does the "size" of a mental image affect thinking? To find out, first picture a cat sitting beside a housefly. Now try to "zoom in" on the cat's ears so you see them clearly. Next, picture a rabbit sitting beside an elephant. How quickly can you "see" the rabbit's front feet? Did it take longer than picturing the cat's ears?

When a rabbit is pictured with an elephant, the rabbit's image must be small because the elephant is large. Using such tasks, Stephen Kosslyn (1985) found that the smaller an image is, the harder it is to "see" its details. To put this finding to use, try forming oversize images of things you want to think about. For example, to understand electricity, picture the wires as large pipes with electrons the size of golf balls moving through them; to understand the human ear, explore it (in your mind's eye) like a large cave; and so forth.

Kinesthetic Imagery

Do muscular responses relate to thinking? In a sense, we think with our bodies as well as our heads. *Kinesthetic images* are created from muscular sensations (Holmes & Collins, 2001). Such images help us think about movements and actions.

As you think and talk, kinesthetic sensations can guide the flow of ideas. For example, if a friend calls and asks you the combination of a lock you lent her, you may move your hands as if twirling the dial on the lock. Or, try answering this question: Which direction do you turn the hot-water tap in your kitchen to shut off the water? Most people haven't simply memorized the words "Turn it clockwise" or "Turn it counterclockwise." Instead you will probably "turn" the tap in your imagination before answering. You may even make a turning motion with your hand before answering.

Kinesthetic images are especially important in music, sports, dance, skateboarding, martial arts, and other movement-oriented skills. People with good kinesthetic imagery learn such skills faster than do those with poor imagery (Glisky, Williams, & Kihlstrom, 1996).

CONCEPTS—I'M POSITIVE, IT'S A WHATCHAMACALLIT

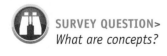

SURVEY QUESTION>
What are concepts?

A concept is an idea that represents a category of objects or events. Concepts help us identify important features of the world. That's why experts in various areas of knowledge are good at classifying objects. Birdwatchers, tropical fish fanciers, five-year-old dinosaur enthusiasts, and other experts all learn to look for identifying details that beginners tend to miss. If you are knowledgeable about a topic, such as horses, flowers, or football, you literally see things differently than less well informed people do (Johnson & Mervis, 1997; Ross, 2006).

Forming Concepts

How are concepts learned? **Concept formation** is the process of classifying information into meaningful categories (Ashby & Maddox, 2005). At its most basic, concept formation is based on experience with *positive* and *negative instances* (examples that belong, or do not belong, to the concept class). Concept formation is not as simple as it might seem. Imagine a child learning the concept of *dog*:

Dog Daze

A child and her father go for a walk. At a neighbour's house, they see a medium-sized dog. The father says, "See the dog." As they pass the next yard, the child sees a cat and says, "Dog!" Her father corrects her, "No, that's a *cat.*" The child now thinks, "Aha, dogs are large and cats are small." In the next yard, she sees a Pekingese and says, "Cat!" "No, that's a dog," replies her father.

The child's confusion is understandable. At first she might even mistake a Pekingese for a dust mop. However, with more positive and negative instances, the child will eventually recognize everything from Great Danes to Chihuahuas as members of the same category—dogs.

As adults, we often acquire concepts by learning or forming rules. A **conceptual rule** is a guideline for deciding whether objects or events belong to a concept class. For example, a triangle must be a closed shape with three sides made of straight lines. Rules are an efficient way to learn concepts, but examples remain important. It's unlikely that memorizing rules would allow a new listener to accurately categorize punk, hip-hop, fusion, salsa, metal, country, and rap music. Learning concepts by rule puts significant demands on working memory, which is why young children aren't very good at that sort of learning. Working at Western University in London, Ontario, psychologist Paul Minda and his colleagues have distinguished between rule-governed and "family resemblance" concepts. The latter are concepts for which it is difficult to specify a rule but for which "you know it when you see it." Minda, Desroches, and Church (2008) found that young children were good at learning family resemblance categories—even three-year-olds could do that—but very bad at learning rule-based categories. To strengthen the case that working memory is crucial for learning rule-based categories, Miles and Minda (2011) gave adults a concurrent task (i.e., asked them to look at concept exemplars and learn the concept rule while at the same time doing a second task that required working memory capacity). Adult performance was much poorer in this situation.

Types of Concepts

Are there different kinds of concepts? Yes, **conjunctive concepts,** or "and concepts," are defined by the presence of two or more features (Reed, 2010). In other words, an item must have "this feature and this feature *and* this feature." For example, a *motorcycle* must have two wheels *and* an engine *and* handlebars.

Relational concepts are based on how an object relates to something else, or how its features relate to one another. All of the following are relational concepts: *larger, above, left, north,* and *upside down.* Another example is *brother,* which is defined as "a male considered in his relation to another person having the same parents."

A study found that rock climbers use kinesthetic imagery to learn climbing routes and to plan their next few moves (Smyth & Waller, 1998).

Brian Bailey/Getty Images

Concept formation The process of classifying information into meaningful categories.

Conceptual rule A formal rule for deciding whether an object or event is an example of a particular concept.

Conjunctive concept A class of objects that have two or more features in common. (For example, to qualify an object must be both red *and* triangular.)

Relational concept A concept defined by the relationship between features of an object or between an object and its surroundings (for example, "greater than," "lopsided").

Disjunctive concepts have *at least one* of several possible features. These are "either/or" concepts. To belong to the category, an item must have "this feature *or* that feature *or* another feature." For example, in baseball, a *strike* is *either* a swing and a miss *or* a pitch over the plate *or* a foul ball if there are not two strikes already. The either/or quality of disjunctive concepts makes them hard to learn.

Exemplar Theories

A group of Canadian psychologists at McMaster University in Hamilton, Ontario, have argued for the role of exemplars (stored representations of individual experiences) in our ability to identify concepts. To see how exemplar theory would explain our use of concepts in real life, suppose that you are responsible for deciding whether a particular person has a mental disorder. How would you do this? McMaster psychologists Lee Brooks and Geoffrey Norman believe that clinical diagnosis often involves matching the current patient to a previously treated patient who was similar. That is, when trying to understand a patient's problem, experienced clinicians search memory for a similar case. They do this because that is how they store information about the concepts they work with (the various disorders they can identify)—in terms of exemplars (Norman, Young, & Brooks, 2007).

Prototypes

When you think of the concept *bird*, do you mentally list the features that birds have? Probably not. In addition to rules and features, we use **prototypes,** or ideal models, to identify concepts (Burnett et al., 2005; Rosch, 1977). A robin, for example, is a prototypical bird; an ostrich is not. In other words, some items are better examples of a concept than others are. Which of the drawings in Figure 8.6 best represents a cup? At some point, as a cup grows taller or wider, it becomes a vase or a bowl. How do we know when the line is crossed? Probably, we mentally compare objects to an "ideal" cup, like Number 5. That's why it's hard to identify concepts when we can't come up with relevant prototypes. What, for example, are the objects shown in Figure 8.7? As you can see, prototypes are especially helpful when we try to categorize complex stimuli (Minda & Smith, 2001).

▶▶**FIGURE 8.6** When does a cup become a bowl or a vase? Deciding if an object belongs to a conceptual class is aided by relating it to a prototype, or ideal example. Subjects in one experiment chose Number 5 as the "best" cup. (After Labov, 1973.)

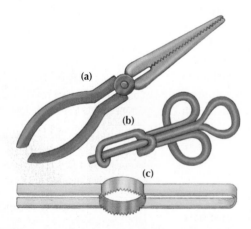

▶▶**FIGURE 8.7** Use of prototypes in concept identification. Even though its shape is unusual, item (a) can be related to a model (an ordinary set of pliers) and thus recognized. But what are items (b) and (c)? If you don't recognize them, look ahead to Figure 8.9. (Adapted from Bransford, J. D., McCarrell, N. S., A sketch of cognitive approach to comprehension: some thoughts about understanding what it means, Figures b & d on p. 381, in Johnson-Laird, P. N., and Watson, P. C., *Thinking: Readings in Cognitive Sciences.* Copyright © 1977, Cambridge University Press.)

Rate this word: **JAZZ**

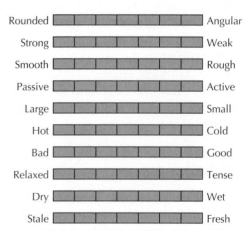

Rounded							Angular
Strong							Weak
Smooth							Rough
Passive							Active
Large							Small
Hot							Cold
Bad							Good
Relaxed							Tense
Dry							Wet
Stale							Fresh

▶▶**FIGURE 8.8** This is an example of Osgood's (1952) semantic differential. The connotative meaning of the word *jazz* can be established by rating it on the scales. Mark your own rating by placing dots or X's in the spaces. Connect the marks with a line; then have a friend rate the word and compare your responses. It might be interesting to do the same for *rock and roll, classical,* and *rap.* You might also want to try the word *psychology.* (From *Psychological Bulletin,* Vol. 49, No. 3, May 1952.)

Connotative Meaning

Generally speaking, concepts have two types of meaning. The **denotative meaning** of a word or concept is its exact definition. The **connotative meaning** is its emotional or personal meaning. The denotative meaning of the word *naked* (having no clothes) is the same for a nudist as it is for a movie censor, but we could expect their connotations to differ. Connotative differences can influence how we think about important issues. For example, the term *enhanced radiation device* has a more positive connotation than *neutron bomb* does (Gruner & Tighe, 1995).

Can you clarify what a connotative meaning is? Yes, connotative meaning can be measured with a technique called the *semantic differential,* as shown in Figure 8.8. When we rate words or concepts, most of their connotative meaning boils down to the dimensions *good/bad, strong/weak,* and *active/passive.* These dimensions give words very different connotations, even when their denotative meanings are similar. For example, I am *conscientious;* you are *careful;* he is *nitpicky!*

FIGURE 8.9 Context can substitute for a lack of appropriate prototypes in concept identification.

LANGUAGE—DON'T LEAVE HOME WITHOUT IT

As we have seen, thinking may occur without language. Everyone has searched for a word to express an idea that exists as a vague image or feeling. Nevertheless, most thinking relies heavily on language, because words *encode* (translate) the world into symbols that are easy to manipulate (Figure 8.10).

The study of taste sensations, described in Chapter 4, depends to some extent on the vocabulary available to describe tastes. While we have lots of words to describe aspects of our visual experience, we have fewer words to use for talking about flavours. Recently, wine experts have developed a new vocabulary for talking about the "mouthfeel" of wines. Researchers at Brock University—taking advantage of their location in the middle of Ontario's winemaking country—have created the "White Wine Mouthfeel Wheel" (Pickering & Demiglio, 2008). This wheel presents the technical vocabulary of taste as a segmented wheel, with 33 discrete sensations and 21 integrated perceptual experiences named on the wheel. Its purpose is to aid both research on wine taste and the training of wine professionals.

The study of meaning in words and language is known as **semantics.** It is here that the link between words and thinking becomes most evident. Suppose, on an intelligence test, you were asked to circle the word that does not belong in this series:

Skyscraper   Cathedral   Temple   Prayer

If you circled prayer, you answered as most people do. Now try another problem, again circling the odd item:

Cathedral   Prayer   Temple   Skyscraper

Did you circle *skyscraper* this time? The new order subtly alters the meaning of the last word (Mayer, 1995). This occurs because words get much of their meaning from *context.* For example, the word *shot* means different things when we are thinking of target practice, bartending, medicine, photography, or golf (Carroll, 2008; Miller, 1999).

Likewise, the words we use can greatly affect our thinking: Is the martini glass "half full" or "half empty"? Would you rather eat "rare prime beef" or "bloody slab of dead cow"? More subtle effects also occur. For example, most people have difficulty quickly naming the colour of the ink used to print the words in the bottom two rows of Figure 8.11. The word meanings are just too strong to ignore.

<SURVEY QUESTION
What is the role of language in thinking?

Commercial Eye/Stone/Getty Images

FIGURE 8.10 Wine tasting illustrates the encoding function of language. To communicate their experiences to others, wine connoisseurs must put taste sensations into words. The wine you see here is "marked by deeply concentrated nuances of plum, blackberry, and currant, with a nice balance of tannins and acid, building to a spicy oak finish." (Don't try this with a Timbit!)

Bilingualism—*Ja oder Nein, Oui ou Non*, Yes or No?

Are there advantages to being able to speak more than one language? Definitely. **Bilingualism** is the ability to speak two languages. It's no surprise that Canada, an officially bilingual country, should be a leader in research on bilingualism. At York University in Toronto, Ellen Bialystok has found that students who learn to speak two languages well have better executive control (Bialystok et al., 2009). This means they are better able to select from among a set of stimuli to respond to, or inhibit a response, or assign mental capacity to a particular process. This is true even in toddlers (Poulin-Dubois et al., 2011). Bialystok (2011) argued that when bilingual children speak they face a cognitive challenge not faced by monolingual children: In addition to all the other linguistic tasks involved in speaking, they have to select the language appropriate to the occasion. To meet this challenge, they recruit working memory resources (see Chapter 7).

PURPLE   BLUE   GREEN   GREEN

RED   PURPLE   RED   GREEN

▶▶**FIGURE 8.11** The Stroop interference task. Test yourself by naming the colours in the top two rows as quickly as you can. Then name the colours of the *ink* used to print the words in the bottom two rows (do not read the words themselves). Was it harder to name the ink colours in the bottom rows? (Adapted from MacLeod, 2005.)

Because the words we use can affect our thinking, language also plays a major role in defining ethnic communities and other social groups. To make this point, it might help to illustrate just how different from your own language other languages can be. Consider the Algonquian language called East Cree, which is spoken in northern Quebec. Mary-Odile Junker, of Carleton University in Ottawa, has analyzed the vocabulary of East Cree and maintains the East Cree Language Web at *http://www.eastcree.org/cree/en/*. Junker (2003) reported that East Cree has no adjectives. Eighty-one percent of the words in the East Cree lexicon are verbs, because the people who speak the language characterize most things as processes rather than as objects. For example, Junker suggests that integral to the Cree concept of *mind* is the feature "you can do things with it." The East Cree people see thinking as a skill, so *not thinking properly* means not using your skill rather than lacking skill. In fact, East Cree contains no words for "stupid," "idiot," or "lack of intelligence." Junker (2003) reports there are no insult words in East Cree at all—which really makes the point about how different languages can be!

Language also plays a major role in defining ethnic communities and other social groups. Thus, language can be a bridge or a barrier between cultures. Translating languages can cause a rash of semantic problems. However, in important situations, such as in international business and diplomacy, avoiding semantic confusion may be vital. (See Human Diversity "Bilingualism—*Ja oder Nein, Oui ou Non*, Yes or No?")

The Structure of Language

What does it take to make a language? First, a language must provide *symbols* that stand for objects and ideas (Jay, 2003). The symbols we call words are built out of **phonemes** (FOE-neems: basic speech sounds) and **morphemes** (MOR-feems: speech sounds collected into meaningful units, such as syllables or words). For instance, in English the sounds *m, b, w,* and *a* cannot form a syllable *mbwa*. In Swahili, they can. (Also see Figure 8.12.)

Next, a language must have a **grammar,** or set of rules for making sounds into words and words into sentences (Reed, 2010). One part of grammar, known as **syntax,** concerns rules for word order. Syntax is important because rearranging words almost always changes the meaning of a sentence: "Dog bites man" versus "Man bites dog."

Traditional grammar is concerned with "surface" language—the sentences we actually speak. Linguist Noam Chomsky has focused instead on the unspoken rules we use to change core ideas into various sentences. Chomsky (1986) believes that we do not learn all the sentences we might ever say. Rather, we actively *create* them by applying **transformation rules** to universal, core patterns. We use these rules to change a simple declarative sentence to

Albanian	mak, mak
Chinese	gua, gua
Dutch	rap, rap
English	quack, quack
French	coin, coin
Italian	qua, qua
Spanish	cuá, cuá
Swedish	kvack, kvack
Turkish	vak, vak

▶▶**FIGURE 8.12** Animals around the world make pretty much the same sounds. Notice, however, how various languages use slightly different phonemes to express the sound a duck makes.

other voices or forms (past tense, passive voice, and so forth). For example, the core sentence "Dog bites man" can be transformed to these patterns (and others as well):

Past: The dog bit the man.

Passive: The man was bitten by the dog.

Negative: The dog did not bite the man.

Question: Did the dog bite the man?

Children seem to be using transformation rules when they say things such as "I runned home." That is, the child applied the normal past tense rule to the irregular verb *to run*.

A true language is also *productive*—it can generate new thoughts or ideas. In fact, words can be rearranged to produce an infinite number of sentences. Some are silly: "Please don't feed me to the goldfish." Some are profound: "The heart never knows the colour of the skin." In either case, the productive quality of language makes it a powerful tool for thinking.

Gestural Languages

Contrary to common belief, language is not limited to speech. Consider the case of Ildefonso, a young man who was born deaf. At age 24, Ildefonso had never communicated with another human, except by mime. Then, at last, Ildefonso had a breakthrough: After much hard work with a sign language teacher, he understood the link between a cat and the gesture for it. At that magic moment, he grasped the idea that "cat" could be communicated to another person, just by signing the word.

American Sign Language (ASL), a gestural language, made Ildefonso's long-awaited breakthrough possible. ASL is not pantomime or a code. It is a true language, like German, Spanish, or Japanese (Liddell, 2003). In fact, those who use other gestural languages, such as French Sign, Mexican Sign, or Old Kentish Sign, may not easily understand ASL (Quinto-Pozos, 2008).

Although ASL has a *spatial* grammar, syntax, and semantics all its own (Figure 8.13), both speech and signing follow similar universal language patterns. Signing children pass through the stages of language development at about the same age as speaking children do. Some psychologists now believe that speech evolved from gestures, far back in human history (Corballis, 2002). Gestures help us string words together as we speak (Morsella & Krauss, 2004). Some people would have difficulty speaking with their hands tied to their sides. Do you ever make hand gestures when you are speaking on the phone? If so, you may be displaying a remnant of the gestural origins of language. Perhaps that's also why the same brain areas become more active when a person speaks or signs (Emmorey et al., 2003).

As further evidence of the origin of language in gesture, people rely on gesture when they have difficulty expressing themselves. For example, if you are bilingual, you may use more gestures when speaking in your second language. University of Alberta psychologist Elena

Bilingualism The ability to speak two languages.

Phonemes The basic speech sounds of a language.

Morphemes The smallest meaningful units in a language, such as syllables or words.

Grammar A set of rules for combining language units into meaningful speech or writing.

Syntax Rules for ordering words when forming sentences.

Transformation rules Rules by which a simple declarative sentence may be changed to other voices or forms (past tense, passive voice, and so forth).

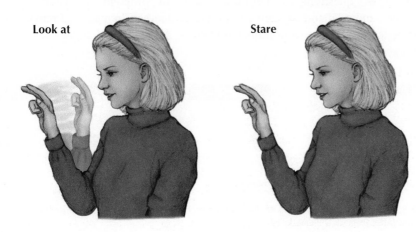

Look at   **Stare**

▶▶**FIGURE 8.13** ASL has only 3000 root signs, compared with roughly 600 000 words in English. However, variations in signs make ASL a highly expressive language. For example, the sign LOOK AT can be varied in ways to make it mean look at me, look at her, look at each, stare at, gaze, watch, look for a long time, look at again and again, reminisce, sightsee, look forward to, predict, anticipate, browse, and many more variations.

Infants can express the idea "pick me up" in gestures before they can make the same request in words. Their progression from gestures to speech may mirror the evolution of human language abilities (Stokoe, 2001).

Nicoladis asked some Chinese–English bilinguals to watch a brief cartoon and then tell the story back to her in each of their two languages. Participants told longer stories in Chinese (their first language) but used more gestures when telling the story in English (Nicoladis et al., 2007). The same Alberta group found a similar result with Hindi–English bilinguals: They used more gestures when telling a story in their second language (Nagpal, Nicoladis, & Marentette, 2011). But in this study, there was a stronger effect of individual differences in first-language skill, so that the rate of gesture use in the first language predicted the rate when speaking the second language. This suggests that some people are just better storytellers than others.

Sign languages naturally arise out of a need to communicate visually. But they also embody a personal identity and define a distinct community. Those who "speak" sign share not just a language but a rich culture as well (Singleton & Newport, 2004).

Animal Language

Do animals use language? Animals do communicate. The cries, gestures, and mating calls of animals have broad meanings that are typically responded to appropriately by other animals of the same species (Searcy & Nowicki, 2005). For the most part, however, natural animal communication is quite limited. Even apes and monkeys make only a few dozen distinct cries, which carry messages such as "attack," "flee," or "food here." More important, animal communication lacks the productive quality of human language. For example, when a monkey gives an "eagle distress call," it means something like, "I see an eagle." The monkey has no way of saying, "I don't see an eagle," or "Thank heavens that wasn't an eagle," or "That sucker I saw yesterday was some huge eagle" (Pinker & Jackendoff, 2005). Let's consider some of psychology's experiences in trying to teach chimpanzees to use language.

Chimp Language

In the late 1960s, Beatrix and Allen Gardner used operant conditioning and imitation to teach a female chimp named Washoe to use ASL. Washoe learned to put together primitive sentence strings like "Come-gimme sweet," "Gimme tickle," and "Open food drink." At her peak, Washoe could construct six-word sentences and use about 240 signs (Gardner & Gardner, 1989).

At around the same time, David Premack taught Sarah the chimpanzee to use 130 "words" consisting of plastic chips arranged on a magnetized board (Figure 8.14). From the beginning of her training, Sarah was required to use proper word order. She learned to answer questions; to label things "same" or "different"; to classify objects by colour, shape, and size; and to form compound sentences (Premack & Premack, 1983). Sarah even learned to use conditional sentences. A *conditional statement* contains a

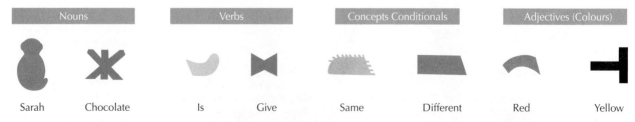

Nouns		Verbs		Concepts Conditionals		Adjectives (Colours)	
Sarah	Chocolate	Is	Give	Same	Different	Red	Yellow

▶▶**FIGURE 8.14** Here is a sample of some of the word-symbols that Sarah the chimpanzee used to communicate with humans. (After Premack & Premack, 1972.)

qualification, often in the if/then form: "If Sarah take apple, then Mary give Sarah chocolate." "If Sarah take banana, then Mary no give Sarah chocolate" (Figure 8.15).

Can it be said with certainty that the chimps understand such interchanges? Most researchers working with chimps believe that they have indeed communicated with them, though of course those researchers can hardly be considered neutral observers.

Criticisms

While the interchanges listed above are impressive, communication and real language usage are different things. Even untrained chimps use simple gestures to communicate with humans. For example, a chimp will point at a banana that is out of reach, while glancing back and forth between the banana and a person standing nearby (Leavens & Hopkins, 1998). (The meaning of the gesture is clear. The meaning of the exasperated look on the chimp's face is less certain, but it probably means, "Give me the banana, you idiot.")

Also, problems with syntax (word order) have plagued almost all animal language studies. For example, when a chimp named Nim Chimpsky (no relation to Noam Chomsky) wanted an orange, he would typically signal a grammarless string of words: "Give orange me give eat orange me eat orange give me eat orange give me you." This might be communication, but it is not language.

Kanzi's Lexigrams

In the 1980s, Duane Rumbaugh and Sue Savage-Rumbaugh taught Kanzi, a pygmy chimpanzee, to communicate by pushing buttons on a computer keyboard. Each of the 250 buttons is marked with a *lexigram*, or geometric word-symbol (Figure 8.16). Using the lexigrams, Kanzi can create primitive sentences several words long. He can also understand about 650 spoken sentences.

Kanzi's sentences consistently follow correct word order. Like a child learning language, Kanzi picked up some rules from his caregivers (Segerdahl, Fields, & Savage-Rumbaugh, 2005). However, he has developed other patterns on his own. For example, Kanzi usually places action symbols in the order he wants to carry them out, such as "chase tickle" or "chase hide." In this respect, Kanzi's grammar is on a par with that of a two-year-old child. Kanzi's ability is interesting, but you should note that it is now almost 30 years since Kanzi first started pushing those buttons. That's enough time for many other chimpanzees to have been given the opportunity to learn as he did—but we're still talking only about Kanzi. As Chomsky pointed out, if chimps were biologically capable of language, they would use it on their own.

FIGURE 8.15 After reading the message "Sarah insert apple pail banana dish" on the magnetic board, Sarah performed the actions as directed. (From "Teaching Language to an Ape," by Ann J. Premack and David Premack. © 1972 Scientific American, Inc. Reprinted by permission of Eric Mose Jr.)

The Great Ape Trust of Iowa

FIGURE 8.16 Kanzi's language learning has been impressive. He can comprehend spoken English words. He can identify lexigram symbols when he hears corresponding words. He can use lexigrams when the objects they refer to are absent, and he can, if asked, lead someone to the object. All these skills were acquired through observation, not conditioning (Savage-Rumbaugh et al., 1990).

STUDY BREAK Imagery, Concepts, and Language

Reflect

Name some ways in which you have used imagery in the thinking you have done today.

Write a conceptual rule for the following idea: *unicycle*. Were you able to define the concept with a rule? Would positive and negative instances help make the concept clearer for others?

A true sports car has two seats, a powerful engine, good brakes, and excellent handling. What kind of a concept is the term *sports car*? What do you think of as a prototypical sports car?

You must learn to communicate with an alien life form whose language cannot be reproduced by the human voice. Do you think it would be better to use a gestural language or lexigrams? Why?

Learning Check

1. List three primary units of thought: _____
2. Our reliance on imagery in thinking means that problem solving is impaired by the use of language or symbols. T or F?
3. Humans appear capable of forming three-dimensional images that can be moved or rotated in mental space. T or F?

4. A *mup* is defined as anything that is small, blue, and hairy. *Mup* is a _____ concept.
5. The connotative meaning of the word *naked* is "having no clothes." T or F?
6. True languages are _____ because they can be used to generate new possibilities.
7. The basic speech sounds are called _____; the smallest meaningful units of speech are called _____.

Critical Thinking

8. A Francophone and an Anglophone are asked to rate the word *bilingual* on the semantic differential. Under what conditions would their ratings be most alike?
9. Chimpanzees and other apes are intelligent and entertaining animals. If you were doing language research with a chimp, what major problem would you have to guard against?

Answers: 1. images, concepts, language or symbols (others could be listed) 2. F 3. T 4. conjunctive 5. F 6. productive 7. phonemes, morphemes 8. If they are both bilingual, they are likely to have experienced positive aspects of being able to converse in two languages and to have experienced interactions with people from the other language group. 9. The problem of anthropomorphizing (ascribing human characteristics to animals) is especially difficult to avoid when researchers spend many hours "conversing" with chimps.

PROBLEM SOLVING—GETTING AN ANSWER IN SIGHT

SURVEY QUESTION>
What do we know about problem solving?

We all solve many problems every day. Problem solving can be as commonplace as figuring out how to make a non-poisonous meal out of leftovers or as significant as developing a cure for cancer. How do we solve such problems? A good way to start a discussion of problem solving is to solve a problem. Give this one a try:

> A famous ocean liner (the *Queen of Hearts*) is steaming toward port at 30 kilometres per hour. The ocean liner is 80 kilometres from shore when a seagull takes off from its deck and flies toward port. At the same instant, a speedboat leaves port at 50 kilometres per hour. The bird flies back and forth between the speedboat and the *Queen of Hearts* at a speed of 60 kilometres per hour. How far will the bird have flown when the two boats pass?

If you don't immediately see the answer to this problem, read it again. (The answer is revealed in the "Insightful Solutions" section.)

Mechanical Solutions

Mechanical solution A problem solution achieved by trial and error or by a fixed procedure based on learned rules.

Algorithm A learned set of rules that always leads to the correct solution of a problem.

For routine problems, a **mechanical solution** may be adequate. Mechanical solutions are achieved by trial and error or by rote. If you forget the combination to your bike lock, you may be able to discover it by trial and error. In an era of high-speed computers, many trial-and-error solutions are best left to machines. A computer could generate all possible combinations of the five numbers on the lock in a split second. (Of course, it would take a long time to try them all.) When a problem is solved by *rote*, thinking is guided by an **algorithm,** or learned set of rules that always leads to a correct solution. A simple example of an algorithm is the steps needed to divide one number into another.

If you have a good background in math, you may have solved the problem of the bird and the boats by rote. (Your authors hope you didn't. There is an easier solution.)

Solutions by Understanding

Many problems cannot be solved mechanically. In that case, **understanding** (deeper comprehension of a problem) is necessary. Try this problem:

> A person has an inoperable stomach tumour. A device is available that produces rays that at high intensity will destroy tissue (both healthy and diseased). How can the tumour be destroyed without damaging surrounding tissue? (Also see the sketch in Figure 8.17.)

What does this problem show about problem solving? German psychologist Karl Duncker gave college students this problem in a classic series of studies. Duncker asked them to think aloud as they worked. He found that successful students first had to discover the *general properties* of a correct solution. A **general solution** defines the requirements for success, but not in enough detail to guide further action. This phase was complete when students realized that the intensity of the rays had to be lowered on their way to the tumour. Then, in the second phase, they proposed a number of **functional** (workable) **solutions** and selected the best one (Duncker, 1945). (One solution is to focus weak rays on the tumour from several angles. Another is to rotate the person's body, to minimize exposure of healthy tissue.)

It might help to summarize with a more familiar example. Almost everyone who has tried to play a poker game like Texas Hold'em begins at the mechanical, trial-and-error level. If you want to take the easy (i.e., rote) route, printed odds tables are available for every stage of play. In time, those who persist begin to understand the general properties of the game. After that, they can play fast enough to keep up with other players.

Heuristics

"You can't get there from here," or so it often seems when facing a problem. Solving problems often requires a strategy. If the number of alternatives is small, a **random search strategy** may work. This is another example of trial-and-error thinking in which all possibilities are tried, more or less randomly. Imagine that you are travelling and you decide to look up an old friend, Janet Smith, in a city you are visiting. You open the phone book and find 47 J. Smiths listed. Of course, you could dial each number until you find the right one. "Forget it," you say to yourself. "Is there any way I can narrow the search?" "Oh, yeah! I remember hearing that Janet lives by the beach." Then you take out a map and call only the numbers with addresses near the waterfront (Hunt & Ellis, 2004).

The approach used in this example is a **heuristic** (hew-RIS-tik: a strategy for identifying and evaluating problem solutions). Typically, a heuristic is a "rule of thumb" that *reduces the*

Understanding In problem solving, a deeper comprehension of the nature of the problem.

General solution A solution that correctly states the requirements for success but not in enough detail for further action.

Functional solution A detailed, practical, and workable solution.

Random search strategy Trying possible solutions to a problem in a more or less random order.

Heuristic Any strategy or technique that aids problem solving, especially by limiting the number of possible solutions to be tried.

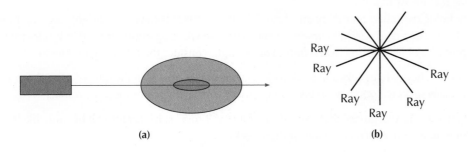

(a)   (b)

▸▸ **FIGURE 8.17** A schematic representation of Duncker's tumour problem. The dark spot represents a tumour surrounded by healthy tissue. How can the tumour be destroyed without injuring surrounding tissue? (Adapted from Duncker, 1945.)

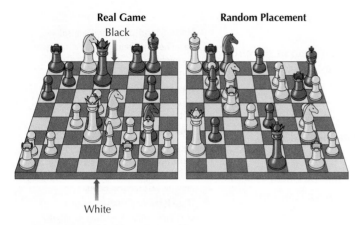

Real Game **Random Placement**

Black

White

▶▶**FIGURE 8.18** The left chessboard shows a realistic game. The right chessboard is a random arrangement of pieces. Expert chess players can memorize the left board at a glance, yet they are no better than beginners at memorizing the random board (Ross, 2006). Expert performance at most thinking tasks is based on acquired strategies and knowledge. If you would like to excel at a profession or a mental skill, plan on adding to your knowledge every day (Goldstein, 2008).

Insight A sudden mental reorganization of a problem that makes the solution obvious.

Fixation The tendency to repeat wrong solutions or faulty responses, especially as a result of becoming blind to alternatives.

■ Table 8.3 **Solutions to Insight Problems**

Water lilies: Day 19

Twenty dollars: $10

How many pets?: Three (one bird, one cat, and one dog)

Between 2 and 3: A decimal point

One word: ONE WORD (You may object that the answer is two words, but the problem called for the answer to be "one word," and it is.)

See Figure 8.19 for the problems.

number of alternatives thinkers must consider (Solso, MacLin, & MacLin, 2008). Although this raises the odds of success, it does not guarantee a solution. Here are some heuristic strategies that often work:

- Try to identify how the current state of affairs differs from the desired goal. Then find steps that will reduce the difference.
- Try working backward from the desired goal to the starting point or current state.
- If you can't reach the goal directly, try to identify an intermediate goal or subproblem that at least gets you closer.
- Represent the problem in other ways—with graphs, diagrams, or analogies, for instance.
- Generate a possible solution and test it. Doing so may eliminate many alternatives, or it may clarify what is needed for a solution.

Experts and Novices

Research has shown that expert skills are based on *acquired strategies* (learned heuristics) and specific *organized knowledge* (systematic information). Experts are better able to see the true nature of problems and to define them in terms of general principles (Anderson, 2005). For example, chess experts are much more likely than novices to have heuristics available for solving problems. However, what really sets master players apart is their ability to intuitively recognize *patterns* that suggest what lines of play should be explored next. This helps eliminate a large number of possible moves. The chess master, therefore, does not waste time exploring unproductive pathways (Ross, 2006).

In other words, becoming a star performer does not come from some general strengthening of the mind. Master chess players don't necessarily have better memories than beginners (except for realistic chess positions) (Gobet & Simon, 1996; Solso, MacLin, & MacLin, 2008). (See Figure 8.18.) And, typically, they don't explore more moves ahead than lesser players.

Insightful Solutions

A thinker who suddenly solves a problem has experienced **insight.** Insight is so rapid and clear that we may wonder why we didn't see the solution sooner (Schilling, 2005). Insights are usually based on reorganizing a problem. This allows us to see problems in new ways and makes their solutions seem obvious (Robertson, 2001).

Let's return now to the problem of the boats and the bird. The best way to solve it is by insight. Because the boats will cover the 80-kilometre distance in exactly 1 hour, and the bird flies 60 kilometres per hour, the bird will have flown 60 kilometres when the boats meet. Very little math is necessary if you have insight into this problem. Figure 8.19 lists some additional insight problems you may want to try. (The answers can be found in Table 8.3.)

The Nature of Insight

Psychologists Robert Sternberg and Janet Davidson (1982) believe that insight involves three abilities. The first is *selective encoding*, which refers to selecting information that is relevant to a problem while ignoring distractions. For example, consider the following problem:

If you have white socks and black socks in your drawer, mixed in the ratio of 4 to 5, how many socks will you have to take out to ensure you have a pair of the same colour?

A person who recognizes that "mixed in a ratio of 4 to 5" is irrelevant will be more likely to come up with the correct answer of three socks.

Water lilies

Problem: Water lilies growing in a pond double in area every 24 hours. On the first day of spring, only one lily pad is on the surface of the pond. Twenty days later, the pond is entirely covered. On what day is the pond half-covered?

Twenty dollars

Problem: Jessica and Blair both have the same amount of money. How much must Jessica give Blair so that Blair has $20 more than Jessica?

How many pets?

Problem: How many pets do you have if all of them are birds except two, all of them are cats except two, and all of them are dogs except two?

Between 2 and 3

Problem: What one mathematical symbol can you place between 2 and 3 that results in a number greater than 2 and less than 3?

One word

Problem: Rearrange the letters NEWDOOR to make one word.

Solutions to these problems are listed in ▲*Table 8.3, on page 334.*

Bank of Canada

⏩FIGURE 8.19

Insight also relies on *selective combination,* or bringing together seemingly unrelated bits of useful information. Try this sample problem:

> With a 7-minute hourglass and an 11-minute hourglass, what is the simplest way to time the boiling of an egg for 15 minutes?

The answer requires using both hourglasses in combination. First, the 7-minute and the 11-minute hourglasses are started. When the 7-minute hourglass runs out, it's time to begin boiling the egg. At this point, 4 minutes remain on the 11-minute hourglass. Thus, when it runs out, it is simply turned over. When it runs out again, 15 minutes will have passed.

A third source of insights is *selective comparison.* This is the ability to compare new problems with old information or with problems already solved. A good example is the hat rack problem, in which subjects must build a structure that can support an overcoat in the middle of a room. Each person is given only two long sticks and a C-clamp to work with. The solution, shown in Figure 8.20, is to clamp the two sticks together so that they are wedged between the floor and the ceiling. If you were given this problem, you would be more likely to solve it if you first thought of how pole lamps are wedged between floor and ceiling.

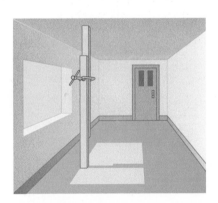

⏩FIGURE 8.20 Solution to the hat rack problem.

Fixations

One of the most important barriers to problem solving is **fixation,** the tendency to get "hung up" on wrong solutions or to become blind to alternatives. Usually this occurs when we place unnecessary restrictions on our thinking (German & Barrett, 2005). How, for example, could you plant four small trees so that each is an equal distance from all the others? (The answer is shown in Figure 8.21.)

⏩FIGURE 8.21 Four trees can be placed equidistant from one another by piling dirt into a mound. Three of the trees are planted equal distances apart around the base of the mound. The fourth tree is planted on top of the mound. If you were fixated on arrangements that involve level ground, you may have been blind to this three-dimensional solution.

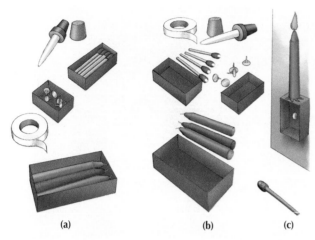

(a) **(b)** **(c)**

» **FIGURE 8.22** Materials for solving the candle problem were given to subjects in boxes (a) or separately (b). Functional fixedness caused by condition (a) interfered with solving the problem. The solution to the problem is shown in (c).

A prime example of restricted thinking is **functional fixedness.** This is an inability to see new uses (functions) for familiar objects or for things that were used in a particular way (German & Barrett, 2005). If you have ever used a dime as a screwdriver, you've overcome functional fixedness.

How does functional fixedness affect problem solving? Karl Duncker illustrated the effects of functional fixedness by asking students to mount a candle on a vertical board so the candle could burn normally. Duncker gave each student three candles, some matches, some cardboard boxes, some thumbtacks, and other items. Half of Duncker's subjects received these items *inside* the cardboard boxes. The others were given all the items, including the boxes, spread out on a tabletop.

Duncker found that when the items were in the boxes, solving the problem was very difficult. Why? If students saw the boxes as *containers*, they didn't realize the boxes might be part of the solution. (If you haven't guessed the solution, check Figure 8.22.) Undoubtedly, we could avoid many fixations by being more flexible in categorizing the world (Langer, 2000). For instance, creative thinking could be facilitated in the container problem by saying "This *could* be a box," instead of "This *is* a box."

When tested with the candle problem, five-year-old children show no signs of functional fixedness. Apparently, this is because they have had less experience with the use of various objects. It is sometimes said that to be more creative, you should try to see the world without preconceptions, as if through the eyes of a child. In the case of functional fixedness, that may actually be true (German & Defeyter, 2000).

Common Barriers to Problem Solving

Functional fixedness is just one of the mental blocks that prevent insight. Here's an example of another: A $5 bill is placed on a table and a stack of objects is balanced precariously on top of the bill. How can the bill be removed without touching or moving the objects? One answer is to split the bill on one of its edges. Gently pulling from opposite ends will tear the bill in half and remove it without toppling the objects. Many people fail to suggest this solution because tearing a bill seems destructive (Adams, 2001). Of course, in this example, functional fixedness may be a good thing—the suggested solution would damage a perfectly good $5 bill. That makes the point that few aspects of human psychology evolved without conferring *some* adaptive advantage. Other common mental blocks can hinder problem solving, too, as listed here:

1. **Emotional barriers:** inhibition and fear of making a fool of oneself, fear of making a mistake, inability to tolerate ambiguity, excessive self-criticism
   Example: An architect is afraid to try an unconventional design because she fears that other architects will think it is frivolous.
2. **Cultural barriers:** values that hold that fantasy is a waste of time; that playfulness is for children only; that reason, logic, and numbers are good; that feelings, intuitions, pleasure, and humour are bad or have no value in the serious business of problem solving
   Example: A corporate manager wants to solve a business problem but becomes stern and angry when members of his marketing team joke playfully about possible solutions.
3. **Learned barriers:** conventions about uses (functional fixedness), meanings, possibilities, taboos
   Example: A cook doesn't have any clean mixing bowls and fails to see that he could use a frying pan as a bowl.
4. **Perceptual barriers:** habits leading to a failure to identify important elements of a problem
   Example: A beginning artist concentrates on drawing a vase of flowers without seeing that the "empty" spaces around the vase are part of the composition, too.

Functional fixedness A rigidity in problem solving caused by an inability to see new uses for familiar objects.

Inductive thought Thinking in which a general rule or principle is gathered from a series of specific examples; for instance, inferring the laws of gravity by observing many falling objects.

Deductive thought Thought that applies a general set of rules to specific situations; for example, using the laws of gravity to predict the behaviour of a single falling object.

Logical thought Drawing conclusions on the basis of formal principles of reasoning.

Illogical thought Thought that is intuitive, haphazard, or irrational.

Fluency In tests of creativity, the total number of solutions produced.

STUDY BREAK Problem Solving

Reflect

Identify at least one problem you have solved mechanically or by rote. Now identify a problem you solved by understanding. Did the second problem involve finding a general solution or a functional solution? Or both? What heuristics did you use to solve the problem?

What is the best insightful solution you've ever come up with? Did it involve selective encoding, combination, or comparison?

Can you think of a time when you overcame functional fixedness to solve a problem?

Learning Check

1. Insight refers to rote, or trial-and-error, problem solving. T or F?
2. The first phase in problem solving by understanding is to discover the general properties of a correct solution. T or F?
3. Problem-solving strategies that guide the search for solutions are called _____.

4. A common element underlying insight is that information is encoded, combined, and compared _____.
   a. mechanically   b. by rote
   c. functionally   d. selectively
5. The term fixation refers to the point at which a helpful insight becomes fixed in one's thinking. T or F?
6. Organized knowledge, acquired strategies, and the ability to recognize patterns are all characteristics of human expertise. T or F?

Critical Thinking

7. Do you think that it is true that "a problem clearly defined is a problem half solved"?
8. Sea otters select suitably sized rocks and use them to hammer shellfish loose for eating. They then use the rock to open the shell. Does this qualify as thinking?

Answers

1. F 2. T 3. heuristics 4. d 5. F 6. T 7. Although this might be an overstatement, it is true that clearly defining a starting point and the desired goal can serve as a heuristic in problem solving. 8. Psychologist Donald Griffin (1992) believes it does because thinking is implied by actions that appear to be planned with an awareness of likely results.

CREATIVE THINKING—DOWN ROADS LESS TRAVELLED

Original ideas have changed the course of human history. Much of what we now take for granted in art, medicine, music, technology, and science was once regarded as radical or impossible. How do creative thinkers like Stephen Hawking achieve the breakthroughs that advance us into new realms? Psychologists have learned a great deal about how creativity occurs and how to promote it, as you will soon learn.

<**SURVEY QUESTION**
What is creative thinking?

We have seen that problem solving may be mechanical, insightful, or based on understanding. To this we can add that thinking may be **inductive** (going from specific facts or observations to general principles) or **deductive** (going from general principles to specific situations). Thinking may also be **logical** (proceeding from given information to new conclusions on the basis of explicit rules) or **illogical** (intuitive, associative, or personal).

What distinguishes creative thinking from more routine problem solving? Creative thinking involves all these thinking styles, plus *fluency, flexibility,* and *originality.* Let's say that you would like to find creative uses for the billions of plastic containers discarded each year. The creativity of your suggestions could be rated in this way: **Fluency** is defined as the total number of suggestions you are able to make. **Flexibility** is the number of times you shift from one class

John Bryson/Sygma/Corbis

Fluency is an important part of creative thinking. Mozart produced more than 600 pieces of music. Shakespeare wrote 154 sonnets. Salvador Dalí (shown here) created more than 1500 paintings as well as sculptures, drawings, illustrations, books, and even an animated cartoon. Not all of these works were masterpieces. However, a fluent outpouring of ideas fed the creative efforts of each of these geniuses.

Flexibility In tests of creativity, the number of different types of solutions produced.

Originality In tests of creativity, how novel or unusual solutions are.

Convergent thinking Thinking directed toward discovery of a single established correct answer; conventional thinking.

Divergent thinking Thinking that produces many ideas or alternatives; a major element in original or creative thought.

■ Table 8.4 **Convergent and Divergent Problems**

Convergent Problems

- What is the area of a triangle that is 3 metres wide at the base and 2 metres tall?
- Erica is shorter than Zoey but taller than Carlo, and Carlo is taller than Jared. Who is the second tallest?
- If you simultaneously drop a baseball and a bowling ball from a tall building, which will hit the ground first?

Divergent Problems

- What objects can you think of that begin with the letters BR?
- How could discarded aluminum cans be put to use?
- Write a poem about fire and ice.

of possible uses to another. **Originality** refers to how novel or unusual your ideas are. By counting the number of times you showed fluency, flexibility, and originality, we could rate your creativity, or capacity for *divergent thinking* (Baer, 1993; Runco, 2004).

In routine problem solving or thinking, there is one correct answer, and the problem is to find it. This leads to **convergent thinking** (lines of thought converge on the answer). **Divergent thinking** is the reverse, in which many possibilities are developed from one starting point (Cropley, 2006). (See Table 8.4 for some examples.) Rather than repeating learned solutions, creative thinking produces new answers, ideas, or patterns (Davidovitch & Milgram, 2006).

Tests of Creativity

Divergent thinking can be measured in several ways. In the *Unusual Uses Test*, you would be asked to think of as many uses as possible for some object, such as the plastic containers mentioned earlier. In the *Consequences Test*, you would list the consequences that would follow a basic change in the world. For example, you might be asked, "What would happen if everyone suddenly lost their sense of balance and could no longer stay upright?" People try to list as many reactions as possible. If you were to take the *Anagrams Test*, you would be given a word such as *creativity* and asked to make as many new words as possible by rearranging the letters. Each of these tests can be scored for fluency, flexibility, and originality. (For an example of other tests of divergent thinking, see Figure 8.23.) Tests of divergent thinking seem to tap something quite different from intelligence. Generally, there is little correlation between creativity tests and IQ test scores (Preckel, Holling, & Wiese, 2006).

Isn't creativity more than divergent thought? What if a person comes up with a large number of useless answers to a problem? A good question. Divergent thinking is an important part of creativity, but there is more to it. To be creative, the solution to a problem must be more than novel, unusual, or original. It must also be *practical* if it is an invention and *sensible* if it is an idea. This is the dividing line between a "harebrained scheme" and a "stroke of genius." In other words, the creative person brings reasoning and critical thinking to bear on new ideas once they are produced (Runco, 2003).

Stages of Creative Thought

Is there any pattern to creative thinking? Typically, five stages occur during creative problem solving:

1. **Orientation.** As a first step, the person defines the problem and identifies its most important dimensions.

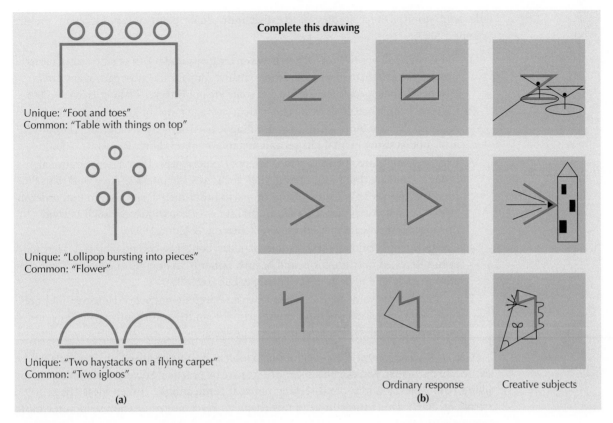

Complete this drawing

Unique: "Foot and toes"
Common: "Table with things on top"

Unique: "Lollipop bursting into pieces"
Common: "Flower"

Unique: "Two haystacks on a flying carpet"
Common: "Two igloos"

(a)

Ordinary response   Creative subjects

(b)

▸▸**FIGURE 8.23** Some tests of divergent thinking. Creative responses are more original and more complex. [(a) Adapted from Wallach & Kogan, 1965; (b) adapted from Barron, 1958.]

2. **Preparation.** In the second stage, creative thinkers saturate themselves with as much information about the problem as possible.

3. **Incubation.** Most major problems produce a period during which all attempted solutions will be futile. At this point, problem solving may proceed on a subconscious level: Although the problem seems to have been set aside, it is still "cooking" in the background.

4. **Illumination.** The stage of incubation is often ended by a rapid insight or series of insights. These produce the "Aha!" experience, often depicted in cartoons as a light bulb appearing over the thinker's head.

5. **Verification.** The final step is to test and critically evaluate the solution obtained during the stage of illumination. If the solution proves faulty, the thinker reverts to the stage of incubation.

Of course, creative thought is not always so neat. Nevertheless, the stages listed are a good summary of the most typical sequence of events.

Some authors believe that truly exceptional creativity requires a rare combination of thinking skills, personality, and a supportive social environment. This mix, they believe, accounts for creative giants such as Edison, Freud, Mozart, Picasso, and others (Runco, 2004; Tardif & Sternberg, 1988).

Positive Psychology: The Creative Personality

What makes a person creative? According to the popular stereotype, highly creative people are eccentric, introverted, neurotic, socially inept, unbalanced in their interests, and on the edge of madness. Although some artists and musicians cultivate this public image, there is

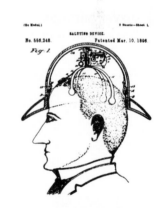

Hat-tipping device. According to the patent, it is for "automatically effecting polite salutations by the elevation and rotation of the hat on the head of the saluting party when said person bows to the person or persons saluted." In addition to being original or novel, a creative solution must fit the demands of the problem. Is this a creative solution to the "problem" of hat tipping? (U.S. Patent No. 556,248. From *Absolutely Mad Inventions*, by A. E. Brown and H. A. Jeffcott [1970].)

little truth to it. Direct studies of creative individuals paint a very different picture (Winner, 2003):

1. There is a small positive correlation between creativity and IQ. In other words, smarter people have a slight tendency to be more creative. But, for the most part, at any given level of IQ, some people are creative and some are not (Preckel, Holling, & Wiese, 2006).

2. Creative people usually have a greater-than-average range of knowledge and interests, and they are more fluent in combining ideas from various sources. They are also good at using mental images and metaphors in thinking (Riquelme, 2002).

3. Creative people are open to a wide variety of experiences. They accept irrational thoughts and are uninhibited about their feelings and fantasies. They tend to use broad categories, to question assumptions, to break mental sets, and to find order in chaos. They also experience more unusual states of consciousness, such as vivid dreams and mystical experiences (Ayers, Beaton, & Hunt, 1999).

4. Creative people enjoy symbolic thought, ideas, concepts, and possibilities. They tend to be interested in truth, form, and beauty, rather than in fame or success. Their creative work is an end in itself (Sternberg & Lubart, 1995).

5. Creative people value their independence and prefer complexity. However, they are unconventional and non-conforming primarily in their work; otherwise, they do not have unusual, outlandish, or bizarre personalities.

Can creativity be learned? It is beginning to look as if some creative thinking skills can be learned. In particular, you can become more creative by practising divergent thinking and by taking risks, analyzing ideas, and seeking unusual connections between ideas (Baer, 1993; Sternberg, 2001). Don't forget to read this chapter's Psychology in Action section for more on creativity.

INTUITIVE THOUGHT—MENTAL SHORTCUT? OR DANGEROUS DETOUR?

SURVEY QUESTION>
How accurate is intuition?

At the same time that irrational, intuitive thought may contribute to creative problem solving, it can also lead to thinking errors. To see how this can happen, try the following problems:

Problem 1: An epidemic breaks out, and 600 people are about to die. Doctors have two choices. If they give drug A, 200 lives will be saved. If they give drug B, there is a one-third chance that 600 people will be saved, and a two-thirds chance that none will be saved. Which drug should they choose?

Problem 2: Again, 600 people are about to die, and doctors must make a choice. If they give drug A, 400 people will die. If they give drug B, there is a one-third chance that no one will die, and a two-thirds chance that 600 will die. Which drug should they choose?

Most people choose drug A for the first problem and drug B for the second. This is fascinating because the two problems are identical. The only difference is that the first is stated in terms of lives saved, the second in terms of lives lost. Yet, even people who realize that their answers are contradictory find it difficult to change them (Kahneman & Tversky, 1972, 1973).

Intuition

As the example shows, we often make decisions intuitively, rather than logically or rationally. **Intuition** is quick, impulsive thought. It may provide fast answers, but it can also be misleading and sometimes disastrous. (But see Critical Thinking "Have You Ever Thin-Sliced Your Teacher?")

Two noted psychologists, Daniel Kahneman and Amos Tversky (1937–1996), studied how we make decisions in the face of uncertainty. They found that human judgment is often

Intuition Quick, impulsive thought that does not make use of formal logic or clear reasoning.

Have You Ever Thin-Sliced Your Teacher?

Think back to your least favourite teacher (not your current one, of course!). How long did it take you to figure out that he or she wasn't going to make your list of star teachers?

In an intriguing study, psychologist Nalini Ambady asked people to watch video clips of teachers they did not know. After watching three 10-second segments, participants were asked to rate the teachers. Amazingly, their ratings correlated highly with year-end course evaluations made by actual students (Ambady & Rosenthal, 1993). Ambady obtained the same result when she presented an even thinner "slice" of teaching behaviour, just three two-second clips. A mere six seconds is all that participants needed to form intuitive judgments of the instructors' teaching!

In his book *Blink,* Malcolm Gladwell (2005) argues that this was not a case of hurried irrationality. Instead, it was "thin-slicing," or

quickly making sense of thin slivers of experience. According to Gladwell, these immediate, intuitive reactions can sometimes form the basis of more carefully reasoned judgments. They are a testament to the power of the cognitive unconscious, which is the part of the brain that does automatic, unconscious processing (Wilson, 2002). Far from being irrational, intuition may be an important part of how we think.

The trick, of course, is figuring out when thin-slicing can be trusted and when it can't. After all, first impressions aren't always right. For example, have you ever had a teacher you came to appreciate only after classes were well under way or only after the course was over? In many circumstances, quick impressions are most valuable when you take the time to verify them through further observation.

---

not rational (Kahneman, 2003; Kahneman, Slovic, & Tversky, 1982). Let's explore some common intuitive thinking errors, so you will be better prepared to avoid them.

Representativeness

One very common pitfall in judgment is illustrated by the question "Which is more probable? "

A. Team Canada will not be in the lead after the first period of a hockey game but will win the game.

B. Team Canada will not be in the lead after the first period of a hockey game.

Tversky and Kahneman (1982) found that most people regard statements like A as more probable than B. However, this intuitive answer overlooks an important fact: The likelihood of two events occurring together is lower than the probability of either one alone. For example, the probability of getting one head when flipping a coin is one half, or 0.5. The probability of getting two heads when flipping two coins is one fourth, or 0.25. Therefore, A is less likely to be true than B.

According to Tversky and Kahneman, such faulty conclusions are based on the **representativeness heuristic.** That is, we tend to give a choice greater weight if it seems to be representative of what we already know. Thus, you probably compared the information about Team Canada with your mental model of what our national hockey team's behaviour should be like. Answer A seems to better represent the model. Therefore, it seems more likely than answer B, even though it isn't.

Hot Cognition

Feelings also tend to affect good judgment. When we must make a choice, our emotional reactions to various alternatives can determine what intuitively seems to be the right answer. Emotions such as fear, hope, anxiety, liking, or disgust can eliminate possibilities from consideration or promote them to the top of the list (Kahneman, 2003).

Underlying Odds

A second common error in judgment involves ignoring the **base rate,** or underlying probability, of an event. People in one experiment were told that they would be given descriptions of 100 people—70 lawyers and 30 engineers. Subjects were then asked to guess, without knowing anything about a person, whether she or he was an engineer or a lawyer. All

> **Representativeness heuristic** A tendency to select wrong answers because they seem to match preexisting mental categories.
>
> **Base rate** The basic rate at which an event occurs over time; the basic probability of an event.

Framing In thought, the terms in which a problem is stated or the way that it is structured.

correctly stated the probabilities as 70 percent for lawyer and 30 percent for engineer. Participants were then given this description:

> Eric is a 30-year-old man. He is married with no children. A man of high ability and high motivation, he promises to be quite successful in his field. He is well liked by his colleagues.

Notice that the description gives no new information about Eric's occupation. He could still be either an engineer or a lawyer. Therefore, the odds should again be estimated as 70–30. However, most people changed the odds to 50–50. Intuitively it seems that Eric has an equal chance of being either an engineer or a lawyer. But this guess completely ignores the underlying odds.

Perhaps it is fortunate that we do at times ignore underlying odds. Were this not the case, how many would start high-risk businesses? On the other hand, people who smoke, drink and then drive, or don't wear seat belts ignore rather high odds of injury or illness. In many high-risk situations, ignoring base rates is the same as thinking you are an exception to the rule.

Framing

The most general conclusion about intuition is that the way a problem is stated, or **framed**, affects decisions (Tversky & Kahneman, 1981). As the first example in this discussion revealed, people often give different answers to the same problem if it is stated in slightly different ways. To gain some added insight into framing, try another thinking problem:

> A couple are divorcing. Both parents seek custody of their only child, but custody can be granted to just one parent. If you had to make a decision based on the following information, to which parent would you award custody of the child?

> **Parent A:** average income, average health, average working hours, reasonable rapport with the child, relatively stable social life.

> **Parent B:** above-average income, minor health problems, lots of work-related travel, very close relationship with the child, extremely active social life.

STUDY BREAK   Creative Thinking and Intuition

Reflect

Make up a question that would require convergent thinking to answer. Now do the same for divergent thinking.

Which of the tests of creativity described in the text do you think you would do best on? (Look back if you can't remember them all.)

To better remember the stages of creative thinking, make up a short story that includes these words: *orient, prepare, in Cuba, illuminate, verify.*

Explain in your own words how representativeness and base rates contribute to thinking errors.

Learning Check

1. Fluency, flexibility, and originality are characteristics of
   a. convergent thought   b. deductive thinking
   c. creative thought   d. trial-and-error solutions
2. List the typical stages of creative thinking in the correct order.

3. Reasoning and critical thinking tend to block creativity; these are non-creative qualities. T or F?

4. To be creative, an original idea must also be practical or feasible. T or F?

5. Intelligence and creativity are highly correlated; the higher a person's IQ, the more likely he or she is to be creative. T or F?

6. Kate is single, outspoken, and very bright. As a college student, she was deeply concerned with discrimination and other social issues and participated in several protests. Which statement is more likely to be true?
   a. Kate is a bank teller.
   b. Kate is a bank teller and a feminist.

Critical Thinking

7. A coin is flipped four times with one of the following results: (a) H T T H, (b) T T T T, (c) H H H H, (d) H H T H. Which sequence would most likely precede getting a head on the fifth coin flip?

Answers

1. c 2. orientation, preparation, incubation, illumination, verification 3. F 4. T 5. F 6. a 7. The chance of getting a head on the fifth flip is the same in all four cases. Each time you flip a coin, the chance of getting heads is 50 percent, no matter what happened before. However, many people intuitively think that (b) is the answer because heads is "overdue," or that (c) is correct because the coin is "on a roll" for heads.

Most people choose to award custody to Parent B, the parent who has some drawbacks but also several advantages (such as above-average income). That's because people tend to look for *positive qualities* that can be *awarded* to the child. However, how would you choose if you were asked this question: Which parent should be *denied* custody? In this case, most people choose to deny custody to Parent B. Why is Parent B a good choice one moment and a poor choice the next? It's because the second question asked who should be denied custody. To answer this question, people tend to look for *negative qualities* that would *disqualify* a parent. As you can see, the way a question is framed can channel us down a narrow path so we attend to only part of the information provided, rather than weighing all the pros and cons (Shafir, 1993).

Usually, the *broadest* way of framing or stating a problem produces the best decisions. However, we sometimes state problems in increasingly narrow terms until a single, seemingly "obvious" answer emerges. For example, to select a career, it would be wise to consider pay, working conditions, job satisfaction, needed skills, future employment outlook, and many other factors. Instead, such decisions are often narrowed to thoughts such as, "I like to write, so I'll be a journalist"; "I want to make good money, and law pays well"; or "I can be creative in photography." Framing decisions so narrowly greatly increases the risk of making a poor choice. If you would like to think more critically and analytically, it is important to pay attention to how you are defining problems before you try to solve them. Remember, shortcuts to answers often short-circuit clear thinking.

Psychology in Action

ENHANCING CREATIVITY—BRAINSTORMS

Thomas Edison explained his creativity by saying, "Genius is 1 percent inspiration and 99 percent perspiration." Many studies of creativity show that "genius" and "eminence" owe as much to persistence and dedication as they do to inspiration (Glueck, Ernst, & Unger, 2002; Winner, 2003). Once it is recognized that creativity can be hard work, then something can be done to enhance it. Here are some suggestions:

<SURVEY QUESTION
What can be done to improve thinking and promote creativity?

1. Break Mental Sets and Challenge Assumptions
A *mental set* is the tendency to perceive a problem in a way that blinds us to possible solutions. Mental sets are a major barrier to creative thinking. Usually, they lead us to see a problem in preconceived terms that impede our problem-solving attempts. (Fixations and functional fixedness, which were described earlier, are specific types of mental sets.)

Try the problems pictured in Figure 8.24. If you have difficulty, try asking yourself what assumptions you are making. The problems are designed to demonstrate the limiting effects of a mental set. (The answers to these problems, along with an explanation of the sets that prevent their solution, are found in Figure 8.26.)

Now that you have been forewarned about the danger of faulty assumptions, see if you can correctly answer the following questions. If you get caught on any of them, consider it an additional reminder of the value of actively challenging the assumptions you are making in any instance of problem solving.

1. A farmer had 19 sheep. All but 9 died. How many sheep did the farmer have left?
2. It is not unlawful for a man living in Manitoba to be buried in Saskatchewan. T or F?
3. I have two coins that together total 30 cents. One of the coins is not a nickel. What are the two coins?

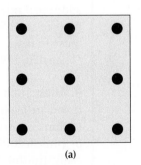
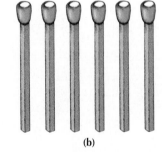

(a)   (b)

▸▸**FIGURE 8.24** (a) Nine dots are arranged in a square. Can you connect them by drawing four continuous straight lines without lifting your pencil from the paper? (b) Six matches must be arranged to make four triangles. The triangles must be the same size, with each side equal to the length of one match. (The solutions to these problems appear in Figure 8.26.)

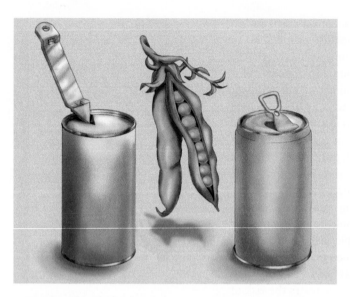

▶▶ **FIGURE 8.25** Example of "opening."

These questions are designed to cause thinking errors. Here are the answers:

> 1. Nineteen—9 alive and 10 dead. 2. F. It is against the law to bury a living person anywhere. 3. A quarter and a nickel. One of the coins is not a nickel, but the other one is!

2. Define Problems Broadly

An effective way to break mental sets is to enlarge the definition of a problem. For instance, assume that your problem is to design a better doorway. This is likely to lead to ordinary solutions. Why not change the problem to design a better way to get through a wall? Now your solutions will be more original. Best of all might be to state the problem as follows: Find a better way to define separate areas for living and working. This could lead to truly creative solutions (Adams, 2001).

Let's say you are leading a group that's designing a new can opener. Wisely, you ask the group to think about *opening* in general, rather than about can openers. This was just the approach that led to the pop-top can (see Figure 8.25). As the design group discussed the concept of opening, one member suggested that nature has its own openers, like the soft seam on a pea pod. Instead of a new can-opening tool, the group invented the self-opening can (Stein, 1974).

3. Restate the Problem in Different Ways

Stating problems in novel ways also tends to produce more creative solutions. See if you can cross out six letters to make a single word out of the following:

C S R I E X L E A T T T E R E S

If you're having difficulty, it may be that you need to restate the problem. Were you trying to cross out six letters? The real solution is to cross out the letters in the words "six letters," which yields the word CREATE.

One way to restate a problem is to imagine how another person would view it. What would a child, engineer, professor, mechanic, artist, psychologist, judge, or minister ask about the problem? Also, don't be afraid to ask "silly" or playful questions such as: If the problem were alive, what would it look like? If the problem were edible, how would it taste?

At the very least, you should almost always ask the following questions: What information do I have? What don't I know? Have I used all of the information? What additional information do I need? What are the parts of the problem? How are the parts related? How could the parts be related? Remember, to think more creatively you must find ways to jog yourself out of mental sets and habitual modes of thought (Michalko, 1998).

4. Allow Time for Incubation

If you are feeling hurried by a sense of time pressure, you are almost always less likely to think creatively (Amabile, Hadley, & Kramer, 2002). You need to be able to revise or embellish initial solutions, even those based on rapid insight. Incubation is especially fruitful when you are exposed to external cues that relate to the problem (remember Archimedes' bath?). For example, Johannes Gutenberg, creator of the printing press, realized while at a wine harvest that the mechanical pressure used to crush grapes could also be used to imprint letters on paper (Dorfman, Shames, & Kihlstrom, 1996).

5. Seek Varied Input

Remember, creativity requires divergent thinking. Rather than digging deeper with logic, you are attempting to shift your mental "prospecting" to new areas. As an example of this strategy, Edward de Bono (1992) recommends that you randomly look up words in the dictionary and relate them to the problem. Often the words will trigger a fresh perspective or open a new avenue. For instance, let's say you are asked to come up with new ways to clean oil off a beach. Following de Bono's suggestion, you would read a list of randomly selected words such as the following, relate each to the problem, and see what thoughts are triggered: *weed, rust, poor, magnify, foam, gold, frame, hole, diagonal, vacuum, tribe, puppet, nose, link, drift, portrait, cheese, coal.* You may get similar benefits from relating various objects to a problem. Or, take a walk, skim through a newspaper, or look through a stack of photographs to see what thoughts they trigger (Michalko, 1998). Exposing yourself to a wide variety of information is a good way to encourage divergent thinking (Clapham, 2001).

6. Look for Analogies

Many "new" problems are really old problems in new clothing (Siegler, 1989). Representing a problem in a variety of ways is often the key to solution. Most problems become easier to solve when they are effectively represented. For example, consider this problem:

> Two backpackers start up a steep trail at 6 a.m. They hike all day, resting occasionally, and arrive at the top at 6 p.m. The next day they start back down the trail at 6 a.m. On the way down, they stop several times and vary their pace. They arrive back at 6 p.m. On the way down, one of the hikers, who is a mathematician, tells the other that she has realized that they will pass a point on the trail at exactly the same time as they did the day before. Her non-mathematical friend finds this hard to believe, since on both days they have stopped and started many times and changed their pace. The problem: Is the mathematician right?

Perhaps you will see the answer to this problem immediately. If not, think of it this way: What if there were two pairs of backpackers, one going up the trail, the second coming down, and both hiking *on the same day?* As one pair of hikers goes up the trail and the other goes down, they *must* pass each other at some point on the trail, right? Therefore, at that point they will be at the same place at the same time. Now, would your conclusion change if one of the pairs was going up the trail one day and the other was coming down the trail the next? If you mentally draw their path up the mountain and then visualize them coming back down it the next day, do you see that at some point the two paths will meet at the same point at the same time on both days? Well, what if the same pair of hikers were going up one day and coming back down the next? As you can now see, the mathematician was right.

7. Delay Evaluation

Various studies suggest that people are most likely to be creative when they are given the freedom to play with ideas and solutions without having to worry about whether they will be evaluated. In the first stages of creative thinking, it is important to avoid criticizing your efforts. Worrying about the correctness of solutions tends to inhibit creativity (Basadur, Runco, & Vega, 2000).

Living More Creatively

Many conventional thinkers live intelligent, successful, and fulfilling lives. Just the same, creative thinking can add spice to life and lead to exciting personal insights. Psychologist

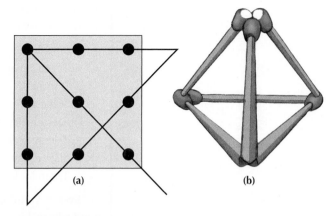

(a)   (b)

▸▸**FIGURE 8.26** Problem solutions. (a) The dot problem can be solved by extending the lines beyond the square formed by the dots. Most people assume incorrectly that they may not do this. (b) The match problem can be solved by building a three-dimensional pyramid. Most people assume that the matches must be arranged on a flat surface. If you remembered the four-tree problem from earlier in the chapter, the match problem may have been easy to solve.

Mihalyi Csikszentmihalyi (sik-sent-me-HALE-yee) (1997) makes these recommendations about how to become more creative:

- Find something that surprises you every day.
- Try to surprise at least one person every day.
- If something sparks your interest, follow it.
- Make a commitment to doing things well.
- Seek challenges.
- Take time for thinking and relaxing.
- Start doing more of what you really enjoy, and less of what you dislike.
- Try to look at problems from as many viewpoints as you can.

Even if you don't become more creative by following these suggestions, they are still good advice. Life is not a standardized test with a single set of correct answers. It is much more like a blank canvas on which you can create designs that uniquely express your talents and interests. To live more creatively, you must be ready to seek new ways of doing things. Try to surprise at least one person today—yourself, if no one else.

 STUDY BREAK Enhancing Creativity

Reflect

Review the preceding pages and note which methods you could use more often to improve the quality of your thinking. Now mentally summarize the points you especially want to remember.

Learning Check

1. Fixations and functional fixedness are specific types of mental sets. T or F?
2. The incubation period in creative problem solving usually lasts just a matter of minutes. T or F?

3. Exposure to creative models has been shown to enhance creativity. T or F?
4. One way to live more creatively is to surprise yourself every day. T or F?

Critical Thinking

5. Do you think there is any connection between your mood and your creativity?

Answers

1. T 2. F 3. T 4. T 5. In general, more intense moods are associated with higher creativity (Davis, 2009).

CHAPTER IN REVIEW

Major Points

- Intelligence is often defined as a single general human quality and operationally defined as performance on an IQ test.

- Simplistic definitions of intelligence have been questioned. IQ is influenced by nurture as well as nature.

- Thinking, problem solving, language, and creativity are the origins of intelligent behaviour.

- Thinking is influenced by the form in which information is represented—as images, concepts, or symbols.

- Language is an especially powerful way to encode information and manipulate ideas.

- Understanding problem solving can make you more effective at finding solutions.

- Expert problem solving is based on acquired knowledge and strategies.

- Creative thinking is novel, divergent, and tempered with a dash of practicality.

- Some thinking errors can be avoided if you know the pitfalls of intuitive thought.

- Creativity can be enhanced by strategies that promote divergent thinking.

Summary

How is human intelligence defined and measured?

- Intelligence refers to the general capacity (or *g*-factor) to act purposefully, think rationally, and deal effectively with the environment.

- In practice, intelligence is operationally defined by intelligence tests, which provide a useful but narrow estimate of real-world intelligence.

- Artificial intelligence refers to any artificial system that can perform tasks that require intelligence when done by people. Two principal areas of artificial intelligence research on particular human skills are computer simulations and expert systems.

- The first intelligence test was assembled by Alfred Binet. A modern version of Binet's test is the Stanford-Binet Intelligence Scale.

- Another major intelligence test is the Wechsler Adult Intelligence Scale (WAIS). The WAIS measures both verbal and performance intelligence. Group intelligence tests are also available.

- Intelligence is expressed as an intelligence quotient (IQ), defined in terms of how a person's test scores relate to

those of other people in the same age group. The distribution of IQ scores approximates a normal curve.

How much does intelligence vary from person to person?

- Most people score in the mid-range on intelligence tests. Only a small percentage of people have exceptionally high or low IQ scores.

- People with IQs in the gifted or "genius" range of above 140 tend to be superior in many respects. However, by criteria other than IQ, many children can be considered gifted or talented in one way or another.

- The term *intellectually disability* is applied to those whose IQ falls below 70 or who lack various adaptive behaviours. About 50 percent of the cases of intellectual disability are organic. Many of the remaining cases are thought to reflect familial intellectual disability.

What are some controversies in the study of intelligence?

- Traditional IQ tests often suffer from a degree of cultural and racial bias. For this and other reasons, it is wise to remember that IQ is merely an index of intelligence and that intelligence is narrowly defined by most tests.

- Many psychologists have begun to forge new, broader definitions of intelligence. Howard Gardner's theory of multiple intelligences is a good example, although it is not unproblematic.

- Intelligence is partially determined by heredity. However, environment is also important, as revealed by IQ increases induced by education and stimulating environments.

What is the nature of thought?

- Thinking is an internal representation of external stimuli or situations.

- Three basic units of thought are images, concepts, and language (or symbols).

In what ways are images related to thinking?

- Images may be stored in memory or created to solve problems.

- Images can be three-dimensional, they can be rotated in space, and their size may change.

- Kinesthetic images are used to represent movements and actions. Kinesthetic sensations help structure the flow of thoughts for many people.

What are concepts?

- A concept is a generalized idea of a class of objects or events.

- Concept formation may be based on positive and negative instances or rule learning.

- In practice, concept identification frequently makes use of prototypes, or ideal models.

- Concepts may be conjunctive ("and" concepts), disjunctive ("either/or" concepts), or relational.

- The denotative meaning of a word or concept is its dictionary definition. Connotative meaning is personal or emotional.

What is the role of language in thinking?

- Language encodes events into symbols, for easy mental manipulation. The study of meaning in language is called *semantics.*

- Bilingualism is a valuable ability. Students who learn to speak two languages well have better executive control.

- Language carries meaning by combining a set of symbols according to a set of rules (grammar), which includes rules about word order (syntax).

- True languages are productive and can be used to generate new ideas or possibilities.

- Complex gestural systems, such as American Sign Language, are true languages.

- Chimpanzees and other primates have been taught American Sign Language and similar systems. This suggests to some that primates are capable of very basic language use. Others question this conclusion.

What do we know about problem solving?

- The solution to a problem may be arrived at mechanically (by trial and error or by rote application of rules), but mechanical solutions are often inefficient.

- Solutions by understanding usually begin with discovery of the general properties of an answer, followed by a functional solution.

- Problem solving is aided by heuristics, which narrow the search for solutions.

- When understanding leads to a rapid solution, insight has occurred. Three elements of insight are selective encoding, selective combination, and selective comparison.

- Insight can be blocked by fixations. Functional fixedness is a common fixation, but emotional blocks, cultural values, learned conventions, and perceptual habits are also problems.

What is creative thinking?

- To be creative, a solution must be practical and sensible as well as original. Creative thinking requires divergent thought, characterized by fluency, flexibility, and originality. Tests of creativity measure these qualities.

- Five stages often seen in creative problem solving are orientation, preparation, incubation, illumination, and verification. Not all creative thinking fits this pattern.

- Studies suggest that the creative personality has a number of characteristics, most of which contradict popular stereotypes. There is only a very small correlation between IQ and creativity.

- Some creative thinking skills can be learned.

How accurate is intuition?

- Intuitive thinking can be fast and accurate but also often leads to errors. Wrong conclusions may be drawn when an answer seems highly representative of what we already believe is true.

- Emotions also lead to intuitive thinking and poor choices.

- A second problem is ignoring the base rate (or underlying probability) of an event.

- Clear thinking is usually aided by stating or framing a problem in broad terms.

What can be done to improve thinking and promote creativity?

- Various strategies that promote divergent thinking tend to enhance creative problem solving.

- In group situations, brainstorming may lead to creative solutions. The principles of brainstorming can also be applied to individual problem solving.

Interactive Learning www
Please visit http://www.psychologyjourney4ce.nelson.com for a list of weblinks to relevant psychology sites.

CourseMate
Access an interactive e-book and chapter-specific interactive learning tools, including flashcards, quizzes, videos, and more, in your psychology CourseMate. Visit Nelsonbrain.com to use CourseMate.

psyk.trek 6. Memory, 7. Cognition and Intelligence, Psyk.Trek Simulations: 1. Experimenting with the Stroop Test, 7. Problem Solving, 8. Psychological testing: Measuring your creativity.

The questions that follow are only a sample of what you need to know. If you miss any of the items, review the entire chapter and the Study Breaks. Another way to prepare for tests is to use the Study Guide and the Practice Exams that are available with this text.

1. What basic unit of thought is used when a person does mental rotation?
   a. concepts   **b.** language   **c.** images   **d.** symbols

2. A triangle must be a closed shape with three sides that are straight lines. What type of concept is a triangle?
   a. a conjunctive concept   **b.** a relational concept
   c. a disjunctive concept   **d.** a connotative concept

3. Which of the following is *not* an element of spoken language?
   a. grammar   **b.** syntax   **c.** phonemes   **d.** lexigrams

4. To what is functional fixedness a major barrier?
   a. insightful problem solving   **b.** using random search strategies
   c. mechanical problem solving   **d.** achieving fixations through problem solving

5. What area uses computer simulations and expert systems as primary research tools?
   a. psycholinguistics   **b.** the field of artificial intelligence (AI)
   c. studies of divergent thinking   **d.** studies of the semantic differential

6. By definition, when does a person have average intelligence?
   a. when mental age (MA) = chronological age (CA)
   b. when chronological age (CA) = 100
   c. when mental age (MA) = 100
   d. when mental age (MA) × chronological age (CA) = 100

7. What one thing is common to people who are mentally gifted and people who have an intellectual disability?
   a. a tendency to suffer from metabolic disorders
   b. testing with the Wechsler Adult Intelligence Scale (WAIS) rather than the Stanford-Binet Intelligence Scales, Fifth Edition (SB5)
   c. mental ages (MAs) that are higher than their chronological ages (CAs)
   d. extreme intelligence quotient (IQ) scores

8. What is a deviation IQ?
   a. a measure of intelligence based on comparison of mental and chronological ages
   b. a measure of intelligence in deviant populations
   c. a measure of intelligence based on a person's standing relative to their age group
   d. a measure of intelligence among people suffering from cognitive delay

9. A test is scored for fluency and flexibility. What is the test designed to measure?
   a. intuitive thinking   **b.** convergent thinking
   c. divergent thinking   **d.** base rates and framing

10. What is increased by seeking varied information, delaying evaluation, and looking for analogies?
    a. intuitive thinking   **b.** convergent thinking
    c. divergent thinking   **d.** functional fixedness

11. How does the size of a mental image affect our thinking of that same image?
    a. the larger the image, the harder it is to see details
    b. mental images do not vary in size
    c. the size of a mental image is always proportional to the size of the object imaged
    d. the smaller the image, the harder it is to see details

12. Which of the following statements best applies to transformation rules?
    a. they are used in problem solving
    b. they are applied to representations of intended meanings to produce spoken sentences
    c. they prevent functional fixedness
    d. they turn collections of phonemes into morphemes

13. One person loves cats and another person hates cats. What meaning does the word *cat* have for these people?
    a. the same connotative meaning
    b. the same meaning connotatively and denotatively
    c. the same denotative meaning but different connotative meanings
    d. the same connotative meaning but different denotative meanings

14. What is American Sign Language (ASL)?
    a. a language acquired by children in the same way that spoken languages are acquired
    b. a coded form of communication but not a real language
    c. the original form of human communication
    d. a language used spontaneously by apes

15. Which of the following is *not* a type of barrier to problem solving discussed in the chapter?
    a. emotional   **b.** cultural   **c.** perceptual   **d.** physical

16. In studies of concepts, what is an exemplar?
    a. a measure of connotative meaning
    b. a formal rule for deciding whether an object is an example of a concept
    c. a stored representation of an individual experience
    d. an ideal model used as a prime example of a particular concept

17. What is a heuristic?
    a. a strategy for reducing the number of alternatives that thinkers must consider
    b. a method of reasoning by analogy
    c. a comparison between a target concept and another, very different, concept
    d. a sudden mental reorganization of a problem

18. According to Norman and Brooks, what are experienced clinicians most likely to do when classifying a patient's mental disorder?
    a. consult their mental representations of generic patients
    b. search their memory for similar patients
    c. use the Stanford-Binet test results
    d. use a formal rule for deciding whether the patient belongs in a given category

19. What is a mental set?
    a. a tendency to perceive a problem in a way that blinds access to potential solutions
    b. a pair of images related on some dimension
    c. a tendency to select wrong answers because they are familiar
    d. the terms in which a problem is stated

20. The contribution of environment to intelligence is thought to be which of the following?
    a. the same throughout the lifespan
    b. larger in adolescents than in young children
    c. larger in young children than in adolescents
    d. non-existent

ANSWERS   1. c 2. a 3. d 4. a 5. b 6. a 7. d 8. c 9. c 10. c 11. d 12. b 13. c 14. a 15. d 16. c 17. a 18. b 19. a 20. c

NEL

chapter 9

Motivation and Emotion

JOURNEY INTO PSYCHOLOGY: I'LL DO IT TOMORROW!

I'm finally getting around to writing this introduction to the Motivation and Emotion chapter. I've been meaning to do it for some time, but something always got in the way until now. You know how that is—you're a student and almost all students procrastinate. Some procrastinate so much that it becomes a significant problem associated with emotional distress and lower grades.

No culture or society is immune to the attractions of putting work off to another day (e.g., Ferrari et al., 2007). Researchers at the University of Alberta recently partnered with colleagues in Singapore to see whether Canadian and Singaporean students differ in how much they procrastinate, what they do while procrastinating, and what effect the behaviour has on their mental state (Klassen et al., 2010).

Klassen and his colleagues found that students in Canada were somewhat more likely to report procrastinating with respect to academic work, while students in Singapore reported slightly higher self-regulation skills. But beyond that, the picture was very similar: Students who procrastinated the most reported the biggest effects on their grade point average, and in both countries the best predictor of procrastination was students' belief in their ability to manage their own learning activities. When it comes to buckling down to work, in other words, you can if you think you can.

Procrastination can be a serious problem. If you have experienced such a problem, take heart: Research at Carleton University in Ottawa offers a possible solution. Michael Wohl and his colleagues suggested that one thing that produces procrastination is negative feelings about the subject being avoided. For example, suppose you have a midterm coming up and you fear you might not do well on it. You might put off studying just because thinking about the exam produces negative feelings. If, as a result, you do poorly on the exam, you might get mad at yourself. What happens before the next midterm in that course—do you change your ways, or do you procrastinate again?

According to Wohl, Pychyl, and Bennett (2010), you would be *less* likely to procrastinate on the second exam if you forgave yourself for procrastinating on the first exam. The idea is that after doing badly on the first exam, you have negative feelings. Those feelings are connected to the topic of studying for exams in that course, including the next midterm. To avoid those negative feelings, you try not to think about their source—midterms in that course—and, as a result, you don't study. A solution is to forgive yourself for procrastinating last time. If you forgive yourself, you are less likely to have those negative feelings—so you will have less reason to avoid studying for the next midterm in that course. In fact, that's how things worked when Wohl and his colleagues studied a large first-year psychology class at Carleton: Students who procrastinated on their first midterm but then forgave themselves were less likely to put off studying for the second midterm and as a result did better than students who did not forgive themselves.

The lesson is clear. If you procrastinated when you should have been studying for an exam, don't linger on the negative thoughts about yourself. Resolve to do better next time—and then forgive yourself.

 Survey Questions

- What is motivation? Are there different types of motives?
- What causes hunger? Overeating? Eating disorders?
- Is there more than one type of thirst? In what ways are pain avoidance and the sex drive unusual?
- What are the typical patterns of human sexual response?
- How does arousal relate to motivation?
- What are social motives? Why are they important?
- Are some motives more basic than others?
- What happens during emotion?
- What physiological changes underlie emotion? Can lie detectors really detect lies?
- How accurately are emotions expressed by the face and body language?
- How do psychologists explain emotions?
- What does it mean to have emotional intelligence?

MOTIVATION—PUSH ME, PULL ME

What are your goals? Why do you pursue them? When are you satisfied? When do you give up? **Motivation** refers to the dynamics of behaviour—the ways in which our actions are *initiated, sustained, directed,* and *terminated* (Franken, 2007).

Can you clarify that? Yes. Imagine that Kayleigh is studying biology in the library. Her stomach begins to growl and she can't concentrate. She grows restless and decides to buy an apple from a vending machine. The machine is empty, so she goes to the cafeteria. Closed. Kayleigh walks to a nearby fast food outlet, where she finally eats. Her hunger satisfied, she resumes studying. Notice how Kayleigh's food seeking was *initiated* by a bodily need. Her search was *sustained* because her need was not immediately met, and her actions were *directed* by possible sources of food. Finally, achieving her goal *terminated* her food seeking.

A Model of Motivation

Many motivated activities begin with a **need,** or internal deficiency. The need that initiated Kayleigh's search was a shortage of key substances in her body. Needs cause a **drive** (an energized motivational state) to develop. The drive was hunger, in Kayleigh's case. Drives activate a *response* (an action or series of actions) designed to push us toward a **goal** (the "target" of motivated behaviour). Reaching a goal that satisfies the need will end the chain of events. Thus, a simple model of motivation can be shown in this way:

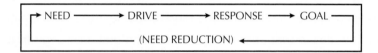

NEED ⟶ DRIVE ⟶ RESPONSE ⟶ GOAL ⟶ (NEED REDUCTION) ⟵

Aren't needs and drives the same thing? No, because the strength of needs and drives can differ (Beck, 2004). For example, it is not uncommon for older people to suffer from dehydration (a bodily need for water) despite experiencing a lack of thirst (the drive to drink) (Farrell et al., 2008).

Now let's observe Kayleigh again. It's a holiday weekend and she's home from school: For dinner, Kayleigh has soup, salad, a large steak, a baked potato, two pieces of cheesecake, and three cups of coffee. After dinner, she complains that she is "too full to move." Soon after, Kayleigh's aunt arrives with a strawberry pie. Kayleigh exclaims that strawberry pie is her favourite and eats three large pieces! Is this hunger? Certainly, Kayleigh's dinner already satisfied her biological needs for food.

How does that change the model of motivation? Kayleigh's "pie lust" illustrates that motivated behaviour can be energized by the "pull" of external stimuli, as well as by the "push" of internal needs.

Incentives

The "pull" of a goal is called its **incentive value** (the goal's appeal beyond its ability to fill a need). Some goals are so desirable (e.g., strawberry pie) that they can motivate behaviour in the absence of an internal need. Other goals are so low in incentive value that they may be rejected even if they meet the internal need. Fresh silkworms, for instance, are highly nutritious. However, it is doubtful that you would eat one no matter how hungry you were. Regardless, because they are also easy to grow and produce few waste products, silkworms may become the preferred food for astronauts on long space voyages (Yang et al., 2009).

Usually, our actions are energized by a mixture of internal needs *and* external incentives. That's why a strong need may change an unpleasant incentive into a desired goal. We'll bet you've eaten some pretty horrible leftovers when the refrigerator was otherwise bare. The incentive value of goals also helps explain motives that don't seem to come from internal needs, such as drives for success, status, or approval (Figure 9.1).

Motivation An internal process that initiates, sustains, directs, and terminates activities.

Need An internal deficiency that may energize behaviour.

Drive The psychological expression of internal needs or valued goals; for example, hunger, thirst, or a drive for success.

Goal The target or objective of motivated behaviour.

Incentive value The value of a goal above and beyond its ability to fill a need.

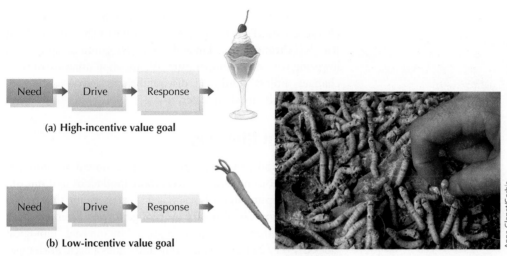

Anna Clopet/Corbis

(a) High-incentive value goal

(b) Low-incentive value goal

▸▸**FIGURE 9.1** Needs and incentives interact to determine drive strength. (a) Moderate need combined with a high-incentive goal produces a strong drive. (b) Even when a strong need exists, drive strength may be moderate if a goal's incentive value is low. It is important to remember, however, that incentive value lies in the eye of the beholder. No matter how hungry, few people would be able to eat the pictured silkworms.

Types of Motives

For our purposes, motives can be divided into three major categories:

1. **Biological motives** are based on biological needs that must be met for survival. The most important biological motives are hunger; thirst; pain avoidance; and needs for air, sleep, elimination of wastes, and regulation of body temperature. Biological motives are innate.

2. **Stimulus motives** express our needs for stimulation and information. Examples include activity, curiosity, exploration, manipulation, and physical contact. Although such motives also appear to be innate, they are not strictly necessary for survival.

3. **Learned motives** are based on learned needs, drives, and goals. Learned motives, which are often social in nature, help explain many human activities, such as standing for election or auditioning for *American Idol.* Many learned motives are related to learned needs for power, affiliation (the need to be with others), approval, status, security, and achievement.

Biological Motives and Homeostasis

How important is air in your life? Water? Sleep? Food? Temperature regulation? For most of us, satisfying biological needs is so routine that we tend to overlook how much of our behaviour they direct. But exaggerate any of these needs through famine, shipwreck, poverty, near drowning, or bitter cold, and their powerful grip on behaviour becomes evident.

Biological drives are essential because they maintain *homeostasis* (HOE-me-oh-STAY-sis), or bodily equilibrium (Cooper, 2008). The term **homeostasis** means "standing steady," or "steady state." Optimal levels exist for body temperature, for chemicals in the blood, for blood pressure, and so forth (Levin, 2006). When the body deviates from these "ideal" levels, automatic reactions begin to restore equilibrium (Deckers, 2005). Thus, it might help to think of homeostasis as being similar to a thermostat set at a particular temperature. (As we'll see in the section on pain below, Ronald Melzack suggests that pain is a neural response to disruption of equilibrium by injury.)

A (Very) Short Course on Thermostats

The thermostat in your house constantly compares the actual room temperature to a *set point,* or ideal temperature, which you can control. When room temperature falls below the set point, the heat is automatically turned on to warm the room. When the heat equals or slightly exceeds the set point, it is automatically turned off or the air conditioning is turned on. In this way, room temperature is kept in a state of equilibrium hovering around the set point.

Biological motives Innate motives based on biological needs.

Stimulus motives Innate needs for stimulation and information.

Learned motives Motives based on learned needs, drives, and goals.

Homeostasis A steady state of bodily equilibrium.

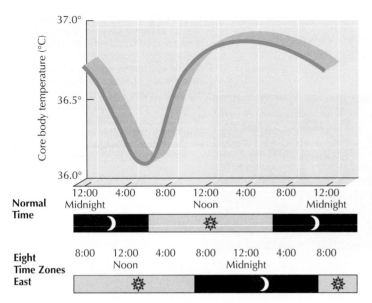

▸▸FIGURE 9.2 Core body temperature is a good indicator of a person's circadian rhythm. Most people reach a low point two to three hours before their normal waking time. Rapid travel to a different time zone, shift work, depression, and illness can throw sleep and waking patterns out of synchronization with the body's core rhythm. Mismatches of this kind are very disruptive (Reinberg & Ashkenazi, 2008).

The first reactions to disequilibrium in the human body are also automatic. For example, if you become too hot, more blood will flow through your skin and you will begin to perspire, thus lowering your body temperature. We are often unaware of such changes, unless continued disequilibrium drives us to seek shade, warmth, food, or water.

Circadian Rhythms

Our needs and drives can change from moment to moment. After eating, our motivation to eat more food tends to diminish, and a few minutes in the hot sun can leave us feeling thirsty. But our motivation can also vary over longer cycles. Scientists have long known that body activity is guided by internal "biological clocks." Every 24 hours, your body undergoes a cycle of changes called **circadian** (*circa*: about; *diem*: a day) **rhythms** (Beersma & Gordijn, 2007). Throughout the day, activities in the liver, kidneys, and endocrine glands undergo large changes. Body temperature, blood pressure, and amino acid levels also shift from hour to hour. These activities, and many others, peak once a day (Figure 9.2). People are usually more motivated and alert at the high point of their circadian rhythms (Antle & Mistlberger, 2005).

Jet Lag and Shift Work

Circadian rhythms are most noticeable after a major change in time schedules. Business people, athletes, and other time zone travellers tend to perform poorly when their body rhythms are disturbed. If you travel great distances east or west, the peaks and valleys of your circadian rhythms will be out of phase with the Sun and clocks. For example, you might be wide awake at midnight and feel like you're sleepwalking during the day. (Return to Figure 9.2.) Shift work has the same effect, causing fatigue, irritability, upset stomach, and depression (Garbarino et al., 2002; Shen et al., 2006).

How fast do people adapt to rhythm changes? For major time zone shifts (five hours or more) it can take up to two weeks to resynchronize. The *direction* of travel also affects adaptation (Herxheimer & Waterhouse, 2003). Let's say that you live in Vancouver and fly east to Toronto. If you get up at 7 a.m. in Toronto, it's 4 a.m. back in Vancouver—and your body knows it. If you fly west, the Sun comes up later. In this case, it is easier for you to "advance" (stay up later and sleep in).

Adjusting to jet lag is slowest when you stay indoors, where you can sleep and eat on "home time." Getting outdoors speeds adaptation. A few intermittent five-minute periods of exposure to bright light early in the morning are also helpful for resetting your circadian rhythm (Duffy & Wright, 2005). Bright light affects the timing of body rhythms by reducing the amount of melatonin produced by the pineal gland. When melatonin levels rise late in the evening, it's bedtime as far as the brain is concerned.

Canadian Forces personnel often have to travel long distances east or west, so the Forces have an enduring interest in mitigating the effects of jet lag. The problem has been studied at the Defence Research & Development establishment in Toronto. There, Michel Paul compared the beneficial effects of a dose of melatonin and of morning exposure to bright light (Paul et al., 2011). The best result came from combining the two treatments, with melatonin taken before going to sleep and light exposure upon waking up.

How does this affect those of us who are not world travellers? There are few college students who have not at one time or another "burned the midnight oil," especially for final exams. At such times it is wise to remember that departing from your regular schedule usually costs more than it's worth. You may be motivated to do as much during one hour in the morning as you could have done in three hours of work after midnight. You might just as well go to sleep two hours earlier.

Circadian rhythms Cyclical changes in bodily functions and arousal levels that vary on a schedule approximating a 24-hour day.

Reflect

Motives help explain why we do what we do. See if you can think of something you do that illustrates the concepts of need, drive, response, and goal. Does the goal in your example vary in incentive value? What effects do high- and low-incentive-value goals have on your behaviour?

Mentally list some biological motives you have satisfied today.

Learning Check

1. Motives _____, sustain, _____, and terminate activities.
2. Needs provide the _____ of motivation, whereas incentives provide the _____.

Classify the following needs or motives by placing the correct letter in the blank.
A. Biological motive
B. Stimulus motive
C. Learned motive

3. _____ curiosity
4. _____ status
5. _____ sleep
6. _____ thirst
7. _____ achievement
8. _____ physical contact
9. The maintenance of bodily equilibrium is called thermostasis. T or F?
10. A goal high in incentive value may create a drive in the absence of any internal need. T or F?

Critical Thinking

11. Many people mistakenly believe that they suffer from *hypoglycemia* (low blood sugar), which is often blamed for fatigue, difficulty concentrating, irritability, and other symptoms. Why is it unlikely that many people actually have hypoglycemia?

Answers

1. initiate, direct 2. push, pull 3. B 4. C 5. A 6. A 7. C 8. B 9. F 10. T 11. Because of homeostasis: Blood sugar is normally maintained within narrow bounds. While blood sugar levels fluctuate enough to affect hunger, true hypoglycemia is an infrequent medical problem.

In general, if you can anticipate an upcoming body rhythm change, it is best to preadapt to your new schedule. *Preadaptation* refers to gradually matching your sleep–waking cycle to a new time schedule. Before travelling, for instance, you should go to sleep one hour later (or earlier) each day until your sleep cycle matches the time at your destination.

HUNGER—PARDON ME, MY HYPOTHALAMUS IS GROWLING

<SURVEY QUESTION
What causes hunger? Overeating? Eating disorders?

You get hungry, you find food, and you eat: Hunger might seem like a "simple" motive, but we have only recently begun to understand it. Hunger provides a good model of how both internal and external factors direct our behaviour.

Internal Factors in Hunger

Don't feelings of hunger originate in the stomach? To find out, Walter Cannon and A. L. Washburn (1912) decided to see if stomach contractions cause hunger. In an early study, Washburn trained himself to swallow a balloon, which could be inflated through an attached tube. (You, too, will do anything for science, right?) This allowed Cannon to record the movements of Washburn's stomach (Figure 9.3). When Washburn's stomach contracted, he reported that he felt "hunger pangs." In view of this, the two scientists concluded that hunger is caused by the contractions of an empty stomach.

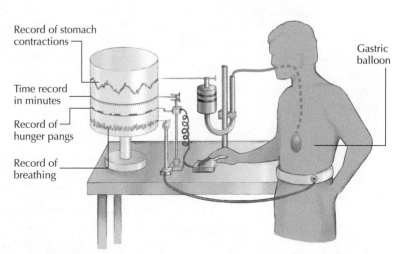

Record of stomach contractions

Time record in minutes

Record of hunger pangs

Record of breathing

Gastric balloon

▶▶**FIGURE 9.3** In Walter Cannon's early study of hunger, a simple apparatus was used to simultaneously record hunger pangs and stomach contractions. (After Cannon, 1934.)

Hypothalamus A small area at the base of the brain that regulates many aspects of motivation and emotion, especially hunger, thirst, and sexual behaviour.

Set point (for fat) The proportion of body fat that tends to be maintained by changes in hunger and eating.

Of course, hunger is not simply an issue for science; it's also a practical problem. Food insecurity exists when the availability of nutritionally adequate and safe foods is limited. Canadian Community Health Survey data from 2004 (Health Canada, 2007) show that food insecurity is particularly common in some groups in Canadian society: One in four families headed by a single mother experience food insecurity, while one-third of Aboriginal households living on reserve and more than half of Aboriginal families living off reserve also do (Willows et al., 2009). This condition produces a variety of negative psychological effects, including anxiety, depression, and cognitive impairments. Zheng Wu of the University of Victoria found food insufficiency to be strongly related to depression. In fact, Wu and Schimmele (2005) found that food insufficiency was a better predictor of depression risk than either income or education.

For many people, hunger produces an overall feeling of weakness or shakiness, rather than a "growling" stomach. Of course, eating *does* slow when the stomach is stretched or distended (full). (Remember last Thanksgiving?) However, we now know that the stomach is not essential for feeling hunger. Even people who have had their stomachs removed for medical reasons continue to feel hungry and eat regularly (Woods et al., 2000).

Then what does cause hunger? Many different factors combine to promote and suppress hunger. The brain receives many signals from parts of the digestive system, ranging from the tongue and stomach to the intestines and the liver.

Brain Mechanisms

What part of the brain controls hunger? Although no single "hunger thermostat" exists, the **hypothalamus** is especially important because it regulates many motives, including hunger, thirst, and the sex drive (Figure 9.4).

The hypothalamus is sensitive to levels of sugar in the blood (and other substances described in a moment). It also receives neural messages from the liver and stomach. When combined, these signals determine whether you are hungry or not (Woods et al., 2000).

One part of the hypothalamus acts as a feeding system that initiates eating. If the *lateral hypothalamus* is "turned on" with an electrified probe, even a well-fed animal will immediately begin eating. (The term *lateral* simply refers to the *sides* of the hypothalamus. See Figure 9.5.) If the same area is destroyed, the animal may never eat again.

The lateral hypothalamus is normally activated in a variety of ways. For example, when you are hungry, your stomach lining produces *ghrelin* (GREL-in), a hormone that activates your lateral hypothalamus (Olszewski et al., 2003). (If your stomach is growlin', it's probably releasing ghrelin.) Ghrelin also activates parts of your brain involved in learning. This means you should consider studying before you eat, not immediately afterward (Diano et al., 2006).

How do we know when to stop eating? A second area in the hypothalamus is part of a satiety system, or "stop mechanism" for eating. If the *ventromedial* (VEN-tro-MEE-dee-al) *hypothalamus* is destroyed, dramatic overeating results. (*Ventromedial* refers to the bottom middle of the hypothalamus.) Rats with such damage will eat until they balloon up to weights of 1000 grams or more (Figure 9.6). A normal rat weighs about 180 grams. To put this weight gain in human terms, picture someone you know who weighs 180 pounds (80 kilograms) growing to a weight of 1000 pounds (450 kilograms).

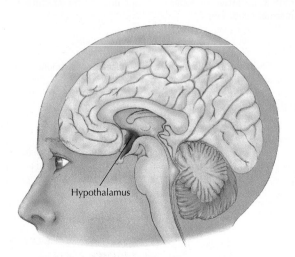

▸▸**FIGURE 9.4** Location of the hypothalamus in the human brain.

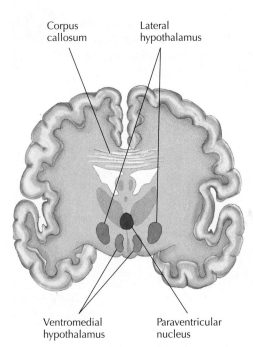

▸▸**FIGURE 9.5** This is a cross section through the middle of the brain (viewed from the front of the brain). Indicated areas of the hypothalamus are associated with hunger and the regulation of body weight.

Corpus callosum

Lateral hypothalamus

Ventromedial hypothalamus

Paraventricular nucleus

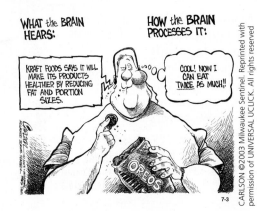

WHAT the BRAIN HEARS:

KRAFT FOODS SAYS IT WILL MAKE ITS PRODUCTS HEALTHIER BY REDUCING FAT AND PORTION SIZES.

HOW the BRAIN PROCESSES IT:

COOL! NOW I CAN EAT TWICE AS MUCH!!

OREOS

7-3

Your Brain's "Fat Point"

Like a thermostat, your brain maintains a **set point** in order to control your weight over the long term. It does this by monitoring the amount of fat stored in your body in specialized *fat cells* (Ahima & Osei, 2004).

Your set point is the weight you maintain when you are making no effort to gain or lose weight. When your body weight goes below its set point, you will feel hungry most of the time. On the other hand, fat cells release a substance called *leptin* when your "spare tire" is well inflated. Leptin is carried in the bloodstream to the hypothalamus, where it tells us to eat less (Williams et al., 2004).

Can you change your fat set point? Your leptin levels are partly under genetic control. In rare cases mice (and we humans) inherit a genetic defect that reduces leptin levels in the body, leading to obesity. In such cases, taking leptin can help (Williamson et al., 2005).

For the rest of us, the news is not so encouraging because there is currently no known way to lower your set point for fat, since the number of fat cells remains unchanged throughout adult life (Spalding et al., 2008). To make matters worse, radical diets do not help. They may even raise the set point for fat, resulting in *diet-induced obesity* (Ahima & Osei, 2004). You may not be able to lose weight by resetting your hypothalamus, but psychologists have studied more effective approaches to weight loss. We will examine some later in this chapter.

The mouse on the left has a genetic defect that prevents its fat cells from producing normal amounts of leptin. Without this chemical signal, the mouse's body acts as if its set point for fat storage is, shall we say, rather high.

The *paraventricular* (PAIR-uh-ven-TRICK-you-ler) *nucleus* of the hypothalamus also affects hunger. This area helps keep blood sugar levels steady by both starting and stopping eating. The paraventricular nucleus is sensitive to a substance called neuropeptide Y (NPY). If NPY is present in large amounts, an animal will eat until it cannot hold another bite (Williams et al., 2004).

A chemical called glucagon-like peptide 1 (GLP-1) is also involved in causing eating to cease. After you eat a meal, GLP-1 is released by the intestines. From there, it travels in the bloodstream to the brain. When enough GLP-1 arrives, your desire to eat ends (Nori, 1998). By the way, it takes at least 10 minutes for the hypothalamus to respond after you begin eating. That's why you are less likely to overeat if you eat slowly, which gives your brain time to get the message that you've had enough (Liu et al., 2000).

In addition to knowing when to start eating, and when meals are over, your brain also controls your weight over long periods of time. (See Brainwaves: "Your Brain's 'Fat Point.'")

The substances we have reviewed are only some of the chemical signals that start and stop eating (Geary, 2004). Others continue to be discovered. In time, they may make it possible to artificially control hunger. If so, better treatments for both extreme obesity and self-starvation could follow (Batterham et al., 2003).

External Factors in Hunger and Obesity

As we have seen, "hunger" is affected by more than just our biological needs for food. In fact, if internal needs alone controlled eating, many fewer people would overeat (Stroebe, Papies, & Aarts, 2008). In 2011, the Canadian and U.S. governments released a joint report detailing rates of

▶▶**FIGURE 9.6** Damage to the hunger satiety system in the hypothalamus can produce a very fat rat, a condition called hypothalamic *hyperphagia* (HI-per-FAGE-yah: overeating). This rat weighs 1080 grams. (The pointer has gone completely around the dial and beyond.)

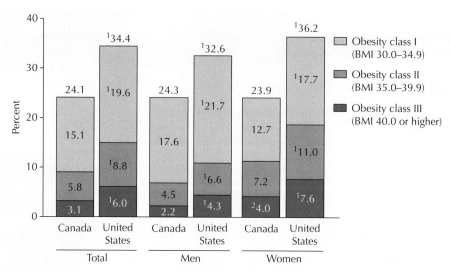

▶▶**FIGURE 9.7** An increasing incidence of obesity has occurred in Canada during the last 20 years, with 59 percent of adult Canadians now classified as overweight or obese (Foulds, Bredin, & Warburton, 2011).

[1]Significantly different from estimate for Canada ($p < 0.05$).
[2]Use with caution (coefficient of variation 16.6%–33.3%).

Notes: BMI is body mass index. Estimates were age-standardized by the direct method to the 2000 United States Census population using age groups 20–39, 40–59, and 60–79. Pregnant women are excluded. Obesity class estimates do not sum to exact totals due to rounding. (CDC/NCHS, 2007-2008 National Health and Nutrition Examination Survey and 2007-2009 Canadian Health Measures Survey.)

overweight and obesity in the two countries. Although Canadians are not doing as well as we might, we're doing better than our neighbours to the south. The report provides data from surveys in the period 2007 to 2009 showing that in the age range 20 to 79 years old, 34.4 percent of Americans and 24.1 percent of Canadians were obese, defined as having a body mass index (BMI) of 30 or more (see Figure 9.7). An astounding 6 percent of Americans had a BMI greater than 40, which in an adult 5 feet 4 inches (162 cm) tall is equivalent to a weight greater than 232 pounds (105 kg).

Part of the reason for the difference between the two countries may be that Canadians eat more fruit and vegetables than Americans do. Federal government data for 2009 indicate that on average Canadians eat 43 percent more fruit and 68 percent more vegetables per person than do Americans. Canadians are more likely to think about nutrition and health when selecting foods, while Americans are more likely to think about "fuelling the body." As a result, obesity is overtaking smoking as a cause of needless deaths (Murray, 2001). Let's consider some external influences on hunger and their role in obesity, a major health risk and, for many, a source of social stigma and low self-esteem.

Which Canadian city has the highest proportion of overweight adults? One of the consequences of moves to discourage smoking in Canada over the last 10 years appears to have been a widespread (no pun intended) increase in weight. The problem varies in severity by city and province, with the lowest rate of obesity found in Vancouver (12 percent of the adult population obese and a further 40 percent overweight) and the highest in St. John's, Newfoundland and Labrador (36 percent obese and another 34 percent overweight). People in Ontario and Quebec are close to the national average (presumably because they have so much of the population), but within Ontario there is significant variation: Hamilton (34.6 percent of adults obese), Windsor (33.2 percent), and Thunder Bay (32.6 percent) have relatively high proportions of obese adults, while the situation is better in Toronto (15.6 percent) and Ottawa (19.7 percent). The Statistics Canada report can be found at http://www.statcan.gc.ca/ads-annonces/82-003-x/pdf/4225223-eng.pdf.

External Eating Cues

Most of us are sensitive to *external eating cues:* signs and signals linked with food. In cultures like ours, where food is plentiful, eating cues add greatly to the risk of overeating (Woods et al., 2000). Many first-year college students gain weight rapidly during their first three months on campus. Patricia Pliner interviewed students at the University of Toronto early in their first year and then again five months later (Pliner & Saunders, 2008). Each student's weight was measured on both occasions. The average gain in weight for students living at home and for unrestrained (non-dieting) students in residence was 1.2 kilograms (2.6 pounds). For restrained eaters living in residence, in contrast, the average gain was 4.1 kilograms (9 pounds). Pliner and Saunders noted that the major finding in this study is that first-year weight gain is not a function simply of starting university studies—it varies with residence and dietary restraint status.

In a related study by researchers in Toronto, Janet Polivy tested restrained eaters (dieters) and unrestrained eaters (Polivy, Herman, & Deo, 2010). Participants saw two different-sized slices of pizza—one given to them and one they were told was for a participant in another room. In both conditions, the actual size of the slice participants ate was the same—it was only the comparison slice that varied, being either larger or smaller. A little later, they were provided with plates of cookies for a taste test and told they could eat as many as they wanted. Restrained eaters whose pizza slice was larger than the other slice ate 35 percent more cookies (by weight) than those whose slice was the smaller one. Note that the actual size of the slice they had eaten was the same for all participants. What mattered for dieters was how *they saw* their slice—as big or small. Polivy and colleagues explained this by suggesting that when dieters ate the "larger" slice, they saw that as ruining their diet, at least for the day, so they felt less restraint when offered cookies. The moral of the story: If you are on a diet, don't look at what other people are eating.

Taste

The availability of a variety of tasty foods can also lead to overeating and obesity in societies where such foods are plentiful. Normally, tastes for foods vary considerably. For example, if you are well fed, leptin dulls the tongue's sensitivity to sweet tastes (Kawai et al., 2000). If you have noticed that you lose your "sweet tooth" when you are full, you may have observed this effect. Actually, if you eat too much of any particular food, it will become less appealing. This probably helps us maintain variety in our diets.

Emotional Eating

Is it true that people also overeat when they are emotionally upset? Yes. People with weight problems are prone to overeat when they are anxious, angry, or sad (Geliebter & Aversa, 2003). Since obese individuals are often unhappy, the result is overeating that leads to emotional distress and still more overeating (Rutledge & Linden, 1998).

Cultural Factors

Learning to think of some foods as desirable and others as revolting has a large impact on what we eat. In North America we would never consider eating the eyes out of the steamed head of a monkey, but in some parts of the world they are considered a delicacy. In short, cultural values greatly affect the *incentive value* of foods.

One reason cultural factors matter is that obesity is a risk factor for several health problems, including type 2 diabetes. Some groups in Canadian society are more at risk than others. Obesity is a particular problem in some Aboriginal groups. A recent study at the University of British Columbia reported that 48 percent of British Columbia Aboriginal adults were obese (Foulds et al., 2011). Noreen Willows tracked weight in Cree preschool children in northern Quebec (Willows, Johnson, & Ball, 2007). Using the International Obesity Task Force standards for weight and age, she found that 52.9 percent of these five-year-olds were obese. The Canadian government reported the prevalence of type 2 diabetes to be almost three times as high among First Nations people living on reserve as in the general population (Public Health Agency of Canada, 2011).

Dieting

A diet is not just a way to lose weight. Your current diet is defined by the types and amounts of food you regularly eat. Some diets actually encourage overeating. In one classic experiment, rats were given meals of chocolate chip cookies, salami, cheese, bananas,

Anorexia nervosa Active self-starvation or a sustained loss of appetite that has psychological origins.

marshmallows, milk chocolate, peanut butter, and fat. These pampered rodents overate, gaining almost three times as much weight as rats that ate only laboratory chow (Sclafani & Springer, 1976). (Rat chow is a dry mixture of several bland grains.)

People are also sensitive to dietary content. In general, *sweetness*, high *fat content*, and *variety* tend to encourage overeating (Lucas & Sclafani, 1990). The easy availability of calorie-rich foods in North America makes willpower an important component of a healthy lifestyle. For example, restaurant and fast food meals tend to be higher in fat and calories than meals made at home (Brownell, 2003). Far fewer people are obese in France, most likely because they simply eat less. Food portions at restaurants in the United States are at least 25 percent larger than portions in France. The French also take longer to eat a meal, which discourages overeating (Rozin et al., 2003).

An added problem faced by people who want to control their weight concerns "yo-yo" dieting.

Actress Valerie Bertinelli has been a lifelong yo-yo dieter who tried many different diets. As a spokeswoman for an American weight-loss program, Valerie lost about 40 pounds (20 kilograms). Will she maintain her weight loss after she reaches her target weight?

Anorexia nervosa is a dangerous disorder. This haunting Italian anti-anorexia poster shows 68-pound (30 kg) model Isabelle Caro, who struggled with anorexia for 15 years and, tragically, passed away in November 2010. Many celebrities have struggled with eating disorders, including Karen Carpenter (who died of starvation-induced heart failure), Paula Abdul, Kirstie Alley, Fiona Apple, and Victoria Beckham (Posh Spice).

The Paradox of Yo-Yo Dieting

If dieting doesn't work, why are hundreds of "new" diets published each year? The answer is that although dieters do lose weight, most regain it soon after they stop dieting. In fact, many people end up weighing even more than before. Why should this be so? Toronto researchers Patricia Pliner and Tracy Saunders (2008) cautioned against assuming that dieting causes weight gain—it may be that obesity-proneness causes people to diet and also to gain weight. On the other hand, we know that dieting slows the body's metabolism (the rate at which energy is used up). In effect, a dieter's body may become highly efficient at *conserving* calories and storing them as fat (Pinel, Assanand, & Lehman, 2000).

To summarize, eating and overeating are related to internal and external influences, diet, emotions, genetics, exercise, and many other factors. People become obese in different ways and for different reasons. We live in a culture that provides inexpensive, good-tasting food everywhere, and we have a brain that evolved to say "Eat whenever food is available." Nevertheless, many people have learned to take control of eating by applying psychological principles (see Discovering Psychology: "Behavioural Dieting").

Eating Disorders

Under the sheets of her hospital bed, Krystal looks like a skeleton. People with anorexia, who are mostly adolescent females, lose devastating amounts of weight from severe, self-inflicted dieting (Cooper, 2005). If she cannot overcome her **anorexia nervosa** (AN-uh-REK-see-yah ner-VOH-sah: self-starvation), Krystal may die of malnutrition.

Do anorexics lose their appetite? Although a compulsive attempt to lose weight causes them to not seek or desire food, they usually still feel physical hunger. Often, anorexia starts with "normal" dieting that slowly begins to dominate the person's life. In time, anorexics suffer debilitating health problems. From 5 to 8 percent (more than 1 in 20) die of malnutrition (Polivy & Herman, 2002). Table 9.1 lists the symptoms of anorexia nervosa.

Behavioural Dieting

As we have noted, dieting is usually followed by rapid weight gains. If you really want to lose weight, you must overhaul your eating and exercise habits, an approach called **behavioural dieting**. Here are some helpful behavioural techniques:

1. **Commit to weight loss.** Involve other people in your efforts. Programs such as Overeaters Anonymous or Take Off Pounds Sensibly can be a good source of social support.

2. **Exercise.** No diet can succeed for long without an increase in exercise. To lose weight, you must use more calories than you take in. Burning just 200 extra calories a day can help prevent rebound weight gains. Add activity to your routine in every way you can think of. Stop saving steps and riding elevators. Buy a step counter to track the number of steps you take every day. Walking 10 000 steps per day will burn between 2000 and 3500 calories a week (depending on your weight). The more frequently and vigorously you exercise, the more weight you will lose (Jeffery & Wing, 2001).

3. **Learn your eating habits by observing yourself and keeping a "diet diary."** Begin by making a complete, two-week record of when and where you eat, what you eat, and the feelings and events that occur just before and after eating. Is a roommate, relative, or spouse encouraging you to overeat? What are your most "dangerous" times and places for overeating?

4. **Learn to weaken your personal eating cues.** When you have learned when and where you do most of your eating, avoid these situations. Try to restrict your eating to one room, and do not read, watch TV, study, or talk on the phone while eating. Require yourself to interrupt what you are doing in order to eat.

5. **Count calories, but don't starve yourself.** To lose weight, you must eat less, and counting calories allows you to keep a record of your food intake. If you have trouble eating less every day, try dieting four days a week. People who diet intensely every other day lose as much as those who diet moderately every day (Viegener et al., 1990).

6. **Develop techniques to control the act of eating.** Whenever you can, check for nutritional information and buy groceries and meals lower in calories and fats. Begin to take smaller portions. Carry to the table only what you plan to eat. Put all other food away before leaving the kitchen. Eat slowly, sip water between bites of food, leave food on your plate, and stop eating before you are completely full. Be especially wary of the extra-large servings at fast-food restaurants (Murray, 2001).

7. **Avoid snacks.** It is generally better to eat more small meals a day than fewer large ones because more calories are burned (Assanand, Pinel, & Lehman, 1998). (No, we don't mean high-calorie snacks *in addition to* meals.) If you have an impulse to snack, set a timer for 20 minutes and see if you are still hungry then. Delay the impulse to snack several times if possible. Dull your appetite by filling up on raw carrots, bouillon, water, coffee, or tea.

8. **Chart your daily progress.** Record your weight, the number of calories eaten, and whether you met your daily goal. Set realistic goals by cutting down calories gradually. Losing about a pound per week is realistic, but remember, you are changing habits, not just dieting. "Diets" don't work!

9. **Set a "threshold" for weight control.** Maintaining weight loss can be even more challenging than losing weight. It is easier to maintain weight losses if you set a regain limit of 3 pounds (1.5 kilograms) or less. In other words, if you gain more than 2 or 3 pounds (1.5 or 2 kilograms), you immediately begin to make corrections in your eating habits and amount of exercise (Brownell, 2003).

Be patient. It takes years to develop eating habits. You can expect it to take at least several months to change them. If you are unsuccessful at losing weight with these techniques, you might find it helpful to seek the aid of a psychologist familiar with behavioural weight-loss techniques.

Bulimia (bue-LIHM-ee-yah) **nervosa** is a second major eating disorder. Bulimic persons gorge on food, then vomit or take laxatives to avoid gaining weight (see Table 9.1). As with anorexia, most victims of bulimia are girls or women. Approximately 5 percent of college women are bulimic. Bingeing and purging can seriously damage health. Typical risks include sore throat, hair loss, muscle spasms, kidney damage, dehydration, tooth erosion, swollen salivary glands, menstrual irregularities, loss of sex drive, and even heart attack.

Causes

What causes anorexia and bulimia? It's difficult to say what causes eating disorders, though we know about some conditions that are associated with them. For example, people who suffer from eating disorders are extremely dissatisfied with their bodies (Crisp et al., 2006). Usually, they have distorted views of themselves, exaggerated fears of becoming fat, and low self-esteem. Many overestimate their body size by 25 percent or more. As a result, they think

Behavioural dieting Weight reduction based on changing exercise and eating habits, rather than temporary self-starvation.

Bulimia nervosa Excessive eating (gorging) usually followed by self-induced vomiting and/or taking laxatives.

■ Table 9.1   **Recognizing Eating Disorders**

Table A Criteria for anorexia nervosa

A. Refusal to maintain body weight at or above a minimally normal weight for age and height (e.g., weight loss leading to maintenance of body weight less than 85 percent of that expected or failure to make expected weight gain during period of growth, leading to body weight less than 85 percent of that expected).

B. Intense fear of gaining weight or becoming fat, even though underweight.

C. Disturbance in the way in which body weight or shape is experienced; undue influence of body weight or shape on self-evaluation, or denial of the seriousness of the current low body weight.

D. In postmenarcheal females, amenorrhea—the absence of at least three consecutive menstrual cycles. (A woman is considered to have amenorrhea if her periods occur only following hormone, e.g., estrogen, administration.)

Specify type:

Restricting type: During the episode of anorexia nervosa, the person does not regularly engage in binge eating or purging behaviour (i.e., self-induced vomiting or the misuse of laxatives or diuretics).

Binge-eating/purging type: During the episode of anorexia nervosa, the person has regularly engaged in binge eating or purging behaviour (i.e., self-induced vomiting or the misuse of laxatives or diuretics).

Table B Criteria for Bulimia Nervosa

A. Recurrent episodes of binge eating. An episode of binge eating is characterized by both of the following:

   1. Eating, in a discrete period of time (e.g., within any two-hour period), an amount of food that is definitely larger than most people would eat during a similar period of time and under similar circumstances.

   2. A sense of lack of control over eating during the episode (e.g., a feeling that one cannot stop eating or control what or how much one is eating).

B. Recurrent inappropriate compensatory behaviour in order to prevent weight gain, such as self-induced vomiting; misuse of laxatives, diuretics or other medications; fasting; or excessive exercise.

C. The binge eating and inappropriate compensatory behaviours both occur, on average, at least twice a week for three months.

D. Self-evaluation is unduly influenced by body shape and weight.

E. The disturbance does not occur exclusively during episodes of anorexia nervosa.

Specify type:

Purging type: During the current episode of bulimia nervosa, the person has regularly engaged in self-induced vomiting or the misuse of laxatives, diuretics, or enemas.

Nonpurging type: During the current episode of bulimia nervosa, the person has used other inappropriate compensatory behaviours, such as fasting or exercise, but has not regularly engaged in self-induced vomiting or the misuse of laxatives, diuretics, or enemas.

(Reprinted with permission from the Diagnostic and Statistical Manual of Mental Disorders, Fourth Edition, Text Revision, (Copyright © 2000). American Psychiatric Association.)

they are disgustingly "fat" when they are actually wasting away (Figure 9.8) (Polivy & Herman, 2002). Do all of these qualities contribute to eating disorders, or only some of them? We don't yet know.

Girls who spend a lot of time reading fashion magazines are more likely to have distorted body images and unrealistic ideas about how they compare with others (Martinez-Gonzalez et al., 2003). It is not possible to say on the basis of survey data which comes first—are girls with distorted body images drawn to fashion magazines, do fashion magazines promote unrealistic ideas about body size, or are both influences at work? Nonetheless, if information from the media does influence young women's satisfaction with their bodies, we can provide other information to counter that effect. In a recent study, a team led by psychologist Gail

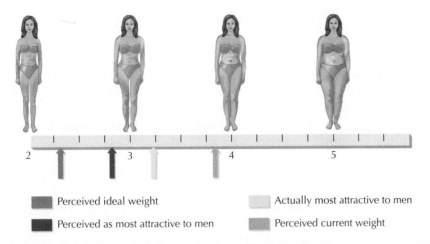

Perceived ideal weight

Actually most attractive to men

Perceived as most attractive to men

Perceived current weight

▸▸**FIGURE 9.8** Women with abnormal eating habits were asked to rate their body shape on a scale similar to the one you see here. As a group, they chose ideal figures much thinner than what they thought their current weights were. (Most women say they want to be thinner than they currently are, but to a lesser degree than women with eating problems.) Notice that the women with eating problems chose an ideal weight that was even thinner than what they thought men prefer. This is not typical of most women. In this study, only women with eating problems wanted to be thinner than what they thought men find attractive (Zellner, Harner, & Adler, 1989).

McVey of The Hospital for Sick Children in Toronto offered students at three Canadian universities a three-hour intervention focused on media literacy, self-esteem, and stress management. Compared to baseline measures, the mostly female students reported improved body satisfaction after the program (McVey et al., 2010). It's not clear how long such improvements last after the intervention ends, but this study is a promising beginning.

More recently, McVey and Joanne Gusella of the IWK Health Care Centre in Halifax developed an Internet-based teacher-training module called the *Student Body*. Their goal is to increase teachers' awareness of things that trigger unhealthy dieting in children, and of how to prevent such dieting (McVey et al., 2009). The website is http://research .aboutkidshealth.ca/thestudentbody/home.asp. A similar online program from Australia is *BodyThink*, at http://www.kidsmatter.edu.au/primary/programs-guide/bodythink/.

The popularity of fitness, exercise, and sports may also contribute to eating disorders. Today, more people are changing their diets in search of a lean, muscular look. People engaged in sports that require low body fat or extreme weight loss (such as wrestling, gymnastics, pole vaulting, high jumping, and even cycling) are particularly likely to develop eating disorders (Weltzin et al., 2005). Note once again that we cannot say that participation in a sport causes the extreme weight loss in such cases: An underlying psychological condition may cause some people both to lose weight and to be drawn to such sports.

Treatment

Most people suffering from eating disorders will not seek help on their own. Typically, it takes strong urging by family or friends to get sufferers into treatment.

Treatment for anorexia usually begins with giving drugs to relieve obsessive fears of gaining weight. Then a medical diet is used to restore weight and health. Next, a counsellor may help patients work on the distress that led to weight loss. For bulimia, behavioural counselling may include self-monitoring of food intake. A related cognitive-behavioural approach focuses on changing the thinking patterns and beliefs about weight and body shape that perpetuate eating disorders (Byrne & McLean, 2002; Cooper, 2005).

BIOLOGICAL MOTIVES REVISITED—THIRST, PAIN, AND SEX

Is there more than one type of thirst? In what ways are pain avoidance and the sex drive unusual?

Most biological motives work in ways that are similar to hunger. For example, thirst is only partially controlled by dryness of the mouth. If you were to take a drug that made your mouth constantly wet, or dry, your water intake would remain normal. Like hunger, thirst is regulated by separate *thirst* and *thirst satiety* systems in the hypothalamus. Also like hunger, thirst is strongly affected by learning and cultural values.

Thirst

You may not have noticed, but there are actually two kinds of thirst. **Extracellular thirst** occurs when water is lost from the fluids surrounding the cells of your body. Bleeding, vomiting, diarrhea, sweating, and drinking alcohol cause this type of thirst (Franken, 2007). When a person loses both water and minerals in any of these ways—especially by perspiration—a slightly salty liquid may be more satisfying than plain water.

Why would a thirsty person want to drink salty water? Before the body can retain water, minerals lost through perspiration (mainly salt) must be replaced. In lab tests, animals greatly prefer saltwater after salt levels in their bodies are lowered (Strickler & Verbalis, 1988).

A second type of thirst occurs when you eat a salty meal. In this instance your body does not lose fluid. Instead, excess salt causes fluid to be drawn out of cells. As the cells "shrink," **intracellular thirst** is triggered. Thirst of this type is best quenched by plain water.

The drives for food, water, air, sleep, and elimination are all similar in that they are generated by a combination of activities in the body and the brain, and they are influenced by various external factors. However, the drive to avoid pain and the sex drive are different.

> **Extracellular thirst** Thirst caused by a reduction in the volume of fluids found between body cells.
>
> **Intracellular thirst** Thirst triggered when fluid is drawn out of cells due to an increased concentration of salts and minerals outside the cell.
>
> **Episodic drive** A drive that occurs in distinct episodes.

Pain

How is the drive to avoid pain different? Hunger, thirst, and sleepiness come and go in a fairly regular cycle each day. Pain avoidance, by contrast, is an **episodic drive.** That is, it occurs in distinct episodes when bodily damage takes place or is about to occur. Most drives prompt us to actively seek a desired goal (food, drink, warmth, and so forth). Pain prompts us to *avoid* or *eliminate* sources of discomfort.

A leading Canadian pain researcher, McGill University's Ronald Melzack, argues for a significant psychological component of pain. That is, he suggests that it is not simply a matter of damaged tissue in the body—a burned finger, a scraped knee—sending a "pain signal" to the brain. Rather, Melzack claims that we must understand pain as a system in the brain (a "neuromatrix") responsible for regulating the body's physical state (homeostasis again). This system, given somatosensory information about an injury to the body, plus other information (such as what the wound looks like, memory, and a stress-coping mechanism), produces the experience of pain as part of its response to the wound (Melzack, 1999; Melzack & Katz, 2006).

Given the strong psychological component of pain, it's not surprising that some people feel they must be "tough" and not show any distress. Others complain loudly at the smallest ache or pain. The first attitude raises pain tolerance, and the second lowers it. As this suggests, the drive to avoid pain is partly learned. That's why members of some societies endure cutting, burning, whipping, tattooing, and piercing of the skin that would agonize most people (but apparently not devotees of

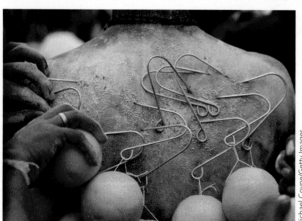

Tolerance for pain and the strength of a person's motivation to avoid discomfort are greatly affected by cultural practices and beliefs.

Michael Coyne/Getty Images

piercing and body art). In general, we learn how to react to pain by observing family members, friends, and other role models (McMahon & Koltzenburg, 2005).

The Sex Drive

Sex is unlike other biological motives because sex (contrary to anything your personal experience might suggest) is not necessary for *individual* survival. It is necessary, of course, for *group* survival.

The term **sex drive** refers to the strength of one's motivation to engage in sexual behaviour. In lower animals, the sex drive is directly related to hormones. Female mammals (other than humans) are interested in mating only when their fertility cycles are in the stage of **estrus,** or "heat." Estrus is caused by a release of **estrogen** (a female sex hormone) into the bloodstream. Hormones are important in males as well. In most animals, castration will abolish the sex drive. But in contrast to females, the normal male animal is almost always ready to mate. His sex drive is aroused primarily by the behaviour and scent of a receptive female. Therefore, in many species, mating is closely tied to female fertility cycles.

How much do hormones affect human sex drives? Hormones affect the human sex drive, but not as directly as in animals (Crooks & Baur, 2008). The sex drive in men is related to the amount of **androgens** (male hormones such as testosterone) provided by the testes. When the supply of androgens dramatically increases at puberty, so does the male sex drive. Likewise, the sex drive in women is related to their estrogen levels (Hyde & DeLamater, 2006). However, "male" hormones also affect the female sex drive. In addition to estrogen, a woman's body produces small amounts of androgens. When their androgen levels increase, many women experience a corresponding increase in sex drive (Van Goozen et al., 1995). Testosterone levels decline with age, and various medical problems can lower sexual desire. In some instances, taking testosterone supplements can restore the sex drive in both men and women (Crooks & Baur, 2008).

Does alcohol increase the sex drive? In general, no. Alcohol is a *depressant.* As such, it may, in small doses, stimulate erotic desire by lowering inhibitions. This effect no doubt accounts for alcohol's reputation as an aid to seduction. However, in larger doses alcohol suppresses orgasm in women and erection in men. Getting drunk *decreases* sexual desire, arousal, pleasure, and performance (McKay, 2005).

Numerous other drugs are reputed to be *aphrodisiacs* (substances that increase sexual desire or pleasure). However, like alcohol, many other drugs actually impair sexual response, rather than enhance it (McKay, 2005). Some examples are amphetamines, amyl nitrite, barbiturates, cocaine, Ecstasy, LSD, and marijuana.

Perhaps the most interesting fact about the sex drive is that it is largely *non-homeostatic* (relatively independent of bodily need states). In humans, the sex drive can be aroused at virtually any time by almost anything. It therefore shows no clear relationship to deprivation (the amount of time since the drive was last satisfied). Certainly, an increase in desire may occur as time passes. But recent sexual activity does not prevent sexual desire from occurring again. Notice, too, that people may seek to arouse the sex drive as well as to reduce it. This unusual quality makes the sex drive capable of motivating a wide range of behaviours. It also explains why sex is used to sell almost everything imaginable.

Let's explore human sexuality in a little more detail.

SEXUAL BEHAVIOUR—MAPPING THE EROGENOUS ZONES

Human sexual arousal is complex. It may, of course, be produced by direct stimulation of the body's **erogenous** (eh-ROJ-eh-nus: productive of pleasure or erotic desire) **zones.** Human erogenous zones include the genitals, mouth, breasts, ears, anus, and, to a lesser degree, the

Sex drive The strength of one's motivation to engage in sexual behaviour.

Estrus Changes in the sexual drives of animals that create a desire for mating; particularly used to refer to females in heat.

Estrogen Any of a number of female sex hormones.

Androgen Any of a number of male sex hormones, especially testosterone.

Erogenous zones Areas of the body that produce pleasure and/or provoke erotic desire.

<SURVEY QUESTION
What are the typical patterns of human sexual response?

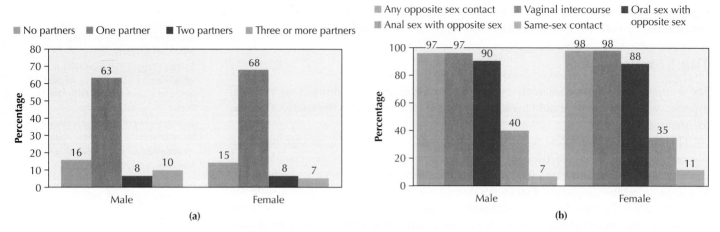

►►**FIGURE 9.9** These graphs show the pattern of sexual behaviour for American adults. (a) Men and women do not differ in their average number of sexual partners or (b) in their overall pattern of sexual activity. (Adapted from Mosher, Chandra, & Jones, 2005.)

entire surface of the body. It is clear, however, that more than physical contact is involved: A urological or gynecological exam rarely results in any sexual arousal. Likewise, an unwanted sexual advance may produce only revulsion. Human sexual arousal obviously includes a large mental element.

Sexual Arousal

Based on the frequency of orgasm (from masturbation or intercourse), the peak of male sexual activity is at age 18. The peak rate of female sexual activity appears to occur a little later (Janus & Janus, 1993). However, male and female sexual patterns are rapidly becoming more alike. Figure 9.9 presents some of the data on sexual behaviour from a major national health survey of American men and women ages 25 to 44. As you can see, in any given year American men and women do not differ in their average number of opposite-sex partners or in their overall pattern of sexual activity (Mosher, Chandra, & Jones, 2005).

Analogous data for Canada are difficult to find because surveys in Canada tend to focus on select subpopulations, such as teens or gays (Barrett et al., 2003). A 2008 Statistics Canada report showed data from a 2005 study of sexual activity in a representative sample of Canadian adolescents 15 to 19 years old (Rotermann, 2008). The report compared findings from 2005 and 1996/1997. Overall, there was a decrease in the number of girls reporting that they had had sexual intercourse at least once in the previous year, from 51 percent of the sample to 43 percent. For boys, the rate was unchanged at 43 percent. The proportions were higher in the older range, with 65 percent of 18- to 19-year-olds having had intercourse at least once in the previous year, compared to 29 percent of 15- to 17-year-olds. The Canadian Community Health Survey for 2009–2010 provides information about the frequency of sexual intercourse for Canadian adults without any breakdown by age. In this survey, 93 percent of males and 92 percent of females reported having had intercourse in the previous year. The vast majority of respondents (83 percent of males and 89 percent of females) reported having only one partner in the previous year.

Human Sexual Response

The pioneering work of gynecologist William Masters and psychologist Virginia Johnson greatly expanded our understanding of sexual response (Masters & Johnson, 1966, 1970). In a series of

Excitement phase The first level of sexual response, indicated by initial signs of sexual arousal.

Plateau phase The second phase of sexual response during which physical arousal is further heightened.

Orgasm A climax and release of sexual excitement.

Resolution The fourth phase of sexual response, involving a return to lower levels of sexual tension and arousal.

experiments, interviews, and controlled observations, Masters and Johnson directly studied sexual intercourse and masturbation in nearly 700 males and females. According to Masters and Johnson, sexual response can be divided into four phases: (1) **excitement,** (2) **plateau,** (3) **orgasm,** and (4) **resolution** (Figures 9.10 and 9.11). These four phases, which are the same for people of all sexual orientations (Garnets & Kimmel, 1991), can be described as follows:

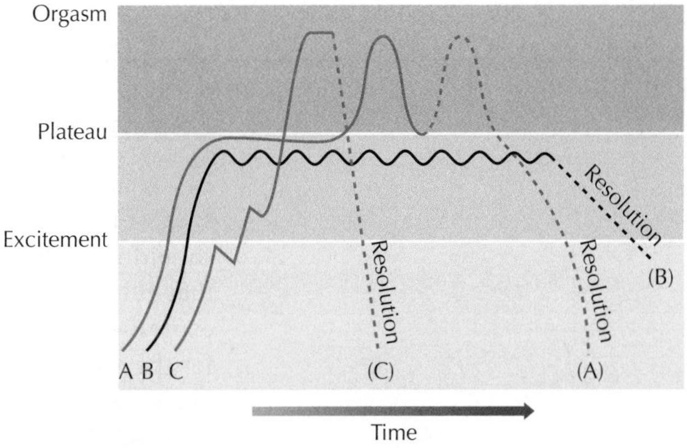

Female Response

In women, the excitement phase is marked by a complex pattern of changes in the body. The vagina is prepared for intercourse, the nipples become erect, pulse rate rises, and the skin may become flushed or reddened. If sexual stimulation ends, the excitement phase will gradually subside. If a woman moves into the plateau phase, physical changes and subjective feelings of arousal become more intense. Sexual arousal that ends during this phase tends to ebb more slowly, which may produce considerable frustration. Occasionally, women skip the plateau phase (see Figure 9.10). For some women, this is almost always the case. Orgasm is usually followed by resolution, a return to lower levels of sexual tension and arousal. After orgasm, about 15 percent of all women return to the plateau phase and may have one or more additional orgasms (Mah & Binik, 2001).

Male Response

Sexual arousal in the male is signalled by erection of the penis during the excitement phase. A rise in heart rate, increased blood flow to the genitals, enlargement of the testicles, erection of the nipples, and numerous other body changes also occur. As is true of female sexual response, continued stimulation moves the male into the plateau phase. Again, physical changes and subjective feelings of arousal become more intense. Further stimulation during the plateau phase brings about a reflex release of sexual tension, resulting in orgasm.

In the mature male, orgasm is usually accompanied by *ejaculation* (release of sperm and seminal fluid). Afterwards, it is followed by a short *refractory period* during which a second orgasm is impossible. Only rarely is the male refractory period immediately followed by a second orgasm. Both orgasm and resolution in the male usually do not last as long as they do for females.

Comparing Male and Female Responses

Although male and female sexual responses are generally quite similar, the differences that do exist can affect sexual compatibility. For example, women typically go through the sexual phases more slowly than do men. However, during masturbation, 70 percent of females reach orgasm in four minutes or less. This is quite comparable to male response times. It suggests again that women are no less physically responsive than men.

Researchers at the University of New Brunswick have been studying the sexual experiences of young women and men and finding some significant differences. For example, Sandra Byers and her colleagues found that men were twice as likely as women to have engaged in solitary online sexual activity (OSA), such as viewing explicit videos or photos, in the previous month, with 85.8 percent of men and 39 percent of women in the sample reporting such activity (Shaughnessy, Byers, & Walsh, 2011). Men were also almost twice as

▶▶FIGURE 9.10 Female sexual response cycle. The green line shows that sexual arousal rises through the excitement phase and levels off for a time during the plateau phase. Arousal peaks during orgasm and then returns to pre-excitement levels. In pattern A, arousal rises from excitement, through the plateau phase, and peaks in orgasm. Resolution may be immediate, or it may first include a return to the plateau phase and a second orgasm (dotted line). In pattern B, arousal is sustained at the plateau phase and slowly resolved without sexual climax. Pattern C shows a fairly rapid rise in arousal to orgasm. Little time is spent in the plateau phase, and resolution is fairly rapid. (From Frank A. Beach, ed., *Sex and Behavior*. New York: John Wiley & Sons, Inc., 1965. Reproduced by permission of the author's estate)

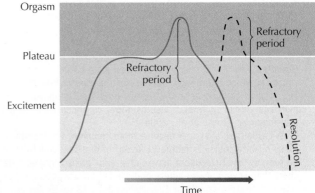

▶▶FIGURE 9.11 Male sexual response cycle. The green line shows that sexual arousal rises through the excitement phase and levels off for a time during the plateau phase. Arousal peaks during orgasm and then returns to pre-excitement levels. During the refractory period, immediately after orgasm, a second sexual climax is typically impossible. However, after the refractory period has passed, there may be a return to the plateau phase, followed by a second orgasm (dotted line). (From Frank A. Beach, ed., *Sex and Behavior*. New York: John Wiley & Sons, Inc., 1965. Reproduced by permission of the author's estate.)

Sexual script An unspoken mental plan that defines a "plot," dialogue, and actions expected to take place in a sexual encounter.

likely as women to have engaged in partnered OSA (men: 25.0 percent, women: 13.0 percent) in the previous month.

Sexual Scripts

In a restaurant we commonly expect certain things to occur. It could even be said that each of us has a restaurant "script" that defines a plot, dialogue, roles, and actions that should take place. We also learn a variety of **sexual scripts,** or unspoken mental plans that guide our sexual behaviour. Such scripts determine when and where we are likely to express sexual feelings, and with whom (Lenton & Bryan, 2005). They provide a "plot" for the order of events in lovemaking and they outline "approved" actions, motives, and outcomes.

Psychologist Eleanor Maticka-Tyndale, of the University of Windsor, is leading a Canadian-funded study aimed at HIV prevention for Rural Youth (HP4RY) in Nigeria, along with Nigerian researchers Adenike Esiet and Dr. Andrew Onokerhoraye. Maticka-Tyndale and her team analyzed sexual scripts in children in the Nigerian equivalent of Grades 7 and 9 (Barnett et al., 2011). Their analysis suggested that the sexual exchange script is both empowering and restricting for girls: It is empowering because girls are not devalued for engaging in such exchanges and are entitled to initiate exchange encounters, but restricting because if a girl refuses an offer she might suffer a violent response. If the boy is seen as giving the girl money or "stuff," another script presents him as entitled to sex in return.

To read more about contemporary sexual scripts, see Human Diversity "What's Love Got to Do with It?"

HUMAN DIVERSITY

What's Love Got to Do with It?

Younger Americans are shifting toward scripts favouring casual sex (Hughes, Morrison, & Asada, 2005). One such script includes sex in a friendship, without traditional romance. According to one survey, more than half of all college students have been *friends with benefits* (friends who have sex but aren't romantically involved) (Puentes, Knox, & Zusman, 2008). Even more casual is the *hook-up* script, in which two people having sex are more or less strangers. In contrast, traditional sexual scripts stress courtship, romance, and marriage. Sex in such relationships might be premarital, but it is still romantic (Roese et al., 2006).

As casual sexual scripts become more common, the traditional focus on intercourse is fading in favour of oral sex, which tends to be seen as less risky, more acceptable, and "not a big deal." Data show that among young adults oral sex is now about as common as intercourse. In a sample of 181 women aged 18 to 25, for example, University of Alberta researchers Brea Malacad and Gretchen Hess found that 73 percent had experienced intercourse at least once, 74 percent had given oral sex to a male partner, and 73 percent had received oral sex (Malacad & Hess, 2010). In general, these women reported substantially more positive than negative emotions in connection with their experiences of oral sex.

Casual sex is not without its own risks. It is usually associated with alcohol use and unsafe sexual behaviours, such as

unprotected sex (Grello, Welsh, & Harper, 2006). Although oral sex is safer than intercourse, a significant chance of getting a sexually transmitted disease remains (Boskey, 2008). Another downside of casual sex is the letdown that can occur when one person follows a romantic script and the other follows a casual script ("he or she is just not that into you"). For example, young women who are having casual sex are more likely to be depressed (Grello, Welsh, & Harper, 2006).

Since the decision to have casual sex is usually made without much thought—that's what makes it casual—it's perhaps not surprising that it can be a source of regret. Recently, psychologists at Saint Mary's University in Halifax surveyed 200 Canadian university students about their experience of regret following uncommitted sexual encounters (i.e., casual sex) (Fisher et al., 2012). They found that the majority of men (72 percent) and women (78 percent) had experienced regret following a casual sex encounter. For both sexes, being intoxicated led them to feel regret after such an encounter, but regret was less likely if the sex was good than if it was bad.

Adolescents and young adults have always engaged in experimentation and exploration. Most young people emerge unscathed from their explorations if they clearly understand that their encounters are casual and practise safe sex.

Sexual Orientation—Whom Do You Love?

Another aspect of sexuality is **sexual orientation,** your degree of emotional and erotic attraction to members of the same sex, opposite sex, or both sexes. *Heterosexuals* are romantically and erotically attracted to members of the opposite sex. *Homosexuals* are attracted to people whose sex matches their own. *Bisexuals* are attracted to both men and women.

What determines a person's sexual orientation? Available evidence suggests that sexual orientation is mainly genetic and biological, although social, cultural, and psychological influences are also involved (LeVay & Valente, 2006).

Healthy Sexual Relationships

Regardless of sexual responsiveness or sexual orientation, as a shared pleasure, a form of intimacy, a means of communication, and a haven from everyday tensions, a positive sexual relationship can do much to enhance a couple's mutual understanding and caring. People are most likely to value their sexuality when they develop a respectful, trusting, and intimate relationship with their partner. A sense of closeness helps maintain sexual interest and mutually satisfying lovemaking, especially in long-term relationships (McCarthy, 1995; McCarthy & Fucito, 2005).

Sexual Problems—When Pleasure Fades

Most people who seek sexual counselling have one or more of the following types of problems (Crooks & Baur, 2008; American Psychiatric Association, 2000):

Desire disorders: The person has little or no sexual motivation or desire.

Arousal disorders: The person desires sexual activity but does not become sexually aroused.

Orgasm disorders: The person does not have orgasms or experiences orgasm too soon or too late.

Sexual pain disorders: The person experiences pain that makes lovemaking uncomfortable or impossible.

Sexual orientation One's degree of emotional and erotic attraction to members of the same sex, opposite sex, or both sexes.

✓ STUDY BREAK Hunger, Thirst, Pain, and Sex

Reflect

Think of the last meal you ate. What caused you to feel hungry? What internal signals told your body to stop eating? How sensitive are you to external eating cues? How were you influenced by portion size?

A friend of yours seems to be engaging in yo-yo dieting. Can you tell your friend why such dieting is ineffective and summarize how behavioural dieting is done?

In what ways are sexual responses of members of the opposite sex similar to your own? In what ways are they different?

Learning Check

1. The hunger satiety system in the hypothalamus signals the body to start eating when it receives signals from the liver or detects changes in blood sugar. T or F?
2. People who diet frequently tend to benefit from practice: They lose weight more quickly each time they diet. T or F?

3. Bulimia nervosa is also known as the binge–purge syndrome. T or F?
4. In addition to burning calories, physical exercise can lower the body's set point. T or F?
5. Thirst may be either intracellular or_____.
6. Pain avoidance is a(n) _____ drive.
7. Sexual behaviour in animals is largely controlled by estrogen levels in the female and the occurrence of estrus in the male. T or F?
8. List the four phases of sexual response identified by Masters and Johnson:

_____, _____, _____, _____.

Critical Thinking

9. Kim, who is overweight, is highly sensitive to external eating cues. How might her wristwatch contribute to her overeating?

Answers 1. F 2. F 3. T 4. F 5. extracellular 6. episodic 7. F 8. excitement, plateau, orgasm, resolution 9. The time of day can influence eating, especially for externally cued eaters, who tend to get hungry at mealtimes, regardless of their internal needs for food.

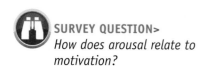

Arousal theory People prefer to maintain ideal, or comfortable, levels of arousal.

In recent years effective treatments have been found for many complaints. Medical treatments or drugs (such as Viagra and Cialis for men) may be helpful for sexual problems that clearly have physical causes. In other cases, counselling or psychotherapy may be the best approach.

For example, many patients benefit from a technique called *sensate focus.* In sensate focus, distressed couples begin by taking turns caressing each other in non-sexual ways. They are told to concentrate on giving pleasure and on signalling what feels good to them. This relieves the pressure to perform and it builds communication skills. Slowly, the couple moves on to mutually satisfying lovemaking, as natural arousal begins to replace fear and anger. In most communities, professional help can be obtained from appropriately trained psychologists, physicians, or counsellors.

STIMULUS MOTIVES—MONKEY BUSINESS

SURVEY QUESTION>
How does arousal relate to motivation?

Are you full of energy right now? Or are you tired? Clearly, the level of arousal you are experiencing is closely linked to your motivation. Are there ideal levels of arousal for different people and different activities? Let's find out.

Most people enjoy a steady "diet" of new movies, novels, tunes, fashions, games, news, websites, and adventures. Yet, *stimulus motives,* which reflect needs for information, exploration, manipulation, and sensory input, go beyond mere entertainment. Stimulus drives also help us survive. As we scan our surroundings, we constantly identify sources of food, danger, shelter, and other key details. The drive for stimulation is already present during infancy. By the time a child can walk, there are few things in the home that have not been tasted, touched, viewed, or handled.

Stimulus drives are readily apparent in animals as well as humans. For example, monkeys will quickly learn to solve a mechanical puzzle made up of interlocking metal pins, hooks, and latches (Butler, 1954) (Figure 9.12). No food treats or other external rewards are needed to get them to explore and manipulate their surroundings. The monkeys seem to work for the sheer fun of it.

Arousal Theory

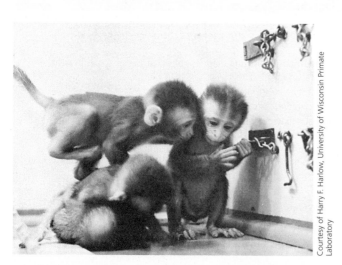

Are stimulus drives homeostatic? Yes. According to **arousal theory** we try to keep arousal at an optimal level (Franken, 2007; Hancock & Ganey, 2003). In other words, when your level of arousal is too low or too high, you will seek ways to raise or lower it.

What do you mean by arousal? Arousal refers to activation of the body and nervous system. Arousal is zero at death; low during sleep; moderate during normal daily activities; and high at times of excitement, emotion, or panic. Arousal theory suggests that we become uncomfortable when arousal is too low ("I'm bored") or when it is too high, as in fear, anxiety, or panic ("The dentist will see you now"). Most adults engage in a mixture of music, parties, sports, hobbies, conversation, sleep, surfing the Web, and the like, to keep arousal at moderate levels. The right mix of activities prevents boredom *and* overstimulation (Csikszentmihalyi, Abuhamdeh, & Nakamura, 2005).

Courtesy of Harry F. Harlow, University of Wisconsin Primate Laboratory

▸▸FIGURE 9.12 Monkeys happily open locks that are placed in their cage. Because no reward is given for this activity, it provides evidence for the existence of stimulus needs.

Sensation Seekers

Do people vary in their needs for stimulation? Arousal theory also suggests that people learn to seek particular levels of arousal. Where would you prefer to go on your next summer vacation? Your backyard? How about a week with your best friends at a cottage on a nearby lake? Or a shopping and museum trip to New York City? How about cage diving with great white sharks in South Africa? If the shark adventure attracts you, you are probably high in sensation seeking and would be interested in a vacation that includes activities like bungee-jumping, scuba diving, skiing, skydiving, and white-water rafting (Pizam et al., 2004).

Sensation seeking is a trait of people who prefer high levels of stimulation (Gray & Wilson, 2007). Whether you are high or low in sensation seeking reflects how your body responds to new, unusual, or intense stimulation (Zuckerman, 2002). People high in sensation seeking tend to be bold and independent, and value change. They also report more sexual partners; are more likely to smoke; and prefer spicy, sour, and crunchy foods over bland foods. High sensation seekers are more likely to engage in high-risk behaviours such as substance abuse (Horvath et al., 2004) and casual unprotected sex (Gullette & Lyons, 2005). Low sensation seekers are orderly, nurturing, and giving, and enjoy the company of others.

Thrill seeking is an element of the sensation-seeking personality.

Levels of Arousal

Is there an ideal level of arousal for peak performance? If we set aside individual differences, most people perform best when their arousal level is *moderate*. Let's say that you have to take an essay exam. If you are feeling sleepy or lazy (arousal level too low), your performance will suffer. If you are in a state of anxiety or panic about the test (arousal level too high), you will also perform below par. Thus, the relationship between arousal and performance forms an *inverted U function* (a curve in the shape of an upside-down U) (Figure 9.13) (Hancock & Ganey, 2003).

The inverted U tells us that at very low levels of arousal, you're not sufficiently energized to perform well. Performance will improve as your arousal level increases, up to the middle of the curve. Then it begins to drop off as you become emotional, frenzied, or disorganized. For example, imagine trying to start a car stalled on a railroad track, with a speeding train bearing down on you.

Is performance always best at moderate levels of arousal? No, the ideal level of arousal depends on the complexity of a task. If a task is relatively simple, it is best for arousal to be high (see Figure 9.13b). When a task is more complex, your best performance will occur at lower levels of arousal (see Figure 9.13c). This relationship is called the **Yerkes-Dodson law.** It applies to a wide variety of tasks and to measures of motivation other than arousal.

Yerkes-Dodson law A summary of the relationships among arousal, task complexity, and performance.

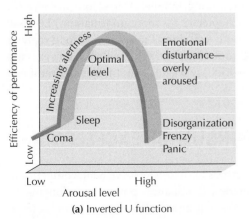

(a) Inverted U function

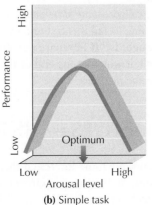

(b) Simple task

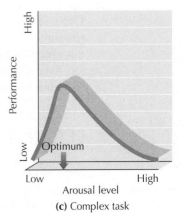

(c) Complex task

▸▸**FIGURE 9.13** (a) The general relationship between arousal and efficiency can be described by an inverted U curve. The optimal level of arousal or motivation is higher for a simple task (b) than for a complex task (c).

Test anxiety High levels of arousal and worry that seriously impair test performance.

Social motives Learned motives acquired as part of growing up in a particular society or culture.

For example, at a track meet, it is almost impossible for sprinters to get too aroused for a race. The task is direct and simple: Run as fast as you can for a short distance. On the other hand, a golfer making a tournament-deciding putt faces a more sensitive and complex task. Excessive arousal is almost certain to hurt his or her performance. Many students have experienced "test anxiety," a familiar example of how too much arousal can lower performance.

Coping with Test Anxiety

Then is it true that by learning to calm down, a person could do better on tests? Not always. To begin with, some arousal is healthy; it focuses us on the task at hand. It is only when arousal interferes with performance that we refer to anxiety. **Test anxiety** is a mixture of psychological states, including *heightened physiological arousal* (nervousness, sweating, pounding heart) and *excessive worry*. This combination—arousal plus worry—tends to distract students with a rush of upsetting thoughts and feelings (Stipek, 2001).

Here are some suggestions for coping with test anxiety:

Preparation

Hard work is the most direct antidote for test anxiety. Many test-anxious students simply study too little, too late. That's why improving your study skills is a good way to reduce test anxiety (Cassady, 2004). If test anxiety is a problem for you, it would be wise to return to the Introduction in this book and review the learning and test-taking skills described there. The best solution is to *overprepare* by studying long before the "big day." Well-prepared students score higher, worry less, and are less likely to panic (Zohar, 1998).

Relaxation

Learning to relax is another way to lower test anxiety (Powell, 2004). You can learn self-relaxation skills by looking at Chapters 12 and 13, where some relaxation techniques are described. Emotional support also helps (Stöber, 2004). If you are test anxious, discuss the problem with your professors or study for tests with a supportive classmate.

Rehearsal

To reduce nervousness, rehearse how you will cope with upsetting events. Before taking a test, imagine yourself going blank, running out of time, or feeling panicked. Then calmly plan how you will handle each situation—by keeping your attention on the task, by focusing on one question at a time, and so forth (Watson & Tharp, 2007).

Restructuring Thoughts

Another helpful strategy involves listing the upsetting thoughts you have during exams. Then you can learn to combat these worries with calming, rational replies (Jones & Petruzzi, 1995). (These are called *coping statements*; see Chapter 12 for more information.) Let's say you think, "I'm going to fail this test and everybody will think I'm stupid." A good reply to this upsetting thought is, "If I prepare well and control my worries, I will probably pass the test. Even if I don't, it won't be the end of the world. My friends will still like me, and I can try to improve on the next test."

LEARNED MOTIVES—THE PURSUIT OF EXCELLENCE

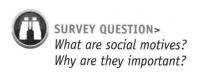

SURVEY QUESTION>
What are social motives? Why are they important?

Some of your friends are more interested than others in success, achievement, competition, money, possessions, status, love, approval, grades, dominance, power, or belonging to groups—all of which are *social motives* or goals. We acquire **social motives** in complex ways, through socialization and cultural conditioning (Franken, 2007). The behaviour of outstanding artists, scientists, athletes, educators, and leaders can be understood in terms of such learned needs, particularly the need for achievement.

The Need for Achievement

To some people, being "motivated" means being interested in achievement (Wigfield & Eccles, 2002). In Chapter 14 we will investigate aggression, helping, affiliation, seeking approval, and other social motives. For now, let's focus on the **need for achievement (nAch),** which is a desire to meet an internal standard of excellence (McClelland, 1961). People with a high need for achievement strive to do well any time they are evaluated.

Characteristics of Achievers

Using a simple measure, David McClelland (1965) found that he could predict the behaviour of high and low achievers. Here's a test: In front of you are five targets. Each is placed at an increasing distance from where you are standing. You are given a beanbag to toss at the target of your choice: Target A, anyone can hit; target B, most people can hit; target C, some people can hit; target D, very few people can hit; target E is rarely if ever hit. If you hit A, you will receive $2; B, $4; C, $8; D, $16; and E, $32. You get only one toss. Which one would you choose? McClelland's research suggests that if you have a high need for achievement, you will select C or perhaps D. Those high in nAch are *moderate* risk takers. When faced with a problem or a challenge, persons high in nAch avoid goals that are too easy.

Why do they pass up the easiest and most difficult goals? Easy goals offer no sense of satisfaction, and "winning" a long shot would be due to luck rather than skill. In contrast, persons low in nAch select sure things or impossible goals. Either way, they don't have to take any responsibility for failure.

People high in nAch complete difficult tasks, they earn better grades, and they tend to excel in their occupations. College students high in the nAch attribute success to their own ability and failure to insufficient effort. Thus, high-nAch students are more likely to renew their efforts when they perform poorly. When the going gets tough, high achievers get going.

© Reuters/Corbis

The person with high need for achievement strives to do well in any situation in which evaluation takes place.

The Key to Success

What does it take to achieve extraordinary success? Psychologist Benjamin Bloom (1985) studied the United States' top concert pianists, Olympic swimmers, sculptors, tennis players, mathematicians, and research neurologists. He found that drive and determination, not great natural talent, led to exceptional success.

The first steps toward high achievement began when parents exposed their children to music, swimming, scientific ideas, and so forth, just for fun. At first, many of the children had very ordinary skills. One Olympic swimmer, for instance, remembers repeatedly losing races as a 10-year-old. At some point, however, the children began to actively cultivate their abilities. Before long, parents noticed their child's rapid progress and found an expert instructor or coach. After more successes, the youngsters began "living" for their talent and practised many hours daily. This continued for many years before they reached truly outstanding heights of achievement.

Bloom's conclusion was that talent is nurtured by dedication and hard work (R. C. Beck, 2004). It blossoms when parents actively support a child's special interest and emphasize doing one's best at all times. Studies of child prodigies and eminent adults also show that intensive practice and expert coaching are common ingredients of high achievement. Elite performance in music, sports, chess, the arts, and many other pursuits requires at least 10 years of dedicated practice (Ericsson & Charness, 1994; Ross, 2006).

Need for achievement (nAch) The desire to excel or meet some internalized standard of excellence.

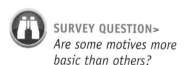

Hierarchy of human needs Abraham Maslow's ordering of needs, based on their presumed strength or potency.

Self-Confidence

You may be able to improve your motivation the way elite athletes do, by increasing your self-confidence (Hanton, Mellalieu, & Hall, 2004). People with self-confidence believe they can successfully carry out an activity or reach a goal. To enhance self-confidence, it is wise to do the following (Druckman & Bjork, 1994):

- Set goals that are specific and challenging, but attainable.
- Visualize the steps you need to take to reach your goal.
- Advance in small steps.
- When you first acquire a skill, your goal should be to make progress in learning.
- Get expert instruction that helps you master the skill.
- Find a skilled model (someone good at the skill) to emulate.
- Get support and encouragement from an observer.
- If you fail, regard it as a sign that you need to try harder, not that you lack ability.

Self-confidence affects motivation by influencing the challenges you will undertake, the effort you will make, and how long you will persist when things don't go well. Self-confidence is worth cultivating.

MOTIVES IN PERSPECTIVE—THE VIEW FROM THE PYRAMID

SURVEY QUESTION>
Are some motives more basic than others?

Are all these motives equally important? Abraham Maslow proposed a **hierarchy of human needs,** in which some needs are more basic or powerful than others. (As you may recall from Chapter 1, Maslow called the full use of personal potential *self-actualization.*) Think about the needs that influence your own behaviour. Which seem strongest? Which do you spend the most time and energy satisfying? Now look at Maslow's hierarchy (Figure 9.14).

Note that biological needs are at the base of the pyramid. Because these needs must be met if we are to survive, they tend to be *prepotent,* or dominant over the higher needs. That's why, when you are really hungry, you can think of little else but food. Maslow believed that higher, more fragile needs are expressed only after we satisfy our biological needs. This is also true of needs for safety and security. Until they are met, we may have little interest in

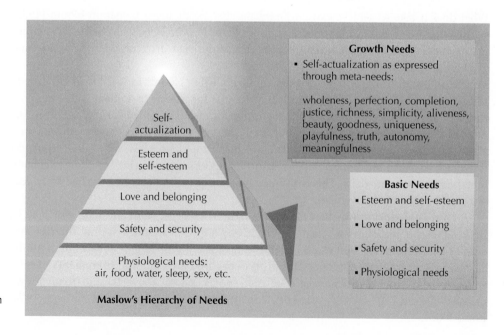

▶▶FIGURE 9.14 Maslow believed that lower needs in the hierarchy are dominant. Basic needs must be satisfied before growth motives are fully expressed. Desires for self-actualization are reflected in various meta-needs (see text).

higher pursuits. For instance, a person who is feeling threatened might have little interest in writing poetry or even talking with friends. For this reason, Maslow described the first four levels of the hierarchy as **basic needs.** Other basic needs are for love and belonging (family, friendship, caring) and esteem and self-esteem (recognition and self-respect).

All the basic needs are *deficiency* motives. That is, they are activated by a *lack* of food, water, security, love, esteem, or other basic needs. At the top of the hierarchy we find **growth needs,** which are expressed as a need for self-actualization. The need for self-actualization is not based on deficiencies. Rather, it is a positive, life-enhancing force for personal growth (Reiss & Havercamp, 2005). Like other humanistic psychologists, Maslow believed that people are basically good. If our basic needs are met, he said, we will tend to move on to actualizing our potentials.

CP Photo/Kevin Frayer

Wheelchair athletes engage in vigorous competition. Maslow considered such behaviour an expression of the need for self-actualization.

How are needs for self-actualization expressed? Maslow also called the less powerful but humanly important actualization motives **meta-needs** (Maslow, 1970). Meta-needs are an expression of tendencies to fully develop your personal potentials. The meta-needs are

1. Wholeness (unity)
2. Perfection (balance and harmony)
3. Completion (ending)
4. Justice (fairness)
5. Richness (complexity)
6. Simplicity (essence)
7. Aliveness (spontaneity)
8. Beauty (rightness of form)
9. Goodness (benevolence)
10. Uniqueness (individuality)
11. Playfulness (ease)
12. Truth (reality)
13. Autonomy (self-sufficiency)
14. Meaningfulness (values)

According to Maslow, we tend to move up through the hierarchy of needs, toward the meta-needs. When the meta-needs are unfulfilled, people fall into a "syndrome of decay" marked by despair, apathy, and alienation. Maslow's point is that mere survival or comfort is usually not enough to make a full and satisfying life. *Are many people motivated by meta-needs?* Maslow estimated that few people are motivated primarily by needs for self-actualization. Most of us are more concerned with esteem, love, or security. When was the last time you met a meta-need?

Intrinsic and Extrinsic Motivation

Some people cook for a living and consider it hard work. Others cook for pleasure and dream of opening a restaurant. For some people, mountain biking, gardening, writing, photography, or jewellery making is fun. For others the same activities are drudgery they must be paid to do. How can the same activity be "work" for one person and "play" for another?

When you do something for enjoyment or to improve your abilities, your motivation is usually *intrinsic*. **Intrinsic motivation** occurs when we act without any obvious external rewards. We simply enjoy an activity or see it as an opportunity to explore, learn, and actualize our potentials. In contrast, **extrinsic motivation** stems from external factors, such as pay, grades, rewards, obligations, and approval. Most of the activities we think of as "work" are extrinsically rewarded (Baard, Deci, & Ryan, 2004; Ryan & Deci, 2000).

Basic needs The first four levels of needs in Maslow's hierarchy; lower needs tend to be more potent than higher needs.

Growth needs In Maslow's hierarchy, the higher-level needs associated with self-actualization.

Meta-needs In Maslow's hierarchy, needs associated with impulses for self-actualization.

Intrinsic motivation Motivation that comes from within, rather than from external rewards; motivation based on personal enjoyment of a task or activity.

Extrinsic motivation Motivation based on obvious external rewards, obligations, or similar factors.

People who are intrinsically motivated feel free to explore creative solutions to problems. *(Left)* Dean Kaman, inventor of the Segway personal transportation device. *(Right)* "Extreme Makeover," an entrant in The Great Arcata to Ferndale World Championship Cross Country Kinetic Sculpture Race.

An interesting example of intrinsic motivation is provided by skateboarders. Recently, Tim Seifert of Memorial University in Newfoundland and Labrador studied a group of teenage boys at a skateboarding park in St. John's (Seifert & Hedderson, 2010). These boys demonstrated persistence—they would try a new trick and fail, and then try again and again until they succeeded. Achieving a new trick was accompanied by expressions of great happiness. But then the typical skateboarder would set himself a new challenge. The skateboarders Seifert observed demonstrated a mastery orientation, focusing on learning the new trick rather than on how they were being perceived by others. Skateboarders in general do not want coaches or organized leagues or rules. They want to operate independently, for their own internal satisfaction. Seifert observed that it is not unusual at the skateboard park to see a 15-year-old boy engrossed for hours, trying a new trick, reflecting on his performance, then trying again, continuing until he masters the trick. Many a parent would no doubt be amazed to think that their 15-year-old child was capable of such concentration and mental toughness!

Turning Play into Work

Don't extrinsic incentives strengthen motivation? Yes, they can, but not always. In fact, *excessive* rewards can decrease intrinsic motivation and spontaneous interest. For instance, in one classic study, children who were lavishly rewarded for drawing with felt-tip pens later showed little interest in playing with the pens again (Greene & Lepper, 1974). Apparently, "play" can be turned into "work" by *requiring* people to do something they would otherwise enjoy. When we are coerced or "bribed" to act, we tend to feel as if we are "faking it." Employees who lack initiative and teenagers who reject school and learning are good examples of those who have such a reaction (Ryan & Deci, 2000).

Creativity

People are more likely to be creative when they are intrinsically motivated. On the job, for instance, salaries and bonuses may increase the amount of work done. However, work *quality* is affected more by intrinsic factors, such as personal interest and freedom of choice (Nakamura & Csikszentmihalyi, 2003). When a person is intrinsically motivated, a certain amount of challenge, surprise, and complexity makes a task rewarding. When extrinsic motivation is stressed, people are less likely to solve tricky problems or come up with innovative ideas (Amabile et al., 2002).

STUDY BREAK Stimulus Motives, Learned Motives, Maslow, and Intrinsic Motivation

Reflect

Does arousal theory seem to explain any of your own behaviour? Think of at least one time when your performance was impaired by arousal that was too low or too high. Now think of some personal examples that illustrate the Yerkes-Dodson law.

Are you high or low in your need for stimulation?

In situations involving risk and skill, do you like to "go for broke"? Or do you prefer sure things? Do you think you are high, medium, or low in nAch?

Which levels of Maslow's hierarchy of needs occupy most of your time and energy?

Name an activity you do that is intrinsically motivated and one that is extrinsically motivated. How do they differ?

Learning Check

1. Exploration, manipulation, and curiosity provide evidence for the existence of _____ drives.

2. Sensation seekers tend to be extroverted, independent, and individuals who value change. T or F?
3. Two key elements of test anxiety that must be controlled are _____ and excessive _____.
4. People high in nAch are attracted to "long shots" and "sure things." T or F?
5. According to Maslow, meta-needs are the most basic and pre-potent sources of human motivation. T or F?
6. Intrinsic motivation is often undermined in situations in which obvious external rewards are applied to a naturally enjoyable activity. T or F?

Critical Thinking

7. Many first-year U.S. college students say that "being well-off financially" is an essential life goal and that "making more money" was a very important factor in their decision to attend college. Which meta-needs are fulfilled by making more money?

Answers

1. stimulus 2. T 3. arousal, worry 4. F 5. F 6. T 7. None of them.

Should extrinsic motivation always be avoided? No, but extrinsic motivation shouldn't be overused, especially with children. In general, (1) if there's no intrinsic interest in an activity to begin with, you have nothing to lose by using extrinsic rewards; (2) if basic skills are lacking, extrinsic rewards may be necessary at first; (3) extrinsic rewards can focus attention on an activity so that real interest will develop; and (4) if extrinsic rewards are used, they should be small and phased out as soon as possible (Buckworth et al., 2007; Cameron & Pierce, 2002).

At work, it is valuable for managers to find out what each employee's interests and career goals are. People are not motivated solely by money. A chance to do challenging, interesting, and intrinsically rewarding work is often important. In many situations it is important to encourage intrinsic motivation, especially when children are learning new skills.

INSIDE AN EMOTION—HOW DO YOU FEEL?

Picture the faces of terrified people fleeing a tornado, and it's easy to see that motivation and emotion are closely related. Emotions shape our relationships and colour our daily activities. **Emotion** is characterized by physiological arousal and changes in facial expressions, gestures, posture, and subjective feelings. As mentioned earlier, the word *emotion* derives from the Latin word meaning "to move."

What "moves" during an emotion? First of all, your body is physically aroused during emotion. Such bodily stirrings are what cause us to say we were "moved" by a play, a funeral, or an act of kindness. Second, we are often motivated, or moved to take action, by emotions such as fear, anger, or joy. Many of the goals we seek make us feel good. Many of the activities we avoid make us feel bad. We feel happy when we succeed and sad when we fail (Kalat & Shiota, 2007).

Emotions are linked to many basic **adaptive behaviours,** such as attacking, fleeing, seeking comfort, helping others, and reproducing. Such behaviours help us survive and adjust to changing conditions (Plutchik, 2003). However, it is also apparent that emotions can have negative effects. Stage fright or "choking" in sports can spoil performances. Hate, anger, contempt, disgust, and fear disrupt behaviour and relationships. But more often, emotions aid survival. As social animals, it would be impossible for humans to live in groups, cooperate in raising children, and defend one another without positive emotional bonds of love, caring, and friendship (Buss, 2000).

<SURVEY QUESTION
What happens during emotion?

Emotion A state characterized by physiological arousal and changes in facial expression, gestures, posture, and subjective feelings.
Adaptive behaviours Actions that aid attempts to survive and adapt to changing conditions.

Physiological changes (in emotion) Alterations in heart rate, blood pressure, perspiration, and other involuntary responses.

Emotional expressions Outward signs that an emotion is occurring.

Emotional feelings The private, subjective experience of having an emotion.

Primary emotions According to Robert Plutchik's theory, the most basic emotions of fear, surprise, sadness, disgust, anger, anticipation, joy, and trust.

Mood A low-intensity, long-lasting emotional state.

A pounding heart, sweating palms, "butterflies" in the stomach, and other bodily reactions are major elements of fear, anger, joy, and other emotions. Typical **physiological changes** take place in heart rate, blood pressure, perspiration, and other bodily stirrings. Most are caused by activity in the sympathetic nervous system and by the hormones *adrenaline* and *noradrenaline,* which the adrenal glands release into the bloodstream.

Emotional expressions, or outward signs of what a person is feeling, are another ingredient of emotion. For example, when you are intensely afraid, your hands tremble, your face contorts, your posture becomes tense and defensive, and your voice changes. In general, these expressions serve to tell others what emotions you are experiencing (Hortman, 2003). **Emotional feelings** (a person's private emotional experience) are a final major element of emotion. This is the part of emotion with which we are usually most familiar.

Primary Emotions

Are some emotions more basic than others? Yes—Robert Plutchik (2003) has identified eight **primary emotions.** These are anticipation, joy, trust, fear, surprise, sadness, disgust, and anger. If the list seems too short, it's because each emotion can vary in *intensity.* When you're angry, for instance, you may feel anything from rage to simple annoyance (see Figure 9.15).

As shown in Figure 9.15, each pair of adjacent primary emotions can be mixed to yield a third, more complex emotion. Other mixtures are also possible. For example, five-year-old Tommy feels both joy and fear as he eats a cookie he took from Mom's cookie jar. The result? Guilt—as you may recall from your own childhood. Likewise, jealousy could be a mixture of love, anger, and fear.

A **mood** is the mildest form of emotion (Figure 9.16). Moods are low-intensity emotional states that can last for many hours, or even days. Moods often affect day-to-day behaviour by preparing us to act in certain ways. For example, when your neighbour Roseanne is in an irritable mood, she may react angrily to almost anything you say. When she is in a happy mood, she can easily laugh off an insult. Happy, positive moods tend to make us more adaptable in several ways. For example, when you are in a good mood, you are likely to make better decisions and you will be more helpful, efficient, creative, and peaceful (Compton, 2005).

Like our motives, our moods are closely tied to circadian rhythms. When your body temperature is at its daily low point, you are more likely to feel "down" emotionally. When body temperature is at its peak, your mood is likely to be positive—even if you missed a night of sleep (Boivin, Czeisler, & Waterhouse, 1997).

Emotion and the Brain

Emotions can be either positive or negative. Ordinarily, we might think that positive and negative emotions are mutually exclusive. But this is not the case. As Tommy's "cookie guilt" implies, you can have positive and negative emotions at the same time. How is that possible? In the brain, positive emotions are processed mainly in the left hemisphere. In contrast, negative emotions are processed in the right hemisphere (Simon-Thomas, Role, & Knight, 2005). The fact that positive and negative emotions are based in different brain areas helps explain why we can feel happy and sad at the same time (Canli et al., 1998). It also explains why your right foot is more ticklish than your left foot! The left hemisphere controls the right side of the body and processes positive emotions (Smith & Cahusac, 2001).

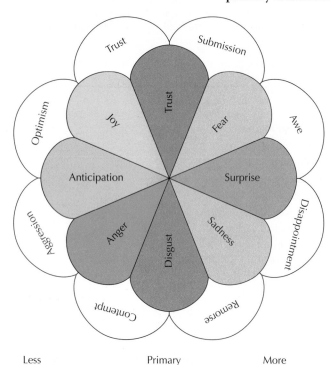

Less intense	Primary emotion	More intense
Interest	Anticipation	Vigilance
Serenity	Joy	Ecstasy
Acceptance	Trust	Admiration
Apprehension	Fear	Terror
Distraction	Surprise	Amazement
Pensiveness	Sadness	Grief
Boredom	Disgust	Loathing
Annoyance	Anger	Rage

▶▶**FIGURE 9.15** Primary and mixed emotions. In Robert Plutchik's model, there are eight primary emotions, as listed in the inner areas. Adjacent emotions may combine to give the emotions listed around the perimeter. Mixtures involving more widely separated emotions are also possible. For example, fear plus anticipation produces anxiety. (Adapted from Plutchik, 2003.)

Thus, most people are more ticklish on their right side. If you really want to tickle someone, be sure to "do it right."

Scientists used to think that all emotions are processed by the cerebral cortex. However, this is not always the case. Imagine this test of willpower: Go to a zoo and place your face close to the glass in front of a rattlesnake display. Suddenly, the rattlesnake strikes at your face. Do you flinch? Even though you know you are safe, Joseph LeDoux predicts that you will recoil from the snake's attack (LeDoux, 2000).

LeDoux and other researchers have found that the amygdala specializes in producing fear (Figure 9.17). (See Chapter 2 for more information.) The amygdala receives sensory information very directly and quickly, bypassing the cortex (Walker & Davis, 2008). As a result, it allows us to respond to potential danger before we really know what's happening. This primitive fear response is not under the control of higher brain centres. The role of the amygdala in emotion may explain why people who suffer from phobias and disabling anxiety often feel afraid without knowing why (Fellous & LeDoux, 2005).

People who suffer damage to the amygdala become "blind" to emotion. An armed robber could hold a gun to a person's head and the person wouldn't feel fear. Such people are also unable to "read" or understand other people's emotional expressions, especially as conveyed by their eyes (Adolphs, 2008). Many lose their ability to relate normally to friends, family, and co-workers (Goleman, 1995).

Later we will attempt to put all the elements of emotion together into a single picture. But first we need to look more closely at bodily arousal and emotional expressions.

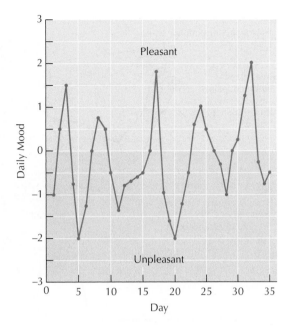

▸▸**FIGURE 9.16** Folklore holds that people who work or attend school on a weekly schedule experience their lowest moods on "Blue Monday." Actually, moods tend to be generally lower for *most* weekdays than they are on weekends. The graph shown here plots the average daily moods of a group of college students over a five-week period. As you can see, many people find that their moods rise and fall on a seven-day cycle. For most students, a low point tends to occur around Monday or Tuesday and a peak on Friday or Saturday. In other words, moods are shaped by weekly schedules. (Adapted from Larsen & Kasimatis, 1990.)

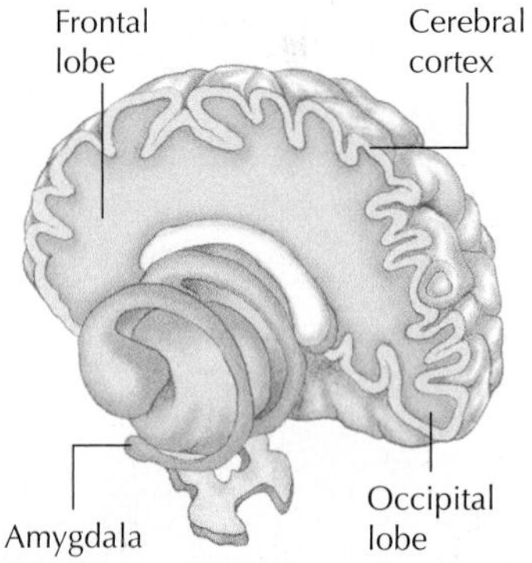

▸▸**FIGURE 9.17** An amygdala can be found buried within the temporal lobes on each side of the brain (see Chapter 2). The amygdala appears to provide "quick and dirty" processing of emotional stimuli that allows us to react involuntarily to danger.

PHYSIOLOGY AND EMOTION—AROUSAL, SUDDEN DEATH, AND LYING

An African Bushman frightened by a lion and a city dweller frightened by a prowler will react in much the same way. Such encounters usually produce muscle tension, a pounding heart, irritability, dryness of the throat and mouth, sweating, butterflies in the stomach, frequent urination, trembling, restlessness, sensitivity to loud noises, and numerous other body changes. These reactions are nearly universal because they are innate. Specifically, they are caused by the **autonomic nervous system (ANS)** (the neural system that connects the brain with internal organs and glands). As you may recall from Chapter 2, activity of the ANS is *automatic*, rather than voluntary (Kalat & Shiota, 2007).

Fight or Flight

The ANS has two divisions, the sympathetic branch and the parasympathetic branch. The two branches are active at all times. Whether you are relaxed or aroused at any moment depends on the relative activity of both branches.

What does the ANS do during emotion? In general, the **sympathetic branch** activates the body for emergency action—for "fighting or fleeing." It does this by arousing some body

<**SURVEY QUESTION**
What physiological changes underlie emotion? Can lie detectors really detect lies?

Autonomic nervous system (ANS)
The system of nerves that connects the brain with the internal organs and glands.
Sympathetic branch The part of the ANS that activates the body at times of stress.

▸▸**FIGURE 9.18** The parasympathetic branch of the ANS calms and quiets the body. The sympathetic branch arouses the body and prepares it for emergency action.

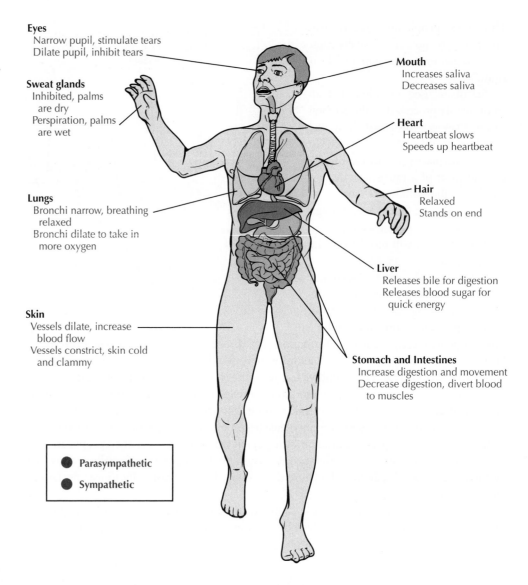

Eyes
Narrow pupil, stimulate tears
Dilate pupil, inhibit tears

Sweat glands
Inhibited, palms
 are dry
Perspiration, palms
 are wet

Lungs
Bronchi narrow, breathing
 relaxed
Bronchi dilate to take in
 more oxygen

Skin
Vessels dilate, increase
 blood flow
Vessels constrict, skin cold
 and clammy

Mouth
Increases saliva
Decreases saliva

Heart
Heartbeat slows
Speeds up heartbeat

Hair
Relaxed
Stands on end

Liver
Releases bile for digestion
Releases blood sugar for
 quick energy

Stomach and Intestines
Increase digestion and movement
Decrease digestion, divert blood
 to muscles

● **Parasympathetic**
● **Sympathetic**

systems and inhibiting others (Figure 9.18). Sugar is released into the bloodstream for quick energy, the heart beats faster to supply blood to the muscles, digestion is temporarily slowed, blood flow in the skin is restricted to reduce bleeding, and so forth. Such reactions improve the chances of surviving an emergency.

The **parasympathetic branch** reverses emotional arousal. This calms and relaxes the body. After a period of high emotion, the heart is slowed, the pupils return to normal size, blood pressure drops, and so forth. In addition to restoring balance, the parasympathetic system helps build up and conserve the body's energy.

The parasympathetic system responds much more slowly than the sympathetic system. That's why a pounding heart, muscle tension, and other signs of arousal don't fade for 20 or 30 minutes after you feel an intense emotion, such as fear. Moreover, after a strong emotional shock, the parasympathetic system may overreact and lower blood pressure too much. This can cause you to become dizzy or faint after seeing something shocking, such as a horrifying accident.

Sudden Death

Strong emotions can kill you in two ways. The first can occur if the sympathetic system becomes too active, resulting in excessive stress. For older persons or those with heart problems, stress-related sympathetic effects may be enough to bring about heart attack and collapse. For example, five times as many people as usual died of heart attacks on the day of a major 1994 earthquake in Los Angeles (Leor, Poole, & Kloner, 1996).

Parasympathetic branch The part of the autonomic system that quiets the body and conserves energy.

Second, the **parasympathetic rebound** to sympathetic arousal can also be severe enough to cause death. In times of war, for instance, combat can be so savage that some soldiers literally die of fear (Moritz & Zamchech, 1946). Apparently, such deaths occur because the parasympathetic nervous system slows the heart to a stop.

Lie Detectors

You undoubtedly know that criminals are not always truthful. But what you may not know is that up to 25 percent of all wrongful convictions include false confessions as evidence (Kassin, 2005). If you can't count on someone's word, what can you trust? The most popular method for detecting falsehoods measures the bodily changes that accompany emotion. However, the accuracy of lie detector tests is doubtful, and they can be a serious invasion of privacy (Lykken, 2001; National Academy of Sciences, 2002).

What is a lie detector? Do lie detectors really detect lies? The lie detector is more accurately called a **polygraph**, a word that means "many writings" (Figure 9.19). Although popularly known as a lie detector because the police use it for that purpose, in reality the polygraph is not a lie detector at all (Bunn, 2007). A suspect is questioned while hooked up to a polygraph, which typically records changes in heart rate, blood pressure, breathing, and the galvanic skin response (GSR). The GSR is recorded from the hand by electrodes that measure skin conductance, or, more simply, sweating. Because the device records only general emotional arousal, it can't tell the difference between lying and fear, anxiety and excitement (Iacono, 2008).

Wouldn't a person be nervous just from being questioned? Yes, but to minimize this problem, skilled polygraph examiners use the *comparison questions test* (Honts & Alloway, 2007). A series of neutral questions is asked interspersed with relevant items. For example, the polygraph operator may ask some neutral (irrelevant, non-emotional) questions, such as, "Is your name [person's name]?" "Did you eat lunch today?" and so forth, along with relevant items like "Did you murder Hensley?" or "Was it $52 000 you took from that bank?" An innocent person may respond emotionally to the whole procedure, but only a guilty person is supposed to respond more to relevant questions than to neutral ones (Iacono, 2008).

Even when questioning is done properly, lie detection may be inaccurate (Grubin & Madsen, 2005). Psychologist David Lykken (1998, 2001) has documented many cases in which innocent people were convicted on the basis of polygraph evidence.

Proponents of lie detection claim it is 95 percent accurate. But in one study, accuracy was dramatically lowered when people thought about past emotional experiences as they answered irrelevant questions (Ben-Shakhar & Dolev, 1996). Similarly, the polygraph may be thrown off by self-inflicted pain, by tranquilizing drugs, or by people who can lie without anxiety (Waid & Orne, 1982). Worst of all, the test is much more likely to label an innocent person guilty, rather than a guilty person innocent. In studies involving real crimes, an average of one innocent person in five were rated as guilty by the lie detector (Lykken, 2001).

Parasympathetic rebound Excess activity in the parasympathetic nervous system following a period of intense emotion.

Polygraph A device for recording heart rate, blood pressure, respiration, and galvanic skin response; commonly called a lie detector.

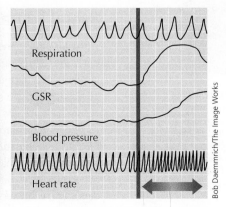

➤➤**FIGURE 9.19** *(Left)* A typical polygraph measures heart rate, blood pressure, respiration, and galvanic skin response. Pens mounted on the top of the machine record bodily responses on a moving strip of paper. *(Right)* Changes in the area marked by the arrow indicate emotional arousal. If such responses appear when a person answers a question, he or she may be lying, but arousal may have other causes.

Bob Daemmrich/The Image Works

STUDY BREAK Emotion and Physiological Arousal

Reflect

How did your most emotional moment of the past week affect your behaviour, expressions, feelings, and bodily state? Could you detect both sympathetic and parasympathetic effects?

Make a list of the emotions you consider to be most basic. To what extent do they agree with Plutchik's list?

What did you think about lie detectors before reading this chapter? What do you think now?

Learning Check

1. Many of the physiological changes associated with emotion are caused by secretion of the hormone
   a. atropine
   b. adrenaline
   c. attributine
   d. amoduline
2. Emotional _____ often serve to communicate a person's emotional state to others.

3. Awe, remorse, and disappointment are among the primary emotions listed by Robert Plutchik. T or F?
4. Emotional arousal is closely related to activity of the _____ nervous system.
5. The sympathetic system prepares the body for "fight or flight" by activating the parasympathetic system. T or F?
6. The parasympathetic system inhibits digestion and raises blood pressure and heart rate. T or F?
7. What body changes are measured by a polygraph? _____ _____ _____ _____

Critical Thinking

8. Can you explain why people "cursed" by shamans or "witch doctors" sometimes actually die?

Answers

1. b 2. expressions 3. F 4. autonomic 5. F 6. F 7. heart rate, blood pressure, breathing rate, galvanic skin response 8. In cultures where there is deep belief in magic or voodoo, a person who thinks that she or he has been cursed may become uncontrollably emotional. After several days of intense terror, a parasympathetic rebound is likely. If the rebound is severe enough, it can lead to physical collapse and death.

On the basis of such evidence, the National Academy of Sciences (2002) has concluded that polygraph tests should not be used to screen employees. Despite the lie detector's flaws, you may be tested for employment or for other reasons. Should this occur, the best advice is to remain calm; then actively challenge the results if the machine wrongly questions your honesty.

SURVEY QUESTION>
How accurately are emotions expressed by the face and body language?

▶▶**FIGURE 9.20** Is anger expressed the same way in different cultures? Masks that are meant to be frightening or threatening are strikingly similar around the world. Most have an open, downward-curved mouth and diagonal or triangular eyes, eyebrows, nose, cheeks, and chin. (Keep this list in mind next Halloween.) Obviously, the pictured mask is not meant to be warm and cuddly. Your ability to "read" its emotional message suggests that basic emotional expressions have universal biological roots (Adolphs, 2008).

Photodisc/Getty Images

EXPRESSING EMOTIONS—MAKING FACES AND TALKING BODIES

Next to our own feelings, the expressions of others are the most familiar part of emotion. Are emotional expressions a carryover from human evolution? Charles Darwin thought so. Darwin (1872) observed that angry tigers, monkeys, dogs, and humans all bare their teeth in the same way. Psychologists believe that emotional expressions evolved to communicate our feelings to others, which aids survival. Such messages give valuable hints about what other people are likely to do next (Kalat & Shiota, 2007).

Facial Expressions

Are emotional expressions the same for all people? Basic expressions appear to be fairly universal (Figure 9.20). Facial expressions of fear, anger, disgust, sadness, surprise, and happiness (enjoyment) are recognized around the world (Smith et al., 2005). Expressions of contempt and interest may also be universal, but researchers are less certain of this (Ekman, 1993). Notice that this list covers most of the primary emotions described earlier. Children who are born blind have little opportunity to learn emotional expressions from others. Even so, they also display basic expressions in the same way sighted people do (Galati, Scherer, & Ricci-Bitti, 1997). It's also nice to note that a smile is the most universal and easily recognized facial expression of emotion.

There are more than a few facial expressions, aren't there? Yes. Your face can produce some 20 000 different expressions, which makes it the most expressive part of your body. Most of these are *facial blends* (a mixture of two or more basic expressions). Imagine, for example, that you just received an F on a test you strongly felt was unfair. Quite likely, your eyes, eyebrows, and forehead would reveal anger, and your mouth would be turned downward in a sad frown.

Most of us believe we can fairly accurately tell what others are feeling by observing their facial expressions. If thousands of facial blends occur, how do we make such judgments? The answer is that facial expressions can be boiled down to three basic dimensions: *pleasantness–unpleasantness, attention–rejection,* and *activation* (or arousal) (Schlosberg, 1954). By smiling when you give a friend a hard time, you add an emotional message of acceptance to the verbal insult, which changes its meaning. As they say in movie Westerns, it makes a big difference to "smile when you say that, pardner."

Cultural Differences in Expressing Emotion

Some facial expressions are shaped by learning and may be found only in specific cultures. Among the Chinese, for example, sticking out the tongue is a gesture of surprise, not of disrespect or teasing. If a person comes from another culture, it is wise for each of you to remember that you may easily misunderstand the other person's expressions. At such times, knowing the social *context* in which an expression occurs helps clarify its meaning (Carroll & Russell, 1996; Kalat & Shiota, 2007).

How many times have you expressed anger this week? If it was more than once, you're not unusual. Anger is commonly expressed in Western cultures. Very likely this is because our culture emphasizes personal independence and a free expression of individual rights and needs. In North America, anger is widely viewed as a "natural" reaction to feeling that you have been treated unfairly.

In contrast, many Asian cultures place a high value on group harmony. In Asia, expressing anger in public is less common, and anger is regarded as less "natural." The reason for this is that anger tends to separate people. Thus, while feeling anger may be common around the world, culture influences the probability that anger will be expressed. Culture also influences positive emotions. In North America, we tend to have positive feelings such as pride and happiness, which reflect our role as *individuals.* In Japan, positive feelings are more often linked with membership in groups (friendly feelings, closeness to others, and respect) (Kitayama, Markus, & Kurokawa, 2000; Markus et al., 2006).

It is common to think of emotion as an individual event. However, as you can see, emotion is shaped by cultural ideas, values, and practices (Mesquita & Markus, 2004).

Gender and Emotional Expression

Women have a reputation for being more emotional than men. Are they? Compared with women, men in Western cultures are less likely to express their emotions. According to psychologist Ronald Levant and colleagues (2006), although male babies start out life more emotionally expressive than female babies, little boys soon learn to toughen up, beginning in early childhood. As a result, men have learned to curtail the expression of most of their emotions.

Body Language

If a friend walked up to you and said, "Hey, ugly, what are you doing?" would you be offended? Probably not, because such remarks are usually delivered with a big grin. The facial and bodily gestures of emotion speak a language all their own and add to what a person says.

The expression of emotion is strongly influenced by learning. As you have no doubt observed, women cry more often, longer, and more intensely than men do. Men begin learning early in childhood to suppress crying—possibly to the detriment of their emotional health (Williams & Morris, 1996). Many men are especially unwilling to engage in public displays of emotion, in contrast to these women, who are grieving for the victims of a 2005 school siege in Breslan, Russia, which left hundreds of children dead.

Amy Etra/PhotoEdit

Emotions are often unconsciously revealed by gestures and body positioning.

Kinesics (kih-NEEZ-iks) is the study of communication through body movement, posture, gestures, and facial expressions (Harrigan, 2006). Informally, we call such communication body language. To see a masterful use of body language, turn off the sound on a television and watch a popular entertainer or politician at work.

What kinds of messages are sent with body language? The posture you adopt sends messages not just to others but also to yourself. In fact, different poses have an effect on your endocrine system—particularly on testosterone and cortisol levels. Testosterone rises as a result of dominance behaviours, and in turn cues those behaviours. Among athletes, testosterone rises after a win and falls after a defeat. Cortisol is a stress hormone. It is lower in more powerful individuals and higher in people who feel powerless. Dana Carney and her colleagues recently assessed these two hormones in men and women who adopted either high-power or low-power poses (Carney, Cuddy, & Yap, 2010). High-power poses involve taking up space and keeping the limbs open. Low-power poses involve the reverse: bringing the limbs in and taking up less space. Men and women who adopted high-power poses showed elevated levels of testosterone and decreased levels of cortisol. Those who adopted low-power poses showed the reverse. In addition, the two groups differed both in their reported feelings of being powerful and "in charge" and in their willingness to accept a gamble. The lesson is, if you want to feel powerful, take up some space—stand or sit in a power pose.

THEORIES OF EMOTION—SEVERAL WAYS TO FEAR A BEAR

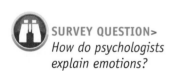

SURVEY QUESTION>
How do psychologists explain emotions?

Is it possible to explain what takes place during emotion? Theories of emotion offer different answers to these questions. Let's explore some prominent views. Each appears to contain part of the truth, so we will try to put them all together in the end.

The James-Lange Theory

You're hiking in the woods when a bear steps onto the trail. What will happen next? Common sense tells us that we will then feel fear, become aroused, and run (and sweat and yell). But is this the true order of events? In the 1880s, William James and Carl Lange (LON-geh) proposed that common sense had it backwards. According to the **James-Lange theory,** bodily arousal (such as increased heart rate) does not *follow* a feeling such as fear. Instead, they argued, *emotional feelings follow bodily arousal*. Thus, we see a bear, run, are aroused, and *then* feel fear as we become aware of our bodily reactions (Figure 9.21).

To support his ideas, James pointed out that we often do not experience an emotion until after reacting. For example, imagine that you are driving. Suddenly a car pulls out in front of you. You swerve and skid to an abrupt halt. Only then do you notice your pounding heart, rapid breathing, and tense muscles—and recognize your fear.

The Cannon-Bard Theory

Walter Cannon (1932) and Phillip Bard disagreed with the James-Lange theory. According to the **Cannon-Bard theory,** emotional feelings and bodily arousal *occur at the same time*. Cannon and Bard believed that seeing a bear activates the thalamus in the brain. The

Kinesics The study of the meaning of body movements, posture, hand gestures, and facial expressions; commonly called body language.

James-Lange theory Emotional feelings follow bodily arousal and come from awareness of such arousal.

Cannon-Bard theory Activity in the thalamus causes emotional feelings and bodily arousal to occur simultaneously.

thalamus, in turn, alerts the cortex and the hypothalamus for action. The cortex produces our emotional feelings and emotional behaviour. The hypothalamus triggers a chain of events that arouses the body. Thus, if you see a dangerous-looking bear, brain activity will simultaneously produce bodily arousal, running, and a feeling of fear (Figure 9.21).

Schachter's Cognitive Theory of Emotion

The previous theories are concerned mostly with our physical responses. Stanley Schachter realized that cognitive (mental) factors also enter into emotion. According to **Schachter's cognitive theory,** emotion occurs when we apply a particular *label* to general physiological *arousal.* We likely choose the appropriate label through a process of **attribution,** by deciding which source is leading to the arousal (Valins, 1967).

Suppose, for instance, that someone sneaks up behind you on a dark street and says, "Boo!" Your body is now aroused (pounding heart, sweating palms, and so on). If you attribute your arousal to a total stranger, you might label your arousal as fear; if you attribute your arousal to a close friend, you may experience surprise or delight. The label (such as anger, fear, or happiness) you apply to bodily arousal is influenced by your past experiences, the situation, and the reactions of others (Figure 9.21).

Support for the cognitive theory of emotion comes from an experiment in which people watched a slapstick movie (Schachter & Wheeler, 1962). Before viewing the movie, everyone got an injection but no one was told what he or she was injected with. One-third of the people received an arousing injection of adrenaline, one-third got a placebo (salt water) injection, and one-third received a tranquilizer. People who received the adrenaline rated the movie funniest and laughed the most while watching it. In contrast, those given the tranquilizer were least amused. The placebo group fell in between.

According to the cognitive theory of emotion, individuals who received adrenaline had a stirred-up body, but no explanation for what they were feeling. By attributing their arousal to the movie, they became happy and amused. This and similar experiments make it clear that emotion is much more than just an agitated body. Perception, experience, attitudes, judgment, and many other mental factors also affect the emotions we feel. Schachter's theory would predict, then, that if you met a bear, you would be aroused. If the bear seemed unfriendly, you would interpret your arousal as fear, and if the bear offered to shake your "paw," you would be happy, amazed, and relieved!

Misattribution

We now move from slapstick movies and fear of bear bodies to an appreciation of bare bodies. There is no guarantee that we always make the correct attributions about our emotions. For example, Valins (1966) showed male college students a series of photographs of nude females. While watching the photographs, each student heard an amplified heartbeat that he believed was his own. In reality, students were listening to a recorded heartbeat carefully designed to beat *louder* and *stronger* when some (but not all) of the slides were shown.

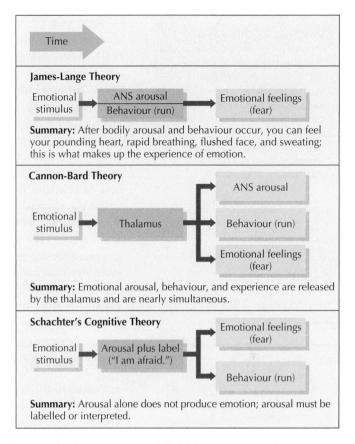

Summary: After bodily arousal and behaviour occur, you can feel your pounding heart, rapid breathing, flushed face, and sweating; this is what makes up the experience of emotion.

Summary: Emotional arousal, behaviour, and experience are released by the thalamus and are nearly simultaneous.

Summary: Arousal alone does not produce emotion; arousal must be labelled or interpreted.

▸▸**FIGURE 9.21** Theories of emotion.

Which theory of emotion best describes the reactions of these people? Given the complexity of emotion, each theory appears to possess an element of truth.

After watching the slides, each student was asked to say which was most attractive. Students who heard the false heartbeat consistently rated slides paired with a "pounding heart" as the most attractive. In other words, when a student saw a slide and heard his heart beat louder, he attributed his "emotion" to the slide. His attribution seems to have been, "Now that one I like!" His next reaction, perhaps, was "But why?" Later research suggests that subjects persuaded themselves that the slide really was more attractive in order to explain their apparent arousal (Truax, 1983).

That seems somewhat artificial. Does it really make any difference what arousal is attributed to? Yes. Attribution theory predicts that you are most likely to "love" someone who gets you stirred up emotionally (Foster et al., 1998). This is true even when fear, anger, frustration, or rejection is part of the formula. In a well-known study by University of British Columbia psychologists Don Dutton and Arthur Aron, a female psychologist interviewed men in a park in Vancouver. Some were on a swaying suspension bridge 230 feet (70 metres) above a river. The rest were on a solid wooden bridge just 10 feet (3 metres) above the ground. After the interview, the psychologist gave each man her telephone number, so he could "find out about the results" of the study. Men interviewed on the suspension bridge were much more likely to give the "lady from the park" a call (Dutton & Aron, 1974). Apparently, these men experienced heightened arousal, which they interpreted as attraction to the experimenter—a clear case of love at first fright!

Emotional Appraisal

According to Richard Lazarus (1991a, 1991b), the role of cognition in experiencing emotions is not restricted to making attributions about arousal *after* it has occurred. Rather, emotions you experience are greatly influenced by how you think about an event *in the first place*. **Emotional appraisal** refers to evaluating the personal meaning of a stimulus: Is it good/bad, threatening/supportive, relevant/irrelevant, and so on. Some examples of emotional appraisals and the emotions they give rise to can be found in Table 9.2.

The Facial Feedback Hypothesis

Schachter and Lazarus added thinking and interpretation (cognition) to our view of emotion, but the picture still seems incomplete. What about expressions? How do they influence emotion? As Charles Darwin observed, the face is very central to emotion—perhaps it is more than just an "emotional billboard."

■ Table 9.2   Appraisals and Corresponding Emotions

Appraisal	Emotion
You have been slighted or demeaned.	Anger
You feel threatened.	Anxiety
You have experienced a loss.	Sadness
You have broken a moral rule.	Guilt
You have not lived up to your ideals.	Shame
You desire something another has.	Envy
You are near something repulsive.	Disgust
You fear the worst but yearn for better.	Hope
You are moving toward a desired goal.	Happiness
You are linked with a valued object or accomplishment.	Pride
You have been treated well by another.	Gratitude
You desire affection from another person.	Love
You are moved by someone's suffering.	Compassion

Source: Paraphrased from Lazarus, 1991a.

Dennis Coon

▸▸**FIGURE 9.22** Facial feedback and emotion. Participants in Ekman's study formed facial expressions like those normally observed during emotion. When they did this, emotion-like changes took place in their bodily activity. (After Ekman, Levenson, & Friesen, 1983.)

Psychologist Carrol Izard (1977, 1990) was among the first to suggest that the face does, indeed, affect emotion. According to Izard, emotions cause innately programmed changes in facial expression. Sensations from the face then provide cues to the brain that help us determine what emotion we are feeling. This idea is known as the **facial feedback hypothesis** (Soussignan, 2002). Stated another way, it says that having facial expressions and becoming aware of them influences our private emotional experience. Exercise, for instance, arouses the body, but we don't experience this arousal as emotion because it does not trigger emotional expressions.

Psychologist Paul Ekman takes this idea one step further. He believes that "making faces" can actually cause emotion (Ekman, 1993). In one study, participants were guided as they arranged their faces, muscle by muscle, into expressions of surprise, disgust, sadness, anger, fear, and happiness (Figure 9.22). At the same time, each person's bodily reactions were monitored.

Contrary to what you might expect, "making faces" can affect the autonomic nervous system, as shown by changes in heart rate and skin temperature. In addition, each facial expression produces a different pattern of activity. An angry face, for instance, raises heart rate and skin temperature, whereas disgust lowers both (Ekman et al., 1983). Other studies have confirmed that posed expressions alter emotions and bodily activity (Duclos & Laird, 2001; Soussignan, 2002).

In a fascinating experiment on facial feedback, people rated how funny they thought cartoons were while holding a pen crosswise in their mouths. Those who held the pen in their teeth thought the cartoons were funnier than did people who held the pen in their lips. Can you guess why? The answer is that if you hold a pen with your teeth, you are forced to form a smile. Holding it with the lips makes a frown. As predicted by the facial feedback hypothesis, emotional experiences were influenced by the facial expressions that people made (Strack, Martin, & Stepper, 1988).

It appears, then, that not only do emotions influence expressions, but expressions influence emotions, as shown here (Duclos & Laird, 2001):

Contracted Facial Muscles	Felt Emotion
Forehead	Surprise
Brow	Anger
Mouth (down)	Sadness
Mouth (smile)	Joy

This could explain an interesting effect you have probably observed. When you are feeling "down," forcing yourself to smile will sometimes be followed by an actual improvement in your mood (Kleinke, Peterson, & Rutledge, 1998).

Facial feedback hypothesis
Sensations from facial expressions help define what emotion a person feels.

Suppressing Emotion—Don't Turn the Music Off

According to popular media, we are supposed to be happy all the time (Hecht, 2007). Yet real emotional life has its ups and downs. Often we try to appear less emotional than we really are, especially when we are feeling negative emotions. Have you ever been angry with a friend in public? Embarrassed by someone's behaviour at a party? Disgusted by someone's table manners? In such circumstances, people are quite good at suppressing outward signs of emotion.

However, restraining emotion can actually increase activity in the sympathetic nervous system. In other words, hiding emotion requires a lot of effort. Suppressing emotions can also impair thinking and memory, as you devote energy to self-control. Thus,

while suppressing emotion allows us to appear calm and collected on the outside, this cool appearance comes at a high cost (Richards & Gross, 2000).

People who express their emotions generally experience better emotional and physical health than people who suppress their emotions (Lumley, 2004; Pennebaker, 2004). Paying attention to our negative emotions can also lead us to think more clearly about the positive *and* the negative. The end result is better decision making, which can increase our overall happiness in the long run (Norem, 2002). Usually, it's better to manage emotions than it is to suppress them. You will find some suggestions for managing emotions in the upcoming Psychology in Action section.

If smiling can improve a person's mood, is it a good idea to inhibit negative emotions? For an answer, see Clinical File: "Suppressing Emotion—Don't Turn the Music Off."

A Contemporary Model of Emotion

To summarize, James and Lange were right that feedback from arousal and behaviour adds to our emotional experiences. Cannon and Bard were right about the timing of events. Schachter showed us that cognition is important. In fact, psychologists are increasingly aware that how you *appraise* a situation greatly affects your emotions (Strongman, 2003). Richard Lazarus stressed the importance of emotional appraisal. Carrol Izard focused on facial expressions. Let's put these ideas together in a single model of emotion (Figure 9.23).

Imagine that a large snarling dog lunges at you with its teeth bared. A modern view of your emotional reactions goes something like this: An *emotionally toned stimulus* (the dog) is *appraised* (judged) as a threat or other cause for emotion. (You think to yourself, "Uh oh, big trouble!") Your appraisal gives rise to *ANS arousal* (your heart pounds and your body becomes stirred up) and *cognitive labelling*. At the same time, your appraisal leads to *adaptive behaviour* (you run from the dog). The appraisal also releases *innate emotional expressions* (your face twists into a mask of fear). It also causes a change in consciousness that you recognize as the subjective experience of fear. (The intensity of this *emotional feeling* is directly related to the amount of ANS arousal taking place in your body.)

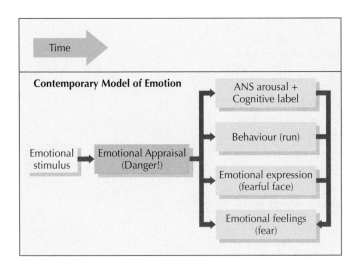

▸▸FIGURE 9.23 A contemporary model of emotion. Appraisal gives rise to arousal and cognitive labelling, behaviour, facial/postural expressions, and emotional feelings. Arousal, attribution, behaviour, and expressions add to emotional feelings. Emotional feelings influence appraisal, which further affects arousal, behaviour, expressions, and feelings.

Each element of emotion—ANS arousal, labelling, adaptive behaviour, subjective experience, and your emotional expressions—may further alter your emotional appraisal of the situation, as well as your thoughts, judgments, and perceptions. Thus, according to the facial feedback hypothesis, your facial expression may further influence your emotion. Such changes affect each of the other reactions, which then alter your appraisal and interpretation of events. Thus, emotion may blossom, change course, or diminish as it proceeds. Note too that the original emotional stimulus can be external, like the attacking dog, or internal, such

STUDY BREAK   Emotional Expression and Theories of Emotion

Reflect

Write a list of emotions that you think you can accurately detect from facial expressions. Does your list match Paul Ekman's? Would you be more confident in rating pleasantness–unpleasantness, attention–rejection, and activation? Why?

Try frowning or smiling for five minutes. Did facial feedback have any effect on your mood?

Cover the left column of Table 9.2. Read each emotional label in the right column. What appraisal do you think would lead to the listed emotion?

Learning Check

1. Charles Darwin held that emotional expressions aid survival for animals. T or F?
2. A formal term for the study of "body language" is _____.
3. Which three dimensions of emotion are communicated by facial expressions?
   a. pleasantness–unpleasantness
   b. complexity
   c. attention–rejection
   d. anger
   e. curiosity–disinterest
   f. activation

4. According to the James-Lange theory, emotional experience precedes physical arousal and emotional behaviour. (We see a bear, are frightened, and run.) T or F?
5. The Cannon-Bard theory of emotion says that bodily arousal and emotional experience occur _____.
6. According to Schachter's cognitive theory, bodily arousal must be labelled or interpreted for an emotional experience to occur. T or F?
7. As you try to wiggle your ears, you keep pulling the corners of your mouth back into a smile. Each time you do, you find yourself giggling. Which of the following provides the best explanation for this reaction?
   a. attribution   b. the Cannon-Bard theory
   c. appraisal   d. facial feedback

Critical Thinking

8. People with high spinal injuries may feel almost no signs of physiological arousal from their bodies. Nevertheless, they still feel emotion, which can be intense at times. What theory of emotion does this observation contradict?

Answers

1. T 2. kinesics 3. a, c, f 4. F 5. simultaneously 6. T 7. d 8. The James-Lange theory and Schachter's cognitive theory. The facial feedback hypothesis also helps explain the observation.

as a memory of being chased by a dog, rejected by a lover, or praised by a friend. That's why mere thoughts and memories can make us fearful, sad, or happy (Strongman, 2003).

A Look Ahead

In the Psychology in Action section of this chapter, we will look further at the impact of emotional appraisals through an examination of *emotional intelligence*. Before we continue, you might want to appraise your learning with the exercises that follow.

Psychology in Action

EMOTIONAL INTELLIGENCE—THE FINE ART OF SELF-CONTROL

The Greek philosopher Aristotle had a recipe for handling relationships smoothly: "Be angry with the right person, to the right degree, at the right time, for the right purpose, and in the right way." Psychologists Peter Salovey and John Mayer call such self-control **emotional intelligence,** the ability to perceive, use, understand, and manage emotions (Salovey & Mayer, 1997). In general, being emotionally intelligent means accepting that emotions are an essential part of who we are and how we survive.

People who excel in life tend to be emotionally intelligent (Mehrabian, 2000). If our emotions are the music of life, then emotionally intelligent people are good musicians. They do not stifle their emotions or overindulge in them. Instead they compose them into sustaining life rhythms that mesh well with other people. They are more *agreeable* than people with low emotional skills (Haas et al., 2007).

<SURVEY QUESTION
What does it mean to have emotional intelligence?

Emotional intelligence Emotional competence, including empathy, self-control, self-awareness, and other skills.

Peter Beavis/Getty Images

Indeed, the costs of poor emotional skills can be high. They range from problems in marriage and parenting to poor physical health. A recent study of how emotional intelligence is related to smoking used data from the Canadian National Longitudinal Survey of Children and Youth (NLSCY) (Hill & Maggi, 2011). This study found that the stress management aspect of emotional intelligence—basically, the ability to control your impatience, anger, and impulses—was an important predictor of smoking. People who score higher on stress management are less likely to smoke daily or occasionally.

A lack of emotional intelligence can ruin careers and sabotage achievement. Perhaps the greatest toll falls on children and teenagers. For them, having poor emotional skills can contribute to depression, eating disorders, unwanted pregnancy, aggression, violent crime, and poor academic performance (Parker, 2005). Thus, in many life circumstances, emotional intelligence is as important as IQ (Dulewicz & Higgs, 2000).

Are there specific skills that make up emotional intelligence? Many elements contribute to emotional intelligence (Larsen & Prizmic, 2004; Mayer et al., 2001). A description of some of the most important skills follows:

Perceiving Emotions The foundation of emotional intelligence is the ability to perceive emotions in yourself and others. Emotionally intelligent people are tuned in to their own feelings (Taylor & Taylor-Allan, 2007). They are able to recognize quickly if they are angry, envious, feeling guilty, or depressed. This is valuable because many people have disruptive emotions without being able to pinpoint why they are uncomfortable. At the same time, emotionally intelligent people have *empathy.* They accurately perceive emotions in others and sense what others are feeling. They are good at "reading" facial expressions, tone of voice, and other signs of emotion.

Using Emotions People who are emotionally intelligent use their feelings to enhance thinking and decision making. For example, if you can remember how you reacted emotionally in the past, it can help you react better to new situations. You can also use emotions to promote personal growth and improve relationships with others. For instance, you may have noticed that helping someone else makes you feel better, too. Likewise, when good fortune comes their way, people who are emotionally smart share the news with others. Almost always, doing so strengthens relationships and increases emotional well-being (Gable et al., 2004).

Understanding Emotions Emotions contain useful information. For instance, anger is a cue that something is wrong, anxiety indicates uncertainty, embarrassment communicates shame, depression means we feel helpless, and enthusiasm tells us we're excited. People who are emotionally intelligent know what causes various emotions, what they mean, and how they affect behaviour.

Managing Emotions Emotional intelligence involves an ability to manage your own emotions and those of others. For example, you know how to calm down when you are angry and you also know how to calm others. As Aristotle noted so long ago, people who are emotionally intelligent can amplify or restrain emotions, depending on the situation (Bonanno et al., 2004).

Positive Psychology and Your Emotions

It's obvious that joy, interest, contentment, love, and similar emotions are pleasant and rewarding. There is a natural tendency to enjoy positive emotions while treating negative emotions as unwelcome misery. Make no mistake, though. Negative emotions can also be valuable and constructive. For example, persistent distress may motivate a person to seek help, mend a relationship, or find a new direction in life (Plutchik, 2003). Negative emotions are associated with actions that probably helped our ancestors save their skins: escaping, attacking, expelling poison, and the like. As useful as these reactions may be, they tend to narrow our focus of attention and limit our ideas about possible actions.

In contrast, positive emotions tend to broaden our focus (Fredrickson & Branigan, 2005). This opens up new possibilities and builds up our personal resources. For instance, emotions such as joy, interest, and contentment create an urge to play, to be creative, to explore, to savour life, to seek new experiences, to integrate, and to grow.

In short, positive emotions are not just a pleasant side effect of happy circumstances. They also encourage personal growth and social connection. Happiness can be cultivated by using the strengths we already possess—including kindness, originality, humour, optimism, and generosity. Such strengths are natural buffers against misfortune, and they can help people live more positive, genuinely happy lives (Seligman, 2002). A capacity for having positive emotions is a basic human strength, and cultivating good feelings is a part of emotional intelligence (Fredrickson, 2003).

Becoming Emotionally Smart

How would a person learn the skills that make up emotional intelligence? Emotional skills can be learned. Accepting that emotions are valuable is an important first step. There are many valuable lessons to learn from paying close attention to your emotions and the emotions of others. It's a good bet that many of the people you admire the most are not just smart, but also emotionally smart. They are people who know how to offer a toast at a wedding, tell a joke at a roast, comfort the bereaved at a funeral, add to the fun at a party, or calm a frightened child. These are skills worth cultivating.

 STUDY BREAK   **Emotional Intelligence**

Reflect

Think of a person you know who is smart, but low in emotional intelligence. Think of another person who is smart cognitively *and* emotionally. How does the second person differ from the first? Which person do you think would make a better parent, friend, supervisor, roommate, or teacher?

Learning Check

1. People who rate high in emotional intelligence tend to be highly aware of their own feelings and unaware of emotions experienced by others. T or F?
2. Using the information imparted by emotional reactions can enhance thinking and decision making. T or F?
3. Positive emotions may be pleasant, but they tend to narrow our focus of attention and limit the range of possible actions we are likely to consider. T or F?
4. Which of the following is *not* an element of emotional intelligence?
   a. empathy
   b. self-control
   c. misattribution
   d. self-awareness

Critical Thinking

5. You are angry because a friend borrowed money from you and hasn't repaid it. What would be an emotionally intelligent response to this situation?

Answers

1. F 2. T 3. F 4. c 5. There's no single right answer. Rather than being angry, it might be better to reflect on whether friendship or money is more important in life. If you appreciate your friend's virtues, accept that no one is perfect, and reappraise the loan as a gift, you could save a valued relationship and reduce your anger at the same time. Alternatively, if you become aware that your friend persistently manipulates other people with emotional appeals for support, it may be worth reappraising your friendship.

CHAPTER IN REVIEW

Major Points

- Motives and goals greatly influence what we do and how we expend our energies.

- The brain monitors various internal signals to control basic motives, such as hunger and thirst.

- Motivated behaviour is also influenced by learned habits, external cues, and cultural values.

- Many activities are related to needs for stimulation and our efforts to maintain desired levels of arousal.

- Emotions can be disruptive, but overall they help us to adapt and survive.

- Emotional intelligence involves managing emotions, not suppressing them.

Summary

What is motivation? Are there different types of motives?

- Motives initiate, sustain, direct, and terminate activities. Motivation typically involves the following sequence: need, drive, goal, and goal attainment (need reduction).

- Behaviour can be activated either by needs (push) or by goals (pull).

- The attractiveness of a goal and its ability to initiate action are related to its incentive value.

- Three principal types of motives are biological motives, stimulus motives, and learned motives.

- Most primary motives operate to maintain homeostasis.

- Circadian rhythms are closely tied to sleep, activity, and energy cycles. Time zone travel and shift work can seriously disrupt motivation, sleep, and bodily rhythms.

What causes hunger? Overeating? Eating disorders?

- Hunger is influenced by a complex interplay between fullness of the stomach, blood sugar levels, metabolism in the liver, and fat stores in the body.

- The most direct control of eating is effected by the hypothalamus, which has areas that act like feeding and satiety systems. The hypothalamus is sensitive to both neural and chemical messages, which affect eating.

- Other factors influencing hunger are the body's set point, external eating cues, the attractiveness and variety of diet, emotions, learned taste preferences and aversions, and cultural values.

- Obesity is the result of internal and external influences, diet, emotions, genetics, and exercise.

- The most effective way to lose weight is behavioural dieting, which is based on techniques that change eating patterns and exercise habits.

- Anorexia nervosa and bulimia nervosa are two prominent eating disorders. Both tend to involve conflicts about self-image, self-control, and anxiety.

Is there more than one type of thirst? In what ways are pain avoidance and the sex drive unusual?

- Like hunger, thirst and other basic motives are primarily under the central control of the hypothalamus.

- Thirst may be either intracellular or extracellular.

- Pain avoidance is unusual because it is episodic as opposed to cyclic. Pain avoidance and pain tolerance are partially learned.

- The sex drive is also unusual because it is non-homeostatic.

What are the typical patterns of human sexual response?

- Sexual arousal is related to the body's erogenous zones, but mental and emotional reactions are the ultimate source of sexual responsiveness.

- Human sexual response can be divided into four phases: excitement, plateau, orgasm, and resolution.

- Overall, male and female sexual responses are similar. However, males experience a refractory period after orgasm, and only 5 percent of men are multiorgasmic. Fifteen percent of women are multiorgasmic.

- Sexual orientation refers to one's degree of emotional and erotic attraction to members of the same sex, opposite sex, or both sexes.

- A combination of hereditary, biological, social, and psychological influences produces one's sexual orientation.

How does arousal relate to motivation?

- Drives for stimulation are partially explained by arousal theory, which states that an ideal level of bodily arousal will be maintained if possible.

- The desired level of arousal or stimulation varies from person to person.

- Optimal performance usually occurs at *moderate* levels of arousal, as described by an inverted U function. The Yerkes-Dodson law further states that for simple tasks, the ideal arousal level is higher, and for complex tasks it is lower.

What are social motives? Why are they important?

- Social motives are learned through socialization and cultural conditioning.

- Such motives account for much of the diversity of human motivation.

- A high need for achievement (nAch) is correlated with success in many situations, with career choice, and with *moderate* risk taking.

- Self-confidence greatly affects motivation in everyday life.

Are some motives more basic than others?

- Maslow's hierarchy of motives categorizes needs as either basic or growth oriented. Lower needs are assumed to be prepotent (dominant) over higher needs. Self-actualization, the highest and most fragile need, is reflected in meta-needs.

- Meta-needs are closely related to intrinsic motivation. In some situations, external rewards can undermine intrinsic motivation, enjoyment, and creativity.

What happens during emotion?

- An emotion consists of physiological changes, adaptive behaviour, emotional expressions, and emotional feelings.

- The primary emotions of fear, surprise, sadness, disgust, anger, anticipation, joy, and acceptance can be mixed to produce more complex emotional experiences.

- The left hemisphere of the brain primarily processes positive emotions. Negative emotions are processed in the right hemisphere.

- The amygdala provides a "quick and dirty" pathway for the arousal of fear that bypasses the cerebral cortex.

What physiological changes underlie emotion? Can lie detectors really detect lies?

- Physical changes associated with emotion are caused by the hormone adrenaline and by activity in the autonomic nervous system (ANS).

- The sympathetic branch of the ANS is responsible primarily for arousing the body; the parasympathetic branch, for quieting it.

- The polygraph, or lie detector, measures emotional arousal (rather than lying) by monitoring heart rate, blood pressure, breathing rate, and the galvanic skin response (GSR).

- The accuracy of the lie detector can be quite low.

How accurately are emotions expressed by the face and body language?

- Basic facial expressions of fear, anger, disgust, sadness, and happiness are universally recognized.

- Facial expressions reveal pleasantness versus unpleasantness, attention versus rejection, and a person's degree of emotional activation.

- The formal study of body language is known as kinesics. Body gestures and movements (body language) also express feelings, mainly by communicating emotional tone rather than specific universal messages.

- Body positioning expresses relaxation or tension and liking or disliking.

How do psychologists explain emotions?

- The James-Lange theory says that emotional experience follows bodily reactions. In contrast, the Cannon-Bard theory says that bodily reactions and emotional experiences occur at the same time.

- Schachter's cognitive theory emphasizes that labelling bodily arousal can determine what emotion you feel. Appropriate labels are chosen by attribution (ascribing arousal to a particular source).

- Contemporary views of emotion place greater emphasis on the effects of emotional appraisals.

- The facial feedback hypothesis holds that facial expressions help define the emotions we feel.

- Contemporary views of emotion emphasize that all of the elements of emotion are interrelated and interact with each other.

What does it mean to have emotional intelligence?

- Emotional intelligence is the ability to consciously make your emotions work for you in a wide variety of life circumstances.

- People who are "smart" emotionally are self-aware and empathic; know how to use emotions to enhance thinking, decision making, and relationships; and can understand and manage emotions.

- Positive emotions are valuable because they tend to broaden our focus and they encourage personal growth and social connection.

Interactive Learning

Please visit http://www.psychologyjourney4ce.nelson.com for a list of weblinks to relevant psychology sites.

CourseMate

Access an interactive e-book and chapter-specific interactive learning tools, including flashcards, quizzes, videos, and more, in your psychology CourseMate. Visit Nelsonbrain.com to use CourseMate.

psyk.trek 8. Motivation and Emotion.

TEST YOUR KNOWLEDGE

The questions that follow are only a sample of what you need to know. If you miss any of the items, review the entire chapter and the Study Breaks. Another way to prepare for tests is to use the Study Guide and the Practice Exams that are available with this text.

1. Why do we find desirable goals motivating?
   a. because they are high in secondary value
   b. because they are high in stimulus value
   c. because they are high in homeostatic value
   d. because they are high in incentive value

2. Maintaining your body's set point for fat is closely linked with the amount of which of the following in the bloodstream?
   a. hypothalamic factor-1   b. ventromedial peptide-1
   c. neuropeptide Y (NPY)   d. leptin

3. Binging and purging are characteristic of people who have which of the following?
   a. taste aversions   b. anorexia
   c. bulimia   d. strong sensitivity to external eating cues

4. What is a similarity of men's and women's sex drives?
   a. They are affected by androgens.
   b. They are extracellular.
   c. They are controlled by estrogen.
   d. They are homeostatic and episodic.

5. What are the typical phases of human sexual arousal?
   a. estrus, refractory period, orgasm, resolution
   b. excitement, orgasm, resolution, refractory period
   c. estrus, orgasm, plateau, resolution
   d. excitement, plateau, orgasm, resolution

6. Complex tasks, such as taking a classroom test, tend to be disrupted by high levels of arousal. What predicts this effect?
   a. the attribution theory
   b. the Yerkes-Dodson law
   c. studies of circadian arousal patterns
   d. studies of the need for achievement

7. Which of the following applies to people high in need for achievement (nAch)?
   a. they prefer long shots   b. they prefer sure things
   c. they are moderate risk takers   d. they prefer change and high levels of stimulation

8. Which needs are at the highest level of Maslow's hierarchy of motives?
   a. meta-needs   b. needs for safety and security
   c. needs for love and belonging   d. extrinsic needs

9. Which component of emotion do polygraph operators try to use to detect deception?
   a. adaptive behaviours   b. physiological changes
   c. emotional expressions   d. the parasympathetic rebound

10. What concept predicts that holding a pen crosswise in your mouth is likely to improve your mood?
    a. the Cannon-Bard theory   b. attribution theory
    c. the facial feedback hypothesis   d. Schachter's cognitive theory

11. People tend to be happy if they are meeting which type of personal goals?
    a. those that satisfy extrinsic needs
    b. those that are personally meaningful
    c. those that lead to celebrity and wealth
    d. those that satisfy most of a person's deficiency motives

12. What is the definition of a drive?
    a. an internal deficiency
    b. a series of actions designed to attain a goal
    c. an energized motivational state
    d. the target of motivated behaviour

13. What is incentive value?
    a. the appeal of a resource beyond its ability to fill a need
    b. the value of a goal based on biological needs
    c. a preference for high levels of stimulation
    d. an object's value based on learned needs

14. What is the body trying to accomplish when it works toward homeostasis?
    a. a low body temperature
    b. avoid equilibrium
    c. consistency throughout all biological motives
    d. optimal levels for physiological characteristics

15. Which of the following will occur when the lateral hypothalamus is stimulated?
    a. A well-fed animal will begin eating.
    b. A hungry animal will stop eating.
    c. A well-fed animal will stop eating.
    d. A hungry animal will begin eating.

16. Which of the following is a way in which pain avoidance differs from other drives?
    a. Pain avoidance rarely occurs in distinct episodes.
    b. Pain avoidance involves an unconscious effort to seek high levels of stimulation.
    c. Pain avoidance is part of homeostasis.
    d. Pain avoidance is an episodic drive.

17. What is a stimulus drive?
    a. the overall level of activation in the body and nervous system
    b. a personality characteristic of people who want high levels of stimulation
    c. a reflection of the need for information, exploration, and sensory input
    d. a curve that relates performance to arousal

18. What is the best antidote for test anxiety?
    a. overpreparation
    b. leptin, prescribed by a physician
    c. higher arousal
    d. writing exams in the evening, when biorhythms peak

19. Why would a thirsty person want to drink salty water?
    a. because excess salt causes fluid to be drawn out of cells, quenching intracellular thirst
    b. because before the body can retain water it must replace salt lost through perspiration
    c. because salty water prevents diarrhea
    d. because some people do not respond adaptively to thirst

20. Why do many dieters who stop dieting end up weighing more than they did before their diet?
    a. diets slow metabolic rate, and their bodies store more calories as fat
    b. dieters typically quit smoking
    c. nutritional guidelines call for weight gain in response to weight cycling
    d. the "supermarket diet" leads to obesity

ANSWERS 1.d 2.d 3.c 4.a 5.d 6.b 7.c 8.c 9.a 10.d 11.b 12.c 13.a 14.d 15.a 16.d 17.c 18.a 19.b 20.a

chapter 10

Elena Elisseeva/Shutterstock

Personality

JOURNEY INTO PSYCHOLOGY: THE HIDDEN ESSENCE

One sunny afternoon Genevieve is seen consoling a distraught woman. Genevieve helps run a women's shelter in the working-class Saint-Henri area of Montreal. But she has not always been a social worker. In fact, she attended an exclusive private school in New Brunswick, went on to study at a prestigious European university, and spent many years pleading cases on behalf of a law firm in Vancouver.

Four years ago, Genevieve decided to devote her life to a higher cause. Against the well-meaning advice of her family, friends, and colleagues, she gave up her job and comfortable life, bicycled most of the way across the country, and ended up in Montreal. If Genevieve's old friends were to meet her now, would they recognize the outgoing and ambitious person who once played basketball like a pro and dreamed of a career in politics? Has her personality changed so drastically that they would no longer connect with her? Chances are she's still very much like her old self. What's really changed in her life are her surroundings and her choice of work.

Perhaps you have had a similar experience. After several years of separation, it is always intriguing to see an old friend. At first you may be struck by how the person has changed. Soon, however, you will probably be delighted to discover that the semi-stranger before you is still the person you once knew. It is exactly this core of consistency that psychologists have in mind when they use the term *personality*.

Without a doubt, personality touches our daily lives. Falling in love, choosing friends, getting along with co-workers, voting in elections, or coping with your zaniest relatives—all raise questions about personality.

What is personality? How does it differ from temperament, character, or attitudes? Is it possible to measure personality? These and related questions are the focus of this chapter.

 Survey Questions

- What do psychologists mean by the term *personality*? What core concepts make up the field of personality?
- What are personality traits? Are some traits more basic than others? Do traits predict how someone will act in the future?
- How do psychodynamic theories explain personality?
- What do behaviourists emphasize in their approach to personality?
- How do humanistic theories differ from other perspectives on personality?
- How do psychologists measure personality?
- What causes shyness? What can be done about it?

THE PSYCHOLOGY OF PERSONALITY—DO YOU HAVE PERSONALITY?

 SURVEY QUESTION>
What do psychologists mean by the term personality? What core concepts make up the field of personality?

"Jim's not handsome, but he has a great personality." "Tom's business friends think he's a nice guy. They should see him at home, where his real personality comes out." "It's hard to believe Tanya and Nikki are sisters. They have such opposite personalities." "Genevieve has a very optimistic personality."

We all frequently use the term *personality*. But if you think that personality means "charm," "charisma," or "style," you have misused the term. Psychologists regard **personality** as a person's unique pattern of thinking, emotions, and behaviour (Feist & Feist, 2006). In other words, personality refers to the consistency in who you are, have been, and will become. It also refers to the special blend of talents, attitudes, values, hopes, loves, hates, and habits that makes each of us a unique person.

How is that different from the way most people use the term? Many people confuse personality with *character*. The term **character** implies that a person has been evaluated, not just described (Skipton, 1997). If, by saying someone has "personality," you mean the person is friendly, outgoing, and attractive, you are really referring to what we regard as good character in our culture. But in some cultures, it is deemed good for people to be fierce, warlike, and cruel. So, while everyone in a particular culture has personality, not everyone has character—or at least not good character. (Do you know any good characters?)

Personality A person's unique and relatively stable behaviour pattern.

Character Personal characteristics that have been judged or evaluated; a person's desirable or undesirable qualities.

Personality is also distinct from *temperament.* Temperament is the "raw material" from which personality is formed, such as your sensitivity, irritability, distractibility, and typical mood (Kagan, 2004). **Temperament** refers to the hereditary aspects of personality. Temperamental differences are readily apparent in infants, who vary in sensitivity, activity levels, prevailing mood, irritability, and adaptability (Kagan, 1989). Knowing Genevieve's adult personality, we would guess that she was an active, happy baby.

Psychologists use a large number of terms to describe and explain personality. It might be wise, therefore, to start with a few key concepts. These ideas should help you keep your bearings as you read this chapter.

Traits

We use the idea of traits every day to talk about the personalities of others. For instance, Dan is *sociable, orderly,* and *intelligent.* His sister Kayla is *shy, sensitive,* and *creative.* In general, **personality traits** are stable qualities that a person shows in most situations (Matthews, Deary, & Whiteman, 2003). Typically, traits are inferred from behaviour. If you see Dan talking to strangers—first at a supermarket and later at a party—you might deduce that he is sociable. Identifying this trait might then lead you to predict that Dan will be sociable at school or at work. In fact, a study of women who appeared to be happy in their college yearbook photos (they had genuine smiles) found that most were still happy people 30 years later (Harker & Keltner, 2001).

When Is the Plaster Set?

As we observed with Genevieve, personality traits are usually quite stable (Gustavsson et al., 1997; Hergenhahn & Olson, 2007). Think about how little the traits of your best friends have changed in the last five years. It would be strange indeed to feel like you were talking with a different person every time you met a friend or acquaintance.

At what age are personality traits firmly established? Personality starts to stabilize at around age 30 and continues to "harden" through age 50 (Caspi, Roberts, & Shiner, 2005). However, older individuals can still undergo change in their personality characteristics (Roberts & Mroczek, 2008). Nevertheless, personality slowly matures during old age as most people continue to become more conscientious and agreeable. It appears that stereotypes of the "grumpy old man" and "cranky old woman" are largely unfounded (Srivastava et al., 2003).

Types

Have you ever asked the question "What type of person is she (or he)?" A **personality type** refers to people who have *several traits in common* (Larsen & Buss, 2005). Informally, your own thinking might include categories such as the executive type, the athletic type, the motherly type, the hip-hop type, the techno geek, and so forth. If we asked you to define these informal types, you would probably list a different collection of traits for each one.

How valid is it to speak of personality "types"? Over the years, psychologists have proposed many ways to categorize personalities into types. For example, Swiss psychiatrist Carl Jung proposed that people are either *introverts* or *extroverts.* An

Does this man have personality? Do you?

Temperament The hereditary aspects of personality, including sensitivity, activity levels, prevailing mood, irritability, and adaptability.

Personality trait A stable, enduring quality that a person shows in most situations.

Personality type A style of personality defined by a group of related traits.

Chosen as Canada's top newsmaker of the 20th century, Prime Minister Pierre Elliott Trudeau (1919–2000) had a major impact on our social and political life. Trudeau brought in many progressive laws, championed the patriation of the Constitution, and helped in the adoption of the Charter of Rights and Freedoms. A fashion-conscious man, he dated several well-known, glamorous women of his time. Many people thought he had a very charismatic and charming personality, but some believed he was arrogant and insensitive.

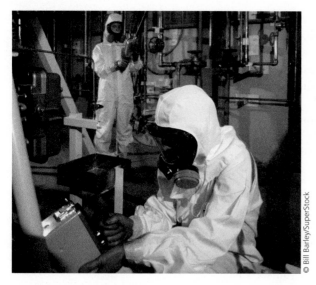

Psychologists and employers are especially interested in the personality traits of individuals who hold high-risk, high-stress positions involving public safety, such as police officers, air-traffic controllers, and nuclear power plant employees.

Introvert A person whose attention is focused inward; a shy and reserved person.

Extrovert A person whose attention is directed outward; an outgoing person.

introvert is a shy person, whose attention is focused inward. An **extrovert** is an outgoing person, whose attention is directed outward. These terms are so widely used that you may think of yourself and your friends as being one type or the other. However, the wildest, wittiest, most party-loving "extrovert" you know is introverted at times. Likewise, extremely introverted persons are assertive and sociable in some situations. In short, two categories (or even several) are often inadequate to fully capture differences in personality. That's why rating people on a list of traits tends to be more informative than classifying them into two or three types.

Given that human beings differ markedly from each other in personality, it is no surprise to find such differences in other animals. Canadian researchers have noted many interesting personality characteristics in such varied species as octopuses, bighorn sheep, chipmunks, and squirrels. Some individual members are aggressive and others shy, some are active and others passive, and some become stressed easily and others don't (Dingemanse & Réale, 2005; Martin & Réale, 2008; Mather & Anderson, 1993). Possessing unique personality traits can have major consequences for the survival of the individual animals themselves as well as for their young. For example, in the Yukon Territory, among the red squirrel population, some females are described as very active; some, as aggressive; and others rate lower on these variables. When the food is plentiful, the pups of the more active mothers thrive very well, but when the food supplies are meagre, the pups of the less active mothers fare better. Similarly, during winter, the pups of the aggressive mothers are more likely to survive as they compete for resources, but only when there is much to eat. During hard times, it is the young of the less aggressive mothers who have better survival rates. Why do these differences exist? It may be because when there is much to go around, the progeny of the aggressive mothers inherit certain characteristics that allow them to survive and reproduce more effectively. But during times of hardship, those who inherit less aggressive tendencies may be able to spend their time more wisely and cautiously, looking for and using whatever limited resources they can find. In sum, different personality types fare better in different environments, which is why varied personalities manage to survive in the wild (Boon, Réale, & Boutin, 2007).

Besides human beings, individual members of many other species show unique personality patterns. The four species of animals featured here are a good example of variation in personality (see the text for an explanation).

Self-Concept

The rough outlines of your self-concept would be revealed by this request: "Please tell us about yourself." In other words, your **self-concept** consists of all your ideas, perceptions, and feelings about who you are.

Self-concepts have a major impact on behaviour. We creatively build our self-concepts out of daily experiences. Then we slowly revise them as we have new experiences. Once a stable self-concept exists, it tends to guide what we pay attention to, remember, and think about (Markus & Nurius, 1986).

Self-concepts can greatly affect personal adjustment—especially when they are negative (Larsen & Buss, 2005). For example, Maryanne thinks she is stupid, worthless, and a failure, despite getting good grades in college. With such a negative self-concept, Maryanne feels depressed regardless of how well she does in school.

© CORBIS

Self-concepts can be remarkably consistent. In an interesting study, very old people were asked how they had changed over the years. Almost all thought they were essentially the same person they were when they were young (Troll & Skaff, 1997).

Self-Esteem

Note that Maryanne also suffers from low self-esteem (how she evaluates herself). A person with high self-esteem is confident, proud, and self-respecting. One who is insecure, lacking in confidence, and self-critical has low self-esteem. Like Maryanne, people with low self-esteem are usually anxious and unhappy.

Self-esteem tends to rise when we experience success. It is also enhanced by praise from others. Thus, a person who is competent and effective and who is loved, admired, and respected by others will almost always have high self-esteem (Baumeister, 1994).

The reasons for having high self-esteem can vary in different cultures. (See Human Diversity: "Self-Esteem and Culture—Hotshot or Team Player?") For example, researchers have found that the Japanese tend to have a lower self-esteem than do Canadians. Living in Canada boosts the self-esteem of Japanese persons, and if Canadians make Japan their home for a while, their self-esteem tends to decline. Does this mean that the Japanese culture has a negative impact on people's perception of themselves? The answer is, Not necessarily. It is likely that the meaning of what it is to be a person depends on where you live and whether you accept the values and beliefs of another culture (Heine et al., 1999). In other words, what Westerners may think is low self-esteem may not be seen as such in other cultures.

> **Self-concept** A person's perception of his or her own personality traits.

HUMAN DIVERSITY

Self-Esteem and Culture—Hotshot or Team Player?

You and some friends are playing an informal game of volleyball. Your team wins, in part because you make some good plays. After the game, you bask in the glow of having performed well. You don't want to brag about being a hotshot, but your self-esteem does get a boost from your personal success.

In Japan, Shinobu is playing volleyball with some friends. His team wins, in part because he makes some good plays. After the game, Shinobu is happy because his team did well. However, Shinobu also dwells on the ways in which he let his team down. He thinks about how he could improve in the future and he resolves to be a better team player.

These sketches illustrate a basic difference in Eastern and Western psychology. In individualistic cultures such as Canada and the United States, self-esteem is based on success, competence, and outstanding performance; the path to higher self-esteem lies in self-enhancement. We are pumped up by our successes and tend to ignore our faults and failures (Ross et al., 2005).

Japanese culture and many other Asian cultures place a greater emphasis on collectivism or mutual interdependence among people. In such cultures, self-esteem is related to group success. It is also based on identifying personal failures and correcting them. Doing so contributes to the welfare of the group. As a result, Japanese people tend to be more self-critical than we are in North America. For them, self-esteem is based on a secure sense of belonging to social groups. This makes self-criticism a way of contributing to the success and well-being of the entire group.

Perhaps self-esteem is still based on success in both Eastern and Western cultures, and it is fascinating that cultures define success in such different ways (Schmitt & Allik, 2005). The North American emphasis on winning and the Japanese stress on belongingness appear to be two different ways to feel good about oneself. (Sources: Heine & Lehman, 1999; Kitayama et al., 1997; Lay & Verkuyten, 1999.)

Personality theory A system of concepts, assumptions, ideas, and principles used to understand and explain personality.

Trait theorist A psychologist interested in classifying, analyzing, and interrelating traits to understand personality.

There is a strange fact about how we see ourselves as we get older. Canadian researchers tell us that, as we age, we find faults with the way we were in the past and believe we are developing better personalities, even when we don't change very much over the years (Wilson & Ross, 2001). Why do we resort to this illusion? Could it be because as humans, we want to believe that as time passes, everything is supposed to improve? Alternatively, by seeing ourselves in a positive light compared to our past, we may find it easier to live with ourselves and to accept our current situation.

Personality Theories

It would be easy to get lost without a framework for understanding personality. How do our thoughts, actions, and feelings relate to one another? How does personality develop? Why do some people suffer from psychological problems? How can they be helped? To answer such questions, psychologists have created a number of theories. A **personality theory** is a system of concepts, assumptions, ideas, and principles proposed to explain personality.

Many personality theories exist, so it is possible to introduce only a few here. The five major perspectives we will consider are *trait theories, psychodynamic theories, behaviouristic theories, social learning theories*, and *humanistic theories*.

THE TRAIT APPROACH—DESCRIBE YOURSELF IN 18 000 WORDS OR LESS

SURVEY QUESTION>
What are personality traits? Are some traits more basic than others? Do traits predict how someone will act in the future?

How many words can you think of to describe the personality of a close friend? Your list might be long: Over 18 000 English words refer to personal characteristics. As you know, traits are stable and enduring qualities that a person shows in most situations. For example, if you are usually optimistic, reserved, and friendly, these qualities could be traits of your personality.

What if you are sometimes pessimistic, uninhibited, or shy? The original three qualities are still traits as long as they are most typical of your behaviour. Let's say our friend Genevieve approaches most situations with optimism, but tends to expect the worst each time she applies for a job. If her pessimism is limited to this situation or a few others, it is still accurate and useful to describe her as an optimistic person.

Predicting Behaviour

As we have noted, separating people into broad types, such as "introvert" or "extrovert," may oversimplify personality. However, introversion/extroversion can also be thought of as a trait. Knowing how you rate on this single dimension would allow us to predict how you will behave in a variety of settings. Researchers have found that students high in the trait of introversion are more likely to prefer the Internet because they find it easier to talk with people online (Koch & Pratarelli, 2004). (Other interesting links exist between traits and behaviour. See Using Psychology: "What's Your Musical Personality?")

Describing People

In general, psychologists try to identify traits that best describe a person. Take a moment to check the traits in Table 10.1 that describe your personality. Are the traits you checked of equal importance? Are some stronger or more basic than others? Do any overlap? For example, if you checked "dominant," did you also check "confident" and "bold"? Answers to these questions would interest a trait theorist. To better understand personality, **trait theorists** attempt to analyze, classify, and interrelate traits.

What's Your Musical Personality?

Even if you like all kinds of music, you probably prefer some styles to others. Of the styles listed here, which three do you enjoy the most? (Circle your choices.)

heavy alternative rock folk classical jazz blues country metal electronic/dance soul/funk rap/hip-hop pop religious soundtrack

In one study, Peter Rentfrow and Samuel Gosling found that the types of music people prefer tend to be associated with their personality characteristics. See if your musical tastes match their findings (Rentfrow & Gosling, 2003).

- People who value aesthetic experiences, have good verbal abilities, and are liberal and tolerant of others tend to like

music that is reflective and complex (blues, jazz, classical, and folk music).
- People who are curious about new experiences, enjoy taking risks, and are physically active prefer intense, rebellious music (rock, alternative, and heavy metal music).
- People who are cheerful, conventional, extroverted, reliable, helpful, and conservative tend to enjoy upbeat conventional music (country, soundtrack, religious, and pop music).
- People who are talkative, full of energy, forgiving, and physically attractive, and who reject conservative ideals, tend to prefer energetic, rhythmic music (rap/hip-hop, soul/funk, and electronic/dance music).

Classifying Traits

Are there different types of traits? Yes. Psychologist Gordon Allport (1961) identified several kinds. **Common traits** are characteristics shared by most members of a culture. Common traits tell us how people from a particular nation or culture are similar, or which traits a culture emphasizes. In Western cultures, for example, competitiveness is a fairly common trait. Among the Hopi of Northern Arizona, however, it is relatively rare. Newfoundlanders are described as hospitable, generous, and friendly, so we could say that the culture of Newfoundland is marked by these common traits.

Of course, common traits tell us little about individuals. While many people are competitive in our culture, each person may rate high, medium, or low on this trait. Usually we are also interested in these **individual traits,** which define a person's unique personal qualities.

Here's an analogy to help you separate common traits from individual traits: If you decide to buy a pet dog, you will want to know the general characteristics of the dog's breed (its common traits). In addition, you will want to know about the "personality" of a specific dog (its individual traits) before you decide to take it home.

■ Table 10.1   Adjective Checklist

Check the traits you feel are characteristic of your personality. Are some more basic than others?

aggressive	organized	ambitious	clever
confident	loyal	generous	calm
warm	bold	cautious	reliable
sensitive	mature	talented	jealous
sociable	honest	funny	religious
dominant	dull	accurate	nervous
humble	uninhibited	visionary	cheerful
thoughtful	serious	helpful	emotional
orderly	anxious	conforming	good-natured
liberal	curious	optimistic	kind
meek	neighbourly	passionate	compulsive

Common traits Personality traits that are shared by most members of a particular culture.

Individual traits Personality traits that define a person's unique individual qualities.

Cardinal trait A personality trait so basic that all of a person's activities relate to it.

Central traits The core traits that characterize an individual personality.

Secondary traits Traits that are inconsistent or relatively minor.

Surface traits The visible or observable traits of one's personality.

Source traits Basic underlying traits of personality; each source trait is reflected in a number of surface traits.

Factor analysis A statistical technique used to correlate multiple measurements and identify general underlying factors.

Trait profile A graph of the scores obtained on several personality traits.

Five-factor model There are five universal dimensions of personality.

Allport also made distinctions between *cardinal traits, central traits,* and *secondary traits.* A **cardinal trait** is so basic that all of a person's activities can be traced to the trait. For instance, an overriding factor in the life of Mother Teresa was compassion for the poor. Likewise, the personality of Terry Fox was dominated by the cardinal traits of courage and determination. According to Allport, few people have cardinal traits.

How do central and secondary traits differ from cardinal traits? **Central traits** are the core qualities or basic building blocks of personality. A surprisingly small number of central traits can capture the essence of a person. For instance, just six traits would provide a good description of Genevieve's personality: dominant, sociable, honest, cheerful, intelligent, and optimistic. When college students were asked to describe someone they knew well, they mentioned an average of seven central traits (Allport, 1961).

Secondary traits are the less consistent, relatively superficial aspects of a person. Any number of secondary traits could be listed in a personality description. Your own secondary traits include such things as food preferences, attitudes, political opinions, musical tastes, and so on. In Allport's terms, a personality description might therefore include the following items:

Name: Jane Doe

Age: 22

Cardinal traits: None

Central traits: Possessive, autonomous, artistic, dramatic, self-centred, trusting

Secondary traits: Prefers colourful clothes, likes to work alone, politically liberal, always late

Source Traits

A second major approach to traits is illustrated by the work of Raymond B. Cattell (1906–1998). Cattell wanted to dig deeper into personality to learn how traits are interlinked. He began by studying features that make up the visible areas of personality. He called these **surface traits**. Through the use of questionnaires, direct observations, and life records, Cattell assembled data on the surface traits of a large number of people. He then noted that surface traits often appear in *clusters,* or groups. In fact, some traits appeared together so often that they seemed to represent a single more basic trait. Cattell called such underlying personality characteristics **source traits** (Cattell, 1965).

How do source traits differ from Allport's central traits? The main difference is that Allport classified traits subjectively, whereas Cattell used a statistical technique called *factor analysis* to reduce surface traits to source traits. In a **factor analysis**, psychologists look at the correlations among several variables. If patterns emerge in these correlations, they are assumed to reflect general, underlying factors. Using this approach, Cattell developed a list of 16 source traits. He considered this the basic number necessary to describe a personality.

Cattell's source traits are measured by a test called the *Sixteen Personality Factor Questionnaire* (the 16 PF). Like many tests of its type, the 16 PF can be used to produce a **trait profile**, or graph of a person's score on each trait. Trait profiles draw a "picture" of individual personalities, which makes it easier to compare them (see Figure 10.1).

The Big Five

Noel is outgoing and friendly, conscientious, emotionally stable, and smart. His brother Joel is introverted, hostile, irresponsible, emotionally unpredictable, and uninterested in ideas. You will be spending a week in a space capsule with either Noel or Joel. Whom would you choose? If the answer seems obvious, it's because Noel and Joel were described with the **five-factor model,** a system that identifies the five most basic dimensions of personality.

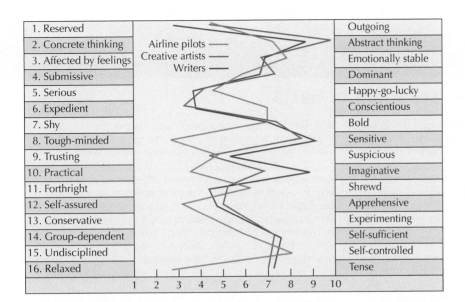

1. Reserved	Outgoing
2. Concrete thinking	Abstract thinking
3. Affected by feelings	Emotionally stable
4. Submissive	Dominant
5. Serious	Happy-go-lucky
6. Expedient	Conscientious
7. Shy	Bold
8. Tough-minded	Sensitive
9. Trusting	Suspicious
10. Practical	Imaginative
11. Forthright	Shrewd
12. Self-assured	Apprehensive
13. Conservative	Experimenting
14. Group-dependent	Self-sufficient
15. Undisciplined	Self-controlled
16. Relaxed	Tense

Airline pilots ——
Creative artists ——
Writers ——

1 2 3 4 5 6 7 8 9 10

▸▸**FIGURE 10.1** The 16 source traits measured by Cattell's 16 PF are listed beside the graph. Scores can be plotted as a profile for an individual or a group. The profiles shown here are group averages for airline pilots, creative artists, and writers. Notice the similarity between artists and writers and the difference between these two groups and pilots. (After Cattell, 1973.)

The "Big Five" factors listed in Figure 10.2 attempt to further reduce Cattell's 16 factors to just 5 universal dimensions (Costa & McCrae, 2006). The Big Five may be the best answer of all to the question "What is the essence of human personality?" (McCrae & Terracciano, 2005).

Five Key Dimensions

If you would like to compare the personalities of two people, try rating them informally on the five dimensions shown in Figure 10.2. For factor 1, *extroversion,* rate how introverted or extroverted each person is. Factor 2, *agreeableness,* refers to how friendly, nurturing, and caring a person is, as opposed to cold, indifferent, self-centred, or spiteful. A person who is *conscientious* (factor 3) is self-disciplined, responsible, and achieving. People low on this factor are irresponsible, careless, and undependable. Factor 4, *neuroticism,* refers to negative, upsetting emotions. People who are high in neuroticism tend to be anxious, emotionally "sour," irritable, and unhappy. Finally, people who rate high on factor 5, *openness to experience,* are intelligent and open to new ideas (McCrae & Costa, 2001). The beauty of this model is that almost any trait you can name will be related to one of the five factors. If you were selecting a roommate, hiring an employee, or answering a singles ad, you would probably like to know all of the personal dimensions covered by the Big Five. Now, try rating yourself as you read *Discovering Psychology:* "Which Personality Are You (and Which Is Best)?"

The Big Five traits predict how people will act in various circumstances. For example, people who score high in conscientiousness tend to perform well at work, do well in school, and rarely have automobile accidents (Arthur & Doverspike, 2001; Barrick, Moun, & Judge, 2001; Chamorro-Premuzic & Furnham, 2003). They even live longer (Martin, Friedman, & Schwartz, 2007).

Another interesting example of the usefulness of the Big Five theory comes to us from the University of Alberta. Researchers tried to establish which personality variables are related to exercise practices. According to their results, people who are high on extroversion or conscientiousness are more frequent exercisers, whereas those high on neuroticism are less likely to work out. People high on neuroticism exercise because of their concerns with being overweight or appearance, people with high scores on extroversion and conscientiousness are driven by the motivation of health and fitness, and people with high scores on extroversion and openness like exercising because of fun and enjoyment. Extroverts prefer to work out with others over exercising alone;

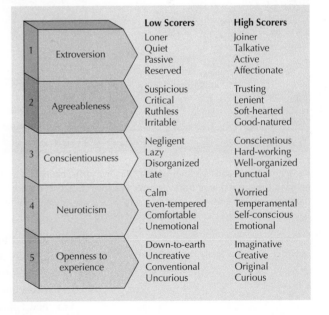

		Low Scorers	High Scorers
1	Extroversion	Loner Quiet Passive Reserved	Joiner Talkative Active Affectionate
2	Agreeableness	Suspicious Critical Ruthless Irritable	Trusting Lenient Soft-hearted Good-natured
3	Conscientiousness	Negligent Lazy Disorganized Late	Conscientious Hard-working Well-organized Punctual
4	Neuroticism	Calm Even-tempered Comfortable Unemotional	Worried Temperamental Self-conscious Emotional
5	Openness to experience	Down-to-earth Uncreative Conventional Uncurious	Imaginative Creative Original Curious

▸▸**FIGURE 10.2** The Big Five. According to the five-factor model, basic differences in personality can be boiled down to the dimensions shown here. The five-factor model answers these essential questions about a person: Is she or he extroverted or introverted? Agreeable or difficult? Conscientious or irresponsible? Emotionally stable or unstable? Smart or unintelligent?

Which Personality Are You (and Which Is Best)?

According to the *five-factor model*, your rating on each of five basic personality dimensions, or factors, gives a good overall de scription of your personality. Try it (see Figure 10.2). How well do you think your ratings describe you?

When you were rating yourself, did you notice that some of the traits in Figure 10.2 don't seem very attractive? After all, who would want to score low in *extroversion*? What could be good about being quiet, inward-looking, and reserved? In other words, aren't some personality patterns better than others?

What is the best personality pattern? You might be surprised to learn that there is no one "best" personality pattern. For example, extroverts tend to earn more during their careers than introverts, and they have more sexual partners. But they are also more likely to take risks than introverts (and to land in the hospital with an injury). Extroverts are also more likely to divorce. Because of this, extroverted men are less likely to live with their children. In other words, extroversion tends to open the doors to some life experiences and close doors to others (Nettle, 2005).

The same is true for *agreeableness*. Agreeable people attract more friends and enjoy strong social support from others. But agreeable people often put the interests of friends and family ahead of their own. This leaves agreeable people at a disadvantage. To do creative, artistic work or to succeed in the business world often involves putting your own interests first (Nettle, 2008).

How about conscientiousness? Up to a point, being conscientious is associated with high achievement. However, having impossibly high standards, a trait called *perfectionism,* can be a problem. As you might expect, college students who are perfectionists tend to get good grades. Yet some students cross the line into maladaptive perfectionism, which typically *lowers* performance at school and elsewhere (Accordino, Accordino, & Slaney, 2000). Authentic Navajo rugs always have a flaw in their intricate designs. Navajo weavers intentionally make a "mistake" in each rug as a reminder that humans are not perfect. There is a lesson in this: It is not always necessary, or even desirable, to be perfect. To learn from your experiences you must feel free to make mistakes (Castro & Rice, 2003). Success, in the long run, is more often based on seeking excellence rather than perfection (Enns, Cox, & Clara, 2005).

Except for very extreme personality patterns, which are often maladaptive, most personalities involve a mixture of costs and benefits. We all face the task of pursuing life experiences that best suit our own unique personality patterns (Nettle, 2008).

Knowing where a person stands on the "Big Five" personality factors helps in the prediction of behaviour. For example, people who score high on conscientiousness tend to be safe drivers who are unlikely to have automobile accidents (Arthur & Doverspike, 2001).

people high on openness preferred working out outdoors; and people who are fond of competitive exercises are low on agreeableness, whereas people who enjoy routine exercise programs are low on openness but have high conscientiousness scores (Courneya & Hellsten, 1998). Do these findings describe you or your friends and family in any way? They are certainly true of your textbook authors!

In recent years, Canadian psychologists have identified a sixth personality factor called honesty/humility. They have conducted research in many countries, especially taking into account various unique terms for personality characteristics that are commonly used in various languages. Their results point to the need of adding an additional factor to the Big Five model. The reason, they argue, is that the dimension of honesty/humility stands out on its own, separate from the five factors in the traditional scheme. It has been termed the HEXACO model, where each of the six letters stands for a separate factor (Ashton & Lee, 2007).

People who obtain high scores for honesty are high on the traits of sincerity and fairness, whereas low scores indicate greediness and dishonesty. Researchers using the HEXACO model have found that people scoring low on honesty/humility are more likely to engage in criminal activity; be more unethical in their business practices—accepting or offering bribes; seek status and power for its own sake; and engage in sexual harassment (Ashton & Lee, 2008).

This new Canadian model with six rather than the usual five factors is becoming more widely accepted, but it still needs further research corroboration to be adopted as a true description of human personality.

Before you read the next section, take a moment to answer the questions that follow. Doing so will add to your understanding of a long-running controversy in the psychology of personality.

Rate Yourself: How Do You View Personality?

1. My friends' actions are fairly consistent from day to day and in different situations. T or F?

2. Whether a person is honest or dishonest, kind or cruel, a hero or a coward, depends mainly on circumstances. T or F?

3. Most people I have known for several years have pretty much the same personalities now as they did when I first met them. T or F?

4. The reason that people in some professions (such as teachers, lawyers, or doctors) seem so much alike is that their work requires that they act in particular ways. T or F?

5. One of the first things I would want to know about a potential roommate is what the person's personality is like. T or F?

6. I believe that immediate circumstances usually determine how people act at any given time. T or F?

7. To be comfortable in a particular job, a person's personality must match the nature of the work. T or F?

8. Almost anyone would be polite at a wedding reception; it doesn't matter what kind of personality the person has. T or F?

Now count the number of times you marked true for the odd-numbered items. Do the same for the even-numbered items.

If you agreed with most of the odd-numbered items, you tend to view behaviour as strongly influenced by personality traits or lasting personal dispositions.

If you agreed with most of the even-numbered items, you view behaviour as strongly influenced by external situations and circumstances.

If the number of times you answered true is nearly equal for odd and even items, you place equal weight on traits and situations as sources of behaviour. This is the view now held by many personality psychologists (Funder, 2006; Mischel & Shoda, 1998).

Traits, Consistency, and Situations

To predict how a person will act, is it better to focus on personality traits or external circumstances? Actually, it's best to take both into account. Personality traits are quite consistent (Roan, 1992). Yet, situations also greatly influence our behaviour. For instance, it would be unusual for you to dance at a movie or read a book at a football game. Likewise, few people sleep on roller coasters or tell off-colour jokes at funerals. However, your personality traits may predict whether you choose to read a book, go to a movie, or attend a football game in the first place. Typically, traits interact with situations to determine how we will act (Mischel, 2004).

Trait–situation interactions occur when external circumstances influence the expression of personality traits. For instance, imagine what would happen if you moved from a place of worship to a classroom to a party to a football game. As the setting changed, you would probably become louder and more boisterous. This change would demonstrate situational effects on behaviour. At the same time, your personality traits would also be apparent: If you were quieter than average in class, you would probably be quieter than average in the other settings too. Where do such differences come from? The next section explores one source of personality traits.

Do We Inherit Personality?

How much does heredity affect personality traits? Some breeds of dogs have reputations for being friendly, aggressive, intelligent, calm, or emotional. Such differences fall in the realm of **behavioural genetics**—the study of inherited behavioural traits. We know that facial features, eye colour, body type, and many other physical characteristics are inherited. So, too, are many behavioural tendencies (Bouchard, 2004). Genetic studies have shown that intelligence, some mental disorders, temperament, and other complex qualities are influenced by

Trait–situation interaction The influence that external settings or circumstances have on the expression of personality traits.

Behavioural genetics The study of inherited behavioural traits and tendencies.

heredity. In view of such findings, it would not be surprising to find that genes affect personality as well (Nettle, 2006). *Wouldn't comparing the personalities of identical twins help answer the question?* It would indeed—especially if the twins were separated at birth or soon after.

Twins and Traits

For over three decades, psychologists at the University of Minnesota have been studying identical twins who grew up in different homes. Reunited twins take a wide range of medical and psychological tests. These tests show that identical twins are very much alike, even when they are reared apart (Bouchard et al., 1990). They may even be similar in appearance, voice quality, facial gestures, hand movements, and nervous tics, such as nail biting. Separated twins also tend to have similar talents. If one twin excels at art, music, dance, drama, or athletics, the other is likely to as well—despite wide differences in childhood environment. However, as Critical Thinking: "Amazing Twins" explains, it's wise to be cautious about some reports of extraordinary similarities in reunited twins.

CRITICAL THINKING

Amazing Twins

Many reunited twins in the Minnesota study have displayed similarities far beyond what would be expected on the basis of heredity. A good example is provided by the "Jim twins," James Lewis and James Springer. Both Jims had married and divorced women named Linda. Both had undergone police training. Both had named their firstborn sons James Allan. Both drove Chevrolets and vacationed at the same beach each summer. Both listed carpentry and mechanical drawing among their hobbies. Both had built benches around trees in their yards. And so forth (Holden, 1980).

Does heredity actually control such details of our lives? Are there child-naming genes and bench-building genes? Of course, the idea is preposterous. How, then, do we explain the eerie similarities in separated twins' lives?

Decades of research have revealed that identical twins are similar to each other in their personality, style of thinking, and IQ, much more so than fraternal twins and unrelated siblings brought up together. At the same time, however, some marked differences may arise even when two identical twins grow up together.

Consider identical twins Carolyn Spiro and Pamela Spiro Wagner, who, unlike the "Jim Twins," lived together throughout their childhood. While in sixth grade, they found out that U.S. President John F. Kennedy had been assassinated. Carolyn wasn't sure why everyone was so upset. Pamela heard voices announcing that she was responsible for his death. After years of hiding her voices from everyone, Pamela tried to commit suicide while the twins were attending Brown University. She was diagnosed with schizophrenia. Never to be cured, she has gone on to write award-winning poetry. Carolyn eventually became a Harvard psychiatrist (Spiro Wagner & Spiro, 2005).

On the other hand, completely unrelated persons can occasionally also have some similarities (Wyatt et al., 1984). Why might this be so? It's because people of the same age and sex live in the same historical times and select from similar societal options.

Imagine that you have just struck up a friendship at school with someone of the same age, sex, and race. Over the next few weeks, you begin to compare and contrast similarities in behaviour and preferences with the new chum. To the astonishment of both parties, there seems to be much in common. For example, both of you use the same brand of toothpaste; are passionate about baseball; cannot start the day without coffee; and, most surprisingly, have mothers named Samantha! You begin to wonder why you have so much in common

with your friend, though you know there is no genetic shared heritage. Research suggests that unrelated people who grow up in a given culture may manifest similarities at the surface level, while being different in their personalities, their styles of thinking, and the way they approach their environment. Identical twins, on the other hand, seem to be much closer to each other at a deeper level, whether or not they grow up in the same household (Segal et al., 2008).

There are two messages here: 1. Two unrelated persons from the same society might discover similarity in certain details of their lives. 2. Identical twins are more similar to each other in the ways they think and act because they have the same genes, but identical does not always mean thinking and behaving identically.

Courtesy of Pam Wagner

Identical twins Pam (left) and Carolyn (right) were raised together. Regardless, Carolyn became a psychiatrist, and Pamela developed schizophrenia and went on to become an award-winning poet (Spiro Wagner & Spiro, 2005). Their story illustrates the complex interplay of forces that shape our adult personalities.

STUDY BREAK   Personality and Trait Theories

Reflect

List six or seven traits that best describe your personality. Which system of traits seems to best match your list: Allport's, Cattell's, or the Big Five?

Choose a prominent trait from your list. Does its expression seem to be influenced by specific situations? Do you think that heredity contributed to the trait?

Learning Check

1. _____ refers to the hereditary aspects of a person's emotional nature.
2. The term _____ refers to the presence or absence of desirable personal qualities.
   a. personality   b. source trait
   c. character   d. temperament
3. A system that classifies all people as either introverts or extroverts is an example of a _____ approach to personality.

4. An individual's perception of his or her own personality constitutes that person's _____.
5. Central traits are those shared by most members of a culture. T or F?
6. Which of the following is not one of the Big Five personality factors?
   a. submissiveness   b. agreeableness
   c. extroversion   d. neuroticism
7. What is the sixth personality factor proposed by Canadian researchers in addition to the Big Five factors?
8. To understand personality, it is wise to remember that traits and situations _____ to determine our behaviour.

Critical Thinking

9. In what way would memory contribute to the formation of an accurate or inaccurate self-concept?
10. Are situations equally powerful in their impact on behaviour?

Answers

1. temperament 2. c 3. type 4. self-concept 5. F 6. a 7. honesty/humility 8. interact 9. As discussed in Chapter 7, memory is highly selective, and long-term memories are often distorted by recent information. Such properties add to the mouldability of self-concept. 10. No. Circumstances can have a strong or weak influence. In some situations, almost everyone will act the same, no matter what their personality traits are. In other situations, traits may be of greater importance.

Another large-scale project involving twins is being carried out at the University of British Columbia under the directorship of Kerry Jang, who has collected data on close to 1500 twins. Jang and associates study the genetics of personality, psychological disorders, attitudes, and talents. One surprising result to emerge from this lab is that attitudes toward abortion, political adherence (liberal versus conservative), and physical exercise are influenced by our genes (CBC, 2008). Such findings challenge a long-held view by many that only the environment determines how we behave, think, and feel about various issues of importance in our lives.

Psychoanalytic theory The Freudian theory of personality that emphasizes unconscious forces and conflicts.

Summary

Studies of twins make it clear that heredity has a sizable effect on each of us. All told, it seems reasonable to conclude that heredity is responsible for about 25 to 50 percent of the variation in many personality traits (Caspi, Roberts, & Shiner, 2005). Notice, however, that the same figures imply that personality is shaped by environment as much as, or more than, it is by heredity.

Each personality is a unique blend of heredity and environment, biology, and culture. We are not—thank goodness—genetically programmed robots whose behaviour and personality traits are "wired in" for life. Where you go in life is the result of the choices you make. To a degree, these choices are influenced by inherited tendencies (Funder, 2006).

PSYCHOANALYTIC THEORY—ID CAME TO ME IN A DREAM

Psychodynamic theorists don't busy themselves with studying traits. Instead, they try to probe under the surface of personality—to learn what drives, conflicts, and energies animate us. **Psychoanalytic theory,** the best-known psychodynamic approach, grew out of the work

<SURVEY QUESTION
How do psychodynamic theories explain personality?

id The primitive part of personality that remains unconscious, supplies energy, and demands pleasure.

pleasure principle A desire for immediate satisfaction of wishes, desires, or needs.

psyche The mind, mental life, and personality as a whole.

libido In Freudian theory, the force, primarily pleasure oriented, that energizes the personality.

eros Freud's name for the "life instinct."

thanatos The death instinct.

of Sigmund Freud, a Viennese physician. As a doctor, Freud was fascinated by patients whose problems seemed to be more emotional than physical. From about 1890 until he died in 1939, Freud evolved a theory of personality that deeply influenced modern thought. Let's consider some of its main features.

The Structure of Personality

How did Freud view personality? Freud's model portrays personality as a dynamic system directed by three mental structures: the *id*, the *ego*, and the *superego*. According to Freud, most behaviour involves activity of all three systems. (Freud's theory includes a large number of concepts. For your convenience, they are defined in Table 10.2 rather than in page margins.)

The Id

The **id** is made up of innate biological instincts and urges. It is self-serving, irrational, impulsive, and totally unconscious. The id operates on the **pleasure principle.** That is, it seeks to freely express pleasure-seeking urges of all kinds. If we were solely under control of the id, the world would be chaotic beyond belief.

The id acts as a well of energy for the entire **psyche** (sigh-KEY), or personality. This energy, called **libido** (lih-BEE-doe), flows from the life instincts (or **Eros**). According to Freud, libido underlies our efforts to survive, as well as our sexual desires and pleasure seeking. Freud also described a death instinct. **Thanatos,** as he called it, produces aggressive and destructive urges. Freud offered humanity's long history of wars and violence as evidence of such urges. Most id energies, then, are aimed at discharging tensions related to sex and aggression.

■ Table 10.2   Key Freudian Concepts

Anal stage The psychosexual stage corresponding roughly to the period of toilet training (ages one to three years).

Anal-expulsive personality A disorderly, destructive, cruel, or messy person.

Anal-retentive personality A person who is obstinate, stingy, or compulsive, and who generally has difficulty "letting go."

Conscience The part of the superego that causes guilt when its standards are not met.

Conscious The region of the mind that includes all mental contents a person is aware of at any given moment.

Ego The executive part of personality that directs rational behaviour.

Ego ideal The part of the superego representing ideal behaviour; a source of pride when its standards are met.

Electra conflict A girl's sexual attraction to her father and feelings of rivalry with her mother.

Erogenous zones Areas of the body that produce pleasure and/or erotic desire.

Eros Freud's name for the "life instinct."

Fixation A lasting conflict developed as a result of frustration or overindulgence.

Genital stage The period of full psychosexual development, marked by the attainment of mature adult sexuality.

Id The primitive part of personality that remains unconscious, supplies energy, and demands pleasure.

Latency According to Freud, the period in childhood when psychosexual development is more or less dormant.

Libido In Freudian theory, the force, primarily pleasure oriented, that energizes the personality.

Moral anxiety Apprehension felt when thoughts, impulses, or actions conflict with the superego's standards.

Neurotic anxiety Apprehension felt when the ego struggles to control id impulses.

Oedipus conflict A boy's sexual attraction to his mother, and feelings of rivalry with his father.

Oral stage The psychosexual stage (roughly birth to one year of age) when infants are preoccupied with the mouth as a source of pleasure and means of expression.

Oral-aggressive personality A person who uses the mouth to express hostility by shouting, cursing, biting, and so forth. Also, one who actively exploits others.

Oral-dependent personality A person who wants to passively receive attention, gifts, love, and so forth.

Phallic personality A person who is vain, exhibitionistic, sensitive, and narcissistic.

Phallic stage The psychosexual stage (roughly age three to six years) when a child is preoccupied with the genitals.

Pleasure principle A desire for immediate satisfaction of wishes, desires, or needs.

Preconscious The area of the mind containing information that can be voluntarily brought to awareness.

Psyche The mind, mental life, and personality as a whole.

Psychosexual stages The oral, anal, phallic, and genital stages, during which various personality traits are formed.

Reality principle Delaying action (or pleasure) until it is appropriate.

Superego A judge or censor for thoughts and actions.

Thanatos The death instinct.

Unconscious The region of the mind that is beyond awareness—especially impulses and desires not directly known to a person.

The Ego

The **ego** is sometimes described as the "executive," because it directs energies supplied by the id. The id is like a tyrannical king or queen whose power is awesome but who must rely on others to carry out orders. The id can only form mental images of things it desires. The ego wins power to direct behaviour by relating the desires of the id to external reality.

The ego is guided by the **reality principle.** That is, it delays action until it is practical or appropriate. The ego is the system of thinking, planning, problem solving, and deciding. It is in conscious control of the personality.

The Superego

What is the role of the superego? The **superego** acts as a judge or censor for the thoughts and actions of the ego. One part of the superego, called the **conscience,** reflects actions for which a person has been punished. When standards of the conscience are not met, you are punished internally by *guilt* feelings.

A second part of the superego is the **ego ideal**. The ego ideal reflects all behaviour one's parents approved of or rewarded. The ego ideal is a source of goals and aspirations. When its standards are met, we feel *pride*.

The superego acts as an "internalized parent" to bring behaviour under control. A person with a weak superego will have a delinquent, criminal, or antisocial personality. In contrast, an overly strict or harsh superego may cause inhibition, rigidity, or unbearable guilt.

The Dynamics of Personality

How do the id, ego, and superego interact? Freud didn't strictly picture the id, ego, and superego as parts of the brain or as "little people" running the human psyche. Instead, they are conflicting mental processes. Freud theorized a delicate balance of power among the three. For example, the id's demands for immediate pleasure often clash with the superego's moral restrictions. Perhaps an example will help to clarify the role of each part of the personality.

> **Freud in a Nutshell**
>
> Let's say you are sexually attracted to an acquaintance. The id clamours for immediate satisfaction of its sexual desires but is opposed by the superego (which finds the very thought of sex shocking). The id says, "Go for it!" The superego icily replies, "Never even think that again!" And what does the ego say? The ego says, "I have a plan!"

Of course, this is a drastic simplification, but it does capture the core of Freudian thinking. To reduce tension, the ego could begin actions leading to friendship, romance, courtship, and marriage. If the id is unusually powerful, the ego may give in and attempt a seduction. If the superego prevails, the ego may be forced to displace or sublimate sexual energies to other activities (sports, music, dancing, push-ups, cold showers). According to Freud, much of this activity occurs at the unconscious level.

Is the ego always caught in the middle? Freud argued that the answer was yes, and the pressures on it can be intense. In addition to meeting the conflicting demands of the id and superego, the overworked ego must deal with external reality.

According to Freud, you feel anxiety when your ego is threatened or overwhelmed. Impulses from the id cause **neurotic anxiety** when the ego can barely keep them under control. Threats of

ego The executive part of personality that directs rational behaviour.

reality principle Delaying action (or pleasure) until it is appropriate.

superego A judge or censor for thoughts and actions.

conscience The part of the superego that causes guilt when its standards are not met.

ego ideal The part of the superego representing ideal behaviour; a source of pride when its standards are met.

neurotic anxiety Apprehension felt when the ego struggles to control id impulses.

Freud considered personality an expression of two conflicting forces, the life instinct and the death instinct. Both are symbolized in this drawing by Allan Gilbert. (If you don't immediately see the death symbolism, stand farther from the drawing.)

"All Is Vanity" by Allan Gilbert

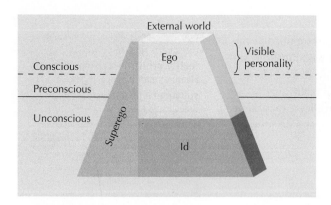

▶▶**FIGURE 10.3** The approximate relationship between the id, ego, and superego, and the levels of awareness.

moral anxiety Apprehension felt when thoughts, impulses, or actions conflict with the superego's standards.

unconscious The region of the mind that is beyond awareness—especially impulses and desires not directly known to a person.

conscious The region of the mind that includes all mental contents a person is aware of at any given moment.

preconscious The area of the mind containing information that can be voluntarily brought to awareness.

psychosexual stages The oral, anal, phallic, and genital stages, during which various personality traits are formed.

oral The psychosexual stage (roughly birth to one year of age) when infants are preoccupied with the mouth as a source of pleasure and means of expression.

anal The psychosexual stage corresponding roughly to the period of toilet training (ages one to three years).

phallic The psychosexual stage (roughly age three to six years) when a child is preoccupied with the genitals.

genital The period of full psychosexual development, marked by the attainment of mature adult sexuality.

erogenous zone Areas of the body that produce pleasure and/or erotic desire.

fixations A lasting conflict developed as a result of frustration or overindulgence.

punishment from the superego cause **moral anxiety** (guilt). Each person develops habitual ways of calming these anxieties, and many resort to using *ego-defence mechanisms* to lessen internal conflicts. Defence mechanisms are mental processes that deny, distort, or otherwise block out sources of threat and anxiety. The ego-defence mechanisms that Freud identified are used as a form of protection against stress, anxiety, and threatening events (see Chapter 12, pages 493). In addition, Freud argued that it is the repressed unconscious thoughts, wishes, and feelings that can potentially cause maladaptive behaviours or mental disorders.

Levels of Awareness

Freud believed that our behaviour often expresses unconscious (or hidden) internal forces. The **unconscious** holds repressed memories and emotions, plus the instinctual drives of the id. Even though they are beyond awareness, unconscious thoughts, feelings, or urges may slip into behaviour in disguised or symbolic form. For example, if you meet someone you would like to know better, you may unconsciously leave a book or a jacket at that person's house to ensure another meeting.

Earlier you said that the id is completely unconscious. Are the actions of the ego and superego unconscious? At times, yes, but they also operate on two other levels of awareness (see Figure 10.3). The **conscious** level includes everything you are aware of at a given moment, including thoughts, perceptions, feelings, and memories. The **preconscious** contains material that can be easily brought to awareness. If you stop to think about a time when you felt angry or rejected, you will be moving this memory from the preconscious to the conscious level of awareness.

The superego's activities also reveal differing levels of awareness. At times we consciously try to live up to moral codes or standards. Yet, at other times a person may feel guilty without knowing why. Psychoanalytic theory credits such guilt to unconscious workings of the superego. Indeed, Freud believed that the unconscious origins of many feelings cannot be easily brought to awareness.

Personality Development

How does psychoanalytic theory explain personality development? Freud hypothesized that the core of personality is formed by the age of six years in a series of **psychosexual stages.** He believed that erotic childhood urges have lasting effects on development. As you might expect, this is a controversial idea. However, Freud used the terms *sex* and *erotic* very broadly to refer to many physical sources of pleasure.

A Freudian Fable?

Freud identified four psychosexual stages: the **oral, anal, phallic**, and **genital.** (He also described a period of "latency" between the phallic and genital stages. Latency is explained in a moment.) At each stage, a different part of the body becomes a child's primary **erogenous zone** (an area capable of producing pleasure). Each area then serves as the main source of pleasure, frustration, and self-expression. Freud believed that many adult personality traits can be traced to **fixations** in one or more of the stages.

What is a fixation? A fixation is an unresolved conflict or emotional hang-up caused by overindulgence or by frustration. As we describe the psychosexual stages, you'll see why Freud considered fixations important.

The Oral Stage

During the first year of life, most of an infant's pleasure comes from stimulation of the mouth. If a child is overfed or frustrated, oral traits may be created. Adult expressions of oral needs include gum chewing, nail biting, smoking, kissing, overeating, and alcoholism.

What if there is an oral fixation? Fixation early in the oral stage produces an **oral-dependent** personality. Oral-dependent persons are gullible (they swallow things easily!) and passive, and they need lots of attention (they want to be mothered and showered with gifts). Frustrations later in the oral stage may cause aggression, often in the form of biting. Fixations here create cynical, **oral-aggressive** adults who exploit others. They also like to argue ("biting sarcasm" is their forte!).

The Anal Stage

Between the ages of one and three years, the child's attention shifts to the process of elimination. When parents attempt toilet training, the child can gain approval or express rebellion or aggression by "holding on" or by "letting go." Therefore, harsh or lenient toilet training can cause an anal fixation that may lock such responses into personality. Freud described the **anal-retentive** (holding-on) personality as obstinate, stingy, orderly, and compulsively clean. The **anal-expulsive** (letting-go) personality is disorderly, destructive, cruel, or messy.

The Phallic Stage

Adult traits of the **phallic personality** are vanity, exhibitionism, sensitive pride, and narcissism (self-love). Freud thought that phallic fixations develop between the ages of three and six years. At this time, increased sexual interest causes the child to be physically attracted to the parent of the opposite sex. In males this attraction leads to an **Oedipus** (ED-eh-pes) **conflict**. In it, the boy feels a rivalry with his father for the affection of his mother. Freud believed that the male child feels threatened by the father (specifically, the boy fears castration). To ease his anxieties, the boy must *identify* with the father. Their rivalry ends when the boy seeks to become more like his father. As he does, he begins to accept the father's values and form a conscience. His love for his mother is repressed or pushed back into the unconscious.

What about the female child? Girls experience an **Electra conflict.** In this case, the girl loves her father and competes with her mother. However, according to Freud, the girl identifies with her mother more gradually than the boy does with his father.

Freud believed that females already feel castrated. Because of this, they are less driven to identify with their mothers than boys are with their fathers. This, he said, is less effective in creating a conscience. This particular part of Freudian thought has been thoroughly rejected by modern feminists. It is probably best understood as a reflection of the male-dominated times in which Freud lived.

Latency

According to Freud, there is a period of **latency** from age six years to puberty. Latency is not actually a stage. Rather, it is a quiet time during which psychosexual development is dormant. Freud's belief that psychosexual development is "on hold" at this time is hard to accept. Nevertheless, Freud saw latency as a relatively quiet time compared to the stormy first six years of life.

The Genital Stage

At puberty an upswing in sexual energies activates all the unresolved conflicts of earlier years. This upsurge, according to Freud, is the reason adolescence can be filled with emotion and turmoil. It is marked, during adolescence, by a growing capacity for responsible social-sexual relationships. The genital stage ends with a mature capacity for love and the realization of full adult sexuality.

Critical Comments

As bizarre as Freud's theory might seem, it has been influential for several reasons. First, it emphasized the idea that the first years of life help to shape adult personality. Second, it identified feeding, toilet training, and early sexual experiences as critical events in personality

Was Freud's ever-present cigar a sign of an oral fixation? Was it a phallic symbol? Was it both? Or was it neither? Once, when he was asked, Freud himself apparently replied, "Sometimes a cigar is just a cigar." An inability to say for sure is one of the shortcomings of psychoanalytic theory.

oral-dependent A person who wants to passively receive attention, gifts, love, and so forth.

oral-aggressive A person who uses the mouth to express hostility by shouting, cursing, biting, and so forth. Also, one who actively exploits others.

anal-retentive A person who is obstinate, stingy, or compulsive, and who generally has difficulty "letting go."

anal-expulsive A disorderly, destructive, cruel, or messy person.

phallic personality A person who is vain, exhibitionistic, sensitive, and narcissistic.

Oedipus conflict A boy's sexual attraction to his mother, and feelings of rivalry with his father.

Electra conflict A girl's sexual attraction to her father and feelings of rivalry with her mother.

latency According to Freud, the period in childhood when psychosexual development is more or less dormant.

Reflect

Try to think of at least one time when your thoughts, feelings, or actions seemed to reflect the workings of each of the following: the id, the ego, and the superego.

Do you know anyone who seems to have oral, anal, or phallic personality traits? Do you think Freud's concept of fixation explains their characteristics?

Do any of your personal experiences support the existence of an Oedipus conflict or an Electra conflict? If not, is it possible that you have repressed feelings related to these conflicts?

Learning Check

1. List the three divisions of personality postulated by Freud.

_____ _____ _____

2. Which division is totally unconscious? _____

3. Which division is responsible for moral anxiety? _____
4. Freud proposed the existence of a life instinct known as Thanatos. T or F?
5. Freud's view of personality development is based on the concept of _____ stages.
6. Arrange these stages in the proper order: phallic, anal, genital, oral. _____ _____ _____ _____
7. Freud considered the anal-retentive personality to be obstinate and stingy. T or F?

Critical Thinking

8. Many adults would find it embarrassing or humiliating to drink from a baby bottle. Can you explain why?

Answers

1. id, ego, superego 2. id 3. superego 4. F 5. psychosexual 6. oral, anal, phallic, genital 7. T 8. A psychoanalytic theorist would say that it is because the bottle rekindles oral conflicts and feelings of vulnerability and dependence.

formation. Third, Freud was among the first to propose that development proceeds through a series of stages. (Erik Erikson's psychosocial stages, which cover development from birth to old age, are a modern offshoot of Freudian thinking. See Chapter 3, pages 121–123.)

Is the Freudian view of development widely accepted? Few psychologists wholeheartedly embrace Freud's theory today. In some cases Freud was clearly wrong. His portrayal of the elementary school years (latency) as free from sexuality and unimportant for personality development is hard to believe. His idea of the role of a stern or threatening father in the development of a strong conscience in males has also been challenged. Studies show that a son is more likely to develop a strong conscience if his father is affectionate and accepting, rather than stern and punishing. Freud also overemphasized sexuality in personality development. Other motives and cognitive factors are of equal importance.

Freud has also been criticized for his views of patients who believed they were sexually molested as children. Freud assumed that such events were merely childhood fantasies. This view led to a long-standing tendency to disbelieve children who have been molested and women who have been raped (Brannon, 1996).

Many more criticisms of Freud could be listed, but the fact remains that his theory contains some grains of truth. At the same time, a major remaining problem with Freud's theory is insurmountable: Whatever value it may have clinically, it has been difficult to verify scientifically. Some go so far as to claim that his ideas have been sufficiently tested, but the results of these studies do not confirm Freud's conjectures about personality development (Erwin, 1996).

LEARNING THEORIES OF PERSONALITY—HABIT I SEEN YOU BEFORE?

 SURVEY QUESTION>
What do behaviourists emphasize in their approach to personality?

How do behaviourists approach personality? According to some critics, as if people are robots like R2D2 of *Star Wars* fame. Actually, the behaviourist position is not nearly that mechanistic, and its value is well established. Behaviourists have shown repeatedly that children can learn things like kindness, hostility, generosity, or destructiveness. What does this have to do with personality? Everything, according to the behavioural viewpoint.

Behavioural personality theories emphasize that personality is a collection of learned behaviour patterns. Like other acquired behaviours, personality develops as a result of classical and operant conditioning, observational learning, reinforcement, extinction, generalization, and discrimination. When Mother says, "It's not nice to make mud pies with Mummy's blender. If we want to grow up to be a big boy, we won't do it again, will we?" she serves as a model and in other ways shapes her son's personality.

Strict **learning theorists** reject the idea that personality is made up of traits. They would assert, for instance, that there is no such thing as a trait of "honesty" (Mischel, 2004).

Certainly some people are honest while others are not. How can honesty not be a trait? A learning theorist would agree that some people are honest more often than others. But knowing this does not allow us to predict for certain whether a person will be honest in a specific situation. It would not be unusual, for example, to find that a person honoured for returning a lost wallet had cheated on a test, bought a term paper, or broken the speed limit. If you were to ask a learning theorist, "Are you an honest person?" the reply might be, "In what situation?"

A good example of how situations influence behaviour is shown by a study in which people were intentionally overpaid for doing an assigned task. Under normal circumstances, 80 percent kept the extra money without saying anything about it. But as few as 17 percent were dishonest if the situation was restructured. For instance, if people thought the money was coming out of the pocket of the person doing the study, far fewer were dishonest (Bersoff, 1999).

As you can see, learning theorists are especially interested in the **situational determinants** (external causes) of our actions. However, this does not entirely remove the person from the picture. Situations always interact with a person's prior learning history to activate behaviour.

Situations vary greatly in their impact. Some are powerful. Others are trivial and have little effect on behaviour. The more powerful the situation, the easier it is to see what is meant by situational determinants. For example, each of the following situations would undoubtedly have a strong influence on behaviour: A lion walks into a supermarket; you accidentally sit on a lit cigarette; you find your lover in bed with your best friend. Yet, even these situations could provoke very different reactions from different personalities. That's why behaviour is always a product of both prior learning and the situations in which we find ourselves (Mischel, Shoda, & Smith, 2004).

Personality = Behaviour

How do learning theorists view the structure of personality? The behavioural view of personality can be illustrated with an early theory proposed by John Dollard and Neal Miller (1950). In their view, **habits** (learned behaviour patterns) make up the structure of personality. As for the dynamics of personality, habits are governed by four elements of learning: *drive, cue, response,* and *reward.* A **drive** is any stimulus strong enough to goad a person to action (such as hunger, pain, lust, frustration, or fear). **Cues** are signals from the environment. These signals guide **responses** (actions) so that they are most likely to bring about **reward** (positive reinforcement).

How does that relate to personality? Let's say a child named Kindra is frustrated by her older brother Kelvin, who takes a toy from her. Kindra could respond in several ways: She could throw a temper tantrum, hit Kelvin, tell a parent, and so forth. The response she chooses is guided by available cues and the previous effects of each response. If telling a parent has paid off in the past, and a parent is present, telling again may be her immediate response. If a different set of cues exists (if the parent is absent or if Kelvin looks particularly menacing), Kindra may select some other response. To an outside observer, Kindra's actions seem to reflect her personality. To a learning theorist, they simply express the combined effects of drive, cue, response, and reward.

Behavioural personality theory Any model of personality that emphasizes learning and observable behaviour.

Learning theorist A psychologist interested in variables affecting learning and in theories of learning.

Situational determinants External conditions that strongly influence behaviour.

Habit A deeply ingrained, learned pattern of behaviour.

Drive Any stimulus (especially an internal stimulus such as hunger) strong enough to provoke a person to action.

Cue Any external stimulus that guides responses, especially by signalling the presence or absence of reinforcement.

Response Any behaviour, either observable or internal.

Reward Anything that produces pleasure or satisfaction; a positive reinforcer.

Freud believed that aggressive urges are "instinctual." In contrast, behavioural theories assume that personal characteristics such as aggressiveness are learned. Is this child's aggression the result of observational learning, harsh punishment, or prior reinforcement?

Doesn't this analysis leave out a lot? Yes. Learning theorists first set out to provide a simple, clear model of personality. But in recent years they have had to face a fact that they originally tended to overlook. The fact is this: People think. The new breed of behavioural psychologists—who include perception, thinking, expectations, and other mental events in their views—are called *social learning theorists.* Learning principles, modelling, thought patterns, perceptions, expectations, beliefs, goals, emotions, and social relationships are combined in **social learning theory** to explain personality (Mischel et al., 2004).

Social Learning Theory

The "cognitive behaviourism" of social learning theory can be illustrated by three concepts proposed by Julian Rotter. They are the psychological situation, expectancy, and reinforcement value (Rotter & Hochreich, 1975). Let's examine each.

Someone trips you. How do you respond? Your reaction probably depends on whether you think it was intentional or accidental. It is not enough to know the setting in which you respond. We also need to know your **psychological situation** (how a person interprets or defines the situation). As another example, let's say you score low on an exam. Do you consider it a challenge to work harder, a sign that you should drop the class, or an excuse to get drunk? Again, your interpretation is important.

An **expectancy** refers to your anticipation that making a response will lead to reinforcement. To continue the example, if working harder has paid off in the past, it is a likely reaction to a low test score. But to predict your response, we would also have to know if you expect your efforts to pay off in the present situation. In fact, expected reinforcement may be more important than actual past reinforcement. And what about the value you attach to grades, school success, or personal ability? Rotter's third concept, **reinforcement value**, states that humans attach different subjective values to various activities or rewards. This, too, must be taken into account to understand personality.

Self-Efficacy

The ability to control your own life is the essence of what it means to be human. Because of this, Albert Bandura believes that one of the most important expectancies we develop concerns **self-efficacy** (a capacity for producing a desired result). You're attracted to someone in your anthropology class. Will you ask him or her out? You're thinking about learning to snowboard. Will you try it this winter? You're beginning to consider a career in psychology. Will you take the courses you need to get into graduate school? You'd like to exercise more on the weekends. Will you join a hiking club? In these and countless other situations, efficacy beliefs play a key role in shaping our lives by influencing the activities and environments we choose to get into (Bandura, 2001).

Self-Reinforcement

Another idea deserves mention. At times, we all evaluate our actions and may reward ourselves with special privileges or treats for good behaviour. With this in mind, social learning theory adds the concept of self-reinforcement to the behaviouristic view. **Self-reinforcement** refers to praising or rewarding yourself for having made a particular response (such as completing a school assignment). Thus, habits of self-praise and self-blame become an important part of personality. In fact, self-reinforcement can be thought of as the behaviourist's counterpart to the superego.

Self-reinforcement is closely related to high self-esteem. The reverse is also true: Mildly depressed college students tend to have low rates of self-reinforcement. It is not known

Social learning theory An explanation of personality that combines learning principles, cognition, and the effects of social relationships.

Psychological situation A situation as it is perceived and interpreted by an individual, not as it exists objectively.

Expectancy Anticipation about the effect a response will have, especially regarding reinforcement.

Reinforcement value The subjective value a person attaches to a particular activity or reinforcer.

Self-efficacy Belief in your capacity to produce a desired result.

Self-reinforcement Praising or rewarding oneself for having made a particular response (such as completing a school assignment).

whether low self-reinforcement leads to depression, or vice versa. In either case, self-reinforcement is associated with less depression and greater life satisfaction (Seybolt & Wagner, 1997; Wilkinson, 1997). From a behavioural viewpoint, there is value in learning to be "good to yourself."

Behaviouristic View of Development

How do learning theorists account for personality development? Many of Freud's ideas can be restated in terms of learning theory. Dollard and Miller (1950) agree with Freud that the first six years are crucial for personality development, but for different reasons. Rather than thinking in terms of psychosexual urges and fixations, they ask, "What makes early learning experiences so lasting in their effects?" Their answer is that childhood is a time of urgent drives, powerful rewards and punishments, and crushing frustrations. Also important is **social reinforcement,** which is based on praise, attention, or approval from others. These forces combine to shape the core of personality.

Critical Situations

Miller and Dollard believe that during childhood four **critical situations** are capable of leaving a lasting imprint on personality. These are (1) feeding, (2) toilet or cleanliness training, (3) sex training, and (4) learning to express anger or aggression.

Why are these of special importance? Feeding serves as an illustration. If children are fed when they cry, it encourages them to actively manipulate their parents. The child allowed to cry without being fed learns to be passive. Thus, a basic active or passive orientation toward the world may be created by early feeding experiences. Feeding can also affect later social relationships because the child learns to associate people with pleasure or with frustration and discomfort.

Toilet and cleanliness training can be a particularly strong source of emotion for both parents and children. Tom's parents were aghast the day they found him smearing feces about with joy. They reacted with sharp punishment, which frustrated and confused Tom. Many attitudes toward cleanliness, conformity, and bodily functions are formed at such times. Studies also show that severe, punishing, or frustrating toilet training can have undesirable effects on personality development (Sears, Maccoby, & Levin, 1957). Because of this, toilet and cleanliness training demands patience and a sense of humour.

What about sex and anger? When, where, and how a child learns to express anger and sexual feelings can leave an imprint on personality. Specifically, permissiveness for sexual and aggressive behaviour in childhood is linked to adult needs for power (McClelland & Pilon, 1983). This link probably occurs because permitting such behaviours allows children to get pleasure from asserting themselves. Sex training also involves learning socially defined "male" and "female" gender roles—which also affect personality (Pervin, Cervone, & John, 2005).

Becoming Male or Female

From birth onward, children are labelled as boys or girls and encouraged to learn sex-appropriate behaviour (Denmark et al., 2005). According to social learning theory, identification and imitation contribute greatly to personality development and to sex training. **Identification** refers to the child's emotional attachment to admired adults, especially those who provide love and care. Identification typically encourages **imitation,** a desire to act like the admired person. Many "male" or "female" traits come from children's attempts to imitate a same-sex parent with whom they identify.

Adult personality is influenced by identification with parents and imitation of their behaviour.

> **Social reinforcement** Praise, attention, approval, and/or affection from others.
>
> **Critical situations** Situations during childhood that are capable of leaving a lasting imprint on personality.
>
> **Identification** Feeling emotionally connected to a person and seeing oneself as like him or her.
>
> **Imitation** An attempt to match one's own behaviour to another person's behaviour.

Instrumental behaviours
Behaviours directed toward the achievement of some goal; behaviours that are instrumental in producing some effect.

Expressive behaviours Behaviours that express or communicate emotion or personal feelings.

Bem Sex Role Inventory (BSRI)
A list of 60 personal traits including "masculine," "feminine," and "neutral" traits; used to rate one's degree of androgyny.

Androgyny The presence of both "masculine" and "feminine" traits in a single person (as masculinity and femininity are defined within one's culture).

If children are around parents of both sexes, why don't they imitate behaviour typical of the opposite sex as well as of the same sex? Recall from Chapter 6 (page 239) that learning takes place vicariously as well as directly. This means that we can learn by observing and remembering the actions of others. But the actions we choose to imitate depend on their outcomes. For example, boys and girls have equal chances to observe adults and other children acting aggressively. However, girls are less likely than boys to imitate directly aggressive behaviour (shouting at or hitting). Instead, girls are more likely to rely on indirectly aggressive behaviour (excluding others from friendship, spreading rumours). One possible reason for this may be that the expression of direct aggression is thought to be inappropriate for girls. As a consequence, girls rarely see female aggression rewarded or approved (Richardson & Green, 1999). In other words, "girlfighting" could be a culturally reinforced pattern (Brown, 2005). Intriguingly, over the past few years, girls have become more willing to engage in direct aggression as popular culture presents more and more images of directly aggressive women (Artz, 2005).

Historically, parents and other adults in Western countries tended to encourage boys to engage in **instrumental** (goal-directed) **behaviours,** to be directly aggressive, to hide their emotions, and to prepare for the world of work. Girls, on the other hand, were encouraged in **expressive** (emotion-oriented) **behaviours** and, to a lesser degree, were socialized for indirect aggression and for motherhood. Thus, from an early age males and females tended to grow up in different, gender-defined cultures (Martin & Fabes, 2001). But these differences are becoming less and less noticeable as traditional male and female gender roles have been called into question.

Androgyny—Are You Masculine, Feminine, or Androgynous?

Are you aggressive, ambitious, analytical, assertive, athletic, competitive, decisive, dominant, forceful, independent, individualistic, self-reliant, and willing to take risks? If so, you are quite "masculine." Are you affectionate, cheerful, childlike, compassionate, flatterable, gentle, gullible, loyal, sensitive, shy, soft-spoken, sympathetic, tender, understanding, warm, and yielding? If so, then you are quite "feminine." What if you have traits from both lists? In that case, you may be *androgynous* (an-DROJ-ih-nus).

The two lists you just read are from the work of psychologist Sandra Bem. By combining 20 "masculine" traits (self-reliant, assertive, and so forth), 20 "feminine" traits (affectionate, gentle), and 20 neutral traits (truthful, friendly), Bem created the **Bem Sex Role Inventory (BSRI).** Next, she and her associates gave the BSRI to thousands of people, asking them to say whether each trait applied to them. Of those surveyed, 50 percent fell into traditional feminine or masculine categories; 15 percent scored higher on traits of the opposite sex; and 35 percent were androgynous, getting high scores on both feminine and masculine items.

The word **androgyny** (an-DROJ-ih-nee) literally means "man-woman." It refers to having both feminine and masculine traits. Bem is convinced that our complex society requires flexibility with respect to gender-related traits. It is necessary, she believes, for men to be gentle, compassionate, sensitive, and yielding and for women to be forceful, self-reliant, independent, and ambitious—as the situation requires. In short, Bem feels that more people should be androgynous.

Adaptability

Bem has shown that androgynous individuals are more adaptable because they are less hindered by images of "feminine" or "masculine" behaviour. In contrast, rigid gender stereotypes and gender roles can seriously restrict behaviour (Bem, 1975, 1981). For example, in one study people were given the choice of doing either a "masculine" activity (oil a hinge, nail boards together, and so forth) or a "feminine" activity (prepare a baby bottle, wind yarn

Androgynous individuals adapt easily to both traditionally "feminine" and traditionally "masculine" situations.

into a ball, and so on). Masculine men and feminine women consistently chose to do gender-appropriate activities, even when the opposite choice paid more!

Bem has concluded that masculine males tend to have great difficulty expressing warmth, playfulness, and concern—even when they are appropriate. They view such feelings as too "feminine." Masculine men also find it hard to accept emotional support from others, particularly from women (Levant, 2001). Highly feminine women face opposite problems. For them, being independent and assertive is difficult, even when these qualities are desirable (see Figure 10.4). In contrast, more androgynous individuals are higher in emotional intelligence (Guastello & Guastello, 2003).

Gender in Perspective

Androgyny has been hotly debated over the years. Now, as the dust begins to settle, the picture looks like this:

- Having "masculine" traits primarily means that a person is independent and assertive. Scoring high in "masculinity," therefore, is related to high self-esteem and to success in many situations (Long, 1989).

- Having "feminine" traits primarily means that a person is nurturant and interpersonally oriented. People who score high in "femininity," therefore, tend to seek and receive social support. They tend to experience greater social closeness with others and more happiness in marriage (Reevy & Maslach, 2001).

In sum, there are advantages to possessing both "feminine" *and* "masculine" traits (Woodhill & Samuels, 2004). In general, androgynous persons are more flexible when it comes to coping with difficult situations (Hittner & Daniels, 2002). Androgynous persons also tend to be more satisfied with their lives because they can use both instrumental and emotionally expressive capacities to enhance their lives and relationships (Lefkowitz & Zeldow, 2006).

It is worth saying again that many people remain comfortable with traditional views of gender. Nevertheless, "feminine" traits and "masculine" traits can readily exist in the same person, and androgyny can be a highly adaptive balance.

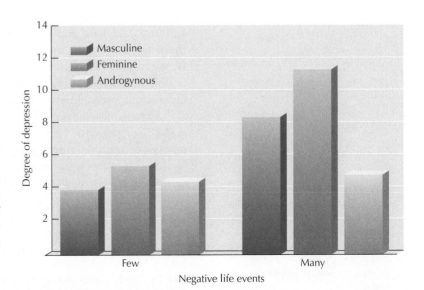

▸▸**FIGURE 10.4** Another indication of the possible benefits of androgyny is found in a study of reactions to stress. When confronted with an onslaught of negative events, strongly masculine or feminine persons become more depressed than androgynous individuals do. (Adapted from Roos & Cohen, 1987.)

STUDY BREAK Behavioural and Social Learning Theories

Reflect

What is your favourite style of food? Can you relate Dollard and Miller's concepts of habit, drive, cue, response, and reward to explain your preference?

Some people love to shop. Others hate it. How have the psychological situation, expectancy, and reinforcement value affected your willingness to "shop 'til you drop"?

Whom did you identify with as a child? What aspects of that person's behaviour did you imitate?

Think of three people you know, one who is androgynous, one who is traditionally feminine, and one who is traditionally masculine. What advantages and disadvantages do you see in each collection of traits? How do you think you would be classified if you took the BSRI?

Learning Check

1. Learning theorists believe that personality "traits" are really _____ acquired through prior learning. They also emphasize _____ determinants of behaviour.
2. Dollard and Miller consider cues the basic structure of personality. T or F?

3. To explain behaviour, social learning theorists include mental elements, such as _____ (the anticipation that a response will lead to reinforcement).
4. Self-reinforcement is to behaviouristic theory as superego is to psychoanalytic theory. T or F?
5. Which of the following is not a "critical situation" in the behaviourist theory of personality development?
   a. feeding   b. sex training
   c. language training   d. anger training
6. In addition to basic rewards and punishments, a child's personality is shaped by _____ reinforcement.
7. Social learning theories of development emphasize the impact of identification and _____.
8. A person who is aggressive, ambitious, analytical, and assertive would be rated as androgynous on the BSRI. T or F?

Critical Thinking

9. Julian Rotter's concept of reinforcement value is closely related to a motivational principle discussed in Chapter 9. Can you name it?

Answers

1. habits, situational 2. F 3. expectancies 4. T 5. c 6. social 7. imitation 8. F 9. incentive value

HUMANISTIC THEORY—PEAK EXPERIENCES AND PERSONAL GROWTH

SURVEY QUESTION>
How do humanistic theories differ from other perspectives on personality?

Humanism focuses on human experience, problems, potentials, and ideals. It is a reaction to the static quality of traits, the pessimism of psychoanalytic theory, and the mechanical nature of learning theory. At its core is a positive image of what it means to be human. Humanists reject the Freudian view of personality as a battleground for instincts and unconscious forces. Instead, they view human nature as inherently good. (**Human nature** consists of the traits, qualities, potentials, and behaviour patterns most characteristic of the human species.) Humanists also oppose the mechanical, "thinglike" overtones of the behaviourist viewpoint. We are not, they say, merely a bundle of mouldable responses. Rather, we are creative beings capable of **free choice** (an ability to choose that is not controlled by genetics, learning, or unconscious forces). In short, humanists seek ways to encourage our potentials to blossom.

To a humanist, the person you are today is largely the product of all the choices you have made. The humanistic view also emphasizes immediate **subjective experience** (private perceptions of reality), rather than prior learning. Humanists believe that there are as many "real worlds" as there are people. To understand behaviour, we must comprehend how a person subjectively views the world—what is "real" for him or her.

Who are the major humanistic theorists? Many psychologists have added to the humanistic tradition. Of these, the best known are Carl Rogers (1902–1987) and Abraham Maslow (1908–1970). Since Maslow's idea of self-actualization was introduced in Chapter 1 (page 22), let's begin with a more detailed look at this facet of his thinking.

Maslow and Self-Actualization

Abraham Maslow became interested in people who were living unusually effective lives. How were they different? To find an answer, Maslow began by studying the lives of great men and women, such as Albert Einstein, William James, Jane Addams, Eleanor Roosevelt,

Human nature Those traits, qualities, potentials, and behaviour patterns most characteristic of the human species.

Free choice The ability to freely make choices that are not controlled by genetics, learning, or unconscious forces.

Subjective experience Reality as it is perceived and interpreted, not as it exists objectively.

Abraham Lincoln, John Muir, and Walt Whitman. From there he moved on to directly studying living artists, writers, poets, and other creative individuals.

Along the way, Maslow's thinking changed radically. At first he studied only people of obvious creativity or high achievement. However, it eventually became clear that a homemaker, clerk, student, or someone like Genevieve could live a rich, creative, and satisfying life. Maslow referred to the process of fully developing personal potentials as self-actualization (Maslow, 1954). The heart of self-actualization is a continuous search for personal fulfillment (Ewen, 2003; Reiss & Havercamp, 2005).

Self-actualizer One who is living creatively and making full use of his or her potential.

Characteristics of Self-Actualizers

A **self-actualizer** is a person who is living creatively and fully using his or her potential. In his studies, Maslow found that self-actualizers have many similarities. Whether famous or unknown, well schooled or uneducated, rich or poor, self-actualizers tend to fit the following profile:

1. *Efficient perceptions of reality.* Self-actualizers are able to judge situations correctly and honestly. They are very sensitive to the fake and dishonest.

2. *Comfortable acceptance of self, others, and nature.* Self-actualizers accept their own human nature with all its flaws. The shortcomings of others and the contradictions of the human condition are accepted with humour and tolerance.

3. *Spontaneity.* Maslow's subjects extended their creativity into everyday activities. Actualizers tend to be unusually alive, engaged, and spontaneous.

4. *Task centring.* Most of Maslow's subjects had a mission to fulfill in life or some task or problem outside of themselves to pursue. Humanitarians such as Albert Schweitzer and Mother Teresa represent this quality.

5. *Autonomy.* Self-actualizers are free from reliance on external authorities or other people. They tend to be resourceful and independent.

6. *Continued freshness of appreciation.* Self-actualizers seem to constantly renew appreciation of life's basic goods. A sunset or a flower will be experienced as intensely time after time as it was at first. There is an "innocence of vision," like that of an artist or a child.

7. *Fellowship with humanity.* Maslow's subjects felt a deep identification with others and the human situation in general.

8. *Profound interpersonal relationships.* The interpersonal relationships of self-actualizers are marked by deep, loving bonds.

9. *Comfort with solitude.* Despite their satisfying relationships with others, self-actualizing persons value solitude and are comfortable being alone (Sumerlin & Bundrick, 1996).

10. *Non-hostile sense of humour.* This refers to the wonderful capacity to laugh at oneself. It also describes the sense of humour a man like Abraham Lincoln had. Lincoln probably never made a joke that hurt anybody. His wry comments were a gentle prodding of human shortcomings.

11. *Peak experiences.* All of Maslow's subjects reported the frequent occurrence of peak experiences (temporary moments of self-actualization). These occasions were marked by feelings of ecstasy, harmony, and deep meaning. Self-actualizers reported feeling at one with the universe, stronger and calmer than ever before, filled with light, beautiful and good, and so forth.

In summary, self-actualizers feel safe, calm, accepted, loved, loving, and alive. There seems to be good agreement among humanistic psychologists from a number of different countries, including Canada, the United States, Belgium, and France, about the essential features of the concept of self-actualization (Leclerc et al., 1998). (See Using Psychology: "Steps Toward Self-Actualization" for some specific suggestions to experience self-actualization.)

Steps Toward Self-Actualization

There is no magic formula for leading a more creative life. Self-actualization is primarily a *process,* not a goal or an end point. As such, it requires hard work, patience, and commitment. Here are some ways to begin:

1. *Be willing to change.* Begin by asking yourself, "Am I living in a way that is deeply satisfying to me and that truly expresses me?" If not, be prepared to make changes in your life. Indeed, ask yourself this question often and accept the need for continual change.
2. *Take responsibility.* You can become an architect of self by acting as if you are personally responsible for every aspect of your life. Shouldering responsibility in this way helps end the habit of blaming others for your own shortcomings.
3. *Examine your motives.* Self-discovery involves an element of risk. If your behaviour is restricted by a desire for safety or security, it may be time to test some limits. Try to make each life decision a choice for growth, not a response to fear or anxiety.
4. *Experience honestly and directly.* Wishful thinking is another barrier to personal growth. Self-actualizers trust themselves enough to accept all kinds of information without distorting it to fit their fears and desires. Try to see yourself as others do. Be willing to admit, "I was wrong" or "I failed because I was irresponsible."

5. *Make use of positive experiences.* Maslow considered peak experiences temporary moments of self-actualization. Therefore, you might actively repeat activities that have caused feelings of awe, amazement, exaltation, renewal, reverence, humility, fulfillment, or joy.
6. *Be prepared to be different.* Maslow felt that everyone has a potential for "greatness," but most fear becoming what they might. As part of personal growth, be prepared to trust your own impulses and feelings; don't automatically judge yourself by the standards of others. Accept your uniqueness.
7. *Get involved.* With few exceptions, self-actualizers tend to have a mission or calling in life. For these people, "work" is done not just to fill deficiency needs but to satisfy higher yearnings for truth, beauty, community, and meaning. Get personally involved and committed. Turn your attention to problems outside yourself.
8. *Assess your progress.* There is no final point at which one becomes self-actualized. It's important to gauge your progress frequently and to renew your efforts. If you feel bored at school, at a job, or in a relationship, consider it a challenge. Have you been taking responsibility for your own personal growth? Almost any activity can be used as a chance for self-enhancement if it is approached creatively. (Based on Maslow, 1954, 1967, 1971.)

Fully functioning person A person living in harmony with his or her deepest feelings, impulses, and intuitions.

Self A continuously evolving conception of one's personal identity.

Self-image The total subjective perception of oneself (another term for self-concept).

Symbolization The process of bringing an experience into awareness.

Despite the intuitive appeal of Maslow's ideas, critics have pointed out numerous problems with his approach. First, although Maslow tried to investigate self-actualization empirically, his choice of people for study was based on highly subjective criteria. Second, there are many ways to make full use of personal potential, not just limited to the way Maslow outlined them in his theory. But coming to Maslow's defence, we can safely say that his primary contribution was to draw our attention to the possibility of lifelong personal growth.

Carl Rogers's Self Theory

Carl Rogers, another well-known humanist, based his theory on clinical experience with unhappy people. Nevertheless, he emphasized the human capacity for inner peace and happiness. The **fully functioning person,** he said, lives in harmony with her or his deepest feelings and impulses. Such people are open to their experiences, and they trust their inner urges and intuitions (Rogers, 1961). Rogers believed that this attitude is most likely to occur when a person receives ample amounts of love and acceptance from others.

Personality Structure and Dynamics

Rogers's theory emphasizes the **self,** a flexible and changing perception of personal identity. Much behaviour can be understood as an attempt to maintain consistency between our *self-image* and our actions. (Your **self-image** is the total subjective perception of your body and personality.) For example, people who think of themselves as kind tend to be considerate in most situations.

Let's say you know a person who thinks she is kind, but she really isn't. How does that fit Rogers's theory? According to Rogers, experiences that match the self-image are **symbolized** (admitted to awareness) and contribute to gradual changes in the self. Information or feelings inconsistent with your self-image are said to be incongruent. Thus, a person who thinks she is kind, but really isn't, is in a psychological state of **incongruence.** That is, there is a discrepancy between her experiences and her self-image. As another example, it would be incongruent to believe that you are a person who never gets angry if you spend much of each day seething inside.

Experiences seriously incongruent with the self-image can be threatening. Because of this, we often distort or deny such experiences, preventing the self from changing. In time, a gulf develops between self-image and reality. As the self-image grows more inaccurate and unrealistic, the **incongruent person** becomes confused, vulnerable, dissatisfied, or seriously maladjusted (see Figure 10.5). Interestingly, a study of college students confirmed that being authentic is vital for healthy functioning. Basically, to be happy, we need to feel that our behaviour accurately expresses who we are (Sheldon et al., 1997). Please note, however, that being authentic doesn't mean you can do whatever you want. Being true to yourself is no excuse for acting irresponsibly or ignoring the feelings of others (Kernis & Goldman, 2005).

When your self-image is consistent with what you really think, feel, do, and experience, you are best able to actualize your potentials. Rogers also considered it essential to have congruence between the self-image and the **ideal self.** The ideal self is similar to Freud's ego ideal. It is an image of the person you would most like to be.

Is it really incongruent not to live up to your ideal self? Rogers was aware that we never fully attain our ideals. Nevertheless, the larger the gap between the way you see yourself and the way you would like to be, the more tension and anxiety you will experience.

Rogers emphasized that to maximize our potential, we must accept information about ourselves as honestly as possible. In accord with this, researchers have found that people with a close match between their self-image and their ideal self tend to be socially poised, confident, and resourceful. Those with a poor match tend to be depressed, anxious, and insecure (Boldero et al., 2005).

According to psychologists Hazel Markus and Paula Nurius (1986), our ideal self is only one of a number of *possible selves* (persons we could become or are afraid of becoming). Genevieve, who was described earlier, is an interesting personality, to say the least. She is one of those people who seems to have lived many lives in the time that most of us manage only one. Like Genevieve, you may have pondered many possible personal identities. (See Clinical File: "Telling Stories about Ourselves.") Possible selves translate our hopes, fears, fantasies, and goals into specific images of who we *could* be. Thus, a beginning law student might picture herself as a successful lawyer, an enterprising college

Humanists consider self-image a central determinant of behaviour and personal adjustment.

Incongruence A state that exists when there is a discrepancy between one's experiences and self-image or between one's self-image and ideal self.

Incongruent person A person who has an inaccurate self-image or whose self-image differs greatly from the ideal self.

Ideal self An idealized image of oneself (the person one would like to be).

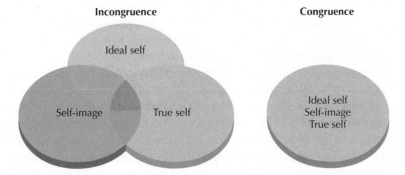

►► FIGURE 10.5 Incongruence occurs when there is a mismatch between any of these three entities: your ideal self (the person you would like to be), your self-image (the person you think you are), and your true self (the person you actually are). Self-esteem suffers when there is a large difference between one's ideal self and one's self-image. Anxiety and defensiveness are common when the self-image does not match the true self.

Telling Stories about Ourselves

You know these two student types: the carefree party animal and the conscientious bookworm. Perhaps you even think of yourself as one or the other. Is there any truth to these (stereo)types? Can you change your type?

College life often creates a conflict between opportunities for fun with friends and the need to study hard. In general, our personality traits are relatively stable characteristics (McAdams & Pals, 2006). As a result, a person high in the Big Five traits of extroversion and agreeableness will tend to embrace a carefree college lifestyle. In comparison, someone high in conscientiousness will find it easier to hit the books (McGregor, McAdams, & Little, 2006).

Does that mean a partier can't become a bookworm (or vice versa)? It depends: Do you mean over a week? Or a lifetime? Personality traits do slowly change as we age. In particular, we tend to become more agreeable, conscientious, and emotionally stable as we grow older (Roberts & Mroczek, 2008).

Oh, you need to change by the end of the term? That's a taller order. In that case, you might want to try telling yourself stories about possible selves you could become. The *narrative approach* to personality asserts that our personalities are shaped by the stories we tell about ourselves (Lodi-Smith et al., 2009; Pals, 2006). In

other words, alternative life stories are not just fantasies or daydreams. They actually influence who we are and who we become.

So, if you feel that you are being too careless and carefree at school, start imagining yourself studying more, getting to classes on time, and getting good grades. Listen to the stories of successful students and use them to revise your own story. Visit your campus counselling centre to learn more about how to succeed at school. In other words, imagine yourself as a bit more of a bookworm. (Don't worry, your carefree nature won't desert you!)

If you feel you are too conscientious and working too hard, imagine yourself going out with friends more often. Listen to the stories of your extroverted classmates. Imagine the benefits of balancing work and play in your life. If you are shy or perfectionistic, visit your campus counselling centre to learn how to become more sociable or relaxed. And, again, don't worry: Having more fun won't make you irresponsible.

Whatever possible self you choose to pursue, you are more likely to become what you imagine if you elaborate your story, making it more detailed and "real" as you gradually adopt new patterns. You *can* create a new narrative identity for yourself (Bauer, McAdams, & Pals, 2008).

---

student might imagine himself as an Internet entrepreneur, and a person on a diet might imagine both slim and grossly obese possible selves. Such images tend to direct our future behaviour (Oyserman et al., 2004).

Of course, almost everyone over age 30 has probably felt the anguish of realizing that some cherished possible selves will never be realized. Nevertheless, there is value in asking yourself not just "Who am I?" but also "Who would I like to become?" As you do, remember Maslow's advice that everyone has a potential for greatness, but most fear becoming what they might.

Humanistic View of Development

Why do mirrors, photographs, video cameras, and the reactions of others hold such fascination and threat for many people? Carl Rogers's theory suggests it is because they provide information about one's self. The development of a self-image depends greatly on information from the environment. It begins with a sorting of perceptions and feelings: my body, my toes, my nose, I want, I like, I am, and so on. Soon, it expands to include self-evaluation: I am a good person, I did something bad just now, and so forth.

How does development of the self contribute to later personality functioning? Rogers believed that positive and negative evaluations by others cause children to develop internal standards of evaluation called **conditions of worth.** In other words, we learn that some actions win our parents' love and approval, whereas others are rejected. More important, parents may label some feelings as bad or wrong. For example, a child might be told that it is wrong to feel angry toward a brother or sister—even when anger is justified. Likewise, a little boy might be told that he must not cry or show fear, two very normal emotions.

Learning to evaluate some experiences or feelings as "good" and others as "bad" is directly related to a later capacity for self-esteem, positive self-evaluation, or **positive self-regard,** to use Rogers's term. To think of yourself as a good, lovable, worthwhile person,

Conditions of worth Internal standards used to judge the value of one's thoughts, actions, feelings, or experiences.

Positive self-regard Thinking of oneself as a good, lovable, worthwhile person.

your behaviour and experiences must match your internal conditions of worth. The problem is that this can cause incongruence by leading to the denial of many true feelings and experiences.

To put it simply, Rogers blamed many adult emotional problems on attempts to live by the standards of others. He believed that congruence and self-actualization are encouraged by replacing conditions of worth with **organismic valuing** (a natural, undistorted, full-body reaction to an experience). Organismic valuing is a direct, gut-level response to life that avoids the filtering and distortion of incongruence. It involves trusting one's own feelings and perceptions. Organismic valuing is most likely to develop, Rogers felt, when children (or adults) receive **unconditional positive regard** (unshakable love and approval) from others—that is, when they are "prized" as worthwhile human beings, just for being themselves, without any conditions or strings attached. Although this may be a luxury few people enjoy, a recent study confirmed that we are more likely to move toward our ideal selves if we receive affirmation and support from a close partner (Drigotas et al., 1999).

> **Organismic valuing** A natural, undistorted, full-body reaction to an experience.
>
> **Unconditional positive regard** Unshakable love and approval given without qualification.

PERSONALITY THEORIES—OVERVIEW AND COMPARISON

Which personality theory is right? Each theory has added to our understanding by organizing observations of human behaviour. Theories can never be fully proved or disproved. We can only ask, "Does the evidence tend to support this theory or disconfirm it?" The best way to judge a theory is by its usefulness. Does the theory adequately explain behaviour? Does it stimulate new research? Does it suggest how to treat psychological disorders? Each theory has fared differently in these areas (Pervin et al., 2005).

Table 10.3 provides an overview of the four principal approaches to personality. In the final analysis, the challenge now facing personality theorists is how to integrate the four major perspectives into a unified, systematic explanation of personality (Mayer, 2005).

<SURVEY QUESTION
How do psychologists measure personality?

■ Table 10.3 **Comparison of Four Views of Personality**

	Trait Theories	Psychoanalytic Theory	Behaviouristic Theory	Humanistic Theory
View of human nature	neutral	negative	neutral	positive
Is behaviour free or determined?	determined	determined	determined	free choice
Principal motives	depends on one's traits	sex and aggression	drives of all kinds and the environment	self-actualization
Personality structure	traits	id, ego, superego	habits	self
Role of unconscious	minimized	maximized	practically non-existent	minimized
Conception of conscience	traits of honesty, etc.	superego	self-reinforcement, punishment history	ideal self, valuing process
Developmental emphasis	combined effects of heredity and environment	psychosexual stages	critical learning situations, identification and imitation	development of self-image
Barriers to personal growth	unhealthy traits	unconscious conflicts, fixations	maladaptive habits, unhealthy environment	conditions of worth, incongruence

PERSONALITY ASSESSMENT—PSYCHOLOGICAL YARDSTICKS

How is personality "measured"? Psychologists use interviews, observation, questionnaires, and projective tests to assess personality (Derlega, Winstead, & Jones, 2005). Each method has strengths and limitations. For this reason, they are often used in combination.

Formal personality measures are refinements of more casual ways of judging a person. At one time or another, you have probably "sized up" a potential date, friend, or roommate by engaging in conversation (interview). Perhaps you have asked a friend, "When I am delayed I get angry. Do you?" (questionnaire). Maybe you watch your professors when they are angry or embarrassed to learn what they are "really" like (observation). Or possibly you have noticed that when you say, "I think people feel …," you may be expressing your own feelings (projection). Let's see how psychologists apply each of these methods to probe personality.

The Interview

In an **interview,** psychologists use questioning to learn about a person's life history, personality traits, or current mental state. In an **unstructured interview,** conversation is informal and topics are taken up freely as they arise. In a **structured interview,** the interviewer obtains information by asking a planned series of questions.

How are interviews used? Interviews are used to identify personality disturbances; to select people for jobs, universities, or special programs; and to study the dynamics of personality. Interviews also provide information for counselling or therapy. For instance, a counsellor might ask a depressed person, "Have you ever contemplated suicide? What were the circumstances?" The counsellor might then follow by asking, "How did you feel about it?" or "How is what you are feeling now different from what you felt then?"

In addition to providing information, interviews make it possible to observe a person's tone of voice, hand gestures, posture, and facial expressions. Such body language cues are important because they may radically alter the message sent, as when a person claims to be completely calm but trembles uncontrollably.

Limitations

Interviews give rapid insight into personality, but they have certain limitations. For one thing, interviewers can be swayed by preconceptions. A person identified as a "homemaker,"

Interview (personality) A face-to-face meeting held for the purpose of gaining information about an individual's personal history, personality traits, current psychological state, and so forth.

Unstructured interview An interview in which conversation is informal and topics are taken up freely as they arise.

Structured interview An interview that follows a prearranged plan in which a series of questions are asked.

"college student," "high school athlete," "punk," or "ski bum" may be misjudged because of an interviewer's bias toward a particular lifestyle. Second, an interviewer's own personality or even gender may influence a client's behaviour. When this occurs, it can accentuate or distort the person's apparent traits (Pollner, 1998). A third problem is that people sometimes try to deceive interviewers. For example, a person accused of a crime might pretend to have a mental disability to avoid punishment.

A fourth problem is the **halo effect,** which is the tendency to generalize a favourable or unfavourable first impression to unrelated details of personality. A person who is likable or physically attractive may be rated more mature, intelligent, or adjusted than she or he actually is. The halo effect is something to keep in mind when interviewing for employment. First impressions do make a difference (Lance, LaPointe, & Stewart, 1994).

Even with their limitations, interviews are a respected method of assessment. In many cases, interviews are the first step in evaluating personality and an essential prelude to therapy. Nevertheless, interviews often may not be enough. Usually, they must be supplemented by other measures and tests (Meyer et al., 2001).

What is your initial impression of the person on the right? If you think that she looks friendly, attractive, or neat, your subsequent perceptions might be altered by a positive first impression. Interviewers are often influenced by the halo effect (see text).

Direct Observation and Rating Scales

Are you fascinated by airports, bus depots, parks, bars, subway stations, or other public places? Many people relish a chance to observe the actions of others. When used as an assessment procedure, **direct observation** (looking at behaviour) is a simple extension of this natural interest in people watching. For instance, a psychologist might arrange to observe a disturbed child as he plays with other children. Is the child withdrawn? Does he become hostile or aggressive without warning? By careful observation, the psychologist can identify personality traits and clarify the nature of his problems.

Wouldn't observation be subject to the same problems of misperception as an interview? Yes. Misperceptions can be a problem. A solution is to use **rating scales** (see Figure 10.6) to evaluate a person. A rating scale is a list of personality traits or specific aspects of behaviour that can be used to evaluate a person. Rating scales reduce the risk that some traits will be

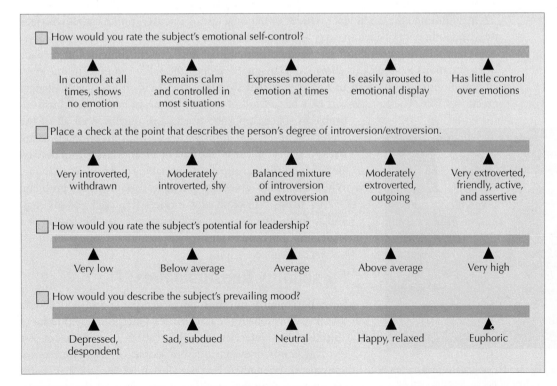

▸▸**FIGURE 10.6** Sample rating scale items. To understand how the scale works, imagine someone you know well. Where would you place check marks on each of the scales to rate that person's characteristics?

Halo effect The tendency to generalize a favourable or unfavourable first impression to unrelated details of personality.

Direct observation Assessing behaviour through direct surveillance.

Rating scale A list of personality traits or aspects of behaviour on which a person is rated.

Behavioural assessment Recording the frequency of various behaviours.

Situational test A simulation of real-life conditions so that a person's reactions may be directly observed.

In-basket test A testing procedure that simulates the individual decision-making challenges that executives face.

Leaderless group discussion A test of leadership that simulates group decision making and problem solving.

Personality questionnaire A paper-and-pencil test consisting of questions that reveal aspects of personality.

Objective test A test that gives the same score when different people correct it.

overlooked while others are exaggerated (Synhorst et al., 2005). Perhaps they should be a standard procedure for choosing a roommate, spouse, or lover!

An alternative is to do a **behavioural assessment** by recording the frequency of specific behaviours. In this case, observers record actions, not what traits they think a person has (Ramsay, Reynolds, & Kamphaus, 2002). For example, a psychologist working with hospitalized patients with psychological disorders might record the frequency of the patients' aggression, self-care, speech, and unusual behaviours.

Behavioural assessments can also be used to probe thought processes. In one study, for example, couples were assessed while communicating with each other about their sexuality. Couples with sexual difficulties were less likely to be receptive to talking about their sexuality and more likely to blame each other than were couples with no sexual difficulties (Kelly, Strassberg, & Turner, 2006).

Situational Testing

In **situational testing**, real-life conditions are simulated so that a person's spontaneous reactions can be observed. Such tests assume that the best way to learn how people react is to put them in realistic situations and watch what happens. Situational tests expose people to frustration, temptation, pressure, boredom, or other conditions capable of revealing personality characteristics (Weekley & Jones, 1997). Some of the popular reality TV programs, such as *Survivor,* bear some similarity to situational tests—which may account for their ability to attract millions of viewers.

How are situational tests done? An interesting example of situational testing is the judgmental firearms training provided by many police departments. At times, police officers must make split-second decisions about using their weapons. A mistake could be fatal. In a typical shoot–don't shoot test, actors play the part of armed criminals. As various high-risk scenes are acted out live or on video, officers must decide to shoot or hold fire. A newspaper reporter who once took the test (and failed it) gives this account (Gersh, 1982):

> I judged wrong. I was killed by a man in a closet, a man with a hostage, a woman interrupted when kissing her lover, and a man I thought was cleaning a shotgun. . . . I shot a drunk who reached for a comb, and a teenager who pulled out a black water pistol. Looked real to me.

In addition to the training it provides, situational testing uncovers police cadets who lack the good judgment needed to carry a gun out on the street.

When selecting people for employment, situational tests present difficult but realistic work situations to applicants (Borman, Hanson, & Hedge, 1997). For example, in one exercise applicants are given an **in-basket test** that simulates the decision-making challenges executives face. The test consists of a basket full of memos, requests, and typical business problems. Each applicant is asked to quickly read all of the materials and take appropriate action. In another, more stressful test, applicants take part in a **leaderless group discussion** that requires group decision making and problem solving. While the group grapples with a realistic business problem, "clerks" bring in price changes, notices about delayed supplies, and so forth. By observing applicants, it is possible to evaluate leadership skills and to see how job candidates cope with stress.

David McNew/Newsmakers/Getty Images

A police officer undergoes judgmental firearms training. Variations on this situational test are used by a growing number of police departments. All officers must score a passing grade.

Personality Questionnaires

Most **personality questionnaires** are paper-and-pencil tests that reveal personality characteristics. Questionnaires are more objective than interviews or observation. (An **objective test** gives the same score when different people correct it.) Questions, administration, and scoring are all standardized so that scores are unaffected by the opinions or prejudices of the examiner. However, this is not enough to ensure a test's accuracy. A good test must also be reliable and valid. A test is **reliable** if it yields close to the same score each time it is given to the same person. A test has **validity** if it measures what it claims to measure. Unfortunately, many personality tests you will encounter, such as those in magazines or on the Internet, have little or no validity.

Many personality tests have been devised, including the *Jackson Personality Inventory* (developed by Western University psychologist Douglas Jackson), the *Guilford-Zimmerman Temperament Survey*, the *California Psychological Inventory*, the *Allport-Vernon Study of Values*, the 16 PF, and many more. One of the best-known and most widely used objective tests is the **Minnesota Multiphasic Personality Inventory (MMPI-2)** (Butcher, 2005). The MMPI-2 is composed of 567 items to which a test taker must respond "true" or "false." Items include statements such as the following:

- Everything tastes the same.
- There is something wrong with my mind.
- I am made nervous by certain animals.
- Whenever possible I avoid being in a crowd.
- I have never indulged in any unusual sex practices.
- Someone has been trying to poison me.
- I daydream very little.*

How can these items show anything about personality? For instance, what if a person has a cold so that "everything tastes the same"? For an answer (and a little bit of fun), read the following items. Answer "Yes," "No," or "Don't bother me, I can't cope!"

- I would enjoy the work of a chicken flicker.
- My eyes are always cold.
- Frantic screaming makes me nervous.
- I believe I smell as good as most people.
- I use shoe polish to excess.
- The sight of blood no longer excites me.
- As an infant I had very few hobbies.
- Dirty stories make me think about sex.
- I stay in the bathtub until I look like a raisin.
- I salivate at the sight of mittens.
- I never finish what I

Reliability The ability of a test to yield nearly the same score each time it is given to the same person.

Validity The ability of a test to measure what it purports to measure.

Minnesota Multiphasic Personality Inventory-2 (MMPI-2) One of the best-known and most widely used objective personality questionnaires.

■ Table 10.4 **MMPI-2 Basic Clinical Subscales**

1. *Hypochondriasis (HI-po-kon-DRY-uh-sis).* Exaggerated concern about one's physical health.
2. *Depression.* Feelings of worthlessness, hopelessness, and pessimism.
3. *Hysteria.* The presence of physical complaints for which no physical basis can be established.
4. *Psychopathic deviation.* Emotional shallowness in relationships and a disregard for social and moral standards.
5. *Masculinity/femininity.* One's degree of traditional "masculine" aggressiveness or "feminine" sensitivity.
6. *Paranoia.* Extreme suspiciousness and feelings of persecution.
7. *Psychasthenia (sike-as-THEE-nee-ah).* The presence of obsessive worries, irrational fears (phobias), and compulsive (ritualistic) actions.
8. *Schizophrenia.* Emotional withdrawal and unusual or bizarre thinking and actions.
9. *Mania.* Emotional excitability, manic moods or behaviour, and excessive activity.
10. *Social introversion.* A tendency to be socially withdrawn.

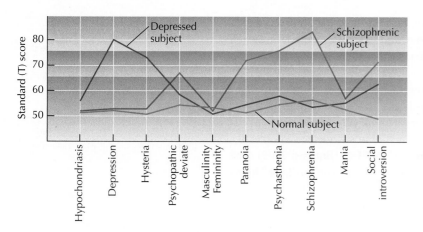

» **FIGURE 10.7** An MMPI-2 profile showing hypothetical scores indicating normality, depression, and psychosis. High scores begin at 66 and very high scores at 76. An unusually low score (40 and below) may also reveal personality characteristics or problems.

MMPI-2 profile A graphic representation of an individual's scores on each of the primary scales of the MMPI-2.

Validity scales Scales that tell whether test scores should be invalidated for lying, inconsistency, "faking good," or "faking bad."

Honesty test A paper-and-pencil test designed to detect attitudes, beliefs, and behaviour patterns that predispose a person to dishonest behaviour.

These items were written by humorist Art Buchwald (1965) and psychologist Carol Sommer to satirize personality questionnaires. Such questions may seem ridiculous, but they are not very different from the real thing. How, then, do the items on tests such as the MMPI-2 reveal anything about personality? The answer is that a single item tells little about personality. For example, a person who agrees that "everything tastes the same" might simply have a cold. It is only through patterns of response that personality dimensions are revealed.

Items on the MMPI-2 were selected for their ability to correctly identify people with particular psychological problems (Butcher, 2005). For instance, if a series of items is consistently answered in a particular way by depressed persons, it is assumed that others who answer the same way are also prone to depression. As silly as the gag items might seem, it is possible that some could actually work in a legitimate test. But before an item could be part of a test, it would have to correlate highly with some trait or dimension of personality.

The MMPI-2 measures 10 major aspects of personality (listed in Table 10.4). After the MMPI-2 is scored, results are charted graphically as an **MMPI-2 profile** (see Figure 10.7). By comparing a person's profile to scores produced by typical, normal adults, a psychologist can identify various personality disorders (Butcher, 2005). Additional scales identify substance abuse, eating disorders, Type A (heart-attack prone) behaviour, repression, anger, cynicism, low self-esteem, family problems, inability to function in a job, and other problems (Butcher, 2006).

How accurate is the MMPI-2? Personality questionnaires are accurate only if people tell the truth about themselves. Because of this, the MMPI-2 has additional **validity scales** that reveal whether a person's scores should be discarded. The validity scales detect attempts by test takers to "fake good" (make themselves look good) or "fake bad" (make it look like they have problems). Other scales uncover defensiveness or tendencies to exaggerate shortcomings and troubles. When taking the MMPI-2, it is best to answer honestly, without trying to second-guess the test.

A clinical psychologist trying to decide if a person has emotional problems would be wise to take more than the MMPI-2 into account. Test scores are informative, but they can incorrectly label some people (Cronbach, 1990). (Critical Thinking: "Honesty Tests—Do

CRITICAL THINKING

Honesty Tests—Do They Tell the Truth?

Each year, millions of anxious job seekers take honesty tests given by companies that hope to avoid hiring dishonest workers (Spector, 2005). **Honesty tests** (also known as *integrity tests*) assume that poor attitudes toward dishonest acts predispose a person to dishonest behaviour. Examples include attitudes toward taking office supplies home or leaving work early. Most of the tests also ask people how honest they think the average person is and how honest they are in comparison. Surprisingly, many job applicants willingly rate their own honesty as below average (Neuman & Baydoun, 1998). (You have to admire them for being honest about it!) Honesty tests also ask about prior brushes with the law, past acts of theft or deceit, and attitudes toward alcohol and drug use.

Is honesty testing valid? This question is still very much in dispute. Some psychologists believe that the best honesty tests are sufficiently valid to be used for making hiring decisions (Ones &

Viswesvaran, 2001). Others, however, remain unconvinced. Most studies have failed to demonstrate that honesty tests can accurately predict if a person will be a poor risk on the job (Horn, Nelson, & Brannick, 2004; Ones, Viswesvaran, & Schmidt, 2003). Psychologists are also concerned because honesty tests are often administered by untrained people. Yet another cause for concern is the fact that 96 percent of test takers who fail are *falsely labelled* as dishonest (Camara & Schneider, 1994). In North America alone, that means well over a million workers a year are wrongly accused of being dishonest (Rieke & Guastello, 1995).

In some jurisdictions, the use of honesty tests as the sole basis for deciding whether to hire a person has been banned. Yet, it's easy to understand why employers want to do whatever they can to reduce theft and dishonesty in the workplace. The pressures to use honesty tests are intense. No doubt, the debate about honesty testing will continue. Honest.

They Tell the Truth?" discusses a related problem.) Fortunately, clinical judgments usually rely on information from interviews, tests, and other sources. Also, despite their limitations, it is reassuring to note that psychological assessments are at least as accurate as commonly used medical tests (Meyer et al., 2001).

PROJECTIVE TESTS OF PERSONALITY—INKBLOTS AND HIDDEN PLOTS

Projective tests take a different approach to personality. Interviews, observation, rating scales, and inventories try to directly identify overt, observable traits (Leichtman, 2004). By contrast, projective tests seek to uncover deeply hidden or unconscious wishes, thoughts, and needs.

As a child you may have delighted in finding faces and objects in cloud formations. Or perhaps you have learned something about your friends' personalities from their reactions to movies or paintings. If so, you will have some insight into the rationale for projective tests. In a **projective test,** a person is asked to describe ambiguous stimuli or make up stories about them. Describing an unambiguous stimulus (a picture of an automobile, for example) tells little about your personality. But when you are faced with an unstructured stimulus, you must organize what you see in relation to your own life experiences. Everyone sees something different in a projective test, and what is perceived is believed to reveal the inner workings of personality.

Projective tests have no right or wrong answers, making them difficult to fake (Leichtman, 2004). Moreover, projective tests can be a rich source of information, since responses are not restricted to simple true/false or yes/no answers.

The Rorschach Inkblot Test

The inkblot test, or **Rorschach Technique** (ROR-shack), is one of the oldest and most widely used projective tests. Developed by Swiss psychiatrist Hermann Rorschach in the 1920s, it consists of 10 standardized inkblots. These vary in colour, shading, form, and complexity.

How does the test work? First, a person is shown each blot and asked to describe what she or he sees in it (see Figure 10.8). Later the psychologist may return to a blot, asking the person to identify specific sections of it, to expand previous descriptions, or to give new impressions about what it contains. Obvious differences in content—such as "blood

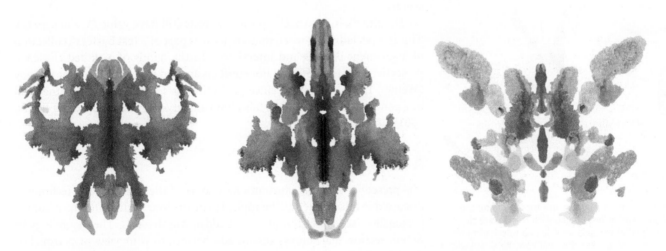

▶▶**FIGURE 10.8** Inkblots similar to those used on the Rorschach. What do you see?

Thematic Apperception Test (TAT) A projective test consisting of 20 different scenes and life situations about which respondents make up stories.

Test battery A group of tests and interviews given to the same individual.

dripping from a dagger" versus "flowers blooming in a field"—are important for identifying personal conflicts and fantasies. But, surprisingly, content is less important than what parts of the inkblot are used to organize images. These factors allow psychologists to detect emotional disturbances by observing how a person perceives the world. The Rorschach is especially good at detecting psychosis, one of the most serious of all mental disorders (Ganellen, 1996).

The Thematic Apperception Test

Another popular projective test is the **Thematic Apperception Test (TAT),** developed by personality theorist Henry Murray (1893–1988).

How does the TAT differ from the Rorschach? The TAT consists of 20 sketches depicting various scenes and life situations (see Figure 10.9). During testing, a person is shown each sketch and asked to make up a story about the people in it. Later, the person looks at each sketch a second or a third time and elaborates on previous stories or creates new stories.

To score the TAT, psychologists analyze the content of the stories. Interpretations focus on how people feel, how they interact, what events led up to the incidents depicted in the sketch, and how the story will end. For example, TAT stories told by bereaved college students typically include themes of death, grief, and coping with loss (Balk et al., 1998).

A psychologist might also count the number of times the central figure in a TAT story is angry, overlooked, apathetic, jealous, or threatened. Here is a story written by a student to describe Figure 10.9:

> The girl has been seeing this guy her mother doesn't like. The mother is telling her that she better not see him again. The mother says, "He's just like your father." The mother and father are divorced. The mother is smiling because she thinks she is right. But she doesn't really know what the girl wants. The girl is going to see the guy again, anyway.

As this example implies, the TAT is especially good at revealing feelings about a person's social relationships (Alvarado, 1994).

Limitations of Projective Testing

Although projective tests have been popular, their validity is considered lowest among tests of personality (Lilienfeld, 1999). Objectivity and reliability (consistency) are also low for different users of the TAT and Rorschach. Note that after a person interprets an ambiguous stimulus, the scorer must interpret the person's (sometimes) ambiguous responses. In a sense, the interpretation of a projective test may be a projective test for the scorer!

Despite their drawbacks, projective tests still have value (Weiner, 1997). This is especially true when they are used as part of a **test battery** (collection of assessment devices and interviews). In the hands of a skilled clinician, projective tests can detect major conflicts and aid in setting goals for therapy (Weiner, 1997). Moreover, since projective tests are unstructured, they can be a good way to get clients to talk about anxiety-provoking topics (O'Roark, 2001).

A Look Ahead

The preceding example illustrates how some of the concepts and techniques discussed in this chapter can be applied to further our understanding of human personality (see also Clinical File: "Sudden Murderers"). The Psychology in Action section that follows should add balance to your view of personality. Don't be shy. Read on!

▶▶**FIGURE 10.9** This is a picture like those used for the Thematic Apperception Test. If you wish to simulate the test, tell a story that explains what led up to the pictured situation, what is happening now, and how the action will end.

Sudden Murderers

Personality assessments provide us with clues to some of the most perplexing human events. Consider Fred Cowan, a model student in school and described by those who knew him as quiet, gentle, and a man who loved children. Despite his size (he was quite a large man), Fred was described by a co-worker as "someone you could easily push around."

Fred Cowan represents a puzzling phenomenon: We occasionally read in the news about sudden murderers—gentle, quiet, shy, good-natured people who explode without warning into violence (Pontius, 2000; Lee, Zimbardo, & Bertholf, 1977). Two weeks after he was suspended from his job, Fred returned to work determined to get even with his supervisor. Unable to find the man, he killed four co-workers and a policeman before taking his own life.

Isn't such behaviour contrary to the idea of personality traits? It might seem that sudden murderers are newsworthy simply because they are unlikely candidates for violence. On the contrary, research conducted by Melvin Lee, Philip Zimbardo, and Minerva Bertholf suggests that sudden murderers explode into violence *because* they are shy, restrained, and inexpressive, not in spite of it. These researchers studied a group of murderers at a prison. Of all the inmates they observed, ten had committed homicides that were unexpected first offences. Nine were criminals with a record of habitual violence prior to murder. Sixteen were inmates convicted of non-violent crimes.

Did the inmates differ in personality makeup? Each of the inmates took a battery of tests, including the MMPI-2, a measure of shyness, and an adjective checklist. Personal interviews were also done with each inmate. As expected, the sudden murderers were passive, shy, and overcontrolled (restrained) individuals. The habitually violent inmates were "masculine" (aggressive), undercontrolled (impulsive), and less likely to view themselves as shy than the average person (Lee et al., 1977).

Psychologists have learned that quiet, overcontrolled individuals are likely to be especially violent if they ever lose control. Their attacks are usually triggered by a minor irritation or frustration, but the attack reflects years of unexpressed feelings of anger and belittlement. When sudden murderers finally release the strict controls they have maintained on their behaviour, a furious and frenzied attack ensues. Usually it is totally out of proportion to the offence against them, and many have amnesia concerning their violent actions.

In comparison, the previously violent murderers showed very different reactions. Although they killed, their violence was moderate—usually only enough to do the necessary damage. Typically, they felt they had been cheated or betrayed and that they were doing what was necessary to remedy the situation or maintain their manhood (Lee et al., 1977).

STUDY BREAK Personality Assessment

Reflect

How do you assess personality? Do you informally make use of any of the methods described in this chapter?

You are a candidate for a desirable job. Your personality will be assessed by a psychologist. What method (or methods) would you prefer that she or he use? Why?

Learning Check

1. The halo effect is the tendency of an interviewer to influence what is said by the interviewee. T or F?
2. Which of the following is considered the most objective measure of personality?
   a. rating scales   b. personality questionnaires
   c. projective tests   d. TAT
3. Situational testing allows direct _____ of personality characteristics.
4. A psychotic person would probably score highest on which MMPI-2 scale?
   a. depression   b. hysteria
   c. schizophrenia   d. mania

5. The use of ambiguous stimuli is most characteristic of
   a. interviews   b. projective tests
   c. personality inventories d. direct observation
6. The content of one's responses to the MMPI-2 is considered an indication of unconscious wishes, thoughts, and needs. T or F?
7. Doing a behavioural assessment requires direct observation of the person's actions or a direct report of the person's thoughts. T or F?
8. A surprising finding is that sudden murderers are usually under-controlled, very masculine, and more impulsive than average. T or F?
9. A test is considered valid if it consistently yields the same score when the same person takes it on different occasions. T or F?

Critical Thinking

10. Can you think of one more reason why personality traits may not be accurately revealed by interviews?
11. Which type of personality theorist would be most interested in projective tests?

Answers

1. F 2. b 3. observation 4. c 5. b 6. F 7. T 8. F 9. F 10. Because of trait–situation interactions, a person may not behave in a normal fashion while being evaluated in an interview. 11. Psychodynamic, because projective testing is designed to uncover unconscious thoughts, feelings, and conflicts.

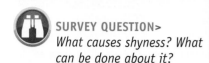

What causes shyness? What can be done about it?

Psychology in Action

BARRIERS AND BRIDGES—UNDERSTANDING SHYNESS

As a personality trait, **shyness** refers to a tendency to avoid others, as well as feelings of anxiety, preoccupation, and social inhibition (uneasiness and strain when socializing) (Bruch, 2001). Shy persons fail to make eye contact, retreat when spoken to, speak too quietly, and display little interest or animation in conversations. Do you

- find it hard to talk to strangers?
- lack confidence with people?
- feel uncomfortable in social situations?
- feel nervous with people who are not close friends?

Mild shyness may be no more than a nuisance. However, extreme shyness is often associated with depression, loneliness, fearfulness, social anxiety, inhibition, and low self-esteem (Derlega et al., 2005; Jackson et al., 2002).

Elements of Shyness

What causes shyness? To begin with, shy persons often lack **social skills** (proficiency at interacting with others). Many simply have not learned how to meet people or how to start a conversation and keep it going. **Social anxiety** (a feeling of apprehension in the presence of others) is also a factor in shyness. Almost everyone feels nervous in some social situations (such as meeting an attractive stranger). Typically, this is a reaction to **evaluation fears** (fears of being inadequate, embarrassed, ridiculed, or rejected). Although fears of rejection are common, they are much more frequent or intense for shy persons (Bradshaw, 2006; Jackson, Towson, & Narduzzi, 1997). A third problem for shy persons is a **self-defeating bias** (distortion) in their thinking. Specifically, shy persons almost always blame themselves when a social encounter doesn't go well. They are unnecessarily self-critical in social situations (Lundh et al., 2002).

Situational Causes of Shyness

Shyness is most often triggered by *novel* or *unfamiliar* social situations. A person who does fine with family or close friends may become shy and awkward when meeting a stranger. Shyness is also magnified by formality, by meeting someone of higher status, by being noticeably different from others, or by being the focus of attention (as in giving a speech) (Larsen & Buss, 2005).

Don't most people become cautious and inhibited in such circumstances? Yes. That's why we need to see how the personalities of shy and non-shy persons differ.

Dynamics of the Shy Personality

There is a tendency to think that shy persons are wrapped up in their own feelings and thoughts. But, surprisingly, researchers Jonathan Cheek and Arnold Buss (1979) found no connection between shyness and **private self-consciousness** (attention to inner feelings, thoughts, and fantasies). Instead, they discovered that shyness is linked to **public self-consciousness** (acute awareness of oneself as a social object). Persons who rate high in public self-consciousness worry about what others think of them (Cowden, 2005).

They worry about saying the wrong thing or appearing foolish. In public, they may feel "naked" or as if others can "see through them." Such feelings trigger anxiety or outright fear during social encounters,

Shyness A tendency to avoid others plus uneasiness and strain when socializing.

Social skills Proficiency at interacting with others.

Social anxiety A feeling of apprehension in the presence of others.

Evaluation fears Fears of being inadequate, embarrassed, ridiculed, or rejected.

Self-defeating bias A distortion of thinking that impairs behaviour.

Private self-consciousness Preoccupation with inner feelings, thoughts, and fantasies.

Public self-consciousness Intense awareness of oneself as a social object.

© David Young-Wolff / PhotoEdit

leading to awkwardness and inhibition (Cowden, 2005). The shy person's anxiety, in turn, often causes him or her to misperceive others in social situations (Schroeder, 1995).

As mentioned, almost everyone feels anxious in at least some social situations. But there is a key difference in the way shy and non-shy persons label this anxiety. Shy persons tend to consider their social anxiety a lasting personality trait. Shyness, in other words, becomes part of their self-concept. In contrast, non-shy persons believe that external situations cause their occasional feelings of shyness. When non-shy persons feel anxiety or "stage fright," they assume that almost anyone would feel as they do under the same circumstances (Zimbardo, Pilkonis, & Norwood, 1978).

Labelling is important because it affects *self-esteem*. In general, non-shy persons tend to have higher self-esteem than shy persons. This is because non-shy persons give themselves credit for their social successes and they recognize that failures are often due to circumstances. In contrast, shy people blame themselves for social failures and never give themselves credit for successes (Girodo, 1978).

Shy Beliefs

What can be done to reduce shyness? Shyness is often maintained by unrealistic or self-defeating beliefs (Antony, 2004; Butler, 2001). Here's a sample of such beliefs:

1. If you wait around long enough at a social gathering, something will happen. Comment: This is really a cover-up for fear of starting a conversation. For two people to meet, at least one has to make an effort, and it might as well be you.
2. Other people who are popular are just lucky when it comes to being invited to social events or asked out. Comment: Except for times when a person is formally introduced to someone new, this is false. People who are more active socially typically make an effort to meet and spend time with others. They join clubs, invite others to do things, strike up conversations, and generally leave little to luck.
3. The odds of meeting someone interested in socializing are always the same, no matter where I am. Comment: This is another excuse for inaction. It pays to seek out situations that have a higher probability of leading to social contact, such as clubs, teams, and school events.
4. If someone doesn't seem to like you right away, she or he really doesn't like you and never will. Comment: This belief leads to much needless shyness. Even when a person doesn't show immediate interest, it doesn't mean the person dislikes you. Liking takes time and opportunity to develop.

Unproductive beliefs like the preceding can be replaced with statements such as the following:

1. I've got to be active in social situations.
2. I can't wait until I'm completely relaxed or comfortable before taking a social risk.
3. I don't need to pretend to be someone I'm not; it just makes me more anxious.
4. I may think other people are harshly evaluating me, but actually I'm being too hard on myself.
5. I can set reasonable goals for expanding my social experience and skills.
6. Even people who are very socially skilful are never successful 100 percent of the time. I shouldn't get so upset when an encounter goes badly. (Adapted from the work of Canadian psychologist Michel Girodo (1978), as well as Antony (2004) and Butler (2001).)

Social Skills

Learning social skills takes practice. There is nothing "innate" about knowing how to meet people or start a conversation. Social skills can be directly practised in a variety of ways. It can be helpful, for instance, to record and listen to several of your conversations. You may be surprised by the way you pause, interrupt, miss cues, or seem uninterested. Similarly, it can be useful to look at yourself in a mirror and exaggerate facial expressions of surprise, interest, dislike, pleasure, and so forth. By such methods, most people can learn to put more animation and skill into their self-presentation. (For a discussion of related skills, see the section on self-assertion in Chapter 14, page 573.)

Conversation

One of the simplest ways to make better conversation is by learning to ask questions. A good series of questions shifts attention to the other person and shows you are interested. Nothing fancy is needed. You can do fine with questions such as "Where do you (work, study, live)? Do you like (dancing, travel, music)? How long have you (been at this school, worked here, lived here)?" After you've broken the ice, the best questions are often those that are open-ended (they can't be answered yes or no):

- "What parts of the country have you seen?" (as opposed to "Have you ever been to Banff National Park?")
- "What's it like living on the west side?" (as opposed to "Do you like living on the west side?")
- "What kinds of food do you like?" (as opposed to "Do you like Chinese cooking?")

It's easy to see why open-ended questions are helpful. In replying to open-ended questions, people often give "free information" about themselves. This extra information can be used to ask other questions or to lead into other topics of conversation.

Overcoming shyness requires a real effort to learn new skills and test old beliefs and attitudes. It may even require the help of a counsellor or therapist. At the very least, a shy person must be willing to take social risks. Breaking down the barriers of shyness will always include some awkward or unsuccessful encounters. Nevertheless, the rewards are powerful: human companionship and personal freedom.

 STUDY BREAK **Shyness and Social Skills**

Reflect

If you are shy, see if you can summarize how social skills, social anxiety, evaluation fears, self-defeating thoughts, and public self-consciousness contribute to your social inhibition. If you're not shy, imagine how you would explain these concepts to a shy friend.

Learning Check

1. Social anxiety and evaluation fears are seen almost exclusively in shy individuals; the non-shy rarely have such experiences. T or F?
2. Unfamiliar people and situations most often trigger shyness. T or F?

3. Public self-consciousness plus a tendency to label oneself as shy are major characteristics of the shy personality. T or F?
4. Changing personal beliefs and practising social skills can be helpful in overcoming shyness. T or F?

Critical Thinking

5. Shyness is a trait of Vonda's personality. Like most shy people, Vonda is most likely to feel shy in unfamiliar social settings. Vonda's shy behaviour demonstrates that the expression of traits is governed by what concept?

Answers

1. F 2. T 3. T 4. T 5. Trait–situation interactions (again).

CHAPTER IN REVIEW

Major Points

- Each of us displays consistent behaviour patterns that define our own personalities and allow us to predict how other people will act.

- Personality can be understood by identifying traits, by probing mental conflicts and dynamics, by noting the effects of prior learning and situations, and by knowing how people perceive themselves.

- Psychologists use interviews, direct observation, questionnaires, and projective tests to measure and assess personality.

- Shyness is related to public self-consciousness and other psychological factors that can be altered, which makes it possible for some people to overcome shyness.

Summary

What do psychologists mean by the term personality? What core concepts make up the field of personality?

- Personality is made up of one's unique and enduring behaviour patterns.

- Character may be defined as personality evaluated, or the possession of desirable qualities.

- Temperament refers to the hereditary and physiological aspects of one's emotional nature.

- Personality traits are lasting personal qualities that are inferred from behaviour.

- Personality types group people into categories on the basis of shared traits.

- Behaviour is influenced by self-concept, which is a perception of one's own personality traits.

- A positive self-evaluation leads to high self-esteem. Low self-esteem is associated with stress, unhappiness, and depression.

- Personality theories combine interrelated assumptions, ideas, and principles to explain personality.

What are personality traits? Are some traits more basic than others? Do traits predict how someone will act in the future?

- Trait theories identify qualities that are most lasting or characteristic of a person.

- Allport made useful distinctions between common traits and individual traits and between cardinal, central, and secondary traits.

- Cattell's theory attributes visible surface traits to the existence of 16 underlying source traits.

- Source traits are measured by the *Sixteen Personality Factor Questionnaire* (16 PF).

- The five-factor model identifies five universal dimensions of personality: extroversion, agreeableness, conscientiousness, neuroticism, and openness to experience. Recently, Canadian psychologists have made a proposal of adding a sixth dimension, that of honesty/humility.

- Traits interact with situations to explain our behaviour.

- Behavioural genetics and studies of identical twins suggest that heredity contributes significantly to adult personality traits.

How do psychodynamic theories explain personality?

- Like other psychodynamic approaches, Sigmund Freud's psychoanalytic theory emphasizes unconscious forces and conflicts within the personality.

- In Freud's theory, personality is made up of the id, ego, and superego.

- Libido, derived from the life instincts, is the primary energy running the personality. Conflicts within the personality may cause neurotic anxiety or moral anxiety and motivate us to use ego-defence mechanisms.

- The personality operates on three levels: the conscious, preconscious, and unconscious.

- The Freudian view of personality development is based on a series of psychosexual stages: the oral, anal, phallic, and genital stages. Fixation at any stage can leave a lasting imprint on personality.

What do behaviourists emphasize in their approach to personality?

- Behavioural theories of personality emphasize learning, conditioning, and immediate effects of the environment (situational determinants).

- Learning theorists Miller and Dollard consider habits the basic core of personality. Habits express the combined effects of drive, cue, response, and reward.

- Social learning theory adds cognitive elements to the behavioural view of personality. Examples include the psychological situation, expectancies, and reinforcement value.

- The behaviouristic view of personality development holds that social reinforcement in four situations is critical. The situations are feeding, toilet or cleanliness training, sex training, and anger or aggression training.

- Identification and imitation are of particular importance in learning to be "male" or "female."
- Psychological androgyny is related to greater behavioural adaptability and flexibility.

How do humanistic theories differ from other perspectives on personality?

- Humanistic theory emphasizes subjective experience and needs for self-actualization.
- Abraham Maslow found that self-actualizers share characteristics that range from efficient perceptions of reality to frequent peak experiences.
- Carl Rogers viewed the self as an entity that emerges from personal experience. We tend to become aware of experiences that match our self-image, while excluding those that are incongruent with it.
- The incongruent person has a highly unrealistic self-image and/or a mismatch between the self-image and the ideal self. The congruent or fully functioning person is flexible and open to experiences and feelings.
- As parents apply conditions of worth to children's behaviour, thoughts, and feelings, children begin to do the same. Internalized conditions of worth then contribute to incongruence, which disrupts the organismic valuing process.

How do psychologists measure personality?

- Techniques typically used for personality assessment are interviews, observation, questionnaires, and projective tests.
- Structured and unstructured interviews provide much information, but they are subject to interviewer bias and misperceptions. The halo effect may also lower the accuracy of an interview.
- Direct observation, sometimes involving situational tests, behavioural assessment, or the use of rating scales, allows evaluation of a person's actual behaviour.

- Personality questionnaires, such as the Minnesota Multiphasic Personality Inventory-2 (MMPI-2), are objective and reliable, but their validity is open to question.
- Projective tests ask a person to project thoughts or feelings to an ambiguous stimulus or unstructured situation.
- The Rorschach Technique, or inkblot test, is a well-known projective technique. A second is the Thematic Apperception Test (TAT).
- Projective tests are low in validity and objectivity. Nevertheless, they are considered useful by many clinicians, particularly as part of a test battery.

What causes shyness? What can be done about it?

- Shyness is a mixture of social inhibition and social anxiety. It is marked by heightened public self-consciousness and a tendency to regard one's shyness as a lasting trait.
- Shyness can be lessened by changing self-defeating beliefs and by improving social skills.

Interactive Learning

Please visit http://www.psychologyjourney4ce.nelson.com for a list of weblinks to relevant psychology sites.

CourseMate

Access an interactive e-book and chapter-specific interactive learning tools, including flashcards, quizzes, videos, and more, in your psychology CourseMate. Visit Nelsonbrain.com to use CourseMate.

psyk.trek   10. Personality theory

TEST YOUR KNOWLEDGE

The questions that follow are only a sample of what you need to know. If you miss any of the items, review the entire chapter and the Study Breaks. Another way to prepare for tests is to use the Study Guide and the Practice Exams that are available with this text.

1. What is being judged when someone's personality is evaluated?
   a. temperament
   b. character
   c. extroversion
   d. self-esteem

2. A personality type is usually defined by the presence of which of the following?
   a. all five personality dimensions
   b. a stable self-concept
   c. several specific traits
   d. a source trait

3. Using factor analysis, what 16 items did personality theorist Raymond Cattell identify?
   a. common traits
   b. source traits
   c. cardinal traits
   d. trait–situation interactions

4. Which of the following is *not* one of the Big Five personality dimensions?
   a. extroversion
   b. agreeableness
   c. neuroticism
   d. androgyny

5. Research methods within which of the following have been used to study the extent to which we inherit personality characteristics?
   a. behavioural genetics
   b. social learning theory
   c. factor analysis
   d. trait profiling

6. According to Freud, which division of personality is governed by the reality principle?
   a. ego
   b. id
   c. ego ideal
   d. superego

7. Freud stated that the mind functions on three levels: the conscious, unconscious, and which of the following?
   a. psyche
   b. preconscious
   c. superego
   d. subconscious

8. According to Freudian theory, where is a fixation most likely for a person who is passive, dependent, and needs lots of attention?
   a. in the oral stage
   b. in the superego
   c. in the Oedipal stage
   d. in the genital stage

9. Who is most likely to have a special interest in the situational determinants of our actions?
   a. psychodynamic theorists
   b. humanistic theorists
   c. learning theorists
   d. behavioural geneticists

10. Which of the following is *not* a concept of social learning theory?
    a. incongruence
    b. expectancy
    c. self-efficacy
    d. reinforcement value

11. Maslow thought of peak experiences as temporary moments of which of the following?
    a. congruence
    b. positive self-regard
    c. self-actualization
    d. self-reinforcement

12. According to Carl Rogers, what replaces conditions of worth to encourage personal growth?
    a. self-efficacy
    b. instrumental worth
    c. latency
    d. organismic valuing

13. The halo effect can be a serious problem in accurate personality assessment that is based on
    a. projective testing
    b. behavioural recording
    c. interviewing
    d. the Thematic Apperception Test (TAT)

14. Situational testing is primarily an example of using _____ to assess personality.
    a. direct observation
    b. structured interviewing
    c. cardinal traits
    d. projective techniques

15. Which of the following items does *not* belong with the others?
    a. Rorschach Technique
    b. Thematic Apperception Test (TAT)
    c. MMPI-2
    d. projective testing

16. By definition, what term describes a test that measures what it claims to measure?
    a. valid
    b. situational
    c. objective
    d. reliable

17. Which of the following is an objective personality questionnaire?
    a. the Thematic Apperception Test (TAT)
    b. the in-basket test
    c. the leaderless group discussion test
    d. the Minnesota Multiphasic Personality Inventory-2 (MMPI-2)

18. Which clinical subscale of the Minnesota Multiphasic Personality Inventory-2 (MMPI-2) is designed to detect phobias and compulsive actions?
    a. hysteria
    b. paranoia
    c. psychasthenia
    d. mania

19. Which of the following is shyness *not* related to?
    a. private self-consciousness
    b. social anxiety
    c. self-esteem
    d. blaming oneself for social failures

20. How do shy persons tend to consider their social anxiety?
    a. as a situational reaction
    b. as a personality trait
    c. as a public efficacy
    d. as a habit

ANSWERS 1.b 2.c 3.b 4.d 5.a 6.a 7.b 8.a 9.c 10.a 11.c 12.d 13.c 14.a 15.c 16.a 17.d 18.c 19.a 20.b

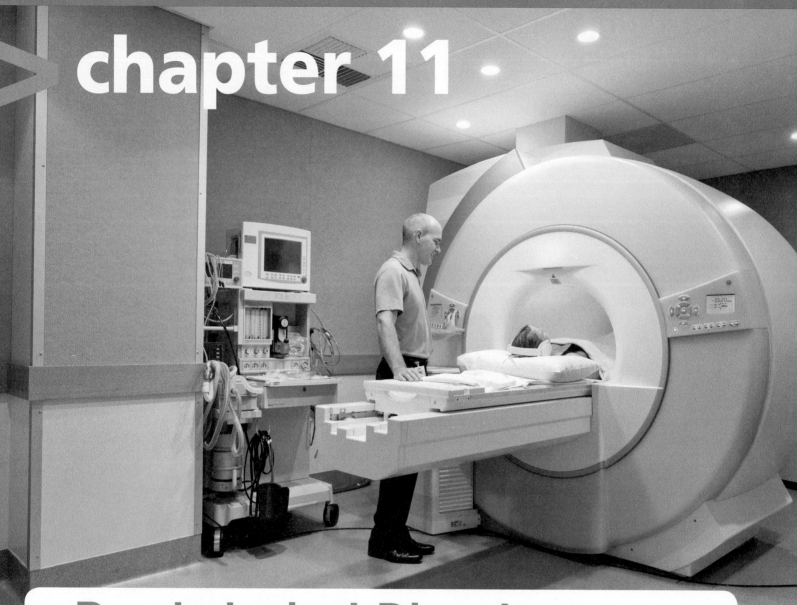

Psychological Disorders

JOURNEY INTO PSYCHOLOGY: A HERO'S ODYSSEY

In a far-off land in April 1994, under the hot African sun, a colossal tragedy was about to take place. One man whose fate it was to witness this event was a Canadian, General Roméo Dallaire (pictured on the right), commander of the United Nations forces in Rwanda. His job was to keep the peace following the end of a civil war in that country. But as he remarked later, peace was murdered ruthlessly as a vicious campaign of mass killings broke out. In just 100 days, nearly 800 000 (mostly Tutsi) Rwandans were ruthlessly slaughtered by the Hutu, making it one of the worst genocides of our time. Dallaire asked his bosses at the United Nations for 5000 soldiers to stop the butchery from spiralling out of control, but his request was not granted. He could do nothing but watch helplessly as the sounds, sights, and horror of death engulfed the country. After the carnage had ceased and a semblance of peace was restored, Dallaire returned to Canada.

He received tremendous praise for his valiant efforts to deal with an impossible situation and was given numerous honours. Dallaire, however, was far from being in a celebratory mood. He was relentlessly tormented by the memories of the horrors he had witnessed. He experienced terrifying spells of anxiety and nightmares, became suicidal, and was forced to take time off work to seek therapy. He was guilt-ridden because he blamed himself for not doing enough to prevent the slaughter. At the lowest point in his life, he was found in a drunken stupor by the police under a park bench in Ottawa. What Dallaire was going through was diagnosed as post-traumatic stress disorder. Courageously, he began to face the demons that were haunting him and managed to turned his life around completely. He relived the difficult events of the war by writing a book called *Shake Hands with the Devil— The Failure of Humanity in Rwanda.* He went on to testify against those who had perpetrated ethnic hatred and violence. At present, Dallaire serves in the Canadian Senate and campaigns tirelessly against the use of child soldiers in wars around the world.

Sandy Young/WireImage/Getty Images

Post-traumatic stress disorder is an incapacitating condition that brings untold pain to its sufferers and their families. Besides this condition, we will discuss numerous other psychological disorders in this chapter. For now, here are some facts you may find surprising as well as interesting:

- About 20 percent of Canada's adult population suffers from a mental disorder or drug abuse in any given year.
- One out of every 100 persons will become so severely disturbed as to require hospitalization at some point in his or her lifetime.
- Schizophrenia affects over 200 000 Canadians.
- Twelve percent of Canada's population develops depression, and 10 percent of people have an anxiety disorder.
- One out of every eight school-age children is seriously maladjusted.
- Each year in North America, over 2 million people are admitted to general hospitals for psychiatric treatment.
- Twenty-five percent of all hospital days in Canada are spent in caring for patients with a mental illness.

What does it mean to be "crazy"? In the 1800s, doctors and non-professionals alike used terms such as "crazy," "insane," "cracked," and "lunatic" quite freely. The "insane" were thought of as bizarre and definitely different from the rest of the population. Today, our understanding of psychological disorders is more sophisticated. To draw the line between normal and abnormal, we must weigh some complex issues. In this chapter, we will explore some of those issues, as well as an array of psychological problems.

psychopathology The scientific study of mental, emotional, and behavioural disorders; also, abnormal or maladaptive behaviour.

Subjective discomfort Personal, private feelings of discomfort, unhappiness, or emotional distress.

Statistical abnormality Abnormality defined on the basis of an extreme score on some dimension, such as IQ or anxiety.

Survey Questions

- How is normality defined, and what are the major psychological disorders?
- What is a personality disorder?
- What problems result when a person experiences high levels of anxiety?
- How do psychologists explain anxiety-based disorders?
- What are the major characteristics of schizophrenia? What causes it?
- What are mood disorders? What causes them?
- Why do people commit suicide? Can suicide be prevented?

NORMALITY—WHAT IS NORMAL?

SURVEY QUESTION>

How is normality defined, and what are the major psychological disorders?

"That guy is really wacko. His porch lights are dimming." "Yeah, the butter's sliding off his waffle. I think he's ready to go postal." Informally, it's tempting to make snap judgments about mental health. However, to seriously classify people as psychologically unhealthy raises complex and age-old issues. The scientific study of mental, emotional, and behavioural disorders is known as **psychopathology.** The term also refers to mental or psychological disorders themselves, such as schizophrenia or depression, and to behaviour patterns that make people unhappy and impair personal growth (Butcher, Mineka, & Hooley, 2007).

Defining abnormality can be tricky. We might begin by saying that psychopathology is characterized by **subjective discomfort** (anxiety, depression, or other signs of emotional distress).

But couldn't a person be seriously disturbed without feeling discomfort? Yes. Psychopathology doesn't always cause personal anguish. A person suffering from mania might feel "on top of the world." Also, a lack of discomfort may reveal a problem. For example, if you showed no signs of grief after the death of a close friend, we might suspect psychopathology. In practice, subjective discomfort explains most instances in which people voluntarily seek professional help.

Some psychologists use statistics to define normality more objectively. **Statistical abnormality** refers to scoring very high or low on some dimension, such as intelligence, anxiety, or depression. Anxiety, for example, is a feature of several psychological disorders. To measure it, we could create a test to learn how many people show low, medium, or high levels of anxiety. Usually, the results of such tests will form a normal (bell-shaped) curve, as shown in Figure 11.1. (Normal in this case is a statistical concept. It refers only to the shape of the curve.) Notice that most people score in the central region of such curves. A person who deviates from the average by being anxious all the time (high anxiety) might be abnormal. So, too, might a person who never feels anxiety.

Then a statistical definition of abnormality tells us nothing about the meaning of deviations from the norm? Right. It is as statistically "abnormal" (unusual) for a person to score above 145 on an IQ test as it is to score below 55. However, only the lower score is regarded as "abnormal" or undesirable (Wakefield, 1992).

Statistical definitions also can't tell us where to draw the line between normality and abnormality. To

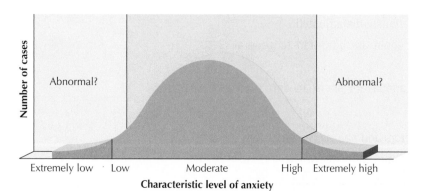

▶▶**FIGURE 11.1** The number of people displaying a personal characteristic may help define what is statistically abnormal.

take a new example, we could obtain the average frequency of sexual intercourse for persons of a particular age, sex, sexual orientation, and marital status. Clearly, a person who feels driven to have sex dozens of times a day has a problem. But as we move back toward the norm we face the statistical problem of drawing lines. How often does a normal behaviour have to occur before it becomes abnormal? As you can see, statistical boundary lines tend to be somewhat arbitrary (Comer, 2011).

Nonconformity may also underlie psychological disorders. **Social nonconformity** refers to disobeying social standards for acceptable conduct. Extreme nonconformity can lead to destructive or self-destructive behaviour. (Think, for instance, of a drug abuser or a prostitute.) However, we must be careful to separate unhealthy nonconformity from creative lifestyles. Many eccentric "characters" are charming and emotionally stable. Note, too, that strictly following social norms is no guarantee of mental health. In some cases, psychopathology involves rigid conformity. (See Discovering Psychology: "Crazy for a Day.")

A young woman ties a thick rubber cord around her ankles, screams hysterically, and jumps headfirst off a bridge. Thirty years ago, the woman's behaviour might have seemed completely crazy. Today, it is a routine form of entertainment (called bungee jumping).

Before any behaviour can be defined as abnormal, we must consider the **situational context** (social situation, behavioural setting, or general circumstances) in which it occurs. Is it normal to stand outside and water a lawn with a hose? It depends on whether it is raining. Is it abnormal for a grown man to remove his pants and expose himself to another man or woman in a place of business? It depends on whether the other person is a bank clerk or a doctor! Almost any imaginable behaviour can be considered normal in some contexts. In mid-October 1972, an airplane carrying a rugby team called the Old Christians crashed in the snow-capped Andes of South America. Incredibly, 16 of the 45 people who had been aboard at the time of the crash survived 73 days in deep snow and subfreezing temperatures. They were forced to use extremely grim measures to do so—they ate the bodies of those who had died in the crash.

Culture is one of the most influential contexts in which any behaviour is judged. In some cultures it is considered normal to defecate or urinate in public or to appear naked in public. In our culture, such behaviours would be considered unusual or abnormal. In some Muslim cultures, women who remain completely housebound are considered normal or even virtuous. In Western cultures they might be diagnosed as suffering from a disorder called agoraphobia (Fabrega, 2004). (Agoraphobia is described later in this chapter.)

Social nonconformity does not automatically indicate psychopathology.

Social nonconformity Failure to conform to societal norms or the usual minimum standards for social conduct.
Situational context The social situation, behavioural setting, or general circumstances in which an action takes place.

USING PSYCHOLOGY

Crazy for a Day

Performing a mildly abnormal behaviour is a good way to get a sense of how social norms define "normality" in daily life. Here's your assignment: Do something strange in public and observe how people react to you. (Please don't do anything dangerous, harmful, or offensive—and don't get arrested!) Here are some deviant behaviours that other students have staged:

- Sit in the dining area of a fast-food restaurant and loudly carry on a conversation with an imaginary companion.
- Stand in a busy hallway on campus and adopt a kung fu stance. Remain in that position for 10 minutes.
- Walk around campus on a sunny day while wearing a raincoat and carrying an open umbrella. Keep the umbrella over your head when you are inside buildings.

- Stick one finger in your nose and another in your ear. Walk through a busy shopping mall.
- Cover your head with aluminum foil for a day.

Does the idea of performing any of these actions make you uncomfortable? If so, you may not need to do anything more to appreciate how powerfully social norms constrain our actions. As we have noted, social nonconformity is just one facet of abnormal behaviour. Nevertheless, actions that are regarded as "strange" within a particular culture are often the first sign to others that a person has a problem.

The Politics of Madness

The year is 1840. You are a slave in the U.S. South who has tried repeatedly to escape from a cruel and abusive master. An expert is consulted about your "abnormal" behaviour. His conclusion? You are suffering from "drapetomania," a mental "disorder" that causes slaves to run away (Wakefield, 1992).

As this example suggests, psychiatric terms are easily abused. Historically, some have been applied to culturally disapproved behaviours that are not really disorders. For example, all of the following were once considered disorders: childhood masturbation, lack of vaginal orgasm, self-defeating personality (applied mainly to women), and nymphomania (being a woman with a healthy sexual appetite) (Wakefield, 1992). Even today, race, gender, and social class continue to affect the diagnosis of various disorders (Durand, Barlow, & Stewart, 2007).

Gender is probably the most common source of bias in judging normality because standards tend to be based on males

(Nolen-Hoeksema & Rector, 2008; Widiger, 2005). According to well-known Canadian psychologist Paula Caplan (1995) and others, women are penalized both for conforming to female stereotypes and for ignoring them. If a woman is independent, aggressive, and unemotional, she may be considered "unhealthy." Yet, at the same time, a woman who is vain, emotional, irrational, and dependent on others (all "feminine" traits in our culture) may be classified as a histrionic or dependent personality (Bornstein, 1996). Indeed, a majority of persons classified as having dependent personality disorder are women. In view of this, Paula Caplan asks, why isn't there a category called "delusional dominating personality disorder" for obnoxious men (Caplan, 1995)?

The differences we have reviewed illustrate the subtle influence that culture can have on perceptions of disorder and normality. Be cautious before you leap to conclusions about the mental health of others.

Cultural relativity Perceptions and judgments made relative to the values of one's culture.

Maladaptive behaviour Behaviour that makes it difficult to adapt to the environment and meet the demands of day-to-day life.

Mental (or psychological) disorder A significant impairment in psychological functioning.

Thus, **cultural relativity** (the idea that judgments are made relative to the values of one's culture) can affect the diagnosis of psychological disorders (Alarcon, 1995). (See Human Diversity: "The Politics of Madness.") Still, all cultures classify people as abnormal if they fail to communicate with others or are consistently unpredictable in their actions.

Core Features of Disordered Behaviour

If abnormality is so hard to define, how are judgments of psychopathology made? It's clear that all the standards we have discussed are relative. However, abnormal behaviour does have two core features. First, it is **maladaptive.** Rather than helping people cope successfully, abnormal behaviour makes it more difficult for them to meet the demands of day-to-day life. Second, people suffering from psychological disorders have much less control than others over their ability to control thoughts, behaviours, or feelings. For example, gambling is not a problem if people bet for entertainment and can maintain self-control. However, compulsive gambling is a sign of psychopathology. In the most extreme cases, people become a danger to themselves or others, which is clearly maladaptive (Hansell, 2007).

In practice, deciding that a person needs help usually occurs when the person does something (hits someone, hallucinates, stares into space, collects rolls of toilet paper, and so forth) that annoys or gains the attention of a person in a position of power in the person's life (an employer, teacher, parent, spouse, or the person himself or herself). That person then does something about it. (A police officer may be called, the person may be urged to see a psychologist, a relative may start commitment proceedings, or the person may voluntarily seek help.)

Classifying Mental Disorders—Problems by the Book

Up until recently, in Canada and the United States, psychological problems have been classified by using the Diagnostic and Statistical Manual of Mental Disorders (DSM-IV-TR) (American Psychiatric Association [APA], 2000). A new edition of this manual, called DSM-5, is being published in 2013. The DSM is designed to help mental health professionals with the correct identification of psychological disorders. This process then leads them to select the best therapies for their clients.

A **mental (or psychological) disorder** is a significant impairment in psychological functioning (Comer, 2011). If you were to glance through the DSM manual, you would see many

Courtesy of Ulrike Kantor, Ulrike Kantor Gallery.

The self-portraits shown here were painted by Andy Wilf between 1978 and 1981. During that time, Wilf is said to have increasingly abused drugs and alcohol. This dramatic series of images is a record of his self-destructive descent into a private hell. The third painting shows a shrouded skull—and foretells the artist's fate. Wilf died of a drug overdose. Drug abuse is but one of the many psychopathologies, or "problems in living," psychologists seek to alleviate.

disorders organized in different categories. Table 11.1 lists some common psychological disorders together with some examples of the types of problems people suffering from these disorders would experience.

In addition to the formal mental disorders we have mentioned, many cultures have names for "unofficial" psychological "disorders." See Human Diversity: "Running Amok with Cultural Maladies" for some samples.

General Risk Factors

What causes psychological disorders like those listed in Table 11.1? We will soon explore the causes of some specific problems. For now, it is worth noting that a variety of risk factors contribute to psychopathology. This means that if you have had exposure to one or more of

■ Table 11.1 Some Categories of Psychopathology

Type of Disorder	Primary Symptom	Typical Signs of Trouble
Psychotic disorders	Loss of contact with reality	You hear or see things that others don't; your mind has been playing tricks on you.
Mood disorders	Mania or depression	You feel sad and hopeless, or you talk too loud and too fast and have a rush of ideas and feelings that others think are unreasonable.
Anxiety disorders	High anxiety or anxiety-based disorders	You have anxiety attacks and feel like you are going to die, or you are afraid to do things that most people can do, or you spend unusual amounts of time doing things like washing your hands or counting your heartbeats.
Somatoform disorders	Bodily complaints without an organic (physical) basis	You feel physically sick, but your doctor says nothing is wrong with you, or you suffer from pain that has no physical basis, or you are preoccupied with thoughts about being sick.
Dissociative disorders	Amnesia, feelings of unreality, multiple identities	There are major gaps in your memory of events; you feel like you are a robot or a stranger to yourself; others tell you that you have done things that you don't remember doing.
Personality disorders	Unhealthy personality patterns	Your behaviour patterns repeatedly cause problems at work, at school, and in your relationships with others.
Sexual disorder	Deviant sexual behaviour, problems in sexual adjustment	You can gain sexual satisfaction only by engaging in highly atypical sexual behaviour, or you have problems with sexual desire, arousal, or performance.
Substance-related disorders	Problems related to drug use	You have been drinking too much, using illegal drugs, or taking prescription drugs more often than you should.

Running Amok with Cultural Maladies

Every culture recognizes the existence of psychopathology, and most have at least a few folk names for afflictions. Here are some examples from around the world:

- *Amok.* Men in Malaysia, Laos, the Philippines, and Polynesia who believe they have been insulted are sometimes known to go amok. After a period of brooding they erupt into an outburst of violent, aggressive, or homicidal behaviour randomly directed at people and objects.
- *Susto.* Among Latin Americans, the symptoms of susto include insomnia, irritability, phobias, and an increase in sweating and heart rate. Susto can result if someone is badly frightened by a black magic curse. In extreme cases, voodoo death can result, as the person is literally scared to death.
- *Ghost sickness.* Among many North American Aboriginal groups, people who become preoccupied with death and the deceased are said to suffer from ghost sickness. The symptoms of ghost sickness include bad dreams, weakness, loss of appetite, fainting, dizziness, fear, anxiety, hallucinations, loss of consciousness, confusion, feelings of futility, and a sense of suffocation.
- *Koro.* In south and east Asia, a man may experience sudden and intense anxiety that his penis (or, occasionally in females, the vulva and nipples) will recede into the body. In addition to the terror this incites, victims also believe that advanced cases of koro can cause death. A similar fear of shrinking genitals has also been reported from West Africa (Dzokoto & Adams, 2005).
- *Pibloktoq (or Arctic hysteria).* In the Arctic region, an Inuit person may experience mild irritation and isolation, followed by a spell involving highly unusual behaviours. The person may yell obscenities, break objects, tear off clothing, eat feces, or perform other irrational acts. This period of wild excitement is followed by seizures and coma. Interestingly, the affected person typically remembers nothing about the intense episode.
- *Dhat.* In Indian society, dhat is the fear of the loss of semen during nocturnal emissions. A man suffering from dhat will feel anxious and perhaps also guilty. He may also experience fatigue, loss of appetite, weakness, anxiety, and sexual dysfunction.
- *Zar.* In North African and Middle Eastern societies, zar is said to occur when spirits possess an individual. Zar is marked by shouting, laughing, hitting the head against a wall, singing, or weeping. Victims may become withdrawn, and they may refuse to eat or carry out daily tasks.

The existence of such terms emphasizes that people have a need to label and categorize disturbed behaviour. As you can see, however, folk terminology tends to be vague. Most of the problems listed here include symptoms from more than one of the psychological disorders described in DSM-IV-TR. As a result they provide little guidance about the true nature of a person's problems or the best ways to treat them. That's why the DSM is based on empirical data and clinical observations. Otherwise, psychologists and psychiatrists would be no better than folk healers or shamans when making diagnoses. By the way, culture-bound disorders occur in all societies. For example, American psychologists Pamela Keel and Kelly Klump believe that bulimia is primarily a syndrome of Western cultures (Keel & Klump, 2003). (Sources: Durand et al., 2007; López & Guarnaccia, 2000; Sumathipala, Siribaddana, & Bhugra, 2004.)

these factors, your chances of developing a psychological disorder increase more than those of someone who has not been subjected to these variables.

- **Biological/physical factors:** genetic defects or inherited vulnerabilities, poor prenatal care, very low birth weight, chronic physical illness or disability, exposure to toxic chemicals or drugs, head injuries.
- **Psychological factors:** stress, low intelligence, lack of control or mastery.
- **Family factors:** parents who are immature, have a history of mental illness, or are criminal or abusive; severe marital strife; extremely poor child discipline; disordered family communication patterns.
- **Social conditions:** poverty, stressful living conditions, homelessness, social disorganization, overcrowding.

Insanity

Which of the psychological disorders causes insanity? None. **Insanity** is a legal term. It refers to an inability to manage one's affairs or foresee the consequences of one's actions. People who are declared insane are not legally responsible for their actions. If necessary, they can be involuntarily committed to a psychiatric hospital. The Canadian Criminal Code uses the expression "criminally not responsible on account of mental disorder" instead of insanity.

Legally, insanity is established by testimony from expert witnesses (psychologists and psychiatrists). An **expert witness** is a person recognized by a court of law as being qualified to give opinions on a specific topic. People who are involuntarily committed are usually

Insanity A legal term that refers to a mental inability to manage one's affairs or to be aware of the consequences of one's actions.

Expert witness A person recognized by a court of law as being qualified to give expert testimony on a specific topic.

judged to be a danger to themselves or to others, or they have a severe mental disability (Luchins et al., 2004). Involuntary commitments happen most often when people are brought to emergency rooms. Then, if two doctors agree that the person will either commit suicide or hurt someone else, she or he is admitted to the hospital (Gorman, 1996).

> **Antisocial personality** A person who lacks a conscience; is emotionally shallow, impulsive, and selfish; and tends to manipulate others.

PERSONALITY DISORDERS—BLUEPRINTS FOR MALADJUSTMENT

<SURVEY QUESTION
What is a personality disorder?

"Get out of here and leave me alone so I can die in peace," Judy screamed at her nurses in the seclusion room of the psychiatric hospital. On one of her arms, long, dark red marks mingled with the scars of previous suicide attempts. Judy once bragged that her record was 67 stitches. Today, the nurses had to strap her into restraints to keep her from gouging out her own eyes. She was given a sedative and slept for 12 hours. She woke calmly and asked for her therapist—even though her latest outburst began when he cancelled a morning appointment and changed it to the afternoon.

Judy has a borderline personality disorder. Although she is capable of working, Judy has repeatedly lost jobs because of her turbulent relationships with other people. At times she can be friendly and a real charmer. At other times she is extremely unpredictable, moody, and even suicidal. Being a friend to Judy can be a fearsome challenge. Cancelling an appointment, forgetting a special date, a wrong turn of phrase—these and similar small incidents may trigger Judy's anger or, worse yet, a suicide attempt.

Maladaptive Personality Patterns

As stated earlier, a person with a personality disorder has a very maladaptive personality pattern. For example, people who have paranoid personality disorder are suspicious, hypersensitive, and wary of others. Narcissistic persons need constant admiration, and they are lost in fantasies of power, wealth, brilliance, beauty, or love. Celebrities appear more likely to be narcissistic than non-celebrities, perhaps because they receive so much attention (Young & Pinsky, 2006). The dependent personality has an extreme lack of self-confidence. Dependent persons allow others to run their lives, and they place everyone else's needs before their own. People with a histrionic personality disorder constantly seek attention by dramatizing their emotions and actions.

Typically, patterns such as the ones just described begin during adolescence or even childhood. The list of personality disorders is long, so let's focus on a single, frequently misunderstood problem, the antisocial personality.

Antisocial Personality

What are the characteristics of an antisocial personality? A person with an **antisocial personality** lacks a conscience. Such people are impulsive, selfish, dishonest, emotionally shallow, and manipulative (Lykken, 1995). Antisocial persons, who are sometimes called sociopaths or psychopaths, are poorly socialized and seem to be incapable of having deep feelings, such as guilt, shame, fear, loyalty, or love (APA, 2000).

What causes sociopathy? People with antisocial personalities show similar problems in childhood (Burt et al., 2007). Typically, people with antisocial personalities were emotionally deprived, neglected, and physically abused as children (Pollock et al., 1990). Adult sociopaths also display subtle neurological problems (see Figure 11.2). For example, they have unusual brain activity patterns that suggest underarousal of the brain. This may explain why sociopaths tend to be thrill-seekers. Quite likely, they are searching for stimulation strong enough to overcome their chronic underarousal and feelings of "boredom" (Hare, 2006).

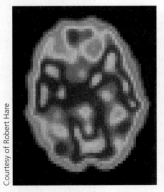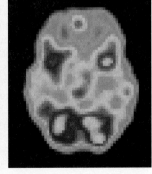

Courtesy of Robert Hare

▶▶**FIGURE 11.2** Using a sophisticated brain-scanning technique, Canadian psychologist Robert Hare found that the normally functioning brain (*left*) lights up with activity when a person sees emotion-laden words such as "maggot" and "cancer." But the brain of a person with antisocial personality disorder (*right*) remains inactive, especially in areas associated with feelings and self-control. When Dr. Hare showed the right image to several neurologists, one asked, "Is this person from Mars?"

In a revealing study, sociopaths were shown extremely grisly and unpleasant photographs. The photos are so upsetting that normal people are visibly startled by them. The sociopaths, however, showed no startle response to the photos. (They didn't bat an eye.) Those with antisocial personalities might therefore be described as emotionally cold. They simply do not feel normal pangs of conscience, guilt, or anxiety (Blair et al., 2006). This coldness seems to account for an unusual ability to calmly lie, cheat, steal, or take advantage of others (Lykken, 1995).

The case of Paul Bernardo fits the definition of antisocial personality disorder perfectly. Known as the Scarborough rapist, Bernardo sexually assaulted many young women in the late 1980s in the Toronto suburb of Scarborough. Together with his wife, Karla Homolka, acting as a willing accomplice, Bernardo went on to kidnap, brutally torture, rape, and murder teenaged girls in the Niagara region. Homolka's own sister was one of their victims. The videotapes showing Bernardo's sadistic torture were so horrific that even some lawyers could not bring themselves to watch them. Bernardo has allegedly confessed to having no conscience. He planned and carried out gruesome acts without regard for others' feelings or their right to exist. You would not be able to guess any of this if you had met him at a social gathering—he may have appeared very charming and proven to be delightful company.

Are sociopaths dangerous? Sociopaths tend to have a long history of conflict with society. Many are delinquents or criminals who may be a threat to the general public (Ogloff, 2006). One study found that psychopaths are unaware of signs of disgust in others. This may add to their capacity for cruelty and their ability to use others (Kosson et al., 2002).

Bernardo was clearly a very dangerous criminal. Not all individuals with antisocial personality disorder commit rape or murder, however. Some may be successful business people, entertainers, or politicians. They attain success by lying, cheating, and coldly taking advantage of others (Ogloff, 2006). The defining feature of their personality is that they feel no remorse over their deceitful tendencies.

Does Russell Williams (pictured below) have antisocial personality disorder? Psychologists are unsure. Unlike Bernardo and his type, who display antisocial tendencies early in life, Russell began inflicting pain on others in his mid-40s, which is quite late for someone with this disorder. Usually, by the time they reach their 40s, such people begin to slow down and decrease their

Studies show that more than 65 percent of all persons with antisocial personalities have been arrested, usually for crimes such as robbery, vandalism, or rape. You may have heard about a recent case of a former decorated soldier of the Canadian Air Force who was convicted of very gruesome crimes. Russell Williams seemed to be leading a double life, one in which he was a married family man and held a very responsible job. In his other role, he was a sexual predator who not only stole copious quantities of women's underwear to satisfy his perverted desires but had assaulted many females. Subsequently, he turned to murdering his victims after raping them first. Upon being charged with these heinous crimes, Russell confessed to everything and led the police to places where his victims' bodies could be recovered.

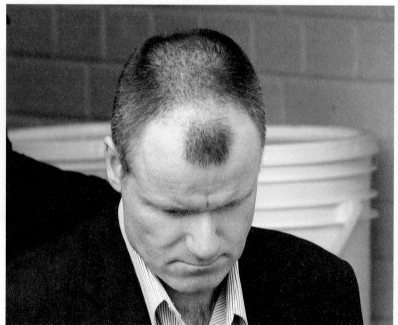

Nathan Denette / Associated Press Images

STUDY BREAK   Normality, Psychopathology, and Personality Disorders

Reflect

Think of an instance of abnormal behaviour you have witnessed. By what formal standards would the behaviour be regarded as abnormal? In what way was the behaviour maladaptive?

Many of the characteristics that define personality disorders exist to a minor degree in normal personalities. Try to think of a person you know who has some of the characteristics described for each type of personality disorder.

Learning Check

1. Statistical definitions of abnormality successfully avoid the limitations of other approaches. T or F?
2. One of the most powerful contexts in which judgments of normality and abnormality are made is
   - a. the family
   - b. occupational settings
   - c. religious systems
   - d. culture
3. Amnesia, multiple identities, and depersonalization are possible problems in
   - a. mood disorders
   - b. somatoform disorders
   - c. psychosis
   - d. dissociative disorders
4. Which one of the following is not a major psychological problem listed in the DSM system?
   - a. mood disorders
   - b. personality disorders
   - c. insanity
   - d. anxiety disorders
5. People who hear voices and experience bizarre thoughts would have which psychological disorder?
   - a. psychotic disorder
   - b. anxiety disorder
   - c. personality disorder
   - d. mood disorder
6. Which of the following personality disorders is associated with an inflated sense of self-importance and a constant need for attention and admiration?
   - a. narcissistic
   - b. antisocial
   - c. paranoid
   - d. manipulative
7. Antisocial personality disorder is difficult to treat, but there is typically a decline in psychopathic behaviour a year or two after adolescence. T or F?

Critical Thinking

8. Brian, a fan of grunge rock, occasionally wears a skirt in public. Does Brian's cross-dressing indicate that he has a mental disorder?

Answers

1. F 2. d 3. d 4. c 5. a 6. a 7. F 8. Probably not. Undoubtedly, Brian's cross-dressing is socially disapproved of by many people. Nevertheless, to be classified as a mental disorder it must cause him to feel disabling shame, guilt, depression, or anxiety. The cultural relativity of behaviour like Brian's is revealed by the fact that it is fashionable and acceptable for women to wear men's clothing.

---

devious activities (Tavshunsky, 2010). There is certainly more to Russell Williams than meets the eye, so psychologists have their work cut out for them before such an intricate case can be understood more thoroughly.

Can psychopathy be treated? Antisocial personality disorder is rarely treated successfully (Hare, 2006). All too often, psychopaths manipulate therapy, just like any other situation. If it is to their advantage to act "cured," they will do so. However, they return to their former behaviour patterns as soon as possible. On a more positive note, psychopathic tendencies do tend to decline somewhat after age 40, even without treatment.

> **Anxiety** Apprehension, dread, or uneasiness similar to fear but based on a perceived sense of threat.

ANXIETY-BASED DISORDERS—WHEN ANXIETY RULES

Anxiety refers to feelings of apprehension, dread, or uneasiness. We all feel anxiety, but anxiety that is out of proportion to a situation or does not subside when the threat (or perceived threat) is over may reveal a problem. Tim, a college student, became unbearably anxious whenever he took exams. By the time he went to see a counsellor, Tim had skipped several tests and was in danger of dropping out of school. In general, anxiety-related problems like Tim's involve

<SURVEY QUESTION
What problems result when a person experiences high levels of anxiety?

- high levels of anxiety and/or restrictive, self-defeating behaviour patterns
- a tendency to employ elaborate schemes to deal with perceived threats or to use avoidance responses to get through the day
- pervasive feelings of stress, insecurity, inferiority, unhappiness, and dissatisfaction with life

Typically, people with anxiety-related problems are afraid that something bad will happen to them, and they are unable to do anything constructive about it. They struggle to preserve control, but their efforts are ineffective and they remain unhappy (Rachman, 2004).

Adjustment disorder An emotional disturbance caused by ongoing stressors within the range of common experience.

Generalized anxiety disorder A chronic state of tension and worry about work, relationships, ability, or impending disaster.

If anxiety is a normal emotion, when does it signify a problem? A problem exists when intense anxiety prevents people from doing what they want or need to do. Also, their anxieties are out of control—they simply cannot stop worrying.

Adjustment Disorders

Do such problems cause a "nervous breakdown"? People suffering from anxiety-based problems may be miserable, but they rarely experience a "breakdown." Actually, the term *nervous breakdown* has no formal meaning. Nevertheless, a problem known as an adjustment disorder does come close to what many people have in mind when they say someone had a breakdown.

Adjustment disorders occur when ordinary stresses push people beyond their ability to cope with life. Examples of such stresses are prolonged unemployment, intense marital strife, and chronic physical illness. People suffering from an adjustment disorder may be extremely irritable, anxious, apathetic, or depressed. They also have trouble sleeping, lose their appetite, and suffer from various physical complaints (APA, 2000). Often, their problems can be relieved by rest, sedation, supportive counselling, and a chance to talk through fears and anxieties.

How is an adjustment disorder different from an anxiety disorder? The outward symptoms are similar. However, adjustment disorders disappear when a person's life circumstances improve. People suffering from anxiety disorders experience a sense of misery, regardless of what's happening around them, even when they have no obvious external pressures. They feel that they must be on guard against *future* situations that *could* happen at any time (Barlow, 2000).

Anxiety Disorders

In most anxiety disorders, distress seems greatly out of proportion to a person's circumstances. For example, consider the following description of Adrian H:

> She becomes very anxious that her children "might have been hurt or killed if they were out of the neighbourhood playing and she hadn't heard from them in a couple of hours." She also worries all the time about her job performance and her relationships with men. Adrian believes that men rarely call back after a date or two because "they can sense I'm not a fun person." She never really relaxes, has difficulty focusing at work, has frequent headaches, and suffers from insomnia. (Adapted from Brown & Barlow, 2007.)

Distress like Adrian H's is a key ingredient in anxiety disorders. Many psychologists believe it also underlies dissociative and somatoform disorders, where maladaptive behaviour serves to reduce anxiety and discomfort. To deepen your understanding, let's first examine the anxiety disorders themselves. Then we will see how anxiety contributes to other problems.

Generalized Anxiety Disorder

A person with a **generalized anxiety disorder** has experienced at least six months of excessive anxiety and worry (Dugas et al., 1998). Sufferers typically complain of sweating, a racing heart, clammy hands, dizziness, upset stomach, rapid breathing, irritability, and poor concentration. Most of us may spend some time worrying about one thing or another at various points in our lives, but people with generalized anxiety disorder are consumed by numerous insignificant matters that take up much of their time and energy. They are not able to turn off the worry process. Overall, more women than men have generalized anxiety disorder (Brown & Barlow, 2007).

Was Adrian H's problem a generalized anxiety disorder? Yes. However, if she also experienced *anxiety attacks,* then she would be diagnosed with panic disorder. It is estimated that 3.7 percent of Canadians develop panic disorder at some time in their lives (Ramage-Morin, 2004).

Panic Disorder (without Agoraphobia)

In **panic disorder (without agoraphobia),** people are highly anxious and also have moments when they feel sudden, intense, unexpected panic. During a panic attack, victims experience a racing heart, chest pain, choking, dizziness, feelings of unreality, trembling, or fears of losing control. Many believe that they are having a heart attack, are going insane, or are about to die. This pattern leaves victims unhappy and uncomfortable much of the time. Again, the majority of people who suffer from panic disorder are women (Foot & Koszycki, 2004).

To get an idea of how a panic attack feels, imagine that you are trapped in your stateroom on a sinking ocean liner (the *Titanic*?). The room fills with water. When only a small air space remains near the ceiling and you are gasping for air, you'll know what a panic attack feels like.

Panic Disorder (with Agoraphobia)

In a **panic disorder (with agoraphobia),** people suffer from chronic anxiety and brief moments of sudden panic. In addition, they have agoraphobia (ah-go-rah-FOH-bee-ah), which is an intense, irrational fear that a panic attack will occur in a public place or unfamiliar situation. That is, agoraphobics intensely fear leaving their home and familiar surroundings. Typically, they find ways of avoiding places that frighten them—such as crowds, open roads, supermarkets, automobiles, and so on. As a result, some people with agoraphobia become prisoners in their own homes (APA, 2000).

Agoraphobia

Agoraphobia can also occur **without panic disorder.** In this case, people fear that something extremely embarrassing will happen or that they won't be able to escape an uneasy situation if they leave home or enter unfamiliar surroundings. For example, someone with agoraphobia may refuse to go outside because he or she fears having a sudden attack of dizziness, diarrhea, or shortness of breath. Going outside the home alone, being in a crowd, standing in line, crossing a bridge, or riding in a car can be impossible for these people (APA, 2000). About 4.2 percent of all adults suffer from agoraphobia (with or without panic disorder) during their lifetime (Grant et al., 2006).

Specific Phobia

As we noted earlier, phobias are intense, irrational fears that a person cannot shake off, even when there is no real danger. In a **specific phobia,** the person's fear, anxiety, and avoidance are focused on particular objects, activities, or situations. In descending order of prevalence (Stinson et al., 2007), the most common specific phobias are

- Fear of insects, birds, snakes, or other animals (including, of course, arachnophobia, the fear of spiders, and zoophobia, the fear of animals)
- Acrophobia—fear of heights
- Astraphobia—fear of storms, thunder, and lightning
- Aquaphobia—fear of being on or in water
- Aviophobia—fear of airplanes
- Claustrophobia—fear of closed spaces
- Agoraphobia—fear of crowds

Specific phobias can be linked to nearly any object or situation. By combining the appropriate root word with the word *phobia,* any number of unlikely fears can be named. Some of these include acarophobia, fear of itching; zemmiphobia, fear of the great mole rat; phobosophobia, fear of fear; arachibutyrophobia, fear of peanut butter sticking to the roof of the mouth; and hippopotomonstrosesquipedaliophobia, fear of long words!

People affected by phobias recognize that their fears are unreasonable, but they cannot control them. For example, a person with a spider phobia would find it impossible to ignore a picture of a spider, even though a photograph can't bite anyone (Miltner et al., 2004). Specific phobias can be linked to nearly any object or situation.

Almost everyone has a few mild fears, such as fears of heights, closed spaces, or bugs and crawly things. A phobic disorder differs from such garden-variety fears in that it produces

For a person with a fear of snakes (ophidophobia), merely looking at this picture may be unsettling.

Panic disorder (without agoraphobia) A chronic state of anxiety with brief moments of sudden, intense, unexpected panic.

Panic disorder (with agoraphobia) A chronic state of anxiety and brief moments of sudden panic. The person fears that these panic attacks will occur in public places or unfamiliar situations.

Agoraphobia (without panic disorder) The person fears that something extremely embarrassing will happen to him or her if he or she leaves the house or enters unfamiliar situations.

Specific phobia An intense, irrational fear of specific objects, activities, or situations.

Social phobia An intense, irrational fear of being observed, evaluated, embarrassed, or humiliated by others in social situations.

Obsessive-compulsive disorder An extreme preoccupation with certain thoughts and/or repetitive performance of certain behaviours.

Obsession Recurring irrational or disturbing thoughts or mental images that a person cannot prevent.

Compulsion An act an individual feels driven to repeat, often against his or her will.

Stress disorder A significant emotional disturbance caused by stresses outside the range of normal human experience.

overwhelming anxiety. True phobias may lead to vomiting, wild climbing and running, or fainting. For a phobic disorder to exist, the person's fear must disrupt his or her daily life. Persons with a phobic disorder are so threatened that they will go to almost any length to avoid the feared object or situation. About 12 percent of all adults have phobic disorders during their lifetime (Comer, 2011).

Social Phobia

In a **social phobia,** people fear social situations in which they can be observed, evaluated, embarrassed, or humiliated by others. This leads them to avoid certain social situations, such as eating, writing, using the washroom, or speaking in public. Many individuals with this disorder are extremely shy and inhibited in the presence of groups of people. When such situations cannot be avoided, people endure them with intense anxiety or distress. It is common for them to have uncomfortable physical symptoms, such as a pounding heart, shaking hands, sweating, diarrhea, mental confusion, and blushing. Social phobias greatly impair functioning at work, at school, and in personal relationships (APA, 2000). About 8 percent of Canadians are affected by social phobias at one time or another (Shields, 2005a).

Obsessive-Compulsive Disorder

People who suffer from **obsessive-compulsive disorder** are preoccupied with certain distressing thoughts and may also feel compelled to perform certain behaviours. You have probably experienced a mild obsessional thought, such as a song or stupid commercial jingle that repeats over and over in your mind. This may be irritating, but it's usually not terribly disturbing. True **obsessions** are images or thoughts that force their way into awareness against a person's will. They are so disturbing that they cause intense anxiety. The most common obsessions are about violence or harm (such as poisoning one's spouse or being hit by a car), about being "dirty" or "unclean," about whether one has performed some action (such as turning off the stove), and about committing immoral acts (Grabill et al., 2008).

Obsessions usually give rise to **compulsions.** These are irrational acts that people feel driven to repeat. Often, compulsive acts help control or block out anxiety caused by an obsession. For example, a minister who finds profanities popping into her mind might start compulsively counting her heartbeats. Doing this would prevent her from thinking "dirty" words.

Many compulsive people are checkers or cleaners. For instance, people who feel guilty and unclean because they masturbate or "think dirty thoughts" may be driven to wash their hands hundreds of times a day. Typically, such compulsive behaviour will continue even after the person's hands become raw and painful (Tallis, 1996). Likewise, a young mother who repeatedly pictures a knife plunging into her baby might check once an hour to make sure all the knives in her house are locked away. Doing so may reduce her anxieties, but it will probably also take over her life.

Of course, not all obsessive-compulsive behaviours are so dramatic. Many simply involve extreme orderliness and rigid routine. Compulsive attention to detail and rigid following of rules help keep activities totally under control and make the highly anxious person feel more secure.

Stress Disorders

Stress disorders occur when stresses outside the range of normal human experience cause a major emotional disturbance (APA, 2000). They also affect many political hostages; combat veterans; prisoners of war; victims of terrorism, violent crime, child molestation, rape; and people who witness the death or injury of another person (Brown & Barlow, 2007).

Symptoms of stress disorders include repeatedly reliving the traumatic event, avoiding reminders of the event, and blunted emotions.

The severe obsessions and compulsions of billionaire Howard Hughes led him to live as a recluse for over 20 years. Hughes had an intense fear of contamination. He constructed sterile environments in which his contact with people and objects was strictly limited by complicated rituals. For instance, before handling a spoon Hughes had the handle wrapped in tissue paper and sealed with tape. A second piece of tissue had to be wrapped around the first before he would touch it.

Also common are insomnia, nightmares, wariness, poor concentration, irritability, and explosive anger or aggression. If such reactions last less than a month after a traumatic event, the problem is called an **acute stress disorder.** If they last more than a month, the person is suffering from **post-traumatic stress disorder (PTSD)** (APA, 2000).

PTSD may persist for years after the stress has passed—as has happened to many veterans of various wars around the world. Canadians gained knowledge of PTSD as they became aware of the tragedy affecting one of their heroes, General Roméo Dallaire, whose story was mentioned in the opening vignette of this chapter.

The experience of Dallaire is not unique. A survey conducted with regular armed forces personnel showed that the chances of suffering from post-traumatic stress disorder increased with the number of missions served. For example, 4.7 percent of those with three or more deployments, 2.7 percent with up to two missions, and 1.7 percent who did not serve on any missions were experiencing symptoms of post-traumatic stress disorder (Statistics Canada, 2003). To deal effectively with this increasing problem, the Canadian military has set up a special program to help those who have developed PTSD as a result of their overseas duties in the theatre of war.

Another event that has become embedded in the minds of millions of people and has caused many to develop PTSD is the terrorist attacks of September 11, 2001. For many who helped in the rescue operations and those who managed to escape the burning fires and the collapsing World Trade Center buildings, the terrifying images were very intense and disturbing. To cite yet another event, in December 2004, a tsunami killed more than 250 000 people in southern Asia. In the aftermath of such disasters, many survivors suffer from acute stress reactions. For some, the flare-up of anxiety and distress occurs months or years after the stressful event, an example of a post-traumatic stress reaction.

Dissociative Disorders

In dissociative reactions we see striking episodes of amnesia, fugue, or multiple identity. **Dissociative amnesia** is an inability to recall one's name, address, or past. **Dissociative fugue** (fyoog) involves a loss of memory, sudden travel away from home, and confusion about personal identity. Dissociations are often triggered by highly traumatic events (McLewin & Muller, 2006). In such cases, forgetting personal identity and fleeing unpleasant situations can serve as defences against intolerable anxiety.

A person suffering from a **dissociative identity disorder** has two or more separate identities or personality states (APA, 2000). (Note that identity disorders are not the same as schizophrenia. Schizophrenia, which is a psychotic disorder, is discussed later in this chapter.) A dramatic example of multiple identity is described in the book *Sybil* (Schreiber, 1973). Sybil reportedly had 16 different personality states. Each identity had a distinct voice, vocabulary, and posture. One personality could play the piano (not Sybil), but the others could not.

When an identity other than Sybil was in control, Sybil experienced a "time lapse," or memory blackout. Sybil's amnesia and separate identities first appeared during childhood. As a girl she was beaten, locked in closets, perversely tortured, sexually abused, and almost killed. Sybil's first dissociations allowed her to escape by creating another person who would suffer torture in her place. Dissociative identity disorder often begins with unbearable childhood experiences, like those Sybil endured. A history of childhood trauma, especially sexual abuse, is found in over 95 percent of persons whose personalities split into multiple identities (McLewin & Muller, 2006; Simeon et al., 2002).

Please note, however, that while people with multiple personalities are very likely to have suffered sexual trauma, it does not mean that anyone who experiences this kind of trauma will develop dissociative identity disorder.

Flamboyant cases like Sybil's have led some experts to question the existence of multiple personalities (Rieber, 1999). Based on newly discovered recordings of therapy sessions between Sybil and her psychiatrists, Rieber claims that Sybil's multiple selves were not real;

Acute stress disorder A psychological disturbance lasting up to one month following stresses that would produce anxiety in anyone who experienced them.

Post-traumatic stress disorder (PTSD) A psychological disturbance lasting more than one month following stresses that would produce anxiety in anyone who experienced them.

Dissociative amnesia Loss of memory (partial or complete) for important information related to personal identity.

Dissociative fugue A disorder involving some loss of memory, sudden travel away from home, plus confusion about one's personal identity.

Dissociative identity disorder The presence of two or more distinct personalities (multiple personality).

Hypochondriasis A preoccupation with fears of having a serious disease. Ordinary physical signs are interpreted as proof of disease, but no physical abnormality can be found.

Somatization disorder Afflicted persons have numerous physical complaints. Typically, they have consulted many doctors, but no organic problems can be identified.

Uncontrollable sneezing, which may continue for days or weeks, is often a conversion disorder. In such cases, sneezing is atypical in rate and rhythm. In addition, the person's eyes do not close during a sneeze, and sneezing does not occur during sleep. (A normal sneeze is shown here.) All these signs suggest that the cause of the sneezing is psychological, not physical (Fochtmann, 1995).

they were the products of her therapists' beliefs in the existence of multiple personality disorder and their use of hypnosis to persuade and encourage Sybil to produce lots of different identities. Nevertheless, many psychologists think that multiple identity is a real, if rare, problem (Cormier & Thelen, 1998).

Therapy for dissociative identity disorder may make use of hypnosis, which allows contact with the various personality states. The goal of therapy is integration and fusion of the identities into a single, balanced personality. Fortunately, multiple identity disorders are far rarer in real life than they are in TV dramas!

Somatoform Disorders

Have you ever known someone who seemed to be obsessed by fears of having a serious disease? These people are preoccupied with bodily functions, such as their heartbeat or breathing or digestion. Minor physical problems—even a small sore or an occasional cough—may convince them that they have cancer or some other dreaded disease. Typically, they can't give up their fears of illness, even if doctors can find no medical basis for their complaints (Korol, Craig, & Firestone, 2003).

Are you describing hypochondria? Yes. In **hypochondriasis** (HI-po-kon-DRY-uh-sis), people interpret normal bodily sensations as proof that they have a terrible disease. (See Clinical File: "Sick of Being Sick" for a related disorder with a curious twist.) In a related problem called **somatization disorder** (som-ah-tuh-ZAY-shun), people express their anxieties through various bodily complaints. That is, they suffer from problems such as vomiting or nausea, shortness of breath, or difficulty swallowing. Typically, the person complains about numerous bodily problems, feels ill much of the time, and visits doctors repeatedly. Most sufferers take medicines or other treatments, but no physical cause can be found for their distress (Ford, 1995). Similarly, a person with **pain disorder** is disabled by pain that has no identifiable physical basis (APA, 2000).

A rarer somatoform disorder is called *conversion disorder*. In this condition, severe emotional conflicts are believed to be "converted" into symptoms that actually disturb physical

Pain disorder Pain that has no identifiable physical cause and appears to be of psychological origin.

Munchausen syndrome by proxy An affected person fakes the medical problems of someone in her or his care in order to gain attention.

Munchausen syndrome An affected person fakes his or her own medical problems in order to gain attention.

THE CLINICAL FILE

Sick of Being Sick

At 14, Ben was in the hospital again for his sinus problem. He had already undergone 40 surgeries since the age of eight. In addition, he had been diagnosed at various times with bipolar disorder, oppositional defiant disorder, and attention deficit hyperactivity disorder. Ben was taking 19 different medications, and his mother said she desperately wanted him to be "healed." She sought numerous tests and never missed an appointment. But at long last, it became clear that there was nothing wrong with Ben. Left alone with doctors, Ben revealed that he was "sick of being sick."

In reality, it was Ben's mother who was sick. She was eventually diagnosed as suffering from **Munchausen syndrome by proxy** (Awadallah et al., 2005). This is a pattern in which a person fakes the medical problems of someone in his or her care. (In **Munchausen syndrome**, the person fakes her or his own medical problems.) As in Ben's case, most people with the syndrome are

mothers who fabricate their children's illnesses. Sometimes they even deliberately harm their children. For example, one mother injected her son with 7-Up (Reisner, 2006).

But why? People who suffer from Munchausen syndrome and Munchausen syndrome by proxy appear to have a pathological need to seek attention and sympathy from medical professionals. They may also win praise for being health conscious or a good parent (APA, 2000).

This case illustrates another point about psychological disorders: Ben's mother was eventually diagnosed with several disorders, including Munchausen by proxy, schizoaffective disorder, and borderline personality disorder. As this suggests, many disturbed people are *comorbid*. That is, they suffer from more than one disorder at a time. Not only does comorbidity increase their misery, it also makes it more difficult for health care providers to diagnose and treat them.

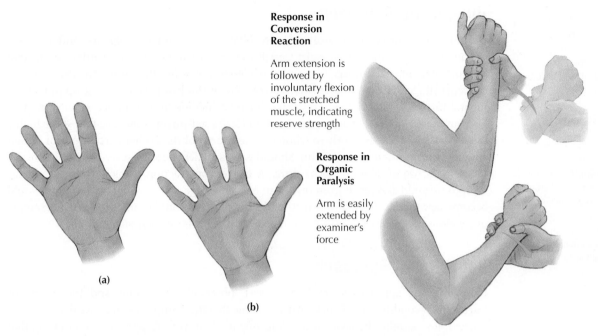

Response in Conversion Reaction

Arm extension is followed by involuntary flexion of the stretched muscle, indicating reserve strength

Response in Organic Paralysis

Arm is easily extended by examiner's force

(a)

(b)

▸▸**FIGURE 11.3** (*Left*) Glove anaesthesia is a conversion reaction involving loss of feeling in areas of the hand that would be covered by a glove (a). If the anaesthesia were physically caused, it would follow the pattern shown in (b). (*Right*) To test for organic paralysis of the arm, an examiner can suddenly extend the arm, stretching the muscles. A conversion reaction is indicated if the arm pulls back involuntarily. (Adapted from Weintraub, 1983.)

functioning or closely resemble a physical disability. For instance, a soldier might become deaf or lame or develop "glove anaesthesia" just before a battle.

What is glove anaesthesia? Glove anaesthesia is a loss of sensitivity in the areas of the skin that would normally be covered by a glove. Glove anaesthesia shows that conversion symptoms often contradict known medical facts. The system of nerves in the hands does not form a glovelike pattern and could not cause such symptoms (see Figure 11.3).

If symptoms disappear when a victim is asleep, hypnotized, or anaesthetized, a conversion reaction must be suspected (Russo et al., 1998). Another sign to watch for is that victims of conversion reactions may be strangely unconcerned about their sudden disability.

ANXIETY AND DISORDER—THREE PATHWAYS TO TROUBLE

What causes the problems described in the preceding discussion? Susceptibility to anxiety-based disorders appears to be partly inherited (Rachman, 2004). Studies of parents suffering from panic disorder, for instance, show that an unusually large number (60 percent) of their children are born with a fearful, inhibited temperament. Such children are irritable and wary as infants, shy and fearful as toddlers, and quiet and cautious introverts in elementary school. By the time they reach adulthood, they are at high risk for anxiety problems, such as panic attacks (Barlow, 2000; Durand et al., 2007).

Biological explanations don't provide a complete picture of the causes of anxiety-based disorders. Not everyone who develops these problems has parents with high levels of anxiety. So what other explanations do psychologists offer to account for these disorders?

Many theories exist to explain the causes of dissociative, anxiety, and somatoform disorders, but we will mention only three. These are (1) the humanistic approach, (2) the behavioural approach, and (3) the cognitive approach.

<SURVEY QUESTION
How do psychologists explain anxiety-based disorders?

Humanistic Approach

Humanistic theories emphasize subjective experience, human problems, and personal potentials. Humanistic psychologist Carl Rogers regarded emotional disorders as the end product of a faulty self-image (your total perception of yourself, in other words, your self-concept) (Rogers, 1959). Rogers believed that anxious individuals have built up unrealistic mental images of themselves. This leaves them vulnerable to contradictory information. Let's say, for example, that an essential part of Carli's self-image is the idea that she is highly intelligent. If Carli does poorly in school, she may deny or distort her perceptions of herself and her perceptions of the situation. Should Carli's anxiety become severe, she might resort to the rigid use of defence mechanisms. A conversion reaction, panic attacks, or similar symptoms could also result from threats to her self-image. These symptoms, in turn, would become new threats that provoke further distortions. We would soon have a classic example of a vicious cycle of maladjustment and anxiety that feeds on itself once started.

Behavioural Approach

Behaviouristic approaches emphasize overt, observable behaviour and the effects of learning and conditioning. Behaviourists assume that the "symptoms" we have discussed are learned, just as other behaviours are. You might recall from Chapter 6, for instance, that phobias can be acquired through classical conditioning. Similarly, panic attacks may reflect conditioned emotional responses that generalize to new situations. As another example, the "sickness behaviour" of someone who suffers from hypochondriasis may be reinforced by the sympathy and attention he or she gets.

One point that all theorists agree on is that disordered behaviour is ultimately self-defeating and paradoxical. A paradox is a contradiction. The contradiction in self-defeating behaviour is that it makes the person more miserable in the long run, even though it temporarily lowers anxiety.

But if the person becomes more miserable in the long run, how does the pattern get started? The behavioural explanation is that self-defeating behaviour begins with avoidance learning (described in Chapter 6). **Avoidance learning** occurs when making a particular response delays or prevents the onset of a painful or unpleasant stimulus. Here's a quick review to refresh your memory:

> An animal is placed in a special cage called a shuttle box. After a few minutes a light comes on, followed a moment later by a painful shock. Quickly, the animal escapes into a second chamber. After a few minutes, a light comes on in this chamber, and the shock is repeated. Soon the animal learns to avoid pain by moving before the shock occurs. Once an animal learns to avoid the shock, it can be turned off altogether. A well-trained animal may avoid the non-existent shock indefinitely.

The same analysis can be applied to human behaviour. A behaviourist would say that the powerful reward of immediate relief from anxiety keeps self-defeating avoidance behaviour alive. This view, known as the **anxiety reduction hypothesis,** seems to explain why the behaviour patterns we have discussed often look very "stupid" to outside observers.

Cognitive Approach

The **cognitive view** is that distorted thinking causes people to magnify ordinary threats and failures, which leads to distress (Provencher, Dugas, & Ladouceur, 2004). For example, Pierre, who has social phobia, constantly has upsetting thoughts about being evaluated. One reason for this is that people with social phobia tend to be perfectionists. Like others with social phobia, Pierre is excessively concerned about mistakes. He also perceives criticism where none exists (Brown & Barlow, 2007). Pierre tends to focus too much attention on himself, which intensifies his anxiety in social situations. Even when persons with social

STUDY BREAK Anxiety-Based Disorders

Reflect

Which of the anxiety disorders would you least want to suffer from? Why?

What minor obsessions or compulsions have you experienced?

What is the key difference between a stress disorder and an adjustment disorder? (Review both discussions if you don't immediately know the answer.)

Which of the three main explanations of anxiety-based disorders do you find most convincing?

Learning Check

1. Excessive anxiety over ordinary life stresses is characteristic of which of the following disorders?
   a. PTSD
   b. agoraphobia
   c. hypochondriasis
   d. adjustment disorder

2. Panic disorder can occur with or without agoraphobia, but agoraphobia cannot occur alone, without the presence of a panic disorder. T or F?

3. A person who intensely fears eating, writing, or speaking in public suffers from _____ _____.

4. "Checkers" and "cleaners" suffer from which disorder?
   a. acarophobia
   b. panic disorder with agoraphobia
   c. generalized anxiety disorder
   d. obsessive-compulsive disorder

5. The symptoms of acute stress disorders last less than one month; post-traumatic stress disorders last more than one month. T or F?

6. Which of the following is not a dissociative disorder?
   a. fugue   b. amnesia
   c. conversion reaction   d. multiple identity

7. The humanistic theorists' explanation of anxiety-based disorder is based on the avoidance learning hypothesis. T or F?

Critical Thinking

8. Many of the physical complaints associated with anxiety disorders are closely related to activity of what part of the nervous system?

9. Why would you expect the rate of PTSD to be especially high among Canadian soldiers who witnessed the genocide in Rwanda?

Answers

1. d 2. F 3. social phobia 4. d 5. T 6. c 7. F 8. The autonomic nervous system (ANS), especially the sympathetic branch of the ANS. 9. In addition to the unusual stresses they experienced, Canadian soldiers had neither the resources nor the mandate from the United Nations to take any decisive actions to stop the genocide, which further increased their sense of helplessness.

---

phobia are successful, distorted thinking leads them to think they have failed (Barlow, 2002). In short, changing the thinking patterns of anxious individuals like Pierre can greatly lessen their fears (Hall, 2006).

Implications

There is probably a core of truth to all three psychological explanations. For this reason, understanding anxiety-based disorders may be aided by combining parts of each perspective. Each viewpoint also suggests a different approach to treatment. Because there are many possibilities, therapy is discussed later, in Chapter 13.

> **Schizophrenia** A psychosis characterized by delusions, hallucinations, apathy, and emotional problems.

PSYCHOTIC DISORDERS—THE DARK SIDE OF THE MOON

Schizophrenia (SKIT-soh-FREE-nee-uh) is among the most serious of all psychological problems. It is classified as a psychotic disorder. The disorder is marked by delusions, hallucinations, apathy, thinking abnormalities, and emotional problems. One person in 100 will develop schizophrenia.

A person who is psychotic undergoes a number of striking changes in thinking, behaviour, and emotion. Basic to all of these changes is the fact that schizophrenia reflects a loss of contact with shared views of reality. The following comments, made by two patients with schizophrenia, illustrate what is meant by a break from reality (Torrey, 1988):

> Everything is in bits. You put the picture up bit by bit into your head. It's like a photograph that's torn in bits and put together again. If you move it's frightening.

> Last week I was with a girl and suddenly she seemed to get bigger and bigger, like a monster coming nearer and nearer.

<SURVEY QUESTION
What are the major characteristics of schizophrenia? What causes it?

Delusion A false belief held against all contrary evidence.

Flat affect An extreme lack of emotional expressiveness.

Disturbed verbal communication Speech that is disorganized, garbled, or unintelligible.

Personality disintegration A shattering of the coordination among thoughts, actions, and emotions normally found in personality.

Disorganized schizophrenia Schizophrenia marked by incoherence, grossly disorganized behaviour, bizarre thinking, and flat affect or grossly inappropriate emotions.

Catatonic schizophrenia Schizophrenia marked by stupor; rigidity; unresponsiveness; posturing; mutism; and sometimes agitated, purposeless behaviour.

Paranoid schizophrenia Schizophrenia marked by a preoccupation with delusions or by frequent auditory hallucinations related to a single theme, especially grandeur or persecution.

What are the major symptoms of schizophrenia? Unlike many psychological disorders, there is no one symptom that all patients with schizophrenia manifest. However, certain symptoms are more likely to occur than others. We will describe the most common features of this disorder.

Delusions and hallucinations are two symptoms that occur quite frequently. People who suffer from **delusions** hold false beliefs that they insist are true, regardless of how much the facts contradict them. An example is a 43-year-old man with schizophrenia who was convinced he was pregnant (Mansouri & Adityanjee, 1995). People with other common delusions may believe that they have committed a sinful deed, that their body is diseased or rotting away, that they are a famous historical figure, or that others are out to get them (APA, 2000).

Other delusions may include the idea that their thoughts and actions are being controlled, that their thoughts are being broadcast (so others can hear them), that thoughts have been inserted into their mind, or that their thoughts have been removed.

Hallucinations are imaginary sensations, such as seeing, hearing, or smelling things that don't exist in the real world. The most common psychotic hallucination is hearing voices, like the voice that told a Toronto man to push a person into the path of an oncoming subway train. Sometimes these voices command patients to hurt themselves. Unfortunately, sometimes people obey (Barrowcliff & Haddock, 2006). More rarely, psychotic people may feel "insects crawling under their skin," taste "poisons" in their food, or smell "gas" that their "enemies" are using to "get" them. Sensory changes, such as anaesthesia (numbness, or a loss of sensation) or extreme sensitivity to heat, cold, pain, or touch, can also occur.

During a psychotic episode, emotions are often severely disturbed. A person may be wildly elated, depressed, hyperemotional, or apathetic. If a man with schizophrenia is told his mother just died, he might smile, or giggle, or show no emotion at all. Sometimes patients display **flat affect,** a condition in which the face is frozen in a blank expression. Brain-imaging studies of psychotic patients with "frozen masks" reveal abnormal functioning of the brain areas responsible for processing emotions (Fahim et al., 2005).

However, behind their "frozen masks," people continue to feel emotions just as strongly as ever, though these feelings are not translated into facial expressions (Sison et al., 1996).

Disturbed verbal communication is a common symptom of psychotic disorders. In fact, psychotic speech tends to be so garbled and chaotic that it sometimes sounds like a "word salad."

Major disturbances such as those just described—as well as added problems in thought, memory, and attention—bring about personality disintegration and a break with reality. **Personality disintegration** occurs when a person's thoughts, actions, and emotions are no longer coordinated. Personality disintegration seriously impairs a person's work, social relations, and self-care.

Remember the person with psychosis who said, "Everything is in bits .... It's like a photograph that's torn in bits and put together again"? Many symptoms of schizophrenia appear to be related to problems with selective attention. In other words, it is hard for people with schizophrenia to focus on one item of information at a time. Having an impaired "sensory filter" in their brains may be why they are overwhelmed by a jumble of thoughts, sensations, images, and feelings (Heinrichs, 2001).

Is there more than one type of schizophrenia? Schizophrenia appears to be a group of related disturbances. It has three major subtypes (APA, 2000):

- **Disorganized schizophrenia** is marked by incoherence, grossly disorganized behaviour, bizarre thinking, and flat affect or grossly inappropriate emotions.
- **Catatonic schizophrenia** is marked by stupor; rigidity; unresponsiveness; posturing; mutism; and sometimes agitated, purposeless behaviour.
- **Paranoid schizophrenia** is marked by a preoccupation with delusions or by frequent auditory hallucinations related to a single theme, especially grandeur or persecution.

Some patients don't fit into any of the three subtypes, so they are given the diagnosis of **undifferentiated schizophrenia**—lacking the specific features of catatonic, disorganized, or paranoid types.

Disorganized Schizophrenia

The disorder known as *disorganized schizophrenia* comes close to matching the stereotyped images of "madness" seen in movies. In disorganized schizophrenia, personality disintegration is almost complete: Emotions, speech, and behaviour are all highly disorganized. The result is silliness, laughter, and bizarre or obscene behaviour, as shown by this intake interview of a patient named Edna:

Doctor: I am Dr. _____. I would like to know something more about you.

Patient: You have a nasty mind. Lord! Lord! Cat's in a cradle.

Doctor: Tell me, how do you feel?

Patient: London's bell is a long, long dock. Hee! Hee! (Giggles uncontrollably.)

Doctor: Do you know where you are now?

Patient: D_____n! S_____t on you all who rip into my internals! The grudgerometer will take care of you all! (Shouting) I am the Queen, see my magic, I shall turn you all into smidgelings forever!

Doctor: Your husband is concerned about you. Do you know his name?

Patient: (Stands, walks to and faces the wall) Who am I, who are we, who are you, who are they, (turns) I … I … I … I! (Makes grotesque faces.)

Edna was placed in the women's ward where she proceeded to masturbate. Occasionally, she would scream or shout obscenities. At other times she giggled to herself. She was known to attack other patients. She began to complain that her uterus was attached to a "pipeline to the Kremlin" and that she was being "infernally invaded" by communism (Suinn, 1975).

Disorganized schizophrenia typically develops in early adolescence or young adulthood. It is often preceded by serious personality disorganization in earlier years. Chances of improvement are limited, and social impairment is usually extreme (APA, 2000).

In disorganized schizophrenia, behaviour is marked by silliness, laughter, and bizarre or obscene behaviour.

Catatonic Schizophrenia

Catatonic schizophrenia brings about a stuporous condition in which odd positions may be held for hours or even days. These periods of immobility may be similar to the tendency to "freeze" at times of great emergency or panic. Occasionally, the stupor may give way to agitated outbursts or violent behaviour. The following excerpt describes a catatonic episode:

Manuel appeared to be physically healthy upon examination. Yet he did not regain his awareness of his surroundings. He remained motionless, speechless, and seemingly unconscious. One evening an aide turned him on his side to straighten out the sheet, was called away to tend another patient, and forgot to return. Manuel was found the next morning, still on his side, his arm tucked under his body, as he had been left the night before. His arm was turning blue from lack of circulation, but he seemed to be experiencing no discomfort. (Suinn, 1975)

Undifferentiated schizophrenia
Schizophrenia lacking the specific features of catatonic, disorganized, or paranoid types.

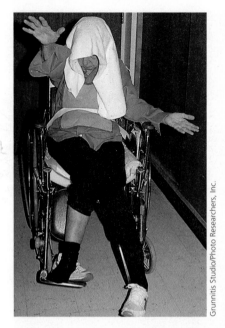

Can the characteristic catatonic features of rigid postures and stupor be understood in terms of abnormal body chemistry? Environment? Heredity?

Psychological trauma A psychological injury or shock, such as that caused by violence, abuse, neglect, separation, and so forth.
Disturbed family environment Stressful or unhealthy family relationships, communication patterns, and emotional atmosphere.
Deviant communication Patterns of communication that cause guilt, anxiety, confusion, anger, conflict, and emotional turmoil.

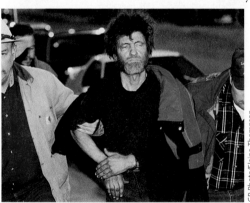

▶▶**FIGURE 11.4** Over a period of years, Theodore Kaczynski mailed bombs to unsuspecting victims, many of whom were maimed or killed. As a young adult, Kaczynski was a brilliant mathematician. At the time of his arrest, he had become the Unabomber—a reclusive "loner" who deeply mistrusted other people and modern technology. After his arrest in 1996, Kaczynski was judged to be suffering from paranoid schizophrenia.

Notice that Manuel did not speak. Mutism, along with a marked decrease in responsiveness to the environment, makes the patient difficult to "reach." Fortunately, this bizarre form of schizophrenia has become rare in Europe and North America because of drug treatment.

Paranoid Schizophrenia

Paranoid schizophrenia is the most common subtype of schizophrenia. As in paranoid delusional disorders, paranoid schizophrenia centres on delusions of grandeur and persecution. However, people with paranoid schizophrenia also hallucinate, but their delusions are more bizarre and unconvincing than those in a delusional disorder (Freeman & Garety, 2004).

Thinking that their minds are being controlled by God, the government, or "cosmic rays from space," or that someone is trying to poison them, people suffering from paranoid schizophrenia may feel forced into violence to "protect" themselves (see Figure 11.4). An example is James Huberty, who brutally murdered 21 people at a McDonald's restaurant in San Ysidro, California, in 1984. Huberty suffered from paranoid schizophrenia and felt persecuted and cheated by life. Shortly before he announced to his wife that he was "going hunting humans," Huberty had been hearing voices.

How dangerous are the mentally ill? Depictions in the news certainly give the impression that practically everyone who is mentally ill is dangerous. But are they? You might be surprised by the answer, found in Critical Thinking: "Are the Mentally Ill Prone to Violence?"

The Causes of Schizophrenia

Former British Prime Minister Winston Churchill once described a question that perplexed him as "a riddle wrapped in a mystery inside an enigma." The same words might describe the causes of schizophrenia.

Environment

What causes schizophrenia? An increased risk of developing schizophrenia may begin at birth or even before. Women who are exposed to the influenza (flu) virus during the first half of pregnancy have children who are more likely to develop schizophrenia than the children of women exposed to the virus later in pregnancy (Brown et al., 2004). Malnutrition during pregnancy and complications at the time of birth can have a similar impact. Possibly, such events disturb brain development, leaving people more vulnerable to a psychotic break with reality (Walker et al., 2004).

Early **psychological trauma** (a psychological injury or shock) may also add to the risk. Often, the victims of schizophrenia were exposed to violence, sexual abuse, death, divorce, separation, or other stresses in childhood (Walker et al., 2004). Living in a troubled family is a related risk factor. In a **disturbed family environment,** stressful relationships, communication patterns, and negative emotions prevail. **Deviant communication** patterns cause anxiety, confusion, anger, conflict, and turmoil. Typically, disturbed families interact in ways that are laden with guilt, prying, criticism, negativity, and emotional attacks (Bressi, Albonetti, & Razzoli, 1998; Docherty et al., 1998).

Although they are attractive, environmental explanations alone are not enough to account for schizophrenia. For example, when the children of parents with schizophrenia are raised away from their chaotic home environment, they are still more likely to become psychotic (Walker et al., 2004).

Heredity

Does that mean that heredity affects the risk of developing schizophrenia? Evidence has grown stronger in recent years that heredity is a factor in schizophrenia. It is clear that some individuals inherit a potential for developing schizophrenia. They are, in other words, more vulnerable to the disorder than others are (Harrison & Weinberger, 2005; Walker et al., 2004).

Are the Mentally Ill Prone to Violence?

News reports and television programs tend to greatly exaggerate the connection between mental illness and violence (Corrigan et al., 2005). Such media reports both create and reflect deeply held beliefs about mental disorders in our society. Such beliefs are important because they affect laws and personal attitudes toward the mentally ill. For example, people who strongly believe that the mentally ill are prone to violence are typically afraid to have former mental patients as neighbours, co-workers, or friends (Corrigan & Watson, 2005).

The reality is just the opposite. According to the largest study ever conducted on this question, mentally ill individuals who are not also substance abusers are no more prone to violence than are normal individuals (Monahan et al., 2001). There are only a few exceptions to this conclusion, and, in those cases, the risk is not very large (Noble, 1997; Rice, 1997).

- Only persons who are *actively psychotic* are more violence prone than non-patients. That is, if a person is experiencing delusions

and hallucinations, the risk of violence is elevated. Other mental problems are unrelated to violence.
- Only persons *currently* experiencing psychotic symptoms are at increased risk for violence. Violent behaviour is not related to having been a mental patient or having had psychotic symptoms *in the past*.

Thus, most news stories give a false impression. Even when we consider people who are actively psychotic, we find that the vast majority are not violent. The risk of violence from mental patients is actually a small fraction of that posed by persons who have the following attributes: young, male, poor, and intoxicated (Corrigan & Watson, 2005).

As you can see, only a small minority of the actively mentally ill pose an increased risk. Former mental patients, in particular, are no more likely to be violent than people in general. No matter how disturbed a person may have been, she or he merits respect and compassion. Note that the overwhelming majority of violent crimes are committed by people who are not mentally ill.

How has that been shown? If one identical twin develops schizophrenia (remember, identical twins have identical genes), then the other twin has a 48 percent chance of also having the disorder (Lenzenweger & Gottesman, 1994). The figure for twins can be compared to the risk of schizophrenia for the population in general, which is 1 percent. (See Figure 11.5 for other relationships.) In general, it is clear that schizophrenia is more common among close relatives and it tends to run in families (Plomin & Rende, 1991). There's even a case on record of four identical quadruplets all developing schizophrenia (Mirsky et al., 2000). In light of such evidence, researchers are beginning to search for specific genes related to schizophrenia (Gershon et al., 1998).

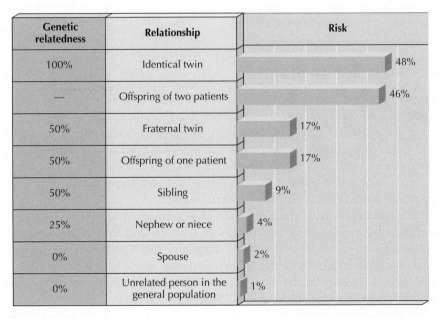

Genetic relatedness	Relationship	Risk
100%	Identical twin	48%
—	Offspring of two patients	46%
50%	Fraternal twin	17%
50%	Offspring of one patient	17%
50%	Sibling	9%
25%	Nephew or niece	4%
0%	Spouse	2%
0%	Unrelated person in the general population	1%

▸▸**FIGURE 11.5** Lifetime risk of developing schizophrenia is associated with how closely a person is genetically related to a person with schizophrenia. A shared environment also increases the risk. (Estimates from Lenzenweger & Gottesman, 1994.)

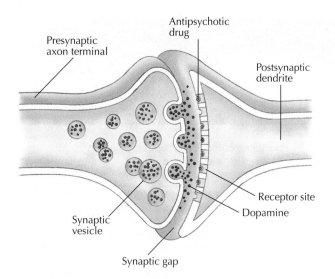

FIGURE 11.6 Dopamine normally crosses the synapse between two neurons, activating the second cell. Antipsychotic drugs bind to the same receptor sites as dopamine does, blocking its action. In people suffering from schizophrenia, a reduction in dopamine activity can quiet their agitation and psychotic symptoms.

One possible answer is suggested by the fact that the older a man is when he fathers a child, the more likely it is that the child will develop schizophrenia. Apparently, genetic mutations occur in aging male reproductive cells and increase the risk of schizophrenia (as well as other medical problems) (Malaspina et al., 2005; Sipos et al., 2004).

Brain Chemistry

Amphetamine, LSD, PCP ("angel dust"), and similar drugs produce effects that partially mimic the symptoms of schizophrenia. Also, the same drugs (phenothiazines) used to treat LSD overdoses tend to alleviate psychotic symptoms. Facts such as these suggest that **biochemical abnormalities** (disturbances in brain chemicals or neurotransmitters) may occur in people with schizophrenia. It is possible that the affected brain produces some substance similar to a psychedelic (mind-altering) drug. At present, one likely candidate is **dopamine** (DOPE-ah-meen), an important chemical messenger found in the brain.

Many researchers believe that schizophrenia is related to overactivity in brain dopamine systems (Durand et al., 2007; Kapur & Lecrubier, 2003). Another possibility is that dopamine receptors become super-responsive to normal amounts of dopamine (Port & Seybold, 1995). Dopamine appears to trigger a flood of unrelated thoughts, feelings, and perceptions, which may account for the hallucinations and delusions of schizophrenia (Gottesman, 1991). The implication is that individuals with schizophrenia may be on a sort of drug trip caused by their own bodies (see Figure 11.6).

Dopamine is not the only brain chemical that has caught scientists' attention. The neurotransmitter glutamate also appears to be related to schizophrenia (van Elst et al., 2005). People who take the hallucinogenic drug PCP, which affects glutamate, have symptoms that closely mimic schizophrenia (Murray, 2002). This occurs because glutamate influences brain activity in areas that control emotions and sensory information (Tsai & Coyle, 2002). Another tantalizing connection is the fact that stress alters glutamate levels, which in turn alter dopamine systems (Moghaddam, 2002). The story is far from complete, but it appears that dopamine, glutamate, and other brain chemicals partly explain the devastating symptoms of schizophrenia (Walker et al., 2004).

The Schizophrenic Brain

Medical researchers have long hoped for a way to directly observe the schizophrenic brain. Three medical techniques are now making it possible. One, the CT scan, provides an X-ray picture of the brain. (CT stands for computed tomography, or computer-enhanced X-ray images.) When John Hinkley, Jr. (who shot U.S. president Ronald Reagan and three other men in 1981), had a CT scan taken of his brain, it showed that his brain differed from the norm. Specifically, it had wider surface fissuring, as is seen in the brains of people with schizophrenia. In his trial, Hinkley was declared insane.

MRI (magnetic resonance imaging) scans allow researchers to peer inside the schizophrenic brain. What they find is that people with schizophrenia tend to have enlarged ventricles (fluid-filled spaces within the brain), suggesting that surrounding brain tissue has withered (Barkataki et al., 2006). Other brain regions also appear to be abnormal. It is telling that the affected areas are crucial for regulating motivation, emotion, perception, actions, and attention (Gur et al., 1998; Walker et al., 2004).

Other techniques, including fMRI (functional MRI) and positron emission tomography (PET) provide an image of brain activity. To make a PET scan, a radioactive sugar solution is injected into a vein. When the sugar reaches the brain, an electronic device measures how

Biochemical abnormality A disturbance of the body's chemical systems, especially in brain chemicals or neurotransmitters.

Dopamine An important transmitter substance found in the brain—especially in the limbic system, an area associated with emotional response.

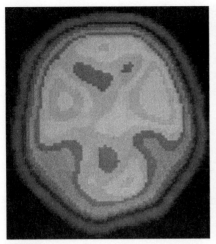
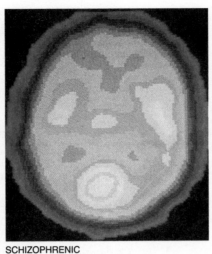
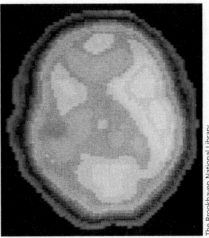

NORMAL   SCHIZOPHRENIC   MANIC-DEPRESSIVE

The Brookhaven National Library

▸▸**FIGURE 11.7** Positron emission tomography produces PET scans of the human brain. In the scans shown here, red, pink, and orange indicate lower levels of brain activity; white and blue indicate higher activity levels. Notice that activity in the brain of someone with schizophrenia is quite low in the frontal lobes (top area of each scan) (Velakoulis & Pantelis, 1996). Activity in the brain of someone with bipolar disorder is low in the left brain hemisphere and high in the right brain hemisphere. The reverse is more often true in schizophrenia. Researchers are trying to identify consistent patterns like these to aid diagnosis of mental disorders.

much is used in each area. These data are then translated into a colour map, or scan, of brain activity (see Figure 11.7).

Researchers are finding patterns in such scans that are consistently linked with schizophrenia, mood disorders, and other problems. For instance, activity tends to be abnormally low in the frontal lobes of the brains of people with schizophrenia (Velakoulis & Pantelis, 1996) (see Chapter 2, page 74, for a discussion of the frontal lobes). In the future, PET scans may be used to diagnose schizophrenia more accurately.

Implications

In summary, the emerging picture of schizophrenia takes this form: Anyone subjected to enough stress may be pushed to a psychotic break. However, some people inherit a difference in brain chemistry or brain structure that makes them more susceptible—even to normal life stresses.

Thus, the right mix of inherited potential and environmental stress brings about mind-altering changes in brain chemicals and brain structure. This explanation is called a **stress-vulnerability model** (Walker & Tessner, 2008). It attributes psychotic disorders to a blend of environmental stress and inherited susceptibility. The model seems to apply to other forms of psychopathology as well, such as depression (Walker et al., 2004) (see Figure 11.8). Just

> **Stress-vulnerability model**
> Attributes psychosis to a combination of environmental stress and inherited susceptibility.

The Stress-Vulnerability Model

Vulnerability ▢
Stress ▢

Low   Medium   High
Degree of psychopathology

▸▸**FIGURE 11.8** Various combinations of vulnerability and stress may produce psychological problems. The top bar shows low vulnerability and low stress. The result? No problem. The same is true of the next bar down, where low vulnerability is combined with moderate stress. Even high vulnerability (third bar) may not lead to problems if stress levels remain low. However, when high vulnerability combines with moderate or high stress (bottom two bars), the person "crosses the line" and suffers from psychopathology.

✔ STUDY BREAK   Schizophrenia

Reflect

What did you think psychosis was like before you read about it? How has your understanding changed?

If you were writing a "recipe" for psychosis, what would the main "ingredients" be?

If you were asked to play the role of a paranoid person for a theatre production, what symptoms would you emphasize?

You have been asked to explain the causes of schizophrenia to the parents of a teenager with schizophrenia. What would you tell them?

Learning Check

1. Carol wrongly believes that her body is "rotting away." She is suffering from
   a. depressive hallucinations   b. a delusion
   c. flat affect   d. Alzheimer's disease
2. Jean, who has suffered a psychotic break, is hearing voices. This symptom is referred to as
   a. flat affect   b. hallucination
   c. a word salad   d. organic delusions
3. Flat affect means
   a. a sense of sadness   b. a sense of elation
   c. inappropriate emotions   d. lack of emotional expression

4. Hallucinations and delusions are the principal features of paranoid schizophrenia. T or F?
5. Environmental explanations of schizophrenia emphasize emotional trauma and
   a. manic parents   b. schizoaffective interactions
   c. psychedelic interactions   d. disturbed family relationships
6. The _____ _____ of a person with schizophrenia runs a 48 percent chance of also developing schizophrenia.
7. Offspring of women who develop antibodies to the flu virus during pregnancy have an increased probability of suffering from schizophrenia as adults. T or F?

Critical Thinking

8. Researchers have found nearly double the normal number of dopamine receptor sites in the brains of people with schizophrenia. Why might that be important?
9. Enlarged surface fissures and ventricles are frequently found in the brains of people with chronic schizophrenia. Why is it a mistake to conclude that such features cause schizophrenia?

Answers

1. b 2. b 3. d 4. T 5. d 6. identical twin 7. T 8. Because of the extra receptors, people with schizophrenia may get psychedelic effects from normal levels of dopamine in the brain. 9. Because correlation does not confirm causation. Structural brain abnormalities are merely correlated with schizophrenia. They could be additional symptoms, rather than causes, of the disorder.

the same, psychosis remains "a riddle wrapped in a mystery inside an enigma." Let us hope the recent advances that we have so briefly explored will turn out to be very fruitful.

MOOD DISORDERS—PEAKS AND VALLEYS

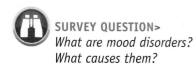

SURVEY QUESTION>
What are mood disorders? What causes them?

Nobody loves you when you're down and out—or so it seems. Psychologists have come to realize that **mood disorders** (major disturbances in emotion) are among the most common of all. Two general types of mood disorders are depressive disorders and bipolar disorders. In **depressive disorders,** sadness and despondency are exaggerated, prolonged, or unreasonable. Signs of a depressive disorder are feelings of dejection, hopelessness, and an inability to feel pleasure or to take interest in anything. Other common symptoms are fatigue, disturbed sleep and eating patterns, feelings of worthlessness, a very negative self-image, and thoughts of suicide. Depression is also known as unipolar disorder. In **bipolar disorders** people usually go both "up" and "down" emotionally (APA, 2000).

Depending on where you happen to live in the world, your chances of developing depression can vary markedly. For example, the lifetime rate of major depression is as low as 0.9 percent in urban Taiwan and as high as 19 percent in Beirut. In the United States, 4.6 percent of people can be expected to develop major depression. In Edmonton, 8.6 percent; in Christchurch, New Zealand, 12.6 percent; and in Paris, about 16 percent of the population suffers from this disorder (Bland, 1997).

Some mood disorders are long-lasting but relatively moderate problems. If a person is mildly depressed for at least two years, the problem is called a **dysthymic** (dis-THIGH-mik) **disorder.** If depression alternates with periods when the person's mood is cheerful, expansive, or irritable, the problem is a **cyclothymic** (SIKE-lo-THIGH-mik) **disorder** (APA,

Mood disorder Major disturbances in mood or emotion.

Depressive disorders Emotional disorders involving sadness and depression.

Bipolar disorders Emotional disorders involving both depression and mania.

Dysthymic disorder Mild to moderate depression that persists for two years or more.

Cyclothymic disorder Mild to moderate manic and depressive behaviour that persists for two years or more.

2000). Even at this level, mood disorders can be debilitating. However, major mood disorders are much more damaging.

Major Mood Disorders

Major mood disorders are marked by extreme emotions. About 14 percent of patients admitted to psychiatric hospitals suffer from major mood disorders. The person who only goes "down" emotionally suffers from a **major depressive disorder.** During major depressive episodes, people reach an extreme low point emotionally. Everything looks bleak and hopeless, and the person's suffering is intense. Feelings of failure, sinfulness, worthlessness, and total despair are dominant. The person becomes extremely subdued or withdrawn and may be intensely suicidal. Depressive reactions pose a serious threat. Suicide attempted during a major depression is rarely a plea for help.

In a **bipolar I disorder,** people experience both extreme mania and deep depression. During manic episodes, the person is loud, elated, hyperactive, grandiose, and energetic. Manic patients may go bankrupt in a matter of days, get arrested, or go on a binge of promiscuous sex. During periods of depression, the person is deeply despondent and possibly suicidal. Approximately 2.4 percent of Canadians develop this debilitating disorder during their lifetime (Wilkins, 2004).

In a **bipolar II disorder,** the person is intensely depressed and guilt-ridden, but experiences only mild manic episodes (called hypomania). That is, both elation and depression occur, but the person's mania is not as extreme as it is in a bipolar I disorder. Bipolar II patients who are hypomanic usually manage to irritate everyone around them. They are excessively cheerful, aggressive, or irritable, and they may brag, talk too fast, interrupt conversations, or spend too much money (Gorman, 1996).

In serious cases of depression, it is impossible for a person to function at work or at school. Sometimes, depressed individuals cannot even feed or dress themselves. In cases of depression and/or mania that are even more severe, the person may also lose touch with reality and display various psychotic symptoms.

In major depressive disorders, suicidal impulses can be intense and despair total.

Causes of Mood Disorders

How is depression explained? Depression and other mood disorders are very complicated and do not have a single causal agent. Some scientists have focused on the biology of mood changes. They are interested in brain chemicals and transmitter substances, especially serotonin, norepinephrine, and dopamine (Ricci & Wellman, 1990). Their findings are incomplete, but progress has been made. For instance, low concentrations of serotonin are thought to play a major role in depression. The newer class of antidepressant drugs work by giving a boost to serotonin levels by making it harder for the vesicles to reabsorb serotonin molecules back into the neurons (see Chapter 2), thus uplifting mood in the process (Jacobs, 2004).

Genetics do appear to play a major role in mood disorders, especially in bipolar disorders (Gershon et al., 1998). As a case in point, if one identical twin has bipolar disorder, the other has an 80 percent chance of developing the same disorder. For non-twin siblings, the probability is 35 percent. This difference may be related to the recent finding that people who have a particular version of a gene are more likely to become depressed when they are stressed (Caspi et al., 2003). As we will discuss below, psychological causes are important in many cases of depression. But for major mood disorders, biological factors seem to play a larger role. (For an interesting look at another cause of depression, see Using Psychology: "Feeling Sad? Could be SAD.")

In addition to determining the biological bases of mood disorders, researchers have also sought psychological explanations. Behavioural theories of depression emphasize learned helplessness, whereas cognitive theories stress self-criticism and negative, distorted, or self-defeating thoughts. The two theories don't oppose each other; they are merely two sides of the same coin, providing explanations of depression from slightly different angles.

Major mood disorders Disorders marked by lasting extremes of mood or emotion and sometimes accompanied by psychotic symptoms.

Major depressive disorder A mood disorder in which the person has suffered one or more intense episodes of depression.

Bipolar I disorder A mood disorder in which a person has episodes of mania (excited, hyperactive, energetic, grandiose behaviour) and also periods of deep depression.

Bipolar II disorder A mood disorder in which a person is mostly depressed (sad, despondent, guilt-ridden) but has also had one or more episodes of mild mania (hypomania).

Feeling Sad? Could Be SAD

Unless you have experienced a winter of "cabin fever" in the Far North, you may be surprised to learn that the rhythms of the seasons underlie certain types of depression and bipolar disorders. Researchers have found that some people suffer from **seasonal affective disorder (SAD),** or depression that typically occurs during the fall and winter months. Almost anyone can get a little depressed when days are short, dark, and cold. But when a person's symptoms are lasting and disabling, the problem may be SAD. Here are some of the major symptoms of SAD, according to Swedish psychiatrist Åsa Westrin and Canadian neuroscientist Raymond Lam (Westrin & Lam, 2007):

- *Oversleeping and difficulty staying awake.* Your sleep patterns may be disturbed, and waking very early in the morning is common.
- *Fatigue.* You feel too tired to maintain a normal routine.
- *Craving.* You hunger for carbohydrates and sweets, leading to overeating and weight gain.
- *Inability to cope.* You feel irritable and stressed.
- *Social withdrawal.* You become unsocial in the winter but are socially active during other seasons.

Starting in the fall, people with SAD sleep longer but more poorly. During the day they feel tired and drowsy, and they tend to overeat. With each passing day they become more sad, anxious, irritable, and socially withdrawn.

Although their depression is not severe, many victims of SAD face each winter with a sense of foreboding. SAD is believed to be especially prevalent in northern latitudes, where days are very short during the winter (Booker & Hellekson, 1992). However, the problem may be worse for people who relocate from southern to more northern latitudes. For example, 13 percent of college students living in northern New England were found to have signs of SAD. The students most likely to be affected were those who had moved from the south to attend college (Low & Feissner, 1998). Similarly, research conducted in a northern community in Canada found that SAD was more common among people who had moved there from more southern latitudes (Williams & Schmidt, 1993).

Studies also support the idea that some northern people may be genetically protected against SAD. For example, the rate of SAD has been found to be quite low among people of Iceland, as well as among the descendents of Icelandic settlers living in Manitoba (Magnusson & Axelsson, 1993).

Generally speaking, seasonal depression is related to the release of more melatonin during the winter. This hormone, which is secreted by the pineal gland, regulates the body's response to changing light conditions. That's why 80 percent of SAD patients can be helped by extra doses of bright light, a remedy called phototherapy (see Figure 11.9). **Phototherapy** involves exposing SAD patients to one or more hours of very bright fluorescent light each day (Neumeister, 2004). This is best done early in the morning, when it simulates dawn in the summer (Avery et al., 2001). For many SAD sufferers, a hearty dose of light appears to be the next best thing to vacationing in the tropics.

Dan McCoy/Rainbow

▶▶**FIGURE 11.9** An hour or more of bright light a day can dramatically reduce the symptoms of seasonal affective disorder. Treatment is usually necessary from fall through spring. Light therapy typically works best when it is used early in the morning (Lewy et al., 1998).

Learned Helplessness

Martin Seligman studied the case of a young marine who seemed to have adapted to the stresses of being held prisoner in Vietnam. The marine's health was related to a promise made by his captors: If he cooperated, they said, he would be released on a certain date. As the date approached, his spirits soared. Then came a devastating blow. He had been deceived. His captors had no intention of ever releasing him. He immediately lapsed into a deep depression, refused to eat or drink, and died shortly thereafter.

This seems like an extreme example. Does anything similar occur outside of prison camps? Apparently so. For example, researchers in Finland found that even in everyday life, people who feel a sense of hopelessness die at a younger age than those who are more optimistic (Everson, Goldberg, & Salonen, 1996). Even very mild levels of depression or the blues can slow us down and cause plenty of misery. (See Using Psychology: "Depression—A Problem for Everyone" for an explanation and to learn some strategies for coping with such feelings.)

How can we explain such patterns? Psychologists have focused on the concept of learned helplessness (Seligman, 1989). **Learned helplessness** is an acquired inability to overcome

Seasonal affective disorder (SAD) Depression that occurs only during fall and winter; presumably related to decreased exposure to sunlight.

Phototherapy A treatment for seasonal affective disorder that involves exposure to bright, full-spectrum light.

Learned helplessness A learned inability to overcome obstacles or to avoid punishment; learned passivity and inaction to aversive stimuli.

Depression—A Problem for Everyone

Canadian college and university students have reported elevated levels of psychological distress (Adlaf et al., 2001).

During the school year, up to 78 percent of all college students suffer some symptoms of depression. At any given time, from 16 to 30 percent of the student population is depressed (McLennan, 1992; Wong & Whitaker, 1993). A study of 7800 Canadian university students also found that students were more likely to report higher rates of distress than the general population (Adlaf et al., 2001).

Depression can take a toll on academic performance. In one study, students diagnosed with depression scored half a grade point below non-depressed students (Hysenbegasi, Hass, & Rowland, 2005). Why do students get "blue"? Various problems contribute to depressive feelings. Here are some of the most common:

1. Stresses from school work and pressures to choose a career can leave students feeling that they are missing out on fun or that all their hard work is meaningless.
2. Isolation and loneliness are common when students leave their support groups behind. In the past, family, a circle of high school friends, and often a boyfriend or girlfriend could be counted on for support and encouragement.
3. Problems with studying and grades frequently trigger depression. Many students start college with high aspirations and little prior experience with failure. At the same time, many lack the basic skills necessary for academic success and are afraid of failure (Martin & Marsh, 2003).
4. Another common problem is the breakup of an intimate relationship, either with a former boyfriend or girlfriend or with a newly formed romance.
5. Students who find it difficult to live up to their idealized images of themselves are especially prone to depression (Scott & O'Hara, 1993).
6. An added danger is that depressed students are more likely to abuse alcohol, which itself is a depressant (Weitzman, 2004).

Recognizing Depression

Most people know, obviously enough, when they are "down." Aaron Beck, an authority on depression, suggests you should assume that more than a minor fluctuation in mood is involved when five conditions exist:

1. You have a consistently negative opinion of yourself.
2. You engage in frequent self-criticism and self-blame.
3. You place negative interpretations on events that usually wouldn't bother you.
4. The future looks bleak and negative.
5. You feel that your responsibilities are overwhelming.

Coping with Depression

If you don't do well on a test or a class assignment, how do you react? If you see it as a small, isolated setback, you probably won't feel too bad. However, if you feel like you have blown it in a big way, depression may follow. Students who strongly link everyday events to long-term goals (such as a successful career or high income) tend to overreact to day-to-day disappointments (McIntosh, Harlow, & Martin, 1995).

What does the preceding tell us about the college blues? The implication is that it's important to take daily tasks one step at a time and chip away at them. That way, you are less likely to feel overwhelmed, helpless, or hopeless. Beck and Greenberg (1974) suggest that when you feel blue, you should make a daily schedule for yourself. Try to schedule activities to fill up every hour during the day. It is best to start with easy activities and progress to more difficult tasks. Check off each item as it is completed. That way, you will begin to break the self-defeating cycle of feeling helpless and falling further behind. (Depressed students spend much of their time sleeping.) A series of small accomplishments, successes, or pleasures may be all that you need to get going again. However, if you are lacking skills needed for success in college, ask for help in getting them. Don't remain "helpless."

Feelings of worthlessness and hopelessness are usually supported by self-critical or negative thoughts. Beck and Greenberg recommend writing down such thoughts as they occur, especially those that immediately precede feelings of sadness. After you have collected these thoughts, write a rational answer to each. For example, the thought "No one loves me" should be answered with a list of those who do care. One more point to keep in mind is this: When events begin to improve, try to accept it as a sign that better times lie ahead. Positive events are most likely to end depression if you view them as stable and continuing, rather than temporary and fragile (Needles & Abramson, 1990). Do not hesitate to ask for help in coping with feelings of depression. Your school's counselling or health service, or your family physician, can all provide you with information and support.

Attacks of the college blues are common and should be distinguished from more serious cases of depression. Severe depression is a serious problem that can lead to suicide or a major impairment of emotional functioning. In such cases it would be wise to seek professional help.

obstacles and avoid aversive stimuli. To observe learned helplessness, let's return to the animals tested in a shuttle box in avoidance learning (see Figure 11.10). If placed in one side of a divided box, dogs will quickly learn to leap to the other side to escape an electric shock. If they are given a warning before the shock occurs (for example, a light that dims),

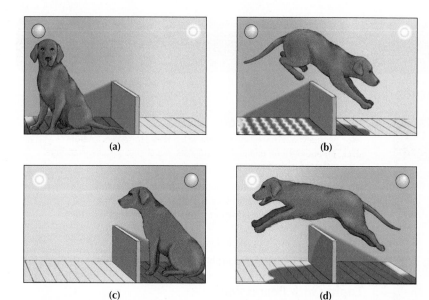

(a) **(b)**

(c) **(d)**

▶▶**FIGURE 11.10** In the normal course of escape and avoidance learning, a light dims shortly before the floor is electrified (a). Since the light does not yet have meaning for the dog, the dog receives a shock (non-injurious, by the way) and leaps the barrier (b). Dogs soon learn to watch for the dimming of the light (c) and to jump before receiving a shock (d). Dogs made to feel "helpless" rarely even learn to escape shock, much less to avoid it.

most dogs learn to avoid the shock by leaping the barrier before the shock arrives. This is true of most dogs, but not those that have learned to feel helpless (Overmier & LoLordo, 1998).

How is a dog made to feel helpless? Before being tested in the shuttle box, a dog can be placed in a harness (from which the dog cannot escape). The dog is then given several painful shocks. The animal is helpless to prevent these shocks. When placed in the shuttle box, dogs prepared this way react to the first shock by crouching, howling, and whining. None of them try to escape. They helplessly resign themselves to their fate. After all, they have already learned that there is nothing they can do about shock.

As the shuttle box experiments suggest, helplessness is a psychological state that occurs when events appear to be uncontrollable (Seligman, 1989). Helplessness also afflicts humans. It is a common reaction to repeated failure and to unpredictable or unavoidable punishment. A prime example is students who feel helpless about their school work. Such students tend to procrastinate and give up easily (McKean, 1994; Perry, 2003).

Seligman and others have pointed out the similarities between learned helplessness and depression. Both are marked by feelings of despondency, powerlessness, and hopelessness. "Helpless" animals display decreased activity, lowered aggression, blunted appetite, and a loss of sex drive. Humans suffer from similar effects and also tend to see themselves as failing, even when they're not (LoLordo, 2001; Seligman, 1989).

Learned helplessness seems to explain many cases of depression and hopelessness. For example, Seligman (1972) describes the fate of Archie, a 15-year-old boy. For Archie, school is an unending series of shocks and failures. Other students treat him as if he's stupid; in class he rarely answers questions because he doesn't know some of the words. He feels knocked down everywhere he turns. These may not be electric shocks, but they are certainly emotional "shocks," and Archie has learned to feel helpless to prevent them. When he leaves school, his chances of success will be poor. He has learned to passively endure whatever shocks life has in store for him. Archie is not alone in this regard. Hopelessness is almost always a major element of depression (Alloy & Clements, 1998; Ciarrochi, Dean, & Anderson, 2002).

People who experience failure in one situation are more likely to act helpless in other situations if they attribute their failure to lasting, general factors. An example would be concluding "I must be stupid" after failing to solve a series of puzzles. In contrast, attributing failure to specific factors in the original situation ("I'm not too good at puzzles" or "I wasn't really interested") tends to prevent helplessness from spreading (Alloy et al., 1984; Anderson et al., 1984; Peterson & Vaidya, 2001).

Learned helplessness and a sense of hopelessness may also explain why women are twice as likely as men to experience depression (Culertson, 1997; Kuehner, 2003). Social and environmental conditions are the main reason for this difference (Winstead & Sanchez, 2005). Factors that contribute to women's greater risk of depression include work and parenting, the strain of providing emotional support for others, and conflicts about birth control and pregnancy. Marital strife, sexual and physical abuse, and poverty are also important. Nationwide, women and children are most likely to live in poverty. As a result, poor women frequently suffer the stresses associated with single parenthood, loss of control over their lives, poor housing, and dangerous neighbourhoods (Stoppard & McMullen, 2003).

The Cognitive Theory of Depression

Aaron Beck (1991) believes that negative, self-defeating thoughts underlie depression. According to him, depressed persons see themselves, the world, and the future in negative terms. This occurs because of major distortions in thinking. He points out that depressed people engage in automatic negative thinking, characterized by cognitive errors. One such error is **selective perception,** which refers to perceiving only certain stimuli in a larger array. If five good things and three bad things happen during the day, depressed people focus only on the bad. Another cognitive error is **overgeneralization,** the tendency to let upsetting events affect unrelated situations. An example would be considering yourself a total failure, or completely worthless, if you were to lose a part-time job or fail a test. To complete the picture, depressed persons tend to magnify the importance of undesirable events by engaging in **all-or-nothing thinking.** That is, they see events as completely good or bad, right or wrong, and themselves as either successful or failing miserably (Beck, 1985).

Both the learned helplessness and cognitive views of depression are useful ways of explaining many cases of depression, but they don't tell us why some people develop a sense of hopelessness or negative ways of thinking and others don't. For example, all of us have heard of individuals who grow up in extremely difficult family environments, marked by poverty, abuse, and neglect. Yet they seem to rise above all adversity and manage to become socially productive and well-adjusted. Despite their challenging past, they don't develop a sense of hopelessness or show signs of what Beck calls cognitive errors. On the other hand, there are those who come from relatively advantaged family backgrounds, yet grow up to view themselves, their world, and their future in a negative light. Given such differences in human experience, how, then, can we explain depression?

As we did with schizophrenia, we will use the stress-vulnerability model here to understand depression. It is likely that depression is a product of many factors interacting in complex ways. One possibility is that genetic predisposition to depression makes some people more vulnerable than others, and environmental factors then act upon a genetic weakness to cause depression. If you lack a genetic predisposition to depression, environmental stresses would have to be very intense in order for you to experience this disorder. On the other hand, if you have inherited a genetic predisposition, the environmental stresses don't have to be too strong for depression to emerge.

Selective perception Perceiving only certain stimuli among a larger array of possibilities.

Overgeneralization Blowing a single event out of proportion by extending it to a large number of unrelated situations.

All-or-nothing thinking Classifying objects or events as absolutely right or wrong, good or bad, acceptable or unacceptable, and so forth.

✔ STUDY BREAK   Mood Disorders

Reflect

Review the stress-vulnerability model of mental disorders. To what extent does the model relate to mood disorders?

We all occasionally engage in negative thinking. Can you remember a time recently when you engaged in selective perception? Overgeneralization? All-or-nothing thinking?

Learning Check

1. Dysthymic disorder is to depression as cyclothymic disorder is to bipolar disorder. T or F?
2. Hypomania means
   a. mild levels of elation and irritation
   b. high levels of elation and irritation
   c. mild levels of depression and hopelessness
   d. increased levels of depression and hopelessness

3. Major mood disorders, especially bipolar disorders, may run in families. T or F?
4. Learned helplessness is emphasized by _____ theories of depression.
   a. humanistic
   b. biological
   c. behaviouristic
   d. psychoanalytic
5. Serotonin levels appear to be low in depression. T or F?
6. The acronym SAD stands for schizotypal affective disorder. T or F?

Critical Thinking

7. In Aaron Beck's terms, a belief such as "I must perform well or I am a rotten person" involves two thinking errors. What are these errors?

Answers   1. T 2. a 3. T 4. c 5. T 6. F 7. Overgeneralization and all-or-nothing thinking.

SURVEY QUESTION>
Why do people commit suicide? Can suicide be prevented?

Psychology in Action

SUICIDE—LIVES ON THE BRINK

"Suicide: A permanent solution to a temporary problem."

Suicide ranks as the seventh most common cause of death in North America. Roughly 1 person out of 100 attempts suicide during his or her life. We tend to be very concerned about the seemingly high rate of murder. However, for every person who dies by homicide in Canada, seven will kill themselves (Langlois & Morrison, 2002). Sooner or later, you are likely to be affected by the suicide attempt of someone you know. Check your knowledge of suicide against the following information.

Factors

What factors affect suicide rates? Suicide rates vary greatly, but some general patterns do emerge.

Sex

Men have the questionable honour of being better at suicide than women. Three times as many men as women complete suicide (see Figure 11.11), but women make more attempts. Male suicide attempts are more lethal because men typically use a gun or an equally fatal method (Garland & Zigler, 1993). Women most often attempt a drug overdose, so there's a better chance of help arriving before death occurs. Sadly, women are beginning to use more deadly methods and may soon equal men in their risk of death by suicide.

Age

Age is also a factor in suicide. Suicide rates gradually rise during adolescence. They then sharply increase during young adulthood (ages 20 to 24) (Statistics Canada, 2000). About half of all suicide cases are over 44 years of age. There is a decline in numbers around age 60, but they pick up again around the age of 75. Unfortunately, as Figure 11.11 shows, even children are not immune from the risk of suicide.

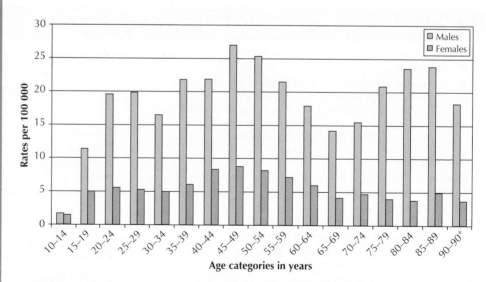

▶▶**FIGURE 11.11** As this bar graph shows, in each age category more males die from suicide than females do. In general, rates tend to increase with an advance in age, reaching a peak between 45 and 49. Even children and adolescents are not immune from the risk of suicide, and many elderly people also kill themselves. (Data for 2007; adapted from the Statistics Canada CANSIM database, Table 102-0551.)

Of special concern is the rate of suicide among younger people. Between 1950 and 1990, suicide rates for adolescents and young adults doubled (Durand & Barlow, 2010). Among college students, suicide is the third leading cause of death (Jamison, 2001).

School is a factor in some suicides, but only in the sense that suicidal students were not living up to their own extremely high standards. Many were good students. Other important factors in student suicide are cocaine or alcohol use (Garlow, Purselle, & Heninger, 2007); chronic health problems (real or imagined); and interpersonal difficulties (some suicides are rejected lovers, but others are simply withdrawn and friendless people).

Ethnicity

Suicide rates vary dramatically from country to country. The rate in the United States is almost ten times as high as the rate in Azerbaijan, and in turn the rate in Hungary is more than three times the U.S. rate (Lester & Yang, 2005).

In Canada, the suicide rate among Aboriginal people is about three times the national average; however, wide fluctuations are seen across different groups. According to Michael Chandler and Christopher Lalonde (1998), some First Nations groups in British Columbia have extremely elevated suicide rates, especially among youth, whereas in other groups suicide is a rare phenomenon. Suicide is relatively low among those First Nations groups that have taken steps toward self-government and the preservation of cultural heritage. Note also that suicide rates are equally high among the Aboriginal peoples of Australia and New Zealand (Goldston et al., 2008; McKenzie, Serfaty, & Crawford, 2003).

Among Canada's growing immigrant population, the rate of suicide is about 50 percent lower than among those who are born in this country. However, the pattern of suicide tends to reflect the countries from which the immigrants arrive. For example, people coming from Europe have higher rates than those immigrating from Africa and Asia (Malenfant, 2004).

What accounts for such a large difference in rates? It is possible that immigrants have been socialized, by their original cultures, to view suicide differently from the way it is seen by the native-born population of Canada. Additionally, immigrants may be tapping into a close-knit social network of persons from their own cultures, which might be very important during a time of crisis.

Place of Residence

Ontario can claim the honour of being the province with the lowest suicide rate in Canada. Nova Scotia shows low rates as well (see Figure 11.12). The provinces with the highest figures are Quebec, Saskatchewan, and Alberta. Until the late 1990s, Quebec exhibited extremely elevated rates—over one-third of all annual Canadian suicides used to be recorded there. In recent years, however, there has been a welcome positive change in the numbers. The province has seen a drop of about 22 percent from 2000 to 2007. Finally, it should be noted that

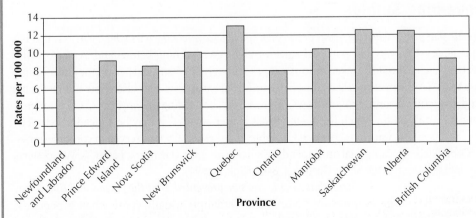

▶▶**FIGURE 11.12** Provincial suicide rates per 100 000 population (data for 2007; adapted from the Statistics Canada CANSIM database, Table 102-0551.)

■ Table 11.2 Suicide Warning Signs

- Withdrawal from contact with others
- Sudden swings in mood
- Recent occurrence of life crisis or emotional shock
- Personality change
- Gift giving of prized possessions
- Depression/hopelessness
- Aggression and/or risk taking
- Single-car accident
- Preoccupation with death
- Drug use
- Death imagery in art
- Direct threats to commit suicide

two of the three territories have the highest suicide rates in the country (Yukon is the exception), but their rates are somewhat difficult to interpret and compare with the provinces because of their extremely small population sizes.

Marital Status

Marriage (when successful) may be the best natural guard against suicidal impulses. Married individuals have lower rates than the divorced, the widowed, and single persons (Yip & Thorburn, 2004).

Immediate Causes of Suicide

Why do people try to kill themselves? The best explanation for suicide may simply come from a look at the conditions that precede it. The following are all major risk factors for suicide (National Institute of Mental Health, 2003; Rudd, Joiner, & Rajab, 2001):

- A prior suicide attempt
- Drug or alcohol abuse
- Depression or other mood disorder
- Feelings of hopelessness, worthlessness
- Antisocial, impulsive, or aggressive behaviour
- Severe anxiety, panic attacks
- Family history of suicidal behaviour
- Shame, humiliation, failure, or rejection
- Availability of a firearm

Suicidal people usually have a history of trouble with family, a lover, or a spouse. Often they have drinking or drug abuse problems, or job difficulties. Depression is a factor in 70 percent of all suicides (Lecomte & Fornes, 1998). Of the 129 persons who committed suicide in the Montreal metro system between 1986 and 1996, 105 had a serious mental illness and 27 percent were under hospital care at the time of death (Mishara, 1999). Mental problems can lead to a preoccupation with death as a way to end the person's suffering.

Typically, suicidal people isolate themselves from others; feel worthless, helpless, and misunderstood; and want to die. An extremely negative self-image and severe feelings of hopelessness are warnings that the risk of suicide is very high (Heisel, Flett, & Hewitt, 2003). A long history of such conditions is not always necessary to produce a desire for suicide. Anyone may temporarily reach a state of depression severe enough to attempt suicide. Most dangerous for the average person are times of divorce, separation, rejection, failure, and bereavement. Each situation can seem intolerable and motivate an intense desire to die, to escape, or to obtain relief (Boergers, Spirito, & Donaldson, 1998). For young people, feelings of anger and hostility add to the danger.

Preventing Suicide

Is it true that people who talk about or threaten suicide are rarely the ones who try it? No, this is a major fallacy. Of every ten potential suicides, eight give warning beforehand. A person who threatens suicide should be taken seriously. (See Figure 11.13.) A suicidal person may say nothing more than "I feel sometimes like I'd be better off dead." Warnings may also come indirectly. If a friend gives you a favourite ring and says, "Here, I won't be needing this any more," or comments, "I guess I won't get my watch fixed—it doesn't matter anyway," it may be a plea for help. The warning signs listed in Table 11.2—especially if observed in combination—can signal an impending suicide attempt (Leenaars, Lester, & Wenckstern, 2005; Slaby, Garfinkel, & Garfinkel, 1994).

Is it true that suicide can't be prevented, that the person will find a way to do it anyway? No. Suicide attempts usually come when a person is alone, depressed, and unable to view matters objectively. You should intervene if someone seems to be threatening suicide.

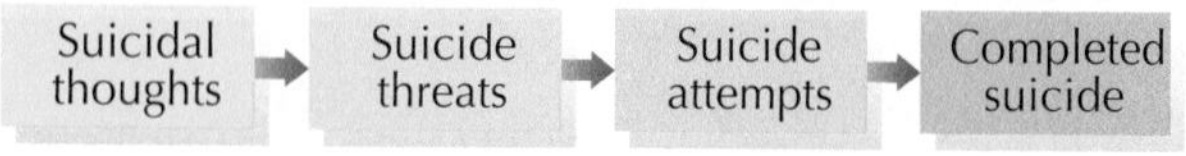

| Suicidal thoughts | → | Suicide threats | → | Suicide attempts | → | Completed suicide |

FIGURE 11.13 Suicidal behaviour usually progresses from suicidal thoughts, to threats, to attempts. A person is unlikely to make an attempt without first making threats. Thus, suicide threats should be taken seriously (Garland & Zigler, 1993).

It is estimated that about two-thirds of all suicide attempts are made by people who do not really want to die. Almost a third more are characterized by a "to be or not to be" attitude. These people are ambivalent or undecided about dying.

Only 3 to 5 percent of suicide cases involve people who really want to die. Most people, therefore, are relieved when someone comes to their aid. Remember that suicide is almost always a cry for help and that you can help. As suicide expert Edwin Shneidman (1987a) puts it, "Suicidal behavior is often a form of communication, a cry for help born out of pain, with clues and messages of suffering and anguish and pleas for response."

How to Help

What is the best thing to do if someone hints they are thinking about suicide? It helps to know some of the common characteristics of suicidal thoughts and feelings (Shneidman, 1987b; Leenaars et al., 2005).

1. *Escape.* Everyone at times feels like running away from an upsetting situation. Running away from home, quitting school, abandoning a marriage—these are all departures. Suicide, of course, is the ultimate escape. It helps when suicidal persons see that the natural wish for escape doesn't have to be expressed by ending it all.

2. *Unbearable psychological pain.* Emotional pain is what the suicidal person is seeking to escape. A goal of anyone hoping to prevent suicide should be to reduce the pain in any way possible. Ask the person, "Where does it hurt?" Suicide occurs when pain exceeds a person's resources for coping with pain.

3. *Frustrated psychological needs.* Often, suicide can be prevented if a distressed person's frustrated needs can be identified and eased. Is the person deeply frustrated in his or her search for love, achievement, trust, security, or friendship?

4. *Constriction of options.* The suicidal person feels helpless and decides that death is the only solution. The person has narrowed all her or his options solely to death. The rescuer's goal, then, is to help broaden the person's perspective. Even when all the choices are unpleasant, suicidal persons can usually be made to see that their least unpleasant option is better than death.

Knowing these patterns will give some guidance in talking to a suicidal person. In addition, your most important task may be to establish rapport (a harmonious connection) with the person. You should offer support, acceptance, and legitimate caring.

Remember that a suicidal person feels misunderstood. Try to accept and understand the feelings the person is expressing. Acceptance should also extend to the idea of suicide itself. It is completely acceptable to ask, "Are you thinking of suicide?"

Establishing communication with suicidal persons may be enough to carry them through a difficult time. You may also find it helpful to get day-by-day commitments from them to meet for lunch, share a ride, and the like. Let the person know you expect him or her to be there. Such commitments, even though small, can be enough to tip the scales when a person is alone and thinking about suicide.

Don't end your efforts too soon. A dangerous time for suicide is when a person suddenly seems to get better after a severe depression. This often means the person has finally decided to end it all. The improvement in mood is deceptive because it comes from an anticipation that suffering is about to end.

Crisis Intervention

Most cities have mental health crisis intervention teams or centres for suicide prevention. Both have staff members trained to talk with suicidal persons over the phone. Give a person who seems to be suicidal the number of one of these services. Urge the person to call you or the other number if she or he becomes frightened or impulsive. Or better yet, help the person make an appointment to get psychological treatment (Weishaar, 2006).

The preceding applies mainly to persons who are having mild suicidal thoughts. If a person actually threatens suicide, you must act more quickly. Ask how the person plans to carry out the suicide. A person who has a specific, workable plan, and the means to carry it out, should be asked to accompany you to the emergency ward of a hospital.

If a person seems on the verge of attempting suicide, don't worry about overreacting. Call the police, crisis intervention, or a rescue unit. Of course, you should call immediately if a person is in the act of attempting suicide or if a drug has already been taken. The majority of suicide attempts come at temporary low points in a person's life and may never be repeated. Get involved—you may save a life!

A final note: If used carelessly, the terms discussed in this chapter can hurt people. Everyone has felt or acted "crazy" during brief periods of stress or high emotion. People with psychological disorders have problems that are more severe or longer lasting than most of us experience. Otherwise, they may not be that different from ourselves or our friends. Generally, it is better to label problems than to label people. Think of the difference between saying, "You have schizophrenia" and saying, "You are a schizophrenic." Which would you prefer to have said about you?

Patients with mental illnesses tend to be stigmatized, rejected, and disgraced. People who have been labelled mentally ill (at any time in their lives) are less likely to be hired. They also tend to be denied housing, and they are more likely to be falsely accused of crimes. Thus, people who are grappling with mental illness may be harmed as much by social stigma as they are by their psychological problems (Corrigan & Penn, 1999). One former patient told one of us the following story:

> After I got back from the hospital, my friends tried to act like nothing had changed. But I could tell they weren't being honest. For instance, a friend invited me to dinner and everything went fine until I dropped my fork. Both my friend and his wife jumped up and stared at me like they thought I might explode. I was quite embarrassed.

Fortunately, a growing number of people recognize that individuals with psychological disorders should be treated with respect and kindness. Remember, it's entirely possible that you, or someone you love, will some day be the one who needs compassion.

 STUDY BREAK **Suicide and Suicide Prevention**

Reflect

You're working at a suicide hotline and you take a call from a very distressed young man. What risk factors will you look for as he tells you about his anguish?

What are the common characteristics of suicidal thoughts and feelings identified by Edwin Shneidman? If a friend of yours were to express any of these thoughts or feelings, how would you respond?

Learning Check

1. More women than men use guns in their suicide attempts. T or F?
2. While the overall suicide rate has remained about the same, there has been a decrease in adolescent suicides. T or F?

3. Suicide is equally a problem of the rich and the poor. T or F?
4. The highest suicide rates are found among the divorced. T or F?
5. The majority (two-thirds) of suicide attempts fall in the "to be" (or cry for help) category. T or F?

Critical Thinking

6. If you follow popular music, see if you can answer this question: What two major risk factors contributed to the 1994 suicide of Kurt Cobain, lead singer for the rock group Nirvana?

Answers

1. F 2. F 3. T 4. T 5. T 6. Drug or alcohol abuse and availability of a firearm.

CHAPTER IN REVIEW

Major Points

- Judgments of normality are relative, but physiological disorders clearly exist and need to be classified, explained, and treated.

- Psychopathology, which involves identifying, classifying, and explaining psychological disorders, is worthwhile and necessary.

- Psychologically unhealthy behaviour is maladaptive and involves a loss of adequate control over thoughts, feelings, and actions.

- Maladaptive behaviour patterns, unhealthy personality types, and excessive levels of anxiety underlie many mental disorders.

- The most severe forms of psychopathology involve emotional extremes and/or a break with reality.

- Psychological disorders are complex and have multiple causes.

- Suicide is a relatively frequent cause of death that can, in many cases, be prevented.

Summary

How is normality defined, and what are the major psychological disorders?

- Psychopathology refers to maladaptive behaviour and to the scientific study of mental disorders.

- Definitions of normality usually take into account the following: subjective discomfort, statistical abnormality, social nonconformity, and the cultural or situational context of behaviour.

- Two key elements in judgments of disorder are that a person's behaviour must be maladaptive and it must involve a loss of control.

- In Canada, the phrase "criminally not responsible on account of mental disorder" defines whether a person may be held responsible for his or her actions. This is determined in court on the basis of testimony by expert witnesses.

What is a personality disorder?

- Personality disorders are deeply ingrained maladaptive personality patterns.

- Antisocial personality or sociopathy is a common personality disorder. Antisocial persons seem to lack a conscience. They are manipulative, emotionally shallow, and dishonest.

What problems result when a person experiences high levels of anxiety?

- Anxiety disorders, dissociative disorders, and somatoform disorders are characterized by high levels of anxiety, rigid defence mechanisms, and self-defeating behaviour patterns.

- The term *nervous breakdown* has no formal meaning. However, emotional breakdowns do correspond somewhat to the occurrence of an adjustment disorder.

- Anxiety disorders include generalized anxiety disorder, panic disorder with or without agoraphobia, agoraphobia (without panic), specific phobias, social phobia, obsessive-compulsive disorders, post-traumatic stress disorder, and acute stress disorder.

- Dissociative disorders may take the form of dissociative amnesia, dissociative fugue, or dissociative identity disorder.

- Somatoform disorders centre on physical complaints that mimic disease or disability. Four examples of somatoform disorders are hypochondriasis, somatization disorder, somatoform pain disorder, and conversion disorder.

How do psychologists explain anxiety-based disorders?

- The humanistic approach emphasizes the effects of a faulty self-image.

- The behaviourists emphasize the effects of previous learning, particularly avoidance learning.

- Cognitive theories of anxiety focus on distorted thinking, judgment, and attention.

What are the major characteristics of schizophrenia? What causes it?

- Schizophrenia is a break in contact with reality that is marked by delusions, hallucinations, sensory changes, disturbed emotions, disturbed communication, and personality disintegration.

- Disorganized schizophrenia is marked by extreme personality disintegration and silly, bizarre, or obscene behaviour. Social impairment is usually extreme.

- Catatonic schizophrenia is associated with stupor, mutism, and odd postures. Sometimes violent and agitated behaviour also occurs.

- In paranoid schizophrenia (the most common type), outlandish delusions of grandeur and persecution are coupled with psychotic symptoms and personality breakdown.

- Current explanations of schizophrenia emphasize a combination of inherited susceptibility, early trauma, environmental stress, and abnormalities in the brain.

- Environmental factors that increase the risk of schizophrenia include viral infection or malnutrition during the mother's pregnancy, birth complications, early psychological trauma, and a disturbed family environment.

- Heredity is a major factor in schizophrenia.

- Recent biochemical studies have focused on the brain transmitter dopamine and its receptor sites.

- The dominant explanation of schizophrenia, and other problems as well, is the stress-vulnerability model.

What are mood disorders? What causes them?

- Mood disorders primarily involve disturbances of mood or emotion, producing manic or depressive states.

- Depression that is long-lasting, though relatively moderate, is called a dysthymic disorder. Chronic, though moderate, swings in mood between depression and elation are called a cyclothymic disorder.

- Bipolar disorders combine mania and depression. In a bipolar I disorder, the person swings between major episodes of mania and depression. In a bipolar II disorder, the person experiences episodes of major depression, but has had periods of mild mania.

- A major depressive disorder involves extreme sadness and despondency but no evidence of mania.

- Seasonal affective disorder (SAD), which occurs during the winter months, is another common form of depression. SAD is typically treated with phototherapy.

- Biological and psychological theories of depression have been proposed. Heredity is clearly a factor in susceptibility to mood disorders.

- Psychological explanations of depression include the learned helplessness model and the cognitive theory of depression. The former emphasizes the importance of lacking control over one's life and feelings of hopelessness, and the latter stresses the role of negative thinking.

- The college blues are a relatively mild form of depression. Learning to manage school work and to challenge self-critical thinking can help in dealing with the college blues.

Why do people commit suicide? Can suicide be prevented?

- Suicide is statistically related to such factors as age, sex, and marital status.

- In individual cases, the potential for suicide is best identified by a desire to escape, unbearable psychological pain, frustrated psychological needs, and a constriction of options.

- Suicide can often be prevented by the efforts of family, friends, and mental health professionals.

Interactive Learning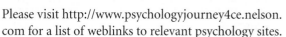

Please visit http://www.psychologyjourney4ce.nelson.com for a list of weblinks to relevant psychology sites.

CourseMate

Access an interactive e-book and chapter-specific interactive learning tools, including flashcards, quizzes, videos, and more, in your psychology CourseMate. Visit Nelsonbrain.com to use CourseMate.

psyk.trek 11. Abnormal Behaviour and Therapy.

TEST YOUR KNOWLEDGE

The questions that follow are only a sample of what you need to know. If you miss any of the items, review the entire chapter and the Study Breaks. Another way to prepare for tests is to use the Study Guide and the Practice Exams that are available with this text.

1. What is the core feature of abnormal behaviour?
   a. behaviour that is statistically frequent
   b. behaviour that is maladaptive
   c. behaviour that is socially conforming
   d. behaviour that is a source of feeling guilty

2. What is the most widely used standard for classifying mental disorders in North America?
   a. The Diagnostic and Statistical Manual of Mental Disorders (DSM-II-TR)
   b. The Diagnostic and Statistical Manual of Mental Disorders (DSM-IIII-TR)
   c. The Diagnostic and Statistical Manual of Mental Disorders (DSM-IV-TR)
   d. Psychiatrist's Desk Reference

3. James is addicted to heroin. He is unable to work, study, or lead a productive life as a result of his habit. What type of disorder does James have?
   a. a substance-related disorder   b. a psychotic disorder
   c. a mood-related disorder   d. a fictitious disorder

4. Who experiences Pibloktoq?
   a. the people of Brazil   b. Inuit people
   c. People from Latin America   d. Chinese people

5. Which of the following is *not* a type of personality disorder?
   a. schizoid   b. borderline
   c. neurotic   d. dependent

6. Jane is extremely unpredictable, moody, and manipulative, and she has had a number of turbulent relationships that have ended abruptly. What type of personality disorder does she most likely have?
   a. antisocial   b. borderline
   c. dependent   d. histrionic

7. What type of personality disorder is described by a person who is impulsive, dishonest, emotionally cold, and manipulative?
   a. antisocial   b. histrionic
   c. dependent   d. obsessive-compulsive

8. Prolonged unemployment, a bad marriage, or physical illness can push a person beyond his or her ability to cope. Which of the following problems will most likely occur?
   a. a dissociative disorder
   b. agoraphobia
   c. an adjustment disorder
   d. a conversion disorder

9. Which disorder includes agoraphobia?
   a. adjustment disorder   b. panic disorder
   c. post-traumatic stress disorder (PTSD)   d. obsessive-compulsive disorder

10. Which view suggests that anxiety disorders are the result of a faulty self-image?
    a. genetic   b. humanistic
    c. behaviouristic   d. cognitive

11. What disorder is characterized by delusions and hallucinations?
    a. bipolar disorder   b. schizophrenia
    c. panic disorder   d. post-traumatic stress disorder

12. Which of the following is not one of the subtypes of schizophrenia?
    a. erotomanic type   b. catatonic type
    c. paranoid type   d. disorganized type

13. Biochemical explanations of schizophrenia have focused on which overactive system in the brain?
    a. radioactive sugar   b. webs and tangles
    c. "angel dust" (PCP)   d. dopamine

14. Enlarged ventricles characterize some patients with which of the following?
    a. bipolar disorder   b. schizophrenia
    c. depression   d. antisocial personality disorder

15. The stress-vulnerability model of psychosis explains mental disorders as a product of two factors, one being environmental stressors. What is the other factor?
    a. psychological trauma   b. deviant communication
    c. exposure to the flu virus during pregnancy   d. heredity

16. What is the name of the disorder that is similar to, yet not as severe as, bipolar disorder?
    a. endogenous disorder   b. cyclothymic disorder
    c. seasonal affective disorder   d. dysthymic disorder

17. What disorder refers to depression that is not too severe?
    a. endogenous disorder   b. cyclothymic disorder
    c. seasonal affective disorder   d. dysthymic disorder

18. One biochemical explanation of depression suggests low amounts of which substance in the brain?
    a. dopamine   b. norepinephrine
    c. serotonin   d. GABA

19. In the development of depression, learned helplessness theory emphasizes a lack of control. What does cognitive theory emphasize?
    a. lack of frustration   b. positive beliefs
    c. negative thinking   d. lack of fulfillment

20. Which person has the greatest risk of attempting suicide?
    a. a person who has a concrete, workable plan for committing suicide
    b. a person who has had a recent life crisis
    c. a person who has withdrawn from contact
    d. a person who is frustrated psychologically with others' needs

ANSWERS   1.b 2.c 3.a 4.b 5.c 6.b 7.a 8.c 9.b 10.b 11.b 12.a 13.d 14.b 15.d 16.b 17.d 18.c 19.c 20.a

chapter 12

Health, Stress, and Coping

JOURNEY INTO PSYCHOLOGY: TAYLOR'S (NOT SO VERY) FINE ADVENTURE

Somehow, Taylor had managed to survive the rush of make-or-break term papers, projects, and classroom presentations. Then it was on to final exams, where his tests seemed perfectly timed to inflict as much suffering as possible. His two hardest exams fell on the same day! Great.

On the last day of exams, Taylor got a late start. Then he got caught in traffic on his way to school. Two drivers cut him off, and another gave him the finger. He ran a red light right in front of a cop. When Taylor finally got to school, the parking lots were swarming with frantic students. Most of them, like him, were within minutes of missing a final exam. At last, Taylor spied an empty space. As he started toward it, a Toyota Prius cut in front of him and grabbed the spot. The driver of the car behind him began to honk impatiently. For a moment, Taylor was seized by a colossal desire to run over anything in sight.

Finally, after a week and a half of stress, pressure, and frustration, Taylor's exams were over. Sleep deprivation, litres of coffee, too much junk food, and equal portions of cramming and complaining had carried him through. He was off for the summer. At last, he could relax and have some fun. Or could he? Just four days later, Taylor got a bad cold, followed by bronchitis that lasted nearly a month.

Was this just more bad luck? Or does Taylor's experience illustrate what happens when stress, emotion, personal habits, and health collide? While the timing of his cold might have been a coincidence, odds are it wasn't. Periods of stress are frequently followed by illness (Lyons & Chamberlain, 2006).

Stress occurs whenever a challenge or a threat forces a person to adjust or adapt. Stress is a normal part of life. But when stress is chronic or severe, it can damage health. Stress, in other words, is a behavioural factor that directly affects personal well-being.

In the first part of this chapter, we will explore a variety of behavioural health risks. Then we will look more closely at what stress is and how it affects us. After that, we will address ways of coping with stress. In addition, we will look at the work of Hans Selye (SEL-yay), who spent most of his career at the University of Montreal and is considered one of the pioneers of stress research.

> **Health psychology** The study of how behavioural principles can be used to prevent illness and promote health.

Survey Questions

- What is health psychology? How does behaviour affect health?
- What is stress? What factors determine its severity?
- What is frustration? What are the major causes of frustration? How do people react to it?
- What is conflict? Are there different types of conflict? How do people react to conflict?
- What are defence mechanisms? How do defence mechanisms help us to cope with stress?
- How is stress related to health and disease?
- What are the best strategies for managing stress?

HEALTH PSYCHOLOGY—HERE'S TO YOUR GOOD HEALTH

Most people agree that health is important—especially their own. Yet, almost one-half of all deaths in North America are primarily due to unhealthy behaviour. **Health psychology** aims to do something about such deaths. Health psychologists use behavioural principles to promote health and prevent illness (Mokdad et al., 2004). Psychologists working in the allied

<SURVEY QUESTION
What is health psychology? How does behaviour affect health?

field of **behavioural medicine** apply psychology to manage medical problems, such as diabetes and asthma. Their interests include pain control, helping people cope with chronic illness and stress-related diseases, self-screening for diseases (such as breast cancer), and similar topics (Brannon & Feist, 2010).

Behavioural Risk Factors

Around the turn of the 20th century, people died primarily from infectious diseases and accidents. Today, people are more likely to die from **lifestyle diseases,** which are related to health-damaging personal habits. Examples include heart disease, stroke, and lung cancer (Mokdad et al., 2004) (see Figure 12.1). Clearly, some lifestyles promote health, whereas others lead to illness or can seriously reduce a person's quality of life.

What kinds of behaviour are you referring to as unhealthy? Some causes of poor health are beyond our control. Nevertheless, a number of behavioural risk factors can be controlled.

Behavioural risk factors are behaviours that increase the chances of disease, injury, or early death. For example, the Canadian Cancer Society estimates that over 20 000 people died from lung cancer in 2011 (Canadian Cancer Society Steering Committee on Cancer Statistics, 2011). Similarly, being overweight is enough to affect a person's chance of dying from cancer or heart disease. Roughly 37 percent of all Canadian adults are overweight, while another 24 percent are obese (Canada Health Measures Survey 2007–2009, 2010).

Being fat is not just a matter of fashion—in the long run it could kill you. A person who is overweight at 20 can anticipate to lose 5 to 20 years of life expectancy (Fontaine et al., 2003).

Each of the following factors is a major behavioural risk (Baum & Posluszny, 1999): high levels of stress, untreated high blood pressure, cigarette smoking, abuse of alcohol or other drugs, overeating, inadequate exercise, unsafe sexual behaviour, exposure to toxic substances, violence, excess sun exposure, reckless driving, and disregarding personal safety (avoidable accidents). The personal habits you have by the time you are 18 or 19 greatly affect your health, happiness, and life expectancy years later (Gurung, 2010; Vaillant & Mukamal, 2001).

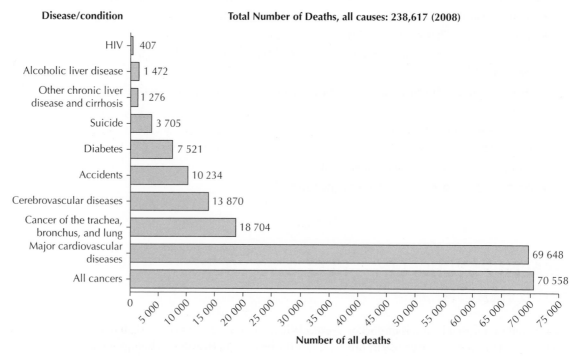

▶▶**FIGURE 12.1** Some of the leading causes of death in Canada are shown in this figure. Many of them, including some cancers, other lung diseases, heart disease, and liver disease, are related to behavioural risk factors such as alcohol use, smoking, lack of exercise, and risky sexual behaviours. (Adapted from Statistics Canada, "Mortality, summary list of causes," 2004. This does not constitute an endorsement by Statistics Canada of this product.)

In the long run, behavioural risk factors and lifestyles do make a difference in health and life expectancy.

In addition to specific risk factors, a general **disease-prone personality** type also exists. Such people tend to be chronically depressed, anxious, hostile—and frequently ill. People who are intellectually resourceful, compassionate, optimistic, and non-hostile tend to enjoy good health (Taylor, 2006; Taylor et al., 2000). Depression, especially, is likely to be harmful to health. People who are depressed tend to sleep poorly, eat poorly, smoke more, fail to use a seat belt, and so on (Allgower, Wardle, & Steptoe, 2001; Luppa et al., 2007).

Lifestyle

In your mind's eye, fast-forward an imaginary film of your life all the way to old age. Do it twice—once with a lifestyle including a large number of behavioural risk factors, and again without them. It should be obvious that countless small risks can add up to dramatically raising the chance of illness. If stress is a frequent part of your life, visualize your body seething with emotion, day after day. If you smoke, picture a lifetime's worth of cigarette smoke blown through your lungs in a week. If you drink, take a lifetime of alcohol's assaults on the brain, stomach, and liver and squeeze them into a month: Your body would be poisoned, ravaged, and soon dead. If you eat a high-fat, high-cholesterol diet, fast-forward a lifetime of heart-killing plaque clogging your arteries.

This discussion is not meant to be a sermon. It is merely a reminder that risk factors do make a difference. To make matters worse, unhealthy lifestyles almost always create multiple risks. That is, people who smoke are also likely to drink excessively. Those who drink excessively are also more likely to be passengers in cars driven by drunk drivers (Mokdad et al., 2004, Straub, 2006). And so on.

Health-Promoting Behaviours

To prevent disease, health psychologists first try to remove behavioural risk factors. All the medicine in the world may not be enough to restore health without changes in behaviour. We all know someone who has had a heart attack or lung disease who couldn't change the habits that led to the illness.

In some cases, lifestyle diseases can be treated or prevented by making specific, minor changes in behaviour. For example, hypertension (high blood pressure) can be deadly. Yet, consuming less sodium (salt) can help fend off this "silent killer" (losing weight, using alcohol sparingly, and getting more exercise will also help) (Georgiades et al., 2000).

In addition to removing specific risk factors, psychologists are also interested in getting people to increase behaviours that promote health. **Health-promoting behaviours** include such obvious practices as getting regular exercise, controlling smoking and alcohol use,

Disease-prone personality A personality type associated with poor health, marked by persistent negative emotions.

Health-promoting behaviour Any practice that tends to maintain or enhance good health.

■ Table 12.1	Major Health-Promoting Behaviours
Source	**Desirable Behaviours**
Nutrition	Eating a balanced diet, low in saturated and trans fats, and at an appropriate caloric intake; maintaining a healthy body weight
Exercise	Performing at least 30 minutes of aerobic exercise, five days per week
Blood pressure	Lowering blood pressure with diet and exercise, or medicine if necessary
Alcohol and drugs	Consuming no more than two drinks per day; abstaining from using drugs
Tobacco	Not smoking; not using smokeless tobacco
Sleep and relaxation	Avoiding sleep deprivation; providing for periods of relaxation every day
Sex	Practising safer sex; avoiding unplanned pregnancy
Injury	Curbing dangerous driving habits, using seat belts; minimizing sun exposure; forgoing dangerous activities
Stress	Learning stress management; lowering hostility

Health Canada's second-hand smoke campaign aims to raise awareness of the dangers of second-hand smoke.

CP PHOTO/Dave Chidley

maintaining a balanced diet, getting good medical care, and managing stress (Zarcadoolas, Pleasant, & Greer, 2006).

Health-promoting behaviours don't have to be restrictive or burdensome. For instance, maintaining a healthy diet doesn't mean surviving on tofu and wheat grass. And you don't need to exercise like an Olympic athlete to benefit from physical activity.

What about alcohol? Moderation in drinking doesn't mean that you must be a teetotaller. Consuming one or two alcoholic drinks per day is generally safe for most people, especially if you remain alcohol-free two or three days a week. However, having three or more drinks a day greatly increases the risk of stroke, cirrhosis of the liver, cancer, high blood pressure, heart disorders, and other diseases (Knoops et al., 2004).

To summarize, a small number of behavioural patterns account for many common health problems (Grunbaum et al., 2004). Table 12.1 lists several major ways to promote good health. (To explore an interesting social factor underlying common health problems, see Using Psychology: "Unhealthy Birds of a Feather.")

USING PSYCHOLOGY

Unhealthy Birds of a Feather

Would you like to eat better, exercise more, or quit smoking? Researchers Nicholas Christakis and James Fowler believe they know why it can be difficult to alter unhealthy behaviours. Often, social factors are a barrier to change. If you are a smoker, do your friends also smoke? Are your family members fast-food junkies just like you? Unhealthy behaviours such as overeating and smoking seem to spread almost like a "mental virus."

One study of social contagion found that people were 57 percent more likely to become obese if they had a friend who became fat first (Christakis & Fowler, 2007). Another study noted that smokers tend to hang out with other smokers (Christakis & Fowler, 2008). Apparently, we tend to flock together with like-minded people and adopt many of their habits.

Does that mean I am doomed to be unhealthy if my family and friends have unhealthy habits? Not necessarily. Social networks can also spread healthful behaviours. If one smoker in a group of smokers quits, others are more likely to follow suit. If your spouse quits smoking, you are 67 percent more likely to quit. If a good friend quits smoking, your chances of abandoning tobacco go up by 36 percent (Christakis & Fowler, 2008). The growing social unpopularity of smoking may explain why fewer adults and teens are smoking today.

The implication? Don't wait for your friends or family to adopt healthier habits. Take the lead and get them to join you. Failing that, start hanging out with a healthier crowd. You might catch something healthy.

Early Prevention

Smoking is one of the largest preventable causes of death and the single most lethal behavioural risk factor (Mokdad et al., 2004). As such, it illustrates the prospect for preventing illness.

What have health psychologists done to lessen the risks? Attempts to "immunize" youths against pressures to start smoking provide a good example. The smoker who says, "Quitting is easy, I've done it dozens of times," states a basic truth—not all smokers who do quit smoking quit for good. In fact, according to Statistics Canada, although the percentage of smokers who quit smoking rose from 10 percent to 17 percent between 1994 and 2004, the percentage of quitters who started smoking again remained stable at 4 percent (Shields, 2005b). Thus, the best way to deal with smoking is to prevent it before it becomes a lifelong habit.

What have health psychologists done to help lessen the risks of smoking? Prevention programs in schools discourage smoking with quizzes about the effects of smoking, antismoking art contests, poster and T-shirt giveaways, antismoking pamphlets for parents, and student quizzes of parents (Zarcadoolas et al., 2006). Such efforts persuade kids that smoking is dangerous and "uncool." Apparently, teens are getting the message, as attitudes toward smoking are more negative than they were 20 years ago (Chassin et al., 2003), and the number of teens who reported they smoked dropped substantially from 2001 to 2011, to 9.4% from 20.8% among teens 15 to 17 and to 19.1% from 33.7% for 18- to 19-year-olds. In fact, smoking among all Canadians aged 12 and over declined to 19.9% from 25.9% of the population over the years 2001 to 2011 (Statistics Canada, 2012).

Some of the best antismoking programs include **refusal skills training.** In this case, youths learn to resist pressures to begin smoking (or using other drugs) (Botvin et al., 1997). For example, students in Grades 6, 7, and 8 can role-play ways to resist smoking pressures from peers, adults, and cigarette ads (although cigarette advertisements are banned in Canada, U.S. magazines, which are available in Canada, still carry such advertising). Similar methods can be applied to other health risks, such as sexually transmitted infections and unplanned pregnancy (Wandersman & Florin, 2003).

The latest health programs also teach students general life skills. The idea is to give people skills that will help them cope with day-to-day stresses. That way, they will be less tempted to escape problems through drug use or other destructive behaviours. **Life skills training** includes practice in stress reduction, self-protection, decision making, self-control, and social skills (Tobler et al., 2000).

And these programs seem to be working—the percentage of Canadians who smoke declined from 24 percent in 2001 to 20.8 percent in 2010 (Statistics Canada, 2011).

STIs AND SAFER SEX—RISK AND RESPONSIBILITY

Unsafe sex is one area in which relatively small changes in behaviour can almost completely eliminate a major health hazard. Attempts to change eating or exercise habits or to quit smoking can be very difficult. Avoiding risky sex should be far easier—but is it?

Sexually Transmitted Infections

A **sexually transmitted infection (STI)** is passed from one person to another by intimate physical contact. Sexually active people run a high risk of getting chlamydia (klah-MID-ee-ah), gonorrhea, hepatitis B, herpes, syphilis, and other STIs. Many people who have an STI remain **asymptomatic.** It is easy to be infected without knowing it. Nearly 75 percent of women with chlamydia have no noticeable symptoms, and 80 percent of women with gonorrhea have no symptoms in the early stages of infection (Rathus et al., 2004). Because of this, it is often impossible to tell if a sexual partner is infectious.

A major problem is that people who are sexually active may have indirect contact with many other people. One study of high school students' sexual relationships found long chains of sexual contacts. A student at the end of the chain might have had sex with only one person, but in reality he or she has had indirect contact with dozens of others (Bearman, Moody, & Stovel, 2004).

Refusal skills training A program that teaches youths how to resist pressures to begin smoking. (Can also be applied to other drugs and health risks.)

Life skills training A program that teaches stress reduction, self-protection, decision making, self-control, and social skills.

Sexually transmitted infection (STI) An infection that is typically passed from one person to the next by intimate physical contact.

Asymptomatic Having a disease while lacking obvious symptoms of illness.

Human immunodeficiency virus (HIV) A sexually transmitted virus that disables the immune system.

Wellness A positive state of good health; more than the absence of disease.

For sexually active people, the **human immunodeficiency virus (HIV)** is an added issue. HIV is a sexually transmitted virus that disables the immune system. Whereas most other STIs are treatable, HIV infections can be lethal. Even with advances in treatment, HIV is still a serious problem.

Behavioural Risk Factors

Sexually active people can do much to protect their own health. Because the organisms that cause STIs are "equal-opportunity germs," the behaviours listed here are risky when performed with any infected person—male or female, young or old, gay or straight.

Risky Behaviours

- Sharing drug needles and syringes
- Anal sex, with or without a condom
- Vaginal or oral sex with someone who injects drugs or engages in anal sex with other partners
- Having sex with someone you don't know well, or with someone you know has had several sexual partners
- Unprotected sex (without a condom) with an infected partner
- Having two or more sex partners (additional partners further increase the risk)

It's important to remember that you can't tell from appearance if a person is infected with an STI. Many people would be surprised to learn that their partners have engaged in behaviour that places them both at risk (Seal & Palmer-Seal, 1996).

The preceding high-risk behaviours can be contrasted with the following list of safer sexual practices:

Safer Sex Practices

- Not having vaginal, anal, or oral sex
- Using a condom
- Sex with one mutually faithful, uninfected partner
- Not injecting drugs
- Discussing contraception and safer sex practices with partner
- Being selective regarding sexual partners
- Reducing the number of sexual partners
- Discussing a partner's sexual health prior to engaging in sex
- Limiting the consumption of alcohol
- Getting tested for HIV and other STIs with a partner

In a survey of over 18 000 sexually active Canadians between the ages of 15 and 24, 32.7 percent of the males and 43.5 percent of the females reported that they had not used a condom the last time they had sexual intercourse, and more than one-third had had more than one partner (Rotermann, 2005). One chilling study of HIV patients—who knew they were infectious—found that 41 percent of those who were sexually active did not always use condoms (Sobel et al., 1996)! Thus, responsibility for safer sex rests with each sexually active individual. It is unwise to count on a sexual partner for protection against HIV infection, or any STI, for that matter.

WELLNESS

Health is not just an absence of disease. People who are truly healthy enjoy a positive state of **wellness** or well-being. Maintaining wellness is a lifelong pursuit and, hopefully, a labour of love. People who attain optimal wellness are both physically and psychologically healthy. They are happy, optimistic, self-confident individuals who can bounce back emotionally from adversity (Tugade, Fredrickson, & Barrett, 2004).

STUDY BREAK Health Psychology

Reflect

If you were to work as a health psychologist, would you be more interested in preventing disease or managing it?

Make a list of the major behavioural risk factors that apply to you. Are you laying the foundation for a lifestyle disease?

Which of the health-promoting behaviours listed in Table 12.1 would you like to increase?

Learning Check

1. Adjustment to chronic illness and the control of pain are topics that would more likely be of interest to a specialist in _____ _____ rather than a health psychologist.

2. With respect to health, which of the following is not a major behavioural risk factor?
   a. overexercise
   b. cigarette smoking
   c. stress
   d. high blood pressure

3. Health psychologists tend to prefer _____ rather than modifying habits (like smoking) that become difficult to break once they are established.

4. The disease-prone personality is marked by _____, anxiety, and hostility.

Critical Thinking

5. The general public is increasingly well informed about health risks and healthful behaviour. Can you apply the concept of reinforcement to explain why so many people fail to act on this information?

Answers

1. behavioural medicine 2. a 3. prevention 4. depression 5. Many health payoffs are delayed by months or years, greatly lessening the immediate rewards for healthful behaviour.

People who enjoy a sense of well-being also have supportive relationships with others, do meaningful work, and live in a clean environment. Many of these aspects of wellness are addressed elsewhere in this book. In this chapter, we will give special attention to the effect that stress has on health and sickness. Understanding stress and learning to control it can improve not only your health but also the quality of your life. For these reasons, a discussion of stress and stress management follows.

STRESS—THRILL OR THREAT?

Although stress is a natural part of life, it can be a major behavioural risk factor if it is prolonged or severe. It might seem that stressful events "happen to" people. Although this is sometimes the case, more often stress is a matter of how we perceive events and react to them. Because of this, stress can often be managed or controlled. Let's look into how stress occurs and typical reactions to it.

Stress can be dangerous if it is prolonged or severe, but it isn't always bad. Stress researcher Hans Selye (1956/1976), who worked at the University of Montreal for over 50 years, once observed, "To be totally without stress is to be dead." **Stress** is the mental and physical condition that occurs when a person must adjust or adapt to the environment. Unpleasant events, such as work pressures, marital problems, or financial woes, naturally produce stress. But so do travel, sports, a new job, mountain climbing, dating, and other positive activities. Even if you aren't a thrill seeker, a healthy lifestyle may include a fair amount of *eustress* (good stress). Eustress can be energizing. Activities that provoke "good stress" are usually experienced as challenging and rewarding.

A **stress reaction** begins with the same autonomic nervous system arousal that occurs during emotion. Imagine you are standing at the top of a wind-whipped ski jump for the first time. Internally, there would be a rapid surge in your heart rate, blood pressure, respiration, muscle tension, and other ANS responses. Short-term stresses of this kind can be uncomfortable, but they rarely do any damage. (Your landing might be another matter, however.) *Long-term* stresses are another matter entirely.

<SURVEY QUESTION
What is stress? What factors determine its severity?

Stress The mental and physical condition that occurs when a person must adjust or adapt to the environment.

Stress reaction The physical response to stress, consisting mainly of bodily changes related to autonomic nervous system arousal.

The General Adaptation Syndrome

The impact of long-term stresses can best be understood by examining the body's defences against stress, a pattern Selye named the *general adaptation syndrome.*

The **general adaptation syndrome (GAS)** is a series of bodily reactions to prolonged stress. Selye (1956/1976) noticed that the first symptoms of almost any disease or trauma (poisoning, infection, injury, or stress) are almost identical. The body responds in the same way to any stress, be it infection, failure, embarrassment, a new job, trouble at school, or a stormy romance.

How does the body respond to stress? The GAS consists of three stages: an alarm reaction, a stage of resistance, and a stage of exhaustion (Selye, 1956/1976).

In the **alarm reaction,** the body mobilizes its resources to cope with added stress. The pituitary gland signals the adrenal glands to produce more adrenaline, noradrenaline, and cortisol. As these stress hormones are dumped into the bloodstream, some bodily processes are speeded up and others are slowed. This allows bodily resources to be applied where they are needed (Lyons & Chamberlain, 2006).

We should all be thankful that our bodies automatically respond to emergencies. But brilliant as this emergency system is, it can also cause problems. In the first phase of the alarm reaction, people have such symptoms as headache, fever, fatigue, sore muscles, shortness of breath, diarrhea, upset stomach, loss of appetite, and a lack of energy. Notice that these are also the symptoms of being sick, of stressful travel, of high-altitude sickness, of final exams, and (possibly) of falling in love!

During the **stage of resistance,** bodily adjustments to stress stabilize. As the body's defences come into balance, symptoms of the alarm reaction disappear. Outwardly, everything seems normal. However, this appearance of normality comes at a high cost. The body is better able to cope with the original stressor, but its resistance to other stresses is lowered. For example, animals placed in extreme cold become more resistant to the cold, but more susceptible to infection. It is during the stage of resistance that the first signs of psychosomatic disorders begin to appear.

Continued stress leads to the **stage of exhaustion,** in which the body's resources are drained and stress hormones are depleted. Some of the typical signs or symptoms of impending exhaustion are as follows (Friedman, 2002):

Emotional signs: Anxiety, apathy, irritability, mental fatigue

Behavioural signs: Avoidance of responsibilities and relationships, extreme or self-destructive behaviour, self-neglect, poor judgment

Physical signs: excessive worry about illness, frequent illness, exhaustion, overuse of medicines, physical ailments and complaints

The GAS may sound melodramatic if you are young and healthy or if you've never endured prolonged stress. However, stress should not be taken lightly. Unless a way of relieving stress is found, the result will be a psychosomatic disease, a serious loss of health, or a complete collapse. When Selye examined animals in the later stages of the GAS, he found that their adrenal glands were enlarged and discoloured. There was intense shrinkage of internal organs such as the thymus, spleen, and lymph nodes, and many animals had stomach ulcers. In addition to such direct effects, stress can disrupt the body's immune system, as described in Clinical File: "Stress, Illness, and the Immune System."

When Is Stress a Strain?

It goes almost without saying that some events are more likely to cause stress than others. A **stressor** is a condition or event that challenges or threatens a person. Police officers, for instance, suffer from a high rate of stress-related diseases. The threat of injury or death, plus occasional confrontations with drunk or belligerent citizens, takes a toll. A major factor here is the unpredictable nature of police work. An officer who stops a car to issue a traffic ticket never knows if a cooperative citizen or an armed gang member is waiting inside.

General adaptation syndrome (GAS) A series of bodily reactions to prolonged stress; occurs in three stages: alarm, resistance, and exhaustion.

Alarm reaction The first stage of the GAS, during which bodily resources are mobilized to cope with a stressor.

Stage of resistance The second stage of the GAS, during which bodily adjustments to stress stabilize, but at a high physical cost.

Stage of exhaustion The third stage of the GAS, at which time the body's resources are exhausted and damage occurs.

Stressor A specific condition or event in the environment that challenges or threatens a person.

THE CLINICAL FILE

Stress, Illness, and the Immune System

How else might stress affect health? An answer can be found in the **immune system,** which mobilizes defences (such as white blood cells) against invading microbes and other disease agents (Ader & Cohen, 1993). The immune system is regulated, in part, by the brain. Because of this link, stress and upsetting emotions can affect the immune system in ways that increase susceptibility to disease (Miller, Cohen, & Ritchey, 2002). The study of links among behaviour, stress, disease, and the immune system is called **psycho-neuroimmunology** (Daruna, 2004).

Studies show that the immune system is weakened in students during major exam times. Immunity is also lowered by divorce, bereavement, a troubled marriage, job loss, depression, and similar stresses (Deinzer et al., 2000; Segerstrom & Miller, 2004; Motivala & Irwin, 2007). Lowered immunity explains why the "double whammy" of getting sick when you are trying to cope with prolonged or severe stress is so common (Lyons & Chamberlain, 2006). Stress causes the body to release substances that increase inflammation.

This is part of the body's self-protective response to threats, but it can prolong infections and delay healing (Kiecolt-Glazer et al., 2002; Wargo, 2007).

Could reducing stress help prevent illness? Yes. Psychological approaches, such as support groups, relaxation exercises, guided imagery, and stress management training, can actually boost immune system functioning (Dougall & Baum, 2003). By doing so, they help promote and restore health. There is even evidence that such measures improve the chances of survival following life-threatening diseases, such as cancer, heart disease, and HIV/AIDS (Schneiderman et al., 2001). With some successes to encourage them, psychologists are now searching for the best combination of treatments to help people resist disease (Miller & Cohen, 2001).

No one is immune to stress. Nevertheless, it's reassuring to know that managing stress can help protect your immune system and your health.

An interesting study shows how unpredictability adds to stress. College students breathed air through a mask in a series of one-minute trials. On some trials, the air contained 20 percent more carbon dioxide (CO_2) than normal. If you were to breathe this air, you would feel anxious, stressed, and a little like you were suffocating. Students hated the "surprise" doses of CO_2. They found it much less stressful to be told in advance that this would occur (Lejuez et al., 2000).

Pressure is another element in stress, especially job stress. **Pressure** occurs when a person must meet urgent external demands or expectations (Weiten, 1998). For example, we feel pressured when activities must be speeded up, when deadlines must be met, when extra work is added unexpectedly, or when we must work near maximum capacity for long periods. Most students who have survived final exams are familiar with the effects of pressure. And we generally feel more stress in situations we can't control (Taris et al., 2005).

To summarize, when emotional "shocks" are intense or repeated, unpredictable, uncontrollable, and linked to pressure, stress will be magnified and damage is likely to result. At work, chronic stress sometimes results in burnout, a pattern of emotional exhaustion described in Clinical File: "Burnout—The High Cost of Caring."

Appraising Stressors

External events are not the whole story of stress. As noted in Chapter 9 (page 386), our emotions are greatly affected by how we appraise situations. That's why some people are distressed by events that others view as a thrill or a challenge (eustress). Ultimately, stress depends on how a situation is perceived. For example, a middle-aged woman may find it stressful to listen to five of her son's gangsta rap albums in a row. Her son, on the other hand, may find it stressful to listen to one of his mother's classic rock albums. To know if you are stressed, we must know what meaning you place on events. As we will see in a moment, whenever a stressor is appraised as a **threat** (potentially harmful), a powerful stress reaction follows (Folkman & Moskowitz, 2004; Lazarus, 1991a).

Immune system The system that mobilizes bodily defences against invading microbes and other disease agents.

Psychoneuroimmunology The study of the links among behaviour, stress, disease, and the immune system.

Pressure A stressful condition that occurs when a person must meet urgent external demands or expectations.

Threat An event or situation perceived as potentially harmful.

Although it may not seem so, assembly line work can be quite stressful because of the lack of control employees have over the pace of work.

Burnout—The High Cost of Caring

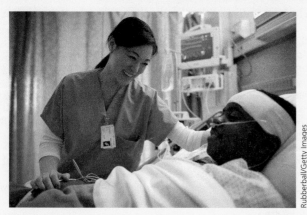

Rubberball/Getty Images

The helping professions require empathy, caring, and emotional involvement. As a result, caregivers risk depleting their emotional resources and ability to cope. Over time, this can lead to burnout.

Margo, a young nurse, realizes with dismay that she has "lost all patience with her patients" and wishes they would "go somewhere else to be sick." Margo's feelings are clearly a sign of job **burnout,** a condition in which workers are physically, mentally, and emotionally drained (Greenglass, Burke, & Moore, 2003). Burnout has three aspects (Maslach, Schaufeli & Leiter, 2001):

• Emotional exhaustion: Affected persons are fatigued, tense, and apathetic, and suffer from physical ailments. They feel "used up" and empty.

• Cynicism or detachment: Burned-out workers have an "I don't give a damn any more" attitude, and they treat clients coldly, as if they were objects.

• Feelings of reduced personal accomplishment: Burned-out workers do poor work and feel helpless, hopeless, or angry. Their self-esteem slumps, and they yearn to change jobs or careers.

Burnout may occur in any job, but it is a special problem in emotionally demanding helping professions, such as nursing, teaching, social work, child care, counselling, and police work. Often the most idealistic and caring workers are the ones who burn out first (Maslach et al., 2001).

If we wish to keep caring people in the helping professions, it may be necessary to adjust workloads, rewards, and the amount of control people have in their jobs (Leiter & Maslach, 2005).

Can college students experience burnout? Yes, they can. If you have a negative attitude toward your studies and feel that your college workload is too heavy, you may be vulnerable to burnout (Jacobs & Dodd, 2003). On the other hand, if you have a positive attitude toward your studies, participate in extracurricular activities, and enjoy good social support from your friends, rock on!

Building stronger social support systems could also help prevent burnout. A good example is the growing use of support groups for nurses and other caregivers. In a **support group,** workers give and receive emotional encouragement as they talk about feelings, problems, and stresses (Greenglass et al., 2003).

Burnout A job-related condition of mental, physical, and emotional exhaustion.

Support group A group formed to provide emotional support for its members through discussion of stresses and shared concerns.

Primary appraisal Deciding if a situation is relevant to oneself and if it is a threat.

Secondary appraisal Deciding how to cope with a threat or challenge.

"Am I Okay or in Trouble?"

Situation: You have been selected to give a speech to 300 people. Or a doctor tells you that you must undergo a dangerous and painful operation. Or the one true love of your life walks out the door. What would your emotional response to these events be? How do you cope with an emotional threat?

According to Richard Lazarus (1991a), there are two important steps in managing a threat. The first is a **primary appraisal,** in which you decide whether a situation is relevant or irrelevant, positive or threatening. In essence, this step answers the question, "Am I okay or in trouble?" Then you make a **secondary appraisal,** in which you assess your resources and choose a way to meet the threat or challenge. ("What can I do about this situation?") Thus, the way a situation is "sized up" greatly affects one's ability to cope with it (see Figure 12.2). Public speaking, for instance, can be appraised as an intense threat or as a chance to perform. Emphasizing the threat—by imagining failure, rejection, or embarrassment—obviously invites disaster (Strongman, 2003).

The Nature of Threat

What does it mean to feel threatened by a stressor? Certainly in most day-to-day situations it doesn't mean you think your life is in danger. Threat has more to do with the idea of control. We are particularly prone to feel stressed when we can't—or think we can't—control our immediate environment. In short, a perceived lack of control is just as threatening as an actual lack of control. For example, college students who *feel* overloaded experience stress even though their workload may not actually be heavier than that of their classmates (Jacobs & Dodd, 2003).

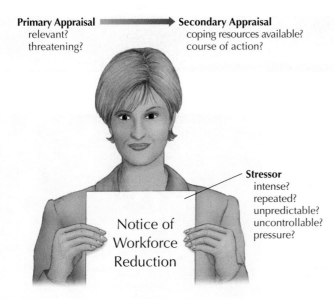

Primary Appraisal ➝ Secondary Appraisal
relevant?   coping resources available?
threatening?   course of action?

Stressor
intense?
repeated?
unpredictable?
uncontrollable?
pressure?

Notice of
Workforce
Reduction

▸▸**FIGURE 12.2** Stress is the product of an interchange between a person and the environment.

A sense of control also comes from believing you can reach desired goals. It is threatening to feel that we lack competence to cope with life's demands (Bandura, 2001). Because of this, the intensity of the body's stress reaction often depends on what we think and tell ourselves about stressors. That's why it's valuable to learn to think in ways that ward off the body's stress response. (Some strategies for controlling upsetting thoughts are described in this chapter's Psychology in Action section.)

Coping with Threat

You have appraised a situation as threatening. What will you do next? There are two major choices. **Problem-focused coping** is aimed at managing or altering the distressing situation itself, perhaps by making a plan of action or concentrating on your next step. This contrasts with **emotion-focused coping,** where we try to control our emotional reactions to the situation. For example, a distressed person may try to distract herself by listening to music, taking a walk, or seeking emotional support from others (Folkman & Moskowitz, 2004).

Couldn't both types of coping occur together? Yes. Sometimes the two types of coping aid one another. For instance, quieting your emotions may make it easier for you to find a way to solve a problem. Say, for example, that a woman feels anxious as she steps to the podium to give a speech. If she does some deep breathing to reduce her anxiety (emotion-focused coping), she will be better able to glance over her notes to improve her delivery (problem-focused coping).

It is also possible for coping efforts to clash. For instance, if you have to make a difficult decision, you may suffer intense emotional distress. In such circumstances there is a temptation to make a quick and ill-advised choice, just to end the suffering. Doing so may allow you to cope with your emotions, but it shortchanges problem-focused coping.

In general, problem-focused coping tends to be especially useful when you are facing a controllable stressor—that is, a situation you can actually do something about. Emotion-focused efforts are best suited to managing stressors that you cannot control (Folkman & Moskowitz, 2004). To improve your chances of coping effectively, the stress-fighting strategies described in this chapter include a mixture of both techniques.

So far, our discussion has focused on everyday stresses. How do people react to the extreme stresses imposed by war, violence, or disaster? Clinical File: "Coping with Traumatic Stress" discusses this important topic.

Problem-focused coping Directly managing or remedying a stressful or threatening situation.

Emotion-focused coping Managing or controlling one's emotional reaction to a stressful or threatening situation.

THE CLINICAL FILE

Coping with Traumatic Stress

Traumatic experiences produce psychological injury or intense emotional pain. Victims of **traumatic stresses,** such as war, torture, rape, assassination, plane crashes, natural disasters, or street violence, may suffer from nightmares, flashbacks, insomnia, irritability, nervousness, grief, emotional numbing, and depression. Time will tell whether the 2011 earthquake and tsunami in Japan will have similar effects. Like most traumatic stresses, the impact of natural disasters can be overwhelming.

People who personally witness or survive a disaster are most affected by traumatic stress. Thirty percent of the students, staff, and faculty who witnessed the September 13, 2006, shooting at Dawson College in Montreal reported some mental health problem in the aftermath of the shooting, including post-traumatic stress disorder (PTSD) (2 percent), major depression (5 percent), alcohol dependency (5 percent), and social phobia (3 percent). Seven percent of those surveyed still showed signs of distress 18 months after the shooting (Boyer et al., 2010).Traumatic stress produces feelings of helplessness and vulnerability (Fields & Margolin, 2001). Victims realize that disaster could strike again without warning. In addition to feeling threatened, many victims sense that they are losing control of their lives (Scurfield, 2002).

What can people do about such reactions? Psychologists recommend the following:

- Identify what you are feeling and talk to others about your fears and concerns.
- Think about the skills that have helped you overcome adversity in the past and apply them to the present situation.
- Continue to do the things that you enjoy and that make life meaningful (LeDoux & Gorman, 2001).
- Get support from others. This is a major element in recovery from all traumatic events.
- Give yourself time to heal. Fortunately, most people are more resilient than they think.

CP PHOTO/Ryan Remiorz

There can be little doubt that the shooting at Dawson College in Montreal on September 13, 2006, was a traumatically stressful event. Even those who witnessed the disaster on television suffered from stress symptoms.

When traumatic stresses are severe or repeated, some people have even more serious symptoms. They suffer from crippling anxiety or become emotionally numb. Typically, they can't stop thinking about the disturbing event; they anxiously avoid anything associated with the event; and they are constantly fearful or nervous. (These are the symptoms of *stress disorders,* which are discussed in Chapter 11.) Such reactions can leave victims emotionally handicapped for months or years after a disaster. If you feel that you are having trouble coping with a severe emotional shock, consider seeking help from a psychologist or other professional.

FRUSTRATION—BLIND ALLEYS AND LEAD BALLOONS

SURVEY QUESTION>
What is frustration? What are the major causes of frustration? How do people react to it?

Traumatic stresses Extreme events that cause psychological injury or intense emotional pain.

Frustration A negative emotional state that occurs when one is prevented from reaching a goal.

External frustration Distress caused by external conditions that hinder progress toward a goal.

Do you remember how frustrated Taylor was when he couldn't find a parking place? **Frustration** is a negative emotional state that occurs when people are prevented from reaching desired goals. In Taylor's case, the goal of finding a parking space was blocked by another car.

Obstacles of many kinds cause frustration. A useful distinction can be made between external and personal sources of frustration. **External frustration** is based on conditions outside the individual that impede progress toward a goal. All of the following are external frustrations: getting stuck with a flat tire, having a marriage proposal rejected, finding the cupboard bare when you go to get your poor dog a bone, and being chased out of the house by your starving dog. In other words, external frustrations are based on delays, failure, rejection, loss, and other direct blocking of motivated behaviour.

Notice that external obstacles can be either social (slow drivers, tall people in theatres, people who cut into lines) or non-social (stuck doors, a dead battery, rain on the day of the game). If you ask 10 of your friends what has frustrated them recently, most will probably mention someone's behaviour ("My sister wore one of my dresses when I wanted to wear it,"

"My supervisor is unfair," "My psychology teacher grades too hard"). As social animals, we humans are highly sensitive to social sources of frustration (Taylor, 2006).

Frustration usually increases as the strength, urgency, or importance of a blocked motive increases. Taylor was especially frustrated in the parking lot because he was late for an exam. Likewise, an escape artist submerged in a tank of water and bound with 100 kilograms of chain would become quite frustrated if a trick lock jammed. Remember, too, that motivation becomes stronger as we near a goal. As a result, frustration is more intense when a person runs into an obstacle very close to a goal. If you've ever missed an A grade by 5 points, you were probably very frustrated. If you've missed an A by 1 point—well, frustration builds character, right?

A final factor affecting frustration is summarized by the old phrase "the straw that broke the camel's back." The effects of repeated frustrations can accumulate until a small irritation sets off an unexpectedly violent response. A case in point is the fact that people with long commutes are more likely to display "road rage" (angry, aggressive driving) (Harding et al., 1998).

Personal frustrations are based on personal characteristics. If you are 1.2 metres (4 feet) tall and aspire to be a professional basketball player, you very likely will be frustrated. If you want to sing professionally but can't stay on pitch, you will likewise be frustrated. In both examples, frustration is actually based on personal limitations. Yet failure may be perceived as externally caused. We will return to this point in the Psychology in Action section. In the meantime, let's look at some typical reactions to frustration.

Reactions to Frustration

Aggression is any response made with the intent of harming a person or an object. It is one of the most persistent and frequent responses to frustration (Anderson & Bushman, 2002).

Does frustration always cause aggression? Aren't there other reactions? Although the connection is strong, frustration does not always provoke aggression. More often, frustration is met first with persistence. This is characterized by more vigorous efforts and varied responses (see Figure 12.3). For example, if you put your last loonie in a vending machine and pressing the button has no effect, you will probably press harder and faster (vigorous effort). Then you will press all the other buttons (varied response). Persistence may help you get around a barrier in order to reach your goal. However, if the machine still refuses either to deliver or to return your loonie, you may become aggressive and kick the machine (or at least tell it what you think of it).

Persistence can be very adaptive. Overcoming a barrier ends the frustration and allows the need or motive to be satisfied. The same is true of aggression that removes or destroys a barrier. Picture a small band of nomadic humans, parched by thirst but separated from a water hole by a menacing animal. It is easy to see that attacking the animal might ensure their survival. In modern society such direct aggression is seldom acceptable. If you find a long line at the drinking fountain, aggression is hardly appropriate. Because direct aggression is discouraged, it is frequently displaced.

How is aggression displaced? Does displaced aggression occur often? Directing aggression toward a source of frustration may be impossible, or it may be too dangerous. If you are frustrated by your boss at work or by a teacher at school, the cost of direct aggression may be too high (losing your job or failing a class). Instead, the aggression may be displaced, or redirected, toward whoever or whatever is available. Targets of **displaced aggression** tend to be perceived as safer, or less likely to retaliate, than the original source of frustration (Miller et al., 2003).

Psychologists attribute much hostility and violence to displaced aggression. A disturbing example is the finding that unemployment and divorce are associated with increased child abuse (Weissman, Jogerst, & Dawson, 2003). In a pattern known as **scapegoating,** a person or group of people are blamed for conditions not of their making. A scapegoat is a person who has become a habitual target of displaced aggression. Despite recent progress, many visible minorities continue to suffer from hostility based on scapegoating. Think, for

Personal frustration Distress caused by personal characteristics that impede progress toward a goal.
Aggression Any response made with the intent of causing harm.
Displaced aggression Redirecting aggression to a target other than the actual source of one's frustration.
Scapegoating Blaming a person or a group of people for conditions not of their making.

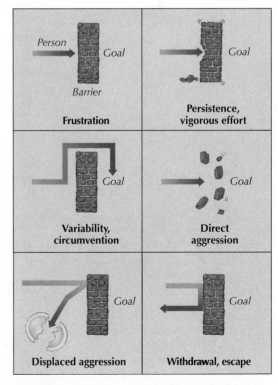

▶▶**FIGURE 12.3** Frustration and common reactions to it.

example, about the hostility expressed toward recent immigrants during times of economic hardship. In many communities, layoffs and job losses have been associated with increases in violence (Catalano, Novaco, & McConnell, 1997).

I have a friend who dropped out of school to hitchhike around the country. He seemed very frustrated before he quit. What type of response to frustration is that? Another major reaction to frustration is escape, or withdrawal. It is stressful and unpleasant to be frustrated. If other reactions do not reduce feelings of frustration, a person may try to escape. **Escape** may mean actually leaving a source of frustration (dropping out of school, quitting a job, ending an unhappy relationship), or it may mean psychologically escaping. Two common forms of psychological escape are apathy (pretending not to care) and the use of drugs such as cocaine, alcohol, marijuana, or narcotics. (See Figure 12.4 for a summary of common reactions to frustration.) The Psychology in Action section at the end of this chapter provides information on how to cope with frustration.

CONFLICT—YES, NO, YES, NO, YES, NO, WELL, MAYBE

SURVEY QUESTION>
What is conflict? Are there different types of conflict? How do people react to conflict?

Conflict occurs whenever a person must choose between contradictory needs, desires, motives, or demands. Choosing between school and work, marriage and single life, or study and failure are common conflicts. There are four general forms of conflict. As we will see, each has its own properties (see Figures 12.4 and 12.5).

Types of Conflict

Approach–Approach Conflicts

A simple **approach–approach conflict** comes from having to choose between two positive, or desirable, alternatives. Choosing between coconut-mocha-champagne and orange-marmalade-swirl ice cream may throw you into a temporary conflict. However, if you really like both choices, your decision will be quickly made. Even when more important decisions are at stake, approach–approach conflicts tend to be the easiest to resolve. When both options are positive, the scales of decision are easily tipped in one direction or the other.

Avoidance–Avoidance Conflicts

Being forced to choose between two negative, or undesirable, alternatives creates an **avoidance–avoidance conflict.** A person in an avoidance conflict is caught between "the devil and the deep blue sea" or "between a rock and a hard place." In real life, avoidance–avoidance conflicts involve dilemmas such as choosing between an unplanned pregnancy and an

Escape Reducing discomfort by leaving frustrating situations or by psychologically withdrawing from them.

Conflict A stressful condition that occurs when a person must choose between incompatible or contradictory alternatives.

Approach–approach conflict Choosing between two positive, or desirable, alternatives.

Avoidance–avoidance conflict Choosing between two negative, or undesirable, alternatives.

▶▶**FIGURE 12.4** The three most basic forms of conflict. For this woman, choosing between pie and ice cream is a minor approach–approach conflict, deciding whether to take a job that will require weekend work is an approach–avoidance conflict, and choosing between paying higher rent and moving is an avoidance–avoidance conflict.

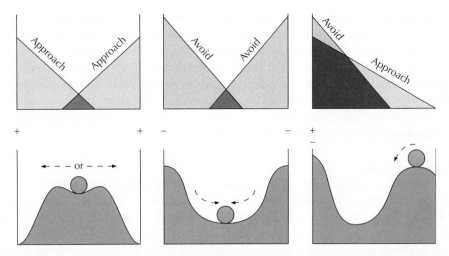

▶▶**FIGURE 12.5** Conflict diagrams. As shown by the coloured areas in the graphs, desires to approach and to avoid increase near a goal. The effects of these tendencies are depicted below each graph. The "behaviour" of the ball in each example illustrates the nature of the conflict above it. An approach conflict *(top left)* is easily decided. Moving toward one goal will increase its attraction *(bottom left)* and will lead to a rapid resolution. (If the ball moves in either direction, it will go all the way to one of the goals.) In an avoidance conflict *(top centre)*, tendencies to avoid are deadlocked, resulting in inaction. In an approach–avoidance conflict *(top right)*, approach proceeds to the point where desires to approach and avoid cancel each other. Again, these tendencies are depicted *(bottom right)* by the action of the ball. (Graphs after Miller, 1944.)

abortion, the dentist and tooth decay, a monotonous job and poverty, or residence food and starvation.

Suppose I don't object to abortion. Or suppose that I consider any pregnancy sacred and not to be tampered with? Like many other stressful situations, these examples can be defined as conflicts only on the basis of personal needs and values. If a woman wants to end a pregnancy and does not object to abortion, she experiences no conflict. If she would not consider abortion under any circumstances, there is no conflict.

Avoidance conflicts often have a "damned if you do, damned if you don't" quality. In other words, both choices are negative, but not choosing may be impossible or equally undesirable. When faced with two equally unpleasant choices, it is easy to see why people often freeze, finding it impossible to decide or take action.

Indecision, inaction, and freezing are not the only reactions to avoidance–avoidance conflicts. Since these conflicts are stressful and rarely solved, people sometimes pull out of them entirely. This reaction, called *leaving the field,* is another form of escape. It may explain the behaviour of a student who could not attend school unless he worked. However, if he worked he could not earn passing grades. His solution after much conflict and indecision? He joined the Canadian Forces.

Approach–Avoidance Conflicts

Approach–avoidance conflicts are also difficult to resolve. In some ways they are more troublesome than avoidance–avoidance conflicts because people seldom escape them. A person in an **approach–avoidance conflict** is "caught" by being attracted to, and repelled by, the same goal or activity. Attraction keeps the person in the situation, but its negative aspects cause turmoil and distress. For example, a high school student arrives to pick up his date for the first time. He is met at the door by her father, who is a professional wrestler—over 2 metres tall and 150 kilograms (or so it seems to him). The father gives the boy a crushing handshake and growls that he will break him in half if the girl is not home on time. The student considers the girl attractive and has a good time. But does he ask her out again? It depends on the relative strengths of his attraction and his fear. Almost certainly he will feel ambivalent about asking her out again, knowing that another encounter with her father awaits him.

Approach–avoidance conflict
Being attracted to and repelled by the same goal or activity.

Ambivalence Mixed positive and negative feelings or simultaneous attraction and repulsion.

Double approach–avoidance conflict Being simultaneously attracted to and repelled by each of two alternatives.

Ambivalence (mixed positive and negative feelings) is a central characteristic of approach–avoidance conflicts. Ambivalence is usually translated into partial approach (Miller, 1944). Since our student is still attracted to the girl, he may spend time with her at school and elsewhere. But he may not actually date her again. Some more realistic examples of approach–avoidance conflicts are dating someone your parents strongly disapprove of, wanting to be in a play but suffering stage fright, wanting to buy a car but not wanting to make monthly payments, and wanting to eat when overweight. Many of life's important decisions have approach–avoidance dimensions.

Multiple Conflicts

Aren't real-life conflicts more complex than the ones described here? Yes. Conflicts are rarely as clear-cut as those described. People in conflict are usually faced with several dilemmas at once, so several types of conflict may be intermingled. The fourth type of conflict moves us closer to reality. In **double approach–avoidance conflicts,** each alternative has both positive and negative qualities. For example, you are offered two jobs: One has good pay but poor hours and dull work; the second has interesting work and excellent hours, but low pay. Which do you select? This situation is more typical of the choices we must usually make. It offers neither completely positive nor completely negative options.

As with single approach–avoidance conflicts, people faced with double approach–avoidance conflicts feel ambivalent about each choice. This causes them to *vacillate,* or waver between the alternatives. Just as you are about to choose one such alternative, its undesirable aspects tend to loom large. So what do you do? You swing back toward the other choice. If you have ever been

---

 STUDY BREAK   **Stress, Frustration, and Conflict**

Reflect

What impact did pressure, control, predictability, repetition, and intensity have on your last stress reaction?

What type of coping do you tend to use when you face a stressor such as public speaking or taking an important exam?

Think of a time when you were frustrated. What was your goal? What prevented you from reaching it? Was your frustration external or personal?

Have you ever displaced aggression? Why did you choose another target for your hostility?

Review the major types of conflict and think of a conflict you have faced that illustrates each type. Did your reactions match those described in the text?

Learning Check

1. Emotional exhaustion, depersonalization, and reduced accomplishment are characteristics of job _____.
2. Stress tends to be greatest when a situation is appraised as a _____ and a person does not feel _____ to cope with the situation.
3. The first stage of the GAS is called the _____ reaction.
4. According to Lazarus, coping with threatening situations can be both problem focused and _____ focused.

5. Which of the following is not a common reaction to frustration?
   a. ambivalence   b. aggression
   c. displaced aggression   d. persistence
6. Samson Goliath is 2 metres tall and weighs 150 kilograms. He has failed miserably in his aspirations to become a jockey. The source of his frustration is mainly _____.
7. Inaction and freezing are most characteristic of avoidance-avoidance conflicts. T or F?
8. Approach–avoidance conflicts produce mixed feelings called _____.

Critical Thinking

9. Which do you think would produce more stress: (a) appraising a situation as mildly threatening but feeling like you are totally incompetent to cope with it, or (b) appraising a situation as very threatening but feeling that you have the resources and skills to cope with it?
10. Being frustrated is unpleasant. If some action, including aggression, ends frustration, why might we expect the action to be repeated on other occasions?

Answers

1. burnout 2. threat, competent 3. alarm 4. emotion 5. a 6. personal 7. T 8. ambivalence 9. There is no correct answer here because individual stress reactions vary greatly. However, the secondary appraisal of a situation often determines just how stressful it is. Feeling incapable of coping with discomfort, the response has been negatively reinforced. This makes it more likely to occur in the future (see Chapter 6).

---

romantically attracted to two people at once—each having qualities you like and dislike—then you have probably experienced **vacillation.** Another example that may be familiar is trying to decide between two areas of study, each with advantages and disadvantages.

In real life it is common to face **multiple approach–avoidance conflicts,** in which several alternatives each have positive and negative features. An example would be trying to choose which college to attend. On a day-to-day basis, most multiple approach–avoidance conflicts are little more than an annoyance. But when they involve major life decisions, such as choosing a career, a school, a life partner, or a job, they can add greatly to the amount of stress we experience.

One common multiple approach–avoidance conflict faced by many young people concerns the decision to become sexually active. The perceived advantages—getting closer to the other person, strengthening the relationship, and satisfaction of sexual desires—may be offset by the possible disadvantages, such as the risk of unplanned pregnancy and sexually transmitted infections or disappointment at failing to live up to one's religious, family, or moral values. One way to deal with this situation that is common with many younger teens is to avoid making a decision and to "just let it happen." The consequence: an increased risk of pregnancy and STIs because condoms are not used.

PSYCHOLOGICAL DEFENCE—MENTAL KARATE?

<SURVEY QUESTION
What are defence mechanisms? How do defence mechanisms help us to cope with stress?

Threatening situations tend to produce anxiety. A person who is anxious feels tense, uneasy, apprehensive, worried, and vulnerable. This can lead to emotion-focused coping that is defensive in nature (Lazarus, 1991b). Since anxiety is unpleasant and uncomfortable, we are usually motivated to avoid it. Psychological defence mechanisms allow us to reduce feelings of anxiety caused by stressful situations or by our shortcomings.

What are psychological defence mechanisms, and how do they reduce anxiety? A **defence mechanism** is any mental process used to avoid, deny, or distort sources of threat or anxiety, including threats to one's self-image. Many of these defence mechanisms were first identified by Sigmund Freud, who assumed they operated unconsciously. Often, defence mechanisms create large blind spots in awareness. For instance, an extremely stingy person might be completely unaware that she is a tightwad.

Everyone has at one time or another used defence mechanisms. Let's consider some of the most common.

Defence Mechanisms

Denial
One of the most basic defences is **denial** (protecting oneself from an unpleasant reality by refusing to accept it or believe it). Denial is closely linked with death, illness, and similar painful and threatening events. For instance, if you were told that you had only three months to live, how would you react? Your first thoughts might be "Aw, come on, someone must have mixed up the X-rays" or "The doctor must be mistaken" or simply "It can't be true!" Similar denial and disbelief are common reactions to the unexpected death of a friend or relative. People may also deny or underestimate the real risks posed by a situation—"I can still pass the test even if I don't study" or "I can have unprotected sex and not get pregnant, or catch an infection."

Repression
Freud noticed that his patients had tremendous difficulty recalling shocking or traumatic events from childhood. It seemed that powerful forces were holding these painful memories from awareness. Freud called this repression (see Chapter 1). He believed that we protect ourselves by repressing threatening thoughts and impulses. Feelings of hostility toward a family member, the names of people we dislike, and past failures are common targets of repression. Research suggests that we are most likely to repress information that threatens our self-image (Mendolia, 2002).

Vacillation Wavering in intention or feelings.
Multiple approach–avoidance conflict Being simultaneously attracted to and repelled by each of several alternatives.
Defence mechanism A habitual and often unconscious psychological process used to reduce anxiety.
Denial Protecting oneself from an unpleasant reality by refusing to perceive it or believe it.

Reaction formation Preventing dangerous impulses from being expressed in behaviour by exaggerating opposite behaviour.

Regression Retreating to an earlier level of development or to earlier, less demanding habits or situations.

Projection Attributing one's own feelings, shortcomings, or unacceptable impulses to others.

Rationalization Justifying your behaviour by giving reasonable and "rational," but false, reasons for it.

Reaction Formation

In a **reaction formation,** impulses are not just repressed; they are also held in check by exaggerating opposite behaviour. For example, a mother who unconsciously resents her children may, through reaction formation, become extremely overprotective and overindulgent. Her real thoughts of "I hate them" and "I wish they were gone" are replaced by "I love them" and "I don't know what I would do without them." The mother's hostile impulses are traded for "smother" love, so that she won't have to admit she hates her children. Thus, the basic idea in a reaction formation is that the individual acts out an opposite behaviour to block threatening impulses or feelings.

Regression

In its broadest meaning, **regression** refers to any return to earlier, less demanding situations or habits. Most parents who have a second child have to put up with at least some regression by the older child. Threatened by a new rival for affection, an older child may regress to childish speech, bedwetting, or infantile play after the new baby arrives, as well as being more clingy and demanding. If you've ever seen a child get homesick at summer camp or on a vacation, you've observed regression. An adult who throws a temper tantrum or a married adult who goes back home to his or her parents is also regressing.

Projection

Projection is an unconscious process that protects us from the anxiety we would feel if we were to discern our faults. A person who is projecting tends to see his or her own feelings, shortcomings, or unacceptable impulses in others. **Projection** lowers anxiety by exaggerating negative traits in others. This justifies one's own actions and directs attention away from personal failings.

Rationalization

Every teacher is familiar with this strange phenomenon: On the day of an exam, an incredible wave of disasters sweeps through the city. Mothers, fathers, sisters, brothers, aunts, uncles, grandparents, friends, other relatives, and pets become ill or die. Engines suddenly fall out of cars. Books are lost or stolen. Alarm clocks go belly-up and ring no more.

The making of excuses comes from a natural tendency to explain our behaviour. **Rationalization** refers to justifying personal actions by giving "rational" but false reasons for them. When the explanation you give for your behaviour seems reasonable and convincing—but is not the real reason—you are rationalizing. For example, our hapless Taylor (remember him?) failed to turn in an assignment given at the beginning of the term in one of his classes. Here's the explanation he gave his professor:

> My car broke down two days ago, and I couldn't get to the library until yesterday. Then I couldn't get all the books I needed because some were checked out, but I wrote what I could. Then last night, as the last straw, the ink cartridge in my printer ran out, and since all the stores were closed, I couldn't finish the paper on time.

When asked why he left the assignment until the last minute (the real reason it was late), Taylor offered another set of rationalizations. Like many people, Taylor had difficulty seeing himself without the protection of his rationalizations.

All of the defence mechanisms described seem pretty undesirable. Do they have a positive side? People who overuse defence mechanisms become less adaptable, because they consume great amounts of emotional energy to control anxiety and maintain an unrealistic self-image. Defence mechanisms do have value, though. Often, they help keep us from being overwhelmed by immediate threats. This can provide time for a person to learn to cope in a more effective, problem-focused manner. If you recognize some of your own behaviour in the descriptions here, it is hardly a sign that you are hopelessly defensive. As noted earlier, most people occasionally use defence mechanisms.

Two defence mechanisms that have a decidedly more positive quality are *compensation* and *sublimation.*

Compensation

Compensatory reactions are defences against feelings of inferiority. A person who has a defect or weakness (real or imagined) may go to unusual lengths to overcome the weakness or to compensate for it by excelling in other areas. Consider the case of André Roussimoff (1946–1993), who had a hormonal abnormality that caused him to grow to 2.3 metres tall. Some professional wrestlers saw him working out in a gym in Paris and persuaded him to join them on the circuit. He came to Montreal and became well known as André the Giant. There are dozens of examples of **compensation** at work. Stevie Wonder, Jeff Healey, Andrea Bocelli, and a number of other well-known musicians are blind.

For some players, computer games may allow for the sublimation of aggressive urges.

Sublimation

The defence called **sublimation** (sub-lih-MAY-shun) is defined as working off frustrated desires (especially sexual desires) through socially acceptable activities. Freud believed that art, music, dance, poetry, scientific investigation, and other creative activities could re-channel sexual energies into productive behaviour. Freud also felt that almost any strong desire can be sublimated. For example, a very aggressive person may find social acceptance as a professional soldier, boxer, or football player. Greed may be refined into a successful business career. Lying may be sublimated into storytelling, creative writing, or politics.

STRESS AND HEALTH—UNMASKING A HIDDEN KILLER

Disaster, depression, and sorrow often precede illness (Brannon & Feist, 2010). More surprising is the finding that major life changes—both good and bad—can increase susceptibility to accidents or illness. Major changes in our surroundings or routines require us to be vigilant, on guard, and ready to react. Over long time periods, this can be quite stressful (Sternberg, 2000).

Compensation Counteracting a real or imagined weakness by emphasizing desirable traits or seeking to excel in the area of weakness or in other areas.

Sublimation Working off unmet desires, or unacceptable impulses, in activities that are constructive or socially acceptable.

Social Readjustment Rating Scale (SRRS) A scale that rates the impact of various life events on the likelihood of illness.

Life change units (LCUs) Numerical values assigned to each life event on the SRRS.

<SURVEY QUESTION
How is stress related to health and disease?

Life Events and Stress

How can I tell if I am subjecting myself to too much stress? Some 45 years ago, Thomas Holmes and his associates developed a rating scale to estimate the health hazards faced when life stresses add up (Holmes & Rahe, 1967; Holmes & Masuda, 1972). More recently, Mark Miller and Richard Rahe updated the scale for use today (Miller & Rahe, 1997). The **Social Readjustment Rating Scale (SRRS)** is reprinted in Table 12.2. Notice that the effect of life events is expressed in **life change units (LCUs)** (numerical values assigned to each life event).

As you read the scale, note again that positive life events may be as costly as disasters. Marriage rates 50 life change units, even though it is usually a happy event. You'll also see many items that read "Change in...." This means that an improvement in life conditions can be as costly as a decline. A stressful adjustment may be required in either case.

To use the scale, add up the LCUs for all life events you have experienced during the last year and compare the total to the following standards.

0–150	No significant problems
150–199	Mild life crisis (33 percent chance of illness)
200–299	Moderate life crisis (50 percent chance of illness)
300 or more	Major life crisis (80 percent chance of illness)

According to Holmes, there is a high chance of illness or accident when your LCU total exceeds 300 points. A more conservative rating of stress can be obtained by totalling LCU points for only the previous six months.

Marriage is usually considered a positive life event. Nevertheless, the many changes it brings can be stressful.

skodonnell/iStockPhoto

■ Table 12.2 The Social Readjustment Rating Scale (SRRS)

Rank	Life Event	Life Change Units	Rank	Life Event	Life Changes Units
1	Death of spouse or child	119	23	Mortgage or loan greater than $10 000	44
2	Divorce	98	24	Change in responsibilities at work	43
3	Death of close family member	92	25	Change in living conditions	42
4	Marital separation	79	26	Change in residence	41
5	Fired from work	79	27	Begin or end school	38
6	Major personal injury or illness	77	28	Trouble with in-laws	38
7	Jail term	75	29	Outstanding personal achievement	37
8	Death of close friend	70	30	Change in work hours or conditions	36
9	Pregnancy	66	31	Change in schools	35
10	Major business readjustment	62	32	Christmas	30
11	Foreclosure on a mortgage or loan	61	33	Trouble with boss	29
12	Gain of new family member	57	34	Change in recreation	29
13	Marital reconciliation	57	35	Mortgage or loan less than $10 000	28
14	Change in health or behaviour of family member	56	36	Change in personal habits	27
15	Change in financial state	56	37	Change in eating habits	27
16	Retirement	54	38	Change in social activities	27
17	Change to different line of work	51	39	Change in number of family get-togethers	26
18	Change in number of arguments with spouse	51	40	Change in sleeping habits	26
19	Marriage	50	41	Vacation	25
20	Spouse begins or ends work	46	42	Change in church activities	22
21	Sexual difficulties	45	43	Minor violations of the law	22
22	Child leaving home	44			

(Reprinted from *Journal of Psychosomatic Research*, Vol. 43(3), M.A. Miller & R.H. Rahe, "Life changes scaling for the 1990s," p. 279-292, Table II, p. 282, copyright © 1997, with permission from Elsevier.)

Many of the listed life changes don't seem relevant to young adults or college students. Does the SRRS apply to these people? The SRRS tends to be more appropriate for older, more established adults. However, research has shown that the health of university students is also affected by stressful events, such as entering unversity, changing majors, or the breakup of a steady relationship.

People differ greatly in their reactions to the same event. For such reasons, the SRRS is at best a rough index of stress. Nevertheless, it's hard to ignore a study in which people were deliberately exposed to the virus that causes common colds. The results were nothing to sneeze at: If a person had a high stress score, he or she was much more likely to actually get a cold (Cohen, Tyrell, & Smith, 1993). In view of such findings, a high LCU score should be taken seriously. If your score goes much over 300, an adjustment in your activities or lifestyle may be needed.

> **Acculturative stress** Stress caused by the many changes and adaptations required when a person moves to a foreign culture.

The Hazards of Hassles

There must be more to stress than major life changes. Isn't there a link between ongoing stresses and health? In addition to having a direct impact, major life events spawn countless daily frustrations and irritations (Pillow, Zautra, & Sandler, 1996). Also, many of us face ongoing stresses at work or at home that do not involve major life changes (Pett & Johnson, 2005).

HUMAN DIVERSITY

Acculturative Stress—Strangers in a Strange Land

Around the world, an increasing number of emigrants and refugees must adapt to dramatic changes in language, dress, values, and social customs. For many, the result is a period of culture shock or **acculturative stress** (stress caused by adapting to a foreign culture). Typical reactions to acculturative stress are anxiety, hostility, depression, alienation, physical illness, and identity confusion (Rummens, Beiser, & Noh, 2003). For many young immigrants, acculturative stress is a major source of mental health problems (Yeh, 2003).

The severity of acculturative stress is related, in part, to how a person adapts to a new culture. Four main patterns are (Berry, 1990; Berry et al., 2005) as follows:

Integration—maintain your old cultural identity but participate in the new culture

Separation—maintain your old cultural identity and avoid contact with the new culture

Assimilation—adopt the new culture as your own and have contact with its members

Marginalization—reject your old culture but suffer rejection by members of the new culture

To illustrate each pattern, let's consider a family that has immigrated to Canada from the imaginary country of Farlandia.

The father favours integration. He is learning English and French and wants to get involved in Canadian life. At the same time, he is a leader in the Farlandian-Canadian community and spends much of his leisure time with other Farlandian-Canadians. His level of acculturative stress is low.

The mother only speaks Farlandish and only interacts with other Farlandian-Canadians. She remains almost completely separate from Canadian society. Her stress level is high.

The teenage daughter is annoyed by hearing Farlandish spoken at home, by her mother's serving only Farlandian food, and by having to spend her leisure time with her extended Farlandian family. She would prefer to speak English or French and to be with her Canadian friends. Her desire to assimilate creates moderate stress.

The son doesn't particularly value his Farlandian heritage, yet his schoolmates reject him because he speaks with a Farlandian accent. He feels trapped between two cultures. His position is marginal and his stress level is high.

To summarize, those who feel marginalized tend to be highly stressed; those who seek to remain separate are also highly stressed; those who pursue integration into their new culture are minimally stressed; and those who assimilate are moderately stressed.

As you can see, integration and assimilation are the best options. However, a big benefit of assimilating is that people who embrace their new culture experience fewer social difficulties. For many, this justifies the stress of adopting new customs and cultural values (Gurung 2010; Ward & Rana-Deuba, 1999).

© Janine Wiedel Photolibrary/Alamy

One of the best antidotes for acculturative stress is a society that tolerates or even celebrates ethnic diversity. Although some people find it hard to accept new immigrants, the fact is, nearly everyone's family tree includes people who were once strangers in a strange land.

Microstressor Any distressing, day-to-day annoyance; also called a *hassle*.

Psychosomatic disorders Illnesses in which psychological factors contribute to bodily damage.

Hypochondriac A person who complains about illnesses that appear to be imaginary.

Such minor but frequent stresses are called *hassles*, or **microstressors.** Parents' expectations, driving to school, feeling discriminated against, communication problems with friends, and too many things to do are common hassles among college and university students (Pett & Johnson, 2005). Hassles range from traffic jams to losing classroom notes; from an argument with a roommate to an employer's unrealistic demands. (See also Human Diversity: "Acculturative Stress—Strangers in a Strange Land.")

In a year-long study, 100 men and women recorded their daily hassles. Participants also reported on their physical and mental health. Frequent and severe hassles turned out to be better predictors of day-to-day health than major life events were (Lazarus, 1981). However, major life events did predict changes in health one or two years after the events took place. It appears that daily hassles are closely linked to immediate health and psychological well-being (Crowther et al., 2001). Major life changes have more of a long-term impact.

What can be done about a high LCU score or feeling excessively hassled? A good response is to use stress management skills. For serious problems, stress management should be learned directly from a therapist or a stress clinic. When ordinary stresses are involved, there is much you can do on your own. This chapter's Psychology in Action section will give you a start. In the meantime, take it easy!

Psychosomatic Disorders

As we have seen, chronic or repeated stress can damage physical health, as well as upset emotional well-being. Prolonged stress reactions are closely related to a large number of psychosomatic (SIKE-oh-so-MAT-ik) illnesses. In **psychosomatic disorders** (psyche: mind; soma: body), psychological factors contribute to actual bodily damage or to damaging changes in bodily functioning. Psychosomatic problems, therefore, are not the same as hypochondria. **Hypochondriacs** (HI-po-KON-dree-aks) imagine that they suffer from diseases. There is nothing imaginary about asthma, a migraine headache, or high blood pressure. Severe psychosomatic disorders can be fatal. The person who says, "Oh, it's just psychosomatic" misunderstands how serious stress-related diseases really are. (See Critical Thinking: "It's All in Your Mind.")

The most common psychosomatic problems are gastrointestinal and respiratory (stomach pain and asthma, for example), but many others exist. Typical problems include eczema (skin rash), hives, migraine headaches, rheumatoid arthritis, hypertension (high blood pressure), colitis (ulceration of the colon), and heart disease. Actually, these are only the major problems.

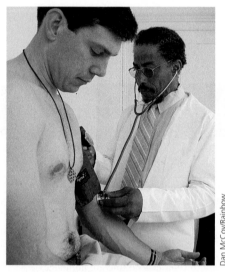

Dan McCoy/Rainbow

It is estimated that at least half of all patients who see a doctor have a psychosomatic disorder or an illness that is complicated by psychosomatic symptoms.

CRITICAL THINKING

It's All in Your Mind

Have you ever had someone dismiss a health concern by saying, "It's all in your mind," as if your problem might be imaginary? For centuries, the medical model has dominated Western thinking. From this perspective, health is an absence of illness, and your body is a complex biological machine that can break down and become ill. Sometimes, you inflict the damage yourself through poor lifestyle choices, such as smoking or overeating. Sometimes, an external cause, such as a virus, is the culprit. In either event, the problem is physical, and your mind has little to do with it. Moreover, physical problems call for physical treatments ("Take your medicine"), so your mind has little to do with your recovery. In the medical model, any impact of the mind on health was dismissed as a mere placebo effect. (To remind yourself about placebo effects, see Chapter 1.)

Over the past 50 years, the medical model has slowly given way to the biopsychosocial model. This view states that diseases are caused by a combination of biological, psychological, and social factors. Most important, the biopsychosocial model defines health as a state of well-being that we can actively attain and maintain (Oakley, 2004). Under this model, instead of passively getting treatments from a doctor, you play a role in fostering your own health. Thus, it may no longer be inaccurate to say, "It's all in your mind," if you mean that a person's beliefs—which affect behaviour—can have a dramatic impact on health (Brooks, 2008). It is becoming clear that medicine works best when doctors help people make sense of their medical condition, to maximize healing (Moerman, 2002). So, as you take responsibility for your own well-being, remember that in some ways health is all in your mind!

Lesser health complaints are also frequently stress related. Typical examples are sore muscles, headaches, neckaches, backaches, indigestion, constipation, chronic diarrhea, fatigue, insomnia, premenstrual problems, and sexual dysfunctions (Taylor, 2006). For some of these problems, biofeedback may be helpful. The next section explains how.

Biofeedback

Psychologists have discovered that people can learn to control bodily activities once thought to be involuntary. This is done by applying informational feedback to bodily control, a process called **biofeedback.** (See Figure 12.6.) If someone were to say to you, "Raise the temperature of your right hand," you probably couldn't because you wouldn't know if you were succeeding. To make your task easier, we could attach a sensitive thermometer to your hand. The thermometer could be wired so that an increase in temperature would activate a signal light. Then all you would have to do is try to keep the light on as much as possible. With practice and the help of biofeedback, you could learn to raise your hand temperature at will.

Biofeedback is an effective way to treat some psychosomatic problems. For instance, people have been trained to prevent migraine headaches with biofeedback. Sensors are taped to patients' hands and foreheads. They then learn to redirect blood flow away from the head to their extremities. Since migraine headaches in part involve excessive blood flow to the head, biofeedback helps reduce the frequency of their headaches (Andrasik, 2003; Larsson et al., 2005).

Early successes led many to predict that biofeedback would offer a cure for psychosomatic illnesses, anxiety, phobias, drug abuse, and a long list of other problems. In reality, biofeedback has proven helpful, but not an instant cure (Schwartz & Andrasik, 2003). Biofeedback can help relieve muscle-tension headaches, migraine headaches, chronic pain (Middaugh & Pawlick, 2002), and motion sickness (Yucha & Montgomery, 2008). It shows promise for lowering blood pressure and controlling heart rhythms (Rau, Bührer, & Weitkunat, 2003). The technique has been used with success to control epileptic seizures and hyperactivity in children (Demos, 2005). Insomnia also responds to biofeedback therapy (Gathchel & Oordt, 2003).

How does biofeedback help? Some researchers believe that many of its benefits arise from general relaxation. Others stress that there is no magic in biofeedback itself. The method simply acts as a "mirror" to help a person perform tasks involving self-regulation. Just as a mirror does not comb your hair, biofeedback does not do anything by itself. It can, however, help people make desired changes in their behaviour (Weems, 1998).

The Cardiac Personality

It would be a mistake to assume that stress is the sole cause of psychosomatic diseases. Genetic differences, organ weaknesses, and learned reactions to stress combine to do damage. Personality also enters the picture. As mentioned earlier, a general disease-prone personality type exists. To a degree, there are also "headache personalities," "asthma personalities," and so on. The best documented of such patterns is the "cardiac personality"—a person at high risk for heart disease.

Cardiologists Meyer Friedman and Ray Rosenman offer a glimpse of how some people create stress for themselves. In a landmark study of heart problems, Friedman and Rosenman (1983) classified people as either **Type A personalities** (those who run a high risk of heart attack) or **Type B personalities** (those who are unlikely to have a heart attack). In an eight-year follow-up, they found more than twice the rate of heart disease in Type A individuals than in Type Bs (Rosenman et al., 1983).

> **Biofeedback** Information given to a person about his or her ongoing bodily activities; aids voluntary regulation of bodily states.
> **Type A personality** A personality type with an elevated risk of heart disease; characterized by time urgency, anger, and hostility.
> **Type B personality** All personality types other than Type A; a low cardiac-risk personality.

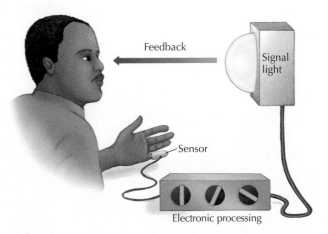

▸▸ **FIGURE 12.6** In biofeedback training bodily processes are monitored and processed electronically. A signal is then routed back to the patient through headphones, signal lights, or other means. This information helps the patient alter bodily activities not normally under voluntary control.

Individuals with Type A personalities feel a continuous sense of anger, irritation, and hostility.

Type A

What is the Type A personality like? Type A people are hard-driving, ambitious, highly competitive, achievement oriented, and striving. Type A people believe that with enough effort they can overcome any obstacle, and they "push" themselves accordingly.

Perhaps the most telltale signs of a Type A personality are *time urgency* and chronic *anger* or *hostility*. Type A people hurry from one activity to another, racing the clock in self-imposed urgency. As they do, they feel a constant sense of frustration and anger. Feelings of anger and hostility, in particular, are strongly related to increased risk of heart attack (Boyle et al., 2004; Bunde & Suls, 2006). One study found that 15 percent of a group of 25-year-old doctors and lawyers who scored high on a hostility test were dead by age 50. The most damaging pattern may occur in hostile persons who keep their anger "bottled up." This increases their pulse rate and blood pressure and puts a tremendous strain on the heart (Bongard, al'Absi, & Lovallo, 1998).

To summarize, there is growing evidence that anger or hostility may be the core lethal factor of Type A behaviour (Krantz & McCeney, 2002; Niaura et al., 2002). To date, hundreds of studies have supported the validity of the Type A concept, although the original research has been criticized. In view of this, Type A individuals would be wise to take their increased health risks seriously.

How are Type A people identified? Characteristics of Type A people are summarized in the short self-identification test presented in Table 12.3. If most of the list applies to you, you may be a Type A. However, confirmation of your type would require more powerful testing methods. Also, remember that the original definition of Type A behaviour was probably too broad, and that people with Type B personalities may show some of the same behaviours. The key psychological factors that increase heart disease risk appear to be anger, hostility, and mistrust (Krantz & McCeney, 2002; Smith et al., 2004).

Because our society places a premium on achievement, competition, and mastery, it is not surprising that many people develop Type A personalities. The best way to avoid the self-made stress this causes is to adopt behaviour that is the opposite of that listed in Table 12.3 (Williams, Barefoot, & Schneiderman, 2003).

■ Table 12.3 **Characteristics of the Type A Person**

Check the items that apply to you. Do you:

____ Have a habit of explosively accentuating various key words in ordinary speech even when there is no need for such accentuation?

____ Finish other persons' sentences for them?

____ Always move, walk, and eat rapidly?

____ Quickly skim reading material and prefer summaries or condensations of books?

____ Become easily angered by slow-moving lines or traffic?

____ Feel an impatience with the rate at which most events take place?

____ Tend to be unaware of the details or beauty of your surroundings?

____ Frequently strive to think of or do two or more things simultaneously?

____ Almost always feel vaguely guilty when you relax, vacation, or do absolutely nothing for several days?

____ Tend to evaluate your worth in quantitative terms (number of A's earned, amount of income, number of games won, and so forth)?

____ Have nervous gestures or muscle twitches, such as grinding your teeth, clenching your fists, or drumming your fingers?

____ Attempt to schedule more and more activities into less time and in so doing make fewer allowances for unforeseen problems?

____ Frequently think about other things while talking to someone?

____ Repeatedly take on more responsibilities than you can comfortably handle?

Shortened and adapted from Meyer Friedman and Ray H. Rosenman, *Type A Behavior and Your Heart* (New York: Knopf, 1983).

Strategies for Reducing Hostility

According to Redford Williams, reducing hostility involves three goals. First, you must stop mistrusting the motives of others. Second, you must find ways to reduce how often you feel anger, indignation, irritation, and rage. Third, you must learn to be kinder and more considerate. Based on his clinical experience, Williams (1989) recommends 12 strategies for reducing hostility and increasing trust.

1. Become aware of your angry, hostile, and cynical thoughts by logging them in a notebook. Record what happened, what you thought and felt, and what actions you took. Review your hostility log at the end of each week.
2. Admit to yourself and to someone you trust that you have a problem with excessive anger and hostility.
3. Interrupt hostile, cynical thoughts whenever they occur. (The Psychology in Action section of Chapter 13, page 544, explains a thought-stopping method you can use for this step.)
4. When you have an angry, hostile, or cynical thought about someone, silently look for the ways in which it is irrational or unreasonable.

5. When you are angry, try to mentally put yourself in the other person's shoes.
6. Learn to laugh at yourself and use humour to defuse your anger.
7. Learn reliable ways to relax. Two methods are described in this chapter's Psychology in Action section. Another can be found in the Psychology in Action discussion of Chapter 13, page 544.
8. Practise trusting others more. Begin with situations where no great harm will be done if the person lets you down.
9. Make an effort to listen more to others and to really understand what they are saying.
10. Learn to be assertive, rather than aggressive, in upsetting situations. (See Chapter 14, page 573, for information about self-assertion skills.)
11. Rise above small irritations by pretending that today is the last day of your life.
12. Rather than blaming people for mistreating you, and becoming angry over it, try to forgive them. We all have shortcomings.

It is entirely possible to succeed in life without sacrificing your health or happiness in the process. People who frequently feel angry and hostile toward others may benefit from the advice of Redford Williams, a physician interested in Type A behaviour. Using Psychology: "Strategies for Reducing Hostility" summarizes his advice.

The Hardy Personality

How do Type A people who do not develop heart disease differ from those who do? Psychologist Salvatore Maddi and others have studied people who have a **hardy personality.** Such people seem to be unusually resistant to stress. The first study of hardiness began with two groups of managers at a large utility company. All the managers held high-stress positions. Yet, some tended to get sick after stressful events, while others were rarely ill. How did the people who were thriving differ from their "stressed-out" colleagues? Both groups seemed to have traits typical of the Type A personality, so that wasn't the explanation. They were also quite similar in most other respects. The main difference was that the hardy group seemed to hold a world view that consisted of three traits (Maddi, 2006):

1. They had a sense of personal commitment to self, work, family, and other stabilizing values.
2. They felt that they had control over their lives and their work.
3. They had a tendency to see life as a series of challenges, rather than as a series of threats or problems.

How do such traits protect people from the effects of stress? Persons strong in commitment find ways of turning whatever they are doing into something that seems interesting and important. They tend to get involved rather than feeling alienated.

Persons strong in control believe that they can more often than not influence the course of events around them. This prevents them from passively seeing themselves as victims of circumstance.

Hardy personality A personality style associated with superior stress resistance.

Finally, people strong in challenge believe that fulfillment is found in continual growth. They seek to learn from their experiences, rather than accepting easy comfort, security, and routine (Maddi, 2006). Indeed, many "negative" experiences can actually enhance personal growth—if you have support from others and the skills needed to cope with challenge (Armeli, Gunthert, & Cohen, 2001).

Positive Psychology: Hardiness and Happiness

Good and bad events occur in all lives. What separates happy people from those who are unhappy is largely a matter of attitude. Happy people tend to see their lives in more positive terms, even when trouble comes their way. For example, happier people tend to find humour in disappointments. They look at setbacks as challenges. They are strengthened by losses (Lyubomirsky & Tucker, 1998). In short, happiness tends to be related to hardiness (Maddi, 2006). Why is there a connection? As psychologist Barbara Fredrickson has pointed out, positive emotions tend to broaden our mental focus. Emotions such as joy, interest, and contentment create an urge to play, to be creative, to explore, to savour life, to seek new experiences, to integrate, and to grow. When you are stressed, experiencing positive emotions can make it more likely that you will find creative solutions to your problems. Positive emotions also tend to reduce the bodily arousal that occurs when we are stressed, possibly limiting stress-related damage (Fredrickson, 2003).

A Look Ahead

The work we have reviewed here has drawn new attention to the fact that each of us has a personal responsibility for maintaining and promoting health. In the Psychology in Action section that follows, we will look at what you can do to better cope with stress and the health risks that it entails. But first, the questions in the Study Break box may help you maintain a healthy grade on your next psychology test.

 STUDY BREAK Stress and Health

Reflect

Pick a year from your life that was unusually stressful. Use the SRRS to find your LCU score for that year. Do you think there was a connection between your LCU score and your health? Or have you observed more of a connection between microstressors and your health?

Mindy complains about her health all the time, but she actually seems to be just fine. An acquaintance of Mindy's dismisses her problems by saying, "Oh, she's not really sick. It's just psychosomatic." What's wrong with this use of the term psychosomatic?

Do you think you are basically a Type A or a Type B personality? To what extent do you possess traits of the hardy personality?

Learning Check

1. Holmes's SRRS appears to predict long-range changes in health, whereas the frequency and severity of daily microstressors is closely related to immediate ratings of health. T or F?
2. Ulcers, migraine headaches, and hypochondria are all frequently psychosomatic disorders. T or F?
3. Which of the following is not classified as a psychosomatic disorder?
   a. hypertension
   b. colitis
   c. eczema
   d. thymus

4. Two major elements of biofeedback training appear to be relaxation and self-regulation. T or F?
5. Evidence suggests that the most important feature of the Type A personality is a sense of time urgency rather than feelings of anger and hostility. T or F?
6. A sense of commitment, challenge, and control characterizes the hardy personality. T or F?
7. Whereas stressful incidents suppress the immune system, stress management techniques have almost no effect on immune system functioning. T or F?

Critical Thinking

8. People with a hardy personality type appear to be especially resistant to the harmful effects of stress. Why do you think this is the case?

Answers
1. T 2. F 3. d 4. T 5. F 6. T 7. F 8. They are able to see the positive aspects of difficult or unpleasant situations.

Psychology in Action

STRESS MANAGEMENT

Stress management is the use of behavioural strategies to reduce stress and improve coping skills. As promised, this section describes strategies for managing stress. Before you continue reading, you may want to assess your level of stress again, this time using a scale developed for undergraduate students (see Table 12.4). Like the SRRS, high scores on the College Life Stress Inventory suggest that you have been exposed to health-threatening levels of stress (Renner & Mackin, 1998).

The College Life Stress Inventory is scored by adding the ratings for all of the items that have happened to you in the last year. The scale below is an approximate guide to the meaning of your score. But remember, stress is an internal state. If you are good at coping with stressors, a high score may not be a problem for you.

2351+	Extremely high
1911–2350	Very high
1471–1910	High
1031–1470	Average

<SURVEY QUESTION
What are the best strategies for managing stress?

Stress management The application of behavioural strategies to reduce stress and improve coping skills.

■ Table 12.4   **College Life Stress Inventory**

Circle the "stress rating" number for any event that has happened to you in the last year, and then add the numbers.

Event	Stress Rating	Event	Stress Rating
Being sexually assaulted	100	Talking in front of a class	72
Finding out that you are HIV-positive	100	Lack of sleep	69
Being accused of rape	98	Change in housing situation (hassles, moves)	69
Death of a close friend	97	Competing or performing in public	69
Death of a close family member	96	Getting in a physical fight	66
Contracting a sexually transmitted infection (other than AIDS)	94	Difficulties with a roommate	66
		Job changes (applying, new job, work hassles)	65
Concerns about being pregnant	91	Declaring a major or concerns about future plans	65
Final exams	90	A class you hate	62
Concerns about your partner being pregnant	90	Drinking or use of drugs	61
Oversleeping for an exam	89	Confrontations with professors	60
Flunking a class	89	Starting a new semester	58
Having a boyfriend or girlfriend cheat on you	85	Going on a first date	57
Ending a steady dating relationship	85	Registration	55
Serious illness in a close friend or family member	85	Maintaining a steady dating relationship	55
Financial difficulties	84	Commuting to campus or work, or both	54
Writing a major term paper	83	Peer pressures	53
Being caught cheating on a test	83	Being away from home for the first time	53
Drunk driving	82	Getting sick	52
Sense of overload in school or work	82	Concerns about your appearance	52
Two exams in one day	80	Getting straight A's	51
Cheating on your boyfriend or girlfriend	77	A difficult class that you love	48
Getting married	76	Making new friends; getting along with friends	47
Negative consequences of drinking or drug use	75	Fraternity or sorority rush	47
Depression or crisis in your best friend	73	Falling asleep in class	40
Difficulties with parents	73	Attending an athletic event (e.g., football game)	20

("A life stress instrument for classroom use," from *Teaching of Psychology,* 25(1), 1996, p. 47, by M.J. Renner and R.S. Mackin. Sage Publications.)

591–1030	Below average
151–590	Low
0–150	Very low

Now that you have a picture of your current level of stress, what can you do about it? The simplest way of coping with stress is to modify or remove its source—by leaving a stressful job, for example. Obviously this is often impossible, which is why learning to manage stress is so important.

As shown in Figure 12.7, stress triggers bodily effects, upsetting thoughts, and ineffective behaviour. Also shown is the fact that each element worsens the others in a vicious circle. Indeed, the basic idea of the "Stress Game" is that once it begins, you lose—unless you take action to break the cycle. The information that follows tells how.

Managing Bodily Reactions

Much of the immediate discomfort of stress is caused by fight-or-flight emotional responses. The body is ready to act, with tight muscles and a pounding heart. If action is prevented, we merely remain "uptight." A sensible remedy is to learn a reliable, drug-free way of relaxing.

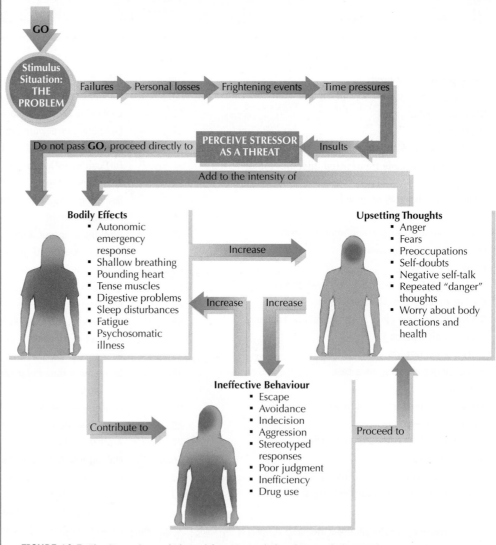

▸▸**FIGURE 12.7** The Stress Game. (Adapted from Rosenthal and Rosenthal, 1980.)

Exercise

Stress-based arousal can be dissipated by using the body. Any full-body exercise can be effective. Swimming, dancing, jumping rope, yoga, most sports, and especially walking are valuable outlets. Regular exercise alters hormones, circulation, muscle tone, and a number of other aspects of physical functioning. Together, such changes can lower the risks for disease (Linden, 2005; Salmon, 2001).

Be sure to choose activities that are vigorous enough to relieve tension, yet enjoyable enough to be done repeatedly. Exercising for stress management is most effective when it is done daily. As little as 30 minutes of total exercise per day, even if it occurs in short 10- to 20-minute sessions, can improve mood and energy (Hansen, Stevens, & Coast, 2001).

Meditation

Many stress counsellors recommend meditation for quieting the body and promoting relaxation. Meditation and its effects were discussed in Chapter 5, page 203. Here, it is enough to restate that meditation is easy to learn—taking an expensive commercial course is unnecessary. It is also one of the most effective ways to relax (Deckro et al., 2002). But be aware that listening to or playing music, taking nature walks, enjoying hobbies, and the like can be meditations of sorts. Anything that reliably interrupts upsetting thoughts and promotes relaxation can be helpful.

Tension Release

It is possible to relax systematically, completely, and by choice. To learn the details of how this is done, consult Chapter 13, page 546, of this book. The basic idea of the **tension-release method** is to tighten all the muscles in a given area of your body (the arms, for instance) and then voluntarily relax them. By first tensing and relaxing each area of the body, you can learn what muscle tension feels like. Then, when each area is relaxed, the change is more noticeable and more controllable. In this way it is possible, with practice, to greatly reduce tension.

Guided Imagery

In a technique called **guided imagery,** people visualize images that are calming, relaxing, or beneficial in other ways. Relaxation, for instance, can be promoted by visualizing peaceful scenes. Pick several places where you feel safe, calm, and at ease. Typical locations might be a beach or lake, the woods, floating on an air mattress in a warm pool, or lying in the sun at a quiet park. To relax, vividly imagine yourself in one of these locations. In the visualized scene, you should be alone and in a comfortable position. It is important to visualize the scene as realistically as possible. Try to feel, taste, smell, hear, and see what you would actually experience in the calming scene. Practise forming such images several times a day for about five minutes each time. When your scenes become familiar and detailed, they can be used to reduce anxiety and encourage relaxation (Rosenthal, 1993). Remember, too, that imagining that a supportive friend or a loving pet is nearby can reduce tension and anxiety (Allen, Blascovich, & Mendes, 2002; Smith, Ruiz, & Uchino, 2004).

Modifying Ineffective Behaviour

Stress is often made worse by our misguided responses to it. The following suggestions may help you deal with stress more effectively.

Slow Down

Remember that stress can be self-generated. Try to do things at a slower pace, especially if your pace has speeded up over the years. Tell yourself, "What counts most is not if I get there first, but if I get there at all" or "It's a marathon, not a sprint."

Tension-release method A procedure for systematically achieving deep relaxation of the body.

Guided imagery Intentional visualization of images that are calming, relaxing, or beneficial in other ways.

Social support Close, positive relationships with other people.

Organize

Disorganization creates stress. Try to take a fresh look at your situation and get organized. Setting priorities can be a real stress fighter. Ask yourself what's really important and concentrate on the things that count. Learn to let go of trivial but upsetting irritations. And above all, when you are feeling stressed, remember to KIS: Keep It Simple (or KISS: Keep It Simple, Stupid).

Strike a Balance

Work, school, family, friends, interests, hobbies, recreation, community, religion—there are many important elements in a satisfying life. Damaging stress often comes from letting one element—especially work or school—get blown out of proportion. Many students are part-time and have an even more precarious balancing act to perform—juggling work, school, family, and so on. Your goal should be quality in life, not quantity. Try to strike a balance between challenging "good stress" and relaxation. Remember, when you are "doing nothing" you are actually doing something very important: Set aside time for "me acts" such as loafing, browsing, puttering, playing, and napping.

Recognize and Accept Your Limits

Many of us set unrealistic and perfectionist goals. Given that no one can ever be perfect, this attitude leaves many people feeling inadequate, no matter how well they have performed. Set gradual, achievable goals for yourself. Also, set realistic limits on what you try to do on any given day. Learn to say no to added demands or responsibilities.

Seek Social Support

Social supports (close, positive relationships with others) facilitate good health and morale (Manne, 2003). People with close, supportive relationships have better immune responses and better health (Kiecolt-Glaser et al., 2002). One reason for this is that support from family and friends serves as a buffer to cushion the impact of stressful events. Women tend to make better use of social support than men do. Women who are stressed seek support and nurture others. Men are more likely to become aggressive or to withdraw emotionally (Taylor et al., 2000). This may be why "manly men" won't ask for help, whereas women in trouble call their friends! Where stress is concerned, many men could benefit from adopting women's tendency to tend and befriend others.

How else might social support help? Most people share positive events, such as marriages, births, graduations, and birthdays, with others. When things go well, we like to tell others. Sharing such events tends to amplify positive emotions and to further increase social support. In many ways, the sharing of good news is an important means by which positive events contribute to individual well-being (Gable et al., 2004).

Write about Your Feelings

If you don't have someone you can talk to about stressful events, you might try expressing your thoughts and feelings in writing. Several studies have found that students who write about their upsetting experiences, thoughts, and feelings are better able to cope with stress, experience fewer illnesses, and get better grades (Pennebaker, 2004). Writing about your feelings tends to leave your mind clearer. This makes it easier to pay attention to life's challenges and come up with effective coping strategies (Klein & Boals, 2001a, 2001b). Thus, after you write about your feelings, it helps to make specific plans for coping with upsetting experiences (Cameron & Nicholls, 1998).

As an alternative, you might want to try writing about positive experiences. In one study, college students who wrote about intensely positive experiences had fewer illnesses over the next three months. Writing for just 20 minutes a day for three days improved the students' moods and had a surprisingly long-lasting effect on their health (Burton & King, 2004).

Avoiding Upsetting Thoughts

Assume you are taking a test. Suddenly you realize that you are running short of time. If you say to yourself, "Oh, no, this is terrible. Now I've blown it," your body's response will probably be sweating, tenseness, and a knot in your stomach. On the other hand, if you say, "I should have watched the time, but getting upset won't help. I'll just take one question at a time," your stress level will be much lower.

As stated earlier, stress is greatly affected by the views we take of events. Physical symptoms and a tendency to make poor decisions are increased by negative thoughts or "self-talk." In many cases, what you say to yourself can be the difference between coping and collapsing (Matheny et al., 1996).

Coping Statements

University of Waterloo Emeritus Professor Donald Meichenbaum has popularized a technique called **stress inoculation.** In it, clients learn to fight fear and anxiety with an internal monologue of positive coping statements. First, clients learn to identify and monitor **negative self-statements** (self-critical thoughts that increase anxiety). Negative thoughts are a problem because they tend to directly elevate physical arousal. To counter this effect, clients learn to replace negative statements with coping statements from a supplied list. Eventually they are encouraged to make their own lists (Saunders et al., 1996).

How are coping statements applied? **Coping statements** are reassuring and self-enhancing. They are used to block out, or counteract, negative self-talk in stressful situations. Before giving a short speech, for instance, you would replace "I'm scared," "I can't do this," "My mind will go blank and I'll panic," or "I'll sound stupid and boring" with "I'll give my speech on something I like," "I'll breathe deeply before I start my speech," or "My pounding heart just means I'm psyched up to do my best." Additional examples of coping statements follow.

Preparing for a Stressful Situation:

- I'll just take things one step at a time.
- If I get nervous, I'll just pause a moment.
- Tomorrow I'll be through it.
- I've managed to do this before.
- What exactly do I have to do?

Confronting the Stressful Situation:

- Relax now; this can't really hurt me.
- Stay organized; focus on the task.
- There's no hurry; take it step by step.
- Nobody's perfect; I'll just do my best.
- It will be over soon; just be calm.

Meichenbaum cautions that saying the "right" things to yourself may not be enough to improve stress tolerance. You must practise this approach in actual stress situations. Also, it is important to develop your own personal list of coping statements by finding what works for you. Ultimately, the value of learning this and other stress management skills ties back into the idea that much stress is self-generated. Knowing that you can manage a demanding situation is in itself a major antidote for stress.

In one study, students who learned stress inoculation techniques had not only less anxiety and depression but also better self-esteem (Schiraldi & Brown, 2001).

Lighten Up

Humour is worth cultivating as a way to reduce stress. A good sense of humour can lower your distress/stress reaction to difficult events (Lefcourt, 2003). In addition, an ability to

Stress inoculation The use of positive coping statements to control fear and anxiety.

Negative self-statements Self-critical thoughts that increase anxiety and lower performance.

Coping statements Reassuring, self-enhancing statements that are used to stop self-critical thinking.

laugh at life's ups and downs is associated with better immunity to disease (McCelland & Cheriff, 1997). Don't be afraid to laugh at yourself and at the many ways in which we humans make things difficult for ourselves. Humour is one of the best antidotes for anxiety and emotional distress because it puts things into perspective (Henman, 2001; Szabo, 2003).

Coping with Frustration and Conflict

In a classic experiment, a psychologist studying frustration placed rats on a small platform at the top of a tall pole. Then he forced them to jump off the platform toward two elevated doors, one locked and the other unlocked. If the rat chose the correct door, it swung open and the rat landed safely on another platform. Rats that chose the locked door bounced off it and fell into a net far below.

The problem of choosing the open door was made unsolvable and very frustrating by randomly alternating which door was locked. After a time, most rats chose the same door every time. This door was then locked. All the rats had to do was to jump to the other door to avoid a fall, but they did not (Maier, 1949).

Isn't that an example of persistence? No. Persistence that is inflexible can turn into stereo-typed behaviour like that of the rats. When dealing with frustration, you must know when to change direction. Here are some suggestions to help you avoid needless frustration.

1. Try to identify the source of your frustration. Is it external or personal?
2. Can the source of frustration be changed? How hard would you have to work to change it? Is it under your control at all?
3. If the source of your frustration can be changed or removed, is the effort worth it?

The answers to these questions help determine if persistence will not work. There is value in learning to accept gracefully those things that cannot be changed.

It is also important to distinguish between real and imagined barriers. Too often we create our own imaginary barriers. For example, Anita wants a part-time job to earn extra money. At the first place she applies, she is told that she doesn't have enough experience. Now she says she is frustrated because she needs experience to work but can't get experience without working. She has quit looking for a job.

Is Anita's need for experience a real barrier? Unless she applies for many jobs, we can't tell if she has overestimated its importance. For her the barrier is real enough to prevent further efforts, but with persistence she might locate an "unlocked door." If a reasonable amount of effort does show that experience is essential, it might be obtained in other ways— through temporary volunteer work, for instance.

How can I handle conflicts more effectively? Most of the suggestions just made also apply to conflicts. However, here are some additional things to remember when you are in conflict or must make a difficult decision:

1. Slow down when making important decisions. Take time to collect information and to weigh pros and cons. Hasty decisions are often regretted. Even if you do make a faulty decision, it will trouble you less if you know that you did everything possible to avoid a mistake.
2. Try out important decisions partially when possible. If you are thinking about moving to a new town, try to spend a few days there first. If you are choosing between schools, do the same. If classes are in progress, sit in on some. If you want to learn to scuba dive, rent equipment for a reasonable length of time before buying.
3. Look for workable compromises. Again it is important to get all available information. If you think that you have only one or two alternatives and they are undesirable or unbearable, seek the aid of a teacher, counsellor, clergyperson, or social service agency. You may be overlooking possible alternatives these people will know about.

4. When all else fails, make a decision and live with it. Indecision and conflict exact a high cost. Sometimes it is best to select a course of action and stick with it unless you find that it is very obviously wrong after you have taken it.

In class you may want to describe some of the frustrations and conflicts you have experienced and how you handled them. Prepare to discuss frustrations and conflicts you have resolved in an unusually effective manner or that you might have handled better. Do you have some additional hints to share with other students?

 STUDY BREAK   Coping with Stress

Reflect

If you were going to put together a "tool kit" for stress management, what items would you include?

Learning Check

1. Exercise, meditation, and progressive relaxation are considered effective ways of countering negative self-statements. T or F?
2. Research shows that social support from family and friends has little effect on the health consequences of stress. T or F?

3. One element of stress inoculation is training in the use of positive coping statements. T or F?
4. Stereotyped responding can be particularly troublesome in coping with frustration. T or F?

Critical Thinking

5. Steve always feels extremely pressured when the due date arrives for his major term papers. How could he reduce stress in such instances?

Answers

1. F 2. F 3. T 4. T 5. The stress associated with doing term papers can be almost completely eliminated by making a long-term assignment into many small daily or weekly assignments. Students who habitually leave things to the last minute are often amazed at how pleasant college work can be once they renounce procrastination.

CHAPTER IN REVIEW

Major Points

- A variety of personal habits and behaviour patterns affect health.
- Maintaining good health is a personal responsibility, not a matter of luck. Wellness is based on minimizing risk factors and engaging in health-promoting behaviours.
- Stress is a normal part of life; however, it is also a major risk factor for illness and disease.
- Although some events are more stressful than others, stress always represents an interaction between people and the environments in which they live.
- Personality characteristics affect the amount of stress a person experiences and the subsequent risk of illness.
- The body's reactions to stress can directly damage internal organs and impair the body's immune system, increasing susceptibility to disease.
- The damaging effects of stress can be reduced with stress management techniques.

Summary

What is health psychology? How does behaviour affect health?

- Health psychologists are interested in behaviour that helps maintain and promote health.
- Studies of health and illness have identified a number of behavioural risk factors and health-promoting behaviours.
- Many sexually active people continue to take unnecessary risks with their health by failing to follow safer sex practices.
- Health psychologists have pioneered efforts to prevent the development of unhealthy habits and to improve well-being through community health campaigns.

What is stress? What factors determine its severity?

- Stress occurs when demands are placed on an organism to adjust or adapt.
- The stages of the GAS are alarm, resistance, and exhaustion. The GAS appears to explain how psychosomatic disorders develop.
- Studies of psychoneuroimmunology show that stress also lowers the body's immunity to disease.
- Stress is more damaging in situations involving pressure, a lack of control, unpredictability of the stressor, and intense or repeated emotional shocks.

- Stress is intensified when a situation is perceived as a threat and when a person does not feel competent to cope with it.
- In work settings, prolonged stress can lead to burnout.
- The primary appraisal of a situation greatly affects our emotional response to it.
- During a secondary appraisal, a problem-focused or emotion-focused way of coping is selected.

What is frustration? What are the major causes of frustration? How do people react to it?

- Frustration is the negative emotional state that occurs when progress toward a goal is blocked.
- External frustrations are based on delay, failure, rejection, loss, and other direct blocking of motives. Personal frustration is related to personal characteristics over which one has little control.
- Frustrations of all types become more intense as the strength, urgency, or importance of the blocked motive increases.
- Major behavioural reactions to frustration include persistence, more vigorous responding, circumvention, direct aggression, displaced aggression (including scapegoating), and escape or withdrawal.

What is conflict? Are there different types of conflict? How do people react to conflict?

- Conflict occurs when one must choose between contradictory alternatives.
- Five types of conflict are approach–approach, avoidance–avoidance, approach–avoidance, double approach–avoidance, and multiple approach–avoidance.
- Approach–approach conflicts are usually the easiest to resolve.
- Avoidance conflicts are difficult to resolve and are characterized by inaction, indecision, freezing, and a desire to escape.
- People usually remain in approach–avoidance conflicts, but fail to fully resolve them, which leads to ambivalence and partial approach.
- Vacillation is a common reaction to double approach–avoidance conflicts.

What are defence mechanisms? How do defence mechanisms help us to cope with stress?

- Anxiety, threat, or feelings of inadequacy frequently lead to the use of defence mechanisms that reduce anxiety.

- Many defence mechanisms have been identified, including compensation, denial, fantasy, intellectualization, isolation, projection, rationalization, reaction formation, regression, repression, and sublimation.

How is stress related to health and disease?

- Work with the Social Readjustment Rating Scale (SRSS) indicates that multiple life changes tend to increase long-range susceptibility to accident or illness.
- Immediate psychological and mental health is more closely related to the intensity and severity of daily hassles (microstressors).
- Intense or prolonged stress may cause damage in the form of psychosomatic problems.
- During biofeedback training, bodily processes are monitored and converted to a signal that tells what the body is doing. This allows people to control some bodily activities and alleviate some psychosomatic illnesses.
- People with Type A personalities are competitive, striving, hostile, and impatient. These characteristics—especially hostility—double the risk of heart attack.
- People who have traits of the hardy personality seem to be unusually resistant to stress.

- The body reacts to stress in a series of stages called the general adaptation syndrome (GAS).

What are the best strategies for managing stress?

- A sizable number of coping skills can be applied to manage stress. Most of these focus on one of three areas: bodily effects, ineffective behaviour, and upsetting thoughts.

Interactive Learning

Please visit http://www.psychologyjourney4ce.nelson .com for a list of weblinks to relevant psychology sites.

CourseMate

Access an interactive e-book and chapter-specific interactive learning tools, including flashcards, quizzes, videos, and more, in your psychology CourseMate. Visit Nelsonbrain.com to use CourseMate.

psyk.trek 11f. Types of Stress, 11g. Responding to Stress.

The questions that follow are only a sample of what you need to know. If you miss any of the items, review the entire chapter and the Study Breaks. Another way to prepare for tests is to use the Study Guide and the Practice Exams that are available with this text.

1. Health-promoting behaviours that combat hypertension include the following: lose weight, consume less sodium, use alcohol sparingly, and get more of which of the following?
   a. sleep
   b. exercise
   c. life change units (LCUs)
   d. cholesterol

2. Which of the following is *not* a sexually transmitted infection?
   a. herpes
   b. eczema
   c. chlamydia
   d. hepatitis B

3. According to Richard Lazarus, during which stage do we choose a way to meet a threat or challenge?
   a. primary stress reaction
   b. secondary stress reaction
   c. primary appraisal
   d. secondary appraisal

4. What is aggression is an especially common reaction to?
   a. frustration
   b. scapegoating
   c. approach conflicts
   d. ambivalence

5. In what type of situation are you most likely to experience vacillation?
   a. an approach–approach conflict
   b. an avoidance–avoidance conflict
   c. a double approach–avoidance conflict
   d. the condition called emotion-focused coping

6. What term refers to justifying your actions by making excuses that appear to explain your behaviour?
   a. sublimation
   b. reaction formation
   c. compensation
   d. rationalization

7. The existence of which of the following provides a good indication that stress is a normal part of life?
   a. sublimation
   b. reaction formation
   c. hypochondria
   d. eustress

8. Ratings on the Social Readjustment Rating Scale (SRRS) are based on the total number of which of the following possibilities, during the past year?
   a. hassles
   b. life change units (LCUs)
   c. sexually transmitted infections (STIs)
   d. psychosomatic illnesses

9. What type of person is the opposite of a person who has a hardy personality?
   a. a person with a high sexually transmitted infection (STI) score
   b. a person with a low life change unit (LCU) score
   c. a person with Type A traits
   d. a person with Type B traits

10. In which of the general adaptation syndrome (GAS) stages is a person least likely to be helped by exercise, meditation, progressive relaxation, and guided imagery?
    a. alarm
    b. resistance
    c. exhaustion
    d. adaptation

11. Marianne is interested in a career in psychology. She wants to apply her psychological knowledge to medical problems. What is Marianne interested in studying?
    a. behavioural medicine
    b. psychoneurology
    c. health psychology
    d. neurophysiology

12. What condition has the symptoms of emotional exhaustion, depersonalization, and reduced feelings of personal accomplishment?
    a. grief
    b. unemployment
    c. job burnout
    d. sensory deprivation

13. When is stress likely to occur?
    a. when anger or rage is present
    b. when persistent or stereotyped responding is required of an organism
    c. when an organism is forced to distinguish between real and imagined barriers
    d. when demands are placed on an organism to adjust or adapt

14. What occurs during the "primary appraisal" stage of emotional adjustment?
    a. The means of meeting a threat is chosen.
    b. The pros and cons of a particular course of action are weighed.
    c. One decides whether a situation is threatening or not.
    d. Vague feelings of anxiety begin.

15. What types of conflicts are most often encountered in everyday life?
    a. approach–approach
    b. approach–avoidance
    c. avoidance–avoidance
    d. multiple approach–avoidance

16. When Johnny's new baby sister came home from the hospital, Johnny started to wet the bed again. What is Johnny's bedwetting an example of?
    a. compensation
    b. repression
    c. denial
    d. regression

17. Upsetting thoughts and emotions may have negative influences on health through their link with which of the following?
    a. sensory systems
    b. thalamic projection system
    c. brain and immune system
    d. stages of alarm and resistance

18. Which general adaptation syndrome (GAS) response leads to fatigue, loss of appetite, and lack of energy?
    a. alarm reaction
    b. stage of resistance
    c. stage of exhaustion
    d. stage of avoidance

19. What is one of the most effective techniques for calming the body?
    a. exercise
    b. progressive relaxation
    c. guided imagery
    d. meditation

20. Joanne is failing her psychology course, but when her mother asks how she is doing, she says, "Fine." What is Joanne's response an example of?
    a. intellectualization
    b. rationalization
    c. denial
    d. reaction formation

ANSWERS   1.b 2.b 3.d 4.a 5.c 6.d 7.d 8.b 9.c 10.c 11.c 12.c 13.d 14.c 15.d 16.d 17.c 18.a 19.b 20.c

Therapies

JOURNEY INTO PSYCHOLOGY: DISABLING FEARS

Imagine not being able to do something as simple as attend your classes because you fear losing control, having a racing heart and butterflies in your stomach, and thinking that you will make a total fool of yourself. This is exactly what a student of one of the authors feared. Michelle approached her teacher one day and explained her condition. She suffered from panic disorder with agoraphobia (see Chapter 11).

It was terrifying for her to leave her home by herself, remain in school for long hours, and sit in a classroom full of strangers. She expressed a strong desire to attend class but preferred to sit in the front row near the door. This was so that if her symptoms got the better of her, she would be able to make a quick exit from the classroom. Rajesh told Michelle that he would make all necessary accommodations to help her deal with her situation. However, her condition became so severe that she had to discontinue her studies and enrol in an intensive therapy program to treat the crippling

Thinkstock

anxieties that had made her life simply miserable. A cognitive therapist, who was the type of professional most likely to treat Michelle, would help her to focus on the way she thinks about her problems and would assist her in acquiring effective techniques of coping with her fears.

This chapter discusses methods used to alleviate problems like Michelle's. First, we will describe therapies that emphasize the value of gaining insight into personal problems. Then, we will focus on behaviour therapies and cognitive therapies, which directly change troublesome actions and thoughts. Later, we will conclude with medical therapies, which are based on psychiatric drugs and other physical treatments.

 Survey Questions

- What is psychotherapy and why is it undertaken? How did psychotherapy originate?
- How is Freudian psychoanalysis conducted?
- What are the major humanistic therapies?
- What is behaviour therapy?
- How is behaviour therapy used to treat phobias and anxieties?
- What role does reinforcement play in behaviour therapy?
- What is cognitive therapy? How does it change thoughts and emotions?
- How is psychotherapy done with groups of people?
- What do various therapies have in common?
- How do psychiatrists treat psychological disorders?
- How are behavioural principles applied to everyday problems?
- How can a person find professional help?

PSYCHOTHERAPY—GETTING BETTER BY THE HOUR

 SURVEY QUESTION>
What is psychotherapy and why is it undertaken? How did psychotherapy originate?

You may wonder what sort of help would be available to you if you ever experienced a problem like Michelle's. In most cases, it would be some form of **psychotherapy.** For the most part, psychotherapy involves verbal interaction between trained mental health professionals and their clients. Some therapists also use learning principles to directly alter troublesome behaviours. Basically, psychotherapy refers to any psychological technique that can bring about positive changes in personality, behaviour, or adjustment.

Dimensions of Therapy

Psychotherapy Any psychological technique used to facilitate positive changes in an individual's personality or behaviour.

Psychotherapists have many approaches to choose from: psychoanalysis, cognitive therapy, Gestalt therapy, client-centred therapy, reality therapy, and behaviour therapy—to name but a few. With so many therapies in use, some confusion may exist about how they differ. It is helpful to recognize that therapies vary widely in emphasis. For this reason, the best approach for a particular person or problem may also vary (Trull, 2005). Subsequent sections of this chapter will detail the main features of many psychotherapies in use today.

Myths

Psychotherapy has been depicted as producing a complete personal transformation—a sort of "major overhaul" of the psyche. But therapy is not equally effective for all problems. Chances of improvement are fairly good for phobias, low self-esteem, some sexual problems, and marital conflicts. Complex problems, such as a general tendency to be extremely fearful in social situations, can be difficult to solve. For many people, the major benefit of therapy is that it provides comfort, support, and a way to make constructive changes (Hellerstein et al., 1998).

It is often unrealistic to expect psychotherapy to undo a person's entire history. Yet, even when problems are severe, therapy may help a person gain a new perspective or learn behaviours to better cope with life. Psychotherapy can be hard work for both clients and therapists. But when it succeeds, few activities are more worthwhile.

It is also worth noting that psychotherapy is not always undertaken to solve problems or end a crisis. Therapy can promote personal growth for people who are already doing well (Bloch, 2006). Therapists in the positive psychology movement are developing ways to help people make use of their personal strengths. Rather than trying to fix what is "wrong" with a person, they seek to nurture positive traits and actively solve problems (Compton, 2005).

Table 13.1 lists some of the elements of positive mental health that therapists seek to restore or promote.

How often do people turn to psychologists, and who uses their services? In the mid-1990s, 2.15 percent of Canadians over the age of 11 years had consulted a psychologist during a 12-month period. This translates to about 515 000 persons. People from all walks of life visit psychologists, but some use their services more than others. For example, two-thirds of the clients seen by psychologists are female. Users also tend to be middle-aged and single, separated, or widowed, and have higher education and income (Hunsley, Lee, & Aubry, 1999). Sadly, the same study also found that a significant proportion of the Canadian population with mental health problems was not receiving any help from psychologists. Reasons for underutilization of services include the following:

- People are often unaware of what psychologists do.
- Many potential clients do not know how to look for a psychologist.
- Many people lack the financial resources to pay for psychological services.
- In recent years, governments have cut funding of publicly funded services.
- Many individuals believe that people ought to be able to solve their own problems (Farberman, 1997; Hunsley et al., 1999).

Whatever the reason, it is unfortunate that many people with serious mental health problems are not receiving proper treatment, especially when effective ways of addressing such issues are available.

ORIGINS OF THERAPY—BORED SKULLS AND HYSTERIA ON THE COUCH

Early treatments for mental problems give ample reason for appreciating modern therapies. Archaeological findings dating to the Stone Age suggest that many ancient approaches were marked by fear and superstitious belief in demons, witchcraft, and magic. One of the more dramatic "cures" practised by ancient "therapists" was a process called trepanning (treh-PAN-ing; also sometimes spelled trephining). In modern usage, **trepanning** is any surgical procedure in which a hole is bored in the skull. In the hands of ancient therapists it meant boring, chipping, or bashing holes into a patient's head. Presumably this was done to relieve pressure or release evil spirits (see Figure 13.1).

> **Trepanning** In modern usage, any surgical procedure in which a hole is bored in the skull; historically, the chipping or boring of holes in the skull to "treat" mental disturbance.

■ Table 13.1 **Elements of Positive Mental Health**

- Personal autonomy and independence
- A sense of identity
- Feelings of personal worth
- Skills in interpersonal communication
- Sensitivity, nurturance, and trust
- Genuineness and honesty with self and others
- Self-control and personal responsibility
- Commitment and love in personal relationships
- Capacity to forgive others and oneself
- Personal values and a purpose in life
- Self-awareness and motivation for personal growth
- Adaptive coping strategies for managing stresses and crises
- Fulfillment and satisfaction in work
- Good habits of physical health

(Adapted from Bergin, 1991; Bloch, 2006).

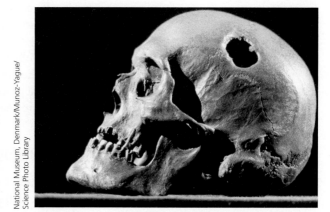

National Museum, Denmark/Munoz-Yague/Science Photo Library

▸▸**FIGURE 13.1** Ancient "treatment" for mental disorders sometimes took the form of boring a hole in the skull. This example shows signs of healing, which means the patient survived the treatment. Many didn't.

Many early asylums were no more than prisons with inmates held in chains.

© Bettman/CORBIS

During the Middle Ages, treatments for mental illness in Europe focused on **demonology,** the study of demons and persons plagued by spirits. Medieval "therapists" commonly blamed abnormal behaviour on supernatural forces, such as possession by the devil, or on curses from witches and wizards. As a cure, they used **exorcism** to "cast out evil spirits." For the fortunate, exorcism was a religious ritual. More often, physical torture was used to make the body an inhospitable place for the devil to reside. Modern analyses of "demonic possession" suggest that many victims were suffering from epilepsy, schizophrenia (Mirsky & Duncan, 2005), dissociative disorders (van der Hart, Lierens, & Goodwin, 1996), or depression (Thase, 2006).

It wasn't until 1793 that the emotionally disturbed were regarded as "mentally ill" and given compassionate treatment. That was the year a French doctor named **Philippe Pinel** changed the Bicêtre asylum in Paris from a squalid "madhouse" into a psychiatric hospital by personally unchaining inmates. Although over 200 years have passed since Pinel began humane treatment, the process of improving psychiatric care continues today.

When was psychotherapy developed? Sigmund Freud was among the pioneers who developed the first true psychotherapy around the late 1800s. As a physician in Vienna, Freud was intrigued by cases of **hysteria,** in which physical symptoms (such as paralysis or numbness) occur without known physical causes. As you may recall, such problems are now called somatoform disorders (see Chapter 11, pages 452–453). Slowly, Freud became convinced that hysteria was caused by deeply hidden unconscious conflicts. Based on this insight, Freud developed a therapy called *psychoanalysis.* Since it is the "grandparent" of more modern therapies, let's examine psychoanalysis in some detail.

PSYCHOANALYSIS—EXPEDITION INTO THE UNCONSCIOUS

SURVEY QUESTION>
How is Freudian psychoanalysis conducted?

Freud's patients usually reclined on a couch during therapy, while he sat out of sight taking notes and offering interpretations. This arrangement was supposed to encourage a free flow of thoughts and images from the unconscious. However, it is the least important characteristic of psychoanalysis, and many modern analysts have abandoned it.

How did Freud treat emotional problems? Freud's theory stressed that neurosis and hysteria are caused by repressed memories, motives, and conflicts—particularly those stemming from instinctual drives for sex and aggression. Although they are hidden, these factors remain active in the personality. This forces the person to develop rigid ego-defence mechanisms and to engage in compulsive and self-defeating behaviour. Thus, the main goal of psychoanalysis (see also Chapter 1) is to resolve internal conflicts that lead to emotional suffering (Wolitzky, 1995).

Freud relied on four basic techniques to uncover the unconscious roots of neuroses or psychological problems (Freud, 1949). These are free association, dream analysis, analysis of resistance, and analysis of transference.

Freud's Techniques

Free Association

The process of **free association** involves saying whatever comes to mind. Patients must speak without concern for whether ideas are painful, embarrassing, or illogical. Thoughts are simply allowed to move freely from one to the next, without self-censorship. The purpose of free association is to lower defences so that unconscious material can emerge (Hoffer & Youngren, 2004).

Demonology In medieval Europe, the study of demons and the treatment of persons "possessed" by demons.

Exorcism The practice of driving off an "evil spirit," especially from the body of a person who is "possessed."

Philippe Pinel The French physician who initiated humane treatment of mental patients in 1793.

Hysteria Wild emotional excitability sometimes associated with the development of apparent physical disabilities (numbness, blindness, and the like) without known physical cause.

Free association In psychoanalysis, the technique of having a client say anything that comes to mind, regardless of how embarrassing or unimportant it may seem.

Dream Analysis

Freud believed that dreams provide a "royal road to the unconscious" because they express forbidden desires and unconscious feelings. Such feelings are found in the **latent content** (hidden, symbolic meaning) of dreams. A dream's **manifest content** (obvious, visible meaning) tends to disguise information from the unconscious.

Freud was very interested in unconscious messages revealed by **dream symbols** (images that have personal or emotional meanings). Let's say a young man reports a dream in which he pulls a pistol from his waistband and aims at a target while his wife watches. The pistol repeatedly fails to discharge, and the man's wife laughs at him. Freud might have seen this as an indication of repressed feelings of sexual impotence, with the gun serving as a disguised image of the penis.

Pioneering psychotherapist Sigmund Freud's famous couch.

Analysis of Resistance

When free associating or describing dreams, patients may resist talking about or thinking about certain topics. Such **resistances** (blockages in the flow of ideas) are said to reveal particularly important unconscious conflicts. As analysts become aware of resistances, they bring them to the patient's awareness so the patient can deal with them realistically (Wolitzky, 1995). Rather than being roadblocks in therapy, resistances can be challenges and guides (Engle & Arkowitz, 2006).

Analysis of Transference

Transference is the tendency to transfer to a therapist feelings that match those the patient had for important persons in his or her past. At times, the patient may act as if the analyst is a rejecting father or an unloving or overprotective mother. As the patient re-experiences repressed emotions, the therapist can help the patient recognize and understand them. Troubled persons often provoke anger, rejection, boredom, criticism, and other negative reactions from others. Effective therapists learn to avoid reacting as others do and playing the patient's habitual "games." This, too, contributes to therapeutic change (Strupp, 1989).

Psychoanalysis Today

What is the status of psychoanalysis today? Traditional psychoanalysis called for three to five therapy sessions a week, often for many years. Today, most patients are seen only once or twice per week, but treatment may still go on for years (Friedman et al., 1998). Because of the huge amounts of time and money this requires, psychoanalysts have become relatively rare.

Many therapists have switched to doing **brief psychodynamic therapy,** which uses direct questioning to reveal unconscious conflicts (Binder, 2004). Modern therapists also actively provoke emotional reactions to lower defences and provide insights (Davanloo, 1995). Interestingly, brief therapy seems to accelerate recovery. It is as if patients realize that they need to get to the heart of their problems quickly (Messer & Kaplan, 2004).

Interpersonal Psychotherapy

One example of a brief dynamic therapy is **interpersonal psychotherapy (IPT),** which was first developed to help depressed people improve their relationships with others (Prochaska & Norcross, 2010). This treatment approach is significantly different from traditional Freudian psychoanalysis, however. Research has confirmed that IPT is effective for depressive disorders, as well as eating disorders, substance abuse, social phobias, and personality disorders (Fiore et al., 2008; Hoffart, 2005; Prochaska & Norcross, 2010; Talbot & Gamble, 2008).

Liona's therapy is a good example of IPT (Brown & Barlow, 2007). Liona was suffering from depression that a therapist helped her trace to a conflict with her parents. When her father was absent, Liona adopted the role of her mother's protector and friend. However, when her father was home, she was expected to resume her role as a daughter. She was angry at her father for frequently abandoning her mother and upset about having to

Latent dream content The hidden or symbolic meaning of a dream, as revealed by dream interpretation and analysis.

Manifest dream content The surface, "visible" content of a dream; dream images as they are remembered by the dreamer.

Dream symbols Images in dreams whose personal or emotional meanings differ from their literal meanings.

Resistance A blockage in the flow of free association; topics the client unconsciously resists thinking or talking about.

Transference The tendency of patients to transfer to a therapist feelings that correspond to those the patient had for important persons in his or her past.

Brief psychodynamic therapy A modern therapy based on psychoanalytic theory but designed to produce insights more quickly.

Interpersonal psychotherapy (IPT) A brief dynamic psychotherapy designed to help people by improving their relationships with other people.

STUDY BREAK   Psychotherapy and Psychoanalysis

Reflect

How has your understanding of psychotherapy changed? How many types of therapy can you name?

Make a list describing what you think it means to be mentally healthy. How well does your list match the items in Table 13.1?

The use of trepanning, demonology, and exorcism all implied that the mentally ill are "cursed." To what extent are the mentally ill rejected and stigmatized today?

Try to free associate (aloud) for 10 minutes. How difficult was it? Did anything interesting surface?

Explain, in your own words, the role of dream analysis, resistances, and transference in psychoanalysis.

Learning Check

1. Which one of the following is not an element of positive mental health?
   a. depending on others for making day-to-day decisions
   b. being committed and loving in personal relationships
   c. having adaptive coping strategies for managing stresses and crises
   d. having good habits of physical health

2. One reason that many people do not use the services of psychologists is because of a common belief that human beings should be able to solve their own problems. T or F?

3. Who turns to psychologists more often for treatment, men or women?

4. Pinel is famous for his use of exorcism. T or F?

5. In psychoanalysis, what is an emotional attachment to the therapist by the patient called?
   a. free association   b. manifest association
   c. resistance   d. transference

Critical Thinking

6. Waiting-list control groups help separate the effects of therapy from improvement related to the mere passage of time. What other type of control group might be needed to learn if therapy is truly beneficial?

Answers

1. a 2. T 3. women 4. F 5. d 6. Placebo therapy is sometimes used to assess the benefits of real therapy. Placebo therapy superficially resembles the real thing but lacks key elements that are thought to be therapeutic.

Spontaneous remission The disappearance of a psychological disturbance without the aid of therapy.

switch roles so often. Liona's IPT sessions (which sometimes included her mother) focused on clarifying Liona's family roles. Her mood improved a lot after her mother urged her to "stick to being herself."

Is Traditional Psychoanalysis Effective?

The development of newer, more streamlined dynamic therapies is in part due to questions about the effectiveness of traditional psychoanalysis. One critic, Hans Eysenck (1967, 1994), suggested that psychoanalysis simply takes so long that patients experience **spontaneous remission.**

How seriously should the possibility of spontaneous remission be taken? It is true that problems ranging from hyperactivity to anxiety improve with the passage of time. However, researchers have confirmed that psychodynamic therapies do, in fact, produce improvement in some patients (Doidge, 1997).

The real value of Eysenck's critique is that it encouraged psychologists to try new ideas and techniques. Researchers began to ask, "When does psychoanalysis work, and why does it work? What procedures are essential, and which are unnecessary?" Modern therapists have given surprisingly varied answers to these questions. Upcoming sections will acquaint you with some of the other therapies currently in use.

HUMANISTIC THERAPIES—RESTORING HUMAN POTENTIAL

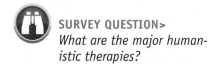

SURVEY QUESTION>
What are the major humanistic therapies?

The goal of traditional psychoanalysis is adjustment. Freud claimed that his patients could expect only to change their "hysterical misery into common unhappiness"! Humanistic therapies are generally more optimistic. Most assume that it is possible for people to fully use their potentials and live rich, rewarding lives. Psychotherapy is seen as a way to give natural tendencies toward mental health a chance to emerge.

Client-Centred Therapy

Psychotherapist Carl Rogers, 1902–1987, who originated client-centred therapy.

What is client-centred therapy? How is it different from psychoanalysis? Psychoanalysts delve into the unconscious. Psychologist Carl Rogers (1902–1987) found it more beneficial to explore *conscious* thoughts and feelings. The psychoanalyst tends to take a position of authority, stating what dreams, thoughts, or memories mean. In contrast, Rogers believed that what is right or valuable for the therapist may be different for the client. (Rogers preferred the term *client* to *patient* because "patient" implies a person is "sick" and needs to be "cured.") Consequently, the client determines what will be discussed during each session. Thus, **client-centred therapy** (also called person-centred therapy) is non-directive and based on insights from conscious thoughts and feelings (Bohart, 1995).

If the client runs things, what does the therapist do? The therapist's job is to create an "atmosphere of growth." The therapist provides opportunities for change, but the client must actively seek to solve his or her problems. The therapist cannot "fix" the client (Bohart & Tallman, 1996).

Health-Promoting Conditions

Rogers believed that effective therapists maintain four basic conditions. First, the therapist offers the client unconditional positive regard (unshakable personal acceptance). The therapist refuses to react with shock, dismay, or disapproval to anything the client says or feels. Total acceptance by the therapist is the first step to self-acceptance by the client.

Second, the therapist attempts to achieve genuine **empathy** by trying to see the world through the client's eyes and feeling some part of what the client is feeling.

As a third essential condition, the therapist strives to be **authentic** (genuine and honest). The therapist must not hide behind a professional role. Rogers believed that phony fronts destroy the growth atmosphere sought in client-centred therapy.

Fourth, the therapist does not make interpretations, propose solutions, or offer advice. Instead, the therapist **reflects** (rephrases, summarizes, or repeats) the client's thoughts and feelings. This allows the therapist to act as a psychological "mirror" so clients can see themselves more clearly. Rogers hypothesized that a person armed with a realistic self-image and greater self-acceptance will gradually discover solutions to life's problems.

Existential Therapy

According to the existentialists, "being in the world" (existence) creates deep conflicts. Each of us must deal with the realities of death. We must face the fact that we create our private world by making choices. We must overcome isolation on a vast and indifferent planet. Most of all, we must confront feelings of meaninglessness.

What do these concerns have to do with psychotherapy? **Existential therapy** focuses on the problems of existence, such as meaning, choice, and responsibility. Like client-centred therapy, it promotes self-knowledge and self-actualization. However, there are important differences. Client-centred therapy seeks to uncover a "true self" hidden behind a screen of defences. In contrast, existential therapy emphasizes **free will**, the human ability to make choices. Accordingly, existential therapists believe you can choose to become the person you want to be.

Existential therapists try to give clients the courage to make rewarding and socially constructive choices. Typically, therapy focuses on **death, freedom, isolation,** and

Client-centred therapy A non-directive therapy based on insights gained from conscious thoughts and feelings; emphasizes accepting one's true self.

Empathy A capacity for taking another's point of view; the ability to feel what another is feeling.

Authenticity In Carl Rogers's terms, the ability of a therapist to be genuine and honest about his or her own feelings.

Reflection In client-centred therapy, the process of rephrasing or repeating thoughts and feelings expressed by clients so they can become aware of what they are saying.

Existential therapy An insight therapy that focuses on the elemental problems of existence, such as death, meaning, choice, and responsibility; emphasizes making courageous life choices.

Free will The presumed ability of humans to freely make choices not determined by heredity, past conditioning, or other concerns.

Death, freedom, isolation, meaninglessness The universal challenges of existence, including an awareness that everyone will die, the responsibility that comes with freedom to choose, the fact that each person is ultimately isolated and alone in her or his private world, and the reality that meaning must be created in life.

Confrontation In existential therapy, the process of confronting clients with their own values and with the need to take responsibility for the quality of their existence.

Gestalt therapy An approach that focuses on immediate experience and awareness to help clients rebuild thinking, feeling, and acting into connected wholes; emphasizes the integration of fragmented experiences.

meaninglessness, the "ultimate concerns" of existence (Yalom, 1980). These universal human challenges include an awareness of one's mortality, the responsibility that comes with freedom to choose, being alone in one's private world, and the reality that meaning must be created in life.

What does the existential therapist do? The therapist helps clients to discover self-imposed limitations in personal identity. To be successful, the client must fully accept the challenge of changing his or her life (Bretherton & Orner, 2004). A key aspect of existential therapy is **confrontation,** in which clients are challenged to examine their values and choices and to take responsibility for the quality of their existence (Gerwood, 1998).

An important part of confrontation is the unique, intense, here-and-now encounter between two human beings. When existential therapy is successful, it brings about a renewed sense of purpose and a reappraisal of what's important in life. Some clients even experience an emotional rebirth like that seen after people survive a close brush with death. As Marcel Proust wrote, "The real voyage of discovery consists not in seeing new landscapes but in having new eyes."

Gestalt Therapy

Gestalt therapy, which is most often associated with Frederick (Fritz) Perls (1969), is built around the idea that perception, or awareness, is disjointed and incomplete in the maladjusted individual. The German word *Gestalt* means "whole" or "complete." **Gestalt therapy** helps individuals rebuild thinking, feeling, and acting into connected wholes. This is achieved by expanding personal awareness; by accepting responsibility for one's thoughts, feelings, and actions; and by filling in gaps in experience (Yontef, 1995).

What do you mean by gaps in experience? Gestalt therapists believe that we often shy away from expressing or "owning" upsetting feelings. This creates a gap in self-awareness that may become a barrier to personal growth. For example, a person who feels anger after the death of a parent might go for years without fully expressing it. This and similar threatening gaps may impair emotional health.

The Gestalt approach is more directive than client-centred therapy, and it emphasizes immediate experience. Working either one-to-one or in a group setting, the Gestalt therapist encourages clients to become more aware of their moment-to-moment thoughts, perceptions, and emotions (Staemmler, 2004). Rather than discussing why clients feel guilt, anger, fear, or boredom, clients are encouraged to have these feelings in the "here and now" and become fully aware of them. The therapist promotes awareness by drawing attention to a client's posture, voice, eye movement, and hand gestures. Clients may also be asked to exaggerate vague feelings until they become clear. Gestalt therapists believe that expressing such feelings allows people to take care of unfinished business and break through emotional impasses.

In all his writings, Perls's basic message comes through clearly: Emotional health comes from knowing what you *want* to do, not dwelling on what you should do or should want to do. Another way of stating this idea is that emotional health comes from taking full responsibility for one's feelings and actions. For example, it means changing "I can't" to "I won't" or "I must" to "I choose to."

How does Gestalt therapy help people discover their real wants? Above all else, Gestalt therapy emphasizes present experience. Clients are urged to stop intellectualizing and talking about feelings. Instead, they learn to live now; live here; stop imagining; experience the real; stop unnecessary thinking; taste and see; express rather than explain, justify, or judge; give in to unpleasantness and pain just as to pleasure; and surrender to being as you are (Naranjo, 1970). Gestalt therapists believe that, paradoxically, the best way to change is to become who you really are (Yontef, 1995).

Because of their emphasis on verbal interaction, humanistic therapies may be conducted at a distance, by telephone or over the Internet. Let's investigate this possibility.

PSYCHOTHERAPY AT A DISTANCE—PSYCH JOCKEYS AND CYBERTHERAPY

How valid are psychological services offered over the phone and on the Internet? For better or worse, high-tech psychotherapy and counselling are rapidly becoming more common (Ormay, 2006). Today, psychological services are available through radio, telephone, video-conferencing, email, and Internet chat rooms (Maheu et al., 2004). What are the advantages and disadvantages of getting help at a distance?

Media Psychologists

By now, you have probably heard a phone-in radio psychologist. On a typical program, callers describe problems arising from child abuse, loneliness, love affairs, phobias, sexual adjustment, or depression. The radio psychologist then offers reassurance, advice, or suggestions for getting help. Talk-radio psychology and similar television programs may seem harmless, but they raise some important questions. For instance, is it reasonable to give advice without knowing anything about a person's background? Might the advice do harm? What good can a psychologist do in three minutes or even an hour?

In defence of themselves, media psychologists point out that listeners may learn solutions to their problems by hearing others talk. Many also stress that their work is educational, not therapeutic. The well-known media psychologist Dr. Phil McGraw has even been awarded a President's Citation from the American Psychological Association for his work in publicizing mental health issues (Meyers, 2006).

Nevertheless, the question arises, "When does advice become therapy?" The American Psychological Association urges media psychologists to discuss problems only of a general nature, instead of actually counselling anyone. For example, if a caller complains about insomnia, the radio psychologist should talk about insomnia in general, not probe the caller's personal life.

By giving information, advice, and social support, media psychologists probably do help some listeners (Levy, 1989). Even so, a good guide for anyone tempted to call a radio psychologist or one on TV might be "buyer beware."

The same caution applies to commercial telephone and Internet therapists. A key feature of successful face-to-face therapy is the establishment of a continuing *relationship* between two people. In this regard, distance therapies are more or less limited by a lack of inter-personal cues, such as facial expressions and body language. For example, brief email messages are no way to make a diagnosis. And forget about facial expressions or body language—not even tone of voice reaches the email therapist. Typing emotional icons (called *emoticons*) like little smiley faces (☺) or frowns (☹) is a poor substitute for real human interaction.

Of special concern is the fact that distance therapists may or may not be trained professionals (Bloom, 1998). And even if they are, questions exist about whether a psychologist licensed in one province or territory can legally do therapy in another via the telephone or the Internet.

Regardless, distance counselling and therapy services do have some advantages. For one thing, clients can more easily remain anonymous. (But beware that email counselling may not be completely confidential and could be intercepted and misused.) Thus, a person who might hesitate to see a psychologist can seek help privately, on the phone or online. Likewise, people who live in rural areas can more easily work with psychologists living in large cities. And, compared with traditional office visits, distance therapies are less expensive.

Media psychologists have been urged to educate without actually doing therapy on the air. Some overstep this boundary, however.

STUDY BREAK Humanistic Therapies

Reflect

Here's a mnemonic for the elements of client-centred therapy: Picture a therapist saying "I ear u" to a client. E stands for empathy, A for authenticity, R for reflection, and U for unconditional positive regard.

What would an existential therapist say about the choices you have made so far in your life? Should you be choosing more "courageously"?

You are going to play the role of a therapist for a classroom demonstration. How would you act if you were a client-centred therapist? An existential therapist? A Gestalt therapist?

A neighbour of yours is thinking about getting counselling on the Internet. What would you tell her about the pros and cons of distance therapy?

Learning Check

Match:

____ 1. Client-centred therapy   A. Electronic advice
____ 2. Gestalt therapy   B. Unconditional positive regard
____ 3. Existential therapy   C. Gaps in awareness
____ 4. Cybertherapy   D. Choice and becoming

5. The Gestalt therapist tries to reflect a client's thoughts and feelings. T or F?
6. Client-centred therapy is directive. T or F?
7. Confrontation and encounter are concepts of existential therapy. T or F?

Critical Thinking

8. How might using the term *patient* affect the relationship between an individual and a therapist?

Answers

1. B 2. C 3. D 4. A 5. F 6. F 7. T 8. The terms *doctor* and *patient* imply a large gap in status and authority between the individual and his or her therapist. Client-centred therapy attempts to narrow this gap by making the person the final authority concerning solutions to her or his problems. Also, the word *patient* implies that a person is "sick" and needs to be "cured." Many regard this as an inappropriate way to think about human problems.

Under the right circumstances, distance therapies can be successful (Day & Schneider, 2002). For example, in one study, telephone counselling helped improve success rates for smokers who wanted to quit (Rabius et al., 2004). Other studies have shown that depressed people benefit from telephone therapy (Mohr et al., 2005; Simon et al., 2004). Psychologists have also demonstrated success providing therapy over the Internet, at least for certain types of problems (Carlbring et al., 2007; Chester & Glass, 2006; Klein, Richards, & Austin, 2006).

The Ever-Evolving Internet

The Internet continues to provide new communication tools that blend voice, text, graphics, and video. Widely available and inexpensive technologies, such as Skype, make it easy to create two-way audio-video links that allow a client and therapist to see one another on computer monitors and to talk via speakerphones. Doing therapy this way still lacks the close personal contact of face-to-face interaction. However, it does remove many of the objections to doing therapy at a distance. It's very likely that distance services will continue to evolve (Riva & Wiederhold, 2006) and become a major source of mental health care in coming years (Schopp, Demiris, & Glueckauf, 2006).

BEHAVIOUR THERAPY—HEALING BY LEARNING

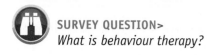

SURVEY QUESTION>
What is behaviour therapy?

Five times a day, for several days, Brooks Workman stopped what she was doing and vividly imagined opening a soft-drink can. She then pictured herself bringing the can to her mouth and placing her lips on it. Just as she was about to drink, hordes of roaches poured out of the can and scurried into her mouth—writhing, twitching, and wiggling their feelers (Williams & Long, 1991).

Why would anyone imagine such a thing? Brooks Workman's behaviour is not as strange as it may seem. Her goal was self-control: Brooks was drinking too many colas and she wanted to cut down. The method she chose (called *covert sensitization*) is a form of behaviour therapy (Cautela & Kearney, 1986). **Behaviour therapy** is the use of learning principles to make constructive changes in behaviour. Behavioural approaches include behaviour modification, aversion therapy, desensitization, and token economies.

Behaviour therapists believe that deep insight into one's problems is often unnecessary for improvement. Instead, they try to directly alter troublesome thoughts and actions. Brooks Workman didn't need to probe into her past or her emotions and conflicts; she simply wanted to break her habit of drinking too many colas. Even when more serious problems are at stake, techniques like the one she used have proven valuable.

In general, how does behaviour therapy work? Behaviour therapists assume that people have learned to be the way they are. If they have learned responses that cause problems, then they can change them by relearning more appropriate responses. Broadly speaking, **behaviour modification** refers to any use of classical or operant conditioning to directly alter human behaviour (Miltenberger, 2004; Spiegler & Guevremont, 2003).

How does classical conditioning work? (I'm not sure I remember.) Classical conditioning is a form of learning in which simple responses (especially reflexes) are associated with new stimuli. Here is a brief review of conditioning principles:

A neutral stimulus is followed by an unconditioned stimulus (US) that consistently produces an unlearned reaction, called the unconditioned response (UR). Eventually, the previously neutral stimulus begins to produce this response directly. The response is then called a conditioned response (CR), and the stimulus becomes a conditioned stimulus (CS). Thus, for a child the sight of a hypodermic needle (CS) is followed by an injection (US), which causes anxiety or fear (UR). Eventually the sight of a hypodermic (the conditioned stimulus) may produce anxiety or fear (a conditioned response) before the child gets an injection.

What does classical conditioning have to do with behaviour modification? Classical conditioning can be used to associate discomfort with a bad habit, as Brooks Workman did. A more powerful version of this approach is called aversion therapy.

Aversion Therapy

Imagine that you are eating an apple. Suddenly you discover that you just bit a large green worm in half. You vomit. Months pass before you can eat an apple again without feeling ill. You now have a conditioned aversion to apples. (A **conditioned aversion** is a learned dislike or negative emotional response to some stimulus.)

How are conditioned aversions used in therapy? In **aversion therapy,** an individual learns to associate a strong aversion with an undesirable habit such as smoking, drinking, or gambling. Aversion therapy has been used to cure hiccups; sneezing; stuttering; vomiting; nail biting; bedwetting; compulsive hair pulling; alcoholism; and addictions to tobacco, marijuana, and crack cocaine. (To learn how aversion therapy can help people quit smoking, see Using Psychology: "Puffing Up an Aversion.") Actually, aversive conditioning is an everyday occurrence. For example, not many physicians who treat lung cancer are smokers, nor do many emergency room doctors drive without using their seat belts (Rosenthal & Steffek, 1991).

Curt Gunther/Camera 5

Aversion therapy for drinking. The sights, smells, and tastes of drinking are associated with unpleasant electric shocks applied to the hand.

> **Behaviour therapy** Any therapy designed to actively change behaviour.
>
> **Behaviour modification** The application of learning principles to change human behaviour, especially maladaptive behaviour.
>
> **Conditioned aversion** A learned dislike or conditioned negative emotional response to a particular stimulus.
>
> **Aversion therapy** Suppressing an undesirable response by associating it with aversive (painful or uncomfortable) stimuli.

Puffing Up an Aversion

The fact that nicotine is toxic makes it easy to create an aversion to smoking. Behaviour therapists have found that electric shock, nauseating drugs, and similar aversive stimuli are not required to make smokers uncomfortable. All that is needed is for the smoker to smoke—rapidly and for a long time.

Rapid smoking (prolonged smoking at a forced pace) is the most widely used aversion therapy for smoking (Lichtenstein, 1982). In this method, clients are told to smoke continuously, taking a puff every six to eight seconds. Rapid smoking continues until the smoker is miserable and can stand it no more. By then, most people are thinking, "I never want to see another cigarette for the rest of my life."

Studies suggest that rapid smoking is one of the most effective behaviour therapies for smoking (Tiffany, Martin, & Baker, 1986).

Anyone tempted to try rapid smoking should realize that it is very unpleasant. Without the help of a therapist, most people quit too soon for the procedure to succeed. (An alternative method that is more practical is described in the Psychology in Action section of this chapter.)

One problem with rapid smoking—as with other stop-smoking methods—is that about one-half of those who quit smoking begin again. During at least the first year after quitting, there is no "safe point" after which relapse becomes less likely (Swan & Denk, 1987).

Because the "evil weed" calls so strongly to former smokers, support from a stop-smoking group or a close, caring person can make a big difference. Former smokers who get encouragement from others are much more likely to stay smoke-free (Gruder et al., 1993).

Rapid smoking Prolonged smoking at a forced pace; used in aversion therapy to produce discomfort from smoking.

Response-contingent consequences Reinforcement, punishment, or other consequences that are applied only when a certain response is made.

Hierarchy A rank-ordered series of higher and lower amounts, levels, degrees, or steps.

Reciprocal inhibition The presence of one emotional state inhibiting the occurrence of another, such as joy preventing fear or anxiety inhibiting pleasure.

An excellent example of aversion therapy is provided by the work of Roger Vogler and his associates (1977). Vogler works with alcoholics who are unable to stop drinking. For many clients, aversion therapy is a last chance. While drinking an alcoholic beverage, clients receive a painful (although non-injurious) electric shock to the hand. Most of the time, these shocks occur as the client is beginning to take a drink of alcohol.

This **response-contingent** (response-connected) shock obviously takes the pleasure out of drinking. Shocks also cause the alcohol abuser to develop a conditioned aversion to drinking. Normally, the misery caused by alcohol abuse comes long after the act of drinking—too late to have much effect. But if alcohol can be linked with immediate discomfort, then drinking will begin to make the individual very uncomfortable.

Is it really acceptable to treat clients this way? People are often disturbed (shocked?) by such methods. However, clients usually volunteer for aversion therapy because it helps them overcome a destructive habit. Indeed, commercial aversion programs for overeating, smoking, and alcohol abuse have attracted many willing customers. And, more important, aversion therapy can be justified by its long-term benefits. As behaviourist Donald Baer put it, "A small number of brief, painful experiences is a reasonable exchange for the interminable pain of a lifelong maladjustment."

Desensitization

SURVEY QUESTION>
How is behaviour therapy used to treat phobias and anxieties?

Assume that you are a swimming instructor who wants to help a child named Jamie overcome fear of the high diving board. How might you proceed? Directly forcing Jamie off the high board could be a psychological disaster. Obviously, a better approach would be to begin by teaching him to dive off the edge of the pool. Then he could be taught to dive off the low board, followed by a platform two metres above the water and then a three-metre platform. As a last step, Jamie could try the high board.

Who's Afraid of a Hierarchy?

This rank-ordered series of steps is called a **hierarchy.** The hierarchy allows Jamie to undergo adaptation. Gradually, he adapts to the high dive and overcomes his fear, much as one adapts to a cool swimming pool on a hot day. When Jamie has conquered his fear, we can say that *desensitization* has occurred (Spiegler & Guevremont, 2003).

Desensitization is also based on **reciprocal inhibition** (using one emotional state to block another) (Heriot & Pritchard, 2004). For instance, it is impossible to be anxious and relaxed at the same time. If we can get Jamie onto the high board in a relaxed state, his anxiety and fear will be inhibited. Repeated visits to the high board should cause fear in this situation to disappear. Again we would say that Jamie has been desensitized. Typically, **systematic desensitization** (a guided reduction in fear, anxiety, or aversion) is attained by gradually approaching a feared stimulus while maintaining relaxation.

What is desensitization used for? Desensitization is primarily used to help people unlearn or countercondition phobias (intense, unrealistic fears) or strong anxieties. For example, each of these people might be a candidate for desensitization: a teacher with stage fright, a student with test anxiety, or a salesperson who fears people.

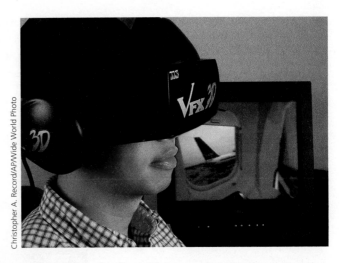

Programs for treating fears of flying combine relaxation, systematic desensitization, group support, and lots of direct exposure to airplanes.

Performing Desensitization

How is desensitization done? First, the client and the therapist construct a hierarchy. This is a list of fear-provoking situations, arranged from least disturbing to most frightening. Second, the client is taught exercises that produce deep relaxation. (These are described in this chapter's Psychology in Action section.) Once the client is relaxed, she or he proceeds to the third step by trying to perform the least disturbing item on the list. For a fear of heights (acrophobia), this might be: "(1) Stand on a chair." The first item is repeated until no anxiety is felt. Any change from complete relaxation is a signal that clients must repeat the relaxation process before continuing. Slowly, clients move up the hierarchy: "(2) Climb to the top of a small stepladder"; "(3) Look down a flight of stairs"; and so on, until the last item is performed without fear: "(20) Fly in an airplane."

For many phobias, desensitization works best when people are directly exposed to the stimuli and situations they fear (Bourne, 2005). For something like a simple spider phobia, this exposure can even be done in groups (Ost, 1996). Also, for some fears (such as fear of riding an elevator), desensitization may be completed in a single session (Sturges & Sturges, 1998).

Programs for treating fear of flying combine relaxation, systematic desensitization, group support, and lots of direct exposure to airplanes. Many such programs conclude with a brief flight, so that participants can "test their wings" (Roberts, 1989). Several private companies offer this type of program in Canada. Such training seminars are given by a pilot and a psychologist. Lasting about 15 to 20 hours, the programs can cost between $800 and $1000.

Vicarious Desensitization

I understand how some fears could be desensitized by a gradual approach—as in the case of the child on the high dive. But how would a therapist use desensitization to combat fear of heights? For a person with a fear of heights, the steps of the hierarchy might be acted out. Often, however, this is impractical. In some cases the problem can be handled by having clients observe models who are performing the feared behaviour (see Figure 13.2) (Rosenthal & Steffek, 1991). A **model** is a person who serves as an example for observational learning. If such **vicarious desensitization** (second-hand learning) is not practical, there is yet another option. Fortunately, desensitization works almost as well when a person vividly imagines each step in the hierarchy (Deffenbacher & Suinn, 1988). If the steps can be visualized without anxiety, fear in the actual situation is reduced.

Virtual Reality Exposure

In an important new development, psychologists are beginning to use virtual reality to treat phobias. Virtual reality is a computer-generated, three-dimensional "world" that viewers enter by wearing a head-mounted video display. **Virtual reality exposure**

Systematic desensitization A reduction in fear, anxiety, or aversion brought about by planned exposure to aversive stimuli.

Model A person who serves as an example in observational learning.

Vicarious desensitization A reduction in fear or anxiety that takes place vicariously ("second-hand") when a client watches models perform the feared behaviour.

Virtual reality exposure Use of computer-generated images to present fear stimuli. The virtual environment responds to a viewer's head movements and other inputs.

Eye movement desensitization and reprocessing (EMDR) A technique for reducing fear or anxiety; based on holding upsetting thoughts in mind while rapidly moving the eyes from side to side.

presents computerized fear stimuli to patients in a controlled fashion (Wiederhold & Wiederhold, 2005). It has already been used to treat acrophobia (fear of heights); fears of flying, driving, and public speaking; spider phobias; and claustrophobia (Arbona et al., 2004; Giuseppe, 2005; Hoffman et al., 2003; Lee et al., 2002; Wald and Taylor, 2000). (See Figure 13.3.)

Desensitization has been one of the most successful behaviour therapies. A second new technique may provide yet another way to lower fears, anxieties, and psychological pain. The Clinical File: "Eye Movement Desensitization" has the details.

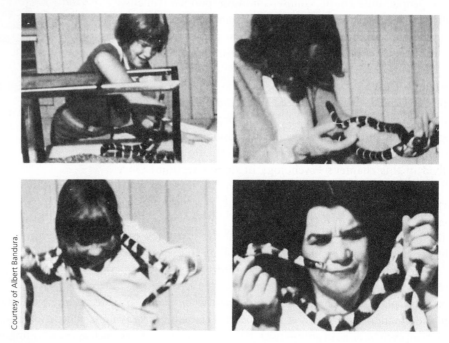

Courtesy of Albert Bandura.

▶▶**FIGURE 13.2** Treatment of a snake phobia by vicarious desensitization. The photographs show models interacting with snakes. To overcome their own fears, people with phobias observed the models. (Bandura, Blanchard, & Ritter, 1969.)

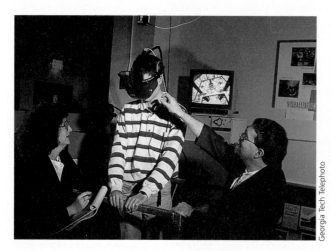

Georgia Tech Telephoto

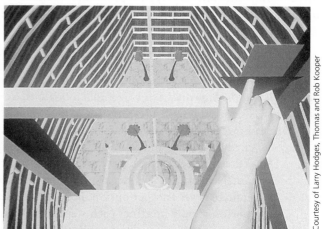

Courtesy of Larry Hodges, Thomas and Rob Kooper

▶▶**FIGURE 13.3** *(Left)* Dr. Barbara Rothbaum and Dr. Larry Hodges show how a virtual reality system is used to expose people to feared stimuli. Many patients say that they would rather face exposure to feared stimuli in a virtual environment than in a real physical environment. *(Right)* A computer image from a virtual elevator. Over an eight-week period, patients who suffered from acrophobia "rode" in the elevator. Each session took them to greater heights. (Image courtesy of Larry Hodges, Thomas Meyer, and Rob Kooper.)

Eye Movement Desensitization—Watching Trauma Fade?

Traumatic events produce painful memories. Victims of accidents, disasters, molestations, muggings, rapes, or emotional abuse are often haunted by disturbing flashbacks. Dr. Francine Shapiro has developed **eye movement desensitization and reprocessing (EMDR)** to help ease traumatic memories and post-traumatic stress.

In a typical EMDR session, the client is asked to visualize the images that most upset her or him. At the same time, a pencil (or other object) is moved rapidly from side to side in front of the person's eyes. Watching the moving object causes the person's eyes to dart swiftly back and forth. After about 30 seconds, patients describe any memories, feelings, and thoughts that emerged and discuss them with the therapist. These steps are repeated until troubling thoughts and emotions no longer surface (Shapiro, 2001; Shapiro & Forrest, 2004).

A number of studies indicate that EMDR lowers anxiety and takes the pain out of traumatic memories (Ironson et al., 2002; Silver et al., 2005). However, EMDR is highly controversial. Some studies, for example, have found that eye movements add nothing to the treatment. The apparent success of EMDR may simply be based on gradual exposure to upsetting stimuli, as in other forms of desensitization (Cahill, Carrigan, & Frueh, 1999; Davidson & Parker, 2001; Lohr, Tolin, & Lilienfeld, 1998; Muris & Merckelbach, 1999). On the other hand, some researchers continue to find that EMDR is superior to traditional therapies (Greenwald, 2006; Rogers & Silver, 2002).

Is EMDR a breakthrough? Or will it prove to be a case of wishful thinking? Given the frequency of traumas in modern society, it shouldn't be long before we find out.

✔ STUDY BREAK Behaviour Therapy

Reflect

Can you describe three problems for which you think behaviour therapy would be an appropriate treatment?

A friend of yours has a dog that goes berserk during thunderstorms. You have an audio recording of a thunderstorm. How could you use the recording to desensitize the dog? (Hint: The player has a volume control.)

Have you ever become naturally desensitized to a stimulus or situation that at first made you anxious (e.g., heights, public speaking, or driving on highways)? How would you explain your reduced fear?

Learning Check

1. What two types of conditioning are used in behaviour modification? _____ and _____
2. Shock, pain, and discomfort play what role in conditioning an aversion?
   a. conditioned stimulus   b. unconditioned response
   c. unconditioned stimulus   d. conditioned response
3. If shock is used to control drinking, it must be _____ contingent.

4. What two principles underlie systematic desensitization? _____ and _____
5. When desensitization is carried out through the use of live or filmed models, it is called
   a. cognitive therapy   b. flooding
   c. covert desensitization   d. vicarious desensitization
6. The three basic steps in systematic desensitization are construct a hierarchy, flood the person with anxiety, and imagine relaxation. T or F?
7. In EMDR therapy, computer-generated virtual reality images are used to expose patients to fear-provoking stimuli. T or F?

Critical Thinking

8. Alcoholics who take a drug called Antabuse become ill after drinking alcohol. Why, then, don't they develop an aversion to drinking?
9. A natural form of desensitization often takes place in hospitals. Can you guess what it is?

Answers

1. classical (or respondent), operant   2. c   3. response   4. adaptation, reciprocal inhibition   5. d   6. F   7. F   8. Their discomfort is delayed enough to prevent it from being closely associated with drinking. Fortunately, there are safer, better ways to do aversion therapy (Wilson, 1987).   9. Doctors and nurses learn to relax and remain calm at the sight of blood because of their frequent exposure to it.

OPERANT THERAPIES—ALL THE WORLD IS A SKINNER BOX?

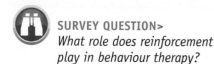

SURVEY QUESTION>
What role does reinforcement play in behaviour therapy?

Aversion therapy and desensitization are based on classical conditioning. Where does operant conditioning fit in? As you may recall, **operant conditioning** refers to learning based on the consequences of making a response. The operant principles most often used by behaviour therapists to deal with human behaviour are the following:

1. *Positive reinforcement.* Responses that are followed by reward tend to occur more frequently. If children whine and get attention, they will whine more frequently. If you get A's in your psychology class, you may become a psychology major.

2. *Non-reinforcement.* A response that is not followed by reward will occur less frequently.

3. *Extinction.* If a response is not followed by reward after it has been repeated many times, it will go away. After winning 3 times, you press the button on a slot machine 30 times more without a payoff. What do you do? You go away. So does the response of button pressing (for that particular machine, at any rate).

4. *Punishment.* If a response is followed by discomfort or an undesirable effect, the response will be suppressed (but not necessarily extinguished).

5. *Shaping.* Shaping means rewarding actions that are closer and closer approximations to a desired response. For example, if you want to reward a child with an intellectual disability for saying "ball," you might begin by rewarding the child for saying anything that starts with a b sound.

6. *Stimulus control.* Responses tend to come under the control of the situation in which they occur. If you set your clock 10 minutes fast, you can get to work on time in the morning. Your departure is under the stimulus control of the clock, even though you know it is fast.

7. *Time out.* A time-out procedure usually involves removing the individual from a situation in which reinforcement occurs. Time out is a variation of non-reinforcement: It prevents reward from following an undesirable response. For example, children who fight with each other can be sent to separate rooms and allowed out only when they are able to behave more calmly (Olson & Roberts, 1987). (For a more thorough review of operant learning, return to Chapter 6, page 242.)

As simple as these principles may seem, they have been used very effectively to overcome difficulties in work, home, school, and industrial settings. Let's see how.

Non-Reinforcement and Extinction

An extremely overweight, mentally ill patient had a persistent and disturbing habit: She stole food from other patients. No one could persuade her to stop stealing or to diet. For the sake of her health, a behaviour therapist assigned her a special table in the ward dining room. If she approached any other table, she was immediately removed from the dining room. Since her attempts to steal food went unrewarded, they rapidly disappeared. Additionally, any attempt to steal from others caused the patient to miss her own meal (Ayllon, 1963).

What operant principles did the therapist in this example use? The therapist used nonreward to produce extinction. The most frequently occurring human behaviours lead to some form of reward. An undesirable response can be eliminated by identifying and removing the rewards that maintain it. But people don't always do things for food, money, or other obvious rewards. Most of the rewards maintaining human behaviour are more subtle. Attention, approval, and concern are common yet powerful reinforcers for humans (see Figure 13.4).

Non-reward and extinction can eliminate many problem behaviours, especially in schools, hospitals, and institutions. Often, difficulties centre on a limited number of particularly disturbing responses. Time out is a good way to remove such responses, usually by refusing to pay attention to a person who is misbehaving. For example, 14-year-old Zeke

Operant conditioning Learning based on the consequences of responding.

periodically appeared in the nude in the activity room of a training centre for disturbed adolescents. This behaviour always generated a great deal of attention from staff and other patients. Usually Zeke was returned to his room and confined there. During this "confinement," he often missed doing his usual chores. As an experiment he was placed on time out. The next time he appeared nude, counsellors and other staff members greeted him normally and then ignored him. Attention from other patients rapidly subsided. Sheepishly he returned to his room and dressed.

Reinforcement and Token Economies

A distressing problem therapists sometimes face is how to break through to severely ill patients who won't talk. Conventional psychotherapy offers little hope of improvement for such patients.

What can be done for them? One widely used approach is based on **tokens** (symbolic rewards, such as plastic chips, that can be exchanged for real rewards). Tokens may be printed slips of paper, check marks, points, or gold stars. Whatever form they take, tokens serve as rewards because they may be exchanged for candy, food, cigarettes, recreation, outings, or watching TV. Tokens are used in psychiatric hospitals, halfway houses, schools for people with intellectual disabilities, programs for delinquents, and ordinary classrooms. They usually produce dramatic improvements in behaviour (Dickerson, Tenhula, & Green-Paden, 2005; Reitman et al., 2004).

By using tokens, a therapist can *immediately reward* positive responses. For maximum impact, therapists select specific **target behaviours** (actions or other behaviours the therapist seeks to modify). Target behaviours are then reinforced with tokens. For example, a mute mentally ill patient might first be given a token each time he or she says a word. Next, tokens may be given for speaking a complete sentence. Later, the patient could gradually be required to speak more often, then to answer questions, and eventually to carry on a short conversation in order to receive tokens. In this way, deeply withdrawn patients have been returned to the world of normal communication.

Full-scale use of tokens in an institutional setting produces a *token economy*. In a **token economy** patients are rewarded with tokens for a wide range of socially desirable or productive activities (Spiegler & Guevremont, 2003). They must pay tokens for privileges and for engaging in problem behaviours (see Figure 13.5). For example, tokens are given to patients who get out of bed, dress themselves, take required medication, arrive for meals on time, and so on. Constructive activities, such as gardening, cooking, or cleaning, may also earn tokens. Patients can exchange tokens for meals and private rooms, movies, passes, off-ward activities, and other privileges. They are charged tokens for staying in bed, disrobing in public, talking to themselves, fighting, crying, and similar target behaviours (Morisse et al., 1996).

Token economies can radically change a patient's overall adjustment and morale. Patients are given an incentive to change, and they are held responsible for their actions. The use of tokens may seem manipulative, but it actually empowers patients. Many people with severe intellectual disability or mental illness and people who display delinquent behaviour have been returned to productive lives by means of token economies (Corrigan, 1997). By the time they are ready to leave, patients may be earning tokens on a weekly basis for maintaining socially desirable behaviours (Miltenberger, 2004). Typically, the most effective token economies are those that gradually switch from tokens to social rewards such as praise, recognition, and approval. Such rewards are what patients will receive when they return to family, friends, and the community.

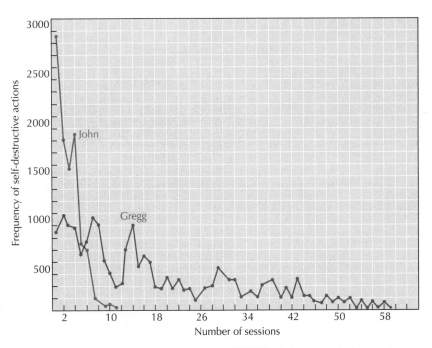

▶▶**FIGURE 13.4** This graph shows extinction of self-destructive behaviour in two autistic boys. Before extinction began, the boys received attention and concern from adults for injuring themselves. During extinction, self-damaging behaviour was ignored. (Adapted from Lovaas & Simmons, 1969.)

Tokens Symbolic rewards, or secondary reinforcers (such as plastic chips, gold stars, or points) that can be exchanged for real reinforcers.

Target behaviours Actions or other behaviours (such as speech) that a therapist selects as the focus for behaviour modification efforts.

Token economy A therapeutic program in which desirable behaviours are reinforced with tokens that can be exchanged for goods, services, activities, and privileges.

Credit Card

OXNARD DAY TREATMENT CENTRE CREDIT INCENTIVE SYSTEM			
EARN CREDITS BY		**SPEND CREDITS FOR**	
MONITOR DAILY	15	COFFEE	5
MENU PLANNING CHAIRMAN	50	LUNCH	10
PARTICIPATE	5	EXCEPT THURSDAY	15
BUY FOOD AT STORE	10	BUS TRIP	5
COOK FOR/PREPARE LUNCH	5	BOWLING	8
WIPE OFF KITCHEN TABLE	3	GROUP THERAPY	5
WASH DISHES	5-10	PRIVATE STAFF TIME	5
DRY AND PUT AWAY DISHES	5	DAY OFF	5-20
MAKE COFFEE AND CLEAN URN	15	WINDOW SHOPPING	5
CLEAN REFRIGERATOR	20	REVIEW WITH DR.	10
ATTEND PLANNING CONFERENCE	1	DOING OWN THING	1
OT PREPARATION	1-5	LATE 1 PER EVERY 10 MIN	
COMPLETE OT PROJECT	5	PRESCRIPTION FROM DR.	10
RETURN OT PROJECT	2		
DUST AND POLISH TABLES	5		
PUT AWAY GROCERIES	3		
CLEAN TABLE	5		
CLEAN 6 ASH TRAYS	2		
CLEAN SINK	5		
CARRY OUT CUPS & BOTTLES	5		
CLEAN CHAIRS	5		
CLEAN KITCHEN CUPBOARDS	5		
ASSIST STAFF	5		
ARRANGE MAGAZINES NEATLY	3		
BEING ON TIME	5		
MONITOR-ANN			

▸▸**FIGURE 13.5** Shown here is a token used in one token economy system; also pictured is a list of credit values for various activities. Tokens may be exchanged for items or for privileges listed on the board. (After photographs by Robert P. Liberman.)

COGNITIVE THERAPY—THINKING CONSTRUCTIVELY!

SURVEY QUESTION>
What is cognitive therapy? How does it change thoughts and emotions?

How would a behaviour therapist treat a problem like depression? None of the techniques described seem to apply. As we have discussed, behaviour therapists usually try to change troublesome actions. However, therapists have also become interested in what people think, believe, and feel, as well as how they act, according to Canadian psychologist Donald Meichenbaum (1993). In general, **cognitive therapy** helps clients change thinking patterns that lead to troublesome emotions or behaviours (Hall, 2006). For example, compulsive hand washing can be greatly reduced by changing a client's thoughts and beliefs about dirt and contamination (Jones & Menzies, 1998).

Cognitive Therapy for Depression

Cognitive therapy has been especially effective for treating depression. As you may recall from Chapter 11, Aaron Beck (1991) proposed that negative, self-defeating thoughts contribute to the development of depression. Depressed persons view themselves, the world, and the future in negative terms. This occurs because of major distortions in thinking. He points out that depressed people engage in automatic negative thinking, characterized by a number of cognitive errors.

How do cognitive therapists alter such negative thinking patterns? Cognitive therapists make a step-by-step effort to correct negative thoughts that lead to depression or similar problems. At first, a client is taught to recognize and keep track of her or his own thoughts. The client and therapist then look for ideas and beliefs that cause depression, anger, and avoidance. For example, here's how a therapist might challenge all-or-nothing thinking (Burns & Persons, 1982):

Patient: I'm feeling even more depressed. No one wants to hire me, and I can't even clean up my apartment. I feel completely incompetent!

Cognitive therapy A therapy directed at changing the maladaptive thoughts, beliefs, and feelings that underlie emotional and behavioural problems.

Therapist: I see. The fact that you are unemployed and have a messy apartment proves that you are completely incompetent?

Patient: Well … I can see that doesn't add up.

Next, clients are asked to gather information to test their beliefs. For instance, a depressed person might list his or her activities for a week. The list is then used to challenge all-or-nothing thoughts, such as "I had a terrible week" or "I'm a complete failure." With more coaching, clients learn to alter their thoughts in ways that improve their moods, actions, and relationships.

Cognitive therapy is as effective as drugs for treating many cases of depression. More important, according to Canadian psychologists, people who have adopted new thinking patterns are less likely to become depressed again—a benefit that drugs can't impart (Dozois & Dobson, 2004).

In an alternative approach, cognitive therapists look for an absence of effective coping skills and thinking patterns, not for the presence of self-defeating thoughts (Dobson, Backs-Dermott, & Dozois, 2000). The aim is to teach clients how to cope with anger, depression, shyness, stress, and similar problems. Stress inoculation, which was described in Chapter 12 (page 507), is a good example of this approach.

Cognitive therapy is a rapidly expanding specialty. Before we leave the topic, let's explore another widely used cognitive therapy.

Rational-Emotive Behaviour Therapy

Rational-emotive behaviour therapy (REBT) attempts to change irrational beliefs that cause emotional problems. According to Albert Ellis (1995, 2004), the basic idea of rational-emotive behaviour therapy is as easy as A-B-C. Ellis assumes that people become unhappy and develop self-defeating habits because they have unrealistic or faulty beliefs.

How are beliefs important? Ellis analyzes problems in this way: The letter A stands for an activating experience, which the person assumes to be the cause of C, an emotional consequence. For instance, a person who is rejected (the activating experience) feels depressed, threatened, or hurt (the consequence). Rational-emotive behaviour therapy shows the client that the real problem is what comes between A and C: In between is B, the client's irrational and unrealistic beliefs. In this example, an unrealistic belief leading to unnecessary suffering is "I must be loved and approved by almost everyone at all times." REBT holds that events do not cause us to have feelings. We feel as we do because of our beliefs (Kottler, 2004). (For some examples, see Using Psychology: "Ten Irrational Beliefs.")

Ellis (1979, 2004) says that most irrational beliefs come from three core ideas, each of which is unrealistic:

1. I must perform well and be approved of by significant others. If I don't, then it is awful, I cannot stand it, and I am a rotten person.
2. You must treat me fairly. When you don't, it is horrible, and I cannot bear it.
3. Conditions must be the way I want them to be. It is terrible when they are not, and I cannot stand living in such an awful world.

It's easy to see that such beliefs can lead to much grief and needless suffering in a less-than-perfect world. Rational-emotive behaviour therapists are very directive in their attempts to change clients' irrational beliefs and "self-talk." The therapist may directly attack clients' logic, challenge their thinking, confront them with evidence contrary to their beliefs, and even assign "homework." Here, for instance, are some examples of statements that dispute irrational beliefs (after Kottler, 2004):

- "Where is the evidence that you are a loser just because you didn't do well this one time?"
- "Who said the world should be fair? That's your rule."
- "What are you telling yourself to make you feel so upset?"
- "Is it really terrible that things aren't working out as you would like? Or is it just inconvenient?"

Rational-emotive behaviour therapy (REBT) An approach that states that irrational beliefs cause many emotional problems and that such beliefs must be changed or abandoned.

Ten Irrational Beliefs—Which Do You Hold?

Rational-emotive behaviour therapists have identified numerous beliefs that commonly lead to emotional upsets and conflicts. See if you recognize any of the following irrational beliefs:

1. I must be loved and approved by almost every significant person in my life or it's awful and I'm worthless. *Example:* "One of my roommates doesn't seem to like me. I must be a total zero."

2. I should be completely competent and achieving in all ways to be a worthwhile person. *Example:* "I don't understand my chemistry class. I guess I really am a stupid person."

3. Certain people I must deal with are thoroughly bad and should be severely blamed and punished for it. *Example:* "The old man next door is such a pain. I'm going to play my stereo even louder the next time he complains."

4. It is awful and upsetting when things are not the way I would very much like them to be. *Example:* "I should have gotten an A in that class. The teacher is unfair."

5. My unhappiness is always caused by external events; I cannot control my emotional reactions. *Example:* "You make me feel awful. I would be happy if it weren't for you."

6. If something unpleasant happens, I should keep dwelling on it. *Example:* "I'll never forget the time my boss insulted me. I think about it every day at work."

7. It is easier to avoid difficulties and responsibilities than to face them. *Example:* "I don't know why my wife seems angry. Maybe it will just pass by if I ignore it."

8. I should depend on others who are stronger than I am. *Example:* "I couldn't survive if he left me."

9. Because something once strongly affected my life, it will do so indefinitely. *Example:* "My girlfriend dumped me during my first year in university. I don't know if I can ever trust a woman again."

10. There is always a perfect solution to human problems and it is awful if this solution is not found. *Example:* "I'm so depressed about politics in this country. It all seems hopeless." (Adapted from Beck, 2002; Ellis, 2004; Rohsenow & Smith, 1982.)

If any of the listed beliefs sound familiar, you may be creating unnecessary emotional distress for yourself by holding on to unrealistic expectations.

Many of us would probably do well to give up our irrational beliefs. Improved self-acceptance and a tolerance of daily annoyances are the benefits of doing so. (See Clinical File: "Overcoming the Gambler's Fallacy.")

Overcoming the Gambler's Fallacy

Seventeen-year-old Jonathan just lost his shirt again. This time he did it playing online blackjack. Jonathan started out making $5 bets and then doubled his bet over and over. Surely, he thought, his luck would eventually change. However, he ran out of money after just eight hands, having lost more than $1000. Last week he lost a lot of money playing Texas Hold'em. Now Jonathan is in tears—he has lost most of his summer earnings, and he is worried about having to drop out of school and tell his parents about his losses. Jonathan has had to admit that he is part of the growing ranks of underage gambling addicts (LaBrie & Shaffer, 2007; Wilber & Potenza, 2006).

Like many problem gamblers, Jonathan suffers from several cognitive distortions related to gambling. Here are some of his mistaken beliefs (adapted from Toneatto, 2002):

Magnified gambling skill: Your self-confidence is exaggerated, despite the fact that you lose persistently.

Attribution errors: You ascribe your wins to skill but blame losses on bad luck.

Gambler's fallacy: You believe that a string of losses must soon be followed by wins.

Selective memory: You remember your wins but forget your losses.

Overinterpretation of cues: You put too much faith in irrelevant cues such as bodily sensations or a feeling that your next bet will be a winner.

Luck as a trait: You believe that you are a "lucky" person in general.

Probability biases: You have incorrect beliefs about randomness and chance events.

Do you have any of these mistaken beliefs? Taken together, Jonathan's cognitive distortions created an illusion of control. That is, he believed that if he worked hard enough, he could figure out how to win. Fortunately, a cognitive therapist helped Jonathan *cognitively restructure* his beliefs. He now no longer believes he can control chance events. Jonathan still gambles a bit, but he does so only recreationally, keeping his losses within his budget and enjoying himself in the process.

The value of cognitive approaches is further illustrated by three techniques (covert sensitization, thought stopping, and covert reinforcement) described in this chapter's Psychology in Action section. A little later on you can see what you think of them.

GROUP THERAPY—PEOPLE WHO NEED PEOPLE

Group therapy is psychotherapy done with more than one person. Most of the therapies we have discussed can be adapted for use in groups. Psychologists first tried working with groups because there was a shortage of therapists. Surprisingly, group therapy has turned out to be just as effective as individual therapy. In addition, it offers some special advantages (McRoberts, Burlingame, & Hoag, 1998).

What are the advantages of group therapy? In group therapy, a person can act out or directly experience problems. Doing so often produces insights that might not occur from merely talking about a person's difficulties. In addition, other group members with similar problems can offer support and useful input (McCluskey, 2002). For reasons such as these, a number of specialized groups have emerged. Because they range from Alcoholics Anonymous to Marriage Encounter, we will look at only a few examples.

Psychodrama

One of the first groups was developed by Jacob L. Moreno (1953), who called his technique psychodrama. In **psychodrama,** clients act out personal conflicts with others who play supporting roles. Through **role-playing** the client re-enacts incidents that cause problems in real life. For example, Don, a troubled teenager, might act out a typical family fight, with the therapist playing his mother and with other clients playing his father, brothers, and sisters. Moreno believed that insights gained in this way transfer to real-life situations.

Therapists using psychodrama often find role reversals especially helpful. A **role reversal** involves taking the part of another person to learn how she or he feels. For instance, Don might role-play his father or mother in order to better understand their feelings. A related method is

<SURVEY QUESTION
How is psychotherapy done with groups of people?

Group therapy Psychotherapy conducted in a group setting to make therapeutic use of group dynamics.

Psychodrama A therapy in which clients act out personal conflicts and feelings in the presence of others who play supporting roles.

Role-playing The dramatic enactment or re-enactment of significant life events.

Role reversal Taking the role of another person to learn how one's own behaviour appears from the other person's perspective.

A group therapy session. Group members offer mutual support while sharing problems and insights.

the **mirror technique,** in which clients observe another person re-enact their behaviour. Thus, Don might briefly join the audience and watch as another group member plays his role. This would allow him to see himself as others do. Later, the group may summarize what happened and reflect on its meaning (Turner, 1997).

Family Therapy

Family relationships are the source of great pleasure and, all too often, of great pain for many people. In **family therapy,** parents and children work as a group to resolve the problems of each family member. Family therapy tends to be brief and focused on specific problems, such as frequent fights or a depressed teenager. For some types of problems, family therapy may be superior to other approaches (Pinsof, Wynne, & Hambright, 1996).

Family therapists believe that a problem experienced by one family member is really the whole family's problem. If the entire pattern of behaviour in a family doesn't change, improvements in any single family member may not last. Thus, family members work together to improve communication, to change destructive patterns, and to see themselves and each other in new ways. This helps them reshape distorted perceptions and interactions directly, with the very persons with whom they have troubled relationships (Goldenberg & Goldenberg, 2004).

Does the therapist work with the whole family at once? Family therapists treat the family as a unit, but they may not meet with the entire family at each session. If a family crisis is at hand, the therapist may first try to identify the most resourceful family members, who can help solve the immediate problem. The therapist and family members may then work on resolving more basic conflicts and on improving family relationships (Dies, 1995).

Group Awareness Training

During the 1960s and 1970s, the human potential movement led many people to seek personal growth experiences. Often, their interest was expressed by participation in sensitivity training or encounter groups.

What is the difference between sensitivity groups and encounter groups? Sensitivity groups tend to be less confrontive than encounter groups. Participants in **sensitivity groups** take part in exercises that gently enlarge self-awareness and sensitivity to others. For example, in a "trust walk," participants expand their confidence in others by allowing themselves to be led around while blindfolded.

Encounter groups are based on an honest expression of feelings, and intensely personal communication may take place. Typically, the emphasis is on tearing down defences and false fronts. Because there is a danger of hostile confrontation, participation is safest when members are carefully screened and a trained leader guides the group. Encounter group "casualties" are rare, but they do occur (Shaffer & Galinsky, 1989).

In business settings, psychologists still use the basic principles of sensitivity and encounter groups—truth, self-awareness, and self-determination—to improve employee relationships. Specially designed encounter groups for married couples are also widely held (Harway, 2004).

There has also been much public interest in various forms of large-group awareness training (Finkelstein, Wenegrat, & Yalom, 1982). **Large-group awareness training** refers to programs that claim to increase self-awareness and facilitate constructive personal change. Lifespring, Actualizations, the Forum, and similar commercial programs are well-known examples. Like the smaller groups that preceded them, large-group training combines psychological exercises, confrontation, new viewpoints, and group dynamics to promote personal change.

Are sensitivity, encounter, and awareness groups really psychotherapies? These experiences tend to be positive, but they produce only moderate benefits (Faith, Wong, & Carpenter,

Mirror technique Observing another person re-enact one's own behaviour, like a character in a play; designed to help persons see themselves more clearly.

Family therapy A technique in which all family members participate, both individually and as a group, to change destructive relationships and communication patterns.

Sensitivity group A group experience consisting of exercises designed to increase self-awareness and sensitivity to others.

Encounter group A group experience that emphasizes intensely honest interchanges among participants regarding feelings and reactions to one another.

Large-group awareness training Any of a number of programs (many of them commercialized) that claim to increase self-awareness and facilitate constructive personal change.

1995). Moreover, many of the claimed benefits may result from the **placebo effect,** in which improvement is based on a client's belief that therapy will help. Positive expectations, a break in daily routine, and an excuse to act differently can have quite an impact. Also, less ambitious goals may be easier to attain. For example, one program succeeded in teaching stress-management techniques in a large-group setting (Timmerman, Emmelkamp, & Sanderman, 1998). Because of their versatility, groups will undoubtedly continue to be a major tool for solving problems and improving lives (Corey, 2008).

> **Therapy placebo effect**
> Improvement caused not by the actual process of therapy but by a client's expectation that therapy will help.

PSYCHOTHERAPY—AN OVERVIEW

How effective is psychotherapy? Judging the outcome of therapy is tricky. The findings of one survey indicated that nearly nine out of ten people who have sought mental health care say their lives improved as a result of the treatment (Kotkin, Daviet, & Gurin, 1996). Unfortunately, you can't just take people's word for it. (See Critical Thinking: "How Do We Know Therapy Actually Works?") Nevertheless, there is ample evidence that therapy is beneficial. Hundreds of studies show a strong pattern of positive effects for psychotherapy and counselling (Barlow, 2004; Lambert & Ogles, 2004).

<SURVEY QUESTION
What do various therapies have in common?

More specific benefits of psychotherapy include the following:

- For certain psychological disorders, psychotherapy provides just as good results as drug treatment, but psychotherapy is 10 to 50 percent less expensive.
- Fewer people drop out during treatment with psychotherapy than they do with drug therapy.
- Psychotherapy can also help people who suffer from a variety of medical conditions, such as headaches, hypertension, arthritis, diabetes, and chronic low-back pain.
- After successful treatment with psychotherapy, people reduce their use of medical services, which saves the overburdened health care system a considerable sum of money (Canadian Psychological Association, 2002).

In general, then, psychotherapy works (Kopta et al., 1999). Of course, results vary in individual cases. For some people therapy is immensely helpful; for others it is unsuccessful; overall it is effective for more people than not. Speaking more subjectively, a real success, in which a person's life is changed for the better, can be worth the frustration of several cases in which little progress is made.

CRITICAL THINKING

How Do We Know Therapy Actually Works?

Why is it risky to believe people who say their therapy was effective? An old joke among doctors is that a cold lasts a week without treatment and seven days with it. Perhaps the same is true of therapy. Someone who feels better after six months of therapy may have experienced a spontaneous remission—they just feel better because so much time has passed. Or perhaps the crisis that triggered the therapy is now nearly forgotten. Or maybe some sort of therapy placebo effect has occurred. Also, it's possible that the person has received help from other people, such as family, friends, or clergy.

To find out if therapy works, we could randomly place clients in an experimental group that receives therapy and a control group that does not. When this is done, the control group may show some improvement, even without receiving therapy (Lambert & Ogles,

2004). Thus, we can conclude that the therapy is effective only if people in the experimental group improve more than those in the control group.

But isn't it unethical to withhold treatment from someone who really needs therapy? One way to deal with this is to use a *waiting-list control group*. In this case, people who are waiting to see a therapist are compared with those who receive therapy. Later, those on the waiting list will eventually also receive some sort of therapy.

If we combine the results of many experiments, it becomes clear that therapy *is* effective (Lipsey & Wilson, 1993). In addition, studies have revealed that some therapies work best for specific problems (Bradley et al., 2005; Eddy et al., 2004). For example, cognitive-behavioural and drug therapies are most helpful in treating obsessive-compulsive disorder.

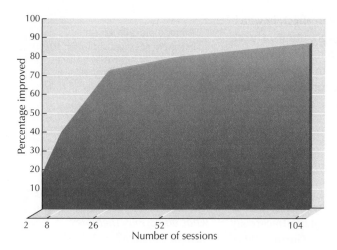

»**FIGURE 13.6** The dose–improvement relationship in psycho-therapy. This graph shows the percentage of patients who improved after varying numbers of therapy sessions. Notice that the most rapid improvement took place during the first six months of once-a-week sessions. (From Howard et al., 1986.)

It is common to think of therapy as a long, slow process. But this is not always the case. Research shows that about 50 percent of all patients feel better after only eight therapy sessions. After 26 sessions, roughly 75 percent improve (Howard et al., 1986) (see Figure 13.6). The typical "dose" of therapy is one hourly session per week. This means that the majority of patients improve after six months of therapy, and half feel better in just two months. Keep in mind, however, that people often suffer for several years before seeking help. In view of this, such rapid improvement is impressive.

Core Features of Psychotherapy

What do psychotherapies have in common? We have sampled only a few of the many therapies in use today. For a summary of major differences among psychotherapies, see Table 13.2. To add to your understanding, let's briefly summarize what all techniques have in common.

All the psychotherapies we have discussed include some combination of the following goals: restoring hope, courage, and optimism; gaining insight; resolving conflicts; improving one's sense of self; changing unacceptable patterns of behaviour; finding purpose; mending interpersonal relationships; and learning to approach problems rationally (Frank & Frank, 2004; Seligman, 1998). To accomplish these goals, psychotherapies offer the following:

1. Therapy provides a caring relationship between the client and therapist, called a therapeutic alliance. Emotional rapport, warmth, friendship, understanding, acceptance, and empathy are the basis for this relationship. The **therapeutic alliance** unites the client and therapist as they work together to solve the client's problems. The strength of this alliance has a major impact on whether therapy succeeds (Kozart, 2002; Meier et al., 2006).

2. Therapy offers a protective setting in which emotional catharsis (release) can take place. Therapy is a sanctuary in which the client is free to express fears, anxieties, and personal secrets without fearing rejection or loss of confidentiality (Weiss, 1990).

3. All therapies to some extent offer an explanation or rationale for the client's suffering. Additionally, they propose a line of action that will end this suffering.

Therapeutic alliance A caring relationship that unites a therapist and a client in working to solve the client's problems.

■ Table 13.2   **Comparison of Psychotherapies**

	Insight or Action?	Directive or Non-directive?	Individual or Group?	Therapy's Strength*
Psychoanalysis	Insight	Directive	Individual	Searching for root causes of problems
Brief psychodynamic therapy	Insight	Directive	Individual	Productive use of conflict
Client-centred therapy	Insight	Non-directive	Both	Acceptance, empathy
Existential therapy	Insight	Both	Individual	Personal empowerment
Gestalt therapy	Insight	Directive	Both	Focus on immediate awareness
Behaviour therapy	Action	Directive	Both	Observable changes in behaviour
Cognitive therapy	Action	Directive	Individual	Constructive guidance
Rational-emotive behaviour therapy	Action	Directive	Individual	Clarity of thinking and goals
Psychodrama	Insight	Directive	Group	Constructive re-enactments
Family therapy	Both	Directive	Group	Shared responsibility for problems

*This column based in part on Andrews (1989).

4. Therapy provides clients with a new perspective about themselves and their situations and a chance to practise new behaviours (Crencavage & Norcross, 1990). Insights gained during therapy can bring about lasting changes in clients' lives (Grande et al., 2003).

If you recall that our discussion began with trepanning and demonology, it is clear that therapies for people with psychological problems have come a long way. Still, the search for ways to improve psychotherapy remains an urgent challenge for those who devote their lives to helping others.

Basic Counselling Skills

A number of general helping skills can be distilled from the various approaches to therapy. These are points to keep in mind if you would like to comfort a person in distress, such as a troubled friend or relative (see Table 13.3).

Active Listening
People frequently talk "at" each other without really listening. A person with problems needs to be heard. Make a sincere effort to listen to and understand the person. Try to accept the person's message without judging it or leaping to conclusions. Let the person know you are listening, through eye contact, posture, your tone of voice, and your replies (Kottler, 2004).

Clarify the Problem
People who have a clear idea of what is wrong in their lives are more likely to discover solutions. Try to understand the problem from the person's point of view. As you do, check your understanding often. For example, you might ask, "Are you saying that you feel depressed just at school? Or in general?" Remember, a problem well defined is often half solved.

Focus on Feelings
Feelings are neither right nor wrong. By focusing on feelings, you can encourage the outpouring of emotion that is the basis for catharsis. Passing judgment on what is said just makes people defensive. For example, a friend confides that she has failed a test. Perhaps you know that she studies very little. If you say, "Just study more and you would do better," she will probably become defensive or hostile. Much more can be accomplished by saying, "You must feel very frustrated" or simply "How do you feel about it?" (Ivey & Galvin, 1984).

Avoid Giving Advice
Many people mistakenly think that they must solve problems for others. Remember that your goal is to provide understanding and support, not solutions. Of course, it is reasonable to give advice when you are asked for it, but beware of the trap of the "Why don't you …? Yes, but…" game. According to psychotherapist Eric Berne (1964), this "game" follows a pattern: Someone says, "I have this problem." You say, "Why don't you do thus and so?" The person replies, "Yes, but …" and then tells you why your suggestion won't work. If you make a new suggestion, the reply will once again be "Yes, but. …" Obviously, the person either knows more about his or her personal situation than you do or he or she has reasons for avoiding your advice. The student described earlier knows she needs to study. Her problem is to understand why she doesn't want to study.

Accept the Person's Frame of Reference
W. I. Thomas said, "Things perceived as real are real in their effects." Try to resist imposing your views on the problems of others. Since we all live in different psychological worlds, there is no "correct" view of a life situation. A person who feels that her or his viewpoint has been understood feels freer to examine it objectively and to question it. Accepting and understanding the perspective of another person can be especially difficult when cultural differences exist (Draguns et al., 2004). (See Human Diversity: "Therapy and Culture—A Bad Case of *Ifufunyane*.")

■ Table 13.3 **Helping Behaviours**

To help another person gain insight into a personal problem, it is valuable to keep the following comparison in mind.

Behaviours That Help	Behaviours That Hinder
Active listening	Probing painful topics
Acceptance	Judging/moralizing
Reflecting feelings	Criticism
Open-ended questioning	Threats
Supportive statements	Rejection
Respect	Ridicule/sarcasm
Patience	Impatience
Genuineness	Placing blame
Paraphrasing	Opinionated statements

(Adapted from Kottler, 2004.)

Therapy and Culture—A Bad Case of *Ifufunyane*

At the age of 23, the patient was clearly suffering from *ifufunyane,* a form of bewitchment common in the Xhosa culture of South Africa. However, he was treated at a local hospital by psychiatrists, who said he had schizophrenia and gave him antipsychotic drugs. The drugs helped, but his family shunned his fancy medical treatment and took him to a traditional healer who gave him herbs for his ifufunyane. Unfortunately, he got worse and was readmitted to the hospital. This time, the psychiatrists included the patient's family in his treatment. Together, they agreed to treat him with a combination of antipsychotic drugs *and* traditional herbs. This time, the patient got much better and his ifufunyane was alleviated too (Niehaus et al. 2005).

As this example illustrates, **culturally skilled therapists** are adept at working with clients from various cultural backgrounds. To be culturally skilled, a counsellor must be able to do all of the following (American Psychological Association, 2003; Draguns et al., 2004; Fowers & Davidov, 2006):

- Adapt traditional theories and techniques to meet the needs of clients from non-European ethnic or racial groups.

- Be aware of his or her own cultural values and biases.
- Establish rapport with a person from a different cultural background.
- Be open to cultural differences without resorting to stereotypes.
- Treat members of people from minority groups as individuals.
- Be aware of a client's ethnic identity and degree of acculturation to the majority society.
- Use existing helping resources within a cultural group to support efforts to resolve problems.

Let's illustrate this with an example. Rod McCormick has looked at how psychotherapy can best be adapted to suit the unique needs and cultural requirements of the First Nations peoples of British Columbia. He notes that to First Nations peoples, healing means having a sense of balance, feeling interconnected, and being spiritual. Therapists should take this particular world view into account if they are to achieve success in therapy (McCormick, 1996). One successful program, designed to treat alcohol and drug abuse problems of First Nations peoples, fosters a sense of meaning and encourages traditional cultural values (McCormick, 2000).

Culturally skilled therapist A therapist who has the awareness, knowledge, and skills necessary to treat clients from diverse cultural backgrounds.

Teams of psychologists and counsellors are often assembled to provide support to victims of major accidents and natural disasters. Because their work is stressful and often heart-wrenching, relief workers also benefit from on-site counselling. Expressing emotions and talking about feelings are major elements of disaster counselling. The counsellor shown here is supporting a victim of the tornado that touched down in Pine Lake, Alberta, in July 2000.

Reflect Thoughts and Feelings

One of the best things you can do when offering support to another person is to give feedback by simply restating what is said. This is also a good way to encourage a person to talk. If your friend seems to be at a loss for words, restate or paraphrase her or his last sentence. Here's an example:

> **Friend:** I'm really down about school. I can't get interested in any of my classes. I flunked my French test, and somebody stole my notebook for psychology.
>
> **You:** You're really upset about school, aren't you?
>
> **Friend:** Yeah, and my parents are hassling me about my grades again.
>
> **You:** You're feeling pressured by your parents?
>
> **Friend:** Yeah, damn.
>
> **You:** It must make you angry to be pressured by them.

As simple as this sounds, it is very helpful to someone trying to sort out feelings. Try it. If nothing else, you'll develop a reputation as a fantastic conversationalist!

Silence

Studies show that counsellors tend to wait longer before responding than do people in everyday conversations. Pauses of five seconds or more are not unusual, and interrupting is rare. Listening patiently lets the person feel unhurried and encourages him or her to speak freely (Goodman, 1984).

Questions

Because your goal is to encourage free expression, open questions tend to be the most helpful (Goodman, 1984). A closed question is one that can be answered yes or no. Open questions call for an open-ended reply. Say, for example, that a friend tells you, "I feel like my boss has it in for me at work." A closed question would be "Oh yeah? So, are you going to quit?" Open questions, such as "Do you want to tell me about it?" or "How do you feel about it?" are more likely to be helpful.

Maintain Confidentiality

Your efforts to help will be wasted if you fail to respect the privacy of someone who has confided in you. Put yourself in the person's place. Don't gossip.

These guidelines are not an invitation to play "junior therapist." Professional therapists are trained to approach serious problems with skills far exceeding those described here. However, the points made help define the qualities of a therapeutic relationship. They also emphasize that each of us can supply two of the greatest mental health resources available at any cost: friendship and honest communication.

MEDICAL THERAPIES—PSYCHIATRIC CARE

Psychotherapy may be applied to anything from a brief crisis to a full-scale psychosis. However, most psychotherapists do not treat patients with major mood disorders, schizophrenia, or other severe conditions. Major mental disorders are more often treated medically.

Three main types of **somatic** (bodily) **therapy** are pharmacotherapy, electrical stimulation therapy, and psychosurgery. Somatic therapy is often done in the context of psychiatric hospitalization. All the somatic approaches have a strong medical slant and are typically administered by psychiatrists.

<SURVEY QUESTION
How do psychiatrists treat psychological disorders?

Drugs

The atmosphere in psychiatric wards and hospitals changed radically in the mid-1950s with the widespread adoption of pharmacotherapy (FAR-meh-koe-THER-eh-pee). **Pharmacotherapy** refers to the use of drugs to treat emotional disturbances. Drugs may relieve the anxiety attacks and other discomforts of milder psychological disorders. They are also used to combat schizophrenia and major mood disorders.

What sorts of drugs are used in pharmacotherapy? Three major types of drugs are used. **Minor tranquillizers** (such as Valium) produce relaxation or reduce anxiety. **Antidepressants** are mood-elevating drugs that combat depression. **Antipsychotics** (also called major tranquillizers) have tranquillizing effects and reduce hallucinations and delusions. (See Table 13.4 for examples of some drugs used to treat mental disorders.) In addition, lithium, which functions as a mood stabilizer, is the preferred mode of treatment for bipolar disorder.

Are drugs a valid approach to treatment? Drugs have shortened hospital stays, and they have greatly improved the chances that people will recover from major psychological disorders. Drug therapy has also made it possible for many people to return to the community, where they can be treated on an outpatient basis.

Somatic therapy Any bodily therapy, such as drug therapy, electroconvulsive therapy, or psychosurgery.

Pharmacotherapy The use of drugs to alleviate the symptoms of emotional disturbance.

Minor tranquillizers Drugs (such as Valium) that produce relaxation or reduce anxiety.

Antidepressants Mood-elevating drugs.

Antipsychotics Drugs that, in addition to having tranquillizing effects, tend to reduce hallucinations and delusional thinking. (Also called major tranquillizers.)

■ Table 13.4	**Commonly Prescribed Psychiatric Drugs**	
Class	**Examples (Trade Names)**	**Effects**
Minor tranquillizers (anti-anxiety drugs)	Ativan, Halcion, Librium, Restoril, Valium, Xanax	Reduce anxiety, tension, fear
Antidepressants	Anafranil, Elavil, Nardil, Norpramin, Parnate, Paxil, Prozac, Tofranil, Zoloft	Counteract depression
Antipsychotics (major tranquillizers)	Clozaril, Haldol, Mellaril, Navane, Risperdal, Thorazine	Reduce agitation, delusions, hallucinations, thought disorders

Electroconvulsive therapy (ECT) A treatment for severe depression, consisting of an electric shock passed directly through the brain, which induces a convulsion.

Limitations of Drug Therapy

Regardless of their benefits, all drugs involve risks. For example, 15 percent of patients taking major tranquillizers for long periods develop a neurological disorder that causes rhythmic facial and mouth movements (Chakos et al., 1996). Similarly, the drug Clozaril (clozapine) can relieve the symptoms of schizophrenia in some previously untreatable cases, but 2 out of 100 patients taking the drug develop a potentially fatal blood disease (Ginsberg, 2006).

Antidepressants and minor tranquillizers also produce side effects. For example, Fluoxetine, or Prozac, which belongs to a class of drugs called the selective serotonin reuptake inhibitors (SSRIs), is used in the treatment of depression, panic disorder, and obsessive-compulsive disorder. It may lead some people to feel extremely uneasy or hyper, and can cause nausea, stomach problems, lowered sex drive, decreased appetite, insomnia, and other discomforting symptoms. Finally, minor tranquillizers such as diazepam and Valium are used in the management of severe levels of anxiety, and their intake is linked to drowsiness and problems with motor coordination and balance (Nolen-Hoeksema & Rector, 2008).

Given these side effects, is the risk worth it? Many experts think it is, because major psychological disorders can be very disabling and affect almost all aspects of life. It's possible, of course, that newer drugs will improve the risk-benefit ratio in the treatment of severe problems like schizophrenia. For example, the drug Risperdal (risperidone) appears to be as effective as Clozaril, without the lethal risk. But even the best new drugs are not cure-alls. They help some people and relieve some problems, but not all. It is noteworthy that for serious mental disorders a combination of medication and psychotherapy almost always works better than drugs alone. Nevertheless, where schizophrenia and major mood disorders are concerned, drugs will undoubtedly remain the primary mode of treatment (Vasa, Carlino, & Pine, 2006; Walker et al., 2004).

Electrical Stimulation Therapy

In contrast to drug therapies, electrical stimulation therapies achieve their effects by altering the electrical activity of the brain. Electroconvulsive therapy is the first, and most dramatic, of these therapies.

Electroshock

In **electroconvulsive therapy (ECT),** a 150-volt electrical current is passed through the brain for slightly less than a second. This rather drastic medical treatment for severe depression triggers a convulsion and causes the patient to lose consciousness for a short time. Muscle relaxants and sedative drugs are given before ECT to soften its impact. Treatments are given in a series of six to eight sessions spread over three to four weeks.

How does shock help? Actually, it is the seizure activity that is believed to be helpful. Proponents of ECT claim that shock-induced seizures alter the biochemical balance in the brain, bringing an end to severe depression and suicidal behaviour (Fink, 2000) as well as improving long-term quality of life (McCall et al., 2006). Others have charged that ECT works only by confusing patients so they can't remember why they were depressed (Kohn, 1988).

The ECT Debate

Many people consider ECT a distasteful procedure, and not all professionals support its use. However, most experts seem to agree on the following: (1) At best, ECT produces only temporary improvement—it gets the patient out of a bad spot, but it must be combined with other treatments. (2) ECT can cause memory losses in some patients. (3) ECT should be used only as a last resort after other treatments have failed. (4) To lower the chance of a relapse, ECT should be followed by antidepressant drugs (Sackeim et al., 2001). All told, ECT is considered by many to be a valid treatment for selected cases of depression—especially for highly suicidal patients (Pagnin et al., 2004). It's interesting to note that most ECT patients feel that the treatment helped them. Most, in fact, would have it done again (Bernstein et al., 1998).

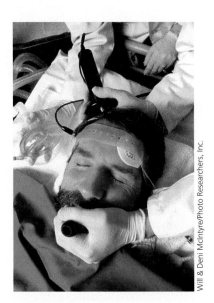

In electroconvulsive therapy, electrodes are attached to the head and a brief electrical current is passed through the brain. ECT is used in the treatment of severe depression.

Will & Deni McIntyre/Photo Researchers, Inc.

Implanted Electrodes

Unlike ECT, implanting electrodes requires surgery but allows for electrical stimulation of precisely targeted brain regions. (See Chapter 2 for more information about electrical stimulation of the brain.) In one study, depressed patients who hadn't benefited from drug therapy and ECT improved when a specific brain region was stimulated (Mayberg et al., 2005). This treatment procedure has been pioneered by researchers in Toronto. Stimulating pleasure centres in the brains of another group of patients also relieved depression (Schlaepfer et al., 2008). Also unlike ECT, implanted electrodes can be used to treat disorders other than depression, such as obsessive-compulsive disorder (Nuttin et al., 1999).

Psychosurgery

The most extreme medical treatment is **psychosurgery** (any surgical alteration of the brain). The best-known psychosurgery is the lobotomy. In the **prefrontal lobotomy,** the frontal lobes were surgically disconnected from other brain areas. This procedure was supposed to calm persons who didn't respond to any other type of treatment.

When the lobotomy was first introduced in the 1930s, there were enthusiastic claims for its success. But later studies suggested that some patients were calmed, some showed no change, and some became "vegetables." Lobotomies also produced a high rate of undesirable side effects, such as seizures, extreme lack of emotional response, major personality changes, and stupor. At about the same time that such problems became apparent, the first antipsychotic drugs became available. Soon after that, the lobotomy was abandoned (Mashour, Walker, & Martuza, 2005).

To what extent is psychosurgery used now? Psychosurgery is still considered valid by many neurosurgeons. However, most now use **deep lesioning,** in which small target areas are destroyed in the brain's interior. The appeal of deep lesioning is that it can have fairly specific effects. Patients suffering from a severe type of obsessive-compulsive disorder may be helped by psychosurgery (Dougherty et al., 2002).

It is worth remembering that psychosurgery cannot be reversed. A drug can be given or taken away and electrical stimulation can be turned off. You can't take back psychosurgery. Many critics argue that psychosurgery should be banned altogether. Others continue to report success with brain surgery. All things considered, it is perhaps most accurate, even after decades of use, to describe psychosurgery as an experimental technique. Nevertheless, it may have value as a remedy for some very specific disorders (Fenton, 1998; Mashour et al., 2005).

Hospitalization

For major psychological disorders, therapy is often best done in a controlled setting, such as a psychiatric hospital. Hospitalization involves placing a person in a protected, therapeutic environment staffed by mental health professionals. This, by itself, can be a form of treatment. Staying in a hospital removes patients from situations that may be provoking or maintaining their problems. For example, people with drug addictions may find it nearly impossible to resist the temptations for drug abuse in their daily lives. Hospitalization can help them make a clean break from their former self-destructive behaviour patterns (André et al., 2003).

At its best, the hospital is a sanctuary that provides diagnosis, support, refuge, and therapy. This is generally true of psychiatric units in general hospitals. At worst, confinement to an institution can be a brutalizing experience that leaves people less prepared to face the world than they were before they arrived.

Psychosurgery Any surgical alteration of the brain designed to bring about desirable behavioural or emotional changes.

Prefrontal lobotomy An antiquated surgery in which portions of the frontal lobes were destroyed or disconnected from other brain areas.

Deep lesioning The use of an electrode (electrified wire) to destroy small areas deep within the brain.

© Peter Turnley/CORBIS

Depending on the quality of the institution, hospitalization may be a refuge or a brutalizing experience.

Partial hospitalization An approach in which patients receive treatment at a hospital during the day, but return home at night.

Deinstitutionalization Reduced use of full-time commitment to mental institutions to treat mental disorders.

Halfway house A community-based facility for individuals making the transition from an institution (psychiatric hospital, prison, and so forth) to independent living.

Community mental health centre A facility offering a wide range of mental health services, such as prevention, counselling, consultation, and crisis intervention.

Crisis intervention Skilled management of a psychological emergency.

In most instances, hospitals are best used as a last resort, after other forms of treatment within the community have been exhausted. Actually, most psychiatric patients do as well with short-term hospitalization as they do with longer periods. For this reason, the average stay in psychiatric hospitals is now just 20 days, rather than 3 to 4 months, as it was 20 years ago.

A new trend in psychiatric treatment is **partial hospitalization.** In this approach, patients spend only part of their time at the hospital. Even for the acutely ill, overnight hospital stays are becoming less common. For example, some patients spend their days in the hospital, but go home at night. Others attend therapy sessions during the evening. A major advantage of partial hospitalization is that patients can go home and practise what they've been learning. Gradually, the amount of time patients spend at the hospital is reduced. Eventually, most people return to normal life. Overall, partial hospitalization is comparable to full hospitalization in its effectiveness (Kiser, Heston, & Paavola, 2006).

Deinstitutionalization

In the past 35 years, the population in large psychiatric hospitals has dropped by two-thirds. This is largely a result of **deinstitutionalization,** or reduced use of full-time commitment to mental institutions. Long-term "institutionalization" can lead to dependency, isolation, and continued emotional disturbance (Chamberlin & Rogers, 1990). Deinstitutionalization was meant to remedy this problem.

How successful has deinstitutionalization been? In truth, its success has been limited (Talbott, 2004). Many provinces have reduced psychiatric hospital populations primarily as a way to save money. The upsetting result is that many chronic patients have been discharged to hostile communities without adequate care. Many former patients have joined the ranks of the homeless. Sadly, patients who trade hospitalization for unemployment, homelessness, and social isolation all too often end up re-hospitalized or in jail (Goldman, 1998).

Large psychiatric hospitals may no longer be warehouses for society's unwanted, but many former patients are no better off in bleak nursing homes, single-room hotels, board-and-care homes, shelters, or jails. Many people who are in jail or prison are mentally ill—three times the number who are in psychiatric hospitals (Human Rights Watch, 2003). These figures suggest that jails are replacing hospitals as our society's "solution" for mental illness. Yet, ironically, high-quality care is available in almost every community. As much as anything, a simple lack of money prevents large numbers of people from getting the help they need (Torrey, 1996).

Halfway houses may be a better way to ease a patient's return to the community (Anthony, Cohen, & Kennard, 1990). **Halfway houses** are short-term group living facilities for people making the transition from an institution (hospital, prison, and so forth) to independent living. Typically, they offer supervision and support, without being as restricted and medically oriented as hospitals. They also keep people near their families. Most important, halfway houses can reduce a person's chances of being readmitted to a hospital (Coursey, Ward-Alexander, & Katz, 1990).

Community Mental Health Programs

Community mental health centres are a bright spot in the area of mental health care. **Community mental health centres** offer a wide range of mental health services and psychiatric care. Such centres try to help people avoid hospitalization and find answers to mental health problems (Burns, 2004). Typically, they do this by providing short-term treatment, counselling, outpatient care, emergency services, and suicide prevention.

If it is like most, the primary aim of the mental health centre in your community is to directly aid troubled citizens. Its second goal is likely to be *prevention.* Consultation, education, and **crisis intervention** (skilled

A well-run halfway house can be a humane and cost-effective way to ease former psychiatric patients back into the community (Coursey et al., 1990).

© Ed Kashi/CORBIS

management of a psychological problem) are used to prevent problems before they become serious. Also, some centres attempt to raise the general level of mental health in a community by combating unemployment, delinquency, and drug abuse (Tausig, Michello, & Subedi, 2004).

How have community mental health centres done in meeting their goals? In practice, they have concentrated much more on providing clinical services than they have on preventing problems. This appears to be primarily the result of wavering government support (translation: money). Overall, community mental health centres have succeeded in making psychological services more accessible than ever before. Many of their programs rely on **paraprofessionals** (individuals who work in a near-professional capacity under the supervision of more highly trained staff). Some paraprofessionals are recovering addicts, recovering alcoholics, or ex-patients who have "been there." Many more are persons (paid or volunteer) who have skills in tutoring, crafts, or counselling or who are simply warm, understanding, and skilled at communication. Often, paraprofessionals are more approachable than doctors. This encourages people to seek mental health services that they might otherwise be reluctant to use (Everly, 2002).

> **Paraprofessional** An individual who works in a near-professional capacity under the supervision of a more highly trained person.

A Look Ahead

In the Psychology in Action section that follows, we will return briefly to behavioural approaches. There you will find a number of useful techniques that you may be able to apply to your own behaviour. You'll also find a discussion of when to seek professional help and how to find it. Here's your authors' professional advice: This is information you won't want to skip.

✓ STUDY BREAK Group Therapies, Psychotherapy Skills, and Medical Therapies

Reflect

Would you rather participate in individual therapy or group therapy? What advantages and disadvantages do you think each has?

Based on your own experience, how valid do you think it is to say that within families "a problem for one is a problem for all"?

What lies at the "heart" of psychotherapy? How would you describe it to a friend?

Which of the basic counselling skills do you already use? Which would improve your ability to help a person in distress?

If a family member of yours became severely depressed, what therapies would be available to him or her? What are the pros and cons of each choice?

Learning Check

1. In psychodrama, people attempt to form meaningful wholes out of disjointed thoughts, feelings, and actions. T or F?
2. Most large-group awareness trainings make use of Gestalt therapy. T or F?
3. Which therapy places great emphasis on role-playing?
   a. psychodrama
   b. awareness training
   c. family therapy
   d. encounter

4. Emotional _____ (release) in a protected setting is an element of most psychotherapies.
5. To aid a troubled friend, you should focus on facts rather than feelings, and you should critically evaluate what the person is saying to help him or her grasp reality. T or F?
6. ECT is a modern form of pharmacotherapy. T or F?
7. Currently, the frontal lobotomy is the most widely used form of psychosurgery. T or F?
8. Partial hospitalization refers to the practice of placing mental patients in halfway houses. T or F?

Critical Thinking

9. In your opinion, do psychologists have a duty to protect others who may be harmed by their clients? For example, if a patient has homicidal fantasies about his ex-wife, should she be informed?
10. In 1982, residents of Berkeley, California, voted on a referendum to ban the use of ECT within city limits. Do you think that the use of certain psychiatric treatments should be controlled by law?

Answers

1. F 2. F 3. a 4. catharsis 5. F 6. F 7. F 8. F 9. According to the law, there is a duty to protect others where a therapist could, with little effort, prevent serious harm. However, this duty can conflict with a client's rights to confidentiality and with client–therapist trust. Therapists must often make difficult choices in such situations. 10. The question of who can prescribe drugs, do surgery, and administer ECT is controlled by law. However, psychiatrists strongly object to residents, city councils, or government agencies making medical decisions.

SELF-MANAGEMENT AND SEEKING PROFESSIONAL HELP

"Throw out the snake oil, ladies and gentlemen, and throw away your troubles. Doctor B. Haviour Modification is here to put an end to all human suffering."

True? Well, not quite. Behaviour therapy is not a cure-all. Its use is often quite complicated and requires a great deal of expertise. Still, behaviour therapy offers a straightforward solution to many problems.

As mentioned elsewhere in this book, you should seek professional help when a significant problem exists. For lesser difficulties you may want to try applying behavioural principles yourself (Watson & Tharp, 2007). Let us see how this might be done.

Applying Reward and Punishment to Boost Your Willpower

"Have you ever decided to quit smoking cigarettes, watching television too much, eating too much, drinking too much, or driving too fast?"

"Well, one of those applies. I have decided several times to quit smoking."

"When have you decided?"

"Usually after I am reminded of how dangerous smoking is—like when I heard that my uncle had died of lung cancer. He smoked constantly."

"If you have decided to quit 'several times,' I assume you haven't succeeded."

"No, the usual pattern is for me to become upset about smoking and then to cut down for a day or two."

"You forget the disturbing image of your uncle's death, or whatever, and start smoking again."

"Yes, I suppose if I had an uncle die every day or so, I might actually quit!"

The use of electric shock to condition an aversion seems remote from everyday problems. Even naturally aversive actions are difficult to apply to personal behaviour. As mentioned earlier, for instance, rapid smoking is difficult for most smokers to carry out on their own. And what about a problem like overeating? It would be difficult indeed to eat enough to create a lasting aversion to overeating. (Although it's sometimes tempting to try.)

In view of such limitations, psychologists have developed an alternative procedure that can be used to curb smoking, overeating, and other habits (Cautela & Kearney, 1986; Watson & Tharp, 2007).

Covert Sensitization

In **covert sensitization,** aversive imagery is used to reduce the occurrence of an undesired response. Here's how it's done: Obtain six index cards and on each write a brief description of a scene related to the habit you wish to control. The scene should be so disturbing or disgusting that thinking about it would temporarily make you very uncomfortable about indulging in the habit. For smoking, some of the cards might read:

- I am in a doctor's office. The doctor looks at some reports and tells me I have lung cancer. He says a lung will have to be removed and sets a date for the operation.
- I am in bed under an oxygen tent. My chest feels caved in. There is a tube in my throat. I can barely breathe.
- I wake up in the morning and smoke a cigarette. I begin coughing up blood.

Other cards would continue along the same line.

For overeating, some of the cards might read:

- I am at the beach. I get up to go for a swim and I overhear people whispering to each other, "Isn't that fat disgusting?"

Covert sensitization Use of aversive imagery to reduce the occurrence of an undesired response.

- I am at a store buying clothes. I try on several things that are too small. The only things that fit look like rumpled sacks. Salespeople are staring at me.

Other cards would continue along the same line.

The trick, of course, is to get yourself to imagine or picture vividly each of these disturbing scenes several times a day. Imagining the scenes can be accomplished by placing them under stimulus control. Simply choose something you do frequently each day (such as getting a cup of coffee or getting up from your chair). Next make a rule: Before you can get a cup of coffee or get up from your chair, or whatever you have selected as a cue, you must take out your cards and vividly picture yourself engaging in the action you wish to curb (overeating or smoking, for example). Then vividly picture the scene described on the top card. Imagine the scene for 30 seconds.

After visualizing the top card, move it to the bottom so the cards are rotated. Make up new cards each week. The scenes can be made much more upsetting than the samples given here. The samples are toned down to keep you from being "grossed out."

Covert sensitization can also be used directly in situations that test your self-control. If you are trying to lose weight, for instance, you might be able to turn down a tempting dessert in this way: As you look at the dessert, visualize maggots crawling all over it. If you make this image as vivid and nauseating as possible, losing your appetite is almost a certainty. If you want to apply this technique to other situations, be aware that vomiting scenes are especially effective. Covert sensitization may sound as if you are playing games with yourself, but it can be a great help if you want to cut down on a bad habit (Cautela & Kearney, 1986; Watson & Tharp, 2007). Try it!

Thought Stopping

As discussed earlier, behaviour therapists accept that thoughts, like visible responses, can also cause trouble. Think of times when you have repeatedly put yourself down mentally or when you have been preoccupied by needless worries, fears, or other negative and upsetting thoughts. If you would like to gain control over such thoughts, thought stopping may help you do it.

In **thought stopping,** aversive stimuli are used to interrupt or prevent upsetting thoughts. The simplest thought-stopping technique makes use of mild punishment to suppress upsetting mental images and internal "talk." Simply place a large, flat elastic band around your wrist. As you go through the day, apply this rule: Each time you catch yourself thinking the upsetting image or thought, pull the elastic band away from your wrist and snap it. You need not make this terribly painful. Its value lies in drawing your attention to how often you form negative thoughts and in interrupting the flow of thoughts. Strong punishment is not required.

It seems like this procedure might be abandoned rapidly. Is there an alternative? A second thought-stopping procedure requires only that you interrupt upsetting thoughts each time they occur. Begin by setting aside time each day during which you will deliberately think the unwanted thought. As you begin to form the thought, shout "Stop!" aloud, with conviction. (Obviously, you should choose a private spot for this part of the procedure!)

Repeat the thought-stopping procedure 10 to 20 times for the first 2 or 3 days. Then switch to shouting "Stop!" covertly (to yourself) rather than aloud. Thereafter, thought stopping can be carried out throughout the day, whenever upsetting thoughts occur (Williams & Long, 1991). After several days of practice, you should be able to stop unwanted thoughts whenever they occur.

Covert Reinforcement

Earlier we discussed how punishing images can be used to decrease undesirable responses, such as smoking or overeating. Many people also find it helpful to covertly reinforce desired actions. **Covert reinforcement** is the use of positive imagery to reinforce desired behaviour. For example, suppose your target behaviour is, once again, not eating dessert. If this were the case, you could do the following (Cautela & Kearney, 1986):

> **Thought stopping** Use of aversive stimuli to interrupt or prevent upsetting thoughts.
>
> **Covert reinforcement** Using positive imagery to reinforce desired behaviour.

> Imagine that you are standing at the dessert table with your friends. As dessert is passed, you politely refuse and feel good about staying on your diet.

These images would then be followed by imagining a pleasant, reinforcing scene:

> Imagine that you are your ideal weight. You look really slim in your favourite colour and style. Someone you like says to you, "Gee, you've lost weight. I've never seen you look so good."

For many people, of course, actual direct reinforcement (as described in the Psychology in Action section of Chapter 6, page 263) is the best way to alter behaviour. Nevertheless, covert reinforcement can have similar effects. To make use of covert reinforcement, choose one or more target behaviours and rehearse them mentally. Then follow each rehearsal with a vivid, rewarding image.

Self-Directed Desensitization—Overcoming Common Fears

You have prepared for two weeks to give a speech in a large class. As your turn approaches, your hands begin to tremble. Your heart pounds and you find it difficult to breathe. You say to your body, "Relax!" What happens? Nothing!

Relaxation

The key to desensitization is relaxation. To inhibit fear, one must learn to relax. Here is a description of how the tension-release method can be used to achieve deep-muscle relaxation.

> Tense the muscles in your right arm until they tremble. Hold them tight for about five seconds and then let go. Allow your hand and arm to go limp and to relax completely. Repeat the procedure. Releasing tension two or three times will allow you to feel whether your arm muscles have relaxed. Repeat the tension-release procedure with your left arm. Compare it with your right arm. Repeat until the left arm is equally relaxed. Apply the tension-release technique to your right leg; to your left leg; to your abdomen; to your chest and shoulders. Clench and release your chin, neck, and throat. Wrinkle and release your forehead and scalp. Tighten and release your mouth and face muscles. As a last step, curl your toes and tense your feet. Then release.

Practise the tension-release method until you can achieve complete relaxation quickly (five to ten minutes).

After you have practised relaxation once a day for a week or two, you will begin to be able to tell when your body (or a group of muscles) is tense. Also, you will begin to be able to relax on command. As an alternative, you might want to try imagining a very safe, pleasant, and relaxing scene. Some people find such images as relaxing as the tension-release method (Rosenthal, 1993). Once you have learned to relax, the next step is to identify the fear you would like to control and construct a hierarchy.

Procedure for Constructing a Hierarchy

Make a list of situations (related to the fear) that make you anxious. Try to list at least 10 situations. Some should be very frightening and others only mildly frightening. Write a short description of each situation on a separate index card. Place the cards in order from the least disturbing situation to the most disturbing. Here is a sample hierarchy for a student afraid of public speaking:

1. Being given an assignment to speak in class
2. Thinking about the topic and the date the speech must be given
3. Writing the speech; thinking about delivering the speech
4. Watching other students speak in class the week before my speech date

5. Rehearsing the speech alone; pretending to give it to the class
6. Delivering the speech to my roommate; pretending my roommate is the teacher
7. Reviewing the speech on the day it is to be presented
8. Entering the classroom; waiting and thinking about the speech
9. Being called; standing up; facing the audience
10. Delivering the speech

Using the Hierarchy

When you have mastered the relaxation exercises and have the hierarchy constructed, set aside time each day to work on reducing your fear. Begin by performing the relaxation exercises. When you are completely relaxed, visualize the scene on the first card (the least frightening scene). If you can vividly picture and imagine yourself in the first situation twice without a noticeable increase in muscle tension, proceed to the next card. Also, as you progress, relax yourself between cards.

Each day, stop when you reach a card that you cannot visualize without becoming tense in three attempts. Each day, begin one or two cards before the one on which you stopped the previous day. Continue to work with the cards until you can visualize the last situation without experiencing tension (techniques are based on Wolpe, 1974).

By using this approach, you should be able to reduce the anxiety associated with things such as public speaking, entering darkened rooms, asking questions in large classes, heights, talking to people you are attracted to, and taking tests (Watson & Tharp, 2007). Even if you are not always able to reduce a fear, you will have learned to place relaxation under voluntary control. This alone is valuable because controlling unnecessary tension can increase energy and efficiency.

Seeking Professional Help—When, Where, and How?

How would I know if I should seek professional help at some point in my life? Although there is no simple answer to this question, the following guidelines may be helpful:

<SURVEY QUESTION
How can a person find professional help?

1. If your level of psychological discomfort (unhappiness, anxiety, or depression, for example) is comparable to a level of physical discomfort that would cause you to see a doctor or dentist, you should consider seeing a psychologist or a psychiatrist.
2. Another signal to watch for is significant changes in behaviour, such as the quality of your work (or schoolwork), your rate of absenteeism, your use of drugs (including alcohol), or your relationships with others.
3. Perhaps you have urged a friend or relative to seek professional help and were dismayed because she or he refused to do so. If you find friends or relatives making a similar suggestion, recognize that they may be seeing things more clearly than you are.
4. If you have persistent or disturbing suicidal thoughts or impulses, you should seek help immediately.

Locating a Therapist

How would I go about looking for a right therapist? Canada has about 13 000 psychologists and 3600 psychiatrists (Goering, Wasylenki, & Durbin, 2000). Here are some suggestions that could help you find the right therapist:

1. *Getting a referral from someone you know.* Many people find doctors, lawyers, and other professionals by word of mouth. If you know that a friend or relative has had a positive experience with a mental health professional, you may consider contacting him or her.
2. *Community mental health centres.* In many parts of Canada, mental health services may be provided by public mental health facilities. (These may be listed in the

phone book or online.) Public mental health centres usually provide counselling and therapy services directly, and they can refer you to private therapists.

3. *Mental health associations.* Many cities have mental health associations organized by concerned citizens. Groups such as these usually keep listings of qualified therapists and other services and programs in the community. For example, the Canadian Mental Health Association (CMHA) has offices throughout the country and provides useful information about mental health issues and treatment. You can contact the CMHA branch in your province or territory to obtain a list of therapists in your area.

4. *Colleges and universities.* If you are a student, you could make use of the counselling services offered by a student health centre or special student counselling facilities. They can often address the issue you are grappling with or refer you to a mental health professional.

5. *Newspaper and radio advertisements.* Some therapists advertise their services in newspapers or on the radio. However, you should carefully inquire into a therapist's training and qualifications. Without the benefit of a referral from a trusted person, it is wise to be cautious.

6. *The Yellow Pages.* Some psychologists are listed in the telephone book under "Psychologist" or in some cases under "Counselling Services." Psychiatrists are generally listed as a subheading under "Physicians." Counsellors may be found under the heading "Marriage and Family Counsellors." These listings will usually put you in touch with individuals in private practice. But, as we said above, caution is the operative word when seeking help from someone for whom you do not have a direct referral.

7. *Crisis hotlines.* The typical crisis hotline is a telephone service staffed by community volunteers to provide support to people who may wish to discuss personal issues on the phone. These people are trained to provide information concerning a wide range of mental health problems. They also have lists of organizations, services, and other resources in the community where you can go for help.

Table 13.5 summarizes all the sources for psychotherapy, counselling, and referrals we have discussed, as well as some additional possibilities.

Options

How would I know what kind of a therapist to see? How would I pick one? The choice between a psychiatrist and a psychologist is somewhat arbitrary. Both are trained to do psychotherapy. While a psychiatrist can administer somatic therapy and prescribe drugs, a psychologist can work in conjunction with a physician if such services are needed. Psychologists and psychiatrists are equally effective as therapists (*Consumer Reports*, 1995; Seligman, 1995).

■ Table 13.5   Mental Health Resources

- Family doctors
- Mental health specialists, such as psychiatrists, psychologists, social workers, and mental health counsellors
- Community mental health centres
- Hospital psychiatry departments and outpatient clinics
- University or medical school affiliated programs
- Family service/social agencies
- Private clinics and facilities
- Employee assistance programs
- Local medical, psychiatric, or psychological societies

Visits to psychiatrists are covered under your province or territory's medicare program. The average fee charged by psychologists in Canada is about $125 an hour and may range from roughly $60 to $180 (Stephens & Joubert, 2001). These visits are not covered by medicare. Group therapy costs even less because the therapist's fee is divided among several people. If you are covered under a private health insurance plan, chances are good that it covers the cost of psychotherapy with a registered psychologist. This is why you need to be certain that a therapist is a registered psychologist with your provincial or territorial licensing agency. Almost anyone can use the label "therapist" or "psychotherapist," but the designation of "psychologist" can only be used by someone who has a master's or a doctorate degree in psychology and has duly obtained a licence to conduct therapy.

If fees are a problem, keep in mind that many therapists charge on a sliding scale, or ability-to-pay basis, and that community mental health centres almost always charge on a sliding scale.

Some communities and university or college campuses have counselling services staffed by sympathetic paraprofessionals or peer counsellors. These services are free or very low cost. As mentioned earlier, paraprofessionals are people who work in a near-professional capacity under professional supervision. **Peer counsellors** are non-professional persons who have learned basic counselling skills. There is a natural tendency, perhaps, to doubt the abilities of paraprofessionals. However, many studies have shown that paraprofessional counsellors are often as effective as professionals (Christensen & Jacobson, 1994).

Also, don't overlook self-help groups, which can add valuable support to professional treatment. Members of a self-help group typically share a particular type of problem, such as eating disorders or coping with an alcoholic parent. **Self-help groups** offer members mutual support and a chance to discuss problems. In many instances, helping others also serves as therapy for those who give help (Burlingame & Davies, 2002). For some problems, self-help groups may be the best choice of all (Fobair, 1997; Galanter et al., 2005).

Qualifications

You can usually find out about a therapist's qualifications simply by asking. A reputable therapist will be glad to reveal her or his background. If you have any doubts, credentials may be checked and other helpful information can be obtained from your provincial or territorial licensing agency. You can also contact the following organizations:

- Canadian Psychiatric Association (http://www.cpa-apc.org/index.php; 613-234-2815)
- Canadian Psychological Association (http://www.cpa.ca/; 1-888-472-0657)
- Canadian Counselling and Psychotherapy Association (http://www.ccpa-accp.ca/; 1-877-765-5565)

The question of how to pick a particular therapist remains. The best way is to start with a short consultation with a respected psychiatrist, psychologist, or counsellor. This will allow the person you consult to evaluate your difficulty and recommend a type of therapy or a therapist who is likely to be helpful. As an alternative, you might ask the person teaching this course for a referral.

Evaluating a Therapist

How would I know whether to quit or ignore a therapist? A balanced look at psychotherapies suggests that all techniques are about equally successful (Wampold et al., 1997). However, all therapists are not equally successful. Far more important than the approach used are the therapist's personal qualities (Luborsky et al., 1997). The most consistently successful therapists are those who are willing to use whatever method seems most helpful for a client. They are also marked by personal characteristics of warmth, integrity, sincerity, and empathy (Patterson, 1989; Strupp, 1989).

Peer counsellor A non-professional person who has learned basic counselling skills.

Self-help group A group of people who share a particular type of problem and provide mutual support to one another.

The relationship between a client and therapist is the therapist's most basic tool (Hubble, Duncan, & Miller, 1999). This is why you must trust and easily relate to a therapist for therapy to be effective. Here are some danger signals to watch for in psychotherapy:

- Therapist makes sexual advances
- Therapist makes repeated verbal threats or is physically aggressive
- Therapist is excessively blaming, belittling, hostile, or controlling
- Therapist makes excessive small talk; talks repeatedly about his or her own problems
- Therapist encourages prolonged dependence on her or him
- Therapist demands absolute trust or tells client not to discuss therapy with anyone else

Clients who like their therapist are generally more successful in therapy (Talley, Strupp, & Morey, 1990). An especially important part of the therapeutic alliance is agreement about the goals of therapy. It is therefore a good idea to think about what you would like to accomplish by entering therapy. Write down your goals and discuss them with your therapist during the first session (Goldfried, Greenberg, & Marmar, 1990). Your first meeting with a therapist should also answer all of the following questions (Somberg, Stone, & Claiborn, 1993):

- Will the information I reveal in therapy remain confidential?
- What risks do I face if I begin therapy?
- How long do you expect treatment to last?
- What form of treatment do you expect to use?
- Are there alternatives to therapy that might help me as much or more?

It's always tempting to avoid facing up to personal problems. With this in mind, you should give a therapist a fair chance and not give up too easily. But don't hesitate to change therapists or to terminate therapy if you lose confidence in the therapist or if you don't relate well to the therapist as a person.

 STUDY BREAK   Self-Management and Finding Professional Help

Reflect

How could you use covert sensitization, thought stopping, and covert reinforcement to change your behaviour? Try to apply each technique to a specific example.

Just for practice, make a fear hierarchy for a situation you find frightening. Does vividly picturing items in the hierarchy make you tense or anxious? If so, can you intentionally relax using the tension-release method?

Assume that you want to seek help from a psychologist or other mental health professional. How would you proceed? Take some time to actually find out what mental health services are available to you.

Learning Check

1. Covert sensitization and thought stopping combine aversion therapy and cognitive therapy. T or F?
2. Like covert aversion conditioning, covert reinforcement of desired responses is also possible. T or F?
3. Exercises that bring about deep-muscle relaxation are an essential element in covert sensitization. T or F?
4. Items in a desensitization hierarchy should be placed in order from the least disturbing to the most disturbing. T or F?
5. The first step in desensitization is to place the visualization of disturbing images under stimulus control. T or F?
6. Persistent emotional discomfort is a clear sign that professional psychological counselling should be sought. T or F?
7. Community mental health centres rarely offer counselling or therapy themselves; they only do referrals. T or F?
8. In many instances, a therapist's personal qualities have more of an effect on the outcome of therapy than does the type of therapy used. T or F?

Critical Thinking

9. Would it be acceptable for a therapist to urge a client to break all ties with a troublesome family member?

Answers

1. T 2. T 3. F 4. T 5. F 6. T 7. F 8. T 9. Such decisions must be made by clients themselves. Therapists can help clients evaluate important decisions and feelings about significant persons in their lives. However, actively urging a client to sever a relationship borders on unethical behaviour.

CHAPTER IN REVIEW

Major Points

- Psychotherapy facilitates positive changes in personality, behaviour, or adjustment.

- Before the development of modern therapies, superstition dominated attempts to treat psychological problems.

- Five major categories of psychotherapy are psychodynamic, humanistic, behavioural, cognitive, and group therapies.

- Psychotherapy is generally effective, although no single form of therapy is superior to others.

- All medical treatments for psychological disorders have pros and cons. Overall, however, their effectiveness is improving.

- Some personal problems can be successfully treated using self-management techniques.

- Everyone should know how to obtain high-quality mental health care in his or her community.

Summary

What is psychotherapy and why is it undertaken? How did psychotherapy originate?

- Psychotherapy is a technique that aims to facilitate positive changes in an individual's personality or behaviour.

- Ancient approaches to mental illness were often based on belief in supernatural forces.

- Demonology attributed mental disturbance to demonic possession and prescribed exorcism as the cure.

- More humane treatment began in 1793 with the work of Philippe Pinel in Paris.

How is Freudian psychoanalysis conducted?

- Freud's psychoanalysis was the first formal psychotherapy. Psychoanalysis seeks to release repressed thoughts and emotions from the unconscious.

- The psychoanalyst uses free association, dream analysis, and analysis of resistance and transference to reveal health-producing insights.

- Some critics argue that traditional psychoanalysis is ineffective and wrongly receives credit for spontaneous remissions of symptoms.

- Brief psychodynamic therapy (which relies on psychoanalytic theory but is brief and focused) is as effective as other major therapies.

What are the major humanistic therapies?

- Client-centred (or person-centred) therapy is non-directive and is dedicated to creating an atmosphere of growth.

- Unconditional positive regard, empathy, authenticity, and reflection are combined to give the client a chance to solve her or his own problems.

- Existential therapies focus on the end result of the choices one makes in life. Clients are encouraged through confrontation and encounter to exercise free will and to take responsibility for their choices.

- Gestalt therapy emphasizes immediate awareness of thoughts and feelings. Its goal is to rebuild thinking, feeling, and acting into connected wholes and to help clients break through emotional blockages.

- Media psychologists, telephone counsellors, and cybertherapists may, on occasion, do some good. However, each has serious drawbacks, and the effectiveness of telephone counselling and cybertherapy has not been established.

- Therapy by videoconferencing shows promise as a way to provide mental health services at a distance.

What is behaviour therapy?

- Behaviour therapists use various behaviour modification techniques that apply learning principles to change human behaviour.

- In aversion therapy, classical conditioning is used to associate maladaptive behaviour (such as smoking or drinking) with pain or other aversive events in order to inhibit undesirable responses.

How is behaviour therapy used to treat phobias and anxieties?

- Classical conditioning underlies systematic desensitization, a technique used to overcome fears and anxieties. In desensitization, gradual adaptation and reciprocal inhibition break the link between fear and particular situations.

- Typical steps in desensitization are these: Construct a fear hierarchy; learn to produce total relaxation; and perform items on the hierarchy (from least to most disturbing).

- Desensitization may be carried out with real settings or it may be done by vividly imagining the fear hierarchy or by watching models perform the feared responses.

- In some cases, virtual reality exposure can be used to present fear stimuli in a controlled manner.

- A new technique called eye movement desensitization and reprocessing (EMDR) shows promise as a treatment for traumatic memories and stress disorders. At present, however, EMDR is highly controversial.

What role does reinforcement play in behaviour therapy?

- Behaviour modification also makes use of operant principles, such as positive reinforcement, non-reinforcement, extinction, punishment, shaping, stimulus control, and time out. These principles are used to extinguish undesirable responses and to promote constructive behaviour.

- Non-reward can extinguish troublesome behaviours. Often this is done by simply identifying and eliminating reinforcers, particularly attention and social approval.

- To apply positive reinforcement and operant shaping, tokens are often used to reinforce selected target behaviours.

- Full-scale use of tokens in an institutional setting produces a token economy. Toward the end of a token economy program, patients are shifted to social rewards such as recognition and approval.

What is cognitive therapy? How does it change thoughts and emotions?

- Cognitive therapy emphasizes changing thought patterns that underlie emotional or behavioural problems. Its goals are to correct distorted thinking and/or teach improved coping skills.

- In a variation of cognitive therapy called rational-emotive behaviour therapy (REBT), clients learn to recognize and challenge their own irrational beliefs.

How is psychotherapy done with groups of people?

- Group therapy may be a simple extension of individual methods or it may be based on techniques developed specifically for groups.

- In psychodrama, individuals enact roles and incidents resembling their real-life problems. In family therapy, the family group is treated as a unit.

- Although they are not literally psychotherapies, sensitivity and encounter groups attempt to encourage positive personality change. In recent years, commercially offered large-group awareness training has become popular. However, the therapeutic benefits of such programs are questionable.

What do various therapies have in common?

- To alleviate personal problems, all psychotherapies offer a caring relationship, emotional rapport, a protected setting, catharsis, explanations for the client's problems, a new perspective, and a chance to practise new behaviours.

- Many basic counselling skills underlie a variety of therapies. These include listening actively, helping to clarify the problem, focusing on feelings, avoiding the giving of unwanted advice, accepting the person's

perspective, reflecting thoughts and feelings, being patient during silences, using open questions when possible, and maintaining confidentiality.

- The culturally skilled counsellor must be able to establish rapport with a person from a different cultural background and adapt traditional theories and techniques to meet the needs of clients from non-European ethnic or racial groups.

How do psychiatrists treat psychological disorders?

- Three medical, or somatic, approaches to treatment are pharmacotherapy, electroconvulsive therapy (ECT), and psychosurgery. All three techniques are controversial to a degree because of questions about effectiveness and side effects.

- Community mental health centres seek to avoid or minimize hospitalization. They also seek to prevent mental health problems through education, consultation, and crisis intervention.

How are behavioural principles applied to everyday problems?

- In covert sensitization, aversive images are used to discourage unwanted behaviour.

- Thought stopping uses mild punishment to prevent upsetting thoughts.

- Covert reinforcement is a way to encourage desired responses by mental rehearsal.

- Desensitization pairs relaxation with a hierarchy of upsetting images in order to lessen fears.

How can a person find professional help?

- In most communities, a competent and reputable therapist can be located with public sources of information or through a referral.

- Practical considerations such as cost and qualifications enter into choosing a therapist. However, the therapist's personal characteristics are of equal importance.

Interactive Learning

Please visit http://www.psychologyjourney4ce.nelson.com for a list of weblinks to relevant psychology sites.

CourseMate

Access an interactive e-book and chapter-specific interactive learning tools, including flashcards, quizzes, videos, and more, in your psychology CourseMate. Visit Nelsonbrain.com to use CourseMate.

psyk.trek 11. Abnormal Behaviour and Therapy.

TEST YOUR KNOWLEDGE

The questions that follow are only a sample of what you need to know. If you miss any of the items, review the entire chapter and the Study Breaks. Another way to prepare for tests is to use the Study Guide and the Practice Exams that are available with this text.

1. Which of the following is *not* one of the reasons why people may be hesitant to seek the services of a psychologist?
   a. a lack of financial resources
   b. being unaware of what psychologists do
   c. believing that people should be able to solve their own problems
   d. believing that psychologists are cold and rejecting

2. The prehistoric treatment of mental health issues, trepanning, involved which of the following?
   a. casting a spell of magic
   b. boring holes in skulls
   c. administering drugs
   d. deep lesioning

3. Which of the following is a psychoanalytic concept?
   a. behaviour therapy
   b. reinforcement
   c. transference
   d. trepanning

4. When evaluating a therapy, we should consider which type of control group to be used, to avoid being misled by a spontaneous remission of symptoms?
   a. non-directive
   b. latent
   c. psychodynamic
   d. waiting-list

5. Which of the following is in contrast with Carl Rogers's approach to therapy?
   a. empathy
   b. authenticity
   c. reflection
   d. confrontation

6. What has the principal goal of filling in gaps in immediate self-awareness?
   a. rational-emotive behavioural therapy (REBT)
   b. existential therapy
   c. person-centred therapy
   d. Gestalt therapy

7. To date, what is the most acceptable type of distance therapy?
   a. media psychology
   b. commercial telephone counselling
   c. Internet-based cybertherapy
   d. telehealth

8. Which of the following is based on classical conditioning principles?
   a. aversion therapy
   b. time out
   c. token economies
   d. eye movement desensitization and reprocessing (EMDR)

9. Which of the following includes the principle of reciprocal inhibition?
   a. eye movement desensitization and reprocessing (EMDR)
   b. rational-emotive behavioural therapy (REBT)
   c. desensitization
   d. the design of a token economy

10. Which treatment approach is most likely used by a psychologist who is interested in helping someone dealing with overgeneralization and irrational beliefs?
    a. exposure therapy
    b. token economies
    c. systematic desensitization
    d. cognitive therapy

11. What is the B in the A-B-C of rational-emotive behavioural therapy (REBT)?
    a. behaviour
    b. belief
    c. being
    d. backward

12. Which treatment approach frequently uses the mirror technique?
    a. exposure therapy
    b. psychodrama
    c. family therapy
    d. eye movement desensitization and reprocessing (EMDR)

13. According to research, about half of all patients feel better after how many therapy sessions?
    a. 8
    b. 16
    c. 24
    d. 26

14. Which of the following has at its core emotional rapport, warmth, understanding, acceptance, and empathy?
    a. the therapeutic alliance
    b. large-group awareness training
    c. role reversals
    d. action therapies

15. Which of the following is inconsistent with a culturally skilled therapists approach?
    a. being aware of the client's degree of acculturation
    b. using helping resources within the client's cultural group
    c. adapting standard techniques to match cultural stereotypes
    d. being aware of their own cultural values

16. What is another term for major tranquillizers?
    a. anti-anxiety drugs
    b. antipsychotics
    c. antidepressants
    d. prefrontal sedatives

17. For which disorder is lithium the preferred method of treatment?
    a. bipolar disorder
    b. schizophrenia
    c. panic disorder
    d. marital problems

18. What is electroconvulsive therapy (ECT) classified as a type of?
    a. somatic therapy
    b. pharmacotherapy
    c. psychosurgery
    d. deep lesioning

19. Which self-management technique uses mild punishment?
    a. thought stopping
    b. desensitization
    c. rational-emotive behavioural therapy (REBT)
    d. time outs

20. What is the tension-release method an important part of?
    a. covert reinforcement
    b. thought stopping
    c. desensitization
    d. peer counselling

chapter 14

Social Behaviour

JOURNEY INTO PSYCHOLOGY: THE ROOTS OF EMPATHY

If you were ever the target of bullying as a child, you know that it can make life very unpleasant. If you were ever the bully, you may know that being the bully really isn't much fun, either. Bullying is a common occurrence during childhood in every part of the world where it has been looked for. It is associated with a number of undesirable outcomes, such as increased risk of depression and anxiety for both the victim and the bully. Bullies also have a higher than normal risk of getting into trouble with the law. There really isn't anything good to say for being a bully or a victim, so it would be wonderful if we could develop a simple, practical method for reducing the occurrence of bullying in our schools.

If you think that reducing bullying is a very difficult challenge, we've got news for you. It may turn out to be child's play. Or to be more precise, baby play—as in, playing with a baby. Canadian teacher Mary Gordon has become famous for her work promoting empathy and emotional skills in children. Gordon had previously founded a network of parenting centres in response to her experiences working with neglectful and abusive parents. She realized that many of these parents lacked empathy for other people, even their own children. The tactic she chose to deal with this problem is, to say the least, forward-looking: She resolved to help a new generation of parents be more empathic by reaching them when they were still children themselves.

In 1996, Gordon founded a program called *Roots of Empathy* (RoE), which teaches children to think about other people's feelings. This celebrated program has expanded across Canada and, recently, into the United States and the United Kingdom, with pilot programs in Australia and other parts of the world. The basic tool in this program is a regular visit to the classroom by a baby and the baby's mother or father. Children in the class are encouraged to think about the baby's and parent's perspectives—what does she need? How can she communicate her needs? What does it feel like to be a parent when your baby is teething or otherwise upset?

The baby and his or her parent visit the classroom once a month throughout the school year, with visits by an RoE trainer each month before and after the baby comes to the classroom as well as during the baby's visit. Children sit on a blanket with the baby and the parent and practise their empathy skills. Teachers report substantial changes in the behaviour of difficult, disruptive children. It's not just the teachers' impression: University of British Columbia researcher Kimberly Schonert-Reichl has documented significant changes in the behaviour of children who participate in the RoE program. One study involved 28 schools in British Columbia and Ontario. Half the schools got the RoE program in Grades 4 through 7 (Schonert-Reichl et al., 2012). Children in the RoE schools showed increased prosocial behaviours and decreased aggression (both proactive and relational aggression) at the end of the school year. The reduction in aggression is particularly noteworthy because children in the control schools actually *increased* in proactive and relational aggression during the year.

As Dr. Schonert-Reichl told the *New York Times,* "Do kids become more empathic and understanding? Do they become less aggressive and kinder to each other? The answer is yes and yes." So if you want to become more empathic yourself, try spending time with a baby!

 Survey Questions

- Why do people affiliate? What factors influence interpersonal attraction?
- How does group membership affect our behaviour?
- What have social psychologists learned about social influence?
- How does self-assertion differ from aggression?
- How are attitudes acquired and changed?
- What causes prejudice and intergroup conflict?
- How do psychologists explain human aggression?
- Why are bystanders so often unwilling to help in an emergency?
- How can we promote social harmony?

AFFILIATION AND ATTRACTION—COME TOGETHER

SURVEY QUESTION>
Why do people affiliate? What factors influence interpersonal attraction?

Each of us is immersed in a complex social world of communities, families, clans, crowds, tribes, companies, parties, troops, bands, sects, gangs, crews, teams, and nations. **Social psychology** is the scientific study of how individuals behave, think, and feel in social situations (i.e., in the presence, actual or implied, of others) (Baron, Byrne, & Branscombe, 2009).

But what brings us together in the first place? We are social beings with a *need to affiliate* (a desire to associate with other people) based on basic human desires for approval, support, security, friendship, and information (Baumeister & Bushman, 2008).

Information? Yes. Other people provide information that helps us evaluate our own reactions. Whenever we are in doubt, we tend to rely on *social comparisons* to guide our behaviour (Kulik, Mahler, & Moore, 2003).

Social Comparison Theory

If you want to know how heavy you are, you simply get on a scale. But how do you know if you are a good athlete, worker, parent, or friend? How do you know if your views on politics, religion, or music are unusual or widely shared? When there are no objective standards, the only available yardstick is provided by comparing yourself with others (Miller, 2006).

Social psychologist Leon Festinger (1919–1989) theorized that group membership fills needs for **social comparison** (comparing your own actions, feelings, opinions, or abilities to those of others). Have you ever "compared notes" with other students after taking an exam? ("How did you do?" "Wasn't that last question hard?") If you have, Festinger (1957) would say that you were satisfying needs for social comparison.

Typically, we don't make social comparisons randomly or on some absolute scale. Meaningful evaluations are based on comparing yourself with people of similar backgrounds, abilities, and circumstances (Stapel & Marx, 2007). To illustrate, let's ask a student named Wendy if she is a good tennis player. If Wendy compares herself with a professional, the answer will be no. But within her tennis group, Wendy is regarded as an excellent player. On a fair scale of comparison, Wendy knows she is good, and she takes pride in her tennis skills. In the same way, thinking of yourself as successful, talented, responsible, or fairly paid depends entirely on whom you choose for comparison. Thus, a desire for social comparison provides a motive for associating with others and influences which groups we join (Franzoi & Klaiber, 2007).

Social psychology The scientific study of how individuals behave, think, and feel in social situations.

Social comparison Making judgments about ourselves through comparison with others.

As the Wendy example suggests, how you feel following a comparison may depend strongly on whom you compare yourself with. University of Toronto psychologists Penelope Lockwood and Rebecca Pinkus have shown that effects found with social comparisons to generic others change when the comparison is made either to a past or future self or to a romantic partner. We'll come back to the romantic partner case below. Lockwood and Pinkus (2008) argued that comparisons to a past or future self activate "alternative selves" that influence our emotions and self-perceptions. They can also change our goals and thus our actions. These selves might include "counterfactual selves." As an example, suppose you got 77 on an exam. It's probably easy to imagine an alternative you who did a few things differently and got an A. In such alternative-self comparisons, you extract from the comparison how things might be different and then either work toward that different state or (if it's negative) work proactively to prevent it.

Don't people also affiliate out of attraction for one another? Of course they do. Let's see why.

High school class reunions are notorious for the rampant social comparison they often encourage. Apparently it's hard to resist comparing yourself with former classmates to see how you are doing in life.

Digital Vision Ltd/SuperStock

Interpersonal Attraction

"Birds of a feather flock together." "Familiarity breeds contempt." "Opposites attract." "Absence makes the heart grow fonder." Are these statements true? Actually, the folklore about friendship is, at best, a mixture of fact and fiction.

What does attract people to each other? **Interpersonal attraction** (affinity to another person) is the basis for most voluntary social relationships (Berscheid & Regan, 2005). As you might expect, we look for friends and lovers who are kind and understanding, who have attractive personalities, and who like us in return (Sprecher, 1998). Deciding whether you would like to know another person can happen very quickly, sometimes within just minutes of meeting (Sunnafrank, Ramirez, & Metts, 2004). In addition, several less obvious factors influence attraction.

Attraction in Children

How do children choose their friends? Young children make unsophisticated judgments in many areas, so we might ask what characteristics draw them to other people. Whom children are attracted to has important consequences, as shown by a number of large-scale, longitudinal studies by researchers in Montreal. Frank Vitaro, Mara Brendgen, and Richard Tremblay reported links between a child's delinquency and her or his best friend's delinquency (Vitaro, Brendgen, & Tremblay, 2000). One study began when the children involved were 6 years old and followed them until they were 23 (Véronneau et al., 2008). Disruptive and aggressive children had friends who shared those characteristics. Having aggressive-disruptive friends was associated with lower likelihood of graduating from high school.

Physical Proximity

Our choice of friends (and even lovers) is based more on *physical proximity* (nearness) than we might care to believe. For example, the closer people live to each other, the more likely they are to become friends. Likewise, lovers like to think they have found the "one and only" person in the universe for them. In reality, they have probably found the best match in a 10-kilometre radius! (Buss, 1985). Marriages are not made in heaven—they are made in local schools, businesses, churches, bars, clubs, and neighbourhoods.

Proximity promotes attraction by increasing the *frequency of contact* between people. In general, we are attracted to people we see often. (That's one reason why actors co-starring in movies often become romantically involved.) In short, there does seem to be a "boy-next-door" or "girl-next-door" effect in romantic attraction, and a "folks-next-door" effect in friendship. Notice, however, that the Internet is making it increasingly easier to stay in constant "virtual contact," which is leading to more and more long-distance friendships and romances (Lawson & Leck, 2006; Ridings & Gefen, 2004).

Physical Attractiveness

People who are *physically attractive* are regarded as good-looking by others. Beautiful people are generally rated as more appealing than average. This is due, in part, to the *halo effect,* a tendency to generalize a favourable impression to unrelated personal characteristics (see Chapter 10). Because of it, we assume that beautiful people are also likable, intelligent, warm, witty, mentally healthy, and socially skilled. In reality, physical attractiveness has almost no connection to intelligence, talents,

What attracts people to each other? Proximity and frequency of contact have a surprisingly large impact.

Interpersonal attraction Social attraction to another person.

Physical beauty can be socially advantageous because of the widespread belief that what is beautiful is good. However, physical beauty is generally unrelated to actual personal traits and talents.

or abilities. Perhaps that's why beauty affects mainly our initial interest in getting to know others (Keller & Young, 1996).

Humour

Another basis for liking someone, or making them like you, is humour. Most people like to be amused so will enjoy the company of a funny friend. But there's more to the use of humour in relationships than just the occasional knee-slapper. One of the world's leading experts on the psychology of humour is Rod Martin of Western University in London, Ontario. Together with his students and colleagues, Martin developed a model of humour styles that distinguishes four separate kinds of humour: two positive and two negative (Martin et al., 2003). The positive styles are affiliative (facilitating relationships by making other people laugh) and self-enhancing (coping with stress by being cheerful). The negative approaches are aggressive (using humour to disparage and manipulate others) and self-defeating (making jokes at your own expense in order to be liked).

Research by the team at Western has investigated how humour styles are related to the Big Five personality characteristics (Chapter 10). The two positive humour styles are positively correlated with Extroversion and Openness, and the two negative humour styles are negatively correlated with Agreeableness and Conscientiousness (e.g., Vernon et al., 2008). Given these associations, it seemed likely that the humour styles would also be correlated with the so-called Dark Triad of personality (Veselka et al., 2010). The Dark Triad is a set of socially aversive traits consisting of narcissism (excessive self-love), psychopathy (high thrill-seeking paired with low empathy), and Machiavellianism (manipulative behaviours). Veselka and her colleagues found that narcissism correlated positively with affiliative and self-enhancing humour styles. In contrast, psychopathy and Machiavellianism correlated positively with aggressive and self-defeating humour. Thus, humour is an integral part of human relationships, which can be used in either a positive way or a negative way.

Similarity

Make a list of your closest friends. What do they have in common (other than the joy of knowing you)? It is likely that their ages are similar to yours and they are of the same sex and ethnicity. There will be exceptions, of course. But similarity on these three dimensions is the general rule for friendships.

Similarity refers to how alike you and another person are in background, age, interests, attitudes, beliefs, and so forth. In everything from casual acquaintance to marriage, similar people are attracted to each other (Figueredo, Sefcek, & Jones, 2006; Miller, Perlman, & Brehm, 2007). McGill University researchers Frances Aboud and Morton Mendelson found that for young children, similarities in sex, age, race, and preferred activity were more important in determining attraction than attitudes, values, or self-esteem (Aboud & Mendelson, 1998).

Does similarity also influence mate selection? Yes, we tend to select as a mate someone who is like us in almost every way, a pattern called *homogamy* (huh-MOG-ah-me) (Blackwell & Lichter, 2004). Both married and unmarried couples who are living together are highly similar in age, education, ethnicity, and religion. To a lesser degree, they are also similar in attitudes and opinions, mental abilities, status, height, weight, and eye colour. Homogamy is probably a good thing. The risk of divorce is highest among couples with sizable differences in age and education (Tzeng, 1992).

Self-Disclosure

How do people who are not yet friends learn whether they are similar? To get acquainted, you must be willing to talk about more than just the weather, sports, or nuclear physics. At some point you must begin to share private thoughts and feelings and reveal yourself to others. This process, which is called **self-disclosure,** is essential for developing close relationships. In general, as friends talk, they gradually deepen the level of liking, trust, and self-disclosure (Levesque, Steciuk, & Ledley, 2002).

Self-disclosure The process of revealing private thoughts, feelings, and one's personal history to others.

It's not surprising that some people have more difficulty with self-disclosure than others. For example, people with low self-esteem are hampered in their relationships with other people by their focus on avoiding disapproval or embarrassment (Wood & Forest, 2010). That focus prevents the self-disclosure that might develop other people's interest in them. With this in mind, two researchers at the University of Waterloo, Amanda Forest and Joanne Wood, asked whether people with low self-esteem might find it easier to talk about themselves on Facebook (Forest & Wood, 2012). They also asked whether that greater willingness to disclose would lead to greater social success. To find out, they asked large numbers of college students to provide their 10 most recent Facebook posts and the counts of how many people commented on or "Liked" each post. The answers to their questions were clear: Low self-esteem participants saw Facebook as a safe venue for talking about their feelings and thought that they would benefit from doing so using that venue. But, unfortunately, their posts were rated as generally more negative and less positive than what high self-esteem people posted. Forest and Wood also analyzed the responses from other people—a count of comments and Likes. These counts provided an important lesson: Other people responded more when high self-esteem people made highly negative posts. Forest and Wood suggested that these people were generally positive, so when they did post something negative, it recruited responses from their friends, who wanted to support them when they were uncharacteristically down. In contrast, other people responded more when low self-esteem individuals made highly positive posts. Forest and Wood suggested that this was an effort by friends to encourage such posts from people who were ordinarily too negative on Facebook.

Excessive self-disclosure is a staple of many television talk shows. Guests frequently reveal intimate details about their personal lives, including private family matters, sex and dating, physical or sexual abuse, major embarrassments, and criminal activities. Viewers probably find such intimate disclosures entertaining, rather than threatening, because they don't have to reciprocate.

Self-disclosure is governed by unspoken rules about what's acceptable. Moderate self-disclosure leads to *reciprocity* (a return in kind). In contrast, *overdisclosure* exceeds what is appropriate for a relationship or social situation, giving rise to suspicion and reducing attraction. For example, imagine standing in line at a store and having the stranger in front of you say, "Lately I've been thinking about how I really feel about myself. I think I'm pretty well adjusted, but I occasionally have some questions about my sexual adequacy." It's interesting to note that on the Internet (and especially on social networking websites like Facebook and MySpace), people often feel freer to express their true feelings, which can lead to genuine, face-to-face friendships (Bargh, McKenna, & Fitzsimons, 2002). However, it can also lead to some very dramatic over-disclosure (George, 2006).

LIKING AND LOVING—DATING, RATING, MATING

How does love differ from interpersonal attraction? It depends on what you mean by the word "love." **Romantic love,** for example, is based on interpersonal attraction, but it also involves high levels of passion, that is, emotional arousal and/or sexual desire (Berscheid & Regan, 2005; Miller et al., 2007). Before going further, a cautionary note: Most research on romantic love is conducted in a particular cultural context—typically in North America. University of Toronto psychologists Karen Dion and her late husband Kenneth argued that the social context in which personal relationships develop is central to understanding these relationships (Dion & Dion, 2006). Social context, of course, includes culture.

Romantic love Love that is associated with high levels of interpersonal attraction, heightened arousal, mutual absorption, and sexual desire.

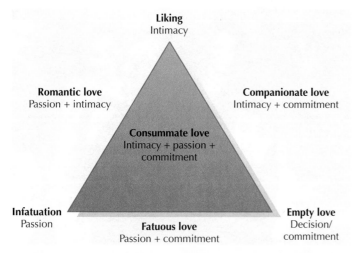

FIGURE 14.1 The Triangle of Love. Each of the three basic components of love (intimacy, passion, and commitment) appears at one corner of the triangle and is associated with a form of love. Pairs of components and their associated form of love appear on lines of the triangle. Consummate love, which involves all three components, is pictured at the centre of the triangle. (Adapted from Sternberg, 1988.)

To get another (tri?)angle on love, psychologist Robert Sternberg (1988) created his influential *triangular theory of love*. According to Sternberg, different forms of love arise from different combinations of three basic components (Figure 14.1). **Intimacy** refers to feelings of connectedness and affection. **Passion** refers to deep emotional and/or sexual feelings. **Commitment** involves the determination to stay in a long-term relationship with another person.

How does the system work? Try it for yourself. Think of a person you love. Now read Table 14.1 as you ask yourself three yes/no questions: Do I feel intimate with this person? Do I feel passion for this person? Am I committed to this person? Find the kind of love that fits your answers. For example, if you answered *yes* to intimacy but *no* to passion and commitment, you **like** that person; you are friends. Alternatively, if you answered *yes* to intimacy and commitment but *no* to passion, then you are feeling **companionate love.** This form of love is more common among couples who have been together for a long time. According to Sternberg, **consummate love** is an ideal reached by couples who combine all three basic components.

Romantic love differs from friendship in two other interesting ways. In contrast to simple liking, romantic love usually involves deep *mutual absorption.* In other words, lovers (unlike friends) attend almost exclusively to one another. Second, recall that social comparisons can be either upward—to someone doing better than you are—or downward—to someone worse off than you. We saw above that a person typically feels better after downward social comparisons to others and worse after upward comparisons. However, University of Toronto psychologists Rebecca Pinkus and Penelope Lockwood found that that isn't true if the comparison is to a romantic partner. A study by Pinkus and her colleagues (2012) found that people felt better following an upward comparison (to a dating partner or spouse who was more successful) than after a downward comparison (to a dating partner or spouse who was less successful). The basis for this effect was a form of empathy—people feel happy for a successful partner and sad for an unsuccessful partner. In the case of married people, it also mattered that one spouse stands to benefit from the other spouse's success and suffer a cost when the other spouse is unsuccessful.

Evolution and Mate Selection

Evolutionary psychology is the study of the evolutionary origins of human behaviour patterns. Many psychologists believe that evolution left an imprint on men and women that

Intimacy Feelings of connectedness and affection for another person.

Passion Deep emotional and/or sexual feelings for another person.

Commitment The determination to stay in a long-term relationship with another person.

Liking A relationship based on intimacy but lacking passion and commitment.

Companionate love A form of love characterized by intimacy and commitment but not passion.

Consummate love A form of love characterized by intimacy, passion, *and* commitment.

Evolutionary psychology The study of the evolutionary origins of human behaviour patterns.

■ Table 14.1	Sternberg's Triangular Theory of Love		
Combinations of intimacy, passion, and commitment			
Type Of Love	Intimacy	Passion	Commitment
Non-love			
Liking	Yes		
Infatuated love		Yes	
Empty love			Yes
Romantic love	Yes	Yes	
Companionate love	Yes		Yes
Fatuous love		Yes	Yes
Consummate love	Yes	Yes	Yes

(Sternberg, R. J. (1988). *The Triangle of Love.* Yale University Press.)

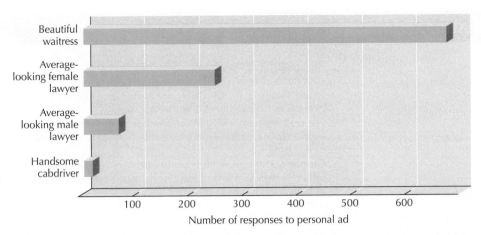

FIGURE 14.2 What do people look for when considering potential dating partners? Here are the results of a study in which personal ads were placed in newspapers. As you can see, men were more influenced by looks, and women by success (Goode, 1996).

influences everything from sexual attraction and infidelity to jealousy and divorce. According to David Buss, the key to understanding human mating patterns is to understand how evolved behaviour patterns guide our choices (Buss, 2004, 2007).

In a study of 37 cultures on six continents, Buss found the following patterns: Compared with women, men are more interested in casual sex; they prefer younger, more physically attractive partners; and they get more jealous over real or imagined sexual infidelities than they do over a loss of emotional commitment. Compared with men, women prefer slightly older partners who appear to be industrious, higher in status, or economically successful, and are more upset by a partner who becomes emotionally involved with someone else, rather than one who is sexually unfaithful (Buss, 2000; Regan et al., 2000) (Figure 14.2).

Why do such differences exist? Buss and others believe that mating preferences evolved in response to the differing reproductive challenges faced by men and women. Since women are more limited than men in the number of children they can have, women must invest more time and energy in reproduction and nurturing children than men have to. Consequently, women evolved an interest in whether their partners will stay with them and whether their mates have the resources to provide for their children (Buss, 2004, 2007; Regan et al., 2000).

In contrast, the reproductive success of men depends on their mates' fertility. Men, therefore, tend to look for health, youth, and beauty in a prospective mate, as signs of suitability for reproduction (Buss, 2007). This preference, perhaps, is why some older men abandon their first wives in favour of young, beautiful "trophy wives." Evolutionary theory further proposes that the male emphasis on mates' sexual fidelity is based on concerns about the paternity of offspring. From a biological perspective, men do not benefit from investing resources in another man's children (Buller, 2005).

Whatever the outcome of the debate about evolution and mate selection, it is important to remember this: Potential mates are rated as most attractive if they are kind, secure, intelligent, and supportive (Klohnen & Luo, 2003; Regan et al., 2000). These qualities are love's greatest allies.

Needs for affiliation and interpersonal attraction inevitably bring people together in groups. In the next section, we will explore several interesting aspects of group membership. But first, here's a chance to review what you have learned.

According to evolutionary psychologists, women tend to be concerned with whether mates will devote time and resources to a relationship. Men place more emphasis on physical attractiveness and sexual fidelity.

STUDY BREAK   Affiliation, Friendship, and Love

Reflect

How has social comparison affected your behaviour? Has it influenced whom you associate with?

Think of three close friends. Which of the attraction factors described earlier apply to your friendships?

To what extent does Sternberg's triangular theory of love apply to your own loving relationships with others?

Learning Check

1. Interpersonal attraction is increased by all but which one of the following?
   a. physical proximity   b. competence
   c. similarity   d. overdisclosure

2. High levels of self-disclosure are reciprocated in most social encounters. T or F?
3. In Sternberg's triangular theory, infatuated love involves passion but not commitment or intimacy. T or F?
4. The most striking finding about marriage patterns is that most people choose mates whose personalities are quite unlike their own. T or F?
5. Compared with men, women tend to be more upset by sexual infidelity than by a loss of emotional commitment on the part of their mates. T or F?

Critical Thinking

6. How has the Internet altered the effects of proximity on interpersonal attraction?

Answers

1. d 2. F 3. T 4. F 5. F 6. As mentioned earlier, it is, of course, possible to interact with another person through the Internet. This makes actual physical proximity less crucial in interpersonal attraction, because frequent contact is possible even at great distances. Internet romances are a good example of this possibility.

HUMANS IN A SOCIAL CONTEXT—PEOPLE, PEOPLE, EVERYWHERE

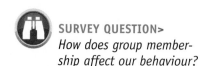

SURVEY QUESTION>
How does group membership affect our behaviour?

We all belong to many overlapping social groups, and in each, we occupy a *position* in the *structure* of the group. **Social roles** are patterns of behaviour expected of persons in various social positions (Breckler, Olson, & Wiggins, 2006). For instance, the roles of mother, boss, and student involve different sets of behaviours and expectations. Some roles are *ascribed* (they are assigned to a person or are not under personal control): male or female, son, adolescent, inmate. *Achieved* roles are voluntarily attained by special effort: spouse, teacher, scientist, bandleader, criminal.

What effect does role-playing have on behaviour? Roles streamline daily interactions by allowing us to anticipate what others will do. When a person is acting as a doctor, mother, clerk, or police officer, we expect certain behaviours. However, roles have a negative side too. Many people experience **role conflicts,** in which two or more roles make conflicting demands on them. Consider, for example, a teacher who must flunk a close friend's daughter, a mother who has a full-time job, or a soccer coach whose son is on the team but isn't a very good athlete. Likewise, the clashing demands of work, family, and school create role conflicts for many students (Hammer, Grigsby, & Woods, 1998; Senécal, Julien, & Guay, 2003). Role conflicts at work (such as being a good team player versus being a strong manager) lead to job burnout (Jawahar, Stone, & Kisamore, 2007) and negative health outcomes (Pomaki, Supeli, & Verhoeven, 2007).

Group Structure, Cohesion, and Norms

Are there other dimensions of group membership? Two important dimensions of any group are its structure and its cohesiveness. **Group structure** consists of the network of roles, communication pathways, and power in a group. Organized groups such as an army or an athletic team have a high degree of structure. Informal friendship groups may or may not be very structured.

Roles have a powerful impact on social behaviour. What kinds of behaviour do you expect from your teachers? What behaviours do they expect from you? What happens if either of you fails to match the other's expectations?

SuperStock

Group cohesiveness refers to the degree of attraction among group members or the strength of their desire to remain in the group. Members of cohesive groups stick together: They tend to stand or sit close together, they pay more attention to one another, and they show more signs of mutual affection. Also, their behaviour tends to be closely coordinated (Chansler, Swamidass, & Cammann, 2003). Cohesiveness is the basis for much of the power that groups exert over us. Therapy groups, businesses, sports teams, and the like seek to increase cohesion because it helps people work together better (Craig & Kelly, 1999; Marmarosh, Holtz, & Schottenbauer, 2005).

Clare Brant, a Mohawk psychiatrist from the Bay of Quinte, Ontario, has written about the extent to which values and attitudes that promote group cohesion still influence the behaviour of Aboriginal peoples (Brant, 1990, 1995). Group cohesion was historically important for Aboriginal peoples. They could not survive in a harsh environment without being in a group. To live together in close quarters all their lives, they developed a value system that discouraged conflict. The group-promotion values include non-interference, non-competitiveness, emotional restraint, and sharing. In addition, Aboriginal culture developed teasing, shaming, and ridiculing as tools to police behaviours that reduced conformity.

In-groups

Cohesiveness is particularly strong for **in-groups** (groups with which a person mainly identifies). Very likely, your own in-groups are defined by a combination of prominent social dimensions, such as nationality, ethnicity, age, education, religion, income, political values, gender, sexual orientation, and so forth. In-group membership helps define who we are socially. Predictably, we tend to attribute positive characteristics to our in-group and negative qualities to **out-groups** (groups with which we do not identify). We also tend to exaggerate differences between members of out-groups and our own groups. This sort of "us-and-them" thinking seems to be a basic fact of social life. It also sets the stage for conflict between groups and for racial and ethnic prejudice—topics we will explore later in this chapter.

Status

In addition to defining roles, a person's social position within groups determines his or her **status,** or level of social power and importance. Higher status bestows special privileges and respect. For example, in one experiment, a man walked into a number of bakeries and asked for a pastry while claiming he did not have enough money to pay for it. Half the time he was well dressed and half the time he was poorly dressed. If the man was polite when he asked, he was equally likely to be given a free pastry no matter how he was dressed (95 percent for well dressed versus 90 percent for poorly dressed). But if he was impolite when he asked, he was much less likely to get a pastry if he was poorly dressed than if he was well dressed (20 versus 75 percent) (Guéguen & Pascual, 2003). You don't have to be in a bakery for this to work. In most situations, we are more likely to comply with a request made by a high-status (well-dressed) person (Guéguen, 2002).

Norms

Our behaviour also responds to group norms. **Norms** are widely accepted (but often unspoken) standards for appropriate behaviour. If you have the slightest doubt about the power of norms, try this test: Walk into a crowded supermarket, get in a checkout line, and begin singing loudly in your fullest voice. Are you the 1 person in 100 who could actually carry out these instructions?

The impact of norms is shown by an interesting study of littering. The question was, "Does the amount of trash in an area affect littering?" To find out, people were given flyers as they walked into a public parking garage. As you can see in Figure 14.3, the more litter there was on the floor, the more likely people were to add to it by dropping their flyer. Apparently, seeing that others had already littered implied a lax

Social role Expected behaviour patterns associated with particular social positions (such as daughter, worker, student).

Role conflict Trying to occupy two or more roles that make conflicting demands on behaviour.

Group structure The network of roles, communication pathways, and power in a group.

Group cohesiveness The degree of attraction among group members or their commitment to remaining in the group.

In-group A group with which a person identifies.

Out-group A group with which a person does not identify.

Status An individual's position in a social structure, especially with respect to power, privilege, or importance.

Norms Widely accepted (but often unspoken) standards of conduct for appropriate behaviour.

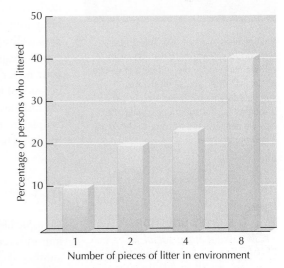

▶▶**FIGURE 14.3** Results of an experiment on norms concerning littering. The prior existence of litter in a public setting implies that littering is acceptable. This encourages others to "trash" the area. (Cialdini, Reno, Kallgren (1990). A focus theory of normative conduct: Recycling the concept of norms to reduce littering in public places. *Journal of Personaliy and Social Psychology*, 58(6), 1015–1026.)

Attribution The process of making inferences about the causes of one's own behaviour and that of others.

Fundamental attribution error The tendency to attribute the behaviour of others to internal causes (personality, likes, and so forth).

Actor–observer bias The tendency to attribute the behaviour of others to internal causes while attributing one's own behaviour to external causes (situations and circumstances).

Social influence Changes in a person's behaviour induced by the presence or actions of others.

Madonna has adopted two children from Malawi. Do you attribute her actions to selfless concern for the suffering of children in Malawi? Or do you think she was motivated by a selfish desire to hog the limelight? Such attributions greatly affect how we perceive and respond to the social behaviour of others.

SURVEY QUESTION>
What have social psychologists learned about social influence?

norm about whether littering is acceptable. The moral? The cleaner a public area is kept, the less likely are people to "trash" it (Cialdini, Reno, & Kallgren, 1990).

Making Attributions

Valerie just insulted Sasha. But why? Every day we must guess how people will act, and why, often from small shreds of evidence. We do this through a process called **attribution.** As we observe others, we make inferences about them. Why did Nick change his college major? Why does Kristi talk so fast when she's around men? In answering such questions, we *attribute* people's behaviour to various causes. It doesn't matter whether we are right or wrong about the causes of their behaviour, our conclusions still affect how *we act.* To learn how we fill in the "person behind the mask," let's explore the making of attributions.

Two people enter a restaurant and order different meals. Nell tastes her food, then salts it. Bert salts his food before he tastes it. How would you explain their behaviour? In Nell's case, you might assume that the *food* needed salt. If so, you have attributed her actions to an *external cause* (one that lies outside a person). With Bert, you might be more inclined to conclude that he must really *like* salt. If so, the cause of his behaviour is internal. *Internal causes,* such as needs, personality traits, and Bert's taste for salt, lie within the person.

What effects do such interpretations have? It is difficult to fully understand social behaviour without considering the attributions that we make. For instance, let's say that at the last five parties you've been to, you've seen a woman named Marcy. Based on this, you assume that Marcy likes to socialize. You see Marcy at yet another gathering and mention that she seems to like parties. She says, "Actually, I hate these parties, but I get invited to play my tuba at them. My music teacher says I need to practise in front of an audience, so I keep attending these dumb events. Want to hear a Sousa march?"

We seldom know the real reasons for others' actions. That's why we tend to infer causes from *circumstances.* However, in doing so, we often make mistakes like the one with Marcy. The most common error is to attribute the actions of others to internal causes (Follett & Hess, 2002; Jones & Nisbett, 1971). This mistake is called the **fundamental attribution error.** We tend to think the actions of others have internal causes even if they are actually caused by external forces or circumstances.

Where our own behaviour is concerned, we are more likely to think that external causes explain our actions. In other words, there is an **actor–observer bias** in how we explain behaviour. As *observers,* we attribute the behaviour of others to their wants, motives, and personality traits (this is the fundamental attribution error). As *actors,* we tend to find external explanations for our own behaviour (Gordon & Kaplar, 2002). No doubt you chose your major in school because of what it has to offer. Other students choose *their* majors because of the kind of people they are. Other people who don't leave tips in restaurants are cheapskates. If you don't leave a tip, it's because the service was bad. And, of course, other people are always late because they are irresponsible. You are late because you were held up by events beyond your control.

SOCIAL INFLUENCE—FOLLOW THE LEADER

No topic lies nearer the heart of social psychology than **social influence** (changes in behaviour induced by the actions of others). When people interact, they almost always affect one another's behaviour (Crano, 2000; Kassin, Fein, & Markus, 2008). For example, in a sidewalk experiment, various numbers of people stood on a busy New York City street. On cue they all looked at a sixth-floor window across the street. A camera recorded how many passersby also stopped to stare. The larger the influencing group, the more people were swayed to join in staring at the window (Milgram, Bickman, & Berkowitz, 1969).

Are there different kinds of social influence? Social influence ranges from mild to strong. The gentlest form of social influence is *mere presence* (changing behaviour just because other people are nearby). We *conform* when we spontaneously change our behaviour to bring it into agreement with others. Compliance is a more directed form of social influence. We *comply* when we change our behaviour in response to another person who has little or no social power, or authority. Obedience is an even stronger form of social influence. We *obey* when we change our behaviour in direct response to the demands of an authority. The strongest form of social influence is *coercion* (changing behaviour because you are forced to).

Mere Presence

Suppose you just happened to be alone in a room, playing air guitar enthusiastically. Would you continue if a stranger entered the room? **Mere presence** refers to the tendency for people to change their behaviour just because of the presence of other people. Let's explore some of the ways mere presence can induce us to modify our behaviour.

Imagine you are out riding your mountain bike when another rider pulls up beside you. Will you pick up your pace? Slow down? Completely ignore the other rider? Psychologist Norman Triplett's 1898 investigation of just such a social situation was the first published social psychology experiment (Strube, 2005). According to Triplett, you are more likely to speed up. This is **social facilitation,** the tendency to perform better when in the presence of others.

Does mere presence always improve performance? No. If you are confident in your abilities, your behaviour will most likely be facilitated in the presence of others. If you are not, then your performance is more likely to be impaired (Uziel, 2007). Another classic study focused on college students shooting pool at a student union. Good players who were confident (sharks?) normally made 71 percent of their shots. Their accuracy improved to 80 percent when they were being watched by others. Less confident, average players (marks?), who normally made 36 percent of their shots, dropped to 25 percent accuracy when someone was watching them (Michaels et al., 1982).

Social loafing is another consequence of having other people nearby. People tend to work less hard (loaf) when they are part of a group than they do when they are solely responsible for their work. In one study, people playing tug-of-war while blindfolded pulled harder if they thought they were competing alone. When they thought others were on their team, they made less of an effort (Ingham et al., 1974).

Conformity

When Harry met Sally, they fell in love and were not shy about expressing themselves around campus. Some students in Harry's classes advised him to be a bit more discreet. Increasingly, Sally noticed other students staring at her and Harry when they were, well, expressing their love. Although they never made a conscious decision to conform, in another week their publicly intimate moments were a thing of the past. Like it or not, life is filled with instances of conformity.

Daily behaviour is probably most influenced by group pressures for conformity (Baron, Byrne, & Branscombe, 2007). We all **conform** to a degree. In fact, some uniformity is a necessity. Imagine being totally unable to anticipate the actions of others. In stores, schools, and homes this would be frustrating and disturbing. On the highways it would be lethal. And there is an evolutionary advantage to conforming: The advantage accrues from doing the safe thing (what other people have done) rather than the risky thing (choosing a new, untried behaviour that might get you killed).

Mere presence The tendency for people to change their behaviour just because of the presence of other people.

Social facilitation The tendency to perform better when in the presence of others.

Social loafing The tendency for people to work less hard when part of a group than when they are solely responsible for their work.

Conformity Bringing one's behaviour into agreement or harmony with norms or with the behaviour of others in a group in the absence of any direct pressure.

Conformity is a subtle dimension of daily life. Notice the similarities in clothing and hairstyles among these couples.

© Roy Morsch/Corbis

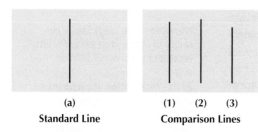

(a)
Standard Line

(1) (2) (3)
Comparison Lines

▸▸**FIGURE 14.4** Stimuli used in Solomon Asch's conformity experiments.

Groupthink A compulsion by members of decision-making groups to maintain agreement, even at the cost of critical thinking.

The Asch Experiment

How strong are group pressures for conformity? One of the first experiments on conformity was staged by Solomon Asch (1907–1996). To fully appreciate it, imagine yourself as a subject. Assume that you are seated at a table with six other students. Your task is actually quite simple. On each trial, you are shown three lines. Your job is to select the line that matches a "standard" line (Figure 14.4).

As the testing begins, each person announces an answer for the first card. When your turn comes, you agree with the others. "This isn't hard at all," you say to yourself. For several more trials your answers agree with those of the group. Then comes a shock. All six people announce that line 1 matches the standard, and you were about to say line 2 matches. Suddenly you feel alone and upset. You nervously look at the lines again. The room falls silent. Everyone seems to be staring at you. The experimenter awaits your answer. Do you yield to the group?

In this study the other "students" were all actors who gave the wrong answer on about a third of the trials to create group pressure (Asch, 1956). Real students conformed to the group on about one-third of the critical trials. Of those tested, 75 percent yielded at least once. People who were tested alone erred in less than 1 percent of their judgments. Clearly, those who yielded to group pressures were denying what their eyes told them.

Are some people more susceptible to group pressures than others? People with high needs for structure or certainty are more likely to conform. So are people who are anxious, low in self-confidence, or concerned with the approval of others. People who live in cultures that emphasize group cooperation (such as many Asian cultures) are also more likely to conform (Bond & Smith, 1996).

In addition to personal characteristics, certain situations tend to encourage conformity—sometimes with disastrous results. Read Critical Thinking: "Groupthink—Agreement at Any Cost" for a prime example.

Group Factors in Conformity

How do groups enforce norms? In most groups, we have been rewarded with acceptance and approval for conformity and threatened with rejection or ridicule for nonconformity. These reactions are called *group sanctions*. Negative sanctions range from laughter, staring, or

CRITICAL THINKING

Groupthink—Agreement at Any Cost

Yale psychologist Irving Janis (1918–1990) first proposed the concept of groupthink in an attempt to understand a series of disastrous decisions made by government officials (Janis, 1989). The core of **groupthink** is misguided loyalty—an urge by decision makers to maintain each other's approval, even at the cost of critical thinking (Singer, 2005). Group members are hesitant to rock the boat, question sloppy thinking, or tolerate alternative views. This self-censorship leads people to believe they agree more than they actually do (Henningsen et al., 2006; Whyte, 2000).

Groupthink has been blamed for contributing to many crises, such as the invasion and occupation of Iraq (Houghton, 2008; Singer, 2005); the *Columbia* space shuttle disaster in 2003; and the loss, in 1999, of the $165 million *Mars Climate Orbiter*. An analysis of 19 international crises found that groupthink contributed to most (Schafer & Crichlow, 1996).

To prevent groupthink, group leaders should take the following steps:

- Define each group member's role as a "critical evaluator."
- Avoid revealing any personal preferences in the beginning.
- State the problem factually, without bias.
- Invite a group member or outside person to play devil's advocate.
- Make it clear that group members will be held accountable for decisions.
- Encourage open inquiry and a search for alternative solutions (Baron, 2005; Chen et al., 1996).

In fairness to our decision makers, it is worth noting that the presence of too many alternatives can lead to *deadlock*, which can delay taking necessary action (Kowert, 2002). Regardless, in an age clouded by the threat of war and terrorism, even stronger solutions to the problem of groupthink would be welcome. Perhaps we should form a group to think about it!

social disapproval to complete rejection or formal exclusion. If you've ever felt the sudden chill of disapproval by others, you will understand the power of group sanctions—just as Harry and Sally did.

Wouldn't the effectiveness of group sanctions depend on the importance of the group? Yes. The more important group membership is to a person, the more he or she will be influenced by other group members. The risk of being rejected can be a threat to our sense of personal identity (Crano, 2000). That's why the Asch experiments are impressive. Because these were only temporary groups, sanctions were informal and rejection had no lasting importance. So in one view, the power of the group was evident in the conforming responses. Of course, these same factors mean that there was very little reason for the students in Asch's experiment not to conform, and since the groups were temporary, participants had little investment in whether their group reached a correct decision. Perhaps you can imagine a student in a contemporary rerun of Asch's experiment, witnessing their confederates make obviously wrong responses, then saying "Whatever!" and going along with the crowd. What would you do?

What other factors, besides importance of the group, affect the degree of conformity? In the sidewalk experiment described earlier, we noted that large groups had more influence. In Asch's face-to-face groups, the size of the majority also made a difference, but a surprisingly small one. In other studies, the number of people who conformed increased dramatically as the majority grew from two to three people. However, a majority of three produced about as much yielding as a majority of eight. The next time you want to talk someone into (or out of) something, take two friends along and see what a difference it makes!

Even more important than the size of the majority is its *unanimity* (total agreement). Having at least one person in your corner can greatly reduce pressures to conform. When Asch gave subjects an ally (who also opposed the majority by giving the correct answer), conformity was lessened. In terms of numbers, a unanimous majority of three is more powerful than a majority of eight with one dissenting.

Compliance—A Foot in the Door

Pressures to "fit in" and conform are usually indirect. In contrast, the term **compliance** refers to situations in which one person bends to the requests of another person who has little or

> **Compliance** Bending to the requests of a person who has little or no authority or other form of social power.

✔ STUDY BREAK Groups, Attribution, Mere Presence, and Conformity

Reflect

How do you feel about participating in group projects at college? Have you ever encountered a social loafer? (*You* were never one, right?) How did you react?

Do you commit the fundamental attribution error? Try to think of a specific example that illustrates the concept.

Identify a recent time when you conformed in some way. How did norms, group pressure, sanctions, and unanimity contribute to your tendency to conform?

Learning Check

1. Status refers to a set of expected behaviours associated with a social position. T or F?
2. The fundamental attribution error is to attribute the actions of others to internal causes. T or F?

3. The effect one person's behaviour has on another is called _____ _____.
4. The mere presence of others always improves performance. T or F?
5. Subjects in Solomon Asch's conformity study yielded on about 75 percent of the critical trials. T or F?
6. Nonconformity is punished by negative group _____.
7. Janis used the term _____ to describe a compulsion among decision-making groups to maintain an illusion of unanimity.

Critical Thinking

8. Would it be possible to be completely nonconforming (i.e., to not conform to any group norm)?

Answers

1. F 2. T 3. social influence 4. F 5. F 6. sanctions 7. groupthink 8. A person who did not follow at least some norms concerning normal social behaviour would very likely be perceived as extremely bizarre, disturbed, or psychotic.

Foot-in-the-door effect The tendency for a person who has first complied with a small request to be more likely later to fulfill a larger request.

Door-in-the-face effect The tendency for a person who has refused a major request to subsequently be more likely to comply with a minor request.

Low-ball technique A strategy in which commitment is gained first to reasonable or desirable terms, which are then made less reasonable or desirable.

no authority. These more direct pressures to comply are quite common. For example, a stranger might ask to borrow your cell phone so he can make a call, a salesperson might suggest that you buy a more expensive watch than you had planned on, or a co-worker might ask you for money to buy a cappuccino.

What determines whether a person will comply with a request? Many factors could be listed, but three stand out as especially interesting.

The Foot-in-the-Door Effect

People who sell door to door have long recognized that once they get a foot in the door, a sale is almost a sure thing. To state the **foot-in-the-door effect** more formally, a person who first agrees to a small request is later more likely to comply with a larger demand (Pascual & Guéguen, 2005). For instance, if someone asked you to put a large, ugly sign in your front yard to promote safe driving, you would probably refuse. If, however, you had first agreed to put a small sign in your window, you would later be much more likely to allow the big sign in your yard.

Apparently, the foot-in-the-door effect is based on observing one's own behaviour. Seeing yourself agree to a small request helps convince you that you didn't mind doing what was asked. After that, you are more likely to comply with a larger request (Pascual & Guéguen, 2005).

The Door-in-the-Face Effect

Let's say that a neighbour comes to your door and asks you to feed his dogs, water his plants, and mow his lawn while he is out of town for a month. This is quite a major request—one that most people would probably turn down. Feeling only slightly guilty, you tell your neighbour that you're sorry but you can't help him. Now, what if the same neighbour returns the next day and asks if you would at least pick up his mail while he is gone. Chances are very good that you would honour this request, even if you might have originally turned it down, too.

Psychologist Robert Cialdini coined the term **door-in-the-face effect** to describe the tendency for a person who has refused a major request to agree to a smaller request. In other words, after a person has turned down a major request ("slammed the door in your face"), he or she may be more willing to comply with a lesser demand. This strategy works because a person who abandons a large request appears to have given up something. In response, many people feel that they must repay her or him by giving in to the smaller request (Cialdini & Goldstein, 2004). In fact, a good way to get another person to comply with a request is to first do a small favour for the person.

The Low-Ball Technique

Anyone who has purchased an automobile will recognize a third way of inducing compliance. Automobile dealers are notorious for convincing customers to buy cars by offering "low-ball" prices that undercut the competition. The dealer first gets the customer to agree to buy at an attractively low price. Then, once the customer is committed, various techniques are used to bump the price up before the sale is concluded.

The **low-ball technique** consists of getting a person committed to act and then making the terms of acting less desirable (Guéguen, Pascual, & Dagot, 2002). Here's another example: A fellow student asks to borrow $25 for a day. This seems reasonable and you agree. However, once you have given your classmate the money, he explains that it would be easier to repay you after payday, in two weeks. If you agree, you've succumbed to the low-ball technique.

CALVIN AND HOBBES © 1985 Watterson. Dist. by UNIVERSAL UCLICK. Reprinted with permission. All rights reserved.

Obedience—Would You Electrocute a Stranger?

A person who has social power in one situation may have very little in another. In those situations where a person has power, she or he is described as an *authority*. When an authority commands **obedience,** the pressure to conform is greater than when someone with little or no authority requests compliance. Let's investigate obedience, a special type of conformity to the demands of an authority.

The question is this: If ordered to do so, would you shock a man with a heart condition who is screaming and asking to be released? Certainly, few people would obey. Or would they? In Nazi Germany, obedient soldiers helped slaughter more than 6 million people in concentration camps. Do such inhumane acts reflect deep character flaws? Are they the acts of heartless psychopaths or crazed killers? Or are they simply the result of obedience to authority? These are questions that puzzled social psychologist Stanley Milgram (1965) when he began a provocative series of studies on obedience.

How did Milgram study obedience? As was true of the Asch experiments, Milgram's research is best appreciated by imagining yourself as a subject. Place yourself in the following situation.

Milgram's Obedience Studies

Imagine answering a newspaper ad to take part in a "learning" experiment at Yale University. When you arrive, a coin is flipped and a second person, a pleasant-looking man in his 50s, is designated the "learner." By chance you have become the "teacher."

Your task is to read a list of word pairs. The learner's task is to memorize them. You are to punish him with an electric shock each time he makes a mistake. The learner is taken to an adjacent room and you watch as he is seated in an "electric chair" apparatus. Electrodes are attached to his wrists. You are then escorted to your position in front of a "shock generator." On this device is a row of 30 switches marked from 15 to 450 volts. Corresponding labels range from "Slight Shock" to "Extreme Intensity Shock" and finally "Danger: Severe Shock." Your instructions are to shock the learner each time he makes a mistake. You must begin with 15 volts and then move one switch (15 volts) higher for each additional mistake (Figure 14.5).

The experiment begins, and the learner soon makes his first error. You flip a switch. More mistakes. Rapidly you reach the 75-volt level. The learner moans after each shock. At 100 volts he complains that he has a heart condition. At 150 volts he says he no longer wants to continue and demands to be released. At 300 volts he screams and says he can no longer give answers.

▶▶**FIGURE 14.5** Scenes from Stanley Milgram's classic study of obedience: the "shock generator," strapping a "learner" into his chair, and a "teacher" being told to administer a severe shock to the learner. (From the film "Obedience" © 1968 by Stanley Milgram, © renewed by Alexandra Milgram, and distributed by The Pennsylvania State University Media Sales. Permission granted by Alexandra Milgram.)

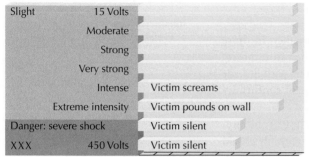

Slight	15 Volts	
	Moderate	
	Strong	
	Very strong	
	Intense	Victim screams
	Extreme intensity	Victim pounds on wall
Danger: severe shock		Victim silent
XXX	450 Volts	Victim silent

10 20 30 40 50 60 70 80 90 100
Percentage of subjects obeying
command at each shock level

▶▶**FIGURE 14.6** Results of Milgram's obedience experiment. Only a minority of subjects refused to provide shocks, even at the most extreme intensities. The first substantial drop in obedience occurred at the 300-volt level (Milgram, 1963).

At some point, you begin to protest to the experimenter. "That man has a heart condition," you say. "I'm not going to kill that man." The experimenter says, "Please continue." Another shock and another scream from the learner and you say, "You mean I've got to keep going up the scale? No, sir. I'm not going to give him 450 volts!" The experimenter says, "The experiment requires that you continue." For a time the learner refuses to answer any more questions and screams with each shock (Milgram, 1965). Then he falls chillingly silent for the rest of the experiment.

It's hard to believe many people would do this. What happened? Milgram also doubted that many people would obey his orders. When he polled a group of psychiatrists before the experiment, they predicted that less than 1 percent of those tested would obey. The astounding fact is that 65 percent obeyed completely by going all the way to the 450-volt level. Virtually no one stopped short of 300 volts ("Severe Shock") (Figure 14.6).

Was the learner injured? No. The "learner" was actually an actor who turned a tape recorder on and off in the shock room. No shocks were ever administered, but the dilemma for the "teacher" was quite real. Subjects protested, sweated, trembled, stuttered, bit their lips, and laughed nervously. Clearly they were disturbed by what they were doing. Nevertheless, most obeyed the experimenter's orders. You may doubt that Milgram's study of obedience applies to you. If so, take a moment to read Discovering Psychology: "Quack Like a Duck."

Milgram's Follow-Up

Why did so many people obey? Some have suggested that the prestige of Yale University added to subjects' willingness to obey. Could it be that they assumed that the professor running the experiment would not really allow anyone to be hurt? To test this possibility, the study was rerun in a shabby office building in nearby Bridgeport, Connecticut. Under these conditions, fewer people obeyed (48 percent).

Milgram was disturbed by the willingness of people to knuckle under to authority and senselessly shock someone. In later experiments, he tried to reduce obedience. He found that the distance between the teacher and the learner was important. When subjects were in the *same room* as the learner, only 40 percent obeyed fully. When they were *face-to-face* with the learner and were required to force his hand down on a simulated "shock plate," only 30 percent obeyed (Figure 14.7). Distance from the authority also had an effect. When the experimenter gave his orders over the phone, only 22 percent obeyed.

USING PSYCHOLOGY

Quack Like a Duck

Imagine your response to the following events. On the first day of class, your psychology professor begins to establish the basic rules of behaviour for the course. Draw a line under the first instruction you think you would refuse to carry out.

1. Seats are assigned and you are told to move to a new location.
2. You are told not to talk during class.
3. Your professor tells you that you must have permission to leave early.
4. You are told to bring your textbook to class at all times.
5. Your professor tells you to use only a pencil for taking notes.
6. You are directed to take off your watch.

7. The professor tells you to keep both hands on your desktop at all times.
8. You are instructed to keep both of your feet flat on the floor.
9. You are told to stand up and clap your hands three times.
10. Your professor says, "Stick two fingers up your nose and quack like a duck."

At what point would you stop obeying such orders? In reality, you might find yourself obeying a legitimate authority long after that person's demands had become unreasonable (Aronson, Wilson, & Akert, 2007).

Implications

Milgram's research raises nagging questions about our willingness to commit antisocial or inhumane acts commanded by a "legitimate authority." Milgram suggested that when directions come from an authority, people rationalize that they are not personally responsible for their actions. In locales as diverse as Cambodia, Rwanda, Bosnia, Vietnam, Darfur, Sri Lanka, Syria, and Iraq, the tragic result has been "sanctioned massacres" of chilling proportions. Even in everyday life, crimes of obedience are common (Zimbardo, 2007). In order to keep their jobs, some people obey orders to do things that they know are dishonest, unethical, or harmful (Hamilton & Sanders, 1995).

Let's end on a more positive note. In one of his experiments, Milgram found that group support can greatly reduce destructive obedience. When real subjects saw two other "teachers" (both actors) resist orders and walk out of the experiment, only 10 percent continued to obey. Thus, a personal assertion of courage or moral fortitude by one or two members of a group may free others to disobey misguided or unjust authority.

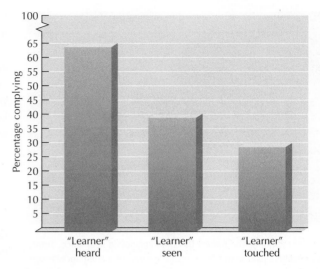

▸▸**FIGURE 14.7** Physical distance from the "learner" had a significant effect on the percentage of subjects obeying orders.

Coercion—Brainwashing and Cults

We close this section on social influence by examining some forms of *coercion,* the most extreme type of social influence. You are being **coerced** if you are forced to change your beliefs or your behaviour against your will.

If you're a history enthusiast, you may associate *brainwashing* with techniques used by the Communist Chinese on prisoners during the Korean War. Through various types of "thought reform," the Chinese were able to coerce some of these prisoners to sign false confessions. More recently, the mass murder/suicide at Jonestown, the Branch Davidian tragedy at Waco, the Heaven's Gate group suicide in San Diego, and Osama bin Laden's al-Qaeda movement have heightened public interest in forced attitude change.

How does coercion differ from other forms of social influence? Brainwashing requires a captive audience. If you are offended by a television commercial, you can change the channel. Prisoners in prisoner-of-war camps are completely at the mercy of their captors. Complete control over the environment allows a degree of psychological manipulation that would be impossible in a normal setting.

Brainwashing

How does captivity facilitate coercion? Brainwashing typically begins by making the target person feel completely helpless. Physical and psychological abuse, lack of sleep, humiliation, and isolation serve to *unfreeze,* or loosen, former values and beliefs. When exhaustion, pressure, and fear become unbearable, *change* occurs as the person begins to abandon former beliefs. Prisoners who reach the breaking point may sign a false confession or cooperate to gain relief. When they do, they are suddenly rewarded with praise, privileges, food, or rest. From that point on, a mixture of hope and fear, plus pressures to conform, serves to *refreeze* (solidify) new attitudes (Taylor, 2004).

How permanent are changes caused by brainwashing? In most cases, the dramatic shift in attitudes brought about by brainwashing is temporary. Most "converted" prisoners who returned to the United States after the Korean War eventually reverted to their original beliefs. Nevertheless, brainwashing can be powerful, as shown by the success of cults in recruiting new members.

Cults

Exhorted by their leader, some 900 members of the Reverend Jim Jones's People's Temple picked up paper cups and drank purple Kool-Aid laced with the deadly poison cyanide.

Coercion Being forced to change your beliefs or your behaviour against your will.

In the tragic fire at the Branch Davidian compound near Waco, Texas, some members paid with their lives for giving total allegiance to cult leader David Koresh.

Psychologically the mass suicide at Jonestown in 1978 is not so incredible as it might seem (Dein & Littlewood, 2005). The inhabitants of Jonestown were isolated in the jungles of Guyana, intimidated by guards, and lulled with sedatives. They were also cut off from friends and relatives and totally accustomed to obeying rigid rules of conduct, which primed them for Jones's final "loyalty test." Of greater psychological interest is the question of how people reach such a state of commitment and dependency.

Why do people join groups such as the People's Temple? The People's Temple was a classic example of a **cult,** an authoritarian group in which the leader's personality is more important than the beliefs she or he preaches. Cult members give their allegiance to this person, who is regarded as infallible, and they follow his or her dictates without question. Almost always, cult members are victimized by their leaders in one way or another.

For example, in April 1993, David Koresh and members of his Branch Davidian group perished in a fire at their Waco, Texas, compound. Like Jim Jones had done years before in Jonestown, Koresh took nearly total control of his followers' lives. He told them what to eat, dictated sexual mores, and had errant followers paddled. Followers were persuaded to surrender money, property, and even their children and wives. And like other cult leaders, Jones and Koresh demanded absolute loyalty and obedience to themselves and to their cult, with tragic results (Dein & Littlewood, 2005; Reiterman, 1993).

Psychologist and pioneering brainwashing expert Margaret Singer (1921–2003) studied and aided hundreds of former cult members. Her interviews reveal that in recruiting new members, cults use a powerful blend of guilt, manipulation, isolation, deception, fear, and escalating commitment. In this respect, cults employ high-pressure indoctrination techniques not unlike those used in brainwashing (Singer, 2003; Singer & Addis, 1992).

Cult A group that professes great devotion to some person and follows that person almost without question; cult members are typically victimized by their leaders in various ways.

Recruitment

Some people studied by Singer were seriously distressed when they joined a cult. Most, however, were simply undergoing a period of mild depression, indecision, or alienation from family and friends (Hunter, 1998). Cult members try to catch potential converts at a time of need—especially when a sense of belonging will be attractive to converts. For instance, many people were approached just after a romance had broken up or when they were struggling with exams or were trying to become independent from their families (Sirkin, 1990). At such times, people are easily persuaded that joining the group is all they need to do to be happy again (Hunter, 1998). Adolescents are especially vulnerable to recruitment into cults as they may be seeking a cause to conform to as a replacement for the parental authority they are rebelling against (Richmond, 2004).

Conversion

How is conversion achieved? Often it begins with intense displays of affection and understanding ("love bombing"). Next comes isolation from people who are not cult members, and drills, discipline, and rituals (all-night meditation or continuous chanting, for instance). These rituals wear down physical and emotional resistance, discourage critical thinking, and generate feelings of commitment (Langone, 2002).

Many cults make clever use of the foot-in-the-door technique, described earlier. At first, recruits make small commitments (to stay after a meeting, for example). Then larger commitments are encouraged (to stay an extra day, to call in sick at work, and so forth). Making a major commitment is usually the final step. The new devotee signs over a bank account or property to the group, moves in with the group, and so forth.

Aftermath of the mass suicide at Jonestown, in Guyana. How do cultlike groups recruit new devotees?

Making such major public commitments creates a powerful cognitive dissonance effect. Before long, it becomes virtually impossible for converts to admit they have made a mistake.

Once in the group, members are cut off from family and friends (former reference groups), and the cult can control the flow and interpretation of information to them. Members are isolated from their former value systems and social structures. Conversion is complete when they come to think of themselves more as group members than as individuals. At this point obedience is nearly total (Wexler, 1995).

Assertiveness Training—Standing Up for Your Rights

Most of us have been rewarded, first as children and later as adults, for compliant, obedient, or "good" behaviour. Perhaps this is why so many people find it difficult to assert themselves. Or perhaps not asserting yourself is related to anxiety about making a scene or feeling disliked by others. Whatever the causes, some people suffer anguish in any situation requiring poise, self-confidence, or self-assertion. Have you ever done any of the following?

- Hesitated to question an error on a restaurant bill because you were afraid of making a scene?
- Backed out of asking for a raise or a change in working conditions?
- Said yes when you wanted to say no?
- Been afraid to question a grade that seemed unfair?

If you've ever had trouble with similar situations, *assertiveness training* (instruction in how to be self-assertive) may offer a solution. The first step in assertiveness training is to convince yourself of three basic rights: You have the right to refuse, to request, and to right a wrong. **Self-assertion** involves standing up for these rights by speaking out on your own behalf.

Is self-assertion just getting things your own way? Not at all. A basic distinction can be made between *self-assertion* and *aggressive* behaviour. Self-assertion is a direct, honest expression of feelings and desires. It is not exclusively self-serving. People who are non-assertive are usually patient to a fault. In contrast to assertive behaviour, **aggression** involves hurting another person or achieving one's goals at the expense of another. Aggression does not take into account the feelings or rights of others. It is an attempt to get one's own way no matter what. Assertion techniques emphasize firmness, not attack (Table 14.2).

The basic idea in assertiveness training is that each assertive action is practised until it can be repeated even under stress. For example, let's say it really angers you when a store clerk waits on several people who arrived after you did. To improve your assertiveness in this situation, you would begin by *rehearsing* the dialogue, posture, and gestures you

Self-assertion A direct, honest expression of feelings and desires.
Aggression Hurting another person or achieving one's goals at the expense of another person.

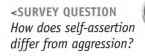
<SURVEY QUESTION
How does self-assertion differ from aggression?

Associated Press photographer Jeff Widener snapped this timeless photo of a lone protester literally standing up on his own behalf while he halted a column of tanks during the 1989 pro-democracy rallies in Tiananmen Square in Beijing, China. How many of us would find the courage to assert ourselves against such direct expressions of authority?

■ Table 14.2 **Comparison of Assertive, Aggressive, and Non-assertive Behaviour**

	Actor	Receiver of Behaviour
Non-assertive behaviour	Self-denying, inhibited, hurt, and anxious; lets others make choices; goals not achieved	Feels sympathy, guilt, or contempt for actor; achieves goals at actor's expense
Aggressive behaviour	Achieves goals at others' expense; expresses feelings, but hurts others; chooses for others or puts them down	Feels hurt, defensive, humiliated, or taken advantage of; does not meet own needs
Assertive behaviour	Self-enhancing; acts in own best interests; expresses feelings; respects rights of others; goals usually achieved; self-respect maintained	Needs respected and feelings expressed; may achieve goal; self-worth maintained

STUDY BREAK Compliance, Obedience, Coercion, and Self-Assertion

Reflect

Return to the description of various types of social power. Can you think of a setting in which you have (to a greater or lesser degree) each type of power?

You would like to persuade people to donate to a deserving charity. How, specifically, could you use compliance techniques to get people to donate?

Are you surprised that so many people obeyed orders in Milgram's experiments? Do you think you would have obeyed? How actively do you question authority?

To what extent are governments entitled to use coercion to modify the attitudes or behaviour of their citizens?

Learning Check

1. The term *compliance* refers to situations in which a person complies with commands made by a person who has authority. T or F?
2. Obedience in Milgram's experiments was related to
   a. distance between learner and teacher
   b. distance between experimenter and teacher
   c. obedience of other teachers
   d. all of these

3. By repeating his obedience experiment in a downtown office building, Milgram demonstrated that the prestige of Yale University was the main reason for subjects' willingness to obey in the original experiment. T or F?
4. Brainwashing differs from other persuasive attempts in that brainwashing requires a _____ _____.
5. In assertiveness training, people learn techniques for getting their way in social situations and angry interchanges. T or F?
6. Non-assertive behaviour causes hurt, anxiety, and self-denial in the actor and sympathy, guilt, or contempt in the receiver. T or F?

Critical Thinking

7. Modern warfare allows killing to take place impersonally and at a distance. How does this relate to Milgram's experiments?

Answers

1. F 2. d 3. F 4. captive audience 5. T 6. T 7. There is a big difference between killing someone in hand-to-hand combat and killing someone by lining up images on a video screen. Milgram's research suggests that it would be easier for a person to follow orders to kill another human when the victim is at a distance and removed from personal contact.

would use to confront the clerk or the other customer. Working in front of a mirror can be very helpful. Rehearsal and role-playing should also be used when you expect a possible confrontation with someone—for example, if you are going to ask for a raise, challenge a grade, or confront a landlord.

Self-assertion does not supply instant poise, confidence, or self-assurance. However, it is a way of combating anxieties associated with life in a sometimes intimidating society. If you are interested in more information, you can consult the book titled *Your Perfect Right,* by Robert Alberti and Michael Emmons (2008).

ATTITUDES—BELIEF + EMOTION + ACTION

SURVEY QUESTION>
How are attitudes acquired and changed?

Attitude A learned tendency to respond to people, objects, or institutions in a positive or negative way.

What is your attitude toward affirmative action, euthanasia, environmental groups, the death penalty, legalized abortion, junk food, psychology? Your answers can have far-reaching effects on your behaviour. Attitudes are intimately woven into our actions and views of the world. Our tastes, friendships, votes, preferences, goals, and behaviour in many other situations are all touched by attitudes (Baumeister & Bushman, 2008).

What specifically is an attitude? An **attitude** is a mixture of belief and emotion that predisposes a person to respond to other people, objects, or groups in a positive or negative way. Attitudes summarize your *evaluation* of objects (Oskamp & Schultz, 2005). As a result, they predict or direct future actions.

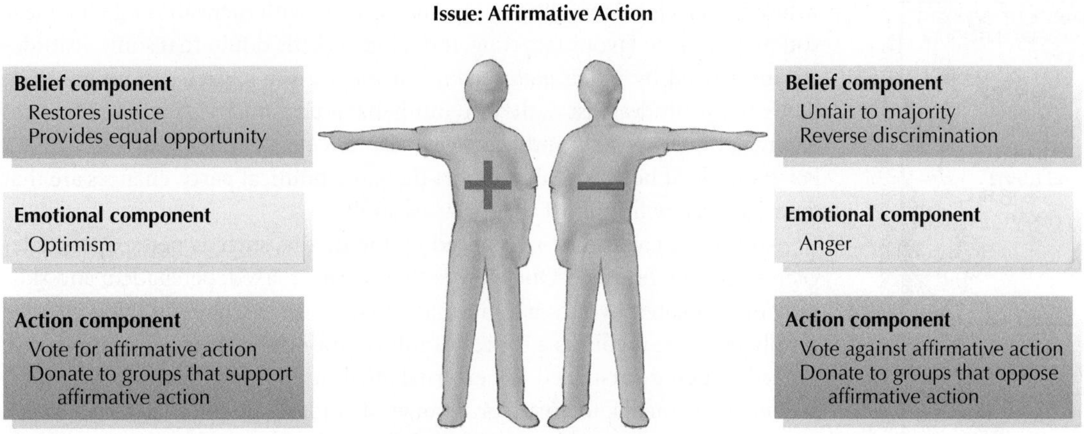

Issue: Affirmative Action

Belief component
Restores justice
Provides equal opportunity

Emotional component
Optimism

Action component
Vote for affirmative action
Donate to groups that support
    affirmative action

Belief component
Unfair to majority
Reverse discrimination

Emotional component
Anger

Action component
Vote against affirmative action
Donate to groups that oppose
    affirmative action

▸▸**FIGURE 14.8** Elements of positive and negative attitudes toward affirmative action.

"Your attitude is showing," is sometimes said. Actually, attitudes are expressed through beliefs, emotions, and actions. The *belief component* of an attitude is what you believe about a particular object or issue. The *emotional component* consists of your feelings toward the attitudinal object. The *action component* refers to your actions toward various people, objects, or institutions. Consider, for example, your attitude toward gun control. You will have beliefs about whether gun control affects rates of crime or violence. You will respond emotionally to guns, finding them either attractive and desirable or threatening and destructive. And you will have a tendency to seek out or avoid gun ownership. The action component of your attitude may well include support of organizations that support or oppose gun control. As you can see, attitudes orient us to the social world. In doing so, they prepare us to act in certain ways (Albarracín, Johnson, & Zanna, 2005). (For another example, see Figure 14.8.)

Forming Attitudes

How do people acquire attitudes? In fact, attitudes are not always acquired—they can be influenced by biological and genetic factors. James Olson and his colleagues at Western University studied attitudes to a large number of targets (objects, processes, and ideas) among identical and fraternal twins (Olson et al., 2001). They found that differences in attitudes among their respondents were partially determined by genetics—so that identical twins were more similar in attitude than fraternal twins. Those attitudes that were most heritable were most strongly held and resistant to pressure to conform. Olson and his colleagues discussed a number of personality traits and other variables that might explain how attitudes could be partially genetically determined: For example, people who are more physically coordinated might be better at athletic activities and so have a more positive attitude to those activities.

Of course, attitudes can also be acquired in a number of ways. Sometimes, attitudes come from *direct contact* (personal experience) with the object of the attitude—such as opposing pollution when a nearby factory ruins your favourite river (Ajzen, 2005). As Western's James Olson and his colleague Mark Zanna of the University of Waterloo have pointed out, some attitudes are simply formed through *chance conditioning* (learning that takes place by chance or coincidence) (Olson & Zanna, 1993). Let's say, for instance, that you have had three encounters in your lifetime with psychologists. If all three were negative, you might take an unduly dim view of psychology. In the same way, people often develop strong attitudes toward cities, foods, or parts of the country on the basis of one or two unusually good or bad experiences.

Attitudes are also learned through *interaction with others,* that is, through discussion with people holding a particular attitude. For instance, if three of your good friends are

volunteers at a local recycling centre and you talk with them about their beliefs, you may come to favour recycling, too. There is little doubt that some attitudes are influenced by *group membership.* In most groups, pressures to conform shape our attitudes, just as they do our behaviour. *Child rearing* (the effects of parental values, beliefs, and practices) also affects attitudes (Bartram, 2006). For example, if both parents support the same political party, chances are that their children will support that party as adults.

Attitudes may also be influenced by the media, such as newspapers, television, and the Internet. One view is that we are coaxed, persuaded, and skilfully manipulated by messages in mass media. An alternative view is that we simply treat the media as a source of information. The latter view argues that instead of being persuaded (an external attribution) we evaluate information provided by media to form or change attitudes (an internal attribution). Ninety-nine percent of North American homes have a television set. According to recent Canadian and U.S. government data, the average person in either country watches just under three hours of television per day. Does the information brought into homes this way have an impact? It may well. For instance, frequent viewers mistrust others and overestimate their own chances of being harmed. One possible explanation is that a steady diet of TV violence leads some people to develop a *mean worldview,* in which they regard the world as a dangerous and threatening place (Eschholz, Chiricos, & Gertz, 2003). An alternative explanation, which may be just as likely, is that mistrustful or fearful people choose to watch more television rather than be out among people they don't trust. With correlational data, of course, you simply can know which way the cause goes.

Attitudes and Behaviour

Why are some attitudes acted on, while others are not? To answer this question, let's consider an example. Assume that a woman named Lorraine knows that automobiles are expensive to operate and add to air pollution, and she hates smog. Why would Lorraine continue to drive to work every day? Probably it is because the *immediate consequences* of our actions weigh heavily on the choices we make. No matter what Lorraine's attitude may be, it is difficult for her to resist the immediate convenience of driving. Our expectations of how *others will evaluate* our actions are also important. Lorraine may resist taking public transit to work for fear that her co-workers will be critical of her environmental stand. By taking this factor into account, researchers have been able to predict family planning choices, alcohol use by teenagers, re-enlistment in the U.S. National Guard, voting on a nuclear power plant initiative, and so forth (Cialdini, 2001). Finally, we must not overlook the effects of long-standing *habits* (Oskamp & Schultz, 2005). Let's say that after years of driving to work Lorraine finally vows to shift to public transit. Despite her good intentions, it would not be unusual if she found herself driving again two months later because of habit.

In short, there are often large differences between attitudes and behaviour—particularly between privately held attitudes and public behaviour. However, barriers to action typically fall when a person holds an attitude with *conviction.* If you have conviction about an issue, it evokes strong feelings, you think about it and discuss it often, and you are knowledgeable about it. Attitudes held with passionate conviction often lead to major changes in personal behaviour (Oskamp & Schultz, 2005).

ATTITUDE CHANGE—MEET THE "SEEKERS"

Reference group Any group that an individual uses as a standard for social comparison.

Although attitudes are fairly stable, they do change. Some attitude change can be understood in terms of **reference groups** (any group an individual uses as a standard for social comparison). It is not necessary to have face-to-face contact with other people for them to be a reference group. It depends instead on whom you identify with or whose attitudes and values you care about (Ajzen, 2005).

Persuasion

What about advertising and other direct attempts to change attitudes? Are they effective? **Persuasion** is any deliberate attempt to change attitudes or beliefs through information and arguments (Brock & Green, 2005). Businesses, politicians, and others who seek to persuade us obviously believe that attitudes can be changed. Billions of dollars are spent yearly on television advertising in the United States and Canada alone. Persuasion can range from the daily blitz of media commercials to personal discussion among friends. In most cases, the success or failure of persuasion can be understood if we consider the *communicator*, the *message*, and the *audience*.

At a community meeting, let's say you have a chance to promote an issue important to you (for or against building a new mall nearby, for instance). Whom should you choose to make the presentation, and how should that person present it? Research suggests that attitude change is encouraged when the following conditions are met. You should have little trouble seeing how these principles are applied to selling everything from underarm deodorants to politicians:

1. The communicator is likable, expressive, trustworthy, an expert on the topic, and similar to the audience in some respect.
2. The communicator appears to have nothing to gain if the audience accepts the message.
3. The message appeals to emotions, particularly to fear or anxiety.
4. The message also provides a clear course of action that will, if followed, reduce fear or produce personally desirable results.
5. The message states clear-cut conclusions.
6. The message is backed up by facts and statistics.
7. The message is repeated as frequently as possible.
8. Both sides of the argument are presented in the case of a well-informed audience.
9. Only one side of the argument is presented in the case of a poorly informed audience (Aronson, 1992; Oskamp & Schultz, 2005).

As we have just seen, we sometimes change our attitudes in response to external persuasion (Gass & Seiter, 2007). Sometimes, however, the internal process of *cognitive dissonance* can also lead to attitude change.

Cognitive Dissonance Theory

Cognitions are thoughts. Dissonance means clashing. The influential theory of **cognitive dissonance** states that contradicting or clashing thoughts cause discomfort. That is, we have a need for *consistency* in our thoughts, perceptions, and images of ourselves (Cooper, Mirabile, & Scher, 2005; Festinger, 1957). Inconsistency, then, can motivate people to make their thoughts or attitudes agree with their actions (Oskamp & Schultz, 2005).

For example, smokers are told on every pack of cigarettes that smoking endangers their lives. They light up and smoke anyway. How do they resolve the tension between this information and their actions? They could quit smoking, but it

> **Persuasion** A deliberate attempt to change attitudes or beliefs with information and arguments.
> **Cognitive dissonance** An uncomfortable clash between self-image, thoughts, beliefs, attitudes, or perceptions and one's behaviour.

CP Photo/Jonathan Hayward

Persuasion. Would you be likely to be swayed by this group's message? Successful persuasion is related to characteristics of the communicator, the message, and the audience.

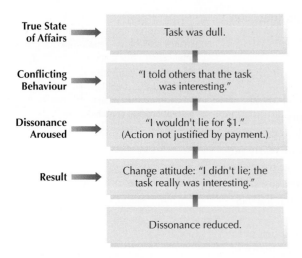

True State of Affairs →	Task was dull.
Conflicting Behaviour →	"I told others that the task was interesting."
Dissonance Aroused →	"I wouldn't lie for $1." (Action not justified by payment.)
Result →	Change attitude: "I didn't lie; the task really was interesting."
	Dissonance reduced.

▸▸**FIGURE 14.9** Summary of the Festinger and Carlsmith (1959) study from the viewpoint of a person experiencing cognitive dissonance.

may be easier to convince themselves that smoking is not really so dangerous. To do this, a smoker might seek examples of heavy smokers who have lived long lives, spend time with other smokers, and avoid information about the link between smoking and cancer. According to cognitive dissonance theory, we also tend to reject new information that contradicts ideas we already hold.

Acting contrary to one's attitudes doesn't always bring about change. How does cognitive dissonance explain that? The amount of justification for acting contrary to your attitudes and beliefs affects how much dissonance you feel. (*Justification* is the degree to which a person's actions are explained by rewards or other circumstances.) In a classic study, college students did an extremely boring task (turning wooden pegs on a board) for a *long* time. Afterwards, they were asked to help lure others into the experiment by pretending that the task was interesting and enjoyable. Students paid $20 for lying to others did not change their own negative opinion of the task: "That was *really* boring!" Those who were paid only $1 later rated the task as "pleasant" and "interesting." How can we explain these results? Apparently, students paid $20 experienced no dissonance. These students could reassure themselves that anybody would tell a little white lie for $20. Those paid $1 were faced with the conflicting thoughts: "I lied" and "I had no good reason to do it." Rather than admit to themselves that they had lied, these students changed their attitude toward what they had done (Festinger & Carlsmith, 1959) (Figure 14.9).

For another example of cognitive dissidence, consider Celia, a college student and self-professed environmental activist. Recently, Celia "inherited" a car from her parents, who were replacing the family clunker. In the past, Celia biked or used public transportation to get around. Her parents' old car is an antiquated gas guzzler, but she has begun to drive it every day. How might Celia reduce the cognitive dissonance created by the clash between her environmentalism and her use of an inefficient automobile? See Table 14.3 for possible strategies.

■ Table 14.3 **Strategies for Reducing Cognitive Dissonance**

Celia, who is a college student, has always thought of herself as an environmental activist. Recently, Celia "inherited" a car from her parents, who were replacing the family clunker. In the past, Celia biked or used public transportation to get around. Her parents' old car is an antiquated gas guzzler, but she has begun to drive it every day. How might Celia reduce the cognitive dissonance created by the clash between her environmentalism and her use of an inefficient automobile?

Strategy	Example
Change your attitude.	"Cars are not really a major environmental problem."
Add consonant thoughts.	"This is an old car, so keeping it on the road makes good use of the resources consumed when it was manufactured."
Change the importance of the dissonant thoughts.	"It's more important for me to support the environmental movement politically than it is to worry about how I get to school and work."
Reduce the amount of perceived choice.	"My schedule has become too hectic. I really can't afford to bike or take the bus any more."
Change your behaviour.	"I'm only going to use the car when it's impossible to bike or take the bus."

Source: After Franzoi, 2002.

STUDY BREAK **Attitudes and Attitude Change**

Reflect

Describe an attitude that is important to you. What are its three components?

Which of the various sources of attitudes best explain your own attitudes?

Who belongs to your most important reference group?

Imagine that you would like to persuade voters to support an initiative to preserve a small wilderness area by converting it to a park. Using research on persuasion as a guide, what could you do to be more effective?

How would you explain cognitive dissonance theory to a person who knows nothing about it?

Learning Check

1. Attitudes have three parts: a _____ component, an _____ component, and an _____ component.
2. Which of the following is associated with attitude formation?
   a. group membership
   b. mass media
   c. chance conditioning
   d. child rearing
   e. all of the preceding
   f. a and d only

3. In presenting a persuasive message, it is best to give both sides of the argument if the audience is already well informed on the topic. T or F?
4. Much attitude change is related to a desire to avoid clashing or contradictory thoughts, an idea summarized by _____ _____ theory.

Critical Thinking

5. Students entering a college gym are asked to sign a banner promoting water conservation. Later, the students shower at the gym. What effect would you expect signing the banner to have on how long students stay in the showers?
6. Cognitive dissonance theory predicts that false confessions obtained during brainwashing are not likely to bring about lasting changes in attitudes. Why?

Answers

1. belief, emotional, action   2. e   3. T   4. cognitive dissonance   5. Cognitive dissonance theory predicts that students who sign the banner will take shorter showers, to be consistent with their publicly expressed support of water conservation. This is exactly the result observed in a study done by social psychologist Elliot Aronson.   6. Because there is strong justification for such actions. As a result, little cognitive dissonance is created when a prisoner makes statements that contradict her or his beliefs.

PREJUDICE—ATTITUDES THAT INJURE

Love and friendship bring people together. Prejudice, which is marked by suspicion, fear, or hatred, has the opposite effect. **Prejudice** is a negative emotional attitude held toward members of specific social groups. The phenomenon—members of one group holding negative emotional attitudes toward members of a different group—is found all over the world. Prejudices may be reflected in the policies of police departments, schools, or government institutions (Dovidio, Glick, & Rudman, 2005). In such cases, prejudice is referred to as *racism, sexism, ageism,* or *heterosexism,* depending on the group affected. In Canada, research on prejudice has typically focused on the experiences of different ethnic groups. The first psychologist to study prejudice from the point of view of the victim was the Univeristy of Toronto's Kenneth Dion. You can learn more about his work in Human Diversity: "Experiencing Prejudice."

Many studies of the experience of prejudice in Canada rely on a large-scale survey carried out by the Canadian government in 2002 and known as the Ethnic Diversity Survey. This survey of approximately 47 000 people of various ethnicities included questions about the extent to which respondents felt part of society, and also questions about their experience of prejudice. Twenty-four percent of visible minority respondents said that they felt uncomfortable or out of place in Canada because of their ethnicity or religion. The survey also provided data about actual experiences of discrimination. **Discrimination** refers to unequal treatment of people who should have the same rights as others. About 20 percent of visible minority respondents reported suffering such discrimination sometimes or often over the previous five years. The reported experience rate did vary noticeably by subgroup: It was highest for Blacks at 32 percent, followed by South Asians at 21 percent and Chinese

<SURVEY QUESTION
What causes prejudice and intergroup conflict?

Prejudice A negative emotional attitude held against members of a particular group of people.
Discrimination Treating members of various social groups differently in circumstances where their rights or treatment should be identical.

Experiencing Prejudice

What does psychological research tell us about the experience of prejudice in Canada? Research on prejudice originally focused largely on the psychology of the prejudiced person, asking why he or she held such views. The impetus to change that approach and consider the experience of prejudice from the victim's perspective came to a large extent from the late Kenneth Dion, a psychologist at the University of Toronto (e.g., Dion & Earn, 1975; Dion, Earn, & Yee, 1978). Through his work, what it feels like to be the victim of prejudice became an important research topic.

Dion developed a theory of the experience of prejudice as a psychosocial stressor. If we see prejudice as producing stress, then all that we know about the effects of stress becomes applicable to the experience of prejudice. To test this stressor theory, Dion, Dion, and Banerjee (2009) analyzed data from the Canadian Ethnic Diversity Survey, referred to above. They considered three indices of well-being: a sense of belonging to Canadian society, a sense of trust of people encountered in the local community, and satisfaction with life. They also asked whether experiencing discrimination

on multiple bases—e.g., skin colour, religion, language, and accent—made the effect on well-being worse compared with experiencing discrimination only on a single basis. They called this the "multiple jeopardy" hypothesis.

Reported discrimination was negatively related to well-being on all three measures: sense of belonging, trust, and life satisfaction (Dion et al., 2009). The effect was strongest for visible minorities but was found for all groups studied. However, the multiple jeopardy hypothesis was supported only for Anglophones outside of Quebec. Dion and his colleagues suggested that for the Anglophone majority group, discrimination was unusual and therefore had a stronger effect when it did occur. It's important to note that this does not mean that visible minority people don't feel the effects of discrimination. The argument, based on self-reports made by visible minority respondents, is that it's already horrible to be discriminated against on the basis of skin colour. It doesn't get much more horrible when discrimination on some other basis, such as accent, is added to the mix.

at 18 percent. A report on this survey by Statistics Canada is available at http://www.statcan .gc.ca/pub/89-593-x/89-593-x2003001-eng.pdf.

Becoming Prejudiced

How do prejudices develop? One major theory suggests that prejudice is a form of *scapegoating* (blaming a person or a group for the actions of others or for conditions not of their making). Scapegoating is a type of *displaced aggression* in which hostilities triggered by frustration are redirected at "safer" targets (Nelson, 2006).

At times, the development of prejudice (like other attitudes) can be traced to direct experiences with members of the rejected group. A child who is repeatedly bullied by members of a particular ethnic group might develop a lifelong dislike for all members of the group. Yet, even subtle influences, such as parents' attitudes, the depiction of people in books and on TV, and exposure to children of other races, may have an impact.

Distinguished psychologist Gordon Allport (1958) concluded that there are two important sources of prejudice. *Personal prejudice* occurs when members of another ethnic group are perceived as a threat to one's own interests. For example, members of another group may be viewed as competitors for jobs. *Group prejudice* occurs when a person conforms to group norms. Let's say, for instance, that you have no personal reason for disliking out-group members. Nevertheless, your friends, acquaintances, or co-workers expect it of you.

The Prejudiced Personality

Other research suggests that prejudice can be a general personality characteristic. Theodore Adorno and his associates (1950) carefully probed what they called the *authoritarian personality.* These researchers started out by studying anti-Semitism. In the process, they found that people who are prejudiced against one out-group tend to be prejudiced against *all* out-groups (Perreault & Bourhis, 1999).

What are the characteristics of the prejudice-prone personality? The **authoritarian personality** is marked by rigidity, inhibition, prejudice, and oversimplification. Authoritarians also

Authoritarian personality A personality pattern characterized by rigidity; inhibition; prejudice; and an excessive concern with power, authority, and obedience.

tend to be very *ethnocentric.* **Ethnocentrism** refers to placing one's own group at the centre, usually by rejecting all other groups. Put more simply, authoritarians consider their own ethnic group superior to others.

Even if we discount the obvious bigotry of the authoritarian personality, racial prejudice runs deep in many nations. Let's probe deeper to find the roots of such prejudiced behaviour.

Ethnocentrism Placing one's own group or race at the centre—that is, tending to reject all other groups but one's own.
Social stereotypes Oversimplified images of the traits of individuals who belong to a particular social group.
Symbolic prejudice Prejudice that is expressed in disguised fashion.

INTERGROUP CONFLICT—THE ROOTS OF PREJUDICE

An unfortunate by-product of group membership is that it often limits contact with people in other groups. Additionally, groups themselves may come into conflict. Both events tend to foster hatred and prejudice toward the out-group. The bloody clashes of opposing forces in various parts of the world are reminders that intergroup conflict is widespread. Daily, we read of jarring strife between political, religious, or ethnic groups. These conflicts are almost always amplified by stereotyped images of out-group members (Bar-Tal & Labin, 2001).

What exactly is a stereotype? **Social stereotypes** are oversimplified images of people in various groups. There is a good chance that you have stereotyped images of some of the following: Anglo-Canadians, French Canadians, Haitians, Jews, women, Christians, old people, men, social conservatives, blue-collar workers, politicians, business executives, teenagers, and billionaires (Figure 14.10). In general, the top three categories on which most stereotypes are based are sex, age, and race (Fiske et al., 2002).

When a prejudiced person meets a pleasant or likable member of a rejected group, the out-group member tends to be perceived as an exception to the rule, not as evidence against the stereotype. This prevents prejudiced persons from changing their stereotyped beliefs (Wilder, Simon, & Faith, 1996).

Some researchers argue that racism today is often disguised by **symbolic prejudice.** The idea is that people who realize that crude and obvious racism is socially unacceptable may express prejudice in thinly veiled forms, for example, when they state their opinions about affirmative action, immigration, crime, and so on. On this view, modern racists find ways to rationalize their prejudice so that it seems to be based on issues other than raw racism. While it is possible that such an effect exists, we should not assume that opposition to affirmative action or immigration is necessarily racist. It is possible to make principled arguments against those processes. In recent research at the University of Guelph in Ontario, Leanne Son Hing and colleagues (Son Hing et al., 2011) investigated attitudes to the merit principle, the belief that outcomes should be distributed on the basis of merit. This belief that can be used to argue against affirmative action policies, so some researchers assume that the belief is racist. Is that a reasonable assumption?

Son Hing and her colleagues distinguished two different kinds of belief in the merit principle, which they called prescriptive and descriptive. The difference is that some people believe that society *should* be run on the basis of merit (prescriptive), while others believe that it *is* run on the basis of merit (descriptive). An example of the latter view is that poor people are poor because they are lazy or incompetent. In Son Hing's study, people who believed in the descriptive merit principle also had other *hierarchy-legitimizing* views. That is, their view was that things are as they should be in society and that we don't need to change. People who believed, instead, that the merit principle is how society should be organized rather than how it is organized did not show the same hierarchy-legitimizing views. Such people opposed affirmative action policies only when those violated the merit principle, not in general.

▸▸**FIGURE 14.10** Racial stereotypes are common in sports. For example, a study confirmed that many people actually do believe that "white men can't jump." This stereotype implies that African-American basketball players are naturally superior in athletic ability. European-American players, in contrast, are falsely perceived as smarter and harder working than African Americans. Such stereotypes set up expectations that distort the perceptions of fans, coaches, and sportswriters. The resulting misperceptions, in turn, help perpetuate the stereotypes (Stone, Perry, & Darley, 1997).

Ethnic pride is slowly replacing stereotypes and discrimination. However, despite affirmations of ethnic heritage, the problem of prejudice is far from solved.

EPphoto/Shutterstock

Two experiments, both in unlikely settings and both using children, offer some additional insights into how stereotypes and intergroup tensions develop.

Experiments in Prejudice

What is it like to be discriminated against? In an interesting experiment conducted in North Carolina in 1973, Caucasian elementary school children were given direct experience with prejudice (Weiner & Wright, 1973). On the first day of the experiment, children were randomly assigned to the Orange or Green group and given coloured armbands. Orange children were treated better than Green children—they were given privileges, and the teacher announced to the class that Orange children were smarter, cleaner, and better behaved. Throughout the day, the teacher praised the Orange children and criticized the Green children. On day 2, the roles were reversed, so that Green children were treated better. On the third day of the experiment and again two weeks later, children were given a test of racial prejudice and asked to commit themselves to interaction with Black people. Compared to a control group—another class in the same grade in the same school—children who had the experience of discrimination held less prejudiced beliefs about Black people and were more willing to commit to a social interaction with them, both on the third day and two weeks later.

The colour of an armband might seem like a trivial basis for creating prejudices. However, people primarily use skin colour to make decisions about the race of another person (Brown, Dane, & Durham, 1998). Surely, this is just as superficial a way of judging people as armband colour is, especially given recent biological evidence that it does not even make genetic sense to talk about "races" (Bonham, Warshauer-Baker, & Collins, 2005). (See "Understand That Race Is a Social Construction" later in this chapter.)

Equal-Status Contact

What can be done to combat prejudice? According to Canadian psychologists James Olson and Mark Zanna, more frequent *equal-status contact* between groups in conflict should reduce prejudice and stereotyping (Olson & Zanna, 1993; Wernet et al., 2003). Equal-status contact refers to interacting on an equal footing, without obvious differences in power or status. In various studies, mixed-race groups have been formed at work, in the laboratory, and at schools. The conclusion from such research is that personal contact with a disliked group tends to induce friendly behaviour, respect, and liking. However, these benefits occur only when personal contact is cooperative and on an equal footing (Grack & Richman, 1996). But personal contact may not be enough—especially for people who are not in fact prejudiced against members of other groups. For more on this somewhat surprising observation, see Critical Thinking: "The Pitfalls of Empathy."

Superordinate Goals

Let us now consider a revealing study done with 11-year-old boys. When the boys arrived at a summer camp, they were split into two groups and housed in separate cabins. At first the groups were kept apart to build up separate

Yuri Arcurs/Shutterstock

The Pitfalls of Empathy

Empathy refers to the sharing of experience or the understanding of how another person feels or what they are thinking. Most of us think of empathy as a good thing. So consider this question: Do you think that feeling empathy for minority group members who have experienced racism would lead you to respond in a warmer, friendlier way to a member of that minority group? You might be tempted to say, "Of course!" After all, that's the whole idea behind the advice to "walk a mile in someone else's shoes before you criticize them." And obviously that was the inspiration for the Weiner and Wright (1973) study with the orange and green armbands: Give children an experience that will help them feel what the person suffering discrimination feels.

Unfortunately, life is seldom as simple as this recipe suggests. Psychologist Jacquie Vorauer of the University of Manitoba has found that trying to be empathic can have the opposite effect to that intended (Vorauer & Sasaki, 2009, 2012). The problem has to do with what are called metaperceptions. Think about your professor for a moment. How do you think your professor sees you? Perhaps you think that she or he sees you as a hard-working, capable student. That's a metaperception—it's your perception of someone else's perception of you. Now consider what happens in an intergroup interaction. In this situation, you're dealing with a particular person. Vorauer says that you are probably going to think about how that person evaluates you. So your metaperceptions are now important.

Vorauer distinguished between low-prejudice (LP) and high-prejudice (HP) persons on the basis of responses to a questionnaire. Vorauer believes that LPs and HPs have different metaperceptions. LPs expect to be seen in a positive light, to be seen as unprejudiced. Because they are not worried about being seen as prejudiced, they "slack off" in the communication of their attitude. HPs, in contrast, are concerned that in an intergroup interaction they will be seen as prejudiced—so they work harder to prevent that perception. The ironic result is that in an actual interaction with a visible minority person, an HP may behave more favourably than an LP.

In fact, this result is made more likely by encouraging empathy. Remember the Weiner and Wright orange/green armbands study? What was the point of that intervention? To get children to think about what it feels like to be discriminated against. Suppose that you are interacting with a person who belongs to some other group. You want to be fair so you try to see things from his or her perspective. What's the first thing you see? The first thing you see is—you. That's who the other person is interacting with. Thus, being empathic in this situation makes you more likely to be influenced by your own metaperceptions about the other group (Vorauer & Sasaki, 2012).

How can we prevent such counterintuitive effects? It turns out that the unfortunate influence of empathy on intergroup interactions can be eliminated if the minority group member just talks about some hardship or distress he or she has suffered as a consequence of prejudice. In that case, instead of empathy leading you to see yourself from the other person's perspective, it draws your attention to *their* experience and *their* feelings, and then empathy does what we expect it to do.

So here are the important ideas we get from Vorauer's research: First, being with an out-group person introduces your metaperceptions—your ideas about how that person will evaluate you. Second, people who are confident that they do not have racist attitudes may assume that an out-group interaction partner will know that and thus not work very hard to communicate their attitude. Third, when you encourage someone to be empathic, to take the other person's perspective in an intergroup interaction, you encourage them to think about themselves—to focus on how they look from the interaction partner's perspective. Fourth, empathy in intergroup interaction has a beneficial effect if the out-group person reduces the in-group person's self-focus, for example, by talking about hardships she has suffered. As we said—intergroup interaction isn't simple. But then, not much to do with human psychology is.

group identities and friendships. Soon each group had a flag and a name (the "Rattlers" and the "Eagles") and each had staked out its territory. At this point the two groups were placed in competition with each other. After a number of clashes, disliking between the groups bordered on hatred: The boys baited each other, started fights, and raided each other's cabins (Sherif et al., 1961).

Were they allowed to go home hating each other? As an experiment in reducing intergroup conflict, and to prevent the boys from remaining enemies, various strategies to reduce tensions were tried. Holding meetings between group leaders did nothing. When the groups were invited to eat together, the event turned into a free-for-all. Finally, emergencies that required *cooperation* among members of both groups were staged at the camp. For example, the water supply was damaged so that all the boys had to work together to repair it. Creating this and other **superordinate goals** helped restore peace between the two groups. (A superordinate goal exceeds or overrides other, lesser goals.)

Cooperation and shared goals seem to help reduce conflict by encouraging people in opposing groups to see themselves as members of a single, larger group (Gaertner et al., 2000). Superordinate goals, in other words, have a "we're all in the same boat" effect on perceptions of group membership (Olson & Zanna, 1993). The power of superordinate goals

Superordinate goal A goal that exceeds or overrides all others; a goal that renders other goals relatively less important.

STUDY BREAK Prejudice and Intergroup Conflict

Reflect

Mentally scan over the events of the last week. How would they have changed if prejudices of all types ceased to exist?

Think of the most rigid person you know. Does she or he match the profile of the authoritarian personality?

Stereotypes exist for many social categories, even ordinary ones such as "college student" and "unmarried young adult." What stereotypes do you think you face in daily life?

Learning Check

1. As a basis for prejudice, _____ is frequently related to frustration and displaced _____.
2. The authoritarian personality tends to be prejudiced against all out-groups, a quality referred to as _____.
3. The stereotypes underlying racial and ethnic prejudice tend to evolve from the superordinate goals that often separate groups. T or F?

4. The term *symbolic prejudice* refers to racism or prejudice that is expressed in disguised or hidden form. T or F?
5. Jane Elliot's classroom experiment in prejudice showed that children could be made to dislike one another by imposing status inequalities. T or F?
6. Research suggests that prejudice and intergroup conflict may be reduced by _____ interaction and _____ goals.

Critical Thinking

7. In court trials, defence lawyers sometimes try to identify and eliminate prospective jurors who have authoritarian personality traits. Can you guess why?

Answers

1. scapegoating, aggression 2. ethnocentrism 3. F 4. T 5. T 6. equal-status, superordinate 7. Because authoritarians tend to believe that punishment is effective, they are more likely to vote for conviction.

---

can be seen in the unity that prevailed in the United States (and throughout much of the rest of the world) for months after the September 11 terrorist attacks.

To summarize, prejudice will be reduced when:

- Members of different groups have equal status *within the situation* that brings them together.
- Members of all groups seek a common goal.
- Group members must cooperate to reach the goal.
- Group members spend enough time together for cross-group friendships to develop.

Sports teams are an excellent example of a situation in which all of these conditions apply. The close contact and interdependent effort required in team sports often creates lifelong friendships and breaks down the walls of prejudice.

AGGRESSION—THE WORLD'S MOST DANGEROUS ANIMAL

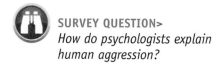

SURVEY QUESTION>
How do psychologists explain human aggression?

"I know not with what weapons World War III will be fought, but World War IV will be fought with sticks and stones."
—Albert Einstein

For a time, the City Zoo of Los Angeles, California, had on display two examples of the world's most dangerous animal—the only animal capable of destroying the Earth and all other animal species. Perhaps you have already guessed which animal it was. In the cage were two college students, representing the species *Homo sapiens*!

About 58 million humans were killed by other humans (an average of nearly one person per minute) during the 125-year period ending with World War II. War, homicide, riots, family violence, assassination, rape, assault, forcible robbery, and other violent acts offer testimony to human aggression. Still, it would be wrong to overstate our capacity for aggression. To give you some perspective, the Population Reference Bureau estimates that during that same 125-year period, a total of perhaps 7 billion people were born. So, during that period, about 1 in every 121 people died due to human aggression—but 120 out of 121 died of some other cause. How do you feel about that number?

What causes aggression? Aggression refers to any action carried out with the intention of harming another person. Aggression has many potential causes. Brief descriptions of some of the major possibilities follow.

Instincts

Some ethologists argue that we are naturally aggressive creatures, having inherited a "killer instinct" from our animal ancestors (Blanchard & Blanchard, 2003). (An *ethologist* is a person who studies the natural behaviour patterns of animals.) Noted ethologist Konrad Lorenz (1966, 1974) also believed that humans lack certain innate patterns that inhibit aggression in animals. For example, in a dispute, two wolves may growl, lunge, bare their teeth, and fiercely threaten each other. In most instances, though, neither is killed or even wounded. One wolf, recognizing the dominance of the other, will typically bare its throat in a gesture of submission. The dominant wolf could kill in an instant, but it is inhibited by the other wolf's submissive gesture. In contrast, human confrontations of equal intensity often end in injury or death.

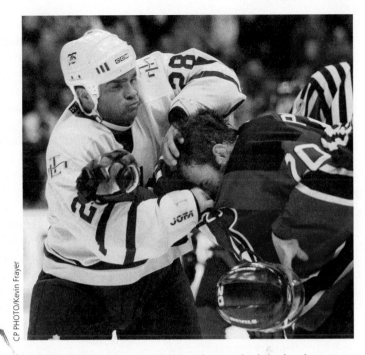

CP PHOTO/Kevin Frayer

Ritualized human aggression. Violent and aggressive behaviour is so common it may be viewed as entertainment. How "natural" is aggressive behaviour?

The idea that humans are "naturally" aggressive has an intuitive appeal, but many psychologists question it. Many of Lorenz's "explanations" of aggression are little more than loose comparisons between human and animal behaviour. Just labelling a behaviour "instinctive" does little to explain it. More important, we are left with the question of why some individuals or human groups (the Arapesh, the Senoi, the Navajo, the Inuit, and others) show little hostility or aggression. And, thankfully, the vast majority of humans *do not* kill or harm others.

Recently, there has been even more reason to doubt that humans are naturally aggressive. Cushman and his colleagues (2012) found that people asked to simulate a harmful action suffered a strong stress reaction, even before doing the action and even though they knew it was only pretend. An example action is drawing a rubber knife across a person's throat—simulating murder. No harm was done, but the behaviour caused a stress reaction compared with a control condition (e.g., using the rubber knife to simulate carving a cardboard loaf of bread). The implication is that we are "wired" to have an aversion to doing harm to other people. For an ordinary person to go to war, he or she must overcome that aversion, which may later be a source of distress.

Biology

Despite problems with the instinctive view, aggression does have biological roots. Physiological studies have shown that some brain areas are capable of triggering or ending aggressive behaviour. Mara Brendgen and her colleagues at the University of Montreal evaluated genetic and environmental contributions to both reactive and proactive aggression in 172 pairs of six-year-old twins (Brendgen et al., 2006, 2008). They concluded that variability in both kinds of aggression is due to both genetic and environmental factors. Much of the genetic contribution was common to both forms of violence, suggesting that they reflect some underlying characteristic. Genetic factors that may influence aggression include, for example, a low physiological arousal threshold in the brain. An example of an environmental factor is a harsh, threatening, and unpredictable home environment.

Brendgen and her colleagues concluded that while genetic effects are important, whether a child uses more reactive or more proactive aggression is largely determined by specific aspects of his or her environment. In a more recent study, the same Montreal group assessed a twin sample at age seven. Slightly more than 50 percent of the variability in reputation for being aggressive was traced to genetic influences (Brendgen et al., 2011).

If violence has a biological cause, we might expect even very young children to be violent (even if they haven't had time to learn violent responses). Richard Tremblay and his colleagues at the University of Montreal have been studying violence in children for some time (Tremblay, 2012). Perhaps the most remarkable idea this group has advanced is that, contrary to long-held views, children do not learn violent responses in adolescence, as suggested by the "age-crime curve" (Blumstein, Cohen, & Farrington, 1988). Rather, they start life as violent beings, with aggressive behaviour peaking between 24 and 42 months, after which most children learn to control aggression and solve problems in other ways. As Donald Hebb put it, children do not need to learn how to have a temper tantrum. In Tremblay's words, "children do not need to learn to use physical aggression from their environment; they rather learn not to use physical aggression" (p. 2). Recall the discussion above of Mara Brendgen's twin studies, which showed both genetic and environmental influences on children's aggression. It's possible that more violent children don't experience the kind of environment that teaches people not to use physical aggression.

The effects of alcohol and other drugs provide another indication of the role of the brain and biology in violence and aggression. A variety of studies show that alcohol is involved in large percentages of murders and violent crimes. Intoxicating drugs also seem to lower inhibitions to act aggressively—often with tragic results (Anderson & Bushman, 2002; Quigley & Leonard, 2000). Alcohol and drugs may also have something to do with dating violence among students. How serious is this problem? One study interviewed students at 31 universities in Europe, North America, Latin America, Asia, the Middle East, Australia, and New Zealand (Straus, 2004). The researchers involved are all members of the International Dating Violence Research Consortium (http://pubpages.unh.edu/~mas2/ID.htm). A total of 8666 students responded, of whom two-thirds were women (because most of the classes surveyed were courses in psychology or sociology, which usually have a majority of women students). Considering just severe assaults (punching and attacks with objects), about one in ten students had attacked their partner in the previous year. There was little effect of geography: All regions were represented among the more violent and less violent universities.

Women committed a larger number of severe assaults than men at 18 of the 31 universities. However, the injury data tell a different story: Men had a higher rate of causing severe injury at 26 universities. In a smaller-scale study of dating violence at four universities in Mexico, Texas, and New Hampshire, reports of violence varied from 30 to 46 percent of participating couples (Straus & Ramirez, 2007). In these samples, the most common finding was for women and men to be equally likely to be violent.

How do students compare to other groups? For context, in a recent study of violence by men against their female partners in Quebec, 16.7 percent of the 18- to 24-year-old women interviewed reported that their male partners had severely physically assaulted them in the previous year (Rinfret-Raynor et al., 2004). In the Straus (2004) study, the corresponding number for men at Montreal universities severely assaulting a dating partner was 7.9 percent.

To summarize, the fact that we are biologically *capable* of aggression does not mean that aggression is inevitable or "part of human nature." Twenty eminent scientists who studied the question concluded: "Biology does not condemn humanity to war.... Violence is neither in our evolutionary legacy nor in our genes. The same species that invented war is capable of inventing peace" (Scott & Ginsburg, 1994; UNESCO, 1990). Humans are fully capable of learning to inhibit aggression. For example, North American Quakers and Amish adopt non-violence as a way of life (Bandura, 2001).

Frustration

Step on a dog's tail and you may get nipped. Frustrate a human and you may get insulted. The **frustration-aggression hypothesis** states that frustration tends to lead to aggression.

Does frustration always produce aggression? Although the connection is strong, a moment's thought will show that frustration does not *always* lead to aggression. Frustration, for instance, may lead to stereotyped responding or perhaps to a state of "learned helplessness" (see Chapter 11). Also, aggression can occur in the absence of frustration. This possibility is illustrated by sports spectators who start fights, throw bottles, tear down goal posts, and so forth, after their team has *won*.

Road rage and some highway shootings may be a reaction to the frustration of traffic congestion. The fact that automobiles provide anonymity, or a loss of personal identity, may also encourage aggressive actions that would not otherwise occur.

Aversive Stimuli

Frustration probably encourages aggression because the former is uncomfortable. Various *aversive stimuli*, which produce discomfort or displeasure, can heighten hostility and aggression (Anderson, Anderson, & Deuser, 1996; Morgan, 2005) (Figure 14.11). Examples include insults, high temperatures, pain, and even disgusting scenes or odours. Such stimuli probably raise overall arousal levels so that we become more sensitive to *aggression cues* (signals that are associated with aggression) (Carlson, Marcus-Newhall, & Miller, 1990). Aversive stimuli also tend to activate ideas, memories, and expressions associated with anger and aggression (Morgan, 2005).

Some cues for aggression are internal (angry thoughts, for instance). Many are external: Certain words, actions, and gestures made by others are strongly associated with aggressive responses. A raised middle finger, for instance, is an almost universal invitation to aggression in North America.

Social Learning

One of the most widely accepted explanations of aggression is also the simplest. Social learning theory holds that we learn to be aggressive by observing aggression in others (Bandura, 2001). **Social learning theory** combines learning principles with cognitive processes, socialization, and modelling to explain behaviour. According to this view, there is no instinctive human programming for fist-fighting, pipe bombing, knife wielding, gun loading, 95-mile-an-hour (150-kilometre-per-hour) "bean balls," or other violent or aggressive behaviours. Hence, aggression must be learned (Figure 14.12).

You may recall Richard Tremblay's (2012) finding that violent behaviour peaks before the fourth birthday, declining as children learn alternatives. If Tremblay is right, must social learning theory be wrong as an account of the origins of aggression? In fact, a social learning account of violent behaviour might begin with the role of social learning in providing alternatives to violence. In this case, the small percentage of children who continue to be violent into adolescence and adulthood do not have good role models—their environment does not include strong people who resolve disputes non-violently. It's quite

Frustration-aggression hypothesis Frustration tends to lead to aggression.
Social learning theory Combines learning principles with cognitive processes, socialization, and modelling to explain behaviour.

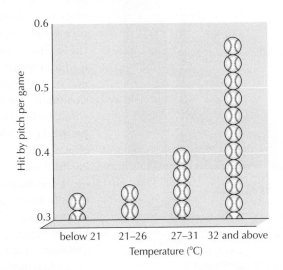

▶▶ **FIGURE 14.11** Personal discomfort caused by aversive (unpleasant) stimuli can make aggressive behaviour more likely. For example, studies of crime rates show that the incidence of highly aggressive behaviour, such as murder, rape, and assault, rises as the air temperature goes from warm to hot to sweltering (Anderson, 1989). The results you see here further confirm the heat–aggression link. The graph shows that there is a strong association between the temperatures at Major League Baseball games and the number of batters hit by a pitch during those games. When the temperature goes over 90 degrees Fahrenheit (32 degrees Celsius), watch out for that fastball! (Reifman, Larrick, & Fein, 1991).

▸▸**FIGURE 14.12** Violent behaviour among delinquent boys doesn't appear overnight. Usually, their capacity for violence develops slowly, as they move from minor aggression to increasingly brutal acts. Overall aggression increases dramatically in early adolescence as boys gain physical strength and more access to weapons (Loeber & Hay, 1997).

possible, then, that learning could increase or decrease aggression. In the ordinary case, young children learn to work out their conflicts with other people peacefully, and not to be violent. But that trend could be counterbalanced by other influences.

Media Violence

Every day, mainstream media provide an endless stream of bad models, especially concerning violence. TV, movies, computer games, and even music lyrics all contain violence. According to the organization Adults and Children Together (ACT) Against Violence, young children spend about 35 hours a week in front of TV or computer screens. By the end of elementary school, children will have seen about 8000 murders and 100 000 other violent acts depicted on TV. Eighty percent of popular video games contain violent content. And, of course, teenagers and young people are also chronically exposed to violence in the media.

How much does media violence affect children? As Albert Bandura showed in his studies of imitation (see Chapter 6), children may learn new aggressive actions by watching violent or aggressive behaviour, or they may learn that violence is "okay." Either way, they are more likely to act aggressively—toward a Bo-Bo doll, at least. Heroes on TV are as violent as the villains, and they usually receive praise for their violence. Boys and girls who watch a lot of violence on TV or play violent video games are much more likely to be aggressive as adults (Huesmann et al., 2003; Bartholow, Bushman, & Sestir, 2006). (See Figure 14.13.) Of course, one cannot say that this is a case of cause and effect. Boys and girls who choose to watch a lot of television violence or play violent video games may already be different from other children in ways that influence their aggressive behaviour. That is, there may be something different about them that causes them both to watch more television violence and to be more aggressive as adults.

In addition to teaching new antisocial actions, media such as TV and video games may disinhibit dangerous impulses that viewers already have. *Disinhibition* (the removal of inhibition) results in acting out behaviour that would normally be restrained. For example, many TV programs give the message that violence is acceptable behaviour that leads to success and popularity. For some people, this message may lower inhibitions against acting out hostile feelings (Anderson et al., 2003). But will it actually lead to violence? Think back to the paper by Cushman and his colleagues (2012) on aversion to doing harm. Cushman reported that people showed stress effects when anticipating their turn to carry out a simulated harmful act. Those same people did not show stress effects when watching someone else simulate the harmful acts. So watching and doing are not the same.

It has been argued that exposure to media violence tends to lower sensitivity to violent acts (Funk, 2005). The argument is as follows: As anyone who has seen a real street fight or mugging can tell you, TV violence is sanitized and unrealistic. The real thing is gross, ugly, and gut-wrenching. Even when media violence is graphic, as it is in many video

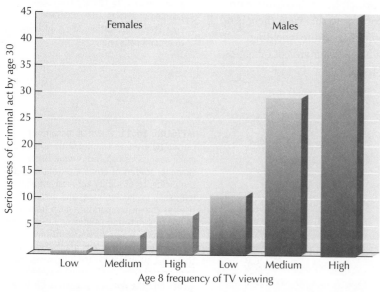

▸▸**FIGURE 14.13** The likelihood of committing criminal acts by age 30 is related to the amount of TV watching a person did when he or she was a child (Eron, 1987). (L.D. Eron, "The Development of Aggressive Behavior from the Perspective of a Developing Behaviorism," *American Psychologist*, p. 435-442, May 1987, Copyright © American Psychological Association, reprinted with permission.)

games, it is experienced in the relaxed and familiar setting of the home. For at least some viewers, this combination diminishes emotional reactions to violent scenes. The argument, then, says that sanitized violence in the media does not produce the revulsion that real violence occasions. Instead, it *desensitizes* people (reduces emotional sensitivity) to violence (Huesmann et al., 2003). But the essence of this argument is that media violence is not realistic. The argument suggests that the reason violent TV shows are popular is because they don't show "blood and guts," but somehow this is evidence that people are drawn to violence. An alternative to Huesmann et al.'s interpretation is that violence depicted on television shows is sanitized precisely because ordinary people are not comfortable with graphic violence. In this view, the causal relation runs from the audience to the television networks, rather than the other way around.

Parents as Media Guides

Other than pulling the plug, what can parents do about media's possible negative effects on children? Actually, quite a lot. Parents can make a big difference if they do the following (ACT Against Violence, 2005; Frydman, 1999):

1. Start by creating a safe, warm environment at home and school and by modelling positive ways of getting along in the world. Children typically model parents' behaviour, including their media viewing habits, and they are guided by parents' reactions to media.
2. Limit total media time so that TV and computer games do not dominate your child's view of the world. If necessary, set schedules for when watching TV or playing video games is allowed. Don't use media as a babysitter.
3. Closely monitor what your child does experience. Change channels or turn off the TV if you object to a program. Be prepared to offer games and activities that stimulate your child's imagination and creativity as well as model positive behaviour and social attitudes.
4. Explore media with your child so that you can counter what is shown. Help your child distinguish between reality and fantasy in media. Reply to distortions, stereotypes, and violence as they appear on screen. Encourage the child to propose more mature, realistic, and positive responses to situations.
5. Show by your own disapproval that violent TV and computer game heroes are not the ones to emulate.

By following these guidelines you can help children learn to enjoy media without being overly influenced by programs and advertisers. One study found that elementary school children become less aggressive when they decrease the amount of time they spend watching TV and playing video games (Robinson et al., 2001).

For the immediate future, it is clear that we need more people who are willing to engage in helpful, altruistic, **prosocial behaviour** (actions that are constructive, altruistic, or helpful to others). In the next section, we will examine some of the forces that prevent people from helping others and look at how to encourage prosocial behaviour.

PROSOCIAL BEHAVIOUR—HELPING OTHERS

In May 2001, employees in a Montreal office building noticed a young woman lying in the rain, naked from the waist down and apparently in pain. They did nothing for three hours, with their supervisor telling them not to get involved. The supervisor, who was subsequently fired, claimed he thought the woman was a vagrant and that he did not know she was in distress at first. When she had not moved three hours later, he asked employees to call the police. The comatose woman was taken to hospital.

This case evoked memories of the murder of Kitty Genovese in Queens, New York, in 1964. Kitty Genovese's murder took more than 30 minutes, but none of her neighbours tried to help. None even called the police until after the attack had ended. Perhaps it is understandable that

> **Prosocial behaviour** Behaviour toward others that is helpful, constructive, or altruistic.

<SURVEY QUESTION
Why are bystanders so often unwilling to help in an emergency?

Does this person need help? What factors determine whether a person in trouble will receive help in an emergency? Surprisingly, more potential helpers tend to lower the chances that help will be given.

no one wanted to get involved. After all, it could have been a violent lovers' quarrel. Or helping might have meant risking personal injury. But what prevented these people from at least calling the police? Although many details of the Kitty Genovese murder have been called into question, the episode was instrumental in launching research into *bystander apathy* (Manning, Levine, & Collins, 2007).

Isn't this an example of the alienation of city life? News reports treated this incident as evidence of a breakdown in social ties caused by the impersonality of the city. Although it is true that urban living can be dehumanizing, this does not fully explain such *bystander apathy* (the unwillingness of bystanders to offer help during emergencies is also referred to as the *bystander effect*). According to landmark work by psychologists John Darley and Bibb Latané (1968), failure to help is related to the number of people present. Over the years many studies have shown that the *more* potential helpers are present, the *less* likely people are to help (Latané, Nida, & Wilson, 1981; Miller, 2006).

Why would people be less willing to help when others are present? In Kitty Genovese's case, the answer is that everyone thought *someone else* would help. The dynamics of this effect are easily illustrated: Suppose that two motorists have stalled by the roadside, one on a sparsely travelled country road and the other on a busy highway. Who gets help first?

On the highway, where hundreds of cars pass every minute, each driver can assume that someone else will help. Personal responsibility for helping is spread so thin that no one takes action. On the country road, one of the first few people to arrive will probably stop, since the responsibility is clearly theirs. In general, Darley and Latané assume that bystanders are not apathetic or uncaring; they are inhibited by the presence of others.

Bystander Intervention

People must pass through four decision points before giving help. First they must notice that something is happening. Next they must define the event as an emergency. Then they must take responsibility. Finally, they must select a course of action (Figure 14.14). Laboratory experiments have shown that each step can be influenced by the presence of other people.

Noticing

What would happen if you fainted and collapsed on the sidewalk? Would someone stop to help? Would people think you were drunk? Would they even notice you? Darley and Latané suggest that if the sidewalk is crowded, few people will even see you. This has nothing to do with people blocking each other's vision. Instead, it is related to widely accepted norms against staring at others in public. People in crowds typically keep their eyes to themselves.

Is there any way to show that this is a factor in bystander apathy? To test this idea, students were asked to fill out a questionnaire either alone or in a room full of people. While the students worked, a thick cloud of smoke was blown into the room through a vent.

▶▶**FIGURE 14.14** This decision tree summarizes the steps a person must take before making a commitment to offer help, according to Darley and Latané's model.

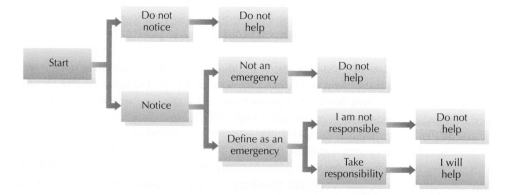

Most students left alone in the room noticed the smoke immediately. Few of the people in groups noticed the smoke until it actually became difficult to see through it. Subjects working in groups politely kept their eyes on their papers and avoided looking at others (or the smoke). In contrast, those who were alone scanned the room from time to time.

Defining an Emergency

The smoke-filled room also shows the influence others have on defining a situation as an emergency. When subjects in groups finally noticed the smoke, they cast sidelong glances at others in the room. (Remember *social comparison*?) Apparently, they were searching for clues to help interpret what was happening. No one wanted to overreact or act like a fool if there was no emergency. However, as subjects coolly surveyed the reactions of others, they were themselves being watched. In real emergencies, people sometimes "fake each other out" and underestimate the need for action because each person attempts to appear calm. In short, until someone acts, no one acts.

Taking Responsibility

Perhaps the most crucial step in helping is assuming responsibility. In this case, groups limit helping by causing a *diffusion of responsibility* (spreading responsibility among several people).

Is that like the unwillingness of drivers to offer help on a crowded highway? Exactly. It is the feeling that no one is personally responsible for helping. This problem was demonstrated in an experiment in which students took part in a group discussion over an intercom system. Actually, there was only one real subject in each group; the others were tape-recorded actors. Each subject was placed in a separate room (supposedly to maintain confidentiality), and discussions of college life were begun. During the discussion, one of the "students" simulated an epileptic-like seizure and called out for help. In some cases, subjects thought they were alone with the seizure victim. Others believed they were members of three- or six-person groups.

People who thought they were alone with the "victim" of this staged emergency reported it immediately or tried to help. Some subjects in the three-person groups failed to respond, and those who did were slower. In the six-person groups, over a third of the subjects took no action at all. People in this experiment were obviously faced with a conflict like that in many real emergencies: Should they be helpful and responsible, or should they mind their own business? Many were influenced toward inaction by the presence of others.

People do help in some emergencies. How are these different? It is not always clear what makes the difference. Helping behaviour is complex and influenced by many variables. One naturalistic experiment staged in a New York City subway gives a hint of the kinds of things that may be important. When a "victim" (actor) "passed out" in a subway car, he received more help when carrying a cane than when carrying a liquor bottle (Piliavin, Rodin, & Piliavin, 1969).

To better answer the question, we need to consider some factors not included in Darley and Latané's account of helping.

Who Will Help Whom?

Many studies suggest that when we see a person in trouble, it tends to cause *heightened arousal* (Dovidio & Penner, 2001). This aroused, keyed-up feeling can motivate us to give aid, but only if the rewards of helping outweigh the costs. Higher costs (such as great effort, personal risk, or possible embarrassment) almost always decrease helping. In addition to general arousal, potential helpers may also feel **empathic arousal.** This means they empathize with the person in need or feel some of the person's pain, fear, or anguish. Helping is much more likely when we are able to take the perspective of others and feel sympathy for their plight (Batson & Powell, 2003).

Empathic arousal is especially likely to motivate helping when the person in need seems to be similar to ourselves (Batson & Powell, 2003). In fact, a feeling of connection to the victim may be one of the most important factors in helping. This, perhaps, is why being in a good mood also increases helping. When we are feeling successful, happy, or fortunate, we may also feel more connected to others (Dovidio & Penner, 2001). In summary, there is a strong

> **Empathic arousal** Emotional arousal that occurs when you feel some of another person's pain, fear, or anguish.

Empathy–helping relationship We are most likely to help someone else when we feel emotions such as empathy and compassion.

empathy–helping relationship: We are most likely to help someone in need when we "feel for" that person and experience emotions such as empathy, sympathy, and compassion (Batson, 2006).

Is there anything that can be done to encourage prosocial behaviour? People who see others helping are more likely to offer help themselves. Also, people who give help in one situation tend to perceive themselves as helpful people. This change in self-image encourages them to help in other situations. One more point is that norms of fairness encourage us to help others who have helped us (Dovidio & Penner, 2001). For all these reasons, helping others not only assists them directly, it encourages others to help too.

"De-victimize" Yourself

If you should find yourself in need of help during an emergency, what can you do to avoid being a victim of bystander apathy? The work we have reviewed here suggests that you should make sure that you are noticed, that people realize there's an emergency, and that they need to take action. Being noticed can be promoted in some situations by shouting "Fire!" Bystanders who might run away from a robbery or an assault may rush to see where the fire is. At the very least, remember to not just scream. Instead, you should call out "Help!" or "I need help right now!" Whenever possible, define your situation for bystanders. Say, for instance, "I'm being attacked; call the police." Or, "Stop that man; he has my purse." You can also directly assign responsibility to a bystander by pointing to someone and saying, "You, call the police," or, "I'm injured; I need you to call an ambulance" (Cummins, 1995).

A Look Ahead

The Psychology in Action section of this chapter returns to the topic of prejudice for some further thoughts about how to promote tolerance. Don't miss this interesting conclusion to our discussion of social psychology.

 STUDY BREAK **Aggression and Prosocial Behaviour**

Reflect

Most people have been angry enough at some time to behave aggressively. Which concepts or theories do you think best explain your own aggressive actions?

An elderly man is at the side of the road, trying to change a flat tire. He obviously needs help. You are approaching him in your car. What must happen before you are likely to stop and help him?

Learning Check

1. The position of ethologists is that there is no biological basis for aggression. T or F?
2. Higher levels of testosterone are associated with more aggressive behaviour. T or F?
3. Frustration and aversive stimuli are more likely to produce aggression when cues for aggressive behaviour are present. T or F?
4. Social learning theory holds that exposure to aggressive models helps drain off aggressive energies. T or F?
5. Heavy exposure to media results in lowered emotional sensitivity to violence. T or F?
6. _____ behaviour refers to actions that are constructive, altruistic, or helpful to others.
7. Seeing that a person in need is similar to ourselves tends to increase empathetic arousal and the likelihood that help will be given. T or F?

Critical Thinking

8. If media violence contributes to aggressive behaviour in our society, do you think it is possible that the media could also promote prosocial behaviour?

Answers

1. F 2. T 3. T 4. F 5. T 6. prosocial 7. T 8. Yes. The media could be used to promote helping, cooperation, charity, and community feeling in the same way that it has encouraged aggression. Numerous studies show that portraying prosocial behaviour in the media increases it in real life (Gretemeyer, 2009). Of course, television can promote prosocial behaviour such as helping, but also by informing viewers about particular needs. It's important to not just see ordinary people as slaves to whatever media offer them, becoming violent in response to media violence and kind in response to examples of kindness. Rather, people take in information, think about it, and respond in the way that makes sense to them. That effect is seen in the remarkable outpouring of generous donations in response to heavily televised disasters such as the Southeast Asian tsunami in December 2004, Hurricane Katrina in August 2005, and the Haiti earthquake in 2010.

Psychology in Action

LIVING WITH DIVERSITY

Breaking the Prejudice Habit

Most people publicly support policies of equality and fairness. Yet, many still have lingering biases and negative images of people of African, Asian, Aboriginal, or other ethnic minority descent. How can we make sense of such conflicting attitudes?

For many people, becoming less prejudiced begins by accepting the value of *openness to the other*, the ability to genuinely appreciate those who differ from us culturally (Fowers & Davidov, 2006). It is important to remember that being open to someone else does not mean that you have to agree with that person or turn your back on your own culture. Openness, in turn, leads to the acceptance of the values of tolerance and equality. Typically, it requires repeated efforts to learn to think, feel, and act differently. Despite the effort required, many people have succeeded in overcoming the "prejudice habit" and becoming more open to life experiences in general (Fowers & Davidov, 2006). If you would like to be more open and tolerant, the following points may be helpful to you.

Beware of Stereotyping

Stereotypes make the social world more manageable. But placing people in categories almost always causes them to appear more similar than they really are. As a result, we tend to see out-group members as very much alike, even when they are as varied as our friends and family. People who are not prejudiced work hard to actively inhibit stereotyped thoughts and to emphasize fairness and equality.

Seek Individuating Information

A good way to tear down stereotypes is to get to know individuals from various ethnic and cultural groups (Giliovich, Keltner, & Nisbett, 2005). Typically, we are most tempted to apply stereotypes when we have only minimal information about a person. Stereotypes help us guess what a person is like and how she or he will act. Unfortunately, these inferences are often wrong.

One of the best antidotes for stereotypes is **individuating information** (information that helps us see a person as an individual, rather than as a member of a group) (Cameron & Trope, 2004). Anything that keeps us from placing a person in a particular social category tends to negate stereotyped thinking. When you meet individuals from various backgrounds, focus on the *person*, not the *label* attached to her or him.

A good example of the effects of individuating information comes from a Canadian study of English-speaking students in a French language program. Students who were "immersed" (spent most of their waking hours with French Canadians) became more positive toward them. Immersed students were more likely to say they had come to appreciate and like French Canadians, they were more willing to meet and interact with them, and they saw themselves as less different from French Canadians (Lambert, 1987).

Don't Fall Prey to Just-World Beliefs

Do you believe that the world is basically fair? Even if you don't, you may believe that the world is sufficiently just so that people generally get what they deserve. It may not be obvious, but such beliefs can directly increase prejudiced thinking (Hafer & Bègue, 2005).

As a result of discrimination, social conditions, and circumstances (such as recent immigration), minorities may occupy lower socioeconomic positions. **Just-world beliefs** (beliefs that people generally get what they deserve) can lead us to assume that minority group members wouldn't be in such positions if they weren't inferior in some way. This bit of faulty thinking amounts to blaming people who are *victims* of prejudice and discrimination for their plight. For example, assuming that a poor person is lazy may overlook the fact that discrimination in hiring has made it very difficult for him or her to find a good job.

<SURVEY QUESTION
How can we promote social harmony?

Individuating information
Information that helps define a person as an individual, rather than as a member of a group or social category.
Just-world beliefs Beliefs that people generally get what they deserve.

Social competition Rivalry among groups, each of which regards itself as superior to others.

Be Aware of Self-Fulfilling Prophecies

You may recall from Chapter 1 that people tend to act in accordance with the behaviour expected by others. If you hold strong stereotypes about members of various groups, a vicious cycle can occur. When you meet someone who is different from yourself, you may treat her or him in a way that is consistent with your stereotypes. If the other person is influenced by your behaviour, she or he may act in ways that seem to match your stereotype. For example, a person who believes that members of another ethnic group are hostile and unfriendly will probably treat people in that group in ways that provoke a hostile and unfriendly response. This creates a self-fulfilling prophecy and reinforces belief in the stereotype.

Remember, Different Does Not Mean Inferior

Some conflicts between groups cannot be avoided. What *can* be avoided is unnecessary **social competition** (rivalry among groups, each of which regards itself as superior to others). The concept of social competition refers to the fact that some individuals seek to enhance their self-esteem by identifying with a group. However, this works only if the group can be seen as superior to others. Because of social competition, groups tend to view themselves as better than their rivals (Baron et al., 2009).

A person who has high self-esteem does not need to treat others as inferior in order to feel good about himself or herself. Similarly, it is not necessary to degrade other groups in order to feel positive about one's own group identity (Fowers & Davidov, 2006). In fact, each ethnic group has strengths that members of other groups could benefit from emulating. For instance, people of African, Asian, and Latin American descent emphasize family networks that help buffer them from some of the stresses of daily life (Suinn, 1999).

Understand That Race Is a Social Construction

From the viewpoint of modern genetics, the concept of race has absolutely no meaning (Bonham et al., 2005; Sternberg et al., 2005). Members of various groups are so varied genetically and human groups have intermixed for so many centuries that it is impossible to tell, biologically, what "race" any given individual belongs to. Thus, race is an illusion based on superficial physical differences and learned ethnic identities. Certainly people *act* as if different races exist. But this is a matter of social labelling, not biological reality. To assume that any human group is biologically superior or inferior is simply wrong. In fact, the best available evidence suggests that all people are descended from the same ancient ancestors. The origins of our species lie in Africa, about 100 000 years ago. Among early human populations, darker skin was a protective adaptation to sun exposure near the equator (Jablonski & Chaplin, 2000). Biologically, we are all brothers and sisters under the skin (Graves, 2001; Smedley & Smedley, 2005).

Look for Commonalities

Competing with others can foster desires to demean, defeat, and vanquish them. When we cooperate with others we tend to share their joys and to suffer when they are in distress (Aronson, 2008). If we don't find ways to cooperate and live in greater harmony, everyone will suffer. That, if nothing else, is one thing that we all have in common. Everyone knows what it feels like to be different. Greater tolerance comes from remembering that feeling.

Tolerance and Cultural Awareness

Living comfortably in a multicultural society means being open to other groups. Getting acquainted with a person whose cultural background is different from your own can be a wonderful learning experience (Matsumoto & Juang, 2008). No one culture has all the answers or the best ways of doing things. Multicultural populations enrich a community's food, music, arts, and philosophy. Likewise, openness toward different racial, cultural, and ethnic groups can be personally rewarding (Fowers & Davidov, 2006).

The importance of cultural awareness often lies in subtleties and details. For example, in large North American cities, many small stores are owned by Korean immigrants. Some of these merchants have been criticized for being cold and hostile to their customers. Refusing to place change directly in customers' hands, for instance, helped trigger an African-American boycott of Korean grocers in New York City. The core of the problem was a lack of cultural awareness on both sides.

In North America, if you walk into a store, you expect the clerk to be courteous to you. One way of showing politeness is by smiling. But in the Confucian-steeped Korean culture, a smile is reserved for family members and close friends. If a Korean or an immigrant from Korea has no reason to smile, he or she just doesn't smile. There's a Korean saying: "If you smile a lot, you're silly." Expressions such as "thank you" and "excuse me" are also used sparingly, and strangers rarely touch each other—not even to return change.

The Journey Continues—Psychology and You

The technological advances of the last 50 years have dramatically changed what is humanly possible. Yet, as a species we still have much in common with people who lived many hundreds and thousands of years ago. Although we might like to think otherwise, we cannot count on technology to solve all of our problems. The threat of war, social conflict, crime, prejudice, infectious disease, overpopulation, environmental damage, famine, homicide, economic disaster—these and most other major dilemmas facing us are *behavioural.* Will the human family endure? It's a psychological question.

At the beginning of this book we described psychology as a journey of self-discovery. It is our sincere hope that you have found enough relevance and value here to spark a lifelong interest in psychology. As your personal journey continues, one thing is certain: Many of your greatest challenges and most treasured moments will involve other people. You would be wise to continue adding to your understanding of human behaviour. Psychology's future looks exciting. What role will it play in your life?

STUDY BREAK   Diversity

Reflect

Which strategies for breaking the prejudice habit do you already use? How could you apply the remaining strategies to becoming more tolerant?

Learning Check

1. We are just as likely to help someone who seems quite different from us as to help someone who seems very similar. T or F?
2. Many people who don't have prejudiced beliefs still have prejudiced thoughts and feelings in the presence of minority group individuals. T or F?

3. Individuating information tends to be a good antidote for stereotypes. T or F?
4. Just-world beliefs are the primary cause of social competition. T or F?

Critical Thinking

5. Why is it valuable to learn the terms by which members of various groups prefer to be addressed (for example, Black, Inuit, First Nations, or Caucasian)?

Answers

1. F 2. T 3. T 4. F 5. Because labels might have negative meanings that are not apparent to persons outside the group. People who are culturally aware allow others to define their own identities, rather than imposing labels on them.

CHAPTER IN REVIEW

Major Points

- Social psychology studies humans as social animals enmeshed in complex networks of social relationships.

- We are attracted to other people for reasons that are fairly universal.

- To understand social behaviour, we must know what roles people play, their status, the norms they follow, and the attributions they make.

- Everyone is affected by social influence, ranging from mild (mere influence, conformity, and compliance) to strong (obedience and coercion). There are times when it is valuable to resist such pressures.

- Attitudes subtly affect nearly all aspects of social behaviour.

- To persuade others, you must be aware of your role as a communicator, the nature of the audience, and messages that will appeal to them.

- Prejudice is reduced by equal-status contact and mutual interdependence.

- Aggression is a fact of life, but humans are not inevitably aggressive.

- We can encourage helping and altruism by removing barriers to prosocial behaviour.

- Multicultural harmony can be attained through conscious efforts to be more tolerant of others.

Summary

Why do people affiliate? What factors influence interpersonal attraction?

- Affiliation is tied to needs for approval, support, friendship, and information.

- Social comparison theory holds that we affiliate to evaluate our actions, feelings, and abilities.

- Interpersonal attraction is increased by proximity, frequent contact, beauty, competence, and similarity.

- Mate selection is characterized by a large degree of similarity on many dimensions.

- Self-disclosure follows a reciprocity norm: Low levels of self-disclosure are met with low levels in return; moderate self-disclosure elicits more personal replies. However, overdisclosure tends to inhibit self-disclosure by others.

- In comparison with liking, romantic love involves higher levels of emotional arousal and is accompanied by mutual absorption between lovers. Consummate love, involving intimacy, passion, *and* commitment, is the most complete form of love.

- Evolutionary psychology attributes human mating patterns to the differing reproductive challenges faced by men and women during the course of evolution.

How does group membership affect our behaviour?

- Social roles, which may be achieved or ascribed, are particular behaviour patterns associated with social positions. When two or more contradictory roles are held, role conflict may occur.

- Higher status within groups is associated with special privileges and respect.

- Group structure refers to the organization of roles, communication pathways, and power within a group. Group cohesiveness is basically the degree of attraction among group members.

- Norms are standards of conduct enforced (formally or informally) by groups.

- Attribution theory is concerned with how we make inferences about behaviour.

- The fundamental attribution error is to ascribe the actions of others to internal causes. Because of actor–observer differences, we tend to attribute our own behaviour to external causes.

What have social psychologists learned about social influence?

- Social influence refers to alterations in behaviour brought about by the behaviour of others. Social influence ranges from mild (mere influence, conformity, and compliance) to strong (obedience and coercion).

- The presence of others may facilitate (or inhibit) performance. People may also engage in social loafing: working less hard when they are part of a group.

- The famous Asch experiments demonstrated that various group sanctions encourage conformity. Victims of groupthink seek to maintain each other's approval, even at the cost of critical thinking.

- Three strategies for gaining compliance are the foot-in-the-door technique, the door-in-the-face approach, and the low-ball technique.

- Obedience in Milgram's studies decreased when the victim was in the same room, when the victim and subject were face to face, when the authority figure was absent, and when others refused to obey.

- Coercion involves forcing people to change their beliefs or behaviour against their will. Forced attitude change (brainwashing) is sometimes used by cults and other coercive groups.

How does self-assertion differ from aggression?

- Self-assertion involves standing up for yourself, while aggression involves achieving your goals at the expense of another.

How are attitudes acquired and changed?

- Attitudes are learned dispositions made up of a belief component, an emotional component, and an action component.
- Attitudes may be formed by direct contact, interaction with others, child-rearing practices, and group pressures. Peer group influences, reference group membership, the media, and chance conditioning also appear to be important in attitude formation.
- Effective persuasion occurs when characteristics of the communicator, the message, and the audience are well matched.
- In general, a likable and believable communicator who repeats a credible message that arouses emotion in the audience and states clear-cut conclusions will be persuasive.
- Maintaining and changing attitudes is closely related to cognitive dissonance and our needs to be consistent in our thoughts and actions.

What causes prejudice and intergroup conflict?

- Prejudice is a negative attitude held toward members of various out-groups. One theory attributes prejudice to scapegoating. A second account says that prejudices may be held for personal reasons (personal prejudice) or simply through adherence to group norms (group prejudice).
- Prejudiced individuals tend to have an authoritarian or dogmatic personality, characterized by rigidity, inhibition, intolerance, oversimplification, and ethnocentrism.
- Intergroup conflict gives rise to hostility and the formation of social stereotypes. Status inequalities tend to build prejudice. Equal-status contact tends to reduce it.
- Superordinate goals are a key to reducing intergroup conflict.

How do psychologists explain human aggression?

- Ethological explanations of aggression attribute it to inherited instincts. Biological explanations emphasize

brain mechanisms and physical factors related to thresholds for aggression.

- According to the frustration-aggression hypothesis, frustration and aggression are closely linked.
- Frustration is only one of many aversive stimuli that can arouse a person and make aggression more likely. Aggression is especially likely to occur when aggression cues are present.
- Social learning theory has focused attention on the role of aggressive models in the development of aggressive behaviour.

Why are bystanders so often unwilling to help in an emergency?

- Four decision points that must be passed before a person gives help are noticing, defining an emergency, taking responsibility, and selecting a course of action. Helping is less likely at each point when other potential helpers are present.
- Helping is encouraged by general arousal, empathic arousal, being in a good mood, low effort or risk, and perceived similarity between the victim and the helper. For several reasons, giving help tends to encourage others to help too.

How can we promote social harmony?

- Social harmony is attainable through conscious efforts to be more tolerant.
- Greater tolerance can be encouraged by neutralizing stereotypes with individuating information; by looking for commonalities with others; and by avoiding the effects of just-world beliefs, self-fulfilling prophecies, and social competition.
- Cultural awareness is a key element in promoting greater social harmony.

Interactive Learning

Please visit http://www.psychologyjourney4ce.nelson.com for a list of weblinks to relevant psychology sites.

CourseMate

Access an interactive e-book and chapter-specific interactive learning tools, including flashcards, quizzes, videos, and more, in your psychology CourseMate. Visit Nelsonbrain.com to use CourseMate.

psyk.trek 12. Social Psychology.

TEST YOUR KNOWLEDGE

The questions that follow are only a sample of what you need to know. If you miss any of the items, review the entire chapter and the Study Breaks. Another way to prepare for tests is to use the Study Guide and the Practice Exams that are available with this text.

1. The pattern known as homogamy shows the powerful effect that _____ has on interpersonal attraction.
   a. physical beauty   b. similarity
   c. competence   d. physical proximity

2. The fact that men tend to prefer younger, more physically attractive partners is predicted by
   a. evolutionary psychology
   b. the overdisclosure hypothesis
   c. social comparison theory
   d. studies of mutual absorption

3. Away from the office, Jan has become friends with Fran, a woman she supervises at work. Jan must do an evaluation of Fran, who hasn't been very efficient lately. It is most likely that Jan will experience
   a. groupthink   b. role conflict
   c. group sanctions   d. overdisclosure

4. A common error we all make is to attribute the actions of others to internal causes. This is known as the fundamental
   a. reciprocity norm   b. role conflict
   c. social comparison   d. attribution error

5. In Solomon Asch's conformity experiment, subjects yielded to group pressure on about _____ of the critical trials.
   a. 1 percent   b. 10 percent
   c. one-third   d. two-thirds

6. Groupthink is an example of the danger that lies in powerful pressures for group
   a. cohesion   b. conformity
   c. attribution   d. reciprocity

7. Which compliance technique involves getting a person committed to act and then making the terms of acting less desirable?
   a. foot-in-the-door   b. low-ball
   c. door-in-the-face   d. groupthink

8. In Milgram's experiments, the lowest level of obedience occurred when subjects
   a. saw another person refuse to obey
   b. were in the same room with the "learner"
   c. were face-to-face with the "learner"
   d. received orders over the phone

9. "Achieving one's goals without taking into account the rights of others." This statement describes
   a. self-assertion   b. overdisclosure
   c. cognitive dissonance   d. aggression

10. The three parts of an attitude are
    a. internal, external, group
    b. conviction, attribution, absorption
    c. status, norm, cohesion
    d. belief, emotion, action

11. Which of the following is *not* one of the factors that typically determines whether our attitudes are expressed as actions?
    a. empathic arousal
    b. existing habits
    c. immediate consequences
    d. anticipated evaluations by others

12. If you are trying to persuade a poorly informed audience, it is usually best to present
    a. one side of the argument
    b. both sides of the argument
    c. the unfreezing, change, refreezing cycle
    d. negative sanctions

13. The amount of cognitive dissonance a person feels is related to how much _____ exists for his or her actions.
    a. reciprocity
    b. justification
    c. chance conditioning
    d. reference

14. Some expressions of prejudice can be thought of as scapegoating or
    a. displaced aggression
    b. empathic arousal
    c. reference group reversal
    d. external attribution

15. One of the reasons that superordinate goals tend to reduce prejudice is that they require cooperation and
    a. social stereotyping
    b. ethnocentrism
    c. unfreezing
    d. equal-status contact

16. The actor–observer bias is
    a. an actor's concern that her or his unselfish acts will be seen as suspect by observers
    b. the change in an actor's behaviour when the actor knows he or she is being observed
    c. a problem that arises when observers make biased reports of other people's behaviour
    d. the tendency to attribute the behaviour of others to internal causes and one's own behaviour to internal causes

17. Self-assertion is different from aggression because self-assertion
    a. involves continuous violence, not sudden, explosive violence
    b. involves being patient to a fault
    c. is an attempt to get one's own way no matter what
    d. is a direct, honest expression of feelings and desires

18. The point of view most at odds with the idea that humans are instinctively aggressive is
    a. social learning theory
    b. the frustration-aggression hypothesis
    c. ethology
    d. the aversive stimuli effect

19. People are more likely to help another who is in trouble if
    a. many other helpers are present
    b. a diffusion of responsibility occurs
    c. they experience empathic arousal
    d. desensitization has taken place

20. One of the best antidotes for stereotypes is
    a. accepting just-world beliefs
    b. individuating information
    c. accepting self-fulfilling prophecies
    d. honest social competition

Behavioural Statistics

STATISTICS FROM "HEADS" TO "TAILS"

Let's say a friend of yours invites you to try your hand at a game of chance. He offers to flip a coin and pay you a loonie if the coin comes up heads. If the coin shows tails, you must give him a loonie. He flips the coin: tails—you pay him. He flips it again: tails. Again: tails. And again: tails. And again: tails. Suddenly, you are five dollars in the hole.

At this point you are faced with a choice. Should you continue the game in an attempt to recoup your losses? Or should you assume that the coin is biased and quit before you really get "skinned"? Taking out a pocket calculator (and the statistics book you carry with you at all times), you compute the odds of obtaining five tails in a row from an unbiased coin. The probability is 0.031 (roughly three times out of 100).

If the coin really is honest, five consecutive tails is a rare event. Wisely, you decide that the coin is probably biased and refuse to

Descriptive statistics Mathematical tools used to describe and summarize numeric data.

Inferential statistics Mathematical tools used for decision making, for generalizing from small samples, and for drawing conclusions.

Graphical statistics Techniques for presenting numbers pictorially, often by plotting them on a graph.

Frequency distribution A table that divides an entire range of scores into a series of classes and then records the number of scores that fall into each class.

Histogram A graph of a frequency distribution in which the number of scores falling in each class is represented by a vertical bar.

play again. (Unless, of course, your "friend" is willing to pay you for tails for the next five tosses!)

Perhaps a decision could have been made in this hypothetical example without using statistics. But notice how much clearer the situation becomes when it is expressed statistically.

Psychologists try to extract and summarize useful information from the observations they make. To do so, they use two major types of statistics. **Descriptive statistics** summarize or boil down numbers so they become more meaningful and easier to communicate to others. In comparison, **inferential statistics** are used for decision making, for generalizing from small samples, and for drawing conclusions. As was the case in the coin-flipping example, psychologists must often base decisions on limited data. Such decisions are much easier to make with the help of inferential statistics. Let's see how statistics are used in psychology.

Survey Questions

- What are descriptive statistics?
- How are statistics used to identify an average score?
- What statistics do psychologists use to measure how much scores differ from one another?
- What are inferential statistics?
- How are correlations used in psychology?

DESCRIPTIVE STATISTICS—PSYCHOLOGY BY THE NUMBERS

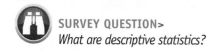

SURVEY QUESTION>
What are descriptive statistics?

Let's say you have completed a study on human behaviour. You measured the willingness of hundreds of men and women to take risks with a risk-taking questionnaire. The results seem interesting, but can you really tell what your data reveal just by looking at a jumble of numbers? To get a clear picture of how people behaved, you will probably turn to descriptive statistics. By summarizing the results of your study, statistics will help you draw valid conclusions about what you observed.

Statistics bring greater clarity and precision to psychological thought and research (Gravetter & Wallnau, 2010). To see how, let's begin by considering three basic types of descriptive statistics: *graphical statistics*, measures of *central tendency*, and measures of *variability*. Let's start with **graphical statistics,** which present numbers pictorially so they are easier to visualize.

Graphical Statistics

Table A.1 shows simulated scores on a test of hypnotic susceptibility given to 100 college students. With such disorganized data, it is hard to form an overall picture of the differences in hypnotic susceptibility. But by using a frequency distribution, large amounts of information can be neatly organized and summarized. A **frequency distribution** is made by breaking down the entire range of possible scores into classes of equal size. Next, the number of scores falling in each class is recorded. In Table A.2, the raw data from Table A.1 have been condensed into a frequency distribution. Notice how much clearer the pattern of scores for the entire group becomes.

Frequency distributions are often shown graphically to make them more visual. A **histogram,** or graph of a frequency distribution, is made by labelling class intervals on the abscissa

■ Table A.1 Raw Scores of Hypnotic Susceptibility									
55	86	52	17	61	57	84	51	16	64
22	56	25	38	35	24	54	26	37	38
52	42	59	26	21	55	40	59	25	57
91	27	38	53	19	93	25	39	52	56
66	14	18	63	59	68	12	19	62	45
47	98	88	72	50	49	96	89	71	66
50	44	71	57	90	53	41	72	56	73
57	38	55	49	87	59	36	56	48	70
33	69	50	50	60	35	67	51	50	52
11	73	46	16	67	13	71	47	25	77

■ Table A.2 Frequency Distribution of Hypnotic Susceptibility Scores	
Class Interval	Number of Persons in Class
0–19	10
20–39	20
40–59	40
60–79	20
80–99	10

(horizontal line) and frequencies (the number of scores in each class) on the ordinate (vertical line). Next, bars are drawn for each class interval; the height of each bar is determined by the number of scores in each class (see Figure A.1). An alternative way of graphing scores is the more familiar **frequency polygon** (see Figure A.2). Here, a point is placed at the centre of each class interval to indicate the number of scores. Then the dots are connected by straight lines.

Measures of Central Tendency

Notice in Table A.2 that more scores fall in the range of 40 to 59 than elsewhere. How can we show this fact? A measure of **central tendency** is simply a number describing a typical score around which other scores fall. A familiar measure of central tendency is the mean, or "average." But, as we shall see in a moment, other types of "averages" can be used. To illustrate each, we need an example. Table A.3 shows the raw data for an imaginary experiment in which two groups of subjects were given a test of memory. Assume that one group was given a drug that might improve memory (let's call the drug Rememberine). The second group received a placebo. Is there a difference in memory scores between the two groups? It's difficult to tell without computing an average.

As one type of average, the **mean** is calculated by adding all the scores for each group and then dividing by the total number of scores. Notice in Table A.3 that the means reveal a difference between the two groups.

The mean is sensitive to extremely high or low scores in a distribution. For this reason, it is not always the best measure of central tendency. (Imagine how distorted it would be to calculate

<SURVEY QUESTION
How are statistics used to identify an average score?

Frequency polygon A graph of a frequency distribution in which the number of scores falling in each class is represented by a point on a line.

Central tendency The tendency for a majority of scores to fall in the midrange of possible values.

Mean A measure of central tendency calculated by adding a group of scores and then dividing by the total number of scores.

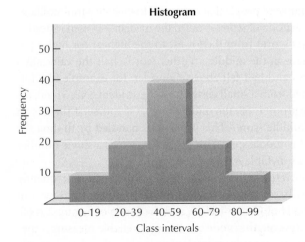

Histogram

▶▶**FIGURE A.1** Frequency histogram of hypnotic susceptibility scores contained in Table A.2.

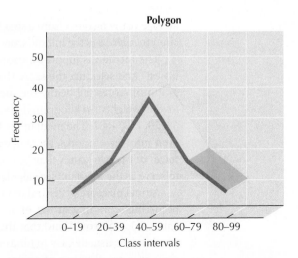

Polygon

▶▶**FIGURE A.2** Frequency polygon of hypnotic susceptibility scores contained in Table A.2.

Median A measure of central tendency found by arranging scores from the lowest to the highest (or highest to lowest) and selecting the score that falls in the middle. That is, half the values in a group of scores fall above the median and half fall below.

Mode A measure of central tendency found by identifying the most frequently occurring score in a group of scores.

■ **Table A.3** Raw Scores on a Memory Test for Subjects Taking Rememberine or a Placebo

Subject	Group 1 Rememberine	Group 2 Placebo
1	65	54
2	67	60
3	73	63
4	65	33
5	58	56
6	55	60
7	70	60
8	69	31
9	60	62
10	68	61
Sum	650	540
Mean	65	54
Median	66	60

$$\text{Mean} = \frac{\Sigma X}{N} \text{ or } \frac{\text{Sum of all scores, X}}{\text{number of scores}}$$

$$\text{Mean Group 1} = \frac{65 + 67 + 73 + 65 + 58 + 55 + 70 + 69 + 60 + 68}{10}$$
$$= \frac{650}{10} = 65$$

$$\text{Mean Group 2} = \frac{54 + 60 + 63 + 33 + 56 + 60 + 60 + 31 + 62 + 61}{10}$$
$$= \frac{540}{10} = 54$$

Median = the middle score or the mean of the two middle scores*
Median = 55 58 60 65 $\boxed{65 \quad 67}$ 68 69 70 73

$$\text{Group 1} = \frac{65 + 67}{2} = 66$$

Median = 31 33 54 56 $\boxed{60 \quad 60}$ 60 61 62 63

$$\text{Group 2} = \frac{60 + 60}{2} = 60$$

* $\boxed{}$ indicates middle score(s)

average yearly incomes from a small sample of people that happened to include a multimillionaire.) In such cases the middle score in a group of scores—called the median—is used instead.

The **median** is found by arranging scores from the lowest to the highest (or highest to lowest) and selecting the score that falls in the middle. In other words, half the values in a group of scores fall below the median and half fall above. Consider, for example, the following weights (in kilograms) obtained from a small class of college students: 48, 51, 60, 62, 68, 70, 71, 74, 82. The median for the group is 68, the middle score. Of course, if there is an even number of scores, there is no "middle score." This problem is handled by finding the mean of the two scores that "share" the middle spot. This procedure yields a single number to serve as the median (see calculations in Table A.3).

A final measure of central tendency is the mode. The **mode** is simply the most frequently occurring score in a group of scores. If you were to take the time to count the scores in Table A.3, you would find that the mode of Group 1 is 65, and the mode of Group 2 is 60. The mode is usually easy to obtain. However, the mode can be an unreliable measure, especially in a small group of scores. The mode's advantage is that it gives the score actually obtained by the greatest number of people.

Measures of Variability

<SURVEY QUESTION
What statistics do psychologists use to measure how much scores differ from one another?

Let's say a researcher discovers two drugs that lower anxiety in agitated patients. However, let's also assume that one drug consistently lowers anxiety by moderate amounts, whereas the second sometimes lowers it by large amounts, sometimes has no effect, and sometimes may even increase anxiety. Overall, there is no difference in the average (mean) amount of anxiety reduction. Even so, an important difference exists between the two drugs. As this example shows, it is not enough to simply know the average score in a distribution. We would usually also like to know if scores are grouped closely together or scattered widely.

Measures of **variability** provide a single number that tells how spread out scores are. When the scores are widely spread, this number gets larger. When they are close together, it gets smaller. If you look again at the example in Table A.3, you will notice that the scores within each group vary widely. How can we show this fact?

The simplest way would be to use the **range,** which is the difference between the highest and lowest scores. In Group 1 of our experiment, the highest score is 73, and the lowest is 55; thus, the range is 18 ($73 - 55 = 18$). In Group 2, the highest score is 63, and the lowest is 31; this makes the range 32. Scores in Group 2 are more spread out than those in Group 1.

A better measure of variability is the **standard deviation** (an index of how much a typical score differs from the mean of a group of scores). To obtain the standard deviation, we find the deviation (or difference) of each score from the mean and then square it (multiply it by itself). These squared deviations are then added and averaged (the total is divided by the number of deviations). (Squaring the difference compensates for the fact that some of the deviations will be negative numbers.) Taking the square root of this average yields the standard deviation (see Table A.4). Notice again that the variability for Group 1 (5.4) is smaller than that for Group 2 (where the standard deviation is 11.3).

■ Table A.4 Computation of the Standard Deviation

Group 1 Mean = 65

Score Mean	Deviation (d)	Deviation Squared (d^2)
$65 - 65 =$	0	0
$67 - 65 =$	2	4
$73 - 65 =$	8	64
$65 - 65 =$	0	0
$58 - 65 =$	-7	49
$55 - 65 =$	-10	100
$70 - 65 =$	5	25
$69 - 65 =$	4	16
$60 - 65 =$	-5	25
$68 - 65 =$	3	9
		292

$$SD = \sqrt{\frac{\text{sum of } d^2}{n}} = \sqrt{\frac{292}{10}} = \sqrt{29.2} = 5.4$$

Group 2 Mean = 54

Score Mean	Deviation (d)	Deviation Squared (d^2)
$54 - 54 =$	0	0
$60 - 54 =$	6	36
$63 - 54 =$	9	81
$33 - 54 =$	-21	441
$56 - 54 =$	2	4
$60 - 54 =$	6	36
$60 - 54 =$	6	36
$31 - 54 =$	-23	529
$62 - 54 =$	8	64
$61 - 54 =$	7	49
		1276

$$SD = \sqrt{\frac{\text{sum of } d^2}{n}} = \sqrt{\frac{1276}{10}} = \sqrt{127.6} = 11.3$$

Variability The tendency for a group of scores to differ in value. Measures of variability indicate the degree to which scores within a group differ from one another.

Range The difference between the highest and lowest scores in a group of scores.

Standard deviation An index of how much a typical score differs from the mean of a group of scores.

■ Table A.5 Computation of a z-Score

$$z = \frac{X - \overline{X}}{SD} = \text{or} \frac{\text{score} - \text{mean}}{\text{standard deviation}}$$

$$\text{Susan: } z = \frac{110 - 100}{10} = \frac{+10}{10}$$
$$= +1.0$$

$$\text{John: } z = \frac{118 - 100}{18} = \frac{+18}{18}$$
$$= +1.0$$

Standard Scores

A particular advantage of the standard deviation is that it can be used to "standardize" scores in a way that gives them greater meaning. For example, John and Susan both took psychology midterms, but in different classes. John earned a score of 118, and Susan scored 110. Who did better? It is impossible to tell without knowing what the average score was on each test, and whether John and Susan scored at the top, middle, or bottom of their classes. We would like to have one number that gives all this information. A number that does this is the z-score.

To convert an original score to a **z-score,** we subtract the mean from the score. The resulting number is then divided by the standard deviation for that group of scores. To illustrate, Susan had a score of 110 in a class with a mean of 100 and a standard deviation of 10. Therefore, her z-score is 1.0 (see Table A.5). John's score of 118 came from a class with a mean of 100 and a standard deviation of 18; thus, his z-score is also 1.0 (see Table A.5). Originally it looked as if John did better on his midterm than Susan did. But we now see that relatively speaking, their scores were equivalent. Compared with other students, each was an equal distance above average.

The Normal Curve

When chance events are recorded, we find that some outcomes have a high probability and occur very often; others have a low probability and occur infrequently; still others have little probability and occur rarely. As a result, the distribution (or tally) of chance events typically resembles a normal curve (see Figure A.3). A normal curve is bell-shaped, with a large number of scores in the middle, tapering to very few extremely high and low scores. Most psychological traits or events are determined by the action of a large number of factors. Therefore, like chance events, measures of psychological variables tend to roughly match a normal curve. For example, direct measurement has shown such characteristics as height, memory span, and intelligence to be distributed approximately along a normal curve. In other words, many people have average height, memory ability, and intelligence. However, as we move above or below average, fewer and fewer people are found.

It is very fortunate that so many psychological variables tend to form a normal curve, because much is known about the curve. One valuable property concerns the relationship between the standard deviation and the normal curve. Specifically, the standard deviation measures off fixed proportions of the curve above and below the mean. For example, in Figure A.4, notice

z-score A number that tells how many standard deviations above or below the mean a score is.

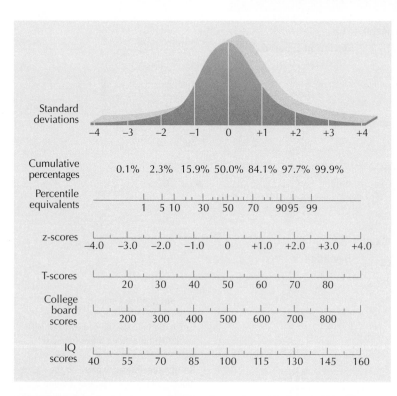

▶▶**FIGURE A.3** The normal curve. The normal curve is an idealized mathematical model. However, many measurements in psychology closely approximate a normal curve. The scales you see here show the relationship of standard deviations, z-scores, and other measures to the curve.

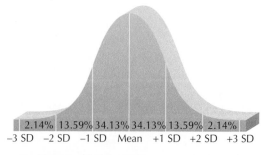

▶▶**FIGURE A.4** Relationship between the standard deviation and the normal curve.

■ Table A.6 **Area Under the Normal Curve as a Percentage of Total Area for a Variety of z-Scores**

z-Score	Percentage of Area to the Left of This Value	Percentage of Area to the Right of This Value
−3.0 SD	0.1	99.9
−2.5 SD	0.6	99.4
−2.0 SD	2.3	97.7
−1.5 SD	6.7	93.3
−1.0 SD	15.9	84.1
−0.5 SD	30.9	69.1
0.0 SD	50.0	50.0
+0.5 SD	69.1	30.9
+1.0 SD	84.1	15.9
+1.5 SD	93.3	6.7
+2.0 SD	97.7	2.3
+2.5 SD	99.4	0.6
+3.0 SD	99.9	0.1

that roughly 68 percent of all cases (IQ scores, memory scores, heights, or whatever) fall between 1 standard deviation above and below the mean (±1 SD), 95 percent of all cases fall between +2 SD and −2 SD, and 99 percent of the cases can be found between +3 SD and −3 SD from the mean.

Table A.6 gives a more complete account of the relationship between z-scores and the percentage of cases found in a particular area of the normal curve. Notice, for example, that 93.3 percent of all cases fall below a z-score of +1.5. A z-score of 1.5 on a test (no matter what the original, or "raw," score was) would be a good performance, since roughly 93 percent of all scores fall below this mark. Relationships between the standard deviation (or z-scores) and the normal curve do not change. This makes it possible to compare various tests or groups of scores if they come from distributions that are approximately normal.

✔ STUDY BREAK Descriptive Statistics

Reflect

Let's say you ask 100 people how long they sleep each night and record their answers. How could you show these scores graphically?

To find the average amount of sleep for your subjects, would you prefer to know the most frequent score (the mode), the middle score (the median), or the arithmetic average (the mean)?

How could you determine how much sleep times vary? That is, would you prefer to know the highest and lowest scores (the range), or the average amount of variation (the standard deviation)?

How would you feel about receiving your scores on classroom tests in the form of z-scores?

Do you think the distribution of scores in your study of sleep would form a normal curve? Why or why not?

Learning Check

1. _____ statistics summarize numbers so they become more meaningful or easier to communicate; _____ statistics are used for decision making, generalizing, or drawing conclusions.

2. Histograms and frequency polygons are graphs of frequency distributions. T or F?

3. Three measures of central tendency are the mean, the median, and the _____.

4. If scores are placed in order, from the smallest to the largest (or largest to smallest), the median is defined as the middle score. T or F?

5. As a measure of variability, the standard deviation is defined as the difference between the highest and lowest scores. T or F?

6. A z-score of −1 tells us that a score fell 1 standard deviation below the mean in a group of scores. T or F?

7. In a normal curve, 99 percent of all scores can be found between +1 and −1 standard deviations from the mean. T or F?

Answers

1. descriptive, inferential 2. T 3. mode 4. T 5. F 6. T 7. F

INFERENTIAL STATISTICS—SIGNIFICANT NUMBERS

You would like to know if girls are more verbally aggressive than boys. You observe a group of five-year-old girls and boys on a playground. After collecting data for a week, you find that the girls committed more acts of verbal aggression than the boys. Could this difference just be a meaningless fluctuation in verbal aggression? Or does it show conclusively that girls are more verbally aggressive than boys? Inferential statistics were created to answer just such questions (Sprinthall, 2007).

As stated earlier, *inferential statistics* are techniques that allow us to make inferences. That is, they allow us to generalize from the behaviour of small groups of subjects to that of the larger groups they represent. For, example, let's say that a researcher studies the effects of a new therapy on a small group of depressed individuals. Is she or he interested only in these particular individuals? Usually not, since except in rare instances, psychologists seek to discover general laws of behaviour that apply widely to humans and animals. Undoubtedly the researcher would like to know if the therapy holds any promise for all depressed people.

Samples and Populations

In any scientific study, we would like to observe the entire set, or population, of subjects, objects, or events of interest. However, this is usually impossible or impractical. Observing all Liberals, all cancer patients, or all mothers-in-law could be both impractical (since all are large populations) and impossible (since people change political views, may be unaware of having cancer, and change their status as relatives). In such cases, **samples** (smaller cross sections of a population) are selected, and observations of the sample are used to draw conclusions about the entire population.

For any sample to be meaningful, it must be representative. That is, the sample group must truly reflect the membership and characteristics of the larger population. In our earlier hypothetical study of a memory drug, it would be essential for the sample of 20 people to be representative of the general population. A very important aspect of representative samples is that their members be chosen at **random.** In other words, each member of the population must have an equal chance of being included in the sample.

Significant Differences

In our imaginary drug experiment, we found that the mean memory score was higher for the group given the drug than it was for persons who didn't take the drug (the placebo group). Certainly this result is interesting, but could it have occurred by chance? If two groups were repeatedly tested (with neither receiving any drug), their mean memory scores would sometimes differ. How much must two means differ before we can consider the difference "real" (not due to chance)?

Notice that the question is similar to the one at the beginning of the Appendix: How many tails in a row must we obtain when flipping a coin before we can conclude that the coin is biased? In the case of the coin, we noted that obtaining five tails in a row is a rare event. Thus, it became reasonable to assume that the coin was biased. Of course, it is possible to get five tails in a row when flipping an honest coin. But since this outcome is unlikely, we have good reason to suspect that something other than chance (a loaded coin, for instance) caused the results. Similar reasoning is used in tests of statistical significance.

Tests of **statistical significance** provide an estimate of how often experimental results could have occurred by chance alone. The results of a significance test are stated as a probability. This probability gives the odds that the observed difference was due to chance. In psychology, any experimental result that could have occurred by chance 5 times (or fewer) out of 100 (in other words, a probability of 0.05 or less) is considered significant. In our memory experiment, the probability is 0.025 ($p = 0.025$) that the group means would differ as they do by chance alone. This allows us to conclude with reasonable certainty that the drug actually did improve memory scores.

Sample A smaller subpart of a population.

Random selection Choosing a sample so that each member of the population has an equal chance of being included in the sample.

Statistical significance The degree to which an event (such as the results of an experiment) is unlikely to have occurred by chance alone.

CORRELATION—RATING RELATIONSHIPS

Psychologists are very interested in detecting relationships between events: Are children from single-parent families more likely to misbehave at school? Is wealth related to happiness? Is there a relationship between childhood exposure to the Internet and IQ at age 20? Is the chance of having a heart attack related to having a hostile personality? All of these are questions about correlation (Silverthorne, 2004).

Many of the statements that psychologists make about behaviour do not result from the use of experimental methods. Rather, they come from keen observations and measures of existing phenomena. A psychologist might note, for example, that the higher a couple's socioeconomic and educational status, the smaller the number of children they are likely to have. Or that grades in high school are related to how well a person is likely to do in college. Or even that as rainfall levels increase within a given metropolitan area, crime rates decline. In these instances, we are dealing with the fact that two variables are correlating (varying together in some orderly fashion), or there is a correlation between them.

The simplest way of visualizing a correlation is to construct a **scatter diagram.** In a scatter diagram, two measures (grades in high school and grades in college, for instance) are obtained. One measure is indicated by the X-axis and the second by the Y-axis. The scatter diagram plots the intersection (crossing) of each pair of measurements as a single point. Many such measurement pairs give pictures like those shown in Figure A.5.

Figure A.5 also shows scatter diagrams of three basic kinds of relationships between variables (or measures). Graphs *a*, *b*, and *c* show positive relationships of varying strength. As you can see, in a positive correlation, increases in the X measure (or score) are matched by increases in the Y measure (or score). An example is finding that higher IQ scores (X) are associated with higher college grades (Y). A **zero correlation** suggests that no relationship exists between two measures (see graph *d*). This might be the result of comparing subjects' hat sizes (X) to their college grades (Y). Graphs *e* and *f* both show a negative correlation. Notice that as values of one measure increase, those of the second become smaller. An example is the relationship between amount of alcohol consumed and scores on a test of coordination: Higher alcohol levels are correlated with lower coordination scores.

The strength of a correlation can also be expressed as a coefficient of correlation. This coefficient is simply a number falling somewhere between +1.00 and −1.00. If the number is zero or close to zero, it indicates a weak or non-existent relationship. If the correlation is +1.00, a **perfect positive relationship** exists; if the correlation is −1.00, a **perfect negative relationship** has been discovered. The most commonly used correlation coefficient is called the Pearson *r*. Calculation of the Pearson *r* is relatively simple, as shown in Table A.7. (The numbers shown are hypothetical.)

As stated in Chapter 1, correlations in psychology are rarely perfect. Most fall somewhere between zero and +1.00 or −1.00. The closer the correlation coefficient is to +1.00 or −1.00, the stronger the relationship. An interesting example of some typical correlations is provided by a study that compared the IQs of adopted children with the IQs of their biological mothers. At age four, the children's IQs correlated 0.28 with their mothers' IQs. By age seven the correlation was 0.35. And by age 13 it had grown to 0.38. Over time, the IQs of adopted children became more similar to the IQs of their biological mothers.

<SURVEY QUESTION
How are correlations used in psychology?

Scatter diagram A graph that plots the intersection of paired measures, that is, the points at which paired X and Y measures cross.

Zero correlation The absence of a (linear) mathematical relationship between two measures.

Perfect positive relationship A mathematical relationship in which the correlation between two measures is +1.00.

Perfect negative relationship A mathematical relationship in which the correlation between two measures is −1.00.

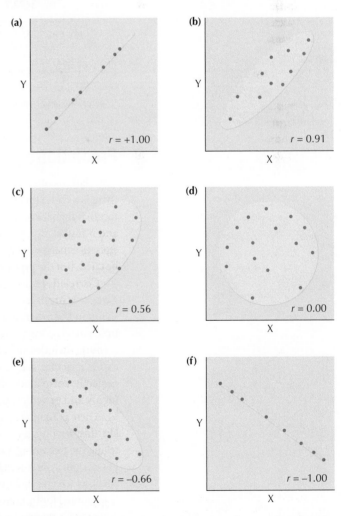

▸▸**FIGURE A.5** Scatter diagrams showing various degrees of relationship for a positive, zero, and negative correlation.

Percent of variance A portion of the total amount of variation in a group of scores.

■ Table A.7   **IQ and Grade Point Average for Computing Pearson _r_**

Student No.	IQ (X)	Grade Point Average (Y)	X Score Squared (X^2)	Y Score Squared (Y^2)	X Times Y (XY)
1	110	1.0	12 100	1.00	110.0
2	112	1.6	12 544	2.56	179.2
3	118	1.2	13 924	1.44	141.6
4	119	2.1	14 161	4.41	249.9
5	122	2.6	14 884	6.76	317.2
6	125	1.8	15 625	3.24	225.0
7	127	2.6	16 129	6.76	330.2
8	130	2.0	16 900	4.00	260.0
9	132	3.2	17 424	10.24	422.4
10	134	2.6	17 956	6.76	348.4
11	136	3.0	18 496	9.00	408.0
12	138	3.6	19 044	12.96	496.8
Total	1503	27.3	189 187	69.13	3488.7

$$r = \frac{\Sigma XY - \frac{(\Sigma X)(\Sigma Y)}{N}}{\left[\Sigma X^2 - \frac{(\Sigma X)^2}{N}\right]\left[\Sigma Y^2 - \frac{(\Sigma Y)^2}{N}\right]}$$

$$= \frac{3488.7 - \frac{1503(27.3)}{12}}{\left[189\,187 - \frac{(1503)^2}{12}\right]\left[69.13 - \frac{(27.3)^2}{12}\right]}$$

$$= \frac{69.375}{81.085} = 0.856 = 0.86$$

Source: Adapted from Pagano, 1981.

Prediction

Correlations often provide highly useful information. For instance, it is valuable to know that there is a correlation between cigarette smoking and lung cancer rates. Another example is the fact that higher consumption of alcohol during pregnancy is correlated with lower birth weight and a higher rate of birth defects. There is a correlation between the number of recent life stresses experienced and the likelihood of emotional disturbance. Many more examples could be cited, but the point is, correlations help us to identify relationships that are worth knowing.

Correlations are particularly valuable for making _predictions_. If we know that two measures are correlated, and we know a person's score on one measure, we can predict his or her score on the other. For example, most universities and colleges have formulas that use multiple correlations to decide which applicants have the best chances for success. Usually the formula includes such predictors as high school or community college GPA, teacher ratings, extracurricular activities, and scores on standardized tests. Although no single predictor is perfectly correlated with post-secondary success, together the various predictors correlate highly and provide a useful technique for screening applicants.

There is an interesting "trick" you can do with correlations that you may find useful. It works like this: If you square the correlation coefficient (multiply _r_ by itself), you will get a number telling the **percent of variance** (amount of variation in scores) accounted for by the correlation. For example, the correlation between IQ scores and college grade point average is 0.5. Multiplying 0.5 times 0.5 gives 0.25, or 25 percent. This means that 25 percent of the variation in college grades is accounted for by knowing IQ scores. In other words, with a correlation of 0.5, college grades are "squeezed" into an oval like the one shown in graph _c_ of Figure A.5. IQ scores take away some of the possible variation in corresponding grade point averages. If there were no correlation between IQ and grades, grades would be completely free to vary, as shown in graph d of Figure A.5.

Along the same line, a correlation of +1.00 or −1.00 means that 100 percent of the variation in the Y measure is accounted for by knowing the X measure: If you know a person's X score, you can tell exactly what the Y score is. An example that comes close to this state of affairs is the high correlation (0.86) between the IQs of identical twins. In any group of identical twins, 74 percent of the variation in the "Y" twins' IQs is accounted for by knowing the IQs of their siblings (the "X" twins).

Squaring correlations to obtain the percent variance accounted for is a useful tool for interpreting the correlations encountered in the media and the psychological literature. For example, sweeping pronouncements about relationships are occasionally made on the basis of correlations in the 0.25 to 0.30 range even though the values mean that only 6 to 9 percent of the variance is accounted for by the observed correlation. Such correlations may document relationships worth noting, but they are rarely something to get excited about.

Correlation and Causation

It is very important to recognize that finding a correlation between two measures does not automatically mean that one causes the other: Correlation does not demonstrate causation. When a correlation exists, the best we can say is that two variables are related in some systematic way. Of course, this does not mean that it is impossible for two correlated variables to have a cause-and-effect relationship. Rather, it means that we cannot conclude, solely on the basis of correlation, that a causal link exists. To gain greater confidence that a cause-and-effect relationship exists, an experiment must be performed (see Chapter 1).

Often, two correlated measures are related as a result of the influence of a third variable. For example, we might observe that the more hours students devote to studying, the better their grades. Although it is tempting to conclude that more studying produces (causes) better grades, it is possible (indeed, it is probable) that grades and the amount of study time are both related to the amount of motivation or interest a student has.

The difference between cause-and-effect data and data that reveal a relationship of unknown origin is one that should not be forgotten. Since we rarely run experiments in daily life, the information on which we act is largely correlational. This should make us more humble and more tentative in the confidence with which we make pronouncements about human behaviour.

✔ STUDY BREAK   Inferential Statistics

Reflect

Informally, you have probably inferred something about a population of people based on the small sample you have observed directly. How could statistics improve the accuracy of your inferences?

If you were trying to test whether a drug causes birth defects, what level of statistical significance would you use? If you were doing a psychology experiment, what level would you be comfortable with?

See if you can identify at least one positive relationship and one negative relationship involving human behaviour that you have observed. How strong do you think the correlation would be in each case? What correlation coefficient would you expect to see?

A woman you know drinks more coffee in the winter than she does in the summer. She also has more colds in the winter. She decides to reduce the amount of coffee she drinks to help prevent colds. What can you tell her about correlation and causation?

Learning Check

1. In inferential statistics, observations of a _____ are used to make inferences and draw conclusions about an entire _____.
2. A representative sample can be obtained by selecting members of the sample at _____.
3. If the results of an experiment could have occurred by chance alone fewer than 25 times out of 100, the result is considered statistically significant. T or F?
4. A scatter diagram can be used to plot and visualize a _____ between two groups of scores.
5. In a negative relationship, increases in X scores correspond to decreases in Y scores. T or F?
6. A perfect positive correlation exists when the correlation coefficient is 0.00. T or F?
7. It is important to remember that correlation does not demonstrate _____.

Answers   1. sample, population 2. random 3. F 4. correlation 5. T 6. F 7. causation

APPENDIX IN REVIEW

Major Points

- The results of psychological studies are often expressed as numbers, which must be summarized and interpreted before they have any meaning.

- Summarizing numbers visually, by using various types of graphs, makes it easier to see trends and patterns in the results of psychological investigations.

- It is helpful to know the "average" of a group of scores as well as how much they vary.

- Many psychological measures produce scores that form a normal curve. This is useful because the characteristics of normal curves are well known.

- Some statistical techniques can be used to generalize results from samples to populations, to draw conclusions, and to tell if the results of a study could have occurred by chance.

- When there is a correlation, or consistent relationship, between scores on two measures, knowing a person's score on one measure allows us to predict his or her score on the second measure.

Summary

What are descriptive statistics?

- Descriptive statistics organize and summarize numbers.

- Graphical statistics, such as histograms and frequency polygons, are used to represent numbers pictorially.

How are statistics used to identify an average score?

- Measures of central tendency define the "typical score" in a group of scores.

- The mean is found by adding all the scores in a group and then dividing by the total number of scores.

- The median is found by arranging a group of scores from the highest to the lowest (or lowest to highest) and selecting the middle score.

- The mode is the score that occurs most frequently in a group of scores.

What statistics do psychologists use to measure how much scores differ from one another?

- Measures of variability provide a number that shows how much scores vary.

- The range is the difference between the highest score and the lowest score in a group of scores.

- The standard deviation shows how much, on average, all the scores in a group differ from the mean.

- To change an original score into a standard score (or z-score), you must subtract the mean from the score and then divide the result by the standard deviation.

- Standard scores (z-scores) tell, in standard deviation units, how far above or below the mean a score is. This allows meaningful comparisons between scores from different groups.

- Scores that form a normal curve are easy to interpret because the properties of the normal curve are well known.

What are inferential statistics?

- Inferential statistics are used to make decisions, to generalize from samples, and to draw conclusions.

- Most studies in psychology are based on samples. Findings from representative samples are assumed to also apply to entire populations.

- In psychology experiments, differences in the average performance of groups could occur purely by chance. Tests of statistical significance tell us if the observed differences between groups are common or rare. If a difference is large enough to be improbable, it suggests that the results did not occur by chance alone.

How are correlations used in psychology?

- Pairs of scores that vary together in an orderly fashion are said to be correlated.

- The relationship between two variables or measures can be positive or negative.

- Correlation coefficients tell how strongly two groups of scores are related.

- Correlation alone does not demonstrate cause-and-effect links between variables or measures.

Interactive Learning

If you have difficulty finding any of the sites listed here, visit *http://www.psychologyjourney4ce.nelson.com* for an updated list of Internet addresses and direct links to relevant sites.

Statistics to Use   If you enter a series of numbers, this site will calculate basic descriptive statistics and more advanced inferential statistics. *http://www.physics.csbsju.edu/stats/*

CourseMate

Access an interactive e-book and chapter-specific interactive learning tools, including flashcards, quizzes, videos, and more, in your psychology CourseMate. Visit NELSONbrain.com to use CourseMate.

TEST YOUR KNOWLEDGE

The questions that follow are only a sample of what you need to know. If you miss any of the items, review the entire Appendix and the Study Breaks. Another way to prepare for tests is to use the Study Guide and the Practice Exams that are available with this text.

1. A histogram is a graphical representation of
   a. the median
   b. a frequency distribution
   c. the range
   d. positive and negative correlations

2. A widely used measure of variability is the
   a. median
   b. standard deviation
   c. correlation coefficient
   d. mode

3. Given scores of 4, 7, 6, 7, 3, 8, 9, 4, 7, and 6, the mode is
   a. 6.1
   b. 7
   c. 3
   d. 6.5

4. To convert an original score to a z-score you need to know the standard deviation and the
   a. mean
   b. median
   c. mode
   d. range

5. Sixty-eight percent of all scores in a normal curve fall between one standard deviation above and below the
   a. range
   b. correlation
   c. z-score
   d. mean

6. Randomly choosing the members of a sample is one way to ensure that the sample is
   a. correlated
   b. representative
   c. statistically significant
   d. causal

7. A scatter diagram provides a way to visualize
   a. a z-score
   b. central tendency
   c. the normal curve
   d. correlations

8. Typically, the results of an experiment are considered significant if they could have occurred by chance with a probability of
   a. 0.05 or less
   b. 0.5 or less
   c. 5.0 or less
   d. +1.00

9. Using a sample to draw conclusions about a population is a key element of
   a. inferential statistics
   b. measuring central tendency
   c. graphing histograms
   d. constructing accurate frequency polygons

10. Which correlation shows the strongest relationship between two groups of scores?
    a. +0.10
    b. +0.01
    c. −0.50
    d. −0.91

Glossary

Ablation Surgical removal of tissue. (p. 65)

Abstract principles Concepts and ideas removed from specific examples and concrete situations. (p. 114)

Accessibility (in memory) Memories currently stored in memory that can be retrieved when necessary are both available and accessible. (p. 288)

Accommodation (perceptual) Changes in the shape of the lens of the eye. (p. 137)

Accommodation (Piaget) In Piaget's theory, the modification of existing mental patterns to fit new demands (i.e., mental schemes are changed to accommodate new information or experiences). (p. 112)

Acculturative stress Stress caused by the many changes and adaptations required when a person moves to a foreign culture. (p. 497)

Acetylcholine A neurotransmitter released by neurons to activate muscles. (p. 59)

Achieved role A role that is assumed voluntarily. (p. 562)

Acquired strategies Learned tactics for swiftly solving the problems encountered in one's area of expertise. (p. 334)

Acquisition The period in conditioning during which a response is reinforced. (p. 234)

Acromegaly Enlargement of the arms, hands, feet, and face caused by excess growth hormone late in the human growth period. (p. 81)

Action potential The nerve impulse. (p. 56)

Activation-synthesis hypothesis A theory to explain how dream content is affected by random neuronal activity and the brain's own attempt to make sense of it. (p. 198)

Active listener A person who knows how to maintain attention, avoid distractions, and actively gather information from lectures. (p. 3)

Actor–observer bias The tendency to attribute the behaviour of others to internal causes while attributing one's own behaviour to external causes (situations and circumstances). (p. 564)

Acute stress disorder A psychological disturbance lasting up to one month following stresses that would produce anxiety in anyone who experienced them. (p. 451)

Adaptive behaviours Actions that aid attempts to survive and adapt to changing conditions. (p. 377)

Adjustment disorder An emotional disturbance caused by ongoing stressors within the range of common experience. (p. 448)

Adolescence The culturally defined period between childhood and adulthood. (p. 117)

Adrenal cortex The outer layer of the adrenal glands; produces hormones that affect salt intake, reactions to stress, and sexual development. (p. 82)

Adrenal glands Endocrine glands that arouse the body, regulate salt balance, adjust the body to stress, and affect sexual functioning. (p. 82)

Adrenal medulla The inner core of the adrenal glands; a source of epinephrine and norepinephrine. (p. 82)

Adrenaline A hormone produced by the adrenal glands that tends to arouse the body. (p. 82)

Affectional needs Emotional needs for love and affection. (p. 105)

Afterimage Visual sensation that persists after a stimulus is removed. (p. 140)

Ageism Discrimination or prejudice based on a person's age. (p. 124)

Aggression cues Stimuli or signals that are associated with aggression and that tend to elicit it. (p. 587)

Aggression Any response made with the intent of causing harm; hurting another person or achieving one's goals at the expense of another person. (p. 489)

Agnosia The inability to identify seen objects. (p. 75)

Agoraphobia (without panic disorder) The person fears that something extremely embarrassing will happen to him or her if he or she leaves the house or enters unfamiliar situations. (p. 449)

Alarm reaction The first stage of the G.A.S., during which bodily resources are mobilized to cope with a stressor. (p. 484)

Alcohol The common name for ethyl alcohol, the intoxicating element in fermented and distilled liquors. (p. 217)

Algorithm A learned set of rules that always leads to a correct solution of a problem. (p. 332)

All-or-nothing thinking Classifying objects or events as absolutely right or wrong, good or bad, acceptable or unacceptable, and so forth. (p. 467)

Alpha waves Large, slow brainwaves associated with relaxation and falling asleep. (p. 189)

Altered state of consciousness (ASC) A condition of awareness distinctly different in quality or pattern from waking consciousness. (p. 184)

Ambiguous stimuli Patterns that allow more than one perceptual organization. (p. 160)

Ambivalence Mixed positive and negative feelings or simultaneous attraction and repulsion. (p. 492)

Ambivalent/resistant attachment A type of insecure attachment characterized by sever distress on leave-taking coupled with ambivalent behaviour at reunion. (p. 104)

Amphetamine psychosis A severe disruption of psychological functioning caused by abuse of amphetamines. (p. 210)

Amphetamines A class of synthetic drugs having stimulant effects on the nervous system. (p. 210)

Amygdala The part of the limbic system associated with fear responses. (p. 78)

Anal-expulsive personality A disorderly, destructive, cruel, or messy person. (p. 408)

Anal-retentive personality A person who is obstinate, stingy, or compulsive, and who generally has difficulty "letting go." (p. 408)

Anal stage The psychosexual stage corresponding roughly to the period of toilet training (ages one to three years). (p. 408)

Androgen Any of a number of male sex hormones, especially testosterone. (p. 365)

Androgyny The presence of both "masculine" and "feminine" traits in a single person (as masculinity and femininity are defined within one's culture). (p. 416)

Anhedonia An inability to feel pleasure. (p. 211)

Animal model In research, using animal behaviour to discover principles that may apply to human behaviour. (p. 17)

Anorexia nervosa Active self-starvation or a sustained loss of appetite that has psychological origins. (p. 368)

Antecedents Events that precede a response. (p. 232)

Anterograde amnesia Loss of the ability to form or retrieve memories of events that occur after an injury or trauma. (p. 291)

Anthropomorphic error The error of attributing human thoughts, feelings, or motives to animals, especially as a way of explaining their behaviour. (p. 33)

Antidepressants Mood-elevating drugs. (p. 539)

Antipsychotics Drugs that, in addition to having tranquillizing effects, tend to reduce hallucinations and delusional thinking. (Also called major tranquillizers.) (p. 539)

Antisocial personality A person who lacks a conscience; is emotionally shallow, impulsive, and selfish; and tends to manipulate others. (p. 445)

Anxiety Apprehension, dread, or uneasiness similar to fear but based on a perceived sense of threat. (p. 447)

Anxiety reduction hypothesis An explanation of the self-defeating nature of avoidance responses as a result of the reinforcing effects of relief from anxiety. (p. 454)

Aphasia A speech disturbance resulting from brain damage. (p. 75)

Apparent-distance hypothesis An explanation of the Moon illusion stating that the horizon seems more distant than the night sky. (p. 168)

Applied research Scientific study undertaken to solve immediate practical problems. (p. 27)

Approach–approach conflict Choosing between two positive, or desirable, alternatives. (p. 144)

Approach–avoidance conflict Being attracted to and repelled by the same goal or activity. (p. 490)

Arousal The overall level of activation in the body and nervous system of a person or animal.

Arousal theory People prefer to maintain ideal, or comfortable, levels of arousal. (p. 370)

Artificial intelligence (AI) Any artificial system (often a computer program) that is capable of humanlike problem solving or intelligent responding. (p. 312)

Assertiveness training Instruction in how to be self-assertive and self-confident. (p. 573)

Assimilation In Piaget's theory, the application of existing mental patterns to new situations (i.e., the new situation is assimilated to existing mental schemes). (p. 112)

Association cortex All areas of the cerebral cortex that are not primarily sensory or motor in function. (p. 75)

Associative learning The formation of simple associations between various stimuli and responses. (p. 231)

Astigmatism Defects in the cornea, lens, or eye that cause some areas of vision to be out of focus. (p. 137)

Astrology A false system based on the belief that human behaviour is influenced by the position of stars and planets. (p. 44)

Asymptomatic Having a disease while lacking obvious symptoms of illness. (p. 481)

Attitude A learned tendency to respond to people, objects, or institutions in a positive or negative way. (p. 574)

Attribution The process of making inferences about the causes of one's own behaviour and that of others; the mental process of assigning causes to events. In emotion, the process of attributing arousal to a particular source. (p. 385)

Auditory ossicles The three small bones that link the eardrum to the cochlea. (p. 144)

Authenticity In Carl Rogers's terms, the ability of a therapist to be genuine and honest about his or her own feelings. (p. 519)

Authoritarian parents Parents who enforce rigid rules and demand strict obedience to authority. (p. 106)

Authoritarian personality A personality pattern characterized by rigidity; inhibition; prejudice; and an excessive concern with power, authority, and obedience. (p. 500)

Authoritative parents Parents who supply firm and consistent guidance combined with love and affection. (p. 107)

Autonomic nervous system (ANS) The system of nerves that connects the brain with the internal organs and glands. (p. 379)

Autonomic system Nerves carrying information to and from the internal organs and glands. (p. 62)

Autonomy versus shame and doubt A conflict between growing self-control and feelings of shame or doubt. (p. 122)

Availability (in memory) Memories currently stored in memory are available. (p. 288)

Aversion therapy Suppressing an undesirable response by associating it with aversive (painful or uncomfortable) stimuli. (p. 523)

Aversive stimulus A stimulus that is painful or uncomfortable. (p. 255)

Avoidance learning Learning that occurs when making a particular response delays or prevents the onset of a painful or unpleasant stimulus; learning to make a response in order to postpone or prevent discomfort. (p. 255)

Avoidance–avoidance conflict Choosing between two negative, or undesirable, alternatives. (p. 490)

Avoidant attachment A form of insecure attachment characterized by indifference to both leave-taking and reunion with the parent or caregiver. (p. 104)

Axon A thin fibre that carries information away from the cell body of a neuron. (p. 54)

Axon terminals Bulb-shaped structures at the ends of axons that form connections with the dendrites and somas of other neurons. (p. 55)

Babbling The repetition by infants of meaningless language sounds (including both vowel and consonant sounds). (p. 109)

Barbiturate One of a large group of sedative drugs that depress activity in the nervous system. (p. 215)

Barnum effect The tendency to consider a personal description accurate if it is stated in very general terms. (p. 174)

Base rate The basic rate at which an event occurs over time; the basic probability of an event. (p. 341)

Basic emotions The first distinct emotions to emerge in infancy. (p. 102)

Basic needs The first four levels of needs in Maslow's hierarchy; lower needs tend to be more potent than higher needs. (p. 375)

Basic research Scientific study undertaken without concern for immediate practical application. (p. 27)

Basic suggestion effect The tendency of hypnotized persons to carry out suggested actions as if they were involuntary. (p. 200)

Behaviour modification The application of learning principles to change human behaviour, especially maladaptive behaviour. (p. 523)

Behaviour therapy Any therapy designed to actively change behaviour. (p. 523)

Behavioural assessment Recording the frequency of various behaviours. (p. 426)

Behavioural contract A formal agreement stating behaviours to be changed and consequences that apply. (p. 265)

Behavioural dieting Weight reduction based on changing exercise and eating habits, rather than temporary self-starvation. (p. 361)

Behavioural genetics The study of inherited behavioural traits and tendencies. (p. 405)

Behavioural medicine The study of behavioural factors in medicine, physical illness, and medical treatment. (p. 478)

Behavioural personality theory Any model of personality that emphasizes learning and observable behaviour. (p. 413)

Behavioural risk factors Behaviours that increase the chances of disease, injury, or premature death. (p. 478)

Behaviourism The school of psychology that emphasizes the study of overt, observable behaviour. (p. 19)

Behaviouristic Any approach that emphasizes overt, observable behaviour and the effects of learning and conditioning. (p. 454)

Belief component What a person thinks or believes about the object of an attitude. (p. 575)

Bem Sex Role Inventory (BSRI) A list of 60 personal traits including "masculine," "feminine," and "neutral" traits; used to rate one's degree of androgyny. (p. 416)

Beta waves Small, fast brain-waves associated with being awake and alert. (p. 189)

Biased sample A subpart of a larger population that does not accurately reflect characteristics of the whole population. (p. 40)

Bilingualism The ability to speak two languages. (p. 329)

Binge drinking Consuming five or more drinks in a short time. (p. 217)

Binocular depth cue A depth cue that requires two eyes. (p. 164)

Biochemical abnormality A disturbance of the body's chemical systems, especially in brain chemicals or neurotransmitters. (p. 460)

Biofeedback Information given to a person about his or her ongoing bodily activities; aids voluntary regulation of bodily states. (p. 499)

Biological motives Innate motives based on biological needs. (p. 353)

Biological predisposition The presumed hereditary readiness of humans to learn certain skills, such as how to use language, or a readiness to behave in particular ways. (p. 110)

Biological rhythm Any repeating cycle of biological activity, such as sleep and waking cycles or changes in body temperature. (p. 185)

Biopsychologist A psychologist who studies the relationship between behaviour and biological processes, especially activity in the nervous system. (p. 89)

Bipolar disorders Emotional disorders involving both depression and mania. (p. 462)

Bipolar I disorder A mood disorder in which a person has episodes of mania (excited, hyperactive, energetic, grandiose behaviour) and also periods of deep depression. (p. 463)

Bipolar II disorder A mood disorder in which a person is mostly depressed (sad, despondent, guilt-ridden) but has also had one or more episodes of mild mania (hypomania). (p. 463)

Bisexual A person romantically and erotically attracted to both men and women. (p. 369)

Blind spot An area of the retina lacking visual receptors. (p. 138)

Bottom-up processing Organizing perceptions by beginning with low-level features. (p. 158)

Brainstem The lower brain, including the medulla, pons, and reticular formation. (p. 77)

Brief psychodynamic therapy A modern therapy based on psychoanalytic theory but designed to produce insights more quickly. (p. 517)

Brightness The intensity of lights or colours. (p. 162)

Brightness constancy The apparent (or relative) brightness of objects remains the same as long as they are illuminated by the same amount of light. (p. 162)

Broca's area The language area of the brain related to grammar and pronunciation. (p. 75)

Bulimia nervosa Excessive eating (gorging) usually followed by self-induced vomiting and/or taking laxatives. (p. 361)

Burnout A job-related condition of mental, physical, and emotional exhaustion. (p. 486)

Bystander apathy Unwillingness of bystanders to offer help during emergencies or to become involved in others' problems. (p. 590)

Caffeine A natural drug with stimulant properties; found in coffee and tea and added to artificial beverages and medicines. (p. 212)

Caffeinism Excessive consumption of caffeine, leading to dependence and a variety of physical and psychological complaints. (p. 212)

Camouflage Designs that break up figure–ground organization. (p. 160)

Cannon-Bard theory Activity in the thalamus causes emotional feelings and bodily arousal to occur simultaneously. (p. 384)

Carcinogen A substance capable of causing cancer. (p. 213)

Cardinal trait A personality trait so basic that all of a person's activities relate to it. (p. 402)

Case study An in-depth focus on all aspects of a single person. (p. 39)

Catatonic schizophrenia Schizophrenia marked by stupor; rigidity; unresponsiveness; posturing; mutism; and sometimes agitated, purposeless behaviour. (p. 456)

Causation The act of causing some effect. (p. 34)

Central nervous system (CNS) The brain and spinal cord. (p. 62)

Central tendency The tendency for a majority of scores to fall in the midrange of possible values. (p. A-3)

Central traits The core traits that characterize an individual personality. (p. 402)

Cephalocaudal From head to toe. (p. 100)

Cerebellum The brain structure that controls posture and coordination. (p. 77)

Cerebral cortex The outer layer of the brain. (p. 69)

Cerebral hemispheres The right and left halves of the cerebrum. (p. 69)

Cerebrum The two large hemispheres that cover the upper part of the brain. (p. 63)

Chance conditioning Conditioning that takes place by chance or coincidence. (p. 575)

Character Personal characteristics that have been judged or evaluated; a person's desirable or undesirable qualities. (p. 396)

Chemical senses Senses, such as smell and taste, that respond to chemical molecules. (p. 147)

Child rearing In forming attitudes, the effects of parental values, beliefs, and practices. (p. 576)

Chromosomes Threadlike "coloured bodies" in the nucleus of each cell that are made up of DNA. (p. 94)

Chronic insomnia Insomnia that persists for more than three weeks. (p. 194)

Chronological age A person's age in years. (p. 312)

Circadian rhythms Cyclical changes in bodily functions and arousal levels that recur on a schedule of about 24 hours. These cycles are governed by internal biological clocks. One such clock regulates sleep and wakefulness. (p. 354)

Classical conditioning A form of learning in which reflex responses are associated with new stimuli. (p. 233)

Client-centred therapy A non-directive therapy based on insights gained from conscious thoughts and feelings; emphasizes accepting one's true self. (p. 519)

Clinical method Studying psychological problems and therapies in clinical settings. (p. 31)

Clinical psychologist A psychologist who specializes in the treatment of psychological and behavioural disturbances or who does research on such disturbances. (p. 27)

Clinical study An intensive investigation of a single person, especially one suffering from some injury or disease. (p. 65)

Cocaine A crystalline drug derived from coca leaves; used as a central nervous system stimulant and local anaesthetic. (p. 211)

Cochlea The snail-shaped organ that makes up the inner ear. (p. 144)

Coefficient of correlation A statistical index ranging from +1.00 to −1.00 that indicates the direction and degree of correlation. (p. 33)

Coercion Being forced to change your beliefs or your behaviour against your will. (p. 571)

Cognition The process of thinking or mentally processing information (images, concepts, words, rules, and symbols). (p. 321)

Cognitive dissonance An uncomfortable clash between self-image, thoughts, beliefs, attitudes, or perceptions and one's behaviour. (p. 577)

Cognitive interview The use of various cues and strategies to improve the memory of eyewitnesses. (p. 278)

Cognitive learning Higher-level learning involving thinking, knowing, understanding, and anticipation. (p. 232)

Cognitive map Internal images or other mental representations of an area (maze, city, campus, and so forth) that underlie an ability to choose alternative paths to the same goal. (p. 258)

Cognitive psychology The area of psychology concerned with human thinking and information processing. (p. 23)

Cognitive therapy A therapy directed at changing the maladaptive thoughts, beliefs, and feelings that underlie emotional and behavioural problems. (p. 530)

Cognitive view Distorted thinking causes people to magnify ordinary threats and failures, leading to anxiety and distress. (p. 454)

Colour-blindness A total inability to perceive colours. (p. 141)

Colour weakness An inability to distinguish some colours. (p. 141)

Commitment The determination to stay in a long-term relationship with another person. (p. 560)

Common traits Personality traits that are shared by most members of a particular culture. (p. 401)

Communicator In persuasion, the person presenting arguments or information.

Community mental health centre A facility offering a wide range of mental health services, such as prevention, counselling, consultation, and crisis intervention. (p. 542)

Companionate love A form of love characterized by intimacy and commitment but not passion. (p. 560)

Comparative psychologist A psychologist primarily interested in studying and comparing the behaviour of different species, especially animals. (p. 16)

Compensation Counteracting a real or imagined weakness by emphasizing desirable traits or seeking to excel in the area of weakness or in other areas. (p. 495)

Compliance Bending to the requests of a person who has little or no authority or other form of social power. (p. 567)

Compulsion An act an individual feels driven to repeat, often against his or her will. (p. 450)

Computer-assisted instruction (CAI) Learning aided by computer-presented information, exercises, and feedback. (p. 248)

Computer simulations Computer programs that mimic some aspect of human thinking, decision making, or problem solving. (p. 313)

Concentrative meditation Mental exercise based on attending to a single object or thought. (p. 204)

Concept An idea representing a category of related objects or events. (p. 322)

Concept formation The process of classifying information into meaningful categories. (p. 325)

Conception The union of an ovum and a sperm cell. (p. 94)

Conceptual rule A formal rule for deciding if an object or event is an example of a particular concept. (p. 325)

Concrete operational stage The period of intellectual development during which children become able to use the concepts of time, space, volume, and number, but in ways that remain simplified and concrete, rather than abstract. (p. 114)

Conditioned aversion A learned dislike or conditioned negative emotional response to a particular stimulus. (p. 523)

Conditioned emotional response (CER) An emotional response that has been linked to a previously non-emotional stimulus by classical conditioning. (p. 238)

Conditioned response (CR) A reflex response that has become associated with a new stimulus; a learned response elicited by a conditioned stimulus. (p. 234)

Conditioned stimulus (CS) A stimulus that evokes a response because it has been repeatedly paired with an unconditioned stimulus. (p. 233)

Conditioned taste aversion A learned aversive response to a specific food. (p. 239)

Conditioning chamber An apparatus designed to study operant conditioning in animals; a Skinner box. (p. 241)

Conditions of worth Internal standards used to judge the value of one's thoughts, actions, feelings, or experiences. (p. 422)

Conductive hearing loss Poor transfer of sounds from the eardrum to the inner ear. (p. 145)

Cones Visual receptors for colours and daylight visual acuity. (p. 138)

Conflict A stressful condition that occurs when a person must choose between incompatible or contradictory alternatives. (p. 490)

Conformity Bringing one's behaviour into agreement or harmony with norms or with the behaviour of others in a group. (p. 565)

Confrontation In existential therapy, the process of confronting clients with their own values and with the need to take responsibility for the quality of their existence. (p. 520)

Congenital problems Problems or defects that originate during prenatal development in the womb. (p. 97)

Conjunctive concept A class of objects that have two or more features in common. (For example, to qualify an object must be both red and triangular.) (p. 325)

Connector neuron A nerve cell that serves as a link between two other nerve cells. (p. 64)

Connotative meaning The subjective, personal, or emotional meaning of a word or concept. (p. 327)

Conscience The part of the superego that causes guilt when its standards are not met. (p. 408)

Conscious The region of the mind that includes all mental contents a person is aware of at any given moment. (p. 409)

Consciousness Mental awareness of sensations, perceptions, memories, and feelings. (p. 410)

Consequences Effects that follow a response. (p. 432)

Conservation In Piaget's theory, mastery of the concept that the weight, mass, and volume of matter remain unchanged (are conserved), even when the shape or appearance of objects changes. (p. 114)

Consistency With respect to child discipline, the maintenance of stable rules of conduct. (p. 126)

Consolidation The process by which relatively permanent memories are formed in the brain. (p. 291)

Constructive processing Reorganizing or updating memories on the basis of logic, reasoning, or the addition of new information. (p. 276)

Consummate love A form of love characterized by intimacy, passion, and commitment. (p. 560)

Continuous reinforcement A schedule in which every correct response is followed by a reinforcer. (p. 250)

Control Altering conditions that influence behaviour in predictable ways. (p. 18)

Control group In a controlled experiment, the group of subjects exposed to all experimental conditions or variables *except* the independent variable. (p. 36)

Conventional moral reasoning Moral thinking based on a desire to please others or to follow accepted rules and values. (p. 120)

Convergence The simultaneous turning inward of the two eyes. (p. 164)

Convergent thinking Thinking directed toward discovery of a single established correct answer; conventional thinking. (p. 338)

Cooing Spontaneous repetition of vowel sounds by infants. (p. 109)

Cooperative play Play in which two or more children must coordinate their actions; if children don't cooperate, the game ends. (p. 105)

Coping statements Reassuring, self-enhancing statements that are used to stop self-critical thinking. (p. 507)

Cornea Transparent membrane covering the front of the eye. (p. 137)

Corpus callosum The bundle of fibres connecting the cerebral hemispheres. (p. 69)

Correlation The existence of a consistent, systematic relationship between two events, measures, or variables. (p. A-9)

Correlational method Making measurements to discover relationships between events. (p. 31)

Correlational study A non-experimental study designed to measure the degree of relationship (if any) between two or more events, measures, or variables. (p. 33)

Corticalization An increase in the relative size of the cerebral cortex. (p. 69)

Counselling psychologist A psychologist who specializes in the treatment of milder emotional and behavioural disturbances. (p. 27)

Counsellor A mental health professional who specializes in helping people with problems not involving serious mental disorder (e.g., marriage counsellors, career counsellors, and school counsellors). (p. 27)

Counterirritation Using mild pain to block more intense or long-lasting pain. (p. 155)

Courtesy bias The tendency to give "polite" answers—especially the tendency to alter answers so as not to hurt an interviewer's feelings. (p. 40)

Covert behaviour A response that is internal or hidden from view (such as a thought or an emotional reaction). (p. 15)

Covert reinforcement Using positive imagery to reinforce desired behaviour. (p. 545)

Covert sensitization Use of aversive imagery to reduce the occurrence of an undesired response. (p. 544)

Cranial nerves Major nerves that leave the brain without passing through the spinal cord. (p. 64)

Crisis intervention Skilled management of a psychological emergency. (p. 542)

Crista A floating structure that responds to fluid movement

within the semicircular canals. (p. 152)

Critical situations Situations during childhood that are capable of leaving a lasting imprint on personality. (p. 415)

Critical thinking An ability to evaluate, compare, analyze, critique, and synthesize information. (p. 43)

Computed tomographic (CT) scanning A computer-enhanced X-ray image of the brain or body. (p. 67)

Cue Any external stimulus that guides responses, especially by signalling the presence or absence of reinforcement. (p. 413)

Cult A group that professes great devotion to some person and follows that person almost without question; cult members are typically victimized by their leaders in various ways. (p. 572)

Cultural psychologist A psychologist who studies the ways in which culture affects human behaviour. (p. 17)

Cultural relativity Perceptions and judgments made relative to the values of one's culture; the idea that behaviour must be judged relative to the values of the culture in which it occurs. (p. 442)

Cultural values The importance and desirability of various objects and activities as defined by people in a given culture.

Culturally skilled therapist A therapist who has the awareness, knowledge, and skills necessary to treat clients from diverse cultural backgrounds. (p. 538)

Culture-fair test A test (such as an intelligence test) designed to minimize the importance of skills and knowledge that may be more common in some cultures than in others. (p. 318)

Curve of forgetting A graph that shows the amount of memorized information remembered after varying lengths of time. (p. 285)

Cyclothymic disorder Mild to moderate manic and depressive behaviour that persists for two years or more. (p. 462)

Dark adaptation Increased retinal sensitivity to light. (p. 141)

Data Observed facts or evidence (data: plural; *datum*: singular). (p. 15)

Data reduction system Any system that selects, analyzes, or condenses information.

Death, freedom, isolation, meaninglessness The universal challenges of existence, including an awareness that everyone will die, the responsibility that comes with freedom to choose, the fact that each person is ultimately isolated and alone in her or his private world, and the reality that meaning must be created in life. (p. 519)

Declarative memory That part of long-term memory containing specific factual information. (p. 279)

Deductive thought Thought that applies a general set of rules to a specific situation; for example, using the laws of gravity to predict the behaviour of a single falling object. (p. 336)

Deep lesioning Removal of tissue within the brain by use of an electrode; the use of an electrode (electrified wire) to destroy small areas deep within the brain. (p. 541)

Deep sleep Stage 4 sleep; the deepest form of normal sleep. (p. 189)

Defence mechanism A habitual and often unconscious psychological process used to reduce anxiety. (p. 493)

Degradation A chemical process by which neurotransmitter molecules are broken down into other chemicals and thus rendered inactive. (p. 59)

Deinstitutionalization Reduced use of full-time commitment to mental institutions to treat mental disorders. (p. 542)

Delta waves   Large, slow brain-waves that occur in deeper sleep (stages 3 and 4). (p. 189)

Delusion   A false belief held against all contrary evidence. (p. 456)

Demonology   In medieval Europe, the study of demons and the treatment of persons "possessed" by demons. (p. 516)

Dendrites   Neuron fibres that receive incoming messages. (p. 54)

Denial   Protecting oneself from an unpleasant reality by refusing to perceive it or believe it. (p. 493)

Denotative meaning   The exact, dictionary definition of a word or concept; its objective meaning. (p. 326)

Dependent variable   In an experiment, the condition (usually a behaviour) that is affected by the independent variable. (p. 36)

Depressant   A substance that decreases activity in the body and nervous system. (p. 205)

Depressive disorders   Emotional disorders involving sadness and depression. (p. 462)

Deprivation   In development, the loss or withholding of normal stimulation, nutrition, comfort, love, and so forth; a condition of lacking. (p. 97)

Depth cues   Perceptual features that impart information about distance and three-dimensional space. (p. 163)

Depth perception   The ability to see three-dimensional space and to accurately judge distances. (p. 163)

Description   In scientific research, the process of naming and classifying. (p. 17)

Descriptive statistics   Mathematical tools used to describe and summarize numeric data. (p. A-1)

Desensitization   Reducing fear or anxiety by repeatedly exposing a person to emotional stimuli while the person is deeply relaxed. (p. 238)

Determinism   The idea that all behaviour has prior causes that would completely explain one's choices and actions if all such causes were known. (p. 22)

Detoxification   In the treatment of alcoholism, the withdrawal of the patient from alcohol. (p. 219)

Developmental level   An individual's current state of physical, emotional, and intellectual development. (p. 99)

Developmental milestone   A significant turning point or marker in personal development. (p. 120)

Developmental psychologist   A psychologist interested in human growth and development from conception until death. (p. 16)

Developmental psychology   The study of progressive changes in behaviour and abilities from conception to death. (p. 93)

Developmental task   Any personal change that must take place for optimal development. (p. 120)

Deviant communication   Patterns of communication that cause guilt, anxiety, confusion, anger, conflict, and emotional turmoil. (p. 458)

Deviation IQ   An IQ obtained statistically from a person's relative standing in his or her age group, that is, how far above or below average the person's score was relative to other scores. (p. 312)

Difficult child   A child who is temperamentally moody, intense, and easily angered. (p. 95)

Diffusion of responsibility   Spreading the responsibility to act among several people; reduces the likelihood that help will be given to a person in need. (p. 591)

Digit-span test   A test of attention and short-term memory in which a string of numbers is recalled. (p. 274)

Direct observation   Assessing behaviour through direct surveillance. (p. 426)

Discipline   A framework of guidelines for acceptable behaviour. (p. 107)

Discovery learning   Learning based on insight and understanding. (p. 259)

Discrimination   Treating members of various social groups differently in circumstances where their rights or treatment should be identical. (p. 579)

Discriminative stimuli   Stimuli that precede rewarded and non-rewarded responses in operant conditioning. (p. 253)

Disease-prone personality   A personality type associated with poor health, marked by persistent negative emotions. (p. 479)

Dishabituation   The reversal of habituation. (p. 178)

Disinhibition   The removal of inhibition; results in acting out behaviour that normally would be restrained. (p. 588)

Disjunctive concept   A concept defined by the presence of at least one of several possible features. (For example, to qualify an object must be either blue or circular.) (p. 326)

Disorganized schizophrenia   Schizophrenia marked by incoherence, grossly disorganized behaviour, bizarre thinking, and flat affect or grossly inappropriate emotions. (p. 456)

Displaced aggression   Redirecting aggression to a target other than the actual source of one's frustration. (p. 489)

Dissociative amnesia   Loss of memory (partial or complete) for important information related to personal identity. (p. 451)

Dissociative fugue   A disorder involving some loss of memory, sudden travel away from home, plus confusion about one's personal identity. (p. 451)

Dissociative identity disorder   The presence of two or more distinct personalities (multiple personality). (p. 451)

Distractors   False items included with a correct item to form a test of recognition memory (for example, the wrong answers on a multiple-choice test). (p. 283)

Disturbed family environment   Stressful or unhealthy family relationships, communication patterns, and emotional atmosphere. (p. 458)

Disturbed verbal communication   Speech that is disorganized, garbled, or unintelligible. (p. 456)

Disuse   The theory that memory traces weaken when memories are not periodically used or retrieved. (p. 287)

Divergent thinking   Thinking that produces many ideas or alternatives; a major element in original or creative thought. (p. 338)

DNA   Deoxyribonucleic acid, a molecular structure that contains coded genetic information. (p. 94)

Dominant gene   A gene whose influence will be expressed each time the gene is present. (p. 94)

Dominant hemisphere   A term usually applied to the side of a person's brain that produces language. (p. 86)

Door-in-the-face effect   The tendency for a person who has refused a major request to subsequently be more likely to comply with a minor request. (p. 568)

Dopamine   An important transmitter substance found in the brain—especially in the limbic system, an area associated with emotional response; a neurotransmitter implicated in Parkinson's disease and schizophrenia. (p. 59)

Double approach–avoidance conflict   Being simultaneously attracted to and repelled by each of two alternatives. (p. 492)

Double-blind experiment An arrangement in which both subjects and researchers are unaware of whether subjects are in the experimental group or the control group. (p. 38)

Dream symbols Images in dreams that serve as visible signs of hidden ideas, desires, impulses, emotions, relationships, and so forth; images in dreams whose personal or emotional meanings differ from their literal meanings. (p. 197)

Drive The psychological expression of internal needs or valued goals, for example, hunger, thirst, or a drive for success; any stimulus (especially an internal stimulus such as hunger) strong enough to provoke a person to action. (p. 352)

Drug-dependency insomnia Insomnia that follows withdrawal from sleeping pills. (p. 194)

Drug interaction A combined effect of two drugs that exceeds the addition of one drug's effects to the other. (p. 209)

Drug tolerance A reduction in the body's response to a drug. (p. 205)

Dysthymic disorder Mild to moderate depression that persists for two years or more. (p. 462)

Easy child A child who is temperamentally relaxed and agreeable. (p. 95)

Echoic memory A brief continuation of sensory activity in the auditory system after a sound is heard. (p. 271)

Educational simulations Computer programs that simulate real-world settings or situations to promote learning. (p. 249)

Effector cells Cells in muscles and glands that are capable of producing some type of response. (p. 64)

Ego The executive part of personality that directs rational behaviour. (p. 408)

Ego ideal The part of the superego representing ideal behaviour; a source of pride when its standards are met. (p. 408)

Egocentric thought Thought that is self-centred and fails to consider the viewpoints of others. (p. 114)

Eidetic imagery The ability to retain a "projected" mental image long enough to use it as a source of information. (p. 294)

Elaborative encoding Encoding that links new information with existing memories and knowledge. (p. 275)

Electra conflict A girl's sexual attraction to her father and feelings of rivalry with her mother. (p. 408)

Electrical stimulation of the brain (ESB) Direct electrical stimulation and activation of brain tissue. (p. 66)

Electroconvulsive shock An electric current passed directly through the brain, producing a convulsion. (p. 292)

Electroconvulsive therapy (ECT) A treatment for severe depression, consisting of an electric shock passed directly through the brain, which induces a convulsion. (p. 540)

Electrode Any device (such as a wire, needle, or metal plate) used to electrically stimulate nerve tissue or to record its activity. (p. 56)

Electroencephalograph (EEG) A device that records electrical activity in the brain. (p. 188)

Emotion A state characterized by physiological arousal and changes in facial expression, gestures, posture, and subjective feelings. (p. 377)

Emotional appraisal Evaluating the personal meaning of a stimulus or situation. (p. 386)

Emotional attachment An especially close emotional bond that infants form with their parents, caregivers, or others. (p. 103)

Emotional component One's feelings toward the object of an attitude. (p. 575)

Emotional expressions Outward signs that an emotion is occurring. (p. 378)

Emotional feelings The private, subjective experience of having an emotion. (p. 378)

Emotional intelligence Emotional competence, including empathy, self-control, self-awareness, managing emotions, and other skills. (p. 389)

Emotion-focused coping Managing or controlling one's emotional reaction to a stressful or threatening situation. (p. 487)

Empathic arousal Emotional arousal that occurs when you feel some of another person's pain, fear, or anguish. (p. 591)

Empathy A capacity for taking another's point of view; the ability to feel what another is feeling. (p. 519)

Empathy–helping relationship We are most likely to help someone else when we feel emotions such as empathy and compassion. (p. 592)

Empirical evidence Facts or information based on direct observation or experience. (p. 15)

Encoding Converting information into a form in which it will be retained in memory. (p. 271)

Encoding failure Failure to store sufficient information to form a useful memory. (p. 286)

Encounter group A group experience that emphasizes intensely honest interchanges among participants regarding feelings and reactions to one another. (p. 534)

Endocrine system Glands whose secretions pass directly into the bloodstream or lymph system. (p. 80)

Endorphins Chemicals that are similar in structure and painkilling effect to opiate drugs such as morphine. (p. 60)

Enkephalins Opiate-like brain chemicals that regulate reactions to pain and stress. (p. 60)

Enrichment Deliberately making an environment more novel, complex, and perceptually or intellectually stimulating. (p. 97)

Environment ("nurture") The sum of all external conditions affecting development, especially the effects of learning. (p. 95)

Epinephrine An adrenal hormone that tends to arouse the body; epinephrine is associated with fear; also known as *adrenaline*. (p. 82)

Episodic drive A drive that occurs in distinct episodes. (p. 364)

Episodic memory A subpart of declarative memory that records personal experiences that are linked with specific times and places. (p. 280)

Equal-status contact Social interaction that occurs on an equal footing, without obvious differences in power or status. (p. 582)

Erogenous zones Areas of the body that produce pleasure and/or provoke erotic desire. (p. 365)

Eros Freud's name for the "life instinct." (p. 408)

Escape Reducing discomfort by leaving frustrating situations or by psychologically withdrawing from them. (p. 490)

Escape learning Learning to make a response in order to end an aversive stimulus. (p. 255)

Estrogen Any of a number of female sex hormones. (p. 365)

Estrus Changes in the sexual drives of animals that create a desire for mating; particularly used to refer to females in heat. (p. 365)

Ethnocentrism Placing one's own group or race at the centre—that is, tending to reject all other groups but one's own. (p. 581)

Ethologist A person who studies the natural behaviour patterns of animals.

Evaluation fears Fears of being inadequate, embarrassed, ridiculed, or rejected. (p. 432)

Evolutionary psychology The study of the evolutionary origins of human behaviour patterns. (p. 560)

Excitement phase The first level of sexual response, indicated by initial signs of sexual arousal. (p. 366)

Exemplars Stored representations of individual experiences. (p. 326)

Existential therapy An insight therapy that focuses on the elemental problems of existence, such as death, meaning, choice, and responsibility; emphasizes making courageous life choices. (p. 519)

Exorcism The practice of driving off an "evil spirit," especially from the body of a person who is "possessed." (p. 516)

Expectancy An anticipation concerning future events or relationships; anticipation about the effect a response will have, especially regarding reinforcement. (p. 414)

Experiment A formal trial undertaken to confirm a fact or principle. (p. 34)

Experimental group In a controlled experiment, the group of subjects exposed to the independent variable or experimental condition. (p. 36)

Experimental method Investigating behaviour through controlled experimentation. (p. 31)

Experimental subjects Humans or animals whose behaviour is investigated in an experiment. (p. 35)

Expert systems Computer programs designed to respond as a human expert would; programs based on the knowledge and rules that underlie human expertise in specific topics. (p. 313)

Expert witness A person recognized by a court of law as being qualified to give expert testimony on a specific topic. (p. 444)

Explicit memory A memory that a person is aware of having; a memory that is consciously retrieved. (p. 283)

Expressive behaviours Behaviours that express or communicate emotion or personal feelings. (p. 416)

External cause A cause of behaviour that is assumed to lie outside a person. (p. 564)

External eating cue Any external stimulus that tends to encourage hunger or to elicit eating. (p. 358)

External frustration Distress caused by external conditions that hinder progress toward a goal. (p. 488)

Extinction The weakening of a conditioned response through removal of the unconditioned stimulus. (p. 235)

Extracellular thirst Thirst caused by a reduction in the volume of fluids found between body cells. (p. 364)

Extraneous variables Conditions or factors excluded from influencing the outcome of an experiment. (p. 36)

Extrasensory perction (ESP) The purported ability to perceive events in ways that cannot be explained by known capacities of the sensory organs. (p. 173)

Extrinsic motivation Motivation based on obvious external rewards, obligations, or similar factors. (p. 375)

Extrovert A person whose attention is directed outward; an outgoing person. (p. 398)

Eye movement desensitization and reprocessing (EMDR) A technique for reducing fear or anxiety; based on holding upsetting thoughts in mind while rapidly moving the eyes from side to side. (p. 526)

Facial agnosia (prosopagnosia) The inability to perceive familiar faces. (p. 75)

Facial feedback hypothesis Sensations from facial expressions help define what emotion a person feels. (p. 387)

Factor analysis A statistical technique used to correlate multiple measurements and identify general underlying factors. (p. 402)

Fallacy of positive instances The tendency to remember or notice information that fits one's expectations, while forgetting discrepancies. (p. 45)

Family therapy A technique in which all family members participate, both individually and as a group, to change destructive relationships and communication patterns. (p. 534)

Feature detector A sensory system highly attuned to a specific stimulus pattern. (p. 135)

Feedback Information returned to a person about the effects a response has had; also known as knowledge of results. (p. 248)

Feeding system Areas in the hypothalamus that initiate eating when stimulated. (p. 356)

Fetal damage A congenital problem; that is, damage or injury that occurs to the fetus during prenatal development. (p. 316)

Figure–ground organization Part of a stimulus appears to stand out as an object (figure) against a less prominent background (ground). (p. 159)

Five-factor model There are five universal dimensions of personality. (p. 402)

Fixation The tendency to repeat wrong solutions or faulty responses, especially as a result of becoming blind to alternatives; a lasting conflict developed as a result of frustration or over-indulgence. (p. 408)

Fixed-interval (FI) schedule A reinforcer is given only when a correct response is made after a set amount of time has passed since the last reinforced response. Responses made during the time interval are not reinforced. (p. 250)

Fixed-ratio (FR) schedule A set number of correct responses must be made to get a reinforcer. For example, a reinforcer is given for every four correct responses. (p. 250)

Flashbulb memories Memories created at times of high emotion that seem especially vivid. (p. 293)

Flat affect An extreme lack of emotional expressiveness. (p. 456)

Flexibility In tests of creativity, the number of different types of solutions produced. (p. 338)

Fluency In tests of creativity, the total number of solutions produced. (p. 336)

Foot-in-the-door effect The tendency for a person who has first complied with a small request to be more likely later to fulfill a larger request. (p. 568)

Formal operations stage The period of intellectual development characterized by thinking that includes abstract, theoretical, and hypothetical ideas. (p. 114)

Fovea An area at the centre of the retina containing only cones. (p. 138)

Frame of reference A mental perspective used for judging and evaluating events. (p. 22)

Framing In thought, the terms in which a problem is stated or the way that it is structured. (p. 342)

Fraternal twins Twins conceived from two separate eggs. Fraternal twins are no more alike genetically than other siblings. (p. 319)

Free association In psychoanalysis, the technique of having a client say anything that comes to mind, regardless of how embarrassing or unimportant it may seem. (p. 516)

Free choice The ability to freely make choices that are not controlled by genetics, learning, or unconscious forces. (p. 418)

Free will The idea that human beings are capable of freely making choices or decisions; the presumed ability of humans to freely make choices not determined by heredity, past conditioning, or other concerns. (p. 519)

Frequency distribution A table that divides an entire range of scores into a series of classes and then records the number of scores that fall in each class. (p. A-2)

Frequency polygon A graph of a frequency distribution in which the number of scores falling in each class is represented by a point on a line. (p. A-3)

Frequency theory Tones up to 4000 hertz are converted to nerve impulses that match the frequency of each tone. (p. 144)

Frontal lobes The brain area associated with movement, the sense of smell, and higher mental functions. (p. 74)

Frustration A negative emotional state that occurs when one is prevented from reaching a goal. (p. 488)

Frustration-aggression hypothesis Frustration tends to lead to aggression. (p. 587)

Fully functioning person A person living in harmony with his or her deepest feelings, impulses, and intuitions. (p. 420)

Functional fixedness A rigidity in problem solving caused by an inability to see new uses for familiar objects. (p. 336)

Functional MRI (fMRI) scan A scan that records brain activity. (p. 67)

Functional solution A detailed, practical, and workable solution. (p. 333)

Functionalism The school of psychology concerned with how behaviour and mental abilities help people adapt to their environments. (p. 19)

Fundamental attribution error The tendency to attribute the behaviour of others to internal causes (personality, likes, and so forth). (p. 564)

g-factor A general ability factor or core of general intellectual ability that involves reasoning, problem-solving ability, knowledge, memory, and successful adaptation to one's surroundings. (p. 310)

Galvanic skin response (GSR) A change in the electrical resistance (or inversely, the conductance) of the skin, due to sweating. (p. 381)

Gate control theory Pain messages pass through neural "gates" in the spinal cord. (p. 155)

General adaptation syndrome (GAS) A series of bodily reactions to prolonged stress; occurs in three stages: alarm, resistance, and exhaustion. (p. 484)

General solution A solution that correctly states the requirements for success but not in enough detail for further action. (p. 333)

Generalized anxiety disorder A chronic state of tension and worry about work, relationships, ability, or impending disaster. (p. 448)

Generativity versus stagnation A conflict in which stagnant self-interest is countered by interest in guiding the next generation. (p. 123)

Genes Specific areas on a strand of DNA that carry hereditary information. (p. 94)

Genetic disorders Problems caused by defects in the genes or by inherited characteristics. (p. 97)

Genital stage The period of full psychosexual development, marked by the attainment of mature adult sexuality. (p. 408)

Gestalt psychology The school of psychology emphasizing the study of thinking, learning, and perception in whole units, not by analysis into parts. (p. 20)

Gestalt therapy An approach that focuses on immediate experience and awareness to help clients rebuild thinking, feeling, and acting into connected wholes; emphasizes the integration of fragmented experiences. (p. 520)

Giftedness The possession of either a high IQ or special talents or aptitudes. (p. 314)

Gigantism Excessive bodily growth caused by too much growth hormone. (p. 81)

Glucagon-like peptide 1 A substance in the brain that terminates eating. (p. 357)

Goal The target or objective of motivated behaviour. (p. 352)

Grammar A set of rules for combining language units into meaningful speech or writing. (p. 329)

Graphical statistics Techniques for presenting numbers pictorially, often by plotting them on a graph. (p. A-2)

Graphology A false system based on the belief that handwriting can reveal personality traits. (p. 44)

Grasping reflex A neonatal reflex consisting of grasping objects placed in the palms. (p. 99)

Group cohesiveness The degree of attraction among group members or their commitment to remaining in the group. (p. 563)

Group intelligence test Any intelligence test that can be administered to a group of people with minimal supervision. (p. 312)

Group prejudice Prejudice held out of conformity to group views. (p. 580)

Group sanctions Rewards and punishments (such as approval or disapproval) administered by groups to enforce conformity among members. (p. 566)

Group structure The network of roles, communication pathways, and power in a group. (p. 563)

Group therapy Psychotherapy conducted in a group setting to make therapeutic use of group dynamics. (p. 533)

Groupthink A compulsion by members of decision-making groups to maintain agreement, even at the cost of critical thinking. (p. 566)

Growth hormone A hormone secreted by the pituitary gland that promotes bodily growth. (p. 81)

Growth needs In Maslow's hierarchy, the higher-level needs associated with self-actualization. (p. 375)

Guided imagery Intentional visualization of images that are calming, relaxing, or beneficial in other ways. (p. 505)

Gustation The sense of taste. (p. 147)

Habit A deeply ingrained, learned pattern of behaviour. (p. 413)

Habituation A decrease in perceptual response to a repeated stimulus. (p. 177)

Hair cells Receptor cells within the cochlea that transduce vibrations into nerve impulses. (p. 144)

Halfway house A community-based facility for individuals making the transition from an institution (mental hospital, prison, and so forth) to independent living. (p. 542)

Hallucination An imaginary sensation, such as seeing, hearing, or smelling something that does not exist in the external world. (p. 158)

Hallucinogen A substance that alters or distorts sensory impressions. (p. 220)

Halo effect The tendency to generalize a favourable or unfavourable first impression to unrelated details of personality. (p. 426)

Handedness A preference for the right or left hand in most activities. (p. 85)

Hardy personality A personality style associated with superior stress resistance. (p. 501)

Hashish Resinous material scraped from the leaves of the hemp plant; hashish has a high concentration of THC. (p. 220)

Health psychology The study of how behavioural principles can be used to prevent illness and promote health. (p. 477)

Health-promoting behaviour Any practice that tends to maintain or enhance good health. (p. 479)

Heredity ("nature") The transmission of physical and psychological characteristics from parents to offspring through genes. (p. 94)

Heterosexual A person romantically and erotically attracted to members of the opposite sex. (p. 369)

Heuristic Any strategy or technique that aids problem solving, especially by limiting the number of possible solutions to be tried. (p. 333)

Hidden observer A detached part of the hypnotized person's awareness that silently observes events. (p. 202)

Hierarchy A rank-ordered series of higher and lower amounts, levels, degrees, or steps. (p. 524)

Hierarchy of human needs Abraham Maslow's ordering of needs, based on their presumed strength or potency. (p. 374)

Higher-order conditioning Classical conditioning in which a conditioned stimulus is used to bring about further learning; that is, a CS is used as if it were a US. (p. 235)

Hippocampus A brain structure associated with emotion and the transfer of information from short-term memory to long-term memory; the part of the limbic system associated with storing memories. (p. 79, 292)

Histogram A graph of a frequency distribution in which the number of scores falling in each class is represented by a vertical bar. (p. A-2)

Homeostasis A steady state of bodily equilibrium. (p. 353)

Homogamy Mate selection of two people who are similar to one another. (p. 558)

Homosexual A person romantically and erotically attracted to same-sex persons. (p. 369)

Honesty test A paper-and-pencil test designed to detect attitudes, beliefs, and behaviour patterns that predispose a person to dishonest behaviour. (p. 428)

Hormone A glandular secretion that affects bodily functions or behaviour. (p. 80)

Hue Classification of colours into basic categories of red, orange, yellow, green, blue, indigo, and violet. (p. 136)

Human growth sequence The pattern of physical development from conception to death. (p. 94)

Human immunodeficiency virus (HIV) A sexually transmitted virus that disables the immune system. (p. 482)

Human nature Those traits, qualities, potentials, and behaviour patterns most characteristic of the human species. (p. 418)

Humanism An approach to psychology that focuses on human experience, problems, potentials, and ideals. (p. 22)

Humanistic Any system of thought focused on subjective experience and human problems and potentials. (p. 454)

Hyperopia Difficulty focusing nearby objects (farsightedness). (p. 137)

Hyperthyroidism Faster metabolism and excitability caused by an overactive thyroid gland. (p. 81)

Hypnic jerk A reflex muscle twitch throughout the body that often occurs as one is falling asleep. (p. 189)

Hypnosis An altered state of consciousness characterized by narrowed attention and increased suggestibility. (p. 200)

Hypnotic susceptibility One's capacity for becoming hypnotized. (p. 201)

Hypochondriac A person who complains about illnesses that appear to be imaginary. (p. 498)

Hypochondriasis A preoccupation with fears of having a serious disease. Ordinary physical signs are interpreted as proof of disease, but no physical abnormality can be found. (p. 451)

Hypopituitary dwarfism Shortness and smallness caused by too little growth hormone. (p. 81)

Hypothalamus The small area of the brain that regulates emotional behaviours and motives. (p. 78, 356)

Hypothesis The predicted outcome of an experiment or an educated guess about the relationship between variables. (p. 29)

Hypothetical possibilities Suppositions, guesses, or projections. (p. 114)

Hypothyroidism Slower metabolism and sluggishness caused by an underactive thyroid gland. (p. 81)

Hysteria Wild emotional excitability sometimes associated with the development of apparent physical disabilities (numbness, blindness, and the like) without known physical cause. (p. 516)

Iconic memory A mental image or visual representation. (p. 271)

Id The primitive part of personality that remains unconscious, supplies energy, and demands pleasure. (p. 408)

Ideal self An idealized image of oneself (the person one would like to be). (p. 421)

Identical twins Twins who develop from a single egg and therefore have identical genes. (p. 319)

Identification Feeling emotionally connected to a person and seeing oneself as like him or her. (p. 415)

Identity versus role confusion A conflict concerning the need to establish a personal identity. (p. 122)

Illogical thought Thought that is intuitive, haphazard, or irrational. (p. 336)

Illusion A misleading or distorted perception. (p. 157)

Image Most often, a mental representation that has picture-like qualities; an icon. (p. 322)

Imagery rehearsal Mentally rehearsing and changing a nightmare in order to prevent it from reoccurring. (p. 197)

I-message A message that states the effect someone else's behaviour had on you (as in, "I think …" or "I feel…"). (p. 128)

Imitation An attempt to match one's own behaviour to another person's behaviour. (p. 415)

Immune system The system that mobilizes bodily defences against invading microbes and other disease agents. (p. 485)

Implicit memory A memory that a person does not know exists; a memory that is retrieved unconsciously. (p. 284)

Impossible figure A stimulus pattern that cannot be organized into a stable perception. (p. 161)

In-basket test A testing procedure that simulates the individual decision-making challenges that executives face. (p. 426)

Incentive value The value of a goal above and beyond its ability to fill a need. (p. 352)

Incongruence A state that exists when there is a discrepancy between one's experiences and self-image or between one's self-image and ideal self. (p. 421)

Incongruent person A person who has an inaccurate self-image or whose self-image differs greatly from the ideal self. (p. 421)

Independent variable In an experiment, the condition being investigated as a possible cause of some change in behaviour. The values that this variable takes are chosen by the experimenter. (p. 35)

Individual intelligence test A test of intelligence designed to be given to a single individual by a trained specialist. (p. 312)

Individual traits Personality traits that define a person's unique individual qualities. (p. 401)

Individuating information Information that helps define a person as an individual, rather than as a member of a group or social category. (p. 593)

Inductive thought Thinking in which a general rule or principle is gathered from a series of specific examples; for instance, inferring the laws of gravity by observing many falling objects. (p. 336)

Industry versus inferiority A conflict in middle childhood centred on lack of support for industrious behaviour, which can result in feelings of inferiority. (p. 122)

Inferential statistics Mathematical tools used for decision making, for generalizing from small samples, and for drawing conclusions. (p. A-2)

Information bits Meaningful units of information, such as numbers, letters, words, or phrases. (p. 274)

Information chunks Information bits grouped into larger units. (p. 274)

Informational view A perspective that explains learning in terms of information imparted by events in the environment. (p. 235)

In-group A group with which a person identifies. (p. 563)

Initiative versus guilt A conflict between learning to take initiative and overcoming feelings of guilt about doing so. (p. 122)

Insanity A legal term that refers to a mental inability to manage one's affairs or to be aware of the consequences of one's actions. (p. 444)

Insight A sudden mental reorganization of a problem that makes the solution obvious. (p. 334)

Insomnia Difficulty in getting to sleep or staying asleep. (p. 193)

Instructional games Educational computer programs designed to resemble video games in order to motivate learning. (p. 249)

Instrumental behaviours Behaviours directed toward the achievement of some goal; behaviours that are instrumental in producing some effect. (p. 416)

Integrity versus despair A conflict in old age between feelings of integrity and the despair of viewing previous life events with regret. (p. 123)

Intellectual disability (formerly mental retardation) The presence of a developmental disability, a formal IQ score below 70, or a significant impairment of adaptive behaviour. (p. 314)

Intelligence An overall capacity to think rationally, act purposefully, and deal effectively with the environment. (p. 309)

Intelligence quotient (IQ) An index of intelligence defined as a person's mental age divided by his or her chronological age and multiplied by 100. (p. 312)

Interaction with others In forming attitudes, the influence of discussions with others who hold particular attitudes. (p. 575)

Interference The tendency for new memories to impair retrieval of older memories, and the reverse. (p. 289)

Internal cause A cause of behaviour that is assumed to lie within a person—for instance, a need, preference, or personality trait. (p. 564)

Internal images Mental images or visual depictions used in memory and thinking. (p. 294)

Internal representation Any image, concept, precept, symbol, or process used to mentally represent information during thought. (p. 322)

Interpersonal attraction Social attraction to another person. (p. 557)

Interpersonal psychotherapy (IPT) A brief dynamic psychotherapy designed to help people by improving their relationships with other people. (p. 517)

Interview (personality) A face-to-face meeting held for the purpose of gaining information about an individual's personal history, personality traits, current psychological state, and so forth. (p. 424)

Intimacy Feelings of connectedness and affection for another person. (p. 560)

Intimacy versus isolation The challenge of establishing intimacy with others, versus feeling a sense of isolation. (p. 123)

Intracellular thirst Thirst triggered when fluid is drawn out of cells due to an increased concentration of salts and minerals outside the cell. (p. 364)

Intra-cranial stimulation Direct electrical stimulation and activation of brain tissue. (p. 245)

Intrauterine environment The physical and chemical environment within the uterus during prenatal development. (p. 97)

Intrinsic motivation Motivation that comes from within, rather than from external rewards; motivation based on personal enjoyment of a task or activity. (p. 375)

Introspection To look within; to examine one's own thoughts, feelings, or sensations. (p. 19)

Introvert A person whose attention is focused inward; a shy and reserved person. (p. 398)

Intuition Quick, impulsive thought that does not make use of formal logic or clear reasoning. (p. 340)

Intuitive thought Thinking that makes little or no use of reasoning and logic. (p. 114)

Ion channels Tiny holes in the axon membrane. (p. 57)

James-Lange theory Emotional feelings follow bodily arousal and come from awareness of such arousal. (p. 384)

Justification In cognitive dissonance theory, the degree to which one's actions are justified by rewards or other circumstances. (p. 578)

Just-world beliefs Belief that people generally get what they deserve. (p. 593)

Keyword method As an aid to memory, using a familiar word or image to link two items. (p. 301)

Kinesics The study of the meaning of body movements, posture, hand gestures, and facial expressions; commonly called body language. (p. 384)

Kinesthetic senses The senses of body movement and positioning. (p. 150)

Knowledge of results (KR) Informational feedback. (p. 248)

Language Words or symbols, and rules for combining them, that are used for thinking and communication. (p. 322)

Large-group awareness training Any of a number of programs (many of them commercialized) that claim to increase self-awareness and facilitate constructive personal change. (p. 534)

Latency According to Freud, the period in childhood when psychosexual development is more or less dormant. (p. 408)

Latent dream content The hidden or symbolic meaning of a dream, as revealed by dream interpretation and analysis. (p. 517)

Latent learning Learning that occurs without obvious reinforcement and that remains unexpressed until reinforcement is provided. (p. 258)

Lateralization Differences between the two sides of the body; especially, differences in the abilities of the brain hemispheres. (p. 88)

Law of effect Responses that lead to desirable effects are repeated; those that produce undesirable results are not. (p. 240)

Leaderless group discussion A test of leadership that simulates group decision making and problem solving. (p. 426)

Learned helplessness A learned inability to overcome obstacles or to avoid punishment; learned passivity and inaction to aversive stimuli. (p. 464)

Learned motives Motives based on learned needs, drives, and goals. (p. 353)

Learning Any relatively permanent change in behaviour that can be attributed to experience. (p. 231)

Learning theorist A psychologist interested in variables affecting learning and in theories of learning. (p. 16, 413)

Lens Structure in the eye that focuses light rays. (p. 137)

Leptin A substance released by fat cells that inhibits eating. (p. 357)

Lexigram A geometric shape used as a symbol for a word. (p. 331)

Libido In Freudian theory, the force, primarily pleasure oriented, that energizes the personality. (p. 408)

Life change units (LCUs) Numerical values assigned to each life event on the SRRS. (p. 495)

Life skills training A program that teaches stress reduction, self-protection, decision making, self-control, and social skills. (p. 481)

Life stages Widely recognized periods of life corresponding to broad phases of development. (p. 120)

Lifestyle disease A disease related to health-damaging personal habits. (p. 478)

Light sleep Stage 1 sleep, marked by small irregular brainwaves and some alpha waves. (p. 189)

Liking A relationship based on intimacy but lacking passion and commitment. (p. 560)

Limbic system The system in the forebrain that is closely linked with emotional response. (p. 78)

Lobes of the cerebral cortex Areas on the cortex bordered by major fissures or defined by their functions. (p. 73)

Lock and key theory of olfaction Odours are related to the shapes of chemical molecules. (p. 148)

Logical consequences Reasonable consequences that are defined by parents. (p. 128)

Logical thought Drawing conclusions on the basis of formal principles of reasoning. (p. 336)

Long sleeper A person who averages nine hours of sleep or more per night. (p. 188)

Long-term memory (LTM) The memory system used for relatively permanent storage of meaningful information. (p. 272)

Looking chamber An experimental apparatus used to test infant perception by presenting visual stimuli and observing infant responses. (p. 99)

Loudness The intensity of a sound; determined by the amplitude of sound waves. (p. 144)

Low-ball technique A strategy in which commitment is gained first to reasonable or desirable terms, which are then made less reasonable or desirable. (p. 568)

Lucid dream A dream in which the dreamer feels awake and capable of normal thought and action. (p. 225)

Magnetic resonance imaging (MRI) scan A three-dimensional representation of the body, based on its response to a magnetic field. (p. 67)

Maintenance rehearsal Silently repeating or mentally reviewing information to hold it in short-term memory. (p. 275)

Major depressive disorder A mood disorder in which the person has suffered one or more intense episodes of depression. (p. 463)

Major mood disorders Disorders marked by lasting extremes of mood or emotion and sometimes accompanied by psychotic symptoms. (p. 463)

Maladaptive behaviour Behaviour that makes it difficult to adapt to the environment and meet the demands of day-to-day life. (p. 442)

Management techniques Combining praise, recognition, approval, rules, and reasoning to enforce child discipline. (p. 107)

Manifest dream content The surface, "visible" content of a dream; dream images as they are remembered by the dreamer. (p. 517)

Mantra A flowing word or sound repeated silently during concentrative meditation. (p. 204)

Marijuana The leaves and flowers of the hemp plant Cannabis sativa. (p. 220)

Massed practice A practice schedule in which studying continues for long periods, without interruption. (p. 5, 298)

Maternal influences The total of all psychological effects mothers have on their children. (p. 108)

Maturation The physical growth and development of the body and nervous system. (p. 100)

Mean A measure of central tendency calculated by adding a group of scores and then dividing by the total number of scores. (p. A-3)

Mechanical solution A problem solution achieved by trial and error or by a fixed procedure based on learned rules. (p. 332)

Median A measure of central tendency found by arranging scores from the lowest to the highest (or highest to lowest) and selecting the score that falls in the middle. That is, half the values in a group of scores fall above the median and half fall below. (p. A-4)

Meditation A mental exercise for producing relaxation or heightened awareness. (p. 203)

Medulla The structure that connects the brain with the spinal cord and controls vital life functions. (p. 77)

Melatonin The hormone released by the pineal gland in response to daily cycles of light and dark. (p. 81)

Memory The mental system for receiving, encoding, storing, organizing, altering, and retrieving information. (p. 270)

Memory cue Any stimulus associated with a particular memory. Memory cues usually enhance retrieval. (p. 288)

Memory decay The fading or weakening of memories assumed to occur when memory traces become weaker. (p. 287)

Memory structure Patterns of associations among bits of information stored in memory. (p. 277)

Memory task Any task designed to test or assess memory.

Memory traces Physical changes in nerve cells or brain activity that take place when memories are stored. (p. 287)

Mental age The average mental ability people display at a given age. (p. 312)

Mental images Internal images or visual depictions used in memory and thinking. (p. 294)

Mental (or psychological) disorder A significant impairment in psychological functioning. (p. 442)

Mental rotation   A mental process that alters the position and orientation of an image in mental space. (p. 323)

Mere presence   The tendency for people to change their behaviour just because of the presence of other people. (p. 565)

Mesmerize   To hypnotize. (p. 200)

Message   In persuasion, the content of a communicator's arguments or presentation.

Metabolic disorder   Any disorder in metabolism (the rate of energy production and use in the body). (p. 316)

Meta-needs   In Maslow's hierarchy, needs associated with impulses for self-actualization. (p. 375)

Micro-electrode   An electrode small enough to record the activity of a single neuron. (p. 66)

Microsleep   A brief shift in brainwave patterns to those of sleep. (p. 185)

Microstressor   Any distressing, day-to-day annoyance; also called a *hassle*. (p. 498)

Mild punishment   Punishment that has a relatively weak effect—especially punishment that only temporarily slows responding. (p. 255)

Mindfulness meditation   Mental exercise based on widening attention to become aware of everything experienced at any given moment. (p. 204)

Minnesota Multiphasic Personality Inventory-2 (MMPI-2)   One of the best-known and most widely used objective personality questionnaires. (p. 427)

Minor tranquillizers   Drugs (such as Valium) that produce relaxation or reduce anxiety. (p. 539)

Mirror technique   Observing another person re-enact one's own behaviour, like a character in a play; designed to help persons see themselves more clearly. (p. 534)

MMPI-2 profile   A graphic representation of an individual's scores on each of the primary scales of the MMPI-2. (p. 428)

Mnemonic   Any kind of memory system or aid. (p. 5, 301)

Mode   A measure of central tendency found by identifying the most frequently occurring score in a group of scores. (p. A-4)

Model   A person who serves as an example in observational learning. (p. 525, 210)

Monocular depth cue   A depth cue that can be sensed with one eye. (p. 165)

Mood   A low-intensity, long-lasting emotional state. (p. 378)

Mood disorder   Major disturbances in mood or emotion. (p. 462)

Moon illusion   The apparent change in size that occurs as the moon moves from the horizon (large moon) to overhead (small moon). (p. 167)

Moral anxiety   Apprehension felt when thoughts, impulses, or actions conflict with the superego's standards. (p. 408)

Moral development   The development of values, beliefs, and thinking abilities that act as a guide regarding what is acceptable behaviour. (p. 119)

Moro reflex   A neonatal reflex evoked by a sudden loss of support or the sounding of a loud noise; in response, the arms are extended and then brought toward each other. (p. 99)

Morphemes   The smallest meaningful units in a language, such as syllables or words. (p. 329)

Motherese (or parentese)   A pattern of speech used when talking to infants, marked by a higher-pitched voice; short, simple sentences: repetition; slower speech; and exaggerated voice inflections. (p. 112)

Motivation   Internal processes that initiate, sustain, direct, and terminate activities. (p. 352)

Motor cortex   A brain area associated with control of movement. (p. 74)

Motor neuron   A nerve cell that carries motor commands from the CNS to muscles and glands. (p. 64)

Müller-Lyer illusion   Two equal-length lines tipped with inward- or outward-pointing V's appear to be of different lengths. (p. 168)

Multiculturalism   Giving equal status, recognition, and acceptance to different ethnic and cultural groups. (p. 594)

Multiple approach–avoidance conflict   Being simultaneously attracted to and repelled by each of several alternatives. (p. 493)

Multiple intelligences   Howard Gardner's controversial theory that there are several specialized types of intellectual ability. (p. 319)

Munchausen syndrome   An affected person fakes his or her own medical problems in order to gain attention. (p. 452)

Munchausen syndrome by proxy   An affected person fakes the medical problems of someone in his or her care in order to gain attention. (p. 452)

Mutual absorption   With regard to romantic love, the nearly exclusive attention lovers give to one another. (p. 560)

Myelin   A fatty layer coating some axons. (p. 58)

Myopia   Difficulty focusing distant objects (nearsightedness). (p. 137)

Natural clinical test   A natural event that provides data on a psychological phenomenon. (p. 39)

Natural consequences   The effects that naturally tend to follow a particular behaviour. (p. 128)

Natural selection   Darwin's theory that evolution favours those plants and animals best suited to their living conditions. (p. 19)

Natural setting   The environment in which an organism typically lives. (p. 32)

Naturalistic observation   Observing behaviour as it unfolds in natural settings. (p. 31)

Need   An internal deficiency that may energize behaviour. (p. 352)

Need for achievement (nAch)   The desire to excel or meet some internalized standard of excellence. (p. 373)

Need to affiliate   The desire to associate with other people. (p. 556)

Negative after-potential   A drop in electrical charge below the resting potential. (p. 58)

Negative attention seeking   Using misbehaviour to gain attention. (p. 244)

Negative correlation   A statistical relationship in which increases in one measure are matched by decreases in the other. (p. 33)

Negative reinforcement   When a response is followed by an end to discomfort or by the removal of an unpleasant event. (p. 244)

Negative self-statements   Self-critical thoughts that increase anxiety and lower performance. (p. 507)

Neonate   A term used for newborn infants during the first weeks following birth. (p. 99)

Nerve   A bundle of axons or nerve fibres. (p. 62)

Network model   A model of memory that views it as an organized system of linked information. (p. 278)

Neurilemma   A layer of cells that encases many axons. (p. 62)

Neurocognitive dream theory   A proposal that dreams reflect everyday waking thoughts and emotions. (p. 198)

Neurogenesis   The production of new neurons from precursor cells. (p. 60)

Neuron   An individual nerve cell. (p. 54)

Neuropeptide Y   A substance in the brain that initiates eating. (p. 357)

Neuropeptides Brain chemicals, such as enkephalins and endorphins, that regulate the activity of neurons. (p. 59)

Neuroplasticity The capacity of the brain to reorganize its neural pathways by developing new synaptic links. (p. 61)

Neuropsychologist A psychologist who studies the relationship between behaviour and biological processes, especially activity in the nervous system. (p. 17)

Neurotic anxiety Apprehension felt when the ego struggles to control id impulses. (p. 408)

Neurotransmitter Any chemical released by a neuron that alters activity in other neurons. (p. 58)

Neutral stimulus (NS) A stimulus that does not evoke a response. (p. 233)

Nicotine A potent stimulant drug found primarily in tobacco; nicotine is a known carcinogen. (p. 212)

Night terror A state of panic that occurs during NREM sleep. (p. 196)

Nightmare A highly unpleasant and undesirable dream that takes place during REM sleep. (p. 196)

Noise-induced hearing loss Damage caused by exposing the hair cells to excessively loud sounds. (p. 146)

Non-REM (NREM) sleep Non-rapid eye movement sleep characteristic of stages 2, 3, and 4. (p. 191)

Nonsense syllables Invented three-letter words used to test learning and memory. (p. 285)

Norepinephrine An adrenal hormone that tends to arouse the body; norepinephrine is associated with anger; also known as *noradrenaline*. (p. 82)

Norms Widely accepted (but often unspoken) standards of conduct for appropriate behaviour; rules that define acceptable and expected behaviour for members of a group. (p. 563)

Normal curve A bell-shaped curve characterized by a large number of scores in a middle area, tapering to very few extremely high and low scores. (p. 313)

Obedience Conformity to the demands of an authority. (p. 569)

Object permanence The concept, gained in infancy, that objects continue to exist even when they are hidden from view. (p. 114)

Objective test A test that gives the same score when different people correct it. (p. 426)

Observation Gathering data directly by recording facts or events. (p. 29)

Observational learning Learning achieved by watching and imitating the actions of another or noting the consequences of those actions. (p. 260)

Observational record A detailed summary of observed events or a video recording of observed behaviour. (p. 33)

Observer bias The tendency of an observer to distort observations or perceptions to match his or her expectations. (p. 32)

Observer effect Changes in behaviour brought about by an awareness of being observed. (p. 32)

Obsession Recurring irrational or disturbing thoughts or mental images that a person cannot prevent. (p. 450)

Obsessive-compulsive disorder An extreme preoccupation with certain thoughts and/or repetitive performance of certain behaviours. (p. 450)

Occipital lobes The portion of the cerebral cortex where vision registers in the brain. (p. 73)

Oedipus conflict A boy's sexual attraction to his mother, and feelings of rivalry with his father. (p. 408)

Olfaction The sense of smell. (p. 147)

Operant conditioning Learning based on the consequences of responding. (p. 528)

Operant extinction The weakening or disappearance of a non-reinforced operant response. (p. 244)

Operant reinforcer Any event that reliably increases the probability or frequency of responses it follows. (p. 241)

Operant stimulus discrimination The tendency to make an operant response when stimuli previously associated with reward are present and to withhold the response when stimuli associated with non-reward are present. (p. 253)

Operant stimulus generalization The tendency to respond to stimuli similar to those that preceded operant reinforcement. (p. 253)

Operational definition Defining a scientific concept by stating the specific actions or procedures used to measure it. For example, "hunger" might be defined as "the number of hours of food deprivation." (p. 30)

Opponent-process theory The theory of colour vision based on three coding systems (red or green, yellow or blue, black or white). (p. 140)

Oral-aggressive personality A person who uses the mouth to express hostility by shouting, cursing, biting, and so forth. Also, one who actively exploits others. (p. 408)

Oral-dependent personality A person who wants to passively receive attention, gifts, love, and so forth. (p. 408)

Oral stage The psychosexual stage (roughly birth to one year of age) when infants are preoccupied with the mouth as a source of pleasure and means of expression. (p. 408)

Organ of Corti The centre part of the cochlea, containing hair cells, canals, and membranes. (p. 144)

Organismic valuing A natural, undistorted, full-body reaction to an experience. (p. 423)

Organized knowledge Orderly and highly refined information about a particular topic or skill. (p. 334)

Orgasm A climax and release of sexual excitement. (p. 366)

Originality In tests of creativity, how novel or unusual solutions are. (p. 338)

Otolith organs Vestibular structures sensitive to movement, acceleration, and gravity. (p. 152)

Out-group A group with which a person does not identify. (p. 563)

Oval window A membrane on the cochlea connected to the third auditory ossicle. (p. 144)

Overdisclosure Self-disclosure that exceeds what is appropriate for a particular relationship or social situation. (p. 559)

Overgeneralization Blowing a single event out of proportion by extending it to a large number of unrelated situations. (p. 467)

Overlearning Continuing to study and learn after you first think you've mastered a topic. (p. 6)

Overly permissive parents Parents who give little guidance, allow too much freedom, or do not require the child to take responsibility. (p. 106)

Overt behaviour An action or response that is directly observable. (p. 15)

Pain disorder Pain that has no identifiable physical cause and appears to be of psychological origin. (p. 452)

Panic disorder (with agoraphobia) A chronic state of anxiety and brief moments of sudden panic. The person fears that these panic attacks will occur in public places or unfamiliar situations. (p. 449)

Panic disorder (without agoraphobia) A chronic state of anxiety with brief moments of sudden, intense, unexpected panic. (p. 449)

Paranoid schizphrenia Schizophrenia marked by a pre-occupation with delusions or by frequent auditory hallucinations related to a single theme, especially grandeur or persecution. (p. 456)

Paraprofessional An individual who works in a near-professional capacity under the supervision of a more highly trained person. (p. 543)

Parasympathetic branch The part of the autonomic system that quiets the body and conserves energy. (p. 380)

Parasympathetic rebound Excess activity in the parasympathetic nervous system following a period of intense emotion. (p. 381)

Parasympathetic system The branch of the autonomic system that quiets the body. (p. 63)

Parietal lobes The area of the brain where bodily sensations register. (p. 73)

Part learning Separately studying subparts of a larger body of information (such as sections of a textbook chapter). (p. 297)

Partial hospitalization An approach in which patients receive treatment at a hospital during the day, but return home at night. (p. 542)

Partial reinforcement A schedule in which only a portion of responses are reinforced. (p. 250)

Partial reinforcement effect Responses acquired with partial reinforcement are more resistant to extinction. (p. 250)

Passion Deep emotional and/or sexual feelings for another person. (p. 561)

Paternal influences The aggregate of all psychological effects fathers have on their children. (p. 108)

Peer counsellor A non-professional person who has learned basic counselling skills. (p. 549)

Percent of variance A portion of the total amount of variation in a group of scores. (p. A-10)

Perception The mental process of organizing sensations into meaningful patterns. (p. 134)

Perceptual construction A mental model of external events. (p. 157)

Perceptual expectancy (or set) A readiness to perceive in a particular manner, induced by strong expectations. (p. 170)

Perceptual features Basic elements of a stimulus, such as lines, shapes, edges, or colours. (p. 135)

Perceptual habits Well-established patterns of perceptual organization and attention. (p. 172)

Perceptual hypothesis An initial guess regarding how to organize (perceive) a stimulus pattern. (p. 160)

Perceptual learning Changes in perception that can be attributed to prior experience; a result of changes in how the brain processes sensory information. (p. 172)

Perfect negative relationship A mathematical relationship in which the correlation between two measures is −1.00. (p. 33)

Perfect positive relationship A mathematical relationship in which the correlation between two measures is +1.00. (p. 33)

Performance intelligence Intelligence measured by solving puzzles, assembling objects, completing pictures, and other tasks requiring the test taker to do something. (p. 311)

Peripheral nervous system (PNS) All parts of the nervous system outside the brain and spinal cord. (p. 62)

Peripheral vision Vision at the edges of the visual field. (p. 140)

Personal frustration Distress caused by personal characteristics that impede progress toward a goal. (p. 489)

Personal prejudice Prejudicial attitudes held toward persons who are perceived as a direct threat to one's own interests. (p. 580)

Personality disintegration A shattering of the coordination among thoughts, actions, and emotions normally found in personality. (p. 456)

Personality A person's unique and relatively stable behaviour pattern. (p. 396)

Personality questionnaire A paper-and-pencil test consisting of questions that reveal aspects of personality. (p. 426)

Personality theorist A psychologist who studies personality traits, dynamics, and theories. (p. 16)

Personality theory A system of concepts, assumptions, ideas, and principles used to understand and explain personality. (p. 400)

Personality trait A stable, enduring quality that a person shows in most situations. (p. 397)

Personality type A style of personality defined by a group of related traits. (p. 397)

Persuasion A deliberate attempt to change attitudes or beliefs with information and arguments. (p. 577)

PET scan Positron emission tomography scan; a computer-generated colour image of brain activity based on glucose consumption in the brain. (p. 67)

Phallic personality A person who is vain, exhibitionistic, sensitive, and narcissistic. (p. 408)

Phallic stage The psychosexual stage (roughly age three to six years) when a child is preoccupied with the genitals. (p. 408)

Pharmacotherapy The use of drugs to alleviate the symptoms of emotional disturbance. (p. 539)

Philippe Pinel The French physician who initiated humane treatment of mental patients in 1793. (p. 516)

Phobia An intense and unrealistic fear of some specific object or situation. (p. 237)

Phonemes The basic speech sounds of a language. (p. 329)

Photoreceptor A sensory receptor for light. (p. 137)

Phototherapy A treatment for seasonal affective disorder that involves exposure to bright, full-spectrum light. (p. 461)

Physical dependence Physical addiction, as indicated by the presence of drug tolerance and withdrawal symptoms. (p. 205)

Physiological changes (in emotion) Alterations in heart rate, blood pressure, perspiration, and other involuntary responses. (p. 378)

Pictorial depth cues Features found in painting, drawings, and photographs that impart information about space, depth, and distance. (p. 165)

Pineal gland The gland in the brain that helps regulate body rhythms and sleep. (p. 81)

Pinna The visible, external part of the ear. (p. 144)

Pitch Higher or lower tones; related to the frequency of sound waves. (p. 144)

Pituitary gland The "master gland," whose hormones influence other endocrine glands. (p. 81)

Place theory Higher and lower tones excite specific areas of the cochlea. (p. 144)

Placebo An inactive substance given in the place of a drug in psychological research. (p. 37)

Placebo effect Changes in behaviour due to expectations that a drug (or other treatment) will have some effect. (p. 535)

Plateau phase The second phase of sexual response during which physical arousal is further heightened. (p. 366)

Play Any activity done for sheer enjoyment. (p. 105)

Pleasure principle A desire for immediate satisfaction of wishes, desires, or needs. (p. 408)

Polygenic characteristics Personal traits or physical properties that are influenced by many genes working in combination. (p. 94)

Polygraph A device for recording heart rate, blood pressure, respiration, and galvanic skin response; commonly called a lie detector. (p. 381)

Pons The area on the brainstem that acts as a bridge between the medulla and other structures. (p. 77)

Population An entire group of animals, people, or objects belonging to a particular category (for example, all college students or all married women). (p. 40)

Positive correlation A statistical relationship in which increases in one measure are matched by increases in the other (or decreases correspond to decreases). (p. 33)

Positive psychology The study of human strengths, virtues, and optimal behaviour. (p. 25)

Positive reinforcement When a response is followed by a reward or other positive event. (p. 244)

Positive self-regard Thinking of oneself as a good, lovable, worthwhile person. (p. 422)

Postconventional moral reasoning Moral thinking based on carefully examined and self-chosen moral principles. (p. 120)

Post-traumatic stress disorder A psychological disturbance lasting more than one month following stresses that would produce anxiety in anyone who experienced them. (p. 451)

Power assertion The use of physical punishment or coercion to enforce child discipline. (p. 107)

Preadaptation Gradual matching of sleep–waking cycles to a new time schedule. (p. 355)

Preconscious The area of the mind containing information that can be voluntarily brought to awareness. (p. 408)

Preconventional moral reasoning Moral thinking based on the consequences of one's choices or actions (punishment, reward, or an exchange of favours). (p. 120)

Prediction An ability to accurately forecast behaviour. (p. 17)

Prefrontal area The very front of the frontal lobes; involved in sense of self, reasoning, and planning. (p. 74)

Prefrontal lobotomy An antiquated surgery in which portions of the frontal lobes were destroyed or disconnected from other brain areas. (p. 541)

Prejudice A negative emotional attitude held against members of a particular group of people. (p. 579)

Premack principle Any high-frequency response can be used to reinforce a low-frequency response. (p. 263)

Preoperational stage The period of intellectual development during which children begin to use language and think symbolically, yet remain intuitive and egocentric in their thought. (p. 144)

Presbyopia Farsightedness caused by aging. (p. 137)

Pressure A stressful condition that occurs when a person must meet urgent external demands or expectations. (p. 485)

Primary appraisal Deciding if a situation is relevant to oneself and if it is a threat. (p. 486)

Primary auditory cortex The part of the temporal lobe where auditory information is first registered in the brain. (p. 73)

Primary caregiver The person primarily responsible for the care of an infant; usually the infant's mother or father. (p. 103)

Primary emotions According to Robert Plutchik's theory, the most basic emotions of fear, surprise, sadness, disgust, anger, anticipation, joy, and acceptance. (p. 378)

Primary motives Innate motives based on biological needs. (p. 353)

Primary motor cortex The brain area associated with control of movement. (p. 74)

Primary reinforcers Non-learned reinforcers; usually those that satisfy physiological needs. (p. 245)

Primary somatosensory area The receiving areas for bodily sensations. (p. 73)

Priming Facilitating the retrieval of an implicit memory by using cues to activate hidden memories. (p. 285)

Private self-consciousness Preoccupation with inner feelings, thoughts, and fantasies. (p. 432)

Proactive interference The tendency for old memories to interfere with the retrieval of newer memories. (p. 289)

Problem-focused coping Directly managing or remedying a stressful or threatening situation. (p. 487)

Procedural memory Long-term memories of conditioned responses and learned skills. (p. 279)

Programmed instruction Any learning format that presents information in small amounts, gives immediate practice, and provides continuous feedback to learners. (p. 248)

Progressive part method Breaking information into a series of short units and then learning increasingly longer groups of units. (p. 297)

Projection Attributing one's own feelings, shortcomings, or unacceptable impulses to others. (p. 494)

Projective tests Psychological tests making use of ambiguous or unstructured stimuli. (p. 429)

Prosocial behaviour Behaviour toward others that is helpful, constructive, or altruistic. (p. 589)

Prototype An ideal model used as a prime example of a particular concept. (p. 326)

Proximodistal From the centre of the body to the extremities. (p. 100)

Pseudo-psychology Any false and unscientific system of beliefs and practices that is offered as an explanation of behaviour. (p. 44)

Psi phenomena Events that seem to lie outside the realm of accepted scientific laws. (p. 173)

Psyche The mind, mental life, and personality as a whole. (p. 408)

Psychiatric nurse A nurse with specialized training in mental health. (p. 27)

Psychiatric social worker A mental health professional trained to apply social science principles to help patients in clinics and hospitals. (p. 27)

Psychiatrist A medical doctor with additional training in the diagnosis and treatment of mental and emotional disorders. (p. 27)

Psychoactive drug A substance capable of altering attention, memory, judgment, time sense, self-control, mood, or perception. (p. 205)

Psychoanalysis A Freudian approach to psychotherapy emphasizing the exploration of unconscious conflicts. (p. 22)

Psychoanalyst A mental health professional (usually a medical doctor) trained to practise psychoanalysis. (p. 27)

Psychoanalytic dream theory A theory that emphasizes internal conflicts, motives, and unconscious forces. (p. 197)

Psychoanalytic theory The Freudian theory of personality that emphasizes unconscious forces and conflicts. (p. 407)

Psychodrama A therapy in which clients act out personal conflicts and feelings in the presence of others who play supporting roles. (p. 533)

Psychodynamic theory Any theory of behaviour that emphasizes internal conflicts, motives, and unconscious forces. (p. 22)

Psycholinguist A specialist in the psychology of language and language development. (p. 110)

Psychological dependence Drug dependence that is based primarily on emotional or psychological needs. (p. 209)

Psychological situation A situation as it is perceived and interpreted by an individual, not as it exists objectively. (p. 414)

Psychological trauma A psychological injury or shock, such as that caused by violence, abuse, neglect, separation, and so forth. (p. 458)

Psychologist A person highly trained in the methods, factual knowledge, and theories of psychology. (p. 26)

Psychology The scientific study of behaviour and mental processes. (p. 14)

Psychoneuroimmunology The study of the links among behaviour, stress, disease, and the immune system. (p. 485)

Psychopathology The scientific study of mental, emotional, and behavioural disorders; also, abnormal or maladaptive behaviour. (p. 440)

Psychosexual stages The oral, anal, phallic, and genital stages, during which various personality traits are formed. (p. 408)

Psychosocial dilemma A conflict between personal impulses and the social world. (p. 120)

Psychosomatic disorders Illnesses in which psychological factors contribute to bodily damage. (p. 498)

Psychosurgery Any surgical alteration of the brain designed to bring about desirable behavioural or emotional changes. (p. 541)

Psychotherapy Any psychological technique used to facilitate positive changes in an individual's personality or behaviour. (p. 514)

PsycINFO A searchable online database that provides brief summaries of the scientific and scholarly literature in psychology. (p. 10)

Puberty The biologically defined period during which a person matures sexually and becomes capable of reproduction. (p. 117)

Public self-consciousness Intense awareness of oneself as a social object. (p. 432)

Punisher Any event that decreases the probability or frequency of responses it follows. (p. 254)

Punishment Any event that follows a response and decreases its likelihood of occurring again; the process of suppressing a response. (p. 244, 254)

Random assignment The use of chance (e.g., flipping a coin) to assign subjects to experimental and control groups. (p. 36)

Random search strategy Trying possible solutions to a problem in a more or less random order. (p. 333)

Random selection Choosing a sample so that each member of the population has an equal chance of being included in the sample. (p. A-8)

Range The difference between the highest and lowest scores in a group of scores. (p. A-5)

Rapid eye movements (REMs) Swift eye movements during sleep. (p. 190)

Rapid smoking Prolonged smoking at a forced pace; used in aversion therapy to produce discomfort for smoking. (p. 524)

Rating scale A list of personality traits or aspects of behaviour on which a person is rated. (p. 426)

Rational-emotive behaviour therapy (REBT) An approach that states that irrational beliefs cause many emotional problems and that such beliefs must be changed or abandoned. (p. 531)

Rationalization Justifying your behaviour by giving reasonable and "rational," but false, reasons for it. (p. 494)

Reaction formation Preventing dangerous impulses from being expressed in behaviour by exaggerating opposite behaviour. (p. 494)

Readiness A condition that exists when maturation has advanced enough to allow the rapid acquisition of a particular skill. (p. 100)

Reality principle Delaying action (or pleasure) until it is appropriate. (p. 408)

Reality testing Obtaining additional information to check on the accuracy of perceptions. (p. 157)

Recall To supply or reproduce memorized information with a minimum of external cues. (p. 282)

Receptor sites Areas on the surface of neurons and other cells that are sensitive to neurotransmitters or hormones. (p. 59)

Recessive gene A gene whose influence will be expressed only when it is paired with a second recessive gene. (p. 94)

Reciprocal inhibition The presence of one emotional state inhibiting the occurrence of another, such as joy preventing fear or anxiety inhibiting pleasure. (p. 524)

Reciprocity A reciprocal interchange or return in kind. (p. 559)

Recitation As a memory aid, repeating aloud information one wishes to retain. (p. 298)

Recoding Reorganizing or modifying information to assist storage in memory. (p. 274)

Recognition memory An ability to correctly identify previously learned information. (p. 282)

Redintegration The process by which memories are reconstructed or expanded by starting with one memory and then following chains of association to other, related memories. (p. 279)

Reference group Any group that an individual uses as a standard for social comparison. (p. 576)

Reflection In client-centred therapy, the process of rephrasing or repeating thoughts and feelings expressed by clients so they can become aware of what they are saying. (p. 519)

Reflex An innate, automatic response to a stimulus (for example, an eye-blink). (p. 233)

Reflex arc The simplest behaviour, in which a stimulus provokes an automatic response. (p. 64)

Refusal skills training A program that teaches youths how to resist pressures to begin smoking. (Can also be applied to other drugs and health risks.) (p. 481)

Regression Retreating to an earlier level of development or to earlier, less demanding habits or situations. (p. 494)

Rehearsal Silently repeating or mentally reviewing information to improve memory. (p. 275)

Reinforcement Any event that increases the probability that a particular response will occur. (p. 232)

Reinforcement value The subjective value a person attaches to a particular activity or reinforcer. (p. 414)

Relational concept A concept defined by the relationship between features of an object or between an object and its surroundings (for example, "greater than," "lopsided"). (p. 325)

Relaxation response The pattern of internal bodily changes that occurs at times of relaxation. (p. 204)

Relearning Learning again something that was previously learned; used to measure memory of prior learning. (p. 283)

Reliability The ability of a test to yield nearly the same score each time it is given to the same person. (p. 427)

REM behaviour disorder A failure of normal muscle paralysis, leading to violent actions during REM sleep. (p. 192)

REM rebound The occurrence of extra rapid eye movement sleep following REM sleep deprivation. (p. 192)

REM sleep Sleep marked by rapid eye movements and a

return to stage 1 EEG patterns. (p. 190)

Reminding system Pain based on small nerve fibres; reminds the brain that the body has been injured. (p. 151)

Representative sample A small, randomly selected part of a larger population that accurately reflects characteristics of the whole population. (p. 40)

Representativeness heuristic A tendency to select wrong answers because they seem to match preexisting mental categories. (p. 341)

Repression The unconscious process by which memories, thoughts, or impulses are held out of awareness. (p. 21)

Research method A systematic approach to answering scientific questions. (p. 15)

Research participant bias Changes in the participants' behaviour caused by the influence of their expectations. (p. 37)

Researcher bias Changes in subjects' behaviour caused by the unintended influence of a researcher's actions. (p. 38)

Resistance A blockage in the flow of free association; topics the client unconsciously resists thinking or talking about. (p. 517)

Resolution The fourth phase of sexual response, involving a return to lower levels of sexual tension and arousal. (p. 366)

Response Any behaviour, either observable or internal; any muscular action, glandular activity, or other identifiable behaviour. (p. 232, 413)

Response chain A linked series of separate actions that lead to reinforcement. (p. 243)

Response-contingent consequences Reinforcement, punishment, or other consequences that are applied only when a certain response is made. (p. 524)

Response-contingent reinforcement Reinforcement given only when a particular response is made. (p. 242)

Response cost Removal of a positive reinforcer after a response is made. (p. 245)

REST Restricted environmental stimulation therapy. (p. 205)

Resting potential The electrical charge of a neuron at rest. (p. 56)

Reticular activating system (RAS) The part of the reticular formation that activates the cerebral cortex. (p. 78)

Reticular formation A network of neurons in the brainstem associated with attention and alertness. (p. 78)

Retina The light-sensitive layer of cells at the back of the eye. (p. 137)

Retinal disparity Small discrepancies in images on the right and left retinas. (p. 164)

Retrieval Recovering information from storage in memory. (p. 271)

Retroactive interference The tendency for new memories to interfere with the retrieval of old memories. (p. 289)

Retrograde amnesia Loss of memory for events that preceded a head injury or other amnesia-causing event. (p. 291)

Reuptake A process in which neurotransmitter molecules are picked up by synaptic vesicles for reuse. (p. 59)

Reversibility of thought Recognition that relationships involving equality or identity can be reversed (for example, if A = B, then B = A). (p. 114)

Reversible figure A stimulus pattern in which figure–ground organization can be reversed. (p. 159)

Reward Anything that produces pleasure or satisfaction; a positive reinforcer. (p. 413)

Rods Visual receptors for dim light that produce only black and white sensations. (p. 138)

Role conflict Trying to occupy two or more roles that make

conflicting demands on behaviour. (p. 563)

Role-playing The dramatic enactment or re-enactment of significant life events. (p. 533)

Role reversal Taking the role of another person to learn how one's own behaviour appears from the other person's perspective. (p. 533)

Romantic love Love that is associated with high levels of interpersonal attraction, heightened arousal, mutual absorption, and sexual desire. (p. 559)

Rooting reflex A neonatal reflex elicited by a light touch to the cheek, causing the infant to turn toward the object and attempt to nurse. (p. 99)

Rorschach technique A projective test composed of 10 standardized inkblots. (p. 429)

Rote learning Learning that takes place mechanically, through repetition and memorization, or by learning rules. (p. 259)

Run of luck A statistically unusual outcome (as in getting five heads in a row when flipping a coin) that could still occur by chance alone. (p. 175)

Saltatory conduction The process by which nerve impulses conducted down the axons of neurons coated with myelin jump from gap to gap in the myelin layer. (p. 58)

Sample A smaller subpart of a population. (p. 40)

Satiety system Areas in the hypothalamus that terminate eating. (p. 356)

Savings score The amount of time saved (expressed as a percentage) when relearning information. (p. 283)

Scaffolding The process of adjusting instruction so that it is responsive to a beginner's behaviour and supports the beginner's efforts to understand a problem or gain a mental skill. (p. 116)

Scapegoating Blaming a person or a group for the actions

of others or for conditions not of their making. (p. 489)

Scatter diagram A graph that plots the intersection of paired measures, that is, the points at which paired X and Y measures cross. (p. A-9)

Schachter's cognitive theory Emotions occur when physical arousal is labelled or interpreted on the basis of experience and situational cues. (p. 386)

Schedule of reinforcement A rule or plan for determining which responses will be reinforced. (p. 250)

Schizophrenia A psychosis characterized by delusions, hallucinations, apathy, and emotional problems. (p. 455)

Scientific method Testing the truth of a proposition by careful measurement and controlled observation. (p. 29)

Scientific observation An empirical investigation that is structured to answer questions about the world. (p. 15)

Seasonal affective disorder (SAD) Depression that occurs only during fall and winter; presumably related to decreased exposure to sunlight. (p. 464)

Secondary appraisal Deciding how to cope with a threat or challenge. (p. 486)

Secondary reinforcer A learned reinforcer; often one that gains reinforcing properties by association with a primary reinforcer. (p. 246)

Secondary traits Traits that are inconsistent or relatively minor. (p. 402)

Secure attachment A type of attachment characterized by mild distress at leave-taking and being readily soothed at reunion with the parent or caregiver. (p. 104)

Selective attention Giving priority to a particular incoming sensory message; voluntarily focusing on a selected portion of sensory input. (p. 153)

Selective combination In problem solving, the ability to connect seemingly unrelated items of information. (p. 335)

Selective comparison   The ability to relate a present problem to similar problems solved in the past or to prior experience. (p. 335)

Selective encoding   The ability to select information relevant to a problem while ignoring useless or distracting information. (p. 334)

Selective perception   Perceiving only certain stimuli among a larger array of possibilities. (p. 467)

Self   A continuously evolving conception of one's personal identity. (p. 420)

Self-actualization   The process of fully developing one's personal potential. (p. 22)

Self-actualizer   One who is living creatively and making full use of his or her potential. (p. 419)

Self-assertion   A direct, honest expression of feelings and desires. (p. 573)

Self-awareness   Consciousness of oneself as a person. (p. 103)

Self-concept   A person's perception of his or her own personality traits. (p. 399)

Self-confidence   Belief that one can successfully carry out an activity or reach a goal. (p. 374)

Self-defeating bias   A distortion of thinking that impairs behaviour. (p. 432)

Self-disclosure   The process of revealing private thoughts, feelings, and one's personal history to others. (p. 558)

Self-efficacy   Belief in your capacity to produce a desired result. (p. 414)

Self-esteem   Regarding oneself as a worthwhile person; a positive evaluation of oneself. (p. 107)

Self-evaluation   Positive and negative feelings held toward oneself. (p. 22)

Self-fulfilling prophecy   A prediction that prompts people to

act in ways that make the prediction come true. (p. 38)

Self-help group   A group of people who share a particular type of problem and provide mutual support to one another. (p. 549)

Self-hypnosis   A state of hypnosis attained without the aid of a hypnotist; autosuggestion. (p. 200)

Self-image   The total subjective perception of oneself (another term for *self-concept*). (p. 420)

Self-recording   Self-management based on keeping records of response frequencies. (p. 263)

Self-reference effect   Memory works better when you encode for meaning and emphasize personal relevance of the material. (p. 275)

Self-regulated learning   Active, self-guided learning. (p. 6)

Self-reinforcement   Praising or rewarding oneself for having made a particular response (such as completing a school assignment). (p. 414)

Self-testing   Evaluating learning by posing questions to yourself. (p. 5)

Semantic memory   A subpart of declarative memory that records impersonal knowledge about the world. (p. 280)

Semantics   The study of meanings in words and language. (p. 326)

Semicircular canals   Fluid-filled canals containing the sensory organs for balance. (p. 152)

Sensation   A sensory impression; also, the process of detecting physical energies with the sensory organs. (p. 134)

Sensation and perception psychologist   A psychologist who studies the sense organs and the process of perception. (p. 16)

Sensation seeking   A personality characteristic of persons who prefer high levels of stimulation. (p. 371)

Sensitive period   During development, a period of increased sensitivity to environmental influences. Also, a time during which certain events must take place for normal development to occur. (p. 96)

Sensitivity group   A group experience consisting of exercises designed to increase self-awareness and sensitivity to others. (p. 534)

Sensorimotor stage   The stage of intellectual development during which sensory input and motor responses become coordinated. (p. 114)

Sensorineural hearing loss   Loss of hearing caused by damage to the inner ear hair cells or auditory nerve. (p. 146)

Sensory adaptation   A decrease in sensory response to an unchanging stimulus. (p. 153)

Sensory analysis   Separation of sensory information into important elements. (p. 135)

Sensory coding   Codes used by the sense organs to transmit information to the brain. (p. 135)

Sensory conflict theory   Explains motion sickness as the result of a mismatch between information from vision, the vestibular system, and kinesthesis. (p. 153)

Sensory deprivation (SD)   Any major reduction in the amount or variety of sensory stimulation. (p. 205)

Sensory gating   Alteration of sensory messages in the spinal cord. (p. 155)

Sensory localization   The principle that the type of sensation experienced is related to the area of the brain activated. (p. 136)

Sensory memory   The first stage of memory, which holds an exact record of incoming information for a few seconds or less. (p. 271)

Sensory neuron   A nerve cell that carries information from the senses toward the CNS. (p. 64)

Separation anxiety   Distress displayed by infants when they

are separated from their parents or principal caregivers. (p. 103)

Serial position effect   The tendency to make the most errors in remembering the middle items of an ordered list. (p. 282)

Serotonin   A neurotransmitter implicated in depression. (p. 59)

Set point (for fat)   The proportion of body fat that tends to be maintained by changes in hunger and eating. (p. 356)

Severe punishment   Intense punishment; punishment capable of suppressing a response for long periods. (p. 255)

Sex drive   The strength of one's motivation to engage in sexual behaviour. (p. 365)

Sexual orientation   One's degree of emotional and erotic attraction to members of the same sex, opposite sex, or both sexes. (p. 369)

Sexual script   An unspoken mental plan that defines a "plot," dialogue, and actions expected to take place in a sexual encounter. (p. 368)

Sexually transmitted infection (STI)   An infection that is typically passed from one person to the next by intimate physical contact. (p. 481)

Shape constancy   The perceived shape of an object is unaffected by changes in its retinal image. (p. 161)

Shaping   Gradually moulding responses to a final desired pattern. (p. 243)

Short sleeper   A person averaging five hours of sleep or less per night. (p. 188)

Short-term memory (STM)   The memory system used to hold small amounts of information for relatively brief time periods. (p. 272)

Shyness   A tendency to avoid others plus uneasiness and strain when socializing. (p. 432)

Sidedness   A combination of preference for hand, foot, eye, and ear. (p. 86)

Signal   In early language development, any behaviour, such as touching, vocalizing, gazing, or smiling, that allows non-verbal interaction and turn-taking between parent and child. (p. 111)

Similarity   The extent to which two people are alike in background, age, interests, attitudes, beliefs, and so forth. (p. 160)

Single-blind experiment   An arrangement in which subjects remain unaware of whether they are in the experimental group or the control group, although the researcher knows. (p. 37)

Single-word stage   In language development, the period during which a child begins to use single words. (p. 110)

Situational context   The social situation, behavioural setting, or general circumstances in which an action takes place. (p. 441)

Situational determinants   External conditions that strongly influence behaviour. (p. 413)

Situational test   A simulation of real-life conditions so that a person's reactions may be directly observed. (p. 426)

Size constancy   The perceived size of an object remains constant, despite changes in its retinal image. (p. 161)

Size–distance invariance   The strict relationship between the distance an object lies from the eyes and the size of its image. (p. 168)

Skin receptors   Sensory organs for touch, pressure, pain, cold, and warmth. (p. 151)

Skin senses   The senses of touch, pressure, pain, heat, and cold. (p. 150)

Sleep apnea   Repeated interruption of breathing during sleep. (p. 197)

Sleep deprivation   Being prevented from getting desired or needed amounts of sleep. (p. 185)

Sleep-deprivation psychosis   A major disruption of mental and emotional functioning brought about by sleep loss. (p. 188)

Sleep hormone   A sleep-promoting substance found in the brain and spinal cord. (p. 188)

Sleep patterns   The order and timing of daily sleep and waking periods. (p. 188)

Sleep spindles   Distinctive bursts of brainwave activity that indicate a person is asleep. (p. 189)

Sleep stages   Levels of sleep identified by brainwave patterns and behavioural changes. (p. 189)

Sleeptalking   Speaking that occurs during NREM sleep. (p. 196)

Slow-to-warm-up child   A child who is temperamentally restrained and unexpressive. (p. 95)

Social anxiety   A feeling of apprehension in the presence of others. (p. 432)

Social comparison   Making judgments about ourselves through comparison with others. (p. 556)

Social competition   Rivalry among groups, each of which regards itself as superior to others. (p. 594)

Social development   The development of self-awareness, attachment to parents or caregivers, and relationships with other children and adults. (p. 103)

Social facilitation   The tendency to perform better when in the presence of others. (p. 565)

Social influence   Changes in a person's behaviour induced by the presence or actions of others. (p. 564)

Social learning theory   Combines learning principles with cognitive processes, socialization, and modelling to explain behaviour. (p. 414)

Social loafing   The tendency for people to work less hard when part of a group than when they are solely responsible for their work. (p. 565)

Social motives   Learned motives acquired as part of growing up in a particular society or culture. (p. 372)

Social nonconformity   Failure to conform to societal norms or the usual minimum standards for social conduct. (p. 441)

Social phobia   An intense, irrational fear of being observed, evaluated, embarrassed, or humiliated by others in social situations. (p. 450)

Social psychologist   A psychologist particularly interested in human social behaviour. (p. 17)

Social psychology   The scientific study of how individuals behave, think, and feel in social situations. (p. 556)

Social Readjustment Rating Scale (SRRS)   A scale that rates the impact of various life events on the likelihood of illness. (p. 495)

Social reinforcement   Praise, attention, approval, and/or affection from others. (p. 415)

Social reinforcers   Reinforcers, such as attention and approval, provided by other people. (p. 248)

Social role   Expected behaviour patterns associated with particular social positions (such as daughter, worker, student). (p. 563)

Social skills   Proficiency at interacting with others. (p. 432)

Social smile   Smiling elicited by social stimuli, such as seeing a parent's face. (p. 102)

Social stereotypes   Oversimplified images of the traits of individuals who belong to a particular social group. (p. 581)

Social support   Close, positive relationships with other people. (p. 506)

Solitary play   Playing alone. (p. 105)

Soma (or cell body)   The part of a neuron that contains the nucleus, which, in turn, carries the genetic material. (p. 54)

Somatic system   Nerves linking the spinal cord with the body and sense organs. (p. 62)

Somatic therapy   Any bodily therapy, such as drug therapy, electroconvulsive therapy, or psychosurgery. (p. 539)

Somatization disorder   Afflicted persons have numerous physical complaints. Typically, they have consulted many doctors, but no organic problems can be identified. (p. 451)

Somatosensory area   A receiving area for bodily sensations. (p. 73)

Somesthetic senses   Sensations produced by the skin, muscles, joints, viscera, and organs of balance. (p. 150)

Somnambulism   Sleepwalking; occurs during NREM sleep. (p. 195)

Sound wave   Cyclic, wavelike movement of air molecules. (p. 144)

Source traits   Basic underlying traits of personality; each source trait is reflected in a number of surface traits. (p. 402)

Spaced practice   A practice schedule that alternates study periods with brief rests. (p. 5, 298)

Specific goal   A goal with a clearly defined and measurable outcome. (p. 7)

Specific phobia   An intense, irrational fear of specific objects, activities, or situations. (p. 449)

Spinal nerves   Major nerves that carry sensory and motor messages in and out of the spinal cord. (p. 64)

"Split-brain" operation   Cutting the corpus callosum. (p. 71)

Spontaneous recovery   The reappearance of a learned response after its apparent extinction. (p. 235)

Spontaneous remission   The disappearance of a psychological disturbance without the aid of therapy. (p. 518)

SQ4R method   An active study-reading technique based on these steps: survey, question, read, recite, reflect, and review. (p. 3)

Stage hypnosis   The use of hypnosis to entertain; often, merely a simulation of hypnosis for that purpose. (p. 203)

Stage of exhaustion   The third stage of the G.A.S., at which time the body's resources are exhausted and damage occurs. (p. 484)

Stage of resistance   The second stage of the G.A.S., during which bodily adjustments to stress stabilize, but at a high physical cost. (p. 484)

Standard deviation   An index of how much a typical score differs from the mean of a group of scores. (p. A-5)

Stanford-Binet Intelligence Scale   A widely used individual test of intelligence; a direct descendant of Alfred Binet's first intelligence test. (p. 310)

State-dependent learning   Memory influenced by one's bodily state at the time of learning and at the time of retrieval. Improved memory occurs when the bodily states match. (p. 288)

Statistical abnormality   Abnormality defined on the basis of an extreme score on some dimension, such as IQ or anxiety. (p. 440)

Statistical significance   The degree to which an event (such as the results of an experiment) is unlikely to have occurred by chance alone. (p. A-8)

Status   An individual's position in a social structure, especially with respect to power, privilege, or importance. (p. 563)

Stem cells   Immature cells that differentiate into various types of mature cells in the body, including neurons. (p. 61)

Stereocilia   Bristle-like structures on hair cells. (p. 144)

Stereoscopic vision   Perception of space and depth caused chiefly by the fact that the eyes receive different images. (p. 164)

Stimulant   A substance that increases activity in the body and nervous system. (p. 205)

Stimulus   Any physical energy that has some effect on an organism and that evokes a response. (p. 19)

Stimulus control   Stimuli that are present when an operant response is acquired tend to control when and where the response is made; linking a particular response with specific stimuli. (p. 252)

Stimulus discrimination   The learned ability to respond differently to similar stimuli. (p. 236)

Stimulus drives   Drives based on needs for exploration, manipulation, curiosity, and stimulation. (p. 353)

Stimulus generalization   The tendency to respond to stimuli similar but not identical to a conditioned stimulus. (p. 236)

Stimulus motives   Innate needs for stimulation and information. (p. 353)

Storage   Holding information in memory for later use. (p. 271)

Stress   The mental and physical condition that occurs when a person must adjust or adapt to the environment. (p. 483)

Stress disorder   A significant emotional disturbance caused by stresses outside the range of normal human experience. (p. 450)

Stress inoculation   The use of positive coping statements to control fear and anxiety. (p. 507)

Stress management   The application of behavioural strategies to reduce stress and improve coping skills. (p. 503)

Stress reaction   The physical response to stress, consisting mainly of bodily changes related to autonomic nervous system arousal. (p. 483)

Stress-vulnerability model   Attributes psychosis to a combination of environmental stress and inherited susceptibility. (p. 461)

Stressor   A specific condition or event in the environment that challenges or threatens a person. (p. 484)

Structuralism   The school of thought concerned with analyzing sensations and personal experience into basic elements. (p. 19)

Structured interview   An interview that follows a prearranged plan in which a series of questions are asked. (p. 424)

Subcortex   All brain structures below the cerebral cortex. (p. 77)

Subjective discomfort   Personal, private feelings of discomfort, unhappiness, or emotional distress. (p. 440)

Subjective experience   Reality as it is perceived and interpreted, not as it exists objectively. (p. 418)

Sublimation   Working off unmet desires, or unacceptable impulses, in activities that are constructive or socially acceptable. (p. 495)

Successive approximations   A series of steps or ever-closer matches to a desired response pattern. (p. 243)

Sucking reflex   A neonatal reflex elicited by touching the mouth, whereupon the infant makes rhythmic sucking movements. (p. 99)

Superego   A judge or censor for thoughts and actions. (p. 408)

Superordinate goal   A goal that exceeds or overrides all others; a goal that renders other goals relatively less important. (p. 583)

Superstitious behaviour   A behaviour repeated because it seems to produce reinforcement, even though it is actually unnecessary. (p. 243)

Support group   A group formed to provide emotional support for its members through discussion of stresses and shared concerns. (p. 486)

Suppression   A conscious effort to put something out of mind or to keep it from awareness. (p. 290)

Surface traits   The visible or observable traits of one's personality. (p. 402)

Survey method   Using questionnaires and surveys to poll large groups of people; the use of public polling techniques to answer psychological questions. (p. 31)

Symbolic prejudice   Prejudice that is expressed in disguised fashion. (p. 581)

Symbolization   The process of bringing an experience into awareness. (p. 420)

Sympathetic branch   The part of the ANS that activates the body at times of stress. (p. 380)

Sympathetic system   The branch of the autonomic system that arouses the body. (p. 63)

Synapse   The microscopic space between two neurons, over which messages pass. It is also referred to as synaptic cleft. (p. 58)

Syntax   Rules for ordering words when forming sentences. (p. 329)

Systematic desensitization   A reduction in fear, anxiety, or aversion brought about by planned exposure to aversive stimuli. (p. 525)

Target behaviours   Actions or other behaviours (such as speech) that a therapist selects as the focus for behaviour modification efforts. (p. 529)

Taste bud   The receptor organ for taste. (p. 149)

Telegraphic speech   In language development, the formation of simple two-word sentences that "telegraph" (communicate) a simple idea. (p. 110)

Temperament   The hereditary aspects of personality, including sensitivity, activity levels, prevailing mood, irritability, and adaptability. (p. 397)

Temporal lobes   Areas that include the sites where hearing registers in the brain. (p. 73)

Temporary insomnia   A brief episode of insomnia. (p. 194)

Tension-release method   A procedure for systematically achieving deep relaxation of the body. (p. 565)

Teratogen   Radiation, a drug, or any other substance capable of altering fetal development in ways that cause birth defects. (p. 97)

Term schedule A written plan that lists the dates of all major assignments for each of your classes for an entire term. (p. 7)

Test anxiety High levels of arousal and worry that seriously impair test performance. (p. 372)

Test battery A group of tests and interviews given to the same individual. (p. 430)

Thalamus The brain structure that relays sensory information to the cerebral cortex. (p. 78)

Thanatos The death instinct. (p. 408)

THC Tetrahydrocannabinol, the main active chemical in marijuana. (p. 220)

Thematic Apperception Test (TAT) A projective test consisting of 20 different scenes and life situations about which respondents make up stories. (p. 430)

Theory A system of ideas designed to interrelate concepts and facts in a way that summarizes existing data and predicts future observations. (p. 31)

Theory of mind A child's current state of knowledge about the mind, including his or her understanding of desires, beliefs, thoughts, intentions, feelings, and so forth. (p. 114)

Therapeutic alliance A caring relationship that unites a therapist and a client in working to solve the client's problems. (p. 536)

Therapy placebo effect Improvement caused not by the actual process of therapy but by a client's expectation that therapy will help. (p. 535)

Thought stopping Use of aversive stimuli to interrupt or prevent upsetting thoughts. (p. 545)

Threat An event or situation perceived as potentially harmful. (p. 485)

Thyroid gland The endocrine gland that helps regulate the rate of metabolism. (p. 81)

Tip-of-the-tongue (TOT) state The feeling that a memory is available but not quite retrievable. (p. 280)

Token economy A therapeutic program in which desirable behaviours are reinforced with tokens that can be exchanged for goods, services, activities, and privileges. (p. 529)

Token reinforcer A tangible secondary reinforcer such as money, gold stars, poker chips, and the like. (p. 246)

Tokens Symbolic rewards, or secondary reinforcers (such as plastic chips, gold stars, or points) that can be exchanged for real reinforcers. (p. 529)

Top-down processing Applying higher-level knowledge to rapidly organize sensory information into a meaningful perception. (p. 158)

Trait profile A graph of the scores obtained on several personality traits. (p. 402)

Trait–situation interaction The influence that external settings or circumstances have on the expression of personality traits. (p. 405)

Trait theorist A psychologist interested in classifying, analyzing, and interrelating traits to understand personality. (p. 400)

Tranquillizer A drug that lowers anxiety and reduces tension. (p. 216)

Transducers Devices that convert one kind of energy into another. (p. 134)

Transference The tendency of patients to transfer to a therapist feelings that correspond to those the patient had for important persons in his or her past. (p. 517)

Transformation The mental ability to change the shape or form of a substance (such as clay or water) and to perceive that its volume remains the same. (p. 112)

Transformation rules Rules by which a simple declarative sentence may be changed to other voices or forms (past tense, passive voice, and so forth). (p. 329)

Traumatic stresses Extreme events that cause psychological injury or intense emotional pain. (p. 488)

Trepanning In modern usage, any surgical procedure in which a hole is bored in the skull; historically, the chipping or boring of holes in the skull to "treat" mental disturbance. (p. 515)

Trichromatic theory A theory of colour vision based on three cone types: red, green, and blue. (p. 140)

Trust versus mistrust A conflict about learning to trust others and the world. (p. 122)

Turn-taking In early language development, the tendency of parent and child to alternate in the sending and receiving of signals or messages. (p. 111)

Twin study A comparison of the characteristics of twins who were raised together or separated at birth; used to identify the relative impact of heredity and environment. (p. 319)

Tympanic membrane The eardrum. (p. 144)

Type A personality A personality type with an elevated risk of heart disease; characterized by time urgency, anger, and hostility. (p. 499)

Type B personality All personality types other than Type A; a low cardiac-risk personality. (p. 499)

Unanimity Being unanimous or of one mind; agreement. (p. 567)

Unconditional positive regard Unshakable love and approval given without qualification. (p. 423)

Unconditioned response (UR) An innate reflex response elicited by an unconditioned stimulus. (p. 234)

Unconditioned stimulus (US) A stimulus innately capable of eliciting a response. (p. 234)

Unconscious The region of the mind that is beyond awareness—especially impulses and desires not directly known to a person. (p. 408)

Uncritical acceptance The tendency to believe generally positive or flattering descriptions of oneself. (p. 44)

Understanding In psychology, when the causes of a behaviour can be stated; in problem solving, a deeper comprehension of the nature of the problem. (p. 17, 333)

Undifferentiated schizophrenia Schizophrenia lacking the specific features of catatonic, disorganized, or paranoid types. (p. 457)

Unstructured interview An interview in which conversation is informal and topics are taken up freely as they arise. (p. 424)

Vacillation Wavering in intention or feelings. (p. 493)

Validity The ability of a test to measure what it purports to measure. (p. 427)

Validity scales Scales that tell whether test scores should be invalidated for lying, inconsistency, "faking good," or "faking bad." (p. 428)

Variability The tendency for a group of scores to differ in value. Measures of variability indicate the degree to which scores within a group differ from one another. (p. A-5)

Variable Any condition that changes or can be made to change; a measure, event, or state that may vary. (p. 35)

Variable-interval (VI) schedule A reinforcer is given for the first correct response made after a varied amount of time has passed since the last reinforced response. Responses made during the time interval are not reinforced. (p. 252)

Variable-ratio (VR) schedule The number of correct responses that must be made to get a reinforcer varies. For example, a reinforcer is given after three to seven correct responses; the actual number changes randomly. (p. 251)

Verbal intelligence Intelligence measured by answering questions involving vocabulary, general information, arithmetic, and other tasks requiring the test taker to say something. (p. 311)

Vestibular senses   The senses of balance, position in space, and acceleration. (p. 150)

Vicarious classical conditioning   Classical conditioning brought about by observing another person react to a particular stimulus. (p. 239)

Vicarious desensitization   A reduction in fear or anxiety that takes place vicariously ("second-hand") when a client watches models perform the feared behaviour. (p. 525)

Virtual reality exposure   Use of computer-generated images to present fear stimuli. The virtual environment responds to a viewer's head movements and other inputs. (p. 525)

Visible spectrum   That part of the electromagnetic spectrum to which the eyes are sensitive. (p. 136)

Visual acuity   The sharpness of visual perception. (p. 138)

Visual cliff   An apparatus that looks like the edge of an elevated platform or cliff. (p. 163)

Visual pigments   Light-sensitive chemicals found in the rods and cones. (p. 140)

Waiting-list control group   People who receive no treatment as a test of the effectiveness of psychotherapy. (p. 535)

Waking consciousness   A state of normal, alert awareness. (p. 184)

Warning system   Pain based on large nerve fibres; warns that bodily damage may be occurring. (p. 151)

Weapon focus   The tendency of crime victims to fix their attention on an attacker's weapon. (p. 176)

Wechsler Adult Intelligence Scale—Third Edition (WAIS-III)   An adult intelligence test that rates both verbal and performance intelligence. (p. 311)

Wechsler Intelligence Scale for Children—Fourth Edition (WISC-IV)   An intelligence test for children that rates both verbal and performance intelligence. (p. 311)

Weekly time schedule   A written plan that allocates time for study, work, and leisure activities during a one-week period. (p. 379)

Wellness   A positive state of good health; more than the absence of disease. (p. 482)

Wernicke's area   The area of the brain related to language comprehension. (p. 75)

Whole learning   Studying an entire package of information (such as a complete poem) at once. (p. 297)

Wish fulfillment   The Freudian belief that many dreams express unconscious desires. (p. 197)

Withdrawal of love   Withholding affection to enforce child discipline. (p. 107)

Withdrawal symptoms   Physical illness and discomfort following the withdrawal of a drug. (p. 205)

Working memory   Another name for short-term memory, especially when it is used for thinking and problem solving. (p. 272)

Yerkes-Dodson law   A summary of the relationships among arousal, task complexity, and performance. (p. 371)

You-message   Threatening, accusing, bossing, lecturing, or criticizing another person (as in, "you always…" or "you never…"). (p. 128)

z-score   A number that tells how many standard deviations above or below the mean a score is. (p. A-6)

Zero correlation   The absence of a (linear) mathematical relationship between two measures. (p. A-9)

Zone of proximal development   The range of tasks a child cannot yet master alone, but that she or he can accomplish with the guidance of a more capable partner. (p. 116)

References

Aboud, F. E., & Mendelson, M. J. (1998). Determinants of friendship selection and quality: Developmental perspectives. In W. M. Bukowski & A. F. Newcomb (Eds.), *The company they keep: Friendship in childhood and adolescence. Cambridge studies in social and emotional development.* New York: Cambridge University Press.

Abramson, R. (1993, January 8). EPA officially links passive smoke, cancer. *Los Angeles Times*, p. A27.

Accordino, D. B., Accordino, M. P., & Slaney, R. B. (2000). An investigation of perfectionism, mental health, achievement, and achievement motivation in adolescents. *Psychology in the Schools, 37*(6), 535–545.

ACT Against Violence. (2005). *Early violence prevention.* Washington: Adults and Children together against Violence. Retrieved October 18, 2006, from http://www .actagainstviolence.com/violprevent /index.html.

Active Healthy Kids Canada (2011). *Don't let this be the most physical activity our kids get after school. Active Healthy Kids Canada report card on physical activity for children and youth.* Toronto: Author. Retrieved September 25, 2012, from http://dvqdas9jty7g6.cloudfront.net /reportcard2011/ahkc2011 _shortform_eng_final.pdf.

Adair, J. G., Paivio, A., & Ritchie, P. (1996). Psychology in Canada. *Annual Review of Psychology, 47*, 341–370.

Adams, J. (2001). *Conceptual blockbusting* (4th ed.). New York: Basic Books.

Adamson, K. (2004). *Kate's journey: triumph over adversity.* Redondo Beach, CA: Nosmada Press.

Addis, K. M., & Kahana, M. J. (2004). Decomposing serial learning: What is missing from the learning curve? *Psychonomic Bulletin & Review, 11*(1), 118–174.

Ader, R., & Cohen, N. (1993). Psychoneuroimmunology: Conditioning and stress. In L. W. Porter and M. R. Rosenzweig (Eds.), *Annual Review of Psychology, 44*, 53–85.

Adlaf, E. M., Begin, P., & Sawka, E. (Eds.). (2005). Canadian Addiction Survey (CAS): A national survey of Canadians' use of alcohol and other drugs: Prevalence of use and related harms: Detailed report. Ottawa: Canadian Centre on Substance Abuse.

Adlaf, E. M., Gliksman, L., Demers, A., & Newton-Taylor, B. (2001). The prevalence of elevated psychological distress among Canadian undergraduates: Findings from the 1998 Canadian Campus Survey. *Journal of American College Health, 50*, 67–72.

Adler, S. A., & Orprecio, J. (2006). The eyes have it: Visual pop-out in infants and adults. *Developmental Science, 9*, 189–206.

Adolphs, R. (2008). Fear, faces, and the human amygdala. *Current Opinion in Neurobiology, 18*(2), 166–172.

Adorno, T. W., Frenkel-Brunswik, E., Levinson, D. J., & Sanford, R. N. (1950). *The authoritarian personality.* New York: Harper.

Advisory Council on the Misuse of Drugs. (2009). *MDMA ("ecstasy"): A review of its harms and classification under the Misuse of Drugs Act 1971.* Retrieved August 29, 2012, from http://www.homeoffice.gov .uk/publications/agencies-public-bodies /acmd1/mdma-report?view=Binary.

Aguiar, A., & Baillargeon, R. (1998). 8.5-month-old infants' reasoning about containment events. *Child Development, 69*, 636–653.

Aguiar, A., & Baillargeon, R. (1999). 2.5-month-old infants' reasoning about when objects should and should not be occluded. *Cognitive Psychology, 39*, 116–157.

Ahima, R. S., & Osei, S. Y. (2004). Leptin signaling. *Physiology & Behavior, 81*, 223–241.

Ajzen, I. (2005). *Attitudes, personality and behaviour* (2nd ed.). New York: McGraw-Hill.

Åkerstedt, T. (2007). Altered sleep/wake patterns and mental performance. *Physiology & Behavior, 90*(2–3), 209–218.

Alarcon, R. D. (1995). Culture and psychiatric diagnosis: Impact on DSM-IV and ICD-10. *Psychiatric Clinics of North America, 18*(3), 449–465.

Albarracín, D., Johnson, B. T., & Zanna, M. P. (Eds.). (2005). *The handbook of attitudes.* Mahwah, NJ: Erlbaum.

Alberti, R., & Emmons, M. (2008). *Your perfect right* (9th ed.). San Luis Obispo, CA: Impact.

Alberto, P. A., & Troutman, A. C. (2009). *Applied behavior analysis for teachers* (8th ed.). Englewood Cliffs, NJ: Prentice Hall.

Alcock, J. E. (2003). Give the null hypothesis a chance: Reasons to remain doubtful about the existence of psi. *Journal of Consciousness Studies, 10*(6–7), 29–50.

Alcock, J. E., Burns, J., & Freeman, A. (2003). *Psi wars: Getting to grips with the paranormal.* Exeter, U.K.: Imprint Academic Press.

Allen, K., Blascovich, J., & Mendes, W. B. (2002). Cardiovascular reactivity in the presence of pets, friends, and spouses: The truth about cats and dogs. *Psychosomatic Medicine, 64*(5), 727–739.

Allgower, A., Wardle, J., & Steptoe, A. (2001). Depressive symptoms, social support, and personal health behaviors in young men and women. *Health Psychology, 20*(3), 223–227.

Allik, J. (2000). Available and accessible information in memory and vision. In E. Tulving (Ed.), *Memory, consciousness, and the brain: The Tallinn Conference.* Hove, U.K.: Psychology Press.

Alloy, L. B., & Clements, C. M. (1998). Hopelessness theory of depression. *Cognitive Therapy & Research, 22*(4), 303–335.

Alloy, L. B., Peterson, C., Abramson, L. Y., & Seligman, M. E. (1984). Attributional style and the generality of learned helplessness. *Journal of Personality & Social Psychology, 46*, 681–687.

Allport, G. W. (1958). *The nature of prejudice.* Garden City, NY: Anchor Books, Doubleday.

Allport, G. W. (1961). *Pattern and growth in personality.* New York: Holt, Rinehart, and Winston.

Alsaker, F. D. (1995). Is puberty a critical period for socialization? *Journal of Adolescence, 18*(4), 427–444.

Alvarado, N. (1994). Empirical validity of the Thematic Apperception Test. *Journal of Personality Assessment, 63*(1), 59–79.

Alvino, J., & the Editors of Gifted Children Monthly. (1996). *Parents' guide to raising a gifted child.* New York: Ballantine.

Amabile, T., Hadley, C. N., & Kramer, S. J. (2002). Creativity under the gun. *Harvard Business Review, 80*(8), 52–61.

Amato, P. R., & Fowler, F. (2002). Parenting practices, child adjustment, and family diversity. *Journal of Marriage & Family, 64*(3), 703–716.

Ambady, N., & Rosenthal, R. (1993). Half a minute: Predicting teacher evaluations from thin slices of nonverbal behavior and physical attractiveness. *Journal of Personality & Social Psychology, 64*, 431–441.

American Psychiatric Association (APA). (2000). *Diagnostic and statistical manual of mental disorders* (4th ed.). Washington: American Psychiatric Association.

American Psychological Association. (2003). Guidelines on multicultural education, training, research, practice, and organizational change for psychologists. *American Psychologist, 58*(5), 377–402.

Andermann, F., Andermann, E., Joubert, M., Karpati, G., et al. (1972). Familial agenesis of the corpus callosum with anterior horn cell disease: A syndrome of mental retardation, areflexia, and paraplegia. *Transactions of the American Neurological Association, 97*, 242–244.

Anderson, C. A. (1989). Temperature and aggression. *Psychological Bulletin, 106*, 74–96.

Anderson, C. A. (2004). An update on the effects of violent video games. *Journal of Adolescence, 27*, 113–122.

Anderson, C. A., Anderson, K. B., & Deuser, W. E. (1996). Examining an affective aggression framework. *Personality & Social Psychology Bulletin, 22*(4), 366–376.

Anderson, C. A., Berkowitz, L., Donnerstein, E., Huesmann, L. R., et al. (2003). The influence of media violence on youth. *Psychological Science in the Public Interest, 4*(3), 81–110.

Anderson, C. A., & Bushman, B. J. (2002). Human aggression. *Annual Review of Psychology, 53*, 27–51.

Anderson, J. R. (2005). *Cognitive psychology and its implications* (6th ed.). New York: Worth.

Anderson, M. C. (2001). Active forgetting: Evidence for functional inhibition as a source of memory failure. *Journal of Aggression, Maltreatment & Trauma, 4*(2), 185–210.

Anderson, M. C., & Bell, T. (2001). Forgetting our facts: The role of inhibitory processes in the loss of propositional knowledge. *Journal of Experimental Psychology: General, 130*(3), 544–570.

Anderson, M. C., & Green, C. (2001, March 15). Suppressing unwanted memories by executive control. *Nature, 410*, 366–369.

Anderson, M. C., Ochsner, K. N., Kuhl, B., Cooper, J., et al. (2004). Neural systems underlying the suppression of unwanted memories. *Science, 303*, 232–235.

Anderson, R. H., Anderson, K., Flemming, D. E., & Kinghorn, E. (1984). A multidimensional test of the attributional reformulation of learned helplessness. *Bulletin of the Psychonomic Society, 22*, 211–213.

Andrasik, F. (2003). Behavioral treatment approaches to chronic headache. *Neurological Sciences, 24*(Suppl2), S80–S85.

André, C., Jaber-Filho, J. A., Carvalho, M., Jullien, C., et al. (2003). Predictors of recovery following involuntary hospitalization of violent substance abuse patients. *The American Journal on Addictions, 12*(1), 84–89.

Andresen, J. (2000). Meditation meets behavioural medicine: The story of experimental research on meditation. *Journal of Consciousness Studies, 7*(11–12), 17–73.

Andrews, J. D. (1989). Integrating visions of reality. *American Psychologist, 44*(5), 803–817.

Annett, M. (2002). *Handedness and brain asymmetry: The right shift theory.* Hove, U.K.: Psychology Press.

Annett, M., & Manning, M. (1990). Arithmetic and laterality. *Neuropsychologia, 28*(1), 61–69.

Anthony, W. A., Cohen, M., & Kennard, W. (1990). Understanding the current facts and principles of mental health systems planning. *American Psychologist, 45*(11), 1249–1252.

Antle, M. C., & Mistlberger, R. E. (2005). Circadian rhythms. In I. Q. Whishaw & B. Kolb (Eds.), *The behavior of the laboratory rat: A handbook with tests.* London: Oxford.

Antony, M. M. (2004). *10 simple solutions to shyness: How to overcome shyness, social anxiety & fear of public speaking.* Oakland, CA: New Harbinger.

Arbona, C. B., Osma, J., Garcia-Palacios, A., Quero, S., et al. (2004). Treatment of flying phobia using virtual reality: Data from a 1-year follow-up using a multiple baseline design. *Clinical Psychology & Psychotherapy, 11*(5), 311–323.

Arendt, J. (1994). Clinical perspectives for melatonin and its agonists. *Biological Psychiatry, 35*(1), 1–2.

Ariely, D., & Wertenbroch, K. (2002). Procrastination, deadlines, and performance: Self-control by precommitment. *Psychological Science, 13*(3), 219–224.

Armeli, S., Gunthert, K. C., & Cohen, L. H. (2001). Stressor appraisals, coping, and post-event outcomes: The dimensionality and antecedents of stress-related growth. *Journal of Social & Clinical Psychology, 20*(3), 366–395.

Arnett, J. J. (2000). Emerging adulthood. *American Psychologist, 55*(5), 469–480.

Arnett, J. J. (2001). Conceptions of the transition to adulthood. *Journal of Adult Development, 8*(2), 133–143.

Arnett, J. J. (2004). *Emerging adulthood: The winding road from late teens through the twenties.* New York: Oxford University Press.

Arnett, J. J., & Tanner, J. L. (Eds.). (2006). *Emerging adults in America: Coming of age in the 21st century.* Washington: American Psychological Association.

Aronson, E. (1992). *The social animal.* San Francisco: W. H. Freeman.

Aronson, E. (2008). *The social animal* (10th ed.). New York: Worth.

Aronson, E., Wilson, T. D., & Akert, R. M. (2007). *Social psychology* (6th ed.). Englewood Cliffs, NJ: Prentice Hall.

Arthur, W., & Doverspike, D. (2001). Predicting motor vehicle crash involvement from a personality measure and a driving knowledge test. *Journal of Prevention & Intervention in the Community, 22*(1), 35–42.

Artz, S. (2005). To die for: Violent adolescent girls' search for male attention. In D. J. Pepler, K. C. Madsen, C. D. Webster, & K. S. Levene (Eds.), *The development and treatment of girlhood aggression.* Mahwah, NJ: Erlbaum.

Ary, D. V., Duncan, T. E., Biglan, A., Metzler, C. W., et al. (1999). Development of adolescent problem behavior. *Journal of Abnormal Child Psychology, 27*(2), 141–150.

Asch, S. E. (1956). Studies of independence and conformity: A minority of one against a unanimous majority. *Psychological Monographs, 70*(416).

Ash, D. W., & Holding, D. H. (1990). Backward versus forward chaining in the acquisition of a keyboard skill. *Human Factors, 32*(2), 139–146.

Ashby, F. G., & Maddox, W. T. (2005). Human category learning. *Annual Review of Psychology, 56*, 149–78.

Ashton, M. C., & Lee, K. (2007). Empirical, theoretical, and practical advantages of the HEXACO model of personality structure. *Personality and Social Psychology Review, 11*(2), 150–166.

Ashton, M., & Lee, K. (2008). The HEXACO model of personality structure and the importance of the H factor. *Social and Personality Psychology Compass, 2,* 1952–1962.

Assanand, S., Pinel, J. P. J., & Lehman, D. R. (1998). Personal theories of hunger and eating. *Journal of Applied Social Psychology, 28*(11), 998–1015.

Atkinson, R. C., & Schiffrin, R. M. (1968). Human memory: A proposed system and its control processes. In K. W. Spence & J. T. Spence (Eds.), *The psychology of learning and motivation* (Vol. 2). London: Academic Press.

Avery, D. H., Eder, D. N., Bolte, M. A., Hellekson, C. J., et al. (2001). Dawn simulation and bright light in the treatment of SAD. *Biological Psychiatry, 50*(3), 205–216.

Awadallah, N., Vaughan, A., Franco, K., Munir, F., et al. (2005). Munchausen by proxy: A case, chart series, and literature review of older victims. *Child Abuse & Neglect, 29*(8), 931–941.

Ayers, L., Beaton, S., & Hunt, H. (1999). The significance of transpersonal experiences, emotional conflict, and cognitive abilities in creativity. *Empirical Studies of the Arts, 17*(1), 73–82.

Ayllon, T. (1963). Intensive treatment of psychotic behavior by stimulus satiation and food reinforcement. *Behavior Research and Therapy, 1,* 53–61.

Ayllon, T., & Azrin, N. H. (1965). The measurement and reinforcement of behavior of psychotics. *Journal of the Experimental Analysis of Behavior, 8,* 357–383.

Ayotte, J., Peretz, I., & Hyde, K. (2002). Congenital amusia: A group study of adults afflicted with a music-specific disorder. *Brain, 125*(2), 238–251.

Baard, P. P., Deci, E. L., & Ryan, R. M. (2004). Intrinsic need satisfaction: A motivational basis of performance and well-being in two work settings. *Journal of Applied Social Psychology, 34*(10), 2045–2068.

Bachman, J. G., & Johnson, L. D. (1979). The freshmen. *Psychology Today, 13,* 78–87.

Baddeley, A. D. (2003). Working memory: Looking back and looking forward. *Nature Reviews Neuroscience, 4*(10), 829–839.

Baddeley, A., Eysenck, M. W., & Anderson, M. C. (2009). *Memory.* Hove, U.K.: Psychology Press.

Baer, J. M. (1993). *Creativity and divergent thinking.* Hillsdale, NJ: Erlbaum.

Bahrke, M. S., Yesalis, C. E., & Brower, K. J. (1998). Anabolic-androgenic steroid abuse and performance-enhancing drugs among adolescents. *Child & Adolescent Psychiatric Clinics of North America, 7*(4), 821–838.

Bailey, L. M., & McKeever, W. F. (2004). A large-scale study of handedness and pregnancy/birth risk events: Implications for genetic theories of handedness. *Laterality: Asymmetries of Body, Brain & Cognition, 9*(2), 175–188.

Baillargeon, R. (2004). Infants' reasoning about hidden objects: Evidence for event-general and event-specific expectations. *Developmental Science, 7*(4), 391–424.

Bain, S. K., & Allin, J. D. (2005). Stanford-Binet Intelligence Scales, Fifth Edition. *Journal of Psychoeducational Assessment, 23*(1), 87–95.

Baisden, R. H. (1995). Therapeutic uses for neural grafts: Progress slowed but not abandoned. *Behavioral & Brain Sciences, 18*(1), 47–48, 90–107.

Balk, D. E., Lampe, S., Sharpe, B., Schwinn, S., et al. (1998). TAT results in a longitudinal study of bereaved college students. *Death Studies, 22*(1), 3–21.

Bandura, A. (1971). *Social learning theory.* New York: General Learning Press.

Bandura, A. (2001). Social cognitive theory. *Annual Review of Psychology, 52,* 1–26.

Bandura, A., Blanchard, E. B., & Ritter, B. (1969). Relative efficacy of desensitization and modeling approaches for inducing behavioral, affective, and attitudinal changes. *Journal of Personality & Social Psychology, 13*(3), 173–199.

Bandura, A., & Rosenthal, T. L. (1966). Vicarious classical conditioning as a function of arousal level. *Journal of Personality & Social Psychology, 3,* 54–62.

Bandura, A., Ross, D., & Ross, S. A. (1963). Vicarious reinforcement and imitative learning. *Journal of Abnormal and Social Psychology, 67,* 601–607.

Bandura, A., & Walters, R. (1959). *Adolescent aggression.* New York: Ronald.

Bandura, A., & Walters, R. (1963). *Social learning and personality development.* New York: Holt.

Banich, M. T. (2004). *Cognitive neuroscience and neuropsychology* (2nd ed.). Boston: Houghton Mifflin.

Barabasz, A. (2000). EEG markers of alert hypnosis. *Sleep & Hypnosis, 2*(4), 164–169.

Barber, T. X. (2000). A deeper understanding of hypnosis: Its secrets, its nature, its essence. *American Journal of Clinical Hypnosis, 42*(3–4), 208–272.

Bard, C., Fleury, M., & Goulet, C. (1994). Relationship between perceptual strategies and response adequacy in sport situations. *International Journal of Sport Psychology, 25*(3), 266–281.

Bargh, J. A., McKenna, K. Y. A., & Fitzsimons, G. M. (2002). Can you see the real me? Activation and expression of the "true self" on the Internet. *Journal of Social Issues, 58*(1), 33–48.

Barkataki, I., Kumari, V., Das, M., Taylor, P., et al. (2006). Volumetric structural brain abnormalities in men with schizophrenia or antisocial personality disorder. *Behavioural Brain Research, 169*(2), 239–247.

Barlow, D. H. (2000). Unraveling the mysteries of anxiety and its disorders from the perspective of emotion theory. *American Psychologist, 55,* 1247–1263.

Barlow, D. H. (2002). *Anxiety and its disorders* (2nd ed.). New York: Guilford.

Barlow, D. H. (2004). Psychological treatments. *American Psychologist, 59*(9), 869–878.

Barnet, A. B., & Barnet, R. J. (1998). *The youngest minds.* New York: Touchstone.

Barnett, J. P., Matycka-Tyndale, E., and the HP4RY Team (2011). The gift of agency: Sexual exchange scripts among Nigerian youth. *Journal of Sex Research, 48* (4), 349–359.

Baron, I. S. (2005). Test review: Wechsler intelligence scale for children (4th ed.). (WISC-IV). *Child Neuropsychology, 11*(5), 471–475.

Baron, R. A., Byrne, D., & Branscombe, N. R. (2007). *Mastering social psychology.* Boston: Pearson/Allyn & Bacon.

Baron, R. A., Byrne, D., & Branscombe, N. R. (2009). *Mastering social psychology* (12th ed.). Boston: Pearson/Allyn & Bacon.

Barrett, D. (1993). The "committee of sleep": A study of dream incubation for problem solving. *Dreaming, 3*(2), 115–122.

Barrett, D., Greenwood, J. G., & McCullagh, J. F. (2006). Kissing laterality and handedness. *Laterality: Asymmetries of Body, Brain & Cognition, 11*(6), 573–579.

Barrett, D. C., Pollack, L. M., & Tilden, M. L. (2002). Teenage sexual orientation, adult openness, and status attainment in gay males. *Sociological Perspectives, 45*(2), 163–182.

Barrett, R. J. (1985). Behavioral approaches to individual differences in substance abuse. In M. Galizio & S. A. Maisto (Eds.), *Determinants of substance abuse treatment: Biological, psychological, and environmental factors.* New York: Plenum.

Barrick, M. R., Moun, M. K., & Judge, T. A. (2001). Personality and performance at the beginning of the new millennium. *International Journal of Selection & Assessment, 9*(1–2), 9–30.

Barron, F. (1958). The psychology of imagination. *Scientific American, 199*(3), 150–170.

Barrowcliff, A. L., & Haddock, G. (2006). The relationship between command hallucinations and factors of compliance: A critical review of the literature. *Journal of Forensic Psychiatry & Psychology, 17*(2), 266–298.

Bar-Tal, D., & Labin, D. (2001). The effect of a major event on stereotyping: Terrorist attacks in Israel and Israeli adolescents' perceptions of Palestinians, Jordanians and Arabs. *European Journal of Social Psychology, 31*(3), 265–280.

Bartholow, B. D., & Anderson, C. A. (2002). Effects of violent video games on aggressive behavior. *Journal of Experimental Social Psychology, 38*(3), 283–290.

Bartholow, B. D., Bushman, B. J., & Sestir, M. A. (2006). Chronic violent video game exposure and desensitization to violence: Behavioral and event-related brain potential data. *Journal of Experimental Social Psychology, 42*(4), 532–539.

Bartholow, B. D., Sestir, M. A., & Davis, E. B. (2005). Correlates and consequences of exposure to video game violence: Hostile personality, empathy, and aggressive behavior. *Personality & Social Psychology Bulletin, 31*(11), 1573–1586.

Bartram, B. (2006). An examination of perceptions of parental influence on attitudes to language learning. *Educational Research, 48*(2), 211–222.

Bartz, W. R. (2002, September–October). Teaching skepticism via the CRITIC acronym. *Skeptical Inquirer,* 42–44.

Basadur, M., Runco, M. A., & Vega, L. A. (2000). Understanding how creative thinking skills, attitudes and behaviors work together. *Journal of Creative Behavior, 34*(2), 77–100.

Bath, H. (1996). Everyday discipline or control with care. *Journal of Child & Youth Care, 10*(2), 23–32.

Batson, C. D. (2006). "Not all self-interest after all": Economics of empathy-induced altruism. In D. De Cremer, M. Zeelenberg, & J. K. Murnighan (Eds.), *Social psychology and economics.* Mahwah, NJ: Erlbaum.

Batson, C. D., & Powell, A. A. (2003). Altruism and prosocial behavior. In T. Millon & M. J. Lerner (Eds.), *Handbook of psychology: Personality and social psychology* (Vol. 5). New York: Wiley.

Batterham, R. L., Cohen, M. A., Ellis, S. M., Le Roux, C. E., et al. (2003). Inhibition of food intake in obese subjects by peptide YY3–36. *New England Journal of Medicine, 349*, 941–948.

Bauer, J. J., McAdams, D. P., & Pals, J. L. (2008). Narrative identity and eudaimonic well-being. *Journal of Happiness Studies, 9*(1), 81–104.

Baum, A., & Posluszny, D. M. (1999). Health psychology. *Annual Review of Psychology, 50*, 137–163.

Baumeister, R. F. (1994). Self-esteem. *Encyclopedia of human behavior* (Vol. 4). San Diego: Academic.

Baumeister, R. F., & Bushman, B. (2008). *Social psychology and human nature.* Belmont, CA: Cengage Learning/Wadsworth.

Baumrind, D. (1991). The influence of parenting style on adolescent competence and substance use. *Journal of Early Adolescence, 11*(1), 56–95.

Baumrind, D. (2005). Patterns of parental authority and adolescent autonomy. In J. Smetana (Ed.), *New directions for child development: Changes in parental authority during adolescence.* San Francisco: Jossey-Bass.

Bayard, S., Gosselin, N., Manon, R., & Lassonde, M. (2004). Inter and Intra hemispheric processing of visual event-related potentials in the absence of the corpus callosum. *Journal of Cognitive Neuroscience, 16*(3), 401–414.

Bearman, P. S., Moody, J., & Stovel, K. (2004). Chains of affection: The structure of adolescent romantic and sexual networks. *American Journal of Sociology, 110*(1), 44–91.

Beck, A. T. (1985). Cognitive therapy of depression: New perspectives. In P. Clayton (Ed.), *Depression.* New York: Raven.

Beck, A. T. (1991). Cognitive therapy. *American Psychologist, 46*(4), 368–375.

Beck, A. T. (2004). Cognitive patterns in dreams and daydreams. In R. I. Rosner & W. J. Lyddon (Eds.), *Cognitive therapy and dreams.* New York: Springer Publishing.

Beck, A. T., & Greenberg, R. L. (1974). *Coping with depression.* New York: Institute for Rational Living.

Beck, B. L., Koons, S. R., & Milgrim, D. L. (2000). Correlates and consequences of behavioral procrastination. *Journal of Social Behavior & Personality, 15*(5), 3–13.

Beck, J. S. (2002). Beck therapy approach. In M. Hersen & W. H. Sledge (Eds.),

Encyclopedia of psychotherapy. San Diego: Academic Press.

Beck, R. C. (2004). *Motivation: Theories and principles* (5th ed.). Englewood Cliffs, NJ: Prentice Hall.

Beebe, B., Gerstman, L., Carson, B., Dolins, M., et al. (1982). Rhythmic communication in the mother–infant dyad. In M. Davis (Ed.), *Interaction rhythms, periodicity in communicative behavior.* New York: Human Sciences Press.

Beeber, L. S., Chazan-Cohen, R., Squires, J., Harden, B. J., et al. (2007). The Early Promotion and Intervention Research Consortium (E-PIRC): Five approaches to improving infant/toddler mental health in Early Head Start. *Infant Mental Health Journal, 28*(2), 130–150.

Beersma, D. G. M., & Gordijn, M. C. M. (2007). Circadian control of the sleep–wake cycle. *Physiology & Behavior, 90*(2–3), 190–195.

Behrend, D. A., Beike, D. R., & Lampinen, J. M. (2004). *The self and memory.* Hove, U.K.: Psychology Press.

Beirne-Smith, M., Patton, J., & Shannon, K. (2006). *Mental retardation: An introduction to intellectual disability* (7th ed.). Englewood Cliffs, NJ: Prentice Hall.

Bellezza, F. S., Six, L. S., & Phillips, D. S. (1992). A mnemonic for remembering long strings of digits. *Bulletin of the Psychonomic Society, 30*(4), 271–274.

Belsky, J. (1996). Parent, infant, and social-contextual antecedents of father–son attachment security. *Developmental Psychology, 32*(5), 905–913.

Belsky, J. (2006). Determinants and consequences of infant-parent attachment. In L. Balter & C. S. Tamis-LeMonda (Eds.), *Child psychology: A handbook of contemporary issues* (2nd ed.). New York: Psychology Press.

Bem, S. L. (1975). Sex-role adaptability: One consequence of psychological androgyny. *Journal of Personality & Social Psychology, 31*, 634–643.

Bem, S. L. (1981). Gender schema theory. A cognitive account of sex typing. *Psychological Review, 88*, 354–364.

Ben-Shakhar, G., & Dolev, K. (1996). Psychophysiological detection through the guilty knowledge technique: Effect of mental countermeasures. *Journal of Applied Psychology, 81*(3), 273–281.

Benbow, C. P. (1986). Physiological correlates of extreme intellectual precocity. *Neuropsychologia, 24*(5), 719–725.

Bender, H. L., Allen, J. P., McElhaney, K. B., Antonishak, J., et al. (2007). Use of harsh physical discipline and developmental outcomes in adolescence. *Development & Psychopathology 19* (1), 227–242.

Benloucif, S., Bennett, E. L., & Rosenzweig, M. R. (1995). Norephinephrine and neural plasticity: The effects of xylamine on experience-induced changes in brain weight, memory, and behavior. *Neurobiology of Learning & Memory, 63*(1), 33–42.

Bensafi, M., Zelano, C., Johnson, B., Mainland, J., et al. (2004). Olfaction: From sniff to percept. In M. S. Gazzaniga (Ed.), *The cognitive neurosciences* (3rd ed.). Cambridge, MA: MIT Press.

Bensley, L., & Van Eenwyk, J. (2001). Video games and real-life aggression. *Journal of Adolescent Health, 29*(4), 244–257.

Benson, H. (1977). Systematic hypertension and the relaxation response. *New England Journal of Medicine, 296*, 1152–1156.

Bergin, A. E. (1991). Values and religious issues in psychotherapy and mental health. *American Psychologist, 46*(4), 394–403.

Berne, E. (1964). *Games people play.* New York: Grove.

Bernstein, H. J., Beale, M. D., Burns, C., & Kellner, C. H. (1998). Patient attitudes about ECT after treatment. *Psychiatric Annals, 28*(9), 524–527.

Bernthal, M. J. (2003) The effects of professional wrestling viewership on children. *The Sport Journal, 6*(3). Retrieved May 6, 2008, from http://thesportjournal.org /article/effect-professional-wrestling -viewership-children.

Berntsen, D., & Thomsen, D. K. (2005). Personal memories for remote historical events: Accuracy and clarity of flashbulb memories related to World War II. *Journal of Experimental Psychology: General, 134*(2), 242–257.

Berry, J. W. (1990). The psychology of acculturation. In R. A. Dienstbier & J. J. Berman (Eds.), *Nebraska Symposium on Motivation 1989: Cross-cultural perspectives, 37.* Lincoln: University of Nebraska Press.

Berry, J. W., Phinney, J. S., Sam, D. L., & Vedder, P. (2005). *Immigrant youth in cultural transition.* Mahwah, NJ: Erlbaum.

Berscheid, E., & Regan, P. (2005). *The psychology of interpersonal relationships.* Englewood Cliffs, NJ: Prentice Hall.

Bersoff, D. M. (1999). Why good people sometimes do bad things: Motivated reasoning and unethical behavior. *Personality & Social Psychology Bulletin, 25*(1), 28–39.

Bertsch, G. J. (1976). Punishment of consummatory and instrumental behavior: A review. *Psychological Record, 26*, 13–31.

Besner, D., Wartak, S., & Robidoux, S. (2008). Constraints on computational models of basic processes in reading. *Journal of Experimental Psychology: Human Perception and Performance, 34*(1), 242–250.

Betancur, C., Velez, A., Cabanieu, G., le Moal, M., et al. (1990). Association between left-handedness and allergy: A reappraisal. *Neuropsychologia, 28*(2), 223–227.

Bexton, W. H., Heron, W., & Scott, T. H. (1954). Effects of decreased variation in the sensory environment. *Canadian Journal of Psychology, 8*, 70–76.

Bhushan, B., & Khan, S. M. (2006). Laterality and accident proneness: A study of locomotive drivers. *Laterality: Asymmetries of Body, Brain & Cognition, 11*(5), 395–404.

Bialystok, E. (2011). Coordination of executive functions in monolingual and bilingual children. *Journal of Experimental Child Psychology, 110*(3), 461–468.

Bialystok, E., Craik, F. I. M., Green, D. W., & Gollan, T. H. (2009). Bilingual minds. *Psychological Science in the Public Interest, 10*, 89–129.

Binder, J. L. (2004). *Key competencies in brief dynamic psychotherapy: Clinical practice beyond the manual.* New York: Guilford.

Binks, P. G., Waters, W. F., & Hurry, M. (1999). Short-term total sleep deprivation does not selectively impair higher cortical functioning. *Sleep, 22*(3), 328–334.

Birnbaum, M. H. (2004). Human research and data collection via the Internet. *Annual Review of Psychology, 55*, 803–832.

Blackmore, S. (1991). Near-death experiences: In or out of the body? *Skeptical Inquirer, 16*(Fall), 34–45.

Blackmore, S. (2004). *Consciousness: An introduction.* New York: Oxford University Press.

Blackwell, D. L., & Lichter, D. T. (2004). Homogamy among dating, cohabiting, and married couples. *Sociological Quarterly, 45*(4), 719–737.

Blair, K. S., Richell, R. A., Mitchell, D. G. V., Leonard, A., et al. (2006). They know the words, but not the music: Affective and semantic priming in individuals with psychopathy. *Biological Psychology, 73*(2), 114–123.

Blakemore, C., & Cooper, G. (1970). Development of the brain depends on the visual environment. *Nature, 228*, 477–478.

Blanchard, D. C., & Blanchard, R. J. (2003). What can animal aggression research tell us about human aggression? *Hormones & Behavior, 44*(3), 171–177.

Bland, R. C. (1997). Epidemiology of affective disorders: A review. *Canadian Journal of Psychiatry, 42*, 367–377.

Bloch, S. (2006). *Introduction to the psychotherapies* (4th ed.). New York: Oxford University Press.

Blood, A. J., & Zatorre, R. J. (2001). Intensely pleasurable responses to music correlate with activity in brain regions implicated in reward and emotion. *Proceedings of the National Academy of Sciences, 98*(20), 11818–11823.

Bloom, B. (1985). *Developing talent in young people.* New York: Ballantine.

Bloom, C. M., & Lamkin, D. M. (2006). The Olympian struggle to remember the cranial nerves. Mnemonics and student success. *Teaching of Psychology, 33*(2), 128–129.

Bloom, J. W. (1998). The ethical practice of Web counseling. *British Journal of Guidance & Counselling, 26*(1), 53–59.

Blumstein, A., Cohen, J., & Farrington, D. (1988). Criminal career research: Its value for criminology. *Criminology, 26*, 1–35.

Blunt, A., & Pychyl, T. A. (2005). Project systems of procrastinators: A personal project-analytic and action control perspective. *Personality & Individual Differences, 38*(8), 1771–1780.

Boergers, J., Spirito, A., & Donaldson, D. (1998). Reasons for adolescent suicide attempts. *Journal of the American Academy of Child & Adolescent Psychiatry, 37*(12), 1287–1293.

Bohan, J. S. (1990). Social constructionism and contextual history: An expanded approach to the history of psychology. *Teaching of Psychology, 17*(2), 82 -89.

Bohannon, J. N., & Stanowicz, L. B. (1988). The issue of negative evidence: Adult responses to children's language errors. *Developmental Psychology, 24*(5), 684–689.

Bohart, A. C., & Tallman, K. (1996). The active client: Therapy as self-help. *Journal of Humanistic Psychology, 36*(3), 7–30.

Bohart, W. (1995). The person-centered therapies. In A. S. Gurman & S. B. Messer (Eds.), *Essential psychotherapies.* New York: Guilford.

Bohbot, V., & Corkin, S. (2007). Posterior parahippocampal place learning in H.M. *Hippocampus, 17*(9), 863–872.

Boivin, D. B., Czeisler, C. A., & Waterhouse, J. W. (1997). Complex interaction of the sleep–wake cycle and circadian phase modulates mood in healthy subjects. *Archives of General Psychiatry, 54*(2), 145–152.

Boivin, D. B., & James, F. O. (2002). Circadian adjustment to night-shift work by judicious light and darkness exposure. *Journal of Biological Rhythms, 17*(6), 556–567.

Boldero, J. M., Moretti, M. M., Bell, R. C., & Francis, J. J. (2005). Self-discrepancies and negative affect: A primer on when to look for specificity, and how to find it. *Australian Journal of Psychology, 57*(3), 139–147.

Bonanno, G. A., Papa, A., Lalande, K., Westphal, M., et al. (2004). The importance of being flexible. *Psychological Science, 15*(7), 482–487.

Bond, R., & Smith, P. B. (1996). Culture and conformity: A meta-analysis of studies using Asch's (1952b, 1956) line judgment task. *Psychological Bulletin, 119*(1), 111–137.

Bond, T., & Wooten, V. (1996). The etiology and management of insomnia. *Virginia Medical Quarterly, 123*(4), 254–255.

Bongard, S., al'Absi, M., & Lovallo, W. R. (1998). Interactive effects of trait hostility and anger expression on cardiovascular reactivity in young men. *International Journal of Psychophysiology, 28*(2), 181–191.

Bonham, V., Warshauer-Baker, E., & Collins, F. S. (2005). Race and ethnicity in the genome era: The complexity of the constructs. *American Psychologist, 60*(1), 9–15.

Bood, S., Sundequist, U., Kjellgren, A., Norlander, T., et al. (2006). Eliciting the relaxation response with the help of flotation-REST (Restricted Environmental Simulation Technique) in patients with stress-related ailments. *International Journal of Stress Management, 13*(2), 154–175.

Booker, J. M., & Hellekson, C. J. (1992). Prevalence of seasonal affective disorder in Alaska. *American Journal of Psychiatry, 149*(9), 1176–1182.

Boom, J., Wouters, H. & Keller, M. (2007). A cross-cultural evaluation of stage development: A Rasch re-analysis of longitudinal socio-moral reasoning data. *Cognitive Development, 22*(2), 231–229.

Boon, A. K., Réale, D., & Boutin, S. (2007). The interaction between personality, offspring fitness and food abundance in North American red squirrels. *Ecology Letters, 10*(11), 1094–1104.

Bootzin, R. R., & Epstein, D. R. (2000). Stimulus control. In K. L. Lichstein & C. M. Morin, *Treatment of late life insomnia.* Thousand Oaks, CA: Sage.

Borlongan, C. V., Sanberg, P. R., & Freeman, T. B. (1999). Neural transplantation for neurodegenerative disorders. *Lancet, 353*(Suppl. 1), S29–30.

Borman, W. C., Hanson, M. A., & Hedge, J. W. (1997). Personnel psychology. *Annual Review of Psychology, 48*, 299–337.

Bornstein, M. H., & Tamis-LeMonda, C. S. (2001). Mother–infant interaction. In A. Fogel & G. Bremmer (Eds.), *Blackwell handbook of infant development.* London: Blackwell.

Bornstein, R. F. (1996). Sex differences in dependent personality disorder prevalence rates. *Clinical Psychology: Science & Practice, 3*(1), 1–12.

Borod, J. C., Bloom, R. L., Brickman, A. M., Nakhutina, L., et al. (2002). Emotional processing deficits in individuals with unilateral brain damage. *Applied Neuropsychology, 9*(1), 23–36.

Borrie, R. A. (1990–91). The use of restricted environmental stimulation therapy in treating addictive behaviors. *International Journal of the Addictions, 25*(7A–8A), 995–1015.

Boskey, E. (2008). *Is oral sex safe sex?* Retrieved May 16, 2009, from http://std .about.com/od/riskfactorsforstds/a/ oralsexsafesex.htm.

Botvin, G. J., Griffin, K. W., Diaz, T., & Ifill-Williams, M. (1997). School-based drug abuse prevention with inner-city minority youth. *Journal of Child & Adolescent Substance Abuse, 6*(1), 5–19.

Bouchard, T. J., Jr. (1983). Twins—Nature's twice-told tale. *Yearbook of science and the future*, 66–81. Chicago: Encyclopedia Britannica.

Bouchard, T. J., Jr. (2004). Genetic influence on human psychological traits: A survey. *Current Directions in Psychological Science, 13*(4), 148–151.

Bouchard, T. J., Lykken, D. T., McGue, M., Segal, N. L., et al. (1990). Sources of human psychological differences: The Minnesota study of twins reared apart. *Science, 250*, 223–228.

Bourne, E. J. (2005). *The anxiety & phobia workbook* (4th ed.). Oakland, CA: New Harbinger.

Bovbjerg, D. H., Redd, W. H., Jacobsen, P. B., Manne, S. L., et al. (1992). An experimental analysis of classically conditioned nausea during cancer chemotherapy. *Psychosomatic Medicine, 54*(6), 623–637.

Bowd, A. D. (2005). Otitis media: health and social consequences for aboriginal youth in Canada's north. *International Journal of Circumpolar Health, 64*(1), 5–15.

Bower, G. H. (1981). Mood and memory. *American Psychologist, 36*, 129–148.

Bower, G. H., & Springsont, F. (1970). Pauses as recoding points in letter series. *Journal of Experimental Psychology, 83*, 421–430.

Bowers, K. S. & Woody, E. Z. (1996). Hypnotic amnesia and the paradox of intentional forgetting. *Journal of Abnormal Psychology, 105*(3), 381–390.

Boyer, R., Lesage, A., Guay, S., Bleau, P., et al. (2010). *Dawson College Shooting, September 13, 2006:* Report on a study conducted with the students and employees of Dawson College on the psychological impact and the search for support. Second of four reports presented to the ministère de la Justice du Québec on the evaluation of the psychological impact and intervention after the shooting at Dawson College on September 13, 2006.

Boyle, S. H., Williams, R. B., Mark, D., Brummett, B. H., et al. (2004). Hostility as a predictor of survival in patients with coronary artery disease. *Psychosomatic Medicine, 66*(5), 629–632.

Bradley, R. H., & Corwyn, R. F. (2002). Socioeconomic status and child development. *Annual Review of Psychology, 53*, 377–399.

Bradley, R., Greene, J., Russ, E., Westen, D., et al. (2005). A multidimensional meta-analysis of psychotherapy for PTSD. *American Journal of Psychiatry, 162*(2), 214–227.

Bradshaw, S. D. (2006). Shyness and difficult relationships: Formation is just the beginning. In D. C. Kirkpatrick, D. S. Duck, & M. K. Foley (Eds.), *Relating difficulty: The processes of constructing and managing difficult interaction.* Mahwah, NJ: Erlbaum.

Bramerson, A., Johansson, L., Ek, L., Nordin, S., et al. (2004). Prevalence of olfactory dysfunction: The Skovde population-based study. *Laryngoscope, 114*(4), 733–737.

Brannon, L. (1996). *Gender.* Boston: Allyn & Bacon.

Brannon, L., & Feist, J. (2010). *Health psychology: An introduction to behavior and health* (7th ed.). Belmont, CA: Cengage Learning/Wadsworth.

Bransford, J. D., & McCarrell, N. S. (1977). A sketch of cognitive approach to comprehension: Some thoughts about understanding what it means to comprehend. In P. N. Johnson-Laird & P. C. Wason (Eds.), *Thinking: Readings in cognitive science.* Cambridge: Cambridge University Press.

Brant, C. (1990). Native ethics and rules of behaviour. *Canadian Journal of Psychiatry, 35*(6), 534–539.

Brant, C. (1995). Communication patterns in Indians: Verbal and non-verbal. *Annals of Sex Research, 6*(4), 259–269.

Braun, A. R., Balkin, T. J., & Herscovitch, P. (1998). Dissociated pattern of activity in visual cortices and their projections during human rapid eye movement sleep. *Science, 279*(5347), 91–95.

Braun, K. A., Ellis, R., & Loftus, E. F. (2002). Make my memory: How advertising can change memories of the past. *Psychology and Marketing, 19,* 1–23.

Braun, S. (2001). Seeking insight by prescription. *Cerebrum, 3*(2), 10–21.

Breckler, S. J., Olson, J., & Wiggins, E. (2006). *Social psychology alive.* Belmont, CA: Wadsworth.

Brendgen, M., Boivin, M., Dionne, G., Barker, E.D., et al. (2011). Gene-environment processes linking aggression, peer victimization, and the teacher–child relationship. *Child Development, 82*(6), 2021–2036.

Brendgen, M., Boivin, M., Vitaro, F., Bukowski, W. M., et al. (2008). Linkages between children's and their friends' social and physical aggression: Evidence for a gene–environment interaction? *Child Development, 79*(1), 13–29.

Brendgen, M., Vitaro, F., Boivin, M., Dionne, G., et al. (2006). Examining genetic and environmental effects on reactive versus proactive aggression. *Developmental Psychology, 42*(6), 1299–1312.

Bressi, C., Albonetti, S., & Razzoli, E. (1998). "Communication deviance" and schizophrenia. *New Trends in Experimental & Clinical Psychiatry, 14*(1), 33–39.

Bretherton, R., & Orner, R. J. (2004). Positive psychology and psychotherapy: An existential approach. In P. A. Linley & S. Joseph (Eds.), *Positive psychology in practice.* New York: Wiley.

Brewer, K. R., & Wann, D. L. (1998). Observational learning effectiveness as a function of model characteristics. *Social Behavior & Personality, 26*(1), 1–10.

Brewer, N., and Wells, G. L. (2006) The confidence-accuracy relationship in eyewitness identification: Effects of lineup instructions, foil similarity, and target-absent base rates. *Journal of Experimental Psychology: Applied, 12*(1), 11–30.

Bridge, H., Harrold, S., Holmes, E. A., Stokes, M., & Kennard, C. (2011). Vivid visual mental imagery in the absence of the primary visual cortex. *Journal of Neurology, 259*(6), 1062–1070.

Bridges, K. M. B. (1932). Emotional development in early infancy. *Child Development, 3*, 324–334.

Brock, T. C., & Green, M. C. (Eds.). (2005). *Persuasion: Psychological insights and perspectives* (2nd ed.). Thousand Oaks, CA: Sage.

Brooks, M. (2008, August 20). The power of the placebo effect. *New Scientist, 2670*, 36–39.

Brooks-Gunn, J., & Warren, M. P. (1988). The psychological significance of secondary sexual characteristics in nine- to eleven-year-old girls. *Child Development, 59*(4), 1061–1069.

Brothen, T., & Wambach, C. (2001). Effective student use of computerized quizzes. *Teaching of Psychology, 28*(4), 292–294.

Broughton, R., Billings, R., Cartwright, R., Doucette, D., et al. (1994). Homicidal somnambulism: A case report. *Sleep, 17,* 253–264.

Brown, A. E., & Jeffcott, H. A., Jr. (1970). *Absolutely mad inventions.* New York: Dover Publications.

Brown, A. M. (1990). Development of visual sensitivity to light and color vision in human infants: A critical review. *Vision Research, 30*(8), 1159–1188.

Brown, A. S., Begg, M. D., Gravenstein, S., Schaefer, C. A., et al. (2004). Serologic evidence of prenatal influenza in the etiology of schizophrenia. *Archives of General Psychiatry, 61,* 774–780.

Brown, G. M. (1994). Light, melatonin and the sleep–wake cycle. *Journal of Psychiatry & Neuroscience, 19*(5), 345–353.

Brown, L. M. (2005). *Girlfighting: Betrayal and rejection among girls.* New York: New York University Press.

Brown, R., & Kulik, J. (1977). Flashbulb memories. *Cognition, 5*, 73–99.

Brown, R. L., Leonard, T., Saunders, L. A., & Papasouiotis, O. (1997). A two-item screening test for alcohol and other drug problems. *Journal of Family Practice, 44*(2), 151–160.

Brown, S. G., Roy, E., Rohr, L., & Bryden, P. (2006). Using hand performance measures to predict handedness. *Laterality: Asymmetries of Body, Brain & Cognition, 11*(1), 1–14.

Brown, T. A., & Barlow, D. H. (2007). *Casebook in abnormal psychology* (3rd ed.). Belmont, CA: Thomson/Wadsworth.

Brown, T. D., Dane, F. C., & Durham, M. D. (1998). Perception of race and ethnicity. *Journal of Social Behavior & Personality, 13*(2), 295–306.

Browne, N., & Keeley, S. (2007). *Asking the right questions: A guide to critical thinking* (8th ed.). Englewood Cliffs, NJ: Prentice Hall.

Brownell, K. D. (2003). *Food fight.* New York: McGraw-Hill.

Bruch, M. A. (2001). Shyness and social interaction. In R. Crozier, & L. Alden (Eds.), *International handbook of social anxiety.* Sussex, U.K.: Wiley.

Bruner, J. (1983). *Child's talk.* New York: Norton.

Bryan, J. H., & Walbek, N. H. (1970). Preaching and practicing generosity: Children's actions and reactions. *Child Development, 41*, 329–353.

Bryden, P. J., Bruyn, J., & Fletcher, P. (2005). Handedness and health: An examination of the association between different handedness classifications and health disorders. *Laterality: Asymmetries of Body, Brain & Cognition, 10*(5), 429–440.

Buchwald, A. (1965, June 20). Psyching out. *The Washington Post.*

Buckhalt, J. A. (2002). A short history of g: Psychometrics' most enduring and controversial construct. *Learning and Individual Differences, 13*, 101–114.

Buckworth, J., Lee, R. E., Regan, G., Schneider, L. K., et al. (2007). Decomposing intrinsic and extrinsic motivation for exercise: Application to stages of motivational readiness. *Psychology of Sport & Exercise, 8*(4), 441–461.

Buddie, A. M. (2004). Alternatives to twelve-step programs. *Journal of Forensic Psychology Practice, 4*(3), 61–70.

Budney, A. J., & Hughes, J. R. (2006). The cannabis withdrawal syndrome. *Current Opinion in Psychiatry, 19*(3), 233–238.

Buehner, M. J., & May, J. (2003). Rethinking temporal contiguity and the judgement of causality: Effects of prior knowledge, experience, and reinforcement procedure. *Quarterly Journal of Experimental Psychology A: Human Experimental Psychology, 56A*(5), 865–890.

Buller, D. J. (2005). *Adapting minds: Evolutionary psychology and the persistent quest for human nature.* Cambridge, MA: MIT Press.

Bunde, J., & Suls, J. (2006). A quantitative analysis of the relationship between the Cook-Medley hostility scale and traditional coronary artery disease risk factors. *Health Psychology, 25*(4), 493–500.

Bunn, G. C. (2007). Spectacular science: The lie detector's ambivalent powers. *History of Psychology, 10*(2), 156–178.

Burchinal, M. R., Roberts, J. E., Riggins, R., Zeisel, S. A., et al. (2000). Relating quality of center-based child care to early cognitive and language development longitudinally. *Child Development, 71*(2), 339–357.

Burger, J. M., & Lynn, A. L. (2005). Superstitious behavior among American and Japanese professional baseball players. *Basic & Applied Social Psychology, 27*(1), 71–76.

Burgess, C. A., & Kirsch, I. (1999). Expectancy information as a moderator of the effects of hypnosis on memory. *Contemporary Hypnosis, 16*(1), 22–31.

Burlingame, G., & Davies, R. (2002). Self-help groups. In M. Hersen & W. H. Sledge (Eds.), *Encyclopedia of psychotherapy.* San Diego: Academic Press.

Burnett, R. C., Medin, D. L., Ross, N. O., & Blok, S. V. (2005). Ideal is typical. *Canadian Journal of Experimental Psychology. Special Issue on 2003 Festschrift for Lee R. Brooks, 59*(1), 3–10.

Burns, D. D., & Persons, J. (1982). Hope and hopelessness: A cognitive approach. In L. E. Abt & I. R. Stuart (Eds.), *The newer therapies: A sourcebook.* New York: Van Nostrand Reinhold.

Burns, T. (2004). *Community mental health teams: A guide to current practices.* New York: Oxford.

Burt, S. A., McGue, M., Carter, L. A., & Iacono, W. G. (2007). The different origins of stability and change in antisocial personality disorder symptoms. *Psychological Medicine, 37*(1), 27–38.

Burton, C. M., & King, L. A. (2004). The health benefits of writing about intensely positive experiences. *Journal of Research in Personality, 38*(2), 150–163.

Burtt, H. E. (1941). An experimental study of early childhood memory: Final report. *Journal of General Psychology, 58*, 435–439.

Bushman, B. J., & Anderson, C. A. (2001). Media violence and the American public. *American Psychologist, 56*(6/7), 477–489.

Bushnell, L. W., Sai, F., & Mullin, L. T. (1989). Neonatal recognition of the mother's face. *British Journal of Developmental Psychology, 7*(1), 3–15.

Bushnell, M. C., Villemure, C., & Duncan, G. H. (2004). Psychophysical and neurophysiological studies of pain modulation by attention. In D. D. Price & M. C. Bushnell (Eds.), *Psychological methods of pain control: Basic science and clinical perspectives.* Seattle, WA: IASP Press.

Buss, D. M. (1985). Human mate selection. *American Scientist, 73*, 47–51.

Buss, D. M. (2000). The evolution of happiness. *American Psychologist, 55*(1), 15–23.

Buss, D. M. (2004). *Evolutionary psychology: The new science of the mind* (2nd ed.). Boston: Allyn & Bacon.

Buss, D. M. (2007). The evolution of human mating. *Acta Psychologica Sinica, 39*(3), 502–512.

Butcher, J. N. (2005). *A beginner's guide to the MMPI-2* (2nd ed.). Washington: American Psychological Association.

Butcher, J. N. (Ed.). (2006). *MMPI-2: A practitioner's guide.* Washington: American Psychological Association.

Butcher, J. N., Mineka, S., & Hooley, J. (2007). *Abnormal psychology and modern life* (13th ed.). Boston: Allyn & Bacon.

Butler, M. G. (2001). *Overcoming social anxiety and shyness: A self-help guide using cognitive behavioral techniques.* New York: New York University Press.

Butler, R. (1954). Curiosity in monkeys. *Scientific American, 190*(18), 70–75.

Byrne, S. M., & McLean, N. J. (2002). The cognitive-behavioral model of bulimia nervosa: A direct evaluation. *International Journal of Eating Disorders, 31*, 17–31.

Caharel, S., Fiori, N., Bernard, C., Lalonde, R., et al. (2006). The effects of inversion and eye displacements of familiar and unknown faces on early and late-stage ERPs. *International Journal of Psychophysiology, 62*(1), 141–151.

Cahill, L. (2006). Why sex matters for neuroscience. *Nature Reviews Neuroscience, 7*(6), 477–484.

Cahill, S. P., Carrigan, M. H., & Frueh, B. C. (1999). Does EMDR work? and if so, why? *Journal of Anxiety Disorders, 13*(1–2), 5–33.

Cahn, B. R., & Polich, J. (2006). Meditation states and traits: EEG, ERP, and neuroimaging studies. *Psychological Bulletin, 132*(2), 180–211.

Callan, M. J., Kay, A. C., Davidenko, N., & Ellard, J. H. (2009). The effects of justice motivation on memory for self- and other-relevant events. *Journal of Experimental Social Psychology, 45*(4), 614–623.

Camara, W. J., & Schneider, D. L. (1994). Integrity tests. *American Psychologist, 49*(2), 112–119.

Cameron, J., & Pierce, W. D. (2002). *Rewards and intrinsic motivation: Resolving the controversy.* Westport, CO: Bergin & Garvey.

Cameron, J. A., & Trope, Y. (2004). Stereotype-biased search and processing of information about group members. *Social Cognition, 22*(6), 650–672.

Cameron, L. D., & Nicholls, G. (1998). Expression of stressful experiences through writing. *Health Psychology, 17*(1), 84–92.

Canadian Cancer Society's Steering Committee on Cancer Statistics (2011). *Canadian Cancer Statistics 2011.* Toronto, ON: Canadian Cancer Society.

Canadian Code of Ethics for Psychologists. (2000). (3rd ed.) Ottawa, ON: Canadian Psychological Association.

Canadian Health Measures Survey 2007–2009. Statistics Canada, The Daily, January 13, 2010. Catalogue 11-001-XIE (Français 11-001-XIF) ISSN 1205-9137.

Canadian Psychological Association. (2002). *The cost-effectiveness of psychological interventions.* Ottawa: Author. Retrieved July 2, 2002, from http://www.cpa.ca/documents/Cost-Effectiveness.pdf.

Canli, T., Desmond, J. E., Zhao, Z., Glover, G., et al. (1998). Hemispheric asymmetry for emotional stimuli detected with fMRI. *Neuroreport, 9*(14) 3233–3239.

Cannon, W. B. (1932). *The wisdom of the body.* New York: Norton.

Cannon, W. B. (1934). Hunger and thirst. In C. Murchinson (Ed.), *Handbook of general experimental psychology.* Worcester, MA: Clark University Press.

Cannon, W. B., & Washburn, A. L. (1912). An explanation of hunger. *American Journal of Physiology, 29*, 444–454.

Canrinus, M., & Lunsky, Y. (2003). Successful aging of women with intellectual disabilities: The Toronto experience. *Journal on Developmental Disabilities, 10*(1), 73–78.

Caplan, P. J. (1995). *They say you're crazy.* Reading, MA: Addison-Wesley.

Carlbring, P., Gunnarsdóttir, M., Hedensjö, L., Andersson, G., et al. (2007). Treatment of social phobia: Randomised trial of Internet-delivered cognitive-behavioural therapy with telephone support. *British Journal of Psychiatry, 190*(2), 123–128.

Carlson, M., Marcus-Newhall, A., & Miller, N. (1990). Effects of situational aggression cues: A quantitative review. *Journal of Personality & Social Psychology, 58*(4), 622–633.

Carlson, N. R. (2007). *Physiology of behavior* (9th ed.). Boston: Allyn & Bacon.

Carlson, N. R. (2010). *Physiology of behavior* (10th ed.). Boston: Allyn & Bacon.

Carnagey, N. L., & Anderson, C. A. (2004). Violent video game exposure and aggression: A literature review. *Minerva Psichiatrica, 45*(1), 1–18.

Carney, D. R., Cuddy, A. J. C., & Yap, A. J. (2010). Power posing: Brief nonverbal displays affect neuroendocrine levels and risk tolerance. *Psychological Science, 21*(10), 1363–1368.

Carney, P. R., Geyer, J. D., & Berry, R. B. (Eds.). (2005). *Clinical sleep disorders.* Philadelphia, PA: Lippincott Williams & Wilkins.

Carney, R. N., & Levin, J. R. (2001). Remembering the names of unfamiliar animals: Keywords as keys to their kingdom. *Applied Cognitive Psychology, 15*(2), 133–143.

Carney, R. N., & Levin, J. R. (2003). Promoting higher-order learning benefits by building lower-order mnemonic connections. *Applied Cognitive Psychology, 17*(5), 563–575.

Carroll, D. W. (2008). *Psychology of language* (5th ed.). Belmont, CA: Cengage Learning/Wadsworth.

Carroll, J. M., & Russell, J. A. (1996). Do facial expressions signal specific emotions? Judging emotion from the face in context. *Journal of Personality & Social Psychology, 70*(2), 205–218.

Carroll, J. S., Willoughby, B., Badger, S., Nelson, L., et al. (2007). So close, yet so far away: The impact of varying marital horizons on emerging adulthood. *Journal of Adolescent Research, 22*(3), 219–247.

Carskadon, M. A., Acebo, C., & Jenni, O. C. (2004). Regulation of adolescent sleep: Implications for behavior. *Annals of the New York Academy of Science, 1021*, 276–291.

Carter, R. (1998). *Mapping the mind.* Berkeley, CA: University of California Press.

Cartwright, R., & Lamberg, L. (1992). *Crisis dreaming.* New York: HarperCollins.

Caspi, A., Roberts, B. W., & Shiner, R. L. (2005). Personality development: Stability and change. *Annual Review of Psychology, 56,* 453–484.

Caspi, A., Sugden, K., Moffitt, T. E., Taylor, A., et al. (2003). Influence of life stress on depression: Moderation by a polymorphism in the 5–HTT gene. *Science, 301*(5631), 386–389.

Cassady, J. C. (2004). The influence of cognitive test anxiety across the learning-testing cycle. *Learning & Instruction, 14*(6), 569–592.

Castro, J. R., & Rice, K. G. (2003). Perfectionism and ethnicity: Implications for depressive symptoms and self-reported academic achievement. *Cultural Diversity and Ethnic Minority Psychology, 9*(1), 64–78.

Catalano, R., Novaco, R., & McConnell, W. (1997). A model of the net effect of job loss on violence. *Journal of Personality & Social Psychology, 72*(6), 1440–1447.

Cattell, R. B. (1965). *The scientific analysis of personality.* Baltimore: Penguin.

Cattell, R. B. (1973, July). Personality pinned down. *Psychology Today,* 40–46.

Cautela, J. R., & Kearney, A. J. (1986). *The covert conditioning handbook.* New York: Springer.

Cavaco, S., Anderson, S. W., Allen, J. S., Castro-Caldas, A., et al. (2004). The scope of preserved procedural memory in amnesia. *Brain: A Journal of Neurology, 127*(8), 1853–1867.

CBC (2008). Hunting nature's handiwork in identical siblings. Retrieved January 6, 2012, from http://www.cbc.ca/news/background/health/identical-twins.html.

Cecil, H., Evans, R. J., & Stanley, M. A. (1996). Perceived believability among adolescents of health warning labels on cigarette packs. *Journal of Applied Social Psychology, 26*(6), 502–519.

Chakos, M. H., Alvir, J. M. J., Woerner, M., & Koreen, A. (1996). Incidence and correlates of tardive dyskinesia in first episode of schizophrenia. *Archives of General Psychiatry, 53*(4), 313–319.

Chamberlin, J., & Rogers, J. A. (1990). Planning a community-based mental health system. *American Psychologist, 45*(11), 1241–1244.

Chambers, R. A., Taylor, J. R., & Potenza, M. N. (2003). Developmental neurocircuitry of motivation in adolescence: A critical period of addiction vulnerability. *American Journal of Psychiatry, 160*(6), 1041–1052.

Chamorro-Premuzic, T., & Furnham, A. (2003). Personality predicts academic performance. *Journal of Research in Personality, 37*(4), 319–338.

Chan, G. C., Hinds, T. R., Impey, S., & Storm, D. R. (1998). Hippocampal neurotoxicity of Delta-sup-9-tetrahydrocannabi-nol. *Journal of Neuroscience, 18*(14), 5322–5332.

Chance, P. (2006). *Learning and behavior* (5th ed.). Belmont, CA: Wadsworth.

Chance, P. (2009). *Learning and behavior* (6th ed.). Belmont, CA: Cengage Learning/Wadsworth.

Chandler, M. J., & Lalonde, C. (1998). Cultural continuity as a hedge against suicide in Canada's First Nations. *Transcultural Psychiatry, 35,* 191–219.

Chandrashekar, J., Hoon, M. A., Ryba, N. J. P., & Cammann, C. (2006). The receptors and cells for mammalian taste. *Nature, 444*(7117), 288–294.

Chansler, P. A., Swamidass, P. M., & Cammann, C. (2003). Self-managing work teams: An empirical study of group cohesiveness in "natural work groups" at a Harley-Davidson Motor Company plant. *Small Group Research, 34*(1), 101–120.

Chapman, R. A. (Ed.). (2006). *The clinical use of hypnosis in cognitive behavior therapy: A practitioner's casebook.* New York: Springer Publishing.

Chassin, L., Presson, C. C., Sherman, S. J., & Kim, K. (2003). Historical changes in cigarette smoking and smoking-related beliefs after 2 decades in a midwestern community. *Health Psychology, 22*(4), 347–353.

Chaves, J. F. (2000). Hypnosis. In A. Kazdin (Ed.), *Encyclopedia of psychology.* Washington: American Psychological Association.

Cheek, J., & Buss, A. H. (1979). Scales of shyness, sociability and self-esteem and correlations among them. Unpublished research, University of Texas. (Cited by Buss, 1980.).

Chen, K., & Kandel, D. B. (1995). The natural history of drug use from adolescence to the mid-thirties in a general population sample. *American Journal of Public Health, 85*(1), 41–47.

Chen, Z., Lawson, R. B., Gordon, L. R., & McIntosh, B. (1996). Groupthink: Deciding with the leader and the devil. *Psychological Record, 46*(4), 581–590.

Chess, S., & Thomas, A. (1986). *Know your child.* New York: Basic.

Chester, A., & Glass, C. A. (2006). Online counselling: A descriptive analysis of therapy services on the internet. *British Journal of Guidance & Counselling, 34*(2), 145–160.

Cheyne, J. A. (2005). Sleep paralysis episode frequency and number, types, and structure of associated hallucinations. *Journal of Sleep Research, 14*(3), 319–324.

Cheyne, J. A., Rueffer, S. D., & Newby-Clark, I. R. (1999). Hypnagogic and hypnopompic hallucinations during sleep paralysis: Neurological and cultural construction of the night-mare. *Consciousness & Cognition, 8,* 319–337.

Chickering, A. W., & Ehrmann, S. C. (1996). Implementing the seven principles: Technology as lever. *AAHE Bulletin, 49*(2), 3–6.

Chickering, A. W., & Gamson, Z. F. (1987). Seven principles for good practice in undergraduate education. *AAHE Bulletin, 39*(7), 3–7.

Chisholm, K. (1998). A three year follow-up of attachment and indiscriminate friendliness in children adopted from Romanian orphanages. *Child Development, 69,* 1092–1106.

Chisholm, K., Carter, M. C., Ames, E. W., & Morison, S. J. (1995). Attachment security and indiscriminately friendly behavior in children adopted from Romanian orphanages. *Development & Psychopathology, 7*(2), 283–294.

Chisolm, T. H., Willott, J. F., & Lister, J. J. (2003). The aging auditory system: Anatomic and physiologic changes and implications for rehabilitation. *International Journal of Audiology, 42*(Suppl. 2), 2S3–2S10.

Chomsky, N. (1975). *Reflections on language.* New York: Pantheon.

Chomsky, N. (1986). *Knowledge of language.* New York: Praeger.

Christakis, N. A., & Fowler, J. H. (2007). The spread of obesity in a large social network over 32 years. *New England Journal of Medicine, 357*(4), 370–379.

Christakis, N. A., & Fowler, J. H. (2008). The collective dynamics of smoking in a large social network. *New England Journal of Medicine, 358*(21), 2249–2258.

Christensen, A., & Jacobson, N. S. (1994). Who (or what) can do psychotherapy. *Psychological Science, 5*(1), 8–14.

Christian, K. M., & Thompson, R. F. (2005). Long-term storage of an associative memory trace in the cerebellum. *Behavioral Neuroscience, 119*(2), 526–537.

Chua, H. F., Boland, J. E., & Nisbett, R. E. (2005). Cultural variation in eye movements during scene perception. *Proceedings of the National Academy of Sciences of the United States of America, 102*(35), 12629–12633.

Cialdini, R. B. (2001). *Influence: Science and practice* (4th ed.). Boston: Allyn & Bacon.

Cialdini, R. B., & Goldstein, N. J. (2004). Social influence: Compliance and conformity. *Annual Review of Psychology, 55,* 591–621.

Cialdini, R. B., Reno, R. R., & Kallgren, C. A. (1990). A focus theory of normative conduct: Recycling the concept of norms to reduce littering in public places. *Journal of Personality & Social Psychology, 58*(6), 1015–1026.

Ciarrochi, J., Dean, F. P., & Anderson, S. (2002). Emotional intelligence moderates the relationship between stress and mental health. *Personality & Individual Differences, 32*(2), 197–209.

Cinciripini, P. M., Wetter, D. W., & McClure, J. B. (1997). Scheduled reduced smoking. *Addictive Behaviors, 22*(6), 759–767.

Clapham, M. M. (2001). The effects of affect manipulation and information exposure on divergent thinking. *Creativity Research Journal, 13*(3–4), 335–350.

Clark, D., Boutros, N., & Mendez, M. (2005). *The brain and behavior* (2nd ed.). Cambridge, MA: Cambridge University Press.

Clayton, N. S., Yu, K. S., & Dickinson, A. (2001). Scrub jays (*Aphelocoma coerulescens*) form integrated memories of the multiple features of caching episodes. *Journal of Experimental Psychology: Animal Behavior Processes, 27,* 17–29.

Cnattingius, S. (2004). The epidemiology of smoking during pregnancy: Smoking prevalence, maternal characteristics and pregnancy outcomes. *Nicotine & Tobacco Research, 6*(Supp. 12), S125–S140.

Cnattingius, S., Signorello, L. B., Ammerén, G., Clausson, B., et al. (2000). Caffeine intake and the risk of first-trimester spontaneous abortion. *New England Journal of Medicine, 343*(25), 1839–1845.

Cochran, G. M., & Harpending, H. (2009). *The 10,000 year explosion.* New York: Basic Books.

Coelho, C. M. & Purkis, H. (2009). The origins of specific phobias: influential theories and current perspectives. *Review of General Psychology, American Psychological Association, 13*(4), 335–348.

Cohen, S., & Lichtenstein, E. (1990). Partner behaviors that support quitting smoking. *Journal of Consulting & Clinical Psychology, 58*(3), 304–309.

Cohen, S., Tyrrell, D. A., & Smith, A. P. (1993). Negative life events, perceived stress, negative affect, and susceptibility to the common cold. *Journal of Personality and Social Psychology, 64*(1), 131–140.

Colangelo, J. J. (2007). Recovered memory debate revisited: Practice implications for mental health counselors. *Journal of Mental Health Counseling, 29*(2), 93–120.

Colin, A. K., Moore, K., & West, A. N. (1996). Creativity, oversensitivity, and rate of habituation. *EDRA: Environmental Design Research Association, 20*(4), 423–427.

Collins, A. M., & Quillian, M. R. (1969). Retrieval time from semantic memory. *Journal of Verbal Learning and Verbal Behavior, 8,* 240–247.

Collins, W. A., & Gunnar, M. R. (1990). Social and personality development. *Annual Review of Psychology, 41,* 387–416.

Collop, N. A. (2005). Obstructive sleep apnea: Treatment overview and controversies. In P. R. Carney, J. D. Geyer, & R. B. Berry (Eds.), *Clinical sleep disorders.* Philadelphia, PA: Lippincott Williams & Wilkins.

Comer, R. J. (2011). *Fundamentals of abnormal psychology* (6th ed.). New York: WorthPublishers.

Commons, M. L., Galaz-Fontes, J. F., & Morse, J. (2006). Leadership, cross-cultural contact, socio-economic status and formal operational reasoning about moral dilemmas among Mexican non-literate adults and high school students. *Journal of Moral Education 35,* (2), 247–267.

Compton, W. C. (2005). *An introduction to positive psychology.* Belmont, CA: Wadsworth.

Conklin, H. M., & Iacono, W. G. (2002) Schizophrenia: A neurodevelopmental perspective. *Current Directions in Psychological Science, 11*(1), 33–37.

Connor, P. D., Sampson, P. D., Streissguth, A. P., Bookstein, F. L., et al. (2006). Effects of prenatal alcohol exposure on fine motor coordination and balance. A study of two adult samples. *Neuropsychologia, 44*(5), 7744–7751.

Consumer Reports. (1995, November). Mental health: Does therapy help?, 734–739.

Conway, A. R. A., Cowan, N., & Bunting, M. F. (2001). The cocktail party phenomenon revisited. *Psychonomic Bulletin & Review, 8*(2), 331–335.

Conway, M. A., Cohen, G., & Stanhope, N. (1992). Very long-term memory for knowledge acquired at school and university. *Applied Cognitive Psychology, 6*(6), 467–482.

Cooper, G. D., Adams, H. B., & Scott, J. C. (1988). Studies in REST: I. Reduced Environmental Stimulation Therapy (REST) and reduced alcohol consumption. *Journal of Substance Abuse Treatment, 5*(2), 61–68.

Cooper, J., Mirabile, R., & Scher, S. J. (2005). Actions and attitudes: The theory of cognitive dissonance. In T. C. Brock & M. C. Green (Eds.), *Persuasion: Psychological insights and perspectives* (2nd ed.). Thousand Oaks, CA: Sage.

Cooper, M. J. (2005). Cognitive theory in anorexia nervosa and bulimia nervosa: Progress, development and future directions. *Clinical Psychology Review, 25*(4), 511–531.

Cooper, R. P., Abraham, J., Berman, S., & Staska, M. (1997). The development of infants' preference for motherese. *Infant Behavior and Development, 20*(4), 477–488.

Cooper, S. J. (2008). From Claude Bernard to Walter Cannon: Emergence of the concept of homeostasis. *Appetite, 51*(3), 419–427.

Coopersmith, S. (1968). Studies in self-esteem. *Scientific American, 218,* 96–106.

Corballis, M. C. (2002). *From hand to mouth: The origins of language.* Princeton, NJ: Princeton University Press.

Coren, S. (1992). *The left-hander syndrome.* New York: Free Press.

Coren, S. (1996). *Sleep thieves.* New York: Free Press.

Corey, G. (2008). *Theory and practice of group counseling* (7th ed.). Belmont, CA: Thomson/Brooks/Cole.

Corkin, S. (2002). What's new with the amnesic patient H.M.? *Nature Reviews Neuroscience, 3,* 153–160.

Cormier, J. F., & Thelen, M. H. (1998). Professional skepticism of multiple personality disorder. *Professional Psychology: Research and Practice, 29*(2), 163–167.

Correa-Chávez, M., Rogoff, B., & Arauz, R. M. (2005). Cultural patterns in attending to two events at once. *Child Development, 76*(3), 664–678.

Corrigan, P. W. (1997). Behavior therapy empowers persons with severe mental illness. *Behavior Modification, 21*(1), 45–61.

Corrigan, P. W., & Penn, D. L. (1999). Lessons from social psychology on discrediting psychiatric stigma. *American Psychologist, 54*(9), 765–776.

Corrigan, P. W., & Watson, A. C. (2005). Findings from the National Comorbidity Survey on the frequency of violent behavior in individuals with psychiatric disorders. *Psychiatry Research, 136*(2–3), 153–162.

Corrigan, P. W., Watson, A. C., Gracia, G., Slopen, N., et al. (2005). Newspaper stories as measures of structural stigma. *Psychiatric Services, 56*(5), 551–556.

Costa, P. T., Jr., & McCrae, R. R. (2006). Trait and factor theories. In J. C. Thomas, D. L. Segal, & M. Hersen (Eds.), *Comprehensive handbook of personality & psychopathology* (Vol. 1): *Personality and everyday functioning.* New York: Wiley.

Costigan, C. L., Koryzma, C. M, Hua, J. M., & Chance, L. J. (2010). Ethnic identity, achievement, and psychological adjustment: Examining risk and resilience among youth from immigrant Chinese families in Canada. *Cultural Diversity and Ethnic Minority Psychology, 16*(2), 264–273.

Côté, J. E. (2006a). Emerging adulthood as an institutionalized moratorium: Risks and benefits to identity formation. In J. J. Arnett & J. L. Tanner (Eds.), *Emerging adults in America: Coming of age in the 21st century.* Washington: American Psychological Association.

Côté, J. E. (2006b). Identity studies: How close are we to developing a social science of identity? An appraisal of the field. *Identity: An International Journal of Theory & Research, 6,* 3–26.

Côté, J., & Bynner, J. M. (2008). Changes in the transition to adulthood in the U.K. and Canada: The role of structure and agency in emerging adulthood. *Journal of youth studies, 11*(3), 251–268.

Côté, J. E., & Levine, C. (2002). *Identity formation, agency, and culture.* Hillsdale, NJ: Erlbaum.

Courneya, K. S., & Hellsten, L. M. (1998). Personality correlates of exercise behavior, motives, barriers and preferences: An application of the five-factor model. *Personality & Individual Differences, 24*(5), 625–633.

Coursey, R. D., Ward-Alexander, L., & Katz, B. (1990). Cost-effectiveness of providing insurance benefits for posthospital psychiatric halfway house stays. *American Psychologist, 45*(10), 1118–1126.

Court, J. H., & Court, P. C. (2001). Repression: R.I.P. *Australian Journal of Clinical & Experimental Hypnosis, 29*(1), 8–16.

Covell, K., Grusec, J. E., & King, G. (1995). The intergenerational transmission of maternal discipline and standards for behavior. *Social Development, 4*(1), 32–43.

Cowan, N. (2005). *Working memory capacity.* Hove, U.K.: Psychology Press.

Cowden, C. R. (2005). Worry and its relationship to shyness. *North American Journal of Psychology, 7*(1), 59–69.

Cowles, J. T. (1937). Food tokens as incentives for learning by chimpanzees. *Comparative Psychology, Monograph, 14*(5, Whole No. 71).

Cox, J. J., Reimann, F., Nicholas, A. K., Thornton, G., et al. (2006). An SCN9A channelopathy causes congenital inability to experience pain. *Nature, 444,* 894–898.

Craig, L. (2006). Does father care mean fathers share?: A comparison of how mothers and fathers in intact families spend time with children. *Gender & Society, 20*(2), 259–281.

Craig, T. Y., & Kelly, J. R. (1999). Group cohesiveness and creative performance. *Group Dynamics, 3*(4), 243–256.

Craik, F. I. M. (1970). The fate of primary items in free recall. *Journal of Verbal Learning and Verbal Behavior, 9,* 143–148.

Crano, W. D. (2000). Milestones in the psychological analysis of social influence. *Group Dynamics: Theory, Research, and Practice, 4*(1), 68–80.

Cravatt, B. F., Prospero-Garcia O., Siuzdak G., Gilula, N. B., et al. (1995). Chemical characterization of a family of brain lipids that induce sleep. *Science, 268*(5216), 1506–1509.

Crawley, S. B., & Sherrod, K. B. (1984). Parent-infant play during the first year of life. *Infant Behavior & Development, 7,* 65–75.

Crencavage, L. M., & Norcross, J. C. (1990). Where are the commonalities among the therapeutic common factors? *Professional Psychology: Research & Practice, 21*(5), 372–378.

Crisp, A., Gowers, S., Joughin, N., McClelland, L., et al. (2006). The enduring nature of anorexia nervosa. *European Eating Disorders Review, 14*(3), 147–152.

Crombag, H. S., & Robinson, T. E. (2004). Drugs, environment, brain, and behavior. *Current Directions in Psychological Science, 13*(3), 107–111.

Cronbach, L. (1990). *Essentials of psychological testing.* Reading, PA: Addison-Wesley.

Cronk, N. J., Slutske, W. S., Madden, P. A. F., Bucholz, K. K., et al. (2005). Risk for separation anxiety disorder among girls: Paternal absence, socioeconomic disadvantage, and genetic vulnerability. *Journal of Abnormal Psychology, 113*(2), 237–247.

Crooks, R., & Baur, K. (2008). *Our sexuality* (10th ed.). Belmont, CA: Cengage Learning/Wadsworth.

Cropley, A. (2006). In praise of convergent thinking. *Creativity Research Journal, 18,* 391–404.

Crowther, J. H., Sanftner, J., Bonifazi, D. Z., & Shepherd, K. L. (2001). The role of daily hassles in binge eating. *International Journal of Eating Disorders, 29,* 449–454.

Csikszentmihalyi, M. (1997). *Creativity.* New York: HarperCollins.

Csikszentmihalyi, M., Abuhamdeh, S., & Nakamura, J. (2005). Flow. In A. J. Elliot & C. S. Dweck (Eds.), *Handbook of competence and motivation.* New York: Guilford.

Culertson, F. M. (1997). Depression and gender. *American Psychologist, 52*(1), 25–31.

Cull, W. L., Shaughnessy, J. J., & Zechmeister, E. B. (1996). Expanding understanding of the expanding-pattern-of-retrieval mnemonic. *Journal of Experimental Psychology: Applied, 2*(4), 365–378.

Cummings, M. R. (2006). *Human heredity: Principles and issues* (7th ed.). Belmont, CA: Wadsworth.

Cummins, D. D. (1995). *The other side of psychology.* New York: St. Martin's Press.

Curci, A., & Luminet, O. (2006). Follow-up of a cross-national comparison on flashbulb and event memory for the September 11th attacks. *Memory, 14*(3), 329–344.

Currie, J., & Thomas, D. (1995). Does Head Start make a difference? *American Economic Review, 85,* 341–364.

Cushman, F., Gray, K., Gaffey, A., & Mendes, W.B. (2012). Simulating murder: The aversion to harmful action. *Emotion, 12*(1), 2–7.

Cynader, M. S. (1994). Mechanisms of brain development and their role in health and well-being. *Daedalus, 123*(4), 155–165.

Czeisler, C. A., Richardson, G. S., Zimmerman, J. C., Moore-Ede, M. C., et al. (1981). Entrainment of human circadian rhythms by light-dark cycles: A reassessment. *Photochemistry, Photobiology, 34,* 239–247.

Dane, S., & Erzurumluoglu, A. (2003). Sex and handedness differences in eye-hand visual reaction times in handball players. *International Journal of Neuroscience, 113*(7), 923–929.

Daniels, H. (2005). Vygotsky and educational psychology: Some preliminary remarks. *Educational & Child Psychology, 22*(1), 6–17.

Danziger, N., Prkachin, K. M., & Willer, J.-C. (2006). Is pain the price of empathy? The perception of others' pain in patients with congenital insensitivity to pain. *Brain: A Journal of Neurology, 129*(9), 2494–2507.

Darley, J. M. (2000). Bystander phenomenon. In A. E. Kazdin (Ed.), *Encyclopedia of psychology* (Vol. 1). Washington: American Psychological Association.

Darley, J. M., & Latané, B. (1968). Bystander intervention in emergencies: Diffusion of responsibility. *Journal of Personality & Social Psychology, 8,* 377–383.

Darou, W. S. (1992). Native Canadians and intelligence testing. *Canadian Journal of Counselling, 26*(2), 96–99.

Daruna, J. H. (2004). *Introduction to psychoneuroimmunology.* Amsterdam: Elsevier.

Darwin, C. (1872). *The expression of emotion in man and animals.* Chicago: University of Chicago Press.

Das, J. P. (2000). Mental retardation. In A. Kazdin (Ed.), *Encyclopedia of psychology.* Washington: American Psychological Association.

Davanloo, H. (1995). Intensive short-term dynamic psychotherapy. *International Journal of Short-Term Psychotherapy, 10*(3–4), 121–155.

Davidovitch, N., & Milgram, R. M. (2006). Creative thinking as a predictor of teacher effectiveness in higher education. *Creativity Research Journal, 18,* 385–390.

Davidson, P. R., & Parker, K. C. H. (2001). Eye movement desensitization and reprocessing (EMDR): A meta-analysis. *Journal of Consulting and Clinical Psychology, 69,* 305–316.

Davidson, T. L. (2000). Latent learning. In A. E. Kazdin (Ed.), *Encyclopedia of psychology* (Vol. 4). Washington: American Psychological Association.

Davis, M. A. (2009). Understanding the relationship between mood and creativity: A meta-analysis. *Organizational Behavior & Human Decision Processes, 108*(1), 25–38.

Davis, M. R., McMahon, M., & Greenwood, K. M. (2005). The efficacy of mnemonic components of the cognitive interview:

Towards a shortened variant for time-critical investigations. *Applied Cognitive Psychology, 19*(1), 75–93.

Dawson, T. L., (2002). New tools, new insights: Kohlberg's moral development stages revisited. *International Journal of Behavioral Development, 26*(2), 154–166.

Day, S., & Schneider, P. L. (2002). Psychotherapy using distance technology. *Journal of Counseling Psychology, 49*(4), 499–503.

de Bono, E. (1992). *Serious creativity.* New York: HarperCollins.

de Jong, P. J., & Muris, P. (2002). Spider phobia. *Journal of Anxiety Disorders, 16*(1), 51–65.

de las Fuentes, C., & Vasquez, M. J. T. (1999). Immigrant adolescent girls of color. In N. G. Johnson, M. C. Roberts, & J. Worell (Eds.), *Beyond appearance.* Washington: American Psychological Association.

de Leon, C. F. M. (2005). Social engagement and successful aging. *European Journal of Ageing, 2*(1), 64–66.

de Rios, M. D., & Grob, C. S. (2005). Editors' introduction: Ayahuasca use in cross cultural perspective. *Journal of Psychoactive Drugs, 37*(2), 119–121.

Deardorff, J., Hayward, C., Wilson, K. A., Bryson, S., et al. (2007). Puberty and gender interact to predict social anxiety symptoms in early adolescence. *Journal of Adolescent Health, 41*(1), 102–104.

Deckers, L. (2005). *Motivation: Biological, psychological, and environmental* (2nd ed.). Boston: Allyn & Bacon.

Deckro, G. R., Ballinger, K. M., Hoyt, M., Wilcher, M., et al. (2002). The evaluation of a mind/body intervention to reduce psychological distress and perceived stress in college students. *Journal of American College Health, 50*(6), 281–287.

Deeb, S. S. (2004). Molecular genetics of color-vision deficiencies. *Visual Neuroscience, 21*(3), 191–196.

Deffenbacher, J. L., & Suinn, R. M. (1988). Systematic desensitization and the reduction of anxiety. *Counseling Psychologist, 16*(1), 9–30.

Dein, S., & Littlewood, R. (2005). Apocalyptic suicide: From a pathological to an eschatological interpretation. *International Journal of Social Psychiatry, 51*(3), 198–210.

Deinzer, R., Kleineidam, C., Stiller-Winkler, R., Idel, H., et al. (2000). Prolonged reduction of salivary immunoglobulin A (sIgA) after a major academic exam. *International Journal of Psychophysiology, 37*, 219–232.

Delgado, J. M. R. (1969). *Physical control of the mind.* New York: Harper and Row.

Delpero, W. T., O'Neill, H., Casson, E., & Hovis, J. (2005). Aviation-relevent epidemiology of color vision deficiency. *Aviation, Space, and Environmental Medicine, 76*(2), 127–133.

Demos, J. N. (2005). *Getting started with neurofeedback.* New York: Norton.

Denison, S., & Xu, F. (2010). Integrating physical constraints in statistical inference by 11-month-old infants. *Cognitive Science, 34*, 885–908.

Denmark, F. L., Rabinowitz, V. C., & Sechzer, J. A. (2005). *Engendering psychology:*

Women and gender revisited (2nd ed.). Boston: Allyn & Bacon.

Dennis, M., Jewell, D., Drake, J., Misakyan, T., et al. (2007). Prospective, declarative, and non-declarative memory in young adults with *spina bifida. Journal of the International Neuropsychological Society, 13*(2), 312–323.

Derlega, V. J., Winstead, B. A., & Jones, W. H. (2005). *Personality: Contemporary theory and research* (3rd ed.). Belmont, CA: Wadsworth.

Desrosiers, J., Wanet-Defalque, M.-C., Temisjian, K., Gresset, J., et al. (2009). Participation in daily activities and social roles of older adults with visual impairment. *Disability and Rehabilitation, 31*(15), 1227–1234.

Devoto, A., Lucidi, F., Violani, C., & Bertini, M. (1999). Effects of different sleep reductions on daytime sleepiness. *Sleep, 22*(3), 336–343.

Diano, S., Farr, S. A., Benoit, S. C., McNay, E. C., et al. (2006). Ghrelin controls hippocampal spine synapse density and memory performance. *Nature Neuroscience, 9,* 381–388.

Dickens, W. T., & Flynn, J. R. (2001). Heritability estimates versus large environmental effects: The IQ paradox resolved. *Psychological Review, 108,* 346–369.

Dickerson, F. B., Tenhula, W. N., & Green-Paden, L. D. (2005). The token economy for schizophrenia: Review of the literature and recommendations for future research. *Schizophrenia Research, 75*(2–3), 405–416.

Dickinson, D. K., & Tabors, P. O. (Eds.). (2001). *Beginning literacy with language.* Baltimore: Paul H. Brookes.

Dies, R. R. (1995). Group psychotherapies. In A. S. Gurman & S. B. Messer (Eds.), *Essential psychotherapies.* New York: Guilford.

Dieterich, S. E., Assel, M. A., Swank, P., Smith, K. E., et al. (2006). The impact of early maternal verbal scaffolding and child language abilities on later decoding and reading comprehension skills. *Journal of School Psychology, 43*(6), 481–494.

Dingemanse, N. J., & Réale, D. (2005). Natural selection and animal personality. *Behaviour, 142*(9–10), 1159–1184.

Dingus, T. A., Klauer, S. G., Neale, V. L., Petersen, A., et al. (2006). The 100-Car Naturalistic Driving Study, Phase II – Results of the 100-car field experiment. *National Highway Traffic Safety Administration Report No. DOT HS 810 593.* Retrieved September 26, 2012, from http://www.distraction.gov/research/PDF-Files/The-100-Car-Naturalistic-Driving-Study.pdf.

Dinkmeyer, D., Sr., McKay, G. D., & Dinkmeyer, D., Jr. (1997). *The parent's handbook.* Circle Pines, MN: American Guidance Service.

Dion, K. K., & Dion, K. L. (2006). Individualism, collectivism, and the psychology of love. In R. J. Sternberg & K. Weis (Eds.), *The new psychology of love.* New Haven, CT: Yale University Press. 338 pp.

Dion, K. L., Dion, K. K., & Banerjee, R. (2009). Discrimination, ethnic group belonging, and wellbeing. In J. G. Reitz, R.

Breton, K. K. Dion, & K. L. Dion, *Multiculturalism and social cohesion: Potentials and challenges of diversity.* Dordrecht, Netherlands: Springer.

Dion, K. L., & Earn, B. M. (1975). The phenomenology of being a target of prejudice. *Journal of Personality and Social Psychology, 32,* 944–950.

Dion, K. L., Earn, B. M., & Yee, P. H. N. (1978). The experience of being a victim of prejudice: An experimental approach. *International Journal of Psychology, 13,* 197–214.

Distin, K. (2006). *Gifted children: A guide for parents and professionals.* London, U.K.: Jessica Kingsley Publishers.

Dixon, M. J., Smilek, D., & Merikle, P. M. (2004). Not all synaesthetes are created equal: Projector versus associator synaesthetes. *Cognitive, Affective, & Behavioral Neuroscience, 4*(3), 335–343.

Dobelle, W. H. (2000). Artificial vision for the blind by connecting a television camera to the visual cortex. *American Society of Artificial Internal Organs, 46,* 3–9.

Dobson, K. S., Backs-Dermott, G. J., & Dozois, D. J. A. (2000). Cognitive and cognitive-behavioral therapies. In C. R. Snyder & R. E. Ingram (Eds.), *Handbook of psychological change: Psychotherapy processes and practices for the 21st century.* New York: Wiley.

Docherty, N. M., Rhinewine, J. P., Labhart, R. P., & Gordinier, S. W. (1998). Communication disturbances and family psychiatric history in parents of schizophrenic patients. *Journal of Nervous & Mental Disease, 186*(12), 761–768.

Doidge, N. (1997). Empirical evidence for the efficacy of psychoanalytic psychotherapies and psychoanalysis. *Psychoanalytic Inquiry, Suppl.,* 102–150.

Dollard, J., & Miller, N. E. (1950). *Personality and psychotherapy: An analysis in terms of learning, thinking and culture.* New York: McGraw-Hill.

Domhoff, W. (2001). A new neurocognitive theory of dreams. *Dreaming, 11,* 13–33.

Domhoff, W. (2003). *The scientific study of dreams: Neural networks, cognitive development, and content analysis.* Washington: American Psychological Association.

Domingo, R. A., & Goldstein-Alpern, N. (1999). "What dis?" and other toddler-initiated, expressive language-learning strategies. *Infant-Toddler Intervention, 9*(1), 39–60.

Domjan, M. (2006). *The principles of learning and behavior* (5th ed.). Belmont, CA: Wadsworth.

Dooling, D. J., & Lachman, R. (1971). Effects of comprehension on retention of prose. *Journal of Experimental Psychology, 88,* 216–222.

Dorfman, J., Shames, J., & Kihlstrom, J. F. (1996). Intuition, incubation, and insight. In G. Underwood (Ed.), *Implicit cognition.* New York: Oxford University Press.

Dorman, M. F., & Wilson, B. S. (2004). The design and function of cochlear implants. *American Scientist, 92*(Sept-Oct), 436–445.

Dosher, B. A., & Ma, J. (1998). Output loss or rehearsal loop? *Journal of Experimental Psychology: Learning, Memory, & Cognition, 24*(2), 316–335.

Dougall, A. L., & Baum, A. (2003). Stress, coping, and immune function. In M. Gallagher & R. J. Nelson (Eds.), *Handbook of psychology: Biological psychology* (Vol. 3). New York: John Wiley.

Dougherty, D. D., Baer, L., Cosgrove, G. R., Cassem, E. H., et al. (2002). Prospective long-term follow-up of 44 patients who received cingulotomy for treatment-refractory obsessive-compulsive disorder. *American Journal of Psychiatry, 159*(2), 269–275.

Dovidio, J. F., & Penner, L. A. (2001). Helping and altruism. In M. Hewstone & M. Brewer (Eds.), *Handbook of social psychology.* London: Blackwell.

Dovidio, J. F., Glick, P., & Rudman, L. A. (Eds.). (2005). *On the nature of prejudice: Fifty years after Allport.* Malden, MA: Blackwell.

Dowling, K. W. (2005). The effect of lunar phases on domestic violence incident rates. *Forensic Examiner, 14*(4), 13–18.

Dozois, D. J. A., & Dobson, K. S. (Eds.). (2004). *The prevention of anxiety and depression: Theory, research, and practice.* Washington: American Psychological Association.

Draguns, J. G., Gielen, U. P., & Fish, J. M. (2004). Approaches to culture, healing, and psychotherapy. In U. P. Gielen, J. M. Fish, & J. G. Draguns (Eds.), *Handbook of culture, therapy, and healing.* Mahwah, NJ: Lawrence Erlbaum.

Drigotas, S. M., Rusbult, C. E., Wieselquist, J., & Whitton, S. W. (1999). Close partner as sculptor of the ideal self: Behavioral affirmation and the Michelangelo phenomenon. *Journal of Personality & Social Psychology, 77*(2), 293–323.

Drolet, G., Dumont, E. C., Gosselin, I., Kinkead, R., et al. (2001). Role of endogenous opioid system in the regulation of the stress response. *Progress in Neuro-Psychopharmacology & Biological Psychiatry, 25*(4), 729–741.

Druckman, D., & Bjork, R. A. (1994). *Learning, remembering, believing: Enhancing human performance.* Washington: National Academy Press.

Drummond, M., Douglas, J., & Olver, J. (2007). Anosmia after traumatic brain injury: A clinical update. *Brain Impairment, 8*(1), 61–70.

Dubow, E. F., Huesmann, L. R., & Eron, L. D. (1987). Childhood correlates of adult ego development. *Child Development, 58*(3), 859–869.

Duclos, S. E., & Laird, J. D. (2001). The deliberate control of emotional experience through control of expressions. *Cognition and Emotion, 15,* 27–56.

Duffy, J. F., & Wright, K. P., Jr. (2005). Entrainment of the human circadian system by light. *Journal of Biological Rhythms, 20*(4), 326–338.

Dugas, M. J., Freeston, M. H., Ladouceur, R., Rhéaume, J., et al. (1998). Worry themes in primary GAD, secondary GAD, and other anxiety disorders. *Journal of Anxiety Disorders, 12*(3), 253–261.

Dulewicz, V., & Higgs, M. (2000). Emotional intelligence. *Journal of Managerial Psychology, 15*(4), 341–372.

Duncan, J., Seitz, R. J., Kolodny, J., Bor, D., et al. (2000). A neural basis for general intelligence. *Science, 289*, 457–460.

Duncker, K. (1945). On problem solving. *Psychological Monographs, 58*(270).

Durand, V. M., & Barlow, D. H. (2010). *Essentials of abnormal psychology* (5th ed.). Belmont, CA: Cengage Learning/Wadsworth.

Durand, V. M., Barlow, D. H., & Stewart, S. H. (2007). *Essentials of Abnormal Psychology* (1st Canadian ed.). Toronto: Thomson Nelson.

Durham, M. D., & Dane, F. C. (1999). Juror knowledge of eyewitness behavior. *Journal of Social Behavior & Personality, 14*(2), 299–308.

Dutta, T., & Mandal, M. K. (2005). The relationship of handedness and accidents: A meta-analytical review of findings. *Psychological Studies, 50*(4), 309–316.

Dutton, D., & Aron, A. (1974). Some evidence for heightened sexual attraction under conditions of high anxiety. *Journal of Personality & Social Psychology, 30*, 510–517.

Dywan, J., & Bowers, K. S. (1983). The use of hypnosis to enhance recall. *Science, 222*, 184–185.

Dzokoto, V. A., & Adams, G. (2005). Understanding genital-shrinking epidemics in West Africa: Koro, juju, or mass psychogenic illness? *Culture, Medicine and Psychiatry, 29*(1), 53–78.

Ebbinghaus, H. (1885). *Memory: A contribution to experimental psychology.* Translated by H. A. Ruger & C. E. Bussenius, 1913. New York Teacher's College, Columbia University.

Eckerman, D. A. (1999). Scheduling reinforcement about once a day. *Behavioural Processes, 45*(1–3), 101–114.

Eddy, K. T., Dutra, L., Bradley, R., & Westen, D. (2004). A multidimensional meta-analysis of psychotherapy and pharmacotherapy for obsessive-compulsive disorder. *Clinical Psychology Review, 24*(8), 1011–1030.

Eichenbaum, H., & Fortin, N. J. (2005). Bridging the gap between brain and behavior: Cognitive and neural mechanisms of episodic memory. *Journal of the Experimental Analysis of Behavior, 84*(3), 619–629.

Eisenberg, N., Valiente, C., Fabes, R. A., Smith, C. L., et al. (2003). The relations of effortful control and ego control to children's resiliency and social functioning. *Developmental Psychology, 39*(4), 761–776.

Eisler, J. A., Justice, J. B., Jr., & Neill, D. B. (2004). Individual differences in reward sensitivity: Implications for psychostimulant abuse vulnerability. *North American Journal of Psychology, 6*(3), 527–544.

Ekman, P. (1993). Facial expression and emotion. *American Psychologist, 48*(4), 384–392.

Ekman, P., Levenson, R. W., & Friesen, W. V. (1983). Autonomic nervous system activity distinguishes among emotions. *Science, 223*, 1208–1210.

Eliot, L. (1999). What's going on in there? New York: Bantam.

Elkind, D. (2007). The power of play: How spontaneous imaginative activities lead to happier, healthier children. Cambridge, MA: Da Capo Press.

Ellickson, P. L., Martino, S. C., & Collins, R. L. (2004). Marijuana use from adolescence to young adulthood. Health Psychology, 23(3), 299–307.

Ellis, A. (1979). The practice of rational-emotive therapy. In A. Ellis & J. Whiteley (Eds.), *Theoretical and empirical foundations of rational-emotive therapy.* Monterey, CA: Brooks/Cole.

Ellis, A. (1995). Changing rational emotive therapy (RET) to rational emotive behavior therapy (REBT). *Journal of Rational-Emotive & Cognitive-Behavior Therapy, 13*(2), 85–89.

Ellis, A. (2004). Why rational emotive behavior therapy is the most comprehensive and effective form of behavior therapy. *Journal of Rational-Emotive & Cognitive-Behavior Therapy, 22*(2), 85–92.

Emmorey, K., Grabowski, T., McCullough, S., Damasio, H., et al. (2003). Neural systems underlying lexical retrieval for sign language. *Neuropsychologia, 41*(1), 85–95.

Emurian, H. H. (2005). Web-based programmed instruction: Evidence of rule-governed learning. *Computers in Human Behavior, 21*(6), 893–915.

Engle, D. E., & Arkowitz, H. (2006). *Ambivalence in psychotherapy: Facilitating readiness to change.* New York: Guilford.

Enns, J. T., & Coren, S. (1995). The box alignment illusion. *Perception & Psychophysics, 57*(8), 1163–1174.

Enns, M. W., Cox, B. J., & Clara, I. P. (2005). Perfectionism and neuroticism: A longitudinal study of specific vulnerability and diathesis-stress models. *Cognitive Therapy and Research, 29*(4), 463–478.

Erickson, C. D., & al-Timimi, N. R. (2001). Providing mental health services to Arab Americans. *Cultural Diversity and Ethnic Minority Psychology, 7*(4), 308–327.

Ericsson, K. A. (2000). How experts attain and maintain superior performance. *Journal of Aging & Physical Activity, 8*(4), 366–372.

Ericsson, K. A., & Charness, N. (1994). Expert performance. *American Psychologist, 49*(8), 725–747.

Ericsson, K. A., & Chase, W. G. (1982). Exceptional memory. *American Scientist, 70*, 607–615.

Ericsson, K. A., Delaney, P. F., Weaver, G., & Mahadevan, R. (2004). Uncovering the structure of a memorist's superior "basic" memory capacity. *Cognitive Psychology, 49*(3), 191–237.

Erikson, E. H. (1963). *Childhood and society.* New York: Norton.

Erikson, E. H. (1968). *Identity: youth and crisis.* New York: Norton.

Erlacher, D., & Schredl, M. (2004). Dreams reflecting waking sport activities: A comparison of sport and psychology students. *International Journal of Sport Psychology, 35*(4), 301–308.

Eron, L. D. (1987). The development of aggressive behavior from the perspective of a developing behaviorism. *American Psychologist, 42*, 435–442.

Erwin, E. (1996). *A final accounting? Philosophical and empirical issues in Freudian psychology.* Cambridge, MA: MIT Press.

Eschholz, S., Chiricos, T., & Gertz, M. (2003). Television and fear of crime: Program types, audience traits, and the mediating effect of perceived neighborhood racial composition. *Social Problems, 50*(3), 395–415.

Espie, C. A. (2002). Insomnia. *Annual Review of Psychology, 53*, 215–243.

Everly, G. S. (2002). Thoughts on peer (para-professional) support in the provision of mental health services. *International Journal of Emergency Mental Health, 4*(2), 89–92.

Everson, C. A. (1998). Physiological consequences of sleep deprivation. *Journal of Musculoskeletal Pain, 6*(3), 93–101.

Everson, S. A., Goldberg, D. E., & Salonen, J. T. (1996). Hopelessness and risk of mortality and incidence of myocardial infarction and cancer. *Psychosomatic Medicine, 58*(2), 113.

Ewen, R. B. (2003). *An introduction to theories of personality* (6th ed.). Hillsdale, NJ: Lawrence Erlbaum.

Eyer, D. E. (1994). Mother-infant bonding: A scientific fiction. *Human Nature, 5*(1), 69–94.

Eysenck, H. J. (1967, June). New ways in psychotherapy. *Psychology Today, 40.*

Eysenck, H. J. (1994). The outcome problem in psychotherapy: What have we learned? *Behaviour Research & Therapy, 32*(5), 477–495.

Fabrega, Jr., H. (2004). Culture and the origins of psychopathology. In U. P. Gielen, J. M. Fish, & J. G. Draguns (Eds.), *Handbook of culture, therapy, and healing.* Mahwah, NJ: Erlbaum.

Fahim, C., Stip, E., Mancini-Marïe, A., Mensour, B., et al. (2005). Brain activity during emotionally negative pictures in schizophrenia with and without flat affect: An fMRI study. *Psychiatry Research: Neuroimaging, 140*(1), 1–15.

Fahle, M., & Poggio, T. (Eds.). (2002). *Perceptual learning.* Cambridge, MA: MIT Press.

Fain, G. L. (2003). *Sensory transduction.* Sunderland, MA: Sinauer.

Fairclough, S. H., & Graham, R. (1999). Impairment of driving performance caused by sleep deprivation or alcohol. *Human Factors, 41*(1), 118–128.

Faith, M. S., Wong, F. Y., & Carpenter, K. M. (1995). Group sensitivity training: Update, meta-analysis, and recommendations. *Journal of Counseling Psychology, 42*(3), 390–399.

Falkowski, C. (2000). *Dangerous drugs.* Center City, MN: Hazelden Information Education.

Farah, M. (2004). *Visual agnosia* (2nd ed.). Cambridge, MA: MIT Press.

Farberman, R. K. (1997). Public attitudes about psychologists and mental health care: Research to guide the American Psychological Association public education campaign. *Professional Psychology: Research and Practice, 28*, 128–136.

Farrell, M. J., Zamarripa, F., Shade, R., Phillips, P. A., et al. (2008). Effect of aging on regional cerebral blood flow responses associated with osmotic thirst and its satiation by water drinking: A PET study. *PNAS Proceedings of the National Academy of Sciences of the United States of America, 105*(1), 382–387.

Farrimond, T. (1990). Effect of alcohol on visual constancy values and possible relation to driving performance. *Perceptual & Motor Skills, 70*(1), 291–295.

Farroni, T., Massaccesi, S., Pividori, D., & Johnson, M. H. (2004). Gaze following in newborns. *Infancy, 5*(1), 39–60.

Feist, J., & Feist, G. J. (2006). *Theories of personality* (6th ed.). New York: McGraw-Hill.

Feldman, D. H. (2004). Piaget's stages: The unfinished symphony of cognitive development. *New Ideas in Psychology, 22*(3), 175–231.

Feldman, R. S., & Meyer, J. (1996). *Fundamentals of neuropsychopharmacology.* Sunderland, MA: Sinauer Associates.

Fellous, J.-M., & LeDoux, J. E. (2005). Toward basic principles for emotional processing: What the fearful brain tells the robot. In J.-M. Fellous & M. A. Arbib (Eds.), *Who needs emotions?: The brain meets the robot.* New York: Oxford University Press.

Fenn, K. M., Nusbaum, H. C., & Margoliash, D. (2003). Consolidation during sleep of perceptual learning of spoken language. *Nature, 425*(6958), 614–616.

Fenton, G. W. (1998). Neurosurgery for mental disorder. *Irish Journal of Psychological Medicine, 15*(2), 45–48.

Fernald, A. (1989). Intonation and communicative intent in mothers' speech to infants: Is the melody the message? *Child Development, 60*(6), 1497–1510.

Fernald, A., Perfors, A., & Marchman, V. A. (2006). Picking up speed in understanding: Speech processing efficiency and vocabulary growth across the 2nd year. *Developmental Psychology, 42*(1), 98–116.

Féron, F., Perry, C., Cochrane, J., Licina, P., et al. (2005). Autologous olfactory ensheathing cell transplantation in human spinal cord injury. *Brain: A Journal of Neurology, 128*(12), 2951–2960.

Ferrari, J. R., Diaz-Morales, J. F., O'Callaghan, J., Diaz, K., et al. (2007). Frequent behavioral delay tendencies by adults: International prevalence rates of chronic procrastination. *Journal of Cross-Cultural Psychology, 38*(4), 458–464.

Ferrari, J. R., & Scher, S. J. (2000). Toward an understanding of academic and nonacademic tasks procrastinated by students: The use of daily logs. *Psychology in the Schools, 37*(4), 359–366.

Festinger, L. (1957). *A theory of cognitive dissonance.* Stanford, CA: Stanford University Press.

Festinger, L., & Carlsmith, J. M. (1959). Cognitive consequences of forced compliance. *Journal of Abnormal and Social Psychology, 58*, 203–210.

Ficca, G., & Salzarulo, P. (2004). What in sleep is for memory. *Sleep Medicine, 5,* 225–230.

Fichten, C. S., & Sunerton, B. (1983). Popular horoscopes and the "Barnum effect." *The Journal of Psychology, 114,* 123–134.

Fields, R. D. (2007). The shark's electric sense. *Scientific American, 297*(8), 74–81.

Fields, R. M., & Margolin, J. (2001). *Coping with trauma.* Washington: American Psychological Association.

Figueredo, A. J., Sefcek, J. A., & Jones, D. N. (2006). The ideal romantic partner personality. *Personality & Individual Differences, 41*(3), 431–441.

Fink, M. (2000). Electroshock revisited. *American Scientist, 88*(March–April), 162–167.

Finkelstein, P., Wenegrat, B., & Yalom, I. (1982). Large group awareness training. *Annual Review of Psychology, 33,* 515–539.

Fiore, D., Dimaggio, G., Nicoló, G., Semerari, A., et al. (2008). Metacognitive interpersonal therapy in a case of obsessive-compulsive and avoidant personality disorders. *Journal of Clinical Psychology, 64*(2), 168–180.

Fischer, S., & Greenberg, R. (1996). *Freud scientifically appraised.* New York: John Wiley.

Fisher, M. L., Worth, K., Garcia, J. R., & Meredith, T. (2012). Feelings of regret following uncommitted sexual encounters in Canadian university students. *Culture, Health & Sexuality: An International Journal for Research, Intervention and Care, 14*(1), 45–57.

Fisher, R. P., & Geiselman, R. E. (1987). Enhancing eyewitness memory with the cognitive interview. In M. M. Gruneberg, P. E. Morris, & R. N. Sykes (Eds.), *Practical aspects of memory: Current research and issues.* Chichester, U.K.: Wiley.

Fiske, S. T., Cuddy, A. J. C., Glick, P., & Xu, J. (2002). A model of (often mixed) stereotype content. *Journal of Personality & Social Psychology, 82*(6), 878–902.

Flanagan, M. B., May, J. G., & Dobie, T. G. (2004). The role of vection, eye movements and postural instability in the etiology of motion sickness. *Journal of Vestibular Research: Equilibrium & Orientation, 14*(4), 335–346.

Flannery, D. J., Rowe, D. C., & Gulley, B. L. (1993). Impact of pubertal status, timing, and age on adolescent sexual experience and delinquency. *Journal of Adolescent Research, 8*(1), 21–40.

Flavell, J. H. (1992). Cognitive development: Past, present, and future. *Developmental Psychology, 28*(6), 998–1005.

Flavell, J. H. (1999). Cognitive development: Children's knowledge about the mind. *Annual Review of Psychology, 50,* 21–45.

Flowe, H. D., & Ebbese, E. B. (2007). The effect of lineup member similarity on recognition accuracy in simultaneous and sequential lineups. *Law & Human Behavior, 31*(1), 33–52.

Flynn, J. R. (2007). *What is intelligence? Beyond the Flynn effect.* New York: Cambridge University Press.

Fobair, P. (1997). Cancer support groups and group therapies. *Journal of Psychosocial Oncology, 15*(3–4), 123–147.

Fochtmann, L. J. (1995). Intractable sneezing as a conversion symptom. *Psychosomatics, 36*(2), 103–112.

Fogel, S. M., Nader, R., Côté, K. A., & Smith, C. T. (2007). Sleep spindles and learning potential. *Behavioral Neuroscience, 121*(1), 1–10.

Folkman, S., & Moskowitz, J. T. (2004). Coping. *Annual Review of Psychology, 55,* 745–774.

Follett, K., & Hess, T. M. (2002). Aging, cognitive complexity, and the fundamental attribution error. *Journals of Gerontology: Series B: Psychological Sciences and Social Sciences, 57B*(4), 312–323.

Fontaine, K. R., Redden, D. T., Wang, C., Westfall, A. O., et al. (2003). Years of life lost due to obesity. *JAMA, 289,* 187–193.

Fontenelle, D. H. (1989). *How to live with your children.* Tucson, AZ: Fisher Books.

Foo, P., Warren, W. H., Duchon, A., & Tarr, M. J. (2005). Do humans integrate routes into a cognitive map? Map versus landmark-based navigation of novel shortcuts. *Journal of Experimental Psychology: Learning, Memory, & Cognition, 31*(2), 195–215.

Foot, M., & Koszycki, D. (2004). Gender differences in anxiety-related traits in patients with panic disorder. *Depression & Anxiety, 20*(3), 123–130.

Ford, C. V. (1995). Dimensions of somatization and hypochondriasis. *Neurologic Clinics, 13*(2), 241–253.

Forest, A. L., & Wood, J. V. (2012). When social networking is not working: Individuals with low self-esteem recognize but do not reap the benefits of self-disclosure on Facebook. *Psychological Science, 23*(3), 295–302.

Forney, W. S., Forney, J. C., & Crutsinger, C. (2005). Developmental stages of age and moral reasoning as predictors of juvenile delinquents' behavioral intention to steal clothing. *Family & Consumer Sciences Research Journal, 34*(2), 110–126.

Fosse, R., Stickgold, R., & Hobson, J. A. (2001). The mind in REM sleep: Reports of emotional experience. *Sleep: Journal of Sleep & Sleep Disorders Research, 24*(8), 947–955.

Foster, C. A., Witcher, B. S., Campbell, W. K., & Green, J. D. (1998). Arousal and attraction. *Journal of Personality & Social Psychology, 74*(1), 86–101.

Foster, G., & Ysseldyke, J. (1976). Expectancy and halo effects as a result of artificially induced teacher bias. *Contemporary Educational Psychology, 1,* 37–45.

Foulds, H. J. A., Bredin, S. S. D., & Warburton, D. E. R. (2011). The prevalence of overweight and obesity in British Columbian Aboriginal adults. *Obesity Reviews, 12*(5), e4–e11.

Fowers, B. J., & Davidov, B. J. (2006). The virtue of multiculturalism: Personal transformation, character, and openness to the other. *American Psychologist, 61*(6), 581–594.

Foxhall, K. (2000, January). Suddenly, a big impact on criminal justice. *APA Monitor,* 36–37.

Frank, J. D., & Frank, J. (2004). Therapeutic components shared by all psychotherapies. In A. Freeman, M. J. Mahoney, P. DeVito, & D. Martin (Eds.), *Cognition and psychotherapy* (2nd ed.). New York: Springer.

Franken, R. E. (2007). *Human motivation.* Belmont, CA: Wadsworth.

Franzoi, S. L. (2002). *Social psychology.* New York: McGraw-Hill.

Franzoi, S. L., & Klaiber, J. R. (2007). Body use and reference group impact: With whom do we compare our bodies? *Sex Roles, 56*(3–4), 205–214.

Fraser, C. (2002). Fact and fiction: A clarification of phantom limb phenomena. *British Journal of Occupational Therapy, 65*(6), 256–260.

Fredrickson, B. L. (2003). The value of positive emotions. *American Scientist, 91,* 330–335.

Fredrickson, B. L., & Branigan, C. (2005). Positive emotions broaden the scope of attention and thought-action repertoires. *Cognition & Emotion, 19*(3), 313–332.

Freedman, N., Park, Y., Abnet, C., Hollenbeck, A., et al. (2012). Association of coffee drinking with total and cause-specific mortality. *New England Journal of Medicine, 366,* 1891–1904.

Freeman, D., & Garety, P. A. (2004). *Paranoia: the psychology of persecutory delusions.* New York: Routledge.

French, S. E., Kim, T. E., & Pillado, O. (2006). Ethnic identity, social group membership, and youth violence. In N. G. Guerra & E. P. Smith (Eds.), *Preventing youth violence in a multicultural society.* Washington: American Psychological Association.

Freud, S. (1900). *The interpretation of dreams.* London: Hogarth.

Freud, S. (1949). *An outline of psychoanalysis.* New York: Norton.

Frey, M. C., & Detterman, D. K. (2004). Scholastic assessment or g? The relationship between the scholastic assessment test and general cognitive ability. *Psychological Science, 15*(6), 373–378.

Fried, P. A., & Smith, A. M. (2001). A literature review of the consequences of prenatal marijuana exposure. *Neurotoxicology and Teratology, 23*(1), 1–11.

Fried, P., Watkinson, B., James, D., & Gray, R. (2002). Current and former marijuana use: Preliminary findings of a longitudinal study of effects on IQ in young adults. *Canadian Medical Association Journal, 166,* 887–891.

Friedman, H. S. (2002). *Health psychology* (2nd ed.). Englewood Cliffs, NJ: Prentice-Hall.

Friedman, L. J. (2004). Erik Erikson on generativity: A biographer's perspective. In E. de St. Aubin, D. P. McAdams, & T.-C. Kim (Eds.), *The generative society: Caring for future generations.* Washington: American Psychological Association.

Friedman, M., & Rosenman, R. (1983). *Type A behavior and your heart.* New York: Knopf.

Friedman, R. C., Bucci, W., Christian, C., Drucker, P., et al. (1998). Private psychotherapy patients of psychiatrist psychoanalysts. *American Journal of Psychiatry, 155,* 1772–1774.

Fritz, C. O., Morris, P. E., Acton, M., Voelkel, A. R., et al. (2007). Comparing and combining retrieval practice and the keyword mnemonic for foreign vocabulary learning. *Applied Cognitive Psychology, 21*(4), 499–526.

Froufe, M., & Schwartz, C. (2001). Subliminal messages for increasing self-esteem: Placebo effect. *Spanish Journal of Psychology, 4*(1), 19–25.

Frydman, M. (1999). Television, aggressiveness and violence. *International Journal of Adolescent Medicine & Health, 11*(3–4), 335–344.

Fukuda, K., & Ishihara, K. (2001). Age-related changes of sleeping pattern during adolescence. *Psychiatry & Clinical Neurosciences, 55*(3), 231–232.

Funder, D. C. (2006). *The personality puzzle* (4th ed.). New York: Norton.

Funk, J. B. (2005). Children's exposure to violent video games and desensitization to violence. *Child and Adolescent Psychiatric Clinics of North America, 14*(3), 387–404.

Furnham, A., Chamorro-Premuzic, T., & Callahan, I. (2003). Does graphology predict personality and intelligence? *Individual Differences Research, 1*(2), 78–94.

Gable, S. L., Reis, H. T., Impett, E., & Asher, E. R. (2004). What do you do when things go right? The intrapersonal and interpersonal benefits of sharing positive events. *Journal of Personality & Social Psychology, 87,* 228–245.

Gabrieli, J. D. E. (1998). Cognitive neuroscience of human memory. *Annual Review of Psychology, 49,* 87–115.

Gaertner, S. L., Dovidio, J. F., Banker, B. S., Houlette, M., et al. (2000). Reducing intergroup conflict: From superordinate goals to decategorization, recategorization, and mutual differentiation. *Group Dynamics, 4*(1), 98–114.

Gagnon, J., Petit, D., Fantini, M., Rompré, S., et al. (2006). REM sleep behavior disorder and REM sleep without atonia in probable Alzheimer disease. *Sleep: Journal of Sleep and Sleep Disorders Research, 29*(10), 1321–1325.

Galambos, N. L., Barker, E. T., & Tilton-Weaver, L. C. (2003). Who gets caught at maturity gap? A study of pseudomature, immature and mature adolescents. *International Journal of Behavioral Development, 27*(3), 253–263.

Galanter, M., Hayden, F., Castañeda, R., & Franco, H. (2005). Group therapy, self-help groups, and network therapy. In R. J. Frances, S. I. Miller, & A. H. Mack (Eds.), *Clinical textbook of addictive disorders* (3rd ed.). New York: Guilford.

Galati, D., Scherer, K. R., & Ricci-Bitti, P. E. (1997). Voluntary facial expression of emotion: Comparing congenitally blind with normally sighted encoders. *Journal of Personality & Social Psychology, 73*(6), 1363–1379.

Gallagher, S. (2004). Nailing the lie: An interview with Jonathan Cole. *Journal of Consciousness Studies, 11*(2), 3–21.

Ganellen, R. J. (1996). Comparing the diagnostic efficiency of the MMPI, MCMI-II, and Rorschach. *Journal of Personality Assessment, 67*(2), 219–243.

Ganis, G., Thompson, W. L., & Kosslyn, S. M. (2004). Brain areas underlying visual mental imagery and visual perception: An fMRI study. *Cognitive Brain Research, 20*(2), 226–241.

Garbarino, S., Beelke, M., Costa, G., Violani, C., et al. (2002). Brain function and effects of shift work: implications for clinical neuropharmacology. *Neuropsychobiology, 45,* 50–56.

Garbarino, S., Mascialino, B., Penco, M. A., Squarcia, S., et al. (2004). Professional shift-work drivers who adopt prophylactic naps can reduce the risk of car accidents during night work. *Sleep: Journal of Sleep & Sleep Disorders Research, 27*(7), 1295–1302.

Gardner, H. (2003, April). *Multiple intelligences after twenty years.* Invited address at meeting of American Educational Research Association. Retrieved May 10, 2009, from http://www.pz.harvard.edu /PIs/HG_MI_after_20_years.pdf.

Gardner, H. (2004). *Frames of mind* (10th anniversary ed.). New York: Basic.

Gardner, R. A., & Gardner, B. T. (1989). *Teaching sign language to chimpanzees.* Albany, NY: State University of New York Press.

Garland, A. F., & Zigler, E. (1993). Adolescent suicide prevention. *American Psychologist, 48*(2), 169–182.

Garlow, S. J., Purselle, D. C., & Heninger, M. (2007). Cocaine and alcohol use preceding suicide in African American and White adolescents. *Journal of Psychiatric Research, 41*(6), 530–536.

Garnets, L. D., & Kimmel, D. (1991). *Lesbian and gay male dimensions in the psychological study of human diversity. Psychological perspectives on human diversity in America.* Washington: American Psychological Association.

Gass, R. H., & Seiter, J. S. (2007). *Persuasion: Social influence and compliance gaining* (3rd ed.). Boston: Allyn & Bacon.

Gates, A. I. (1958). Recitation as a factor in memorizing. In J. Deese (Ed.), *The psychology of learning.* New York: McGraw-Hill.

Gathchel, R. J., & Oordt, M. S. (2003). Insomnia. In R. J. Gatchel & M. S. Oordt (Eds.), *Clinical health psychology and primary care: Practical advice and clinical guidance for successful collaboration.* Washington: American Psychological Association.

Gazzaniga, M. S. (1970). *The bisected brain.* New York: Plenum.

Gazzaniga, M. S. (1995). On neural circuits and cognition. *Neural Computation, 7*(1), 1–12.

Gazzaniga, M. S. (2005). Forty-five years of split-brain research and still going strong. *Nature Reviews Neuroscience, 6*(8), 653–659.

Geary, N. (2004). Endocrine controls of eating: CCK, leptin, and ghrelin. *Physiology & Behavior, 81*(5), 719–733.

Gegenfurtner, K. R., & Kiper, D. C. (2003). Color vision. *Annual Review of Neuroscience, 26,* 181–206.

Geiselman, R. E., Fisher, R. P., MacKinnon, D. P., & Holland, H. L. (1986). Eyewitness memory enhancement with the cognitive interview. *American Journal of Psychology, 99,* 385–401.

Geliebter, A., & Aversa, A. (2003). Emotional eating in overweight, normal weight, and underweight individuals. *Eating Behaviors, 3*(4), 341–347.

Geoffroy, M.C., Cote, S. M., Giguere, C.E., Dionne, G., et al. (2010). Closing the gap in academic readiness and achievement: The role of early childcare. *Journal of Child Psychology and Psychiatry, 51*(12), 1359–1367.

George, A. (2006). Living online: The end of privacy? *New Scientist, 2659*(Sept 18), 50–51.

Georgiades, A., Serwood, A., Gullette, E. C., Babyak, M. A., et al. (2000). Effects of exercise and weight loss on mental stress-induced cardiovascular responses in individuals with high blood pressure. *Hypertension, 36,* 171–176.

Germain, A., Krakow, B., Faucher, B., Zadra, A., et al. (2004). Increased mastery elements associated with imagery rehearsal treatment for nightmares in sexual assault survivors with PTSD. *Dreaming, 14*(4), 195–206.

German, T. P., & Barrett, H. C. (2005). Functional fixedness in a technologically sparse culture. *Psychological Science, 16*(1), 1–5.

German, T. P., & Defeyter, M. A. (2000). Immunity to functional fixedness in young children. *Psychonomic Bulletin & Review, 7*(4), 707–712.

Gersh, R. D. (1982, June 20). *Learning when not to shoot.* Santa Barbara News Press.

Gershoff, E. T. (2002). Corporal punishment by parents and associated child behaviors and experiences: A meta-analytic and theoretical review. *Psychological Bulletin, 128*(4), 539–579.

Gershon, E. S., Badner, J. A., Goldin, L. R., Sanders, A. R., et al. (1998). Closing in on genes for manic-depressive illness and schizophrenia. *Neuropsychopharmacology, 18*(4), 233–242.

Gerwood, J. B. (1998). The legacy of Viktor Frankl. *Psychological Reports, 82*(2), 673–674.

Geschwind, N. (1979). Specializations of the human brain. *Scientific American, 241,* 180–199.

Gewirtz, J. C., & Davis, M. (1998). Application of Pavlovian higher-order conditioning to the analysis of the neural substrates of fear conditioning. *Neuropharmacology, 37*(4–5), 453–459.

Giarratano, J. C., & Riley, G. (2005). *Expert systems, principles and programming* (4th ed.). Belmont, CA: Cengage Learning/ Wadsworth.

Gibson, E. J., & Walk, R. D. (1960). The "visual cliff." *Scientific American, 202*(4), 67–71.

Gibson, K. R. (2002). Evolution of human intelligence: The roles of brain size and mental construction. *Brain, Behavior & Evolution, 59*(1–2), 10–20.

Gilbert, D. G., Gilbert, B. O., & Schultz, V. L. (1998). Withdrawal symptoms: Individual differences and similarities across addictive behaviors. *Personality & Individual Differences, 24*(3), 351–356.

Giliovich, T., Keltner, D., & Nisbett, R. (2005). *Social psychology.* New York: Norton.

Gillberg, M., & Akerstedt, T. (1998). Sleep loss performance: No "safe" duration of a monotonous task. *Physiology & Behavior, 64*(5), 599–604.

Gilligan, C. (1982). *In a different voice.* Cambridge, MA: Harvard University Press.

Ginet, M., & Py, J. (2001). A technique for enhancing memory in eyewitness testimonies for use by police officers and judicial officials: The cognitive interview. *Travail Humain, 64*(2), 173–191.

Ginott, H. G. (1965). *Between parent and child: New solutions to old problems.* New York: Macmillan.

Ginsberg, D. L. (2006). Fatal agranulocytosis four years after clozapine discontinuation. *Primary Psychiatry, 13*(2), 32–33.

Girodo, M. (1978). *Shy? (You don't have to be!).* New York: Pocket Books.

Giummarra, M. J., Gibson, S. J., Georgiou-Karistianis, N., & Bradshaw, J. L. (2007). Central mechanisms in phantom limb perception: The past, present and future. *Brain Research Reviews, 54*(1), 219–232.

Giuseppe, R. (2005). Virtual reality in psychotherapy: Review. *CyberPsychology & Behavior. Special Use of Virtual Environments in Training and Rehabilitation: International Perspectives, 8*(3), 220–230.

Gladwell, M. (2005). *Blink: The power of thinking without thinking.* New York: Little, Brown.

Glisky, M. L., Williams, J. M., & Kihlstrom, J. F. (1996). Internal and external mental imagery perspectives and performance on two tasks. *Journal of Sport Behavior, 19*(1), 3–18.

Glueck, J., Ernst, R., & Unger, F. (2002). How creatives define creativity. *Creativity Research Journal, 14*(1), 55–67.

Gobet, F. (2005). Chunking models of expertise: Implications for education. *Applied Cognitive Psychology, 19*(2), 183–204.

Gobet, F., & Simon, H. A. (1996). Recall of random and distorted chess positions: Implications for the theory of expertise. *Memory & Cognition, 24*(4), 493–503.

Godnig, E. C. (2003). Tunnel vision: Its causes and treatment strategies. *Journal of Behavioral Optometry, 14*(4), 95–99.

Goel, V., & Dolan, R. J. (2004). Differential involvement of left prefrontal cortex in inductive and deductive reasoning. *Cognition, 93*(3), 109–121.

Goel, V., & Grafman, J. (1995). Are the frontal lobes implicated in "planning" functions? Interpreting data from the Tower of Hanoi. *Neuropsychologia, 33*(5), 623–642.

Goering, P., Wasylenki, D., & Durbin, J. (2000). Canada's mental health system.

International Journal of Law & Psychiatry, 23, 345–359.

Gold, D., Shaw, A. & Wolffe, K. (2010) The social lives of Canadian youths with visual impairments. *Journal of Visual Impairment & Blindness, 104*(7), 431–443.

Goldberg, R. (2006). *Drugs across the spectrum* (5th ed.). Belmont, CA: Cengage Learning/Wadsworth.

Goldenberg, H., & Goldenberg, I. (2004). *Family therapy: An overview* (6th ed.). Pacific Grove, CA: Brooks/Cole.

Goldfried, M. R., Greenberg, L. S., & Marmar, C. (1990). Individual psychotherapy: Process and outcome. *Annual Review of Psychology, 41,* 659–688.

Goldman, H. H. (1998). Deinstitutionalization and community care. *Harvard Review of Psychiatry, 6*(4), 219–222.

Goldstein, E. B. (2008). *Cognitive psychology: Connecting mind, research and everyday experience* (2nd ed.). Belmont, CA: Cengage Learning/Wadsworth.

Goldstein, E. B. (2010). *Sensation and perception* (8th ed.). Belmont, CA: Cengage Learning/Wadsworth.

Goldston, D. B., Molock, S. D., Whitbeck, L. B., Murakami, J. L., et al. (2008). Cultural considerations in adolescent suicide prevention and psychosocial treatment. *American Psychologist, 63*(1), 14–31.

Goleman, D. (1982, March). Staying up: The rebellion against sleep's gentle tyranny. *Psychology Today,* 24–35.

Goleman, D. (1995). *Emotional intelligence.* New York: Bantam.

Gomez, R., & McLaren, S. (2007). The interrelations of mother and father attachment, self-esteem and aggression during late adolescence. *Aggressive Behavior, 33*(2), 160–169.

Goodall, J. (1990). *Through a window: My thirty years with the chimpanzees of the Gombe.* Boston: Houghton Mifflin.

Goode, E. (1996). Gender and courtship entitlement: Responses to personal ads. *Sex Roles, 34*(3–4), 141–169.

Goodman, G. (1984). SASHA tapes: Expanding options for help-intended communication. In D. Larson (Ed.), *Teaching psychological skills.* Monterey, CA: Brooks/Cole.

Goodwin, R. D., Fergusson, D. M., & Horwood, L. J. (2005). Childhood abuse and familial violence and the risk of panic attacks and panic disorder in young adulthood. *Psychological Medicine, 35*(6), 881–890.

Gopnik, A., Meltzoff, A. N., & Kuhl, P. K. (1999). *The scientist in the crib.* New York: William Morrow.

Gopnik, A., Meltzoff, A. N., & Kuhl, P. K. (2000). *The scientist in the crib: What early learning tells us about the mind.* New York: HarperCollins.

Gordon, A. K., & Kaplar, M. E. (2002). A new technique for demonstrating the actor-observer bias. *Teaching of Psychology, 29*(4), 301–303.

Gordon, T. (2000). *Parent effectiveness training: The proven program for raising responsible children.* New York: Three Rivers Press.

Gorman, J. M. (1996). *The essential guide to mental health.* New York: St. Martin's Griffin.

Gottesman, I. I. (1991). *Schizophrenia genesis: The origins of madness.* New York: W. H. Freeman & Company.

Gottfredson, L. (1997). Mainstream science on intelligence: An editorial with 42 signatories, history and bibliography. *Intelligence, 24*(1), 13–23.

Gottfredson, L. S. (2007). Applying double standards to "divisive" ideas. Commentary on Hunt and Carlson (2007). *Perspectives on Psychological Science, 2*(2), 216–220.

Gottleib, B. H., Still, E., & Newby-Clark, I. R. (2007). Types and precipitants of growth and decline in emerging adulthood. *Journal of Adolescent Research, 22*(2), 132–155.

Gottlieb, G. (1998). Normally occurring environmental and behavioral influences on gene activity: From central dogma to probabilistic epigenesis. *Psychological Review, 105*(4), 792–802.

Gould, E., Reeves, A. J., & Gross, C. G. (1999). Neurogenesis in the neocortex of adult primates. *Science, 286*(5439), 548.

Grabe, M. (2006). *Integrating technology for meaningful learning.* Boston: Houghton Mifflin.

Grabill, K., Merlo, L., Duke, D., Harford, K., et al. (2008). Assessment of obsessive-compulsive disorder: A review. *Journal of Anxiety Disorders, 22*(1), 1–17.

Grack, C., & Richman, C. L. (1996). Reducing general and specific heterosexism through cooperative contact. *Journal of Psychology & Human Sexuality, 8*(4), 59–68.

Grande, T., Rudolf, G., Oberbracht, C., & Pauli-Magnus, C. (2003). Progressive changes in patients' lives after psychotherapy. *Psychotherapy Research, 13*(1), 43–58.

Grandner, M. A., & Kripke, D. F. (2004). Self-reported sleep complaints with long and short sleep: A nationally representative sample. *Psychosomatic Medicine, 66,* 239–241.

Granrud, C. E. (2004). Visual metacognition and the development of size constancy. In D. T. Levin (Ed.), *Thinking and seeing: Visual metacognition in adults and children.* Cambridge, MA: MIT Press.

Granrud, C. E. (2006). Size constancy in infants: 4-month-olds' responses to physical versus retinal image size. *Journal of Experimental Psychology: Human Perception & Performance, 32*(6), 1398–1404.

Grant, B. F., & Dawson, D. A. (1997). Age at onset of alcohol use and its association with DSM-IV alcohol abuse and dependence. *Journal of Substance Abuse, 9,* 103.

Grant, B. F., Hasin, D. S., Stinson, F. S., Dawson, D. A., et al. (2006). The epidemiology of DSM-IV panic disorder and agoraphobia in the United States: Results from the National Epidemiologic Survey on Alcohol and Related Conditions. *Journal of Clinical Psychiatry, 67*(3), 363–374.

Graves, J. L. (2001). *The emperor's new clothes.* Piscataway, NJ: Rutgers University Press.

Gravetter, F. J., & Wallnau, L. B. (2010). *Statistics for the behavioral sciences* (8th ed.). Belmont, CA: Cengage Learning/Wadsworth.

Gray, J. M., & Wilson, M. A. (2007). A detailed analysis of the reliability and validity of the sensation seeking scale in a UK sample. *Personality & Individual Differences, 42*(4), 641–651.

Greenberg, D. L. (2004). President Bush's false "flashbulb" memory of 9/11/01. *Applied Cognitive Psychology, 18*(3), 363–370.

Greene, D., & Lepper, M. R. (1974, September). How to turn play into work. *Psychology Today,* 49.

Greenfield, P. M. (1997). You can't take it with you: Why abilities assessments don't cross cultures. *American Psychologist, 52,* 1115–1124.

Greenglass, E. R., Burke, R. J., & Moore, K. A. (2003). Reactions to increased workload: Effects on professional efficacy of nurses. *Applied Psychology: An International Review, 52*(4), 580–597.

Greenwald, R. (2006). Eye movement desensitization and reprocessing with traumatized youth. In N. B. Webb (Ed.), *Working with traumatized youth in child welfare: Social work practice with children and families.* New York: Guilford.

Greenwood, J. G., Greenwood, J. J. D., McCullagh, J. F., Beggs, J., et al. (2006). A survey of sidedness in Northern Irish schoolchildren: The interaction of sex, age, and task. *Laterality: Asymmetries of Body, Brain & Cognition, 12*(1), 1–18.

Gregory, R. L. (1990). *Eye and brain: The psychology of seeing.* Princeton, NJ: Princeton University Press.

Gregory, R. L. (2000). Visual illusions. In A. Kazdin (Ed.), *Encyclopedia of psychology.* Washington: American Psychological Association.

Gregory, R. L. (2003). Seeing after blindness. *Nature Neuroscience, 6*(9), 909–910.

Greitemeyer, T. (2009). Effects of songs with prosocial lyrics on prosocial thoughts, affect, and behavior. *Journal of Experimental Social Psychology, 45*(1), 186–190.

Grello, C. M., Welsh, D. P., & Harper, M. S. (2006). No strings attached: The nature of casual sex in college students. *Journal of Sex Research, 43*(3), 255–267.

Griffin, D. R. (1992). *Animal minds.* Chicago: University of Chicago Press.

Griffith, A. (2007). Healing broken nerves. *Scientific American, 297*(3), 28–30.

Grobstein, P., & Chow, K. L. (1975). Perceptive field development and individual experience. *Science, 190,* 352–358.

Grolnick, W. S., Cosgrove, T. J., & Bridges, L. J. (1996). Age-graded change in the initiative of positive affect. *Infant Behavior & Development, 19*(1), 153–157.

Grubin, D., & Madsen, L. (2005). Lie detection and the polygraph: A historical review. *Journal of Forensic Psychiatry & Psychology, 16*(2), 357–369.

Gruder, C. L., Mermelstein, R. J., Kirkendol, S., Hedeker, D., et al. (1993). Effects of social support and relapse prevention training as adjuncts to a televised smoking-cessation intervention. *Journal*

of Consulting & Clinical Psychology, 61(1), 113–120.

Grunbaum, J. A., Kann, L., Kinchen, S., & Ross, J., et al. (2004). Youth risk behavior surveillance: United States, 2003. *Centers for Disease Control and Prevention Morbidity and Mortality Weekly Report Surveillance Summary, 53*(SS02), 1–96.

Gruner, C. R., & Tighe, M. R. (1995). Semantic differential measurements of connotations of verbal terms and their doublespeak facsimiles in sentence contexts. *Psychological Reports, 77*(3, Pt 1), 778.

Guastello, D. D., & Guastello, S. J. (2003). Androgyny, gender role behavior, and emotional intelligence among college students and their parents. *Sex Roles, 49* (11–12), 663–673.

Guéguen, N. (2002). Status, apparel and touch: Their joint effects on compliance to a request. *North American Journal of Psychology, 4*(2), 279–286.

Guéguen, N., & Pascual, A. (2003). Status and people's tolerance towards an ill-mannered person: A field study. *Journal of Mundane Behavior, 4*(1). Retrieved August 4, 2007, from http://www.mundanebehavior.org/issues/v4n1/gueguen-pascual.htm.

Guéguen, N., Pascual, A., & Dagot, L. (2002). Low-ball and compliance to a request: An application in a field setting. *Psychological Reports, 91*(1), 81–84.

Guerrini, I., Thompson, A. D., & Gurling, H. D. (2007). The importance of alcohol misuse, malnutrition and genetic susceptibility on brain growth and plasticity. *Neuroscience & Biobehavioral Reviews, 31*(2), 212–220.

Gullette, D. L., & Lyons, M. A. (2005). Sexual sensation seeking, compulsivity, and HIV risk behaviors in college students. *Journal of Community Health Nursing, 22*(1), 47–60.

Gur, R. E., Cowell, P., Turetsky, B. I., Gallacher, F., et al. (1998). A follow-up magnetic resonance imaging study of schizophrenia. *Archives of General Psychiatry, 55*(2), 145–152.

Gurung, R. (2010). *Health psychology: A cultural approach* (2nd ed.). Belmont, CA: Cengage Learning/Wadsworth.

Gustavsson, J. P., et al. (1997). Stability and predictive ability of personality traits across 9 years. *Personality & Individual Differences, 22*(6), 783–791.

Haas, B. W., Omura, K., Constable, R. T., & Canli, T. (2007). Is automatic emotion regulation associated with agreeableness? A perspective using a social neuroscience approach. *Psychological Science, 18*(2), 130–132.

Haber, R. N. (1969). Eidetic images; with biographical sketches. *Scientific American, 220*(12), 36–44.

Haber, R. N. (1970, May). How we remember what we see. *Scientific American,* 104–112.

Haber, R. N., & Haber, L. (2000). Eidetic imagery. In A. E. Kazdin, (Ed.), *Encyclopedia of psychology* (Vol. 3). Washington: American Psychological Association.

Hadwin, A. F., Kirby, J. R., & Woodhouse, R. A. (1999). Individual differences in notetaking, summarization and learning

from lectures. *Alberta Journal of Educational Research, 45*(1), 1–17.

Haenschel, C., Vernon, D. J., Dwivedi, P., Gruzelier, J. H., et al. (2005). Event-related brain potential correlates of human auditory sensory memory-trace formation. *Journal of Neuroscience, 25*(45), 10494–10501.

Hafer, C. L., & Bègue, L. (2005). Experimental research on just-world theory: Problems, developments, and future challenges. *Psychological Bulletin, 131*(1), 128–167.

Haier, R. J., Jung, R. E., Yeo, R. A., Head, K., et al. (2004). Structural brain variation and general intelligence. *NeuroImage, 23,* 425–433.

Haier, R. J., Siegel, B. V., Nuechterlein, K. H., Hazlett, E., et al. (1988). Cortical glucose metabolic rate correlates of abstract reasoning and attention studied with positron emission tomography. *Intelligence, 12,* 199–217.

Halbert, J., Crotty, M., & Cameron, I. D. (2002). Evidence for the optimal management of acute and chronic phantom pain. *Clinical Journal of Pain, 18*(2), 84–92.

Hall, C. (1966). *The meaning of dreams.* New York: McGraw-Hill.

Hall, C. (1974). What people dream about. In R. L. Woods & H. B. Greenhouse (Eds.), *The new world of dreams: An anthology.* New York: Macmillan.

Hall, J. (2006). *What is clinical psychology?* (4th ed.). New York: Oxford University Press.

Hall, N. C., Perry, R. P., Goetz, T., Ruthig, J. C., et al. (2007). Attributional retraining and elaborative learning: Improving academic development through writing-based interventions. *Learning & Individual Differences, 17*(3), 280–290.

Hallahan, D. P., & Kauffman, J. M. (2006). *Exceptional learners* (10th ed.). Boston: Allyn & Bacon.

Halpern, D. F. (2003). *Thought and knowledge: An introduction to critical thinking* (4th ed.). Mahwah, NJ: Erlbaum.

Hamilton, V. L., & Sanders, J. (1995). Crimes of obedience and conformity in the workplace. *Journal of Social Issues, 51*(3), 67–88.

Hammer, L. B., Grigsby, T. D., & Woods, S. (1998). The conflicting demands of work, family, and school among students at an urban university. *Journal of Psychology, 132*(2), 220–226.

Hancock, P. A., & Ganey, H. C. N. (2003). From the inverted-U to the extended-U: The evolution of a law of psychology. *Journal of Human Performance in Extreme Environments, 7*(1), 5–14.

Hansell, J. H. (2007). *Abnormal psychology: The enduring issues* (2nd ed.). New York: Wiley.

Hansen, C. J., Stevens, L. C., & Coast, J. R. (2001). Exercise duration and mood state. *Health Psychology, 20*(4), 267–275.

Hanton, S., Mellalieu, S. D., & Hall, R. (2004). Self-confidence and anxiety interpretation: A qualitative investigation. *Psychology of Sport & Exercise, 5*(4), 477–495.

Harding, D. J., Fox, C., & Mehta, J. D. (2002). Studying rare events through qualitative case studies. *Sociological Methods & Research, 31*(2), 174–217.

Harding, R. W., Morgan, F. H., Indermaur, D., Ferrante, A. M., et al. (1998). Road rage and the epidemiology of violence. *Studies on Crime & Crime Prevention, 7*(2), 221–238.

Hare, R. D. (2006). Psychopathy: A clinical and forensic overview. *Psychiatric Clinics of North America, 29*(3), 709–724.

Harel, J., & Sher, A. (2003). Insufficient responsiveness in ambivalent mother-infant relationships: Contextual and affective aspects. *Infant Behavior and Development, 26*(3), 371–383.

Harker, L., & Keltner, D. (2001). Expressions of positive emotion in women's college yearbook pictures and their relationship to personality and life outcomes across adulthood. *Journal of Personality & Social Psychology, 80*(1), 112–124.

Harlow, H. F., & Harlow, M. K. (1962). Social deprivation in monkeys. *Scientific American, 207*, 136–146.

Harlow, J. M. (1868). Recovery from the passage of an iron bar through the head. *Publications of the Massachusetts Medical Society, 2*, 327–347.

Harm, D. L. (2002). Motion sickness neurophysiology, physiological correlates, and treatment. In K. M. Stanney (Ed.), *Handbook of virtual environments: Design, implementation, and applications.* Hillsdale, NJ: Erlbaum.

Harrigan, J. A. (2006). Proxemics, kinesics, and gaze. In J. A. Harrigan, R. Rosenthal, & K. R. Scherer (Eds.), *The new handbook of methods in nonverbal behavior research.* New York: Oxford University Press.

Harrison, P. J., & Weinberger, D. R. (2005). Schizophrenia genes, gene expression, and neuropathology: On the matter of their convergence. *Molecular Psychiatry, 10*(1), 40–68.

Hart, B., & Risley, T. R. (1999). *The social world of children learning to talk.* Baltimore, MD: Paul H. Brookes.

Hart, D., & Carlo, G. (2005). Moral development in adolescence. *Journal of Research on Adolescence. Special Issue: Moral Development, 15*(3), 223–233.

Hartgens, F., & Kuipers, H. (2004). Effects of androgenic-anabolic steroids in athletes. *Sports Medicine, 34*(8), 513–554.

Hartlep, K. L., & Forsyth, G. A. (2000). The effect of self-reference on learning and retention. *Teaching of Psychology, 27*(4), 269–271.

Hartmann, P., Reuter, M., & Nyborg, H. (2006). The relationship between date of birth and individual differences in personality and general intelligence: A large-scale study. *Personality & Individual Differences, 40*(7), 1349–1362.

Harway, M. (Ed.), (2004). *Handbook of couples therapy.* San Francisco, CA: Jossey-Bass.

Hashibe, M., Straif, K., Tashkin, D. P., Morgenstern, H., et al. (2005). Epidemiologic review of marijuana use and cancer risk. *Alcohol, 35*(3), 265–275.

Hashimoto, I., Suzuki, A., Kimura, T., Iguchi, Y., et al. (2004). Is there training-dependent reorganization of digit representations in

area 3b of string players? *Clinical Neurophysiology, 115*(2), 435–447.

Hausfather, A., Toharia, A., LaRoche, C., & Engelsmann, F. (1997). Effects of age of entry, day-care quality and family characteristics on preschool behavior. *Journal of Child Psychology and Psychiatry and Allied Disciplines, 38*, 441–448.

Hawks, J., Wang, E. T., Cochran, G. M., Harpending, H. C., et al. (2007). Recent acceleration of human adaptive evolution. *Proceedings of the National Academy of Sciences, 104*(52), 20753–20758.

Haworth, C. M. A., Wright, M. J., Luciano, M., Martin, N. G., et al. (2010). The heritability of general cognitive ability increases linearly from childhood to young adulthood. *Molecular Psychiatry, 15*, 1112–1120.

Hayne, H., & Rovee-Collier, C. (1995). The organization of reactivated memory in infancy. *Child Development, 66*(3), 893–906.

Health Canada. (n.d.). *Applicant's Guide—Medical Use of Marihuana.* Retrieved September 24, 2012, from http://www.hc-sc.gc.ca/dhp-mps/alt_formats/hecs-sesc/pdf/marihuana/how-comment/applicant-demandeur/applicant-guide-demandeur-eng.pdf.

Health Canada. (2007). *Canadian Community Health Survey, Cycle 2.2, Nutrition (2004).* Retrieved September 15, 2012, from http://www.hc-sc.gc.ca/fn-an/alt_formats/hpfb-dgpsa/pdf/surveill/income_food_sec-sec_alim-eng.pdf.

Health Canada. (2012). *Canadian Alcohol and Drug Use Monitoring Survey: Summary of results for 2010.* Retrieved June 1, 2012, from http://www.hc-sc.gc.ca/hc-ps/drugs-drogues/stat/_2010/summary-sommaire-eng.php.

Heath, R. G. (1963). Electrical self-stimulation of the brain in man. *American Journal of Psychiatry, 120*, 571–577.

Hebb, D. O. (1949). *The organization of behavior.* New York: John Wiley & Sons.

Hecht, J. (2007). *The happiness myth: Why what we think is right is wrong.* New York: HarperCollins.

Heimann, M., & Meltzoff, A. N. (1996, March). Deferred imitation in 9-and 14-month-old infants. *British Journal of Developmental Psychology, 14*, 55–64.

Heine, S. J., & Lehman, D. R. (1999). Culture, self-discrepancies, and self-satisfaction. *Personality & Social Psychology Bulletin, 25*(8), 915–925.

Heine, S. J., Lehman, D. R., Markus, H. R., & Kitayama, S. (1999). Is there a universal need for positive self-regard? *Psychological Review, 106*, 766–794.

Heinrich, A., Schneider, B. A., & Craik, F. I. M. (2008). Investigating the influence of continuous babble on auditory short-term memory performance. *The Quarterly Journal of Experimental Psychology, 61*(5), 735–751.

Heinrichs, R. W. (2001). *In search of madness: Schizophrenia and neuroscience.* New York: Oxford University Press.

Heinze, H. J., Hinrichs, H., Scholz, M., Burchert, W., et al. (1998). Neural mechanisms of global and local processing.

Journal of Cognitive Neuroscience, 10(4), 485–498.

Heisel, M. J., Flett, G. L., & Hewitt, P. L. (2003). Social hopelessness and college student suicide ideation. *Archives of Suicide Research, 7*(3), 221–235.

Hellerstein, D. J., Rosenthal, R. N., Pinsker, H., Samstag, L. W., et al. (1998). A randomized prospective study comparing supportive and dynamic therapies. *Journal of Psychotherapy Practice & Research, 7*(4), 261–271.

Hellige, J. B. (1993). *Hemispheric asymmetry.* Cambridge, MA: Harvard University Press.

Henderson, N. D. (1982). Human behavior genetics. *Annual Review of Psychology, 33*, 403–440.

Henman, L. D. (2001). Humor as a coping mechanism. *Humor: International Journal of Humor Research, 14*(1), 83–94.

Henningsen, D. D., Henningsen, M. L. M., Eden, J., & Cruz, M. G. (2006). Examining the symptoms of groupthink and retrospective sensemaking. *Small Group Research, 37*(1), 36–64.

Hepper, P. G., Wells, D. L., & Lynch, C. (2005). Prenatal thumb sucking is related to postnatal handedness. *Neuropsychologia, 43*(3), 313–315.

Hergenhahn, B. R. (2009). *An introduction to the history of psychology* (6th ed.). Belmont, CA: Cengage Learning/Wadsworth.

Hergenhahn, B. R., & Olson, M. H. (2005). *Introduction to the theories of learning* (7th ed.). Englewood Cliffs, NJ: Prentice Hall.

Hergenhahn, B. R., & Olson, M. (2007). *An introduction to theories of personality* (7th ed.). Englewood Cliffs, NJ: Prentice Hall.

Heriot, S. A., & Pritchard, M. (2004). "Reciprocal Inhibition as the Main Basis of Psychotherapeutic Effects" by Joseph Wolpe (1954). *Clinical Child Psychology & Psychiatry, 9*(2), 297–307.

Hermann, B., Seidenberg, M., Sears, L., Hansen, R., et al. (2004). Cerebellar atrophy in temporal lobe epilepsy affects procedural memory. *Neurology, 63*(11), 2129–2131.

Herrmann, D. J., Yoder, C. Y., Gruneberg, M., & Payne, D. G. (2006). *Applied cognitive psychology: A textbook.* Mahwah, NJ: Erlbaum.

Herxheimer, A., & Waterhouse, J. (2003). The prevention and treatment of jet lag. *British Medical Journal, 326*(7384), 296–297.

Herz, R. S. (2001). Ah sweet skunk! *Cerebrum, 3*(4), 31–47.

Hettich, P. I. (2005). *Connect college to career: Student guide to work and life transition.* Belmont, CA: Wadsworth.

Higbee, K. L., Clawson, C., DeLano, L., & Campbell, S. (1990). Using the link mnemonic to remember errands. *Psychological Record, 40*(3), 429–436.

Higham, P. A., & Gerrard, C. (2005). Not all errors are created equal: Metacognition and changing answers on multiple-choice tests. *Canadian Journal of Experimental Psychology. Special Issue on 2003 Festschrift for Lee R. Brooks, 59*(1), 28–34.

Hilgard, E. R. (1968). *The experience of hypnosis.* New York: Harcourt Brace Jovanovich.

Hilgard, E. R. (1977). *Divided consciousness.* New York: Wiley.

Hilgard, E. R. (1994). Neodissociation theory. In S. J. Lynn & J. W. Rhue (Eds.), *Dissociation: Clinical, theoretical and research perspectives.* New York: Guilford.

Hill, E. M. & Maggi, S. (2011). Emotional intelligence and smoking: Protective and risk factors among Canadian young adults. *Personality and Individual Differences, 51*(1), 45–50.

Hinterberger, T., Kübler, A., Kaiser, J., Neumann, N., et al. (2003). A brain–computer interface (BCI) for the locked-in: Comparison of different EEG classifications for the thought translation device. *Clinical Neurophysiology, 114*(3), 416–425.

Hintzman, D. L. (2005). Memory strength and recency judgments. *Psychonomic Bulletin & Review, 12*(5), 858–864.

Hittner, J. B., & Daniels, J. R. (2002). Gender-role orientation, creative accomplishments and cognitive styles. *Journal of Creative Behavior, 36*(1), 62–75.

Hobson, J. A. (2000). Dreams: Physiology. In A. Kazdin (Ed.), *Encyclopedia of psychology.* Washington: American Psychological Association.

Hobson, J. A. (2001). *The dream drugstore.* Cambridge, MA: MIT Press.

Hobson, J. A. (2005). Sleep is of the brain, by the brain and for the brain. *Nature, 437*(7063), 1254–1256.

Hobson, J. A., Pace-Schott, E. F., & Stickgold, R. (2000). Dream science 2000. *Behavioral & Brain Sciences, 23*(6), 1019–1035; 1083–1121.

Hochstenbach, J., Mulder, T., van Limbeek, J., Donders, R., et al. (1998). Cognitive decline following stroke: A comprehensive study of cognitive decline following stroke. *Journal of Clinical & Experimental Neuropsychology, 20*(4), 503–517.

Hodapp, R. M. (1994). Mental retardation. In V.S. Ramachandran (Ed.), *Encyclopedia of human behavior* (Vol. 3). San Diego: Academic Press.

Hofer, B. K., & Yu, S. L. (2003). Teaching self-regulated learning through a "Learning to Learn" course. *Teaching of Psychology, 30*(1), 30–33.

Hoffart, A. (2005). Interpersonal therapy for social phobia: Theoretical model and review of the evidence. In M. E. Abelian (Ed.), *Focus on psychotherapy research.* Hauppauge, NY: Nova Science Publishers.

Hoffer, A., & Youngren, V. R. (2004). Is free association still at the core of psychoanalysis? *International Journal of Psychoanalysis, 85*(6), 1489–1492.

Hoffman, H. G., Garcia-Palacios, A., Carlin, A., Furness, T. A., et al. (2003). Interfaces that heal: Coupling real and virtual objects to treat spider phobia. *International Journal of Human-Computer Interaction, 16*(2), 283–300.

Hohwy, J. & Rosenberg, R. (2005). Unusual experiences, reality testing and delusions of alien control. *Mind & Language, 20*(2), 141–162.

Holden, C. (1980, November). Twins reunited. *Science, 80,* 55–59.

Holmes, J., & Adams, J. W. (2006). Working memory and children's mathematical skills: Implications for mathematical development and mathematics curricula. *Educational Psychology, 26*(3), 339–366.

Holmes, P. S., & Collins, D. J. (2001). The PETTLEP approach to motor imagery: A functional equivalence model for sport psychologists. *Journal of Applied Sport Psychology, 13*(1), 60–83.

Holmes, T., & Masuda, M. (1972, April). Psychosomatic syndrome. *Psychology Today,* 71.

Holmes, T. H., & Rahe, R. H. (1967). The social readjustment rating scale. *Journal of Psychosomatic Research, 11*(2), 213–218.

Holtzen, D. W. (2000). Handedness and professional tennis. *International Journal of Neuroscience, 105*(1–4), 101–111.

Hölzel, B.K., Lazar, S.W., Gard, T., Schuman-Olivier, Z., et al. (2011). How does mindfulness meditation work? Proposing mechanisms of action from a conceptual and neural perspective. *Perspectives on Psychological Science, 6,* 537–559.

Honts, C. R., & Alloway, W. R. (2007). Information does not affect the validity of a comparison question test. *Legal & Criminological Psychology, 12*(2), 311–320.

Hopkins, R. H., & Edwards, R. E. (1972). Pronunciation effects in recognition memory. *Journal of Verbal Learning and Verbal Behavior, 11,* 534–537.

Horn, J., Nelson, C. E., & Brannick, M. T. (2004). Integrity, conscientiousness, and honesty. *Psychological Reports, 95*(1), 27–38.

Horn, R. R., Williams, A. M., Scott, M. A., & Hodges, N. J. (2005). Visual search and coordination changes in response to video and point-light demonstrations without KR. *Journal of Motor Behavior, 37*(4), 265–274.

Horne, J. A., & Reyner, L. A. (1996). Counteracting driver sleepiness: Effects of napping, caffeine, and placebo. *Psychophysiology, 33*(3), 306–309.

Hortman, G. (2003). What do facial expressions convey? *Emotion, 3*(2), 150–166.

Horton, J. E., Crawford, H. J., Harrington, G., & Downs, J. H. (2004). Increased anterior corpus callosum size associated positively with hypnotizability and the ability to control pain. *Brain, 127,* 1741–1747.

Horvath, L. S., Milich, R., Lynam, D., Leukefeld, C., et al. (2004). Sensation seeking and substance use: A cross-lagged panel design. *Individual Differences Research, 2*(3), 175–183.

Hosch, H. M., & Cooper, D. S. (1982). Victimization as a determinant of eyewitness accuracy. *Journal of Applied Psychology, 67,* 649–652.

Houghton, D. P. (2008). Invading and occupying Iraq: Some insights from political psychology. *Peace & Conflict: Journal of Peace Psychology, 14*(2), 169–192.

Howard, I. P., & Rogers, B. J. (2001a). *Seeing in depth* (Vol. 1): *Depth perception.* Toronto: Porteous.

Howard, I. P., & Rogers, B. J. (2001b). *Seeing in depth* (Vol. 2): *Depth perception.* Toronto: Porteous.

Howard, K. I., Kopta, S. M., Krause, M. S., & Orlinsky, D. E. (1986). The dose-effect relationship in psychotherapy. *American Psychologist, 41,* 159–164.

Howes, C. (1997). Children's experiences in center-based child care as a function of teacher background and adult:child ratio. *Merrill-Palmer Quarterly, 43*(3), 404–425.

Hsia, Y., & Graham, C. H. (1997). Color blindness. In A. Byrne & D. R. Hilbert (Eds.), *Readings on color* (Vol. 2): *The science of color.* Cambridge, MA: The MIT Press.

Hubble, M. A., Duncan, B. L., & Miller, S. D. (Eds.). (1999). *The heart and soul of change: What works in therapy.* Washington: American Psychological Association.

Hubel, D. H., & Wiesel, W. N. (2005). *Brain & visual perception: The story of a 25-year collaboration.* New York: Oxford University Press.

Huebner, R. (1998). Hemispheric differences in global/local processing revealed by same-different judgements. *Visual Cognition, 5*(4), 457–478.

Huesmann, L. R., Moise-Titus, J., Podolski, C., & Eron, L. D. (2003). Longitudinal relations between children's exposure to TV violence and their aggressive and violent behavior in young adulthood: 1977–1992. *Developmental Psychology, 39*(2), 201–221.

Hughes, J. R., Oliveto, A. H., Liguori, A., Carpenter, J., et al. (1998). Endorsement of DSM-IV dependence criteria among caffeine users. *Drug & Alcohol Dependence, 52*(2), 99–107.

Hughes, M., Morrison, K., & Asada, K. J. K. (2005). What's love got to do with it? Exploring the impact of maintenance rules, love attitudes, and network support on friends with benefits relationships. *Western Journal of Communication, 69*(1), 49–66.

Huijbregts, S. C., Séguin, J. R., Zelazo, P. D., Parent, S., et al. (2006). Interrelations between maternal smoking during pregnancy, birth weight and sociodemographic factors in the prediction of early cognitive abilities. *Infant & Child Development, 15*(6), 593–607.

Human Rights Watch. (2003). *Ill-equipped: U.S. prisons and offenders with mental illness.* New York: Holt.

Hunsley, J., Lee, C. M., & Aubry, T. (1999). Who uses psychological services in Canada? *Canadian Psychology, 40,* 232–240.

Hunt, E., & Carlson, J. (2007). Considerations relating to the study of group differences in intelligence. *Perspectives on Psychological Science, 2*(2), 194–213.

Hunt, R. R., & Ellis, H. C. (2004). *Fundamentals of cognitive psychology* (7th ed.). New York: McGraw-Hill.

Hunter, E. (1998). Adolescent attraction to cults. *Adolescence, 33*(131), 709–714.

Hunter, J. P., Katz, J., & Davis, K. D. (2003). The effect of tactile and visual sensory inputs on phantom limb awareness. *Brain, 126*(3), 579–589.

Hutchinson, S., Lee, L. H. L., Gaab, N., & Schlaug, G. (2003). Cerebellar volume of musicians. *Cerebral Cortex, 13*(9), 943–949.

Hutchinson, S. R. (2004). Survey research. In K. deMarrais & S. D. Lapan (Eds.), *Foundations for research: Methods of inquiry in education and the social sciences. Inquiry and pedagogy across diverse contexts.* Mahwah, NJ: Erlbaum.

Hutton, T. (2003). *Childhood aggression and exposure to violence in the home.* Statistics Canada: Canadian Centre for Justice Statistics catalogue #85-561-MIE.

Hyde, J. S. (2004). *Half the human experience: The psychology of women* (6th ed.). Boston: Houghton Mifflin.

Hyde, J. S., & DeLamater, J. D. (2006). *Understanding human sexuality* (9th ed.). New York: McGraw-Hill.

Hyde, K. L., & Peretz, I. (2003). What is specific to music processing? Insights from congenital amusia. *Trends in Cognitive Sciences, 7*(8), 362–367.

Hyde, K. L., & Peretz, I. (2004). Brains that are out of tune but in time. *Psychological Science, 15*(5), 356–360.

Hyde, K. L., & Peretz, I. (2005). Congenital amusia: Impaired musical pitch but intact musical time. In J. Syka & M. M. Merzenich (Eds.), *Plasticity and signal representation in the auditory system.* New York: Springer.

Hyman, R. (1996a). Evaluation of the military's twenty-year program on psychic spying. *Skeptical Inquirer, 20*(2), 21–23.

Hyman, R. (1996b). The evidence for psychic functioning: Claims vs. reality. *Skeptical Inquirer, 20*(2), 24–26.

Hyman, R. (2007). Talking with the dead, communicating with the future and other myths created by cold reading. In S. Della Sala (Ed.), *Tall tales about the mind and brain: Separating fact from fiction.* New York: Oxford University Press.

Hysenbegasi, A., Hass, S. L., & Rowland, C. R. (2005). The impact of depression on the academic productivity of university students. *Journal of Mental Health Policy & Economics, 8*(3), 145–151.

Iacono, W. G. (2008). Effective policing: Understanding how polygraph tests work and are used. *Criminal Justice & Behavior, 35*(10), 1295–1308.

Ida, Y., & Mandal, M. K. (2003). Cultural differences in side bias: Evidence from Japan and India. *Laterality: Asymmetries of Body, Brain & Cognition, 8*(2), 121–133.

Ingham, A. G., Levinger, G., Graves, J., & Peckham, V. (1974). The Ringelmann effect: Studies of group size and group performance. *Journal of Personality & Social Psychology, 10,* 371–384.

Iosif, A., & Ballon, B. (2005). Bad moon rising: The persistent belief in lunar connections to madness. *Canadian Medical Association Journal, 173*(12), 1498–1500.

Ironson, G., Freud, B., Strauss, J. L., & Williams, J. (2002). Comparison for two treatments for traumatic stress: A community-based study of EMDR and pro-longed exposure. *Journal of Clinical Psychology, 58*(1), 113–128.

Iversen, L. (2006). *Speed, Ecstasy, Ritalin: The science of amphetamines.* New York: Oxford University Press.

Ivey, A. E., & Galvin, M. (1984). Microcounseling: A metamodel for counseling, therapy, business, and medical interviews. In D. Larson (Ed.), *Teaching psychological skills.* Monterey, CA: Brooks/Cole.

Izard, C. E. (1977). *Human emotions.* New York: Plenum.

Izard, C. E. (1990). Facial expressions and the regulation of emotions. *Journal of Personality & Social Psychology, 58*(3), 487–498.

Izard, C. E., Fantauzzo, C. A., Castle, J. M., Haynes, O. M., et al. (1995). The ontogeny and significance of infants' facial expressions in the first 9 months of life. *Developmental Psychology, 31*(6), 997–1013.

Jablonski, N. G., & Chaplin, G. (2000). The evolution of human skin coloration. *Journal of Human Evolution, 39*(1), 57–106.

Jackson, S. L. (2008). *Research methods: A modular approach.* Belmont, CA: Cengage Learning/Wadsworth.

Jackson, T., Fritch, A., Nagasaka, T., & Gunderson, J. (2002). Towards explaining the association between shyness and loneliness. *Social Behavior & Personality, 30*(3), 263–270.

Jackson, T., Towson, S., & Narduzzi, K. (1997). Predictors of shyness. *Social Behavior & Personality, 25*(2), 149–154.

Jacob, A., Prasad, S., Boggild, M., & Chandratre, S. (2004). Charles Bonnet syndrome: Elderly people and visual hallucinations. *British Medical Journal, 328*(7455), 1552–1554.

Jacobs, B. L. (2004). Depression: The brain finally gets into the act. *Current Directions in Psychological Science, 13*(3), 103–106.

Jacobs, S. R., & Dodd, D. K. (2003). Student burnout as a function of personality, social support, and workload. *Journal of College Student Development, 44*(3), 291–303.

Jaeggi, S. M., Buschkuehl, M., Jonides, J., & Perrig, W. J. (2008). Improving fluid intelligence with training on working memory. *Proceedings of the National Academy of Sciences.* Retrieved September 26, 2012, from http://www.pnas.org/content /early/2008/04/25/0801268105.full.pdf.

Jaehnig, W., & Miller, M. L. (2007). Feedback types in programmed instruction: A systematic review. *Psychological Record, 57*(2), 219–232.

Jaffe, J., Beatrice, B., Feldstein, S., Crown, C. L., et al. (2001). Rhythms of dialogue in infancy. *Monographs of the Society for Research in Child Development, 66*(2), vi–131.

Jamison, K. R. (2001). Suicide in the young: An essay. *Cerebrum, 3*(3), 39–42.

Janis, I. L. (1989). *Crucial decisions.* New York: Free Press.

Janowiak, J. J., & Hackman, R. (1994). Meditation and college students' self-actualization and rated stress. *Psychological Reports, 75*(2), 1007–1010.

Janssen, S. A., & Arntz, A. (2001). Real-life stress and opioid-mediated analgesia in novice parachute jumpers. *Journal of Psychophysiology, 15*(2), 106–113.

Janus, S. S., & Janus, C. L. (1993). *The Janus report.* New York: Wiley.

Jarvik, M. E. (1995). "The scientific case that nicotine is addictive": Comment. *Psychopharmacology, 117*(1), 18–20.

Jarvin, L., & Sternberg, R. J. (2003). Alfred Binet's contributions to educational psychology. In B. J. Zimmerman & D. H. Schunk (Eds.), *Educational psychology: A century of contributions.* Mahwah, NJ: Erlbaum.

Jawahar, I. M., Stone, T. H., & Kisamore, J. L. (2007). Role conflict and burnout: The direct and moderating effects of political skill and perceived organizational support on burnout dimensions. *International Journal of Stress Management, 14*(2), 142–159.

Jay, T. B. (2003). *Psychology of language.* Upper Saddle River, NJ: Prentice Hall.

Jeffery, R. W., & Wing R. R. (2001). The effects of an enhanced exercise program on long-term weight loss. *Obesity Research, 9*(Suppl. 3), O193.

Jenkins, J. G., & Dallenbach, K. M. (1924). Oblivescence during sleep and waking. *American Journal of Psychology, 35,* 605–612.

Jensen, A. R. (2008). Review of "Howard Gardner Under Fire: The Rebel Psychologist Faces His Critics." *Intelligence, 36*(1), 96–97.

Jerabek, I., & Standing, L. (1992). Imagined test situations produce contextual memory enhancement. *Perceptual & Motor Skills, 75*(2), 400.

Joffe, R. T. (2006). Is the thyroid still important in major depression? *Journal of Psychiatry & Neuroscience, 31*(6), 367–368.

Johnson, K. E., & Mervis, C. B. (1997). Effects of varying levels of expertise on the basic level of categorization. *Journal of Experimental Psychology: General, 126*(3), 248–277.

Johnson, S. (2005). *Everything bad is good for you: How today's popular culture is actually making us smarter.* New York: Riverhead.

Johnson, S. M., & White, G. (1971). Self-observation as an agent of behavioral change. *Behavior Therapy, 2,* 488–497.

Johnson, T. J. (2002)., College students' self-reported reasons for why drinking games end. *Addictive Behaviors, 27*(1), 145–153.

Johnson, W., Jung, R. E., Colom, R., & Haier, R. J. (2008). Cognitive abilities independent of IQ correlate with regional brain structure. *Intelligence, 36*(1), 18–28.

Jones, E. E., & Nisbett, R. E. (1971). The actor and observer: Divergent perceptions of the causes of behavior. In E. E. Jones, D. E. Kanouse, H. H. Kelley, R. E. Nisbett, et al. (Eds.), *Attribution: Perceiving the causes of behavior.* Morristown, NJ: General Learning Press.

Jones, G. V., & Martin, M. (2001). Confirming the X-linked handedness gene as recessive, not additive. *Psychological Review, 108*(4), 811–813.

Jones, L., & Petruzzi, D. C. (1995). Test anxiety: A review of theory and current

treatment. *Journal of College Student Psychotherapy, 10*(1), 3–15.

Jones, M. K., & Menzies, R. G. (1998). Danger ideation reduction therapy (DIRT) for obsessive-compulsive washers. *Behaviour Research & Therapy, 36*(10), 959–970.

Jonides, J., Lewis, R. L., Nee, D. E., Lustig, C. A., et al. (2008). The mind and brain of short-term memory. *Annual Review of Psychology, 59,* 193–224.

Jorgensen, G. (2006). Kohlberg or Gillingan: Duet or duel? *Journal of Moral Education, 35*(2), 179–196.

Jouvet, M. (1999). *The paradox of sleep.* Boston: MIT Press.

Juliano, L. M., & Griffiths, R. R. (2004). A critical review of caffeine withdrawal: Empirical validation of symptoms and signs, incidence, severity, and associated features. *Psychopharmacology, 176*(1), 1–29.

Julien, R. M. (2005). *A primer of drug action: A comprehensive guide to the actions, uses, and side effects* (10th ed.). New York: Worth.

Junker, M.-O. (2003). A Native American view of the "mind" as seen in the lexicon of cognition in East Cree. *Cognitive Linguistics. Special talking about thinking across languages, 14*(2–3), 167–194.

Jussim, L., & Harber, K. D. (2005). Teacher expectations and self-fulfilling prophecies: Knowns and unknowns, resolved and unresolved controversies. *Personality & Social Psychology Review, 9*(2), 131–155.

Kadosh, R. C., & Henik, A. (2007). Can synaesthesia research inform cognitive science? *Trends in Cognitive Sciences, 11*(4), 177–184.

Kagan, J. (1971). *Change and continuity in infancy.* New York: Wiley.

Kagan, J. (1989). Temperamental contributions to social behavior. *American Psychologist, 44*(4), 668–674.

Kagan, J. (1999). Born to be shy? In R. Conlan (Ed.), *States of mind.* New York: Wiley.

Kagan, J. (2004). New insights into temperament. *Cerebrum, 6*(1), 51–66.

Kahneman, D. (2003). A perspective on judgment and choice. *American Psychologist, 58*(9), 697–720.

Kahneman, D., Krueger, A. B., Schkade, D., Schwarz, N., et al. (2004). A survey method for characterizing daily life experience: The day reconstruction method. *Science, 306*(5702), 1776–1780.

Kahneman, D., Slovic, P., & Tversky, A. (1982). *Judgment under uncertainty: Heuristics and biases.* Cambridge, MA: Cambridge University Press.

Kahneman, D., & Tversky, A. (1972). Subjective probability: A judgment of representativeness. *Cognitive Psychology, 3,* 430–454.

Kahneman, D., & Tversky, A. (1973). On the psychology of prediction. *Psychological Review, 80,* 237–251.

Kail, R. V., & Cavanaugh, J. C. (2010). *Human development: A life-span view* (5th ed.). Belmont, CA: Cengage Learning/Wadsworth.

Kaitz, M., Zvi, H., Levy, M., Berger, A., et al. (1995). The uniqueness of mother–own-infant interactions. *Infant Behavior & Development, 18*(2), 247–252.

Kalal, D. M. (1999). Critical thinking in clinical practice: Pseudoscience, fad psychology, and the behavioral therapist. *The Behavior Therapist, 22*(4), 81–84.

Kalat, J. W. (2009). *Biological psychology* (10th ed.). Belmont, CA: Cengage Learning/Wadsworth.

Kalat, J. W. (2013). *Biological psychology* (11th ed.). Belmont, CA: Wadsworth.

Kalat, J. W., & Shiota, M. N. (2007). *Emotion.* Belmont, CA: Wadsworth.

Kallio, S., & Revonsuo, A. (2003). Hypnotic phenomena and altered states of consciousness: A multilevel framework of description and explanation. *Contemporary Hypnosis, 20*(3), 111–164.

Kamimori, G. H., Johnson, D., Thorne, D., & Belenky, G. (2005). Multiple caffeine doses maintain vigilance during early morning operations. *Aviation, Space, & Environmental Medicine, 76*(11), 1046–1050.

Kaplan, P. S. (1998). *The human odyssey.* Pacific Grove, CA: Brooks/Cole.

Kapleau, P. (1966). *The three pillars of Zen.* New York: Harper & Row.

Kapur, S., & Lecrubier, Y. (Eds.) (2003). *Dopamine in the pathophysiology and treatment of schizophrenia: New findings.* Washington: Taylor & Francis.

Karim, A. A., Hinterberger, T., Richter, J., Mellinger, J., et al. (2006). Neural internet: Web surfing with brain potentials for the completely paralyzed. *Neurorehabilitation & Neural Repair, 20*(4), 508–515.

Karon, B. P., & Widener, A. J. (1997). Repressed memories and World War II: Lest we forget! *Professional Psychology: Research & Practice, 28*(4), 338–340.

Kassin, S. M. (2005). On the psychology of confessions: Does innocence put innocents at risk? *American Psychologist, 60*(3), 215–228.

Kassin, S. M., Fein, S., & Markus, H. R. (2008). *Social psychology* (7th ed.). Boston: Houghton Mifflin.

Kassin, S. M., Tubb, V. A., Hosch, H. M., & Memon, A. (2001). On the "general acceptance" of eyewitness testimony research. *American Psychologist, 56*(5), 405–416.

Kataria, S. (2004). A clinical guide to pediatric sleep: Diagnosis and management of sleep problems. *Journal of Developmental & Behavioral Pediatrics, 25*(2), 132–133.

Kaufman, A. S. (2000). Intelligence tests and school psychology: Predicting the future by studying the past. *Psychology in the Schools, 37*(1), 7–16.

Kaufman, L., & Kaufman, J. H. (2000). Explaining the moon illusion. *Proceedings of the National Academy of Sciences, 97*(1), 500–505.

Kawai, K., Sugimoto, K., Nakashima, K., Miura, H., et al. (2000). Leptin as a modulator of sweet taste sensitivities in mice. *Proceedings: National Academy of Sciences, 97*(20), 11044–11049.

Kawasaki, H., Adolphs, R., Oya, H., Kovach, C., et al. (2005). Analysis of single-unit responses to emotional scenes in human

ventromedial prefrontal cortex. *Journal of Cognitive Neuroscience, 17*(10), 1509–1518.

Kazdin, A. E. (1975). *Behavior modification in applied settings.* Homewood, IL: Dorsey Press.

Kebbell, M. R., & Wagstaff, G. F. (1998). Hypnotic interviewing: The best way to interview eyewitnesses? *Behavioral Sciences & the Law, 16*(1), 115–129.

Keefe, F. J., Abernethy, A. P., & Campbell, L. C. (2005). Psychological approaches to understanding and treating disease-related pain. *Annual Review of Psychology, 56,* 601–630.

Keel, P. K., & Klump, K. L. (2003). Are eating disorders culture-bound syndromes? Implications for conceptualizing their etiology. *Psychological Bulletin, 129*(5), 747–769.

Keller, H., Kartner, J., Borke, J., Yovsi, R., et al. (2005). Parenting styles and the development of the categorical self: A longitudinal study on mirror self-recognition in Cameroonian Nso and German families. *International Journal of Behavioral Development, 29*(6), 496–504.

Keller, M. C., & Young, R. K. (1996). Mate assortment in dating and married couples. *Personality & Individual Differences, 21*(2), 217–221.

Kellman, P. J., & Arterberry, M. E. (2006). Infant visual perception. In W. Damon, R. M. Lerner, D. Kuhn, & R. S. Siegler (Eds.), *Handbook of child psychology* (Vol. 2): *Cognition, perception and language* (6th ed.). Hoboken, NJ: Wiley.

Kelly, I. W. (1999). "Debunking the debunkers": A response to an astrologer's debunking of skeptics. *Skeptical Inquirer,* Nov-Dec, 37–43.

Kelly, M. P., Strassberg, D. S., & Turner, C. M. (2006). Behavioral assessment of couples' communication in female orgasmic disorder. *Journal of Sex & Marital Therapy, 32*(2), 81–95.

Kelly, T. H., Foltin, R.W., Emurian, C. S., & Fischman, M. W. (1990). Multidimensional behavioral effects of marijuana. *Progress in Neuro-Psychopharmacology & Biological Psychiatry, 14*(6), 885–902.

Kennedy, P. R., & Bakay, R. A. (1998). Restoration of neural output from a paralyzed patient by a direct brain connection. *Neuroreport, 9*(8), 1707–1711.

Kenneth, M., Carpenter, K. M., & Hasin, D. S. (1998). Reasons for drinking alcohol. *Psychology of Addictive Behaviors, 12*(3), 168–184.

Kensinger, E. A. (2007). Negative emotion enhances memory accuracy: Behavioral and neuroimaging evidence. *Current Directions in Psychological Science, 16*(4), 213–218.

Kernis, M. H., & Goldman, B. M. (2005). Authenticity, social motivation, and psychological adjustment. In J. P. Forgas, K. D. Williams, & S. M. Laham (Eds.), *Social motivation: Conscious and unconscious processes.* New York: Cambridge University Press.

Keysers, C., Xiao, D.-K., Földiák, P., & Perrett, D. I. (2005). Out of sight but not out of mind: The neurophysiology of iconic memory in the superior temporal sulcus. *Cognitive Neuropsychology, 22*(3–4), 316–332.

Kida, T. E. (2006). *Don't believe everything you think.* Buffalo, NY: Prometheus.

Kidd, E., & Bavin, E. L., (2007). Lexical and referential inferences on on-line spoken language comprehension: A comparison of adults and primary-school-age children. *First Language, 27*(1), 29–52.

Kiecolt-Glaser, J. K., McGuire, L. Robles, T. F., & Glaser, R. (2002). Emotions, morbidity, and mortality. *Annual Review of Psychology, 53*, 83–107.

Kihlstrom, J. F. (1985). Hypnosis. *Annual Review of Psychology, 36*, 385–418.

Killen, J. D., & Fortmann, S. P. (1997). Craving is associated with smoking relapse. *Experimental & Clinical Psychopharmacology, 5*(2), 137–142.

Kim-Cohen, J., Moffitt, T. E., Caspi, A., & Taylor, A. (2004). Genetic and environmental processes in young children's resilience and vulnerability to socioeconomic deprivation. *Child Development, 75*(3), 651–668.

Kimura, D. (1996). Sex, sexual orientation and sex hormones influence human cognitive function. *Current Opinion in Neurobiology, 6*, 259–263.

Kimura, D. (1999). Sex differences in the brain. *Scientific American, 10,* Summer Quarterly, 26–31.

Kimura, D. (2002). Sex differences in the brain. *Scientific American Special Edition, 12*(1), 32–37.

Kimura, D. (2004). Human sex differences in cognition, fact, not predicament. *Sexualities, Evolution & Gender, 6*(1), 45–53.

Kimura, D., & Clarke, P. G. (2002). Women's advantage on verbal memory is not restricted to concrete words. *Psychological Reports, 91*(3, Pt. 2), 1137–1142.

King, N. J., Muris, P., & Ollendick, T. H. (2005). Childhood fears and phobias: Assessment and treatment. *Child & Adolescent Mental Health, 10*(2), 50–56.

Kingsley, C. H., & Lambert, K. G. (2006). The maternal brain. *Scientific American, 294*(1), 72–79.

Kirsch, I. (2005). The flexible observer and neodissociation theory. *Contemporary Hypnosis, 22*(3), 121–122.

Kirsch, I., & Lynn, S. J. (1995). The altered state of hypnosis. *American Psychologist, 50*(10), 846–858.

Kirsch, I., & Sapirstein, G. (1998). Listening to Prozac but hearing placebo: A meta-analysis of antidepressant medication. *Prevention & Treatment, 1*(June 26), Article 0002a.

Kirsh, S. J. (2005). *Children, adolescents, and media violence: A critical look at the research.* Newbury Park: Sage.

Kirveskari, E., Salmelin, R., & Hari, R. (2006). Neuromagnetic responses to vowels vs. tones reveal hemispheric lateralization. *Clinical Neurophysiology, 117*(3), 643–648.

Kiser, L. J., Heston, J. D., & Paavola, M. (2006). Day treatment centers/partial hospitalization settings. In T. A. Petti & C. Salguero (Eds.), *Community child & adolescent psychiatry: A manual of clinical practice and consultation.* Washington: American Psychiatric Publishing.

Kisilevsky, B. S., Hains, S. M. J., Jacquet, A. Y., Granier-Deferre, C., et al. (2004). Maturation of fetal responses to music. *Developmental Science, 7*(5), 550–559.

Kitayama, S., Markus, H. R., & Kurokawa, M. (2000). Culture, emotion, and well-being: Good feelings in Japan and the United States. *Cognition and emotion, 14,* 93–124.

Kitayama, S., Markus, H. R., Matsumoto, H., & Norasakkunkit, V. (1997). Individual and collective processes in the construction of the self. *Journal of Personality & Social Psychology, 72*(6), 1245–1267.

Klassen, R. M., Ang, R. P., Chong, W. H., Krawchuk, L. L., et al. (2010). Academic procrastination in two settings: Motivation correlates, behavioral patterns, and negative impact of procrastination in Canada and Singapore. *Applied Psychology, 59*(3), 361–379.

Klaus, M. H., & Kennell, J. H. (1982). *Parent–infant bonding.* St. Louis: Mosby.

Klein, B., Richards, J. C., & Austin, D. W. (2006). Efficacy of internet therapy for panic disorder. *Journal of Behavior Therapy & Experimental Psychiatry, 37*(3), 213–238.

Klein, K., & Boals, A. (2001a). The relationship of life event stress and working memory capacity. *Applied Cognitive Psychology, 15*(5), 565–579.

Klein, K., & Boals, A. (2001b). Expressive writing can increase working memory capacity. *Journal of Experimental Psychology: General, 130*(3), 520–533.

Kleinke, C. L., Peterson, T. R., & Rutledge, T. R. (1998). Effects of self-generated facial expressions on mood. *Journal of Personality and Social Psychology, 74*(1), 272–279.

Klohnen, E. C., & Luo, S. (2003). Interpersonal attraction and personality: What is attractive—self similarity, ideal similarity, complementarity or attachment security? *Journal of Personality & Social Psychology, 85*(4), 709–722.

Knaus, W. J., & Ellis, A. (2002). *The procrastination workbook: Your personalized program for breaking free from the patterns that hold you back.* Oakland, CA: New Harbinger Press.

Knoops, K. T. B., de Groot, L. C., Kromhout, D., Perrin, A., et al. (2004). Mediterranean diet, lifestyle factors, and 10-year mortality in elderly European men and women. *Journal of the American Medical Association, 292*(12), 1433–1439.

Koch, C. (2004). *The quest for consciousness: A neurobiological approach.* Englewood, CO: Roberts and Co.

Koch, W. H., & Pratarelli, M. E. (2004). Effects of intro/extraversion and sex on social internet use. *North American Journal of Psychology, 6*(3), 371–382.

Koepke, J. E., & Bigelow, A. E. (1997). Observations of newborn suckling behavior. *Infant Behavior & Development, 20*(1), 93–98.

Kohlberg, L. (1969). The cognitive-developmental approach to socialization. In A. Goslin (Ed.), *Handbook of socialization theory and research.* Chicago: Rand McNally.

Kohlberg, L. (1981). *Essays on moral development* (Vol. 1): *The philosophy of moral development.* San Francisco: Harper.

Kohn, A. (1988, March 21). Shock therapy makes a comeback. *Los Angeles Times,* Part II, p. 5.

Köke, A., Schouten J. S., Lamerichs-Geelen. M. J. H., Lipsch J. S. M., et al. (2004). Pain reducing effect of three types of transcutaneous electrical nerve stimulation in patients with chronic pain: A randomized crossover trial. *Pain, 108*(1–2), 36–42.

Kolb, B. (1990). Recovery from occipital stroke: A self-report and an inquiry into visual processes. *Canadian Journal of Psychology, 44*(2), 130–147.

Kolb, B., Gibb, R., & Gorny, G. (2003). Experience-dependent changes in dendritic arbor and spine density in neocortex vary with age and sex. *Neurobiology of Learning & Memory, 79*(1), 1–10.

Kolb, B., Robbin, G., & Terry, E. R. (2003). Brain plasticity and behavior. *Current Directions in Psychological Science, 12*(1), 1–5.

Kolers, P. A. (1975). Specificity of operations in sentence recognition. *Cognitive Psychology, 7*(3), 289–306.

Konner, M. (1991). *Childhood.* Boston: Little, Brown.

Kopta, M. S., Lueger, R. J., Saunders, S. M., & Howard, K. I. (1999). Individual psychotherapy outcome and process research. *Annual Review of Psychology, 50,* 441–469.

Korol, C., Craig, K. D., & Firestone, P. (2003). Dissociative and somatoform disorders. In P. Firestone & W. L. Marshall (Eds.), *Abnormal psychology: Perspectives* (2nd ed.). Toronto: Prentice Hall.

Kosslyn, S. M. (1983). *Ghosts in the mind's machine.* New York: Norton.

Kosslyn, S. M. (1985, May). Stalking the mental image. *Psychology Today,* 23–28.

Kosslyn, S. M. (2005). Mental images and the brain. *Cognitive Neuropsychology, 22*(3–4), 333–347.

Kosslyn, S. M., Ball, T. M., & Reiser, B. J. (1978). Visual images preserve metric spatial information: Evidence from studies of image scanning. *Journal of Experimental Psychology: Human Perception and Performance, 4,* 47–60.

Kosslyn, S. M., Thompson, W. L., Costantini-Ferrando, M. F., Alpert, N. M., et al. (2000). Hypnotic visual illusion alters color processing in the brain. *American Journal of Psychiatry, 157*(8), 1279–1284.

Kosson, D. S., Suchy, Y., Mayer, A. R., & Libby, J. (2002). Facial affect recognition in criminal psychopaths. *Emotion, 2*(4), 398–411.

Kotkin, M., Daviet, C., & Gurin, J. (1996). The Consumer Reports mental health survey. *American Psychologist, 51*(10), 1080–1082.

Kottler, J. A. (2004). *Introduction to therapeutic counseling.* Belmont, CA: Wadsworth.

Kowert, P. A. (2002). Groupthink or deadlock: When do leaders learn from their advisors? *SUNY series on the presidency.* Albany: State University of New York Press.

Kozart, M. F. (2002). Understanding efficacy in psychotherapy. *American Journal of Orthopsychiatry, 72*(2), 217–231.

Kozlowski, L. T., Goldberg, M. E., Yost, B. A., White, E., et al. (1998). Smokers' misperceptions of light and ultra-light cigarettes may keep them smoking. *American Journal of Preventive Medicine, 15*(1), 9–16.

Krakow, B., & Krakow, J. K. (2002). *Turning nightmares into dreams.* Albuquerque, NM: New Sleepy-Times.

Krakow, B., & Zadra, A. (2006). Clinical management of chronic nightmares: Imagery rehearsal therapy. *Behavioral Sleep Medicine, 4*(1), 45–70.

Krantz, D. S., & McCeney, M. K. (2002). Effects of psychological and social factors on organic disease. *Annual Review of Psychology, 53,* 341–369.

Ksir, C. J., Hart, C. L., & Ray, O. S. (2006). *Drugs, society, and human behavior* (11th ed.). New York: McGraw-Hill.

Kuehner, C. (2003). Gender differences in unipolar depression: An update of epidemiological findings and possible explanations. *Acta Psychiatrica Scandinavica, 108*(3), 163–174.

Kulik, J., Mahler, H. I. M., & Moore, P. J. (2003). Social comparison affiliation under threat: Effects on recovery from major surgery. In P. Salovey & A. J. Rothman (Eds.), *Social psychology of health: Key readings in social psychology.* New York: Psychology Press.

Kumaran, D., & Maguire, E. A. (2005). The human hippocampus: Cognitive maps or relational memory? *Journal of Neuroscience, 25*(31), 7254–7259.

Kunkel, M. A. (1993). A teaching demonstration involving perceived lunar size. *Teaching of Psychology, 20*(3), 178–180.

La Berge, S. P. (1981, January). Lucid dreaming: Directing the action as it happens. *Psychology Today,* 48–57.

La Berge, S. P. (1985). *Lucid dreaming.* Los Angeles: Tarcher.

LaBar, K. S. (2007). Beyond fear: Emotional memory mechanisms in the human brain. *Current Directions in Psychological Science, 16*(4), 173–177.

LaBar, K. S., & LeDoux, J. E. (2002). Emotional learning circuits in animals and man. In R. J. Davidson, K. R. Scherer, & H. H. Goldsmith (Eds.), *Handbook of affective sciences.* New York: Oxford University Press.

Laberge, L., Petit, D., Simard, C., Vitaro, F., et al. (2001). Development of sleep patterns in early adolescence. *Journal of Sleep Research, 10*(1), 59–67.

Labov, W. (1973). The boundaries of words and their meanings. In C. J. N. Bailey & R. W. Shuy (Eds.), *New ways of analyzing variation in English.* Washington: Georgetown University Press.

LaBrie, R. A., & Shaffer, H. J. (2007). Gambling with adolescent health. *Journal of Adolescent Health, 40*(5), 387–389.

Lacayo, A. (1995). Neurologic and psychiatric complications of cocaine abuse.

Neuropsychiatry, Neuropsychology, & Behavioral Neurology, 8(1), 53–60.

Lachaine, J., Beauchemin, C., & Landry, P. A. (2010). Clinical and economic characteristics of patients with fibromyalgia syndrome. *Clinical Journal of Pain, 26*(4), 284–290.

Lachman, M. E. (2004). Development in midlife. *Annual Review of Psychology, 55,* 305–331.

Lackner, J. R., & DiZio, P. (2005). Vestibular, proprioceptive, and haptic contributions to spatial orientation. *Annual Review of Psychology, 56,* 115–147.

Lacks, P., & Morin, C. M. (1992). Recent advances in the assessment and treatment of insomnia. *Journal of Consulting and Clinical Psychology, 60*(4), 586–594.

Lamb, M. R., & Yund, E. W. (1996). Spatial frequency and attention. *Perception & Psychophysics, 58*(3), 363–373.

Lambert, M. J. (1999). Are differential treatment effects inflated by researcher therapy allegiance? *Clinical Psychology: Science & Practice, 6*(1), 127–130.

Lambert, M. J., & Ogles, B. M. (2004). The efficacy and effectiveness of psychotherapy. In M. J. Lambert (Ed.), *Bergin and Garfield's handbook of psychotherapy and behavior change* (5th ed.). New York: Wiley.

Lambert, W. E. (1987). The effects of bilingual and bicultural experiences on children's attitudes and social perspectives. In P. Homel, M. Palij, & D. Aaronson (Eds.), *Childhood bilingualism.* Hillsdale, NJ: Erlbaum.

Lance, C. E., LaPointe, J. A., & Stewart, A. M. (1994). A test of the context dependency of three causal models of halo rater error. *Journal of Applied Psychology, 79*(3), 332–340.

Landau, J. D., & Bavaria A. J. (2003). Does deliberate source monitoring reduce students's misconceptions about psychology? *Teaching of Psychology, 30,* 311–314.

Landau, J. D., & Leynes, P. A. (2006). Do explicit memory manipulations affect the memory blocking effect? *American Journal of Psychology, 119*(3), 463–479.

Langan, L. A., Sockalingam, R., Caissie, R., and Corsten, G. (2007). Occurrence of otitis media and hearing loss among First Nations elementary school children. *Canadian Journal of Speech-Language Pathology and Audiology, 31*(4), 178–185.

Langer, E. J. (2000). Mindful learning. *Current Directions in Psychological Science, 9,* 220–223.

Langleben, D. D., Loughead, J. W., Bilker, W. B., Ruparel, K., et al. (2005). Telling truth from lie in individual subjects with fast event-related fMRI. *Human Brain Mapping, 26*(4), 262–272.

Langlois, S., & Morrison, P. (2002). Suicide deaths and suicide attempts. *Health Reports, 13,* 9–22 (Statistics Canada, Catalogue No. 82–003–XIE). Retrieved September 26, 2012, from http://www .statcan .gc.ca/pub/82-003-x/2001002 /article /6060-eng.pdf.

Langone, M. D. (2002). Cults, conversion, science, and harm. *Cultic Studies Review, 1*(2), 178–186.

LaPointe, L. L (Ed.). (2005). Feral Children. *Journal of Medical Speech-Language Pathology, 13*(1), vii–ix.

Larsen, R. J., & Buss, D. M. (2005). *Personality psychology* (2nd ed.). New York: McGraw-Hill.

Larsen, R. J., & Kasimatis, M. (1990). Individual differences in entrainment of mood to the weekly calendar. *Journal of Personality & Social Psychology, 58*(1), 164–171.

Larsen, R. J., & Prizmic, Z. (2004). Affect regulation. In R. Baumeister & K. D. Voohs (Eds.), *Handbook of self-regulation: Research, theory, and applications.* London: Guilford.

Larsson, B., Carlsson, J., Fichtel, Å., & Melin, L. (2005). Relaxation treatment of adolescent headache sufferers: Results from a school-based replication series. *Headache: The Journal of Head & Face Pain, 45*(6), 692–704.

Lassonde, M. (1994). Disconnection syndrome in callosal agenesis. In M. Lassonde & M. A. Jeeves (Eds.), *Callosal agenesis: A natural split brain?* (pp. 275–284). New York: Plenum Press.

Latané, L., Nida, S. A., & Wilson, D. W. (1981). The effects of group size on helping behavior. In J. P. Rushton & R. M. Sorrentino (Eds.), *Altruism and helping behavior: Social, personality and developmental perspectives.* Hillsdale, NJ: Erlbaum.

Lau, A. S., Littrownik, A. J., Newton, R. R., Black, M. M., et al. (2006). Factors affecting the link between physical discipline and child externalizing problems in Black and White families. *Journal of Community Psychology, 34*(1), 89–103.

Laurent, G., Stopfer, M., Friedrich, R. W., Rabinovich, M. I., et al. (2001). Odor encoding as an active, dynamical process. *Annual Review of Neuroscience, 24,* 263–297.

Laureys, S, & Boly. M. (2007). What is it like to be vegetative or minimally conscious? *Current Opinion in Neurology, 20,* 609–613.

Lavie, P. (2001). Sleep-wake as a biological rhythm. *Annual Review of Psychology, 52,* 277–303.

Lawson, H. M., & Leck, K. (2006). Dynamics of Internet dating. *Social Science Computer Review, 24*(2), 189–208.

Lay, C., & Verkuyten, M. (1999). Ethnic identity and its relation to personal self-esteem. *Journal of Social Psychology, 139*(3), 288–299.

Lazar, S. W. (2005). Mindfulness research. In C. K. Germer, R. D. Siegel, & P. R. Fulton (Eds.), *Mindfulness and psychotherapy.* New York: Guilford.

Lazar, S. W., Bush, G., Gollub, R. L., Fricchione, G. L., et al. (2000). Functional brain mapping of the relaxation response and meditation. *Neuroreport, 11*(7), 1581–1585.

Lazarus, R. S. (1981, July). Little hassles can be hazardous to health. *Psychology Today,* 12–14.

Lazarus, R. S. (1991a). Progress on a cognitive-motivational-relational theory of emotion. *American Psychologist, 46*(8), 819–834.

Lazarus, R. S. (1991b). Cognition and motivation in emotion. *American Psychologist, 46*(4), 352–367.

Leal, M. C., Shin, Y. J., Laborde, M.-L., Calmels, M.-N., et al. (2003). Music perception in adult cochlear implant recipients. *Acta Oto-Laryngologica, 123*(7), 826–835.

Leary, M. R. (2004). *Introduction to behavioral research methods* (4th ed.). Boston: Allyn & Bacon.

Leatherdale, S. T., & Burkhalter, R. (2012). The substance use profile of Canadian youth: Exploring the prevalence of alcohol, drug and tobacco use by gender and grade. *Addictive Behaviors, 37*(3), 318–322.

Leavens, D. A., & Hopkins, W. D. (1998). Intentional communication by chimpanzees. *Developmental Psychology, 34*(5), 813–822.

LeBlanc, G., & Bearison, D. J. (2004). Teaching and learning as a bi-directional activity: Investigating dyadic interactions between child teachers and child learners. *Cognitive Development, 19*(4), 499–515.

Leclerc, G., Lefrancois, R., Dube, M., Hebert, R., et al. (1998). The self-actualization concept: A content validation. *Journal of Social Behavior & Personality, 13,* 69–84.

Lecomte, D., & Fornes, P. (1998). Suicide among youth and young adults, 15 through 24 years of age. *Journal of Forensic Sciences, 43*(5), 964–968.

LeDoux, J. (1999). The power of emotions. In R. Conlan (Ed.), *States of mind.* New York: Wiley.

LeDoux, J. E. (2000). Emotion circuits in the brain. *Annual Review of Neuroscience, 23,* 155–184.

LeDoux, J. E., & Gorman, J. M. (2001). A call to action: Overcoming anxiety through active coping. *American Journal of Psychiatry. 158*(12), 1953–1955.

Lee, J. M., Ku, J. H., Jang, D. P., Kim, D., et al. (2002). Virtual reality system for treatment of the fear of public speaking using image-based rendering and moving pictures. *CyberPsychology & Behavior, 5*(3), 191–195.

Lee, M., Zimbardo, P. G., & Bertholf, M. (1977, November). Shy murderers. *Psychology Today.*

Leenaars, A. A., Lester, D., & Wenckstern, S. (2005). Coping with: The art and the research. In R. I. Yufit & D. Lester (Eds.), *Assessment, treatment, and prevention of suicidal behavior.* New York: Wiley.

Leeper, R. W. (1935). A study of a neglected portion of the field of learning: The development of sensory organization. *Pedagogical Seminary and Journal of Genetic Psychology, 46,* 41–75.

Lefcourt, H. M. (2003). Humor as a moderator of life stress in adults. In C. E. Schaefer (Ed.), *Play therapy with adults.* New York: Wiley.

Lefkowitz, E. S., & Zeldow, P. B. (2006). Masculinity and femininity predict optimal mental health: A belated test of the androgyny hypothesis. *Journal of Personality Assessment, 87*(1), 95–101.

Lefrançois, G. R. (2006). *Theories of human learning: What the old woman said* (5th ed.). Belmont, CA: Cengage Learning/Wadsworth.

Lehman, D. R., Chiu, C., & Schaller, M. (2004). Psychology and culture. *Annual Review of Psychology, 55,* 689–714.

Leichtman, M. (2004). Projective tests: The nature of the task. In M. J. Hilsenroth & D. L. Segal (Eds.), *Comprehensive handbook of psychological assessment* (Vol. 2): *Personality assessment.* New York: Wiley.

Leiter, M. P., & Maslach, C. (2005). *Banishing burnout: Six strategies for improving your relationship with work.* San Francisco, CA: Jossey-Bass.

Lejuez, C. W., Eifert, G. H., Zvolensky, M. J., & Richards, J. B. (2000). Preference between onset predictable and unpredictable administrations of 20% carbon-dioxide-enriched air. *Journal of Experimental Psychology: Applied, 6*(4), 349–358.

Lenton, A. P., & Bryan, A. (2005). An affair to remember: The role of sexual scripts in perceptions of sexual intent. *Personal Relationships, 12*(4), 483–498.

Lenzenweger, M. F., & Gottesman, I. I. (1994). Schizophrenia. In V. S. Ramachandran (Ed.), *Encyclopedia of human behavior.* San Diego: Academic Press.

Leor, J., Poole, W. K., & Kloner, R. A. (1996). Sudden cardiac death triggered by earthquake. *The New England Journal of Medicine, 334*(7), 413.

Lepore, F. E. (2002). When seeing is not believing. *Cerebrum, 4*(2), 23–38.

Lerner, M. J. (1977). The justice motive: Some hypotheses as to its origins and forms. *Journal of Personality, 45,* 1–52.

Lerner, M. J. (1980). *The belief in a just world: A fundamental delusion.* New York: Plenum Press.

Leslie, K., & Ogilvie, R. (1996). Vestibular dreams: The effect of rocking on dream mentation. *Dreaming: Journal of the Association for the Study of Dreams, 6*(1), 1–16.

Lester, D., & Yang, B. (2005). Regional and time-series studies of suicide in nations of the world. *Archives of Suicide Research, 9*(2), 123–133.

Lettvin, J. Y. (1961). Two remarks on the visual system of the frog. In W. Rosenblith (Ed.), *Sensory communication.* Cambridge, MA: MIT Press.

Levant, R. F. (2001). Men and masculinity. In J. Worell (Ed.), *Encyclopedia of women and gender.* San Diego: Academic Press.

Levant, R. F., Good, G. E., Cook, S. W., O'Neil, J. M., et al. (2006). The Normative Male Alexithymia Scale: Measurement of a gender-linked syndrome. *Psychology of Men & Masculinity, 7*(4), 212–224.

LeVay, S., & Valente, S. M. (2006). *Human sexuality* (2nd ed.). Sunderland, MA: Sinauer Associates.

Levesque, M. J., Steciuk, M., & Ledley, C. (2002). Self-disclosure patterns among well-acquainted individuals. *Social Behavior & Personality, 30*(6), 579–592.

Levi, A. M. (1998). Are defendants guilty if they were chosen in a lineup? *Law & Human Behavior, 22*(4), 389–407.

Levin, B. E. (2006). Metabolic sensing neurons and the control of energy homeostasis. *Physiology & Behavior, 89*(4), 486–489.

Levin, R., & Fireman, G. (2002). Nightmare prevalence, nightmare distress, and self-reported psychological disturbance. *Sleep: Journal of Sleep & Sleep Disorders Research, 25*(2), 205–212.

Levin, R., & Nielsen, T. (2007). Disturbed dreaming, posttraumatic stress disorder, and affect distress: A review and neurocognitive model. *Psychological Bulletin, 133*(3), 482–528.

Levy, D. A. (1989). Social support and the media: Analysis of responses by radio psychology talk show hosts. *Professional Psychology: Research & Practice, 20*(2), 73–78.

Levy, J., & Reid, M. (1976). Cerebral organization. *Science,* 337–339.

Lewis, M. (1995, January–February). Self-conscious emotions. *American Scientist, 83,* 68–78.

Lewy, A. J., Bauer, V. K., Cutler, N. L., Sack, R. L., et al. (1998). Morning vs. evening light treatment of patients with winter depression. *Archives of General Psychiatry, 55*(10), 890–896.

Leyendecker, B., Harwood, R. L., Comparini, L., & Yalçinkaya, A. (2005). Socioeconomic status, ethnicity, and parenting. In T. Luster & L. Okagaki (Eds.), *Parenting: An ecological perspective* (2nd ed.). Mahwah, NJ: Erlbaum.

Lichtenstein, E. (1982). The smoking problem: A behavioral perspective. *Journal of Consulting and Clinical Psychology, 50,* 804–819.

Lichtman, A. H., & Martin, B. R. (2006). Understanding the pharmacology and physiology of cannabis dependence. In R. Roffman & R. S. Stephens (Eds.), *Cannabis dependence. Its nature, consequences and treatment.* New York: Cambridge University Press.

Liddell, S. K. (2003). *Grammar, gesture and meaning in American Sign Language.* Cambridge, MA: Cambridge University Press.

Lilienfeld, S. O. (1999, September/October). Projective measures of personality and psychopathology. *Skeptical Inquirer,* 32–39.

Lilienfeld, S. O., Fowler, K. A., Lohr, J. M., & Lynn, S. (2005). Pseudoscience, non-science & nonsense in clinical psychology: Dangers and remedies. In R. H. Wright & N. A. Cummings (Eds.), *Destructive trends in mental health: The well-intentioned path to harm.* New York: Routledge.

Lindemann, B. (2001). Receptors and transduction in taste. *Nature, 413,* 219–225.

Linden, W. (2005). *Stress management: From basic science to better practice.* Thousand Oaks, CA: Sage.

Linderoth, B., & Foreman, R. D. (2006). Mechanisms of spinal cord stimulation in painful syndromes: Role of animal models. *Pain Medicine, 7*(Suppl. 1), S14–S26.

Lindsay, E. W., Mize, J., & Pettit, G. S. (1997). Differential pay patterns of mothers and fathers of sons and daughters. *Sex Roles, 37*(9–10), 643–661.

Lipps, G., & Yiptong-Avila, J. (1999). *From home to school: How Canadian children cope.* Initial analyses using data from the second cycle of the school component of the National Longitudinal Survey of Children and Youth. Culture, Tourism and the Centre for Education Statistics, Catalogue No. 89F0117XIE.

Lipsey, M. W., & Wilson, D. B. (1993). The efficacy of psychological, educational, and behavioral treatment: Confirmation from meta-analysis. *American Psychologist, 48*(12), 1181–1209.

Liu, X., Matochik, J. A., Cadet, J. L., & London, E. D. (1998). Smaller volume of prefrontal lobe in polysubstance abusers. *Neuropsychopharmacology, 18*(4), 243–252.

Liu, Y., Gao, J., Liu, H., & Fox, P. T. (2000). The temporal response of the brain after eating revealed by functional MRI. *Nature, 405,* 1058–1062.

Lockwood, P., & Pinkus, R. T. (2008). The impact of social comparisons on motivation. In J. Y. Shah & W. L. Gardner (Eds.) *Handbook of Motivation Science.* New York: Guilford Press.

Lodi-Smith, J., Geise, A. C., Roberts, B. W., & Robins, R. W. (2009). Narrating personality change. *Journal of Personality & Social Psychology, 96*(3), 679–689.

Loeber, R., & Hay, D. (1997). Key issues in the development of aggression and violence from childhood to early adulthood. In J. T. Spence (Ed.), *Annual Review of Psychology, 48,* 371–410.

Loftus, E. F. (2003a). Make-believe memories. *American Psychologist, 58*(11), 867–873.

Loftus, E. F. (2003b). Memory in Canadian courts of law. *Canadian Psychology, 44*(3), 207–212.

Loftus, E. F., & Bernstein, D. M. (2005). Rich false memories: The royal road to success. In A.F. Healy (Ed.), *Experimental cognitive psychology and its applications.* Washington: American Psychological Association.

Loftus, E. F., & Ketcham, K. (1994). The myth of repressed memory: False memories and allegations of abuse. New York: St. Martin's Press.

Loftus, E., & Palmer, J. C. (1974). Reconstruction of automobile destruction: An example of interaction between language and memory. *Journal of Verbal Learning and Verbal Behavior, 13,* 585–589.

Lohr, J. M., Tolin, D. F., & Lilienfeld, S. O. (1998). Efficacy of eye movement desensitization and reprocessing. *Behavior Therapy, 29*(1), 123–156.

LoLordo, V. M. (2001). Learned helplessness and depression. In M. E. Carroll & J. B. Overmier (Eds.), *Animal research and human health: Advancing human welfare through behavioral science.* Washington: American Psychological Association.

Long, V. O. (1989). Relation of masculinity to self-esteem and self-acceptance in male professionals, college students, and clients. *Journal of Counseling Psychology, 36*(1), 84–87.

López, S. R., & Guarnaccia, P. J. (2000). Cultural psychopathology: Uncovering the social world of mental illness. *Annual Review of Psychology, 51,* 571–598.

Lorenz, K. (1966). *On aggression.* Translated by M. Kerr-Wilson. New York: Harcourt Brace Jovanovich.

Lorenz, K. (1974). *The eight deadly sins of civilized man.* Translated by M. Kerr-Wilson. New York: Harcourt Brace Jovanovich.

Lovaas, O., & Simmons, J. (1969). Manipulation of self-destruction in three retarded children. *Journal of Applied Behavior Analysis, 2,* 143–157.

Low, K. G., & Feissner, J. M. (1998). Seasonal affective disorder in college students: Prevalence and latitude. *Journal of American College Health, 47*(3), 135–137.

Lubinski, D. (2004). Introduction to the special section on cognitive abilities: 100 years after Spearman's (1904) "'General Intelligence' Objectively Determined and Measured." *Journal of Personality and Social Psychology, 86*(1), 96–111.

Luborsky, L., McLellan, A. T., Diguer, L., Woody, G., et al. (1997). The psychotherapist matters. *Clinical Psychology: Science & Practice, 4*(1), 53–65.

Lucas, F., & Sclafani, A. (1990). Hyperphagia in rats produced by a mixture of fat and sugar. *Physiology & Behavior, 47*(1), 51–55.

Luce, G. G. (1965). Current research on sleep and dreams. Health Service Publication, No. 1389. U. S. Department of Health, Education and Welfare.

Luchins, D. J., Cooper, A. E., Hanrahan, P., & Rasinski, K. (2004). Psychiatrists' attitudes toward involuntary hospitalization. *Psychiatric Services, 55*(9), 1058–1060.

Lumley, M. A. (2004). Alexithymia, emotional disclosure, and health: A program of research. *Journal of Personality. Special Emotions, Personality, and Health, 72*(6), 1271–1300.

Lundh, L., Berg, B., Johansson, H., Nilsson, L., et al. (2002). Social anxiety is associated with a negatively distorted perception of one's own voice. *Cognitive Behaviour Therapy, 31*(1), 25–30.

Lunsky, Y. (2003). Depressive symptoms in intellectual disability: Does gender play a role? *Journal of Intellectual Disability Research, 47*(6), 417–427.

Lunsky, Y. (2004). Suicidality in a clinical and community sample of adults with mental retardation. *Research in Developmental Disabilities, 25*(3), 231–243.

Lunsky, Y., & Gracey, C. (2009). The reported experience of four women with intellectual disabilities receiving emergency psychiatric services in Canada: A qualitative study. *Journal of Intellectual Disabilities, 13*(2), 87–98.

Lunsky, Y., & Palucka, A. M. (2004). Depression in intellectual disability. *Current Opinion in Psychiatry, 17*(5), 359–363.

Luppa, M., Heinrich, S., Angermeyer, M. C., König, H. H., et al. (2007). Cost-of-illness studies of depression: A systematic review. *Journal of Affective Disorders, 98*(1–2), 29–43.

Lustig, C., May, C. P., & Hasher, L. (2001). Working memory span and the role of proactive interference. *Journal of Experimental Psychology: General, 130*(2), 199–207.

Lutz, A., Greischar, L. L., Rawlings, N. B., Ricard, M., et al. (2004). Long-term meditators self-induce high-amplitude gamma synchrony during mental practice. *Proceedings of the National Academy of Sciences, 101,* 1636–1637.

Luyben, P. D., Hipworth, K., & Pappas, T. (2003). Effects of CAI on the academic performance and attitudes of college students. *Teaching of Psychology, 30*(2), 154–158.

Lykken, D. T. (1995). *The antisocial personalities.* Hillsdale, NJ: Erlbaum.

Lykken, D. T. (1998). *A tremor in the blood: Uses and abuses of the lie detector.* New York: Plenum.

Lykken, D. T. (2001). Lie detection. In W. E. Craighead & C. B. Nemeroff (Eds.), *The Corsini encyclopedia of psychology and behavioral science* (3rd ed.). New York: Wiley.

Lynch, K. B., Geller, S. R., & Schmidt, M. G. (2004). Multi-year evaluation of the effectiveness of a resilience-based prevention program for young children. *Journal of Primary Prevention, 24*(3), 335–353.

Lyons, A. C., & Chamberlain, K. (2006). *Health psychology.* Cambridge, MA: Cambridge University Press.

Lyubomirsky, S., & Tucker, K. L. (1998). Implications of individual differences in subjective happiness for perceiving, interpreting, and thinking about life events. *Motivation & Emotion, 22*(2), 155–186.

Lyznicki, J. M., Doege, T. C., Davis, R. M., & Williams, M. A. (1998). Sleepiness, driving, and motor vehicle crashes. *Journal of the American Medical Association, 279*(23), 1908–1913.

Maas, J. (1999). *Power sleep.* New York: HarperCollins.

Mack, A. (2002). Is the visual world a grand illusion? *Journal of Consciousness Studies, 9*(5–6), 102–110.

Macklin, C. B., & McDaniel, M. A. (2005). The bizarreness effect: Dissociation between item and source memory. *Memory, 13*(7), 682–689.

MacLeod, C. M. (2005). The Stroop task in cognitive research. In A. Wenzel & D. C. Rubin (Eds.), *Cognitive methods and their application to clinical research.* Washington: American Psychological Association.

MacLeod, C. M., Gopie, N., Hourihan, K. L., Neary, K. R., et al. (2010). The production effect: Delineation of a phenomenon. *Journal of Experimental Psychology: Learning, Memory, and Cognition, 36*(3), 671–685.

Macmillan, M., & Lena, M. L. (2000). Rehabilitating Phineas Gage. *Neuropsychological rehabilitation, 20*(5), 641–653.

Macmillan, M. (2000). Restoring Phineas Gage: A 150th retrospective. *Journal of the History of the Neurosciences, 9*(1), 46–66.

Maddi, S. R. (2006). Hardiness: The courage to grow from stresses. *Journal of Positive Psychology, 1*(3), 160–168.

Maddock, J., & Glanz, K. (2005). The relationship of proximal normative beliefs and global subjective norms to college students' alcohol consumption. *Addictive Behaviors, 30*(2), 315–323.

Maddock, J. E., Laforge, R. G., Rossi, J. S., & O'Hare, T. (2001). The College Alcohol Problems Scale. *Addictive Behaviors, 26*, 385–398.

Magnusson, A., & Axelsson, J. (1993). The prevalence of seasonal affective disorder is low among descendants of Icelandic emigrants in Canada. *Archives of General Psychiatry, 50*, 947–951.

Maguire, E. A., Frackowiak, R. S. J., & Frith, C. D. (1997). Recalling routes around London: Activation of the hippocampus in taxi drivers. *The Journal of Neuroscience, 17*(8), 7103–7110.

Maguire, E. A., Valentine, E. R., Wilding, J. M., & Kapur, N. (2003). Routes to remembering: The brains behind superior memory. *Nature Neuroscience, 6*(1), 90–95.

Mah, K., & Binik, Y. M. (2001). The nature of human orgasm: A critical review of major trends. *Clinical Psychology Review, 21*(6), 823–856.

Maheu, M. M., Pulier, M. L., Wilhelm, F. H., McMenamin, J. P., et al. (2004). *The mental health professional and the new technologies: A handbook for practice today.* Mahwah, NJ: Lawrence Erlbaum.

Maier, N. R. F. (1949). *Frustration.* New York: McGraw-Hill.

Mailis-Gagnon, A., & Israelson, D. (2005). *Beyond pain: Making the mind-body connection.* Ann Arbor, MI: University of Michigan Press.

Malacad, B. L., & Hess, G. C. (2010). Oral sex: Behaviours and feelings of Canadian young women and implications for sex education. *The European Journal of Contraception and Reproductive Health Care, 15*(3), 177–185.

Malaspina, D., Reichenberg, A., Weiser, M., Fennig, S., et al. (2005). Paternal age and intelligence: Implications for age-related genomic changes in male germ cells. *Psychiatric Genetics, 15*(2), 117–125.

Malenfant, E. C. (2004). Suicide in Canada's immigrant population. *Health Reports, 15* (2), 9–17, (Statistics Canada, Catalogue 82-003).

Manalo, E. (2002). Uses of mnemonics in educational settings: A brief review of selected research. *Psychologia: An International Journal of Psychology in the Orient, 45*(2), 69–79.

Mandler, J. M., & McDonough, L. (1998). On developing a knowledge base in infancy. *Developmental Psychology, 34*(6), 1274–1288.

Mangels, J. A., Picton, T. W., & Craik, F. I. M. (2001). Attention and successful episodic encoding: An event-related potential study. *Brain Research, 11*, 77–95.

Manne, S. (2003). Coping and social support. In A. Nezu, C. Nezu, & P. Geller (Eds.), *Handbook of health psychology* (Vol. 9). New York: Wiley.

Manning, R., Levine, M., & Collins, A. (2007). The Kitty Genovese murder and the social psychology of helping: The parable of the 38 witnesses. *American Psychologist, 62*(6), 555–562.

Mansouri, A., & Adityanjee, A. M. (1995). Delusion of pregnancy in males: A case report and literature review. *Psychopathology, 28*(6), 307–311.

Mantyla, T. (1986). Optimizing cue effectiveness: Recall of 600 incidentally learned words. *Journal of Experimental Psychology: Learning, Memory, & Cognition, 12*(1), 66–71.

Marks, D. F. (2000). *The psychology of the psychic.* Buffalo, NY: Prometheus.

Markus, H. R., & Nurius, P. (1986). Possible selves. *American Psychologist, 41*, 954–969.

Markus, H. R., Uchida, Y., Omoregie, H., Townsend, S. S., et al. (2006). Going for the gold: Models of agency in Japanese and American contexts. *Psychological Science, 17*(2), 103–112.

Marlatt, G. A., Baer, J. S., Donovan, D. M., & Kivlahan, D. R. (1988). Addictive behaviors: Etiology and treatment. *Annual Review of Psychology, 39*, 223–252.

Marmarosh, C., Holtz, A., & Schottenbauer, M. (2005). Group cohesiveness, group-derived collective self-esteem, group-derived hope, and the well-being of group therapy members. *Group Dynamics: Theory, Research, & Practice, 9*(1), 32–44.

Marsiglia, F. F., Kulis, S., Hecht, M. L., & Sills, S. (2004). Ethnicity and ethnic identity as predictors of drug norms and drug use among preadolescents in the US southwest. *Substance Use & Misuse, 39*(7), 1061–1094.

Martin, A. J., & Marsh, H. W. (2003). Fear of failure: Friend or foe? *Australian Psychologist, 38*(1), 31–38.

Martin, C. L., & Fabes, R. A. (2001). The stability and consequences of young children's same-sex peer interactions. *Developmental Psychology, 37*(3), 431–446.

Martin, J. G., & Réale, D. (2008). Temperament, risk assessment and habituation to novelty in eastern chipmunks, *Tamias striatus. Animal Behaviour, 75* (1), 309–318.

Martin, L. R., Friedman, H. S., & Schwartz, J. E. (2007). Personality and mortality risk across the life span: The importance of conscientiousness as a biopsychosocial attribute. *Health Psychology, 26*(4), 428–436.

Martin, R. A., Puhlik-Doris, P., Larsen, G., Gray, J., et al. (2003). Individual differences in uses of humor and their relation to psychological well-being: Development of the Humor Styles Questionnaire. *Journal of Research in Personality, 37*(1), 48–75.

Martin, S. (1995, January). Field's status unaltered by the influx of women. *APA Monitor, 9*.

Martin, W. L. B., & Freitas, M. B. (2002). Mean mortality among Brazilian left-and right-handers: Modification or selective elimination. *Laterality, 7*(1), 31–44.

Martinez-Gonzalez, M. A., Gual, P., Lahortiga, F., Alonso, Y., et al. (2003). Parental factors, mass media influences, and the onset of eating disorders in a prospective population-based cohort. *Pediatrics, 111*, 315–320.

Mashour, G. A., Walker, E. E., & Martuza, R. L. (2005). Psychosurgery: Past, present,

and future. *Brain Research Reviews, 48*(3), 409–419.

Masi, G., Mucci, M., & Millepiedi, S. (2001). Separation anxiety disorder in children and adolescents. *CNS Drugs, 15*(2), 93–104.

Maslach, C., Schaufeli, W. B., & Leiter, M. P. (2001). Job burnout. *Annual Review of Psychology, 52*, 397–422.

Maslow, A. H. (1954). *Motivation and personality.* New York: Harper.

Maslow, A. H. (1967). Self-actualization and beyond. In J. F. T. Bugental (Ed.), *Challenges of humanistic psychology.* New York: McGraw-Hill.

Maslow, A. H. (1969). *The psychology of science.* Chicago: Henry Regnery.

Maslow, A. H. (1970). *Motivation and personality.* New York: Harper & Row.

Maslow, A. H. (1971). *The farther reaches of human nature.* New York: Viking.

Masse, L. C., & Tremblay, R. E. (1997). Behavior of boys in kindergarten and the onset of substance use during adolescence. *Archives of General Psychiatry, 54*(1), 62.

Masten, A. S. (2001). Ordinary magic: Resilience processes in development. *American Psychologist, 56*(3), 227–238.

Masters, J. L., & Holley, L. M. (2006). A glimpse of life at 67: The modified future-self worksheet. *Educational Gerontology, 32*(4), 261–269.

Masters, W. H., & Johnson, V. E. (1966). *Human sexual response.* Boston: Little, Brown.

Masters, W. H., & Johnson, V. E. (1970). *The pleasure bond: A new look at sexuality and commitment.* Boston: Little, Brown.

Masuda, T., Gonzalez, R., Kwan, L., & Nisbett, R. E. (2008). Culture and aesthetic preference: Comparing the attention to context of East Asians and Americans. *Personality & Social Psychology Bulletin, 34*(9), 1260–1275.

Matheny, K. B., Brack, G. L., McCarthy, C. J., & Penick, J. M. (1996). The effectiveness of cognitively-based approaches in treating stress-related symptoms. *Psychotherapy, 33*(2), 305–320.

Mather, G. (2008). *Foundations of sensation and perception.* Hove, U.K.: Psychology Press.

Mather, J. A., & Anderson, R. C. (1993). Personalities of octopuses (*Octopus rubescens*). *Journal of Comparative Psychology, 107*(3), 336–340.

Matson, J. L., Sevin, J. A., Fridley D., & Love, S. R. (1990). Increasing spontaneous language in three autistic children. *Journal of Applied Behavior Analysis, 23*(2), 223–227.

Matsumoto, D., & Juang, L. (2008). *Culture and psychology* (4th ed.). Belmont, CA: Cengage Learning/Wadsworth.

Matthews, G., Deary, I. J., & Whiteman, M. C. (2003). *Personality traits* (2nd ed.). New York: Cambridge University Press.

Mayberg, H., Lozano, A., Voon, V., McNeely, H. E., et al. (2005). Deep brain stimulation for treatment-resistant depression. *Neuron, 45*(5), 651–660.

Mayer, J. D. (2005). A tale of two visions: Can a new view of personality help inte-

grate psychology? *American Psychologist, 60*(4), 294–307.

Mayer, J. D., & Hanson, E. (1995). Mood-congruent judgment over time. *Personality & Social Psychology Bulletin, 21*(3), 237–244.

Mayer, J. D., Salovey, P., Caruso, D. R., & Sitarenios, G. (2001). Emotional intelligence as standard intelligence. *Emotion, 1*(3), 232–242.

Mayer, R. E. (1995). *Thinking, problem solving, and cognition.* New York: Freeman.

Mayer, R. E. (2004). Should there be a three-strikes rule against pure discovery learning? *American Psychologist, 59*(1), 14–19.

Mazur, J. E. (2006). *Learning and behavior* (6th ed.). Englewood Cliffs, NJ: Prentice Hall.

McAdams, D. P., & Pals, J. L. (2006). A new Big Five: Fundamental principles for an integrative science of personality. *American Psychologist, 61*(3), 204–217.

McBride, W. J., Murphy, J. M., & Ikemoto, S. (1999). Localization of brain reinforcement mechanisms. *Behavioural Brain Research, 101*(2), 129–152.

McCall, W. V., Prudic, J., Olfson, M., & Sackeim, H. (2006). Health-related quality of life following ECT in a large community sample. *Journal of Affective Disorders, 90*(2–3), 269–274.

McCann, S. L., & Stewin, L. L. (1988). Worry, anxiety, and preferred length of sleep. *Journal of Genetic Psychology, 149*(3), 413–418.

McCarthy, B. W. (1995). Bridges to sexual desire. *Journal of Sex Education & Therapy, 21*(2), 132–141.

McCarthy, B. W., & Fucito, L. M. (2005). Integrating medication, realistic expectations, and therapeutic interventions in the treatment of male sexual dysfunction. *Journal of Sex & Marital Therapy, 31*(4), 319–328.

McCartney, K., Bernieri, F., & Harris, M. J. (1990). Growing up and growing apart: A developmental meta-analysis of twin studies. *Psychological Bulletin, 107*(2), 226–237.

McClelland, D. C. (1961). *The achieving society.* New York: Van Nostrand.

McClelland, D. C. (1965). Achievement and entrepreneurship. *Journal of Personality & Social Psychology, 1*, 389–393.

McClelland, D. C., & Cheriff, A. D. (1997). The immunoenhancing effects of humor on secretory IgA and resistance to respiratory infections. *Psychology & Health, 12*(3), 329–344.

McClelland, D. C., & Pilon, D. A. (1983). Sources of adult motives in patterns of parent behavior in early childhood. *Journal of Personality & Social Psychology, 44*, 564–574.

McCluskey, U. (2002). The dynamics of attachment and systems-centered group psychotherapy. *Group Dynamics, 6*(2), 131–142.

McCormick, R. (1996). Culturally appropriate means and ends of counselling as described by the First Nations people of British Columbia. *International Journal for the Advancement of Counselling, 18,* 163–172.

McCormick, R. (2000). Aboriginal traditions in the treatment of substance abuse. *Canadian Journal of Counselling, 34,* 25–32.

McCrae, R. R., & Costa, P. T. (2001). A five-factor theory of personality. In L. A. Pervin & O. P. John (Eds.), *Handbook of personality.* New York: Guilford.

McCrae, R. R., & Terracciano, A. (2005). Universal features of personality traits from the observer's perspective: Data from 50 cultures. *Journal of Personality & Social Psychology, 88*(3), 547–561.

McDaniel, M. A., Maier, S. F., & Einstein, G. O. (2002). "Brain-specific" nutrients: A memory cure? *Psychological Science in the Public Interest, 3*(1), 12–38.

McDonald, J. K., Yanchar, S. C., & Osguthorpe, R. (2005). Learning from programmed instruction: Examining implications for modern instructional technology. *Educational Technology Research & Development, 53*(2), 84–98.

McGregor, I., McAdams, D. P., & Little, B. R. (2006). Personal projects, life stories, and happiness: On being true to traits. *Journal of Research in Personality, 40*(5), 551–572.

McGue, M., Bouchard, T. J. Jr., Iacono, W. G., & Lykken, D. T. (1993). Behavioral genetics of cognitive ability: A life-span perspective. In R. Plomin & G. E. McClearn (Eds.), *Nature, nurture, and psychology.* Washington: American Psychological Association.

McIntosh, W. D., Harlow, T. F., & Martin, L. L. (1995). Linkers and nonlinkers: Goal beliefs as a moderator of the effects of everyday hassles on rumination, depression, and physical complaints. *Journal of Applied Social Psychology, 25*(14), 1231–1244.

McKay, A. (2005). Sexuality and substance use: The impact of tobacco, alcohol, and selected recreational drugs on sexual function. *Canadian Journal of Human Sexuality, 14*(1–2), 47–56.

McKean, K. J. (1994). Using multiple risk factors to assess the behavioral, cognitive, and affective effects of learned helplessness. *Journal of Psychology, 128*(2), 177–183.

McKeever, W. F. (2000). A new family handedness sample with findings consistent with X-linked transmission. *British Journal of Psychology, 91*(1), 21–39.

McKeever, W. F., Cerone, L. J., Suter, P. J., & Wu, S. M. (2000). Family size, miscarriage-proneness, and handedness. *Laterality, 5*(2), 111–120.

McKenzie, K., Serfaty, M., & Crawford, M. (2003). Suicide in ethnic minority groups. *British Journal of Psychiatry, 183*(2), 100–101.

McKenzie, S. W. (2011). Personal observation.

McKim, M. K., Cramer, K. M., Stuart, B., & O'Connor, D. L. (1999). Infant care decisions and attachment security: The Canadian Transition to Child Care Study. *Canadian Journal of Behavioural Science, 31,* 92–106.

McKim, W. A. (2007). *Drugs and behavior* (6th ed.). Englewood Cliffs, NJ: Prentice Hall.

McLennan, J. (1992). "University blues": Depression among tertiary students during an academic year. *British Journal of Guidance & Counselling, 20*(2), 186–192.

McLewin, L. A., & Muller, R. T. (2006). Childhood trauma, imaginary companions, and the development of pathological dissociation. *Aggression & Violent Behavior, 11*(5), 531–545.

McMahon, S., & Koltzenburg, M. (2005). *Wall & Melzack's textbook of pain* (5th ed.). London: Churchill Livingstone.

McNally, R. J., & Clancy, S. A. (2005). Sleep paralysis, sexual abuse, and space alien abduction. *Transcultural Psychiatry, 42*(1), 113–122.

McNally, R. J., Clancy, S. A., & Barrett, H. M. (2004). Forgetting trauma? In D. Reisberg & P. Hertel (Eds.), *Memory and emotion.* New York: Oxford University Press.

McNamara, D. S., & Scott, J. L. (2001). Working memory capacity and strategy use. *Memory & Cognition, 29*(1), 10–17.

McRoberts, C., Burlingame, G. M., & Hoag, M. J. (1998). Comparative efficacy of individual and group psychotherapy. *Group Dynamics, 2*(2), 101–117.

McVey, G. L., Gusella, J., Tweed, S., & Ferrari, M. (2009). A controlled evaluation of web-based training for teachers and public health practitioners on the prevention of eating disorders. *Eating Disorders: Journal of Treatment and Prevention, 17*(1), 1–26.

McVey, G., Kirsh, G., Maker, D., Walker, K., et al. (2010) Promoting positive body image among university students: A collaborative pilot study. *Body Image, 7*(3), 200–204.

Mehrabian, A. (2000). Beyond IQ. *Genetic, Social, & General Psychology Monographs, 126,* 133–239.

Meichenbaum, D. (1993). Changing conceptions of cognitive behavior modification: Retrospect and prospect. *Journal of Consulting and Clinical Psychology, 61,* 202–204.

Meier, P. S., Donmall, M. C., McElduff, P., Barrowclough, C., et al. (2006). The role of the early therapeutic alliance in predicting drug treatment dropout. *Drug & Alcohol Dependence, 83*(1), 57–64.

Meltzoff, A. N. (2005). Imitation and other minds: The "Like Me" hypothesis. In S. Hurley & N. Chater (Eds.), *Perspectives on imitation: From neuroscience to social science* (Vol. 2): *Imitation, human development, and culture.* Cambridge, MA: MIT Press.

Meltzoff, A. N., & Prinz, W. (2002). *The imitative mind: Development, evolution, and brain bases.* Cambridge, MA: Cambridge University Press.

Melzack, R. (1999). From the gate to the neuromatrix. *Pain. Special issue: A tribute to Patrick D. Wall* (Suppl. 6), S121–S126.

Melzack, R., & Katz, J. (2004). The gate control theory: Reaching for the brain. In T. Hadjistavropoulos & K. D. Craig (Eds.), *Pain: Psychological perspectives.* Mahwah, NJ: Erlbaum.

Melzack, R., & Katz, J. (2006). Pain in the 21st century: The neuromatrix and beyond. In G. Young, A. W. Kane, & K. Nicholson (Eds.), *Psychological Knowledge in Court: PTSD, pain, and TBI.* New York: Springer.

Melzack, R., & Wall, P. D. (1996). *The challenge of pain.* Harmondsworth, U.K.: Penguin.

Mendolia, M. (2002). An index of self-regulation of emotion and the study of repression in social contexts that threaten or do not threaten self-concept. *Emotion, 2*(3), 215–232.

Merritt, J. M., Stickgold, R., Pace-Schott, E., Williams, J., et al. (1994). Emotion profiles in the dreams of men and women. *Consciousness & Cognition, 3*(1), 46–60.

Mesquita, B., & Markus, H. R. (2004). Culture and emotion: Models of agency as sources of cultural variation in emotion. In A. S. R. Manstead, S. R. Antony, N. Frijda, & A. Fischer (Eds.), *Feelings and emotions: The Amsterdam symposium.* New York: Cambridge University Press.

Messer, S. B., & Kaplan, A. H. (2004). Outcomes and factors related to efficacy of brief psychodynamic therapy. In D. P. Charman (Ed.), *Core processes in brief psychodynamic psychotherapy: Advancing effective practice.* Mahwah, NJ: Lawrence Erlbaum.

Meunier, M., Monfardini, E., & Boussaoud, D. (2007). Learning by observation in rhesus monkeys. *Neurobiology of Learning & Memory, 88*(2), 243–248.

Meyer, G. J., Finn, S. E., Eyde, L. D., Kay, G. G., et al. (2001). Psychological testing and psychological assessment. *American Psychologist, 56*(2) 128–165.

Meyers, L. (2006). Behind the scenes of the "Dr. Phil" show. *Monitor on Psychology, 37*(9), 63.

Michael, D., & Chen, S. (2006). *Serious games: Games that educate, train, and inform.* Boston: Thomson Course Technology.

Michaels, J. W., Blommel, J. M., Brocato, R. M., Linkous, R. A., et al. (1982). Social facilitation and inhibition in a natural setting. *Replications in Social Psychology, 2,* 21–24.

Michalko, M. (1998). *Cracking creativity.* Berkeley, CA: Ten Speed Press.

Middaugh, S. J., & Pawlick, K. (2002). Biofeedback and behavioral treatment of persistent pain in the older adult: A review and a study. *Applied Psychophysiology & Biofeedback, 27*(3), 185–202.

Miles, S. J., & Minda, J. P. (2011). The effects of concurrent verbal and visual tasks on category learning. *Journal of Experimental Psychology: Learning, Memory, and Cognition, 37*(3), 588–607.

Milgram, S. (1963). Behavioral study of obedience. *Journal of Abnormal and Social Psychology, 67,* 371–378.

Milgram, S. (1965). Some conditions of obedience and disobedience to authority. *Human Relations, 18,* 57–76.

Milgram, S., Bickman, L., & Berkowitz, L. (1969). Note on the drawing power of crowds of different size. *Journal of Personality & Social Psychology, 13,* 79–82.

Miller, D. T. (2006). *An invitation to social psychology.* Belmont, CA: Wadsworth.

Miller, E. K., & Cohen, J. D. (2001). An integrative theory of prefrontal cortex function. *Annual Review of Neuroscience, 24,* 167–202.

Miller, G. (1956). The magical number seven, plus or minus two: Some limits on our capacity for processing information. *Psychological Review, 63,* 81–87.

Miller, G. A. (1999). On knowing a word. *Annual Review of Psychology, 50,* 1–19.

Miller, G. E., Cohen, S., & Ritchey, A. K. (2002). Chronic psychological stress and the regulation of pro-inflammatory cytokines. *Health Psychology, 21*(6), 531–541.

Miller, M. A., & Rahe, R. H. (1997). Life changes scaling for the 1990s. *Journal of Psychosomatic Research, 43*(3), 279–292.

Miller, N., Pedersen, W. C., Earleywine, M., & Pollock, V. E. (2003). A theoretical model of triggered displaced aggression. *Personality & Social Psychology Review, 7*(1), 75–97.

Miller, N. E. (1944). Experimental studies of conflict. In J. McV. Hunt (Ed.), *Personality and the behavior disorders* (Vol. I). New York: Ronald Press.

Miller, R., Perlman, D., & Brehm, S. S. (2007). *Intimate relationships* (4th ed.). New York: McGraw-Hill.

Miller, W. R., & Munoz, R. F. (2005). *Controlling your drinking: Tools to make moderation work for you.* New York: Guilford.

Millman, R. B., & Ross, E. J. (2003). Steroid and nutritional supplement use in professional athletes. *American Journal on Addictions, 12*(Suppl 2), S48–S54.

Milne, R., & Bull, R. (2002). Back to basics: A componential analysis of the original cognitive interview mnemonics with three age groups. *Applied Cognitive Psychology, 16*(7), 743–753.

Milner, B. (1965). Memory disturbance after bilateral hippocampal lesions. In P. Milner & S. Glickman (Eds.), *Cognitive processes and the brain.* Princeton, NJ: Van Nostrand.

Miltenberger, R. G. (2004). *Behavior modification* (3rd ed.). Belmont, CA: Wadsworth.

Miltner, W. H. R., Krieschel, S., Hecht, H., Trippe, R., et al. (2004). Eye movements and behavioral responses to threatening and nonthreatening stimuli during visual search in phobic and nonphobic subjects. *Emotion, 4*(4), 323–339.

Milton, J., & Wiseman, R. (1999). A meta-analysis of mass-media tests of extrasensory perception. *British Journal of Psychology, 90*(2), 235–240.

Minda, J. P., Desroches, A. S., & Church, B. A. (2008). Learning rule-described and non-rule-described categories: A comparison of children and adults. *Journal of Experimental Psychology: Learning, Memory, and Cognition, 34*(6), 1518–1533.

Minda, J. P., & Smith, J. D. (2001). Prototypes in category learning: The effects of category size, category structure, and stimulus complexity. *Journal of Experimental Psychology: Learning, Memory, & Cognition, 27,* 775–799.

Minton, H. L. (2000). Psychology and gender at the turn of the century. *American Psychologist, 55*(6), 613–615.

Miotto, K., Darakjian, J., Basch, J., Murray, S., et al. (2001). Gamma-hydroxybutyric acid: Patterns of use, effects and withdrawal. *American Journal on Addictions, 10*(3), 232–241.

Miranda, R., & Kihlstrom, J. F. (2005). Mood congruence in childhood and recent autobiographical memory. *Cognition & Emotion, 19*(7), 981–998.

Mirsky, A. F., Bieliauskas, L. A., French, L. M., Van Kammen D. P., et al. (2000). A 39-year followup on the Genain quadruplets. *Schizophrenia Bulletin, 26*(3), 699–708.

Mirsky, A. F., & Duncan, C. C. (2005). Pathophysiology of mental illness: A view from the fourth ventricle. *International Journal of Psychophysiology, 58*(2–3), 162–178.

Mischel, W. (2004). Toward an integrative science of the person. *Annual Review of Psychology, 55*, 1–22.

Mischel, W., & Shoda, Y. (1998). Reconciling processing dynamics and personality dispositions. *Annual Review of Psychology, 49*, 229–258.

Mischel, W., Shoda, Y., & Smith, R. E. (2004). *Introduction to personality: Toward an integration* (7th ed.). Hoboken, NJ: Wiley.

Mishara, B. (1999). Suicide in the Montreal subway system: Characteristics of the victims, antecedents, and implications for prevention. *Canadian Journal of Psychiatry, 44*, 690–696.

Mistlberger, R. E. (2005). Circadian regulation of sleep in mammals: Role of the suprachiasmatic nucleus. *Brain Research Reviews, 49*(3), 429–454.

Mitchell, D. (1987, February). Firewalking cults: Nothing but hot air. *Laser, 7*–8.

Mitchell, I. A., MacDonald, R. A. R., Knussen, C., et al. (2007). A survey investigation of the effects of music listening on chronic pain. *Psychology of Music, 35*(1), 37–57.

Mitru, G., Millrood, D. L., & Mateika, J. H., Serpell, M. G. (2002). The impact of sleep on learning and behavior in adolescents. *Teachers College Record, 104*(4), 704–726.

Miyake, A. (2001). Individual differences in working memory. *Journal of Experimental Psychology: General, 130*(2), 163–168.

Moerman, D. E. (2002). The meaning response and the ethics of avoiding placebos. *Evaluation & the Health Professions. Special Recent Advances in Placebo Research, 25*(4), 399–409.

Mogg, K., Bradley, B. P., Hyare, H., & Lee, S. (1998). Selective attention to food-related stimuli in hunger. *Behaviour Research & Therapy, 36*(2), 227–237.

Moghaddam, B. (2002). Stress activation of glutamate neurotransmission in the prefrontal cortex. *Biological Psychiatry, 51*(10), 775–787.

Morrison, R. G., & Wallace, B. (2001). Imagery vividness, creativity and the visual arts. *Journal of Mental Imagery, 25*(3–4), 135–152.

Mohr, D. C., Hart, S. L., Julian, L., Catledge, C., et al. (2005). Telephone-administered psychotherapy for depression. *Archives of General Psychiatry, 62*(9), 1007–1014.

Mokdad, A. H., Marks, J. S., Stroup, D. F., & Gerberding, J. L. (2004). Actual causes of death in the United States, 2000. *Journal of the American Medical Association, 291*(March 10), 1238–1245.

Mollon, J. D., Pokorny, J., & Knoblauch, K. (2003). *Normal and defective color vision.* New York: Oxford University Press.

Monahan, J., Steadman, H. J., Silver, E., Appelbaum, P. S., et al. (2001). *Rethinking risk assessment: The MacArthur study of mental disorder and violence.* New York, Oxford University Press.

Montgomery, G. (1989, March). The mind in motion. *Discover,* 58–68.

Montgomery, P., & Dennis, J. (2004). A systematic review of non-pharmacological therapies for sleep problems in later life. *Sleep Medicine Reviews, 8*(1), 47–62.

Montplaisir, J., Petit, D., Lorrain, D., Gauthier, S., & Nielsen, T. (1995). Sleep in Alzheimer's disease: Further considerations on the role of brainstem and forebrain cholinergic populations in sleep–wake mechanisms. *Sleep, 18*, 145–148.

Montreal Declaration on Intellectual Disabilities. (2004). Retrieved May 10, 2009, from http://www.mdri.org/mdri-web -2007/pdf/montrealdeclaration.pdf.

Moor, J. (Ed.). (2003). *The Turing test: The elusive standard of artificial intelligence.* London: Kluwer Academic Publishers.

Moore, S. A., & Zoellner, L. A. (2007). Overgeneral autobiographical memory and traumatic events: An evaluative review. *Psychological Bulletin, 133*(3), 419–437.

Moran, J. M., Macrae, C. N., Heatherton, T. F., Wyland, C. L., et al. (2006). Neuroanatomical evidence for distinct cognitive and affective components of self. *Journal of Cognitive Neuroscience, 18*(9), 1586–1594.

Moreno, J. L. (1953). *Who shall survive?* New York: Beacon.

Morgan, J. P. (Ed.). (2005). *Psychology of aggression.* Hauppauge, NY: Nova Science Publishers.

Morgenstern, J., Labouvie, E., McCrady, B. S., Kahler, C. W., et al. (1997). Affiliation with Alcoholics Anonymous after treatment. *Journal of Consulting & Clinical Psychology, 65*(5), 768–777.

Morin, C., LeBlanc, M., Bélanger, L., Ivers, H., et al. (2011). Prevalence of insomnia and its treatment in Canada. *The Canadian Journal of Psychiatry, 56*, 540–548.

Morisse, D., Batra, L., Hess, L., & Silverman, R. (1996). A demonstration of a token economy for the real world. *Applied & Preventive Psychology, 5*(1), 41–46.

Moritz, A. P., & Zamchem, N. (1946). Sudden and unexpected deaths of young soldiers. *American Medical Association Archives of Pathology, 42*, 459–494.

Moro, V., Berlucchi, G., Lerch, J., Tomaiuolo, F., et al. (2008). Selective deficit of mental visual imagery with intact primary visual cortex and visual perception. *Cortex, 44*(2), 109–118.

Morsella, E., & Krauss, R. M. (2004). The role of gestures in spatial working memory and speech. *American Journal of Psychology, 117*(3), 411–424.

Mosher, W. D., Chandra, C., & Jones, J. (2005). *Sexual behavior and selected health measures: Men and women 15–44 years of age, United States, 2002.* Atlanta: Centers for Disease Control. Retrieved August 25, 2006, from http://www.cdc.gov/nchs /data/ad/ad362.pdf.

Moss, K. (1989). Performing the light-switch task in lucid dreams: A case study. *Journal of Mental Imagery, 13*(2), 135–137.

Most, S. B., Scholl, B. J., Clifford, E. R., & Simons, D. J. (2005). What you see is what you set: Sustained inattentional blindness and the capture of awareness. *Psychological Review, 112*(1), 217–242.

Motivala, S. J., & Irwin, M. R. (2007). Sleep and immunity: Cytokine pathways linking sleep and health outcomes. *Current Directions in Psychological Science, 16*(1), 21–25.

Muris, P., & Merckelbach, H. (1999). Traumatic memories, eye movements, phobia, and panic. *Journal of Anxiety Disorders, 13*(1–2), 209–223.

Murray, B. (2001, November). A daunting unbelievable experience. *Monitor on Psychology,* 18.

Murray, J. B. (2002). Phencyclidine (PCP): A dangerous drug, but useful in schizophrenia research. *Journal of Psychology, 136*(3), 319–327.

Murrell, A. R., Christoff, K. A., & Henning, K. R. (2007). Characteristics of domestic violence offenders: Associations with childhood exposure to violence. *Journal of Family Violence, 22*(7), 523–532.

Mussen, P. H., Conger, J. J., Kagan, J., & Geiwitz, J. (1979). *Psychological development: A life span approach.* New York: Harper & Row.

Musso, M., Weiller, C., Kiebel, S., Müller, S. P., et al. (1999). Training-induced brain plasticity in aphasia. *Brain, 122*, 1781–1790.

Nagel, T. (1974). What is it like to be a bat? *The Philosophical Review, 83*, 435–450.

Nagpal, J., Nicoladis, E., & Marentette, P. (2011). Predicting individual differences in L2 speakers' gestures. *International Journal of Bilingualism, 15*(2), 205–214.

Nairne, J. S. (2002). Remembering over the short-term. *Annual Review of Psychology, 53*, 53–81.

Naitoh, P., Kelly, T. L., & Englund, C. E. (1989). Health effects of sleep deprivation. *U. S. Naval Health Research Center Report,* No. 89–46.

Nakamichi, M. (2004). Tool-use and tool-making by captive, group-living orangutans (*Pongo pygmaeus abelii*) at an artificial termite mound. *Behavioural Processes, 65*(1), 87–93.

Nakamura, J., & Csikszentmihalyi, M. (2003). The motivational sources of creativity as viewed from the paradigm of positive psychology. In L. G. Aspinwall & U. M. Staudinger (Eds.), *A psychology of human strengths: Fundamental questions and future directions for a positive psychology.* Washington: American Psychological Association.

Naranjo, C. (1970). Present-centeredness: Technique, prescription, and ideal. In J. Fagan & I. L. Shepherd (Eds.), *What Is Gestalt Therapy?* New York: Harper & Row.

National Academy of Sciences. (2002). *The polygraph and lie detection.* Washington: Author.

National Institute of Mental Health. (2003). *In harm's way: Suicide in America.* Bethesda, MD: Author.

Nau, S. D., & Lichstein, K. L. (2005). Insomnia: Causes and treatments. In P. R. Carney, J. D. Geyer, & R. B. Berry (Eds.), *Clinical sleep disorders.* Philadelphia, PA: Lippincott Williams & Wilkins.

Navarro, M. (1995, December 9). Drug sold abroad by prescription becomes widely abused in U.S. *The New York Times,* pp. 1, 9.

Naveh-Benjamin, M., Guez, J., & Sorek, S. (2007). The effects of divided attention on encoding processes in memory: Mapping the locus of interference. *Canadian Journal of Experimental Psychology/Revue canadienne de psychologie expérimentale, 61*(1), 1–12.

NCCDPHP (National Center for Chronic Disease Prevention and Health Promotion). (2004). *Health effects of cigarette smoking.* Retrieved September 26, 2012, from http://www.cdc.gov/tobacco /data_statistics/fact_sheets/health_effects /effects_cig_smoking/.

Neath, I., & Surprenant, A. (2003). *Human memory* (2nd ed.). Belmont, CA: Wadsworth.

Needles, D. J., & Abramson, L. Y. (1990). Positive life events, attributional style, and hopefulness: Testing a model of recovery from depression. *Journal of Abnormal Psychology, 99*(2), 156–165.

Nehlig, A. (Ed.). (2004). *Coffee, tea, chocolate, and the brain.* Boca Raton, FL: CRC Press.

Neisser, U., Boodoo, G., Bouchard, T. J., Boykin, A. W., et al. (1996). Intelligence: Knowns & unknowns. *American Psychologist, 51*, 77–101.

Nelson, T. D. (2005). Ageism: Prejudice against our feared future self. *Journal of Social Issues, 61*(2), 207–221.

Nelson, T. D. (2006). *The psychology of prejudice* (2nd ed.). Needham Heights, MA: Allyn & Bacon.

Nemeroff, C. B., Bremner, J. D., Foa, E. B., Mayberg, H. S., et al. (2006). Posttraumatic stress disorder: A state-of-the-science review. *Journal of Psychiatric Research, 40*(1), 1–21.

Neter, E., & Ben-Shakhar, G. (1989). The predictive validity of graphological inferences: A meta-analytic approach. *Personality and Individual Differences, 10*(7), 737–745.

Nettle, D. (2005). An evolutionary perspective on the extraversion continuum. *Evolution & Human Behavior, 26*, 363–373.

Nettle, D. (2006). The evolution of personality variation in humans and other animals. *American Psychologist, 61*(6), 622–631.

Nettle, D. (2008, February 9). The personality factor: What makes you unique? *New Scientist, 2642*, 36–39.

Neuman, G. A., & Baydoun, R. (1998). An empirical examination of overt and covert integrity tests. *Journal of Business & Psychology, 13*(1), 65–79.

Neumeister, A. (2004). Neurotransmitter depletion and seasonal affective disorder: Relevance for the biologic effects of light therapy. *Primary Psychiatry. Special Neurotransmitter Depletion, 11*(6), 44–48.

Newman, A. W., & Thompson, J. W. (2001). The rise and fall of forensic hypnosis in criminal investigation. *Journal of the American Academy of Psychiatry & the Law, 29*(1), 75–84.

Ng, S. H. (2002). Will families support their elders? Answers from across cultures. In T. Nelson (Ed.), *Ageism: Stereotyping and prejudice against older persons.* Cambridge, MA: MIT Press.

Niaura, R., Todaro, J. F., Stroud, L., Spiro, A., et al. (2002). Hostility, the metabolic syndrome, and incident coronary heart disease. *Health Psychology, 21*(6), 588–593.

Nickerson, R. S., & Adams, M. J. (1979). Long-term memory for a common object. *Cognitive Psychology, 11*, 287–307.

Nicoladis, E., Pika, S., Yin, H., & Marentette, P. (2007). Gesture use in story recall by Chinese-English bilinguals. *Applied Psycholinguistics, 28*(4), 721–735.

Niedzwienska, A. (2004). Metamemory knowledge and the accuracy of flashbulb memories. *Memory, 12*(5), 603–613.

Niehaus, D. J. H., Stein, D. J., Koen, L., Lochner, C., et al. (2005). A case of "Ifufunyane": A Xhosa culture-bound syndrome. *Journal of Psychiatric Practice, 11*(6), 411–413.

Nielsen, D. M., & Metha, A. (1994). Parental behavior and adolescent self-esteem in clinical and nonclinical samples. *Adolescence, 29*(115), 525–542.

Nielsen, M., & Dissanayake, C. (2004). Pretend play, mirror self-recognition and imitation: A longitudinal investigation through the second year. *Infant Behavior & Development, 27*(3), 342–365.

Nielsen, T. A., Zadra, A. L., Simard, V., Saucier, S., et al. (2003). The typical dreams of Canadian university students. *Dreaming, 13*, 211–235.

Nisbett, R. E., & Miyamotot, Y. (2005). The influence of culture: Holistic versus analytic perception. *Trends in Cognitive Sciences, 9*(10), 467–473.

Njeri, I. (1991, January 13). Beyond the melting pot. *Los Angeles Times*, pp. E1, E8.

Noble, P. (1997). Violence in psychiatric inpatients. *International Review of Psychiatry, 9*(2–3), 207–216.

Noice, H., & Noice, T. (1999). Long-term retention of theatrical roles. *Memory, 7*(3), 357–382.

Noland, J. S., Singer, L. T., Short, E. J., Minnes, S., et al. (2005). Prenatal drug exposure and selective attention in preschoolers. *Neurotoxicology & Teratology, 27*(3), 429–438.

Nolen-Hoeksema, S., & Rector, N. A. (2008). *Abnormal psychology* (1st Canadian ed.). Toronto: McGraw-Hill.

Norem, J. K. (2002). *The positive power of negative thinking: Using defensive pessimism to harness anxiety and perform at your peak.* New York: Basic Books.

Norenzayan, A., & Nisbett, R.E. (2000). Culture and causal cognition. *Current Directions in Psychological Science, 9*, 132–135.

Nori, G. (1998). Glucagon and the control of meal size. In G. P. Smith (Ed.), *Satiation: From gut to brain.* New York: Oxford University Press.

Norlander, T., Bergman, H., & Archer, T. (1998). Effects of flotation REST on creative problem solving and originality. *Journal of Environmental Psychology, 18*(4), 399–408.

Norlander, T., Bergman, H., & Archer, T. (1999). Primary process in competitive archery performance: Effects of flotation REST. *Journal of Applied Sport Psychology, 11*(2), 194–209.

Norman, G., Young, M., & Brooks, L. (2007). Non-analytical models of clinical reasoning: The role of experience. *Medical Education, 41*(12), 1140–1145.

Northcutt, R. G. (2004). Taste buds: Development and evolution. *Brain, Behavior & Evolution, 64*(3), 198–206.

Nurnberger, J. I., & Zimmerman, J. (1970). Applied analysis of human behaviors: An alternative to conventional motivational inferences and unconscious determination in therapeutic programming. *Behavior Therapy, 1*, 59–69.

Nuttin, B., Cosyns, P., Demeulemeester, H., Gybels, J., et al. (1999). Electrical stimulation in anterior limbs of internal capsules in patients with obsessive-compulsive disorder. *The Lancet, 354*(9189), 1526.

O'Brien, R. M., Figlerski, R. W., Howard, S. R., & Caggiano, J. (1981, August). *The effects of multi-year, guaranteed contracts on the performance of pitchers in major league baseball.* Paper presented at the annual meeting of the American Psychological Association, Los Angeles, CA.

O'Conner, T. G, Marvin, R. S., Rutter, M., Olrick, J. T., et al. (2003). Child-parent attachment following early institutional deprivation. *Development & Psychopathology, 15*(1), 19–38.

O'Connor, M. G., Sieggreen, M. A., Bachna, K., Kaplan, B., et al. (2000). Long-term retention of transient news events. *Journal of the International Neuropsychological Society, 6*(1), 44–51.

O'Craven, K. M., & Kanwisher, N. (2000). Mental imagery of faces and places activates corresponding stimulus-specific brain regions. *Journal of Cognitive Neuroscience, 12*(6), 1013–1023.

O'Keeffe, C., & Wiseman, R. (2005). Testing alleged mediumship: Methods and results. *British Journal of Psychology, 96*(2), 165–179.

O'Neill, B. (2003, March 8). *Don't believe everything you read online.* BBC News. Retrieved September 26, 2012, from http://news.bbc.co.uk/2/hi/uk_news/magazine/3151595.stm.

O'Neill, P. (2005) The ethics of problem definition. *Canadian Psychology, 46*, 13–20.

O'Roark, A. M. (2001). Personality assessment, projective methods and a triptych perspective. *Journal of Projective Psychology & Mental Health, 8*(2), 116–126.

Oakley, R. (2004). How the mind hurts and heals the body. *American Psychologist, 59*(1), 29–40.

Oatley, K., & Jenkins, J. M. (1992). Human emotions: Function and dysfunction. In M. R. Rosenzweig & L. W. Porter (Eds.), *Annual Review of Psychology, 45*, 55–85.

Oberauer, K., & Göthe, K. (2006). Dual-task effects in working memory: Interference between two processing tasks, between two memory demands, and between storage and processing. *European Journal of Cognitive Psychology, 18*(4), 493–519.

Obhi, S. S., & Haggard, P. (2004, July–August). Free will and free won't. *American Scientist, 92*, 358–365.

Ochoa, J. G., & Pulido, M. (2005). Parasomnias. In P. R. Carney, J. D. Geyer, & R. B. Berry (Eds.), *Clinical sleep disorders.* Philadelphia, PA: Lippincott Williams & Wilkins.

Ogloff, J. R. P. (2006). Psychopathy/antisocial personality disorder conundrum. *Australian & New Zealand Journal of Psychiatry, 40*(6), 519–528.

Ohayon, M. M., Guilleminault, C., & Priest, R. G. (1999). Night terrors, sleepwalking, and confusional arousals in the general population. *Journal of Clinical Psychiatry, 60*(4), 268–276.

Olds, M. E., & Fobes, J. L. (1981). The central basis of motivation: Intracranial self-stimulation studies. *Annual Review of Psychology, 32*, 523–574.

Olio, K. A. (2004). The truth about "false memory syndrome." In P. J. Caplan & L. Cosgrove (Eds.), *Bias in psychiatric diagnosis. A project of the association for women in psychology.* Northvale, NJ: Jason Aronson.

Oliwenstein, L. (1993, May). The gene with two faces. *Discover*, 26.

Olson, A. K., Eadie, B. D., Ernst, C., & Christie, B. R. (2006). Environmental enrichment and voluntary exercise massively increase neurogenesis in the adult hippocampus via dissociable pathways. *Hipocampus, 16*, 250–260.

Olson, J. M., Vernon, P. A., Harris, J. A., & Jang, K. L. (2001). The heritability of attitudes: A study of twins. *Journal of Personality & Social Psychology, 80*(6), 845–860.

Olson, J. M., & Zanna, M. P. (1993). Attitudes and attitude change. In L. W. Porter and M. R. Rosenzweig (Eds.), *Annual Review of Psychology, 44*, 117–154.

Olson, R. L., & Roberts, M. W. (1987). Alternative treatments for sibling aggression. *Behavior Therapy, 18*(3), 243–250.

Olsson, A., Nearing, K., & Phelps, E. A. (2007). Learning fears by observing others: The neural systems of social fear transmission. *Social Cognitive & Affective Neuroscience, 2*(1), 3–11.

Olszewski, P. K., Li, D., Grace, M. K., Billington, C. J., et al. (2003). Neural basis of orexigenic effects of ghrelin acting within lateral hypothalamus. *Peptides, 24*(4), 597–602.

Olthof, A., Sutton, J. E., Slumskie, S. W., D'Addetta, J., et al. (1999). In search of the cognitive map: Can rats learn an abstract pattern of rewarded arms on the radial maze? *Journal of Experimental Psychology: Animal Behavior Processes, 25*, 352–362.

Ones, D. S., & Viswesvaran, C. (2001). Integrity tests and other criterion-focused occupational personality scales (COPS) used in personnel selection. *International Journal of Selection & Assessment, 9*(1–2), 31–39.

Ones, D. S.,Viswesvaran, C., & Schmidt, F. L. (2003). Personality and absenteeism: A meta-analysis of integrity tests. *European Journal of Personality. Special Issue: Personality and Industrial, Work and Organizational Applications, 17*(Suppl1), S19–S38.

Onishi, K. & Baillargeon, R. (2005). Do 15-month-old infants understand false beliefs? *Science, 308*(5719), 255–258.

Onwuegbuzie, A. J. (2000). Academic procrastinators and perfectionistic tendencies among graduate students. *Journal of Social Behavior & Personality, 15*(5), 103–109.

Ooki, S. (2005). Genetic and environmental influences on the handedness and footedness in Japanese twin children. *Twin Research and Human Genetics, 8*(6), 649–656.

Ord, T. J., Martins, E. P., Thakur, S., Mane, K. K., et al. (2005). Trends in animal behaviour research (1968–2002): Ethoinformatics and the mining of library databases. *Animal Behaviour, 69*(6), 1399–1413.

Ormay, T. (2006). Cybertherapy: Psychotherapy on the Internet. *International Journal of Psychotherapy, 10*(2), 51–60.

Ormerod, B. K., & Galea, L. A. (2001). Reproductive status influences cell proliferation and cell survival in the dentate gyrus of adult female meadow voles: A possible regulatory role for estradiol. *Neuroscience, 102*, 369–379.

Ornstein, R. (1997). *The right mind.* San Diego: Harcourt Brace.

Osgood, C. E. (1952). The nature and measurement of meaning. *Psychological Bulletin, 49*, 197–237.

Oskamp, S., & Schultz, P. W. (2005). *Attitudes and opinions* (3rd ed.). Mahwah, NJ: Erlbaum.

Ost, L. (1996). One-session group treatment of spider phobia. *Behaviour Research & Therapy, 34*(9), 707–715.

Oster, H. (2005). The repertoire of infant facial expressions: a ontogenetic perspective. In J. Nadel & D. Muir (Eds.), *Emotional development: Recent research advances.* New York: Oxford University Press.

Overmier, J. B., & LoLordo, V. M. (1998). Learned helplessness. In W. T. O'Donohue et al. (Eds.), *Learning and behavior therapy.* Boston: Allyn & Bacon.

Oyserman, D., Bybee, D., Terry, K., & Hart-Johnson, T. (2004). Possible selves as roadmaps. *Journal of Research in Personality, 38*(2), 130–149.

Pagano, R. R. (1981). *Understanding statistics in the behavioral sciences.* St. Paul, MN: West Publishing Company.

Pagano, R. R., & Warrenburg, S. (1983). Meditation. In R. J. Davidson, G. E. Schwartz, & D. Shapiro (Eds.),

Consciousness and self-regulation. New York: Plenum.

Page, M. P. A., Madge, A., Cumming, N., & Norris, D. G. (2007). Speech errors and the phonological similarity effect in long-term memory: Evidence suggesting a common locus. *Journal of Memory & Language, 56*(1), 49–64.

Pagnin, D., de Queiroz, V., Pini, S., & Cassano, G. B. (2004). Efficacy of ECT in depression: A meta-analytic review. *Journal of ECT, 20*(1), 13–20.

Palinkas, L. A., Suedfeld, P., & Steel, G. D. (1995). Psychological functioning among members of a small polar expedition. *Aviation and Space Environmental Medicine, 66*, 943–950.

Palmer, S. E., & Beck, D. M. (2007). The repetition discrimination task: An objective method for studying perceptual grouping. *Perception & Psychophysics, 69*(1), 68–78.

Pals, J. L. (2006). Narrative identity processing of difficult life experiences: Pathways of personality development and positive self-transformation in adulthood. *Journal of Personality, 74*(4), 1079–1110.

Panksepp, J., & Pasqualini, M. S. (2005). The search for the fundamental brain/mind sources of affective experience. In J. Nadel & D. Muir (Eds.), *Emotional development: Recent research advances.* New York: Oxford University Press.

Papanicolaou, A. C. (Ed.). (2006). *The amnesias: A clinical textbook of memory disorders.* New York: Oxford University Press.

Papps, F., Walker, M., Trimboli, A., & Trimboli, C. (1995). Parental discipline in Anglo, Greek, Lebanese, and Vietnamese cultures. *Journal of Cross-Cultural Psychology, 26*(1), 49–64.

Paquette, V., Lévesque, J., Mensour, B., Leroux, J. M., et al. (2003). "Change the mind and you change the brain": Effects of cognitive-behavioral therapy on the neural correlates of spider phobia. *NeuroImage, 18*, 401–409.

Paradis, C. M., Solomon, L. Z., Florer, F., & Thompson, T. (2004). Flashbulb memories of personal events of 9/11 and the day after for a sample of New York City residents. *Psychological Reports, 95*(1), 304–310.

Parker, A., Ngu, H., & Cassaday, H. J. (2001). Odour and Proustian memory. *Applied Cognitive Psychology, 15*(2), 159–171.

Parker, J. D. A. (2005). The relevance of emotional intelligence for clinical psychology. In R. Schulze & R. D. Roberts (Eds.), *Emotional intelligence: An international handbook.* Ashland, OH: Hogrefe & Huber.

Pascual, A., & Guéguen, N. (2005). Foot-in-the-door and door-in-the-face: A comparative meta-analytic study. *Psychological Reports, 96*(1), 122–128.

Patenaude, J., Niyonsenga, T., & Fafard D. (2003). Changes in students' moral development during medical school: A cohort study. *Canadian Medical Association Journal, 168*(7), 840–844.

Patterson, C. H. (1989). Foundations for a systematic eclectic psychotherapy. *Psychotherapy, 26*(4), 427–435.

Patterson, D. R. (2004). Treating pain with hypnosis. *Current Directions in Psychological Science, 13*, 252–255.

Patterson, G. R. (1982). *Coercive family process.* Eugene, OR: Castilia Press.

Paul, M. A., Gray, G. W., Lieberman, H. R., Love, R. J., et al. (2011). Phase advance with separate and combined melatonin and light treatment. *Psychopharmacology, 214*(2), 515–523.

Paulsson, T., & Parker, A. (2006). The effects of a two-week reflection-intention training program on lucid dream recall. *Dreaming, 16*(1), 22–35.

Pavlov, I. P. (1927). *Conditioned reflexes.* Translated by G. V. Anrep. New York: Dover.

Penfield, W. (1957, April 27). Brain's record of past a continuous movie film. *Science News Letter, 265.*

Penfield, W. (1958). *The excitable cortex in conscious man.* Springfield, IL: Charles C. Thomas.

Penfield, W., & Perot, P. (1963). The brain's record of auditory and visual experience. *Brain, 86*, 595–696.

Pennebaker, J. W. (2004). Writing to heal: A guided journal for recovering from trauma and emotional upheaval. Oakland, CA: New Harbinger Press.

Peretz, I., Gosselin, N., Tillmann, B., Cuddy, L. L., et al. (2008). On-line identification of congenital amusia. *Music Perception, 25*(4), 331–343.

Perin, C. T. (1943). A quantitative investigation of the delay of reinforcement gradient. *Journal of Experimental Psychology, 32*, 37–51.

Perkins, D. (1995). *Outsmarting IQ: The emerging science of learnable intelligence.* New York: Free Press.

Perls, F. (1969). *Gestalt therapy verbatim.* Lafayette, CA: Real People.

Perreault, S., & Bourhis, R. Y. (1999). Ethnocentrism, social identification, and discrimination. *Personality & Social Psychology Bulletin, 25*(1), 92–103.

Perry, R. P. (2003). Perceived (academic) control and causal thinking in achievement settings. *Canadian Psychology, 44*(4), 312–331.

Perry, R. P., Hladkyj, S., Pekrun, R. H., & Pelletier, S. T. (2001). Academic control and action control in the achievement of college students: A longitudinal field study. *Journal of Educational Psychology, 93*(4), 776–789.

Perugini, E. M., Kirsch, I., Allen, S. T., Coldwell, E., et al. (1998). Surreptitious observation of responses to hypnotically suggested hallucinations. *International Journal of Clinical & Experimental Hypnosis, 46*(2), 191–203.

Pervin, L. A., Cervone, D., & John, O. P. (2005). *Personality: Theory and research* (9th ed.). Hoboken, NJ: Wiley.

Pesant, N., & Zadra, A. (2006). Dream content and psychological well-being: A longitudinal study of the continuity hypothesis. *Journal of Clinical Psychology, 62*(1), 111–121.

Petersen, S. E., Fox, P. T., Posner, M. I., Mintun, M., et al. (1988). Positron emission tomography studies of the cortical anatomy of single-word processing. *Nature, 331*(6157), 585–589.

Peterson, C., & Vaidya, R. S. (2001). Explanatory style, expectations, and depressive symptoms. *Personality & Individual Differences, 31*(7), 1217–1223.

Peterson, L. R., & Peterson, M. J. (1959). Short-term retention of individual verbal items. *Journal of Experimental Psychology, 58*, 193–198.

Peterson, S. E. (1992). The cognitive functions of underlining as a study technique. *Reading Research & Instruction, 31*(2), 49–56.

Petit, D., Gagnon, J., Fantini, F. L., Ferini-Strambi, L., et al. (2004). Sleep and quantitative EEG in neurodegenerative disorders. *Journal of Psychosomatic Research, 56*, 487–496.

Petitto, L. A., & Marentette, P. F. (1991). Babbling in the manual mode: Evidence for the ontogeny of language. *Science, 251*, 1493–1496.

Pett, M. A., & Johnson, M. J. M. (2005). Development and psychometric evaluation of the Revised University Student Hassles Scale. *Educational & Psychological Measurement, 65*(6), 984–1010.

Peverly, S. T., Brobst, K. E., Graham, M., & Shaw, R. (2003). College adults are not good at self-regulation. *Journal of Educational Psychology, 95*(2), 335–346.

Phinney, J. S. & Alipuria, L. L. (2006). Multiple social categorization and identity among multiracial, multiethnic and multicultural individuals: Processes and implications. In R. J. Crisp & M. Hewstone (Eds.), *Multiple social categorization: Processes, models and applications.* New York: Psychology Press.

Phinney, J. S., & Ong, A. D. (2007). Conceptualization and measurement of ethnic identity: Current status and future directions. *Journal of Counseling Psychology, 54*(3), 271–281.

Piaget, J. (1951, original French, 1945). *The psychology of intelligence.* New York: Norton.

Piaget, J. (1952). *The origins of intelligence in children.* New York: International University Press.

Piccione, C., Hilgard, E. R., & Zimbardo, P. G. (1989). On the degree of stability of measured hypnotizability over a 25-year period. *Journal of Personality & Social Psychology, 56*(2), 289–295.

Pickel, K. L., French, T. A., & Betts, J. M. (2003). A cross-modal weapon focus effect: The influence of a weapon's presence on memory for auditory information. *Memory, 11*(3), 277–292.

Pickering, G. J. & Demiglio, P. (2008). The white wine mouthfeel wheel: A lexicon for describing the oral sensations elicited by white wine. *Journal of Wine Research, 19*(1), 51–67.

Piefke, M., Weiss, P., Markowitsch, H., & Fink, G. (2005). Gender differences in the functional neuroanatomy of emotional episodic autobiographical memory. *Human Brain Mapping, 24*, 313–324.

Piek, J. P. (2006). *Infant motor development.* Champaign, IL: Human Kinetics Publishers.

Pierce, J. P. (1991). Progress and problems in international public health efforts to reduce tobacco usage. *Annual Review of Public Health, 12*, 383–400.

Pierce, W. D., & Cheney, C. D. (2004). *Behavior analysis and learning* (3rd ed.). Mahwah, NJ: Erlbaum.

Pierrehumbert, B., Ramstein, T., Karmaniola, A., Miljkovitch, R., et al. (2002). Quality of child care in the preschool years. *International Journal of Behavioral Development, 26*(5), 385–396.

Piliavin, I. M., Rodin, J., & Piliavin, J. A. (1969). Good samaritanism: An underground phenomenon? *Journal of Personality & Social Psychology, 13*, 289–299.

Pillow, D. R., Zautra, A. J., & Sandler, I. (1996). Major life events and minor stressors: Identifying mediational links in the stress process. *Journal of Personality & Social Psychology, 70*(2), 381–394.

Pinel, J. P. J., Assanand, S., & Lehman, D. R. (2000). Hunger, eating, and ill health. *American Psychologist, 55*(10), 1105–1116.

Pinker, S., & Jackendoff, R. (2005). The faculty of language: What's special about it? *Cognition, 95*(2), 201–236.

Pinkus, R. T., Lockwood, P., Marshall, T. C., & Yoon, H. M. (2012). Responses to comparisons in romantic relationships: Empathy, shared fate, and contrast. *Personal Relationships, 19*(1), 182–201.

Pinsof, W. M., Wynne, L. C., & Hambright, A. B. (1996). The outcomes of couple and family therapy. *Psychotherapy, 33*(2), 321–331.

Pizam, A., Jeong, G.-H., Reichel, A., van Boemmel, H., et al. (2004). The relationship between risk-taking, sensation-seeking, and the tourist behavior of young adults: A cross-cultural study. *Journal of Travel Research, 42*, 251–260.

Plassmann, H., O'Doherty, J., Shiv, B., & Rangel, A. (2008). Marketing actions can modulate neural representations of experienced pleasantness. *Proceedings of the National Academy of Sciences, 105*(3), 1050–1054.

Pliner, P., & Saunders, T. (2008). Vulnerability to freshman weight gain as a function of dietary restraint and residence. *Physiology & Behavior, 93*(1–2), 76–82.

Plomin, R., DeFries, J. C., McClearn, G. E., & McGuffin, P. (2001). *Behavioral Genetics* (4th ed.). New York: Worth.

Plomin, R., Fulker, D. W., Corley, R., & DeFries, J. C. (1997). Nature, nurture, and cognitive development from 1 to 16 years: A parent-offspring adoption study. *Psychological Science, 8*(6), 442–447.

Plomin, R., & Rende, R. (1991). Human behavioral genetics. In M. R. Rosenzweig & L. W. Porter (Eds.), *Annual Review of Psychology, 42*, 161–190.

Plutchik, R. (2003). *Emotions and life: Perspectives from psychology, biology, and evolution.* Washington: American Psychological Association.

Pogatchnik, S. (1990, January 26). Kids' TV gets more violent, study finds. *The Los Angeles Times,* pp. F1, F27.

Polemikos, N., & Papaeliou, C. (2000). Sidedness preference as an index of organization of laterality. *Perceptual & Motor Skills, 91*(3, Pt 2), 1083–1090.

Polivy, J., & Herman, C. P. (2002). Causes of eating disorders. *Annual Review of Psychology, 53,* 187–213.

Polivy, J., Herman, C.P., & Deo, R. (2010). Getting a bigger slice of the pie. Effects on eating and emotion in restrained and unrestrained eaters. *Appetite, 55*(3), 426–430.

Pollner, M. (1998). The effects of interviewer gender in mental health interviews. *Journal of Nervous & Mental Disease, 186*(6), 369–373.

Pollock, V. E., Briere, J., Schneider, L., Knop, J., et al. (1990). Childhood antecedents of antisocial behavior. *American Journal of Psychiatry, 147*(10), 1290–1293.

Pomaki, G., Supeli, A., & Verhoeven, C. (2007). Role conflict and health behaviors: Moderating effects on psychological distress and somatic complaints. *Psychology & Health, 22*(3), 317–335.

Pontius, A. (2000). Comparison between two opposite homicidal syndromes (syndrome E vs. limbic psychotic trigger reaction). *Aggression & Violent Behavior, 5*(4), 423–427.

Pope, H. G., Gruber, A. J., & Yurgelun-Todd, D. (1995). The residual neuropsychological effects of cannabis. *Drug & Alcohol Dependence, 38*(1), 25–34.

Port, R. L., & Seybold, K. S. (1995). Hippocampal synaptic plasticity as a biological substrate underlying episodic psychosis. *Biological Psychiatry, 37*(5), 318–324.

Porter, S., Spencer, L., & Birt, A. R. (2003). Blinded by emotion? Effect of the emotionality of a scene on susceptibility to false memories. *Canadian Journal of Behavioural Science, 35*(3), 165–175.

Posada, G., Jacobs, A., Richmond, M. K., Carbonell, O. A., et al. (2002). Maternal caregiving and infant security in two cultures. *Developmental Psychology, 38*(1), 67–78.

Pougnet, E., Serbin, L. A., Stack, D. M. & Schwartzman, A. E. (2011). Fathers' influence on children's cognitive and behavioural functioning: A longitudinal study of Canadian families. *Canadian Journal of Behavioural Science, 43*(3), 173–182.

Poulin-Dubois, D., Blaye, A., Coutya, J., & Bialystok, E. (2011). The effects of bilingualism on toddlers' executive functioning. *Journal of Experimental Child Psychology, 108*(3), 567–579.

Powell, D. H. (2004). Behavioral treatment of debilitating test anxiety among medical students. *Journal of Clinical Psychology, 60*(8), 853–865.

Powell, R. A., Symbaluk, D. G., & Honey, P. L. (2009). *Introduction to learning and behavior* (3rd ed.). Belmont, CA: Cengage Learning/Wadsworth.

Preckel, F., Holling, H., & Wiese, M. (2006). Relationship of intelligence and creativity in gifted and non-gifted students: An investigation of threshold theory. *Personality & Individual Differences, 40*(1), 159–170.

Premack, A. J., & Premack, D. (1972, October). Teaching language to an ape. *Scientific American,* 92–99.

Premack, D., & Premack, A. J. (1983). *The mind of an ape.* New York: Norton.

Pressley, M. (1987). Are key-word method effects limited to slow presentation rates? An empirically based reply to Hall and Fuson (1986). *Journal of Educational Psychology, 79*(3), 333–335.

Priluck, R., & Till, B. D. (2004). The role of contingency awareness, involvement, and need for cognition in attitude formation. *Journal of the Academy of Marketing Science, 32*(3), 329–344.

Prochaska, J. O., & Norcross, J. C. (2010). *Systems of psychotherapy: A transtheoretical analysis* (7th ed.). Belmont, CA: Cengage Learning/Wadsworth.

Provencher, M. D., Dugas, M. J., & Ladouceur, R. (2004). Efficacy of problemsolving training and cognitive exposure in the treatment of generalized anxiety disorder: A case replication series. *Cognitive & Behavioral Practice, 11*(4), 404–414.

Public Health Agency of Canada. (2011). *Diabetes in Canada: Facts and figures from a public health perspective.* Retrieved September 15, 2012, from http://www .phac-aspc.gc.ca/cd-mc/publications /diabetes-diabete/facts-figures-faits -chiffres-2011/pdf/facts-figures-faits -chiffres-eng.pdf.

Puentes, J., Knox, D., & Zusman, M. E. (2008). Participants in "friends with benefits" relationships. *College Student Journal, 42*(1), 176–180.

Pursch, J. A. (1983, June 12). Cocaine can give you the business. *Los Angeles Times,* Part VII, p. 12.

Pychyl, T. A., Lee, J. M., Thibodeau, R., & Blunt, A. (2000). Five days of emotion: An experience sampling study of undergraduate student procrastination. *Journal of Social Behavior & Personality, 15*(5), 239–254.

Quednow, B. B., Jessen, F., Kühn, K.-W., Maier, W., et al. (2006). Memory deficits in abstinent MDMA (ecstasy) users: Neuropsychological evidence of frontal dysfunction. *Journal of Psychopharmacology, 20*(3), 373–384.

Quigley, B. M., & Leonard, K. E. (2000). Alcohol, drugs, and violence. In V. B. Van Hasselt & M. Hersen (Eds.), *Aggression and violence: An introductory text.* Boston: Allyn & Bacon.

Quinn, P. C., Bhatt, R. S., & Hayden, A. (2008). Young infants readily use proximity to organize visual pattern information. *Acta Psychologica, 127*(2), 289–298.

Quinto-Pozos, D. (2008). Sign language contact and interference: ASL and LSM. *Language in Society, 37*(2), 161–189.

Rabius, V., McAlister, A. L., Geiger, A., Huang, P., et al. (2004). Telephone counseling increases cessation rates among young adult smokers. *Health Psychology, 23*(5), 539–541.

Rachman, S. (2004). *Anxiety* (2nd. ed.), New York: Routledge.

Rahman, S. López-Hernández, G. Y., Corrigall, W. A. & Papke, R. L. (2008). Neuronal nicotinic receptors as brain targets for pharmacotherapy of drug addiction. *CNS & Neurological Disorders—Drug Targets, 7,* 422–441.

Rainville, P. (2004). Pain & emotions. In D. D. Price & M. C. Bushnell (Eds.), *Psychological methods of pain control: Basic science and clinical perspectives.* Seattle, WA: IASP Press.

Rainville, P., Duncan, G., H., Price, D. D., Carrier, B., & Bushnell, M. C. (1997). Pain affect encoded in human anterior cingulate but not somatosensory cortex. *Science, 277*(5328), 968–971.

Rainville, P., Hofbauer, R. K., Bushnell, M. C., Duncan, G. H., et al. (2002). Hypnosis modulates activity in brain structures involved in the regulation of consciousness. *Journal of Cognitive Neuroscience, 14,* 887–901.

Rainville, P., & Price, D. D. (2003). Hypnosis: Phenomenology and the neurobiology of Consciousness. *International Journal of Clinical and Experimental Hypnosis, 51*(2), 105–129.

Ramachandran, V. S. (1995). 2–D or not 2–D—that is the question. In R. Gregory, J. Harris, P. Heard, & D. Rose (Eds.), *The artful eye.* Oxford: Oxford University Press.

Ramage-Morin, P. L. (2004). Panic disorder and coping. *Supplement to Health Reports, 15,* 33–63 (Statistics Canada, Catalogue 82-003).

Ramos, B. M. C., Siegel, S., & Bueno, J. L. O. (2002). Occasion setting and drug tolerance. *Integrative Physiological and Behavioral Science, 37,* 165–177.

Ramsay, M. C., Reynolds, C. R., & Kamphaus, R. W. (2002). *Essentials of behavioral assessment.* New York: Wiley.

Rathus, S. A., Nevid, J. S., Fichner-Rathus, L., McKenzie, S., et al. (2004). *Essentials of Human Sexuality* (2nd Canadian ed.) Toronto: Pearson.

Rathus, S., & Longmuir, S. (2012). *HDEV* (1st Canadian ed.). Toronto: Nelson Education.

Rau, H., Bührer, M., & Weitkunat, R. (2003). Biofeedback of R-wave-to-pulse interval normalizes blood pressure. *Applied Psychophysiology and Biofeedback, 28*(1), 37–46.

Rau, W., & Durand, A. (2000). The academic ethic and college grades: Does hard work help students to "make the grade"? *Sociology of Education, 73*(1), 19–38.

Reed, J. D., & Bruce, D. (1982). Longitudinal tracking of difficult memory retrievals. *Cognitive Psychology, 14,* 280–300.

Reed, S. K. (2010). *Cognition: Theory and applications* (8th ed.). Belmont, CA: Cengage Learning/Wadsworth.

Reevy, G. M., & Maslach, C. (2001). Use of social support: Gender and personality differences. *Sex Roles, 44*(7–8), 437–459.

Regan, P. C., Levin, L., Sprecher, S., Christopher, F. S., et al. (2000). Partner preferences: What characteristics do men and women desire in their short-term sexual and long-term romantic partners? *Journal of Psychology & Human Sexuality, 12*(3), 1–21.

Rehm, J., Baliunas, D., Brochu, S., Fischer, B., et al. (2006). *The costs of substance abuse in Canada 2002.* Ottawa: Canadian Centre on Substance Abuse.

Reid, P. T. (2002). Multicultural psychology. *Cultural Diversity & Ethnic Minority Psychology, 8*(2), 103–114.

Reiff, S., Katkin, E. S., & Friedman, R. (1999). Classical conditioning of the human blood pressure response. *International Journal of Psychophysiology, 34*(2), 135–145.

Reifman, A. S., Larrick, R. P., & Fein, S. (1991). Temper and temperature on the diamond: The heat-aggression relationship in major league baseball. *Personality & Social Psychology Bulletin, 17*(5), 580–585.

Reinberg, A., & Ashkenazi, I. (2008). Internal desynchronization of circadian rhythms and tolerance to shift work. *Chronobiology International, 25*(4), 625–643.

Reisner, A. D. (2006). A case of Munchausen syndrome by proxy with subsequent stalking behavior. *International Journal of Offender Therapy & Comparative Criminology, 50*(3), 245–254.

Reiss, M., Tymnik, G., Kögler, P., Kögler, W., et al. (1999). Laterality of hand, foot, eye, and ear in twins. *Laterality, 4*(3), 287–297.

Reiss, S., & Havercamp, S. M. (2005). Motivation in developmental context: A new method for studying self-actualization. *Journal of Humanistic Psychology, 45*(1), 41–53.

Reiterman, T. (1993, April 23). Parallel roads led to Jonestown, Waco. *The Los Angeles Times,* A-24.

Reitman, D., Murphy, M. A., Hupp, S. D. A., & O'Callaghan, P. M. (2004). Behavior change and perceptions of change: Evaluating the effectiveness of a token economy. *Child & Family Behavior Therapy, 26*(2), 17–36.

Renner, M. J., & Mackin, R. S. (1998). A life stress instrument for classroom use. *Teaching of Psychology, 25*(1), 46–48.

Rentfrow, P. J., & Gosling, S. D. (2003). The do re mi's of everyday life: The structure and personality correlates of music preferences. *Journal of Personality & Social Psychology, 84*(6), 1236–1256.

Rescorla, R. A. (1987). A Pavlovian analysis of goal-directed behavior. *American Psychologist, 42,* 119–126.

Rescorla, R. A. (2004). Spontaneous recovery. *Learning & Memory, 11*(5), 501–509.

Restak, R. M. (2001). *The secret life of the brain.* New York: The Dana Press.

Rhine, J. B. (1953). *New world of the mind.* New York: Sloane.

Ricci, L. C., & Wellman, M. W. (1990). Monamines: Biochemical markers of suicide? *Journal of Clinical Psychology, 46*(1), 106–116.

Rice, M. E. (1997). Violent offender research and implications for the criminal justice system. *American Psychologist, 52*(4), 414–423.

Richards, J. M., & Gross, J. J. (2000). Emotion regulation and memory: The cognitive costs of keeping one's cool. *Journal of Personality & Social Psychology, 79*(3), 410–424.

Richardson, D. R., & Green, L. R. (1999). Social sanction and threat explanations on gender effects in direct and indirect aggression. *Aggressive Behavior, 25*, 425–434.

Richelle, M. N. (1995). *B. F. Skinner: A reappraisal.* Hillsdale: Erlbaum.

Richmond, L. J. (2004). When spirituality goes awry: Students in cults. *Professional School Counseling, 7*(5), 367–375.

Ridenour, T. A., Maldonado-Molina, M., Compton, W. M., Spitznagel, E. L., et al. (2005). Factors associated with the transition from abuse to dependence among substance abusers: Implications for a measure of addictive liability. *Drug & Alcohol Dependence, 80*(1), 1–14.

Ridings, C. M., & Gefen, D. (2004). Virtual community attraction: Why people hang out online. *Journal of Computer-Mediated Communication, 10*(1). Retrieved July 8, 2009, from http://jcmc.indiana.edu/vol10/issue1/ridings_gefen.html.

Rieber, R. W. (1999). Hypnosis, false memory and multiple personality. *History of Psychiatry, 10*(37, Pt 1), 3–11.

Rieke, M. L., & Guastello, S. J. (1995, June). Unresolved issues in honesty and integrity testing. *American Psychologist,* 458–459.

Riley, W., Jerome, A., Behar, A., & Zack, S. (2002). Feasibility of computerized scheduled gradual reduction for adolescent smoking cessation. *Substance Use & Misuse, 37*(2), 255–263.

Rinfret-Raynor, M., Riou, A., Cantin, S., Drouin, C., et al. (2004). A survey on violence against female partners in Québec, Canada. *Violence Against Women, 10*(7), 709–728.

Riquelme, H. (2002). Can people creative in imagery interpret ambiguous figures faster than people less creative in imagery? *Journal of Creative Behavior, 36*(2), 105–116.

Riva, G., & Wiederhold, B. K. (2006). Emerging trends in cybertherapy: Introduction to the special issue. *Psychology Journal, 4*(2), 121–128.

Roan, S. (1992, September 1). Forever set in your ways at 30? *Los Angeles Times,* pp. E1, E2.

Roberts, B. W., & Mroczek, D. (2008). Personality trait change in adulthood. *Current Directions in Psychological Science, 17,* 31–35.

Roberts, R. (1989). Passenger fear of flying: Behavioural treatment with extensive in-vivo exposure and group support. *Aviation, Space, & Environmental Medicine, 60*(4), 342–348.

Roberts, R. E., Phinney, J. S., Masse, L. C., Chen, Y. R., et al. (1999). The structure of ethnic identity of young adolescents from diverse ethnocultural groups. *Journal of Early Adolescence, 19*(3), 301–322.

Roberts, W. A. (2002). Are animals stuck in time? *Psychological Bulletin, 128*(3), 473–489.

Roberts, W. A., Feeney, M. C., MacPherson, K., Petter, M., et al. (2008). Episodic-like memory in rats: Is it based on when or how long ago? *Science, 320*(5872), 113–115.

Roberts, W. A., & Roberts, S. (2002). Two tests of the stuck-in-time hypothesis. *Journal of General Psychology, 129*(4), 415–429.

Robertson, I. S. (2001). *Problem solving.* Hove, U.K.: Psychology Press.

Robertson, L. C. & Sagiv, N. (2005). *Synesthesia: Perspectives from cognitive neuroscience.* New York: Oxford.

Robins, R. W., Gosling, S. D., & Craik, K. H. (1998, July–August). Psychological science at the crossroads. *American Scientist, 86,* 310–313.

Robins, R. W., Gosling, S. D., & Craik, K. H. (1999). An empirical analysis of trends in psychology. *American Psychologist, 54*(2), 117 -128.

Robinson, D. N. (2008). *Consciousness and mental life.* New York: Columbia University Press.

Robinson, T. N., Wilde, M. L., Navracruz, L. C., Haydel, K. F., et al. (2001). Effects of reducing children's television and video game use on aggressive behavior. *Archives of Pediatrics and Adolescent Medicine, 155*(1), 17–23.

Robinson-Riegler, B., & McDaniel, M. (1994). Further constraints on the bizarreness effect: Elaboration at encoding. *Memory & Cognition, 22*(6), 702–712.

Rock, A. (2004). *The mind at night. The new science of how and why we dream.* New York: Basic Books.

Rodd, Z. A., Bell, R. L., McQueen, V. K., Davids, M. R., et al. (2005). Chronic ethanol drinking by alcohol-preferring rats increases the sensitivity of the posterior ventral tegmental area to the reinforcing effects of ethanol. *Alcoholism: Clinical & Experimental Research, 29*(3), 358–366.

Roeckelein, J. E. (2004). *Imagery in psychology: A reference guide.* Westport, CT: Praeger.

Roediger, H. L., & McDermott, K. B. (1995). Creating false memories: Remembering words not presented on lists. *Journal of Experimental Psychology: Learning, Memory, and Cognition, 21*(4), 803–814.

Roediger, III, H. L., & Amir, N. (2005). Implicit memory tasks: Retention without conscious recollection. In A. Wenzel & D. C. Rubin (Eds.), *Cognitive methods and their application to clinical research.* Washington: American Psychological Association.

Roese, N. J., Pennington, G. L., Coleman, J., Janicki, M., et al. (2006). Sex differences in regret: All for love or some for lust? *Personality & Social Psychology Bulletin, 32*(6), 770–780.

Rogers, C. R. (1959). A theory of therapy, personality, and interpersonal relationships, as developed in the client-centered framework. In S. Koch (Ed.), *Psychology: A study of a science* (Vol. 3). New York: McGraw-Hill.

Rogers, C. R. (1961). *On becoming a person: A therapist's view of psychotherapy.* Boston: Houghton Mifflin.

Rogers, S., & Silver, S. M. (2002). Is EMDR an exposure therapy? A review of trauma protocols. *Journal of Clinical Psychology, 58*(1), 43–59.

Rogers, T. B., Kuiper, N. A., & Kirker, W. S. (1977). Self-reference and the encoding of personal information. *Journal of Personality and Social Psychology, 35*(9), 677–688.

Rohsenow, D. J., & Smith R. E. (1982). Irrational beliefs as predictors of negative affective states. *Motivation and Emotion, 6,* 299–301.

Roid, G. H. (2003). *Stanford-Binet Intelligence Scales, Fifth Edition, Examiner's Manual.* Itasca, IL: Riverside.

Rolls, E. T. (2008). Top-down control of visual perception: Attention in natural vision. *Perception, 37*(3), 333–354.

Roos, P. E., & Cohen, L. H. (1987). Sex roles and social support as moderators of life stress adjustment. *Journal of Personality & Social Psychology, 52,* 576–585.

Rosch, E. (1977). Classification of real-world objects: Origins and representations in cognition. In P. N. Johnson-Laird & P. C. Wason (Eds.), *Thinking: Reading in cognitive science.* Cambridge: Cambridge University Press.

Rose, N. S., Olsen, R. K., Craik, F. I. M., & Rosenbaum, R. S. (2011). Working memory and amnesia: The role of stimulus novelty. *Neuropsychologia, 50*(1), 11–18.

Rosen, G., Hugdahl, K., Ersland, L., Lundervold, A., et al. (2001). Different brain areas activated during imagery of painful and non-painful "finger movements" in a subject with an amputated arm. *Neurocase, 7*(3), 255–260.

Rosen, L. A., Booth, S. R., Bender, M. E., McGrath, M. L., et al. (1988). Effects of sugar (sucrose) on children's behavior. *Journal of Consulting & Clinical Psychology, 56*(4), 583–589.

Rosenbaum, R. S., Murphy, K. J., & Rich, J. B. (2012). The amnesias. *Wiley Interdisciplinary Reviews: Cognitive Science, 3*(1), 47–63.

Rosenberg, L. B. (1994, July). The effect of interocular distance upon depth perception when using stereoscopic displays to perform work within virtual and telepresent environments. *USAF AMRL Technical Report* (Wright-Patterson), AL/CF-TR-1994–0052.

Rosenman, R. H., Brand, R. J., Jenkins, C. D., Friedman, M., et al. (1975). Coronary heart disease in the Western Collaborative Group Study: Final follow-up experience of 8 1/2 years. *Journal of the American Medical Association, 233,* 872–877.

Rosenthal, R. (1965). Clever Hans: A case study of scientific method. Introduction to a reissue of *Clever Hans: (The horse of Mr. Von Osten),* by O. Pfungst. New York: Holt.

Rosenthal, R. (1973, September). The Pygmalion effect lives. *Psychology Today,* 56–63.

Rosenthal, R. (1994). Science and ethics in conducting, analyzing, and reporting psychological research. *Psychological Science, 5,* 127–134.

Rosenthal, T. L. (1993). To soothe the savage breast. *Behavior Research & Therapy, 31*(5), 439–462.

Rosenthal, T. L., & Rosenthal, R. (1980). *The vicious cycle of stress reaction.* Copyright Renate & Ted Rosenthal, Stress Management Clinic, Department of Psychiatry, University of Tennessee College of Medicine, Memphis.

Rosenthal, T. L., & Steffek, B. D. (1991). Modeling methods. In F. H. Kanfer & A. P. Goldstein (Eds.), *Helping people change.* Elmsford, NY: Pergamon.

Rosenzweig, M. R., Breedlove, S. M., & Watson, N. V. (2004). Biological psychology: *An introduction to behavioral and cognitive neuroscience* (4th ed.). Sunderland, MA: Sinauer Associates.

Rosnow, R. L. (2006). *Writing papers in psychology: A student guide to research papers, essays, proposals, posters, and handouts* (7th ed.). Belmont, CA: Wadsworth.

Ross, H. E., & Plug, C. (2002). *The mystery of the moon illusion.* Oxford: Oxford University Press.

Ross, M., Heine, S. J., Wilson, A. E., & Sugimori, S. (2005). Cross-cultural discrepancies in self-appraisals. *Personality and Social Psychology Bulletin, 31*(9), 1175–1188.

Ross, P. E. (2006). The expert mind. *Scientific American, 294*(7), 64–71.

Rotermann, M. (2005). Sex, condoms and STDs among young people. *Health Reports, 16*(3), 39–45. Statistics Canada Catalog 82-003XIE. Retrieved September 26, 2012, from http://www.statcan.gc.ca/pub/82-003-x/2004003/article/7838-eng.pdf.

Rotermann, M. (2008). Trends in teen sexual behaviour and condom use. *Statistics Canada Health Reports, 19*(3), 53. Retrieved September 26, 2012, from http://publications.gc.ca/collections/collection_2008/statcan/82-003-X/82-003-XIE2008003.pdf#page=55.

Rothschild, B., & Rand, M. (2006). *Help for the helper: The psychophysiology of compassion fatigue and vicarious trauma.* New York: Norton.

Rotter, J. B., & Hochreich, D. J. (1975). *Personality.* Glenview, IL: Scott, Foresman.

Rowe, B. (2007). College awareness guide: What students need to know to succeed in college. Upper Saddle River, NJ: Prentice Hall.

Roy, S. & Park, N. W. (2010). Dissociating the memory systems mediating complex tool knowledge and skills. *Neuropsychologia, 48*(10), 3026–3036.

Rozin, P., Kabnick, K., Pete, E., Fischler, C., et al. (2003). The ecology of eating: Smaller portion sizes in France than in the United States help explain the French paradox. *Psychological Science, 14*(5), 450–454.

Rubin, D. C. (1985, September). The subtle deceiver: Recalling our past. *Psychology Today,* 38–46.

Rubin, K. H. (1998). Social and emotional development from a cultural perspective. *Developmental Psychology, 34*(4), 611–615.

Rudd, M. D., Joiner, T. E., Jr., & Rajab, M. H. (2001). *Treating suicidal behavior.* New York: Guilford.

Rueckl, J. G., & Galantucci, B. (2005). The locus and time course of long-term morphological priming. *Language & Cognitive Processes, 20*(1), 115–138.

Rummens, J., Beiser, M., & Noh, S. (Eds.). (2003). *Immigration, ethnicity and health.* Toronto: University of Toronto Press.

Runco, M. A. (2003). Idea evaluation, divergent thinking, and creativity. In M. A. Runco (Ed.), *Critical creative processes. Perspectives on creativity research.* Cresskill, NJ: Hampton Press.

Runco, M. A. (2004). Creativity. *Annual Review of Psychology, 55,* 657–687.

Russell, S. (2007, February 13). Medical pot cuts pain, study finds. *San Francisco Chronicle,* B-1.

Russell, S., & Norvig, P. (2003). *Artificial intelligence: A modern approach* (2nd ed.). Englewood Cliffs, NJ: Prentice Hall.

Russo, M. B., Brooks, F. R., Fontenot, J., Halliday, A. W., et al. (1998). Conversion disorder presenting as multiple sclerosis. *Military Medicine, 163*(10), 709–710.

Rutledge, T., & Linden, W. (1998). To eat or not to eat: Affective and physiological mechanisms in the stress-eating relationship. *Journal of Behavioral Medicine, 21*(3), 221–240.

Rutz, C., Bluff, L. A., Weir, A. A. S., & Kacelnik, A. (2007). Video cameras on wild birds. *Science, 318,* 765.

Ruva, C., McEvoy, C., & Bryant, J. B. (2007). Effects of pre-trial publicity and jury deliberation on juror bias and source memory errors. *Applied Cognitive Psychology, 21*(1), 45–67.

Ryan, M. P. (2001). Conceptual models of lecture learning. *Reading Psychology, 22*(4), 289–312.

Ryan, R. M., & Deci, E. L. (2000). Self-determination theory and the facilitation of intrinsic motivation, social development, and well-being. *American Psychologist, 55,* 68–78.

Ryff, C. D. (1995). Psychological well-being in adult life. *Current Directions in Psychological Science, 4*(4), 99–104.

Ryff, C. D., & Singer, B. (2000). Interpersonal flourishing. *Personality and Social Psychology Review, 4,* 30–44.

Ryff, C. D., Singer, B. H., & Palmersheim, K. A. (2004). Social inequalities in health and well-being: The role of relational and religious protective factors. In O. G. Brim, C. D. Ryff, & R. C. Kessler (Eds.), *How healthy are we?: A national study of well-being at midlife.* Chicago, IL: University of Chicago Press.

Sackeim, H. A., Haskett, R. F., Mulsant, B. H., Thase, M. E., et al. (2001). Continuation pharmacotherapy in the prevention of relapse following electroconvulsive therapy. *Journal of the American Medical Association, 285,* 1299–1307.

Sahelian, R. (1998). *5-HTP.* Wakefield, RI: Moyer Bell.

Saksida, L. M., & Wilkie, D. M. (1994). Time-of-day discrimination by pigeons. *Animal Learning & Behavior, 22,* 143–154.

Salmon, P. (2001). Effects of physical exercise on anxiety, depression, and sensitivity to stress: A unifying theory. *Clinical Psychology Review, 21*(1), 33–61.

Salovey, P., & Mayer, J. (1997). *Emotional development and emotional intelligence.* New York: Basic Books.

Salthouse, T. A. (2004). What and when of cognitive aging. *Current Directions in Psychological Science, 13*(4), 140–144.

Santrock, J. W., & Halonen, J. S. (2007). *Connections to college success.* Belmont, CA: Wadsworth.

Saunders, T., Driskell, J. E., Johnston, J. H., & Salas, E. (1996). The effect of stress inoculation training on anxiety and

performance. *Journal of Occupational Health Psychology, 1*(2), 170–186.

Savage-Rumbaugh, S., Sevcik, R. A., Brakke, K. E., Rumbaugh, D. M., et al. (1990). Symbols: Their communicative use, comprehension, and combination by bonobos (*Pan paniscus*). *Advances in Infancy Research, 6,* 221–278.

Saxton, M., Houston-Price, C., & Dawson, N. (2005). The prompt hypothesis: Clarification requests as corrective input for grammatical errors. *Applied Psycholinguistics, 26*(3), 393–414.

Saxvig, I. W., Lundervold, A. J., Gronli, J., Ursin, R., et al. (2008). The effect of a REM sleep deprivation procedure on different aspects of memory function in humans. *Psychophysiology, 45*(2), 309–317.

Scarr, S. (1998). American child care today. *American Psychologist, 53*(2), 95–108.

Schachter, S., & Wheeler, L. (1962). Epinephrine, chlorpromazine and amusement. *Journal of Abnormal and Social Psychology, 65,* 121–128.

Schacter, D. L. (1996). *Searching for memory.* New York: Basic.

Schacter, D. L. (2000). Memory: Memory systems. In A. Kazdin (Ed.), *Encyclopedia of psychology.* Washington: American Psychological Association.

Schacter, D. L. (2001). *The seven sins of memory.* Boston: Houghton Mifflin.

Schacter, D. L., Norman, K. A., & Koutstaal, W. (1998). The cognitive neuroscience of constructive memory. *Annual Review of Psychology, 49,* 289–318.

Schafer, M., & Crichlow, S. (1996). Antecedents of groupthink: A quantitative study. *Journal of Conflict Resolution, 40*(3), 415–435.

Schaie, K. W. (1994). The course of adult intellectual development. *American Psychologist, 49*(4), 304–313.

Schaie, K. W. (2005). *Developmental influences on adult intelligence: The Seattle longitudinal study.* London, U.K.: Oxford University Press.

Scheck, B., Neufeld, P., & Dwyer, J. (2000). *Actual innocence.* New York: Doubleday.

Schenck, C. H., & Mahowald, M. W. (2005). Rapid eye movement and non-REM sleep parasomnias. *Primary Psychiatry, 12*(8), 67–74.

Schick, T., & Vaughn, L. (2001). *How to think about weird things: Critical thinking for a new age.* New York: McGraw-Hill.

Schick, T., & Vaughn, L. (2010). *How to think about weird things: Critical thinking for a new age.* New York: McGraw-Hill.

Schilling, M. A. (2005). A "small-world" network model of cognitive insight. *Creativity Research Journal, 17*(2–3), 131–154.

Schiraldi, G. R., & Brown, S. L. (2001). Primary prevention for mental health: Results of an exploratory cognitive-behavioral college course. *Journal of Primary Prevention, 22*(1), 55–67.

Schlaepfer, T. E., Cohen, M. X., Frick, C., Kosel, M., et al. (2008). Deep brain stimulation to reward circuitry alleviates anhedonia in refractory major depression. *Neuropsychopharmacology, 33*(2), 368–377.

Schlosberg, H. (1954). Three dimensions of emotion. *Psychological Review, 61,* 81–88.

Schmitt, D. P., & Allik, J. (2005). Simultaneous administration of the Rosenberg Self-Esteem Scale in 53 nations: Exploring the universal and culture-specific features of global self-esteem. *Journal of Personality & Social Psychology, 89*(4), 623–642.

Schmolck, H., Buffalo, E. A., & Squire, L. R. (2000). Memory distortions develop over time. *Psychological Science, 11*(1), 39–45.

Schneider, K. J., Bugental, J. F. T., & Pierson, J. F. (2001). Introduction. *The Handbook of Humanistic Psychology.* Thousand Oaks, CA: Sage.

Schneiderman, N., Antoni, M. H., Saab, P. G., & Ironson, G. (2001). Health psychology: Psychological and biobehavioral aspects of chronic disease management. *Annual Review of Psychology, 52,* 555–580.

Schonert-Reichl, K.A., Smith, V., Zaidman-Zait, A., & Hertzman, C. (2012). Promoting children's prosocial behaviors in school: Impact of the "Roots of Empathy" program on the social and emotional competence of school-aged children. *School Mental Health, 4*(1), 1–21.

Schonfeld, A. M., Mattson, S. N., & Riley E. P. (2005). Moral maturity and delinquency after prenatal alcohol exposure. *Journal of Studies on Alcohol. 66*(4), 545–554.

Schopp, L. H., Demiris, G., & Glueckauf, R. L. (2006). Rural backwaters or front-runners? Rural telehealth in the vanguard of psychology practice. *Professional Psychology: Research & Practice, 37*(2), 165–173.

Schoppe-Sullivan, S. J., Mangledorf, S. C., Brown, G. L., & Sokolowski, M. S. (2007). Goodness-of-fit in family context: Infant temperament, marital quality and early co-parenting behavior. *Infant Behavior and Development, 30*(1), 82–96.

Schreiber, E. H., & Schreiber, D. E. (1999). Use of hypnosis with witnesses of vehicular homicide. *Contemporary Hypnosis, 16*(1), 40–44.

Schreiber, F. R. (1973). *Sybil.* Chicago: Regency.

Schroeder, J. E. (1995). Self-concept, social anxiety, and interpersonal perception skills. *Personality & Individual Differences, 19*(6), 955–958.

Schuel, H., Chang, M. C., Burkman, L. J., Picone, R. P., et al. (1999). Cannabinoid receptors in sperm. In G. Nahas, K. M. Sutin, D. Harvey, & S. Agurell (Eds.), *Marijuana and medicine.* Totowa, NJ: Humana Press.

Schultheiss, O. C., Wirth, M. M., & Stanton, S. J. (2004). Effects of affiliation and power motivation arousal on salivary progesterone and testosterone. *Hormones & Behavior, 46*(5), 592–599.

Schultz, D. P., & Schultz, S. E. (2008). *A history of modern psychology* (9th ed.). Belmont, CA: Cengage Learning/Wadsworth.

Schum, T. R., Kolb, T. M., McAuliffe T. L., Simms, M., et al. (2002). Sequential acquisition of toilet-training skills: A descriptive study of gender and age differences in normal children. *Pediatrics, 3,* e48. Retrieved September 26, 2012, from

http://pediatrics.aappublications.org /content/109/3/e48.full.pdf.

Schwartz, B. L. (2002). *Tip-of-the-tongue states: Phenomenology, mechanism, and lexical retrieval.* Hillsdale, NJ: Erlbaum.

Schwartz, M. S., & Andrasik, F. (Eds.). (2003). *Biofeedback: A practitioner's guide* (3rd ed.). New York: Guilford.

Schwartz, S. J. (2008). Self and identity in early adolescence: Some reflections and an introduction to the special issue. *Journal of Early Adolescence, 28*(1), 5–15.

Sclafani, A., & Springer, D. (1976). Dietary obesity in adult rats: Similarities to hypothalamic and human obesity syndromes. *Psychology and Behavior, 17,* 461–471.

Scoboria, A., Mazzoni, G., Kirsch, I., & Milling, L. S. (2002). Immediate and persisting effects of misleading questions and hypnosis on memory reports. *Journal of Experimental Psychology: Applied, 8*(1), 26–32.

Scott, J. P., & Ginsburg, B. E. (1994). The Seville statement on violence revisited. *American Psychologist, 49*(10), 849–850.

Scott, L., & O'Hara, M. W. (1993). Self-discrepancies in clinically anxious and depressed university students. *Journal of Abnormal Psychology, 102*(2), 282–287.

Scurfield, R. M. (2002). Commentary about the terrorist acts of September 11, 2001: Posttraumatic reactions and related social and policy issues. *Trauma Violence & Abuse, 3*(1), 3–14.

Seal, D. W., & Palmer-Seal, D. A. (1996). Barriers to condom use and safer sex talk among college dating couples. *Journal of Community & Applied Social Psychology, 6*(1), 15–33.

Searcy, W. A., & Nowicki, S. (2005). The evolution of animal communication: Reliability and deception in signaling systems. Princeton, NJ: Princeton University Press.

Sears, R. R., Maccoby, E. E., & Levin, H. (1957). *Patterns of child rearing.* Evanston, IL: Row, Peterson.

Seckel, A. (2000). *The art of optical illusions.* London, U.K.: Carlton Books.

Segal, N. L., McGuire, S. A., Miller, S. A., & Havlena, J. (2008). Tacit coordination in monozygotic twins, dizygotic twins and virtual twins: Effects and implications of genetic relatedness. *Personality and Individual Differences, 45*(7), 607–612.

Segerdahl, P., Fields, W., & Savage-Rumbaugh, S. (2005). *Kanzi's primal language: The cultural initiation of primates into language.* New York: Palgrave MacMillan.

Segerstrom, S., & Miller, G. E. (2004). Psychological stress and the human immune system: A meta-analytic study of 30 years of inquiry. *Psychological Bulletin, 130*(4), 601–630.

Seidman, B. F. (2001, January–February). Medicine wars. *Skeptical Inquirer,* 28–35.

Seifert, T. & Hedderson, C. (2010). Intrinsic motivation and flow in skateboarding: An ethnographic study. *Journal of Happiness Studies, 11*(3), 277–292.

Seitz, A., & Watanabe, T. (2005). A unified model for perceptual learning. *Trends in Cognitive Sciences, 9*(7), 329–334.

Seligman, M. E. P. (1972). For helplessness: Can we immunize the weak? In *Readings* in psychology today (2nd ed.). Del Mar, CA: CRM.

Seligman, M. E. P. (1989). Helplessness. New York: Freeman.

Seligman, M. E. P. (1995). The effectiveness of psychotherapy. American Psychologist, 50(12), 965–974.

Seligman, M. E. P. (1998). Why therapy works. APA Monitor, 29(12), 2.

Seligman, M. E. P. (2002). Authentic happiness: Using the new positive psychology to realize your potential for lasting fulfillment. New York: Free Press/Simon and Schuster.

Seligman, M. E. P., & Csikszentmihalyi, M. (2000). Positive psychology: An introduction. American Psychologist, 55, 5–14.

Selye, H. (1956/1976). The stress of life. New York: Knopf.

Senécal, C., Julien, E., & Guay, F. (2003). Role conflict and academic procrastination: A self-determination perspective. European Journal of Social Psychology, 33(1), 135–145.

Seybolt, D. C., & Wagner, M. K. (1997). Self-reinforcement, gender-role, and sex of participant in prediction of life satisfaction. Psychological Reports, 81(2), 519–522.

Shaffer, D. R., & Kipp, K. (2010). Developmental psychology: Childhood and adolescence (8th ed.). Belmont, CA: Cengage Learning/Wadsworth.

Shaffer, J. B., & Galinsky, M. D. (1989). Models of group therapy. Englewood Cliffs, NJ: Prentice Hall.

Shafir, E. (1993). Choosing versus rejecting: Why some options are both better and worse than others. Memory and Cognition, 21, 546–556.

Shafton, A. (1995). Dream reader. Albany, NY: SUNY Press.

Shapiro, C. M., Trajanovic, N. N., & Fedoroff, J. P. (2003). Sexsomnia: A new parasomnia? Canadian Journal of Psychiatry, 48(5), 311–317.

Shapiro, F. (2001). Eye movement desensitization and reprocessing: Basic principles, protocols and procedures (2nd ed.). New York: Guilford.

Shapiro, F., & Forrest, M. S. (2004). EMDR: The breakthrough therapy for overcoming anxiety, stress, and trauma. New York: Basic Books.

Shariff, A. (2009). Ethnic identity and parenting stress in South Asian families: Implications for culturally sensitive counselling. Canadian Journal of Counselling, 43(1), 35–46.

Sharot, T., Martorella, E. A., Delgado, M. R., & Phelps, E. A. (2007). How personal experience modulates the neural circuitry of memories of September 11. PNAS Proceedings of the National Academy of Sciences of the United States of America, 104(1), 389–394.

Shaughnessy, K., Byers, E. S., & Walsh, L. (2011). Online sexual activity experience of heterosexual students: Gender similarities and differences. Archives of Sexual Behavior, 40(2), 419–427.

Shaywitz, B. A., Shaywitz, S. E., Pugh, K. R., Constable, R. T., et al. (1995). Sex differences in the functional organization of the brain for language. Nature, 373, 607–609.

Sheldon, K. M., Ryan, R. M., Rawsthorne, L. J., & Ilardi, B. (1997). Trait self and true self: Cross-role variation in the Big-Five personality traits and its relations with psychological authenticity and subjective well-being. Journal of Personality & Social Psychology, 73(6), 1380–1393.

Shen, J., Botly, L. C. P., Chung, S. A., Gibbs, A. L., et al. (2006). Fatigue and shift work. Journal of Sleep Research, 15(1), 1–5.

Shepard, R. N. (1975). Form, formation, and transformation of internal representations. In R. L. Solso (Ed.), Information processing and cognition: The Loyola Symposium. Hillsdale, NJ: Erlbaum.

Shepherd, G. M. (2006). Smell images and the flavour system in the human brain. Nature, 444(7117), 316–321.

Sherif, M., Harvey, O. J., White, B. J., Hood, W. R., et al. (1961). Intergroup conflict and cooperation: The Robbers Cave experiment. University of Oklahoma, Institute of Group Relations.

Shields, M. (2005a). Social anxiety disorder: Much more than shyness. Canadian Social Trends, Summer, 22–28. Statistics Canada, Catalogue No. 11-008.

Shields, M. (2005b). The journey to quitting smoking. Health Reports, 16(3), 19–36. Statistics Canada Catalogue No. 82-003. Retrieved February 8, 2012, from http://www.statcan.gc.ca/pub /82-003-x/2004003/article/7839-eng.pdf.

Shneerson, J. M. (2005). Sleep medicine: A guide to sleep and its disorders (2nd ed.). London: Blackwell.

Shneidman, E. (1987a, March). At the point of no return. Psychology Today, 54–58.

Shneidman, E. S. (1987b). Psychological approaches to suicide. In G. R. VandenBos & B. K. Bryant (Eds.), Cataclysms, crises, and catastrophes: Psychology in action. Washington: American Psychological Association.

Shurkin, J. N. (1992). Terman's kids. Boston: Little, Brown.

Siegel, R. K. (2005). Intoxication: The universal drive for mind-altering substances. Rochester, VT: Park Street Press.

Siegel, S. (1999). Drug anticipation and drug addiction. The 1998 H. David Archibald Lecture. Addiction, 94, 1113–1124.

Siegel, S. (2002). Pavlovian conditioning and drug overdose: When tolerance fails. Addiction Research & Theory, 9, 503–513.

Siegel, S., Baptista, M. A. S., Kim, J. A., McDonald, R. V., et al. (2000). Pavlovian psychopharmacology: The associative basis of tolerance. Experimental and Clinical Psychopharmacology, 8, 273–276.

Siegler, R. S. (1989). Mechanisms of cognitive development. Annual Review of Psychology, 40, 353–379.

Siegler, R. S. (2004). Children's thinking (4th ed.). Mahwah, NJ: Erlbaum.

Siegler, R. S. & Alibali, M. W. (2005). Children's thinking (4th ed.). Upper Saddle River, NJ: Prentice Hall.

Siegler, R. S., DeLoache, J. S., & Eisenberg, N. (2006). How children develop (2nd ed.). New York: Worth.

Sigelman, C. K., & Rider, E. A. (2009). Life-span human development (6th ed.). Belmont, CA: Cengage Learning/Wadsworth.

Silver, S. M., Rogers, S., Knipe, J., & Colelli, G. (2005). EMDR therapy following the 9/11 terrorist attacks: A community-based intervention project in New York City. International Journal of Stress Management, 12(1), 29–42.

Silverthorne, C. (2004). Common sense statistics (4th ed.). New York: McGraw-Hill.

Simeon, D., Guralnik, O., Knutelska, M., & Schmeidler, J. (2002). Personality factors associated with dissociation: Temperament, defenses, and cognitive schemata. American Journal of Psychiatry, 159, 489–491.

Simister, J., & Cooper, C. (2005). Thermal stress in the U.S.A.: Effects on violence and on employee behaviour. Stress & Health, 21, 3–15.

Simner, M. L., & Goffin, R. D. (2003). A position statement by the international graphonomics society on the use of graphology in personnel selection testing. International Journal of Testing, 3(4), 353–364.

Simon, G. E., Ludman, E. J., Tutty, S., Operskalski, B., et al. (2004). Telephone psychotherapy and telephone care management for primary care patients starting antidepressant treatment. Journal of the American Medical Association, 292, 935–942.

Simon, L. (1998). Genuine reality: A life of William James. Ft. Worth: Harcourt-Brace.

Simon-Thomas, E. R., Role, K. O., & Knight, R. T. (2005). Behavioral and electrophysiological evidence of a right hemisphere bias for the influence of negative emotion on higher cognition. Journal of Cognitive Neuroscience, 17(3), 518–529.

Simons, D. J., & Chabris, C. F. (1999). Gorillas in our midst: Sustained inattentional blindness for dynamic events. Perception, 28, 1059–1074.

Simons, J. S., Dodson, C. S., Bell, D., & Schacter, D. L. (2004). Specific-and partial-source memory: Effects of aging. Psychology & Aging, 19(4), 689–694.

Simonton, D. K., & Baumeister, R. F. (2005). Positive psychology at the summit. Review of General Psychology. Special Positive Psychology, 9(2), 99–102.

Simpson, D. D., Joe, G. W., Fletcher, B. W., Hubbard, R. L., et al. (1999). A national evaluation of treatment outcomes for cocaine dependence. Archives of General Psychiatry, 57(6), 507–514.

Singer, J. D. (2005). Explaining foreign policy: U.S. decision-making and the Persian Gulf War. Political Psychology, 26(5), 831–834.

Singer, M. T. (2003). Cults in our midst: The continuing fight against their hidden menace (rev. ed.). San Francisco: Jossey-Bass.

Singer, M. T., & Addis, M. E. (1992). Cults, coercion, and contumely. Cultic Studies Journal, 9(2), 163–189.

Singleton, J. L., & Newport, E. L. (2004). When learners surpass their models: The acquisition of American Sign Language from inconsistent input. Cognitive Psychology, 49(4), 370–407.

Sinha, R., Garcia, M., Paliwal, P., Kreek, M. J., et al. (2006). Stress-induced cocaine craving and hypothalamic-pituitary-adrenal responses are predictive of cocaine relapse outcomes. Archives of General Psychiatry, 63(3), 324–331.

Sipos, A., Rasmussen, F., Harrison, G., Tynelius, P., et al. (2004). Paternal age and schizophrenia: A population based cohort study. British Medical Journal, 329(7474), 1070.

Sirkin, M. I. (1990). Cult involvement: A systems approach to assessment and treatment. Psychotherapy, 27(1), 116–123.

Sison, C. E., Alpert, M., Fudge, R., & Stern, R. M. (1996). Constricted expressiveness and psychophysiological reactivity in schizophrenia. Journal of Nervous & Mental Disease, 184(10), 589–597.

Skipton, L. H. (1997). The many faces of character. Consulting Psychology Journal: Practice & Research, 49(4), 235–245.

Slaby, A. E., Garfinkel, B. D., & Garfinkel, L. F. (1994). No one say my pain. New York: Norton.

Slater, A., Mattock, A., & Brown, E. (1990). Size constancy at birth: Newborn infants' responses to retinal and real size. Journal of Experimental Child Psychology, 49(2), 314–322.

Slater, A., Mattock, A., Brown, E., & Bremner, J. G. (1991). Form perception at birth: Cohen and Younger (1984) revisited. Journal of Experimental Child Psychology, 51(3), 395–406.

Sloman, A. (2008). The well-designed young mathematician. Artifical Intelligence, 172(18), 2015–2034.

Slot, L. A. B., & Colpaert, F. C. (1999). Recall rendered dependent on an opiate state. Behavioral Neuroscience, 113(2), 337–344.

Smedley, A., & Smedley, B. D. (2005). Race as biology is fiction, racism as a social problem is real. American Psychologist, 60(1), 16–26.

Smith, A. P. (2005). Caffeine at work. Human Psychopharmacology: Clinical & Experimental, 20(6), 441–445.

Smith, A. P., Clark, R., & Gallagher, J. (1999). Breakfast cereal and caffeinated coffee: Effects on working memory, attention, mood and cardiovascular function. Physiology & Behavior, 67(1), 9–17.

Smith, C., Carey, S., & Wiser, M. (1985). On differentiation: A case study of the development of the concepts of size, weight, and density. Cognition, 21(3), 177–237.

Smith, E., & Delargy, M. (2005). Locked-in syndrome. British Medical Journal, 330, 406–409.

Smith, J. C. (1986, September). Meditation, biofeedback, and the relaxation controversy: A cognitive-behavioral perspective. American Psychologist, 1007–1009.

Smith, J. L., & Cahusac, P. M. B. (2001). Right-sided asymmetry in sensitivity to tickle. Laterality, 6(3), 233–238.

Smith, M. L., Cottrell, G. W., Gosselin, F., & Schyns, P. G. (2005). Transmitting and decoding facial expressions. Psychological Science, 16(3), 184–189.

Smith, T. W., Glazer, K., Ruiz, J. M., & Gallo, L. C. (2004). Hostility, anger, aggressiveness, and coronary heart disease: An interpersonal perspective on personality, emotion, and health. *Journal of Personality. Special Emotions, Personality, and Health, 72*(6), 1217–1270.

Smith, T. W., Ruiz, J. M., & Uchino, B. N. (2004). Mental activation of supportive ties, hostility, and cardiovascular reactivity to laboratory stress in young men and women. *Health Psychology, 23*(5), 476–485.

Smith, W. P., Compton, W. C., & West, W. B. (1995). Meditation as an adjunct to a happiness enhancement program. *Journal of Clinical Psychology, 51*(2), 269–273.

Smyth, M. M., & Waller, A. (1998). Movement imagery in rock climbing. *Applied Cognitive Psychology, 12*(2), 145–157.

Snedeker, J., Geren, J., & Shafto, C. L., (2007). Starting over: international adoption as a natural experiment in language development. *Psychological Science, 18*(1), 79–87.

Snyder, A., Bahramali, H., Hawker, T., & Mitchell, D. J. (2006). Savant-like numerosity skills revealed in normal people by magnetic pulses. *Perception, 35*(6), 837–845.

Sobel, E., Shine, D., DiPietro, D., & Rabinowitz, M. (1996). Condom use among HIV-infected patients in South Bronx, New York. *AIDS, 10*(2), 235–236.

Sobolewski, J. M., & Amato, P. R. (2005). Economic hardship in the family of origin and children's psychological well-being in adulthood. *Journal of Marriage and Family, 67*(1), 141–156.

Solso, R. L., MacLin, M. K., & MacLin, O. H. (2008). *Cognitive psychology* (8th ed.). Boston: Allyn & Bacon.

Somberg, D. R., Stone, G., & Claiborn, C. D. (1993). Informed consent: Therapists' beliefs and practices. *Professional Psychology: Research & Practice, 24*(2), 153–159.

Son Hing, L.S., Bobocel, D.R., Zanna, M.P., Garcia, D.M., et al. (2011). The merit of meritocracy. *Journal of Personality and Social Psychology, 101*(3), 433–450.

Soussignan, R. (2002). Duchenne smile, emotional experience, and autonomic reactivity: A test of the facial feedback hypothesis. *Emotion, 2*(1), 52–74.

Soussignan, R., & Schaal, B. (2005). Emotional processes in human newborns: a functionalist perspective. In J. Nadal & D. Muir (Eds.), *Emotional development: recent research advances*. New York: Oxford University Press.

Spafford, M., Rudman, D.L., Leipert, B., Klinger, L. et al. (2010). When self-presentation trumps access: Why older adults with low vision go without low vision services. *Journal of Applied Gerontology, 29*(5), 579–602.

Spalding, K. L., Arner, E., Westermark, P. O., Bernard, S., et al. (2008, May 4). Dynamics of fat cell turnover in humans. *Nature*, doi:10.1038/nature06902.

Spano, R. (2005). Potential sources of observer bias in police observational data. *Social Science Research, 34*(3), 591–617.

Speca, M., Carlson, L. E., Goodey, E., & Angen, M. (2000). A randomized, wait-list controlled clinical trial: The effect of a mindfulness meditation-based stress reduction program on mood and symptoms of stress in cancer outpatients. *Psychosomatic Medicine, 62*, 613–622.

Spector, P. E. (2005). *Industrial and organizational psychology: Research and practice* (4th ed.). New York: Wiley.

Spence, S., & David, A. (Eds.). (2004). *Voices in the brain: The cognitive neuropsychiatry of auditory verbal hallucinations*. London, U.K.: Psychology Press.

Sperry, R. W. (1968). Hemisphere deconnection and unity in conscious awareness. *American Psychologist, 23*, 723–733.

Spiegler, M. D., & Guevremont, D. C. (2003). *Contemporary behavior therapy*. Belmont, CA: Wadsworth.

Spiro Wagner, P., & Spiro, C. S. (2005). *Divided minds: Twin sisters and their journey through schizophrenia*. New York: St. Martin's Press.

Sprecher, S. (1998). Insiders' perspectives on reasons for attraction to a close other. *Social Psychology Quarterly, 61*(4), 287–300.

Springer, S. P., & Deutsch, G. (1998). *Left brain, right brain*. New York: Freeman.

Sprinthall, R. C. (2007). *Basic statistical analysis* (8th ed.). Boston: Allyn & Bacon.

Squire, L. R. (2004). Memory systems of the brain: A brief history and current perspective. *Neurobiology of Learning & Memory, 82*, 171–177.

Srivastava, S., John, O. P., Gosling, S. D., & Potter, J. (2003). Development of personality in early and middle adulthood: Set like plaster or persistent change? *Journal of Personality & Social Psychology, 84*(5), 1041–1053.

Staemmler, F.-M. (2004). Dialogue and interpretation in Gestalt therapy: Making sense together. *International Gestalt Journal, 27*(2), 33–57.

Stanovich, K. E. (2007). *How to think straight about psychology* (8th ed.). Boston: Allyn & Bacon.

Stapel, D. A., & Marx, D. M. (2007). Distinctiveness is key: How different types of self-other similarity moderate social comparison effects. *Personality & Social Psychology Bulletin, 33*(3), 439–448.

Statistics Canada. (2000). Statistical report on the health of Canadians (Catalogue No. 82-570-X1E). Retrieved September 26, 2012, from http://www.statcan.gc.ca/pub/82-570-x/82-570-x1997001-eng.pdf.

Statistics Canada. (2001). You snooze, you lose? Sleep patterns in Canada. *Canadian Social Trends*, Catalogue No. 11-008. Retrieved September 26, 2012, from http://www.statcan.gc.ca/pub/11-008-x/2000004/article/5558-eng.pdf.

Statistics Canada. (2003, September 5). Canadian community health survey: Canadian forces supplement on mental health. *The Daily*.

Statistics Canada. (2007). The amount of TV children and teens watch per week and per province. Retrieved May 5, 2008, from http://www.statcan.ca/english/kits/winner/2004/grade9/TVwatching/Children.htm.

Statistics Canada. (2008, April 2). *The Daily*. Retrieved September 26, 2012, from http://www.statcan.gc.ca/daily-quotidien/080402/dq080402-eng.pdf.

Statistics Canada (2011). *Mortality: summary list of causes, 2008*. Catalogue no. 84F0209X. Retrieved September 26, 2012, from http://www.statcan.gc.ca/pub/84f0209x/2008000/t001-eng.pdf.

Statistics Canada. (2012, June 19). *The Daily*. Retrieved September 19, 2012, from http://www.statcan.gc.ca/daily-quotidien/120619/tdq120619-eng.htm.

Steiger, A. (2007). Neurochemical regulation of sleep. *Journal of Psychiatric Research, 41*, 537–552.

Stein, L. M., & Memon, A. (2006). Testing the efficacy of the cognitive interview in a developing country. *Applied Cognitive Psychology, 20*(5), 597–605.

Stein, M. D., & Friedmann, P. D. (2005). Disturbed sleep and its relationship to alcohol use. *Substance Abuse, 26*(1), 1–13.

Stein, M. I. (1974). *Stimulating creativity* (Vol. 1). New York: Academic.

Stein, M. T., & Ferber, R. (2001). Recent onset of sleepwalking in early adolescence. *Journal of Development, Behavior, and Pediatrics, 22*, 33–35.

Steinberg, L. (2001). Adolescent development. *Annual Review of Psychology, 52*, 83–110.

Stephens, K., Kiger, L., Karnes, F. A., & Whorton, J. E. (1999). Use of nonverbal measures of intelligence in identification of culturally diverse gifted students in rural areas. *Perceptual & Motor Skills, 88*(3, Pt 1), 793–796.

Stephens, T., & Joubert, N. (2001). The economic burden of mental health problems in Canada. *Chronic Diseases in Canada, 22*, 18–23.

Steriade, M., & McCarley, R. W. (1990). *Brainstem control of wakefulness and sleep*. New York: Plenum.

Sternberg, R. J. (1988). *The triangle of love*. New York: Basic.

Sternberg, R. J. (2000). The holy grail of general intelligence. *Science, 289*, 399–401.

Sternberg, R. J. (2001). Is there a heredity-environment paradox? In R. J. Sternberg & E. L. Grigorenko (Eds.), *Environmental effects on cognitive abilities*. Mahwah, NJ: Erlbaum.

Sternberg, R. J. (2004). Culture and intelligence. *American Psychologist, 59*(5), 325–338.

Sternberg, R. J., & Davidson, J. D. (1982, June). The mind of the puzzler. *Psychology Today, 16*, 37–44.

Sternberg, R. J., & Grigorenko, E. L. (2005). Cultural explorations of the nature of intelligence. In A. F. Healy (Ed.), *Experimental cognitive psychology and its applications*. Washington: American Psychological Association.

Sternberg, R. J., Grigorenko, E. L., & Kidd, K. K. (2005). Intelligence, race, and genetics. *American Psychologist, 60*(1), 46–59.

Sternberg, R. J., & Lubart, T. I. (1995). *Defying the crowd*. New York: The Free Press.

Steuer, F. B., & Hustedt, J. T. (2002). *TV or no TV? A primer on the psychology of television*. Lanham, MD: University Press of America.

Stewart, A. J., & Ostrove, J. M. (1998). Women's personality in middle age. *American Psychologist, 53*(11), 1185–1194.

Stewart-Williams, S. (2004). The placebo puzzle: Putting together the pieces. *Health Psychology, 23*(2), 198–206.

Stickgold, R., & Walker, M. (2004). To sleep, perchance to gain creative insight? *Trends in Cognitive Sciences, 8*(5), 191–192.

Stinson, F. S., Dawson, D. A., Chou, S. P., Smith, S., et al. (2007). The epidemiology of DSM-IV specific phobia in the USA: Result from the National Epidemiologic Survey on Alcohol and Related Conditions. *Psychological Medicine, 37*(7), 1047–1059.

Stipek, D. (2001). *Motivation to learn* (4th ed.). Boston: Allyn & Bacon.

Stöber, J. (2004). Dimensions of test anxiety: Relations to ways of coping with pre-exam anxiety and uncertainty. *Anxiety, Stress & Coping: An International Journal, 17*(3), 213–226.

Stokes, D. M. (2001, May–June). The shrinking filedrawer. *Skeptical Inquirer, 25*(3), 22–25.

Stokoe, W. C. (2001). *Language in hand: Why sign came before speech*. Washington: Gallaudet University Press.

Stolerman, I. P., & Jarvis, M. J. (1995). The scientific case that nicotine is addictive. *Psychopharmacology, 117*(1), 2–10.

Stone, J., Perry, Z. W., & Darley, J. M. (1997). "White men can't jump." *Basic and Applied Social Psychology, 19*(3), 291–306.

Stoppard, J. M., & McMullen, L. M. (Eds.). (2003). *Situating sadness: Women and depression in social context*. New York: New York University Press.

Strack, F., Martin, L. L., & Stepper, S. (1988). Inhibiting and facilitating conditions of facial expressions: A non-obtrusive test of the facial feedback hypothesis. *Journal of Personality & Social Psychology, 54*, 768–777.

Straneva, P. A., Maixner, W., Light, K. C., Pedersen, C. A., et al. (2002). Menstrual cycle, beta-endorphins, and pain sensitivity in premenstrual dysphoric disorder. *Health Psychology, 21*(4), 358–367.

Strange, J. R. (1965). *Abnormal psychology*. New York: McGraw-Hill.

Straub, R. (2006). *Health psychology* (2nd ed.). New York: Worth.

Straus, M. A. (2004). Prevalence of violence against dating partners by male and female university students worldwide. *Violence against Women, 10*(7), 790–811.

Straus, M. A., & Ramirez, I. L. (2007). Gender symmetry in prevalence, severity, and chronicity of physical aggression against dating partners by university students in Mexico and USA. *Aggressive Behavior, 33*(4), 281–290.

Strickler, E. M., & Verbalis, J. G. (1988, May–June). Hormones and behavior: The biology of thirst and sodium appetite. *American Scientist*, 261–267.

Stroebe, W., Papies, E. K., & Aarts, H. (2008). From homeostatic to hedonic theories of eating: Self-regulatory failure in food-rich environments. *Applied Psychology: An International Review, 57*, 172–193.

Strongman, K. T. (2003). *The psychology of emotion: From everyday life to theory* (5th ed.). New York: Wiley.

Strote, J., Lee, J. E., & Wechsler, H. (2002). Increasing MDMA use among college students: Results of a national survey. *Journal of Adolescent Health, 30*(1), 64–72.

Strube, M. J. (2005). What did Triplett really find? A contemporary analysis of the first experiment in social psychology. *American Journal of Psychology, 118*(2), 271–286.

Strupp, H. H. (1989). Psychotherapy: Can the practitioner learn from the researcher? *American Psychologist, 44*(4), 717–724.

Sturges, J. W., & Sturges, L. V. (1998). In vivo systematic desensitization in a single-session treatment of an 11-year-old girl's elevator phobia. *Child & Family Behavior Therapy, 20*(4), 55–62.

Stuss, D. T., & Alexander, M. P. (2000). The anatomical basis of affective behavior, emotion and self-awareness: A specific role of the right frontal lobe. In G. Hatano, N. Okada, & H. Tanabe (Eds.), *Affective minds. The 13th Toyota conference.* Amsterdam: Elsevier.

Stuss, D. T., & Levine, B. (2002). Adult clinical neuropsychology. *Annual Review of Psychology, 53,* 401–433.

Suedfeld, P. (1990). Restricted environmental stimulation and smoking cessation. *International Journal of Addictions, 25*(8), 861–888.

Suedfeld, P., & Borrie, R. A. (1999). Health and therapeutic applications of chamber and flotation restricted environmental stimulation therapy (REST). *Psychology & Health, 14*(3), 545–566.

Sugimoto, K., & Ninomiya, Y. (2005). Introductory remarks on umami research: Candidate receptors and signal transduction mechanisms on umami. *Chemical Senses, 30*(Suppl. 1), i21–i22.

Suinn, R. M. (1975). *Fundamentals of behavior pathology* (2nd ed.). New York: Wiley.

Suinn, R. M. (1999, March). Scaling the summit: Valuing ethnicity. *APA Monitor, 2.*

Sumathipala, A., Siribaddana, S. H., & Bhugra, D. (2004). Culture-bound syndromes: The story of dhat syndrome. *British Journal of Psychiatry, 184*(3), 200–209.

Sumerlin, J. R., & Bundrick, C. M. (1996). Brief index of self-actualization: A measure of Maslow's model. *Journal of Social Behavior & Personality, 11*(2), 253–271.

Sunnafrank, M., Ramirez, A., & Metts, S. (2004). At first sight: Persistent relational effects of get-acquainted conversations. *Journal of Social & Personal Relationships, 21*(3), 361–379.

Sutherland, R. J., Lehmann, H., Spanswick, S. C., Sparks, F. T., et al. (2006). Growth points in research on memory and hippocampus. *Canadian Journal of Experimental Psychology, 60*(2), 166–174.

Swaak, J., de Jong, T., & van Joolingen, W. R. (2004). The effects of discovery learning and expository instruction on the acquisition of definitional and intuitive knowledge. *Journal of Computer Assisted Learning, 20*(4), 225–234.

Swan, G. E., & Denk, C. E. (1987). Dynamic models for the maintenance of smoking cessation: Event history analysis of late relapse. *Journal of Behavioral Medicine, 10*(6), 527–554.

Synhorst, L. L., Buckley, J. A., Reid, R., Epstein, M. H., et al. (2005). Cross informant agreement of the Behavioral and Emotional Rating Scale-2nd Edition (BERS-2) parent and youth rating scales. *Child & Family Behavior Therapy, 27*(3), 1–11.

Szabo, A. (2003). The acute effects of humor and exercise on mood and anxiety. *Journal of Leisure Research, 35*(2), 152–162.

Talbot, N. L., & Gamble, S. A. (2008). IPT for women with trauma histories in community mental health care. *Journal of Contemporary Psychotherapy, 38*(1), 35–44.

Talbott, J. A. (2004). Deinstitutionalization: Avoiding the disasters of the past. *Psychiatric Services. Special Issue: A Tribute to John A. Talbott, M.D., 55*(10), 1112–1115.

Talley, P. F., Strupp, H. H., & Morey, L. C. (1990). Matchmaking in psychotherapy: Patient-therapist dimensions and their impact on outcome. *Journal of Consulting & Clinical Psychology, 58*(2), 182–188.

Tallis, F. (1996). Compulsive washing in the absence of phobic and illness anxiety. *Behaviour Research & Therapy, 34*(4), 361–362.

Tamis-LeMonda, C. S., Shannon, J. D., Cabrera, N. J., & Lamb, M. E. (2004). Fathers and mothers at play with their 2- and 3-year-olds: Contributions to language and cognitive development. *Child Development, 75*(6), 1806–1820.

Taraban, R., Rynearson, K., & Kerr, M. (2000). College students' academic performance and self-reports of comprehension strategy use. *Reading Psychology, 21*(4), 283–308.

Tardif, T. Z., & Sternberg, R. J. (1988). What do we know about creativity? In R. J. Sternberg (Ed.), *The nature of creativity.* Cambridge, MA: Cambridge University Press.

Taris, T. W., Bakker, A. B., Schaufeli, W. B., Stoffelsen, J., et al. (2005). Job control and burnout across occupations. *Psychological Reports, 97*(3), 955–961.

Taub, E. (2004). Harnessing brain plasticity through behavioral techniques to produce new treatments in neurorehabilitation. *American Psychologist, 59*(8), 692–704.

Tausig, M., Michello, J., & Subedi, S. (2004). *A sociology of mental illness* (2nd ed.). Englewood Cliffs, NJ: Prentice Hall.

Tavshunsky, A. (Saturday, October 9, 2010). Col. Russell Williams: A serial killer like none police have seen. *The Toronto Star.* Retrieved March 23, 2012 from http://www.thestar.com/news/article /873244--col-russell-williams-a-serial-killer-like-none-police-have-seen.

Taylor, G. J., & Taylor-Allan, H. L. (2007). Applying emotional intelligence in understanding and treating physical and psychological disorders: What we have learned from alexithymia. In R. Bar-On, J. G. Maree, & Maurice J. Elias (Eds.), *Educating people to be emotionally intelligent.* Westport, CT: Praeger.

Taylor, K. (2004). *Brainwashing: The science of thought control.* New York: Oxford University Press.

Taylor, S. E. (2002). Classical conditioning. In M. Hersen & W. H. Sledge (Eds.), *Encyclopedia of psychotherapy.* San Diego: Academic Press.

Taylor, S. E. (2006). *Health psychology* (6th ed.). New York: McGraw-Hill.

Taylor, S. E., Kemeny, M. E., Reed, G. M., Bower, J. E., et al. (2000). Psychological resources, positive illusions, and health. *American Psychologist, 55*(1), 99–109.

Tennesen, M. (2007, March 10). Gone today, hear tomorrow. *New Scientist, 2594,* 42–45.

Terman, L. M., & Merrill, M. A. (1937, revised, 1960). *Stanford-Binet Intelligence Scale.* Boston: Houghton Mifflin.

Terman, L. M., & Oden, M. (1959). *The gifted group in mid-life* (Vol. 5): *Genetic studies of genius.* Stanford, CA: Stanford University Press.

Terry, D. J., & Hogg, M. A. (1996). Group norms and the attitude-behavior relationship. *Personality & Social Psychology Bulletin, 22*(8), 776–793.

Thaler, L., Arnott, S. R., & Goodale, M. A. (2011). Neural correlates of natural human echolocation in early and late blind echolocation experts. *PLoS ONE, 6*(5): e20162.

Thase, M. E. (2006). Major depressive disorder. In F. Andrasik (Ed.), *Comprehensive handbook of personality and psychopathology* (Vol. 2): *Adult psychopathology.* New York: Wiley.

Thelen, E. (2000). Infancy: Perception and motor development. In A. Kazdin (Ed.), *Encyclopedia of psychology.* Washington: American Psychological Association.

Thiessen, E. D., Hill, E. A., & Saffran, J. R. (2005). Infant-directed speech facilitates word segmentation. *Infancy, 7*(1), 53–71.

Thomas, E. M. (2004). *Aggressive behaviour outcomes for young children: Change in parenting environment predicts change in behaviour.* Ottawa, ON: Statistics Canada. Retrieved September 26, 2012, from http://www.statcan.gc.ca/pub /89-599-m/89-599-m2004001-eng.pdf.

Thompson, R. A., Easterbrooks, M. A., & Padilla-Walker, L. M. (2003). Social and emotional development in infancy. In R. M. Lerner, M. A. Easterbrooks, & J. Mistry (Eds.), *Handbook of psychology: Developmental psychology.* New York: Wiley.

Thompson, R. F. (2005). In search of memory traces. *Annual Review of Psychology, 56,* 1–23.

Thomson, D.R., Milliken, B., & Smilek, D. (2010). Long-term conceptual implicit memory: a decade of evidence. *Memory & Cognition, 38*(1), 42–46.

Tierny, J. (1987, September–October). Stitches: Good news; Better health linked to sin, sloth. *Hippocrates,* 30–35.

Tiffany, S. T., Martin, E. M., & Baker, T. B. (1986). Treatments for cigarette smoking: An evaluation of the contributions of aversion and counseling procedures. *Behavior Research & Therapy, 24*(4), 437–452.

Till, B. D., & Priluck, R. L. (2000). Stimulus generalization in classical conditioning: An initial investigation and extension. *Psychology & Marketing, 17*(1), 55–72.

Tillmann, B., Jolicoeur, P., Ishihara, M., Gosselin, N., et al. (2010). The amusic brain: Lost in music, but not in space. *PLoS ONE, 5*(4), e10173.

Tillmann, B., Rusconi, E., Traube, C., Butterworth, B., et al. (2011) Fine-grained pitch processing of music and speech in congenital amusia. *Journal of the Acoustical Society of America, 130,* 4089–4096.

Timmerman, C. K., & Kruepke, K. A. (2006). Computer-assisted instruction, media richness, and college student performance. *Communication Education, 55*(1), 73–104.

Timmerman, I. G. H., Emmelkamp, P. M. G., & Sanderman, R. (1998). The effects of a stress-management training program in individuals at risk in the community at large. *Behaviour Research & Therapy, 36*(9), 863–875.

Tjepkema, M. (2005). Insomnia. *Health Reports, 17*(1): Statistics Canada, Catalogue No. 82-003-XPE2005001.

Tobler, N. S., Roona, M. R., Ocshorn, P., Marshall, D. G., et al. (2000). School-based adolescent drug prevention programs: 1998 meta-analysis. *Journal of Primary Prevention, 20,* 275–337.

Tolman, E. C., & Honzik, C. H. (1930). Introduction and removal of reward and maze performance in rats. *University of California Publications in Psychology, 4,* 257–275.

Tolman, E. C., Ritchie, B. F., & Kalish, D. (1946). Studies in spatial learning: II. Place learning versus response learning. *Journal of Experimental Psychology, 36,* 221–229.

Tomasello, M. (2003). *Constructing a language: A usage-based theory of language acquisition.* Cambridge, MA: Harvard University Press.

Toneatto, T. (2002). Cognitive therapy for problem gambling. *Cognitive & Behavioral Practice, 9*(3), 191–199.

Toneatto, T., Sobell, L. C., Sobell, M. B., & Rubel, E. (1999). Natural recovery from cocaine dependence. *Psychology of Addictive Behaviors, 13*(4), 259–268.

Tononi, G., & Cirelli, C. (2003). Sleep and synaptic homeostasis: A hypothesis. *Brain Research Bulletin, 62*(2), 143–150.

Torrey, E. F. (1988). *Surviving schizophrenia: A family manual.* New York: Harper & Row.

Torrey, E. F. (1996). *Out of the shadows.* New York: John Wiley & Sons.

Tourangeau, R. (2004). Survey research and societal change. *Annual Review of Psychology, 55,* 775–801.

Toyota, H., & Kikuchi, Y. (2005). Encoding richness of self-generated elaboration and spacing effects on incidental memory. *Perceptual & Motor Skills, 101*(2), 621–627.

Trainor, L. J., & Desjardins, R. N. (2002). Pitch characteristics of infant-directed speech affect infants' ability to discriminate vowels. *Psychonomic Bulletin & Review, 9*(2), 335–340.

Travis, F., Arenander, A., & DuBois, D. (2004). Psychological and physiological characteristics of a proposed object-referral/self-referral continuum of self-awareness. *Consciousness & Cognition, 13,* 401–420.

Treffert, D. A., & Christensen, C. D. (2005). Inside the mind of a savant. *Scientific American, 293*(6), 108–113.

Trehub, S. E., Unyk, A. M., Kamenetsky, S. B., Hill, D. S., et al. (1997). Mothers' and fathers' singing to infants. *Developmental Psychology, 33,* 500–507.

Trehub, S. E., Unyk, A. M., & Trainor, L. J. (1993a). Adults identify infant-directed music across cultures. *Infant Behavior & Development, 16*(2), 193–211.

Trehub, S. E., Unyk, A. M., & Trainor, L. J. (1993b). Maternal singing in cross-cultural perspective. *Infant Behavior & Development, 16*(3), 285–295.

Tremblay, R. E. (2012). The development of physical aggression. In R. E. Tremblay, M. Boivin, & R. D. Peters (Eds.), *Encyclopedia on early childhood development* [online]. Montréal: Centre of Excellence for Early Childhood Development and Strategic Knowledge Cluster on Early Child Development, 1–5. Retrieved September 26, 2012, from http://www.child-encyclopedia.com/documents/TremblayANGxp3.pdf.

Troll, L. E., & Skaff, M. M. (1997). Perceived continuity of self in very old age. *Psychology & Aging, 12*(1), 162–169.

Truax, S. R. (1983). Active search, mediation, and the manipulation of cue dimensions: Emotion attribution in the false feedback paradigm. *Motivation and Emotion, 7,* 41–60.

Trull, T. (2005). *Clinical psychology* (7th ed.). Belmont, CA: Wadsworth.

Tsai, G., & Coyle, J. T. (2002). Glutamatergic mechanisms in schizophrenia. *Annual Review of Pharmacology & Toxicology, 42,* 165–179.

Tse, L. (1999). Finding a place to be: Ethnic identity exploration of Asian Americans. *Adolescence, 34*(133), 121–138.

Tugade, M. M., Fredrickson, B. L., & Barrett, L. F. (2004). Psychological resilience and positive emotional granularity: Examining the benefits of positive emotions on coping and health. *Journal of Personality. Special Emotions, Personality, & Health, 72*(6), 1161–1190.

Tulving, E. (1989). Remembering and knowing the past. *American Scientist, 77*(4), 361–367.

Tulving, E. (2002). Episodic memory: From mind to brain. *Annual Review of Psychology, 53*(1), 1–25.

Tulving, E., Schacter, D. L., McLachlan, D. R., & Moscovitch, M. (1988). Priming of semantic autobiographical knowledge: A case study of retrograde amnesia. *Brain & Cognition, 8*(1), 3–20.

Turiel, E. (2006). Thought, emotions, and social interactional processes in moral development. In M. Killen & J. G. Smetana, (Eds.), *Handbook of moral development.* Mahwah, NJ: Erlbaum.

Turkington, C. (1986, August). Pot and the immune system. *APA Monitor,* 22.

Turner, S. J. M. (1997). The use of the reflective team in a psychodrama therapy group. *International Journal of Action Methods, 50*(1), 17–26.

Tversky, A., & Kahneman, D. (1981). The framing of decisions and the psychology of choice. *Science, 211,* 453–458.

Tversky, A., & Kahneman, D. (1982). Judgments of and by representativeness. In D. Kahneman, P. Slovic, & A. Tversky (Eds.), *Judgment under uncertainty: Heuristics and biases.* Cambridge, MA: Cambridge University Press.

Tye-Murray, N., Spencer, L., & Woodworth, G. G. (1995). Acquisition of speech by children who have prolonged cochlear implant experience. *Journal of Speech & Hearing Research, 38*(2), 327–337.

Tzeng, M. (1992). The effects of socioeconomic heterogamy and changes on marital dissolution for first marriages. *Journal of Marriage and Family, 54,* 609–619.

U.S. Department of Energy Office of Science. (2005). *About the Human Genome Project.* Washington: U.S. Department of Energy. Retrieved September 3, 2005, from http://www.ornl.gov/sci/techresources/Human_Genome/project/about.shtml.

Ulett, G. A. (1992). 3000 years of acupuncture: From metaphysics to neurophysiology. *Integrative Psychiatry, 8*(2), 91–100.

Ulrich, R. E., Stachnik, T. J., & Stainton, N. R. (1963). Student acceptance of generalized personality interpretations, *Psychological Reports, 13,* 831–834.

Underwood, B. J. (1957). Interference and forgetting. *Psychological Review, 64,* 49–60.

UNESCO. (1990). The Seville statement on violence. *American Psychologist, 45*(10), 1167–1168.

Unsworth, G., & Ward, T. (2001). Video games and aggressive behaviour. *Australian Psychologist, 36*(3), 184–192.

Uylings, H. B. M. (2006). Development of the human cortex and the concept of "critical" or "sensitive" periods. *Language Learning, 56*(Suppl. 1), S59–S90.

Uziel, L. (2007). Individual differences in the social facilitation effect: A review and meta-analysis. *Journal of Research in Personality, 41*(3), 579–601.

Vaillant, G. E. (2005). Alcoholics Anonymous: Cult or cure? *Australian and New Zealand Journal of Psychiatry, 39*(6), 431–436.

Vaillant, G. E., & Mukamal, K. (2001). Successful aging. *American Journal of Psychiatry, 158*(6), 839–847.

Valins, S. (1966). Cognitive effects of false heart-rate feedback. *Journal of Personality & Social Psychology, 4,* 400–408.

Valins, S. (1967). Emotionality and information concerning internal reactions. *Journal of Personality & Social Psychology, 6,* 458–463.

Vallerand, A. H., Saunders, M. M., & Anthony, M. (2007). Perceptions of control over pain by patients with cancer and their caregivers. *Pain Management Nursing, 8*(2), 55–63.

Van der Hart, O., Lierens, R., & Goodwin, J. (1996). Jeanne Fery: A sixteenth-century case of dissociative identity disorder. *Journal of Psychohistory, 24*(1), 18–35.

van Dierendonck, D., & Te Nijenhuis, J. (2005). Flotation restricted environmental stimulation therapy (REST) as a stress-management tool: A meta-analysis. *Psychology & Health, 20*(3), 405–412.

van Elst, L. T., Valerius, G., Büchert, M., Thiel, T., et al. (2005). Increased prefrontal and hippocampal glutamate concentration in schizophrenia: Evidence from a magnetic resonance spectroscopy study. *Biological Psychiatry, 58*(9), 724–730.

Van Goozen, S. H. M., Cohen-Kettenis, P. T., Gooren, L. J. G., & Frijda, N. H. (1995). Gender differences in behaviour: Activating effects of cross-sex hormones. *Psychoneuroendocrinology, 20*(4), 343–363.

Van Lawick-Goodall, J. (1971). *In the shadow of man.* New York: Houghton Mifflin.

van Lier, P., Vitaro, F., Barker, E., Koot, H., et al. (2009). Developmental links between trajectories of physical violence, vandalism, theft, and alcohol-drug use from childhood to adolescence. *Journal of Abnormal Child Psychology, 37*(4), 481–492.

Van Rooij, J. J. F. (1994). Introversion-extraversion: Astrology versus psychology. *Personality & Individual Differences, 16*(6), 985–988.

Vasa, R. A., Carlino, A. R., & Pine, D. S. (2006). Pharmacotherapy of depressed children and adolescents: Current issues and potential directions. *Biological Psychiatry, 59*(11), 1021–1028.

Vastag, B. (2001). Stem cells step closer to the clinic: Paralysis partially reversed in rats with ALS-like disease. *Journal of the American Medical Association, 285,* 1691–1693.

Velakoulis, D., & Pantelis, C. (1996). What have we learned from functional imaging studies in schizophrenia? *Australian & New Zealand Journal of Psychiatry, 30*(2), 195–209.

Vernon, P. A., Martin, R. A., Schermer, J. A., & Mackie, A. (2008). A behavioral genetic investigation of humor styles and their correlations with the Big-5 personality dimensions. *Personality and Individual Differences, 44*(5), 1116–1125.

Véronneau, M.-H., Vitaro, F., Pedersen, S., & Tremblay, R. E. (2008). Do peers contribute to the likelihood of secondary school graduation among disadvantaged boys? *Journal of Educational Psychology, 100*(2), 429–442.

Veselka, L. Schermer, J.A., Martin, R.A., & Vernon, P.A. (2010). Relations between humor styles and the Dark Triad traits of personality. *Personality and Individual Differences, 48*(6), 772–774.

Vestergaard-Poulsen, P., van Beek, M., Skewes, J., Bjarkam, C. R., et al. (2009). Long-term meditation is associated with increased gray matter density in the brain stem. *NeuroReport, 20,* 170–174.

Videon, T. M. (2005). Parent–child relations and children's psychological well-being: Do dads matter? *Journal of Family Issues, 26*(1), 55–78.

Viegener, B. J., Perri, M. G., Nezu, A. M., Renjilian, D. A., et al. (1990). Effects of an intermittent, low-fat, low-calorie diet in the behavioral treatment of obesity. *Behavior Therapy, 21*(4), 499–509.

Visser, B. A., Ashton, M. C., & Vernon, P. A. (2006). Beyond g: Putting multiple intelligences theory to the test. *Intelligence, 34*(5), 487–502.

Vitaro, F., Brendgen, M., & Tremblay, R. E. (2000). Influence of deviant friends on delinquency: Searching for moderator variables. *Journal of Abnormal Child Psychology, 28*(4), 313–325.

Viveros, M. P., Llorente, R., Moreno, E., & Marco, E. M. (2005). Behavioural and neuroendocrine effects of cannabinoids in critical developmental periods. *Behavioural Pharmacology, 16*(5–6), 353–362.

Vogel, E. K., Woodman, G. F., & Luck, S. J. (2006). The time course of consolidation in visual working memory. *Journal of Experimental Psychology: Human Perception & Performance, 32*(6), 1436–1451.

Vogler, R. E., & Bartz, W. R. (1992). *Teenagers and alcohol.* Philadelphia: Charles Press.

Vogler, R. E., Weissbach, T. A., Compton, J. V., & Martin, G. T. (1977). Integrated behavior change techniques for problem drinkers in the community. *Journal of Consulting and Clinical Psychology, 45,* 267–279.

Volkow, N. D., Gillespie, H., Mullani, N., & Tancredi, L. (1996). Brain glucose metabolism in chronic marijuana users at baseline and during marijuana intoxication. *Psychiatry Research: Neuroimaging, 67*(1), 29–38.

Volterra, M. C., Caselli, O., Capirci, E., & Pizzuto, E. (2004). Gesture and the emergence and development of language. In M. Tomasello & D. I. Slobin (Eds), *Beyond nature-nurture.* Mahwah, NJ: Erlbaum.

Vorauer, J. D. & Sasaki, S. J. (2009). Helpful only in the abstract? Ironic effects of empathy in intergroup interaction. *Psychological Science, 20*(2), 191–197.

Vorauer, J. D. & Sasaki, S. J. (2012). The pitfalls of empathy as a default intergroup interaction strategy: Distinct effects of trying to empathize with a lower status outgroup member who does versus does not express distress. *Journal of Experimental Social Psychology, 48*(2), 519–524.

Vygotsky, L. S. (1962). *Thought and language.* Cambridge, MA: MIT Press.

Vygotsky, L. S. (1978). *Mind in society. The development of higher mental processes.* M. Cole, V. John-Steiner, S. S. Scribner, & E. Souberman (Eds.). Cambridge, MA: Harvard University Press.

Wachs, T. D. (2006). The nature, etiology and consequences of individual differences in temperament. In L. Balter, & C. S. Tamis-LeMonda (Eds.), *Child Psychology: A handbook of contemporary issues* (2nd ed.). New York: Psychology Press.

Wager, T. D., Rilling, J. K., Smith, E. E., Sokolik, A., et al. (2004, February 20). Placebo-induced changes in fMRI in the anticipation and experience of pain. *Science, 303,* 1162–1166.

Wagstaff, G., Brunas-Wagstaff, J., Cole, J., & Wheatcroft, J. (2004). New directions in forensic hypnosis: Facilitating memory with a focused meditation technique. *Contemporary Hypnosis, 21*(1), 14–27.

Waid, W. M., & Orne, M. T. (1982, July/August). The physiological detection of deception. *American Scientist, 70,* 402–409.

Wakefield, J. C. (1992). The concept of mental disorder. *American Psychologist, 47*(3), 373–388.

Wald, J., & Taylor, S. (2000). Efficacy of virtual reality exposure therapy to treat driving phobia. *Journal of Behavior Therapy & Experimental Psychiatry, 31* (3–4), 249–257.

Walker, D. L., & Davis, M. (2008). Role of the extended amygdala in short-duration versus sustained fear: A tribute to Dr. Lennart Heimer. *Brain Structure & Function, 213*(1–2), 29–42.

Walker, E., Kestler, L., Bollini, A., & Hochman, K. M. (2004). Schizophrenia: Etiology and course. *Annual Review of Psychology, 55,* 401–430.

Walker, E., & Tessner, K. (2008). Schizophrenia. *Perspectives on Psychological Science, 3*(1), 30–37.

Walker, M. P., & Stickgold, R. (2006). Sleep, memory, and plasticity. *Annual Review of Psychology, 57,* 139–166.

Wallach, M. A., & Kogan, N. (1965). *Modes of thinking in young children.* New York: Holt.

Walsh, J., & Uestuen, T. B. (1999). Prevalence and health consequences of insomnia. *Sleep, 22*(Suppl 3), S427–S436.

Walsh, R., & Shapiro, S. L., (2006). The meeting of meditative disciplines and Western psychology: A mutually enriching dialogue. *American Psychologist, 61*(3), 227–239.

Walton, C. E., Bower, M. L., & Bower, T. G. (1992). Recognition of familiar faces by newborns. *Infant Behavior & Development, 15*(2), 265–269.

Wampold, B. E., Minami T., Tierney, S. C., Baskin, T. W., et al. (2005). The placebo is powerful: Estimating placebo effects in medicine and psychotherapy from randomized clinical trials. *Journal of Clinical Psychology, 61*(7), 835–854.

Wampold, B. E., Mondin, G. W., Moody, M., Stich, F., et al. (1997). A meta-analysis of outcome studies comparing bona fide psychotherapies. *Psychological Bulletin, 122*(3), 203–215.

Wandersman, A., & Florin, P. (2003). Community interventions and effective prevention. *American Psychologist, 58*(6/7), 441–448.

Wang, Y., Hummer, T., Kronenberger, W, Mosier, K. et al. (2011). One week of violent game play alters prefrontal activity. Paper presented at the 97th meeting of the Radiological Society of North America, December 2, 2011.

Ward, C., & Rana-Deuba, A. (1999). Acculturation and adaptation revisited. *Journal of Cross-Cultural Psychology, 30*(4), 422–442.

Ward, J. (2006). *The student's guide to cognitive neuroscience.* Hove, U.K.: Psychology Press.

Wargo, E. (2007). Understanding the have-knots: The role of stress in just about everything. *APS Observer, 20*(11), 18–23.

Warren, D. J., & Normann, R. A. (2005). Functional reorganization of primary visual cortex induced by electrical stimulation in the cat. *Vision Research, 45,* 551–565.

Waterfield, R. (2002). *Hidden depths: The story of hypnosis.* London: Macmillan.

Watson, D. L., & Tharp, R. G. (2007). *Self-directed behavior* (9th ed.). Belmont, CA: Wadsworth.

Watson, J. B. (1913). Psychology as the behaviorist views it. *Psychological Review, 20,* 158–177.

Watson, J. B. (1994). Psychology as the behaviorist views it. Special Issue: The centennial issue of the Psychological Review. *Psychological Review, 101*(2), 248–253.

Way, I., vanDeusen, K. M., Martin, G., Applegate, B., et al. (2004). Vicarious trauma: A comparison of clinicians who treat survivors of sexual abuse and sexual offenders. *Journal of Interpersonal Violence, 19*(1), 49–71.

Wechsler, H., Molnar, B. E., Davenport, A. E., & Baer, J. S. (1999). College alcohol use: A full or empty glass? *Journal of American College Health, 47*(6), 247–252.

Wedding, D., & Corsini, R. J. (2005). *Case studies in psychotherapy* (4th ed.). Belmont, CA: Wadsworth.

Weekley, J. A., & Jones, C. (1997). Video-based situational testing. *Personnel Psychology, 50*(1), 25–49.

Weems, C. F. (1998). The evaluation of heart rate biofeedback using a multi-element design. *Journal of Behavior Therapy & Experimental Psychiatry, 29*(2), 157–162.

Weiner, I. B. (1997). Current status of the Rorschach inkblot method. *Journal of Personality Assessment, 68*(1), 5–19.

Weiner, M. J., & Wright, F. E. (1973). Effects of undergoing arbitrary discrimination upon subsequent attitudes toward a minority group. *Journal of Applied Social Psychology, 3*(1), 94–102.

Weintraub, M. I. (1983). *Hysterical conversion reactions.* New York: SP Medical & Scientific Books.

Weishaar, M. E. (2006). A cognitive-behavioral approach to suicide risk reduction in crisis intervention. In A. R. Roberts & K. R. Yeager (Eds.), *Foundations of evidence-based social work practice.* New York: Oxford University Press.

Weiss, B., Dodge, K. A., Bates, J. E., & Pettit, G. S. (1992). Some consequences of early harsh discipline. *Child Development, 63*(6), 1321–1335.

Weiss, J. (1990, March). Unconscious mental functioning. *Scientific American,* 103–109.

Weisskirch, R. S. (2005). Ethnicity and perceptions of being a "typical American" in relationship to ethnic identity development. *International Journal of Intercultural Relations, 29*(3), 355–366.

Weissman, A. M., Jogerst, G. J., & Dawson, J. D. (2003). Community characteristics associated with child abuse in Iowa. *Child Abuse & Neglect, 27*(10), 1145–1159.

Weiten, W. (1998). Pressure, major life events, and psychological symptoms. *Journal of Social Behavior & Personality, 13*(1), 51–68.

Weitzenhoffer, A. M., & Hilgard, E. R. (1959). *Stanford Hypnotic Susceptibility Scale, Forms A and B.* Palo Alto, CA: Consulting Psychologists Press.

Weitzman, E. R. (2004). Poor mental health, depression, and associations with alcohol consumption, harm, and abuse in a national sample of young adults in college. *Journal of Nervous & Mental Disease, 192*(4), 269–277.

Wells, G. L. (2001). Police lineups: Data, theory, and policy. *Psychology, Public Policy, & Law, 7*(4), 791–801.

Wells, G. L., Memon, A., & Penrod, S. D. (2006). Eyewitness evidence: Improving its probative value. *Psychological Science in the Public Interest, 7*(2), 45–75.

Wells, G. L., and Olsen, E. A. (2003). Eyewitness testimony. *Annual Review of Psychology, 54,* 277–295.

Weltzin, T. E., Weisensel, N., Franczyk, D., Burnett, K., et al. (2005). Eating disorders in men: Update. *Journal of Men's Health & Gender, 2*(2), 186–193.

Wernet, S. P., Follman, C., Magueja, C., & Moore-Chambers, R. (2003). Building bridges and improving racial harmony: An evaluation of the Bridges Across Racial Polarization Program. In J. J. Stretch, E. M. Burkemper, W. J. Hutchison, & J. Wilson (Eds.), *Practicing social justice.* New York: Haworth Press.

Wertheimer, M. (1959). *Productive thinking.* New York: Harper & Row.

Wessel, I., & Wright, D. B. (Eds.). (2004). *Emotional memory failures.* Hove, U.K.: Psychology Press.

West, T. G. (1991). *In the mind's eye.* Buffalo, NY: Prometheus.

Westen, D. (1998). The scientific legacy of Sigmund Freud: Toward a psychodynamically informed psychological science. *Psychological Bulletin, 124*(3), 333 -371.

Westrin, Å., & Lam, R. W. (2007). Seasonal affective disorder: A clinical update. *Annals of Clinical Psychiatry, 19*(4), 239–246.

Wexler, M. N. (1995). Expanding the groupthink explanation to the study of contemporary cults. *Cultic Studies Journal, 12*(1), 49–71.

Whitaker, B. G. (2007). Internet-based attitude assessment: Does gender affect measurement equivalence? *Computers in Human Behavior, 23*(3), 1183–1194.

White, G. L., & Taytroe, L. (2003). Personal problem-solving using dream incubation: Dreaming, relaxation, or waking cognition? *Dreaming, 13*(4), 193–209.

Whitehouse, A. J. O., Maybery, M. T., & Durkin, K. (2006). The development of the picture-superiority effect. *British Journal of Developmental Psychology, 24*(4), 767–773.

Whyte, G. (2000). Groupthink. In A. E. Kazdin (Ed.), *Encyclopedia of psychology* (Vol. 4). Washington: American Psychological Association.

Widiger, T. A. (2005). Classification and diagnosis: Historical development and contemporary issues. In J. E. Maddux & B. A. Winstead (Eds.), *Psychopathology: Foundations for a contemporary understanding.* Mahwah, NJ: Erlbaum.

Wiederhold, B. K., & Wiederhold, M. D. (2005). Acrophobia. In B. K. Wiederhold & M. D. Wiederhold, *Virtual reality therapy for anxiety disorders: Advances in evaluation and treatment.* Washington: American Psychological Association.

Wigfield, A., & Eccles, J. (Eds.). (2002). *Development of achievement motivation.* San Diego: Academic Press.

Wilber, M. K., & Potenza, M. N. (2006). Adolescent gambling: Research and clinical implications. *Psychiatry, 3*(10), 40–46.

Wilder, D. A., Simon, A. F., & Faith, M. (1996). Enhancing the impact of counterstereotypic information. *Journal of Personality & Social Psychology, 71*(2), 276–287.

Wilding, J., & Valentine, E. (1994). Memory champions. *British Journal of Psychology, 85*(2), 231–244.

Wilkins, K. (2004). Bipolar I disorder: Social support and work. *Supplement to Health Reports,* 15, 23–51. Statistics Canada, Catalogue 82-003.

Wilkinson, D., & Abraham, C. (2004). Constructing an integrated model of the antecedents of adolescent smoking. *British Journal of Health Psychology, 9*(3), 315–333.

Wilkinson, M. (2006). The dreaming mind-brain: A Jungian perspective. *Journal of Analytical Psychology, 51*(1), 43–59.

Wilkinson, R. B. (1997). Interactions between self and external reinforcement in predicting depressive symptoms. *Behaviour Research & Therapy, 35*(4), 281–289.

Willander, J., & Larsson, M. (2006). Smell your way back to childhood: Autobiographical odor memory. *Psychonomic Bulletin & Review, 13*(2), 240–244.

Williams, D. G., & Morris, G. (1996). Crying, weeping or tearfulness in British and Israeli adults. *British Journal of Psychology, 87*(3), 479–505.

Williams, G., Cai, X. J., Elliott, J. C., & Harrold, J. A. (2004). Anabolic neuropeptides. *Physiology & Behavior. Special Issue: Reviews on Ingestive Science, 81*(2), 211–222.

Williams, R. (1989). *The trusting heart: Great news about Type A behavior.* New York: Random House.

Williams, R. B., Barefoot, J. C., & Schneiderman, N. (2003). Psychosocial risk factors for cardiovascular disease: More than one culprit at work. *JAMA: Journal of the American Medical Association, 290*(16), 2190–2192.

Williams, R. J., & Schmidt, G. G. (1993). Frequency of seasonal affective disorder among individuals seeking treatment at a northern Canadian mental health center. *Psychiatry Research, 46,* 41–45.

Williams, R. L., & Eggert, A. (2002). Notetaking predictors of test performance. *Teaching of Psychology, 29*(3), 234–236.

Williams, R. L., & Long, J. D. (1991). *Toward a self-managed life style.* Boston: Houghton Mifflin.

Williams, R. L., Agnew, Jr., H. W., & Webb, W. B. (1964). Sleep patterns in young adults: An EEG study. *Electroencephalography and Clinical Neurophysiology,* 376–381.

Williamson, D. A., Ravussin, E., Wong, M.-L., Wagner, A., et al. (2005). Microanalysis of eating behavior of three leptin deficient adults treated with leptin therapy. *Appetite, 45,* 75–80.

Willoughby, T., Wood, E., Desmarais, S., Sims, S., et al. (1997). Mechanisms that facilitate the effectiveness of elaboration strategies. *Journal of Educational Psychology, 89*(4), 682–685.

Willows, N. D., Johnson, M. S., & Ball, G. D. C. (2007). Prevalence estimates of overweight and obesity in Cree preschool children in Northern Quebec according to international and US reference criteria. *American Journal of Public Health, 97*(2), 311–316.

Willows N. D., Veugelers P., Raine K., Kuhle S. (2009). Prevalence and sociodemographic risk factors related to household food security in Aboriginal peoples in Canada. *Public Health Nutrition,* 1150–1156.

Wilson, A. E., & Ross, M. (2001). From chump to champ: People's appraisals of their earlier and present selves. *Journal of Personality & Social Psychology, 80*(4), 572–584.

Wilson, G. L. (2002). *Groups in context: Leadership and participation in small groups* (6th ed.). New York: McGraw-Hill.

Wilson, G. T. (1987). Chemical aversion conditioning as a treatment for alcoholism: A re-analysis. *Behaviour Research and Therapy, 25*(6), 503–516.

Wingood, G. M., DiClemente, R. J., Bernhardt, J. M., Harrington, K., et al. (2003). A prospective study of exposure to rap music videos and African American female adolescents' health. *American Journal of Public Health, 93,* 437–439.

Winner, E. (2003). Creativity and talent. In M. H. Bornstein, L. Davidson, C. L. M. Keyes, & K. Moore (Eds.), *Well-being: Positive development across the life course.* Mahwah, NJ: Erlbaum.

Winstead, B. A., & Sanchez, J. (2005). Gender and psychopathology. In J. E. Maddux & B. A. Winstead (Eds.), *Psychopathology: Foundations for a contemporary understanding.* Mahwah, NJ: Erlbaum.

Wise, R. A., & Safer, M. A. (2004). What US judges know and believe about eyewitness testimony. *Applied Cognitive Psychology, 18*(4), 427–443.

Wiseman, R., & Watt, C. (2006). Belief in psychic ability and the misattribution hypothesis: A qualitative review. *British Journal of Psychology, 97*(3), 323–338.

Witelson, S. F., Beresh, H., & Kigar, D. L. (2006). Intelligence and brain size in 100 postmortem brains: Sex, lateralization and age factors. *Brain: A Journal of Neurology, 129*(2), 386–398.

Witherington, D. C., Campos, J. J., Anderson, D. I., Lejeune, L., et al. (2005). Avoidance of heights on the visual cliff in newly walking infants. *Infancy, 7*(3), 285–298.

Withers, N. W., Pulvirenti, L., Koob, G. F., & Gillin, J. C. (1995). Cocaine abuse and

dependence. *Journal of Clinical Psychopharmacology, 15*(1), 63–78.

Wixted, J. T. (2004). The psychology and neuroscience of forgetting. *Annual Review of Psychology, 55,* 235–269.

Wohl, M. J. A., Pychyl, T. A., & Bennett, S. H. (2010). I forgive myself, now I can study: How self-forgiveness for procrastinating can reduce future procrastination. *Personality and Individual Differences, 48*(7), 803–808.

Wolfe, J. B. (1936). Effectiveness of token rewards for chimpanzees. *Comparative Psychology Monographs, 12*(5), Whole No. 60.

Wolitzky, D. L. (1995). The theory and practice of traditional psychoanalytic psychotherapy. In A. S. Gurman & S. B. Messer (Eds.), *Essential psychotherapies.* New York: Guilford.

Wolpe, J. (1974). *The practice of behavior therapy* (2nd ed.). New York: Pergamon.

Wolpin, M., Marston, A., Randolph, C., & Clothier, A. (1992). Individual difference correlates of reported lucid dreaming frequency and control. *Journal of Mental Imagery, 16*(3–4), 231–236.

Wong, J. L., & Whitaker, D. J. (1993). Depressive mood states and their cognitive and personality correlates in college students. *Journal of Clinical Psychology, 49*(5), 615–621.

Wood, E., & Willoughby, T. (1995). Cognitive strategies for test-taking. In E. Wood, V. Woloshyn, & T. Willoughby (Eds.), *Cognitive strategy instruction for middle and high schools.* Cambridge, MA: Brookline Books.

Wood, J. M., Bootzin, R. R., Kihlstrom, J. F., & Schacter, D. L. (1992). Implicit and explicit memory for verbal information presented during sleep. *Psychological Science, 3*(4), 236–239.

Wood, J. M., Nezworski, M. T., Lilienfeld, S. O., & Barb, H. N. (2003). The Rorschach inkblot test, fortune tellers, and cold reading. *Skeptical Inquirer, 27*(4), 29–33.

Wood, J. V., & Forest, A. L. (2010). Seeking pleasure and avoiding pain in interpersonal relationships. In M. D. Alicke & C. Sedikides (Eds.), *The handbook of self-enhancement and self-protection.* New York: Guilford Press.

Woodhill, B. M., & Samuels, C. A. (2004). Desirable and undesirable androgyny: A prescription for the twenty-first century. *Journal of Gender Studies, 13*(1), 15–28.

Woodruff-Pak, D. S. (2001). Eyeblink classical conditioning differentiates normal aging from Alzheimer's disease. *Integrative Physiological & Behavioral Science, 36*(2), 87–108.

Woods, S. C., Schwartz, M. W., Baskin, D. G., & Seeley, R J. (2000). Food intake and the regulation of body weight. *Annual Review of Psychology, 51,* 255–277.

Woody, S. R. (1996). Effects of focus of attention on anxiety levels and social performance of individuals with social phobia. *Journal of Abnormal Psychology, 105*(1), 61–69.

Worthen, J. B., & Marshall, P. H. (1996). Intralist and extralist sources of distinctiveness and the bizarreness effect. *Amer-*

ican Journal of Psychology, 109(2), 239–263.

Wraga, M., Shephard, J. M., Church, J. A., Inati, S., et al. (2005). Imagined rotations of self versus objects: An fMRI study. *Neuropsychologia, 43*(9), 1351–1361.

Wu, C. W. H., & Kaas, J. H. (2002). The effects of long-standing limb loss on anatomical reorganization of the somatosensory afferents in the brainstem and spinal cord. *Somatosensory & Motor Research, 19*(2), 153–163.

Wu, Z., & Schimmele, C. M. (2005). Food insufficiency and depression. *Sociological Perspectives, 48*(4), 481–504.

Wyatt, J. W., Posey, A., Welker, W., & Seamonds, C. (1984). Natural levels of similarities between identical twins and between unrelated people. *The Skeptical Inquirer, 9,* 62–66.

Wynne, C. D. L. (2004). The perils of anthropomorphism. *Nature, 428*(6983), 606.

Xu, F. & Denison, S. (2009) Statistical inference and sensitivity to sampling in 11-month-old infants. *Cognition, 112,* 97–104.

Xu, F. & Garcia, V. (2008) Intuitive statistics by 8-month-old infants. *Proceedings of the National Academy of Sciences of the United States of America, 105,* 5012–5015.

Yalom, I. D. (1980). *Existential psychotherapy.* New York: Basic.

Yang, Y., Tang, L., Tong, L., & Liu, H. (2009). Silkworms culture as a source of protein for humans in space. *Advances in Space Research, 43*(2), 1236–1242.

Yarmey, A. D. (2003). Eyewitness identification: Guidelines and recommendations for identification procedures in the United States and in Canada. *Canadian Psychology, 44*(3), 181–189.

Yeh, C. J. (2003). Age, acculturation, cultural adjustment, and mental health symptoms of Chinese, Korean, and Japanese immigrant youths. *Cultural Diversity & Ethnic Minority Psychology, 9*(1), 34–48.

Yip, P. S. F., & Thorburn, J. (2004). Marital status and the risk of suicide: Experience from England and Wales, 1982–1996. *Psychological Reports, 94*(2), 401–407.

Yokota, F., & Thompson, K. M. (2000). Violence in G-rated animated films. *Journal of the American Medical Association, 283*(20), 2716.

Yonas, A., Elieff, C. A., & Arterberry, M. E. (2002). Emergence of sensitivity to pictorial depth cues: Charting development in individual infants. *Infant Behavior & Development. Special Issue: Variability in Infancy, 25*(4), 495–514.

Yontef, G. M. (1995). Gestalt therapy. In A. S. Gurman & S. B. Messer (Eds.), *Essential psychotherapies.* New York: Guilford.

Yoo, C. S. M., & Miller, L. D. (2011) Culture and parenting: psychological adjustment among Chinese-Canadian adolescents. *Canadian Journal of Counselling and Psychotherapy/Revue canadienne de counseling et de psychotherapie, 45*(1), 34–52.

Yoshida, M. (1993). Three-dimensional electrophysiological atlas created by computer mapping of clinical responses elicited on stimulation of human subcortical struc-

tures. *Stereotactic & Functional Neurosurgery, 60*(1–3), 127–134.

Yost, W. A. (2007) *Fundamentals of hearing: An introduction* (5th ed.). San Diego: Elsevier.

Young, R. (2005). Neurobiology of savant syndrome. In C. Stough (Ed.), *Neurobiology of exceptionality.* New York: Kluwer Academic Publishers.

Young, S. M., & Pinsky, D. (2006). Narcissism and celebrity. *Journal of Research in Personality, 40*(5), 463–471.

Yucha, C. & Montgomery, D. (2008). *Evidence-based practice in biofeedback and neurofeedback.* Wheat Ridge, CO: Association for Applied Psychophysiology and Biofeedback.

Yuille, J. C., & Daylen, J. (1998). The impact of traumatic events on eyewitness memory. In C. Thompson, D. Herrmann, D. Bruce, J. D. Read, et al. (Eds.), *Eyewitness memory: Theoretical and applied perspectives.* Mahwah, NJ: Erlbaum.

Zadra, A., & Pihl, R. (1997). Lucid dreaming as a treatment for recurrent nightmares. *Psychotherapy and Psychosomatics, 66,* 50–55.

Zago, S., Corti, S., Bersano, A., Baron, P., et al. (2010). A cortically blind patient with preserved visual imagery. *Cognitive and Behavioral Neurology, 23*(1), 44–48.

Zarcadoolas, C., Pleasant, A., & Greer, D. S. (2006). *Advancing health literacy: A framework for understanding and action.* San Francisco: Jossey-Bass.

Zellner, D. A., Harner, D. E., & Adler, R. L. (1989). Effects of eating abnormalities and gender on perceptions of desirable body shape. *Journal of Abnormal Psychology, 98*(1), 93–96.

Zemishlany, Z., Aizenberg, D., & Weizman, A. (2001). Subjective effects of MDMA ("Ecstasy") on human sexual function. *European Psychiatry, 16*(2), 127–130.

Zentall, T. R. (2005). Animals may not be stuck in time. *Learning and Motivation, 36*(2), 208–225.

Zimbardo, P. (2007). *The Lucifer effect: Understanding how good people turn evil.* New York: Random House.

Zimbardo, P. G., Pilkonis, P. A., & Norwood, R. M. (1978). The social disease called shyness. In *Annual editions, personality and adjustment 78/79.* Guilford, CT: Dushkin.

Zimmerman, S., & Zimmerman, A. M. (1990). Genetic effects of marijuana. *International Journal of Addictions, 25*(1A), 19–33.

Zohar, D. (1998). An additive model of test anxiety: Role of exam-specific expectations. *Journal of Educational Psychology, 90,* 330–340.

Zola, S. M., & Squire, L. R. (2001). Relationship between magnitude of damage to the hippocampus and impaired recognition in monkeys. *Hippocampus, 11,* 92–98.

Zuckerman, M. (2002). Genetics of sensation seeking. In J. Benjamin, R. P. Ebstein, & R. H. Belmaker (Eds.), *Molecular genetics and the human personality.* Washington: American Psychiatric Publishing.

Name Index

Subject Index

Material found within figures is indicated by f. Material found within tables is indicated by t.